Collins

— POCKET —

Korean
Dictionary

한 - 영 영 - 한

HarperCollins Publishers
Westerhill Road
Bishopbriggs
Glasgow
G64 2QT
Great Britain

First Edition 2012

© HarperCollins Publishers 2012

Reprint 10 9 8 7 6 5 4 3 2 1

ISBN 978-0-00-745421-1

www.collinslanguage.com

A catalogue record for this book is
available from the British Library

Typesetting by Davidson Publishing
Solutions, Glasgow and Lingea s.r.o.

Printed in Great Britain by Clays Ltd,
St Ives plc

Acknowledgements
We would like to thank those authors and
publishers who kindly gave permission
for copyright material to be used in the
Collins Word Web. We would also like
to thank Times Newspapers Ltd for
providing valuable data.

Series Editor
Rob Scriven

Managing Editor
Ruth O'Donovan

Project Manager
Morven Dooner

Editor
Susie Beattie

Contributors
Eugene Benoit
Sunyoung Park

For the Publisher
Lucy Cooper
Kerry Ferguson
Elaine Higgleton
Susanne Reichert

목차   CONTENTS

머리말

콜린스 영-한, 한-영 사전을 구매해 주셔서 대단히 감사합니다. 이 사전이 가내와 여행지 혹은 직장에서 유용하게 사용되기를 바랍니다.

INTRODUCTION

We are delighted that you have decided to buy this English-Korean, Korean-English dictionary and hope you will enjoy and benefit from using it at home, on holiday or at work.

축약형   ABBREVIATIONS

형용사	*adj*	adjective
부사	*adv*	adverb
감탄사	*excl*	exclamation
전치사	*prep*	preposition
대명사	*pron*	pronoun
명사	*n*	noun
복수형	*pl*	plural
동사	*v*	verb
자동사	*vi*	intransitive verb
타동사	*vt*	transitive verb

영어발음/ENGLISH PRONUNCIATION

단모음	English example	Explanation
[ɑ:]	father	입을 크게 벌리고 [아]를 길게 발음
[ʌ]	but, come	입을 [아]로 벌리고 [어]라고 발음
[æ]	man, cat	[애]와 [아]의 중간발음
[ə]	father, ago	[으]에 가까운 [어]의 짧은 발음
[ɜ:]	bird, heard	입을 작게 벌리고 [어]를 약하고 길게 발음
[ɛ]	get, bed	[에]를 짧게 발음
[ɪ]	it, big	[이]
[i:]	tea, see	입을 좌우로 벌려 [이]를 길게 발음
[ɒ]	hot, wash	입을 크게 벌리는 [아]에 가까운 [오]의 발음
[ɔ:]	saw, all	입 속에서부터 [오]를 강하고 길게 발음
[ʊ]	put, book	입술을 둥글게 하여 [우]를 발음
[u:]	too, you	입술을 내밀어 [우]를 강하게 발음

이중모음	English example	Explanation
[aɪ]	fly, high	[아]를 강하게 발음한 뒤 [이]를 가볍게 이어 발음
[aʊ]	how, house	[아]를 강하게 발음한 뒤 [우]를 가볍게 이어 발음
[ɛə]	there, bear	입을 넓게 하여 [에] 다음에 [어]를 이어 발음
[eɪ]	day, obey	입을 좌우로 벌려 [에]다음에 [이]를 이어 발음
[ɪə]	here, hear	[에]에가까운 [이]다음에 [어]를 이어 발음
[əʊ]	go, note	[오]에 [우]를 이어 발음
[ɔɪ]	boy, oil	입술을 둥글게 하여 [오]다음에 [이]를 이어 발음
[ʊə]	poor, sure	입술을 내민 [우]다음에 [어]를 이어 발음

자음	English example	Explanation
[b]	big, lobby	다문 입술을 갑자기 벌려 발음하는 유성음 [브]
[d]	mended	혀끝을 윗니의 잇몸에 댔다가 떼면서 내는 유성음 [드]
[g]	go, get, big	혀의 뒷 부분을 입천장에 대고 발음하는 유성음 [그]
[dʒ]	gin, judge	혀끝을 윗니의 잇몸에 댔다가 떼면서 내는 유성음 [쥐]
[f]	fish, cliff	윗니를 아래 입술에 대고 발음하는 무성음 [프]
[ŋ]	sing	혀의 뒷부분을 올려 코로 목청을 울려 내는 유성음 [응]
[h]	house, he	목에서 숨을 강하게 내쉬며 내는 무성음 [흐]
[j]	young, yes	우리말의 [야,여,요,유] 등의 유성음
[k]	come, mock	혀의 뒷 부분을 입천장에 대고 발음하는 무성음 [크]
[l]	let, bill	혀끝을 윗니의 잇몸에 대고 혀의 양쪽으로 공기를 통과시키며 내는 유성음 [르]
[m]	mouse, him	양 입술을 다물고 내는 비음 [므]
[n]	net, bin	혀끝을 윗니의 잇몸에 대고 내는 비음 [느]

[p]	pick, lip	다문 입술을 벌려 발음하는 무성음 [프]
[r]	red, tread	혀끝을 위로 말아 올리며 내는 소리 [르]
[s]	sand, yes	혀끝을 윗니의 잇몸쪽에 접근시키며 음하는 무성음 [스]
[t]	toe, fit	혀끝을 윗니의 잇몸에 댔다가 떼면서 내는 무성음 [트]
[z]	rose, zebra	혀끝을 윗니의 잇몸쪽에 접근시켜 발음하는 유성음 [즈]
[ʃ]	she, machine	혀끝을 입천장 쪽으로 향하고 발음하는 무성음 [슈]
[tʃ]	chin, rich	혀끝을 윗니의 잇몸에 댔다가 떼면서 내는 무성음 [취]
[v]	valley	윗니를 아래 입술에 대고 발음하는 유성음 [브]
[w]	water, which	입술을 내밀고 혀의 뒷부분을 올려 내는 유성음 [우]
[x]	loch	목구멍에서 내는 소리 [크]
[ʒ]	vision	혀끝을 입천장 쪽으로 향하고 발음하는 유성음 [쥬]
[θ]	think, myth	혀끝을 윗니와 아랫니 사이로 가볍게 대어 발음하는 무성음 [쓰]
[ð]	this, the	혀끝을 윗니와 아랫니 사이로 가볍게 대어 발음하는 유성음 [드]

['] 표시는 음절의 강세 표시를 나타낸다.

KOREAN PRONUNCIATION

CONSONANTS

Letter	Symbol	Explanation
ㄱ	[g]	**k** as in **k**ey at the beginning or end of a word, or before ㅂ,ㄷ,ㄱ,ㅋ,ㅌ,ㅊ,ㅍ **ng** as in si**ng** before ㅁ,ㄴ,ㅇ,ㄹ **g** as in **g**irl before a vowel and elsewhere
ㄲ	[kk]	tensed* **k** as in s**k**y
ㄴ	[n]	**n** as in **n**o If followed by ㄹ, like English **l**
ㄷ	[d]	**t** as in **t**in at the beginning or end of a word **d** as in **d**og elsewhere
ㄸ	[tt]	tensed* **t** as in s**t**ar
ㄹ	[r/l]	between English **r** and **l**. before a vowel, rolled like a Scots **r** as in mu**r**der. when preceded or followed by another ㄹ like **l** as in ye**ll**ow
ㅁ	[m]	**m** as in **m**oon
ㅂ	[b]	**p** as in **p**ark at the beginning or end of a word **b** as in **b**ig elsewhere
ㅃ	[pp]	tensed* **p** as in s**p**a
ㅅ	[s]	**s** as in **s**un
	[sh]	before an 'i' or 'ee' sound like **sh** in **sh**ip or **sh**eep
ㅆ	[ss]	tensed* **s** as in **s**ip if followed by ㄴ like **n** as in bi**n**
ㅇ		zero or null consonant at the beginning of a syllable – not pronounced
	[ng]	**ng** as in si**ng** at the end of a syllable
ㅈ	[j]	**ch** as in **ch**arm at the beginning of a word **t** as in ba**t** the end of word if followed by a vowel, **j** as in **j**azz
ㅉ	[jj]	tensed* **ch** as in **j**azz
ㅊ	[ch]	aspirated** **ch** as in ke**tch**up
ㅋ	[k]	aspirated** **k** as in ki**ck** high
ㅌ	[t]	aspirated** **t** as the t in ren**t** house
ㅍ	[p]	aspirated** **p** as in mo**p** handle
ㅎ	[h]	**h** as in **h**ello when followed by ㅁ,ㄴ it is silent.

* tensed sounds are produced by holding the breath while making the sound
** aspirated sounds are produced by producing a puff of air while making the sound

VOWELS

Letter	Symbol	Explanation
ㅏ	[a]	**a** as in **a**rm
ㅑ	[ya]	**ya** as in **ya**rd
ㅐ	[ae]	**a** as in h**a**t
ㅒ	[yae]	**ya** as in **ya**p
ㅓ	[eo]	**u** as in f**u**r
ㅕ	[yeo]	**yea** as in **yea**rn
ㅗ	[o]	**o** as in l**o**ck
ㅛ	[yo]	**yo** as in **yo**ga
ㅜ	[u]	**oo** as in b**oo**t
ㅠ	[yu]	**you** as in **you**
ㅡ	[eu]	no direct English equivalent. Similar to the **u** sound in **u**gh
ㅣ	[i]	**ee** as in f**ee**t
ㅔ	[e]	**e** as in b**e**d
ㅖ	[ye]	**ye** as in **ye**ah

DIPTHONGS

Letter	Symbol	Explanation
ㅘ	[wa]	**ua** as in g**ua**va
ㅙ	[wae]	**wa** as in **wa**g
ㅚ	[oe]	**way** as in **way** sometimes **we** as in **we**t
ㅝ	[weo]	**wo** as in **wo**k
ㅞ	[we]	**way** as in **way**
ㅟ	[wi]	**wi** as in **wi**th
ㅢ	[ui]	**ooee** as in c**ooee** sometimes **yay** as in **yay**

숫자 / NUMBERS

There are two number systems in Korean – Native Korean and Sino-Korean. These
Two systems are used in different circumstances.
Native Korean numbers are used for hours and with counting words
Sino-Korean numbers are used with dates, telephone numbers, money, minutes
and words borrowed from other languages.

Native Korean	Sino-Korean		English
공 [gong]	영 [yeong]	0	zero
하나 [hana]	일 [il]	1	one
둘 [dul]	이 [i]	2	two
셋 [ses]	삼 [sam]	3	three
넷 [net]	사 [sa]	4	four
다섯 [daseot]	오 [o]	5	five
여섯 [yeoseot]	육 [yuk]	6	six
일곱 [ilgop]	칠 [chil]	7	seven
여덟 [yeodeorp]	팔 [pal]	8	eight
아홉 [ahop]	구 [gu]	9	nine
열 [yeor]	십 [sib]	10	ten
열하나 [yeolhana]	십일 [sibil]	11	eleven
열둘 [yeoldul]	십이 [sibi]	12	twelve
열셋 [yeolset]	십삼 [sipsam]	13	thirteen
열넷 [yeollet]	십사 [sipsa]	14	fourteen
열다섯 [yeoldaseot]	십오 [sibo]	15	fifteen
열여섯 [yeollyeoseot]	십육 [sibyuk]	16	sixteen
열일곱 [yeorilgop]	십칠 [sipchil]	17	seventeen
열여덟 [yeollye-odeorp]	십팔 [sippal]	18	eighteen
열아홉 [yeaorahop]	십구 [sipgu]	19	nineteen
스물 [seumur]	이십 [isip]	20	twenty
스물하나 [seumul-hana]	이십일 [isibil]	21	twenty-one
스물둘 [seumuldul]	이십이 [isibi]	22	twenty-two
스물셋 [seumulset]	이십삼 [isipsam]	23	twenty-three
서른 [seoreun]	삼십 [samsip]	30	thirty

서른하나 [seoreun-hana]	삼십일 [samsibil]	31	thirty-one
마흔 [maheun]	사십 [sasip]	40	forty
쉰 [swin]	오십 [osip]	50	fifty
예순 [yesun]	육십 [yuksip]	60	sixty
일흔 [ilheun]	칠십 [chilsip]	70	seventy
여든 [yeodeun]	팔십 [palsip]	80	eighty
아흔 [aheun]	구십 [gusip]	90	ninety
There are no Native Korean numbers above 99	백 [baek]	100	one hundred
	백십 [baeksip]	110	one hundred and ten
	이백 [ibeak]	200	two hundred
	이백오십 [ibeago-sip]	250	two hundred and fifty
	일천 [ilcheon]	1,000	one thousand
	일백만 [ilbaeng-man]	1,000,000	one million

요일	DAYS OF THE WEEK
월요일 [wolloil]	Monday
화요일 [hwayoil]	Tuesday
수요일 [suyoil]	Wednesday
목요일 [mogyoil]	Thursday
금요일 [guemyoil]	Friday
토요일 [toyoil]	Saturday
일요일 [illyoil]	Sunday

달	MONTHS
1월 [ilwol]	January
2월 [iwol]	February
3월 [samwol]	March
4월 [sawol]	April
5월 [owol]	May
6월 [yukwol]	June
7월 [chilwol]	July
8월 [palwol]	August
9월 [guwol]	September
10월 [sibwol]	October
11월 [sibilwol]	November
12월 [sibiwol]	December

KOREAN – ENGLISH
한 – 영

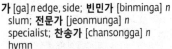

ㄱ

가 [ga] n edge, side; 빈민가 [binminga] n slum; 전문가 [jeonmunga] n specialist; 찬송가 [chansongga] n hymn

가게 [gage] n shop; 담배가게 [dambaegage] n tobacconist's; 선물가게 [seonmulgage] n gift shop; 구두가게 [gudugage] n shoe shop; 가장 가까운 사진 장비 가게는 어디에 있어요? [gajang gakkaun sajin jangbi gageneun eodie isseoyo?] Where is the nearest shop which sells photographic equipment?; 가장 가까운 신문 가게는 어디에 있어요? [gajang gakkaun sinmun gageneun eodie isseoyo?] Where is the nearest shop which sells newspapers?; 가장 가까운 우표 가게는 어디에 있어요? [gajang gakkaun upyo gageneun eodie isseoyo?] Where is the nearest shop which sells stamps?

가격 [gagyeok] n price; 소매가격 [somaegagyeok] n retail price; 가격표 [gagyeokpyo] n price list; 판매가격 [panmaegagyeok] n selling price; 가격에 부츠가 포함되나요? [gagyeoge bucheuga pohamdoenayo?] Does the price include boots?; 가격에 막대가 포함되나요? [gagyeoge makdaega pohamdoenayo?] Does the price include poles?; 가격에 온수가 포함되나요? [gagyeoge onsuga pohamdoenayo?] Is hot water included

in the price?; 가격에 종합 보험료가 포함되나요? [gagyeoge jonghap boheomnyoga pohamdoenayo?] Is fully comprehensive insurance included in the price?; 가격에는 무엇이 포함되나요? [gagyeogeneun mueosi pohamdoenayo?] What is included in the price?; 가격을 적어 주세요 [gagyeogeul jeogeo juseyo] Please write down the price

가구 [gagu] n furniture; 가구장이 [gagujangi] n joiner; 가구가 갖추어진 [gaguga gatchueojin] adj furnished

가급 [gageup] 가급적 [gageupjeok] adv preferably

가까이 [gakkai] adv near; 가까이 있는 [gakkai inneun] adj handy; 가까이에 [gakkaie] adv close

가끔 [gakkeum] 가끔의 [gakkeumui] adj occasional

가나 [gana] n Ghana; 가나 사람 [gana saram] n Ghanaian; 가나의 [ganaui] adj Ghanaian

가난 [ganan] n poverty; 가난한 [gananhan] adj poor

가능 [ganeung] n potential; 불가능한 [bulganeunghan] adj impossible; 예측 가능한 [yecheuk ganeunghan] adj predictable; 가능성 [ganeungseong] n possibility; 가능한 [ganeunghan] adj possible; 가능한 한 빨리 [ganeunghan han ppalli] asap (as soon as possible)

가다 [gada] vi go; 되돌아가다 [doedoragada] v turn back; 앞서 가다 [apseo gada] v go ahead; 금이 가다 [geumi gada] vi crack; ...에 가고 싶어요 [...e gago sipeoyo] We'd like to go to...; ...에 갈 거예요 [...e gal geoyeyo] I'm going to...; ...에 갈까요? [...e galkkayo?] Can we go to...?; 우리는...에 갈 거예요 [urineun...e gal geoyeyo] We're going to...; 저리 가세요! [jeori gaseyo!] Go away!; 집에 가고 싶어요 [jibe gago sipeoyo] I'd like to go home; 쭉 가세요 [jjuk gaseyo] Go straight on

가득 [gadeuk] v fill; 가득한 [gadeukhan] adj full; 가득 넣어 주세요 [gadeuk neoheo juseyo] Fill it up, please

가디건 [gadigeon] n cardigan
가라앉다 [garaantda] vi sink
가라테 [garate] n karate
가래 [garae] n spade
가렵다 [garyeopda] v itch; **가려운**
[garyeoun] adj itchy; **다리가 가려워요**
[dariga garyeowoyo] My leg itches
가로지르다 [garojireuda] v cross;
가로질러서 [garojilleoseo] prep across
가루 [garu] n flour, powder; **빵가루**
[ppanggaru] npl breadcrumbs;
가루비누 [garubinu] n soap powder;
꽃가루 [kkotgaru] n pollen
가르랑거리다 [gareuranggeorida] v purr
가르치다 [gareuchida] v teach; **가르치기**
[gareuchigi] n teaching
가리다 [garida] v sort out, comb, screen;
눈가리개 [nungarigae] n blindfold
가리키다 [garikida] v indicate, point
가명 [gamyeong] adv alias ▷ n
pseudonym
가뭄 [gamum] n drought
가발 [gabal] n wig; **(남성용) 가발**
[(namseongyong) gabal] n toupee
가방 [gabang] n bag; **멜빵 달린 가방**
[melppang dallin gabang] n satchel;
책가방 [chaekgabang] n schoolbag;
서류 가방 [seoryu gabang] n briefcase;
세면가방 [semyeongabang] n toilet
bag; **여행용 가방** [yeohaengyong
gabang] n overnight bag; **여행가방**
[yeohaenggabang] n suitcase; **큰 가방**
[keun gabang] n holdall; **누군가가 제
가방을 훔쳐 갔어요** [nugungaga je
gabangeul humchyeo gasseoyo]
Someone's stolen my bag; **잠깐만 제
가방을 봐 주시겠어요?** [jamkkanman
je gabangeul bwa jusigesseoyo?] Could
you watch my bag for a minute,
please?; **택시에 가방을 두고 내렸어요**
[taeksie gabangeul dugo
naeryeosseoyo] I left my bags in the
taxi
가볍다 [gabyeopda] **가벼운** [gabyeoun]
adj light (not heavy)
가봉 [gabong] n Gabon
가사 [gasa] n housework
가상 [gasang] **가상의** [gasangui] adj
virtual; **가상현실** [gasanghyeonsil] n
virtual reality
가속 [gasok] n acceleration; **가속기**
[gasokgi] n accelerator; **가속하다**
[gasokhada] v accelerate, speed up
가수 [gasu] n singer
가쉽 [gaswip] n gossip
가스 [gaseu] n gas; **배기 가스** [baegi
gaseu] npl exhaust fumes; **최루가스**
[choerugaseu] n teargas; **캠핑 가스**
[kaemping gaseu] n camping gas; **천연
가스** [cheonyeon gaseu] n natural gas;
가스레인지 [gaseureinji] n gas cooker;
가스 냄새가 나요 [gaseu naemsaega
nayo] I can smell gas; **가스 계량기는
어디있어요?** [gaseu gyeryanggineun
eodiisseoyo?] Where is the gas meter?
가슴 [gaseum] n breast, chest (body
part); **여성의 가슴** [yeoseongui
gaseum] n bust; **가슴앓이** [gaseumari]
n heartburn; **가슴이 아파요** [gaseumi
apayo] I have a pain in my chest
가시 [gasi] n thorn
가열 [gayeol] n heating; **가열되다**
[gayeoldoeda] v heat up; **가열하다**
[gayeolhada] v heat
가용 [gayong] **사용할 수 있는**
[sayonghal su inneun] adj available;
가용성 [gayongseong] n availability;
가용성의 [gayongseongui] adj soluble
가위 [gawi] npl scissors; **손톱가위**
[sontopgawi] npl nail scissors; **큰 가위**
[keun gawi] npl clippers
가을 [gaeul] n autumn
가이드 [gaideu] n guide; **영어 가이드
관광이 있어요?** [yeongeo gaideu
gwangwangi isseoyo?] Is there a
guided tour in English?; **영어 하는
가이드 있어요?** [yeongeo haneun
gaideu isseoyo?] Is there a guide who
speaks English?; **가이드 관광은 몇 시에
시작해요?** [gaideu gwangwangeun
myeot sie sijakhaeyo?] What time does
the guided tour begin?; **현지 걷기
가이드가 있어요?** [hyeonji geotgi
gaideuga isseoyo?] Do you have a guide
to local walks?
가이아나 [gaiana] n Guyana

가장 [gajang] adv most; 가장 무도회 의상 [gajang mudohoe uisang] n fancy dress

가장자리 [gajangjari] n edge

가재 [gajae] n crayfish; 바닷가재 [badatgajae] n lobster

가정 [gajeong] adv perhaps ▷ n presumption, home;...이라고 가정하면 [...irago gajeonghamyeon] conj supposing; 가정교사 [gajeonggyosa] n tutor; 가정하다 [gajeonghada] v assume, suppose

가져오다 [gajyeooda] v bring

가족 [gajok] n family, household; 가족과 여기에 왔어요 [gajokgwa yeogie wasseoyo] I'm here with my family

가죽 [gajuk] n leather; 스웨이드 가죽 [seuweideu gajuk] n suede; 양가죽 [yanggajuk] n sheepskin

가지 [gaji] n aubergine, branch; 나뭇가지 [namutgaji] n stick

가지다 [gajida] vt take; 가지고 있다 [gajigo itda] v have

가짜 [gajja] 가짜의 [gajjaui] adj fake

가축 [gachuk] npl cattle

가치 [gachi] n value, worth; 가치 없는 [gachi eomneun] adj worthless; 수리할 가치가 있을까요? [surihal gachiga isseulkkayo?] Is it worth repairing?

가톨릭 [gatollik] 가톨릭교도 [gatollikgyodo] n Catholic; 가톨릭교의 [gatollikgyoui] adj Catholic

가파르다 [gapareuda] 가파른 [gapareun] adj steep; 아주 가파른가요? [aju gapareungayo?] Is it very steep?

각 [gak] n angle

각각 [gakgak] adv respectively

각자 [gakja] pron each; 각자의 [gakjaui] adj each

간 [gan] n liver; 마구간 [magugan] n stable; 저는 간을 못 먹어요 [jeoneun ganeul mot meogeoyo] I can't eat liver

간격 [gangyeok] n gap, interval

간결 [gangyeol] 간결한 [gangyeolhan] adj concise

간과 [gangwa] 간과하다 [gangwahada] v overlook

간단 [gandan] 간단히 [gandanhi] adv briefly, simply

간신히 [gansinhi] adv barely

간염 [ganyeom] n hepatitis

간장 [ganjang] n soy sauce

간접 [ganjeop] 간접의 [ganjeobui] adj indirect

간주 [ganju] 간주하다 [ganjuhada] v reckon, regard

간지럽다 [ganjireopda] 간지러운 [ganjirurun] adj ticklish

간직하다 [ganjikhada] vt keep

간질 [ganjil] n epilepsy; 간질 발작 [ganjilbaljjark] n epileptic fit; 간질 환자 [ganjil hwanja] n epileptic

간질이다 [ganilieda] v tickle

간청 [gancheong] 간청하다 [gancheonghada] v appeal

간호사 [ganhosa] n nurse; 간호사에게 이야기하고 싶어요 [ganhosaege iyagihago sipeoyo] I'd like to speak to a nurse

갈겨쓰다 [galgyeosseuda] v scribble

갈다 [galda] v sharpen;...을 갈아 (가루로) 만들다 [...eul gara (garuro) mandeulda] vt grind

갈대 [galdae] n reed

갈매기 [galmaegi] n seagull

갈아타다 [garatada] v change, transfer;... 가려면 어디에서 갈아타나요? [... garyeomyeon eodieseo garatanayo?] Where do I change for...?; 어디에서 갈아타야 할까요? [eodieseo garataya halkkayo?] Where do I change?;...에서 갈아 타셔야 해요 [... eseo gara tasyeoya haeyo] You have to transfer at...; 갈아 타야 하나요? [gara taya hanayo?] Do I have to change?

갈증 [galjeung] n thirst

갈채 [galchae] n cheer

갈퀴 [galkwi] n rake

감각 [gamgak] n sense; 유머감각 [yumeogamgak] n sense of humour; 감각적인 [gamgakjeogin] adj sensuous

감격 [gamgyeok] 감격적인 [gamgyeokjeogin] adj thrilling

감기 [gamgi] n cold (illness); 감기에 걸렸어요 [gamgie geollyeosseoyo] I have a cold

감기약 [gamgiyak] *n* cold medicine; **감기약 주세요** [gamgiyak juseyo] I'd like something for a cold

감다 [gamda] *v* wind (coil around); **다시 감다** [dasi gamda] *v* rewind

감당 [gamdang] **감당할 수 있는** [gamdanghal su inneun] *adj* affordable

감독 [gamdok] *n* oversight (supervision); **감독자** [gamdokja] *n* supervisor, surveyor; **감독관** [gamdokgwan] *n* invigilator; **감독하다** [gamdokhada] *v* supervise

감동 [gamdong] *n* emotion, feeling; **감동적인** [gamdongjeogin] *adj* touching; **감동한** [gamdonghan] *adj* touched

감리교 [gamnigyo] **감리교 신자의** [gamnigyo sinjaui] *adj* Methodist

감명 [gammyeong] **감명받은** [gammyeongbadeun] *adj* impressed; **감명을 주다** [gammyeongeul juda] *v* impress

감미료 [gammiryo] *n* sweetener; **감미료 있어요?** [gammiryo isseoyo?] Do you have any sweetener?

감사¹ [gamsa] *n* audit; **감사관** [gamsagwan] *n* auditor; **감사하다** [gamsahada] *v* audit

감사² [gamsa] **감사!** [gamsa!] *excl* thanks!; **감사하다** [gamsahada] *v* appreciate, thank; **감사해 하지 않는** [gamsahae haji annneun] *adj* ungrateful; **대단히 감사합니다** [daedanhi gamsahamnida] Thank you very much; **감사합니다** [gamsahamnida] Thank you

감상 [gamsang] *n* **감상적인** [gamsangjeogin] *adj* soppy

감소 [gamso] *n* decrease; **감소하다** [gamsohada] *v* decrease

감시 [gamsi] **감시하다** [gamsihada] *n* spy

감시관 [gamsigwan] **교통감시관** [gyotonggamsigwan] *n* traffic warden

감염 [gamyeom] *n* infection; **물린 곳이 감염됐어요** [mullin gosi gamyeomdwaesseoyo] This bite is infected

감옥 [gamok] *n* jail; **지하감옥** [jihagamok] *n* dungeon

감자 [gamja] *n* potato; **으깬 감자** [eukkaen gamja] *npl* mashed potatoes; **구운 감자** [guun gamja] *n* baked potato; **껍질째 구운 감자** [kkeopjiljjae guun gamja] *n* jacket potato; **감자 벗기는 기구** [gamja beotgineun gigu] *n* potato peeler; **감자칩** [gamjachip] *npl* chips, crisps

감전 [gamjeon] *n* electric shock

감정 [gamjeong] *n* emotion; **감정의** [gamjeongui] *adj* emotional; **감정적인** [gamjeongjeogin] *adj* sentimental

갑옷 [gabot] *n* armour

갑작 [gapjak] **갑자기** [gapjagi] *adv* abruptly, suddenly; **갑작스러운** [gapjakseureoun] *adj* abrupt, sudden

갑판 [gappan] *n* deck; **차 싣는 갑판에 어떻게 갈 수 있어요?** [cha sitneun gappane eotteoke gal su isseoyo?] How do I get to the car deck?; **갑판에 나가도 될까요?** [gappane nagado doelkkayo?] Can we go out on deck?

값 [gabt] *n* value; **값싼** [gapssan] *adj* inexpensive

갓길 [gatgil] **포장 갓길** [pojang gatgil] *n* hard shoulder

강 [gang] *n* river; **강에서 수영해도 될까요?** [gangeseo suyeonghaedo doelkkayo?] Can one swim in the river?; **강에서 하는 보트 여행이 있어요?** [gangeseo haneun boteu yeohaengi isseoyo?] Are there any boat trips on the river?

강간 [ganggan] *n* rape (sexual attack); **강간범** [gangganbeom] *n* rapist; **강간하다** [gangganhada] *v* rape

강도 [gangdo] *n* burglar, robber; **무장 강도** [mujang gangdo] *n* hold-up; **노상 강도** [nosang gangdo] *n* mugger; **강도 행위** [gangdo haengwi] *n* mugging; **강도죄** [gangdojoe] *n* burglary; **강도질** [gangdojil] *n* robbery; **강도질하다** [gangdojilhada] *v* burgle

강력 [gangnyeok] **강력한** [gangnyeokhan] *adj* powerful

강렬 [gangnyeol] 강렬한 [gangnyeolhan] *adj* intense

강사 [gangsa] *n* instructor, lecturer; 운전 강사 [unjeon gangsa] *n* driving instructor

강습 [gangseup] *n* lesson; 재교육 강습 [jaegyoyuk gangseup] *n* refresher course; 스노보드 강습을 해주시나요? [seunobodeu gangseubeul haejusinayo?] Do you organise snowboarding lessons?; 스키 강습을 해주시나요? [seuki gangseubeul haejusinayo?] Do you organise skiing lessons?; 강습을 받을 수 있나요? [gangseubeul badeul su innayo?] Can we take lessons?; 강습을 해주십니까? [gangseubeul haejusimnikka?] Do you give lessons?

강아지 [gangaji] *n* puppy

강연 [gangyeon] *n* talk

강요 [gangyo] 강요된 [gangyodoen] *adj* strained; 강요하다 [gangyohada] *v* force

강의 [gangui] *n* lecture; 강의 시간표 [gangui siganpyo] *n* syllabus; 강의하다 [ganguihada] *v* lecture

강장 [gangjang] 강장제 [gangjangje] *n* tonic

강제 [gangje] 강제적인 [gangjejeogin] *adj* compulsory

강조 [gangjo] *n* stress; 강조하다 [gangjohada] *v* emphasize, highlight, stress, underline

강타 [gangta] *n* bash, blow; 강타하다 [gangtahada] *v* bash

강하다 [ganghada] 강하게 [ganghage] *adv* strongly; 강한 [ganghan] *adj* strong; 더 강한 것이 필요해요 [deo ganghan geosi pillyohaeyo] I need something stronger

강화 [ganghwa] 강화하다 [ganghwahada] *v* strengthen

갖추다 [gatchuda] 갖춘 [gatchun] *adj* equipped

같게하다 [gatgehada] *v* equalize

같다 [gatda] *v* equal;...과 같이 [...gwa gachi] *v* like; 같은 [gateun] *adj* equal, the same; 같음 [gateum] *n* equality;

같이 [gachi] (유사한 것) *conj* as, together

개 [gae] *n* dog; 암캐 [amkae] *n* bitch; 양 지키는 개 [yang jikineun gae] *n* sheepdog; 개집 [gaejip] *n* kennel; 테리어개 [terieogae] *n* terrier

개구리 [gaeguri] *n* frog

개미 [gaemi] *n* ant

개발 [gaebal] *n* development; 개발도상국 [gaebaldosangguk] *n* developing country

개별 [gaebyeol] 개별지도 [gaebyeoljido] *n* tutorial

개선 [gaeseon] *n* improvement; 개선하다 [gaeseonhada] (보다 좋은) *v* improve

개수 [gaesu] 개수대 [gaesudae] *n* sink

개스켓 [gaeseuket] *n* gasket

개신교 [gaesingyo] 개신교도 [gaesingyodo] *n* Protestant; 개신교도의 [gaesingyodoui] *n* Protestant

개암 [gaeam] *n* hazelnut

개업 [gaeeop] 일반 개업의 [ilban gaeeobui] *abbr* GP

개연 [gaeyeon] 개연성 [gaeyeonseong] *n* probability

개요 [gaeyo] *n* outline

개울 [gaeul] *n* stream

개인 [gaein] *n* individual; 비개인적인 [bigaeinjeogin] *adj* impersonal; 개인용 일정 수첩 [gaeinyong iljeong sucheop] *n* personal organizer; 개인의 [gaeinui] *adj* individual, personal; 개인적으로 [gaeinjeogeuro] *adv* personally; 방에 개인 욕실이 있어요? [bange gaein yoksiri isseoyo?] Does the room have a private bathroom?; 개인 소지품이에요 [gaein sojipumieyo] It is for my own personal use; 개인보험을 들고 싶어요 [gaeinboheomeul deulgo sipeoyo] I'd like to arrange personal accident insurance

개장 [gaejang] 개장하다 [gaejanghada] *v* redecorate

개정 [gaejeong] 개정하다 [gaejeonghada] *v* rectify

개조 [gaejo] *n* makeover, remake

개축 [gaechuk] **개축하다** [gaechukhada] v rebuild

객실 [gaeksil] n parlour; **객실 담당 여직원** [gaeksil damdang yeojigwon] n chambermaid; **객실 승무원** [gaeksil seungmuwon] n cabin crew; **객실서비스** [gaeksilseobiseu] n room service

객차 [gaekcha] n carriage

갤럽 [gaelleop] n gallop

갱 [gaeng] n gang; **갱단의 일원** [gaengdanui irwon] n gangster

갱년 [gaengnyeon] **갱년기** [gaengnyeongi] n menopause

갱신 [gaengsin] **갱신하다** [gaengsinhada] v update

거 [geo] n vehicle; **세발자전거** [sebaljajeongeo] n tricycle

거기 [geogi] **거기에** [geogie] adv there

거꾸로 [geokkuro] adv upside down; **거꾸로 하다** [geokkuro hada] v reverse

거나 [geona] **...거나 또는...거나** [...geona ttoneun...geona] conj either... or

거대 [geodae] **거대한** [geodaehan] adj enormous, giant, gigantic, huge, mammoth, mega; **거대한** [geodaehan] adj magnificent

거래 [georae] n bargain, deal; **증권중개인** [jeunggwonjunggaein] n stockbroker; **거대한** [geodaehan] adj tremendous

거래소 [georaeso] **증권거래소** [jeunggwongeoraeso] n stock exchange

거르다 [georeuda] v filter

거름 [georeum] n manure

거리 [geori] n distance, street; **주행거리계** [juhaenggeorigye] n mileometer; **사거리** [sageori] n crossroads; **거리지도** [georijido] n street map

거만 [geoman] **거만한** [geomanhan] adj arrogant, stuck-up

거미 [geomi] n spider; **거미줄** [geomijul] n web; **거미집** [geomijip] n cobweb

거부 [geobu] **거부권** [geobugwon] n veto

거북 [geobuk] n turtle

거북이 [geobugi] n tortoise

거실 [geosil] n living room

거울 [geoul] n mirror

거위 [geowi] n goose

거의 [geoui] adv almost, nearly; **거의... 않다** [geoui...anta] adv hardly

거인 [geoin] n giant

거절 [geojeol] n refusal; **거절하다** [geojeolhada] v refuse, reject, turn down

거주 [geoju] n stay; **거주의** [geojuui] adj residential

거지 [geoji] n beggar, tramp (beggar)

거짓말 [geojitmal] n lie; **거짓말하다** [geojitmalhada] v lie

거짓말쟁이 [geojitmaljaengi] n liar

거치다 [geochida] v pass through; **...을 거쳐** [...eul geochyeo] prep via

거칠다 [geochilda] **거친** [geochin] adj coarse, harsh, rough

거품 [geopum] n bubble; **거품 목욕** [geopum mogyok] n bubble bath; **거품이는** [geopumineun] adj fizzy

걱정 [geokjeong] n concern; **걱정되는** [geokjeongdoeneun] adj worrying; **걱정스러운** [geokjeongseureoun] adj worried; **걱정하는** [geokjeonghaneun] adj concerned; **걱정하다** [geokjeonghada] vi worry

건강 [geongang] n health; **건강이 나쁜** [geongangi nappeun] adj poorly; **건강한** [geonganghan] adj healthy, well; **건강과 미용** [geonganggwa miyong] health and beauty

건널목 [geonneolmok] n level crossing

건막 [geonmak] **건막류** [geonmangnyu] n bunion

건물 [geonmul] n building; **고층 건물** [gocheung geonmul] n high-rise; **건물에 승강기가 있나요?** [geonmure seungganggiga innayo?] Is there a lift in the building?

건배 [geonbae] n toast (tribute); **건배!** [geonbae!] excl cheers!

건설 [geonseol] n construction; **건설적인** [geonseoljeogin] adj constructive; **건설하다** [geonseolhada] v construct

건전 [geonjeon] 건전한 [geonjeonhan] *adj* sound

건조 [geonjo] 식기 건조대 [sikgi geonjodae] *n* draining board; 건조시키다 [geonjosikida] *v* dry; 건조기 [geonjogi] *n* dryer; 건조한 [geonjohan] (젖지 않음) *v* dry; 건초 더미 [geoncho deomi] *n* haystack; 옷을 건조시킬 곳이 있나요? [oseul geonjosikil gosi innayo?] Is there somewhere to dry clothes?; 제 머리카락은 건조해요 [je meorikarageun geonjohaeyo] I have dry hair

건초 [geoncho] *n* hay

건축 [geonchuk] *n* architecture; 건축 부지 [geonchuk buji] *n* building site; 건축업자 [geonchugeopja] *n* builder; 건축가 [geonchukga] *n* architect

건포도 [geonpodo] *n* currant; 씨없는 건포도 [ssieomneun geonpodo] *n* sultana

걷기 [geotgi] *n* walking; 가이드 딸린 걷기가 있어요? [gaideu ttallin geotgiga isseoyo?] Are there any guided walks?; 현지 걷기 가이드가 있어요? [hyeonji geotgi gaideuga isseoyo?] Do you have a guide to local walks?; 힐 워킹을 하고 싶어요 [hil wokingeul hago sipeoyo] I'd like to go hill walking

걷다 [geotda] *v* walk; 빠른걸음으로 걷다 [ppareungeoreumeuro geotda] *v* trot; 발을 끌며 걷다 [bareul kkeulmyeo geotda] *v* shuffle; 걷기 [geotgi] *n* walking, (도보) walk; 몇 킬로미터를 걸어야 하나요? [myeot killomiteoreul georeoya hanayo?] How many kilometres is the walk?; 거기까지 걸어갈 수 있어요? [geogikkaji georeogal su isseoyo?] Can I walk there?

걸다 [geolda] *vt* hang; 걸려 있다 [geollyeo itda] *vi* hang

걸레 [geolle] 대걸레 [daegeolle] *n* mop; 대걸레로 닦다 [daegeollero dakkda] *v* mop up

걸리다 [geollida] (시간) 걸리다 [(sigan) geollida] *v* take (*time*); 오래 걸리나요? [orae geollinayo?] Will it be long?; 거기까지 가는 데 얼마나 걸리나요? [geogikkaji ganeun de eolmana geollinayo?] How long will it take to get there?; ...까지 가는 데 얼마나 걸리나요? [...kkaji ganeun de eolmana geollinayo?] How long will it take to get to...?

걸상 [geolsang] *n* stool

걸쇠 [geolsoe] *n* clasp

걸음 [georeum] *n* step; 걸음걸이 [georeumgeori] *n* footstep

걸이 [geori] 옷걸이 [otgeori] *n* coathanger, hanger

걸작 [geoljak] *n* masterpiece

검 [geom] *n* sword

검다 [geomda] 검댕 [geomdaeng] *n* soot; 검은 [geomeun] *adj* black

검사 [geomsa] *n* check-up; 도말 표본 검사 [domal pyobon geomsa] *n* smear test; 신체검사 [sinchegeomsa] *n* physical; 여권 검사 [yeogwon geomsa] *n* passport control; 정밀검사 [jeongmilgeomsa] *n* scan

검색 [geomsaek] *n* search; 검색 엔진 [geomsaek enjin] *n* search engine; 검색하다 [geomsaekhada] *v* search

검소 [geomso] 검소한 [geomsohan] *adj* thrifty

검표 [geompyo] 검표원 [geompyowon] *n* ticket inspector

겁 [geop] *n* cowardice; 겁나게 하다 [geomnage hada] *v* terrify; 겁많은 [geommanheun] *adj* cowardly; 겁주다 [geopjuda] *v* scare; 겁에 질린 [geobe jillin] *adj* terrified; 겁을 주다 [geobeul juda] *v* frighten; 겁쟁이 [geopjaengi] *n* coward

겁먹다 [geommeokda] 겁먹은 [geommeogeun] *adj* frightened, scared

것 [geot]...라는 것 [...raneun geot] *pron* that; 어느 것 [eoneu geot] *pron* which

게 [ge] *n* crab; 게자리 [gejari] *n* Cancer (*horoscope*)

게다가 [gedaga] *adv* besides, further ▷ *conj* then

게르빌루스쥐 [gereubilluseujwi] *n* gerbil

게시 [gesi] 게시판 [gesipan] n bulletin board, notice board

게으르다 [geeureuda] 게으른 [geeureun] adj lazy

게으름 [geeureum] n laziness; 게으름피우다 [geeureumpiuda] v mess about

게이지 [geiji] n gauge

게임 [geim] n game; 보드 게임 [bodeu geim] n board game; 컴퓨터 게임 [keompyuteo geim] n computer game; 게임 콘솔 [geim konsol] n games console

겔 [gel] n gel

겨 [gyeo] 왕겨 [wanggyeo] n bran

겨냥하다 [gyeonyanghada] v aim

겨드랑이 [gyeodeurangi] n armpit

겨우 [gyeou] adv scarcely

겨우살이 [gyeousari] n mistletoe

겨울 [gyeoul] n winter; 겨울 스포츠 [gyeoul seupocheu] npl winter sports

겨자 [gyeoja] n mustard

격노 [gyeongno] 격노한 [gyeongnohan] adj furious

격동 [gyeokdong] n surge

격려 [gyeongnyeo] n encouragement; 격려가 되는 [gyeongnyeoga doeneun] adj encouraging

격리 [gyeongni] n quarantine; 격리된 [gyeongnidoen] adj isolated

격분 [gyeokbun] n outrage, frenzy; 격분시키는 [gyeokbunsikineun] adj infuriating

격식 [gyeoksik] n formality

격언 [gyeogeon] n proverb

격자 [gyeokja] n grid; 격자무늬의 [gyeokjamunuiui] adj tartan

견과 [gyeongwa] n nut (food); 견과 알레르기 [gyeongwa allereugi] n nut allergy; 견과류가 들어가지 않은 식사를 준비해 주시겠어요? [gyeongwaryuga deureogaji anheun siksareul junbihae jusigesseoyo?] Could you prepare a meal without nuts?

견디다 [gyeondida] v bear up

견본 [gyeonbon] n sample

견습 [gyeonseup] 견습생 [gyeonseupsaeng] n apprentice

견인 [gyeonin] n traction; 견인차 [gyeonincha] n breakdown truck, breakdown van; 정비소까지 견인해 주시겠어요? [jeongbisokkaji gyeoninhae jusigesseoyo?] Can you tow me to a garage?

견적 [gyeonjeok] n estimate

견해 [gyeonhae] n view

결과 [gyeolgwa] n consequence, outcome, result

결국 [gyeolguk] adv eventually

결단 [gyeoldan] n resolve; 결단성이 없는 [gyeoldanseongi eomneun] adj indecisive; 결단을 내리지 못하는 [gyeoldaneul naeriji motaneun] adj undecided

결론 [gyeollon] n conclusion

결말 [gyeolmal] n ending; 결말을 짓다 [gyeolmareul jitda] vt conclude

결석 [gyeolseok] n absence; 병으로 인한 결석 통지 [byeongeuro inhan gyeolseok tongji] n sick note; 무단결석하다 [mudangyeolseokhada] v play truant

결속 [gyeolsok] 결속하다 [gyeolsokhada] v tie up

결승 [gyeolseung] 준결승전 [jungyeolseungjeon] n semifinal; 결승전 [gyeolseungjeon] n final

결심 [gyeolsim] n decision, resolution; 결심하다 [gyeolsimhada] v decide

결점 [gyeoljeom] n defect, flaw; 결점이 있는 [gyeoljeomi inneun] adj faulty

결정 [gyeoljeong] n 결정적인 [gyeoljeongjeogin] adj decisive

결합 [gyeolhap] n combination, conjunction; 결합시키다 [gyeolhapsikida] v combine

결핵 [gyeolhaek] n tuberculosis; 결핵균 [gyeolhaekgyun] n TB

결혼 [gyeolhon] n marriage; 신랑 들러리 [sillang deulleori] n best man; 결혼 증명서 [gyeolhon jeungmyeongseo] n marriage certificate; 결혼 상황 [gyeolhon sanghwang] n marital status; 결혼 전의 성 [gyeolhon jeonui seong] n maiden name; 결혼반지 [gyeolhonbanji] n wedding ring;

결혼식 [gyeolhonsik] n wedding; 결혼기념일 [gyeolhoninyeomil] n wedding anniversary; 결혼하다 [gyeolhonhada] v marry; 기혼의 [gihonui] adj married

겸손 [gyeomson] 겸손한 [gyeomsonhan] adj humble, modest

경 [gyeong] n sir; 망원경 [mangwongyeong] n telescope

경감 [gyeonggam] 경감시키다 [gyeonggamsikida] v relieve

경계 [gyeonggye] n border, boundary; 경계하는 [gyeonggyehaneun] v alert

경고 [gyeonggo] n warning; 위험 경고등 [wiheom gyeonggodeung] npl hazard warning lights; 경고하다 [gyeonggohada] v alert, warn; 오일 경고등이 꺼지지 않아요 [oil gyeonggodeungi kkeojiji anhayo] The oil warning light won't go off

경관 [gyeonggwan] n landscape

경기 [gyeonggi] n match (sport); 단식 경기 [dansik gyeonggi] npl singles; 축구 경기 [chukgu gyeonggi] n football match; 오종 경기 [ojong gyeonggi] n pentathlon; 운동경기 [undonggyeonggi] npl athletics; 원정 경기 [wonjeong gyeonggi] n away match; 경기를 하다 [gyeonggireul hada] n play (in sport); 홈경기 [homgyeonggi] n home match; 축구 경기를 보고 싶어요 [chukgu gyeonggireul bogo sipeoyo] I'd like to see a football match

경기장 [gyeonggijang] n stadium, pitch, playing field; 경기장에 어떻게 갈 수 있을까요? [gyeonggijange eotteoke gal su isseulkkayo?] How do we get to the stadium?

경도 [gyeongdo] n longitude

경력 [gyeongnyeok] n career, work experience

경련 [gyeongnyeon] n spasm

경로 [gyeongno] n route

경리 [gyeongni] n treasurer

경마 [gyeongma] n horse race; 경마기수 [gyeongmagisu] n jockey; 경마 보고 싶어요 [gyeongma bogo sipeoyo] I'd like to see a horse race

경마차 [gyeongmacha] n buggy

경매 [gyeongmae] n auction

경멸 [gyeongmyeol] 경멸하다 [gyeongmyeolhada] v despise

경보 [gyeongbo] 비상 경보 [bisang gyeongbo] n alarm call; 도난 경보기 [donan gyeongbogi] n burglar alarm; 잘못된 경보 [jalmotdoen gyeongbo] n false alarm; 화재 경보 [hwajae gyeongbo] n fire alarm; 화재경보 [hwajaegyeongbo] n smoke alarm

경비 [gyeongbi] n defence; 해안 경비대 [haean gyeongbidae] n coastguard

경비원 [gyeongbiwon] 유흥업소 경비원 [yuheungeopso gyeongbiwon] n bouncer

경상 [gyeongsang] 경상비 [gyeongsangbi] npl overheads

경솔 [gyeongsol] 경솔한 [gyeongsolhan] adj thoughtless

경연 [gyeongyeon] n contest; 경연 참가자 [gyeongyeon chamgaja] n contestant

경영자 [gyeongyeongja] 최고 경영자 [choego gyeongyeongja] abbr CEO

경쟁 [gyeongjaeng] n competition, rivalry; 경쟁 상대 [gyeongjaeng sangdae] n rival; 경쟁의 [gyeongjaengui] adj competitive; 경쟁자 [gyeongjaengja] n competitor; 경쟁하는 [gyeongjaenghaneun] adj rival; 경쟁하다 [gyeongjaenghada] v compete; 경쟁하다 [gyeongjaenghada] v race

경적 [gyeongjeok] n siren

경제 [gyeongje] n economy; 경제적인 [gyeongjejeogin] adj economical; 경제학자 [gyeongjehakja] n economist

경제학 [gyeongjehak] npl economics; 경제학의 [gyeongjehagui] adj economic

경주 [gyeongju] n race (contest); 단거리 경주 [dangeori gyeongju] n sprint; 단거리 경주 선수 [dangeori gyeongju seonsu] n sprinter; 자동차 경주 선수 [jadongcha gyeongju seonsu] n racing driver; 자동차경주

[jadongchagyeongju] n motor racing; 경주마 [gyeongjuma] n racehorse; 경주용차 [gyeongjuyongcha] n racing car; 경주장 [gyeongjujang] n racetrack; 경주자 [gyeongjuja] n racer, runner; 경주코스 [gyeongjukoseu] n racecourse; 크로스컨트리 경주 [keuroseukeonteuri gyeongju] n cross-country

경찰 [gyeongchal] n cop, police; 여자 경찰관 [yeoja gyeongchalgwan] n policewoman; 경찰서 [kyungcharlsur] n police station; 경찰관 [gyeongchalgwan] n police officer, policeman; 보험 처리를 위한 경찰 보고서가 필요해요 [boheom cheorireul wihan gyeongchal bogoseoga pillyohaeyo] I need a police report for my insurance; 경찰! [gyeongchal!] Police!; 경찰서는 어디있어요? [gyeongchalseoneun eodiisseoyo?] Where is the police station?; 경찰에 신고해야 합니다 [gyeongchare singohaeya hamnida] We will have to report it to the police; 경찰을 불러 주세요 [gyeongchareul bulleo juseyo] Call the police; 경찰서를 찾아야 해요 [gyeongchalseoreul chajaya haeyo] I need to find a police station

경첩 [gyeongcheop] n hinge
경축 [gyeongchuk] 경축하다 [gyeongchukhada] v celebrate
경치 [gyeongchi] n scenery
경쾌 [gyeongkwae] 경쾌한 [gyeongkwaehan] adj sporty
경탄 [gyeongtan] 경탄하다 [gyeongtanhada] v wonder
경향 [gyeonghyang] n tendency; 경향이 있다 [gyeonghyangi itda] v tend
경험 [gyeongheom] n experience; 경험하다 [gyeongheomhada] v go through, undergo
경호 [gyeongho] 경호원 [gyeonghowon] n bodyguard, guard, security guard
경화증 [gyeonghwajeung] 다발성경화증 [dabalseonggyeonghwajeung] n multiple sclerosis, MS
곁 [gyeot] n neighbourhood;...곁에서 [...

gyeoteseo] prep by
계 [gye] 속도계 [sokdogye] n speedometer; 온도계 [ondogye] n thermometer; 태양계 [taeyanggye] n solar system
계곡 [gyegok] n ravine, valley
계급 [gyegeup] n class; 노동자 계급의 [nodongja gyegeubui] adj working-class; 중산 계급의 [jungsan gyegeubui] adj middle-class
계기판 [gyegipan] n dashboard
계단 [gyedan] n staircase ▷ npl stairs; 계단식의 [gyedansigui] adj terraced; 현관 계단 [hyeongwan gyedan] n doorstep
계란 [gyeran] n egg; 삶은 달걀 [sarmeun dalgyal] n boiled egg; 저는 생계란을 못 먹어요 [jeoneun saenggyeraneul mot meogeoyo] I can't eat raw eggs; 계란이 들어가지 않은 식사를 준비해 주시겠어요? [gyerani deureogaji anheun siksareul junbihae jusigesseoyo?] Could you prepare a meal without eggs?
계량 [gyeryang] n meter, gauge; 가스 계량기는 어디있어요? [gaseu gyeryanggineun eodiisseoyo?] Where is the gas meter?; 전기 계량기는 어디있어요? [jeongi gyeryanggineun eodiisseoyo?] Where is the electricity meter?
계산 [gyesan] n calculation; 계산대 [gyesandae] n counter, till; 계산기 [gyesangi] n calculator; 계산하다 [gyesanhada] v calculate; 휴대 계산기 [hyudae gyesangi] n pocket calculator
계산서 [gyesanseo] n bill (account); 계산서 갖다 주세요 [gyesanseo gatda juseyo] Please bring the bill; 계산서를 각자 주세요 [gyesanseoreul gakja juseyo] Separate bills, please
계속 [gyesok] 계속되다 [gyesokdoeda] vi continue; 계속하다 [gyesokhada] v carry on, go on; 계속하다 [gyesokhada] v continue
계약 [gyeyak] n contract; 임대차계약 [imdaechagyeyak] n lease; 자유계약으로 [jayugyeyageuro] adv

freelance; 자유계약의 [jayugyeyagui] *adj* freelance; 계약자 [gyeyakja] *n* contractor

계원 [gyewon] 접수계원 [jeopsugyewon] *n* receptionist

계절 [gyejeol] *n* season; 계절적인 [gyejeoljeogin] *adj* seasonal

계좌 [gyejwa] 당좌계좌 [dangjwagyejwa] *n* current account; 은행 계좌 통지서 [eunhaeng gyejwa tongjiseo] *n* bank statement; 은행계좌 [eunhaenggyejwa] *n* account (*in bank*), bank account; 공동 계좌 [gongdong gyejwa] *n* joint account; 계좌번호 [gyejwabeonho] *n* account number; 제 계좌에서 돈을 이체하고 싶어요 [je gyejwaeseo doneul ichehago sipeoyo] I would like to transfer some money from my account

계층 [gyecheung] *n* rank (*status*)

계피 [gyepi] *n* cinnamon

계획 [gyehoek] *n* plan, scheme; 도로계획 [dorogyehoek] *n* street plan; 도시계획 [dosigyehoek] *n* town planning; 배치계획 [baechigyehoek] *n* layout; 계획하다 [gyehoekhada] *v* plan

고객 [gogaek] *n* customer

고고학 [gogohak] *n* archaeology; 고고학자 [gogohakja] *n* archaeologist

고국 [goguk] *n* homeland

고글 [gogeul] *npl* goggles

고기 [gogi] *n* meat; 붉은 고기 [bulgeun gogi] *n* red meat; 돼지고기 [dwaejigogi] *n* pork; 돼지고기 토막 [dwaejigogi tomak] *n* pork chop; 송아지 고기 [songaji gogi] *n* veal; 쇠고기 [soegogi] *n* beef; 쇠고기 햄버거 [soegogi haembeogeo] *n* beefburger; 양 고기 [yang gogi] *n* mutton; 저민 고기 [jeomin gogi] *n* mince; 저는 붉은 고기를 안 먹어요 [jeoneun bulgeun gogireul an meogeoyo] I don't eat red meat; 저는 고기 안 먹어요 [jeoneun gogi an meogeoyo] I don't eat meat; 저는 고기를 좋아하지 않아요 [jeoneun gogireul johahaji anhayo] I don't like meat; 고기 / 생선이 들어가지 않은 요리는 어느 것인가요? [gogi /

saengseoni deureogaji anheun yorineun eoneu geosingayo?] Which dishes have no meat / fish?; 고기 드세요? [gogi deuseyo?] Do you eat meat?; 고기가 상했어요 [gogiga sanghaesseoyo] This meat is off; 고기가 차요 [gogiga chayo] The meat is cold

고대 [godae] 고대의 [godaeui] *adj* ancient

고도 [godo] *n* altitude

고독 [godok] *n* loneliness; 고독한 [godokhan] *adj* lonely

고등 [godeung] 고등교육 [godeunggyoyuk] *n* higher education

고등어 [godeungeo] *n* mackerel

고래 [gorae] *n* whale

고려 [goryeo] ...을 고려하면 [...eul goryeohamyeon] *prep* considering

고르다 [goreuda] *v* pick out

고름 [goreum] *n* pus

고리 [gori] *n* link; 갈고리 [galgori] *n* hook

고릴라 [gorilla] *n* gorilla

고마워하다 [gomawohada] 고마워하는 [gomawohaneun] *adj* grateful

고막 [gomak] *n* eardrum

고맙다 [gomapda] 잘 지내요, 고마워요 [jal jinaeyo, gomawoyo] Fine, thanks; 정말 고마워요 [jeongmal gomawoyo] That's very kind of you

고모 [gomo] 고모, 이모 [gomo, imo] *n* auntie; 고모,이모 [gomo,imo] *n* aunt

고무 [gomu] *n* rubber; 고무 밴드 [gomu baendeu] *n* elastic band; 고무 슬리퍼 [gomu seullipeo] *npl* flip-flops; 고무밴드 [gomubaendeu] *n* rubber band; 고무장갑 [gomujanggap] *npl* rubber gloves; 고무장화 [gomujanghwa] *npl* wellies, wellingtons

고문 [gomun] *n* torture; 고문하다 [gomunhada] *v* torture

고발 [gobal] *n* charge (*accusation*); 고발하다 [gobalhada] *v* charge (*accuse*)

고백 [gobaek] *n* confession; 고백하다 [gobaekhada] *v* confess

고삐 [goppi] *npl* reins

고사리 [gosari] n fern
고상 [gosang] 고상한 [gosanghan] adj tasteful
고소 [goso] n accusation; 고소하다 [gosohada] (법적 조치를 하다) v accuse
고속 [gosok] 고속 모터 보트 [gosok moteo boteu] n speedboat; 고속도로 [gosokdoro] n motorway
고속도로 [gosokdoro] n motorway; 이 고속도로에는 요금소가 있어요? [i gosokdoroeneun yogeumsoga isseoyo?] Is there a toll on this motorway?; 고속도로에 어떻게 갑니까? [gosokdoroe eotteoke gamnikka?] How do I get to the motorway?; 고속도로에 교통이 복잡한가요? [gosokdoroe gyotongi bokjaphangayo?] Is the traffic heavy on the motorway?
고슴도치 [goseumdochi] n hedgehog
고아 [goa] n orphan
고양이 [goyangi] n cat; 새끼고양이 [saekkigoyangi] n kitten
고요 [goyo] 고요한 [goyohan] adj calm
고용 [goyong] n employment, hire; 임시고용 [imsigoyong] n temp; 고용주 [goyongju] n employer; 고용인 [goyongin] n employee; 고용하다 [goyonghada] v employ, hire
고의 [goui] n deliberation; 고의적으로 [gouijeogeuro] adv deliberately; 고의적인 [gouijeogin] adj deliberate, intentional
고장 [gojang] n breakdown; 고장나다 [gojangnada] v break down; 고장난 [gojangnan] adj broken down; 고장 서비스를 불러 주세요 [gojang seobiseureul bulleo juseyo] Call the breakdown service, please
고전 [gojeon] n classic; 고전적인 [gojeonjeogin] adj classical
고정 [gojeong] 고정된 [gojeongdoen] adj fixed; 고정시키다 [gojeongsikida] v fix; 고정관념 [gojeonggwannyeom] n stereotype
고집 [gojip] n tantrum
고찰 [gochal] 고찰하다 [gochalhada] v look at

고체 [goche] 고체의 [gocheui] adj solid
고추냉이 [gochunaengi] n horseradish
고층 [gocheung] 고층 건물 [gocheung geonmul] n high-rise
고치다 [gochida] v mend
고통 [gotong] n agony, pain
고투 [gotu] n struggle
고함 [goham] n shout
고환 [gohwan] n testicle
곡 [gok] 교향곡 [gyohyanggok] n symphony; 곡조 [gokjo] n tune
곡괭이 [gokgwaengi] n pick
곡물 [gongmul] n grain
곡식 [goksik] n corn; 시리얼 [sirieol] n cereal
곡예 [gogye] 곡예사 [gogyesa] n acrobat
곤경 [gongyeong] n difficulty; 곤경에 빠진 [gongyeonge ppajin] adj stuck
곤란 [gollan] n trouble
곤충 [gonchung] n insect
곧 [got] adv presently, shortly, soon
골 [gol] n (골키퍼) goal; 두개골 [dugaegol] n skull; 슬개골 [seulgaegol] n kneecap; 견갑골 [gyeongapgol] n shoulder blade
골기퍼 [golgipeo] 골키퍼 [golkipeo] n goalkeeper
골동 [goldong] 골동품 [goldongpum] n antique; 골동품점 [goldongpumjeom] n antique shop
골목 [golmok] n alley; 골목길 [golmokgil] n side street
골반 [golban] n pelvis
골수 [golsu] n marrow
골절 [goljeol] n fracture
골프 [golpeu] n golf; 골프 코스 [golpeu koseu] n golf course; 골프 클럽 [golpeu keulleop] n golf club (society); 골프채 [golpeuchae] n golf club (game); 티 [ti] n tee; 어디에서 골프를 칠 수 있어요? [eodieseo golpeureul chil su isseoyo?] Where can I play golf?; 이 근처에 대중 골프장이 있나요? [i geuncheoe daejung golpeujangi innayo?] Is there a public golf course near here?; 골프채 빌려 주나요? [golpeuchae billyeo junayo?] Do they

hire out golf clubs?

곰 [gom] n bear; 북극곰 [bukgeukgom] n polar bear

곰팡이 [gompangi] n mould (fungus); 곰팡 슨 [gompang seun] adj mouldy

곱 [gop] 곱하다 [gophada] v multiply

곱셈 [gopsem] n multiplication

곱슬 [gopseul] 곱슬머리의 [gopseulmeoriui] adj curly; 곱슬곱슬한 머리칼 [gopseulgopseulhan meorikal] n curl

곱슬머리 [gopseulmeori] 저는 곱슬머리예요 [jeoneun gopseulmeoriyeyo] My hair is naturally curly

곳 [got] ...하는 곳에 [...haneun gose] conj where; 가 볼 만한 곳을 아세요? [ga bol manhan goseul aseyo?] Do you know a good place to go?

공 [gong] n ball (toy); 배드민턴 공 [baedeuminteon gong] n shuttlecock; 배관공 [baegwangong] n plumber; 작은 공 [jageun gong] n pellet

공간 [gonggan] n space

공격 [gonggyeok] n attack, knock; 공격적인 [gonggyeokjeogin] adj aggressive; 공격하다 [gonggyeokhada] n attack; 테러리스트 공격 [tereoriseuteu gonggyeok] n terrorist attack

공공 [gonggong] 공공의 [gonggongui] adj public

공급 [gonggeup] n supply; 공급자 [gonggeupja] n supplier; 공급품 [gonggeuppum] npl supplies; 공급하다 [gonggeuphada] v supply

공기 [gonggi] n air; 공기를 넣다 [gonggireul neota] v pump up; 공기를 확인해 주시겠어요? [gonggireul hwaginhae jusigesseoyo?] Can you check the air, please?

공동 [gongdong] 공동 계좌 [gongdong gyejwa] n joint account; 공동의 [gongdongui] adj joint; 공동의 [gongdongui] adj common; 공동체 [gongdongche] n community

공동소유 [gongdongsoyu] 휴가시설의 공동 소유 [hyugasiseorui gongdong soyu] n timeshare

공룡 [gongnyong] n dinosaur

공무 [gongmu] 공무원 [gongmuwon] n civil servant

공백 [gongbaek] n blank

공범 [gongbeom] n accomplice

공부 [gongbu] 공부하다 [gongbuhada] v study; 아직 공부하고 있어요 [ajik gongbuhago isseoyo] I'm still studying

공사 [gongsa] 도로 공사 [doro gongsa] npl roadworks

공산주의 [gongsanjuui] n communism; 공산주의의 [gongsanjuuiui] adj communist; 공산주의자 [gongsanjuuija] n communist

공상 [gongsang] 공상하다 [gongsanghada] v fancy

공석 [gongseok] n vacancy

공수 [gongsu] 공수병 [gongsubyeong] n rabies

공식 [gongsik] n formula; 비공식적인 [bigongsikjeogin] adj informal; 공식적인 [gongsikjeogin] adj official

공연 [gongyeon] n performance; 첫 공연 [cheot gongyeon] n premiere; 무슨 연극을 공연하나요? [museun yeongeugeul gongyeonhanayo?] What's on at the theatre?; 얼마동안 공연하나요? [eolmadongan gongyeonhanayo?] How long does the performance last?; 언제 공연이 끝나요? [eonje gongyeoni kkeutnayo?] When does the performance end?; 언제 공연이 시작해요? [eonje gongyeoni sijakhaeyo?] When does the performance begin?; 오늘 밤 콘서트 홀에서 무슨 공연이 있나요? [oneul bam konseoteu horeseo museun gongyeoni innayo?] What's on tonight at the concert hall?

공예 [gongye] n craft

공용 [gongyong] 공용 수영장은 어디있어요? [gongyong suyeongjangeun eodiisseoyo?] Where is the public swimming pool?

공원 [gongwon] n park; 국립 공원 [gungnip gongwon] n national park; 테마 공원 [tema gongwon] n theme park; **이 근처에 놀이 공원이 있어요?** [i geuncheoe nori gongwoni isseoyo?] Is there a play park near here?

공작새 [gongjaksae] n peacock

공장 [gongjang] n factory, plant (site/ equipment); **정유 공장** [jeongyu gongjang] n oil refinery; **공장에서 일해요** [gongjangeseo ilhaeyo] I work in a factory

공제 [gongje] **공제하다** [gongjehada] v deduct

공주 [gongju] n princess

공중 [gongjung] **공중 전화 박스** [gongjung jeonhwa bakseu] n call box; **공중납치하다** [gongjungnapchihada] v hijack; **공중전화** [gongjungjeonhwa] n payphone

공중전화 [gongjungjeonhwa] **카드 공중 전화** [kadeu gongjung jeonhwa] n cardphone

공책 [gongchaek] n notebook

공평 [gongpyeong] **공평한** [gongpyeonghan] adj fair (reasonable), impartial; **공평함** [gongpyeongham] n fairness

공포 [gongpo] n horror, panic; **공포 영화** [gongpo yeonghwa] n horror film; **공포증** [gongpojeung] n phobia; **공포스러운** [gongposeureoun] adj spooky; **공포에 사로잡히다** [gongpoe sarojaphida] v panic; **공포하다** [gongpohada] v issue

공포증 [gongpojeung] **밀실 공포증의** [milsil gongpojeungui] adj claustrophobic

공학 [gonghak] n engineering; **전자공학** [jeonjagonghak] npl electronics

공항 [gonghang] n airport; **공항대기실** [gonghangdaegisil] n departure lounge; **공항버스** [gonghangbeoseu] n airport bus; **공항 가는 버스가 있어요?** [gonghang ganeun beoseuga isseoyo?] Is there a bus to the airport?; **공항에 어떻게 갈 수 있을까요?** [gonghange eotteoke gal su isseulkkayo?] How do I get to the airport?; **공항까지 택시 요금이 얼마예요?** [gonghangkkaji taeksi yogeumi eolmayeyo?] How much is the taxi to the airport?

공허 [gongheo] **공허감** [gongheogam] n void

공화국 [gonghwaguk] n republic; **도미니카 공화국** [dominika gonghwaguk] n Dominican Republic; **체첸 공화국** [chechen gonghwaguk] n Chechnya; **체코 공화국** [cheko gonghwaguk] n Czech Republic

공휴일 [gonghyuil] n bank holiday, public holiday

과감 [gwagam] **과감한** [gwagamhan] adj drastic; **과감한 걸 원하지 않아요** [gwagamhan geol wonhaji anhayo] I don't want anything drastic

과거 [gwageo] n past; **과거의** [gwageoui] adj past

과다 [gwada] n overabundance; **과다 복용** [gwada bogyong] n overdose; **과다한** [gwadahan] adj redundant

과대 [gwadae] n excess, exaggeration; **과대 평가하다** [gwadae pyeonggahada] v overestimate

과도 [gwado] **과도한** [gwadohan] adj excessive

과로 [gwaro] n strain

과부 [gwabu] n widow

과소 [gwaso] **과소 평가하다** [gwaso pyeonggahada] v underestimate

과속 [gwasok] **과속 운전하고 있었어요** [gwasok unjeonhago isseosseoyo] You were driving too fast; **그 남자가 과속했어요** [geu namjaga gwasokhaesseoyo] He was driving too fast

과수 [gwasu] **과수원** [gwasuwon] n orchard

과시 [gwasi] n show-off; **과시하다** [gwasihada] v show off

과식 [gwasik] **과식하다** [gwasikhada] vi cram

과식증 [gwasikjeung] n bulimia

과열 [gwayeol] **엔진이 과열됐어요** [enjini gwayeoldwaesseoyo] The engine is overheating

과일 [gwail] n fruit (botany), fruit (collectively); **과일 주스** [gwail juseu] n fruit juice; **과일 샐러드** [gwail saelleodeu] n fruit salad

과잉 [gwaing] n redundancy

과장 [gwajang] n exaggeration; **과장하다** [gwajanghada] v exaggerate

과정 [gwajeong] n course, process; **정해진 과정** [jeonghaejin gwajeong] n routine; **교육과정** [gyoyukgwajeong] n curriculum; **훈련과정** [hullyeongwajeong] n training course

과제 [gwaje] n task

과테말라 [gwatemalla] n Guatemala

과학 [gwahag] n science; **컴퓨터 과학** [keompyuteo gwahak] n computer science; **공상과학 소설** [gongsanggwahak soseol] n science fiction, scifi; **과학자** [gwahakja] n scientist; **과학적인** [gwahakjeogin] adj scientific

관 [gwan] n coffin, tube, official; **도관** [dogwan] n pipe; **배수관** [baesugwan] n drainpipe; **배기관** [baegigwan] n exhaust pipe; **송유관** [songyugwan] n pipeline; **시험관** [siheomgwan] n examiner, test tube; **외교관** [oegyogwan] n diplomat; **경찰관** [gyeongchalgwan] n police officer, policeman

관계 [gwangye] n relation, relationship; **관계가 없는** [gwangyega eomneun] adj irrelevant; **관계가 있는** [gwangyega inneun] adj related, relevant

관광 [gwangwang] n sightseeing, tourism; **관광 안내소** [gwangwang annaeso] n visitor centre; **관광 안내원** [gwangwang annaewon] n tour guide; **관광객** [gwangwanggaek] n tourist

관광지 [gwangwangji] n (tourist) sights; **여기에는 어떤 관광지를 방문할 수 있을까요?** [yeogieneun eotteon gwangwangjireul bangmunhal su isseulkkayo?] What sights can you visit here?

관념 [gwannyeom] n 고정관념 [gojeonggwannyeom] n stereotype

관대 [gwandae] n generosity, hospitality; **관대한** [gwandaehan] adj tolerant

관련 [gwallyeon] n regard

관료 [gwallyo] n 관료주의 [gwallyojuui] n bureaucracy

관리 [gwalli] n management, mandarin (official); **여성관리자** [yeoseonggwallija] n manageress; **관리인** [gwalliin] n caretaker, warden; **관리자** [gwallija] n manager; **관리자** [gwallija] n director; **관리하다** [gwallihada] v manage; **관리할 수 있는** [gwallihal su inneun] adj manageable

관목 [gwanmok] n bush (shrub), shrub

관세 [gwanse] n tariff ▷ npl customs, (customs) duty; **세관원** [segwanwon] n customs officer; **관습에 얽매이지 않는** [gwanseube eorngmaeiji annneun] adj unconventional; **관세를 내야 합니까?** [gwansereul naeya hamnikka?] Do I have to pay duty on this?

관습 [gwanseup] n custom ▷ npl manners

관심 [gwansim] n interest (curiosity); **미안하지만, 관심없어요** [mianhajiman, gwansimeopseoyo] Sorry, I'm not interested

관악 [gwanak] n 관악대 [gwanakdae] n brass band

관용 [gwanyong] n tolerance; **관용성이 없는** [gwanyongseongi eomneun] adj intolerant

관용구 [gwanyonggu] n idiom; **관용구 숙어집** [gwanyonggu sugeojip] n phrasebook

관절 [gwanjeol] n 관절염 [gwanjeollyeom] n arthritis

관절염 [gwanjeollyeom] n 관절염이 있어요 [gwanjeollyeomi isseoyo] I suffer from arthritis

관점 [gwanjeom] n standpoint, viewpoint

관제 [gwanje] n control; **등화관제** [deunghwagwanje] n blackout; **항공 관제사** [hanggong gwanjesa] n air-traffic controller

관중 [gwanjung] n spectator

관찰 [gwanchal] n 관찰자 [gwanchalja] n observer; **관찰하다** [gwanchalhada] v observe

관측 [gwancheuk] 관측소
[gwancheukso] n observatory

관하여 [gwanhayeo]...에 관하여 [...e
gwanhayeo] prep concerning

관해 [gwanhae]...에 관하여 [...e
gwanhayeo] prep regarding

관현 [gwanhyeon] 관현악단
[gwanhyeonakdan] n orchestra

괄호 [gwalho] npl brackets

광 [gwang] 광산 [gwangsan] n mine

광고 [gwanggo] abbr ad ▷ n advert,
advertisement, advertising,
commercial, commercial break;
광고하다 [gwanggohada] v advertise;
항목별 광고 [hangmokbyeol gwanggo]
npl small ads

광대 [gwangdae] n performer, vastness;
어릿광대 [eoritgwangdae] n clown;
광대역 [gwangdaeyeok] n broadband;
광대한 [gwangdaehan] adj extensive

광물 [gwangmul] 광물성의
[gwangmulseongui] adj mineral

광부 [gwangbu] n miner

광신 [gwangsin] 광신자 [gwangsinja] n
fanatic

광택 [gwangtaek] n gloss; 구두광택제
[gudugwangtaekje] n shoe polish;
광택제 [gwangtaekje] n polish; 사진을
무광택지로 뽑고 싶어요 [sajineul
mugwangtaekjiro ppopgo sipeoyo] I'd
like the photos matt

광택지 [gwangtaekji] 사진을 광택지로
뽑고 싶어요 [sajineul gwangtaekjiro
ppopgo sipeoyo] I'd like the photos
glossy

괜찮다 [gwaenchanta] 괜찮은
[gwaenchanheun] adj okay; 괜찮아요
[gwaenchanhayo] I don't mind, It doesn't
matter, No problem; 괜찮으세요?
[gwaenchanheuseyo?] Are you alright?;
괜찮겠어요? [gwaenchankesseoyo?] Do
you mind?

괴롭다 [goeropda] 괴로워하다
[goerowohada] v suffer

괴롭히다 [goerophida] v bother, pester,
pick on, spite; 괴롭힘 [goerophim] n
harassment

괴물 [goemul] n monster

괴짜 [goejja] n nutter

굉장 [goengjang] 굉장히 좋은
[goengjanghi joheun] adj fabulous

굉장한 [goengjanghan] adj terrific

교감 [gyogam] n deputy head

교과 [gyogwa] 교과서 [gyogwaseo] n
textbook

교과서 [gyogwaseo] n schoolbook

교구 [gyogu] n parish; 교구 목사 [gyogu
moksa] n vicar

교대 [gyodae] 교대로 [gyodaero] adv
alternatively; 교대조 [gyodaejo] n
relay; 교대의 [gyodaeui] adj alternate

교도 [gyodo] 교도관 [gyodogwan] n
prison officer

교도소 [gyodoso] n prison

교복 [gyobok] n school uniform

교사 [gyosa] n schoolteacher, teacher;
보조 교사 [bojo gyosa] n classroom
assistant; 임시교사 [imsigyosa] n
supply teacher; 가정교사
[gajeonggyosa] n tutor; 교사입니다
[gyosaimnida] I'm a teacher

교수 [gyosu] n professor

교습 [gyoseup] 운전 교습 [unjeon
gyoseup] n driving lesson

교신 [gyosin] n correspondence

교실 [gyosil] n classroom

교역 [gyoyeok] n transaction

교외 [gyooe] n suburb; 교외의 [gyooeui]
adj suburban

교육 [gyoyuk] n education; 성인 교육
[seongin gyoyuk] n adult education,
further education; 재교육 강습
[jaegyoyuk gangseup] n refresher
course; 교육받은 [gyoyukbadeun] adj
educated; 교육의 [gyoyugui] adj
educational; 교육과정
[gyoyukgwajeong] n curriculum;
교육하다 [gyoyukhada] v instruct;
고등교육 [godeunggyoyuk] n higher
education

교장 [gyojang] n headteacher, principal

교정 [gyojeong] n campus, proof (for
checking), revision

교차 [gyocha] v crossing; 순환교차로
[sunhwangyocharo] n roundabout;

교차로 [gyocharo] *n* junction; 교차된 [gyochadoen] *adj* cross; 교차시키다 [gyochasikida] *n* cross

교체 [gyoche] *n* replacement

교통 [gyotong] *n* traffic; 대중교통수단 [daejunggyotongsudan] *n* public transport; 교통마비 [gyotongmabi] *n* traffic jam; 교통신호등 [gyotongsinhodeung] *npl* traffic lights; 교통감시관 [gyotonggamsigwan] *n* traffic warden; 교통규칙집 [gyotonggyuchikjip] *n* Highway Code; 고속도로에 교통이 복잡한가요? [gosokdoroe gyotongi bokjaphangayo?] Is the traffic heavy on the motorway?

교향 [gyohyang] 교향곡 [gyohyanggok] *n* symphony

교환 [gyohwan] 교환하다 [gyohwanhada] *v* exchange, switch; 이것을 교환하고 싶어요 [igeoseul gyohwanhago sipeoyo] I'd like to exchange this

교환대 [gyohwandae] 전화교환대 [jeonhwagyohwandae] *n* switchboard

교활 [gyohwal] 교활한 [gyohwalhan] *adj* cunning, sly; 교활해 보이는 [gyohwalhae boineun] *adj* shifty

교황 [gyohwang] *n* pope

교회 [gyohoe] *n* church; 교회를 방문할 수 있어요? [gyohoereul bangmunhal su isseoyo?] Can we visit the church?

구 [gu] *num* nine ▷ *n* globe, limb; 선거구 [seongeogu] *n* constituency; 개찰구 [gaechalgu] *n* ticket barrier

구강 [gugang] 구강청결제 [gugangcheonggyeolje] *n* mouthwash

구걸 [gugeol] 구걸하다 [gugeolhada] *v* beg

구경 [gugyeong] 아파트를 구경시켜 주시겠어요? [apateureul gugyeongsikyeo jusigesseoyo?] Could you show us around the apartment?; 구경시켜 주시겠어요? [gugyeongsikyeo jusigesseoyo?] Could you show us around?

구글 [gugeul] *v* Google®

구급 [gugeup] 구급상자 [gugeupsangja] *n* first-aid kit; 구급차 [gugeupcha] *n* ambulance; 구급차를 불러 주세요 [gugeupchareul bulleo juseyo] Call an ambulance

구더기 [gudeogi] *n* maggot

구독 [gudok] *n* subscription; 정기구독 [jeonggigudok] *n* standing order

구동 [gudong] 사륜구동 [saryungudong] *n* four-wheel drive

구두 [gudu] *n* shoe; 구두끈 [gudukkeun] *n* shoelace; 구두법 [gudubeop] *n* punctuation; 구두의 [guduui] *adj* oral; 구두가게 [gudugage] *n* shoe shop; 구두광택제 [gudugwangtaekje] *n* shoe polish

구두쇠 [gudusoe] *n* miser

구류 [guryu] *n* detention

구르다 [gureuda] *vi* roll; 구르기 [gureugi] *n* roll

구름 [gureum] *n* cloud

구리 [guri] *n* copper

구매 [gumae] 구매자 [gumaeja] *n* buyer

구멍 [gumeong] *n* aperture, hole, puncture; 목구멍 [mokgumeong] *n* throat; 동전 구멍 [dongjeon gumeong] *n* slot; 구멍뚫다 [gumeongttulta] *v* pierce; 구멍을 뚫다 [gumeongeul ttulta] *v* bore *(drill)*; 구멍을 뚫다 [gumeongeul ttulta] *v* drill; 구멍을 뚫은 [gumeongeul ttureun] *adj* pierced; 팬 구멍 [paen gumeong] *n* pothole; 신발에 구멍이 났어요 [sinbare gumeongi nasseoyo] I have a hole in my shoe

구명 [gumyeong] 구명띠 [gumyeongtti] *n* lifebelt; 구명조끼 [gumyeongjokki] *n* life jacket; 구명의 [gumyeongui] *adj* life-saving; 구명정 [gumyeongjeong] *n* lifeboat; 구명보트를 불러요! [gumyeongboteureul bulleoyo!] Call out the lifeboat!

구별 [gubyeol] *n* distinction; 구별하다 [gubyeolhada] *v* distinguish

구보 [gubo] *adj* double-quick; 느린 구보로 달리다 [neurin guboro dallida] *v* canter

구부러지다 [gubureojida] *v* bend, curve, flex; 구부러지지 않는 [gubureojiji annneun] *adj* inflexible

구부리다 [guburida] *v* bend, stoop; **구부릴 수 있는** [guburil su inneun] *adj* flexible

구성 [guseong] *n* composition; **재구성하다** [jaeguseonghada] *v* restructure; **구성되다** [guseongdoeda] *v* consist of; **구성하다** [guseonghada] *v* make up; **구성하고 있는** [guseonghago inneun] *adj* component

구술 [gusul] *n* dictation; **구술시험** [gusulsiheom] *n* oral exam

구슬 [guseul] *n* bead

구식 [gusik] **구식의** [gusigui] *adj* naff, old-fashioned; **구식인** [gusigin] *adj* out-of-date

구역 [guyeok] *n* area; **보행자 전용 구역** [bohaengja jeonyong guyeok] *n* pedestrian precinct; **서비스 구역** [seobiseu guyeok] *n* service area; **작업구역** [jageopguyeok] *n* workstation; **행정 구역** [haengjeong guyeok] *n* ward (area); **금연 구역이 있나요?** [geumyeon guyeogi innayo?] Is there a non-smoking area?

구역질 [guyeokjil] *n* nausea; **구역질나는** [guyeokjillaneun] *adj* disgusting

구입 [guip] **구입한** [guiphan] *adj* bought

구조 [gujo] *n* rescue, structure; **구조하다** [gujohada] *v* rescue

구조대 [gujodae] **가장 가까운 산악 구조대는 어디 있어요?** [gajang gakkaun sanak gujodaeneun eodi isseoyo?] Where is the nearest mountain rescue service post?

구조원 [gujowon] **인명 구조원** [inmyeong gujowon] *n* lifeguard; **구조원을 데려와요!** [gujowoneul deryeowayo!] Get the lifeguard!; **구조원이 있어요?** [gujowoni isseoyo?] Is there a lifeguard?

구직 [gujik] **구직센터** [gujiksenteo] *n* job centre

구체 [guche] *n* sphere; **구체적으로** [guchejeogeuro] *adv* specifically; **구체적인** [guchejeogin] *adj* specific

구충 [guchung] **구충제** [guchungje] *n* insect repellent

구토 [guto] **구토하다** [gutohada] *v* vomit

구하다 [guhada] **구해주다** [guhaejuda] *v* save

국 [guk] *n* bureau, office; **우체국** [ucheguk] *n* post office

국가 [gukga] *n* anthem, country; **애국가** [aegukga] *n* national anthem; **국립 공원** [gungnip gongwon] *n* national park; **국수주의** [guksujuui] *n* nationalism; **국수주의자** [guksujuuija] *n* nationalist; **개발도상국** [gaebaldosangguk] *n* developing country

국가번호 [gukgabeonho] *n* dialling code; **영국 국가번호는 어떻게 되나요?** [yeongguk gukgabeonhoneun eotteoke doenayo?] What is the dialling code for the UK?

국경 [gukgyeong] *n* frontier

국내 [gungnae] **국내의** [gungnaeui] *adj* domestic

국번 [gukbeon] *n* dialling code

국소 [gukso] **국소마취** [guksomachwi] *n* local anaesthetic; **국소적인** [guksojeogin] *adj* local

국수 [guksu] *npl* noodles

국외 [gugoe] *adv* abroad; **국외로 추방하다** [gugoero chubanghada] *v* deport

국유 [gugyu] **국유화하다** [gugyuhwahada] *v* nationalize

국자 [gukja] *n* ladle

국자가리비 [gukjagaribi] *n* scallop

국적 [gukjeok] *n* nationality

국제 [gukje] **국제연합** [gukjeyeonhap] *n* United Nations; **국제연합** [gukjeyeonhap] *n* UN; **국제적인** [gukjejeogin] *adj* international; **어디에서 국제 전화를 할 수 있나요?** [eodieseo gukje jeonhwareul hal su innayo?] Where can I make an international phone call?; **여기에서 국제 전화를 해도 될까요?** [yeogieseo gukje jeonhwareul haedo doelkkayo?] Can I phone internationally from here?; **국제 전화카드 주세요** [gukje jeonhwakadeu juseyo] An international phone card, please; **국제 전화카드 파세요?** [gukje jeonhwakadeu paseyo?] Do you sell international phone cards?

국화 [gukhwa] n chrysanthemum

국회 [gukhoe] n parliament

군 [gun] n army; **공군** [gonggun] n Air Force

군대 [gundae] n army ▷ npl troops; **군대의** [gundaeui] adj military

군인 [gunin] n serviceman, soldier; **여군** [yeogun] n servicewoman

군주 [gunju] n monarch; **군주제** [gunjuje] n monarchy

군중 [gunjung] n crowd

굳도리널 [gutdorineol] n skirting board

굴 [gul] n oyster

굴뚝 [gulttuk] n chimney

굴림대 [gullimdae] n roller

굴복 [gulbok] **굴복하다** [gulbokhada] v kneel down

굴착 [gulchak] **굴착장치** [gulchakjangchi] n rig

굴착기 [gulchakgi] n excavator, digger; **유정의 굴착장치** [yujeongui gulchakjangchi] n oil rig

굵기 [gurkgi] **긁기** [geurkgi] n scratch

굶다 [gurmda] **굶어죽다** [gurmeojukda] v starve

굶주리다 [gurmjurida] **몹시 굶주린** [mopsi gurmjurin] adj ravenous; **굶주림** [gurmjurim] n hunger

굽다 [gupda] v bake; **구운** [guun] adj baked, roast; **굽은** [gubeun] adj bent (not straight); **굽은 부분** [gubeun bubun] n bend; **굽이치는** [gubichineun] adj wavy; **굽기** [gupgi] (요리) n baking; **그릴에 굽다** [geurire gupda] v grill

굽이 [gubi] n sinus

굽히다 [guphida] v bend, bend down, bend over; **앞으로 굽히다** [apeuro guphida] v lean forward

궁 [gung] n palace; **이 궁은 언제 열어요?** [i gungeun eonje yeoreoyo?] When is the palace open?; **이 궁은 일반인에게 개방되나요?** [i gungeun ilbaninege gaebangdoenayo?] Is the palace open

to the public?

궁도 [gungdo] **12궁도** [sibi gungdo] n zodiac

궁리 [gungni] **궁리하다** [gungnihada] v devise

궁수 [gungsu] **궁수자리** [gungsujari] n Sagittarius

궁전 [gungjeon] n palace

궁지 [gungji] n dead end, stalemate

권 [gwon] n circle, ticket; **북극권** [bukgeukgwon] n Arctic Circle; **대기 항공권** [daegi hanggonggwon] n stand-by ticket; **상품권** [sangpumgwon] n voucher; **탑승권** [tapseunggwon] n boarding card, boarding pass; **통행우선권** [tonghaenguseongwon] n right of way

권리 [gwolli] n right; **인권** [ingwon] npl human rights

권총 [gwonchong] n pistol; **회전식 연발 권총** [hoejeonsik yeonbal gwonchong] n revolver

권투 [gwontu] n boxing; **권투 선수** [gwontu seonsu] n boxer

권하다 [gwonhada] v rope in

권한 [gwonhan] n power; **권한을 주다** [gwonhaneul juda] v authorize

궤양 [gweyang] n ulcer

귀 [gwi] n ear; **귀마개** [gwimagae] npl earplugs; **귀앓이** [gwiari] n earache; **귀청이 터질 것 같은** [gwicheongi teojil geot gateun] adj deafening; **귀고리** [gwigori] n earring; **귀가 들리지 않는** [gwiga deulliji annneun] adj deaf; **흡혈귀** [heuphyeolgwi] n vampire

귀기울이다 [gwigiurida] **귀를 기울이다** [gwireul giurida] v listen to

귀뚜라미 [gwitturami] n cricket (insect)

귀리 [gwiri] npl oats

귀엽다 [gwiyeopda] **귀여운** [gwiyeoun] adj cute

귀중 [gwijung] **귀중품** [gwijungpum] npl valuables; **귀중품은 어디에 놓을 수 있을까요?** [gwijungpumeun eodie noheul su isseulkkayo?] Where can I leave my valuables?; **귀중품을 금고에 넣고 싶어요** [gwijungpumeul geumgoe neoko sipeoyo] I'd like to put my valuables in the safe

귀찮다 [gwichanta] 귀찮은 [gwichanheun] adj annoying; 귀찮게 하다 [gwichanke hada] v annoy

귀환 [gwihwan] n return (coming back)

규율 [gyuyul] n discipline

규정 [gyujeong] n regulation; 죄송합니다만, 제가 규정을 몰랐어요 [joesonghamnidaman, jega gyujeongeul mollasseoyo] I'm very sorry, I didn't know the regulations

규칙 [gyuchik] n rule; 불규칙한 [bulgyuchikhan] adj irregular; 교통규칙집 [gyotonggyuchikjip] n Highway Code; 규칙적으로 [gyuchikjeogeuro] adv regularly; 규칙적인 [gyuchikjeogin] adj regular

균열 [gyunyeol] n crack (fracture)

균형 [gyunhyeong] n balance; 균형 잡힌 [gyunhyeong japhin] adj balanced

귤 [gyul] n mandarin (fruit)

그 [geu] adj that ▷ art the; 그들 [geudeul] pron they

그것 [geugeot] pron it; 그것 자체 [geugeot jache] pron itself; 그것들 [geugeotdeul] pron those; 그것들의 [geugeotdeurui] adj those; 그것의 [geugeosui] adj its

그늘 [geuneul] n shade; 그늘지게 하다 [geuneuljige hada] v screen (off)

그들 [geudeul] 그들 자신 [geudeul jasin] pron themselves; 그들을 [geudeureul] pron them; 그들의 [geudeurui] adj their; 그들의 것 [geudeurui geot] pron theirs

그래프 [geuraepeu] n graph

그램 [geuraem] n gramme

그러나 [geureona] adv however ▷ conj but

그러므로 [geureomeuro] adv therefore

그럭저럭 [geureokjeoreok] adv so-so

그런 [geureon] adj such

그렇게 [geureoke] adv so, such

그렇지만 [geureochiman] adv though

그렇지 않다 [geureochi anta] 그렇지 않으면 [geureochi anheumyeon] adv otherwise

그레이비 [geureibi] n gravy

그레이프프루트 [geureipeupeuruteu] n grapefruit

그루지아 [geurujia] 그루지야 [geurujiya] n Georgia (country); 그루지야 사람 [geurujiya saram] n Georgian (inhabitant of Georgia); 그루지야의 [geurujiyaui] adj Georgian

그릇 [geureut] n bowl; 달걀 그릇 [dalgyal geureut] n eggcup

그릇되다 [geureutdoeda] 그릇된 [geureutdoen] adj false

그리고 [geurigo] conj and

그리다 [geurida] vt paint

그리스 [geuriseu] n Greece; 그리스 사람 [geuriseu saram] n Greek (person); 그리스어 [geuriseueo] n Greek (language); 그리스의 [geuriseuui] adj Greek

그리스도 [geuriseudo] n Christ

그리워하다 [geuriwohada] 몹시 그리워하다 [mopsi geuriwohada] v long

그린란드 [geurillandeu] n Greenland

그릴 [geuril] n grill; 그릴에 구운 [geurire guun] adj grilled; 그릴에 굽다 [geurire gupda] v grill

그림 [geurim] n diagram, drawing, painting, picture; 그림붓 [geurimbut] n paintbrush; 그림같은 [geurimgateun] adj picturesque; 그림틀 [geurimteul] n picture frame

그림자 [geurimja] n shadow

그만두다 [geumanduda] vt quit, stop

그저께 [geujeokke] the day before yesterday

극 [geuk] n drama; 북극 [bukgeuk] n Arctic, the Arctic; 남극 [namgeuk] n South Pole, the Antarctic, Antarctica; 남극 대륙 [namgeuk daeryuk] n Antarctic; 연속극 [yeonsokgeuk] n soap opera; 극의 [geugui] adj polar

극단 [geukdan] 극단주의 [geukdanjuui] n extremism; 극단주의자 [geukdanjuuija] n extremist

극도 [geukdo] 극도로 [geukdoro] adv extremely; 극도의 [geukdoui] adj extreme

극복 [geukbok] 극복하다 [geukbokhada]

v overcome

극작가 [geukjakga] n playwright

극장 [geukjang] n theatre

극적 [geukjeok] 극적인 [geukjeogin] *adj* dramatic

극찬 [geukchan] n rave

근거리 [geungeori] 근거리 왕복 [geungeori wangbok] n shuttle

근무 [geunmu] 근무 시간 [geunmu sigan] *npl* office hours; 탄력근무제 [tallyeokgeunmuje] n flexitime

근본 [geunbon] 근본적인 [geunbonjeogin] *adj* essential

근시 [geunsi] 근시의 [geunsiui] *adj* near-sighted, short-sighted; 제 눈은 근시입니다 [je nuneun geunsiimnida] I'm short-sighted

근원 [geunwon] n origin

근육 [geunyuk] n muscle; 근육이 발달한 [geunyugi baldalhan] *adj* muscular

근접 [geunjeop] n proximity; 근접한 [geunjeophan] *prep* near

근처 [geuncheo] n vicinity; 근처에 [geuncheoe] *adv* nearby; 근처의 [geuncheoui] *adj* nearby

근친 [geunchin] 근친자 [geunchinja] n next-of-kin

글라이더 [geullaideo] n glider

글루코오스 [geullukooseu] n glucose

글루텐 [geulluten] n gluten; 글루텐이 없는 요리 있어요? [geulluteni eomneun yori isseoyo?] Do you have gluten-free dishes?

글자 [geulja] n letter (*a, b, c*); 머리글자 [meorigeulja] *npl* initials; 글자 그대로 [geulja geudaero] *adv* literally

긁다 [geurkda] v scratch

긇다 [geurta] 끓어 넘치다 [kkeureo neomchida] v boil over

금 [geum] n gold; 대출금 [daechulgeum] n loan; 장학금 [janghakgeum] n scholarship; 금도금한 [geumdogeumhan] *adj* gold-plated; 금색의 [geumsaegui] *adj* golden; 금이 가다 [geumi gada] vi crack

금간 [geumgan] 금이 간 [geumi gan] *adj* cracked

금고 [geumgo] n safe; 제 장신구를 금고에 넣고 싶어요 [je jangsingureul geumgoe neoko sipeoyo] I would like to put my jewellery in the safe; 귀중품을 금고에 넣고 싶어요 [gwijungpumeul geumgoe neoko sipeoyo] I'd like to put my valuables in the safe; 금고에 넣어 주세요 [geumgoe neoheo juseyo] Put that in the safe, please; 금고에 넣어둔 것이 있어요 [geumgoe neoheodun geosi isseoyo] I have some things in the safe

금기 [geumgi] n taboo

금리 [geumni] n interest rate

금발 [geumbal] 금발인 [geumbarin] *adj* blonde; 저는 금발머리예요 [jeoneun geumbalmeoriyeyo] My hair is naturally blonde

금붕어 [geumbungeo] n goldfish

금속 [geumsok] n metal; 장식용 금속 조각 [jangsigyong geumsok jogak] n tinsel

금연 [geumyeon] 금연 구역이 있나요? [geumyeon guyeogi innayo?] Is there a non-smoking area?; 금연실 좌석을 예약하고 싶어요 [geumyeonsil jwaseogeul yeyakhago sipeoyo] I want to book a seat in a non-smoking compartment; 금연실이 좋겠어요 [geumyeonsiri jokesseoyo] I'd like a no smoking room

금연석 [geumyeonseok] 금연석으로 주세요 [geumyeonseogeuro juseyo] I'd like a non-smoking seat; 금연석이요 [geumyeonseogiyo] Non-smoking, please

금요일 [geumyoil] n Friday; 금요일에 [geumyoire] on Friday; 십이월 삼십일일 금요일에 [sibiwol samsibiril geumyoire] on Friday the thirty first of December

금융 [geumyung] n finance

금잔화 [geumjanhwa] n marigold

금전 [geumjeon] n money; 금전 출납기 [geumjeon chullapgi] n cash register

금주 [geumju] n abstinence; 절대 금주의 [jeoldae geumjuui] *adj* teetotal

금지 [geumji] n ban; 이륙을 금지하다 [iryugeul geumjihada] v ground;

금지된 [geumjidoen] adj banned, forbidden, prohibited, taboo; 금지하다 [geumjihada] v ban, prohibit; 금하다 [geumhada] v forbid

급 [geup] 급히 [geuphi] adv hastily; 급해요 [geuphaeyo] I'm in a hurry

급습 [geupseup] n raid; 급습하다 [geupseuphada] v raid

급여 [geubyeo] 병가 중 지급되는 급여 [byeongga jung jigeupdoeneun geubyeo] n sick pay

긍지 [geungji] n pride

기 [gi] 보청기 [bocheonggi] n hearing aid; 비성수기 [biseongsugi] n low season; 녹음기 [nogeumgi] n tape recorder; 방열기 [bangyeolgi] n radiator; 주사기 [jusagi] n syringe; 살수기 [salsugi] n sprinkler; 선풍기 [seonpunggi] n fan; 세탁기 [setakgi] n washing machine; 수증기 [sujeunggi] n steam; 압축기 [apchukgi] v press; 인쇄기 [inswaegi] n printer (machine); 자동 매표기 [jadong maepyogi] n ticket machine; 제설기 [jeseolgi] n snowplough; 청소기 [cheongsogi] n Hoover®; 건조기 [geonjogi] n dryer; 굴착기 [gulchakgi] n digger; 공기압축기 [gonggiapchukgi] n pneumatic drill; 기화기 [gihwagi] n carburettor; 타자기 [tajagi] n typewriter; 확성기 [hwakseonggi] n loudspeaker; 휴대 계산기 [hyudae gyesangi] n pocket calculator; 사용할 수 있는 팩스기가 있나요? [sayonghal su inneun paekseugiga innayo?] Is there a fax machine I can use?

기각 [gigak] 기각하다 [gigakhada] v overrule

기간 [gigan] n duration, period, session, spell (time); 시용기간 [siyonggigan] n trial period

기계 [gigye] n machine; 기계류 [gigyeryu] n machinery; 기계적인 [gigyejeogin] adj mechanical; 기계공 [gigyegong] n mechanic; 풀베는 기계 [pulbeneun gigye] n mower

기관 [gigwan] n institution, organ (body part); 디젤기관 [dijelgigwan] n diesel

기관지 [gigwanji] 기관지염 [gigwanjiyeom] n bronchitis

기구 [gigu] n apparatus, appliance; 북대서양조약기구 [bukdaeseoyangjoyakgigu] abbr NATO; 요리 기구 [yori gigu] n cooker

기근 [gigeun] n famine

기꺼이 [gikkeoi] adv willingly

기념 [ginyeom] n commemoration; 기념비 [ginyeombi] n monument; 기념물 [ginyeommul] n memorial; 기념품 [ginyeompum] n memento, souvenir

기념일 [ginyeomil] n anniversary; 결혼기념일 [gyeolhonginyeomil] n wedding anniversary

기념품 [ginyeompum] 기념품 있어요? [ginyeompum isseoyo?] Do you have souvenirs?

기니 [gini] n Guinea; 적도 기니 [jeokdo gini] n Equatorial Guinea

기니피그 [ginipigeu] n guinea pig (rodent)

기다 [gida] v crawl

기다리다 [gidarida] v hang on, wait for, wait; 아주 오래 기다렸어요 [aju orae gidaryeosseoyo] We've been waiting for a very long time; 여기서 몇 분만 기다려 주시겠어요? [yeogiseo myeot bunman gidaryeo jusigesseoyo?] Can you wait here for a few minutes?; 기다리는 동안 해 주실 수 있어요? [gidarineun dongan hae jusil su isseoyo?] Can you do it while I wait?; 기다려 주세요 [gidaryeo juseyo] Please wait for me

기대 [gidae] n expectation, hope; 기대하다 [gidaehada] v expect

기대다 [gidaeda] v lean

기도 [gido] n prayer; 기도하다 [gidohada] v pray

기독교 [gidokgyo] 기독교 신앙 [gidokgyo sinang] n Christianity; 기독교도 [gidokgyodo] n Christian; 기독교의 [gidokgyoui] adj Christian

기둥 [gidung] n column, mast, pillar, post (stake); 가로등 기둥 [garodeung gidung] n lamppost

기록 [girok] n record; CD 기록 장치 [CD girok jangchi] n CD burner; DVD 기록 장치 [DVD girok jangchi] n DVD burner; 기록 보관소 [girok bogwanso] n archive; 기록자 [girokja] n recorder (scribe); 기록하다 [girokhada] v record

기류 [giryu] 난기류 [nangiryu] n turbulence

기르기스탄 [gireugiseutan] 키르기스스탄 [kireugiseuseutan] n Kyrgyzstan

기르다 [gireuda] vt grow

기름 [gireum] n grease, oil; 물 위의 기름층 [mul wiui gireumcheung] n oil slick; 등유 [deungyu] n kerosene; 유정 [yujeong] n oil well; 기름에 튀기다 [gireume twigida] v deep-fry; 기름을 바르다 [gireumeul bareuda] v oil; 기름투성이의 [gireumtuseongiui] adj greasy; 이 얼룩은 기름이에요 [i eollugeun gireumieyo] This stain is oil

기린 [girin] n giraffe

기묘 [gimyo] 기묘한 [gimyohan] adj quaint

기밀 [gimil] 기밀의 [gimirui] adj confidential

기반 [giban] 기반시설 [gibansiseol] n infrastructure

기법 [gibeop] n technique

기본 [gibon] 기본 원리 [gibon wolli] npl basics; 기본의 [gibonui] adj basic; 기본적으로 [gibonjeogeuro] adv basically

기분 [gibun] n mood, temper ▷ npl spirits; 기분이 상한 [gibuni sanghan] adj bad-tempered

기뻐하다 [gippeohada] 기뻐하는 [gippeohaneun] adj pleased

기쁘다 [gippeuda] 기쁜 [gippeun] adj glad; 마침내 뵙게 되어 기쁩니다 [machimnae boepge doeeo gippeumnida] I'm delighted to meet you at last

기쁨 [gippeum] n delight, joy, pleasure; 매우 기쁜 [maeu gippeun] adj delightful; 아주 기뻐하는 [aju gippeohaneun] adj delighted

기사 [gisa] n article; 사망기사

[samanggisa] n obituary; 전기 기사 [jeongi gisa] n electrician

기소 [giso] 기소하다 [gisohada] v prosecute

기수 [gisu] 경마기수 [gyeongmagisu] n jockey

기숙 [gisuk] 기숙생 [gisuksaeng] n boarder; 기숙학교 [gisukhakgyo] n boarding school

기숙사 [gisuksa] n dormitory

기술 [gisul] n technology; 정보기술 [jeongbogisul] abbr IT; 기술자 [gisulja] n engineer, technician; 기술적인 [gisuljeogin] adj technical; 기술학상의 [gisulhaksangui] adj technological

기어 [gieo] n gear (mechanism)

기억 [gieok] n memory; 기억하다 [gieokhada] v remember

기업 [gieop] n corporation; 다국적 기업 [dagukjeok gieop] n multinational

기여 [giyeo] n contribution; 기여하다 [giyeohada] v contribute

기운 [giun] n strength; 기운을 잃게 하는 [giuneul irke haneun] adj depressing; 기운이 없는 [giuni eomneun] adj depressed

기울이다 [giurida] vt tip (incline)

기원 [giwon] 기원전 [giwonjeon] abbr BC

기인 [giin] 기인하다 [giinhada] v result in

기입 [giip] n entry; 차변에 기입하다 [chabyeone giiphada] v debit

기자 [gija] n reporter; 기자회견 [gijahoegyeon] n press conference

기재 [gijae] n statement, registration; 목록에 기재하다 [mongnoge gijaehada] v list; 기재하다 [gijaehada] v write down

기저귀 [gijeogwi] n nappy

기적 [gijeok] n miracle

기절 [gijeol] 기절하다 [gijeolhada] v faint

기준 [gijun] n criterion

기중기 [gijunggi] n crane (for lifting)

기증 [gijeung] 기증자 [gijeungja] n donor; 기증하다 [gijeunghada] v donate

기차 [gicha] n train;... 가는 다음 기차는 언제 있어요? [... ganeun daeum gichaneun eonje isseoyo?] When is the next train to...?;... 가는 마지막 기차는 언제 있어요? [... ganeun majimak gichaneun eonje isseoyo?] When is the last train to...?;... 가는 첫 기차는 언제 있어요? [... ganeun cheot gichaneun eonje isseoyo?] When is the first train to...?;... 가는 기차 시간표는 어떻게 되나요? [... ganeun gicha siganpyoneun eotteoke doenayo?] What times are the trains to...?;... 가는 기차는 몇 시에 있어요? [... ganeun gichaneun myeot sie isseoyo?] What time is the train to...?;... 가는 기차는 얼마나 자주 있어요? [... ganeun gichaneun eolmana jaju isseoyo?] How frequent are the trains to...?; 여기가... 가는 기차 승강장 맞아요? [yeogiga... ganeun gicha seunggangjang majayo?] Is this the right platform for the train to...?; 이게...행 기차인가요? [ige...haeng gichaingayo?] Is this the train for...?; 직행 기차인가요? [jikhaeng gichaingayo?] Is it a direct train?; 기차는 몇 시에... 도착해요? [gichaneun myeot sie... dochakhaeyo?] What time does the train arrive in...?; 기차는 몇 시에 떠나요? [gichaneun myeot sie tteonayo?] What time does the train leave?; 기차는 어느 승강장에서 떠나요? [gichaneun eoneu seunggangjangeseo tteonayo?] Which platform does the train leave from?; 기차는 언제 도착해요? [gichaneun eonje dochakhaeyo?] When is the train due?; 기차에 식당칸이 있어요? [gichae sikdangkani isseoyo?] Is there a buffet car on the train?; 기차가 10분 연착되고 있어요 [gichaga 10bun yeonchakdoego isseoyo] The train is running ten minutes late; 기차는... 에서 서나요? [gichaga...eseo seonayo?] Does the train stop at...?; 기차가 연착되고 있어요? [gichaga yeonchakdoego isseoyo?] Is the train running late?; 기차가 제 시간에 있어요? [gichaga je sigane isseoyo?] Is the train on time?;...행 기차는 어느 승강장에서 떠나요? [...haeng gichaneun eoneu seunggangjangeseo tteonayo?] Which platform does the train for... leave from?

기차역 [gichayeok] n train station; 기차역에 가는 가장 좋은 방법은 무엇인가요? [gichayeoge ganeun gajang joheun bangbeobeun mueosingayo?] What's the best way to get to the railway station?

기침 [gichim] n cough; 기침약 [gichimyak] n cough mixture; 기침하다 [gichimhada] vi cough; 기침이 나요 [gichimi nayo] I have a cough

기타 [gita] n guitar

기화 [gihwa] 기화기 [gihwagi] n carburettor

기회 [gihoe] n chance, occasion, opportunity

기획 [gihoek] n planning

기후 [gihu] n climate; 기후 변화 [gihu byeonhwa] n climate change

긴급 [gingeup] n urgency; 긴급한 [gingeuphan] adj urgent

긴장 [ginjang] n tension; 긴장시키다 [ginjangsikida] v strain; 긴장을 풀다 [ginjangeul pulda] vi relax; 긴장감 [ginjanggam] n suspense; 긴장한 [ginjanghan] adj tense, uptight

길 [gil] n path, road; 산책길 [sanchaekgil] n promenade; 오솔길 [osolgil] n pass (in mountains); 좁은 길 [jobeun gil] n lane, lane (driving);...에 가려면 어느 길을 타나요? [...e garyeomyeon eoneu gireul tanayo?] Which road do I take for...?; 이 길은 어디로 이어지나요? [i gireun eodiro ieojinayo?] Where does this path lead?; 길에서 벗어나지 마세요 [gireseo beoseonaji maseyo] Keep to the path; 길이 언제 뚫릴까요? [giri eonje tturilkkayo?] When will the road be clear?

길다 [gilda] 더 길게 [deo gilge] adv longer; 긴 [gin] adj long; 길게 [gilge] adv long

길들여지다 [gildeullyeojida] 길들여진 [gildeullyeojin] adj tame

길이 [giri] n length; 이 길이로 해 주세요 [i giriro hae juseyo] This length, please

길잃다 [girirta] 길잃은 동물 [girireun dongmul] n stray

깁다 [gipda] v stitch; 기운 [giun] (바느질) adj patched

깃털 [gittheol] n feather

깊다 [gipda] 깊은 [gipeun] adj deep; 깊게 [gipge] adv deeply; 물이 얼마나 깊어요? [muri eolmana gipeoyo?] How deep is the water?

깊이 [gipi] n depth

ㄲ

까마귀 [kkamagwi] n crow; 큰까마귀 [keunkkamagwi] n raven

까지 [kkaji]...까지 [...kkaji] conj till, until

까치 [kkachi] n magpie

까페 [kkape] 카페 [kape] n café; 여기에 인터넷 카페가 있나요? [yeogie inteonet kapega innayo?] Are there any Internet cafés here?

깎다 [kkakkda] v trim down; 값을 끈질기게 깎다 [gapseul kkeunjilgige kkakkda] v haggle

깔끔 [kkalkkeum] 깔끔하게 [kkalkkeumhage] adv neatly; 깔끔한 [kkalkkeumhan] adj neat

깔때기 [kkalttaegi] n funnel

깡통 [kkangtong] 작은 깡통 [jageun kkangtong] n canister; 깡통따개 [kkangtongttagae] n can-opener, tin-opener

깨끗하다 [kkaekkeutada] vt clean; 깨끗한 [kkaekkeutan] adj clean; 깨끗한 잔을 주시겠어요? [kkaekkeutan janeul jusigesseoyo?] Can I have a clean glass, please?; 깨끗한 포크를 주시겠어요? [kkaekkeutan pokeureul jusigesseoyo?] Could I have a clean fork please?

깨다 [kkaeda] vt break; 깨어서 [kkaeeoseo] adj awake

깨닫다 [kkaedatda] v realize

깨우다 [kkaeuda] v wake up, awaken; 깨워 드릴까요? [kkaewo deurilkkayo?]

Shall I wake you up?
깨지다 [kkaejida] v chip; 깨지기 쉬운
[kkaejigi swiun] adj fragile; 깨짐
[kkaejim] n break; 제가 창문을
깨뜨렸어요 [jega changmuneul
kkaetteuryeosseoyo] I've broken the
window
깨지지 않다 [kkaejiji anta] 깨지지 않는
[kkaejiji annneun] adj unbreakable
꺼지다 [kkeojida] 안 꺼져요 [an
kkeojyeoyo] It won't turn off
꺽쇠 [kkeoksoe] n staple (wire)
껌 [kkeom] n chewing gum; 풍선껌
[pungseonkkeom] n bubble gum
껍질 [kkeopjil] n peel, shell; 껍질을
벗기다 [kkeopjireul beotgida] vt peel
껴안다 [kkyeoanda] 꼭 껴안다 [kkok
kkyeoanda] v cuddle
꼬리 [kkori] n tail
꼬마 [kkoma] n brat
꼬챙이 [kkochaengi] n skewer
꼭두각시 [kkokdugaksi] n puppet
꽃 [kkot] n blossom, flower; 닮맞이꽃
[dalmajikkot] n primrose; 은방울꽃
[eunbangulkkot] n lily of the valley; 꽃병
[kkotbyeong] n vase; 꽃다발
[kkottabal] n bouquet; 꽃이 피다
[kkochi pida] v blossom, flower;
꽃장수 [kkotchangsu] n florist; 꽃가루
[kkotgaru] n pollen; 꽃가루 알레르기
[kkotgaru allereugi] n hay fever
꽤 [kkwae] adv pretty
꾸러미 [kkureomi] 작은 꾸러미 [jageun
kkureomi] n packet
꾸리다 [kkurida] v (포장) do up
꾸짖다 [kkujitda] v scold, tell off
꿇다 [kkurta] 무릎을 꿇다 [mureupeul
kkurta] v kneel
꿈 [kkum] n dream; 꿈꾸다 [kkumkkuda]
v dream
꿩 [kkwong] n pheasant; 들꿩
[deulkkwong] n grouse (game bird)
꿰매다 [kkwemaeda] v sew; 완전히
꿰매다 [wanjeonhi kkwemaeda] v sew
up
끄다 [kkeuda] v go off, switch off, turn
off, turn out; 불꺼도 돼요? [bulkkeodo
dwaeyo?] Can I switch the light off?;

라디오 꺼도 돼요? [radio kkeodo
dwaeyo?] Can I switch the radio off?
끄덕이다 [kkeudeogida] 머리를
끄덕이다 [meorireul kkeudeogida] v
nod
끈 [kkeun] n strap, string
끈적하다 [kkeunjeokhada] 끈적끈적한
[kkeunjeokkkeunjeokhan] adj sticky
끌 [kkeul] n chisel
끌다 [kkeulda] vt drag; 끌어내다
[kkeureonaeda] v pull out; 끌고가다
[kkeulgogada] v tow away; 이끌다
[ikkeulda] adj direct
끌어당기다 [kkeureodanggida] v attract;
끌어당기기 [kkeureodanggigi] n
attraction; 마음을 끌어당기는
[maeumeul kkeureodanggineun] adj
attractive
끌어올리다 [kkeureoollida] v boost
끓다 [kkeurta] vi boil; 끓는 [kkeurnneun]
adj boiling; 서서히 끓다 [seoseohi
kkeurta] v simmer; 서서히 끓인
[seoseohi kkeurin] adj poached
(simmered gently)
끔찍하다 [kkeumjjikhada] 끔찍한
[kkeumjjikhan] adj horrendous,
horrible; 끔찍한 [kkeumjjikhan] adj
hideous
끝 [kkeut] n end, finish, tip (end of
object); ...을 끝내다 [...eul kkeutnaeda]
n finish; 끝난 [kkeutnan] adj done;
끝낸 [kkeutnaen] adj finished; 끝없는
[kkeuteomneun] adj endless; 끝으로
[kkeuteuro] adv lastly; 발끝 [balkkeut] n
tiptoe
끝나다 [kkeutnada] v end; 언제 공연이
끝나요? [eonje gongyeoni kkeutnayo?]
When does the performance end?
끼다 [kkida] 꼭 끼는 [kkok kkineun] adj
skin-tight
끼이다 [kkiida] 끼여서 못움직이게 된
[kkiyeoseo mosumjigige doen] adj
jammed

나 [na] *pron* I; **나를** [nareul] *pron* me; **나의** [naui] *adj* my; **내 자신** [nae jasin] *pron* myself; **내 것** [nae geot] *pron* mine

나누다 [nanuda] *v* share, divide

나라 [nara] *n* country; **어디 나라에서 오셨어요?** [eodi naraeseo osyeosseoyo?] Where are you from?

나머지 [nameoji] *npl* leftovers

나무 [namu] *n* tree; **나무 줄기** [namu julgi] *n* trunk; **너도밤나무** [neodobamnamu] *n* beech (tree); **느릅나무** [neureumnamu] *n* elm; **단풍나무** [danpungnamu] *n* maple; **대나무** [daenamu] *n* bamboo; **버드나무** [beodeunamu] *n* willow; **산사나무** [sansanamu] *n* hawthorn; **소나무** [sonamu] *n* pine; **야자나무** [yajanamu] *n* palm (tree); **자작나무** [jajangnamu] *n* birch; **전나무** [jeonnamu] *n* fir (tree); **참나무** [chamnamu] *n* oak; **통나무** [tongnamu] *n* log; **호랑가시나무** [horanggasinamu] *n* holly; **지역의 풀과 나무를 보고 싶어요** [jiyeogui pulgwa namureul bogo sipeoyo] We'd like to see local plants and trees

나물 [namul] **콩나물** [kongnamul] *npl* beansprouts

나방 [nabang] *n* moth

나비 [nabi] *n* butterfly

나쁘다 [nappeuda] **몹시 나쁜** [mopsi nappeun] *adj* awful; **나쁘게** [nappeuge] *adv* badly; **나쁜** [nappeun] *adj* bad, vicious; **더 나쁘게** [deo nappeuge] *adv* worse; **더 나쁜** [deo nappeun] *adj* worse; **건강이 나쁜** [geongangi nappeun] *adj* poorly; **가장 나쁜** [gajang nappeun] *adj* worst; **날씨가 아주 나빠요!** [nalssiga aju nappayo!] What awful weather!

나사 [nasa] *n* screw; **나사를 빼다** [nasareul ppaeda] *v* unscrew; **나사못** [nasamot] *n* screw; **나사돌리개** [nasadolligae] *n* screwdriver; **나사가 풀렸어요** [nasaga pullyeosseoyo] The screw has come loose

나아가다 [naagada] *v* head

나이 [nai] *n* age; **나이 제한** [nai jehan] *n* age limit; **나이가 지긋한** [naiga jigeutan] *adj* elderly; **가장 나이 많은** [gajang nai manheun] *adj* eldest

나이지리아 [naijiria] *n* Nigeria; **나이지리아 사람** [naijiria saram] *n* Nigerian; **나이지리아의** [naijiriaui] *adj* Nigerian

나일론 [naillon] *n* nylon

나중 [najung] **나중에** [najunge] *adv* afterwards, later; **나중에 다시 전화하시겠어요?** [najunge dasi jeonhwahasigesseoyo?] Can you try again later?; **지금 지불해야 하나요 아니면 나중에 지불해야 하나요?** [jigeum jibulhaeya hanayo animyeon najunge jibulhaeya hanayo?] Do I pay now or later?

나체 [nache] *n* nude; **나체주의자** [nachejuuija] *n* nudist; **나체의** [nacheui] *adj* nude

나침반 [nachimban] *n* compass

나타나다 [natanada] *v* appear, turn up

낙서 [nakseo] *npl* graffiti

낙원 [nagwon] *n* paradise

낙천 [nakcheon] **낙천주의** [nakcheonjuui] *n* optimism; **낙천적인** [nakcheonjeogin] *adj* optimistic; **낙천가** [nakcheonga] *n* optimist

낙타 [nakta] *n* camel

낙하 [nakha] **낙하산** [nakhasan] *n* parachute

낚다 [nakkda] **낚아채다** [nakkachaeda] v snatch

낚시 [nakksi] **낚싯대** [nakksitdae] n fishing rod; **낚시 도구** [nakksi dogu] n fishing tackle; **낚시질** [nakksijil] n angling; **낚시꾼** [nakksikkun] n angler; **낚시하다** [nakksihada] vi fish; **낚시 허가가 필요한가요?** [nakksi heogaga pillyohangayo?] Do you need a fishing permit?; **어디에서 낚시를 할 수 있어요?** [eodieseo nakksireul hal su isseoyo?] Where can I go fishing?; **여기에서 낚시할 수 있어요?** [yeogieseo nakksihal su isseoyo?] Can we fish here?; **여기에서 낚시해도 될까요?** [yeogieseo nakksihaedo doelkkayo?] Am I allowed to fish here?

난간 [nangan] n banister, rail ▷ npl railings

난관 [nangwan] n dilemma

난독 [nandok] **난독증** [nandokjeung] n dyslexia; **난독증 환자** [nandokjeung hwanja] n dyslexic; **난독증의** [nandokjeungui] adj dyslexic

난로 [nanno] **벽난로** [byeongnanno] n fireplace

난민 [nanmin] n refugee

난방 [nanbang] **중앙 난방** [jungang nanbang] n central heating; **난방이 되지 않아요** [nanbangi doeji anhayo] The heating doesn't work; **난방이 안 켜져요** [nanbangi an kyeojyeoyo] I can't turn the heating on; **난방이 안 꺼져요** [nanbangi an kkeojyeoyo] I can't turn the heating off; **방에 난방 되나요?** [bange nanbang doenayo?] Does the room have heating?; **수영장에 난방이 되나요?** [suyeongjange nanbangi doenayo?] Is the pool heated?; **난방기는 어떻게 작동해요?** [nanbanggineun eotteoke jakdonghaeyo?] How does the heating work?

난소 [nanso] n ovary

난장 [nanjang] **난장판** [nanjangpan] npl shambles

난쟁이 [nanjaengi] n dwarf

난초 [nancho] n orchid

난파 [nanpa] n shipwreck; **난파한** [nanpahan] adj shipwrecked

난폭 [nanpok] **난폭한** [nanpokhan] adj fierce, violent

날 [nal] n blade; **면도날** [myeondonal] n razor blade; **날것의** [nalgeosui] adj raw

날개 [nalgae] n wing

날다 [nalda] vi fly

날씨 [nalssi] n weather; **날씨가 바뀔까요?** [nalssiga bakkwilkkayo?] Is the weather going to change?; **날씨가 아주 나빠요!** [nalssiga aju nappayo!] What awful weather!; **날씨가 좋아졌으면 좋겠어요** [nalssiga johajyeosseumyeon jokesseoyo] I hope the weather improves; **날씨가 계속 이랬으면 좋겠어요** [nalssiga gyesok iraesseumyeon jokesseoyo] I hope the weather stays like this; **내일 날씨가 어떨까요?** [naeil nalssiga eotteolkkayo?] What will the weather be like tomorrow?

날씬하다 [nalssinhada] **날씬한** [nalssinhan] adj slender

날아가다 [naragada] v fly away

날짜 [naljja] n date

날카롭다 [nalkaropda] **날카로운** [nalkaroun] adj sharp

낡다 [narkda] **낡은** [nalgeun] adj worn

남 [nam] n bloke; **미혼남** [mihonnam] n bachelor; **남미** [nammi] n South America; **남미 사람** [nammi saram] n South American; **남미의** [nammiui] adj South American; **남동쪽** [namdongjjok] n southeast; **남쪽** [namjjok] n south; **남쪽으로** [namjjogeuro] adv south; **남쪽으로 가는** [namjjogeuro ganeun] adj southbound; **남쪽의** [namjjogui] adj south, southern; **남서쪽** [namseojjok] n southwest; **남아프리카** [namapeurika] n South Africa; **남아프리카 사람** [namapeurika saram] n South African; **남아프리카의** [namapeurikaui] adj South African; **남극** [namgeuk] n South Pole, the Antarctic, Antarctica; **남극 대륙** [namgeuk daeryuk] n Antarctic

남녀 [namnyeo] **남녀 공용이 아닌 기숙사 있나요?** [namnyeo gongyongi anin gisuksa innayo?] Do you have any single sex dorms?

남다 [namda] v remain; **남아 있는** [nama inneun] adj remaining; **살아남다** [saranamda] v survive

남성 [namseong] n male; **남성의** [namseongui] adj male; **남성적인** [namseongjeogin] adj masculine

남용 [namyong] n abuse; **남용하다** [namyonghada] v abuse

남자 [namja] n chap, guy, man; **남자 배우** [namja baeu] n actor; **남자 친구** [namja chingu] n boyfriend; **남자 턱시도** [namja teoksido] n dinner jacket; **남자 화장실** [namja hwajangsil] n gents'; **그 남자** [geu namja] pron he; **그 남자 자신** [geu namja jasin] pron himself; **그 남자 것** [geu namja geot] pron his; **그 남자를** [geu namjareul] pron him; **그 남자의** [geu namjaui] adj his

남자친구 [namjachingu] **남자친구가 있어요** [namjachinguga isseoyo] I have a boyfriend

남편 [nampyeon] n husband; **전 남편** [jeon nampyeon] n ex-husband; **제 남편이에요** [je nampyeonieyo] This is my husband

납 [nap] n lead (metal); **납이 없는** [nabi eomneun] adj lead-free

납득 [napdeuk] **납득시키다** [napdeuksikida] v convince

납세 [napse] **납세자** [napseja] n tax payer

납치 [napchi] **공중납치범** [gongjungnapchibeom] n hijacker; **공중납치하다** [gongjungnapchihada] v hijack

낫다 [natda] **(상처 등이) 낫다** [(sangcheo deungi) natda] v heal

낭 [nang] **침낭** [chimnang] n sleeping bag

낭비 [nangbi] n waste; **낭비하는** [nangbihaneun] adj extravagant; **낭비하다** [nangbihada] v squander, waste

낮다 [natda] **낮은** [najeun] adj low; **낮게** [natge] adv low; **더 낮은** [deo najeun] adj lower

낮추다 [natchuda] v lower; **소리를 낮춰 주시겠어요?** [sorireul natchwo jusigesseoyo?] Please could you lower the volume?

낯설다 [natseolda] **낯선사람** [natseonsaram] n stranger

내 [nae] **유월 내내** [yuwol naenae] for the whole of June

내기 [naegi] n bet, betting; **내기하다** [naegihada] n bet

내다 [naeda] v pay; **바로 내야 합니까?** [baro naeya hamnikka?] Do I have to pay it straightaway?; **어디에서 벌금을 내야 합니까?** [eodieseo beolgeumeul naeya hamnikka?] Where do I pay the fine?; **언제까지 내야 돼요?** [eonjekkaji naeya dwaeyo?] When is it due to be paid?

내려가다 [naeryeogada] v descend, go down

내려오다 [naeryeooda] v come down

내리다 [naerida] v get off; **언제 내려야 하는지 알려 주세요** [eonje naeryeoya haneunji allyeo juseyo] Please tell me when to get off

내버려둔 [naebeoryeodun] adj unattended

내부 [naebu] n interior; **내부 통신 시스템** [naebu tongsin siseutem] n intercom; **내부에** [naebue] adv inside; **내부의** [naebuui] adj internal; **실내 장식가** [sillae jangsikga] n interior designer; **안쪽** [anjjok] n inside

내선 [naeseon] n extension

내쉬다 [naeswida] v breathe out

내용 [naeyong] n content

내일 [naeil] adv tomorrow; **내일 무엇을 하고 싶어요?** [naeil mueoseul hago sipeoyo?] Would you like to do something tomorrow?; **내일 날씨가 어떨까요?** [naeil nalssiga eotteolkkayo?] What will the weather be like tomorrow?; **내일 다시 전화할게요** [naeil dasi jeonhwahalkkeyo] I'll call back tomorrow; 내일 밤 [naeil bam] tomorrow night; 내일 아침 7시에 모닝콜 부탁해요 [naeil achim 7sie moningkol butakhaeyo] I'd like an alarm call for tomorrow morning at seven o'clock; 내일 아침 [naeil achim] tomorrow morning; 내일 아침에 시간 있어요 [naeil achime sigan isseoyo] I'm free tomorrow morning; 내일 열어요? [naeil yeoreoyo?] Is it open tomorrow?; 내일 오후 [naeil ohu] tomorrow afternoon; 내일 전화하면 될까요? [naeil jeonhwahamyeon doelkkayo?] May I call you tomorrow?; 저는 내일 떠나요 [jeoneun naeil tteonayo] I'm leaving tomorrow; 저는 내일 아침 10 시에 떠나요 [jeoneun naeil achim 10sie tteonayo] I will be leaving tomorrow morning at ten a.m.

내장 [naejang] npl bowels

내전 [naejeon] n civil war

냄비 [naembi] n saucepan

냄새 [naemsae] n scent, smell; 냄새를 맡다 [naemsaereul matda] vi smell; 냄새가 나다 [naemsaega nada] vi smell; 이상한 냄새가 나요 [isanghan naemsaega nayo] There's a funny smell; 가스 냄새가 나요 [gaseu naemsaega nayo] I can smell gas

냅킨 [naepkin] n napkin; 식탁용 냅킨 [siktagyong naepkin] n serviette

냉난방 [naengnanbang] 냉난방 장치를 한 [naengnanbang jangchireul han] adj air-conditioned; 냉난방 장치 [naengnanbang jangchi] n air conditioning

냉동고 [naengdonggo] n freezer

냉장고 [naengjanggo] n fridge, refrigerator

너 [neo] pron you (singular); 너 자신 [neo jasin] pron yourself; 너의 것 [neoui geot] pron yours (singular); 너의 [neoui] adj your (singular)

너구리 [neoguri] n racoon

너그럽다 [neogeureopda] 너그러운 [neogeureoun] adj broad-minded

너머 [neomeo] ...의 너머에 [...ui neomeoe] prep beyond

너트 [neoteu] n nut (device)

넓다 [neorpda] 넓은 [neorbeun] adj wide; 넓게 [neopge] adv wide

넘기 [neomgi] 장애물 뛰어넘기 [jangaemul ttwieoneomgi] n show-jumping

넘어지다 [neomeojida] v fall down, stumble; 걸려 넘어지게 하다 [geollyeo neomeojige hada] v trip (up); 걸려 넘어질 뻔하다 [geollyeo neomeojil ppeonhada] v stumble; 넘어졌어요 [neomeojyeosseoyo] She fell

네글리제 [negeullije] n negligee

네덜란드 [nedeollandeu] n Holland ▷ npl Netherlands; 네덜란드 사람 [nedeollandeu saram] n Dutch, Dutchman; 네덜란드 여자 [nedeollandeu yeoja] n Dutchwoman; 네덜란드의 [nedeollandeuui] adj Dutch

네번째 [nebeonjjae] 네 번째의 [ne beonjjaeui] adj fourth

네온 [neon] n neon

네트워크 [neteuwokeu] n network

네팔 [nepal] n Nepal

넥타이 [nektai] 나비 넥타이 [nabi nektai] n bow tie

년 [nyeon] n year; 1년간의 [illyeonganui] adj yearly; 100년 [baeng nyeon] n centenary; 윤년 [yunnyeon] n leap year; 회계 연도 [hoegye yeondo] n financial year

년간 [nyeongan] 10년간 [sim nyeongan] n decade

노 [no] n oar, paddle

노동 [nodong] n labour; 노동력 [nodongnyeok] n workforce; 노동조합 [nodongjohap] n trade union; 노동조합 [nodongjohap] n pool (resources); 노동조합원 [nodongjohabwon] n trade unionist; 노동자 [nodongja] n labourer, workman; 노동자 계급의 [nodongja gyegeubui] adj working-class; 노동자 [nodongja] n worker; 노동허가증 [nodongheogajeung] n work permit

노래 [norae] n singing, song; 노래하다 [noraehada] v sing

노래방 [noraebang] n karaoke

노력 [noryeok] n effort, try; 열심히 노력하다 [yeolsimhi noryeokhada] v struggle

노련 [noryeon] 노련한 [noryeonhan] adj experienced, veteran

노령연금 [noryeongyeongeum] 노령의 연금수령자 [noryeongui yeongeumsuryeongja] n old-age pensioner

노르웨이 [noreuwei] n Norway; 노르웨이 사람 [noreuwei saram] n Norwegian (person); 노르웨이어 [noreuweieo] n Norwegian (language); 노르웨이의 [noreuweiui] adj Norwegian

노른자 [noreunja] n yolk

노병 [nobyeong] n veteran

노상 [nosang] n highway; 노상 강도 [nosang gangdo] n mugger

노새 [nosae] n mule

노선도 [noseondo] n underground map; 지하철 노선도 있어요? [jihacheol noseondo isseoyo?] Do you have a map of the tube?; 지하철 노선도를 주시겠어요? [jihacheol noseondoreul jusigesseoyo?] Could I have a map of the tube, please?

노예 [noye] n slave

노인 [noin] n senior citizen; 노인병 환자 [noinbyeong hwanja] n geriatric; 노인의 [noinui] adj geriatric

노트북 [noteubuk] n laptop; 여기서 제 노트북을 사용할 수 있을까요? [yeogiseo je noteubugeul sayonghal su isseulkkayo?] Can I use my own laptop here?

노하우 [nohau] n know-how

녹 [nok] n rust

녹다 [nokda] vi melt

녹말 [nongmal] 옥수수 녹말 [oksusu nongmal] n cornflour

녹슬다 [nokseulda] 녹슨 [nokseun] adj rusty

녹음 [nogeum] n recording; 녹음기 [nogeumgi] n tape recorder; 녹음하다 [nogeumhada] v tape

녹이다 [nogida] vt dissolve, melt

논리 [nolli] 논리적인 [nollijeogin] adj logical

논쟁 [nonjaeng] n argument, debate; 논쟁의 [nonjaengui] adj controversial; 논쟁하다 [nonjaenghada] v argue, debate

논평 [nonpyeong] n comment, commentary; 논평하다 [nonpyeonghada] v comment

놀다 [nolda] 놀고 있는 [nolgo inneun] adj idle

놀라다 [nollada] v surprise; 놀라서 멍해진 [nollaseo meonghaejin] adj petrified; 놀라운 [nollaun] adj alarming, amazing, astonishing, marvellous, surprising, wonderful; 놀라게 하다 [nollage hada] v amaze, astonish; 놀란 [nollan] adj amazed, astonished, surprised; 놀람 [nollam] n surprise; 놀랍게도 [nollapgedo] adv surprisingly; 깜짝 놀라게 하다 [kkamjjak nollage hada] v startle; 갑작스러운 놀람 [gapjakseureoun nollam] n fright

놀리다 [nollida] v kid, tease

놀이 [nori] 불꽃놀이 [bulkkotnori] npl fireworks

농가 [nongga] n farmhouse

농구 [nonggu] n basketball

농담 [nongdam] n joke; 농담하다 [nongdamhada] v joke

농부 [nongbu] n farmer

농사 [nongsa] n farming

농업 [nongeop] n agriculture; 농업의 [nongeobui] adj agricultural

농작물 [nongjangmul] n crop

농장 [nongjang] n farm

높다 [nopda] 높은 [nopeun] adj high; 높이 [nopi] adv high; 얼마나 높아요? [eolmana nopayo?] How high is it?

높이 [nopi] n height; 높이뛰기 [nopittwigi] n high jump

높이다 [nopida] v heighten, elevate; 소리를 높여도 될까요? [sorireul nopyeodo doelkkayo?] May I turn the volume up?

놓다 [nota] v put, place

놓치다 [nochida] vt miss; 갈아탈 편을 놓쳤어요 [garatal pyeoneul

nochyeosseoyo] I've missed my connection

뇌 [noe] n brain; **뇌진탕** [noejintang] n concussion

뇌물 [noemul] **뇌물 수수** [noemul susu] n bribery; **뇌물을 주다** [noemureul juda] v bribe

뇌우 [noeu] n thunderstorm

누구 [nugu] pron who; **누구에게** [nuguege] pron whom; **누구의** [nuguui] adj whose; **누구의 것** [nuguui geot] pron whose; **누군가** [nugunga] pron someone; **누구세요?** [nuguseyo?] Who is it?; **누구시죠?** [nugusijyo?] Who's calling?

누군가 [nugunga] pron somebody

누르다 [nureuda] v press; **어느 버튼을 눌러야 하나요?** [eoneu beoteuneul nulleoya hanayo?] Which button do I press?

누이 [nui] **시누이** [sinui] (husband's sister) n sister-in-law

눈 [nun] n eye, snow; **눈 먼** [nun meon] adj blind; **눈보라** [nunbora] n snowstorm; **눈동자** [nundongja] n pupil (eye); **눈뭉치** [nunmungchi] n snowball; **눈사람** [nunsaram] n snowman; **눈송이** [nunsongi] n snowflake; **눈을 깜박이다** [nuneul kkambagida] vi blink; **눈을 가리다** [nuneul garida] v blindfold; **눈이 내리다** [nuni naerida] v snow; **눈꺼풀** [nunkkeopul] n eyelid; **눈가리개** [nungarigae] n blindfold; **아이라이너** [airaineo] n eyeliner; **아이섀도** [aisyaedo] n eye shadow;... **가는 길에 눈이 쌓였나요?** [... ganeun gire nuni ssahyeonnayo?] Is the road to... snowed up?; **눈 상태는 어떤가요?** [nun sangtaeneun eotteongayo?] What are the snow conditions?; **눈에 뭐가 들어갔어요** [nune mwoga deureogasseoyo] I have something in my eye; **눈은 어떤가요?** [nuneun eotteongayo?] What is the snow like?; **눈이 따가워요** [nuni ttagawoyo] My eyes are sore; **눈이 아주 많이 와요** [nuni aju manhi wayo] The snow is

very heavy; **눈이 올 것 같아요?** [nuni ol geot gatayo?] Do you think it will snow?; **눈이 와요** [nuni wayo] It's snowing

눈금 [nungeum] n scale (measure)

눈물 [nunmul] n tear (from eye)

눈보라 [nunbora] **심한 눈보라** [simhan nunbora] n blizzard

눈사태 [nunsatae] **눈사태 위험이 있어요?** [nunsatae wiheomi isseoyo?] Is there a danger of avalanches?

눈썹 [nunsseop] n eyebrow; **속눈썹** [songnunsseop] n eyelash

눕히다 [nuphida] v lay; **여러 각도로 눕힐 수 있는** [yeoreo gakdoro nuphil su inneun] adj reclining; **누워 있어야 하나요?** [nuwo isseoya hanayo?] Do I have to stay in bed?

뉴스 [nyuseu] npl news; **뉴스 캐스터** [nyuseu kaeseuteo] n presenter; **뉴스 아나운서** [nyuseu anaunseo] n newsreader; **뉴스는 언제 해요?** [nyuseuneun eonje haeyo?] When is the news?

뉴질랜드 [nyujillaendeu] n New Zealand; **뉴질랜드 사람** [nyujillaendeu saram] n New Zealander

느긋하다 [neugeutada] **느긋한** [neugeutan] adj easy-going, laid-back

느끼다 [neukkida] v feel

느낌 [neukkim] n feeling; **느낌표** [neukkimpyo] n exclamation mark

느리다 [neurida] **느린** [neurin] adj slow; **연결이 아주 느린 것 같아요** [yeongyeori aju neurin geot gatayo] The connection seems very slow; **제 시계가 느린 것 같아요** [je sigyega neurin geot gatayo] I think my watch is slow

느슨하다 [neuseunhada] **느슨한** [neuseunhan] adj slack

늑골 [neukgol] n rib

늑대 [neukdae] n wolf

늘 [neul] adv always

늘씬하다 [neulssinhada] **늘씬한** [neulssinhan] adj slim

늘어지다 [neureojida] **축 늘어진** [chuk neureojin] adj flabby; **길게 늘어진**

[gilge neullyeojin] *adj* oblong
늙다 [neurkda] 늙은 [neulgeun] *adj*
aged; 늙은 [neulgeun] *adj* old
능가 [neungga] 능가하다
[neunggahada] *v* beat *(outdo)*
능력 [neungnyeok] *n* ability; **...할 능력이**
있는 [...hal neungnyeogi inneun] *adj*
capable
능률 [neungnyul] *n* efficiency;
비능률적인 [bineungnyuljeogin] *adj*
inefficient
늦다 [neutda] 늦은 [neujeun] *adj* late
(delayed); 늦게 [neutge] *adv* late; **너무**
늦어요 [neomu neujeoyo] It's too late;
늦어서 미안해요 [neujeoseo
mianhaeyo] Sorry we're late; **예정보다**
약간 늦고 있어요 [yejeongboda
yakgan neutgo isseoyo] We are slightly
behind schedule; **우리가 십분**
늦었어요 [uriga sipbun neujeosseoyo]
We are ten minutes late
늦잠 [neutjam] *n* have a lie-in, lie in
늪 [neup] *n* bog
니스 [niseu] *n* varnish
니제르 [nijereu] *n* Niger
니카라과 [nikaragwa] *n* Nicaragua;
니카라과 사람 [nikaragwa saram] *n*
Nicaraguan; **니카라과의** [nikaragwaui]
adj Nicaraguan
니커스 [nikeoseu] *npl* knickers
니코틴 [nikotin] *n* nicotine

다가오다 [dagaoda] *v* approach;
다가오는 [dagaoneun] *adj* coming
다과 [dagwa] *npl* refreshments
다국적 [dagukjeok] **다국적 기업**
[dagukjeok gieop] *n* multinational;
다국적의 [dagukjeogui] *adj*
multinational
다닥냉이 [dadangnaengi] *n* cress
다듬다 [dadeumda] 깎아 다듬다 [kkakka
dadeumda] *v* trim; **머리 좀 다듬어**
주시겠어요? [meori jom dadeumeo
jusigesseoyo?] Can I have a trim?
다락 [darak] **다락방** [darakbang] *n* attic
다람쥐 [daramjwi] *n* squirrel
다루다 [daruda] *v* deal with, handle,
tackle
다르다 [dareuda] **...과는 다른** [...
gwaneun dareun] *prep* unlike; **다른**
[dareun] *adj* different, other; **다른 곳에**
[dareun gose] *adv* elsewhere; **다른 거**
없나요? [dareun geo eomnayo?] Have
you anything else?
다리 [dari] *n* bridge, leg; **넓적다리**
[neopjeokdari] *n* thigh; **다리를 저는**
[darireul jeoneun] *adj* lame; **다리를**
다쳤어요 [darireul dachyeosseoyo] She
has hurt her leg; **다리를 움직일 수**
없어요 [darireul umjigil su eopseoyo]
He can't move his leg, I can't move my
leg; **다리에 쥐가 났어요** [darie jwiga
nasseoyo] I've got cramp in my leg;
다리가 가려워요 [dariga garyeoweoyo]

My leg itches

다리다 [darida] v iron; **어디에서 이걸 다릴 수 있을까요?** [eodieseo igeol daril su isseulkkayo?] Where can I get this ironed?

다리미 [darimi] 다리미가 필요해요 [darimiga pillyohaeyo] I need an iron

다림 [darim] 다림질 [darimjil] n ironing; 다리미판 [darimipan] n ironing board; 다림질하다 [darimjilhada] v iron

다만 [daman] 다만...뿐 [daman...ppun] adv only

다물다 [damulda] 입 다물다 [ip damulda] v shut up

다발성 [dabalseong] 다발성경화증 [dabalseonggyeonghwajeung] n multiple sclerosis, MS

다섯 [daseot] number five; 다섯 번째의 [daseot beonjjaeui] adj fifth

다수 [dasu] n host (multitude) ▷ pron many; 대다수 [daedasu] n majority

다스 [daseu] n dozen

다시 [dasi] adv again; 다시 하다 [dasi hada] v redo

다양 [dayang] 다양성 [dayangseong] n variety; 다양한 [dayanghan] adj varied, various

다용도 [dayongdo] 다용도실 [dayongdosil] n utility room

다운로드 [daunnodeu] n download

다운로드하다 [daunnodeuhada] v download

다음 [daeum] 다음에 [daeume] adv next; 다음의 [daeumui] adj following, next

다이버 [daibeo] n diver

다이빙 [daibing] n dive, diving; 다이빙대 [daibingdae] n diving board; 스쿠버 다이빙 [seukubeo daibing] n scuba diving; 다이빙을 하고 싶어요 [daibingeul hago sipeoyo] I'd like to go diving; 다이빙하기 가장 좋은 곳은 어디인가요? [daibinghagi gajang joheun goseun eodiingayo?] Where is the best place to dive?

다이빙하다 [daibinghada] v dive

다이아몬드 [daiamondeu] n diamond

다이어트 [daieoteu] 다이어트하다

[daieoteuhada] v diet; 다이어트 중이에요 [daieoteu jungieyo] I'm on a diet

다재다능 [dajaedaneung] 다재다능한 [dajaedaneunghan] adj versatile

다치다 [dachida] v damage; 다쳤어요 [dachyeosseoyo] He has cut himself, She has hurt herself, She is hurt; 다친 사람들이 있어요 [dachin saramdeuri isseoyo] There are some people injured; 다친 사람이 있어요 [dachin sarami isseoyo] Someone is injured; 그 여자는 크게 다쳤어요 [geu yeojaneun keuge dachyeosseoyo] She is seriously injured; 팔을 다쳤어요 [pareul dachyeosseoyo] He has hurt his arm

다큐멘터리 [dakyumenteori] n documentary

다투다 [datuda] v quarrel, row (to argue)

다행 [dahaeng] 다행히 [dahaenghi] adv luckily

닦다 [dakkda] v polish, wipe, wipe up

단거리 [dangeori] 단거리 경주 [dangeori gyeongju] n sprint; 단거리 경주 선수 [dangeori gyeongju seonsu] n sprinter

단단하다 [dandanhada] 단단한 [dandanhan] adj firm, hard (firm, rigid)

단백질 [danbaekjil] n protein

단속 [dansok] 단속하다 [dansokhada] v crack down on

단수 [dansu] n singular

단순 [dansun] 단순한 [dansunhan] adj mere, simple; 단순화하다 [dansunhwahada] v simplify

단식 [dansik] 단식 경기 [dansik gyeonggi] npl singles

단어 [daneo] n word

단위 [danwi] n unit

단점 [danjeom] n drawback, shortcoming

단정 [danjeong] n correctness; 단정치 못한 [danjeongchi motan] adj untidy; 단정한 [danjeonghan] adj tidy

단조 [danjo] 단조로운 [danjoroun] adj dull, monotonous

단지 [danji] n estate; 산업 단지 [saneop danji] n industrial estate

단체 [danche] n party (group)

단추 [danchu] *n* button; 소매 단추 [somae danchu] *npl* cufflinks

단편 [danpyeon] *n* reply, answer; 단편 소설 [danpyeon soseol] *n* short story

단호 [danho] 단호한 [danhohan] *adj* determined

닫다 [datda] *v* close, shut; 쾅 닫다 [kwang datda] *vt* slam; 몇 시에 닫아요? [myeot sie dadayo?] What time do you close?; 문이 안 닫혀요 [muni an datyeoyo] The door won't close; 상점은 몇 시에 닫아요? [sangjeomeun myeot sie dadayo?] What time do the shops close?; 언제 닫아요? [eonje dadayo?] When does it close?; 은행은 언제 닫나요? [eunhaengeun eonje datnayo?] When does the bank close?; 창을 닫아도 될까요? [changeul dadado doelkkayo?] May I close the window?

닫히다 [dachida] 닫힌 [dachin] *adj* closed

달 [dal] *n* moon; 보름달 [boreumdal] *n* full moon

달걀 [dalgyal] *n* egg; 부활절 달걀 [buhwaljeol dalgyal] *n* Easter egg; 달걀 노른자 [dalgyal noreunja] *n* egg yolk; 달걀 그릇 [dalgyal geureut] *n* eggcup; 달걀 흰자 [dalgyal huinja] *n* egg white; 스크램블드 에그 [seukeuraembeuldeu egeu] *npl* scrambled eggs

달다 [dalda] 단 [dan] (맛이 달콤한) *adj* sweet *(taste)*

달러 [dalleo] *n* dollar; 달러 받으세요? [dalleo badeuseyo?] Do you take dollars?

달력 [dallyeok] *n* calendar

달리기 [dalligi] *n* running

달리다 [dallida] *vi* run; 느린 구보로 달리다 [neurin guboro dallida] *v* canter; (길거리 등을) 달리다 [(gilgeori deungeul) dallida] *vi* run

달성 [dalseong] 달성하다 [dalseonghada] *v* achieve

달아나다 [daranada] *v* flee

달팽이 [dalpaengi] *n* snail; 민달팽이 [mindalpaengi] *n* slug

닭 [dalg] *n* chicken; 수탉 [sutalg] *n* cock;

암탉 [amtalg] *n* hen

닮다 [darmda] *v* resemble, take after

담 [dam] 담석 [damseok] *n* gallstone

담그다 [damgeuda] 매리네이드에 담그다 [maerineideue damgeuda] *v* marinade; 잠깐 담그다 [jamkkan damgeuda] *n* dip

담낭 [damnang] *n* gall bladder

담당자 [damdangja] 말 사육 담당자 [mal sayuk damdangja] *n* groom

담배 [dambae] *n* cigarette, tobacco; 담배가게 [dambaegage] *n* tobacconist's

담보 [dambo] 주택담보 융자 [jutaekdambo yungja] *n* mortgage

담비 [dambi] 흰담비 [huindambi] *n* ferret

담요 [damyo] *n* blanket; 전기 담요 [jeongi damyo] *n* electric blanket; 담요를 하나 더 갖다 주세요 [damyoreul hana deo gatda juseyo] Please bring me an extra blanket; 담요가 더 필요해요 [damyoga deo pillyohaeyo] We need more blankets

담쟁이덩굴 [damjaengideonggul] *n* ivy

답답하다 [dapdaphada] 답답한 [dapdaphan] *adj* stuffy; 답답한 [dapdaphan] *adj* stifling

답변 [dapbyeon] *n* answer; 답변을 문자로 보내 주시겠어요? [dapbyeoneul munjaro bonae jusigesseoyo?] Can you text me your answer?

당 [dang]...당 [...dang] (각각) *prep* per

당구 [danggu] *npl* billiards

당근 [danggeun] *n* carrot

당기다 [danggida] 앞당기다 [apdanggida] *v* bring forward; 잡아당기다 [jabadanggida] *vt* pull

당나귀 [dangnagwi] *n* donkey

당뇨 [dangnyo] 당뇨가 있어요 [dangnyoga isseoyo] I'm diabetic

당뇨병 [dangnyobyeong] *n* diabetes; 당뇨병 환자 [dangnyobyeong hwanja] *n* diabetic; 당뇨병의 [dangnyobyeongui] *adj* diabetic

당밀 [dangmil] *n* treacle

당신 [dangsin] *pron* you *(plural)*, you *(singular polite)*; 당신 자신 [dangsin jasin] *pron* yourself *(intensifier)*, yourself *(polite)*; 당신의 것 [dangsinui geot] *pron* yours *(singular polite)*; 당신의 것 [dangsinui geot] *pron* yours *(plural)*; 당신의 [dangsinui] *adj* your *(plural)*, your *(singular polite)*; 당신은요? [dangsineunyo?] And you?

당의 [dangui] *n* icing

당일 [dangil] 당일 왕복표 [dangil wangbokpyo] *n* day return

당좌 [dangjwa] 당좌 대월 [dangjwa daewol] *n* overdraft; 당좌계좌 [dangjwagyejwa] *n* current account

당황 [danghwang] 당황하게 하는 [danghwanghage haneun] *adj* puzzling; 당황한 [danghwanghan] *adj* baffled, bewildered, confused, puzzled

닻 [dat] *n* anchor

대 [dae]... 대... [... dae...] *prep* versus; 대나무 [daenamu] *n* bamboo; 시간대 [sigandae] *n* time zone; 계산대 [gyesandae] *n* till; 판매대 [panmaedae] *npl* stands

대각 [daegak] 대각선의 [daegakseonui] *adj* diagonal

대구 [daegu] *n* cod, haddock, whiting

대기 [daegi] *n* atmosphere; 대기명단 [daegimyeongdan] *n* waiting list; 대기실 [daegisil] *n* waiting room; 대기하다 [daegihada] *v* wait up

대기실 [daegisil] 공항대기실 [gonghangdaegisil] *n* departure lounge; 환승 대기실 [hwanseung daegisil] *n* transit lounge

대담 [daedam] 대담한 [daedamhan] *adj* daring

대답 [daedap] *n* answer, reply; 대답하다 [daedaphada] *v* answer, reply

대략 [daeryak] *adv* about, approximately, roughly; 대략적인 [daeryakjeogin] *adj* approximate

대량 [daeryang] *pron* much

대령 [daeryeong] 육군 대령 [yukgun daeryeong] *n* colonel

대로 [daero] *n* avenue

대륙 [daeryuk] *n* continent; 남극 대륙 [namgeuk daeryuk] *n* Antarctic

대리 [daeri] *n* substitute; 대리모 [daerimo] *n* surrogate mother; 대리인 [daeriin] *n* agent, attorney

대머리 [daemeori] 대머리의 [daemeoriui] *adj* bald

대명사 [daemyeongsa] *n* pronoun

대변 [daebyeon] 대변인 [daebyeonin] *n* spokesman, spokesperson; 여자 대변인 [yeoja daebyeonin] *n* spokeswoman

대부분 [daebubun] *adv* largely, mostly

대비 [daebi] 대비하다 [daebihada] *v* provide for

대사 [daesa] *n* ambassador; 신진대사 [sinjindaesa] *n* metabolism

대사관 [daesagwan] *n* embassy; 대사관에 전화하고 싶어요 [daesagwane jeonhwahago sipeoyo] I'd like to phone my embassy; 대사관에 전화해야 해요 [daesagwane jeonhwahaeya haeyo] I need to call my embassy

대서양 [daeseoyang] *n* Atlantic

대성당 [daeseongdang] *n* cathedral; 이 대성당은 언제 열어요? [i daeseongdangeun eonje yeoreoyo?] When is the cathedral open?

대신 [daesin] *n* on behalf of;...대신에 [... daesine] *prep* instead of; 대신하다 [daesinhada] *v* replace, substitute; 그 대신에 [geu daesine] *adv* instead

대야 [daeya] *n* basin

대양 [daeyang] *n* ocean

대접 [daejeop] *n* treat; 대접하다 [daejeophada] *v* entertain

대조 [daejo] *n* contrast

대중 [daejung] *n* public; 대중교통수단 [daejunggyotongsudan] *n* public transport

대차대조 [daechadaejo] 대차대조표 [daechadaejopyo] *n* balance sheet

대참사 [daechamsa] *n* catastrophe

대처 [daecheo] 대처하다 [daecheohada] *v* cope (with)

대출 [daechul] 대출금 [daechulgeum] *n* loan

대칭 [daeching] 대칭적인 [daechingjeogin] *adj* symmetrical

대통령 [daetongnyeong] *n* president

대패 [daepae] n plane (tool)

대표 [daepyo] n chief, rep; 대표자 [daepyoja] n delegate; 대표적인 [daepyojeogin] adj representative; 대표하다 [daepyohada] v represent; 대표하다 [daepyohada] v stand for; 판매대표 [panmaedaepyo] n sales rep

대피 [daepi] 대피소 [daepiso] n layby, shelter

대하다 [daehada]...에 대해 [...e daehae] prep about

대학 [daehak] n college, uni, university; 대학 졸업생 [daehak joreopsaeng] n graduate; 대학 재학생 [daehak jaehaksaeng] n undergraduate; 법과대학 [beopgwadaehak] n law school

대학원 [daehagwon] 대학원생 [daehagwonsaeng] n postgraduate

대항 [daehang] 대항자 [daehangja] n opponent

대행 [daehaeng] 대행사 [daehaengsa] n agency; 대행의 [daehaengui] adj acting

대형 [daehyeong] 대형 수송차 [daehyeong susongcha] abbr HGV; 대형 슈퍼마켓 [daehyeong syupeomaket] n hypermarket

대화 [daehwa] n conversation, dialogue; 대화방 [daehwabang] n chatroom

대회 [daehoe] n rally

댐 [daem] n dam

더듬다 [deodeumda] 말을 더듬다 [mareul deodeumda] v stammer, stutter

더듬다 [deodeumda] 손으로 더듬다 [soneuro deodeumda] v grope

더러움 [deoreoum] n smudge

더럽다 [deoreopda] 더러운 [deoreoun] adj dirty, foul; 더러움 [deoreoum] n dirt; 더러워요 [deoreowoyo] It's dirty; 방이 더러워요 [bangi deoreowoyo] The room is dirty; 시트가 더러워요 [siteuga deoreowoyo] The sheets are dirty; 제 시트가 더러워요 [je siteuga deoreowoyo] My sheets are dirty

더미 [deomi] n stack

더블베이스 [deobeulbeiseu] n double bass

더하다 [deohada]...을 더하여 [...eul deohayeo] prep plus

던지다 [deonjida] v fling, pitch ▷ vt throw; 가볍게 던지다 [gabyeopge deonjida] v toss

덤불 [deombul] n bush (thicket)

덥다 [deopda] 너무 더워요 [neomu deowoyo] I'm too hot, It's a bit too hot; 더워서 잠을 잘 수 없어요 [deowoseo jameul jal su eopseoyo] I can't sleep for the heat; 방이 너무 더워요 [bangi neomu deowoyo] The room is too hot; 아주 더워요 [aju deowoyo] It's very hot

덩굴 [deonggul] n vine; 인동덩굴 [indongdeonggul] n honeysuckle

덩어리 [deongeori] n block (solid piece), loaf, lump, mass (amount); 큰 덩어리 [keun deongeori] n chunk

덮개 [deopgae] n cover

덮다 [deopda] v cover

데님 [denim] n denim; 데님제 옷 [denimje ot] npl denims

데모 [demo] n demo

데우다 [deuda] v heat up, warm up; 이걸 데워 주시겠어요? [igeol dewo jusigesseoyo?] Can you warm this up, please?

데이 [dei] 밸런타인데이 [baelleontaindei] n Valentine's Day

데이지 [deiji] n daisy

데이터베이스 [deiteobeiseu] n database

덴마크 [denmakeu] n Denmark; 덴마크 사람 [denmakeu saram] n Dane; 덴마크어 [denmakeueo] n Danish (language); 덴마크의 [denmakeuui] adj Danish

도 [do] 무인도 [muindo] n desert island; 지하도 [jihado] n underpass

도구 [dogu] n instrument, tool; 낚시 도구 [nakksi dogu] n fishing tackle; 도구 한 벌 [dogu han beol] n kit

도기 [dogi] n pottery

도끼 [dokki] n axe

도난 [donan] 도난 경보기 [donan gyeongbogi] n burglar alarm; 도난 신고를 하고 싶어요 [donan singoreul hago sipeoyo] I want to report a theft

도넛 [doneot] n doughnut

도덕 [dodeok] n moral; **부도덕한** [budodeokhan] adj immoral; **도덕적인** [dodeokjeogin] adj moral

도둑 [doduk] n thief; **도둑질** [dodukjil] n theft

도둑맞다 [dodungmatda] 카드를 도둑맞았어요 [kadeureul dodungmajasseoyo] My card has been stolen; 지갑을 도둑맞았어요 [jigabeul dodungmajasseoyo] My wallet has been stolen

도로 [doro] n road; **도로 공사** [doro gongsa] npl roadworks; **도로 표지** [doro pyoji] n road sign, signpost; **도로세** [dorose] n road tax; **도로의 살얼음** [doroui sareoreum] n black ice; **도로지도** [dorojido] n road map; **도로계획** [dorogyehoek] n street plan; **순환도로** [sunhwandoro] n ring road; **자전거 도로** [jajeongeo doro] n cycle lane, cycle path; **중심도로** [jungsimdoro] n main road; **중앙 분리대가 있는 도로** [jungang bullidaega inneun doro] n dual carriageway; **고속도로** [gosokdoro] n motorway;... **도로 지도가 필요해요** [... doro jidoga pilyohaeyo] I need a road map of...; **시내 도로 지도가 필요해요** [sinae doro jidoga pillyohaeyo] I want a street map of the city; **이 지역 도로 지도 있어요?** [i jiyeok doro jido isseoyo?] Do you have a road map of this area?

도망 [domang] 도망가다 [domanggada] v run away

도매 [domae] n wholesale; **도매의** [domaeui] adj wholesale

도미노 [domino] n domino ▷ npl dominoes

도미니카 [dominika] 도미니카 공화국 [dominika gonghwaguk] n Dominican Republic

도박 [dobak] n gambling; **도박을 하다** [dobageul hada] v gamble; **도박장** [dobakjang] n betting shop, casino; **도박꾼** [dobakkkun] n gambler

도보 [dobo] 도보 여행자 [dobo yeohaengja] n rambler; 장거리 도보 [janggeori dobo] n tramp (long walk)

도서관 [doseogwan] n library

도시 [dosi] n city, town; **도심** [dosim] n city centre; **도시계획** [dosigyehoek] n town planning; **도시 특산품 있어요?** [dosi teuksanpum isseoyo?] Have you anything typical of this town?

도시락 [dosirak] n packed lunch

도심 [dosim] n town centre; **도심지에** [dosimjie] adv downtown

도용 [doyong] 명의 도용 [myeongui doyong] n identity theft

도움 [doum] n assistance, help; **도와줘요!** [dowajwoyo!] excl help!; **도움이 되지 않는** [doumi doeji annneun] adj unhelpful

도자기 [dojagi] n china

도장 [dojang] n seal (mark)

도전 [dojeon] n challenge; **도전적인** [dojeonjeogin] adj challenging; **도전하다** [dojeonhada] v challenge

도중 [dojung] 도중에 [dojunge] adv halfway

도착 [dochak] n arrival; **복장 도착자** [bokjang dochakja] n transvestite; **도착하다** [dochakhada] v arrive, get in; **도착하다** [dochakhada] v reach

도착하다 [dochakhada] 우리가 일찍/ 늦게 도착했어요 [uriga iljjik/ neutge dochakhaesseoyo] We arrived early/ late

도청장치 [docheongjangchi] 도청장치 된 [docheongjangchiga doen] adj bugged

도토리 [dotori] n acorn

도표 [dopyo] n chart

독 [dok] n poison; **독버섯** [dokbeoseot] n toadstool; **독주** [dokju] n solo; **독주자** [dokjuja] n soloist; **독액** [dogaek] n venom; **독을 넣다** [dogeul neota] v poison; **해독제** [haedokje] n antidote

독감 [dokgam] n flu; **독감에 걸렸어요** [dokgame geollyeosseoyo] I've got flu; **최근에 독감을 앓았어요** [choegeune dokgameul arasseoyo] I had flu recently

독립 [dongnip] n independence;

독립적인 [dongnipjeogin] adj independent

독서 [dokseo] n reading

독수리 [doksuri] n eagle, vulture

독일 [dogil] n Germany; 독일 사람 [dogil saram] n German (person); 독일어 [dogireo] n German (language); 독일의 [dogirui] adj German

독자 [dokja] n reader

독재 [dokjae] 독재자 [dokjaeja] n dictator

독점 [dokjeom] n monopoly; 독점적으로 [dokjeomjeogeuro] adv exclusively

독창 [dokchang] 독창적인 [dokchangjeogin] adj ingenious

독특 [dokteuk] 독특한 [dokteukhan] adj distinctive, unique

돈 [don] n money; 돈쓰다 [donsseuda] v spend; 돈 좀 빌려 주시겠어요? [don jom billyeo jusigesseoyo?] Could you lend me some money?; 돈을 급히 보내 줄 수 있나요? [doneul geuphi bonae jul su innayo?] Can you arrange to have some money sent over urgently?; 돈이 떨어졌어요 [doni tteoreojyeosseoyo] I have run out of money; 돈이 없어요 [doni eopseoyo] I have no money

돌 [dol] n stone; 조약돌 [joyakdol] n pebble

돌고래 [dolgorae] n dolphin

돌다 [dolda] v go around, turn; 돌아오게 하다 [doraoge hada] v get back;...에 가려면 여기서 돌아야 하나요? [...e garyeomyeon yeogiseo doraya hanayo?] Is this the turning for...?

돌려 [dollyeo] 돌려보내다 [dollyeobonaeda] v send back

돌려주다 [dollyeojuda] v bring back

돌발 [dolbal] n outbreak

돌보다 [dolboda] v care, look after; 돌보는 [dolboneun] adj caring

돌아가다 [doragada] 골고루 돌아가다 [golgoru doragada] v go round

돌아오다 [doraoda] v come back, return

돌진 [doljin] 돌진하다 [doljinhada] vi dash

돕다 [dopda] (남을) 돕다 [(nameul) dopda] n help; 빨리 도와주세요! [ppalli dowajuseyo!] Fetch help quickly!; 도와 주시겠어요? [dowa jusigesseoyo?] Can you help me, please?; 도와주세요! [dowajuseyo!] Help!; 도와주시겠어요? [dowajusigesseoyo?] Can you help me?; 타는 것 좀 도와 주시겠어요? [taneun geot jom dowa jusigesseoyo?] Can you help me get on, please?

동 [dong] 남동쪽 [namdongjjok] n southeast; 동쪽 [dongjjok] n east; 동쪽에 [dongjjoge] adv east; 동쪽으로 가는 [dongjjogeuro ganeun] adj eastbound; 동쪽의 [dongjjogui] adj east, eastern; 극동 [geukdong] n Far East

동굴 [donggul] n cave

동급 [donggeup] 동급생 [donggeupsaeng] n classmate

동기 [donggi] n motive; 동기를 부여 받은 [donggireul buyeo badeun] adj motivated; 동기부여 [donggibuyeo] n motivation

동등 [dongdeung] 동등한 것 [dongdeunghan geot] n equivalent

동료 [dongnyo] n colleague

동맥 [dongmaek] n artery

동맹 [dongmaeng] n alliance

동맹국 [dongmaengguk] n ally

동물 [dongmul] n animal; 동물원 [dongmurwon] n zoo; 동물의 발 [dongmurui bal] n paw; 동물군 [dongmulgun] npl fauna; 동물학 [dongmulhak] n zoology; 설치류 동물 [seolchiryu dongmul] n rodent; 야생 생물 [yasaeng saengmul] n wildlife; 애완 동물 [aewan dongmul] n pet; 길잃은 동물 [girireun dongmul] n stray; 포유동물 [poyudongmul] n mammal

동반 [dongban] 동반자 [dongbanja] n companion; 어린이를 동반해도 될까요? [eorinireul dongbanhaedo doelkkayo?] Is it okay to take children?

동사 [dongsa] n verb

동시 [dongsi] 동시에 [dongsie] adv simultaneously; 동시에 일어나다 [dongsie ireonada] v coincide; 동시의 [dongsiui] adj simultaneous

동안 [dongan]...하는 동안에 [...haneun dongane] *n* while;...동안 [...dongan] *prep* during; 그 동안에 [geu dongane] *adv* meantime, meanwhile; 여름 동안에 [yeoreum dongane] during the summer

동양 [dongyang] *n* Orient; 동양의 [dongyangui] *adj* oriental

동요 [dongyo] *n* nursery rhyme

동의 [dongui] 동의하다 [donguihada] *v* agree

동일 [dongil] 동일한 [dongilhan] *adj* identical, same

동자 [dongja] 눈동자 [nundongja] *n* pupil *(eye)*

동적 [dongjeok] 동적인 [dongjeogin] *adj* dynamic

동전 [dongjeon] *n* coin; 동전 구멍 [dongjeon gumeong] *n* slot; 전화걸기 위해 동전을 바꾸고 싶어요 [jeonhwageolgi wihae dongjeoneul bakkugo sipeoyo] I'd like some coins for the phone, please

동점 [dongjeom] *n* draw *(tie)*

동정 [dongjeong] *n* pity, sympathy; 동정적인 [dongjeongjeogin] *adj* sympathetic; 동정하다 [dongjeonghada] *v* sympathize

동종 [dongjong] 동종 요법 [dongjong yobeop] *n* homeopathy; 동종 요법의 [dongjong yobeobui] *adj* homeopathic

동침 [dongchim] 동침하다 [dongchimhada] *v* sleep together

동행 [donghaeng] 동행하다 [donghaenghada] *v* accompany

동화 [donghwa] *n* fairytale

돛 [dot] *n* sail

돼지 [dwaeji] *n* pig; 돼지 저금통 [dwaeji jeogeumtong] *n* piggybank; 돼지고기 [dwaejigogi] *n* pork; 돼지고기 토막 [dwaejigogi tomak] *n* pork chop

되다 [doeda]...이 되다 [...i doeda] *v* become

되돌리다 [doedollida] *v* put back

되돌아가다 [doedoragada] *v* retrace

되찾다 [doechatda] *v* regain

두건 [dugeon] *n* hood

두근거리다 [dugeungeorida] *v* throb

두꺼비 [dukkeobi] *n* toad; 두꺼비집 [dukkeobijip] *n* fuse box

두껍다 [dukkeopda] 두꺼운 [dukkeoun] *adj* thick

두께 [dukke] *n* thickness

두다 [duda] *v* deposit, lay; 한쪽에 두다 [hanjjoge duda] *v* put aside

두더지 [dudeoji] *n* mole *(mammal)*

두드러지다 [dudeureojida] *v* stand out, stick out

두드리다 [dudeurida] *v* knock; 가볍게 두드리기 [gabyeopge dudeurigi] *n* tap

두려움 [duryeoum] *n* fear, scare

두려워하다 [duryeowohada] *v* fear; 두려워하여 [duryeowohayeo] *adj* afraid

두루미 [durumi] *n* crane *(bird)*

두목 [dumok] *n* godfather *(criminal leader)*

두번 [dubeon] 두 번 [du beon] *adv* twice

두번째 [dubeonjjae] 두번째로 [dubeonjjaero] *adv* secondly; 두번째의 [dubeonjjaeui] *n* second

두통약 [dutongyak] 두통약 주세요 [dutongyak juseyo] I'd like something for a headache

둑 [duk] *n* bank *(ridge)*, embankment

둔감 [dungam] 둔감한 [dungamhan] *adj* insensitive

둘러보다 [dulleoboda] 주변을 둘러보다 [jubyeoneul dulleoboda] *v* look round; 그냥 둘러보는 중이에요 [geunyang dulleoboneun jungieyo] I'm just looking

둘러싸다 [dulleossada] *v* surround

둥글다 [dunggeulda] 둥근 [dunggeun] *adj* round

둥지 [dungji] *n* nest

뒤 [dwi] *n* rear; 뒤로 이동하다 [dwiro idonghada] *v* move back; 뒤쪽으로 [dwijjogeuro] *adv* backwards; 뒤에 [dwie] *adv* behind, back; 뒤의 [dwiui] *adj* back, rear;...의 뒤에 [...ui dwie] *prep* behind

뒤기 [dwigi] 멀리뛰기 [meollittwigi] *n* jump

뒤꿈치 [dwikkumchi] *n* heel

뒤엎다 [dwieopda] *v* upset

뒤집다 [dwijipda] 뒤집히다 [dwijiphida] v capsize

뒤쳐지다 [dwichyeojida] 저만 뒤쳐졌어요 [jeoman dwichyeojyeosseoyo] I've been left behind

뒷면 [dwitmyeon] 뒷면에 계속 [dwitmyeone gyesok] abbr PTO

뒷문 [dwitmun] 뒷문 열쇠는 어느 것인가요? [dwitmun yeolsoeneun eoneu geosingayo?] Which is the key for the back door?

드라이 [deurai] 커트하고 드라이 해주세요 [keoteuhago deurai haejuseyo] A cut and blow-dry, please

드라이브 [deuraibeu] n drive

드라이어 [deuraieo] 헤어 드라이어 [heeo deuraieo] n hairdryer

드라이클리닝 [deuraikeullining] n dry-cleaning

드러내다 [deureonaeda] v bare, disclose, reveal

드러머 [deureomeo] n drummer

드럼 [deureom] n drum; 베이스 드럼 [beiseu deureom] n bass drum

드럽다 [deureopda] 샤워기가 더러워요 [syawogiga deoreowoyo] The shower is dirty; 세면기가 더러워요 [semyeongiga deoreowoyo] The washbasin is dirty

드레스 [deureseu] n dress; 웨딩드레스 [wedingdeureseu] n wedding dress

드릴 [deuril] n drill

드문 [deumun] adj rare (uncommon)

드물다 [deumulda] 드물게 [deumulge] adv rarely, seldom

득점 [deukjeom] n score (game/match); 득점하다 [deukjeomhada] v score

듣다 [deutda] v hear, listen; 듣기 [deutgi] n hearing

들것 [deulgeot] n stretcher

들끓다 [deulkkeurta] 세상을 들끓게 하는 [sesangeul deulkkeurke haneun] adj sensational

들다 [deulda] ...하고 싶은 마음이 드는 [...hago sipeun maeumi deuneun] adj willing; 안에 들이지 않다 [ane deuriji anta] v keep out

들어가다 [deureogada] v go in, enter; 움푹 들어가게 하다 [umpuk deureogage hada] v dent

들어맞다 [deureomatda] v fit in

들어오다 [deureooda] v enter; 들어오세요! [deureooseyo!] Come in!

들여놓다 [deullyeonota] v stock

들이쉬다 [deuriswida] v breathe in

들판 [deulpan] n field

등 [deung] n back; 등뼈 [deungppyeo] n backbone; 안개등 [angaedeung] n fog light; 전조등 [jeonjodeung] n headlamp, headlight; 정지등 [jeongjideung] n brake light; 가로등 [garodeung] n streetlamp; 기타 등등 [gita deungdeung] abbr etc; 등이 아파요 [deungi apayo] I've hurt my back, My back is sore; 등이 안 좋아요 [deungi an johayo] I've got a bad back

등급 [deunggeup] n grade; 2등급의 [ideunggeubui] adj second-rate

등기 [deunggi] 등기소 [deunggiso] n registry office; 등기우편 [deunggiupyeon] n recorded delivery; 등기 우편은 도착하는 데 얼마나 걸려요? [deunggi upyeoneun dochakhaneun de eolmana geollyeoyo?] How long will it take by registered post?

등대 [deungdae] n lighthouse

등록 [deungnok] n register, registration; 등록된 [deungnokdoen] adj registered; 등록하다 [deungnokhada] v register, sign on

등반 [deungban] n climbing; 등반하다 [deungbanhada] v climb; 조랑말 등반 [jorangmal deungban] n pony trekking

등산 [deungsan] n mountaineering; 등산자 [deungsanja] n mountaineer; 등산가 [deungsanga] n climber

등유 [deungyu] n paraffin

등화 [deunghwa] 등화관제 [deunghwagwanje] n blackout

디스켓 [diseuket] n diskette

디스코 [diseuko] n disco

디스크 [diseukeu] n disc, disk; 디스크 드라이브 [diseukeu deuraibeu] n disk drive; 디스크 자키 [diseukeu jaki] abbr disc jockey, DJ; **콤팩트디스크** [kompaekteudiseukeu] n compact disc, CD; **플로피 디스크** [peullopi diseukeu] n floppy disk; **하드 디스크** [hadeu diseukeu] n hard disk

디옥시리보핵산 [dioksiribohaeksan] n DNA

디자인 [dijain] n design; **디자이너** [dijaineo] n designer; **디자인하다** [dijainhada] v design

디저트 [dijeoteu] n dessert; **디저트스푼** [dijeoteuseupun] n dessert spoon

디젤 [dijel] **디젤기관** [dijelgigwan] n diesel; **디젤...어치요** [dijel...eochiyo]... worth of diesel, please

디지털 [dijiteol] **디지털 라디오** [dijiteol radio] n digital radio; **디지털 방식의** [dijiteol bangsigui] adj digital; **디지털 카메라** [dijiteol kamera] n digital camera; **디지털 시계** [dijiteol sigye] n digital watch; **디지털 텔레비전** [dijiteol tellebijeon] n digital television

디지털 카메라 [dijiteol kamera] **이 디지털 카메라에 사용하는 메모리 카드 주세요** [i dijiteol kamerae sayonghaneun memori kadeu juseyo] A memory card for this digital camera, please

딥 [dip] n dip (food/sauce)

따갑다 [ttagapda] **눈이 따가워요** [nuni ttagawoyo] My eyes are sore

따개 [ttagae] **병따개** [byeongttagae] n bottle-opener; **깡통따개** [kkangtongttagae] n can-opener, tin-opener

따뜻하다 [ttatteutada] **따뜻하게 하다** [ttatteutage hada] v warm up; **따뜻한** [ttatteutan] adj warm

따라 [ttara]**...에 따라** [...e ttara] prep according to;**...을 따라** [...eul ttara] prep along

따라서 [ttaraseo] adv accordingly, consequently

따로 [ttaro] **따로따로** [ttarottaro] adv apart

따옴표 [ttaompyo] npl inverted commas

딱딱하다 [ttakttakhada] **딱딱한** [ttakttakhan] adj stiff

딱정벌레 [ttakjeongbeolle] n beetle

딴조 [ttanjo] **단조하다** [danjohada] (금속) v forge

딸 [ttal] n daughter; **의붓딸** [uibutthtal] n stepdaughter; **딸을 잃어버렸어요** [ttareul ireobeoryeosseoyo] My daughter is lost; **딸이 없어졌어요** [ttari eopseojyeosseoyo] My daughter is missing

딸기 [ttalgi] n strawberry; **나무딸기** [namuttalgi] n raspberry; **검은딸기** [geomeunttalgi] n blackberry

딸꾹질 [ttalkkukjil] npl hiccups

땀 [ttam] n perspiration, sweat; 땀을 흘리다 [ttameul heullida] v sweat; 땀투성이의 [ttamtuseongui] adj sweaty

땅 [ttang] n ground, land

땅콩 [ttangkong] n peanut; 땅콩 버터 [ttangkong beoteo] n peanut butter; 땅콩 알레르기 [ttangkong allereugi] n peanut allergy; 땅콩 알레르기가 있어요 [ttangkong allereugiga isseoyo] I'm allergic to peanuts; 땅콩이 들어 있나요? [ttangkongi deureo innayo?] Does that contain peanuts?

땋다 [ttata] 땋은 것 [ttaheun geot] n plait

때 [ttae]...인 때 [...in ttae] conj when; 그 때에 [geu ttaee] adv then

때때로 [ttaettaero] adv occasionally, sometimes

때리다 [ttaerida] v beat (strike) ▷ vt hit; 때려눕히다 [ttaeryeonuphida] v knock down; 세게 때리다 [sege ttaerida] v smack; 찰싹 때리다 [chalssak ttaerida] v slap, spank, swat

때문 [ttaemun]... 때문에 [... ttaemune] prep owing to; 때문에 [ttaemune] conj because

떠나다 [tteonada] v get out, go away, leave; 저는 내일 떠나요 [jeoneun naeil tteonayo] I'm leaving tomorrow

떠돌다 [tteodolda] vi drift

떨다 [tteolda] v shudder, tremble; 덜덜 떨다 [deoldeol tteolda] v shiver

떨리다 [tteollida] 떨리는 [tteollineun] adj shaky

떨어지다 [tteoreojida] vi fall; 멀리 떨어진 [meolli tteoreojin] adj remote; 뒤떨어지다 [dwitteoreojida] v lag behind; 떨어져 [tteoreojyeo] adv away, off

뗏목 [ttetmok] n raft

또는 [ttoneun] conj or

또한 [ttohan] adv also;...도 또한 [...do ttohan] adv too

뚜껑 [ttukkeong] n lid

뚱뚱하다 [ttungttunghada] 뚱뚱한 [ttungttunghan] adj obese

뛰다 [ttwida] v leap, jump; 멀리뛰기 [meollittwigi] n long jump; 높이뛰기 [nopittwigi] n high jump; 뛰어들다 [ttwieodeulda] v plunge; 뛰기 [ttwigi] n run; 가볍게 뛰어넘다 [gabyeopge ttwieoneomda] vt skip

뛰어나다 [ttwieonada] v excel; 아주 뛰어난 [aju ttwieonan] adj excellent

뜨개 [tteugae] 뜨개바늘 [tteugaebaneul] n knitting needle

뜨개질 [tteugaejil] n knitting

뜨겁다 [tteugeopda] 뜨거운 [tteugeoun] adj hot; 음식이 너무 뜨거워요 [eumsigi neomu tteugeowoyo] The food is too hot

뜨다 [tteuda] vi float ▷ vt knit; 뜨는 것 [tteuneun geot] n float; 코바늘로 뜨다 [kobaneullo tteuda] v crochet

뜰 [tteul] 안뜰 [antteul] n courtyard

뜻 [tteut] n meaning; 무슨 뜻인가요? [museun tteusingayo?] What does this mean?

뜻밖 [tteutbakk] 뜻밖의 [tteutbakkui] adj unexpected

뜻밖에 [tteutbakke] adv unexpectedly

띠 [tti] n band (strip); 머리띠 [meoritti] n hairband

ㄹ

라디에이터 [radieiteo] 라디에이터가 새고 있어요 [radieiteoga saego isseoyo] There is a leak in the radiator

라디오 [radio] n radio; 라디오 방송국 [radio bangsongguk] n radio station; 라디오 켜도 돼요? [radio kyeodo dwaeyo?] Can I switch the radio on?; 라디오 꺼도 돼요? [radio kkeodo dwaeyo?] Can I switch the radio off?

라마단 [ramadan] n Ramadan

라벤더 [rabendeo] n lavender

라벨 [rabel] n label

라오스 [raoseu] n Laos

라운지 [raunji] n lounge

라이베리아 [raiberia] n Liberia; 라이베리아 사람 [raiberia saram] n Liberian; 라이베리아의 [raiberiaui] adj Liberian

라이브 [raibeu] adj live; 어디에서 라이브 음악을 들을 수 있어요? [eodieseo raibeu eumageul deureul su isseoyo?] Where can we hear live music?

라이터 [raiteo] n cigarette lighter, lighter

라일락 [raillak] n lilac

라일로 [raillo] 라일로 (에어매트리스) [raillo (eeomaeteuriseu)] n Lilo®

라임 [raim] n lime (fruit)

라켓 [raket] n racquet

라트비아 [rateubia] n Latvia; 라트비아 사람 [rateubia saram] n Latvian (person); 라트비아어 [rateubiaeo] n Latvian (language); 라트비아의 [rateubiaui] adj Latvian

라틴 [ratin] 라틴 아메리카 [ratin amerika] n Latin America; 라틴 아메리카의 [ratin amerikaui] adj Latin American; 라틴어 [ratineo] n Latin

란제리 [ranjeri] n lingerie; 란제리 매장은 어디에 있나요? [ranjeri maejangeun eodie innayo?] Where is the lingerie department?

랍비 [rapbi] n rabbi

래커 [raekeo] n lacquer

램프 [raempeu] n lamp, slip road; 램프의 갓 [raempeuui gat] n lampshade; 침대 맡의 램프 [chimdae matui raempeu] n bedside lamp; 램프가 작동하지 않아요 [raempeuga jakdonghaji anhayo] The lamp is not working

량 [ryang] 복용량 [bogyongnyang] n dose

러스크 [reoseukeu] n rusk

러시아 [reosia] n Russia; 러시아 사람 [reosia saram] n Russian (person); 러시아어 [reosiaeo] n Russian (language); 러시아의 [reosiaui] adj Russian

러시아워 [reosiawo] n rush hour ▷ npl peak hours

럭비 [reokbi] n rugby

런던 [reondeon] n London

레깅스 [regingseu] npl leggings

레모네이드 [remoneideu] n lemonade; 레모네이드 한 잔 주세요 [remoneideu han jan juseyo] A glass of lemonade, please

레몬 [remon] n lemon; 레몬 껍질 [remon kkeopjil] n zest (lemon-peel); 레몬 넣어서요 [remon neoheoseoyo] with lemon

레바논 [rebanon] n Lebanon; 레바논 사람 [rebanon saram] n Lebanese; 레바논의 [rebanonui] adj Lebanese

레슬링 [reseulling] n wrestling; 레슬링 선수 [reseulling seonsu] n wrestler

레오타드 [reotadeu] n leotard

레이더 [reideo] n radar

레이스 [reiseu] n lace

레이저 [reijeo] n laser

레인지 [reinji] n oven; 전자레인지

[jeonjareinji] n microwave oven

레저 [rejeo] n leisure; 레저 센터 [rejeo senteo] n leisure centre

렌즈 [renjeu] n lens; 줌 렌즈 [jum renjeu] n zoom lens

렌치 [renchi] n wrench

렌트카 [renteuka] n hire car, hired car, rental car

력 [ryeok] 노동력 [nodongnyeok] n workforce; 의지력 [uijiryeok] n willpower

로고 [rogo] n logo

로그아웃 [rogeuaut] 로그아웃하다 [rogeuautada] v log out

로그오프 [rogeuopeu] 로그오프하다 [rogeuopeuhada] v log off

로그온 [rogeuon] 로그온하다 [rogeuonhada] v log on

로그인 [rogeuin] 로그인하다 [rogeuinhada] v log in

로마 [roma] 로마의 [romaui] adj Roman

로마네스크 [romaneseukeu] 로마네스크 양식의 [romaneseukeu yangsigui] adj Romanesque

로맨스 [romaenseu] n romance; 로맨틱한 [romaentikhan] adj romantic

로봇 [robot] n robot

로비 [robi] n lobby; 로비에서 만나요 [robieseo mannayo] I'll meet you in the lobby

로서 [roseo]...로서 [...roseo] prep as

로션 [rosyeon] n lotion; 볕에 탄 후 바르는 로션 [byeote tan hu bareuneun rosyeon] n after sun lotion; 면도한 후 바르는 로션 [myeondohan hu bareuneun rosyeon] n aftershave; 클렌징 로션 [keullenjing rosyeon] n cleansing lotion

로제 [roje] n rosé; 좋은 로제 와인을 추천해 주시겠어요? [joheun roje waineul chucheonhae jusigesseoyo?] Can you recommend a good rosé wine?

로즈마리 [rojeumari] 로즈메리 [rojeumeri] n rosemary

로켓 [roket] n rocket

롤 [rol] 헤어롤 [heeorol] n curler

롤러스케이트 [rolleoseukeiteu] npl rollerskates; 롤러스케이트 타기 [rolleoseukeiteu tagi] n rollerskating; 어디에서 롤러 스케이트를 탈 수 있어요? [eodieseo rolleo seukeiteureul tal su isseoyo?] Where can we go roller skating?

롤러코스터 [rolleokoseuteo] n rollercoaster

료 [ryo] 봉사료 [bongsaryo] n cover charge; 조미료 [jomiryo] n seasoning; 수업료 [sueomnyo] npl tuition fees; 감미료 [gammiryo] n sweetener

루마니아 [rumania] n Romania; 루마니아 사람 [rumania saram] n Romanian (person); 루마니아어 [rumaniaeo] n Romanian (language); 루마니아의 [rumaniaui] adj Romanian

룩셈부르크 [ruksembureukeu] n Luxembourg

룰렛 [rullet] n roulette

룸서비스 [rumseobiseu] 룸 서비스가 있어요? [rum seobiseuga isseoyo?] Is there room service?

류머티즘 [ryumeotijeum] n rheumatism

리넨 [rinen] n linen

리놀륨 [rinollyum] n lino

리듬 [rideum] n rhythm

리모컨 [rimokeon] n remote control

리무진 [rimujin] n limousine

리본 [ribon] n ribbon

리비아 [ribia] n Libya; 리비아 사람 [ribia saram] n Libyan; 리비아의 [ribiaui] adj Libyan

리코더 [rikodeo] n recorder (music)

리큐어 [rikyueo] n liqueur; 어떤 리큐어가 있나요? [eotteon rikyueoga innayo?] What liqueurs do you have?

리크 [rikeu] n leek

리터 [riteo] n litre

리투아니아 [rituania] n Lithuania; 리투아니아 사람 [rituania saram] n Lithuanian (person); 리투아니아어 [rituaniaeo] n Lithuanian (language); 리투아니아의 [rituaniaui] adj Lithuanian

리프트 [ripeuteu] n lift; 스키장 리프트 [seukijang ripeuteu] n chairlift; 리프트는 어디있어요? [ripeuteuneun eodiisseoyo?] Where is the lift?;

리프트가 있나요? [ripeuteuga innayo?] Is there a lift?; 마지막 리프트는 언제 가나요? [majimak ripeuteuneun eonje ganayo?] When does the last chair-lift go?; 첫 리프트는 언제 가나요? [cheot ripeuteuneun eonje ganayo?] When does the first chair-lift go?; 휠체어 리프트가 있나요? [hwilcheeo ripeuteuga innayo?] Do you have a lift for wheelchairs?

리히텐슈타인 [rihitensyutain] *n* Liechtenstein

린스 [rinseu] *n* conditioner

릴 [ril] *n* reel

립스틱 [ripseutik] *n* lipstick

마가린 [magarin] *n* margarine

마감 [magam] 마감 시간 [magam sigan] *n* deadline

마개 [magae] *n* plug; 마개 구멍 [magae gumeong] *n* plughole; 마개로 막다 [magaero makda] *v* plug in; 귀마개 [gwimagae] *npl* earplugs

마구 [magu] 마구간 [magugan] *n* stable

마녀 [manyeo] *n* witch

마늘 [maneul] *n* garlic; 속에 마늘이 있나요? [soge maneuri innayo?] Is there any garlic in it?

마다가스카르 [madagaseukareu] *n* Madagascar

마당 [madang] *n* yard (*enclosure*)

마라톤 [maraton] *n* marathon

마루 [maru] 층계 꼭대기의 마루 [cheunggye kkokdaegiui maru] *n* landing

마르다 [mareuda] 마른 [mareun] *adj* skinny

마르크스주의 [mareukeuseujuui] Marxism

마리화나 [marihwana] *n* marijuana

마멀레이드 [mameolleideu] *n* marmalade

마무리하다 [mamurihada] *v* finalize

마법 [mabeop] 마법사 [mabeopsa] *n* sorcerer; 마법의 [mabeobui] *n* magic

마비 [mabi] *n* paralysis; 마비된 [mabidoen] *adj* paralysed; 소아마비 [soamabi] *n* polio; 심장마비

[simjangmabi] *n* heart attack; 교통마비 [gyotongmabi] *n* traffic jam

마사지 [masaji] *n* massage

마술 [masul] *n* magic; 마술사 [masulsa] *n* conjurer, juggler, magician; 마술적인 [masuljeogin] *adj* magical

마스카라 [maseukara] *n* mascara

마스크 [maseukeu] *n* mask; 마스크를 쓴 [maseukeureul sseun] *adj* masked

마시다 [masida] *v* drink; 무엇을 좀 마시겠어요? [mueoseul jom masigesseoyo?] Would you like a drink?; 마실 것 드릴까요? [masil geot deurilkkayo?] Would you like a drink?; 마실 것 좀 갖다 줄까요? [masil geot jom gatda julkkayo?] Can I get you a drink?; 뭘 마시시겠어요? [mwol masisigesseoyo?] What would you like to drink?; 뭘 마시겠어요? [mwol masigesseoyo?] What would you like to drink?; 저는 술 안 마셔요 [jeoneun sul an masyeoyo] I'm not drinking; 저는 술을 안 마셔요 [jeoneun sureul an masyeoyo] I don't drink alcohol; 저는 와인을 절대 마시지 않아요 [jeoneun waineul jeoldae masiji anhayo] I never drink wine; 고맙지만, 마시지 않겠어요 [gomapjiman, masiji ankesseoyo] I'm not drinking, thank you

마약 [mayak] *n* drugs, narcotics; 마약 중독자 [mayak jungdokja] *n* drug addict; 마약상 [mayaksang] *n* drug dealer

마오리 [maori] 마오리 사람 [maori saram] *n* Maori (*person*); 마오리어 [maorieo] *n* Maori (*language*); 마오리의 [maoriui] *adj* Maori

마요네즈 [mayonejeu] *n* mayonnaise

마우스 [mauseu] *n* mouse (*computer*); 마우스패드 [mauseupaedeu] *n* mouse mat

마을 [maeul] *n* village

마음 [maeum] *n* mind;...하고 싶은 마음이 드는 [...hago sipeun maeumi deuneun] *adj* willing; 마음이 내키지 않는 [maeumi naekiji annneun] *adj* reluctant; 마음이 좁은 [maeumi jobeun] *adj* narrow-minded

마이크 [maikeu] *n* microphone, mike; 마이크가 있어요? [maikeuga isseoyo?] Does it have a microphone?

마일 [mail] *n* mile; 시속 마일 수 [sisok mail su] *abbr* mph; 총 마일수 [chong mailsu] *n* mileage

마저럼 [majeoreom] *n* marjoram

마지막 [majimak] 마지막의 [majimagui] *adj* last

마찬가지 [machangaji] 마찬가지로 [machangajiro] *prep* as

마천루 [macheollu] *n* skyscraper

마취 [machwi] 마취제 [machwije] *n* anaesthetic; 전신 마취 [jeonsin machwi] *n* general anaesthetic; 국소마취 [guksomachwi] *n* local anaesthetic

마침내 [machimnae] *adv* finally, last

마침표 [machimpyo] *n* full stop

마카로니 [makaroni] *npl* macaroni

마케팅 [maketing] *n* marketing

마호가니 [mahogani] *n* mahogany

막다 [makda] *v* block

막대 [makdae] *n* bar (*strip*), rod

막연 [magyeon] 막연한 [magyeonhan] *adj* vague

막히다 [makhida] 막힌 [makhin] *adj* blocked; 숨이 막히다 [sumi makhida] *vi* choke; 변기가 막혔어요 [byeongiga makhyeosseoyo] The toilet won't flush; 왜 이렇게 길이 막혀요? [wae ireoke giri makhyeoyo?] What is causing this hold-up?

만 [man] *n* bay

만기 [mangi] 만기일 [mangiil] *n* expiry date; 만기가 된 [mangiga doen] *adj* due; 유통만기일 [yutongmangiil] *n* sell-by date

만나다 [mannada] *v* meet up, meet; 로비에서 만나요 [robieseo mannayo] I'll meet you in the lobby; 나중에 만날까요? [najunge mannalkkayo?] Shall we meet afterwards?; 만나서 반가워요 [mannaseo bangawoyo] Pleased to meet you; 만나서 반가웠습니다 [mannaseo bangawosseumnida] It was a pleasure to meet you; 어디에서 만날까요?

[eodieseo mannalkkayo?] Where can we meet?, Where shall we meet?

만남 [mannam] *n* meeting

만년필 [mannyeonpil] *n* fountain pen

만두 [mandu] *n* dumpling

만들다 [mandeulda] *v* make; 손으로 만든 [soneuro mandeun] *adj* handmade; 집에서 만든 [jibeseo mandeun] *adj* home-made

만료 [mallyo] 만료되다 [mallyodoeda] *v* expire

만성 [manseong] 만성의 [manseongui] *adj* chronic

만세 [manse] 만세! [manse!] *excl* hooray!

만유 [manyu] *n* cruise

만일 [manil] 만일...이면 [manil...imyeon] *conj* if

만장일치 [manjangilchi] 만장일치인 [manjangilchiin] *adj* unanimous

만족 [manjok] *n* satisfaction; 만족스러운 [manjokseureoun] *adj* satisfactory; 만족한 [manjokhan] *adj* satisfied

만지다 [manjida] *v* touch

만찬 [manchan] *n* dinner; 만찬회 [manchanhoe] *n* dinner party

만화 [manhwa] *n* cartoon, comic strip; 만화책 [manhwachaek] *n* comic book

많다 [manta] 보다 많은 양 [boda manheun yang] *pron* more; 더 많은 [deo manheun] *adj* more; 더 많이 [deo manhi] *adv* more; 많은 [manheun] *adj* many, much; 말이 많은 [mari manheun] *adj* talkative; 매우 많은 [maeu manheun] *adj* numerous; 가장 많은 [gajang manheun] *adj* most; 가장 많이 [gajang manhi] *adv* most (*superlative*); 미터기에 나온 것보다 많아요 [miteogie naon geotboda manhayo] It's more than on the meter; ...이 너무 많이 들어갔어요 [...i neomu manhi deureogasseoyo] There's too much... in it

말 [mal] *n* horse; 말 사육 담당자 [mal sayuk damdangja] *n* groom; 말을 못하는 [mareul motaneun] *adj* dumb, speechless; 말이 많은 [mari manheun] *adj* talkative; 주말 [jumal] *n* weekend;

승마 [seungma] *n* horse riding; 암말 [ammal] *n* mare; 얼룩말 [eollungmal] *n* zebra; 경마 [gyeongma] *n* horse racing; 경주마 [gyeongjuma] *n* racehorse; 말을 탈 수 있어요? [mareul tal su isseoyo?] Can we go horse riding?

말괄량이 [malgwallyangi] *n* tomboy

말기 [malgi] **(병이)** 말기의 [(byeongi) malgiui] *n* terminal

말다툼 [maldatum] *n* quarrel, row (*argument*); 쓸데없는 말다툼을 하다 [sseuldeeomneun maldatumeul hada] *v* squabble

말라리아 [mallaria] *n* malaria

말라위 [mallawi] *n* Malawi

말레이시아 [malleisia] *n* Malaysia; 말레이시아 사람 [malleisia saram] *n* Malaysian; 말레이시아의 [malleisiaui] *adj* Malaysian

말려들다 [mallyeodeulda] *v* get into

말리다 [mallida] 말린 [mallin] *adj* dried; 머리를 말려 주시겠어요? [meorireul mallyeo jusigesseoyo?] Can you dye my hair, please?

말썽 [malsseong] 말썽을 일으키는 사람 [malsseongeul ireukineun saram] *n* troublemaker

말썽꾸러기 [malsseongkkureogi] 말썽꾸러기인 [malsseongkkureogiin] *adj* naughty

말씀 [malsseum] 다시 말씀해 주시겠어요? [dasi malsseumhae jusigesseoyo?] Could you repeat that, please?; 천천히 말씀해 주시겠어요? [cheoncheonhi malsseumhae jusigesseoyo?] Could you speak more slowly, please?; 크게 말씀해 주시겠어요? [keuge malsseumhae jusigesseoyo?] Could you speak louder, please?

말총머리 [malchongmeori] *n* ponytail

말하다 [malhada] *v* say, speak, talk to, talk, tell; 말하기 [malhagi] *n* saying

맛 [mat] *n* flavour, taste; 맛보다 [matboda] *v* taste; 맛없는 [maseomneun] *adj* tasteless; 맛있는 [masinneun] *adj* delicious; 맛 좀 볼 수 있을까요? [mat jom bol su isseulkkayo?] Can I taste it?; **맛이 별로예요** [masi byeolloyeyo] It doesn't taste very nice

맛있다 [masitda] **맛있는** [masinneun] *adj* tasty; **맛있어요** [masisseoyo] That was delicious; **맛있었어요** [masisseosseoyo] That was delicious; **맛있게 드세요!** [masitge deuseyo!] Enjoy your meal!

망 [mang] *n* net; **철조망** [cheoljomang] *n* barbed wire

망고 [manggo] *n* mango

망명 [mangmyeong] *n* asylum, exile; **망명자** [mangmyeongja] *n* asylum seeker

망아지 [mangaji] *n* foal

망연 [mangyeon] **망연자실한** [mangyeonjasilhan] *adj* devastated

망원 [mangwon] **망원경** [mangwongyeong] *n* telescope

망치다 [mangchida] *vt* spoil; **망쳐놓다** [mangchyeonota] *v* mess up

맞다 [matda] *v* fit; **저한테 안 맞아요** [jeohante an majayo] It doesn't fit me

맞은편 [majeunpyeon] **...의 맞은편에** [...ui majeunpyeone] *prep* opposite

매끄럽다 [maekkeureopda] **매끄러운** [maekkeureoun] *adj* smooth

매니큐어 [maenikyueo] *n* manicure, nail polish, nail varnish; **매니큐어 제거제** [maenikyueo jegeoje] *n* nail-polish remover; **매니큐어를 하다** [maenikyueoreul hada] *v* manicure

매다 [maeda] *v* tie

매달다 [maedalda] *v* suspend

매듭 [maedeup] *n* knot

매력 [maeryeok] *n* charm; **매력적인** [maeryeokjeogin] *adj* charming; **매력적인** [maeryeokjeogin] *adj* stunning; **성적 매력이 있는** [seongjeok maeryeogi inneun] *adj* sexy; **아주 매력적인** [aju maeryeokjeogin] *adj* lovely

매리네이드 [maerineideu] *n* marinade

매머드 [maemeodeu] *n* mammoth

매복 [maebok] *n* ambush

매우 [maeu] *adv* much, very

매월 [maewol] **매월의** [maeworui] *adj* monthly

매일 [maeil] *adv* daily; **매일의** [maeirui] *adj* daily

매점 [maejeom] *n* buyout

매춘 [maechun] **매춘부** [maechunbu] *n* prostitute

매트 [maeteu] *n* mat

매트리스 [maeteuriseu] *n* mattress

매표 [maepyo] **매표소** [maepyoso] *n* booking office, ticket office

매표기 [maepyogi] **매표기를 어떻게 사용하나요?** [maepyogireul eotteoke sayonghanayo?] How does the ticket machine work?; **매표기는 어디에 있어요?** [maepyogineun eodie isseoyo?] Where is the ticket machine?; **매표기가 고장났어요** [maepyogiga gojangnasseoyo] The ticket machine isn't working

매혹 [maehok] **매혹적인** [maehokjeogin] *adj* fascinating, glamorous

맥락 [maengnak] *n* context

맥박 [maekbak] *n* pulse; **맥박 조정기** [maekbak jojeonggi] *n* pacemaker

맥주 [maekju] *n* beer; **저장맥주** [jeojangmaekju] *n* lager; **맥주 한 잔 더요** [maekju han jan deoyo] another beer; **생맥주 주세요** [saengmaekju juseyo] A draught beer, please

맵다 [maepda] **음식이 너무 매워요** [eumsigi neomu maewoyo] The food is too spicy

맹금 [maenggeum] *n* bird of prey

맹세 [maengse] *n* oath, vow; **맹세하다** [maengsehada] *v* swear

맹인 [maengin] *n* blind person; **맹인 안내견** [maengin annaegyeon] *n* guide dog

맹장 [maengjang] **맹장염** [maengjangyeom] *n* appendicitis

머그 [meogeu] *n* mug

머랭 [meoraeng] *n* meringue

머리 [meori] *n* head *(body part)*; **붉은 머리의** [bulgeun meoriui] *adj* red-haired; **드라이어로 머리를 매만지기** [deuraieoro meorireul maemanjigi] *n* blow-dry; **땋아늘인**

머리 [ttahaneurin meori] n pigtail; 머리 스카프 [meori seukapeu] n headscarf; 머리띠 [meoritti] n hairband; 머리카락 [meorikarak] n hair; 머리솔 [meorisol] n hairbrush; 머리위 공간 [meoriwi gonggan] n headroom; 머리타래 [meoritarae] n lock (hair); 머리핀 [meoripin] n hairgrip; 상고머리 [sanggomeori] n crew cut; 곱슬머리의 [gopseulmeoriui] adj curly

머리카락 [meorikarak] 스트레이트너 [seuteureiteuneo] npl straighteners

머리칼 [meorikal] 곱슬곱슬한 머리칼 [gopseulgopseulhan meorikal] n curl

머리털 [meoriteol] 머리털이 붉은 사람 [meoriteori bulgeun saram] n redhead

머릿글 [meoritgeul] n lead (position)

머무르다 [meomureuda] v stay; 어디에 머무르세요? [eodie meomureuseyo?] Where are you staying?

머플러 [meopeulleo] n muffler

먹다 [meokda] v eat; 먹고 살다 [meokgo salda] v live on; 뭘 드시겠어요? [mwol deusigesseoyo?] What would you like to eat?; 저는 간을 못 먹어요 [jeoneun ganeul mot meogeoyo] I can't eat liver; 테라스에서 먹어도 될까요? [teraseueseo meogeodo doelkkayo?] Can I eat on the terrace?

먹이 [meogi] n prey

먼지 [meonji] n dust; 먼지투성이의 [meonjituseongiui] adj dusty

멀다 [meolda] 멀리 [meolli] adv far; 멀리 떨어진 [meolli tteoreojin] adj remote; 멀리서 [meolliseo] adv remotely; 눈 먼 [nun meon] adj blind; 먼 [meon] adj distant, far; 멀지 않아요 [meolji anhayo] It's not far; 먼가요? [meongayo?] Is it far?; 바닷가가 얼마나 먼가요? [badatgaga eolmana meongayo?] How far is the beach?; 얼마나 먼가요? [eolmana meongayo?] How far is it?; 은행이 얼마나 먼가요? [eunhaengi eolmana meongayo?] How far is the bank?; 꽤 멀어요 [kkwae meoreoyo] It's quite far

멀리 [meolli] 뱃멀미의 [baetmeolmiui] adj seasick; 멀리뛰기 [meollittwigi] n long jump; 멀리뛰기 [meollittwigi] n jump

멀미 [meolmi] n travel sickness; 비행기 멀미가 난 [bihaenggi meolmiga nan] adj airsick

멈추다 [meomchuda] vi stop

멋지다 [meotjida] 멋진 [meotjin] adj cool (stylish); 멋진 [meotjin] adj super

멍하다 [meonghada] 멍한 [meonghan] adj absent-minded

메뉴 [menyu] n menu; 세트 메뉴 [seteu menyu] n set menu; 메뉴 주세요 [menyu juseyo] The menu, please; 세트 메뉴 주세요 [seteu menyu juseyo] We'll take the set menu; 세트 메뉴는 얼마예요? [seteu menyuneun eolmayeyo?] How much is the set menu?; 어린이 메뉴가 있나요? [eorini menyuga innayo?] Do you have a children's menu?; 후식 메뉴 주세요 [husik menyu juseyo] The dessert menu, please

메달 [medal] n medal; 큰 메달 [keun medal] n medallion

메뚜기 [mettugi] n grasshopper

메마르다 [memareuda] 메마른 [memareun] adj bone dry

메모 [memo] n memo, note (message); 메모 용지 [memo yongji] n scrap paper; 메모장 [memojang] n notepad; 메모지 [memoji] n jotter; 메모하다 [memohada] v note down

메모리 카드 [memori kadeu] 이 디지털 카메라에 사용하는 메모리 카드 주세요 [i dijiteol kamerae sayonghaneun memori kadeu juseyo] A memory card for this digital camera, please

메모하다 [memohada] v jot down

메시지 [mesiji] n message; 문자 메시지 [munja mesiji] n text message; 문자 메시지를 보내다 [munja mesijireul bonaeda] v text; 문자메시지 [munjamesiji] n SMS; 메시지를 남겨도 될까요? [mesijireul namgyeodo doelkkayo?] Can I leave a message?; 그의 비서에게 메시지를 남길 수

있을까요? [geuui biseoege mesijireul namgil su isseulkkayo?] Can I leave a message with his secretary?

메신저 [mesinjeo] n messenger

메아리 [meari] n echo

메일 [meil] n email, mail; 스팸 메일 [seupaem meil] n spam, junk mail

메추라기 [mechuragi] n quail

메카 [meka] n Mecca

멕시코 [meksiko] n Mexico; 멕시코 사람 [meksiko saram] n Mexican; 멕시코의 [meksikoui] adj Mexican

멜로디 [mellodi] n melody

멜론 [mellon] n melon

멜빵 [melppang] npl braces, suspenders

며느리 [myeoneuri] n daughter-in-law

며칠 [myeochil] 며칠이죠? [myeochirijyo?] What is the date?

면 [myeon] n cotton; 면봉 [myeonbong] n cotton bud

면담 [myeondam] n interview; 면담하다 [myeondamhada] v interview

면도 [myeondo] 면도날 [myeondonal] n razor blade; 면도칼 [myeondokal] n razor; 면도용 거품 [myeondoyong geopum] n shaving foam; 면도용 크림 [myeondoyong keurim] n shaving cream; 면도하다 [myeondohada] v shave; 면도하지 않은 [myeondohaji anheun] adj unshaven; 면도한 후 바르는 로션 [myeondohan hu bareuneun rosyeon] n aftershave; 전기 면도기 [jeongi myeondogi] n shaver

면세 [myeonse] n duty-free; 면세의 [myeonseui] adj duty-free

면세점 [myeonsejeom] 면세점은 어디에 있어요? [myeonsejeomeun eodie isseoyo?] Where is the duty-free shopping?

면역 [myeonyeok] n immunity; 면역체계 [myeonyeokchegye] n immune system

면접 [myeonjeop] 면접원 [myeonjeobwon] n interviewer

면체 [myeonche] 정육면체 [jeongyungmyeonche] n cube

면허 [myeonheo] n licence; 운전 면허 시험 [unjeon myeonheo siheom] n

driving test; 운전 면허증 [unjeon myeonheojeung] n driving licence; 임시면허 운전자 [imsimyeonheo unjeonja] n learner driver

면허증 [myeonheojeung] 제 운전 면허증 번호는....에요 [je unjeon myeonheojeung beonhoneun....eyo] My driving licence number is...; 제 운전 면허증이에요 [je unjeon myeonheojeungieyo] Here is my driving licence

면회 [myeonhoe] 면회 시간은 언제예요? [myeonhoe siganeun eonjeyeyo?] When are visiting hours?

멸종 [myeoljong] 멸종한 [myeoljonghan] adj extinct

명 [myeong] 네 명 테이블이요 [ne myeong teibeuriyo] A table for four people, please

명단 [myeongdan] 대기명단 [daegimyeongdan] n waiting list; 최종선발 후보자 명단 [choejongseonbal huboja myeongdan] n shortlist

명랑 [myeongnang] 명랑한 [myeongnanghan] adj jolly

명령 [myeongnyeong] n command, order; 명령하다 [myeongnyeonghada] v order (command)

명백 [myeongbaek] 명백한 [myeongbaekhan] adj apparent, undisputed; 명백한 [myeongbaekhan] adj clear

명사 [myeongsa] n noun

명상 [myeongsang] n meditation

명성 [myeongseong] n prestige

명세서 [myeongseseo] 계산 명세서를 주시겠어요? [gyesan myeongseseoreul jusigesseoyo?] Can I have an itemized bill?

명승지 [myeongseungji] n beauty spot

명예 [myeongye] n fame, honour

명함 [myeongham] 명함 있으세요? [myeongham isseuseyo?] Do you have a business card?; 명함 한 장 주시겠어요? [myeongham han jang jusigesseoyo?] Can I have your card?; 제 명함이에요 [je myeonghamieyo] Here's my card

명확 [myeonghwak] **명확한**
[myeonghwakhan] *adj* definite; **명확히**
[myeonghwakhi] *adv* definitely; **명확히**
[myeonghwakhi] *adv* apparently

몇몇 [myeotmyeot] *pron* several; **몇몇의**
[myeotmyeochui] *adj* several

모 [mo] **모직물** [mojingmul] *npl*
woollens; **대리모** [daerimo] *n*
surrogate mother; **대모** [daemo] *n*
godmother

모국 [moguk] **모국어** [mogugeo] *n*
mother tongue

모기 [mogi] *n* midge, mosquito

모나코 [monako] *n* Monaco

모니터 [moniteo] *n* monitor

모뎀 [modem] *n* modem

모두 [modu] *pron* everybody

모듈 [modyul] *n* module

모든 [modeun] *adj* all, every; **모든 사람**
[modeun saram] *pron* everyone; **모든
것** [modeun geot] *pron* everything

모래 [morae] *n* sand; **모래 언덕** [morae
eondeok] *n* sand dune; **모래상자**
[moraesangja] *n* sandpit; **모래성**
[moraeseong] *n* sandcastle; **모래알**
[moraeal] *n* grit; **사암** [saam] *n*
sandstone

모레 [more] *n* the day after tomorrow

모로코 [moroko] *n* Morocco; **모로코
사람** [moroko saram] *n* Moroccan;
모로코의 [morokoui] *adj* Moroccan

모르다 [moreuda] *v* not know, be
ignorant of; **모르겠어요**
[moreugesseoyo] I don't know, I don't
understand

모르타르 [moreutareu] *n* mortar
(*plaster*)

모르핀 [moreupin] *n* morphine

모리셔스 [morisyeoseu] *n* Mauritius

모리타니 [moritani] *n* Mauritania

모방 [mobang] **모방하다** [mobanghada]
v imitate; **모방하다** [mobanghada] *v*
mimic

모범 [mobeom] **모범이 되는** [mobeomi
doeneun] *adj* model

모성 [moseong] **모성의** [moseongui] *adj*
maternal

모스 [moseu] *n* Morse

모양 [moyang] *n* look, shape

모욕 [moyok] *n* contempt, insult;
모욕하다 [moyokhada] *v* insult

모유 [moyu] **모유를 먹이다** [moyureul
meogida] *v* breast-feed

모으다 [moeuda] *vt* collect

모음 [moeum] *n* vowel

모이다 [moida] *v* get together

모임 [moim] **모임약속** [moimyaksok] *n*
rendezvous

모자 [moja] *n* cap, hat; **야구 모자** [yagu
moja] *n* baseball cap

모자이크 [mojaikeu] *n* mosaic

모잠비크 [mojambikeu] *n* Mozambique

모조 [mojo] **모조의** [mojoui] *adj* mock;
모조품 [mojopum] *n* imitation

모터 [moteo] *n* motor

모텔 [motel] *n* motel

모퉁이 [motungi] *n* corner, turning;
모퉁이 근처에 있어요 [motungi
geuncheoe isseoyo] It's round the
corner; **모퉁이에 있어요** [motungie
isseoyo] It's on the corner

모피 [mopi] *n* fur; **모피코트** [mopikoteu]
n fur coat

모험 [moheom] *n* adventure; **모험을
좋아하는** [moheomeul johahaneun]
adj adventurous

모형 [mohyeong] *n* dummy, model,
mould (*shape*); **모형을 만들다**
[mohyeongeul mandeulda] *v* model;
축소 모형 [chukso mohyeong] *n*
miniature

목 [mok] *n* neck; **목구멍** [mokgumeong]
n throat

목걸이 [mokgeori] *n* necklace

목관 [mokgwan] **목관 악기** [mokgwan
akgi] *n* woodwind

목록 [mongnok] *n* list; **목록에 없는**
[mongnoge eomneun] *adj* unlisted;
목록에 기재하다 [mongnoge
gijaehada] *v* list; **우편물 발송 주소
목록** [upyeonmul balsong juso
mongnok] *n* mailing list; **와인 목록
주세요** [wain mongnok juseyo] The
wine list, please

목마 [mongma] **흔들목마**

[heundeulmongma] n rocking horse

목마르다 [mongmareuda] 목마른 [mongmareun] adj thirsty; 목말라요 [mongmallayo] I'm thirsty

목발 [mokbal] n crutch

목사 [moksa] n minister (clergy); 교구 목사 [gyogu moksa] n vicar

목소리 [moksori] n voice

목수 [moksu] n carpenter; 목수일 [moksuil] n carpentry

목요일 [mogyoil] 목요일에 [mogyoire] on Thursday

목욕 [mogyok] 목욕 가운 [mogyok gaun] n bathrobe; 목욕 타월 [mogyok tawol] n bath towel; 목욕하다 [mogyokhada] v bathe; 욕실 [yoksil] n bathroom; 거품 목욕 [geopum mogyok] n bubble bath

목재 [mokjae] n timber, wood (material)

목적 [mokjeok] n aim, objective, purpose; 목적지 [mokjeokji] n destination

목제 [mokje] 목제의 [mokjeui] adj wooden; 목제품 [mokjepum] n woodwork

목차 [mokcha] npl contents (list)

목초 [mokcho] 목초지 [mokchoji] n meadow

몫 [mogt] n share

몰도바 [moldoba] n Moldova; 몰도바 사람 [moldoba saram] n Moldovan; 몰도바의 [moldobaui] adj Moldovan

몰두 [moldu] 몰두한 [molduhan] adj preoccupied

몰타 [molta] n Malta; 몰타 사람 [molta saram] n Maltese (person); 몰타어 [moltaeo] n Maltese (language); 몰타의 [moltaui] adj Maltese

몸 [mom] n body; 몸이 편치 않은 [momi pyeonchi anheun] adj unwell

몸무게 [mommuge] n (body) weight; 몸무게가 얼마인가요? [mommugega eolmaingayo?] How much do you weigh?

몸짓 [momjit] n gesture

몹시 [mopsi] adv awfully

못 [mot] n nail, peg; 장식못 [jangsingmot] n stud

못생긴 [mossaenggin] adj ugly

못하다 [motada] 말을 못하는 [mareul motaneun] adj dumb; 오도가도 못하는 [odogado motaneun] adj stranded

몽골 [monggol] n Mongolia; 몽골 사람 [monggol saram] n Mongolian (person); 몽골어 [monggoreo] n Mongolian (language); 몽골의 [monggorui] adj Mongolian

묘 [myo] 묘비 [myobi] n gravestone; 묘지 [myoji] n graveyard

묘기 [myogi] n stunt

묘사 [myosa] n description; 묘사하다 [myosahada] v describe

묘지 [myoji] n cemetery

무 [mu] n radish; 무분별한 [mubunbyeolhan] adj senseless; 격자무늬의 [gyeokjamunuiui] adj tartan

무겁다 [mugeopda] 무거운 [mugeoun] adj heavy; 무겁게 [mugeopge] adv heavily; 크고 무거운 [keugo mugeoun] adj massive; 이것은 너무 무거워요 [igeoseun neomu mugeowoyo] This is too heavy

무게 [muge] n weight; 무게재다 [mugejaeda] v weigh

무기 [mugi] n club (weapon), weapon

무기물 [mugimul] n mineral

무너뜨리다 [muneotteurida] vt crash

무너지다 [muneojida] v collapse

무능 [muneung] 무능한 [muneunghan] adj incompetent

무늬 [munui] n pattern; 줄무늬 [julmunui] n stripe; 줄무늬의 [julmunuiui] adj striped; 체크 무늬의 [chekeu munuiui] adj checked

무단 [mudan] 무단결석하다 [mudangyeolseokhada] v play truant

무대 [mudae] n stage

무더기 [mudeogi] n heap

무덤 [mudeom] n grave, tomb

무덥다 [mudeopda] 무더운 [mudeoun] adj sweltering

무도 [mudo] 무도회 [mudohoe] n ball (dance)

무도회 [mudohoe] 가장 무도회 의상 [gajang mudohoe uisang] n fancy

dress

무디다 [mudida] 무딘 [mudin] *adj* blunt

무례 [murye] 무례한 [muryehan] *adj* outrageous, rude; 무례한 [muryehan] *adj* cheeky

무료 [muryo] 무료의 [muryoui] *adj* free (*no cost*)

무릎 [mureup] *n* knee, lap; 무릎을 꿇다 [mureupeul kkurta] *v* kneel

무리 [muri] *n* a lot, flock, herd

무보수 [mubosu] 무보수의 [mubosuui] *adj* unpaid

무선 [museon] *adj* wireless; 무선으로 조종되는 [museoneuro jojongdoeneun] *adj* radio-controlled; 무선의 [museonui] *adj* cordless; 방에서 무선 인터넷 있어요? [bangeseo museon inteonet isseoyo?] Does the room have wireless Internet access?

무섭다 [museopda] 무서운 [museoun] *adj* appalling, frightening, horrifying, terrible; 무서운 [museoun] *adj* scary; 무섭게 [museopge] *adv* terribly

무성생식 [museongsaengsik] 무성생식을 하다 [museongsaengsigeul hada] *v* clone

무스 [museu] *n* mousse

무슨 [museun] *adj* what; 무슨 일이죠? [museun irijyo?] What happened?

무시 [musi] *n* neglect; 무시된 [musidoen] *adj* neglected; 무시하다 [musihada] *v* ignore, neglect

무시무시한 [musimusihan] *adj* gruesome

무식 [musik] *n* ignorance; 무식한 [musikhan] *adj* ignorant

무신론 [musinnon] 무신론자 [musinnonja] *n* atheist

무심 [musim] 무심코 [musimko] *adv* inadvertently

무아경 [muagyeong] *n* ecstasy

무안 [muan] 무안케 하는 [muanke haneun] *adj* embarrassing; 무안한 [muanhan] *adj* embarrassed

무알코올 [mualkool] 어떤 무알코올 음료가 있나요? [eotteon mualkool eumnyoga innayo?] What non-alcoholic drinks do you have?

무언 [mueon] 무언극 [mueongeuk] *n* pantomime

무엇 [mueot] *pron* what; 무언가 [mueonga] *pron* something;... 무엇이라고 하나요? [...mueosirago hanayo?] What is the word for...?

무역 [muyeok] *n* trade

무연 [muyeon] *n* unleaded; 무연 휘발유 [muyeon hwiballyu] *n* unleaded petrol; 고급 무연...어치요 [gogeup muyeon... eochiyo]... worth of premium unleaded, please

무용수 [muyongsu] 발레 무용수 [balle muyongsu] *n* ballet dancer

무의식 [muuisik] 무의식의 [muuisigui] *adj* unconscious

무익 [muik] 무익한 [muikhan] *adj* useless

무인 [muin] 무인도 [muindo] *n* desert island

무일푼의 [muilpunui] *adj* broke

무장 [mujang] 무장한 [mujanghan] *adj* armed

무적 [mujeok] 무적의 [mujeogui] *adj* unbeatable

무조건 [mujogeon] 무조건적인 [mujogeonjeogin] *adj* unconditional

무지개 [mujigae] *n* rainbow

무해 [muhae] 무해한 [muhaehan] *adj* harmless

무화과 [muhwagwa] *n* fig

묵다 [mukda] *v* stay; 하룻밤 더 묵고 싶어요 [harutbam deo mukgo sipeoyo] I want to stay an extra night

묶다 [mukkda] 묶는 것 [mukkneun geot] *n* bond

문 [mun] *n* door, gate; 문 손잡이 [mun sonjabi] *n* door handle; 문지기 [munjigi] *n* doorman; 덧문 [deotmun] *n* shutters; 문 손잡이가 빠졌어요 [mun sonjabiga ppajyeosseoyo] The door handle has come off; 문을 잠궈 두세요 [muneul jamgwo duseyo] Keep the door locked; 문이 안 닫혀요 [muni an datyeoyo] The door won't close; 문이 안 열려요 [muni an yeollyeoyo] The door won't open; 문이 안 잠겨요 [muni an jamgyeoyo] The door won't lock

문구 [mungu] 문구점 [mungujeom] n stationer's

문단 [mundan] n paragraph

문맹 [munmaeng] 문맹의 [munmaengui] adj illiterate

문명 [munmyeong] n civilization

문방구 [munbanggu] n stationery

문법 [munbeop] n grammar; 문법의 [munbeobui] adj grammatical

문서 [munseo] n document ▷ npl documents; 문서화 [munseohwa] n documentation

문신 [munsin] n tattoo

문어 [muneo] n octopus

문의 [munui] n inquiry; 문의하다 [munuihada] v enquire, inquire; 전화번호 문의 [jeonhwabeonho munui] npl directory enquiries

문자 [munja] n phrase; 문자 메시지 [munja mesiji] n text message; 문자 메시지를 보내다 [munja mesijireul bonaeda] v text; 문자메시지 [munjamesiji] n SMS; 두문자어 [dumunjaeo] n acronym; 답변을 문자로 보내 주시겠어요? [dapbyeoneul munjaro bonae jusigesseoyo?] Can you text me your answer?

문장 [munjang] n sentence (words); 문구 [mungu] n phrase

문제 [munje] n problem; 문제가 있으면 누구에게 연락해야 할까요? [munjega isseumyeon nuguege yeollakhaeya halkkayo?] Who do we contact if there are problems?; 당신의 팩스에 문제가 있어요 [dangsinui paekseue munjega isseoyo] There is a problem with your fax; 방에 문제가 있어요 [bange munjega isseoyo] There's a problem with the room

문지르다 [munjireuda] v rub, scrub

문학 [munhak] n literature

문화 [munhwa] n culture; 문화의 [munhwaui] adj cultural

묻다 [mutda] v (질문) ask; 캐묻기 좋아하는 [kaemutgi johahaneun] adj inquisitive; 길 묻기 [gil mutgi] Asking the way

물 [mul] n water; 물뿌리개 [mulppurigae] n watering can; 물방울 [mulbangul] n drip; 물주다 [muljuda] v water; 인쇄물 [inswaemul] n printout; 광천수 [gwangcheonsu] n mineral water; 기념물 [ginyeommul] n memorial; 물 한 주전자 [mul han jujeonja] a jug of water; 물 한 잔 [mul han jan] a glass of water; 물을 더 갖다 주세요 [mureul deo gatda juseyo] Please bring more water

물건 [mulgeon] n thing; 어질러진 물건 [eojilleojin mulgeon] n clutter

물고기 [mulgogi] n fish; 물고기자리 [mulgogijari] n Pisces; 민물고기 [minmulgogi] n freshwater fish; 어부 [eobu] n fisherman; 어선 [eoseon] n fishing boat; 어업 [eoeop] n fishing

물냉이 [mullaengi] n watercress

물놀이터 [mulloriteo] 어린이를 위한 물놀이터가 있어요? [eorinireul wihan mulloriteoga isseoyo?] Is there a paddling pool for the children?

물다 [mulda] v bite; 물기 [mulgi] n bite

물려 [mullyeo] 물려받다 [mullyeobatda] v inherit

물리 [mulli] 물리치료사 [mullichiryosa] n physiotherapist; 물리요법 [mulliyobeop] n physiotherapy; 물리학 [mullihak] npl physics; 물리학자 [mullihakja] n physicist

물리다 [mullida] 물렸어요 [mullyeosseoyo] I have been bitten

물병 [mulbyeong] 물병자리 [mulbyeongjari] n Aquarius; 유리 물병 [yuri mulbyeong] n carafe

물속 [mulsok] 물속에서 [mulsogeseo] adv underwater

물정 [muljeong] 세상물정에 밝은 [sesangmuljeonge balgeun] adj streetwise

물질 [muljil] n stuff, substance; 항생 물질 [hangsaeng muljil] n antibiotic

물체 [mulche] n object; 미확인 비행물체 [mihwagin bihaengmulche] abbr UFO

뮤즐리 [myujeulli] n muesli

뮤지컬 [myujikeol] n musical

미 [mi] 남미 [nammi] n South America;

남미 사람 [nammi saram] n South American; 남미의 [nammiui] adj South American

미국 [miguk] n America, United States; 북미 [bungmi] n North America; 북미 사람 [bungmi saram] n North American; 북미의 [bungmiui] adj North American; 미식 축구 [misik chukgu] n American football; 미국 사람 [miguk saram] n American; 미국의 [migugui] adj American

미끄러지다 [mikkeureojida] v skid, slide, slip; 미끄러지기 [mikkeureojigi] n slide; 그 차가 미끄러졌어요 [geu chaga mikkeureojyeosseoyo] The car skidded

미끄럽다 [mikkeureopda] 미끄러운 [mikkeureoun] adj slippery

미나리아재비 [minariajaebi] n buttercup

미디어 [midieo] npl media

미래 [mirae] n future; 미래의 [miraeui] adj future

미로 [miro] n maze

미리 [miri] adv beforehand

미묘 [mimyo] 미묘한 [mimyohan] adj subtle

미사 [misa] n mass (church); 미사는 언제예요? [misaneun eonjeyeyo?] When is mass?

미사일 [misail] n missile

미성년 [miseongnyeon] 미성년의 [miseongnyeonui] adj underage; 미성년자 [miseongnyeonja] n minor

미세 [mise] n minuteness; 미세한 [misehan] n minute

미소 [miso] n smile; 미소짓다 [misojitda] v smile; 환한 미소 [hwanhan miso] n beam

미숙 [misuk] n inexperience; 미숙한 [misukhan] adj immature, inexperienced, unskilled

미술 [misul] 미술관 [misulgwan] n art gallery; 미술품 [misulpum] n work of art

미신 [misin] 미신적인 [misinjeogin] adj superstitious

미안 [mian] 미안! [mian!] excl sorry!; 미안합니다 [mianhamnida] I'm sorry, Sorry; 미안하지만 못 알아 들었어요 [mianhajiman mot ara deureosseoyo] Sorry, I didn't catch that; 미안하지만, 사귀는 사람 있어요 [mianhajiman, sagwineun saram isseoyo] Sorry, I'm in a relationship; 정말 미안합니다 [jeongmal mianhamnida] I'm very sorry; 귀찮게해서 미안합니다 [gwichankehaeseo mianhamnida] I'm sorry to trouble you; 늦어서 미안해요 [neujeoseo mianhaeyo] Sorry we're late

미얀마 [miyanma] n Myanmar

미용 [miyong] 미용 성형외과 [miyong seonghyeongoegwa] n cosmetic surgery; 미용사 [miyongsa] n hairdresser; 미용실 [miyongsil] n beauty salon, hairdresser's; 건강과 미용 [geonganggwa miyong] Health and beauty

미워하다 [miwohada] v hate

미이라 [miira] n mummy (body)

미인 [miin] n beauty

미지근하다 [mijigeunhada] 미지근한 [mijigeunhan] adj lukewarm

미치다 [michida] 미치광이 [michigwangi] n maniac; 미친 [michin] adj crazy, insane, mad (insane); 미친 사람 [michin saram] n madman; 미친듯이 [michindeusi] adv madly; 미칠 듯한 [michil deutan] adj frantic

미터 [miteo] n meter, metre; 미터법의 [miteobeobui] adj metric

미터기 [miteogi] 미터기 있어요? [miteogi isseoyo?] Do you have a meter? (taxi)

미혼 [mihon] 미혼남 [mihonnam] n bachelor; 미혼여성 [mihonyeoseong] n spinster; 미혼의 [mihonui] adj unmarried; 미혼이에요 [mihonieyo] I'm single; 미혼이에요? [mihonieyo?] Are you single?; 예, 미혼이에요 [ye, mihonieyo] Yes, I'm single

믹서 [mikseo] n blender, food processor, liquidizer, mixer

민간 [mingan] 민간의 [minganui] adj civilian; 민간인 [minganin] n civilian;

민간전설 [minganjeonseol] *n* folklore

민감 [mingam] **민감한** [mingamhan] *adj* sensitive

민들레 [mindeulle] *n* dandelion

민속 [minsok] **민속 음악** [minsok eumak] *n* folk music

민족 [minjok] *n* nation; **민족적인** [minjokjeogin] *adj* national

민주 [minju] **민주주의** [minjujuui] *n* democracy; **민주적인** [minjujeogin] *adj* democratic

믿다 [mitda] *v* rely on ▷ *vi* believe

믿음 [mideum] *n* belief, faith; **믿어지지 않는** [mideojiji annneun] *adj* incredible

밀 [mil] *n* wheat; **호밀** [homil] *n* rye

밀가루 [milgaru] *n* flour; **통밀가루의** [tongmilgaruui] *adj* wholemeal

밀감 [milgam] *n* tangerine

밀다 [milda] *vt* push; **밀어 주시겠어요?** [mireo jusigesseoyo?] Can you give me a push?

밀도 [mildo] *n* density

밀랍 [millap] *n* wax

밀렵 [millyeop] **밀렵한** [millyeophan] *adj* poached *(caught illegally)*

밀리미터 [millimiteo] *n* millimetre

밀물 [milmul] **밀물은 언제예요?** [milmureun eonjeyeyo?] When is high tide?

밀수 [milsu] *n* smuggling; **밀수업자** [milsueopja] *n* smuggler; **밀수하다** [milsuhada] *v* smuggle

밀실 [milsil] *n* closet; **밀실 공포증의** [milsil gongpojeungui] *adj* claustrophobic

밀접 [miljeop] **밀접하게** [miljeophage] *adv* closely

밀집 [miljip] **밀집한** [miljiphan] *adj* dense

밀폐 [milpye] **밀폐된** [milpyedoen] *adj* airtight

밍크 [mingkeu] *n* mink

밑 [mit] **밑에** [mite] *adv* underneath;...**의 밑에** [...ui mite] *prep* beneath, under;...**의 바로 밑에** [...ui baro mite] *prep* underneath

바 [ba] *n* bar; **미니 바** [mini ba] *n* minibar; **핸들바** [haendeulba] *npl* handlebars; **멋진 바는 어디에 있어요?** [meotjin baneun eodie isseoyo?] Where is there a nice bar?; **바는 어디에 있어요?** [baneun eodie isseoyo?] Where is the bar?

바가지 [bagaji] *n* rip-off; **바가지 씌우다** [bagaji ssuiuda] *v* overcharge

바구니 [baguni] *n* basket

바깥 [bakkat] **바깥쪽으로** [bakkatjjogeuro] *adv* outside

바꾸다 [bakkuda] *v* swap, alter, change; **바꿀 수 있는** [bakkul su inneun] *adj* convertible

바나나 [banana] *n* banana

바느질 [baneujil] *n* sewing

바늘 [baneul] *n* needle; **뜨개바늘** [tteugaebaneul] *n* knitting needle; **한 바늘** [han baneul] *n* stitch; **바늘과 실 있어요?** [baneulgwa sil isseoyo?] Do you have a needle and thread?

바닐라 [banilla] *n* vanilla

바다 [bada] *n* sea; **바다표범** [badapyobeom] *n* seal *(animal)*; **바닷가재** [badatgajae] *n* lobster; **바다가 보이는 방이 좋겠어요** [badaga boineun bangi jokesseoyo] I'd like a room with a view of the sea; **오늘 바다가 거친가요?** [oneul badaga geochingayo?] Is the sea rough today?

바닥 [badak] *n* bottom; **(방)바닥** [(bang)

badak] n floor; **바닥의** [badagui] adj bottom

바닷가 [badatga] n beach, shore; **이 근처에 좋은 바닷가가 있나요?** [i geuncheoe joheun badatgaga innayo?] Are there any good beaches near here?; **이 근처에 한적한 바닷가가 있나요?** [i geuncheoe hanjeokhan badatgaga innayo?] Is there a quiet beach near here?

바라다 [barada] v hope, want, wish; **바라건대** [barageondae] adv hopefully

바람 [baram] n wind; **바람이 센** [barami sen] adj windy; **산들바람** [sandeulbaram] n breeze

바람둥이 [baramdungi] n flirt

바레인 [barein] n Bahrain

바로 [baro] adv right

바르다 [bareuda] **똑바로** [ttokbaro] adv straight on; **똑바른** [ttokbareun] adj straight

바베이도스 [babeidoseu] n Barbados

바보 [babo] n fool, idiot, twit; **바보같은** [babogateun] adj stupid

바비큐 [babikyu] n barbecue; **바비큐장소는 어디인가요?** [babikyujangsoneun eodiingayo?] Where is the barbecue area?

바쁘다 [bappeuda] **바쁜** [bappeun] adj busy; **미안하지만, 바빠요** [mianhajiman, bappayo] Sorry, I'm busy

바삭 [basak] **바삭바삭한** [basakbasakhan] adj crisp, crispy

바순 [basun] n bassoon

바스크 [baseukeu] **바스크 사람** [baseukeu saram] n Basque (person); **바스크어** [baseukeueo] n Basque (language); **바스크의** [baseukeuui] adj Basque

바위 [bawi] n rock

바이러스 [baireoseu] n virus; **안티바이러스** [antibaireoseu] n antivirus

바이올린 [baiollin] n violin; **바이올리니스트** [baiolliniseuteu] n violinist

바인더 [baindeo] **링바인더** [ringbaindeo]

n ring binder

바지 [baji] npl trousers; **이 바지 입어봐도 될까요?** [i baji ibeobwado doelkkayo?] Can I try on these trousers?

바질 [bajil] n basil

바치 [bachi] **반바지** [banbaji] npl shorts

바퀴 [bakwi] n wheel; **바퀴가 잠겼어요** [bakwiga jamgyeosseoyo] The wheels lock

바퀴벌레 [bakwibeolle] n cockroach

바탕 [batang] n character, background; **...을 바탕으로 한** [...eul batangeuro han] adj based

바텐더 [batendeo] n barman, bartender; **여자 바텐더** [yeoja batendeo] n barmaid

바티칸 [batikan] **바티칸 궁전** [batikan gungjeon] n Vatican

바하마 [bahama] npl Bahamas

박격 [bakgyeok] **박격포** [bakgyeokpo] n mortar (military)

박람 [bangnam] **박람회** [bangnamhoe] n fair

박람회 [bangnamhoe] **박람회장** [bangnamhoejang] n fairground

박물관 [bangmulgwan] n museum; **이 박물관은 매일 열어요?** [i bangmulgwaneun maeil yeoreoyo?] Is the museum open every day?; **이 박물관은 아침에 문 열어요?** [i bangmulgwaneun achime mun yeoreoyo?] Is the museum open in the morning?; **이 박물관은 언제 열어요?** [i bangmulgwaneun eonje yeoreoyo?] When is the museum open?; **이 박물관은 오후에 열어요?** [i bangmulgwaneun ohue yeoreoyo?] Is the museum open in the afternoon?; **이 박물관은 일요일마다 열어요?** [i bangmulgwaneun iryoilmada yeoreoyo?] Is the museum open on Sundays?

박봉 [bakbong] **박봉의** [bakbongui] adj underpaid

박사 [baksa] n PhD

박수 [baksu] n applause; **박수를 치다** [baksureul chida] v applaud; **박수치다** [baksuchida] vi clap

박식 [baksik] 박식한 [baksikhan] adj knowledgeable

박쥐 [bakjwi] n bat (mammal)

박테리아 [bakteria] npl bacteria

박하 [bakha] n mint (herb/sweet); 서양박하 [seoyangbakha] n peppermint

박해 [bakhae] 박해하다 [bakhaehada] v persecute

밖 [bakk]...의 밖에 [...ui bakke] prep outside; 밖으로 [bakkeuro] adv out; 밖으로 기울어지다 [bakkeuro giureojida] v lean out; 밖의 [bakkui] adj out; 그 밖에 [geu bakke] adv else; 밖으로 전화하고 싶은데 전화가 있나요? [bakkeuro jeonhwahago sipeunde jeonhwaga innayo?] I want to make an outside call, can I have a line?

반 [ban] 반쯤 [banjjeum] adv half; 반원 [banwon] n semicircle; 반값으로 [bangapseuro] adv half-price; 반값의 [bangapsui] adj half-price; 반탈지유 [bantaljiyu] n semi-skimmed milk; 절반 [jeolban] n half; 절반의 [jeolbanui] adj half

반갑다 [bangapda] v be pleased; 만나서 반가워요 [mannaseo bangawoyo] Pleased to meet you

반납 [bannap] 나갈 때 어디에서 열쇠를 반납하나요? [nagal ttae eodieseo yeolsoereul bannaphanayo?] Where do we hand in the key when we're leaving?; 언제 자전거를 반납해야 할까요? [eonje jajeongeoreul bannaphaeya halkkayo?] When is the bike due back?; 여기에 차를 반납해야 합니까? [yeogie chareul bannaphaeya hamnikka?] Do I have to return the car here?;...에서 반납하고 싶어요 [...eseo bannaphago sipeoyo] I'd like to leave it in...

반대 [bandae] n contrary, opposition, reverse; 반대로 [bandaero] adv vice versa; 반대쪽의 [bandaejjogui] adj opposite; 반대편에 [bandaepyeone] adv opposite; 반대하는 [bandaehaneun] adj opposing; 반대하다 [bandaehada] v oppose;

반대하여 [bandaehayeo] prep against; 반대한 [bandaehan] adj opposed; 시계 반대 방향으로 [sigye bandae banghyangeuro] adv anticlockwise

반도 [bando] n peninsula

반드시 [bandeusi] adv necessarily

반박 [banbak] n contradiction; 반박하다 [banbakhada] v contradict

반복 [banbok] n repeat; 반복적인 [banbokjeogin] adj repetitive; 반복하다 [banbokhada] v repeat; 반복하여 [banbokhayeo] adv repeatedly

반사 [bansa] n reflection; 반사하다 [bansahada] v reflect; 반사행동 [bansahaengdong] n reflex

반응 [baneung] n feedback, reaction; 반응하다 [baneunghada] v react

반장 [banjang] n prefect

반점 [banjeom] n dot, spot; 반점이 많은 [banjeomi manheun] adj spotty

반주 [banju] 식전 반주를 주세요 [sikjeon banjureul juseyo] We'd like an aperitif

반죽 [banjuk] n batter, dough; 회반죽 [hoebanjuk] n plaster (for wall)

반지 [banji] n ring; 약혼 반지 [yakhon banji] n engagement ring; 결혼반지 [gyeolhonbanji] n wedding ring

반창고 [banchanggo] n Band-Aid®, plaster (for wound); 반창고 주세요 [banchanggo juseyo] I'd like some plasters

반칙 [banchik] n foul

반하다 [banhada] v (매혹되다) fall for

반항 [banhang] 반항적인 [banhangjeogin] adj rebellious

반환 [banhwan] 반환금 [banhwangeum] n refund; 반환하다 [banhwanhada] v refund; 이것을 반환하고 싶어요 [igeoseul banhwanhago sipeoyo] I'd like to return this

받다 [batda] v receive; 물려받다 [mullyeobatda] v inherit; 받아쓰기 [badasseugi] n dictation

받아들이다 [badadeurida] v accept; 받아들일 수 있는 [badadeuril su inneun] adj acceptable

받치다 [batchida] v bear

발 [bal] *n* foot ▷ *npl* feet; 동물의 발 [dongmurui bal] *n* paw; 맨발로 [maenballo] *adv* barefoot; 맨발의 [maenbarui] *adj* barefoot; 발목 [balmok] *n* ankle; 발끝 [balkkeut] *n* tiptoe; 발치료 의사 [balchiryo uisa] *n* chiropodist; 발자국 [baljaguk] *n* footprint; 발이 아파요 [bari apayo] My feet are sore; 제 발은 육 사이즈예요 [je bareun yuk saijeuyeyo] My feet are a size six

발가락 [balgarak] *n* toe

발가벗다 [balgabeotda] 발가벗은 [balgabeoseun] *adj* naked; 발가벗은 [balgabeoseun] *adj* bare

발견 [balgyeon] 발견하다 [balgyeonhada] *v* discover, find out

발레 [balle] *n* ballet; 발레 무용수 [balle muyongsu] *n* ballet dancer; 발레리나 [ballerina] *n* ballerina; 발레화 [ballehwa] *npl* ballet shoes; 어디에서 발레 표를 살 수 있어요? [eodieseo balle pyoreul sal su isseoyo?] Where can I buy tickets for the ballet?

발렌타인 [ballentain] 밸런타인데이 [baelleontaindei] *n* Valentine's Day

발명 [balmyeong] *n* invention; 발명가 [balmyeongga] *n* inventor; 발명하다 [balmyeonghada] *v* invent

발바리 [balbari] *n* Pekinese

발사 [balsa] *n* shot

발생 [balsaeng] *n* occurrence; 다시 발생하는 [dasi balsaenghaneun] *adj* recurring; 발생하다 [balsaenghada] *v* occur

발송 [balsong] 발송인 [balsongin] *n* sender; 우편물 발송 주소 목록 [upyeonmul balsong juso mongnok] *n* mailing list

발신 [balsin] 발신음 [balsineum] *n* dialling tone

발음 [bareum] *n* pronunciation; 발음하다 [bareumhada] *v* pronounce

발작 [baljak] *n* seizure, stroke (*apoplexy*); 간질 발작 [ganjilbaljjark] *n* epileptic fit

발전 [baljeon] 발전기 [baljeongi] *n* generator; 발전하다 [baljeonhada] *vi* develop

발진 [baljin] *n* rash; 입가의 발진 [ipgaui baljin] *n* cold sore

발칸 [balkan] 발칸 여러 나라의 [balkan yeoreo naraui] *adj* Balkan

발코니 [balkoni] *n* balcony; 발코니 있는 방 있어요? [balkoni inneun bang isseoyo?] Do you have a room with a balcony?

발톱 [baltop] *n* claw

발표 [balpyo] *n* announcement, presentation; 발표하다 [balpyohada] *v* announce

발행 [balhaeng] 발행자 [balhaengja] *n* publisher

밝다 [barkda] 밝은 [balgeun] *adj* bright, light (*not dark*)

밝혀지다 [barkhyeojida] *v* come out

밟다 [barpda] *v* tread; 짓밟다 [jitbapda] *n* stamp

밤 [bam] *n* chestnut, night; 오늘밤 [oneulbam] *adv* tonight; 내일 밤 [naeil bam] tomorrow night; 밤에 [bame] at night; 이틀밤 묵고 싶어요 [iteulbam mukgo sipeoyo] I'd like to stay for two nights; 지난 밤 [jinan bam] last night; 밤에 할 수 있는 것이 무엇일까요? [bame hal su inneun geosi mueosilkkayo?] What is there to do in the evenings?

밧줄 [batjul] *n* rope

방 [bang] *n* room; 1인용 방 [il inyong bang] *n* single, single room; 빈 방 [bin bang] *n* spare room; 다락방 [darakbang] *n* loft; 방 번호 [bang beonho] *n* room number; 트윈 룸 [teuwin rum] *n* twin room;... 이름으로 방을 예약했어요 [... ireumeuro bangeul yeyakhaesseoyo] I booked a room in the name of...; 다른 방이 좋겠어요 [dareun bangi jokesseoyo] I'd like another room; 더블 베드가 있는 방이 좋겠어요 [deobeul bedeuga inneun bangi jokesseoyo] I'd like a room with a double bed; 방 있어요? [bang isseoyo?] Do you have a room?; 방에 문제가 있어요 [bange munjega isseoyo] There's a problem with the room; 방에 TV 있어요? [bange TV isseoyo?] Does the room have a TV?; **방에서 인터넷 되나요?** [bangeseo inteonet doenayo?] Is there an Internet connection in the room?; **방을 볼 수 있을까요?** [bangeul bol su isseulkkayo?] Can I see the room?; **방을 빌리고 싶어요** [bangeul billigo sipeoyo] I'd like to rent a room; **방을 바꿀 수 있나요?** [bangeul bakkul su innayo?] Can I switch rooms?; **방이 너무 더워요** [bangi neomu deowoyo] The room is too hot; **방이 너무 추워요** [bangi neomu chuwoyo] The room is too cold; **방이 너무 시끄러워요** [bangi neomu sikkeureowoyo] The room is too noisy; **방이 너무 작아요** [bangi neomu jagayo] The room is too small; **방이 더러워요** [bangi deoreowoyo] The room is dirty; **방이 얼마예요?** [bangi eolmayeyo?] How much is the room?; **방이 깨끗하지 않아요** [bangi kkaekkeutaji anhayo] The room isn't clean; **바다가 보이는 방이 좋겠어요** [badaga boineun bangi jokesseoyo] I'd like a room with a view of the sea; **발코니 있는 방 있어요?** [balkoni inneun bang isseoyo?] Do you have a room with a balcony?; **조용한 방이 좋겠어요** [joyonghan bangi jokesseoyo] I'd like a quiet room; **산이 보이는 방이 좋겠어요** [sani boineun bangi jokesseoyo] I'd like a room with a view of the mountains; **언제 방을 비워야 하나요?** [eonje bangeul biwoya hanayo?] When do I have to vacate the room?; **여기가 당신 방이에요** [yeogiga dangsin bangieyo] This is your room; **오늘 밤 방 있어요?** [oneul bam bang isseoyo?] Do you have a room for tonight?; **제 방으로 청구하세요** [je bangeuro cheongguhaseyo] Please charge it to my room; **트윈 베드가 있는 방이 좋겠어요** [teuwin bedeuga inneun bangi jokesseoyo] I'd like a room with twin beds; **휠체어로 출입할 수 있는 방이 필요해요** [hwilcheeoro churiphal su inneun bangi piryohaeyo] I need a room with wheelchair access

방갈로 [banggallo] n bungalow

방관 [banggwan] **방관자** [banggwanja] n onlooker

방광 [banggwang] n bladder; **방광염** [banggwangyeom] n cystitis

방글라데시 [banggeulladesi] n Bangladesh; **방글라데시 사람** [banggeulladesi saram] n Bangladeshi; **방글라데시의** [banggeulladesiui] adj Bangladeshi

방금 [banggeum] adv just

방망이 [bangmangi] n bat (with ball); **밀방망이** [milbangmangi] n rolling pin

방목 [bangmok] **방목장** [bangmokjang] n range (mountains)

방문 [bangmun] n visit; **방문시간** [bangmunsigan] npl visiting hours; **방문객** [bangmungaek] n visitor; **방문하다** [bangmunhada] v visit; **친구들을 방문하러 왔어요** [chingudeureul bangmunhareo wasseoyo] I'm here visiting friends; **성을 방문할 수 있어요?** [seongeul bangmunhal su isseoyo?] Can we visit the castle?; **시내를 방문할 시간이 있어요?** [sinaereul bangmunhal sigani isseoyo?] Do we have time to visit the town?; **...을(를) 방문하고 싶어요** [...eul(reul) bangmunhago sipeoyo] We'd like to visit...; **정원을 방문할 수 있어요?** [jeongwoneul bangmunhal su isseoyo?] Can we visit the gardens?; **교회를 방문할 수 있어요?** [gyohoereul bangmunhal su isseoyo?] Can we visit the church?; **휠체어로...을 방문할 수 있나요?** [hwilcheeoro...eul bangmunhal su innayo?] Can you visit... in a wheelchair?

방법 [bangbeop] n method, way; **시내 중심가에 가는 가장 좋은 방법은 무엇인가요?** [sinae jungsimgae ganeun gajang joheun bangbeobeun mueosingayo?] What's the best way to get to the city centre?; **이 호텔에 가는 가장 좋은 방법은 무엇인가요?** [i hotere ganeun gajang joheun bangbeobeun mueosingayo?] What's the best way to get to this hotel?; **기차역에 가는 가장**

좋은 방법은 무엇인가요? [gichayeoge ganeun gajang joheun bangbeobeun mueosingayo?] What's the best way to get to the railway station?

방부 [bangbu] **방부제** [bangbuje] n preservative

방빙 [bangbing] **방빙제** [bangbingje] n de-icer

방사성 [bangsaseong] **방사성의** [bangsaseongui] adj radioactive

방송 [bangsong] n broadcast; **라디오 방송국** [radio bangsongguk] n radio station; **방송하다** [bangsonghada] v broadcast

방수 [bangsu] **방수의** [bangsuui] adj showerproof, waterproof; **방수포** [bangsupo] n tarpaulin

방식 [bangsik] n manner; **디지털 방식의** [dijiteol bangsigui] adj digital; **사고 방식** [sago bangsik] n mentality

방앗간 [bangatgan] n mill

방어 [bangeo] **방어자** [bangeoja] n defender; **방어하다** [bangeohada] v defend

방언 [bangeon] n dialect

방열 [bangyeol] **방열기** [bangyeolgi] n radiator

방울 [bangul] n drop; **물방울** [mulbangul] n drip

방위 [bangwi] n defence; **정당방위** [jeongdangbangwi] n self-defence

방전 [bangjeon] n discharge; **금방 방전돼요** [geumbang bangjeondwaeyo] It's not holding its charge

방정식 [bangjeongsik] n equation

방충제 [bangchungje] **방충제 있어요?** [bangchungje isseoyo?] Do you have insect repellent?

방탕 [bangtang] **방탕하다** [bangtanghada] v misbehave

방패 [bangpae] n shield

방학 [banghak] **학기 중의 중간 방학** [hakgi jungui junggan banghak] n half-term

방한 [banghan] **방한용 재킷** [banghanyong jaekit] n anorak

방해 [banghae] n interruption, setback;

방해하다 [banghaehada] v disturb, interrupt, obstruct; **방해행위** [banghaehaengwi] v sabotage

방향 [banghyang] n aroma, direction; **방향요법** [banghyangyobeop] n aromatherapy; **방향 약도를 그려 주시겠어요?** [banghyang yakdoreul geuryeo jusigesseoyo?] Can you draw me a map with directions?

방화 [banghwa] **방화벽** [banghwabyeok] n firewall; **방화죄** [banghwajoe] n arson

배 [bae] n abdomen, belly, boat, pear, tummy; **3배로 하다** [sambaero hada] v treble; **바지선** [bajiseon] n barge; **배를 젓다** [baereul jeotda] v row (in boat); **배의** [baeui] adj coeliac; **배젓기** [baejeotgi] n rowing; **젓는 배** [jeotneun bae] n rowing boat; **마지막 배는 언제 있어요?** [majimak baeneun eonje isseoyo?] When is the last boat?; **배는 어디에서 출발하나요?** [baeneun eodieseo chulbalhanayo?] Where does the boat leave from?; **배에 먹을 곳이 있어요?** [baee meogeul gosi isseoyo?] Is there somewhere to eat on the boat?; **첫 배는 언제 있어요?** [cheot baeneun eonje isseoyo?] When is the first boat?

배경 [baegyeong] n background

배고프다 [baegopeuda] **배고픈** [baegopeun] adj hungry; **배고파요** [baegopayo] I'm hungry; **배고프지 않아요** [baegopeuji anhayo] I'm not hungry

배관 [baegwan] n plumbing; **배관공** [baegwangong] n plumber

배구 [baegu] n volleyball

배기 [baegi] **배기 가스** [baegi gaseu] npl exhaust fumes; **배기관** [baegigwan] n exhaust pipe

배기관 [baegigwan] **배기관이 고장났어요** [baegigwani gojangnasseoyo] The exhaust is broken

배꼽 [baekkop] n belly button, navel

배낭 [baenang] n backpack, rucksack; **배낭여행** [baenangyeohaeng] n backpacking; **배낭여행자**

[baenangyeohaengja] n backpacker

배달 [baedal] 신문배달 [sinmunbaedal] n paper round

배드민턴 [baedeuminteon] n badminton

배부르다 [baebureuda] 배불러요 [baebulleoyo] I'm full

배상 [baesang] 배상금 [baesanggeum] n ransom

배수 [baesu] n drain; 배수관 [baesugwan] n drainpipe

배수구 [baesugu] 배수구가 막혔어요 [baesuguga makhyeosseoyo] The drain is blocked

배신 [baesin] 배신하다 [baesinhada] v betray

배심 [baesim] n jury

배역 [baeyeok] n cast

배영 [baeyeong] n backstroke

배우 [baeu] n performer; 남자 배우 [namja baeu] n actor; 여자 배우 [yeoja baeu] n actress; 영화 배우 [yeonghwa baeu] n film star

배우다 [baeuda] v learn

배우자 [baeuja] n spouse

배지 [baeji] n badge

배출 [baechul] 배출하다 [baechulhada] (방출) n drain; 탄소배출량 [tansobaechullyang] n carbon footprint

배치 [baechi] n placement; 배치계획 [baechigyehoek] n layout

배터리 [baeteori] n battery; 배터리 있어요? [baeteori isseoyo?] Do you have any batteries?; 배터리가 다 됐어요 [baeteoriga da dwaesseoyo] The battery is flat; 이 카메라에 사용하는 배터리 있나요? [i kamerae sayonghaneun baeteori innayo?] Do you have batteries for this camera?

배포 [baepo] 배포하다 [baepohada] v give out

배회하다 [baehoehada] v wander

백 [baek] number (a) hundred; 오백...이요 [obaek...iyo] I'd like five hundred...; 이백...이요 [ibaek...iyo] I'd like two hundred...

백금 [baekgeum] n platinum

백내장 [baengnaejang] n cataract (eye)

백랍 [baengnap] n pewter

백만 [baengman] n million; 백만장자 [baengmanjangja] n millionaire

백발 [baekbal] 백발의 [baekbarui] adj grey-haired

백분율 [baekbunyul] n percentage

백신 [baeksin] v vaccine; 백신 접종이 필요해요 [baeksin jeopjongi pillyohaeyo] I need a vaccination

백조 [baekjo] n swan

백파이프 [baekpaipeu] npl bagpipes

백합 [baekhap] n lily

백혈병 [baekhyeolbyeong] n leukaemia

백화점 [baekhwajeom] n department store

밴조 [baenjo] n banjo

뱀 [baem] n snake; 도마뱀 [domabaem] n lizard; 방울뱀 [bangulbaem] n rattlesnake

버너 [beoneo] 점화용 보조 버너 [jeomhwayong bojo beoneo] n pilot light

버릇 [beoreut] 버릇 없는 [beoreut eomneun] adj spoilt

버리다 [beorida] v ditch, scrap, throw out

버마 [beoma] n Burma; 버마 사람 [beoma saram] n Burmese (person); 버마어 [beomaeo] n Burmese (language); 버마의 [beomaui] adj Burmese

버섯 [beoseot] n mushroom; 독버섯 [dokbeoseot] n toadstool

버스 [beoseu] n bus; 버스 승무원 [beoseu seungmuwon] n bus conductor; 버스 승차권 [beoseu seungchagwon] n bus ticket; 버스 정류장 [beoseu jeongnyujang] n bus station, bus stop; 소형버스 [sohyeongbeoseu] n minibus; 시외버스 [sioebeoseu] n coach (vehicle); 공항버스 [gonghangbeoseu] n airport bus;... 가는 다음 버스는 언제 있어요? [... ganeun daeum beoseuneun eonje isseoyo?] When is the next bus to...?;... 가는 마지막 버스는 언제 있어요? [... ganeun majimak beoseuneun eonje isseoyo?]

When is the last bus to…?;**... 가는 버스는 얼마나 자주 오나요?** [... ganeun beoseuneun eolmana jaju onayo?] How frequent are the buses to…?, How often are the buses to…?;**... 가는 버스는 어디에서 탈수 있어요?** [... ganeun beoseuneun eodieseo talsu isseoyo?] Where do I catch the bus to…?;**... 가는 버스가 있어요?** [... ganeun beoseuga isseoyo?] Is there a bus to…?;**... 가는 첫 버스는 언제 있어요?** [... ganeun cheot beoseuneun eonje isseoyo?] When is the first bus to…?;**... 행 버스는 어디에서 탈 수 있어요?** [... haeng beoseuneun eodieseo tal su isseoyo?] Where do I get a bus for…?;**마지막 버스는 몇 시에 있어요?** [majimak beoseuneun myeot sie isseoyo?] What time is the last bus?;**바닷가 가는 버스가 있어요?** [badatga ganeun beoseuga isseoyo?] Is there a bus to the beach?;**버스 정류장은 어디있어요?** [beoseu jeongnyujangeun eodiisseoyo?] Where is the bus station?;**버스 정류장이 얼마나 먼가요?** [beoseu jeongnyujangi eolmana meongayo?] How far is the bus stop?;**버스 정류장까지 거리가 얼마나 될까요?** [beoseu jeongnyujangkkaji georiga eolmana doelkkayo?] How far are we from the bus station?;**버스를 세워 주세요** [beoseureul sewo juseyo] Please stop the bus;**버스는 몇 시에 떠나요?** [beoseuneun myeot sie tteonayo?] What time does the bus leave?;**버스는 몇 시에 오나요?** [beoseuneun myeot sie onayo?] What time does the bus arrive?;**버스는 이십분마다 와요** [beoseuneun isipbunmada wayo] The bus runs every twenty minutes;**시내 가는 버스가 있어요?** [sinae ganeun beoseuga isseoyo?] Is there a bus to the city?;**실례합니다, 어느 버스가... 에 가나요?** [sillyehamnida, eoneu beoseuga... e ganayo?] Excuse me, which bus goes to…?;**어디에서... 가는 버스를 탈 수 있어요?** [eodieseo... ganeun beoseureul tal su isseoyo?] Where can I get a bus to…?;**어디에서 버스 카드를 살 수 있을까요?** [eodieseo beoseu kadeureul sal su isseulkkayo?] Where can I buy a bus card?;**이 버스... 가나요?** [i beoseu... ganayo?] Does this bus go to…?;**공항 가는 버스가 있어요?** [gonghang ganeun beoseuga isseoyo?] Is there a bus to the airport?;**가장 가까운 버스 정류장은 어디있어요?** [gajang gakkaun beoseu jeongnyujangeun eodiisseoyo?] Where is the nearest bus stop?

버찌 [beojji] n cherry

버클 [beokeul] n buckle

버킷 [beokit] n bucket

버터 [beoteo] n butter

버팀대 [beotimdae] n brace (fastening)

버팔로 [beopallo] n buffalo

번개 [beongae] n lightning

번역 [beonyeok] n translation; **번역사** [beonyeoksa] n translator; **번역하다** [beonyeokhada] v translate

번영 [beonyeong] n prosperity

번지 점프 [beonji jeompeu] **어디에서 번지 점프를 할 수 있나요?** [eodieseo beonji jeompeureul hal su innayo?] Where can I go bungee jumping?

번째 [beonjjae] **세 번째의** [se beonjjaeui] adj third; **여덟 번째의** [yeodeol beonjjaeui] adj eighth; **천 번째의** [cheon beonjjaeui] adj thousandth

번쩍이다 [beonjjeogida] vi flash

번호 [beonho] n number; **방 번호** [bang beonho] n room number; **번호판** [beonhopan] n number plate; **우편번호** [upyeonbeonho] n postcode; **전화번호** [jeonhwabeonho] n phone number; **전화번호 문의** [jeonhwabeonho munui] npl directory enquiries; **전화번호부** [jeonhwabeonhobu] n directory, telephone directory; **참조번호** [chamjobeonho] n reference number; **계좌번호** [gyejwabeonho] n account number; **휴대폰 번호** [hyudaepon beonho] n mobile number; **PIN** [PIN] npl PIN [PIN]; **전화번호가 무엇입니까?**

[jeonhwabeonhoga mueosimnikka?]
What's the telephone number?; 제
운전 면허증 번호는....에요 [je unjeon
myeonheojeung beonhoneun....eyo]
My driving licence number is...; 차
번호는...이에(예)요 [cha beonhoneun...
ie(ye)yo] Registration number...; 팩스
번호가 무엇입니까? [paekseu
beonhoga mueosimnikka?] What is the
fax number?
벌 [beol] n bee, punishment; 도구 한 벌
[dogu han beol] n kit; 말벌 [malbeol] n
wasp; 벌을 주다 [beoreul juda] v
punish; 한 벌 [han beol] n set; 호박벌
[hobakbeol] n bumblebee
벌금 [beolgeum] n fine; 벌금이
얼마예요? [beolgeumi eolmayeyo?]
How much is the fine?; 어디에서
벌금을 내야 합니까? [eodieseo
beolgeumeul naeya hamnikka?] Where
do I pay the fine?
벌꿀 [beolkkul] n honey
벌다 [beolda] v earn
벌레 [beolle] n bug; 무당벌레
[mudangbeolle] n ladybird; 대벌레
[daebeolle] n stick insect; 애벌레
[aebeolle] n caterpillar; 제 방에 벌레가
있어요 [je bange beollega isseoyo]
There are bugs in my room
범 [beom] 흉악범 [hyungakbeom] n
thug
범람 [beomnam] n flooding; 범람하다
[beomnamhada] vi flood; 범람하다
[beomnamhada] vi flood
범선 [beomseon] n sailing boat
범위 [beomwi] n extent, range (limits);
광범위하게 [gwangbeomwihage] adv
extensively
범인 [beomin] n criminal, culprit
범죄 [beomjoe] n crime; 범죄의
[beomjoeui] adj criminal; 사이버 범죄
[saibeo beomjoe] n cybercrime
범주 [beomju] n category
범퍼 [beompeo] n bumper
법 [beop] n law; 요리법 [yoribeop] n
recipe; 구두법 [gudubeop] n
punctuation
법과 [beopgwa] 법과대학

[beopgwadaehak] n law school
법률 [beomnyul] 법률제정
[beomnyuljejeong] n legislation
법안 [beoban] n bill (legislation)
법원 [beobwon] n court
법정 [beopjeong] n tribunal
벗기다 [beotgida] v strip
벗다 [beotda] v take off; 옷을 벗다
[oseul beotda] v undress
벗어나다 [beoseonada] v get away
베개 [begae] n pillow; 베갯잇 [begaesit]
pillowcase; 베개를 하나 더 갖다
주세요 [begaereul hana deo gatda
juseyo] Please bring me an extra pillow
베네수엘라 [benesuella] n Venezuela;
베네수엘라 사람 [benesuella saram] n
Venezuelan; 베네수엘라의
[benesuellaui] adj Venezuelan
베다 [beda] v mow; 얇게 베다 [yapge
beda] v slice
베레모 [beremo] n beret
베리 [beri] n berry; 블루베리 [beulluberi]
n blueberry; 블랙베리 [beullaekberi] n
BlackBerry®; 구스베리 [guseuberi] n
gooseberry; 크란베리 [keuranberi] n
cranberry
베스트셀러 [beseuteuselleo] n bestseller
베이비시트 [beibisiteu] 베이비 시트
있어요? [beibi siteu isseoyo?] Do you
have a baby seat?
베이스 [beiseu] n bass; 베이스 드럼
[beiseu deureom] n bass drum
베이컨 [beikeon] n bacon
베일 [beil] n veil
베트남 [beteunam] n Vietnam; 베트남
사람 [beteunam saram] n Vietnamese
(person); 베트남어 [beteunameo] n
Vietnamese (language); 베트남의
[beteunamui] adj Vietnamese
벤치 [benchi] n bench
벨기에 [belgie] n Belgium; 벨기에 사람
[belgie saram] n Belgian; 벨기에의
[belgieui] adj Belgian
벨로루시 [bellorusi] n Belarus; 벨로루시
사람 [bellorusi saram] n Belarussian
(person); 벨로루시어 [bellorusieo] n
Belarussian (language); 벨로루시의
[bellorusiui] adj Belarussian

벨벳 [belbet] n velvet

벨소리 [belsori] 휴대폰 벨소리 [hyudaepon belsori] n ringtone

벨크로 [belkeuro] n Velcro®

벨트 [belteu] 컨베이어 벨트 [keonbeieo belteu] n conveyor belt; 안전벨트 [anjeonbelteu] n safety belt; 좌석 벨트 [jwaseok belteu] n seatbelt; 팬 벨트 [paen belteu] n fan belt

벼룩 [byeoruk] n flea

벽 [byeok] n wall; 방화벽 [banghwabyeok] n firewall; 벽난로 [byeongnanno] n fireplace

벽돌 [byeokdol] n block (buildings), brick; 벽돌공 [byeokdolgong] n bricklayer

벽지 [byeokji] n wallpaper

변경 [byeongyeong] n alteration; 예약을 변경할 수 있을까요? [yeyageul byeongyeonghal su isseulkkayo?] Can I change my booking?

변기 [byeongi] n toilet; 유아용 변기 [yuayong byeongi] n potty; 변기가 막혔어요 [byeongiga makhyeosseoyo] The toilet won't flush; 유아용 변기 있어요? [yuayong byeongi isseoyo?] Do you have a potty?

변동 [byeondong] 변동하다 [byeondonghada] v range

변두리 [byeonduri] npl outskirts

변명 [byeonmyeong] n excuse; 변명하다 [byeonmyeonghada] v excuse, vary, modify

변비 [byeonbi] n constipation; 변비에 걸린 [byeonbie geollin] adj constipated; 변비가 있어요 [byeonbiga isseoyo] I'm constipated

변상 [byeonsang] 변상하다 [byeonsanghada] v reimburse

변속 [byeonsok] 변속 레버 [byeonsok rebeo] n gear lever, gear stick, gearshift

변위 [byeonwi] 변위 추간판 [byeonwi chuganpan] n slipped disc

변제 [byeonje] 변제하다 [byeonjehada] v pay back

변천 [byeoncheon] n transition

변하다 [byeonhada] vi change; 변하게 하다 [byeonhage hada] vt convert;

변하기 쉬운 [byeonhagi swiun] adj changeable, variable

변형 [byeonhyeong] n transformation; 변형시키다 [byeonhyeongsikida] v transform

변호 [byeonho] 변호사 [byeonhosa] n lawyer, solicitor

변화 [byeonhwa] n change; 시간변화 [siganbyeonhwa] n conjugation; 기후 변화 [gihu byeonhwa] n climate change

별 [byeol] n star (sky); 별자리 [byeoljari] n horoscope

별개 [byeolgae] 별개의 [byeolgaeui] adj separate

별관 [byeolgwan] n pavilion

별나다 [byeollada] 별난 [byeollan] adj eccentric, weird

별명 [byeolmyeong] n nickname

별장 [byeoljang] n holiday home, villa

병 [byeong] n bottle, disease, illness, jar, sickness; 병든 [byeongdeun] adj sick; 병따개 [byeongttagae] n bottle-opener; 병으로 인한 결석 통지 [byeongeuro inhan gyeolseok tongji] n sick note; 병가 [byeongga] n sick leave; 병가 중 지급되는 급여 [byeongga jung jigeupdoeneun geubyeo] n sick pay; 빈 병 수거함 [bin byeong sugeoham] n bottle bank; 서모스 보온병 [seomoseu boonbyeong] n Thermos®; 알츠하이머병 [alcheuhaimeobyeong] n Alzheimer's disease; 일사병 [ilsabyeong] n sunstroke; 잼 병 [jaem byeong] n jam jar; 공수병 [gongsubyeong] n rabies; 꽃병 [kkotbyeong] n vase; 무탄산 생수 한 병 [mutansan saengsu han byeong] a bottle of still mineral water; 생수 한 병 [saengsu han byeong] a bottle of mineral water; 탄산 생수 한 병 [tansan saengsu han byeong] a bottle of sparkling mineral water; 한 병 더 갖다 주세요 [han byeong deo gatda juseyo] Please bring another bottle

병균 [byeonggyun] n germ

병동 [byeongdong] n hospital ward;...은

어느 병동에 있나요? [...eun eoneu byeongdonge innayo?] Which ward is... in?

병실 [byeongsil] n ward (hospital room)

병아리 [byeongari] n chick; **수평아리** [supyeongari] n cockerel

병약 [byeongyak] **병약자** [byeongyakja] n invalid; **병약한** [byeongyakhan] adj unhealthy

병원 [byeongwon] n hospital, infirmary; **산과병원** [sangwabyeongwon] n maternity hospital; **정신 병원** [jeongsin byeongwon] n mental hospital; **병원에 어떻게 가나요?** [byeongwone eotteoke ganayo?] How do I get to the hospital?; **병원에 가야 될까요?** [byeongwone gaya doelkkayo?] Will he have to go to hospital?, Will she have to go to hospital?; **병원에서 일해요** [byeongwoneseo ilhaeyo] I work in a hospital; **병원은 어디에 있나요?** [byeongwoneun eodie innayo?] Where is the hospital?; **그 남자를 병원에 데려가야 해요** [geu namjareul byeongwone deryeogaya haeyo] We must get him to hospital

보 [bo] n pace; **보청기** [bocheonggi] n hearing aid; **침대보** [chimdaebo] n bedspread

보고 [bogo] n account (report), report; **보고하다** [bogohada] v report

보고서 [bogoseo] **보험 처리를 위한 경찰 보고서가 필요해요** [boheom cheorireul wihan gyeongchal bogoseoga pillyohaeyo] I need a police report for my insurance

보관 [bogwan] n custody; **수하물 임시보관소** [suhamul imsibogwanso] n left-luggage office; **임시보관 수하물** [imsibogwan suhamul] n left-luggage; **임시보관 수하물함** [imsibogwan suhamulham] n left-luggage locker; **기록 보관소** [girok bogwanso] n archive

보관소 [bogwanso] **분실물 보관소** [bunsilmul bogwanso] n lost-and-found, lost-property office;

휴대품 보관소 [hyudaepum bogwanso] n cloakroom

보관함 [bogwanham] **짐 보관함이 있어요?** [jim bogwanhami isseoyo?] Are there any luggage lockers?

보급 [bogeup] n refill; **연료를 보급하다** [yeollyoreul bogeuphada] v refuel

보내다 [bonaeda] v send; **내보내다** [naebonaeda] v send out; **돌려보내다** [dollyeobonaeda] v send back; **떠나보내다** [tteonabonaeda] v send off; **돈을 급히 보내 줄 수 있나요?** [doneul geuphi bonae jul su innayo?] Can you arrange to have some money sent over urgently?; **여기에서 팩스를 보낼 수 있을까요?** [yeogiseo paekseureul bonael su isseulkkayo?] Can I send a fax from here?; **이메일 보내도 될까요?** [imeil bonaedo doelkkayo?] Can I send an email?; **팩스 보내는 데 얼마입니까?** [paekseu bonaeneun de eolmaimnikka?] How much is it to send a fax?; **팩스를 보내고 싶어요** [paekseureul bonaego sipeoyo] I want to send a fax

보너스 [boneoseu] n bonus

보닛 [bonit] n bonnet (car)

보다 [boda] v look, see, seem, try; **...보다** [...boda] conj than; **보이다** [boida] v seem; **보이다** [boida] v show, show up; **노려보다** [noryeoboda] v glare; **눈을 가늘게 뜨고 보다** [nuneul ganeulge tteugo boda] v squint; **아기를 보다** [agireul boda] v babysit; **자세히 살피다** [jasehi salpida] v scan; **지켜보다** [jikyeoboda] n watch; **훑어보다** [hurteoboda] vi browse; **흘끗 보다** [heulkkeut boda] v glance; **흘끗 보기** [heulkkeut bogi] n glance; **나중에 뵙겠습니다** [najunge boepgesseumnida] See you later; **방을 볼 수 있을까요?** [bangeul bol su isseulkkayo?] Can I see the room?; **여기서 볼만 한 것이 무엇인가요?** [yeogiseo bolman han geosi mueosingayo?] What is there to see here?; **곧 뵙겠습니다** [got boepgesseumnida] See you soon

보도 [bodo] n footpath, walkway; 횡단
보도 [hoengdan bodo] n pedestrian
crossing; 횡단보도 [hoengdanbodo] n
zebra crossing

보드 [bodeu] n board; 화이트보드
[hwaiteubodeu] n whiteboard

보드카 [bodeuka] n vodka

보디빌딩 [bodibilding] n bodybuilding

보람 [boram] 보람이 있는 [borami
inneun] adj rewarding

보류 [boryu] 보류지 [boryuji] n reserve
(land)

보리 [bori] n barley

보모 [bomo] n childminder, nanny

보물 [bomul] n treasure

보병 [bobyeong] n infantry

보상 [bosang] n compensation, reward;
보상하다 [bosanghada] v compensate

보석 [boseok] n bail, gem, jewel; 보석류
[boseongnyu] n jewellery; 보석상
[boseoksang] n jeweller; 보석점
[boseokjeom] n jeweller's

보수 [bosu] n compensation, fee,
reward; 보수적인 [bosujeogin] adj
conservative; 보수가 좋은 [bosuga
joheun] adj well-paid; 유지보수
[yujibosu] n maintenance

보스니아 [boseunia] n Bosnia; 보스니아
사람 [boseunia saram] n Bosnian
(person); 보스니아의 [boseuniaui] adj
Bosnian

보스니아헤르체고비나
[boseuniahereuchegobina] 보스니아
헤르체고비나 [boseunia
hereuchegobina] n Bosnia
Herzegovina

보습 [boseup] 보습제 [boseupje] n
moisturizer

보안 [boan] n security

보온 [boon] 보온복 [boonbok] n shell
suit; 서모스 보온병 [seomoseu
boonbyeong] n Thermos®

보유 [boyu] n reserve (retention)

보육원 [boyugwon] 사설 보육원 [saseol
boyugwon] n playgroup

보이다 [boida] v show, reveal; 눈에
보이는 [nune boineun] adj visible

보일러 [boilleo] n boiler

보장 [bojang] n guarantee; 보장하다
[bojanghada] v ensure; 사회보장
[sahoebojang] n social security

보조 [bojo] n assistance, pace; 보행
보조기 [bohaeng bojogi] n Zimmer®
frame; 보조가 필요해요 [bojoga
pillyohaeyo] I need assistance

보조금 [bojogeum] n grant, subsidy;
보조금을 지불하다 [bojogeumeul
jibulhada] v subsidize

보존 [bojon] n conservation

보즈—ㅇ [bojeu] 보증 기간이 끝나지
않았어요 [bojeung gigani kkeutnaji
anhasseoyo] It's still under guarantee

보증 [bojeung] n guarantee, warranty;
보증하다 [bojeunghada] v assure,
guarantee, insure; 차 보증 기간이
끝나지 않았어요 [cha bojeung gigani
kkeutnaji anhasseoyo] The car is still
under warranty

보증금 [bojeunggeum] 보증금을
돌려주시겠어요? [bojeunggeumeul
dollyeojusigesseoyo?] Can I have my
deposit back, please?; 보증금이
얼마예요? [bojeunggeumi eolmayeyo?]
How much is the deposit?

보청기 [bocheonggi] 저는 보청기를 껴요
[jeoneun bocheonggireul kkyeoyo] I
have a hearing aid

보충 [bochung] n supplement; 보충하는
[bochunghaneun] adj complementary

보츠와나 [bocheuwana] n Botswana

보통 [botong] adv generally, usually;
보통은 [botongeun] adv usually;
보통의 [botongui] adj ordinary, usual

보트 [boteu] 모터 보트 [moteo boteu] n
motorboat; 작은 보트 [jageun boteu]
n dinghy; 고속 모터 보트 [gosok
moteo boteu] n speedboat

보편 [bopyeon] 보편적 [bopyeonjeok]
adj widespread

보행 [bohaeng] 보행 보조기 [bohaeng
bojogi] n Zimmer® frame; 보행자
[bohaengja] n pedestrian; 보행자 전용
구역 [bohaengja jeonyong guyeok] n
pedestrian precinct; 보행자 전용의
[bohaengja jeonyongui] adj
pedestrianized; 보행자 전용구역

[bohaengja jeonyongguyeok] *n*
precinct

보험 [boheom] *n* insurance; 3자 보험
[samja boheom] *n* third-party
insurance; 보험증서
[boheomjeungseo] *n* insurance
certificate; 보험증권
[boheomjeunggwon] *n* insurance
policy; 보험에 든 [boheome deun] *adj*
insured; 상해보험 [sanghaeboheom] *n*
accident insurance; 생명보험
[saengmyeongboheom] *n* life
insurance; 여행보험
[yeohaengboheom] *n* travel insurance;
자동차 보험 [jadongcha boheom] *n* car
insurance; 보험 정보를 알려 주세요
[boheom jeongboreul allyeo juseyo]
Give me your insurance details, please;
보험 처리를 위한 영수증이 필요해요
[boheom cheorireul wihan
yeongsujeungi pillyohaeyo] I need a
receipt for the insurance; 보험 처리를
위한 경찰 보고서가 필요해요 [boheom
cheorireul wihan gyeongchal
bogoseoga pillyohaeyo] I need a police
report for my insurance; 보험증서를 볼
수 있을까요? [boheomjeungseoreul
bol su isseulkkayo?] Can I see your
insurance certificate please?; 보험사가
지불해 주나요? [boheomsaga jibulhae
junayo?] Will the insurance pay for it?;
보험에 들었어요? [boheome
deureosseoyo?] Do you have
insurance?; 저는 보험에 들었어요
[jeoneun boheome deureosseoyo] I
have insurance; 저는 치과 보험에
들었는지 모르겠어요 [jeoneun chigwa
boheome deureonneunji
moreugesseoyo] I don't know if I have
dental insurance; 저는 치과 보험에
들지 않았어요 [jeoneun chigwa
boheome deulji anhasseoyo] I don't
have dental insurance; 저는 사설
건강보험에 들었어요 [jeoneun saseol
geongangboheome deureosseoyo] I
have private health insurance; 저는
여행자보험에 들지 않았어요 [jeoneun
yeohaengjaboheome deulji

anhasseoyo] I don't have travel
insurance; 저는 건강보험에 들지
않았어요 [jeoneun geongangboheome
deulji anhasseoyo] I don't have health
insurance; 제 보험 정보예요 [je
boheom jeongboyeyo] Here are my
insurance details; 종합 보험료로
얼마를 더 내야 할까요? [jonghap
boheomnyoro eolmareul deo naeya
halkkayo?] How much extra is
comprehensive insurance cover?;
가격에 종합 보험료가 포함되나요?
[gagyeoge jonghap boheomnyoga
pohamdoenayo?] Is fully
comprehensive insurance included in
the price?; 개인보험을 들고 싶어요
[gaeinboheomeul deulgo sipeoyo] I'd
like to arrange personal accident
insurance

보호 [boho] *n* protection; 보호하다
[bohohada] *v* guard, protect; 화면
보호기 [hwamyeon bohogi] *n*
screen-saver

복 [bok] *n* suit, fortune; 보온복
[boonbok] *n* shell suit; 수영복
[suyeongbok] *n* bathing suit,
swimming costume; 야회복
[yahoebok] *n* evening dress; 화장복
[hwajangbok] *n* dressing gown; 새해
복 많이 받으세요! [saehae bok manhi
badeuseyo!] Happy New Year!

복권 [bokgwon] *n* lottery

복도 [bokdo] *n* corridor, hallway

복사 [boksa] *n* photocopy, radiation;
복사기 [boksagi] *n* photocopier;
복사하다 [boksahada] *v* copy,
photocopy; 어디에서 복사할 수
있을까요? [eodieseo boksahal su
isseulkkayo?] Where can I get some
photocopying done?; 이것을
복사하려고요 [igeoseul
boksaharyeogoyo] I'd like a photocopy
of this, please; 이것을 컬러
복사하려고요 [igeoseul keolleo
boksaharyeogoyo] I'd like a colour
photocopy of this, please

복수 [boksu] *n* plural, revenge

복숭아 [boksunga] *n* peach; 승도복숭아

[seungdoboksunga] n nectarine

복용 [bogyong] 복용량 [bogyongnyang] n dose; 과다 복용 [gwada bogyong] n overdose; 얼만큼 복용해야 하나요? [eolmankeum bogyonghaeya hanayo?] How much should I take?; 어떻게 복용해야 하나요 [eotteoke bogyonghaeya hanayo] How should I take it?

복원 [bogwon] 복원하다 [bogwonhada] v restore

복음 [bogeum] n gospel

복잡 [bokjap] n complication; 복잡한 [bokjaphan] adj complicated

복장 [bokjang] n costume; 복장 도착자 [bokjang dochakja] n transvestite

복제 [bokje] 복제품 [bokjepum] n replica

복지 [bokji] n cloth, welfare; 사회복지사 [sahoebokjisa] n social worker

복합 [bokhap] 복합적인 [bokhapjeogin] n complex; 복합체 [bokhapche] n complex

본관 [bongwan] 본관을 잠가 주세요 [bongwaneul jamga juseyo] Turn it off at the mains

본능 [bonneung] n instinct

본래 [bollae] 본래의 [bollaeui] adj original

본문 [bonmun] n text

본부 [bonbu] n abbr HQ ▷ npl headquarters

본사 [bonsa] n head office

본의 [bonui] 본의아닌 [bonuianin] adj unintentional

본토 [bonto] n mainland

볼 [bol] n ball; 네트볼 [neteubol] n netball

볼거리 [bolgeori] n mumps

볼리비아 [bollibia] n Bolivia; 볼리비아 사람 [bollibia saram] n Bolivian; 볼리비아의 [bollibiaui] adj Bolivian

볼링 [bolling] n bowling; 볼링 레인 [bolling rein] n bowling alley; 텐핀 볼링 [tenpin bolling] n tenpin bowling

볼터치 [bolteochi] n blusher

볼트 [bolteu] n volt

볼펜 [bolpen] n ballpoint pen; 볼펜

상표명 [bolpen sangpyomyeong] n Biro®

봄 [bom] n spring (season); 봄철 [bomcheol] n springtime

봉사 [bongsa] 봉사료 [bongsaryo] n cover charge; 봉사자 [bongsaja] n server (person); 자원봉사자 [jawonbongsaja] v volunteer

봉사료 [bongsaryo] 봉사료 포함인가요? [bongsaryo pohamingayo?] Is service included?

봉쇄 [bongswae] n blockage

봉인 [bongin] 봉인하다 [bonginhada] v seal

봉지 [bongji] n bag; 비닐봉지 [binilbongji] n plastic bag, polythene bag; 봉지 하나 주시겠어요? [bongji hana jusigesseoyo?] Can I have a bag, please?

봉투 [bongtu] n envelope

부 [bu] n department, ministry (government), wealth; 부작용 [bujagyong] n side effect; 대부 [daebu] n godfather (baptism)

부가가치 [bugagachi] 부가가치세 [bugagachise] n VAT; 부가가치세 포함인가요? [bugagachise pohamingayo?] Is VAT included?

부과 [bugwa] (대금을) 부과하다 [(daegeumeul) bugwahada] v charge (price)

부끄러워하다 [bukkeureowohada] 부끄러워하는 [bukkeureowohaneun] adj ashamed

부끄럼 [bukkeureom] 부끄럼 타는 [bukkeureom taneun] adj shy

부대 [budae] n sack (container); 부대에 담다 [budaee damda] v sack

부도덕 [budodeok] 부도덕한 [budodeokhan] adj immoral; 부도덕한 행위 [budodeokhan haengwi] n vice

부동 [budong] 부동액 [budongaek] n antifreeze

부동산 [budongsan] n estate ▷ npl premises; 부동산 중개인 [budongsan junggaein] n estate agent

부두 [budu] n dock, jetty, pier

부드럽다 [budeureopda] 부드러운

[budeureoun] adj soft, tender

부딪치다 [buditchida] v ram

부루퉁 [burutung] **부루퉁해지다** [burutunghaejida] v sulk

부루퉁한 [burutunghan] adj sulky

부르다 [bureuda] v page, call

부리 [buri] n beak

부모 [bumo] npl parents; **조부모** [jobumo] npl grandparents; **홀부모** [holbumo] n single parent

부목 [bumok] n splint

부문 [bumun] n sector

부분 [bubun] n part, portion; **부분적으로** [bubunjeogeuro] adv partly; **부분적인** [bubunjeogin] adj partial; **이 부분이 제대로 작동하지 않아요** [i bubuni jedaero jakdonghaji anhayo] This part doesn't work properly

부사 [busa] n adverb

부서지다 [buseojida] vt snap; **부서진** [buseojin] adj broken

부속 [busok] **부속물** [busongmul] n accessory

부수다 [busuda] v break up, demolish, pull down; **산산이 부수다** [sansani busuda] vt smash

부스러기 [buseureogi] n crumb

부여 [buyeo] **동기를 부여 받은** [donggireul buyeo badeun] adj motivated

부유 [buyu] **부유한** [buyuhan] adj rich, wealthy, well-off

부인 [buin] n madam

부재 [bujae] n absence; **부재의** [bujaeui] adj absent

부적당 [bujeokdang] **부적당한** [bujeokdanghan] adj inadequate, unfit, unsuitable

부정 [bujeong] n injustice; **부정적인** [bujeongjeogin] adj negative; **부정적인 말(태도)** [bujeongjeogin mal(taedo)] n negative; **부정하다** [bujeonghada] (부정적) v deny; **부정할 수 없는** [bujeonghal su eomneun] adj undeniable

부정사 [bujeongsa] n infinitive

부정직 [bujeongjik] **부정직한** [bujeongjikhan] adj bent (dishonest), dishonest

부정확 [bujeonghwak] **부정확한** [bujeonghwakhan] adj inaccurate, incorrect

부족 [bujok] n deficit, lack, shortage, shortfall, tribe; **부족한** [bujokhan] adj scarce

부주의 [bujuui] n oversight (mistake); **부주의한** [bujuuihan] adj careless

부지 [buji] **건축 부지** [geonchuk buji] n building site

부지깽이 [bujikkaengi] n poker

부진 [bujin] **식욕부진증** [sigyokbujinjeung] n anorexia; **식욕부진의** [sigyokbujinui] adj anorexic

부처 [bucheo] n Buddha

부추 [buchu] npl chives

부치다 [buchida] v send; **이 주소로 제 편지를 부쳐 주세요** [i jusoro je pyeonjireul buchyeo juseyo] Please send my mail on to this address; **짐을 미리 부쳤어요** [jimeul miri buchyeosseoyo] I sent my luggage on in advance

부탁 [butak] n favour, request; **내일 아침 7시에 모닝콜 부탁해요** [naeil achim 7sie moningkol butakhaeyo] I'd like an alarm call for tomorrow morning at seven o'clock

부탁하다 [butakhada] **부탁합니다** [butakhamnida] Please

부터 [buteo] ...**로부터** [...robuteo] prep from

부패 [bupae] n corruption; **부패한** [bupaehan] adj corrupt

부표 [bupyo] n buoy

부풀다 [bupulda] **부푼** [bupun] adj swollen

부품 [bupum] n part; **예비 부품** [yebi bupum] n spare part; **토요타 부품 있어요?** [toyota bupum isseoyo?] Do you have parts for a Toyota?

부피 [bupi] n volume

부호 [buho] n code; **생략부호** [saengnyakbuho] n apostrophe; **의문부호** [uimunbuho] n question mark; **인용부호** [inyongbuho] npl quotation marks

부활절 [buhwaljeol] n Easter; 부활절
달걀 [buhwaljeol dalgyal] n Easter egg

북 [buk] n north; 북미 [bungmi] n North
America; 북미 사람 [bungmi saram] n
North American; 북미의 [bungmiui]
adj North American; 북동쪽
[bukdongjjok] n northeast; 북쪽
[bukjjok] n north; 북쪽으로
[bukjjogeuro] adv north; 북쪽으로
가는 [bukjjogeuro ganeun] adj
northbound; 북쪽의 [bukjjogui] adj
north, northern; 북서쪽 [bukseojjok] n
northwest; 북아일랜드 [bugaillaendeu]
n Northern Ireland; 북아프리카
[bugapeurika] n North Africa;
북아프리카 사람 [bugapeurika saram]
n North African; 북아프리카의
[bugapeurikaui] adj North African; 북한
[bukhan] n North Korea; 북해 [bukhae]
n North Sea

북경 [bukgyeong] 베이징 [beijing] n
Beijing

북극 [bukgeuk] n (the) Arctic, North
Pole; 북극곰 [bukgeukgom] n polar
bear; 북극권 [bukgeukgwon] n Arctic
Circle; 북극해 [bukgeukhae] n Arctic
Ocean

분 [bun] n minute; 10분의 1 [sim bunui
il] n tenth; 1000분의 1 [cheon bunui il]
n thousandth; 3분의 1 [sambunui il] n
third; 30분 [samsib bun] n half-hour;
4분의 1 [sabunui il] n quarter; 6분의 1
[yukbunui il] adj sixth; 7분의 1
[chilbunui il] n seventh; 8분의 1
[palbunui il] n eighth; 9분의 1
[gubunui il] n ninth; 여기서 몇 분만
기다려 주시겠어요? [yeogiseo myeot
bunman gidaryeo jusigesseoyo?] Can
you wait here for a few minutes?

분개 [bungae] 분개하다 [bungaehada] v
resent; 분개하고 있는 [bungaehago
inneun] adj resentful

분기점 [bungijeom] n junction, fork (in
road); ...에 가려면 어느 분기점인가요?
[...e garyeomyeon eoneu
bungijeomingayo?] Which junction is it
for...?; 차가...호 분기점 근처에 있어요
[chaga...ho bungijeom geuncheoe

isseoyo] The car is near junction
number...

분노 [bunno] n anger, rage; 노상 분노
[nosang bunno] n road rage

분담 [bundam] 분담하다 [bundamhada]
v club together

분량 [bullyang] 어린이 분량이 있나요?
[eorini bullyangi innayo?] Do you have
children's portions?

분류 [bullyu] n assortment

분리 [bulli] n separation; 분리하다
[bullihada] v disconnect; 분리하다
[bullihada] v separate; 분리하여
[bullihayeo] adv separately

분리대 [bullidae] 중앙 분리대가 있는
도로 [jungang bullidaega inneun doro]
n dual carriageway

분명 [bunmyeong] 분명하게
[bunmyeonghage] adv obviously;
분명하게 하다 [bunmyeonghage hada]
v clarify; 분명한 [bunmyeonghan] adj
obvious; 분명한 [bunmyeonghan] adj
blatant; 분명해지다
[bunmyeonghaejida] v come in; 분명히
[bunmyeonghi] adv clearly

분무 [bunmu] n spray; 분무하다
[bunmuhada] v spray

분배 [bunbae] 분배자 [bunbaeja] n
distributor; 분배하다 [bunbaehada] v
distribute, share out

분별 [bunbyeol] n discretion; 무분별한
[mubunbyeolhan] adj senseless

분서 [bunseo] 문서작업 [munseojageop]
n paperwork

분석 [bunseok] n analysis; 분석하다
[bunseokhada] v analyse

분쇄 [bunswae] 후추 분쇄통 [huchu
bunswaetong] n peppermill

분수 [bunsu] n fountain

분실 [bunsil] 수하물이 분실되었어요
[suhamuri bunsildoeeosseoyo] My
luggage has been lost

분실물 [bunsilmul] 분실물 보관소
[bunsilmul bogwanso] n
lost-and-found, lost-property office

분열 [bunyeol] 분열하다 [bunyeolhada]
v split up

분자 [bunja] n molecule

분파 [bunpa] n sect
분필 [bunpil] n chalk
분할 [bunhal] n division
분해 [bunhae] 분해하다 [bunhaehada] v take apart; 생물분해성의 [saengmulbunhaeseongui] adj biodegradable
불 [bul] n fire, light; 불붙이다 [bulbuchida] v light; 불태우다 [bultaeuda] n burn; 비벼 불을 끄다 [bibyeo bureul kkeuda] v stub out; 모닥불 [modakbul] n bonfire; 점화 [jeomhwa] n ignition; 불 있으세요? [bul isseuseyo?] Have you got a light?; 불켜도 돼요? [bulkyeodo dwaeyo?] Can I switch the light on?; 불이야! [buriya!] Fire!; 불꺼도 돼요? [bulkkeodo dwaeyo?] Can I switch the light off?
불가능 [bulganeung] 불가능한 [bulganeunghan] adj impossible
불가리아 [bulgaria] n Bulgaria; 불가리아 사람 [bulgaria saram] n Bulgarian (person); 불가리아어 [bulgariaeo] n Bulgarian (language); 불가리아의 [bulgariaui] adj Bulgarian
불가피 [bulgapi] 불가피한 [bulgapihan] adj unavoidable
불결 [bulgyeol] 불결한 [bulgyeolhan] adj filthy
불경기 [bulgyeonggi] n recession
불공평 [bulgongpyeong] 불공평한 [bulgongpyeonghan] adj unfair
불교 [bulgyo] n Buddhism; 불교도 [bulgyodo] n Buddhist; 불교의 [bulgyoui] adj Buddhist
불구 [bulgu]...임에도 불구하고 [...imedo bulguhago] conj though;...에도 불구하고 [...edo bulguhago] prep despite
불길 [bulgil] 불길한 [bulgilhan] adj grim, sinister
불꽃 [bulkkot] n blaze, flame, spark; 불꽃놀이 [bulkkotnori] npl fireworks
불다 [bulda] vi blow
불도저 [buldojeo] n bulldozer
불량 [bullyang] 불량배 [bullyangbae] n bully; 소화 불량 [sohwa bullyang] n

indigestion; 불량이에요 [bullyangieyo] It's faulty
불리 [bulli] n disadvantage
불리다 [bullida]...라고 불리는 [...rago bullineun] adj dubbed
불만 [bulman] n complaint; 불만스러운 [bulmanseureoun] adj dissatisfied, unsatisfactory; 불만을 제기하고 싶어요. [bulmaneul jegihago sipeoyo.] I'd like to make a complaint; 누구에게 불만을 제기할수 있을까요? [nuguege bulmaneul jegihalsu isseulkkayo?] Who can I complain to?; 서비스에 대해 불만을 제기하고 싶어요 [seobiseue daehae bulmaneul jegihago sipeoyo] I want to complain about the service
불면 [bulmyeon] 불면증 [bulmyeonjung] n insomnia
불명 [bulmyeong] 정체 불명의 [jeongche bulmyeongui] adj unidentified
불명확 [bulmyeonghwak] 불명확한 [bulmyeonghwakhan] adj unclear
불모 [bulmo] 불모의 [bulmoui] adj sterile
불법 [bulbeop] 불법의 [bulbeobui] adj illegal
불변 [bulbyeon] 불변의 [bulbyeonui] adj unchanged
불성실 [bulseongsil] 불성실한 [bulseongsilhan] adj insincere
불신 [bulsin] 불신한 [bulsinhan] adj unbelievable, unreliable
불안 [buran] n anxiety; 불안한 [buranhan] adj apprehensive, insecure, restless
불안정 [buranjeong] n instability; 불안정한 [buranjeonghan] adj unstable, unsteady
불완전 [burwanjeon] 불완전한 [burwanjeonhan] adj incomplete
불운 [burun] n misfortune; 불운한 [burunhan] adj unlucky
불일치 [burilchi] n disagreement
불충분 [bulchungbun] 불충분한 [bulchungbunhan] adj insufficient, sufficient
불충실 [bulchungsil] 불충실한

[bulchungsilhan] *adj* unfaithful
불친절 [bulchinjeol] 불친절한
[bulchinjeolhan] *adj* unfriendly
불쾌 [bulkwae] *n* displeasure, malaise;
불쾌감을 주는 [bulkwaegameul
juneun] *adj* sickening; 불쾌하게 하는
[bulkwaehage haneun] *adj* offensive;
불쾌한 [bulkwaehan] *adj* obnoxious,
repellent, unpleasant; 불쾌한
[bulkwaehan] *adj* nasty
불편 [bulpyeon] *n* inconvenience; 불편한
[bulpyeonhan] *adj* inconvenient,
uncomfortable
불평 [bulpyeong] *n* grouse *(complaint)*;
불평하다 [bulpyeonghada] *v* complain;
불평하기 [bulpyeonghagi] *n* complaint
불필요 [bulpillyo] 불필요한
[bulpillyohan] *adj* unnecessary
불합리 [bulhamni] 불합리한
[bulhamnihan] *adj* unreasonable
불행 [bulhaeng] *n* misfortune, woe;
불행한 사건 [bulhaenghan sageon] *n*
mishap
불확실 [bulhwaksil] *n* uncertainty;
불확실한 [bulhwaksilhan] *adj*
uncertain, unsure
붉다 [burkda] 머리털이 붉은 사람
[meoriteori bulgeun saram] *n* redhead
붐비다 [bumbida] 붐비는 [bumbineun]
adj crowded
붓 [bu] *n* brush; 그림붓 [geurimbut] *n*
paintbrush
붓다 [butda] *vt* pour
붕대 [bungdae] *n* bandage; 붕대를 감다
[bungdaereul gamda] *v* bandage;
붕대를 새로 감아 주세요 [bungdaereul
saero gama juseyo] I'd like a fresh
bandage; 붕대를 감아 주세요
[bungdaereul gama juseyo] I'd like a
bandage
붙이다 [buchida] *v* attach, glue
붙잡다 [butjapda] *v* capture, grasp
뷔페 [bwipe] *n* buffet
브라우저 [beuraujeo] *n* browser
브라질 [beurajil] *n* Brazil; 브라질 사람
[beurajil saram] *n* Brazilian; 브라질의
[beurajirui] *adj* Brazilian
브래지어 [beuraejieo] *n* bra

브랜디 [beuraendi] *n* brandy; 브랜디
주세요 [beuraendi juseyo] I'll have a
brandy
브레이크 [beureikeu] *n* brake;
브레이크를 걸다 [beureikeureul
geolda] *v* brake; 수동 브레이크
[sudong beureikeu] *n* handbrake;
브레이크가 작동하지 않아요
[beureikeuga jakdonghaji anhayo] The
brakes don't work
브로치 [beurochi] *n* brooch
브로콜리 [beurokolli] *n* broccoli
브리프 [beuripeu] *npl* briefs
브리핑 [beuriping] *n* briefing
블라우스 [beullauseu] *n* blouse
블라인드 [beullaindeu] *n* blind
블레이저 [beulleijeo] *n* blazer
블로그 [beullogeu] *n* blog; 블로그를 쓰다
[beullogeureul sseuda] *v* blog
블루스 [beulluseu] *npl* blues
비 [bi] *n* broom, rain; 비내리다
[binaerida] *v* rain; 비옷 [biot] *n*
raincoat; 비가 오는 [biga oneun] *adj*
rainy; 산성비 [sanseongbi] *n* acid rain;
우기 [ugi] *n* monsoon; 이슬비 [iseulbi]
n drizzle; 기념비 [ginyeombi] *n*
monument; 비가 올 것 같아요? [biga
ol geot gatayo?] Do you think it's going
to rain?; 비가 와요 [biga wayo] It's
raining
비계 [bigye] *n* scaffolding
비공식 [bigongsik] 비공식의
[bigongsigui] *adj* unofficial
비관 [bigwan] *n* pessimism; 비관주의자
[bigwanjuuija] *n* pessimist; 비관적인
[bigwanjeogin] *adj* pessimistic
비교 [bigyo] *n* comparison; 비교되는
[bigyodoeneun] *adj* comparable;
비교적 [bigyojeok] *adv* comparatively;
비교하다 [bigyohada] *v* compare
비극 [bigeuk] *n* tragedy; 비극적인
[bigeukjeogin] *adj* tragic
비기다 [bigida] *v* draw *(equal with)*
비난 [binan] *n* blame; 비난하다
[binanhada] *v* blame, condemn
비누 [binu] *n* soap; 비누 그릇 [binu
geureut] *n* soap dish; 가루 세탁 비누
[garu setak binu] *n* washing powder;

가루비누 [garubinu] n soap powder; 비누가 없어요 [binuga eopseoyo] There is no soap

비늘 [bineul] n scale (tiny piece)

비다 [bida] v be empty; 비어 있는 [bieo inneun] adj vacant; 빈 [bin] adj blank, empty; 속이 빈 [sogi bin] adj hollow; 텅 빈 [teong bin] adj void; 이 자리 비었어요? [i jari bieosseoyo?] Is this seat free?

비단 [bidan] n silk

비둘기 [bidulgi] n dove, pigeon

비듬 [bideum] n dandruff

비디오 [bidio] n video; 비디오 카메라 [bidio kamera] n video camera; 비디오 전화 [bidio jeonhwa] n videophone; 이 비디오 카메라에 사용하는 테이프 하나 주시겠어요? [i bidio kamerae sayonghaneun teipeu hana jusigesseoyo?] Can I have a tape for this video camera, please?

비디오 게임 [bidio geim] 비디오 게임을 할 수 있을까요? [bidio geimeul hal su isseulkkayo?] Can I play video games?

비례 [birye] 비례하는 [biryehaneun] adj proportional

비록 [birok] conj although

비료 [biryo] n fertilizer

비명 [bimyeong] n scream; 비명을 지르다 [bimyeongeul jireuda] v shriek; 비명지르다 [bimyeongjireuda] v scream

비밀 [bimil] n confidence (secret), secret; 비밀의 [bimirui] adj secret; 비밀히 [bimilhi] adv secretly; 일급기밀인 [ilgeupgimirin] adj top-secret

비버 [bibeo] n beaver

비범 [bibeom] 비범한 [bibeomhan] adj extraordinary

비상 [bisang] n alarm; 비상 사태 [bisang satae] n emergency; 비상 착륙 [bisang changnyuk] n emergency landing; 비상 경보 [bisang gyeongbo] n alarm call; 비상구 [bisanggu] n emergency exit

비서 [biseo] abbr PA ▷ n personal assistant, secretary

비스킷 [biseukit] n biscuit

비슷하다 [biseutada] 비슷한 [biseutan] adj similar

비슷함 [biseutam] n similarity

비싸다 [bissada] 비싼 [bissan] adj dear (expensive), expensive; 값비싼 [gabbissan] adj valuable; 너무 비싸요 [neomu bissayo] It's too expensive for me; 왜 그렇게 비싸요? [wae geureoke bissayo?] Why are you charging me so much?; 정말 비싸요 [jeongmal bissayo] It's quite expensive

비열 [biyeol] 비열한 [biyeolhan] adj lousy, vile

비옥 [biok] 비옥한 [biokhan] adj fertile

비올라 [biolla] n viola

비용 [biyong] n cost ▷ npl expenses; 비용이 들다 [biyongi deulda] v cost; 생활비 [saenghwalbi] n cost of living; 수리 비용은 얼마예요? [suri biyongeun eolmayeyo?] How much will the repairs cost?

비우다 [biuda] v vacate

비율 [biyul] n proportion, rate, ratio

비자 [bija] n visa; 입국 비자가 있어요 [ipguk bijaga isseoyo] I have an entry visa; 제 비자예요 [je bijayeyo] Here is my visa

비즈니스 [bijeuniseu] 비즈니스 석 [bijeuniseu seok] n business class

비지니스 [bijiniseu] 쇼 비즈니스 [syo bijeuniseu] n show business

비집다 [bijipda] 비집고 들어가다 [bijipgo deureogada] v squeeze in

비참 [bicham] n misery; 비참한 [bichamhan] adj miserable

비키니 [bikini] n bikini

비타민 [bitamin] n vitamin

비탄 [bitan] 비탄에 잠긴 [bitane jamgin] adj heartbroken

비탈 [bital] n slope

비트 [biteu] 비트 뿌리 [biteu ppuri] n beetroot

비틀거리다 [biteulgeorida] v stagger

비틀다 [biteulda] v wrench ▷ vt twist

비평 [bipyeong] n criticism; 비평가 [bipyeongga] n critic; 비평하다 [bipyeonghada] v criticize

비행 [bihaeng] n flight; 비행사

[bihaengsa] *n* pilot; 비행기 [bihaenggi] *n* plane *(aeroplane)*; 미확인 비행물체 [mihwagin bihaengmulche] *abbr* UFO

비행기 [bihaenggi] *n* plane; 비행기 멀미가 난 [bihaenggi meolmiga nan] *adj* airsick; 비행기 승무원 [bihaenggi seungmuwon] *n* flight attendant;... 가는 비행기는 어느 출구인가요? [... ganeun bihaenggineun eoneu chulguingayo?] Which gate for the flight to...?;... 가는 비행기는 어디에서 탑승 수속을 하나요? [... ganeun bihaenggineun eodieseo tapseung susogeul hanayo?] Where do I check in for the flight to...?; 비행기를 놓쳤어요 [bihaenggireul nochyeosseoyo] I've missed my flight; 비행기가 지연되었어요 [bihaenggiga jiyeondoeeosseoyo] The flight has been delayed; 비행기편을 바꾸려고요 [bihaenggipyeoneul bakkuryeogoyo] I'd like to change my flight; 더 이른 비행기편이 좋아요 [deo ireun bihaenggipyeoni johayo] I would prefer an earlier flight; 싼 비행기편이 있어요? [ssan bihaenggipyeoni isseoyo?] Are there any cheap flights?; 제가 탈 비행기는...에서 떠나요 [jega tal bihaenggineun...eseo tteonayo] My plane leaves at...; 비행기편을 취소하려고요 [bihaenggipyeoneul chwisoharyeogoyo] I'd like to cancel my flight

비행사 [bihaengsa] 우주비행사 [ujubihaengsa] *n* astronaut

비현실 [bihyeonsil] *adj* unreal; 비현실적인 [bihyeonsiljeogin] *adj* unrealistic

빈도 [bindo] *n* frequency

빈민 [binmin] 빈민가 [binminga] *n* slum

빈번 [binbeon] 빈번한 [binbeonhan] *adj* frequent

빈약 [binyak] 빈약한 [binyakhan] *adj* skimpy

빈정 [binjeong] 빈정대는 [binjeongdaeneun] *adj* sarcastic

빈혈 [binhyeol] 빈혈의 [binhyeorui] *adj* anaemic

빌라 [billa] *n* villa; 빌라를 빌리고 싶어요 [billareul billigo sipeoyo] I'd like to rent a villa

빌려주다 [billyeojuda] *v* loan

빌리다 [billida] *v* borrow; 빌려주다 [billyeojuda] *v* lend; 펜을 빌려 주시겠어요? [peneul billyeo jusigesseoyo?] Do you have a pen I could borrow?

빗 [bit] *n* comb

빗나가다 [bitnagada] *v* swerve

빗다 [bitda] *v* comb

빗장 [bitjang] *n* bolt

빙고 [binggo] *n* bingo

빙산 [bingsan] *n* iceberg

빙하 [bingha] *n* glacier

빚 [bit] *n* debt; 빚지다 [bitjida] *v* owe

빛 [bit] 빛나는 [bitnaneun] *adj* brilliant, shiny; 빛나다 [bitnada] *v* shine; 빛에 비춰 봐도 될까요? [biche bichwo bwado doelkkayo?] May I take it over to the light?

ㅃㅃ

[ppaenota] *v* leave out;**...을 뺀** [...eul ppaen] *prep* minus

빼앗다 [ppaeatda] *v* rob

뺨 [ppyam] *n* cheek

뻐꾸기 [ppeokkugi] *n* cuckoo

뻗다 [ppeotda] **뻗어 있다** [ppeodeo itda] *vi* stretch

뼈 [ppyeo] *n* bone; **등뼈** [deungppyeo] *n* backbone; **광대뼈** [gwangdaeppyeo] *n* cheekbone

뽑기 [ppopgi] **제비뽑기** [jebippopgi] *n* draw *(lottery)*

뽑다 [ppopda] *v* pull up; **플러그를 뽑다** [peulleogeureul ppopda] *v* unplug

뾰루지 [ppyoruji] *n* pimple

뾰류지 [ppyoryuji] **뾰루지가 났어요** [ppyorujiga nasseoyo] I have a rash

뾰족하다 [ppyojokhada] **뾰족한 끝** [ppyojokhan kkeut] *n* peak

뿌리 [ppuri] *n* root; **비트 뿌리** [biteu ppuri] *n* beetroot; **구근** [gugeun] *n* bulb *(plant)*

뿔 [ppul] *n* horn

삐다 [ppida] *v* sprain

삐삐 [ppippi] *n* bleeper, pager

빠르다 [ppareuda] **빠른** [ppareun] *adj* fast, quick; **빨리** [ppalli] *adv* fast, quickly; **제 시계가 빠른 것 같아요** [je sigyega ppareun geot gatayo] I think my watch is fast

빠지다 [ppajida] *v* drown; **누가 물에 빠졌어요!** [nuga mure ppajyeosseoyo!] Someone is drowning!

빨간 [ppalgan] *adj* red

빨다 [ppalda] *v* suck; **입으로 빨다** [ibeuro ppalda] *v* suck

빨래 [ppallae] **빨랫줄** [ppallaetjul] *n* clothes line, washing line; **빨래 집게** [ppallae jipge] *n* clothes peg; **빨래방** [ppallaebang] *n* Launderette®

빨리 [ppalli] **가능한 한 빨리** [ganeunghan han ppalli] *abbr* asap; **가능한 한 빨리** [ganeunghan han ppalli] as soon as possible

빵 [ppang] *n* bread; **롤 빵** [rol ppang] *n* bread roll; **빵 상자** [ppang sangja] *n* bread bin; **빵집** [ppangjip] *n* bakery; **빵가루** [ppanggaru] *npl* breadcrumbs; **식빵** [sikppang] *n* bread; **작은 빵** [jageun ppang] *n* bun; **토스터** [toseuteo] *n* toaster; **흑빵** [heukppang] *n* brown bread; **빵 좀 드릴까요?** [ppang jom deurilkkayo?] Would you like some bread?; **빵을 더 갖다 주세요** [ppangeul deo gatda juseyo] Please bring more bread

빼다 [ppaeda] *v* subtract; **빼놓다**

사 [sa] *number* four ▷ *n* person; 여행사 [yeohaengsa] *n* tour operator
사생활 [sasaenghwal] *n* privacy
사각형 [sagakhyeong] 정사각형 [jeongsagakhyeong] *n* square; 정사각형의 [jeongsagakhyeongui] *adj* square; 직사각형 [jiksagakhyeong] *n* rectangle; 직사각형의 [jiksagakhyeongui] *adj* rectangular
사거리 [sageori] 다음 사거리에서 오른쪽으로 가세요 [daeum sageorieseo oreunjjogeuro gaseyo] Go right at the next junction; 다음 사거리에서 왼쪽으로 가세요 [daeum sageorieseo oenjjogeuro gaseyo] Go left at the next junction
사건 [sageon] *n* affair, event, incident, matter; 불행한 사건 [bulhaenghan sageon] *n* mishap; 사건이 많은 [sageoni manheun] *adj* eventful
사격 [sagyeok] *n* shooting
사고 [sago] *n* accident; 사교춤 [sagyochum] *n* ballroom dancing; 사고를 당했어요 [sagoreul danghaesseoyo] I've had an accident; 사고가 났어요 [sagoga nasseoyo] I've been in an accident; 사고가 나면 어떻게 해야 할까요? [sagoga namyeon eotteoke haeya halkkayo?] What do I do if I have an accident?; 사고가 있었어요! [sagoga isseosseoyo!] There's been an accident!

사과 [sagwa] *n* apology, apple; 사과 파이 [sagwa pai] *n* apple pie; 사과즙 [sagwajeup] *n* cider; 사과하다 [sagwahada] *v* apologize
사교 [sagyo] 사교적인 [sagyojeogin] *adj* outgoing, sociable
사귀다 [sagwida] 미안하지만, 사귀는 사람 있어요 [mianhajiman, sagwineun saram isseoyo] Sorry, I'm in a relationship
사기 [sagi] *n* fraud, morale, scam; 사기치다 [sagichida] *v* rip off; 사기꾼 [sagikkun] *n* crook, crook (swindler)
사냥 [sanyang] *n* hunting; 사냥꾼 [sanyangkkun] *n* hunter; 사냥하다 [sanyanghada] *v* hunt
사다 [sada] *v* buy, purchase; 사재다 [sajaeda] *v* stock up on
사다리 [sadari] *n* ladder; 접사다리 [jeopsadari] *n* stepladder
사당 [sadang] *n* shrine
사라지다 [sarajida] *v* disappear, vanish; 사라진 [sarajin] *adj* gone; 사라짐 [sarajim] *n* disappearance
사람 [saram] *n* person; 사람들 [saramdeul] *npl* people; 사람이 살지 않는 [sarami salji annneun] *adj* uninhabited; 한 사람 [han saram] *pron* one
사랑 [sarang] *n* love; 사랑스러운 사람 [sarangseureoun saram] *n* darling; 사랑하는 [saranghaneun] *adj* dear (loved); 사랑하다 [saranghada] *v* love; 사랑해요 [saranghaeyo] I love you
사랑니 [sarangni] *n* wisdom tooth
사려 [saryeo] 사려 깊은 [saryeo gipeun] *adj* thoughtful
사례 [sarye] *n* case
사륜 [saryun] 사륜구동 [saryungudong] *n* four-wheel drive
사립 [sarip] 사립 중고교 [sarip junggogyo] *n* public school
사마귀 [samagwi] *n* wart
사막 [samak] *n* desert
사망 [samang] 사망기사 [samanggisa] *n* obituary; 사망한 [samanghan] *adv* late (dead)
사면 [samyeon] *n* ramp

사무실 [samusil] *n* office; **당신 사무실에 어떻게 가지요?** [dangsin samusire eotteoke gajiyo?] How do I get to your office?; **사무실에서 일해요** [samusireseo ilhaeyo] I work in an office

사물 [samul] **사물함** [samulham] *n* locker

사물함 [samulham] **어느 사물함이 제 것인가요?** [eoneu samulhami je geosingayo?] Which locker is mine?; **옷 넣는 사물함은 어디있어요?** [ot neonneun samulhameun eodiisseoyo?] Where are the clothes lockers?

사별 [sabyeol] **남편과 사별했어요** [nampyeongwa sabyeolhaesseoyo] I'm widowed

사보타주 [sabotaju] **사보타주하다** [sabotajuhada] *v* sabotage

사본 [sabon] *n* copy (reproduction), transcript

사상 [sasang] **사상자** [sasangja] *n* casualty

사서 [saseo] *n* librarian

사소 [saso] **사소한** [sasohan] *adj* trivial; **사소한 것** [sasohan geot] *n* trifle

사순절 [sasunjeol] *n* Lent

사슬 [saseul] *n* chain

사슴 [saseum] *n* deer; **사슴 고기** [saseum gogi] *n* venison

사실 [sasil] *n* fact

사악 [saak] **사악한** [saakhan] *adj* evil, wicked

사업 [saeop] *n* business; **사업가** [saeopga] *n* businessman; **사회사업** [sahoesaeop] *npl* social services; **여성 사업가** [yeoseong saeopga] *n* businesswoman; **사업차 왔어요** [saeopcha wasseoyo] I'm here on business; **자영업하고 있어요** [jayeongeophago isseoyo] I run my own business

사역 [sayeok] *n* ministry (religion)

사용 [sayong] *n* use; **사용자** [sayongja] *n* user; **사용하다** [sayonghada] *v* use; **사용하기 쉬운** [sayonghagi swiun] *adj* user-friendly; **재사용하다** [jaesayonghada] *v* reuse; **미터기를**

사용해 주세요 [miteogireul sayonghae juseyo] Please use the meter; **여기서 제 노트북을 사용할 수 있을까요?** [yeogiseo je noteubugeul sayonghal su isseulkkayo?] Can I use my own laptop here?

사우나 [sauna] *n* sauna

사우디아라비아 [saudiarabia] *n* Saudi, Saudi Arabia; **사우디아라비아 사람** [saudiarabia saram] *n* Saudi Arabian; **사우디아라비아의** [saudiarabiaui] *adj* Saudi, Saudi Arabian

사원 [sawon] *n* temple; **이 사원은 언제 열어요?** [i sawoneun eonje yeoreoyo?] When is the temple open?; **이 사원은 일반인에게 개방되었나요?** [i sawoneun ilbaninege gaebangdoeeonnayo?] Is the temple open to the public?

사위 [sawi] *n* son-in-law

사유 [sayu] **사유재산** [sayujaesan] *n* private property; **사유화하다** [sayuhwahada] *v* privatize

사이 [sai]...**사이에** [...saie] *prep* among; **사이에** [saie] *prep* between

사이즈 [saijeu] *n* size; **16 사이즈예요** [yeolyeoseot saijeuyeyo] I'm a size 16; **더 작은 사이즈 있어요?** [deo jageun saijeu isseoyo?] Do you have this in a smaller size?; **더 큰 사이즈 있어요?** [deo keun saijeu isseoyo?] Do you have this in a bigger size?; **아주 큰 사이즈 있어요?** [aju keun saijeu isseoyo?] Do you have an extra large?; **작은 사이즈 있어요?** [jageun saijeu isseoyo?] Do you have a small?; **제 발은 육 사이즈예요** [je bareun yuk saijeuyeyo] My feet are a size six; **중간 사이즈 있어요?** [junggan saijeu isseoyo?] Do you have a medium?; **큰 사이즈 있어요?** [keun saijeu isseoyo?] Do you have a large?

사이클론 [saikeullon] *n* cyclone

사이클링 [saikeulling] *n* cycling

사임 [saim] **사임하다** [saimhada] *v* resign

사자 [saja] *n* lion; **사자자리** [sajajari] *n* Leo; **암사자** [amsaja] *n* lioness

사장 [sajang] *n* head (principal),

사적 [sajeok] | 8o

managing director
사적 [sajeok] **사적인** [sajeogin] *adj*
private
사전 [sajeon] *n* dictionary; **백과 사전**
[baekgwa sajeon] *n* encyclopaedia
사진 [sajin] *n* photo, photograph; **사진
앨범** [sajin aelbeom] *n* photo album;
사진사 [sajinsa] *n* photographer;
사진술 [sajinsul] *n* photography;
사진찍다 [sajinjjikda] *v* photograph;
스냅 사진 [seunaep sajin] *n* snapshot;
사진을 무광택지로 뽑고 싶어요
[sajineul mugwangtaekjiro ppopgo
sipeoyo] I'd like the photos matt;
사진을 광택지로 뽑고 싶어요 [sajineul
gwangtaekjiro ppopgo sipeoyo] I'd like
the photos glossy; **언제 사진이
준비될까요?** [eonje sajini
junbidoelkkayo?] When will the photos
be ready?; **여기로 사진을 다운로드할
수 있을까요?** [yeogiro sajineul
daunnodeuhal su isseulkkayo?] Can I
download photos to here?; **이
사진들을 CD에 저장해 주시겠어요** [i
sajindeureul CDe jeojanghae
jusigesseoyo] Can you put these
photos on CD, please?
사진장비 [sajinjangbi] *n* photographic
equipment; **가장 가까운 사진 장비
가게는 어디에 있어요?** [gajang
gakkaun sajin jangbi gageneun eodie
isseoyo?] Where is the nearest shop
which sells photographic equipment?
사촌 [sachon] *n* cousin
사춘기 [sachungi] *n* adolescence
사치 [sachi] *n* luxury
사탕 [satang] *n* sweet ▷ *npl* sweets;
막대사탕 [makdaesatang] *n* lollipop,
lolly; **솜사탕** [somsatang] *n* candyfloss
사태 [satae] *n* avalanche
사파리 [sapari] *n* safari
사파이어 [sapaieo] *n* sapphire
사포 [sapo] *n* sandpaper
사프란 [sapeuran] *n* saffron
사하라 [sahara] *n* Sahara
사향초 [sahyangcho] *n* thyme
사형 [sahyeong] *n* capital punishment
사회 [sahoe] *n* society; **사회복지사**

[sahoebokjisa] *n* social worker;
사회보장 [sahoebojang] *n* social
security; **사회사업** [sahoesaeop] *npl*
social services; **사회자** [sahoeja] *n*
compere; **사회적인** [sahoejeogin] *adj*
social; **사회학** [sahoehak] *n* sociology
사회자 [sahoeja] *n* host *(entertains)*
사회주의 [sahoejuui] *n* socialism;
사회주의의 [sahoejuuiui] *adj* socialist;
사회주의자 [sahoejuuija] *n* socialist
삭감 [sakgam] *n* cutback; **삭감하다**
[sakgamhada] *v* cut down
삭제 [sakje] **삭제하다** [sakjehada] *v*
delete
산 [san] *n* acid, mountain; **산성비**
[sanseongbi] *n* acid rain; **산악 자전거**
[sanak jajeongeo] *n* mountain bike;
산이 많은 [sani manheun] *adj*
mountainous; **광산** [gwangsan] *n*
mine; **산이 보이는 방이 좋겠어요** [sani
boineun bangi jokesseoyo] I'd like a
room with a view of the mountains
산과 [sangwa] **산과병원**
[sangwabyeongwon] *n* maternity
hospital
산마리노 [sanmarino] *n* San Marino
산만 [sanman] **산만하게 하다**
[sanmanhage hada] *v* distract
산맥 [sanmaek] *n* mountain range;
카프카스 산맥 [kapeukaseu sanmaek]
n Caucasus; **안데스 산맥** [andeseu
sanmaek] *npl* Andes; **알프스 산맥**
[alpeuseu sanmaek] *npl* Alps
산사태 [sansatae] *n* landslide
산소 [sanso] *n* oxygen
산아 [sana] **산아 제한** [sana jehan] *n*
birth control
산악 [sanak] **가장 가까운 산악 구조대는
어디 있어요?** [gajang gakkaun sanak
gujodaeneun eodi isseoyo?] Where is
the nearest mountain rescue service
post?
산업 [saneop] *n* industry; **산업 단지**
[saneop danji] *n* industrial estate;
산업의 [saneobui] *adj* industrial
산장 [sanjang] **가장 가까운 산장은
어디에 있나요?** [gajang gakkaun
sanjangeun eodie innayo?] Where is

the nearest mountain hut?

산책 [sanchaek] n stroll; **산책길** [sanchaekgil] n promenade

산출 [sanchul] **산출하다** [sanchulhada] v yield

산파 [sanpa] n midwife

산호 [sanho] n coral

살 [sal] **열 두 살이에요** [yeol du sarieyo] She is twelve years old; **열 살이에요** [yeol sarieyo] He is ten years old; **오십살 이에요** [osipsal ieyo] I'm fifty years old

살구 [salgu] n apricot

살균 [salgyun] n bactericide; **살균하다** [salgyunhada] v sterilize; **저온살균한** [jeoonsalgyunhan] adj pasteurized; **초고온살균우유** [chogoonsalgyunuyu] n UHT milk; **미살균 우유로 만든 것인가요?** [misalgyun uyuro mandeun geosingayo?] Is it made with unpasteurised milk?

살다 [salda] v live, reside; **함께 살다** [hamkke salda] v live together; **어디에서 사세요?** [eodieseo saseyo?] Where do you live?; **우리는...에 살아요** [urineun...e sarayo] We live in...; **저는...에 살아요** [jeoneun...e sarayo] I live in...

살수 [salsu] **살수기** [salsugi] n sprinkler

살아있다 [saraitda] **살아있는** [sarainneun] v live; **살아있는** [sarainneun] adj alive

살인 [sarin] n murder; **살인자** [sarinja] n killer, murderer; **살인하다** [sarinhada] v murder

살찌다 [saljjida] **살찐** [saljjin] adj fat

살충 [salchung] **살충제** [salchungje] n pesticide

살토막 [saltomakt] n fillet

삶다 [sarmda] **삶은 달걀** [sarmeun dalgyal] n boiled egg; **삶은** [sarmeun] adj boiled

삼각 [samgak] **삼각건** [samgakgeon] n sling; **삼각형** [samgakhyeong] n triangle

삼촌 [samchon] **외삼촌** [oesamchon] (mother's brother) n uncle

삼키다 [samkida] vi swallow

삽 [sap] n shovel

삽입 [sabip] **삽입하다** [sabiphada] v put in

삽화 [saphwa] n illustration

상 [sang] n award, prize, statue; **보석상** [boseoksang] n jeweller; **청과물상** [cheonggwamulsang] n greengrocer's

상거래 [sanggeorae] **전자상거래** [jeonjasanggeorae] n e-commerce

상고 [sanggo] **상고머리** [sanggomeori] n crew cut

상금 [sanggeum] **거액의 상금** [geoaegui sanggeum] n jackpot

상담 [sangdam] **상담전화** [sangdamjeonhwa] n helpline

상당히 [sangdang] **상당히** [sangdanghi] adv quite, rather

상당하다 [sangdanghada] v be proper; **상당히** [sangdanghi] adv fairly

상대 [sangdae] **상대적으로** [sangdaejeogeuro] adv relatively; **경쟁 상대** [gyeongjaeng sangdae] n rival

상륙 [sangnyuk] **지금 상륙해도 될까요?** [jigeum sangnyukhaedo doelkkayo?] Can we go ashore now?

상사 [sangsa] n boss, superior

상상 [sangsang] n imagination; **상상의** [sangsangui] adj imaginary; **상상하다** [sangsanghada] v imagine

상속 [sangsok] n inheritance; **상속녀** [sangsongnyeo] n heiress; **상속인** [sangsogin] n heir

상승 [sangseung] n rise

상식 [sangsik] n common sense; **일반 상식** [ilban sangsik] n general knowledge

상아 [sanga] n ivory

상어 [sangeo] n shark

상업 [sangeop] **상업 은행** [sangeop eunhaeng] n merchant bank

상영 [sangyeong] **무슨 영화를 상영하나요?** [museun yeonghwareul sangyeonghanayo?] What's on at the cinema?; **어떤 영화를 상영하나요?** [eotteon yeonghwareul sangyeonghanayo?] Which film is on at the cinema?

상의 [sangui] **상의하다** [sanguihada] v

consult

상인 [sangin] *n* dealer; **식료품 상인** [singnyopum sangin] *n* grocer

상자 [sangja] *n* box, carton, chest *(storage)*; **작은 상자** [jageun sangja] *n* locket; **구급상자** [gugeupsangja] *n* first-aid kit

상점 [sangjeom] *n* shop, store; **상점 주인** [sangjeom juin] *n* shopkeeper; **상점 절도** [sangjeom jeoldo] *n* shoplifting; **상점 진열장** [sangjeom jinyeoljang] *n* shop window; **자선 상점** [jaseon sangjeom] *n* charity shop

상조 [sangjo] **시기상조의** [sigisangjoui] *adj* premature

상징 [sangjing] *n* symbol

상처 [sangcheo] *n* sore, wound; **부상** [busang] *(상처)* *n* injury; **상처 입은** [sangcheo ibeun] *adj* hurt, injured; **상처를 입히다** [sangcheoreul iphida] *v* wound; **쏘인 상처** [ssoin sangcheo] *n* sting

상추 [sangchu] *n* lettuce

상쾌 [sangkwae] **상쾌한** [sangkwaehan] *adj* refreshing

상태 [sangtae] *n* state; **비상 사태** [bisang satae] *n* emergency

상표 [sangpyo] *n* brand, trademark; **볼펜 상표명** [bolpen sangpyomyeong] *n* Biro®; **상표명** [sangpyomyeong] *n* brand name

상품 [sangpum] *npl* goods; **주요상품** [juyosangpum] *v* staple *(commodity)*; **상품 진열대** [sangpum jinyeoldae] *n* stall; **상품권** [sangpumgwon] *n* gift voucher, voucher

상하다 [sanghada] *v* damage, hurt, be spoiled; **기분이 상한** [gibuni sanghan] *adj* bad-tempered; **고기가 상했어요** [gogiga sanghaesseoyo] This meat is off

상해 [sanghae] **상해보험** [sanghaeboheom] *n* accident insurance

상호 [sangho] **상호간의** [sanghoganui] *adj* mutual

상환 [sanghwan] *n* repayment; **상환하다** [sanghwanhada] *v* repay

상황 [sanghwang] *n* situation

새 [sae] *n* bird; **물총새** [mulchongsae] *n* kingfisher; **백로과의 새** [baengnogwaui sae] *n* heron; **조류 독감** [joryu dokgam] *n* bird flu; **새 관찰** [sae gwanchal] *n* birdwatching; **울새** [ulsae] *n* robin; **제비** [jebi] *(새)* *n* swallow; **지빠귓과의 명금** [jippagwitgwaui myeonggeum] *n* blackbird; **참새** [chamsae] *n* sparrow; **굴뚝새** [gulttuksae] *n* wren; **개똥지빠귀** [gaettongjippagwi] *n* thrush

새기다 [saegida] *vt* carve; **새겨진 것** [saegyeojin geot] *n* inscription

새끼 [saekki] *n* young; **새끼를 낳다** [saekkireul nata] *v* breed; **짐승의 새끼** [jimseungui saekki] *n* cub; **한배의 새끼** [hanbaeui saekki] *n* litter *(offspring)*

새다 [saeda] *vi* leak; **새는 곳** [saeneun got] *n* leak; **라디에이터가 새고 있어요** [radieiteoga saego isseoyo] There is a leak in the radiator

새롭다 [saeropda] **새로운** [saeroun] *adj* new; **새해** [saehae] *n* New Year

새벽 [saebyeok] *n* dawn

새싹 [saessak] *npl* sprouts

새우 [saeu] *n* shrimp; **참새우** [chamsaeu] *n* prawn; **가시발새우** [gasibalsaeu] *npl* scampi

새장 [saejang] *n* cage

새치 [saechi] **황새치** [hwangsaechi] *n* swordfish

새해 [saehae] **새해 복 많이 받으세요!** [saehae bok manhi badeuseyo!] Happy New Year!

색 [saek] *n* colour; **분홍색의** [bunhongsaegui] *adj* pink; **녹색** [noksaek] *n* green; **녹색의** [noksaegui] *adj* green *(colour)*; **노란색의** [noransaegui] *adj* yellow; **라일락색의** [raillaksaegui] *adj* lilac; **밤색의** [bamsaegui] *adj* maroon; **베이지색의** [beijisaegui] *adj* beige; **주홍색의** [juhongsaegui] *adj* scarlet; **색맹의** [saengmaengui] *adj* colour-blind; **연한 자주색의** [yeonhan jajusaegui] *adj* mauve; **엷은 색깔의** [yeorbeun saekkkarui] *adj* tinted; 오렌지색의 [orenjisaegui] *adj* orange; 자줏빛의 [jajutbichui] *adj* purple; 적갈색의 [jeokgalsaegui] *adj* auburn, ginger; **진한 푸른색의** [jinhan pureunsaegui] *adj* navy-blue; **청록색의** [cheongnoksaegui] *adj* turquoise; **갈색의** [galsaegui] *adj* brown; **금색의** [geumsaegui] *adj* golden; **크림색의** [keurimsaegui] *adj* cream; **햇볕에 탄 빛깔** [haetbyeote tan bitkkal] *n* tan; **황갈색의** [hwanggalsaegui] *adj* tanned; **회색의** [hoesaegui] *adj* grey; **다른 색 있어요?** [dareun saek isseoyo?] Do you have this in another colour?; **색이 마음에 들지 않아요** [saegi maeume deulji anhayo] I don't like the colour; **이 색으로 해 주세요** [i saeguro hae juseyo] This colour, please

색맹 [saengmaeng] **색맹의** [saengmaengui] *adj* colour-blind

색소폰 [saeksopon] *n* saxophone

색인 [saegin] *n* index (list)

색채 [saekchae] **색채가 다양한** [saekchaega dayanghan] *adj* colourful

샌드위치 [saendeuwichi] *n* sandwich; **어떤 종류의 샌드위치가 있으세요?** [eotteon jongnyuui saendeuwichiga isseuseyo?] What kind of sandwiches do you have?

샌들 [saendeul] *n* sandal

샐러드 [saelleodeu] *n* salad; **샐러드 드레싱** [saelleodeu deuresing] *n* salad dressing

샘 [saem] *n* gland

생 [saeng] *adj* raw; **저는 생계란을 못 먹어요** [jeoneun saenggyeraneul mot meogeoyo] I can't eat raw eggs

생각 [saenggak] *n* idea, thought; **생각나게 하는 것** [saenggangnage haneun geot] *n* reminder; **생각나게 하다** [saenggangnage hada] *v* remind; **생각하다** [saenggakhada] *v* think

생강 [saenggang] *n* ginger

생도 [saengdo] *n* cadet

생략 [saengnyak] **생략부호** [saengnyakbuho] *n* apostrophe

생리 [saengni] *n* menstruation; **생리대** [saengnidae] *n* sanitary towel

생머리 [saengmeori] **저는 생머리예요** [jeoneun saengmeoriyeyo] My hair is naturally straight

생명 [saengmyeong] *n* life; **생명보험** [saengmyeongboheom] *n* life insurance

생물 [saengmul] **생물 측정학의** [saengmul cheukjeonghagui] *adj* biometric; **생물분해성의** [saengmulbunhaeseongui] *adj* biodegradable

생물학 [saengmulhak] *n* biology; **생물학의** [saengmulhagui] *adj* biological

생산 [saengsan] *n* production; **생산성** [saengsanseong] *n* productivity; **생산자** [saengsanja] *n* manufacturer; **생산하다** [saengsanhada] *v* produce; **재생산** [jaesaengsan] *n* reproduction

생산자 [saengsanja] *n* producer

생선 [saengseon] *n* fish (as food); **생선 장수** [saengseon jangsu] *n* fishmonger; **생선 싱싱한 거예요, 얼린 거예요?** [saengseon singsinghan geoyeyo, eollin geoyeyo?] Is the fish fresh or frozen?; **생선 육수로 요리된 것인가요?** [saengseon yuksuro yoridoen geosingayo?] Is this cooked in fish stock?; **생선을 주세요** [saengseoneul juseyo] I'll have the fish; **생선이 들어가지 않은 식사를 준비해 주시겠어요?** [saengseoni deureogaji anheun siksareul junbihae jusigesseoyo?] Could you prepare a meal without fish?; **어떤 생선 요리가 있나요?** [eotteon saengseon yoriga innayo?] What fish dishes do you have?; **저는 생선 안 먹어요** [jeoneun saengseon an meogeoyo] I don't eat fish; **고기 / 생선이 들어가지 않은 요리는 어느 것인가요?** [gogi / saengseoni deureogaji anheun yorineun eoneu geosingayo?] Which dishes have no meat / fish?

생수 [saengsu] *n* mineral water; **무탄산 생수 한 병** [mutansan saengsu han byeong] a bottle of still mineral water; 생수 한 병 [saengsu han byeong] a bottle of mineral water; 탄산 생수 한 병 [tansan saengsu han byeong] a bottle of sparkling mineral water

생일 [saengil] n birthday; 생일 축하해요! [saengil chukhahaeyo!] Happy birthday!

생존 [saengjon] n survival; 생존자 [saengjonja] n survivor

생태학 [saengtaehak] n ecology; 생태학의 [saengtaehagui] adj ecological

생활 [saenghwal] n living; 사생활 [sasaenghwal] n privacy; 생활비 [saenghwalbi] n cost of living; 생활수준 [saenghwalsujun] n standard of living

샤워 [syawo] n shower; 샤워 캡 [syawo kaep] n shower cap; 샤워 젤 [syawo jel] n shower gel; 샤워시설이 있어요? [syawosiseori isseoyo?] Are there showers?; 샤워기가 작동하지 않아요 [syawogiga jakdonghaji anhayo] The shower doesn't work

샤워기 [syawogi] 샤워기가 더러워요 [syawogiga deoreowoyo] The shower is dirty

샴페인 [syampein] n champagne

샴푸 [syampu] n shampoo; 샴푸 파세요? [syampu paseyo?] Do you sell shampoo?

서 [seo] n west, book, station; 북서쪽 [bukseojjok] n northwest; 남서쪽 [namseojjok] n southwest; 서부 [seobu] n western; 서쪽으로 가는 [seojjogeuro ganeun] adj westbound; 서쪽의 [seojjogui] adj western; 교과서 [gyogwaseo] n textbook; 경찰서 [kyungcharlsur] n police station

서기 [seogi] abbr AD

서늘하다 [seoneulhada] 서늘한 [seoneulhan] adj cool (cold)

서다 [seoda] vi stand

서두르다 [seodureuda] v hurry, hurry up, rush; 서두름 [seodureum] n hurry

서랍 [seorap] n drawer; 서랍장 [seorapjang] n chest of drawers;

서랍이 뻑뻑해요 [seorabi ppeokppeokhaeyo] The drawer is jammed

서류 [seoryu] n document; 서류 가방 [seoryu gabang] n briefcase; 이 서류를 복사하고 싶어요 [i seoryureul boksahago sipeoyo] I want to copy this document; 제 차량 서류예요 [je charyang seoryuyeyo] Here are my vehicle documents

서리 [seori] n frost; 서리가 내릴 만큼 추운 [seoriga naeril mankeum chuun] adj frosty

서명 [seomyeong] n autograph, signature; 머리글자로 서명하다 [meorigeuljaro seomyeonghada] v initial; 서명하다 [seomyeonghada] v sign

서브 [seobeu] n serve; 서버 [seobeo] n server (computer)

서비스 [seobiseu] n service; 서비스 요금 [seobiseu yogeum] n service charge; 서비스 구역 [seobiseu guyeok] n service area; 서비스를 하다 [seobiseureul hada] v service; 객실서비스 [gaeksilseobiseu] n room service; 서비스에 대해 불만을 제기하고 싶어요 [seobiseue daehae bulmaneul jegihago sipeoyo] I want to complain about the service; 서비스가 엉망이었어요 [seobiseuga eongmangieosseoyo] The service was terrible; 고장 서비스를 불러 주세요 [gojang seobiseureul bulleo juseyo] Call the breakdown service, please; 탁아 서비스가 있어요? [taga seobiseuga isseoyo?] Is there a child-minding service?

서약 [seoyak] n oath

서인도제도 [seoindojedo] npl West Indies; 서인도제도 사람 [seoindojedo saram] n West Indian; 서인도제도의 [seoindojedoui] n West Indian

서정 [seojeong] 서정시 [seojeongsi] npl lyrics

서진 [seojin] n paperweight

서쪽 [seojjok] n west; 서쪽으로 [seojjogeuro] adv west; 서쪽의

[seojjogui] *adj* west
서커스 [seokeoseu] *n* circus
서투르다 [seotureuda] 서투른
[seotureun] *adj* awkward, clumsy
서핑 [seoping] *n* surfing; **서핑보드**
[seopingbodeu] *n* surfboard; **서핑하는**
사람 [seopinghaneun saram] *n* surfer
석 [seok] *n* jewel; **비즈니스 석**
[bijeuniseu seok] *n* business class; **담석**
[damseok] *n* gallstone; **대리석**
[daeriseok] *n* marble; **석회석**
[seokhoeseok] *n* limestone; **이코노미**
석 [ikonomi seok] *n* economy class
석류 [seongnyu] *n* pomegranate
석방 [seokbang] 가석방 [gaseokbang] *n*
parole
석탄 [seoktan] *n* coal
석호 [seokho] *n* lagoon
석회 [seokhoe] *n* lime *(compound)*;
석회석 [seokhoeseok] *n* limestone
섞다 [seokkda] *vt* mix
선 [seon] *n* line; **선체** [seonche] *n* hull;
우주선 [ujuseon] *n* spacecraft
선거 [seongeo] *n* election; **선거구**
[seongeogu] *n* constituency; **총선거**
[chongseongeo] *n* general election
선교사 [seongyosa] *n* missionary
선글라스 [seongeullaseu] *npl* sunglasses
선명 [seonmyeong] **선명한**
[seonmyeonghan] *adj* vivid
선물 [seonmul] *n* gift, present *(gift)*;
선물가게 [seonmulgage] *n* gift shop;
남편에게 줄 선물을 찾고 있어요
[nampyeonege jul seonmureul chatgo
isseoyo] I'm looking for a present for
my husband; **선물 포장을 해**
주시겠어요? [seonmul pojangeul hae
jusigesseoyo?] Please can you
gift-wrap it?; **선물이에요**
[seonmurieyo] This is a gift for you;
아내에게 줄 선물을 찾고 있어요
[anaeege jul seonmureul chatgo
isseoyo] I'm looking for a present for
my wife; **아이에게 줄 선물을 찾고**
있어요 [aiege jul seonmureul chatgo
isseoyo] I'm looking for a present for a
child; **어디에서 선물을 살 수 있어요?**
[eodieseo seonmureul sal su isseoyo?]

Where can I buy gifts?
선박 [seonbak] *n* ship
선반 [seonban] *n* rack, shelf; **벽난로 선반**
[byeongnanno seonban] *n*
mantelpiece; **수화물 선반** [suhwamul
seonban] *n* luggage rack
선발 [seonbal] *n* selection; **최종선발**
후보자 명단 [choejongseonbal huboja
myeongdan] *n* shortlist; **선발된**
[seonbaldoen] *adj* chosen
선불 [seonbul] **선불한** [seonbulhan] *adj*
prepaid; **선불인가요?** [seonburingayo?]
Do I pay in advance?
선사 [seonsa] **선사시대의**
[seonsasidaeui] *adj* prehistoric
선수 [seonsu] *n* player *(of sport)*; **단거리**
경주 선수 [dangeori gyeongju seonsu]
n sprinter; **레슬링 선수** [reseulling
seonsu] *n* wrestler; **축구 선수** [chukgu
seonsu] *n* football player, footballer;
역도 선수 [yeokdo seonsu] *n*
weightlifter; **운동 선수** [undong
seonsu] *n* athlete; **자동차 경주 선수**
[jadongcha gyeongju seonsu] *n* racing
driver; **체조 선수** [chejo seonsu] *n*
gymnast; **권투 선수** [gwontu seonsu]
n boxer
선실 [seonsil] *n* cabin
선언 [seoneon] *n* declaration,
proclamation; **선언하다**
[seoneonhada] *v* declare
선원 [seonwon] *n* sailor, seaman
선인장 [seoninjang] *n* cactus
선장 [seonjang] *n* captain
선적 [seonjeok] *n* shipment
선전 [seonjeon] *n* propaganda, publicity
선착 [seonchak] **선착장** [seonchakjang]
n marina
선창 [seonchang] *n* quay
선출 [seonchul] *n* election; **선출하다**
[seonchulhada] *v* elect
선택 [seontaek] *n* choice, selection;
선택권 [seontaekgwon] *n* option;
선택하다 [seontaekhada] *v* choose,
select; **선택하다** [seontaekhada] *v* pick;
자유선택의 [jayuseontaegui] *adj*
optional
선탠 [seontaen] *n* suntan; **선탠 로션**

[seontaen rosyeon] n suntan lotion; 선탠 오일 [seontaen oil] n suntan oil

선풍 [seonpung] 선풍기 [seonpunggi] n fan

선행 [seonhaeng] 선행하는 [seonhaenghaneun] adj preceding

선호 [seonho] 선호도 [seonhodo] n preference; 선호하다 [seonhohada] v prefer

설거지 [seolgeoji] n washing-up; 설거지용 세제 [seolgeojiyong seje] n washing-up liquid; 설거지하다 [seolgeojihada] v wash up

설계 [seolgye] 설계하다 [seolgyehada] v set out

설교 [seolgyo] n sermon

설득 [seoldeuk] n persuasion, conviction; 설득력 있는 [seoldeungnyeok inneun] adj convincing, persuasive; 설득하다 [seoldeukhada] v persuade

설명 [seolmyeong] n explanation; 설명하다 [seolmyeonghada] vi account for, explain

설문 [seolmun] 설문지 [seolmunji] n questionnaire

설비 [seolbi] 최신 설비 [choesin seolbi] npl mod cons

설사 [seolsa] n diarrhoea; 설사를 해요 [seolsareul haeyo] I have diarrhoea

설탕 [seoltang] n sugar; 무설탕의 [museoltangui] adj sugar-free; 설탕을 입힘 [seoltangeul iphim] n frosting; 가루 설탕 [garu seoltang] n icing sugar; 무설탕 [museoltang] no sugar

섬 [seom] n island

섬광 [seomgwang] n flash

섬기다 [seomgida] v serve

섬세 [seomse] 섬세한 [seomsehan] adj delicate

섬유 [seomyu] n fibre; 섬유 유리 [seomyu yuri] n fibreglass

섭씨 [seopssi] n degree centigrade, degree Celsius

성 [seong] n castle, gender, sex, surname; 성별 [seongbyeol] n sexuality; 성적 매력이 있는 [seongjeok maeryeogi inneun] adj sexy; 성차별 [seongchabyeol] n sexism; 성행위 [seonghaengwi] n sexual intercourse; 결혼 전의 성 [gyeolhon jeonui seong] n maiden name; 성을 방문할 수 있어요? [seongeul bangmunhal su isseoyo?] Can we visit the castle?; 이 성은 일반인에게 개방되었나요? [i seongeun ilbaninege gaebangdoeeonnayo?] Is the castle open to the public?

성격 [seonggyeok] n personality

성경 [seonggyeong] n Bible

성공 [seonggong] n achievement, success; 성공적으로 [seonggongjeogeuro] adv successfully; 성공하다 [seonggonghada] v succeed; 성공한 [seonggonghan] adj successful

성급 [seonggeup] 성급하게 [seonggeuphage] adv impatiently; 성급한 [seonggeuphan] adj impatient; 성급함 [seonggeupham] n impatience

성당 [seongdang] 대성당 [daeseongdang] n cathedral

성명 [seongmyeong] 성명서 [seongmyeongseo] n statement

성분 [seongbun] n component, ingredient

성수 [seongsu] 비성수기 [biseongsugi] n low season; 성수기 [seongsugi] n high season

성숙 [seongsuk] 성숙하다 [seongsukhada] v grow up; 성숙한 [seongsukhan] adj mature

성실 [seongsil] n faith, sincerity; 불성실한 [bulseongsilhan] adj insincere; 성실하게 [seongsilhage] adv faithfully; 성실한 [seongsilhan] adj faithful

성애 [seongae] 성애의 [seongaeui] adj erotic

성욕 [seongyok] n eroticism; 아동에 대한 이상 성욕자 [adonge daehan isang seongyokja] n paedophile

성원 [seongwon] 성원하다 [seongwonhada] v cheer

성인 [seongin] n adult, grown-up, saint; 성인 교육 [seongin gyoyuk] n adult education, further education; 성인

학생 [seongin haksaeng] n mature student

성장 [seongjang] n growth; 성장하다 [seongjanghada] vi grow

성적 [seongjeok] 성적인 [seongjeogin] adj sexual; 성적표 [seongjeokpyo] n report card

성찬 [seongchan] 성찬식 [seongchansik] n communion

성취 [seongchwi] 성취하다 [seongchwihada] v fulfil, work out

성폭행 [seongpokhaeng] 성폭행을 당했어요 [seongpokhaengeul danghaesseoyo] I've been raped

성함 [seongham] n name; 전무님 성함이 어떻게 되나요? [jeonmunim seonghami eotteoke doenayo?] What is the name of the managing director?

성형 [seonghyeong] 성형외과 [seonghyeongoegwa] n plastic surgery

성회일 [seonghoeil] n Ash Wednesday

세 [se] number three ▷ n tax; 부가가치세 [bugagachise] abbr VAT; 도로세 [dorose] n road tax; 세 번째의 [se beonjjaeui] adj third; 소득세 [sodeukse] n income tax

세계 [segye] n world; 세계적인 [segyejeogin] adj global; 세계화 [segyehwa] n globalization; 제3세계 [je3segye] n Third World

세금 [segeum] n tax

세기 [segi] 1 세기 [il segi] n century

세네갈 [senegal] n Senegal; 세네갈 사람 [senegal saram] n Senegalese; 세네갈의 [senegarui] adj Senegalese

세다 [seda] v count

세대 [sedae] n generation

세라믹 [seramik] 세라믹의 [seramigui] adj ceramic

세련 [seryeon] 세련된 [seryeondoen] adj sophisticated

세례 [serye] n christening; 세례명 [seryemyeong] n Christian name

세르비아 [sereubia] n Serbia; 세르비아 사람 [sereubia saram] n Serbian (person); 세르비아어 [sereubiaeo] n Serbian (language); 세르비아의 [sereubiaui] adj Serbian

세면 [semyeon] 세면대 [semyeondae] n washbasin; 세면가방 [semyeongabang] n toilet bag

세미콜론 [semikollon] n semicolon

세밀 [semil] 세밀한 [semilhan] adj detailed

세배 [sebae] 3배의 [sambaeui] adj triple

세번째 [sebeonjjae] 세 번째로 [se beonjjaero] adv thirdly

세부 [sebu] n detail

세상 [sesang] n life, people, world; 세상물정에 밝은 [sesangmuljeonge balgeun] adj streetwise; 세상을 들끓게 하는 [sesangeul deulkkeurke haneun] adj sensational

세우다 [seuda] v put up

세입 [seip] n revenue; 세입자 [seipja] n tenant

세정액 [sejeongaek] n screenwash; 콘택트렌즈 세정액이요 [kontaekteurenjeu sejeongaegiyo] cleansing solution for contact lenses

세제 [seje] n detergent; 설거지용 세제 [seolgeojiyong seje] n washing-up liquid

세차 [secha] n car wash; 세차를 하려고요 [sechareul haryeogoyo] I would like to wash the car

세차장 [sechajang] 세차장은 어떻게 이용해요? [sechajangeun eotteoke iyonghaeyo?] How do I use the car wash?

세척 [secheok] 세척제 [secheokje] n cleanser; 식기 세척기 [sikgi secheokgi] n dishwasher

세척액 [secheogaek] 앞유리 세척액을 가득 채워 주시겠어요? [apyuri secheogaegeul gadeuk chaewo jusigesseoyo?] Can you top up the windscreen washers?

세탁 [setak] n washing; 세탁소 [setakso] n dry-cleaner's, laundry; 가루 세탁 비누 [garu setak binu] n washing powder; 기계세탁이 가능한 [gigyesetagi ganeunghan] adj machine washable; 어디에서 세탁을 할 수 있을까요? [eodieseo setageul hal su isseulkkayo?] Where can I do some washing?

세탁기 [setakgi] *n* washing machine;
세탁기는 어디에 있어요? [setakgineun
eodie isseoyo?] Where are the washing
machines?; **세탁기는 어떻게
작동하나요?** [setakgineun eotteoke
jakdonghanayo?] How does the
washing machine work?

세트 [seteu] *n* set; **세트 메뉴 주세요**
[seteu menyu juseyo] We'll take the set
menu; **세트 메뉴는 얼마예요?** [seteu
menyuneun eolmayeyo?] How much is
the set menu?

세포 [sepo] *n* cell

센터 [senteo] **쇼핑센터** [syopingsenteo]
n shopping centre; **콜센터** [kolsenteo]
n call centre

센트 [senteu] *n* cent

센티미터 [sentimiteo] *n* centimetre

셀러리 [selleori] *n* celery

셀로테이프 [selloteipeu] *n* Sellotape®

셀프서비스 [selpeuseobiseu]
셀프서비스의 [selpeuseobiseuui] *adj*
self-service

셔벗 [syeobeot] *n* sorbet

셔츠 [syeocheu] *n* shirt; **(남자용) 속 셔츠**
[(namjayong) sok syeocheu] *n* vest;
스웨트셔츠 [seuweteusyeocheu] *n*
sweatshirt; **티셔츠** [tisyeocheu] *n*
tee-shirt; **폴로 셔츠** [pollo syeocheu]
n polo shirt

소¹ [so] *n* place; **대피소** [daepiso] *n*
shelter; **매표소** [maepyoso] *n* booking
office, ticket office; **조선소** [joseonso] *n*
shipyard; **증류소** [jeungnyuso] *n*
distillery; **안내소** [annaeso] *n*
information office, inquiries office;
진료소 [jillyoso] *n* surgery (doctor's); **이
근처에 세탁소 있어요?** [i geuncheoe
setakso isseoyo?] Is there a launderette
near here?

소² [so] *n* cow; **송아지** [songaji] *n* calf;
쇠고기 [soegogi] *n* beef; **쇠고기 햄버거**
[soegogi haembeogeo] *n* beefburger;
암소 [amso] *n* cow; **황소** [hwangso] *n*
bull

소개 [sogae] *n* introduction; **소개하다**
[sogaehada] (누구를 소개하다) *v*

introduce; **소개하다** [sogaehada] *v*
present

소견 [sogyeon] *n* remark; **의사소견**
[uisasogyeon] *n* medical; **의사소견서**
[uisasogyeonseo] *n* medical certificate

소금 [sogeum] *n* salt; **소금물의**
[sogeummurui] *adj* saltwater; **소금 좀
주세요** [sogeum jom juseyo] Pass the
salt, please

소녀 [sonyeo] *n* girl

소년 [sonyeon] *n* boy

소다 [soda] **위스키 앤 소다요** [wiseuki
aen sodayo] a whisky and soda

소독 [sodok] **소독제** [sodokje] *n*
antiseptic, disinfectant

소동 [sodong] *n* racket (racquet)

소득 [sodeuk] *n* income ▷ *npl* earnings,
takings; **소득세** [sodeukse] *n* income
tax; **소득신고** [sodeuksingo] *n* tax
return

소름 [soreum] *npl* goose pimples

소리 [sori] *n* sound; **덜거덕 소리**
[deolgeodeok sori] *n* rattle; **쾅하는
소리** [kwanghaneun sori] *n* bang;
소리내어 [sorinaeeo] *adv* aloud;
소리치다 [sorichida] *v* shout, yell;
소리의 [soriui] *adj* acoustic; **소리가 큰**
[soriga keun] *adj* loud; **찰깍 소리가
나다** [chalkkak soriga nada] *v* click;
찰깍하는 소리 [chalkkakhaneun sori] *n*
click; **큰 소리로** [keun soriro] *adv*
loudly; **허튼 소리** [heoteun sori] *n*
nonsense

소말리아 [somallia] *n* Somalia; **소말리족**
[somallijok] *n* Somali (person);
소말리아의 [somalliaui] *adj* Somali;
소말리어 [somallieo] *n* Somali
(language)

소망 [somang] **소원** [sowon] (희망) *n*
wish

소매 [somae] *n* retail, sleeve; **반소매의**
[bansomaeui] *adj* short-sleeved; **소매
단추** [somae danchu] *npl* cufflinks;
소매치기 [somaechigi] *n* pickpocket;
소매가 없는 [somaega eomneun] *adj*
sleeveless; **소매가격** [somaegagyeok]
n retail price; **소매하다** [somaehada] *v*
retail

소매업 [somaeeop] 소매업자
[somaeeopja] n retailer
소문 [somun] n rumour
소문자 [somunja] n lower case letter;
모두 소문자예요 [modu somunjayeyo]
all lower case
소방 [sobang] 소방대 [sobangdae] n fire
brigade; 소방관 [sobanggwan] n
fireman
소방대 [sobangdae] 소방대를 불러
주세요 [sobangdaereul bulleo juseyo]
Please call the fire brigade
소변 [sobyeon] n urine
소비 [sobi] 소비자 [sobija] n consumer
소생 [sosaeng] 소생시키다
[sosaengsikida] v revive
소설 [soseol] n fiction, novel; 단편 소설
[danpyeon soseol] n short story; 추리
소설 [churi soseol] n thriller; 소설가
[soseolga] n novelist; 공상과학 소설
[gongsanggwahak soseol] n science
fiction
소송 [sosong] 소송 절차 [sosong
jeolcha] npl proceedings; 소송제기하다
[sosongjegihada] v sue
소수 [sosu] n minority ▷ pron few; 더
소수의 [deo sosuui] adj fewer; 소수의
[sosuui] adj few
소스 [soseu] n sauce; 비네그레트 소스
[binegeureuteu soseu] n vinaigrette
소시지 [sosiji] n sausage; 살라미 소시지
[sallami sosiji] n salami
소아 [soa] 소아마비 [soamabi] n polio
소아과 [soagwa] 소아과 의사를 추천해
주시겠어요? [soagwa uisareul
chucheonhae jusigesseoyo?] Can you
recommend a paediatrician?
소유 [soyu] n possession; 소유자
[soyuja] n owner; 소유하다 [soyuhada]
v own, possess
소음 [soeum] n din, noise; 소음기
[soeumgi] n silencer
소중 [sojung] 소중한 [sojunghan] adj
precious
소지 [soji] 소지품 [sojipum] npl
belongings
소책자 [sochaekja] n catalogue
소켓 [soket] n socket; 전기면도기 소켓은

어디있어요? [jeongimyeondogi
sokeseun eodiisseoyo?] Where is the
socket for my electric razor?
소통 [sotong] 의사소통 [uisasotong] n
communication
소파 [sopa] n couch, settee, sofa; 소파식
침대 [sopasik chimdae] n sofa bed
소포 [sopo] n parcel; 이 소포 보내는 데
얼마예요? [i sopo bonaeneun de
eolmayeyo?] How much is it to send
this parcel?; 이 소포를 보내려고요 [i
soporeul bonaeryeogoyo] I'd like to
send this parcel
소풍 [sopung] n outing, picnic
소프라노 [sopeurano] n soprano
소프트웨어 [sopeuteuweeo] n software
소형 [sohyeong] adj compact, mini; 소형
콜택시 [sohyeong koltaeksi] n
minicab; 소형 트럭 [sohyeong
teureok] n van; 소형버스
[sohyeongbeoseu] n minibus
소화 [sohwa] n digestion; 소화 불량
[sohwa bullyang] n indigestion; 소화기
[sohwagi] n extinguisher, fire
extinguisher; 소화하다 [sohwahada]
(음식) v digest
속기 [sokgi] n shorthand
속도 [sokdo] n speed; 속도내기
[sokdonaegi] n speeding; 속도제한
[sokdojehan] n speed limit; 속도계
[sokdogye] n speedometer; 속도가
떨어지다 [sokdoga tteoreojida] v slow
down
속물 [songmul] n snob
속바지 [sokbaji] npl underpants
속삭이다 [soksagida] v whisper
속어 [sogeo] n slang
속옷 [sogot] n underwear
속이다 [sogida] v cheat, deceive, fool,
trick
속임수 [sogimsu] n cheat, trick
속치마 [sokchima] n underskirt
속하다 [sokhada] v belong, belong
to;...의 [...ui] prep of
손 [son] n hand; 손바닥 [sonbadak] n
palm (part of hand); 손수건
[sonsugeon] n handkerchief, hankie;
손으로 만든 [soneuro mandeun] adj

handmade; 손위의 [sonwiui] *adj* elder; 손을 쓰지 않아도 되는 [soneul sseuji anhado doeneun] *adj* hands-free; 손잡이 [sonjabi] *n* handle, knob; 손전등 [sonjeondeung] *n* torch; 손가락 [songarak] *n* finger; 손톱 [sontop] *n* fingernail; 손흔들다 [sonheundeulda] *v* wave; 엄지손가락 [eomjisongarak] *n* thumb

손녀 [sonnyeo] *n* granddaughter

손님 [sonnim] *n* guest

손상 [sonsang] *n* damage; 손상하다 [sonsanghada] *v* damage; 수하물이 손상되었어요 [suhamuri sonsangdoeeosseoyo] My luggage has been damaged; 제 여행 가방이 손상되어 왔어요 [je yeohaeng gabangi sonsangdoeeo wasseoyo] My suitcase has arrived damaged

손수 [sonsu] 손수 하는 일 [sonsu haneun il] *abbr* DIY

손실 [sonsil] *n* loss

손아래 [sonarae] 손아랫사람 [sonaraessaram] *n* inferior

손자 [sonja] *n* grandson

손잡이 [sonjabi] 문 손잡이 [mun sonjabi] *n* door handle; 문 손잡이가 빠졌어요 [mun sonjabiga ppajyeosseoyo] The door handle has come off; 손잡이가 빠졌어요 [sonjabiga ppajyeosseoyo] The handle has come off

손주 [sonju] *n* grandchild ▷ *npl* grandchildren

손톱 [sontop] *n* fingernail; 손톱 다듬는 줄 [sontop dadeumneun jul] *n* nailfile; 손톱솔 [sontopsol] *n* nailbrush; 손톱가위 [sontopgawi] *npl* nail scissors

손해 [sonhae] 손해보다 [sonhaeboda] *vi* lose

솔 [sol] *n* brush; 머리솔 [meorisol] *n* hairbrush; 칫솔 [chissol] *n* toothbrush

솔기 [solgi] *n* seam

솔직 [soljik] 솔직한 [soljikhan] *adj* outspoken; 솔직히 [soljikhi] *adv* frankly

솔질 [soljil] 솔질하다 [soljilhada] *v* brush

솜 [som] *n* cotton wool

송아지 [songaji] *n* calf; 송아지 고기 [songaji gogi] *n* veal

송어 [songeo] *n* trout

송유 [songyu] 송유관 [songyugwan] *n* pipeline

송이 [songi] *n* (꽃) bunch

송장 [songjang] *n* invoice; 송장을 보내다 [songjangeul bonaeda] *v* invoice

쇄골 [swaegol] *n* collarbone

쇄신 [swaesin] *n* renovation; 쇄신하다 [swaesinhada] *v* renovate

쇠 [soe] *n* iron; 쇠살대 [soesaldae] *v* grate

쇠약 [soeyak] *n* weakness; 신경 쇠약 [singyeong soeyak] *n* nervous breakdown

쇼 [syo] *n* show; 리얼리티 TV 쇼 [rieolliti TV syo] *n* reality TV; 스트립쇼 [seuteuripsyo] *v* strip; 토크쇼 [tokeusyo] *n* chat show; 어디에 가면 쇼를 볼 수 있나요? [eodie gamyeon syoreul bol su innayo?] Where can we go to see a show?

쇼핑 [syoping] *n* shopping; 쇼핑백 [syopingbaek] *n* carrier bag, shopping bag; 쇼핑카트 [syopingkateu] *n* shopping trolley; 쇼핑센터 [syopingsenteo] *n* shopping centre

숄 [syol] *n* shawl

수 [su] 수의사 [suuisa] *n* vet; 음료수 [eumnyosu] *n* drinking water

수갑 [sugap] *npl* handcuffs

수거 [sugeo] 쓰레기 수거장 [sseuregi sugeojang] *n* dump

수거장 [sugeojang] 쓰레기 수거장 [sseuregi sugeojang] *n* rubbish dump

수건 [sugeon] *n* face cloth; 손수건 [sonsugeon] *n* handkerchief, hankie; 유아용 수건 [yuayong sugeon] *n* baby wipe

수군거리다 [sugungeorida] *v* gossip

수납 [sunap] 수납함 [sunapham] *n* glove compartment

수녀 [sunyeo] *n* nun; 수녀원 [sunyeowon] *n* convent

수단 [sudan] *n* Sudan ▷ *npl* means; 수단 사람 [sudan saram] *n* Sudanese; 수단의 [sudanui] *adj* Sudanese

수달 [sudal] n otter

수당 [sudang] 실업 수당 [sireop sudang] n dole

수도 [sudo] n capital

수도승 [sudoseung] n monk

수도원 [sudowon] n monastery; 대수도원 [daesudowon] n abbey; 이 수도원은 일반인에게 개방되나요? [i sudowoneun ilbaninege gaebangdoenayo?] Is the monastery open to the public?

수동 [sudong] 수동 브레이크 [sudong beureikeu] n handbrake; 수동적인 [sudongjeogin] adj passive

수두 [sudu] n chickenpox

수량 [suryang] n quantity

수레 [sure] 손수레 [sonsure] n cart; 수화물 수레 [suhwamul sure] n luggage trolley

수령 [suryeong] 수령인 [suryeongin] n receiver (person), recipient; 연금 수령자 [yeongeum suryeongja] n pensioner

수로 [suro] n ditch

수리 [suri] n repair; 수리도구 [suridogu] n repair kit; 수리하다 [surihada] v repair; 수리 비용은 얼마예요? [suri biyongeun eolmayeyo?] How much will the repairs cost?; 수리할 수 있으세요? [surihal su isseuseyo?] Can you repair it?; 수리할 가치가 있을까요? [surihal gachiga isseulkkayo?] Is it worth repairing?; 수리 공구 있어요? [suri gonggu isseoyo?] Do you have a repair kit?; 수리 공구 주시겠어요? [suri gonggu jusigesseoyo?] Can I have a repair kit?

수리점 [surijeom] n repair shop; 가장 가까운 휠체어 수리점은 어디인가요? [gajang gakkaun hwilcheeo surijeomeun eodiingayo?] Where is the nearest repair shop for wheelchairs?; 가장 가까운 자전거 수리점은 어디에 있어요? [gajang gakkaun jajeongeo surijeomeun eodie isseoyo?] Where is the nearest bike repair shop?

수막 [sumak] 수막염 [sumagyeom] n meningitis

수면 [sumyeon] 수면제 [sumyeonje] n sleeping pill

수박 [subak] n watermelon

수비 [subi] n defence

수상 [susang] n prime minister; 수상자 [susangja] n prizewinner; 수상한 [susanghan] (의심스러운) adj suspicious

수상스키 [susangseuki] n water-skiing; 어디에서 수상 스키를 탈 수 있나요? [eodieseo susang seukireul tal su innayo?] Where can you go water-skiing?; 여기에서 수상 스키를 타도 될까요? [yeogieseo susang seukireul tado doelkkayo?] Is it possible to go water-skiing here?

수색 [susaek] 수색대 [susaekdae] n search party

수소 [suso] n hydrogen

수속 [susok] n check-in;... 가는 비행기는 어디에서 탑승 수속을 하나요? [... ganeun bihaenggineun eodieseo tapseung susogeul hanayo?] Where do I check in for the flight to...?; 어디에서 수하물 수속을 하나요? [eodieseo suhamul susogeul hanayo?] Where do I check in my luggage?; 언제 탑승 수속을 해야 할까요? [eonje tapseung susogeul haeya halkkayo?] When do I have to check in?; 언제까지 탑승 수속을 할 수 있어요? [eonjekkaji tapseung susogeul hal su isseoyo?] When is the latest I can check in?; 탑승 수속을 하고 싶어요 [tapseung susogeul hago sipeoyo] I'd like to check in, please

수송차 [susongcha] 대형 수송차 [daehyeong susongcha] abbr HGV

수수 [susu] 뇌물 수수 [noemul susu] n bribery

수수료 [susuryo] n charge, commission, fee; 은행 수수료 [eunhaeng susuryo] npl bank charges; 수수료를 받나요? [susuryoreul batnayo?] Do you charge commission?; 수수료가 얼마입니까? [susuryoga eolmaimnikka?] What's the commission?; 얼마입니까? [eolmaimnikka?] How much do you charge?; **이체 수수료가 있어요?** [iche susuryoga isseoyo?] Is there a transfer charge?

수술 [susul] n operation, surgery; **수출** [suchul] n export; **수술실** [susulsil] n operating theatre; **수술하다** [susulhada] v operate (to perform surgery)

수신 [susin] **수신기** [susingi] n receiver (electronic)

수신자부담 [susinjabudam] **수신자 부담 전화를 하고 싶어요** [susinja budam jeonhwareul hago sipeoyo] I'd like to make a reverse charge call

수양 [suyang] **자기수양** [jagisuyang] n self-discipline

수업 [sueop] n lesson, tuition; **수업료** [sueomnyo] npl tuition fees; **야간 수업** [yagan sueop] n evening class

수염 [suyeom] npl whiskers; **수염이 난** [suyeomi nan] adj bearded; **콧수염** [kossuyeom] n moustache; **턱수염** [teoksuyeom] n beard

수영 [suyeong] n swimming; **(남자) 수영복** [(namja) suyeongbok] npl swimming trunks; **남자 수영복** [namja suyeongbok] npl trunks; **수영복** [suyeongbok] n bathing suit, swimming costume, swimsuit; **수영하는 사람** [suyeonghaneun saram] n swimmer; **수영하다** [suyeonghada] vi swim; **수영하러 갑시다** [suyeonghareo gapsida] Let's go swimming; **어디에서 수영을 할 수 있을까요?** [eodieseo suyeongeul hal su isseulkkayo?] Where can I go swimming?

수영장 [suyeongjang] n baths, swimming pool; **얕은 수영장** [yateun suyeongjang] n paddling pool; **수영장에 난방이 되나요?** [suyeongjange nanbangi doenayo?] Is the pool heated?; **수영장이 있어요?** [suyeongjangi isseoyo?] Is there a swimming pool?; **야외수영장인가요?** [yaoesuyeongjangingayo?] Is it an outdoor pool?; **어린이 수영장이 있어요?** [eorini suyeongjangi isseoyo?]

Is there a children's pool?; **공용 수영장은 어디있어요?** [gongyong suyeongjangeun eodiisseoyo?] Where is the public swimming pool?

수완 [suwan] n skill

수요일 [suyoil] **수요일에** [suyoire] on Wednesday

수용 [suyong] **수용량** [suyongnyang] n capacity; **피수용자** [pisuyongja] n inmate

수우 [suu] n breast-feeding; **어디에서 수유를 할 수 있나요?** [eodieseo suyureul hal su innayo?] Where can I breast-feed the baby?

수위 [suwi] n janitor

수유 [suyu] **여기에서 수유해도 될까요?** [yeogieseo suyuhaedo doelkkayo?] Can I breast-feed here?

수은 [sueun] n mercury

수익금 [suikgeum] npl proceeds

수입 [suip] n import; **수입하다** [suiphada] v import

수정 [sujeong] n crystal, modification; **수정하다** [sujeonghada] v revise

수제품 [sujepum] **수제품인가요?** [sujepumingayo?] Is this handmade?

수족 [sujok] **수족관** [sujokgwan] n aquarium

수준 [sujun] n level; **생활수준** [saenghwalsujun] n standard of living

수증 [sujeung] **수증기** [sujeunggi] n steam

수지 [suji] n resin; **수지맞는** [sujimatneun] adj lucrative

수직 [sujik] **수직으로** [sujigeuro] adv upright; **수직의** [sujigui] adj vertical

수집 [sujip] n collection; **수집가** [sujipga] n collector

수채 [suchae] **수채화** [suchaehwa] n watercolour

수출 [suchul] **수출하다** [suchulhada] v export

수치 [suchi] **수치스러운** [suchiseureoun] adj disgraceful; **수치심** [suchisim] n shame

수평 [supyeong] **수평의** [supyeongui] adj horizontal

수포 [supo] n blister

수표 [supyo] n cheque; 백지 수표 [baekji supyo] n blank cheque; 수표장 [supyojang] n chequebook; 여행자 수표 [yeohaengja supyo] n traveller's cheque; 누군가가 제 여행자 수표를 훔쳐 갔어요 [nugungaga je yeohaengja supyoreul humchyeo gasseoyo] Someone's stolen my traveller's cheques; 수표로 지불할 수 있나요? [supyoro jibulhal su innayo?] Can I pay by cheque?; 수표를 현금으로 바꿀 수 있을까요? [supyoreul hyeongeumeuro bakkul su isseulkkayo?] Can I cash a cheque?; 수표를 현금으로 바꾸고 싶어요 [supyoreul hyeongeumeuro bakkugo sipeoyo] I want to cash a cheque, please; 여기에서 여행자 수표를 현금으로 바꿀 수 있을까요? [yeogieseo yeohaengja supyoreul hyeongeumeuro bakkul su isseulkkayo?] Can I change my traveller's cheques here?; 여행자 수표 받으세요? [yeohaengja supyo badeuseyo?] Do you accept traveller's cheques?; 이 여행자 수표를 현금으로 바꾸고 싶어요 [i yeohaengja supyoreul hyeongeumeuro bakkugo sipeoyo] I want to change these traveller's cheques

수프 [supeu] n broth, soup; 고형수프 [gohyeongsupeu] n stock cube; 오늘의 수프는 무엇인가요? [oneurui supeuneun mueosingayo?] What is the soup of the day?

수필 [supil] n essay

수하물 [suhamul] n baggage; 수하물 임시보관소 [suhamul imsibogwanso] n left-luggage office; 수하물 허용 중량 [suhamul heoyong jungnyang] n baggage allowance; 수하물 회수 [suhamul hoesu] n baggage reclaim; 임시보관 수하물 [imsibogwan suhamul] n left-luggage; 임시보관 수하물함 [imsibogwan suhamulham] n left-luggage locker; 제한 초과 수하물 [jehan chogwa suhamul] n excess baggage

수학 [suhak] npl mathematics, maths; 수학의 [suhagui] adj mathematical

수행 [suhaeng] n performance (artistic), performance (functioning); 수행하다 [suhaenghada] v perform

수혈 [suhyeol] n transfusion

수화 [suhwa] n sign language

수화물 [suhwamul] n hand luggage, luggage; 수화물 선반 [suhwamul seonban] n luggage rack; 수화물 수레 [suhwamul sure] n luggage trolley;...발 비행기의 수하물은 어디에 있나요? [...bal bihaenggiui suhamureun eodie innayo?] Where is the luggage for the flight from...?; 우리 수하물이 안 왔어요 [uri suhamuri an wasseoyo] Our luggage has not arrived; 제 수하물이 안 왔어요 [je suhamuri an wasseoyo] My luggage hasn't arrived

수확 [suhwak] n harvest, return (yield); 수확하다 [suhwakhada] v harvest

숙고 [sukgo] 숙고하다 [sukgohada] vt consider; 심사숙고하다 [simsasukgohada] v speculate

숙녀 [sungnyeo] n lady

숙련 [sungnyeon] 숙련된 [sungnyeondoen] adj skilful, skilled

숙박 [sukbak] 숙박 시설 [sukbak siseol] n accommodation; 숙박처를 제공하다 [sukbakcheoreul jegonghada] v accommodate; 아침 제공 숙박 [achim jegong sukbak] n bed and breakfast, B&B

숙소 [sukso] n guesthouse

숙어 [sugeo] n phrase; 관용구 숙어집 [gwanyonggu sugeojip] n phrasebook

숙제 [sukje] n homework

숙취 [sukchwi] n hangover

순간 [sungan] n moment; 순간의 [sunganui] adj momentary; 순간적으로 [sunganjeogeuro] adv momentarily

순결 [sungyeol] 순결한 [sungyeolhan] adj innocent

순교 [sungyo] 순교자 [sungyoja] n martyr

순례 [sullye] n pilgrimage; 순례자 [sullyeja] n pilgrim

순록 [sunnok] *n* reindeer

순무 [sunmu] *n* swede, turnip

순수 [sunsu] 순수한 [sunsuhan] *adj* pure

순위 [sunwi] 우선순위 [useonsunwi] *n* priority

순종 [sunjong] *n* obedience; 순종치 않는 [sunjongchi annneun] *adj* disobedient; 순종하는 [sunjonghaneun] *adj* obedient; 순종하다 [sunjonghada] *v* obey; 순종하지 않다 [sunjonghaji anta] *v* disobey

순진 [sunjin] 순진한 [sunjinhan] *adj* naive

순찰 [sunchal] *n* patrol; 순찰차 [sunchalcha] *n* patrol car

순하다 [sunhada] 순한 [sunhan] *adj* mild

순환 [sunhwan] *n* circulation; 순환도로 [sunhwandoro] *n* ring road; 순환교차로 [sunhwangyocharo] *n* roundabout; 순환하다 [sunhwanhada] *v* cycle

숟가락 [sutgarak] *n* spoon; 한 숟가락 가득 [han sutgarak gadeuk] *n* spoonful; 깨끗한 숟가락을 주시겠어요? [kkaekkeutan sutgarageul jusigesseoyo?] Could I have a clean spoon, please?

술 [sul] *n* booze; 럼 [reom] *n* rum; 셰리주 [syeriju] *n* sherry; 술 취하지 않은 [sul chwihaji anheun] *adj* sober; 술취한 [sulchwihan] *adj* drunk, tipsy

술집 [suljip] *n* bar (*alcohol*), pub; 술집 주인 [suljip juin] *n* publican, bartender

숨 [sum] *n* breath; 숨을 쉬다 [sumeul swida] *v* breathe; 숨이 막히다 [sumi makhida] *vi* choke; 한숨 [hansum] *n* sigh

숨기다 [sumgida] 숨바꼭질 [sumbakkokjil] *n* hide-and-seek; 숨겨진 [sumgyeojin] *adj* hidden

숨다 [sumda] *vi* hide; 숨기다 [sumgida] *vi* hide

숫자 [sutja] *n* figure

숭배 [sungbae] 숭배하다 [sungbaehada] *v* worship

숯 [sut] *n* charcoal

숲 [sup] *n* forest, wood (*forest*)

쉬다 [swida] *vi* rest; 쉬지 않고 [swiji anko] *adv* non-stop

쉼표 [swimpyo] *n* comma

쉽다 [swipda] 쉬운 [swiun] *adj* easy; 쉽게 [swipge] *adv* easily; 읽기쉬운 [irkgiswiun] *adj* legible; 가장 쉬운 코스는 어느 건가요? [gajang swiun koseuneun eoneu geongayo?] Which are the easiest runs?

슈트 [syuteu] *n* suit

슈퍼마켓 [syupeomaket] *n* supermarket; 대형 슈퍼마켓 [daehyeong syupeomaket] *n* hypermarket; 슈퍼마켓을 찾아야 해요 [syupeomakeseul chajaya haeyo] I need to find a supermarket

스낵 [seunaek] *n* snack; 스낵 바 [seunaek ba] *n* snack bar

스노보드 [seunobodeu] 스노보드 강습을 해주시나요? [seunobodeu gangseubeul haejusinayo?] Do you organise snowboarding lessons?; 스노보드를 빌리고 싶어요 [seunobodeureul billigo sipeoyo] I want to hire a snowboard

스노체인 [seunochein] 스노 체인이 필요한가요? [seuno cheini pillyohangayo?] Do I need snow chains?

스노클 [seunokeul] *n* snorkel

스노클링 [seunokeulling] 스노클링을 하고 싶어요 [seunokeullingeul hago sipeoyo] I'd like to go snorkelling

스누커 [seunukeo] *n* snooker

스리랑카 [seurirangka] *n* Sri Lanka

스무번 [seumubeon] 스무 번째의 [seumu beonjjaeui] *adj* twentieth

스와질란드 [seuwajillandeu] *n* Swaziland

스웨덴 [seuweden] *n* Sweden; 스웨덴 사람 [seuweden saram] *n* Swede, Swedish; 스웨덴의 [seuwedenui] *adj* Swedish

스웨터 [seuweteo] *n* sweater; 폴로네크 스웨터 [pollonekeu seuweteo] *n* polo-necked sweater

스위스 [seuwiseu] *n* Switzerland; 스위스 사람 [seuwiseu saram] *n* Swiss; 스위스의 [seuwiseuui] *adj* Swiss

스위치 [seuwichi] n switch
스카프 [seukapeu] n scarf
스칸디나비아 [seukandinabia] n
  Scandinavia; **스칸디나비아의**
  [seukandinabiaui] adj Scandinavian
스캐너 [seukaeneo] n scanner
스케이트 [seukeiteu] n skate ▷ npl
  skates; **스케이트 링크** [seukeiteu
  ringkeu] n skating rink; **스케이트 타기**
  [seukeiteu tagi] n skating;
  스케이트링크 [seukeiteuringkeu] n
  rink; **스케이트장** [seukeiteujang] n ice
  rink; **아이스 스케이팅** [aiseu
  seukeiting] n ice-skating; **어디에서**
  스케이트를 빌릴 수 있나요? [eodieseo
  seukeiteureul billil su innayo?] Where
  can we hire skates?
스케이트보드 [seukeiteubodeu] n
  skateboard; **스케이트보드 타기**
  [seukeiteubodeu tagi] n
  skateboarding; **스케이트보드를 타고**
  싶어요 [seukeiteubodeureul tago
  sipeoyo] I'd like to go skateboarding
스케치 [seukechi] n sketch; **스케치하다**
  [seukechihada] v sketch
스코틀랜드 [seukoteullaendeu] n
  Scotland; **스코틀랜드 사람**
  [seukoteullaendeu saram] n Scot,
  Scotsman; **스코틀랜드 여자**
  [seukoteullaendeu yeoja] n
  Scotswoman; **스코틀랜드의**
  [seukoteullaendeuui] adj Scots,
  Scottish
스쿠터 [seukuteo] n scooter
스크린 [seukeurin] n screen; **평판**
  스크린의 [pyeongpan seukeurinui] adj
  flat-screen
스키 [seuki] n ski; **수상 스키** [susang
  seuki] n water-skiing; **스키 리프트**
  [seuki ripeuteu] n ski lift; **스키 타는**
  사람 [seuki taneun saram] n skier;
  스키 타기 [seuki tagi] n skiing; **스키를**
  타다 [seukireul tada] v ski; **스키장**
  시즌권 [seukijang sijeungwon] n ski
  pass; **초보자용 스키코스** [chobojayong
  seukikoseu] n nursery slope; **스키**
  강습을 해주시나요? [seuki
  gangseubeul haejusinayo?] Do you

organise skiing lessons?; **스키 학교가**
있어요? [seuki hakgyoga isseoyo?] Is
there a ski school?; **스키를 빌리고**
싶어요 [seukireul billigo sipeoyo] I
want to hire skis; **스키를 타고 싶어요**
[seukireul tago sipeoyo] I'd like to go
skiing; **스키막대를 빌리고 싶어요**
[seukimakdaereul billigo sipeoyo] I
want to hire ski poles; **어디에서 스키**
장비를 빌릴 수 있나요? [eodieseo
seuki jangbireul billil su innayo?]
Where can I hire skiing equipment?;
여기에서 스키를 빌릴 수 있어요?
[yeogieseo seukireul billil su isseoyo?]
Can we hire skis here?; **크로스컨트리**
스키를 빌리고 싶어요
[keuroseukeonteuri seukireul billigo
sipeoyo] I want to hire cross-country
skis; **크로스컨트리 스키를 탈 수**
있나요? [keuroseukeonteuri seukireul
tal su innayo?] Is it possible to go
cross-country skiing?; **활강 스키를**
빌리고 싶어요 [hwalgang seukireul
billigo sipeoyo] I want to hire downhill
skis
스키장 [seukijang] n ski area, ski slope;
  스키장 리프트 [seukijang ripeuteu] n
  chairlift; **스키장 입장권은 얼마예요?**
  [seukijang ipjanggwoneun
  eolmayeyo?] How much is a ski pass?;
  어디에서 스키장 입장권을 살 수
  있을까요? [eodieseo seukijang
  ipjanggwoneul sal su isseulkkayo?]
  Where can I buy a ski pass?; **일주일**
  스키장 입장권을 사고 싶어요 [iljuil
  seukijang ipjanggwoneul sago
  sipeoyo] I'd like a ski pass for a week;
  하루 스키장 입장권을 사고 싶어요
  [haru seukijang ipjanggwoneul sago
  sipeoyo] I'd like a ski pass for a day
스키해드 [seukihaedeu] **스킨헤드족**
  [seukinhedeujok] n skinhead
스타일 [seutail] n style; **스타일리스트**
  [seutailliseuteu] n stylist; **헤어 스타일**
  [heeo seutail] n hairdo, hairstyle;
  완전히 새로운 스타일을 하고 싶어요
  [wanjeonhi saeroun seutaireul hago
  sipeoyo] I want a completely new

style; 이 스타일로 해 주세요 [i seutaillo hae juseyo] This style, please

스타일링 [seutailling] 스타일링 제품 파세요? [seutailling jepum paseyo?] Do you sell styling products?

스타킹 [seutaking] n stocking

스턴트맨 [seuteonteumaen] n stuntman

스테레오 [seutereo] n stereo

스테로이드 [seuteroideu] n steroid

스테이크 [seuteikeu] n steak; 럼프 스테이크 [reompeu seuteikeu] n rump steak

스테이플 [seuteipeul] 스테이플로 고정시키다 [seuteipeullo gojeongsikida] v staple

스토브 [seutobeu] n stove

스톱워치 [seutobwochi] n stopwatch

스튜 [seutyu] n stew

스튜디오 [seutyudio] n studio

스트레스 [seuteureseu] n stress; 스트레스를 받고 있는 [seuteureseureul batgo inneun] adj stressed; 스트레스를 주는 [seuteureseureul juneun] adj stressful

스트레오 [seutereo] 스테레오가 있어요? [seutereoga isseoyo?] Does it have a stereo?; 차에 스테레오가 있어요? [chae seutereoga isseoyo?] Is there a stereo in the car?

스트리퍼 [seuteuripeo] n stripper

스티커 [seutikeo] n sticker

스파게티 [seupageti] n spaghetti

스파이 [seupai] n mole (infiltrator), spy

스패너 [seupaeneo] n spanner

스팸 [seupaem] 스팸 메일 [seupaem meil] n spam

스펀지 [seupeonji] n sponge (for washing)

스페인 [seupein] n Spain; 스페인 사람 [seupein saram] n Spaniard, Spanish; 스페인의 [seupeinui] adj Spanish

스패니얼 [seupaenieol] n spaniel

스포츠 [seupocheu] n sport; 스포츠맨 [seupocheumaen] n sportsman; 스포츠우먼 [seupocheuumeon] n sportswoman; 겨울 스포츠 [gyeoul seupocheu] npl winter sports; 피를 보는 스포츠 [pireul boneun seupocheu] n blood sports; 어느

스포츠 행사에 갈 수 있을까요? [eoneu seupocheu haengsae gal su isseulkkayo?] Which sporting events can we go to?; 어떤 스포츠 시설이 있어요? [eotteon seupocheu siseori isseoyo?] What sports facilities are there?

스포크 [seupokeu] n spoke

스포트라이트 [seupoteuraiteu] n spotlight

스푼 [seupun] 테이블스푼 [teibeulseupun] n tablespoon

스프레이 [seupeurei] 헤어 스프레이 [heeo seupeurei] n hair spray

슬래시 [seullaesi] 백슬래시 [baekseullaesi] n backslash

슬레이트 [seulleiteu] n slate

슬로바키아 [seullobakia] n Slovakia; 슬로바키아 사람 [seullobakia saram] n Slovak (person); 슬로바키아어 [seullobakiaeo] n Slovak (language); 슬로바키아의 [seullobakiaui] adj Slovak

슬로베니아 [seullobenia] n Slovenia; 슬로베니아 사람 [seullobenia saram] n Slovenian (person); 슬로베니아어 [seullobeniaeo] n Slovenian (language); 슬로베니아의 [seullobeniaui] adj Slovenian

슬롯머신 [seullotmeosin] n fruit machine

슬리퍼 [seullipeo] 고무 슬리퍼 [gomu seullipeo] npl flip-flops

슬립 [seullip] n slip (underwear)

슬프다 [seulpeuda] 슬프게 [seulpeuge] adv sadly; 슬픈 [seulpeun] adj sad, unhappy

슬픔 [seulpeum] n grief

습 [seup] 습지 [seupji] n swamp

습격 [seupgyeok] 습격하다 [seupgyeokhada] v mug; 습격을 당했어요 [seupgyeogeul danghaesseoyo] I've been attacked

습관 [seupgwan] n habit

습기 [seupgi] n humidity, moisture; 습기 찬 [seupgi chan] adj humid

습지 [seupji] n marsh

습진 [seupjin] n eczema

승강기 [seungganggi] n lift; 건물에

승강기가 있나요? [geonmure seungganggiga innayo?] Is there a lift in the building?

승강장 [seunggangjang] 여기가... 가는 기차 승강장 맞아요? [yeogiga... ganeun gicha seunggangjang majayo?] Is this the right platform for the train to...?; 기차는 어느 승강장에서 떠나요? [gichaneun eoneu seunggangjangeseo tteonayo?] Which platform does the train leave from?;...행 기차는 어느 승강장에서 떠나요? [...haeng gichaneun eoneu seunggangjangeseo tteonayo?] Which platform does the train for... leave from?

승객 [seunggaek] n passenger

승리 [seungni] n triumph, victory; 승리의 [seungniui] adj winning; 승리자 [seungnija] n winner; 승리하다 [seungnihada] v triumph

승마 [seungma] n riding; 승마 갑시다 [seungma gapsida] Let's go horse riding

승무원 [seungmuwon] n crew, steward; 비행기 승무원 [bihaenggi seungmuwon] n flight attendant; 비행기 여승무원 [bihaenggi yeoseungmuwon] n air hostess

승인 [seungin] n approval; 승인하다 [seunginhada] v approve

승진 [seungjin] n promotion

승차 [seungcha] 버스 승차권 [beoseu seungchagwon] n bus ticket; 승차 요금 [seungcha yogeum] n fare; 정기 승차권 [jeonggi seungchagwon] n season ticket; 택시 승차장 [taeksi seungchajang] n taxi rank

시 [si] n poem, poetry; 서정시 [seojeongsi] npl lyrics; 시누이 [sinui] (husband's sister) n sister-in-law; 시어머니 [sieomeoni] (husband's mother) n mother-in-law; 시인 [siin] (작가) n poet

시가 [siga] n cigar

시각 [sigak] n perspective; 시각의 [sigagui] adj visual; 시각화하다 [sigakhwahada] v visualize

시간 [sigan] n hour, time; 마감 시간 [magam sigan] n deadline; 방문시간 [bangmunsigan] npl visiting hours; 추가 시간 [chuga sigan] n injury time; 시간대 [sigandae] n time zone; 시간을 엄수하는 [siganeul eomsuhaneun] adj punctual; 시간표 [siganpyo] n timetable; 식사시간 [siksasigan] n mealtime; 여가시간 [yeogasigan] n spare time; 영업 시간 [yeongeop sigan] npl opening hours; 저녁식사 시간 [jeonyeoksiksa sigan] n dinner time; 점심시간 [jeomsimsigan] n lunch break, lunchtime; 초과 근무 시간 [chogwa geunmu sigan] n overtime; 취침 시간 [chwichim sigan] n bedtime; 근무 시간 [geunmu sigan] npl office hours; 타이머 [taimeo] n timer; 폐점 시간 [pyejeom sigan] n closing time; 한 시간마다 [han siganmada] adv hourly; 한 시간마다의 [han siganmadaui] adj hourly; 휴식시간 [hyusiksigan] n playtime, time off; 1시간 접속가격은 얼마예요? [han sigan jeopsokgagyeogeun eolmayeyo?] How much is it to log on for an hour?; 면회 시간은 언제예요? [myeonhoe siganeun eonjeyeyo?] When are visiting hours?; 최소 사용 시간은 얼마입니까? [choso sayong siganeun eolmaimnikka?] What's the minimum amount of time?; 시간당 얼마예요? [sigandang eolmayeyo?] How much is it per hour?; 갈 시간인가요? [gal siganingayo?] Is it time to go?; 기차가 제 시간에 있어요? [gichaga je sigane isseoyo?] Is the train on time?

시간제 [siganje] 시간제로 [siganjero] adv part-time; 시간제의 [siganjeui] adj part-time

시간표 [siganpyo] n timetable; 강의 시간표 [gangui siganpyo] n syllabus;... 가는 기차 시간표는 어떻게 되나요? [... ganeun gicha siganpyoneun eotteoke doenayo?] What times are the trains to...?; 시간표 좀 주시겠어요? [siganpyo jom jusigesseoyo?] Can I have a timetable, please?

시계 [sigye] n clock, visibility, watch; **디지털 시계** [dijiteol sigye] n digital watch; **시계 방향으로** [sigye banghyangeuro] adv clockwise; **시곗줄** [sigyetjul] n watch strap; **알람 시계** [allam sigye] n alarm clock; **새 시계줄이 필요해요** [sae sigyejuri pillyohaeyo] I need a new strap for my watch; **제 시계를 고치실 수 있으세요?** [je sigyereul gochisil su isseuseyo?] Can you repair my watch?; **제 시계가 빠른 것 같아요** [je sigyega ppareun geot gatayo] I think my watch is fast; **제 시계가 멈췄어요** [je sigyega meomchwosseoyo] My watch has stopped; **제 시계가 느린 것 같아요** [je sigyega neurin geot gatayo] I think my watch is slow

시골 [sigol] n countryside; **시골의** [sigorui] adj rural

시금치 [sigeumchi] n spinach

시기 [sigi] n jealousy, time; **시기상조의** [sigisangjoui] adj premature; **시기하는 듯한** [sigihaneun deutan] adj envious

시끄럽다 [sikkeureopda] **시끄러운** [sikkeureoun] adj noisy; **너무 시끄러워요** [neomu sikkeureowoyo] It's too loud; **방이 너무 시끄러워요** [bangi neomu sikkeureowoyo] The room is too noisy; **시끄러워서 잠을 잘 수 없어요** [sikkeureowoseo jameul jal su eopseoyo] I can't sleep for the noise; **시끄러워요** [sikkeureowoyo] It's noisy

시내 [sinae] n town centre, city centre; **시내 도로 지도가 필요해요** [sinae doro jidoga pillyohaeyo] I want a street map of the city; **시내 중심가로 가 주세요** [sinae jungsimgaro ga juseyo] Please take me to the city centre; **시내를 방문할 시간이 있어요?** [sinaereul bangmunhal sigani isseoyo?] Do we have time to visit the town?; **시내지도를 어디에서 살 수 있어요?** [sinaejidoreul eodieseo sal su isseoyo?] Where can I buy a map of the city?; **시내까지 택시 요금이 얼마예요?** [sinaekkaji taeksi yogeumi eolmayeyo?] How much is the taxi fare into town?; **시내 관광 여행이 있어요?** [sinae gwangwang yeohaengi isseoyo?] Are there any sightseeing tours of the town?; **시내 버스 관광은 언제인가요?** [sinae beoseu gwangwangeun eonjeingayo?] When is the bus tour of the town?; **시내 중심가에 가는 가장 좋은 방법은 무엇인가요?** [sinae jungsimgae ganeun gajang joheun bangbeobeun mueosingayo?] What's the best way to get to the city centre?; **시내 중심가까지 거리가 얼마나 되나요?** [sinae jungsimgakkaji georiga eolmana doenayo?] How far are we from the town centre?

시다 [sida] **신** [sin] adj sour

시대 [sidae] n era, period; **동시대의** [dongsidaeui] adj contemporary; **선사시대의** [seonsasidaeui] adj prehistoric

시도 [sido] n attempt; **시도하다** [sidohada] v attempt, try

시동 [sidong] **차 시동이 걸리지 않아요** [cha sidongi geolliji anhayo] The car won't start

시들다 [sideulda] v wilt

시럽 [sireop] n syrup

시력 [siryeok] n eyesight, sight

시련 [siryeon] n ordeal

시리아 [siria] n Syria; **시리아 사람** [siria saram] n Syrian; **시리아의** [siriaui] adj Syrian

시멘트 [simenteu] n cement

시민 [simin] n citizen; **시민권** [simingwon] npl citizenship, civil rights

시베리아 [siberia] n Siberia

시사 [sisa] npl current affairs; **시사적인** [sisajeogin] adj topical

시상 [sisang] n prize-giving

시설 [siseol] npl facilities; **사설 보육원** [saseol boyugwon] n playgroup; **숙박 시설** [sukbak siseol] n accommodation; **기반시설** [gibansiseol] n infrastructure; **편의 시설** [pyeonui siseol] npl amenities

시소 [siso] n seesaw

시속 [sisok] **시속... 킬로미터** [sisok...

killomiteo] *abbr* km/h

시숙 [sisuk] *n* brother-in-law

시스템 [siseutem] *n* system; 시스템 분석가 [siseutem bunseokga] *n* systems analyst

시아파 [siapa] 시아파의 [siapaui] *adj* Shiite

시외 [sioe] 시외버스 [sioebeoseu] *n* coach *(vehicle)*; 시외 버스를 놓쳤어요 [sioe beoseureul nochyeosseoyo]The coach has left without me

시외버스 [sioebeoseu] 시외버스는 아침 언제 떠나요? [sioebeoseuneun achim eonje tteonayo?]When does the coach leave in the morning?

시용 [siyong] 시용기간 [siyonggigan] *n* trial period

시월 [siwol] *n* October; 시월 삼일 일요일이에요 [siwol samil illyoirieyo] It's Sunday the third of October

시인 [siin] 시인하다 [siinhada] *v* admit *(confess)*

시작 [sijak] *n* beginning, kick-off, outset, start; 다시 시작하다 [dasi sijakhada] *v* resume; 시작되다 [sijakdoeda] *vi* start; 시작하다 [sijakhada] *v* begin, kick off; 시작하다 [sijakhada] *v* start; 관광은 약...에 시작합니다 [gwangwangeun yak...e sijakhamnida]The tour starts at about...

시작하다 [sijakhada] 언제 시작해요? [eonje sijakhaeyo?]When does it begin?; 언제 공연이 시작해요? [eonje gongyeoni sijakhaeyo?]When does the performance begin?

시장 [sijang] *n* market, mayor; 벼룩시장 [byeoruksijang] *n* flea market; 증권시장 [jeunggwonsijang] *n* stock market; 시장조사 [sijangjosa] *n* market research; 시장은 언제 열려요? [sijangeun eonje yeollyeoyo?]When is the market on?

시절 [sijeol] 어린 시절 [eorin sijeol] *n* childhood

시제 [sije] *n* tense

시차 [sicha] 시차 때문에 힘들어요 [sicha ttaemune himdeureoyo] I'm suffering from jet lag

시청 [sicheong] *n* town hall

시청자 [sicheongja] *n* viewer

시체 [siche] *n* corpse

시크교 [sikeugyo] 시크교도 [sikeugyodo] *n* Sikh; 시크교도의 [sikeugyodoui] *adj* Sikh

시트 [siteu] *n* sheet; 시트가 더 필요해요 [siteuga deo pillyohaeyo]We need more sheets

시트콤 [siteukom] *n* sitcom

시한 [sihan] 시한폭탄 [sihanpoktan] *n* time bomb

시행 [sihaeng] *n* operation *(undertaking)*

시험 [siheom] *n* exam, examination *(medical)*, examination *(school)*, test; 시험관 [siheomgwan] *n* examiner, test tube; 시험하다 [siheomhada] *v* test; 시험해 보다 [siheomhae boda] *v* try out; 운전 면허 시험 [unjeon myeonheo siheom] *n* driving test; 재시험 치르다 [jaesiheom chireuda] *v* resit; 구술시험 [gusulsiheom] *n* oral; 시험해 볼 수 있어요? [siheomhae bol su isseoyo?]Can I test it, please?

식기 [sikgi] *n* kitchenware, tableware; 식기 세척기 [sikgi secheokgi] *n* dishwasher; 식기 건조대 [sikgi geonjodae] *n* draining board; 식기세트 [sikgiseteu] *n* cutlery; 식기가 더러워요 [sikgiga deoreowoyo] My cutlery is dirty

식당 [sikdang] *n* dining room, restaurant; 식당차 [sikdangcha] *n* buffet car, dining car; 구내 식당 [gunae sikdang] *n* canteen; 야영장에 식당 있어요? [yayeongjange sikdang isseoyo?] Is there a restaurant on the campsite?; 여기에 채식 식당이 있어요? [yeogie chaesik sikdangi isseoyo?]Are there any vegetarian restaurants here?; 좋은 식당을 추천해 주시겠어요? [joheun sikdangeul chucheonhae jusigesseoyo?] Can you recommend a good restaurant?

식당칸 [sikdangkan] 식당칸은 어디에 있어요? [sikdangkaneun eodie isseoyo?]Where is the buffet car?; 기차에 식당칸이 있어요? [gichae sikdangkani isseoyo?] Is there a buffet car on the train?

식료품 [singnyopum] *npl* groceries; **식료품 상인** [singnyopum sangin] *n* grocer; **식료품 저장실** [singnyopum jeojangsil] *n* larder; **식료품점** [singnyopumjeom] *n* grocer's

식물 [singmul] *n* plant, vegetation; **덩굴식물** [deonggulsingmul] *n* vine; **식물군** [singmulgun] *npl* flora; **구과식물** [gugwa singmul] *n* conifer

식사 [siksa] *n* meal; **대륙식의 아침식사** [daeryuksigui achimsiksa] *n* continental breakfast; **식사 손님** [siksa sonnim] *n* diner; **식사시간** [siksasigan] *n* mealtime; **아침 식사** [achim siksa] *n* breakfast; **저녁식사** [jeonyeoksiksa] *n* supper; **가벼운 식사** [gabyeoun siksa] *n* snack; **생선이 들어가지 않은 식사를 준비해 주시겠어요?** [saengseoni deureogaji anheun siksareul junbihae jusigesseoyo?] Could you prepare a meal without fish?; **계란이 들어가지 않은 식사를 준비해 주시겠어요?** [gyerani deureogaji anheun siksareul junbihae jusigesseoyo?] Could you prepare a meal without eggs?; **견과류가 들어가지 않은 식사를 준비해 주시겠어요?** [gyeongwaryuga deureogaji anheun siksareul junbihae jusigesseoyo?] Could you prepare a meal without nuts?; **글루텐이 들어가지 않은 식사를 준비해 주시겠어요?** [geulluteni deureogaji anheun siksareul junbihae jusigesseoyo?] Could you prepare a meal without gluten?; **해산물이 들어가지 않은 식사를 준비해 주시겠어요?** [haesanmuri deureogaji anheun siksareul junbihae jusigesseoyo?] Could you prepare a meal without seafood?

식욕 [sigyok] *n* appetite; **식욕부진증** [sigyokbujinjeung] *n* anorexia; **식욕부진의** [sigyokbujinui] *adj* anorexic

식용 [sigyong] **식용의** [sigyongui] *adj* edible

식이 [sigi] **식이 요법** [sigi yobeop] *n* diet

식중독 [sikjungdok] *n* food poisoning

식초 [sikcho] *n* vinegar; **비네그레트 소스** [binegeureteu soseu] *n* vinaigrette

식탁 [siktak] **식탁보** [siktakbo] *n* tablecloth

식품 [sikpum] *n* food; **조제식품** [jojesikpum] *n* delicatessen; **자연식품** [jayeonsikpum] *npl* wholefoods; **식품 있어요?** [sikpum isseoyo?] Do you have food?

식히다 [sikhida] *v* chill

신 [sin] *n* god; **나막신** [namaksin] *n* clog

신경 [singyeong] *n* nerve *(to/from brain)*; **신경 쇠약** [singyeong soeyak] *n* nervous breakdown; **신경 안정제** [singyeong anjeongje] *n* tranquillizer; **신경증에 걸린** [singyeongjeunge geollin] *adj* neurotic; **신경을 거스르는** [singyeongeul geoseureuneun] *adj* nerve-racking; **신경질적인** [singyeongjiljeogin] *adj* nervous

신고 [singo] *n* declaration; **소득신고** [sodeuksingo] *n* tax return; **도난 신고를 하고 싶어요** [donan singoreul hago sipeoyo] I want to report a theft; **신고할 것이 없어요** [singohal geosi eopseoyo] I have nothing to declare; **신고해야 할 술 한 병이 있어요** [singohaeya hal sul han byeongi isseoyo] I have a bottle of spirits to declare; **경찰에 신고해야 합니다** [gyeongchare singohaeya hamnida] We will have to report it to the police; **허용치의 담배량을 가지고 있어요.** [heoyongchiui dambaeryangeul gajigo isseoyo.] I have the allowed amount of tobacco to declare; **허용치의 술을 가지고 있어요** [heoyongchiui sureul gajigo isseoyo] I have the allowed amount of alcohol to declare

신랑 [sillang] *n* bridegroom, groom; **신랑 들러리** [sillang deulleori] *n* best man

신뢰 [sinnoe] *n* confidence *(trust)*, trust; **신뢰하는** [sinnoehaneun] *adj* trusting, truthful; **신뢰하다** [sinnoehada] *v* trust; **신뢰할수 있는** [sinnoehalsu inneun] *adj* reliable; **진실** [jinsil] *n*

truth

신문 [sinmun] *n* newspaper; 신문 가게 [sinmun gage] *n* newsagent; 신문배달 [sinmunbaedal] *n* paper round; 신문 있어요? [sinmun isseoyo?] Do you have newspapers?; 신문을 사고 싶어요 [sinmuneul sago sipeoyo] I would like a newspaper; 어디에서 신문을 살 수 있어요? [eodieseo sinmuneul sal su isseoyo?] Where can I buy a newspaper?; 가장 가까운 신문 가게는 어디에 있어요? [gajang gakkaun sinmun gageneun eodie isseoyo?] Where is the nearest shop which sells newspapers?

신발 [sinbal] *n* shoe; 신발에 구멍이 났어요 [sinbare gumeongi nasseoyo] I have a hole in my shoe; 신발은 어느 층에 있나요? [sinbareun eoneu cheunge innayo?] Which floor are shoes on?; 이 신발 굽을 갈아 주실 수 있으세요? [i sinbal gubeul gara jusil su isseuseyo?] Can you re-heel these shoes?; 이 신발을 고치실 수 있으세요? [i sinbareul gochisil su isseuseyo?] Can you repair these shoes?

신부 [sinbu] *n* bride, priest; 신부 들러리 [sinbu deulleori] *n* bridesmaid

신분 [sinbun] 신분증 [sinbunjeung] *n* identity card, ID card

신비 [sinbi] *n* mystery; 신비로운 [sinbiroun] *adj* uncanny; 신비한 [sinbihan] *adj* mysterious

신사 [sinsa] *n* gentleman

신상품 [sinsangpum] *adj* brand-new

신선 [sinseon] 신선하지 않은 [sinseonhaji anheun] *adj* stale; 신선한 [sinseonhan] *adj* fresh

신성 [sinseong] 신성한 [sinseonghan] *adj* holy, sacred

신앙 [sinang] *n* belief, faith; 신앙심 깊은 [sinangsim gipeun] *adj* religious

신용 [sinyong] *n* credit; 신용할 수 있는 [sinyonghal su inneun] *adj* credible

신용카드 [sinyongkadeu] *n* credit card; 신용 카드로 현금 서비스를 받을 수 있을까요? [sinyong kadeuro hyeongeum seobiseureul badeul su

isseulkkayo?] Can I get a cash advance with my credit card?; 신용카드 받으세요? [sinyongkadeu badeuseyo?] Do you take credit cards?; 신용카드로 지불할 수 있나요? [sinyongkadeuro jibulhal su innayo?] Can I pay by credit card?

신음 [sineum] 신음하다 [sineumhada] *v* groan

신음소리 [sineumsori] 신음소리를 내다 [sineumsorireul naeda] *v* moan

신임 [sinim] 신임장 [sinimjang] *npl* credentials

신입 [sinip] *n* newcomer

신자 [sinja] *n* believer, devotee; 감리교 신자의 [gamnigyo sinjaui] *adj* Methodist

신장 [sinjang] *n* kidney

신전 [sinjeon] *n* temple

신진 [sinjin] 신진대사 [sinjindaesa] *n* metabolism

신청 [sincheong] *n* application; 신청서 [sincheongseo] *n* application form; 신청자 [sincheongja] *n* applicant; 신청하다 [sincheonghada] *v* apply

신체 [sinche] 신체의 [sincheui] *adj* physical; 신체검사 [sinchegeomsa] *n* physical

신축 [sinchuk] 신축성 있는 [sinchukseong inneun] *adj* stretchy

신학 [sinhak] *n* theology

신호 [sinho] *n* cue (billiards), signal; 신호를 보내다 [sinhoreul bonaeda] *v* signal; 위급신호 [wigeupsinho] *n* SOS; 교통신호등 [gyotongsinhodeung] *npl* traffic lights; 통화 중 신호 [tonghwa jung sinho] *n* busy signal; 통화중 신호음 [tonghwajung sinhoeum] *n* engaged tone

신혼 [sinhon] 신혼 여행 [sinhon yeohaeng] *n* honeymoon

신혼여행 [sinhonyeohaeng] 우리는 신혼여행 중이에요 [urineun sinhonyeohaeng jungieyo] We are on our honeymoon

신화 [sinhwa] *n* myth, mythology

싣다 [sitda] *v* load

실 [sil] *n* thread, room; 2인실 [i insil] *n*

double room; **다용도실** [dayongdosil]
n utility room; **대기실** [daegisil] n
waiting room; **수술실** [susulsil] n
operating theatre; **응접실** [eungjeopsil]
n sitting room; **직원실** [jigwonsil] n
staffroom; **탈의실** [taruisil] n fitting
room; **화장실** [hwajangsil] n loo;
바늘과 실 있어요? [baneulgwa sil
isseoyo?] Do you have a needle and
thread?

실격 [silgyeok] **실격시키다**
[silgyeoksikida] v disqualify

실내 [sillae] **실내에** [sillaee] adv indoors;
실내의 [sillaeui] adj indoor; **실내화**
[sillaehwa] n slipper; **어떤 실내 활동이
있어요?** [eotteon sillae hwaldongi
isseoyo?] What indoor activities are
there?

실례 [sillye] n rudeness; **실례합니다**
[sillyehamnida] Excuse me

실로폰 [sillopon] n xylophone

실리콘 [sillikon] **실리콘 칩** [sillikon chip]
n silicon chip

실마리 [silmari] n clue

실망 [silmang] n disappointment;
실망시키는 [silmangsikineun] adj
disappointing; **실망시키다**
[silmangsikida] v disappoint, let down;
실망한 [silmanghan] adj disappointed

실수 [silsu] n fault (defect), fault (mistake),
mistake, slip (mistake), slip-up;
실수하다 [silsuhada] v mistake, slip up;
큰 실수 [keun silsu] n blunder

실습실 [silseupsil] **어학실습실**
[eohaksilseupsil] n language
laboratory

실시 [silsi] **실시하다** [silsihada] vt
conduct

실신 [silsin] **실신했어요** [silsinhaesseoyo]
She has fainted

실업 [sireop] **실업 수당** [sireop sudang]
n dole; **실업의** [sireobui] adj
unemployed

실용 [sillyong] **비실용적인**
[bisillyongjeogin] adj impractical;
실용적인 [sillyongjeogin] adj practical

실제 [silje] **실제로** [siljero] adv actually,
really; **실제로는** [siljeroneun] adv

practically; **실제의** [siljeui] adj actual

실조 [siljo] **영양실조** [yeongyangsiljo] n
malnutrition

실직 [siljik] n unemployment; **실직의**
[siljigui] adj jobless

실패 [silpae] n failure, flop; **실패하다**
[silpaehada] vi fail; **실패하다**
[silpaehada] vi backfire; **실패한**
[silpaehan] adj unsuccessful

실행 [silhaeng] n execution, practice;
실행위원 [silhaengwiwon] n executive;
실행하다 [silhaenghada] v carry out,
execute, practise; **실행할 수 있는**
[silhaenghal su inneun] adj feasible

실험 [silheom] n experiment; **실험실**
[silheomsil] n lab, laboratory; **실험재료**
[silheomjaeryo] n guinea pig (for
experiment)

싫다 [sirta] **몹시 싫은** [mopsi sireun] adj
dreadful; **살다** [salda] v live

싫어하다 [sirheohada] v dislike; **몹시
싫어하다** [mopsi sireohada] v loathe

싫증 [sircheung] **싫증이 난** [sircheungi
nan] adj fed up

심각 [simgak] **심각하게** [simgakhage]
adv seriously; **심각한** [simgakhan] adj
serious; **심각한가요?** [simgakhangayo?]
Is it serious?

심다 [simda] v plant

심리 [simni] n inquest; **심리요법**
[simniyobeop] n psychotherapy;
심리학 [simnihak] n psychology;
심리학자 [simnihakja] n psychologist;
심리학적인 [simnihakjeogin] adj
psychological

심문 [simmun] **심문하다** [simmunhada]
v interrogate

심벌즈 [simbeoljeu] npl cymbals

심사 [simsa] n judgment; **심사숙고하다**
[simsasukgohada] v speculate

심술 [simsul] **심술이 난** [simsuri nan] adj
grumpy

심장 [simjang] n heart; **심장마비**
[simjangmabi] n heart attack

심장병 [simjangbyeong] n heart disease;
심장병이 있어요 [simjangbyeongi
isseoyo] I have a heart condition

심판 [simpan] n referee, umpire

심하다 [simhada] **심하게** [simhage] *adv* grossly; **심한** [simhan] *adj* gross *(fat)*

십대 [sipdae] *n* teenager ▷ *npl* teens

십이월 [sibiwol] *n* December; **십이월 삼십일일 금요일에** [sibiwol samsibiril geumyoire] on Friday the thirty first of December

십자 [sipja] **십자말풀이** [sipjamalpuri] *n* crossword

십자가 [sipjaga] *n* cross; **십자가상** [sipjagasang] *n* crucifix

십진법 [sipjinbeop] **십진법의** [sipjinbeobui] *adj* decimal

싱어 [singeo] *n* singer; **리드싱어** [rideusingeo] *n* lead singer

싸다 [ssada] **싼** [ssan] *adj* cheap; **값싼** [gapssan] *adj* inexpensive; **더 싼 거 있어요?** [deo ssan geo isseoyo?] Do you have anything cheaper?; **더 싼 거를 사고 싶어요** [deo ssan georeul sago sipeoyo] I want something cheaper; **가장 싼 것이 좋아요** [gajang ssan geosi johayo] I'd like the cheapest option

싸우다 [ssauda] *v* fight

싸움 [ssaum] *n* fight, fighting, scrap *(dispute)*

쌀 [ssal] *n* rice

쌀쌀하다 [ssalssalhada] **쌀쌀한** [ssalssalhan] *adj* chilly

쌍 [ssang] **쌍을 이루는** [ssangeul iruneun] *adj* twinned; **쌍의 한쪽** [ssangui hanjjok] *n* match *(partnership)*; **한 쌍** [han ssang] *n* couple, pair

쌍둥이 [ssangdungi] *n* twin; **세쌍둥이** [sessangdungi] *npl* triplets; **쌍둥이자리** [ssangdungijari] *n* Gemini

써넣다 [sseoneota] *v* fill in

써버리다 [sseobeorida] **다 써버리다** [da sseobeorida] *v* use up

썩다 [sseokda] *v* decay, rot; **썩은** [sseogeun] *adj* rotten

썰매 [sseolmae] *n* sledge, toboggan; **썰매 타기** [sseolmae tagi] *n* sledging; **썰매타기** [sseolmaetagi] *n* tobogganing; **어디에서 썰매 타기를 할**

수 있나요? [eodieseo sseolmae tagireul hal su innayo?] Where can we go sledging?

쏘다 [ssoda] v sting ▷ vt shoot

쏘이다 [ssoida] 쏘였어요 [ssoyeosseoyo] I've been stung

쓰다 [sseuda] v write, use, taste bitter; **받아쓰기** [badasseugi] n dictation; **쓴** [sseun] adj bitter; **글쓰다** [geulsseuda] v write

쓰다듬다 [sseudadeumda] v stroke

쓰러지다 [sseureojida] v fall down

쓰레기 [sseuregi] n garbage, junk, litter, refuse, rubbish; **쓰레받기** [sseurebatgi] n dustpan; **쓰레기 수거장** [sseuregi sugeojang] n dump, rubbish dump; **쓰레기통** [sseuregitong] n bin, dustbin, litter bin; **쓰레기는 어디에 버릴까요?** [sseuregineun eodie beorilkkayo?] Where do we leave the rubbish?

쓸다 [sseulda] v sweep

쓸모없다 [sseulmoeopda] 쓸모 없어진 [sseulmo eopseojin] adj obsolete

씨 [ssi] n Mr, pip, seed; **씨(여성)** [ssi(yeoseong)] n Ms

씹다 [ssipda] v chew

씻다 [ssitda] v wash

아가씨 [agassi] n lass

아교 [agyo] n gum

아기 [agi] n baby; **아기 보기** [agi bogi] n babysitting; **아기 봐주는 사람** [agi bwajuneun saram] n babysitter; **아기 젖병** [agi jeotbyeong] n baby's bottle; **아기를 보다** [agireul boda] v babysit; **아기용 휴대 침대** [agiyong hyudae chimdae] n carrycot; **어디에서 아기 기저귀를 갈 수 있을까요?** [eodieseo agi gijeogwireul gal su isseulkkayo?] Where can I change the baby?

아내 [anae] n wife; **제 아내예요** [je anaeyeyo] This is my wife

아늑하다 [aneukhada] 아늑한 [aneukhan] adj cosy

아는체 [aneunche] 아는 체하는 사람 [aneun chehaneun saram] n know-all

아니다 [anida] **... 아니다** [... anida] adv not; **...도...도 아니다** [...do...do anida] pron neither; **...도 또한...아니다** [...do ttohan...anida] adv either (with negative), neither; **...도 아니고 또한...도 아니다** [...do anigo ttohan...do anida] conj nor; **...이 아니면** [...i animyeon] conj unless; **아무것도 아닌 것** [amugeotdo anin geot] n nothing; **어느 쪽도... 아니다** [eoneu jjokdo... anida] pron neither

아니오 [anio] 아니오! [anio!] excl no!

아동 [adong] 아동에 대한 이상 성욕자 [adonge daehan isang seongyokja] n paedophile; **아동학대** [adonghakdae] n child abuse

아드리아 [adeuria] **아드리아 해** [adeuria hae] n Adriatic Sea; **아드리아 해의** [adeuria haeui] adj Adriatic

아들 [adeul] n son; **의붓아들** [uibusadeul] n stepson; **아들을 잃어버렸어요** [adeureul ireobeoryeosseoyo] My son is lost; **아들이 없어졌어요** [adeuri eopseojyeosseoyo] My son is missing

아라비아 [arabia] **아라비아 사람** [arabia saram] n Arabic (language); **아라비아의** [arabiaui] adj Arabic

아랍 [arap] **아랍 사람** [arap saram] n Arab; **아랍의** [arabui] adj Arab; **아랍어** [arabeo] Arabic

아랍에미리트 연합국 [arabemiriteu yeonhapguk] npl United Arab Emirates

아래 [arae] **...보다 아래에** [...boda araee] prep below; **손아래의** [sonaraeui] adj junior; **아래로** [araero] adv down; **아래쪽에** [araejjoge] adv below; **아래층에** [araecheunge] adv downstairs; **아래층의** [araecheungui] adj downstairs

아르메니아 [areumenia] n Armenia; **아르메니아 사람** [areumenia saram] n Armenian (person); **아르메니아어** [areumeniaeo] n Armenian (language); **아르메니아의** [areumeniaui] adj Armenian

아르바이트 [areubaiteu] n part-time job; **방학 중 아르바이트** [banghak jung areubaiteu] n holiday job

아르헨티나 [areuhentina] n Argentina; **아르헨티나 사람** [areuhentina saram] n Argentinian (person); **아르헨티나의** [areuhentinaui] adj Argentinian

아름답다 [areumdapda] **아름답게** [areumdapge] adv beautifully; **아름다운** [areumdaun] adj beautiful

아마 [ama] adv maybe, perhaps, presumably, supposedly; **아마도** [amado] adv possibly; **아마도** [amado] adv probably

아마추어 [amachueo] n amateur

아메리카 [amerika] **라틴 아메리카** [ratin amerika] n Latin America; **라틴 아메리카의** [ratin amerikaui] adj Latin American; **중앙 아메리카** [jungang amerika] n Central America

아몬드 [amondeu] n almond

아무것도 [amugeotdo] pron anything

아무도 [amudo] pron anybody, anyone

아버지 [abeoji] n father; **시아버지** [siabeoji] (husband's father) n father-in-law; **아빠** [appa] n dad; **아버지** [abeoji] n parent; **의붓아버지** [uibusabeoji] n stepfather

아보카도 [abokado] n avocado

아부다비 [abudabi] n Abu Dhabi

아비 [abi] **홀아비** [horabi] n widower

아빠 [appa] n daddy

아스파라거스 [aseuparageoseu] n asparagus

아스피린 [aseupirin] n aspirin; **아스피린 주세요** [aseupirin juseyo] I'd like some aspirin; **저는 아스피린을 못 먹어요** [jeoneun aseupirineul mot meogeoyo] I can't take aspirin

아시아 [asia] n Asia; **아시아 사람** [asia saram] n Asian; **아시아의** [asiaui] adj Asian, Asiatic

아연 [ayeon] n zinc

아이 [ai] n child, kid; **아장아장 걷는 아이** [ajangajang geotneun ai] n toddler; **아이들이 차 안에 있어요** [aideuri cha ane isseoyo] My children are in the car; **아이에게 안전한가요?** [aiege anjeonhangayo?] Is it safe for children?; **아이가 셋 있어요** [aiga set isseoyo] I have three children; **아이가 없어졌어요** [aiga eopseojyeosseoyo] My child is missing; **아이가 없어요** [aiga eopseoyo] I don't have any children; **아이가 있어요** [aiga isseoyo] I have a child; **이 여권에는 아이들이 등록되어 있어요** [i yeogwoneneun aideuri deungnokdoeeo isseoyo] The children are on this passport; **이 여권에는 아이가 등록되어 있어요** [i yeogwoneneun aiga deungnokdoeeo isseoyo] The child is on this passport

아이스박스 [aiseubakseu] n icebox

아이스크림 [aiseukeurim] n ice cream;

아이스크림 주세요 [aiseukeurim juseyo] I'd like an ice cream

아이슬란드 [aiseullandeu] n Iceland; 아이슬란드 사람 [aiseullandeu saram] n Icelandic; 아이슬란드의 [aiseullandeuui] adj Icelandic

아이콘 [aikon] n icon

아이티 [aiti] n Haiti

아이팟 [aipat] n iPod®

아일랜드 [aillaendeu] n Eire, Ireland; 북아일랜드 [bugaillaendeu] n Northern Ireland; 아일랜드 사람 [aillaendeu saram] n Irish, Irishman; 아일랜드 여자 [aillaendeu yeoja] n Irishwoman; 아일랜드의 [aillaendeuui] adj Irish

아제르바이잔 [ajereubaijan] n Azerbaijan; 아제르바이잔 사람 [ajereubaijan saram] n Azerbaijani; 아제르바이잔의 [ajereubaijanui] adj Azerbaijani

아직 [ajik] adv still, yet (interrogative), yet (nevertheless), yet (with negative)

아첨 [acheom] 아첨하다 [acheomhada] v flatter

아치 [achi] n arch

아침 [achim] n morning; 대륙식의 아침식사 [daeryuksigui achimsiksa] n continental breakfast; 아침 식사 [achim siksa] n breakfast; 아침 제공 숙박 [achim jegong sukbak] n bed and breakfast, B&B; 내일 아침 [naeil achim] tomorrow morning; 아침에 [achime] in the morning; 오늘 아침 [oneul achim] this morning; 저는 내일 아침 10시에 떠나요 [jeoneun naeil achim 10sie tteonayo] I will be leaving tomorrow morning at ten a.m.

아침식사 [achimsiksa] 아침식사 빼고요 [achimsiksa ppaegoyo] without breakfast; 아침식사 포함이요 [achimsiksa pohamiyo] with breakfast; 아침식사를 어디에서 먹어요? [achimsiksareul eodieseo meogeoyo?] Where is breakfast served?; 아침식사는 몇 시인가요? [achimsiksaneun myeot siingayo?] What time is breakfast?; 아침식사가 포함되나요? [achimsiksaga

pohamdoenayo?] Is breakfast included?

아코디언 [akodieon] n accordion

아티초크 [atichokeu] n artichoke

아파트 [apateu] n apartment; 원룸 아파트 [wollum apateu] n studio flat;... 이름으로 아파트를 예약했어요 [... ireumeuro apateureul yeyakhaesseoyo] We've booked an apartment in the name of...; 아파트를 찾고 있어요 [apateureul chatgo isseoyo] We're looking for an apartment; 아파트를 구경시켜 주시겠어요? [apateureul gugyeongsikyeo jusigesseoyo?] Could you show us around the apartment?

아프가니스탄 [apeuganiseutan] n Afghanistan; 아프가니스탄 사람 [apeuganiseutan saram] n Afghan; 아프가니스탄의 [apeuganiseutanui] adj Afghan

아프다 [apeuda] v ache; 아픈 [apeun] adj ill, painful, sore

아프리카 [apeurika] n Africa; 북아프리카 [bugapeurika] n North Africa; 북아프리카 사람 [bugapeurika saram] n North African; 북아프리카의 [bugapeurikaui] adj North African; 남아프리카 [namapeurika] n South Africa; 남아프리카 사람 [namapeurika saram] n South African; 남아프리카의 [namapeurikaui] adj South African; 아프리카 사람 [apeurika saram] n African; 아프리카의 [apeurikaui] adj African; 중앙 아프리카 공화국 [jungang apeurika gonghwaguk] n Central African Republic

아프리카너 [apeurikaneo] n Afrikaner

아프리칸스 [apeurikanseu] 아프리칸스어 [apeurikanseueo] n Afrikaans

아픔 [apeum] n ache

아홉 번째 [ahopbeonjjae] 아홉 번째의 [ahop beonjjaeui] adj ninth

악 [ak] 악한 [akhan] n villain

악기 [akgi] n musical instrument; 목관 악기 [mokgwan akgi] n woodwind

악단 [akdan] 관현악단

[gwanhyeonakdan] n orchestra
악마 [angma] n devil
악몽 [angmong] n nightmare
악보 [akbo] n score (of music)
악어 [ageo] n alligator, crocodile
악의 [agui] n spite; **악의 있는** [agui inneun] adj malicious; **악의적인** [aguijeogin] adj spiteful
악절 [akjeol] n passage (musical)
악취 [akchwi] n odour, stink; **악취가 나는** [akchwiga naneun] adj smelly; **악취가 나다** [akchwiga nada] v stink
악화 [akhwa] **악화되다** [akhwadoeda] v worsen; **악화시키다** [akhwasikida] v deteriorate
안 [an]...**의 안쪽에** [...ui anjjoge] prep within (space), within (term); **안뜰** [antteul] n courtyard; **안에 들이지 않다** [ane deuriji anta] v keep out;...**안으로** [...aneuro] prep into; **안으로 들이다** [aneuro deurida] v let in; **안의** [anui] adj inner;...**의 안쪽에** [...ui anjjoge] prep inside;...**의 안에** [...ui ane] prep in; **안에 있어요** [ane isseoyo] It's inside; **일주일 안에** [iljuil ane] in a week's time; **이 안에는 뭐가 들었죠?** [i aneneun mwoga deureotjyo?] What is in this?; **한 달 안에** [han dal ane] a month's time
안감 [angam] n lining
안개 [angae] n fog, mist; **안개등** [angaedeung] n fog light; **안개가 자욱한** [angaega jaukhan] adj foggy, misty
안경 [angyeong] npl glasses, specs, spectacles; **쌍안경** [ssangangyeong] npl binoculars; **안경사** [angyeongsa] n optician; **이중 초점 안경** [ijung chojeom angyeong] npl bifocals; **제 안경을 고치실 수 있으세요?** [je angyeongeul gochisil su isseuseyo?] Can you repair my glasses?
안내 [annae] n direction, guidance, information; **맹인 안내견** [maengin annaegyeon] n guide dog; **안내 데스크** [annae deseukeu] n enquiry desk; **안내서** [annaeseo] n handbook, manual; **안내소** [annaeso] n

information office, inquiries office; **안내인이 딸린 여행** [annaeini ttallin yeohaeng] n guided tour; **안내자** [annaeja] n guide; **여행 안내서** [yeohaeng annaeseo] n guidebook; **안내 좀 해 주시겠어요?** [annae jom hae jusigesseoyo?] Can you guide me, please?; **영어로 된 안내책 있어요?** [yeongeoro doen annaechaek isseoyo?] Do you have a guide book in English?; **저는 안내견이 있어요** [jeoneun annaegyeoni isseoyo] I have a guide dog
안내소 [annaeso] **관광 안내소** [gwangwang annaeso] n visitor centre; **관광 안내소는 어디있어요?** [gwangwang annaesoneun eodiisseoyo?] Where is the tourist office?
안내원 [annaewon] **관광 안내원** [gwangwang annaewon] n tour guide
안내책 [annaechaek]...**로 된 안내책 있어요?** [...ro doen annaechaek isseoyo?] Do you have a guide book in...?
안녕 [annyeong] **안녕!** [annyeong!] excl bye!, bye-bye!, cheerio!, farewell!, goodbye!, hello!, hi!; **안녕하세요** [annyeonghaseyo] Good afternoon, Good evening, Good morning; **안녕히 주무세요** [annyeonghi jumuseyo] Good night; **안녕히 가세요** [annyeonghi gaseyo] Goodbye
안다 [anda] **껴안다** [kkyeoanda] n hug
안달 [andal] **안달하기** [andalhagi] n fuss
안달나다 [andallada] v fret
안데스 [andeseu] **안데스 산맥** [andeseu sanmaek] npl Andes
안도 [ando] n relief
안도라 [andora] n Andorra
안락 [allak] **안락 의자** [allak uija] n armchair, easy chair
안색 [ansaek] n complexion
안식일 [ansigil] n Sabbath
안심 [ansim] n reassurance, relief; **안심시켜 주는** [ansimsikyeo juneun] adj reassuring; **안심시키다** [ansimsikida] v reassure; **안심한**

[ansimhan] *adj* relieved

안장 [anjang] *n* saddle; **새들백**
[saedeulbaek] *n* saddlebag

안전 [anjeon] *n* safety; **안전벨트**
[anjeonbelteu] *n* safety belt; **안전핀**
[anjeonpin] *n* safety pin; **안전한**
[anjeonhan] *adj* safe, secure

안전핀 [anjeonpin] **안전핀이 필요해요**
[anjeonpini piryohaeyo] I need a safety
pin

안정 [anjeong] **신경 안정제** [singyeong
anjeongje] *n* tranquillizer; **안정된**
[anjeongdoen] *adj* stable, steady;
안정성 [anjeongseong] *n* stability

안초비 [anchobi] *n* anchovy

안테나 [antena] *n* aerial; **위성방송수신
접시 안테나** [wiseongbangsongsusin
jeopsi antena] *n* satellite dish

앉다 [antda] *vi* sit; **앉을 수 있는 곳이
있나요?** [anjeul su inneun gosi innayo?]
Is there somewhere I can sit down?;
어디에 앉을 수 있을까요? [eodie anjeul
su isseulkkayo?] Where can I sit down?;
여기 앉아도 될까요? [yeogi anjado
doelkkayo?] Can I sit here?

않다 [anta] **쉬지 않고** [swiji anko] *adv*
non-stop; **아무데도... 없다(않다)**
[amudedo... eopda(anta)] *adv*
nowhere; **아무도... 않다** [amudo...
anta] *pron* nobody, none; **결코...않다**
[gyeolko...anta] *adv* never

알 [al] **모래알** [moraeal] *n* grit

알다 [alda] *v* know; **알리다** [allida] *v*
inform; **알아차리다** [aracharida] *v*
notice; **알고 있는** [algo inneun] *adj*
aware; **이것을 어떻게 하는지 아세요?**
[igeoseul eotteoke haneunji aseyo?]
Do you know how to do this?; **그
사람을 아세요?** [geu sarameul aseyo?]
Do you know him?

알라 [alla] *n* Allah

알레르기 [allereugi] *n* allergy; **땅콩
알레르기** [ttangkong allereugi] *n*
peanut allergy; **밀 알레르기** [mil
allereugi] *n* wheat intolerance;
알레르기의 [allereuguii] *adj* allergic;
꽃가루 알레르기 [kkotgaru allereugi] *n*
hay fever

알려지다 [allyeojida] **알려진** [allyeojin]
adj known

알루미늄 [alluminyum] *n* aluminium

알리바이 [allibai] *n* alibi

알맞다 [almatda] **알맞은** [almajeun] *adj*
fit

알바니아 [albania] *n* Albania; **알바니아
사람** [albania saram] *n* Albanian
(*person*); **알바니아어** [albaniaeo] *n*
Albanian (*language*); **알바니아의**
[albaniaui] *adj* Albanian

알제리 [aljeri] *n* Algeria; **알제리 사람**
[aljeri saram] *n* Algerian; **알제리의**
[aljeriui] *adj* Algerian

알코올 [alkool] *n* alcohol; **무알코올의**
[mualkoorui] *adj* alcohol-free; **알코올
농도가 낮은** [alkool nongdoga najeun]
adj low-alcohol; **알코올 중독자** [alkool
jungdokja] *n* alcoholic; **알코올의**
[alkoorui] *adj* alcoholic

알파벳 [alpabet] *n* alphabet

알프스 [alpeuseu] **알프스 산맥**
[alpeuseu sanmaek] *npl* Alps

암 [am] *n* cancer (*illness*)

암기 [amgi] **암기하다** [amgihada] *v*
memorize

암벽 [ambyeok] **암벽타기** [ambyeoktagi]
n rock climbing

암시 [amsi] **암시하다** [amsihada] *v* hint

암페어 [ampeeo] *n* amp

암호 [amho] *n* password

압력 [amnyeok] *n* pressure; **압력을
가하다** [amnyeogeul gahada] *v* lean
on, pressure; **타이어 압력이 얼마여야
하나요?** [taieo amnyeogi eolmayeoya
hanayo?] What should the tyre
pressure be?

압자일렌 [apjaillen] **압자일렌을 하고
싶어요** [apjailleneul hago sipeoyo] I'd
like to go abseiling

압정 [apjeong] *n* drawing pin

압축 [apchuk] **압축기** [apchukgi] *v* press;
공기압축기 [gonggiapchukgi] *n*
pneumatic drill

압핀 [appin] *n* thumb tack

앙골라 [anggolla] *n* Angola; **앙골라 사람**
[anggolla saram] *n* Angolan; **앙골라의**
[anggollaui] *adj* Angolan

앞 [ap] n front; 앞쪽에 [apjjoge] adv
ahead; 앞선 [apseon] adj advanced;
앞에 [ape] adv before; 앞으로 [apeuro]
adv forward; 앞으로 이동하다 [apeuro
idonghada] v move forward; 앞으로
굽히다 [apeuro guphida] v lean
forward; 앞의 [apui] adj front
앞문 [ammun] n front door; 앞문 열쇠는
어느 것인가요? [ammun yeolsoeneun
eoneu geosingayo?] Which is the key
for the front door?
앞치마 [apchima] 어린이용 앞치마
[eoriniyong apchima] n pinafore
애국 [aeguk] 애국적인 [aegukjeogin] adj
patriotic
애국주의 [aegukjuui] 열광적애국주의자
[yeolgwangjeogaegukjuuija] n
chauvinist
애도 [aedo] n mourning
애매 [aemae] 애매한 [aemaehan] adj
tricky
애완 [aewan] 애완 동물 [aewan
dongmul] n pet
애정 [aejeong] 애정 어린 [aejeong
eorin] adj affectionate
애착 [aechak] n attachment
액 [aek] 부동액 [budongaek] n
antifreeze
액체 [aekche] n liquid
앨범 [aelbeom] n album
앵무새 [aengmusae] n parrot
야간 [yagan] n night time; 야간 수업
[yagan sueop] n evening class; 야간
교대근무 [yagan gyodaegeunmu] n
nightshift; 야간 활동 [yagan
hwaldong] n nightlife
야구 [yagu] n baseball; 야구 모자 [yagu
moja] n baseball cap
야단법석 [yadanbeopseok]
야단법석하는 [yadanbeopseokhaneun]
adj fussy
야드 [yadeu] n yard (measurement)
야만 [yaman] 야만적인 [yamanjeogin]
adj uncivilized; 야만적인
[yamanjeogin] adj barbaric
야생 [yasaeng] 야생 생물 [yasaeng
saengmul] n wildlife; 야생의
[yasaengui] adj wild; 야생 생물을 보고

싶어요 [yasaeng saengmureul bogo
sipeoyo] We'd like to see wildlife
야심 [yasim] n ambition; 야심적인
[yasimjeogin] adj ambitious
야영 [yayeong] n camping; 야영자
[yayeongja] n camper; 야영지
[yayeongji] n camp, campsite; 야영하다
[yayeonghada] v camp
야영장 [yayeongjang] 야영장에 식당
있어요? [yayeongjange sikdang
isseoyo?] Is there a restaurant on the
campsite?; 여기에 야영장이 있나요?
[yeogie yayeongjangi innayo?] Is there
a campsite here?
야외 [yaoe] 야외수영장인가요?
[yaoesuyeongjangingayo?] Is it an
outdoor pool?; 어떤 야외 활동이
있어요? [eotteon yaoe hwaldongi
isseoyo?] What outdoor activities are
there?
야채 [yachae] n vegetables; 야채 샐러드
[yachae saelleodeu] n green salad;
야채 싱싱한 거예요, 얼린 거예요?
[yachae singsinghan geoyeyo, eollin
geoyeyo?] Are the vegetables fresh or
frozen?; 야채가 들어있어요? [yachaega
deureoisseoyo?] Are the vegetables
included?
야회 [yahoe] 야회복 [yahoebok] n
evening dress
약 [yak] n drug, medicine; 치약 [chiyak]
n toothpaste; 안약 [anyak] npl eye
drops; 알약 [aryak] n pill; 약사 [yaksa]
n pharmacist; 약한 [yakhan] adj weak;
기침약 [gichimyak] n cough mixture;
피임약 [piimyak] n contraceptive; 이미
이 약을 먹고 있어요 [imi i yageul
meokgo isseoyo] I'm already taking
this medicine
약간 [yakgan] adv slightly ▷ pron some;
약간의 [yakganui] adj slight
약국 [yakguk] n chemist('s); 가장 가까운
약국은 어디에 있어요? [gajang
gakkaun yakgugeun eodie isseoyo?]
Where is the nearest chemist?
약도 [yakdo] n sketch; 방향 약도를 그려
주시겠어요? [banghyang yakdoreul
geuryeo jusigesseoyo?] Can you draw

me a map with directions?

약사 [yaksa] n chemist

약속 [yaksok] n engagement, promise; **약속하다** [yaksokhada] v promise

약어 [yageo] n abbreviation

약혼 [yakhon] **약혼 반지** [yakhon banji] n engagement ring; **약혼녀** [yakhonnyeo] n fiancée; **약혼자** [yakhonja] n fiancé; **약혼한** [yakhonhan] adj engaged; **약혼했어요** [yakhonhaesseoyo] I'm engaged

얇다 [yarpda] **얇은** [yarbeun] adj thin

양 [yang] n amount, Miss, sheep; **숫양** [susyang] n ram; **암양** [amyang] n ewe; **양 지키는 개** [yang jikineun gae] n sheepdog; **양 고기** [yang gogi] n mutton; **양치기** [yangchigi] n shepherd; **양자리** [yangjari] n Aries; **양가죽** [yanggajuk] n sheepskin; **양털** [yangteol] n fleece; **어린양** [eorinyang] n lamb; **인도양** [indoyang] n Indian Ocean

양귀비 [yanggwibi] n poppy

양동이 [yangdongi] n pail

양로원 [yangnowon] n nursing home

양말 [yangmal] n sock

양모 [yangmo] n wool; **양모의** [yangmoui] adj woollen

양배추 [yangbaechu] n cabbage; **양배추 샐러드** [yangbaechu saelleodeu] n coleslaw; **양배추의 일종** [yangbaechuui iljong] npl Brussels sprouts

양보 [yangbo] n right of way; **그 여자는 길을 양보하지 않았어요** [geu yeojaneun gireul yangbohaji anhasseoyo] She didn't give way

양성 [yangseong] **HIV 양성이에요** [HIV yangseongieyo] I am HIV-positive

양식 [yangsik] **사는 양식** [saneun yangsik] n lifestyle

양심 [yangsim] n conscience; **양심적인** [yangsimjeogin] adj conscientious

양육 [yangyuk] n upbringing; **양육하다** [yangyukhada] v foster

양자택일 [yangjataegil] n alternative; **양자택일인** [yangjataegirin] n alternative

양조 [yangjo] **양조장** [yangjojang] n brewery

양쪽 [yangjjok] pron both; **양쪽의** [yangjjogui] adj both

양탄자 [yangtanja] n rug

양파 [yangpa] n onion

얕다 [yatda] **얕은** [yateun] adj shallow

어 [eo] **아프리칸스어** [apeurikanseueo] n Afrikaans; **네델란드어** [nedeollandeueo] Dutch; **노르웨이어** [noreuweieo] Norwegian; **덴마크어** [denmakeueo] Danish; **독일어** [dogireo] German; **러시아어** [reosiaeo] Russian; **베트남어** [beteunameo] Vietnamese; **스웨덴어** [seuwedeneo] Swedish; **스페인어** [seupeineo] Spanish; **아랍어** [arabeo] Arabic; **영어** [yeongeo] English; **일본어** [ilboneo] Japanese; **이탈리아어** [italliaeo] Italian; **중국어** [junggugeo] Chinese; **체코어** [chekoeo] Czech; **그리스어** [geuriseueo] Greek; **크로아티어어** [keuroatiaeo] Croatian; **태국어** [taegugeo] Thai; **터키어** [teokieo] Turkish; **포르투갈어** [poreutugareo] Portuguese; **폴란드어** [pollandeueo] Polish; **프랑스어** [peurangseueo] French; **핀란드어** [pillandeueo] Finnish; **한국어** [hangugeo] Korean

어깨 [eokkae] n shoulder; **어깨를 으쓱하다** [eokkaereul eusseukhada] v shrug; **어깨가 아파요** [eokkaega apayo] I've hurt my shoulder

어느 [eoneu] adj which; **어느 것** [eoneu geot] pron which

어댑터 [eodaepteo] n adaptor

어둠 [eodum] n dark, darkness; **어두운** [eoduun] adj dark

어둡다 [eodupda] **어두운** [eoduun] adj dim; **어두워요** [eoduwoyo] It's dark

어디 [eodi] **어디에** [eodie] adv where; **어디에나** [eodiena] adv everywhere; **어딘가에** [eodingae] adv anywhere, someplace, somewhere; **어디가 어떻게 안 좋으시죠?** [eodiga eotteoke an joheusijyo?] What's the matter?, What's wrong?; **...은 어디에 있어요?** [... eun eodie isseoyo?] Where is...?

어떤 [eotteon] adj any, some ▷ pron any
어떻게 [eotteoke] adv how; 어떻게든
[eotteokedeun] adv somehow; 어떻게
지내세요? [eotteoke jinaeseyo?] How
are you?

어렵다 [eoryeopda] 어려운 [eoryeoun]
adj difficult, hard (difficult); 어려움
[eoryeoum] n difficulty; 읽기 어려운
[irkgi eoryeoun] adj illegible; 이
슬로프는 얼마나 어렵나요? [i
seullopeuneun eolmana
eoryeomnayo?] How difficult is this
slope?

어리다 [eorida] 더 어린 [deo eorin] adj
younger; 어린 [eorin] adj young; 가장
어린 [gajang eorin] adj youngest

어리석다 [eoriseokda] 어리석은
[eoriseogeun] adj daft, idiotic, silly,
unwise

어린 [eorin] 어린 시절 [eorin sijeol] n
childhood

어린이 [eorini] n child; 어린이용 높은
의자 [eoriniyong nopeun uija] n
highchair; 두 살짜리 어린이 좌석이
있으면 좋겠어요 [du salijjari eorini
jwaseogi isseumyeon jokesseoyo] I'd
like a child seat for a two-year-old
child; 어린이 분량이 있나요? [eorini
bullyangi innayo?] Do you have
children's portions?; 어린이 메뉴가
있나요? [eorini menyuga innayo?] Do
you have a children's menu?; 어린이
침대 있어요? [eorini chimdae isseoyo?]
Do you have a cot?; 어린이 수영장이
있어요? [eorini suyeongjangi isseoyo?]
Is there a children's pool?; 어린이
좌석이 있어요? [eorini jwaseogi
isseoyo?] Do you have a child's seat?;
어린이 할인 있어요? [eorini harin
isseoyo?] Are there any reductions for
children?; 어린이를 동반해도 될까요?
[eorinireul dongbanhaedo doelkkayo?]
Is it okay to take children?; 어린이를
위한 물놀이터가 있어요? [eorinireul
wihan mulloriteoga isseoyo?] Is there a
paddling pool for the children?;
어린이를 위한 활동이 있나요?
[eorinireul wihan hwaldongi innayo?]

Do you have activities for children?;
어린이가 할 만한 것이 있을까요?
[eoriniga hal manhan geosi
isseulkkayo?] What is there for children
to do?; 어린이표 [eorinipyo] a child's
ticket

어머니 [eomeoni] n mother; 시어머니
[sieomeoni] (husband's mother) n
mother-in-law; 아버지 [abeoji] n
parent; 의붓어머니 [uibuseomeoni] n
stepmother

어울리다 [eoullida] v suit; 어울리는
[eoullineun] adj matching

어제 [eoje] adv yesterday

어지럽다 [eojireopda] 어지러워요
[eojireowoyo] I feel dizzy

어질다 [eojilda] 어질러진 [eojilleojin] adj
messy

어쨌든 [eojjaetdeun] adv anyhow,
anyway

어학 [eohak] n language study;
어학실습실 [eohaksilseupsil] n
language laboratory; 어학원
[eohagwon] n language school

어휘 [eohwi] n vocabulary

억 [eok] 10억 [sibeok] n billion

억제 [eokje] n curb, inhibition

억지 [eokji] 억지로 [eokjiro] adv
reluctantly

언급 [eongeup] n mention, reference;
언급되다 [eongeupdoeda] v come up;
언급하다 [eongeuphada] v mention,
refer

언니 [eonni] n sister

언덕 [eondeok] n hill; 모래 언덕 [morae
eondeok] n sand dune; 언덕 산책
[eondeok sanchaek] n hill-walking

언어 [eoneo] n language, speech; 몽골어
[monggoreo] n Mongolian (language);
라틴어 [ratineo] n Latin; 언어학자
[eoneohakja] n linguist; 언어학적인
[eoneohakjeogin] adj linguistic; 이중
언어의 [ijung eoneoui] adj bilingual;
현대 언어 [hyeondae eoneo] npl
modern languages

언제 [eonje] adv when; 마지막
올라가는 언제인가요? [majimak
ollagagineun eonjeingayo?] When is

the last ascent?; **언제 끝나요?** [eonje kkeutnayo?] When will you have finished?; **언제부터 그래요?** [eonjebuteo geuraeyo?] When did it happen?

언젠가 [eonjenga] *adv* sometime

얻다 [eotda] *v* get, get (*to a place*) ▷ *vt* gain

얼굴 [eolgul] *n* face; **미안술** [miansul] *n* facial; **얼굴의** [eolgurui] *adj* facial; **얼굴이 붉어지다** [eolguri bulgeojida] *v* flush

얼다 [eolda] *vi* freeze; **언** [eon] *adj* frozen

얼룩 [eolluk] *n* stain; **얼룩 제거제** [eolluk jegeoje] *n* stain remover; **얼룩지게 하다** [eollukjige hada] *v* stain; **이 얼룩은 커피예요** [i eollugeun keopiyeyo] This stain is coffee; **이 얼룩은 피예요** [i eollugeun piyeyo] This stain is blood; **이 얼룩을 지울 수 있나요?** [i eollugeul jiul su innayo?] Can you remove this stain?

얼마 [eolma] **시간당 얼마예요?** [sigandang eolmayeyo?] How much is it per hour?; **얼마예요?** [eolmayeyo?] How much does that come to?, How much is it worth?, How much is it?, How much will it be?, What do I owe you?; **이건 얼마예요?** [igeon eolmayeyo?] How much does it cost?; **저건 얼마예요?** [jeogeon eolmayeyo?] How much does that cost?; **하룻밤에 얼마예요?** [harutbame eolmayeyo?] How much is it per night?

얼스터 [eolseuteo] *n* Ulster

얼음 [eoreum] *n* ice; **도로의 살얼음** [doroui sareoreum] *n* black ice; **얼음의** [eoreumui] *adj* icy; **각얼음** [gageoreum] *n* ice cube; **얼음 넣어 주세요** [eoreum neoheo juseyo] With ice, please

엄격 [eomgyeok] **엄격하게** [eomgyeokhage] *adv* strictly; **엄격한** [eomgyeokhan] *adj* strict; **엄격함** [eomgyeokham] *n* austerity

엄마 [eomma] *n* mum, mummy (*mother*)

엄수 [eomsu] **시간을 엄수하는** [siganeul eomsuhaneun] *adj* punctual

엄지 [eomji] **엄지손가락** [eomjisongarak] *n* thumb

엄청나다 [eomcheongnada] **엄청난** [eomcheongnan] *adj* stunned

업자 [eopja] **밀수업자** [milsueopja] *n* smuggler; **인쇄업자** [inswaeeopja] *n* printer (*person*); **건축업자** [geonchugeopja] *n* builder

없다 [eopda] **...없이** [...eopsi] *prep* without; **...이 하나도 없는** [...i hanado eomneun] *adv* no; **아무도... 않다(없다)** [amudo... anta(eopda)] *pron* no one; **집 없는** [jip eomneun] *adj* homeless; **딸이 없어졌어요** [ttari eopseojyeosseoyo] My daughter is missing; **아들이 없어졌어요** [adeuri eopseojyeosseoyo] My son is missing

없어지다 [eobseojida] **아이가 없어졌어요** [aiga eopseojyeosseoyo] My child is missing

엉겅퀴 [eonggeongkwi] *n* thistle

엉덩이 [eongdeongi] *n* backside, behind, bum, hip ▷ *npl* buttocks

엉망 [eongmang] **서비스가 엉망이었어요** [seobiseuga eongmangieosseoyo] The service was terrible

엎지르다 [eopjireuda] *vt* spill

에나멜 [enamel] *n* enamel

에너지 [eneoji] *n* energy; **태양 에너지** [taeyang eneoji] *n* solar power

에리트레아 [eriteurea] *n* Eritrea

에서 [eseo] **...에서** [...eseo] *prep* at

에스컬레이터 [eseukeolleiteo] *n* escalator

에스토니아 [eseutonia] *n* Estonia; **에스토니아 사람** [eseutonia saram] *n* Estonian (*person*); **에스토니아어** [eseutoniaeo] *n* Estonian (*language*); **에스토니아의** [eseutoniaui] *adj* Estonian

에어로빅 [eeorobik] *npl* aerobics

에어로졸 [eeorojol] *n* aerosol

에어백 [eeobaek] *n* airbag

에어컨 [eeokeon] *n* air conditioning; **방에 에어컨 있어요?** [bange eeokeon isseoyo?] Does the room have air conditioning?; **에어컨이 작동하지**

않아요 [eeokeoni jakdonghaji anhayo] The air conditioning doesn't work; 에어컨이있어요? [eeokeoniisseoyo?] Does it have air conditioning?

에이즈 [eijeu] n AIDS

에이커 [eikeo] n acre

에콰도르 [ekwadoreu] n Ecuador

에티오피아 [etiopia] n Ethiopia; 에티오피아 사람 [etiopia saram] n Ethiopian; 에티오피아의 [etiopiaui] adj Ethiopian

엔진 [enjin] n engine; 검색 엔진 [geomsaek enjin] n search engine

여 [yeo] n female; 여학생 [yeohaksaeng] n schoolgirl

여가 [yeoga] 여가시간 [yeogasigan] n spare time

여객선 [yeogaekseon] v think, set down;... 가는 여객선은 어디에서 탈 수 있어요? [... ganeun yeogaekseoneun eodieseo tal su isseoyo?] Where do we catch the ferry to...?;... 가는 여객선이 있어요? [... ganeun yeogaekseoni isseoyo?] Is there a ferry to...?

여과 [yeogwa] 여과기 [yeogwagi] n colander

여권 [yeogwon] n passport; 여권 검사 [yeogwon geomsa] n passport control; 여권을 도둑맞았어요 [yeogwoneul dodungmajasseoyo] My passport has been stolen; 여권을 잃어버렸어요 [yeogwoneul ireobeoryeosseoyo] I've lost my passport; 여권을 깜빡 잊었어요 [yeogwoneul kkamppak ijeosseoyo] I've forgotten my passport; 이 여권에는 아이들이 등록되어 있어요 [i yeogwoneneun aideuri deungnokdoeeo isseoyo] The children are on this passport; 이 여권에는 아이가 등록되어 있어요 [i yeogwoneneun aiga deungnokdoeeo isseoyo] The child is on this passport; 제 여권을 돌려주세요 [je yeogwoneul dollyeojuseyo] Please give me my passport back; 제 여권이에요 [je yeogwonieyo] Here is my passport

여기 [yeogi] 여기에 [yeogie] adv here;

여기가 어디인가요? [yeogiga eodiingayo?] Where are we?

여기다 [yeogida] 불쌍히 여기다 [bulssanghi yeogida] v pity

여덟 [yeodeorp] 여덟 번째의 [yeodeol beonjjaeui] adj eighth

여드름 [yeodeureum] n acne, zit

여러분 [yeoreobun] 여러분 자신 [yeoreobun jasin] pron yourselves (intensifier), yourselves (polite), yourselves (reflexive)

여론 [yeoron] n public opinion; 여론조사 [yeoronjosa] n opinion poll, poll

여름 [yeoreum] n summer; 여름철 [yeoreumcheol] n summertime; 여름휴가 [yeoreumhyuga] npl summer holidays; 여름 동안에 [yeoreum dongane] during the summer; 여름 전에 [yeoreum jeone] before summer; 여름 후에 [yeoreum hue] after summer; 여름에 [yeoreume] in summer

여물 [yeomul] 여물통 [yeomultong] n trough

여물다 [yeomulda] 여문 [yeomun] adj ripe

여분 [yeobun] 여분으로 [yeobuneuro] adv extra; 여분의 [yeobunui] adj extra, spare

여사 [yeosa] n Mrs

여성 [yeoseong] n female; 여성 사업가 [yeoseong saeopga] n businesswoman; 여성만의 모임 [yeoseongmanui moim] n hen night; 여성스러운 [yeoseongseureoun] adj feminine; 여성의 [yeoseongui] adj female

여왕 [yeowang] n queen

여우 [yeou] n fox

여울 [yeoul] npl rapids

여유 [yeoyu] 여유가 있다 [yeoyuga itda] v afford

여인숙 [yeoinsuk] n inn

여자 [yeoja] n woman; 아일랜드 여자 [aillaendeu yeoja] n Irishwoman; 여자 바텐더 [yeoja batendeo] n barmaid; 여자 배우 [yeoja baeu] n actress; 여자 우편집배원 [yeoja upyeonjipbaewon]

n postwoman; **여자 경찰관** [yeoja gyeongchalgwan] *n* policewoman; **여자친구** [yeojachingu] *n* girlfriend; **여자화장실** [yeojahwajangsil] *n* ladies'; **여군** [yeogun] *n* servicewoman; **그 여자** [geu yeoja] *pron* her, she; **그 여자 자신** [geu yeoja jasin] *pron* herself; **그 여자 것** [geu yeoja geot] *pron* hers; **그 여자의** [geu yeojaui] *adj* her

여자친구 [yeojachingu] **여자친구가 있어요** [yeojachinguga isseoyo] I have a girlfriend

여정 [yeojeong] *n* journey, trip; **두 시간 여정이에요** [du sigan yeojeongieyo] The journey takes two hours; **여정은 얼마나 시간이 걸릴까요?** [yeojeongeun eolmana sigani geollilkkayo?] How long is the journey?

여행 [yeohaeng] *n* journey, tour, travel, travelling, trip; **도보 여행자** [dobo yeohaengja] *n* rambler; **배낭여행** [baenangyeohaeng] *n* backpacking; **배낭여행자** [baenangyeohaengja] *n* backpacker; **신혼 여행** [sinhon yeohaeng] *n* honeymoon; **안내인이 딸린 여행** [annaeini ttallin yeohaeng] *n* guided tour; **여행 안내서** [yeohaeng annaeseo] *n* guidebook; **여행보험** [yeohaengboheom] *n* travel insurance; **여행사** [yeohaengsa] *n* tour operator, tourist office, travel agency, travel agent's; **여행사 직원** [yeohaengsa jigwon] *n* travel agent; **여행용 가방** [yeohaengyong gabang] *n* overnight bag; **여행일정표** [yeohaengiljeongpyo] *n* itinerary; **여행자** [yeohaengja] *n* traveller; **여행가방** [yeohaenggabang] *n* suitcase; **여행하다** [yeohaenghada] *vi* tour, travel; **왕복여행** [wangbogyeohaeng] *n* round trip; **고된여행하다** [godoenyeohaenghada] *v* trek; **급사** [geupsa] *n* courier; **길고 고된 여행** [gilgo godoen yeohaeng] *n* trek; **패키지 여행** [paekiji yeohaeng] *n* package tour; **여행 잘 하세요!** [yeohaeng jal haseyo!] Have a good trip!; **일등석으로 여행하고 싶어요** [ildeungseogeuro yeohaenghago sipeoyo] I would like to travel first-class; **저는 여행자보험에 들지 않았어요** [jeoneun yeohaengjaboheome deulji anhasseoyo] I don't have travel insurance; **강에서 하는 보트 여행이 있어요?** [gangeseo haneun boteu yeohaengi isseoyo?] Are there any boat trips on the river?;...**행 당일치기 여행 있어요?** [...haeng dangilchigi yeohaeng isseoyo?] Do you run day trips to...?; **혼자 여행하고 있어요** [honja yeohaenghago isseoyo] I'm travelling alone

여행자 [yeohaengja] *n* traveller; **여행자 수표** [yeohaengja supyo] *n* traveller's cheque; **여행자 수표 받으세요?** [yeohaengja supyo badeuseyo?] Do you accept traveller's cheques?

여호 [yeoho] **여호와의 증인** [yeohowaui jeungin] *n* Jehovah's Witness

역 [yeok] *n* train station; **지하철역** [jihacheollyeok] *n* metro station, tube station; **철도역** [cheoldoyeok] *n* railway station;... **가려면 어느 역인가요?** [... garyeomyeon eoneu yeogingayo?] Which stop is it for...?; **다음 역은 어디인가요?** [daeum yeogeun eodiingayo?] What is the next stop?; **다음 역은...인가요?** [daeum yeogeun...ingayo?] Is the next stop...?; **가장 가까운 지하철역에 어떻게 가나요?** [gajang gakkaun jihacheollyeoge eotteoke ganayo?] How do I get to the nearest tube station?; **가장 가까운 지하철역은 어디에 있어요?** [gajang gakkaun jihacheollyeogeun eodie isseoyo?] Where is the nearest tube station?

역도 [yeokdo] *n* weightlifting; **역도 선수** [yeokdo seonsu] *n* weightlifter

역력 [yeongnyeok] **역력한** [yeongnyeokhan] *adj* glaring

역사 [yeoksa] *n* history; **역사적인** [yeoksajeogin] *adj* historical; **역사가** [yeoksaga] *n* historian

역할 [yeokhal] *n* role

연 [yeon] *n* kite

연결 [yeongyeol] n connection;
연결되어있는 [yeongyeoldoeeoinneun]
adj attached; 연결하다
[yeongyeolhada] v link (up); 연결하다
[yeongyeolhada] v connect; 연결이
아주 느린 것 같아요 [yeongyeori aju
neurin geot gatayo] The connection
seems very slow

연고 [yeongo] n ointment; 입술 연고
[ipsul yeongo] n lip salve

연구 [yeongu] n research

연구소 [yeonguso] n institute

연극 [yeongeuk] n play

연금 [yeongeum] n pension; 연금 수령자
[yeongeum suryeongja] n pensioner

연기 [yeongi] n acting, smoke ▷ npl
fumes; 연기를 뿜다 [yeongireul
ppumda] v smoke; 연기하다
[yeongihada] v postpone, put off

연대 [yeondae] n regiment

연락 [yeollak] n contact; 문제가 있으면
누구에게 연락해야 할까요? [munjega
isseumyeon nuguege yeollakhaeya
halkkayo?] Who do we contact if there
are problems?; 어디로 연락 드리면
될까요? [eodiro yeollak deurimyeon
doelkkayo?] Where can I contact you?

연례 [yeollye] 연례 총회 [yeollye
chonghoe] abbr AGM

연료 [yeollyo] n fuel; 연료를 보급하다
[yeollyoreul bogeuphada] v refuel

연맹 [yeonmaeng] n league

연못 [yeonmot] n pond

연사 [yeonsa] n speaker

연상 [yeonsang] 연상의 [yeonsangui]
adj senior

연석 [yeonseok] n kerb

연설 [yeonseol] n address (speech)

연속 [yeonsok] n round (series),
sequence; 연속적으로
[yeonsokjeogeuro] adv continually;
연속적인 [yeonsokjeogin] adj
consecutive, constant, continual,
continuous; 연속극 [yeonsokgeuk] n
soap opera; 연속하는 [yeonsokhaneun]
adj successive

연쇄 [yeonswae] 연쇄 충돌 [yeonswae
chungdol] n pile-up

연습 [yeonseup] 예행 연습 [yehaeng
yeonseup] n rehearsal; 예행연습하다
[yehaengyeonseuphada] v rehearse

연어 [yeoneo] n salmon

연예인 [yeonyein] n entertainer; 노상
연예인 [nosang yeonyein] n busker

연인 [yeonin] n lover

연장 [yeonjang] n extension; 연장
케이블 [yeonjang keibeul] n extension
cable

연재 [yeonjae] 연재물 [yeonjaemul] n
serial

연주 [yeonju] 독주 [dokju] n solo;
독주자 [dokjuja] n soloist; 연주를 하다
[yeonjureul hada] vt play (music);
연주자 [yeonjuja] n player
(instrumentalist); 어디에서 지역
음악가의 연주를 들을 수 있어요?
[eodieseo jiyeok eumakgaui
yeonjureul deureul su isseoyo?] Where
can we hear local musicians play?

연착 [yeonchak] 기차가 10분 연착되고
있어요 [gichaga 10bun
yeonchakdoego isseoyo] The train is
running ten minutes late; 기차가
연착되고 있어요? [gichaga
yeonchakdoego isseoyo?] Is the train
running late?

연체 [yeonche] 연체된 [yeonchedoen]
adj overdue; 연체금 [yeonchegeum]
npl arrears

연필 [yeonpil] n pencil; 연필깎이
[yeonpilkkakki] n pencil sharpener

연합 [yeonhap] n union; 연합하다
[yeonhaphada] v unite; 유럽연합
[yureobyeonhap] n European Union,
EU; 국제연합 [gukjeyeonhap] n United
Nations; 국제연합 [gukjeyeonhap] n
UN

열 [yeol] n fever, heat, rank (line); 가열기
[gayeolgi] n heater; 열이 있어요 [yeori
isseoyo] He has a fever

열광 [yeolgwang] n mania;
열광적애국주의자
[yeolgwangjeogaegukjuuija] n
chauvinist

열네번째 [yeollebeonjjae] 열네 번째의
[yeolle beonjjaeui] adj fourteenth

열다 [yeolda] *vt* open; (잠긴 것을) **열다**
[(jamgin geoseul) yeolda] *v* unlock;
문이 안 열려요 [muni an yeollyeoyo]
The door won't open; 언제 열어요?
[eonje yeoreoyo?] When does it open?;
우체국은 언제 열어요? [uchegugeun
eonje yeoreoyo?] When does the post
office open?; 은행은 언제 열어요?
[eunhaengeun eonje yeoreoyo?] When
does the bank open?; 창문이 안 열려요
[changmuni an yeollyeoyo] I can't open
the window, The window won't open;
창을 열어도 될까요? [changeul
yeoreodo doelkkayo?] May I open the
window?

열다섯 [yeoldaseot] *number* fifteen;
열다섯 번째의 [yeoldaseot beonjjaeui]
adj fifteenth

열대 [yeoldae] *n* tropics; 열대 우림
[yeoldae urim] *n* rainforest; 열대성의
[yeoldaeseongui] *adj* tropical

열두번 [yeoldubeon] 열두 번째의
[yeoldu beonjjaeui] *adj* twelfth

열리다 [yeollida] 열린 [yeollin] *adj* open

열매 [yeolmae] 시계풀의 열매
[sigyepurui yeolmae] *n* passion fruit

열번째 [yeolbeonjjae] 열 번째의 [yeol
beonjjaeui] *adj* tenth

열세번 [yeolsebeon] 열세 번째의 [yeolse
beonjjaeui] *adj* thirteenth

열쇠 [yeolsoe] *n* key (*for lock*), key (*music/
computer*); 열쇠고리 [yeolsoegori] *n*
keyring;... 열쇠는 어디에서 받을 수
있을까요? [... yeolsoeneun eodieseo
badeul su isseulkkayo?] Where do we
get the key...?; 202호 열쇠요 [ibaek-i
ho yeolsoeyo] the key for room
number two hundred and two; 보조
열쇠가 필요해요 [bojo yeolsoega
pillyohaeyo] We need a second key;
나갈 때 어디에서 열쇠를 반납하나요?
[nagal ttae eodieseo yeolsoereul
bannaphanayo?] Where do we hand in
the key when we're leaving?; 뒷문
열쇠는 어느 것인가요? [dwitmun
yeolsoeneun eoneu geosingayo?]
Which is the key for the back door?;
앞문 열쇠는 어느 것인가요? [ammun
yeolsoeneun eoneu geosingayo?]
Which is the key for the front door?;
열쇠 주세요 [yeolsoe juseyo] The key,
please; 열쇠 주시겠어요? [yeolsoe
jusigesseoyo?] Can I have a key?;
열쇠를 깜빡 잊었어요 [yeolsoereul
kkamppak ijeosseoyo] I've forgotten
the key; 열쇠에 문제가 있어요
[yeolsoee munjega isseoyo] I'm having
trouble with the key; 열쇠가
고장났어요 [yeolsoega
gojangnasseoyo] The key doesn't work;
이 문 열쇠는 어느 것인가요? [i mun
yeolsoeneun eoneu geosingayo?]
Which is the key for this door?; 이
열쇠는 어디 열쇠죠? [i yeolsoeneun
eodi yeolsoejyo?] What's this key for?;
제 열쇠가 고장났어요 [je yeolsoega
gojangnasseoyo] My key doesn't work;
차에 열쇠를 두고 내렸어요 [chae
yeolsoereul dugo naeryeosseoyo] I left
the keys in the car; 차고 열쇠는 어느
것인가요? [chago yeolsoeneun eoneu
geosingayo?] Which is the key for the
garage?

열심 [yeolsim] 열심인 [yeolsimin] *adj*
keen; 열심히 [yeolsimhi] *adv* hard

열아홉 [yeorahop] 열아홉 번째의
[yeorahop beonjjaeui] *adj* nineteenth

열여덟 [yeollyeodeorp] 열여덟 번째의
[yeollyeodeol beonjjaeui] *adj*
eighteenth

열여섯 [yeollyeoseot] 열여섯 번째의
[yeollyeoseot beonjjaeui] *adj* sixteenth

열의 [yeorui] *n* enthusiasm

열일곱 [yeorilgop] 열일곱 번째의
[yeorilgop beonjjaeui] *adj* seventeenth

열정 [yeoljeong] *n* passion; 열정적인
[yeoljeongjeogin] *adj* enthusiastic

열차 [yeolcha] *n* train; 열차할인카드
[yeolchaharinkadeu] *n* railcard; 다음
열차로 주세요 [daeum yeolcharo
juseyo] The next available train, please;
싼 열차 요금 있어요? [ssan yeolcha
yogeum isseoyo?] Are there any cheap
train fares?; 어디에서... 가는 버스를 탈
수 있어요? [eodieseo... ganeun
beoseureul tal su isseoyo?] Where can I

117 | [yeongeo] 영어

get a train to…?; 열차를 놓쳤어요
[yeolchareul nochyeosseoyo] I've
missed my train; 휠체어로 열차에 타고
내릴 수 있을까요? [hwilcheeoro
yeolchae tago naeril su isseulkkayo?] Is
the train wheelchair-accessible?
열한번째 [yeolhanbeonjjae] 열한 번째의
[yeolhan beonjjaeui] adj eleventh
염 [yeom] 방광염 [banggwangyeom] n
cystitis; 기관지염 [gigwanjiyeom] n
bronchitis; 편도선염
[pyeondoseonyeom]n tonsillitis; 후두염
[huduyeom] n laryngitis
염료 [yeomnyo] n dye
염색 [yeomsaek] 염색하다
[yeomsaekhada] v dye; 부분 염색을
했어요 [bubun yeomsaegeul
haesseoyo] My hair is highlighted;
머리를 염색해 주시겠어요? [meorireul
yeomsaekhae jusigesseoyo?] Can you
dye my roots, please?
염소 [yeomso] n chlorine, goat; 염소자리
[yeomsojari] n Capricorn
염증 [yeomjeung] n inflammation;
염증을 일으킨 [yeomjeungeul ireukin]
adj inflamed
엽서 [yeopseo] 우편엽서
[upyeonyeopseo] n postcard;…로
엽서를 네 장 보낼 건데 우표 좀 주세요
[…ro yeopseoreul ne jang bonael
geonde upyo jom juseyo] Can I have
stamps for four postcards to…;
어디에서 엽서를 살 수 있어요?
[eodieseo yeopseoreul sal su isseoyo?]
Where can I buy some postcards?; 엽서
있어요? [yeopseo isseoyo?] Do you
have any postcards?; 엽서를 찾고
있어요. [yeopseoreul chatgo isseoyo.]
I'm looking for postcards
영 [yeong] n nil, nought, zero
영공 [yeonggong] n airspace
영광 [yeonggwang] n glory; 영광스러운
[yeonggwangseureoun] adj glorious
영구 [yeonggu] 영구적인
[yeonggujeogin] adj permanent;
영구히 [yeongguhi] adv permanently
영국 [yeongguk] n Britain, Great Britain,
UK, United Kingdom; 영국 사람

[yeongguk saram] n British; 영국
파운드 [yeongguk paundeu] n pound
sterling; 영국의 [yeonggugui] adj
British; 영국 국가번호는 어떻게
되나요? [yeongguk gukgabeonhoneun
eotteoke doenayo?] What is the
dialling code for the UK?
영리 [yeongni] 영리한 [yeongnihan] adj
clever
영사 [yeongsa] n consul; 영사관
[yeongsagwan] n consulate
영수증 [yeongsujeung] n receipt; 보험
처리를 위한 영수증이 필요해요
[boheom cheorireul wihan
yeongsujeungi pillyohaeyo] I need a
receipt for the insurance; 영수증이
필요해요 [yeongsujeungi piryohaeyo] I
need a receipt, please
영안 [yeongan] 영안실 [yeongansil] n
funeral parlour, morgue
영양 [yeongyang] n antelope; 영양소
[yeongyangso] n nutrition; 영양실조
[yeongyangsiljo] n malnutrition;
영양이 되는 [yeongyangi doeneun] adj
nutritious; 영양제 [yeongyangje] n
nutrient
영어 [yeongeo] n English (language);
영어 가이드 관광이 있어요? [yeongeo
gaideu gwangwangi isseoyo?] Is there
a guided tour in English?; 영어 하는 분
있으신가요? [yeongeo haneun bun
isseusingayo?] Does anyone speak
English?; 영어 하는 의사가 있나요?
[yeongeo haneun uisaga innayo?] Is
there a doctor who speaks English?;
영어 하는 가이드 있어요? [yeongeo
haneun gaideu isseoyo?] Is there a
guide who speaks English?; 영어로 된
소책자 있어요? [yeongeoro doen
sochaekja isseoyo?] Do you have a
leaflet in English?; 영어로 된 안내책
있어요? [yeongeoro doen annaechaek
isseoyo?] Do you have a guide book in
English?; 영어로 된 영화가 있나요?
[yeongeoro doen yeonghwaga
innayo?] Are there any films in English?;
영어하실 수 있으세요? [yeongeohasil
su isseuseyo?] Do you speak English?;

저는 영어 못해요 [jeoneun yeongeo motaeyo] I don't speak English; 저는 영어를 조금 할 수 있어요 [jeoneun yeongeoreul jogeum hal su isseoyo] I speak very little English

영업 [yeongeop] 영업 시간 [yeongeop sigan] npl opening hours; 영업하세요? [yeongeophaseyo?] Are you open?

영웅 [yeongung] n hero; 여자 영웅 [yeoja yeongung] n heroine

영원 [yeongwon] n eternity, newt; 영원한 [yeongwonhan] adj eternal; 영원히 [yeongwonhi] adv forever

영토 [yeongto] n territory

영향 [yeonghyang] n impact, influence ▷ npl repercussions; 영향을 미치다 [yeonghyangeul michida] v affect, influence

영혼 [yeonghon] n soul

영화 [yeonghwa] n film, movie; 영화 배우 [yeonghwa baeu] n film star; 영화관 [yeonghwagwan] n cinema; 공포 영화 [gongpo yeonghwa] n horror film; 어디에 가면 영화를 볼 수 있어요? [eodie gamyeon yeonghwareul bol su isseoyo?] Where can we go to see a film?; 어떤 영화를 상영하나요? [eotteon yeonghwareul sangyeonghanayo?] Which film is on at the cinema?; 영어로 된 영화가 있나요? [yeongeoro doen yeonghwaga innayo?] Are there any films in English?; 영화가 언제 시작해요? [yeonghwaga eonje sijakhaeyo?] When does the film start?

옆 [yeop]...의 옆에 [...ui yeope] prep next to; 옆으로 [yeopeuro] adv sideways; ...의 옆에 [...ui yeope] prep beside

예 [ye] excl yes ▷ n example, instance; 예를 들면 [yereul deulmyeon] abbr e.g.

예감 [yegam] n premonition

예견 [yegyeon] 예견하다 [yegyeonhada] v foresee

예금 [yegeum] n deposit

예매 [yemae] 오늘 밤 두 자리 예매하고 싶어요 [oneul bam du jari yemaehago sipeoyo] We'd like to reserve two seats for tonight; 표를 예매해 주시겠어요? [pyoreul yemaehae jusigesseoyo?] Can you book the tickets for us?

예멘 [yemen] n Yemen

예방 [yebang] n prevention; 예방조치 [yebangjochi] n precaution; 예방접종 [yebangjeopjong] n vaccination; 예방접종을 하다 [yebangjeopjongeul hada] v vaccinate; 예방하다 [yebanghada] v prevent

예배 [yebae] n worship, church service; 유대교 예배당은 어디에 있어요? [yudaegyo yebaedangeun eodie isseoyo?] Where is there a synagogue?

예배당 [yebaedang] n chapel

예보 [yebo] 일기예보 [ilgiyebo] n weather forecast; 일기예보에서 뭐래요? [ilgiyeboeseo mworaeyo?] What's the weather forecast?

예비 [yebi] 예비 부품 [yebi bupum] n spare part; 예비 바퀴 [yebi bakwi] (n) n spare wheel; 예비 타이어 [yebi taieo] n spare tyre

예쁘다 [yeppeuda] 예쁘게 [yeppeuge] adv prettily; 예쁜 [yeppeun] adj pretty

예산 [yesan] n budget

예수 [yesu] n Jesus

예술 [yesul] n art; 예술 학교 [yesul hakgyo] n art school; 예술적인 [yesuljeogin] adj artistic; 예술가 [yesulga] n artist

예약 [yeyak] n advance booking, booking, reservation; 예약되어 있는 [yeyakdoeeo inneun] adj reserved; 예약하다 [yeyakhada] v book, reserve; 예약 비용이 있어요? [yeyak biyongi isseoyo?] Is there a booking fee to pay?, Is there a booking fee?; 예약을 변경할 수 있을까요? [yeyageul byeongyeonghal su isseulkkayo?] Can I change my booking?; 예약을 취소하고 싶어요 [yeyageul chwisohago sipeoyo] I want to cancel my booking; 예약했어요 [yeyakhaesseoyo] I have a reservation; 일곱시 삼십분에 두 명 예약하고 싶어요 [ilgopsi samsipbune du myeong yeyakhago sipeoyo] I'd like to make a reservation for half past seven for two people; 저는 편지로 예약을 확인했어요 [jeoneun pyeonjiro yeyageul hwaginhaesseoyo] I confirmed my booking by letter; 좌석을 예약했어요 [jwaseogeul yeyakhaesseoyo] I have a seat reservation

예외 [yeoe] n exception; 예외적인 [yeoejeogin] adj exceptional

예절 [yejeol] 예절바른 [yejeolbareun] adj decent

예정 [yejeong] 예정보다 약간 늦고 있어요 [yejeongboda yakgan neutgo isseoyo] We are slightly behind schedule; 예정대로 진행되고 있어요 [yejeongdaero jinhaengdoego isseoyo] We are on schedule

예측 [yecheuk] n forecast; 예측 가능한 [yecheuk ganeunghan] adj predictable; 예측하다 [yecheukhada] v predict; 예측할 수 없는 [yecheukhal su eomneun] adj unpredictable

예행 [yehaeng] 예행 연습 [yehaeng yeonseup] n rehearsal

오늘 [oneul] adv today; 오늘밤 [oneulbam] adv tonight; 오늘 며칠이에요? [oneul myeochirieyo?] What is today's date?; 오늘 열어요? [oneul yeoreoyo?] Is it open today?; 오늘 밤에 추울까요? [oneul bame chuulkkayo?] Will it be cold tonight?

오다 [oda] v come; 돌아오다 [doraoda] vi go back; 나중에 다시 올까요? [najunge dasi olkkayo?] Shall I come back later?

오도 [odo] 오도하는 [odohaneun] adj misleading

오두막 [odumak] n hut

오디션 [odisyeon] n audition

오디오 [odio] n audio; 오디오 세트 [odio seteu] n music centre

오락 [orak] n pastime; 오락장 [orakjang] n amusement arcade

오래가다 [oraegada] v last

오레가노 [oraegano] n oregano

오렌지 [orenji] n orange; 오렌지 주스 [orenji juseu] n orange juice; 오렌지색의 [orenjisaegui] adj orange

오류 [oryu] n error

오르가즘 [oreugajeum] 오르가슴 [oreugaseum] n orgasm

오르간 [oreugan] n organ (music)

오르다 [oreuda] v mount

오른손 [oreunson] 오른손잡이의 [oreunsonjabiui] adj right-handed

오른쪽 [oreunjjok] 오른쪽 핸들 [oreunjjok haendeul] n right-hand drive; 오른쪽의 [oreunjjogui] adj right (not left), right-hand; 다음 사거리에서 오른쪽으로 가세요 [daeum sageorieseo oreunjjogeuro gaseyo] Go right at the next junction; 오른쪽으로 꺾으세요 [oreunjjogeuro kkeokkeuseyo] Turn right; 첫 번째 모퉁이에서 오른쪽으로 꺾으세요 [cheot beonjjae motungieseo oreunjjogeuro kkeokkeuseyo] Take the first turning on your right

오리 [ori] n duck

오리발 [oribal] npl flippers

오만 [oman] n Oman; 오만한 [omanhan] adj bossy

오믈렛 [omeullet] n omelette

오보에 [oboe] n oboe

오븐 [obeun] n oven; 오븐에 넣어도 되는 [obeune neoheodo doeneun] adj ovenproof; 오븐용 장갑 [obeunyong janggap] n oven glove

오세아니아 [oseania] n Oceania

오소리 [osori] n badger

오스트랄라시아 [oseuteurallasia] n Australasia

오스트리아 [oseuteuria] n Austria; 오스트리아 사람 [oseuteuria saram] n Austrian; 오스트리아의 [oseuteuriaui] adj Austrian

오식 [osik] n misprint

오아시스 [oasiseu] n oasis

오염 [oyeom] n pollution; 오염된 [oyeomdoen] adj polluted; 오염시키다 [oyeomsikida] v pollute

오이 [oi] n cucumber

오일 [oil] n oil; 오일 경고등이 꺼지지 않아요 [oil gyeonggodeungi kkeojiji anhayo] The oil warning light won't go off

오전 [ojeon] *abbr* a.m.

오존 [ojon] *n* ozone; 오존층 [ojoncheung] *n* ozone layer

오징어 [ojingeo] *n* squid

오토바이 [otobai] *n* motorbike, motorcycle; 오토바이를 타는 사람 [otobaireul taneun saram] *n* motorcyclist; 오토바이를 빌리고 싶어요 [otobaireul billigo sipeoyo] I want to hire a motorbike

오통통하다 [otongtonghada] 오동통한 [odongtonghan] *adj* chubby

오트밀 [oteumil] *n* oatmeal

오페라 [opera] *n* opera; 오늘 밤 무슨 오페라를 공연해요? [oneul bam museun operareul gongyeonhaeyo?] What's on tonight at the opera?

오페어 [opeeo] *n* au pair

오프사이드 [opeusaideu] 오프사이드의 [opeusaideuui] *adj* offside

오픈 [opeun] 오픈카 [opeunka] *n* convertible

오해 [ohae] *n* misunderstanding; 오해하다 [ohaehada] *v* misunderstand; 오해가 있었어요 [ohaega isseosseoyo] There's been a misunderstanding

오후 [ohu] *abbr* p.m. ▷ *n* afternoon; 내일 오후 [naeil ohu] tomorrow afternoon; 오후에 [ohue] in the afternoon

옥수수 [oksusu] *n* maize; 사탕옥수수 [satangoksusu] *n* sweetcorn

온건 [ongeon] *n* moderation; 온건한 [ongeonhan] *adj* moderate

온난 [onnan] *n* warmth; 지구 온난화 [jigu onnanhwa] *n* global warming

온도 [ondo] *n* temperature; 온도계 [ondogye] *n* thermometer; 자동 온도 조절기 [jadong ondo jojeolgi] *n* thermostat; 몇 도예요? [myeot doyeyo?] What is the temperature?

온두라스 [onduraseu] *n* Honduras

온라인 [ollain] 온라인으로 [ollaineuro] *adv* online; 온라인의 [ollainui] *adj* online

온수 [onsu] 온수가 안 나와요 [onsuga an nawayo] There is no hot water; 가격에 온수가 포함되나요? [gagyeoge onsuga pohamdoenayo?] Is hot water included in the price?

온수기 [onsugi] 온수기는 어떻게 작동하나요? [onsugineun eotteoke jakdonghanayo?] How does the water heater work?

온스 [onseu] *n* ounce

온실 [onsil] *n* conservatory, greenhouse

온천 [oncheon] *n* spa

온화 [onhwa] 온화하게 [onhwahage] *adv* gently; 온화한 [onhwahan] *adj* gentle

올가미 [olgami] *n* trap

올라가다 [ollagada] *v* go up

올리다 [ollida] *v* raise ▷ *vt* lift

올리브 [ollibeu] *n* olive; 올리브 나무 [ollibeu namu] *n* olive tree; 올리브 기름 [ollibeu gireum] *n* olive oil

올빼미 [olppaemi] *n* owl

올챙이 [olchaengi] *n* tadpole

옮기다 [ormgida] *v* remove; 차를 옮겨 주시겠어요? [chareul ormgyeo jusigesseoyo?] Could you move your car, please?

옳다 [orta] 옳은 [oreun] *adj* correct, right (*correct*); 올바르게 [olbareuge] *adv* rightly

옷 [ot] *npl* clothes; 비옷 [biot] *n* raincoat; 옷을 벗다 [oseul beotda] *v* undress; 옷을 입다 [oseul ipda] *vi* dress; 옷을 입은 [oseul ibeun] *adj* dressed; 옷입다 [osipda] *vt* wear; 옷걸이 [otgeori] *n* coathanger, hanger; 풀오버 [purobeo] *n* pullover; 옷 넣는 사물함은 어디있어요? [ot neonneun samulhameun eodiisseoyo?] Where are the clothes lockers?; 옷을 건조시킬 곳이 있나요? [oseul geonjosikil gosi innayo?] Is there somewhere to dry clothes?; 옷이 축축해요 [osi chukchukhaeyo] My clothes are damp

옷장 [otjang] *n* wardrobe

와인 [wain] *n* wine; 식탁용 와인 [siktagyong wain] *n* table wine; 와인 리스트 [wain riseuteu] *n* wine list; 와인잔 [wainjan] *n* wineglass; 포트와인 [poteuwain] *n* port (*wine*); 하우스 와인 [hauseu wain] *n* house wine; 레드 와인 한 병 [redeu wain han byeong] a bottle of red wine; 레드 와인 한 카라프 [redeu wain han karapeu] a carafe of red wine; 와인 목록 주세요 [wain mongnok juseyo] The wine list, please; 와인이 찬가요? [waini changayo?] Is the wine chilled?; 이 얼룩은 와인이에요 [i eollugeun wainieyo] This stain is wine; 이 와인이 차지 않아요 [i waini chaji anhayo] This wine is not chilled; 저는 와인을 절대 마시지 않아요 [jeoneun waineul jeoldae masiji anhayo] I never drink wine; 좋은 로제 와인을 추천해 주시겠어요? [joheun roje waineul chucheonhae jusigesseoyo?] Can you recommend a good rosé wine?; 좋은 레드 와인을 추천해 주시겠어요? [joheun redeu waineul chucheonhae jusigesseoyo?] Can you recommend a good red wine?; 좋은 와인을 추천해 주시겠어요? [joheun waineul chucheonhae jusigesseoyo?] Can you recommend a good wine?; 좋은 화이트 와인을 추천해 주시겠어요? [joheun hwaiteu waineul chucheonhae jusigesseoyo?] Can you recommend a good white wine?; 하우스 와인 한 병 [hauseu wain han byeong] a bottle of the house wine; 하우스 와인 한 카라프 [hauseu wain han karapeu] a carafe of the house wine; 화이트 와인 한 병 [hwaiteu wain han byeong] a bottle of white wine; 화이트 와인 한 카라프 [hwaiteu wain han karapeu] a carafe of white wine

와플 [wapeul] n waffle

완고 [wango] 완고한 [wangohan] adj obstinate; 완고한 [wangohan] adj stubborn

완벽 [wanbyeok] n perfection; 완벽하게 [wanbyeokhage] adv perfectly; 완벽한 [wanbyeokhan] adj perfect

완전 [wanjeon] n perfection, wholeness; 불완전한 [burwanjeonhan] adj incomplete; 완전한 [wanjeonhan] adj complete, sheer; 완전히 [wanjeonhi] adv altogether, completely, dead, entirely, fully; 완전히 [wanjeonhi] adv totally; 완전 채식 요리 있나요? [wanjeon chaesik yori innayo?] Do you have any vegan dishes?; 완전 채식주의자가 먹어도 될까요? [wanjeon chaesikjuuijaga meogeodo doelkkayo?] Is this suitable for vegans?

완하 [wanha] 완하제 [wanhaje] n laxative

왈츠 [walcheu] n waltz; 왈츠를 추다 [walcheureul chuda] v waltz

왕 [wang] n king

왕관 [wanggwan] n crown

왕국 [wangguk] n kingdom

왕복 [wangbok] 당일 왕복표 [dangil wangbokpyo] n day return; 왕복여행 [wangbogyeohaeng] n round trip; 왕복표 [wangbokpyo] n return ticket; 근거리 왕복 [geungeori wangbok] n shuttle; 왕복표는 얼마예요? [wangbokpyoneun eolmayeyo?] How much is a return ticket?;...까지 왕복 두 장이요 [...kkaji wangbok du jangiyo] two return tickets to...;...까지 일등석 왕복이요 [...kkaji ildeungseok wangbogiyo] a first-class return to...

왕자 [wangja] n prince

왕족 [wangjok] 왕족의 [wangjogui] adj royal

왕좌 [wangjwa] n throne

왜 [wae] adv why

왜건 [waegeon] n wagon; 스테이션 왜건 [seuteisyeon waegeon] n estate car

외 [oe] 옥외에서 [ogoeeseo] adv out-of-doors, outdoors; 옥외의 [ogoeui] adj outdoor; 외부 [oebu] n outside; 외부의 [oebuui] adj outside

외과 [oegwa] 미용 성형외과 [miyong seonghyeongoegwa] n cosmetic surgery; 성형외과 [seonghyeongoegwa] n plastic surgery; 외과의사 [oegwauisa] n surgeon

외교 [oegyo] 외교의 [oegyoui] adj diplomatic; 외교관 [oegyogwan] n diplomat

외국 [oeguk] 외국의 [oegugui] adj foreign; 외국인 [oegugin] n alien,

외롭다 [oeropda] | 122

foreigner
외롭다 [oeropda] **외로운** [oeroun] *adj* lonesome
외부 [oebu] **외부의** [oebuui] *adj* exterior, external
외설 [oeseol] **외설적인** [oeseoljeogin] *adj* pornographic
외출 [oechul] **외출하다** [oechulhada] *v* go out
외침 [oechim] *n* call
외투 [oetu] *n* overcoat
외풍 [oepung] *n* draught
왼 [oen] **왼쪽의** [oenjjogui] *adj* left
왼손 [oenson] **왼손잡이의** [oensonjabiui] *adj* left-handed
왼쪽 [oenjjok] **왼쪽 핸들** [oenjjok haendeul] *n* left-hand drive; **왼쪽으로** [oenjjogeuro] *adv* left; **왼쪽의** [oenjjogui] *adj* left-hand; **다음 사거리에서 왼쪽으로 가세요** [daeum sageorieseo oenjjogeuro gaseyo] Go left at the next junction; **두 번째 모퉁이에서 왼쪽으로 꺾으세요** [du beonjjae motungieseo oenjjogeuro kkeokkeuseyo] Take the second turning on your left; **왼쪽으로 꺾으세요** [oenjjogeuro kkeokkeuseyo] Turn left
왼쪽 [oenjjuk] **왼쪽** [oenjjok] *n* left
요가 [yoga] *n* yoga
요구 [yogu] *n* claim, demand; **요구하다** [yoguhada] *v* call for, claim, demand; **지나치게 요구하는** [jinachige yoguhaneun] *adj* demanding
요구르트 [yogureuteu] *n* yoghurt
요금 [yogeum] *n* charge (price), fee; **주차요금 징수기** [juchayogeum jingsugi] *n* parking meter; **추가요금** [chugayogeum] *n* surcharge; **서비스 요금** [seobiseu yogeum] *n* service charge; **승차 요금** [seungcha yogeum] *n* fare; **우편요금** [upyeonyogeum] *n* postage; **전화요금 고지서** [jeonhwayogeum gojiseo] *n* phone bill; **주행거리에 따른 요금이 있어요?** [juhaenggeorie ttareun yogeumi isseoyo?] Is there a mileage charge?; **서비스 요금이 있어요?** [seobiseu

yogeumi isseoyo?] Is there a charge for the service?
요금소 [yogeumso] *n* toll; **이 고속도로에는 요금소가 있어요?** [i gosokdoroeneun yogeumsoga isseoyo?] Is there a toll on this motorway?
요람 [yoram] *n* cradle
요르단 [yoreudan] *n* Jordan; **요르단 사람** [yoreudan saram] *n* Jordanian; **요르단의** [yoreudanui] *adj* Jordanian
요리 [yori] *n* cooking; **주 요리** [ju yori] *n* main course; **요리 기구** [yori gigu] *n* cooker; **요리법** [yoribeop] *n* cookery, recipe; **요리책** [yorichaek] *n* cookbook, cookery book; **요리사** [yorisa] *n* chef, cook; **요리하다** [yorihada] *v* cook; **전채요리** [jeonchaeyori] *n* starter; **집에 사가지고 가는 요리** [jibe sagajigo ganeun yori] *n* takeaway
요법 [yobeop] *n* therapy; **물리요법** [mulliyobeop] *n* physiotherapy; **동종 요법** [dongjong yobeop] *n* homeopathy; **동종 요법의** [dongjong yobeobui] *adj* homeopathic; **심리요법** [simniyobeop] *n* psychotherapy; **식이 요법** [sigi yobeop] *n* diet
요새 [yosae] *n* fort
요소 [yoso] *n* element
요약 [yoyak] *n* summary; **요약하다** [yoyakhada] *v* sum up, summarize
요일 [yoil] **목요일** [mogyoil] *n* Thursday; **성 금요일** [seong geumyoil] *n* Good Friday; **수요일** [suyoil] *n* Wednesday; **오순절의 화요일** [osunjeorui hwayoil] *n* Shrove Tuesday; **월요일** [wollyoil] *n* Monday; **일요일** [illyoil] *n* Sunday; **금요일** [geumyoil] *n* Friday; **토요일** [toyoil] *n* Saturday; **화요일** [hwayoil] *n* Tuesday; **오늘 무슨 요일이에요?** [oneul museun yoirieyo?] What day is it today?; **월요일부터 수요일까지 묵고 싶어요** [woryoilbuteo suyoilkkaji mukgo sipeoyo] I want to stay from Monday till Wednesday
요점 [yojeom] *n* point
요정 [yojeong] *n* fairy

요즘 [yojeum] 요즈음 [yojeueum] *adv* lately, nowadays

요청 [yocheong] *n* request; 요청하다 [yocheonghada] *v* request; 요청하다 [yocheonghada] *v* ask for

요트 [yoteu] *n* yacht

욕 [yok] 욕설 [yokseor] *n* swearword; 욕설을 퍼붓는 [yokseoreul peobutneun] *adj* abusive

욕망 [yongmang] *n* desire

욕실 [yoksil] *n* bathroom; 방에 개인 욕실이 있어요? [bange gaein yoksiri isseoyo?] Does the room have a private bathroom?; 욕실 물이 넘쳤어요 [yoksil muri neomchyeosseoyo] The bathroom is flooded; 욕실에 장애인용 손잡이가 있어요? [yoksire jangaeinyong sonjabiga isseoyo?] Are there support railings in the bathroom?

욕심 [yoksim] *n* greed; 욕심 많은 [yoksim manheun] *adj* greedy

욕조 [yokjo] *n* bath, bathtub

용 [yong] *n* dragon

용감 [yonggam] 용감한 [yonggamhan] *adj* brave, courageous

용구 [yonggu] *n* gear (*equipment*); 용구함 [yongguham] *n* gear box

용기 [yonggi] *n* bravery, container, courage, nerve (*boldness*); 용기를 북돋우다 [yonggireul bukdoduda] *v* encourage; 용기를 잃게 하다 [yonggireul irke hada] *v* discourage

용납 [yongnap] 용납할 수 없는 [yongnaphal su eomneun] *adj* unacceptable

용돈 [yongdon] *n* pocket money

용서 [yongseo] *n* pardon; 용서하다 [yongseohada] *v* forgive; 용서하다 [yongseohada] *v* spare

용수철 [yongsucheol] *n* spring (*coil*)

용암 [yongam] *n* lava

용어 [yongeo] *n* term (*description*)

용의 [yongui] 용의자 [yonguija] *n* suspect

용제 [yongje] *n* solvent

용지 [yongji] 메모 용지 [memo yongji] *n* scrap paper; 필기용지 [pilgiyongji] *n* writing paper

우간다 [uganda] *n* Uganda; 우간다 사람 [uganda saram] *n* Ugandan; 우간다의 [ugandaui] *adj* Ugandan

우대 [udae] 경로 할인이 있어요? [gyeongno harini isseoyo?] Are there any reductions for senior citizens?

우라늄 [uranyum] *n* uranium

우루과이 [urugwai] *n* Uruguay; 우루과이 사람 [urugwai saram] *n* Uruguayan; 우루과이의 [urugwaiui] *adj* Uruguayan

우리 [uri] *pron* we; 우리 자신 [uri jasin] *pron* ourselves; 우리 것 [uri geot] *pron* ours; 우리를 [urireul] *pron* us; 우리의 [uriui] *adj* our

우림 [urim] 열대 우림 [yeoldae urim] *n* rainforest

우물 [umul] *n* well

우박 [ubak] *n* hail; 우박이 내리다 [ubagi naerida] *v* hail

우비 [ubi] 레인코트 [reinkoteu] *abbr* mac

우산 [usan] *n* umbrella

우선 [useon] 우선순위 [useonsunwi] *n* priority; 통행우선권 [tonghaenguseongwon] *n* right of way

우선권 [useongwon] 당신에게 통행 우선권이 없었어요 [dangsinege tonghaeng useongwoni eopseosseoyo] It wasn't your right of way

우송 [usong] 우송하다 [usonghada] *v* mail; 우송하다 [usonghada] *v* post

우수 [usu] 우수한 [usuhan] *adj* excellent, superior

우습다 [useupda] 우스운 [useuun] *adj* funny

우아 [ua] 우아한 [uahan] *adj* elegant, graceful

우연 [uyeon] *n* coincidence; 우연의 [uyeonui] *adj* accidental; 우연하게 [uyeonhage] *adv* casually; 우연한 [uyeonhan] *adj* casual; 우연히 [uyeonhi] *adv* accidentally, by chance, by accident; 우연히 만나다 [uyeonhi mannada] *v* bump into

우울 [uul] *n* depression; 우울한 [uulhan] *adj* gloomy; 항우울제 [hanguuljje] *n* antidepressant

우유 [uyu] *n* milk; 밀크 초콜릿 [milkeu chokollit] *n* milk chocolate; 밀크셰이크 [milkeusyeikeu] *n* milkshake; 반탈지유 [bantaljiyu] *n* semi-skimmed milk; 유아용 우유 [yuayong uyu] *n* baby milk; 유제품 [yujepum] *npl* dairy produce, dairy products; 유제품 회사 [yujepum hoesa] *n* dairy; 초고온살균우유 [chogoonsalgyunuyu] *n* UHT milk; 탈지유 [taljiyu] *n* skimmed milk; 미살균 우유로 만든 것인가요? [misalgyun uyuro mandeun geosingayo?] Is it made with unpasteurised milk?; 생우유 있어요? [saenguyu isseoyo?] Have you got real milk?; 우유 마시세요? [uyu masiseyo?] Do you drink milk?; 우유는 따로 주세요 [uyuneun ttaro juseyo] with the milk separate

우익 [uik] 우익의 [uigui] *adj* right-wing

우정 [ujeong] *n* friendship

우주 [uju] *n* universe; 우주비행사 [ujubihaengsa] *n* astronaut; 우주선 [ujuseon] *n* spacecraft

우즈베키스탄 [ujuebekiseutan] *n* Uzbekistan

우쭐하다 [ujjulhada] 우쭐해진 [ujjulhaejin] *adj* flattered

우체 [uche] 여자 우편집배원 [yeoja upyeonjipbaewon] *n* postwoman; 우체국 [ucheguk] *n* post office; 우체통 [uchetong] *n* mailbox, postbox; 우편집배원 [upyeonjipbaewon] *n* postman

우체국 [ucheguk] 우체국은 언제 열어요? [uchegugeun eonje yeoreoyo?] When does the post office open?

우크라이나 [ukeuraina] *n* Ukraine; 우크라이나 사람 [ukeuraina saram] *n* Ukrainian (*person*); 우크라이나어 [ukeurainaeo] *n* Ukrainian (*language*); 우크라이나의 [ukeurainaui] *adj* Ukrainian

우편 [upyeon] *n* post (*mail*); 등기우편 [deunggiupyeon] *n* recorded delivery; 우편물 [upyeonmul] *n* mail; 우편물 발송 주소 목록 [upyeonmul balsong juso mongnok] *n* mailing list; 우편번호 [upyeonbeonho] *n* postcode; 우편엽서 [upyeonyeopseo] *n* postcard; 우편요금 [upyeonyogeum] *n* postage; 우편환 [upyeonhwan] *n* postal order; 항공우편 [hanggongupyeon] *n* airmail; 등기 우편은 도착하는 데 얼마나 걸려요? [deunggi upyeoneun dochakhaneun de eolmana geollyeoyo?] How long will it take by registered post?; 일반 우편은 도착하는 데 얼마나 걸려요? [ilban upyeoneun dochakhaneun de eolmana geollyeoyo?] How long will it take by normal post?; 특급 우편은 도착하는 데 얼마나 걸려요? [teukgeup upyeoneun dochakhaneun de eolmana geollyeoyo?] How long will it take by priority post?

우편물 [upyeonmul] 저한테 우편물 온 것 있어요? [jeohante upyeonmul on geot isseoyo?] Is there any mail for me?

우표 [upyo] *n* stamp; ...로 엽서를 네 장 보낼 건데 우표 좀 주세요 [...ro yeopseoreul ne jang bonael geonde upyo jom juseyo] Can I have stamps for four postcards to...; 어디에서 우표를 살 수 있나요? [eodieseo upyoreul sal su innayo?] Where can I buy stamps?; 우표 파세요? [upyo paseyo?] Do you sell stamps?; 가장 가까운 우표 가게는 어디에 있어요? [gajang gakkaun upyo gageneun eodie isseoyo?] Where is the nearest shop which sells stamps?

우회 [uhoe] *n* detour; 우회로 [uhoero] *n* bypass

우회로 [uhoero] 우회로가 있어요? [uhoeroga isseoyo?] Is there a diversion?

운 [un] 운좋은 [unjoheun] *adj* lucky

운동 [undong] *n* exercise, movement; 운동 선수 [undong seonsu] *n* athlete; 운동복 [undongbok] *n* sportswear, tracksuit; 운동장 [undongjang] *n* playground; 운동경기 [undonggyeonggi] *npl* athletics; 운동화 [undonghwa] *npl* sneakers

운동화 [undonghwa] *npl* trainers

운명 [unmyeong] n destiny, fate
운반 [unban] 운반하다 [unbanhada] vt carry
운석 [unseok] n meteorite
운송 [unsong] n transit, transport; 운송하다 [unsonghada] v transport
운영 [unyeong] 그는 호텔을 운영해요 [geuneun hotereul unyeonghaeyo] He runs the hotel
운전 [unjeon] n driving; 운전 면허 시험 [unjeon myeonheo siheom] n driving test; 운전 교습 [unjeon gyoseup] n driving lesson; 운전 강사 [unjeon gangsa] n driving instructor; 운전 기사 [unjeon gisa] n chauffeur; 운전자 [unjeonja] n operator; 운전하다 [unjeonhada] v drive; 음주운전 [eumjuunjeon] n drink-driving; 임시면허 운전자 [imsimyeonheo unjeonja] n learner driver; 자동차 운전자 [jadongcha unjeonja] n motorist; 택시 운전사 [taeksi unjeonsa] n taxi driver; 과속 운전하고 있었어요 [gwasok unjeonhago isseosseoyo] You were driving too fast
운전면허증 [unjeonmyeonheojeung] n driving licence; 제 운전 면허증 번호는....에요 [je unjeon myeonheojeung beonhoneun....eyo] My driving licence number is...; 제 운전 면허증이에요 [je unjeon myeonheojeungieyo] Here is my driving licence; 저는 운전면허증이 없어요 [jeoneun unjeonmyeonheojeungi eopseoyo] I don't have my driving licence on me
운전사 [unjeonsa] 트럭 운전사 [teureok unjeonsa] n lorry driver, truck driver
운전자 [unjeonja] n driver
운하 [unha] n canal
울다 [ulda] v cry, weep; 빽빽 울다 [ppaekppaek ulda] v squeak
울리다 [ullida] v ring
울음 [ureum] 울음 소리 [ureum sori] n cry
울타리 [ultari] n fence; 생울타리 [saengultari] n hedge
울퉁불퉁 [ultungbultung] 울퉁불퉁한 [ultungbultunghan] adj bumpy
움직이다 [umjigida] vi move; 뒤로 이동하다 [dwiro idonghada] v move back; 앞으로 이동하다 [apeuro idonghada] v move forward; 움직이는 [umjigineun] adj moving; 흔들흔들 움직이다 [heundeulheundeul umjigida] vi swing; 그 남자를 움직이지 마세요 [geu namjareul umjigiji maseyo] Don't move him; 그 여자는 움직일 수 없어요 [geu yeojaneun umjigil su eopseoyo] She can't move
움켜잡다 [umkyeojapda] v grab
웃기다 [utgida] 웃기는 [utgineun] adj ridiculous
웃다 [utda] v laugh; 비웃다 [biutda] v scoff; 낄낄웃다 [kkilkkirutda] v giggle; 싱긋 웃다 [singgeut utda] v grin; 킬킬 웃다 [kilkil utda] v snigger
웃음 [useum] n laugh, laughter; 싱긋 웃음 [singgeut useum] n grin; 웃음 기호 [useum giho] n smiley
웅대 [ungdae] 웅대한 [ungdaehan] adj grand
웅덩이 [ungdeongi] n pool (water); 물웅덩이 [murungdeongi] n puddle
웅크리다 [ungkeurida] v crouch down
워키토키 [wokitoki] n walkie-talkie
원 [won] n circle, official; 동물원 [dongmurwon] n zoo; 반원 [banwon] n semicircle; 원 그래프 [won geuraepeu] n pie chart; 원뿔 [wonppul] n cone; 원하다 [wonhada] v want; 원형 [wonhyeong] n round (circle); 원형의 [wonhyeongui] adj circular; 집표원 [jippyowon] n ticket collector; 검표원 [geompyowon] n ticket inspector; 포도원 [podowon] n vineyard
원격 [wongyeok] 원격통신 [wongyeoktongsin] npl telecommunications
원고 [wongo] n copy (written text), manuscript
원기 [wongi] 원기 왕성한 [wongi wangseonghan] adj athletic
원래 [wollae] 원래는 [wollaeneun] adv originally; 원래대로의 [wollaedaeroui]

adj intact

원상태 [wonsangtae] 원상태로 돌리다
[wonsangtaero dollida] *v* undo

원수 [wonsu] *n* enemy

원숭이 [wonsungi] *n* monkey

원시 [wonsi] 원시적인 [wonsijeogin] *adj*
primitive; 제 눈은 원시입니다 [je
nuneun wonsiimnida] I'm long-sighted

원어 [woneo] 원어민 [woneomin] *n*
native speaker

원예 [wonye] 원예점 [wonyejeom] *n*
garden centre

원인 [wonin] *n* cause *(ideals)*, cause
(reason);...때문에 [...ttaemune] *prep*
due to; 원인이 되다 [wonini doeda] *v*
cause

원자 [wonja] *n* atom; 원자로 [wonjaro]
n reactor; 원자의 [wonjaui] *adj*
atomic; 원자폭탄 [wonjapoktan] *n*
atom bomb

원정 [wonjeong] 원정 경기 [wonjeong
gyeonggi] *n* away match

원조 [wonjo] *n* aid

원칙 [wonchik] *n* principle

원통 [wontong] *n* cylinder

원한 [wonhan] *n* grudge

월 [wol] *n* month; 1월 [irwol] *n* January;
10월 [sirwol] *n* October; 11월 [sibilwol]
n November; 12월 [shibiwol] *n*
December; 2월 [iwol] *n* February; 3월
[samwol] *n* March; 4월 [sawol] *n* April; 5
월 [owol] *n* May; 6월 [yuwol] *n* June; 7월
[chirwol] *n* July; 8월 [parwol] *n* August; 9
월 [guwol] *n* September

월계 [wolgye] 월계수 잎 [wolgyesu ip] *n*
bay leaf

월급 [wolgeup] *n* salary

월요일 [wollyoil] 월요일에 [woryoire] on
Monday; 유월 십오일 월요일이에요
[yuwol siboil woryoirieyo] It's Monday
the fifteenth of June

웨딩 [weding] 웨딩드레스
[wedingdeureseu] *n* wedding dress

웨이터 [weiteo] *n* waiter

웨이트리스 [weiteuriseu] *n* waitress

웨이퍼 [weipeo] *n* wafer

웨일스 [weilseu] *n* Wales; 웨일스 사람
[weilseu saram] *n* Welsh; 웨일스의

[weilseuui] *adj* Welsh

웹 [wep] 웹 브라우저 [wep beuraujeo] *n*
web browser; 웹 주소 [wep juso] *n*
web address; 웹마스터
[wemmaseuteo] *n* webmaster; 웹캠
[wepkaem] *n* webcam; 웹사이트
[wepsaiteu] *n* website; 웹진 [wepjin] *n*
webzine

웹사이트 [wepsaiteu] 웹사이트 주소는...
이에요 [wepsaiteu jusoneun...ieyo] The
website address is...

위 [wi] *n* stomach;... 위에 [... wie] *prep*
over;...의 위에 [...ui wie] *prep* on;...보다
위에 [...boda wie] *prep* above; 맨 위
[maen wi] *n* top; 맨 위의 [maen wiui]
adj top; 위로 [wiro] *adv* up; 위를
향하여 [wireul hyanghayeo] *adv* uphill;
위쪽으로 [wijjogeuro] *adv* upwards;
위에 [wie] *adv* on; 위의 [wiui] *adj* over;
위의 [wiui] *adj* upper; 위층으로
[wicheungeuro] *adv* upstairs; 위통
[witong] *n* stomachache

위급 [wigeup] 위급신호 [wigeupsinho] *n*
SOS

위기 [wigi] *n* crisis

위대 [widae] 위대한 [widaehan] *adj*
great

위도 [wido] *n* latitude

위반 [wiban] *n* offence; 주차위반 딱지
[juchawiban ttakji] *n* parking ticket;
위반하다 [wibanhada] *v* offend

위생 [wisaeng] 위생학 [wisaenghak] *n*
hygiene

위성 [wiseong] *n* satellite; 위성방송수신
접시 안테나 [wiseongbangsongsusin
jeopsi antena] *n* satellite dish;
위성항법 [wiseonghangbeop] *n* sat
nav; 위성항법장치
[wiseonghangbeopjangchi] *abbr* GPS

위스키 [wiseuki] *n* whisky; 몰트 위스키
[molteu wiseuki] *n* malt whisky;
위스키 주세요 [wiseuki juseyo] I'll have
a whisky; 위스키 앤 소다요 [wiseuki
aen sodayo] a whisky and soda

위원 [wiwon] *n* commissioner; 실행위원
[silhaengwiwon] *n* executive

위원회 [wiwonhoe] *n* board *(meeting)*,
committee

위임 [wiim] 위임하다 [wiimhada] v delegate

위장 [wijang] 위장하다 [wijanghada] v disguise

위조 [wijo] n forgery; 위조품 [wijopum] n fake

위증 [wijeung] 위증죄 [wijeungjoe] n perjury

위치 [wichi] n location, position; 위치하다 [wichihada] v rank; 위치한 [wichihan] adj situated; 여기 위치는... 이에(예)요 [yeogi wichineun...ie(ye)yo] My location is...

위하다 [wihada] ...을 위하여 [...eul wihayeo] prep for

위험 [wiheom] n danger, risk; 위험 경고등 [wiheom gyeonggodeung] npl hazard warning lights; 위험에 빠뜨리다 [wiheome ppatteurida] v endanger; 위험을 무릅쓰다 [wiheomeul mureupsseuda] v risk; 위험한 [wiheomhan] adj dangerous, risky; 눈사태 위험이 있어요? [nunsatae wiheomi isseoyo?] Is there a danger of avalanches?

위협 [wihyeop] n threat; 위협적인 [wihyeopjeogin] adj threatening; 위협하다 [wihyeophada] v intimidate, threaten

윈드서핑 [windeuseoping] 윈드서핑을 하고 싶어요 [windeuseopingeul hago sipeoyo] I'd like to go wind-surfing

윙윙 [wingwing] 윙윙거리다 [wingwinggeorida] v hum

윙크 [wingkeu] 윙크하다 [wingkeuhada] v wink

유감 [yugam] n regret; 유감스럽게도 [yugamseureopgedo] adv unfortunately

유괴 [yugoe] 유괴하다 [yugoehada] v abduct, kidnap

유권자 [yugwonja] n electorate

유급 [yugeup] 유급인 [yugeubin] adj paid

유기 [yugi] 유기의 [yugiui] adj organic; 유기체 [yugiche] n organism

유능 [yuneung] 유능한 [yuneunghan] adj competent

유대교 [yudaegyo] 유대교 예배당은 어디에 있어요? [yudaegyo yebaedangeun eodie isseoyo?] Where is there a synagogue?; 유대교도가 먹는 요리 있어요? [yudaegyodoga meongneun yori isseoyo?] Do you have kosher dishes?

유도 [yudo] n judo

유독 [yudok] 유독한 [yudokhan] adj toxic

유량 [yuryang] 유량계 [yuryanggye] n dipstick

유럽 [yureop] n Europe; 유럽 사람 [yureop saram] n European; 유럽연합 [yureobyeonhap] n European Union, EU; 유럽의 [yureobui] adj European

유령 [yuryeong] n ghost; 유령이 나오는 [yuryeongi naoneun] adj haunted

유례 [yurye] 유례없는 [yuryeeomneun] adj unprecedented

유로 [yuro] n euro

유리 [yuri] n glass, glass (vessel); 섬유 유리 [seomyu yuri] n fibreglass; 스테인드 글라스 [seuteindeu geullaseu] n stained glass; 앞유리 [apyuri] n windscreen; 이중 유리 [ijung yuri] n double glazing; 창유리 [changyuri] n window pane; 창유리 닦개 [changyuri dakkgae] n windscreen wiper

유망 [yumang] 전도 유망한 [jeondo yumanghan] adj promising

유머 [yumeo] n humour; 유머가 풍부한 [yumeoga pungbuhan] adj humorous; 유머감각 [yumeogamgak] n sense of humour

유명 [yumyeong] 유명 인사 [yumyeong insa] n celebrity; 유명한 [yumyeonghan] adj famous, prestigious, renowned; 유명한 [yumyeonghan] adj well-known

유모차 [yumocha] n pram, pushchair

유별 [yubyeol] 유별난 [yubyeollan] adj unusual

유사 [yusa] n resemblance

유산 [yusan] n abortion, heritage, miscarriage

유서 [yuseo] n will (document)

유선 [yuseon] n cable; 유선 텔레비전 [yuseon tellebijeon] n cable television

유세 [yuse] 선거유세하다 [seongeoyusehada] v canvass

유스호스텔 [yuseuhoseutel] 근처에 유스호스텔이 있어요? [geuncheoe yuseuhoseuteri isseoyo?] Is there a youth hostel nearby?

유아 [yua] n infant; 유아용 수건 [yuayong sugeon] n baby wipe; 유아용 우유 [yuayong uyu] n baby milk; 유아용 변기 있어요? [yuayong byeongi isseoyo?] Do you have a potty?

유연 [yuyeon] 유연제 있어요? [yuyeonje isseoyo?] Do you have softener?

유용 [yuyong] 유용한 [yuyonghan] adj helpful, useful

유원 [yuwon] 유원지 [yuwonji] n funfair

유월 [yuwol] n June; 유월 십오일 월요일이에요 [yuwol siboil woryoirieyo] It's Monday the fifteenth of June

유월절 [yuwoljeol] n Passover

유일 [yuil] 유일한 [yuilhan] adj only

유전 [yujeon] 유전성의 [yujeonseongui] adj hereditary; 유전의 [yujeonui] adj genetic; 유전학 [yujeonhak] n genetics

유전자 [yujeonja] n gene; 유전자 변형의 [yujeonja byeonhyeongui] abbr GM, genetically-modified

유정 [yujeong] 유정의 굴착장치 [yujeongui gulchakjangchi] n oil rig

유제품 [yujepum] 유제품이 들어가지 않은 요리 있어요? [yujepumi deureogaji anheun yori isseoyo?] Do you have dairy-free dishes?

유죄 [yujoe] n guilt; 유죄를 입증하다 [yujoereul ipjeunghada] v convict; 유죄의 [yujoeui] adj guilty

유지 [yuji] 유지보수 [yujibosu] n maintenance; 유지하다 [yujihada] v keep up, keep up with, maintain; 유지하다 [yujihada] v keep; 얼마나 오래 유지되나요? [eolmana orae yujidoenayo?] How long will it keep?

유창 [yuchang] 유창한 [yuchanghan] adj fluent

유치 [yuchi] 유치한 [yuchihan] adj childish

유치원 [yuchiwon] n infant school, nursery school

유쾌 [yukwae] 유쾌한 [yukwaehan] adj pleasant

유태교 [yutaegyo] 유태교 예배당 [yutaegyo yebaedang] n synagogue

유태인 [yutaein] n Jew; 유태인의 [yutaeinui] adj Jewish; 유태교 규칙에 따라 처리된 [yutaegyo gyuchige ttara cheoridoen] adj kosher

유통 [yutong] 유통만기일 [yutongmangiil] n sell-by date

유해 [yuhae] 유해한 [yuhaehan] adj harmful, poisonous

유행 [yuhaeng] n fashion; 유행에 뒤떨어진 [yuhaenge dwitteoreojin] adj unfashionable; 유행을 좇는 [yuhaengeul jotneun] adj trendy; 유행의 [yuhaengui] adj fashionable

유행병 [yuhaengbyeong] n epidemic

유형 [yuhyeong] n type

유혹 [yuhok] n temptation; 유혹하는 [yuhokhaneun] adj tempting; 유혹하다 [yuhokhada] v tempt

육 [yuk, yeoseot] number six

육군 [yukgun] 육군 대령 [yukgun daeryeong] n colonel

육두구 [yukdugu] n nutmeg

육수 [yuksu] n gravy, stock; 생선 육수로 요리된 것인가요? [saengseon yuksuro yoridoen geosingayo?] Is this cooked in fish stock?; 육수로 요리된 것인가요? [yuksuro yoridoen geosingayo?] Is this cooked in meat stock?

육십 [yuksip, yesun] number sixty

육아 [yuga] n childcare; 아버지의 육아 휴가 [abeojiui yuga hyuga] n paternity leave; 육아실 [yugasil] n nursery

육필 [yukpil] n handwriting

윤리 [yulli] npl morals; 윤리적인 [yullijeogin] adj ethical

융자 [yungja] 주택담보 융자 [jutaekdambo yungja] n mortgage; 주택을 담보로 융자를 받다 [jutaegeul damboro yungjareul batda] v mortgage

으깨다 [eukkaeda] v crush

으로 [euro] ...으로 [...euro] (방향) prep to

으르렁 [eureureong] 으르렁거리다
[eureureonggeorida] v snarl

윽 [euk] excl ugh

은 [eun] n silver

은박 [eunbak] 은박지 [eunbakji] n tinfoil

은행 [eunhaeng] n bank (finance); 상업
은행 [sangeop eunhaeng] n merchant
bank; 은행 수수료 [eunhaeng susuryo]
npl bank charges; 은행 계좌 통지서
[eunhaeng gyejwa tongjiseo] n bank
statement; 은행잔고 [eunhaengjango]
n bank balance; 은행계좌
[eunhaenggyejwa] n account (in bank),
bank account; 은행가 [eunhaengga] n
banker; 여기에 은행이 있나요? [yeogie
eunhaengi innayo?] Is there a bank
here?; ...에 있는 제 거래 은행에서 돈을
이체하고 싶어요 [...e inneun je georae
eunhaengeseo doneul ichehago
sipeoyo] I would like to transfer some
money from my bank in...; 오늘 은행
열어요? [oneul eunhaeng yeoreoyo?] Is
the bank open today?; 은행은 언제
닫나요? [eunhaengeun eonje
datnayo?] When does the bank close?;
은행은 언제 열어요? [eunhaengeun
eonje yeoreoyo?] When does the bank
open?; 은행이 얼마나 먼가요?
[eunhaengi eolmana meongayo?] How
far is the bank?; 근처에 은행이 있나요?
[geuncheoe eunhaengi innayo?] Is
there a bank nearby?

음 [eum] n sound, tone; 발신음
[balsineum] n dialling tone; 음높이
[eumnopi] n pitch (sound)

음료 [eumnyo] n drink; 음료수
[eumnyosu] n drinking water; 청량
음료 [cheongnyang eumnyo] n soft
drink; 어떤 무알코올 음료가 있나요?
[eotteon mualkool eumnyoga innayo?]
What non-alcoholic drinks do you
have?

음모 [eummo] n conspiracy; 음모를
꾸미다 [eummoreul kkumida] v plot
(conspire), plot (secret plan)

음성 [eumseong] 음성메일

[eumseongmeil] n voicemail

음식 [eumsik] n dish (food), grub

음악 [eumak] n music; 민속 음악
[minsok eumak] n folk music; 배경음악
[baegyeongeumak] n soundtrack;
음악단 [eumakdan] n band (musical
group); 음악적인 [eumakjeogin] adj
musical; 음악회 [eumakhoe] n concert;
어디에서 라이브 음악을 들을 수
있어요? [eodieseo raibeu eumageul
deureul su isseoyo?] Where can we
hear live music?

음악가 [eumakga] n musician; 어디에서
지역 음악가의 연주를 들을 수 있어요?
[eodieseo jiyeok eumakgaui
yeonjureul deureul su isseoyo?] Where
can we hear local musicians play?

음절 [eumjeol] n syllable; 어미에서 두
번째(음절)의 [eomieseo du
beonjjae(eumjeol)ui] adj penultimate

음주 [eumju] 음주 측정기 상표명 [eumju
cheukjeonggi sangpyomyeong] n
Breathalyser®; 음주운전
[eumjuunjeon] n drink-driving

음침 [eumchim] 음침한 [eumchimhan]
adj dismal

음탕 [eumtang] 음탕한 [eumtanghan]
adj obscene

음표 [eumpyo] n note (music)

응급 [eunggeup] 응급 치료 [eunggeup
chiryo] n first aid; 응급실 [eunggeupsil]
n accident & emergency department;
응급 의사를 불러 주세요 [eunggeup
uisareul bulleo juseyo] Please call the
emergency doctor

응급 서비스 [eunggeup seobiseu] 어느
약국이 응급 서비스를 제공하나요?
[eoneu yakgugi eunggeup
seobiseureul jegonghanayo?] Which
pharmacy provides emergency
service?

응급실 [eunggeupsil] 응급실에 가야
해요 [eunggeupsire gaya haeyo] I need
to go to casualty; 응급실은 어디에
있나요? [eunggeupsireun eodie
innayo?] Where is casualty?

응답 [eungdap] n response; 응답하다
[eungdaphada] v respond; 자동 응답기

[jadong eungdapgi] n answering machine, answerphone

응시 [eungsi] **응시하다** [eungsihada] v gaze, stare

응접 [eungjeop] **응접실** [eungjeopsil] n sitting room

응축 [eungchuk] n condensation

의견 [uigyeon] n opinion; **의견이 맞지 않다** [uigyeoni matji anta] v disagree

의도 [uido] n intention

의례 [uirye] **의례적인** [uiryejeogin] adj ritual

의뢰 [uiroe] n commission; **의뢰인** [uiroein] n client

의료 [uiryo] **준의료 종사자** [junuiryo jongsaja] n paramedic

의류 [uiryu] **의류목록 좀 보여 주세요** [uiryumongnok jom boyeo juseyo] I'd like a catalogue

의문 [uimun] n query; **의문부호** [uimunbuho] n question mark

의미 [uimi] n meaning; **무의미한** [muuimihan] adj pointless; **의미하다** [uimihada] v mean

의복 [uibok] n clothing, garment; **운동복** [undongbok] n tracksuit

의붓 [uibut] **의붓딸** [uibutthtal] n stepdaughter; **의붓아들** [uibusadeul] n stepson; **의붓아버지** [uibusabeoji] n stepfather; **의붓어머니** [uibuseomeoni] n stepmother; **의붓자매** [uibutjamae] n stepsister; **의붓형제** [uibutyeongje] n stepbrother

의사 [uisa] n doctor; **부인과 의사** [buingwa uisa] n gynaecologist; **발치료 의사** [balchiryo uisa] n chiropodist; **치과의사** [chigwauisa] n dentist; **수의사** [suuisa] n vet; **외과의사** [oegwauisa] n surgeon; **의사소견** [uisasogyeon] n medical; **의사소견서** [uisasogyeonseo] n medical certificate; **정신과 의사** [jeongsingwa uisa] n psychiatrist; **여의사에게 이야기하고 싶어요** [yeouisaege iyagihago sipeoyo] I'd like to speak to a female doctor; **영어 하는 의사가 있나요?** [yeongeo haneun uisaga innayo?] Is there a doctor who

speaks English?; **응급 의사를 불러 주세요** [eunggeup uisareul bulleo juseyo] Please call the emergency doctor; **의사를 불러요!** [uisareul bulleoyo!] Call a doctor!; **의사에게 이야기하고 싶어요** [uisaege iyagihago sipeoyo] I'd like to speak to a doctor; **의사가 필요해요** [uisaga piryohaeyo] I need a doctor

의사소통 [uisasotong] **의사소통하다** [uisasotonghada] v communicate

의상 [uisang] n outfit; **가장 무도회 의상** [gajang mudohoe uisang] n fancy dress

의석 [uiseok] n seat (constituency)

의식 [uisik] n ceremony, consciousness, ritual; **의식을 잃다** [uisigeul irta] v pass out; **의식을 잃게 하다** [uisigeul irke hada] v knock out; **의식을 회복하다** [uisigeul hoebokhada] v come round; **의식하고 있는** [uisikhago inneun] adj conscious

의심 [uisim] n doubt; **의심스러운** [uisimseureoun] adj doubtful, dubious; **의심하다** [uisimhada] v doubt, suspect; **의심할 여지 없이** [uisimhal yeoji eopsi] adv undoubtedly

의약품 [uiyakpum] n remedy

의원 [uiwon] n councillor

의자 [uija] n chair (furniture), seat (furniture); **안락 의자** [allak uija] n armchair, easy chair; **어린이용 높은 의자** [eoriniyong nopeun uija] n highchair; **일광욕 접이의자** [ilgwangyok jeobiuija] n sunbed; **접의자** [jeobuija] n deckchair; **흔들의자** [heundeuruija] n rocking chair; **높은 의자 있어요?** [nopeun uija isseoyo?] Do you have a high chair?

의장 [uijang] n chairman

의제 [uije] n agenda

의존 [uijon] **의존하다** [uijonhada] v depend

의지 [uiji] n will (motivation); **의지력** [uijiryeok] n willpower; **의지하다** [uijihada] v count on; **의지하다** [uijihada] v resort to

의치 [uichi] n dentures, false teeth; 제

의치를 고칠 수 있나요? [je uichireul gochil su innayo?] Can you repair my dentures?

의학 [uihak] 의학의 [uihagui] adj medical; 정신의학의 [jeongsinuihagui] adj psychiatric

이 [i] npl lice; 이의 [iui] n dental; 젖니가 나다 [jeotniga nada] v teethe

이것 [igeot] adj this ▷ pron this; 이것들 [igeotdeul] pron these; 이것들의 [igeotdeurui] adj these; 이것 주세요 [igeot juseyo] I'll have this

이국 [iguk] 이국적인 [igukjeogin] adj exotic

이기다 [igida] v win

이기적 [igijeok] 이기적인 [igijeogin] adj self-centred, selfish

이끼 [ikki] n moss

이다 [ida] ...인지 어떤지 [...inji eotteonji] conj whether; ...이든 (아니면)... [...ideun (animyeon)...] pron either (.. or); ...이에요 [...ieyo] It's worth...

이데올로기 [ideollogi] n ideology

이동 [idong] n move, shift, transfer; 이동 주택 [idong jutaek] n mobile home; 이동성의 [idongseongui] adj migrant; 이동성의 [idongseongui] adj mobile; 이동하다 [idonghada] v shift; 이동할수 있는 [idonghalsu inneun] adj removable

이득 [ideuk] n gain

이라도 [irado] ...이라도 [...irado] adv even

이라크 [irakeu] n Iraq; 이라크 사람 [irakeu saram] n Iraqi; 이라크의 [irakeuui] adj Iraqi

이란 [iran] n Iran; 이란 사람 [iran saram] n Iranian (person); 이란의 [iranui] adj Iranian

이래 [irae] 그 이래 [geu irae] adv since

이력서 [iryeokseo] abbr CV ▷ n curriculum vitae

이론 [iron] n theory

이롭다 [iropda] 이로운 [iroun] adj profitable

이류 [iryu] 2류의 [iryuui] adj second-class

이륙 [iryuk] n takeoff

이르다 [ireuda] 이른 [ireun] adj early

이름 [ireum] n first name, name; 당신의 이름은 무엇인가요? [dangsinui ireumeun mueosingayo?] What's your name?; 제 이름은...이에요 [je ireumeun...ieyo] My name is...

이마 [ima] n forehead

이메일 [imeil] n email; 이메일 주소 [imeil juso] n email address; 이메일 좀 알려 주시겠어요? [imeil jom allyeo jusigesseoyo?] Can I have your email?

이모 [imo] 고모, 이모 [gomo, imo] n auntie; 고모,이모 [gomo,imo] n aunt

이미 [imi] adv already

이미지 [imiji] n image

이민 [imin] n immigration

이발 [ibal] n haircut; 이발사 [ibalsa] n barber

이불 [ibul] 누비이불 [nubiibul] n quilt; 깃털 이불 [gittheol ibul] n duvet

이사 [isa] n move (house); 이사하다 [isahada] v move in; 이삿짐 트럭 [isatjim teureok] n removal van

이상 [isang] 이상적으로 [isangjeogeuro] adv ideally; 이상적인 [isangjeogin] adj ideal; 이상한 [isanghan] adj odd, strange; 정신 이상자 [jeongsin isangja] n lunatic; 정신이상 [jeongsinisang] n madness; 그 이상의 [geu isangui] adj further

이성애 [iseongae] 이성애의 [iseongaeui] adj heterosexual

이스라엘 [iseurael] n Israel; 이스라엘 사람 [iseurael saram] n Israeli; 이스라엘의 [iseuraerui] adj Israeli

이슬 [iseul] 이슬비 [iseulbi] n drizzle

이슬람 [iseullam] 이슬람교 [iseullamgyo] n Islam, Muslim; 이슬람교의 [iseullamgyoui] adj Islamic, Muslim; 이슬람교도가 먹는 요리 있어요? [iseullamgyodoga meongneun yori isseoyo?] Do you have halal dishes?

이슬람 사원 [iseullam sawon] 이슬람 사원은 어디에 있어요? [iseullam sawoneun eodie isseoyo?] Where is there a mosque?

이식 [isik] n transplant

이쑤시개 [issusigae] n toothpick

이야기 [iyagi] n story, tale; 이야기하는

사람 [iyagihaneun saram] n teller
이야기하다 [iyagihada] v speak;
털어놓고 얘기하다 [teoreonoko
yaegihada] v speak up; 당신과 조용히
이야기할 수 있을까요? [dangsingwa
joyonghi iyagihal su isseulkkayo?] Can I
speak to you in private?
이어폰 [ieopon] npl earphones
이용 [iyong] n utilization; 이용하다
[iyonghada] v exploit; 장애인이 이용할
수 있어요? [jangaeini iyonghal su
isseoyo?] Do you provide access for the
disabled?
이웃 [iut] n neighbour, neighbourhood
이유 [iyu] n reason
이의 [iui] n objection
이익 [iik] n benefit, interest (income),
profit; 이익이 되다 [iigi doeda] v
benefit
이전 [ijeon] 이전에는 [ijeoneneun] adv
formerly; 이전의 [ijeonui] adj previous
이점 [ijeom] n advantage
이제 [ije] 이제까지 [ijekkaji] adv ever
이주 [iju] n migration; 이주자 [ijuja] n
immigrant, migrant; 이주하다
[ijuhada] v emigrate
이집트 [ijipteu] n Egypt; 이집트 사람
[ijipteu saram] n Egyptian; 이집트의
[ijipteuui] adj Egyptian
이체 [iche] 자동 이체 [jadong iche] n
direct debit;...에 있는 제 거래 은행에서
돈을 이체하고 싶어요 [...e inneun je
georae eunhaengeseo doneul
ichehago sipeoyo] I would like to
transfer some money from my bank
in...; 이체 수수료가 있어요? [iche
susuryoga isseoyo?] Is there a transfer
charge?; 이체하는 데 얼마나 걸려요?
[ichehaneun de eolmana geollyeoyo?]
How long will it take to transfer?; 제
계좌에서 돈을 이체하고 싶어요 [je
gyejwaeseo doneul ichehago sipeoyo]
I would like to transfer some money
from my account
이치 [ichi] 이치에 맞는 [ichie matneun]
adj reasonable
이코노미 [ikonomi] 이코노미 석
[ikonomi seok] n economy class

이탈리아 [itallia] n Italy; 이탈리아 사람
[itallia saram] n Italian (person);
이탈리아어 [italliaeo] n Italian
(language); 이탈리아의 [italliaui] adj
Italian
이해 [ihae] n comprehension; 독순술로
이해하다 [doksunsullo ihaehada] v
lip-read; 이해심 많은 [ihaesim
manheun] adj considerate; 이해심
있는 [ihaesim inneun] adj
understanding; 이해하다 [ihaehada] v
understand; 이해할 수 있는 [ihaehal
su inneun] adj understandable
이혼 [ihon] n divorce; 이혼한 [ihonhan]
adj divorced; 이혼했어요
[ihonhaesseoyo] I'm divorced
익다 [ikda] 덜 익은 [deol igeun] adj rare
(undercooked); 덜 익었어요 [deol
igeosseoyo] This isn't cooked properly
익명 [ingmyeong] 익명의 [ingmyeongui]
adj anonymous
익사 [iksa] 익사하다 [iksahada] v drown
익숙 [iksuk] 익숙지 않은 [iksukji
anheun] adj unfamiliar; 익숙한
[iksukhan] adj used
익히다 [ikhida] 이미 익혀진 [imi
ikhyeojin] adj ready-cooked
인 [in] 소인 [soin] (편지) n postmark
인간 [ingan] n human being; 인권
[ingwon] npl human rights; 인간의
[inganui] adj human
인계 [ingye] 인계받다 [ingyebatda] v
take over
인공 [ingong] 인공의 [ingongui] adj
man-made; 인공적인 [ingongjeogin]
adj artificial
인구 [ingu] n population; 인구 조사
[ingu josa] n census
인기 [ingi] n popularity; 인기있는
[ingiinneun] adj popular; 인기있는
사람 [ingiinneun saram] v star (person);
인기가 없는 [ingiga eomneun] adj
unpopular
인내 [innae] n patience; 인내심이 있는
[innaesimi inneun] adj patient;
인내하다 [innaehada] v persevere
인도 [indo] n India, pavement; (남을)
인도하다 [(nameul) indohada] n lead;

인도 사람 [indo saram] n Indian; 인도양 [indoyang] n Indian Ocean; 인도의 [indoui] adj Indian

인도네시아 [indonesia] n Indonesia; 인도네시아 사람 [indonesia saram] n Indonesian (person); 인도네시아의 [indonesiaui] adj Indonesian

인도주의자 [indojuuija] adj humanitarian

인동 [indong] 인동덩굴 [indongdeonggul] n honeysuckle

인력 [illyeok] n manpower

인류 [illyu] n mankind; 인류학 [illyuhak] n anthropology

인명 [inmyeong] 인명 구조원 [inmyeong gujowon] n lifeguard

인사 [insa] n greeting; 인사하다 [insahada] v greet, salute

인상 [insang] n impression; 인상적인 [insangjeogin] adj impressive, striking

인색 [insaek] 인색한 [insaekhan] adj mean, stingy

인쇄 [inswae] n print; 인쇄물 [inswaemul] n printout; 인쇄업자 [inswaeeopja] n printer (person); 인쇄기 [inswaegi] n printer (machine); 인쇄하다 [inswaehada] v print; 인쇄하는 데 얼마예요? [inswaehaneun de eolmayeyo?] How much is printing?

인수 [insu] n takeover

인슐린 [insyullin] n insulin

인식 [insik] 인식하다 [insikhada] v recognize; 인식할수 있는 [insikhalsu inneun] adj recognizable

인심 [insim] 인심 좋은 [insim joheun] adj generous

인어 [ineo] n mermaid

인용 [inyong] n quotation, citation; 인용부호 [inyongbuho] npl quotation marks; 인용문 [inyongmun] n quotation; 인용어구 [inyongeogu] n quote; 인용하다 [inyonghada] v quote

인접 [injeop] 인접한 [injeophan] adj adjacent, close by

인정 [injeong] n acknowledgement; 인정하다 [injeonghada] v own up

인종 [injong] n race (origin); 인종 차별주의 [injong chabyeoljuui] n racism; 인종 차별주의자 [injong chabyeoljuuija] n racist; 인종을 차별하는 [injongeul chabyeolhaneun] adj racist; 인종의 [injongui] adj ethnic, racial

인질 [injil] n hostage

인출기 [inchulgi] 현금 인출기 [hyeongeum inchulgi] n cash dispenser; 여기에 현금 인출기가 있나요? [yeogie hyeongeum inchulgiga innayo?] Is there a cash machine here?; 가장 가까운 현금 인출기는 어디있어요? [gajang gakkaun hyeongeum inchulgineun eodiisseoyo?] Where is the nearest cash machine?

인치 [inchi] n inch

인터넷 [inteonet] n Internet, Net; 인터넷 카페 [inteonet kape] n Internet café; 인터넷 사용자 [inteonet sayongja] n Internet user; 인터넷 서비스 제공자 [inteonet seobiseu jegongja] abbr ISP; 방에서 무선 인터넷 있어요? [bangeseo museon inteonet isseoyo?] Does the room have wireless Internet access?; 방에서 인터넷 되나요? [bangeseo inteonet doenayo?] Is there an Internet connection in the room?; 여기에 인터넷 카페가 있나요? [yeogie inteonet kapega innayo?] Are there any Internet cafés here?

인트라넷 [inteuranet] n intranet

인플레이션 [inpeulleisyeon] n inflation

인플루엔자 [inpeulluenja] n influenza

인형 [inhyeong] n doll; 곰인형 [gominhyeong] n teddy bear

인화 [inhwa] 인화성의 [inhwaseongui] adj flammable

일 [il] n work; 만기일 [mangiil] n expiry date; 손수 하는 일 [sonsu haneun il] abbr DIY; 일터 [ilteo] n workplace; 일하다 [ilhada] vi work; 고된 일 [godoen il] n fag; 조만간 다시 함께 일할 수 있기를 바랍니다 [jomangan dasi hamkke ilhal su itgireul baramnida] I hope we can work together again soon; 어디에서 일하세요? [eodieseo ilhaseyo?] Where do you work?;...에서 일해요 [...eseo ilhaeyo] I work for...; 일 때문에 여기 왔어요 [il ttaemune yeogi wasseoyo] I'm here for work; 일해요 [ilhaeyo] I work; 함께 일해서 즐거웠어요 [hamkke ilhaeseo jeulgeowosseoyo] It's been a pleasure working with you

일격 [ilgyeok] 재빠른 일격 [jaeppareun ilgyeok] n jab

일곱 [ilgop] 일곱 번째의 [ilgop beonjjaeui] adj seventh

일관 [ilgwan] 일관된 [ilgwandoen] adj consistent

일관성 [ilgwanseong] 일관성이 없는 [ilgwanseongi eomneun] adj inconsistent

일광 [ilgwang] 일광욕을 하다 [ilgwangyogeul hada] v sunbathe

일광욕 [ilgwangyok] 일광욕 접이의자 [ilgwangyok jeobiuija] n sunbed

일급 [ilgeup] 일급기밀인 [ilgeupgimirin] adj top-secret; 제1급의 [je1geubui] adj first-class

일기 [ilgi] n diary; 일기예보 [ilgiyebo] n weather forecast

일다 [ilda] 읽기쉬운 [irkgiswiun] adj legible

일등 [ildeung] 일등실이요 [ildeungsiriyo] a first-class cabin

일등석 [ildeungseok] 일등석으로 여행하고 싶어요 [ildeungseogeuro yeohaenghago sipeoyo] I would like to travel first-class;...까지 일등석 왕복이요 [...kkaji ildeungseok wangbogiyo] a first-class return to...

일련 [illyeon] n series

일몰 [ilmol] n sunset

일반 [ilban] 일반 상식 [ilban sangsik] n general knowledge; 일반 개업의 [ilban gaeeobui] abbr GP; 일반적으로 [ilbanjeogeuro] adv generally; 일반적인 [ilbanjeogin] adj general; 일반실이요 [ilbansiriyo] a standard class cabin

일반화 [ilbanhwa] 일반화하다 [ilbanhwahada] v generalize

일본 [ilbon] n Japan; 일본 사람 [ilbon saram] n Japanese (person); 일본어 [ilboneo] n Japanese (language); 일본의 [ilbonui] adj Japanese

일사 [ilsa] 일사병 [ilsabyeong] n sunstroke

일어나다 [ireonada] v get up, happen, rise, wake up; 일어서다 [ireoseoda] v stand up; 자지 않고 일어나 있다 [jaji anko ireona itda] v stay up; 몇 시에 일어나세요? [myeot sie ireonaseyo?] What time do you get up?

일요일 [illyoil] n Sunday; 시월 삼일 일요일이에요 [siwol samil illyoirieyo] It's Sunday the third of October; 일요일에 [iryoire] on Sunday

일원 [irwon] 갱단의 일원 [gaengdanui irwon] n gangster

일인당 [irindang] 일인당 얼마예요? [irindang eolmayeyo?] How much is it per person?

일정 [iljeong] n schedule; 여행일정표 [yeohaengiljeongpyo] n itinerary

일주일 [iljuil] 일주일에 얼마예요? [iljuire eolmayeyo?] How much is it per week?

일찍 [iljjik] adv early; 더 일찍 [deo iljjik] adv earlier

일출 [ilchul] n sunrise

일치 [ilchi] n consensus

일화 [ilhwa] n episode

일회용 [ilhoeyong] adj disposable

읽다 [irkda] v read; 소리내어 읽다 [sorinaeeo irkda] v read out; 읽기 어려운 [irkgi eoryeoun] adj illegible; 읽을 수가 없어요 [ilgeul suga eopseoyo] I can't read it

잃다 [irta] vt lose; 잃은 [ireun] adj lost; 잃은 사람 [ireun saram] n loser

임금 [imgeum] n wage

임대 [imdae] 임대료 [imdaeryo] n rent, rental; 임대(임차)하다 [imdae(imcha) hada] v lease; 임대하다 [imdaehada] v rent; 자동차 임대 [jadongcha imdae] n car hire, car rental

임대차 [imdaecha] 임대차계약 [imdaechagyeyak] n lease

임명 [immyeong] 임명하다 [immyeonghada] v appoint

임무 [immu] n assignment, duty

임시 [imsi] 임시의 [imsiui] adj

temporary; 임시교사 [imsigyosa] n supply teacher; 임시고용 [imsigoyong] n temp; 임시로 때워 주시겠어요? [imsiro ttaewo jusigesseoyo?] Can you do a temporary filling?

임신 [imsin] n pregnancy; 불임의 [burimui] adj infertile; 임신중인 [imsinjungin] adj pregnant

입 [ip] n mouth; 입 다물다 [ip damulda] v shut up

입구 [ipgu] n entrance, entry, way in

입국 [ipguk] 입국 비자가 있어요 [ipguk bijaga isseoyo] I have an entry visa

입다 [ipda] 옷입다 [osipda] vt wear; 입어보다 [ibeoboda] v try on; 뭘 입을까요? [mwol ibeulkkayo?] What should I wear?; 이 드레스 입어 볼 수 있어요? [i deureseu ibeo bol su isseoyo?] Can I try on this dress?; 입어 볼 수 있어요? [ibeo bol su isseoyo?] Can I try it on?

입덧 [ipdeot] n morning sickness

입방 [ipbang] 입방의 [ipbangui] adj cubic

입수 [ipsu] 압수하다 [apsuhada] v confiscate

입술 [ipsul] n lip; 입술 연고 [ipsul yeongo] n lip salve

입양 [ibyang] n adoption; 입양된 [ibyangdoen] adj adopted; 입양하다 [ibyanghada] v adopt

입장 [ipjang] n admission, admittance; 입장을 허락하다 [ipjangeul heorakhada] v admit (allow in)

입장권 [ipjanggwon] n entrance ticket, pass; 스키장 입장권은 얼마예요? [seukijang ipjanggwoneun eolmayeyo?] How much is a ski pass?; 어디에서 스키장 입장권을 살 수 있을까요? [eodieseo seukijang ipjanggwoneul sal su isseulkkayo?] Where can I buy a ski pass?; 일주일 스키장 입장권을 사고 싶어요 [iljuil seukijang ipjanggwoneul sago sipeoyo] I'd like a ski pass for a week; 일주일 입장권은 얼마예요? [iljuil ipjanggwoneun eolmayeyo?] How much is a pass per week?; 하루 스키장

입장권을 사고 싶어요 [haru seukijang ipjanggwoneul sago sipeoyo] I'd like a ski pass for a day; 하루 입장권은 얼마예요? [haru ipjanggwoneun eolmayeyo?] How much is a pass for a day?

입장료 [ipjangnyo] n admission charge, entry fee; 입장료는 얼마예요? [ipjangnyoneun eolmayeyo?] How much does it cost to get in?; 입장료가 있어요? [ipjangnyoga isseoyo?] Is there a cover charge?

입증 [ipjeung] 유죄를 입증하다 [yujoereul ipjeunghada] v convict; 입증하다 [ipjeunghada] v prove

입찰 [ipchal] n bid; 입찰하다 [ipchalhada] v bid (at auction)

잇따르다 [itthareuda] vt follow

잇몸 [itmom] npl gums; 잇몸에서 피가 나요 [itmomeseo piga nayo] My gums are bleeding; 잇몸이 아파요 [itmomi apayo] My gums are sore

있다 [itda] 가만히 있는 [gamanhi inneun] adj motionless;… 있어요? [... isseoyo?] Have you got any…?; 미터기 있어요? [miteogi isseoyo?] Do you have a meter? (taxi); 여기에… 하시는 분 있어요? [yeogie... hasineun bun isseoyo?] Does anyone here speak…?;..은 어디에 있어요? [..eun eodie isseoyo?] Where is …?; 점프선 있어요? [jeompeuseon isseoyo?] Do you have any jump leads?

있음직한 [isseumjikhan] adj probable

잉글랜드 [inggeullaendeu] n England; 잉글랜드 사람 [inggeullaendeu saram] n English, Englishman; 잉글랜드 여자 [inggeullaendeu yeoja] n Englishwoman; 잉글랜드의 [inggeullaendeuui] adj English

잉꼬 [ingkko] n budgerigar, budgie

잉여 [ingyeo] n surplus; 잉여의 [ingyeoui] n surplus

잉크 [ingkeu] n ink

잊다 [itda] v forget; 잊은 [ijeun] adj forgotten; 잊을 수 없는 [ijeul su eomneun] adj unforgettable

잎 [ip] n leaf; 잎들 [ipdeul] npl leaves

자 [ja] n ruler (measure), son, person; **노동자** [nodongja] n workman; **대자** [daeja] n godson; **연주자** [yeonjuja] n player (instrumentalist); **자회사** [jahoesa] n subsidiary; **기록자** [girokja] n recorder (scribe)

자갈 [jagal] n gravel

자격 [jagyeok] n qualification; **자격 있는** [jagyeok inneun] adj qualified; **자격을 갖추다** [jagyeogeul gatchuda] v qualify

자고 [jago] n partridge

자금 [jageum] npl funds; **자금을 공급하다** [jageumeul gonggeuphada] v finance

자급 [jageup] **자급식의** [jageupsigui] adj self-contained

자기 [jagi] **자기수양** [jagisuyang] n self-discipline

자녀 [janyeo] **대자녀** [daejanyeo] n godchild; **수양 자녀** [suyang janyeo] n foster child

자다 [jada] v sleep; **너무 자다** [neomu jada] v oversleep; **동침하다** [dongchimhada] v sleep around; **잘 주무셨어요?** [jal jumusyeosseoyo?] Did you sleep well?

자동 [jadong] **자동 매표기** [jadong maepyogi] n ticket machine; **자동 온도 조절기** [jadong ondo jojeolgi] n thermostat; **자동 응답기** [jadong eungdapgi] n answering machine, answerphone; **자동 이체** [jadong iche]

n direct debit; **자동 판매기** [jadong panmaegi] n slot machine; **자동으로** [jadongeuro] adv automatically; **자동의** [jadongui] adj automatic; **자동판매기** [jadongpanmaegi] n dispenser, vending machine

자동차 [jadongcha] n car; **자동차 보험** [jadongcha boheom] n car insurance; **자동차 열쇠** [jadongcha yeolsoe] npl car keys; **자동차 운전자** [jadongcha unjeonja] n motorist; **자동차 임대** [jadongcha imdae] n car hire, car rental; **자동차 경주 선수** [jadongcha gyeongju seonsu] n racing driver; **자동차 편승 여행자** [jadongcha pyeonseung yeohaengja] n hitchhiker; **자동차 핸들** [jadongcha haendeul] n steering wheel; **자동차정비공** [jadongchajeongbigong] n motor mechanic; **자동차경주** [jadongchagyeongju] n motor racing

자두 [jadu] **말린 자두** [mallin jadu] n prune; **서양자두** [seoyangjadu] n plum

자랑 [jarang] **자랑스러워 하는** [jarangseureowo haneun] adj proud; **자랑하다** [jaranghada] v boast

자료 [jaryo] npl data

자르다 [jareuda] v chop; **마구 자르다** [magu jareuda] v hack; **잘게 자르다** [jalge jareuda] v cut up

자리 [jari] n spot (place), constellation, zodiac; **별자리** [byeoljari] n horoscope; **물고기자리** [mulgogijari] n Pisces; **사자자리** [sajajari] n Leo; **쌍둥이자리** [ssangdungijari] n Gemini; **염소자리** [yeomsojari] n Capricorn; **자리잡다** [jarijapda] v settle down; **전갈자리** [jeongaljari] n Scorpio; **처녀자리** [cheonyeojari] n Virgo; **궁수자리** [gungsujari] n Sagittarius; **가장자리** [gajangjari] n fringe, margin; **게자리** [gejari] n Cancer (horoscope)

자막 [jamak] npl subtitles; **자막이 있는** [jamagi inneun] adj subtitled

자만심 [jamansim] **자만심이 강한** [jamansimi ganghan] adj bigheaded

자매 [jamae] n sister; **의붓자매** [uibutjamae] n stepsister; **형제자매**

[hyeongjemae] npl siblings

자메이카 [jameika] 자메이카 사람
[jameika saram] n Jamaican;
자메이카의 [jameikaui] adj Jamaican

자물쇠 [jamulsoe] n lock (door); 맹꽁이
자물쇠 [maengkkongi jamulsoe] n
padlock; 자물쇠 장수 [jamulsoe
jangsu] n locksmith; 자물쇠
주시겠어요? [jamulsoe jusigesseoyo?]
Can I have a lock?; 자물쇠가 고장났어요
[jamulsoega gojangnasseoyo] The lock
is broken

자발 [jabal] 자발적으로 [jabaljeogeuro]
adv voluntarily; 자발적인 [jabaljeogin]
adj spontaneous, voluntary

자본 [jabon] 자본주의 [jabonjuui] n
capitalism

자비 [jabi] n mercy

자산 [jasan] n asset, assets

자살 [jasal] n suicide; 자살폭탄 테러범
[jasalpoktan tereobeom] n suicide
bomber

자서전 [jaseojeon] n autobiography

자석 [jaseok] n magnet; 자석의
[jaseogui] adj magnetic

자선 [jaseon] n charity; 자선 상점
[jaseon sangjeom] n charity shop

자세 [jase] 자세히 살피다 [jasehi
salpida] v scan

자수 [jasu] n embroidery; 자수를 놓다
[jasureul nota] v embroider

자신 [jasin] 너 자신 [neo jasin] pron
yourself; 당신 자신 [dangsin jasin]
pron yourself (intensifier), yourself
(polite); 여러분 자신 [yeoreobun jasin]
pron yourselves (intensifier), yourselves
(polite), yourselves (reflexive); 우리 자신
[uri jasin] pron ourselves; 자신있는
[jasininneun] adj self-assured; 자기
자신의 [jagi jasinui] adj own; 그 남자
자신 [geu namja jasin] pron himself; 그
여자 자신 [geu yeoja jasin] pron herself

자신감 [jasingam] n confidence
(self-assurance)

자실 [jasil] 망연자실한
[mangyeonjasilhan] adj devastated

자연 [jayeon] n nature; 자연주의자
[jayeonjuuija] n naturalist; 자연식품

자연식품 [jayeonsikpum] npl wholefoods;
자연의 [jayeonui] adj natural; 자연히
[jayeonhi] adv naturally

자영업 [jayeongeop] 자영업의
[jayeongeobui] adj self-employed;
자영업을 해요 [jayeongeobeul haeyo]
I'm self-employed

자외선 [jaoeseon] 자외선 차단제
[jaoeseon chadanje] n sunblock,
sunscreen

자원 [jawon] n resource; 자원하다
[jawonhada] v volunteer; 천연 자원
[cheonyeon jawon] npl natural
resources

자유 [jayu] n freedom; 자유로운
[jayuroun] adj free (no restraint);
자유롭게 해주다 [jayuropge haejuda] v
free; 자유선택의 [jayuseontaegui] adj
optional; 자유계약으로
[jayugyeyageuro] adv freelance;
자유계약의 [jayugyeyagui] adj
freelance

자유주의 [jayujuui] 자유주의의
[jayujuuiui] adj liberal

자음 [jaeum] n consonant

자의식 [jauisik] 자의식이 강한 [jauisigi
ganghan] adj self-conscious

자장가 [jajangga] n lullaby

자전 [jajeon] 세발자전거
[sebaljajeongeo] n tricycle

자전거 [jajeongeo] n bicycle, cycle (bike);
2인승 자전거 [i inseung jajeongeo] n
tandem; 모터 달린 자전거 [moteo
dallin jajeongeo] n moped; 산악
자전거 [sanak jajeongeo] n mountain
bike; 자전거 도로 [jajeongeo doro] n
cycle lane, cycle path; 자전거 타는
사람 [jajeongeo taneun saram] n
cyclist; 자전거 펌프 [jajeongeo
peompeu] n bicycle pump; 자전거,
오토바이 [jajeongeo, otobai] n bike; 이
지역 자전거 지도 있어요? [i jiyeok
jajeongeo jido isseoyo?] Is there a cycle
map of this area?; 자전거 타러 갑시다
[jajeongeo tareo gapsida] Let's go
cycling; 자전거를 타고 싶어요
[jajeongeoreul tago sipeoyo] We
would like to go cycling;...까지 가는

자전거 경로는 어디인가요? [...kkaji ganeun jajeongeo gyeongnoneun eodiingayo?] Where is the cycle path to...?

자정 [jajeong] n midnight

자제 [jaje] n self-control

자주 [jaju] adv often; **자주 하는 질문** [jaju haneun jilmun] abbr FAQ

자취 [jachwi] n self-catering, trace

자치 [jachi] **자치의** [jachiui] adj autonomous; **자치권** [jachigwon] n autonomy

작곡 [jakgok] **작곡가** [jakgokga] n composer

작다 [jakda] **보다 작은** [boda jageun] adj minor; **아주 작은** [aju jageun] adj tiny; **작은** [jageun] adj little, small; **작은 꾸러미** [jageun kkureomi] n packet; **너무 작아요** [neomu jagayo] It's too small; **방이 너무 작아요** [bangi neomu jagayo] The room is too small

작동 [jakdong] n work, performance; **작동하다** [jakdonghada] v operate (to function); **브레이크가 작동하지 않아요** [beureikeuga jakdonghaji anhayo] The brakes are not working; **샤워기가 작동하지 않아요** [syawogiga jakdonghaji anhayo] The shower doesn't work; **세탁기는 어떻게 작동하나요?** [setakgineun eotteoke jakdonghanayo?] How does the washing machine work?; **어떻게 작동하나요?** [eotteoke jakdonghanayo?] How does this work?; **에어컨이 작동하지 않아요** [eeokeoni jakdonghaji anhayo] The air conditioning doesn't work; **온수기는 어떻게 작동하나요?** [onsugineun eotteoke jakdonghanayo?] How does the water heater work?; **...이 제대로 작동하지 않아요** [...i jedaero jakdonghaji anhayo] The... doesn't work properly; **이게 작동하지 않아요** [ige jakdonghaji anhayo] This doesn't work; **기어가 작동하지 않아요** [gieoga jakdonghaji anhayo] The gears are not working; **플래시가 작동하지 않아요** [peullaesiga jakdonghaji anhayo] The flash is not working; **헤드라이트가 작동하지 않아요** [hedeuraiteuga jakdonghaji anhayo] The headlights are not working

작업 [jageop] **문서작업** [munseojageop] n paperwork; **작업 구역** [jageop guyeok] n work station; **작업복** [jageopbok] npl overalls; **작업장** [jageopjang] n workshop; **작업구역** [jageopguyeok] n workstation; **작업공간** [jageopgonggan] n workspace

작업복 [jageopbok] **멜빵 작업복** [melppang jageopbok] npl dungarees

작용 [jagyong] **부작용** [bujagyong] n side effect

작위 [jagwi] **무작위의** [mujagwiui] adj random

작정 [jakjeong] **작정이다** [jakjeongida] v intend to

잔 [jan] n glass; **물 한 잔** [mul han jan] a glass of water; **깨끗한 잔을 주시겠어요?** [kkaekkeutan janeul jusigesseoyo?] Can I have a clean glass, please?

잔고 [jango] **은행잔고** [eunhaengjango] n bank balance

잔돈 [jandon] n small change; **미안하지만 잔돈이 없어요** [mianhajiman jandoni eopseoyo] Sorry, I don't have any change; **주차 미터기에 넣을 잔돈 있으세요?** [jucha miteogie neoheul jandon isseuseyo?] Do you have change for the parking meter?; **...을 잔돈으로 바꿔 주시겠어요?** [...eul jandoneuro bakkwo jusigesseoyo?] Could you give me change of...?; **잔돈 있으세요?** [jandon isseuseyo?] Do you have any small change?; **잔돈 좀 바꿔 주시겠어요?** [jandon jom bakkwo jusigesseoyo?] Can you give me some change, please?; **잔돈은 됐어요** [jandoneun dwaesseoyo] Keep the change; **잔돈을 잘못 주신 것 같아요** [jandoneul jalmot jusin geot gatayo] I think you've given me the wrong change; **잔돈이 없어요** [jandoni eopseoyo] I don't have anything smaller

잔디 [jandi] n lawn; 잔디 깎는 기계 [jandi kkakkneun gigye] n lawnmower; 잔디밭 [jandibat] n lawn

잔소리 [jansori] 잔소리하다 [jansorihada] v nag

잔여물 [janyeomul] npl remains

잔인 [janin] 잔인한 [janinhan] adj brutal, ruthless

잔해 [janhae] n wreckage

잔혹 [janhok] 잔혹한 [janhokhan] adj cruel; 잔혹함 [janhokham] n cruelty

잘 [jal] adv all right, well

잘난체하다 [jallanchehada] 잘난체하는 [jallanchehaneun] adj smug

잘못 [jalmot] n error, mistake; 잘못 놓다 [jalmot nota] v mislay; 잘못 알고서 [jalmot algoseo] adv mistakenly; 잘못된 [jalmotdoen] adj mistaken; 잘못된 판단을 하다 [jalmotdoen pandaneul hada] v misjudge; 잘못하여 [jalmotayeo] adv wrong; 잘못 거셨어요 [jalmot geosyeosseoyo] You have the wrong number; 계산서가 잘못됐어요 [gyesanseoga jalmotdwaesseoyo] The bill is wrong; 그건 제 잘못이 아니에요 [geugeon je jalmosi anieyo] It wasn't my fault

잘생기다 [jalsaenggida] 잘 생긴 [jal saenggin] adj handsome; 잘생긴 [jalsaenggin] adj good-looking

잘하다 [jalhada] 잘했어요! [jalhaesseoyo!] excl well done!

잠 [jam] n sleep; 낮잠 [natjam] n nap; 늦잠 자다 [neutjam jada] v sleep in; 선잠 [seonjam] n snooze; 선잠 자다 [seonjam jada] v snooze; 잠들어 [jamdeureo] adj asleep; 잠깨다 [jamkkaeda] v awake; 더워서 잠을 잘 수 없어요 [deowoseo jameul jal su eopseoyo] I can't sleep for the heat; 시끄러워서 잠을 잘 수 없어요 [sikkeureowoseo jameul jal su eopseoyo] I can't sleep for the noise; 잠을 못 자요 [jameul mot jayo] I can't sleep

잠그다 [jamgeuda] vt lock; 문을 잠궈 두세요 [muneul jamgwo duseyo] Keep the door locked; 문이 안 잠겨요 [muni an jamgyeoyo] The door won't lock

잠기다 [jamgida] v soak

잠비아 [jambia] n Gambia, Zambia; 잠비아 사람 [jambia saram] n Zambian; 잠비아의 [jambiaui] adj Zambia

잠수 [jamsu] 잠수복 [jamsubok] n wetsuit; 잠수함 [jamsuham] n submarine

잠시 [jamsi] n while; 잠시의 [jamsiui] adj brief

잠옷 [jamot] n nightdress, nightie

잠자리 [jamjari] n dragonfly

잠재 [jamjae] 잠재성 [jamjaeseong] n potential; 잠재적인 [jamjaejeogin] adj potential

잠정 [jamjeong] 잠정적인 [jamjeongjeogin] adj provisional

잡다 [japda] v seize, catch, hold; 단단히 잡다 [dandanhi japda] v grip; 따라잡다 [ttarajapda] v catch up; 갖가지 잡다한 [gatgaji japdahan] adj miscellaneous; 꽉 잡다 [kkwak japda] v squeeze; 꽉 잡고 있다 [kkwak japgo itda] v hold on; 이것을 잡아 주시겠어요? [igeoseul jaba jusigesseoyo?] Could you hold this for me?

잡담 [japdam] n chat; 잡담하다 [japdamhada] v chat, waffle

잡이 [jabi] 손잡이 [sonjabi] n handle, knob

잡종 [japjong] n mongrel

잡지 [japji] n magazine (periodical); 어디에서 잡지를 살 수 있어요? [eodieseo japjireul sal su isseoyo?] Where can I buy a magazine?

잡초 [japcho] n weed

장 [jang] n chapter; 박람회장 [bangnamhoejang] n fairground; 선착장 [seonchakjang] n marina; 수영장 [suyeongjang] n swimming pool; 양조장 [yangjojang] n brewery; 장티푸스 [jangtipuseu] n typhoid; 정거장 [jeonggeojang] n station; 경기장 [gyeonggijang] n playing field, stadium

장갑 [janggap] n glove; 벙어리 장갑

[beongeori janggap] n mitten; **오븐용
장갑** [obeunyong janggap] n oven
glove; **고무장갑** [gomujanggap] npl
rubber gloves

장관 [janggwan] n minister (government)

장교 [janggyo] n officer

장군 [janggun] n general

장난 [jangnan] n prank

장난감 [jangnangam] n toy

장대 [jangdae] n pole; **장대높이뛰기**
[jangdaenopittwigi] n pole vault;
장대한 [jangdaehan] adj spectacular

장려 [jangnyeo] **장려금** [jangnyeogeum]
n incentive

장례 [jangnye] **장례식** [jangnyesik] n
funeral

장로교 [jangnogyo] **장로교회**
[jangnogyohoe] n Presbyterian;
장로교회의 [jangnogyohoeui] adj
Presbyterian

장미 [jangmi] n rose

장벽 [jangbyeok] n barrier

장비 [jangbi] n equipment, tackle;
어디에서 스키 장비를 빌릴 수 있나요?
[eodieseo seuki jangbireul billil su
innayo?] Where can I hire skiing
equipment?; **장비를 빌릴 수 있나요?**
[jangbireul billil su innayo?] Can we
hire the equipment?

장소 [jangso] n place; **행사 장소**
[haengsa jangso] n venue

장수 [jangsu] n tradesman; **자물쇠 장수**
[jamulsoe jangsu] n locksmith

장식 [jangsik] n decoration, ornament;
장식자 [jangsikja] n decorator; **장식품**
[jangsikpum] n ornament; **장식하다**
[jangsikhada] v decorate

장신구 [jangsingu] **제 장신구를 금고에
넣고 싶어요** [je jangsingureul
geumgoe neoko sipeoyo] I would like
to put my jewellery in the safe

장애 [jangae] n disability, hitch; **장애물**
[jangaemul] n block (obstruction),
hurdle, obstacle; **장애인** [jangaein] npl
disabled; **장애가 있는** [jangaega
inneun] adj disabled, handicapped;
노상 장애물 [nosang jangaemul] n
roadblock; **장애물 뛰어넘기**

[jangaemul ttwieoneomgi] n
show-jumping

장애인 [jangaein] n disabled person;
욕실에 장애인용 손잡이가 있어요?
[yoksire jangaeinyong sonjabiga
isseoyo?] Are there support railings in
the bathroom?; **장애인 할인이 있나요?**
[jangaein harini innayo?] Is there a
reduction for disabled people?; **장애인
화장실이 있어요?** [jangaein
hwajangsiri isseoyo?] Are there any
toilets for the disabled?; **장애인을 위한
어떠한 시설이 있어요?** [jangaeineul
wihan eotteohan siseori isseoyo?]
What facilities do you have for disabled
people?; **장애인이 이용할 수 있어요?**
[jangaeini iyonghal su isseoyo?] Do you
provide access for the disabled?; **저는
시각 장애인이에요** [jeoneun sigak
jangaeinieyo] I'm visually impaired, I'm
blind; **저는 청각 장애인이에요**
[jeoneun cheonggak jangaeinieyo] I'm
deaf

장어 [jangeo] **뱀장어** [baemjangeo] n
eel

장의 [jangui] **장의사** [janguisa] n
undertaker

장인 [jangin] n craftsman

장자 [jangja] **백만장자**
[baengmanjangja] n millionaire

장치 [jangchi] n device, mechanism;
냉난방 장치를 한 [naengnanbang
jangchireul han] adj air-conditioned;
위성항법장치
[wiseonghangbeopjangchi] abbr GPS;
촉매 변환 장치 [chongmae
byeonhwan jangchi] n catalytic
converter; **굴착장치** [gulchakjangchi]
n rig; **핸즈프리 장치** [haenjeupeuri
jangchi] n hands-free kit; **화재 피난
장치** [hwajae pinan jangchi] n fire
escape

장터 [jangteo] n marketplace

장학 [janghak] **장학금** [janghakgeum] n
scholarship

장화 [janghwa] n boot

장황 [janghwang] **장황하다**
[janghwanghada] v mount up

재 [jae] 재조직하다 [jaejojikhada] v reorganize; 재사용하다 [jaesayonghada] v reuse; 재생산 [jaesaengsan] n reproduction; 재시험 치르다 [jaesiheom chireuda] v resit; 재구성하다 [jaeguseonghada] v restructure

재고 [jaego] 재고품 [jaegopum] (재고품 목록) v stock; 재고하다 [jaegohada] v reconsider

재난 [jaenan] n disaster

재능 [jaeneung] n talent; 재능이 있는 [jaeneungi inneun] adj talented; 천부의 재능이 있는 [cheonbuui jaeneungi inneun] adj gifted

재다 [jaeda] v calculate, measure; 치수 좀 재 주시겠어요? [chisu jom jae jusigesseoyo?] Can you measure me, please?

재단 [jaedan] 재단사 [jaedansa] n tailor

재떨이 [jaetteori] n ashtray; 재떨이 있어요? [jaetteori isseoyo?] May I have an ashtray?

재료 [jaeryo] n material; 재료가 무엇인가요? [jaeryoga mueosingayo?] What is the material?

재무 [jaemu] 재무상의 [jaemusangui] adj financial

재미 [jaemi] n fun; 몹시 재미있는 [mopsi jaemiinneun] adj hilarious; 재미있는 [jaemiinneun] adj entertaining, fun, playful

재미있다 [jaemiitda] 재미있으셨어요? [jaemiisseusyeosseoyo?] Did you enjoy yourself?

재봉 [jaebong] 재봉틀 [jaebongteul] n sewing machine

재산 [jaesan] n fortune, property; 사유재산 [sayujaesan] n private property

재생 [jaesaeng] 재생가능한 [jaesaengganeunghan] adj renewable; 재생하다 [jaesaenghada] v renew

재석 [jaeseok] 채석장 [chaeseokjang] n quarry

재연 [jaeyeon] n replay; 재연하다 [jaeyeonhada] v replay

재즈 [jaejeu] n jazz

재채기 [jaechaegi] 재채기하다 [jaechaegihada] v sneeze

재치 [jaechi] n tact, wit; 재치없는 [jaechieomneun] adj tactless; 재치있는 [jaechiinneun] adj tactful, witty

재킷 [jaekit] n jacket; 방한용 재킷 [banghanyong jaekit] n anorak

재판 [jaepan] n trial; 재판관 [jaepangwan] n judge

재해 [jaehae] 대재해의 [daejaehaeui] adj disastrous

재혼 [jaehon] 재혼하다 [jaehonhada] v remarry

재활용 [jaehwallyong] n recycling; 재활용하다 [jaehwallyonghada] v recycle

재회 [jaehoe] n reunion

잭 [jaek] n jack

잼 [jaem] n jam; 잼 병 [jaem byeong] n jam jar

쟁기 [jaenggi] n plough; 쟁기로 갈다 [jaenggiro galda] n plough

쟁반 [jaengban] n tray

쟁점 [jaengjeom] n issue

저 [jeo] 저지방의 [jeojibangui] adj low-fat; 저...이에요 [jeo...ieyo] It's... (calling), This is... (calling)

저것 [jeogeot] pron that

저금 [jeogeum] 돼지 저금통 [dwaeji jeogeumtong] n piggybank

저널리스트 [jeoneolliseuteu] n journalist

저널리즘 [jeoneollijeum] n journalism

저녁 [jeonyeok] n evening; 저녁식사 [jeonyeoksiksa] n supper; 오늘 저녁에 뭐 하실거예요? [oneul jeonyeoge mwo hasilgeoyeyo?] What are you doing this evening?; 저녁에 [jeonyeoge] in the evening

저녁식사 [jeonyeoksiksa] 저녁식사 시간 [jeonyeoksiksa sigan] n dinner time

저리다 [jeorida] 저린 [jeorin] adj numb

저속 [jeosok] 저속한 [jeosokhan] adj vulgar

저수 [jeosu] 저수지 [jeosuji] n reservoir

저온 [jeoon] 저온살균한 [jeoonsalgyunhan] adj pasteurized

저울 [jeoul] *npl* scales

저자 [jeoja] *n* author, writer

저작 [jeojak] 저작권 [jeojakgwon] *n* copyright

저장 [jeojang] *n* storage; 식료품 저장실 [singnyopum jeojangsil] *n* larder; 저장하다 [jeojanghada] *v* store

저주 [jeoju] *n* curse; 저주받은 [jeojubadeun] *adj* damn

저지 [jeoji] *n* jersey

저지르다 [jeojireuda] *v* commit

저쪽 [jeojjok] 저쪽에 있어요 [jeojjoge isseoyo] It's over there

저축 [jeochuk] *npl* savings; 저축하다 [jeochukhada] *v* save up

저택 [jeotaek] 대저택 [daejeotaek] *n* mansion, stately home

저항 [jeohang] *n* resistance; 저항하다 [jeohanghada] *v* resist

적개심 [jeokgaesim] 적개심을 일으키다 [jeokgaesimeul ireukida] *v* antagonize

적게 [jeokge] 더 적게 [deo jeokge] *adv* less

적극 [jeokgeuk] 적극적인 [jeokgeukjeogin] *adj* positive

적다 [jeokda] *v* be few, write down; 보다 적은 양 [boda jeogeun yang] *pron* less; 주소를 적어 주시겠어요? [jusoreul jeogeo jusigesseoyo?] Will you write down the address, please?; 적어 주시겠어요? [jeogeo jusigesseoyo?] Could you write it down, please?, Could you write that down, please?; 가격을 적어 주세요 [gagyeogeul jeogeo juseyo] Please write down the price

적당 [jeokdang] 부적당한 [bujeokdanghan] *adj* inadequate

적대 [jeokdae] 적대적인 [jeokdaejeogin] *adj* hostile

적도 [jeokdo] *n* equator; 적도 기니 [jeokdo gini] *n* Equatorial Guinea

적수 [jeoksu] *n* adversary

적십자 [jeoksipja] *n* Red Cross

적어도 [jeogeodo] *adv* at least

적응 [jeogeung] *n* adaptation; 적응시키다 [jeogeungsikida] *v* adapt

적절 [jeokjeol] 적절하게 [jeokjeolhage] *adv* properly

적합 [jeokhap] 적합성 [jeokhapseong] *n* fit; 적합하다 [jeokhaphada] *vi* fit; 적합한 [jeokhaphan] *adj* appropriate, proper, suitable

전 [jeon] 전 남편 [jeon nampyeon] *n* ex-husband; 전조등 [jeonjodeung] *n* headlamp, headlight;...전에 [...jeone] *prep* before; 전에 [jeone] *adv* previously;...전에 [...jeone] *prep* before; 전의 [jeonui] *adj* former; 전처 [jeoncheo] *n* ex-wife; 전경 [jeongyeong] *n* foreground; 전표 [jeonpyo] *n* slip *(paper)*; 기원전 [giwonjeon] *abbr* BC; 다섯시 전에 [daseossi jeone] before five o'clock; 여름 전에 [yeoreum jeone] before summer; 일주일 전에 [iljuil jeone] a week ago; 한 달 전에 [han dal jeone] a month ago

전갈 [jeongal] *n* scorpion; 전갈자리 [jeongaljari] *n* Scorpio

전구 [jeongu] *n* bulb *(electricity)*, light bulb

전국 [jeonguk] 전국지도를 어디에서 살 수 있어요? [jeongukjidoreul eodieseo sal su isseoyo?] Where can I buy a map of the country?

전기 [jeongi] *n* biography, electricity; 전기 담요 [jeongi damyo] *n* electric blanket; 전기 기사 [jeongi gisa] *n* electrician; 전기의 [jeonguiui] *adj* electric, electrical; 전기 요금을 추가로 내야 하나요? [jeongi yogeumeul chugaro naeya hanayo?] Do we have to pay extra for electricity?; 전기 요금이 포함되나요? [jeongi yogeumi pohamdoenayo?] Is the cost of electricity included?; 전기 계량기는 어디있어요? [jeongi gyeryanggineun eodiisseoyo?] Where is the electricity meter?; 전기가 안 들어와요 [jeongiga an deureowayo] There is no electricity

전단 [jeondan] 전단지 [jeondanji] *n* leaflet

전당포 [jeondangpo] *n* pawnbroker

전대 [jeondae] *n* money belt

전도 [jeondo] *n* future; 전도 유망한

[jeondo yumanghan] *adj* promising

전등 [jeondeung] 손전등 [sonjeondeung] *n* torch; **전등이 작동하지 않아요** [jeondeungi jakdonghaji anhayo] The light doesn't work

전략 [jeollyak] *n* strategy; **전략적인** [jeollyakjeogin] *adj* strategic

전류 [jeollyu] *n* current *(electricity)*

전망 [jeonmang] *n* outlook, prospect

전문 [jeonmun] *n* speciality; **전문으로 하다** [jeonmuneuro hada] *v* specialize; **전문가 [jeonmunga]** *n* expert, professional, specialist

전반 [jeonban] 전반적으로 [jeonbanjeogeuro] *adv* overall

전보 [jeonbo] *n* telegram; **어디에서 전보를 보낼 수 있을까요?** [eodieseo jeonboreul bonael su isseulkkayo?] Where can I send a telegram from?; **여기에서 전보를 보낼 수 있을까요?** [yeogieseo jeonboreul bonael su isseulkkayo?] Can I send a telegram from here?; **전보를 보내고 싶어요** [jeonboreul bonaego sipeoyo] I want to send a telegram

전부 [jeonbu] *pron* all

전분 [jeonbun] *n* starch

전선 [jeonseon] *n* flex

전설 [jeonseol] *n* legend; **민간전설** [minganjeonseol] *n* folklore

전세기 [jeonsegi] *n* charter flight

전소 [jeonso] 전소하다 [jeonsohada] *v* burn down

전속력 [jeonsongnyeok] 전속력으로 달리다 [jeonsongnyeogeuro dallida] *v* sprint

전송 [jeonsong] 전송하다 [jeonsonghada] *v* forward

전술 [jeonsul] *npl* tactics

전시 [jeonsi] *n* display; **전시하다** [jeonsihada] *v* display; **전시회** [jeonsihoe] *n* exhibition, showing

전신 [jeonsin] *n* whole body; **전신 마취** [jeonsin machwi] *n* general anaesthetic

전압 [jeonap] *n* voltage; **전압이 어떻게 되나요?** [jeonabi eotteoke doenayo?]

What's the voltage?

전야 [jeonya] *n* eve

전염 [jeonyeom] *n* infection; **전염성의** [jeonyeomseongui] *adj* contagious; **전염성인 [jeonyeomseongin]** *adj* infectious

전염성 [jeonyeomseong] 전염성의 [jeonyeomseongui] *adj* catching

전용 [jeonyong] 보행자 전용 구역 [bohaengja jeonyong guyeok] *n* pedestrian precinct; **보행자 전용의** [bohaengja jeonyongui] *adj* pedestrianized

전율 [jeonyul] *n* thrill; **전율을 느끼는** [jeonyureul neukkineun] *adj* thrilled

전이 [jeoni] 전임으로 [jeonimeuro] *adv* full-time

전임 [jeonim] 전임의 [jeonimui] *adj* full-time; **전임자 [jeonimja]** *n* predecessor

전자 [jeonja] 전자책 [jeonjachaek] *n* e-book; **전자상거래** [jeonjasanggeorae] *n* e-commerce; **전자의 [jeonjaui]** *adj* electronic; **전자공학 [jeonjagonghak]** *npl* electronics; **전자티켓 [jeonjatiket]** *n* e-ticket; **전류 계통에 문제가 있어요** [jeollyu gyetonge munjega isseoyo] There is something wrong with the electrics

전쟁 [jeonjaeng] *n* war

전지 [jeonji] *n* battery

전진 [jeonjin] *n* advance; **전진시키다** [jeonjinsikida] *v* advance

전차 [jeoncha] *n* tram

전채 [jeonchae] 전채요리 [jeonchaeyori] *n* starter; **전채요리로 파스타를 주세요** [jeonchaeyoriro paseutareul juseyo] I'd like pasta as a starter

전체 [jeonche] *n* whole; **...의 전체에 [...ui jeonchee]** *prep* throughout; **전체의 [jeoncheui]** *adj* entire, total, whole; **전체의 [jeoncheui]** *adj* gross *(income etc.)*

전통 [jeontong] *n* tradition; **전통적인 [jeontongjeogin]** *adj* traditional; **전통적인 [jeontongjeogin]** *adj* conventional

전투 [jeontu] n battle
전하 [jeonha] n charge (electricity)
전하다 [jeonhada] vt deliver
전함 [jeonham] n battleship
전형 [jeonhyeong] 전형적인
[jeonhyeongjeogin] adj classic, typical
전화 [jeonhwa] n phone, phonecall,
telephone; 비디오 전화 [bidio
jeonhwa] n videophone; 다시
전화하다 [dasi jeonhwahada] v call
back, phone back, ring back; 상담전화
[sangdamjeonhwa] n helpline; 잘못
걸린 전화 [jalmot geollin jeonhwa] n
wrong number; 전화 카드 [jeonhwa
kadeu] n phonecard; 전화를 끊다
[jeonhwareul kkeunta] v hang up;
전화를 걸다 [jeonhwareul geolda] v
dial; 전화요금 고지서
[jeonhwayogeum gojiseo] n phone
bill; 전화교환대
[jeonhwagyohwandae] n
switchboard; 전화판매
[jeonhwapanmae] npl telesales;
전화하다 [jeonhwahada] v phone, ring
up; 공중 전화 [gongjung jeonhwa] n
phonebox; 공중 전화 박스 [gongjung
jeonhwa bakseu] n call box; 공중전화
[gongjungjeonhwa] n payphone;
대사관에 전화하고 싶어요
[daesagwane jeonhwahago sipeoyo]
I'd like to phone my embassy; 어디에서
전화를 할 수 있을까요? [eodieseo
jeonhwareul hal su isseulkkayo?]
Where can I make a phone call?;
어디에서 국제 전화를 할 수 있나요?
[eodieseo gukje jeonhwareul hal su
innayo?] Where can I make an
international phone call?; 여기에서
전화를 해도 될까요? [yeogieseo
jeonhwareul haedo doelkkayo?] Can I
phone from here?; 여기에서 국제
전화를 해도 될까요? [yeogieseo gukje
jeonhwareul haedo doelkkayo?] Can I
phone internationally from here?;...에
전화하려면 얼마예요? [...e
jeonhwaharyeomyeon eolmayeyo?]
How much is it to telephone...?; 전화
좀 쓸 수 있을까요? [jeonhwa jom sseul

su isseulkkayo?] Can I use your phone,
please?, May I use your phone?; 전화를
하고 싶어요 [jeonhwareul hago
sipeoyo] I want to make a phone call;
전화를 해야 해요 [jeonhwareul haeya
haeyo] I must make a phone call;
전화번호가 무엇입니까?
[jeonhwabeonhoga mueosimnikka?]
What's the telephone number?; 전화에
문제가 있어요 [jeonhwae munjega
isseoyo] I'm having trouble with the
phone; 집에 전화하시겠어요? [jibe
jeonhwahasigesseoyo?] Would you like
to phone home?; 집에 전화해도
될까요? [jibe jeonhwahaedo
doelkkayo?] May I phone home?; 긴급
전화를 해야 해요 [gingeup
jeonhwareul haeya haeyo] I need to
make an urgent telephone call
전화번호 [jeonhwabeonho] n phone
number; 전화번호 문의
[jeonhwabeonho munui] npl directory
enquiries; 전화번호부
[jeonhwabeonhobu] n directory,
phonebook, telephone directory;
당신의 휴대 전화번호는 몇 번인가요?
[dangsinui hyudae
jeonhwabeonhoneun myeot
beoningayo?] What is the number of
your mobile?; 전화번호 문의는 몇
번인가요? [jeonhwabeonho
munuineun myeot beoningayo?] What
is the number for directory enquiries?;
전화번호 좀 알려 주시겠어요?
[jeonhwabeonho jom allyeo
jusigesseoyo?] Can I have your phone
number?; 제 휴대 전화 번호는...이에요
[je hyudae jeonhwa beonhoneun...
ieyo] My mobile number is...
전화카드 [jeonhwakadeu] n phone card;
25유로짜리 전화카드를 사고 싶어요
[ishibo yurojjari jeonhwakadeureul
sago sipeoyo] I'd like a twenty-five
euro phone card; 어디에서 전화카드를 살
수 있어요? [eodieseo
jeonhwakadeureul sal su isseoyo?]
Where can I buy a phonecard?;
전화카드 주세요 [jeonhwakadeu

juseyo] A phonecard, please; 전화카드
파세요? [jeonhwakadeu paseyo?] Do
you sell phone cards?; 국제 전화카드
주세요 [gukje jeonhwakadeu juseyo]
An international phone card, please;
국제 전화카드 파세요? [gukje
jeonhwakadeu paseyo?] Do you sell
international phone cards?

전환 [jeonhwan] n diversion

절 [jeol] 만우절 [manujeol] n April Fools'
Day

절다 [jeolda] 다리를 절다 [darireul
jeolda] v limp

절단 [jeoldan] n cut, cutting; 절단하다
[jeoldanhada] v cut

절대 [jeoldae] 절대 금주의 [jeoldae
geumjuui] adj teetotal; 절대적으로
[jeoldaejeogeuro] adv absolutely

절도 [jeoldo] n thief; 상점 절도
[sangjeom jeoldo] n shoplifting

절망 [jeolmang] n despair; 절망적인
[jeolmangjeogin] adj desperate

절반 [jeolban] 절반으로 [jeolbaneuro]
adv fifty-fifty; 절반의 [jeolbanui] adj
fifty-fifty

절벽 [jeolbyeok] n cliff

절약 [jeollyak] 절약하다 [jeollyakhada] v
economize

절연 [jeollyeon] n insulation

절차 [jeolcha] 소송 절차 [sosong
jeolcha] npl proceedings

절하 [jeolha] 평가절하 [pyeonggajeolha]
n devaluation

절하다 [jeolhada] v bow

젊은이 [jeormeuni] n lad

점 [jeom] n dot, mole (skin), spot
(blemish); 보석점 [boseokjeom] n
jeweller's; 문구점 [mungujeom] n
stationer's; 원예점 [wonyejeom] n
garden centre

점검 [jeomgeom] 점검하다
[jeomgeomhada] n check

점령 [jeomnyeong] n occupation
(invasion)

점성 [jeomseong] 점성술
[jeomseongsul] n astrology

점심 [jeomsim] n lunch; 점심시간
[jeomsimsigan] n lunch break,

lunchtime; 만나서 점심 먹을까요?
[mannaseo jeomsim meogeulkkayo?]
Can we meet for lunch?; 언제 점심이
준비되나요? [eonje jeomsimi
junbidoenayo?] When will lunch be
ready?; 점심 때 시간 있어요 [jeomsim
ttae sigan isseoyo] I'm free for lunch;
점심 먹으러 어디에서 정차해요?
[jeomsim meogeureo eodieseo
jeongchahaeyo?] Where do we stop for
lunch?; 점심이 훌륭했어요 [jeomsimi
hullyunghaesseoyo] The lunch was
excellent

점원 [jeomwon] n shop assistant

점유 [jeomyu] 점유하다 [jeomyuhada] v
occupy

점진 [jeomjin] 점진적인 [jeomjinjeogin]
adj gradual

점차 [jeomcha] adv gradually,
increasingly

점토 [jeomto] n clay

점퍼 [jeompeo] n jumper

점프 [jeompeu] 번지점프
[beonjijeompeu] n bungee jumping;
점프선 [jeompeuseon] npl jump leads

점호 [jeomho] n roll call

점화 [jeomhwa] n lighting; 점화 플러그
[jeomhwa peulleogeu] n spark plug

접 [jeop] 접사다리 [jeopsadari] n
stepladder

접근 [jeopgeun] n access; 접근하다
[jeopgeunhada] v approach; 접근하기
쉬운 [jeopgeunhagi swiun] adj
accessible

접다 [jeopda] vt fold; 접는 [jeomneun]
adj folding; 접은 자리 [jeobeun jari] n
fold

접속 [jeopsok] 접속하다 [jeopsokhada]
v access; 접속이 안돼요 [jeopsogi
andwaeyo] I can't log on

접수 [jeopsu] 접수창구 [jeopsuchanggu]
n reception; 접수계원 [jeopsugyewon]
n receptionist

접시 [jeopsi] n dish (plate), plate; 받침
접시 [batchim jeopsi] n saucer

접종 [jeopjong] n inoculation,
vaccination; 예방접종
[yebangjeopjong] n vaccination;

예방접종을 하다 [yebangjeopjongeul hada] v vaccinate; **백신 접종이 필요해요** [baeksin jeopjongi pillyohaeyo] I need a vaccination

접질림 [jeopjillim] n sprain

접촉 [jeopchok] **접촉하다** [jeopchokhada] v contact

접합 [jeophap] **접합 부문** [jeophap bumun] n joint (junction)

젓가락 [jeotgarak] npl chopsticks

젓다 [jeotda] vi paddle; **휘젓다** [hwijeotda] vt stir

정강이 [jeonggangi] n shin

정거 [jeonggeo] **정거장** [jeonggeojang] n station

정거장 [jeonggeojang]...**까지 몇 정거장인가요?** [...kkaji myeot jeonggeojangingayo?] How many stops is it to...?

정글 [jeonggeul] n jungle

정기 [jeonggi] **정기 승차권** [jeonggi seungchagwon] n season ticket; **정기 항공편** [jeonggi hanggongpyeon] n scheduled flight; **정기적인** [jeonggijeogin] adj on time; **정기구독** [jeonggigudok] n standing order

정기선 [jeonggiseon] n liner

정당 [jeongdang] **정당방위** [jeongdangbangwi] n self-defence; **정당한** [jeongdanghan] adj valid; **정당화하다** [jeongdanghwahada] v justify

정도 [jeongdo] n degree

정돈 [jeongdon] **정돈하다** [jeongdonhada] v clear up, tidy, tidy up

정량 [jeongnyang] n dose, size; **정량화하다** [jeongnyanghwahada] v quantify

정력 [jeongnyeok] n stamina; **정력적인** [jeongnyeokjeogin] adj energetic

정류장 [jeongnyujang] **버스 정류장** [beoseu jeongnyujang] n bus station, bus stop; **버스 정류장은 어디있어요?** [beoseu jeongnyujangeun eodiisseoyo?] Where is the bus station?; **버스 정류장이 얼마나 먼가요?** [beoseu jeongnyujangi eolmana meongayo?] How far is the bus stop?; **버스 정류장까지 거리가 얼마나 될까요?** [beoseu jeongnyujangkkaji georiga eolmana doelkkayo?] How far are we from the bus station?; **가장 가까운 버스 정류장은 어디있어요?** [gajang gakkaun beoseu jeongnyujangeun eodiisseoyo?] Where is the nearest bus stop?; **택시정류장 어디에 있어요?** [taeksijeongnyujang eodie isseoyo?] Where is the taxi stand?

정리 [jeongni] **정리하다** [jeongnihada] v freshen up

정말 [jeongmal] adv indeed

정맥 [jeongmaek] n vein

정밀 [jeongmil] **정밀검사** [jeongmilgeomsa] n scan

정박 [jeongbak] **정박하다** [jeongbakhada] v moor

정방향 [jeongbanghyang] **정방향 좌석이요** [jeongbanghyang jwaseogiyo] Facing the front, please

정보 [jeongbo] n information; **정보 제공자** [jeongbo jegongja] n grass (informer); **정보를 주는** [jeongboreul juneun] adj informative; **정보기술** [jeongbogisul] abbr IT;...**에 관한 정보를 얻고 싶어요** [...e gwanhan jeongboreul eotgo sipeoyo] I'd like some information about...; **우리 회사에 관한 정보예요** [uri hoesae gwanhan jeongboyeyo] Here's some information about my company; **회사에 관한 정보를 받고 싶어요** [hoesae gwanhan jeongboreul batgo sipeoyo] I would like some information about the company

정복 [jeongbok] **정복하다** [jeongbokhada] v conquer

정부 [jeongbu] n government

정비 [jeongbi] n garage; **자동차정비공** [jadongchajeongbigong] n motor mechanic; **차량 연례 정비** [charyang yeollye jeongbi] abbr MOT

정비사 [jeongbisa] **정비사를 보내 주시겠어요?** [jeongbisareul bonae jusigesseoyo?] Can you send a mechanic?

정비소 [jeongbiso] 이 근처에 정비소가 있나요? [i geuncheoe jeongbisoga innayo?] Is there a garage near here?; 정비소까지 견인해 주시겠어요? [jeongbisokkaji gyeoninhae jusigesseoyo?] Can you tow me to a garage?; 정비소까지 태워 주시겠어요? [jeongbisokkaji taewo jusigesseoyo?] Can you give me a lift to the garage?

정상 [jeongsang] n summit; 비정상적인 [bijeongsangjeogin] adj abnormal; 정상의 [jeongsangui] adj normal; 정상적으로 [jeongsangjeogeuro] adv normally

정신 [jeongsin] n spirit; 정신 병원 [jeongsin byeongwon] n mental hospital; 정신 이상자 [jeongsin isangja] n lunatic; 정신의학의 [jeongsinuihagui] adj psychiatric; 정신이상 [jeongsinisang] n madness; 정신적인 [jeongsinjeogin] adj mental, spiritual; 정신과 의사 [jeongsingwa uisa] n psychiatrist

정신분열 [jeongsinbunyeol] 정신분열증의 [jeongsinbunyeoljeungui] adj schizophrenic

정어리 [jeongeori] n sardine

정오 [jeongo] n midday, noon; 정오 열두시예요 [jeongo yeoldusiyeyo] It's twelve midday; 정오에 [jeongoe] at midday

정욕 [jeongyok] n lust

정원 [jeongwon] n garden; 정원 가꾸기 [jeongwon gakkugi] n gardening; 정원사 [jeongwonsa] n gardener; 정원을 방문할 수 있어요? [jeongwoneul bangmunhal su isseoyo?] Can we visit the gardens?

정유 [jeongyu] 정유 공장 [jeongyu gongjang] n oil refinery

정육점 [jeongyukjeom] n butcher's; 정육점 주인 [jeongyukjeom juin] n butcher

정의 [jeongui] n definition, justice; 정의하다 [jeonguihada] v define

정자 [jeongja] n sperm

정전 [jeongjeon] n power cut

정정 [jeongjeong] n correction; 정정하다 [jeongjeonghada] v correct

정제 [jeongje] n tablet; 정제소 [jeongjeso] n refinery

정중 [jeongjung] 정중하게 [jeongjunghage] adv politely; 정중한 [jeongjunghan] adj polite; 정중함 [jeongjungham] n politeness

정지 [jeongji] n stop, suspension; 정지된 [jeongjidoen] adv still; 정지등 [jeongjideung] n brake light; 정지하다 [jeongjihada] n halt

정직 [jeongjik] n honesty; 정직하게 [jeongjikhage] adv honestly; 정직한 [jeongjikhan] adj honest, straightforward

정차 [jeongcha] ...에서 정차합니까? [... eseo jeongchahamnikka?] Do we stop at...?

정찰 [jeongchal] n scout

정체 [jeongche] n congestion; 정체 불명의 [jeongche bulmyeongui] adj unidentified; 정체성 [jeongcheseong] n identity

정치 [jeongchi] 정치적인 [jeongchijeogin] adj political; 정치가 [jeongchiga] n politician; 정치학 [jeongchihak] npl politics

정탐 [jeongtam] 정탐하기 [jeongtamhagi] n spying

정하다 [jeonghada] v settle

정향 [jeonghyang] n clove

정화 [jeonghwa] 정화조 [jeonghwajo] n septic tank

정확 [jeonghwak] 부정확한 [bujeonghwakhan] adj inaccurate, incorrect; 정확성 [jeonghwakseong] n accuracy; 정확하게 [jeonghwakhage] adv accurately, precisely; 정확하게 [jeonghwakhage] adv correctly; 정확한 [jeonghwakhan] adj accurate, exact, precise; 정확히 [jeonghwakhi] adv exactly

젖 [jeot] 젖을 짜다 [jeojeul jjada] v milk

젖다 [jeotda] 젖은 [jeojeun] adj wet; 함빡 젖은 [hamppak jeojeun] adj soggy; 흠뻑 젖은 [heumppeok jeojeun] adj soaked

제 [je] 얼룩 제거제 [eolluk jegeoje] n
stain remover; 자외선 차단제
[jaoeseon chadanje] n sunblock,
sunscreen; 제초제 [jechoje] n
weedkiller; 강장제 [gangjangje] n
tonic; 광택제 [gwangtaekje] n polish;
유연제 있어요? [yuyeonje isseoyo?] Do
you have softener?
제거 [jegeo] n removal; 매니큐어 제거제
[maenikyueo jegeoje] n nail-polish
remover; 얼룩 제거제 [eolluk jegeoje]
n stain remover; 제거하다 [jegeohada]
v eliminate, take away; 제거하다
[jegeohada] v remove
제공 [jegong] n offer; 1박 2식 제공
[ilbak isik jegong] n half board; 정보
제공자 [jeongbo jegongja] n grass
(informer); 제공하다 [jegonghada] v
offer, provide
제국 [jeguk] n empire
제기 [jegi] 소송제기하다
[sosongjegihada] v sue
제단 [jedan] n altar
제도 [jedo] 제도법 [jedobeop] npl
graphics; 페로스 제도 [peroseu jedo]
npl Faroe Islands
제라늄 [jeranyum] n geranium
제목 [jemok] n title
제발 [jebal] 제발! [jebal!] excl please
제복 [jebok] n uniform
제비 [jebi] 제비뽑기 [jebippopgi] n draw
(lottery)
제빵 [jeppang] 제빵사 [jeppangsa] n
baker
제삼 [jesam] 제3세계 [je3segye] n Third
World
제설 [jeseol] 제설기 [jeseolgi] n
snowplough
제안 [jean] n proposal, suggestion;
제안하다 [jeanhada] v propose,
suggest
제외 [jeoe] n exception, exclusion;...을
제외하고 [...eul jeoehago] prep except,
excluding; 제외하다 [jeoehada] v
exclude, rule out
제작 [jejak] 주문 제작한 [jumun
jejakhan] adj customized
제정 [jejeong] 법률제정

[beomnyuljejeong] n legislation
제조 [jejo] n make; 제조하다 [jejohada]
v manufacture
제쳐두다 [jechyeoduda] 제쳐 놓고
[jechyeo noko] prep apart from
제초 [jecho] 제초제 [jechoje] n
weedkiller
제출 [jechul] 제출하다 [jechulhada] v
put forward
제트기 [jeteugi] n jet; 점보제트기
[jeombojeteugi] n jumbo jet
제트스키 [jeteuseuki] 어디에서 제트
스키를 빌릴 수 있나요? [eodieseo jeteu
seukireul billil su innayo?] Where can I
hire a jet-ski?
제품 [jepum] n product; 배달 [baedal] n
delivery; 유제품 [yujepum] npl dairy
produce, dairy products; 유제품 회사
[yujepum hoesa] n dairy; 화학 제품
[hwahak jepum] n chemical; 스타일링
제품 파세요? [seutailling jepum
paseyo?] Do you sell styling products?
제한 [jehan] n limit; 나이 제한 [nai
jehan] n age limit; 산아 제한 [sana
jehan] n birth control; 속도제한
[sokdojehan] n speed limit; 제한 초과
수하물 [jehan chogwa suhamul] n
excess baggage; 제한하다 [jehanhada]
v restrict
제한속도 [jehansokdo] 이 도로는 제한
속도가 얼마인가요? [i doroneun jehan
sokdoga eolmaingayo?] What is the
speed limit on this road?
제휴 [jehyu] 제휴자 [jehyuja] n
associate
젤 [jel] 헤어 젤 [heeo jel] n hair gel
젤리 [jelli] n jelly
조 [jo] 곡조 [gokjo] n tune
조각 [jogak] n chip (small piece), scrap
(small piece); 조각술 [jogaksul] n
sculpture; 조각가 [jogakga] n sculptor;
조각하다 [jogakhada] v engrave;
색종이 조각 [saekjongi jogak] npl
confetti; 얇은 조각 [yarbeun jogak] n
slice; 장식용 금속 조각 [jangsigyong
geumsok jogak] n tinsel; 작은 조각
[jageun jogak] n bit; 한 조각 [han
jogak] n piece

조개 [jogae] n shellfish; 조개 알레르기가 있어요 [jogae allereugiga isseoyo] I'm allergic to shellfish

조건 [jogeon] n condition;...(이라는) 조건으로 [...(iraneun) jogeoneuro] conj provided, providing; 조건부의 [jogeonbuui] adj conditional; 필요조건 [piryojogeon] n requirement

조깅 [joging] n jogging; 조깅하다 [joginghada] vi jog; 어디에서 조깅을 할 수 있어요? [eodieseo jogingeul hal su isseoyo?] Where can I go jogging?

조끼 [jokki] n waistcoat; 구명조끼 [gumyeongjokki] n life jacket

조랑말 [jorangmal] n pony; 조랑말 여행을 하고 싶어요 [jorangmal yeohaengeul hago sipeoyo] I'd like to go pony trekking

조롱 [jorong] 조롱하다 [joronghada] v mock

조만간 [jomangan] adv sooner

조명 [jomyeong] 투광 조명 [tugwang jomyeong] n floodlight

조물 [jomul] 조물주 [jomulju] n maker

조미 [jomi] 조미료 [jomiryo] n seasoning

조사 [josa] n investigation, survey; 조사관 [josagwan] n inspector; 조사하다 [josahada] v examine, inspect; 시장조사 [sijangjosa] n market research; 여론조사 [yeoronjosa] n opinion poll, poll; 인구 조사 [ingu josa] n census

조상 [josang] n ancestor

조선 [joseon] n shipbuilding; 조선소 [joseonso] n shipyard

조수 [josu] n assistant, tide

조심 [josim] n caution; 조심스러운 [josimseureoun] adj careful; 조심스럽게 [josimseureopge] adv carefully, cautiously; 조심하는 [josimhaneun] adj cautious

조약 [joyak] n treaty; 북대서양조약기구 [bukdaeseoyangjoyakgigu] abbr NATO

조언 [joeon] n advice; 조언하다 [joeonhada] v advise

조용 [joyong] 조용한 [joyonghan] adj silent

조용하다 [joyonghada] v keep quiet, stay silent; 조용하게 [joyonghage] adv quietly; 조용한 [joyonghan] adj quiet

조이다 [joida] 결속 장치를 조여 주시겠어요? [gyeolsok jangchireul joyeo jusigesseoyo?] Can you tighten my bindings, please?

조절 [jojeol] 자동 온도 조절기 [jadong ondo jojeolgi] n thermostat

조정 [jojeong] n adjustment; 맥박 조정기 [maekbak jojeonggi] n pacemaker; 조정하다 [jojeonghada] v adjust; 조정할 수 있는 [jojeonghal su inneun] adj adjustable

조제 [joje] n pharmacy; 조제식품 [jojesikpum] n delicatessen

조종 [jojong] n controls; 무선으로 조종되는 [museoneuro jojongdoeneun] adj radio-controlled; 조종실 [jojongsil] n cockpit; 조종하다 [jojonghada] v manipulate; 조종이 안 돼요 [jojongi an dwaeyo] The controls have jammed; 어떻게 조종하는지 보여주시겠어요? [eotteoke jojonghaneunji boyeojusigesseoyo?] Can you show me how the controls work?

조종간 [jojonggan] n joystick, lever

조지아 [jojia] n Georgia (US state)

조직 [jojik] n organization, tissue (anatomy), tissue (paper); 조직적인 [jojikjeogin] adj systematic; 조직하다 [jojikhada] v organize; 재조직하다 [jaejojikhada] v reorganize

조치 [jochi] 예방조치 [yebangjochi] n precaution

조카 [joka] n nephew; 조카딸 [jokattal] n niece

조타 [jota] n steering

조합 [johap] 노동조합 [nodongjohap] n trade union; 노동조합 [nodongjohap] n pool (resources)

조합원 [johabwon] n mixture, partnership; 노동조합원 [nodongjohabwon] n trade unionist

조항 [johang] n clause

족제비 [jokjebi] n weasel

존경 [jongyeong] n respect; 존경하다

[jongyeonghada] v respect; 존경할
만한 [jongyeonghal manhan] adj
respectable

존엄 [joneom] 존엄성 [joneomseong] n
dignity

존재 [jonjae] n presence; 존재하다
[jonjaehada] v be, exist; 귀찮은 존재
[gwichanheun jonjae] n nuisance

졸다 [jolda] v doze

졸리다 [jollida] 졸리는 [jollineun] adj
drowsy, sleepy

졸업 [joreop] n graduation; 졸업장
[joreopjang] n diploma

졸업생 [joreopsaeng] 대학 졸업생
[daehak joreopsaeng] n graduate

좁다 [jopda] 마음이 좁은 [maeumi
jobeun] adj narrow-minded; 좁은
[jobeun] adj narrow

종 [jong] n bell; 종치기 [jongchigi] n toll

종결 [jonggyeol] n closure

종교 [jonggyo] n religion

종기 [jonggi] n abscess; 종기가 났어요
[jonggiga nasseoyo] I have an abscess

종류 [jongnyu] n kind, sort, species; 어떤
치즈인가요? [eotteon chijeuingayo?]
What sort of cheese?

종말 [jongmal] adv all day long; 종말에
[jongmare] adv terminally

종사 [jongsa] 준의료 종사자 [junuiryo
jongsaja] n paramedic

종양 [jongyang] n tumour

종이 [jongi] n paper; 종이클립
[jongikeullip] n paperclip; 페이퍼 백
[peipeo baek] n paperback

종점 [jongjeom] n terminal

종합 [jonghap] 종합 보험료로 얼마를 더
내야 할까요? [jonghap boheomnyoro
eolmareul deo naeya halkkayo?] How
much extra is comprehensive
insurance cover?

좋다 [jota] 더 좋은 [deo joheun] adj
better; 더 좋게 [deo joke] adv better;
좋아! [joha!] excl okay!, OK!; 좋은
[joheun] adj fine, good, nice; 좋게
[joke] n fine; 굉장히 좋은 [goengjanghi
joheun] adj fabulous; 몸이 안 좋아요
[momi an johayo] He's not well; 날씨가
참 좋아요! [nalssiga cham johayo!]

What a lovely day!; 예, 좋아요 [ye,
johayo] Yes, I'd love to; 이것도 마음에
들지 않아요 [igeotdo maeume deulji
anhayo] I don't like it either; 정말
좋군요 [jeongmal jokunyo] It's quite
good; 좋아요! [johayo!] OK!

좋아하다 [johahada] v like; 캐묻기
좋아하는 [kaemutgi johahaneun] adj
inquisitive; 좋아하는 [johahaneun] adj
favourite; 좋아하는 것 [johahaneun
geot] n favourite; 당신을 아주 많이
좋아해요 [dangsineul aju manhi
johahaeyo] I like you very much;
저는...을 좋아하지 않아요 [jeoneun...
eul johahaji anhayo] I don't like...;
저는...을 좋아해요 [jeoneun...eul
johahaeyo] I like...

좌석 [jwaseok] n seat; 좌석 벨트
[jwaseok belteu] n seatbelt; 창쪽 좌석
[changjjok jwaseok] n window seat;
두 살짜리 어린이 좌석이 있으면
좋겠어요 [du saljjari eorini jwaseogi
isseumyeon jokesseoyo] I'd like a child
seat for a two-year-old child; 어린이
좌석이 있어요? [eorini jwaseogi
isseoyo?] Do you have a child's seat?;
좌석을 예약했어요 [jwaseogeul
yeyakhaesseoyo] I have a seat
reservation; 창쪽 좌석이 좋아요
[changjjok jwaseogi johayo] I'd like a
window seat; 금연실 좌석을 예약하고
싶어요 [geumyeonsil jwaseogeul
yeyakhago sipeoyo] I want to book a
seat in a non-smoking compartment;
통로쪽 좌석이 좋아요 [tongnojjok
jwaseogi johayo] I'd like an aisle seat;
흡연구역 좌석으로 주세요
[heubyeonguyeok jwaseogeuro
juseyo] I'd like a seat in the smoking
area

좌우 [jwau] 앞뒤(좌우)로 흔들다
[apdwi(jwau)ro heundeulda] v rock

좌익 [jwaik] 좌익의 [jwaigui] adj
left-wing

좌절 [jwajeol] 좌절한 [jwajeolhan] adj
frustrated

좌천 [jwacheon] 좌천시키다
[jwacheonsikida] v relegate

죄 [joe] *n* sin; 위증죄 [wijeungjoe] *n* perjury

죄다 [joeda] 단단히 죄다 [dandanhi joeda] *v* tighten

죄수 [joesu] *n* prisoner

주 [ju] *n* week; 주 요리 [ju yori] *n* main course; 주로 [juro] *adv* mainly, primarily; 주된 [judoen] *adj* principal; 주말 [jumal] *n* weekend; 식전 반주 [sikjeon banju] *n* aperitif; 다다음 주 [dadaeum ju] the week after next; 다음 주 [daeum ju] next week; 일주일 안에 [iljuil ane] in a week's time; 일주일 전에 [iljuil jeone] a week ago; 지난 주 [jinan ju] last week; 지지난주 [jijinanju] the week before last

주간 [jugan] *n* daytime

주걱 [jugeok] *n* spatula

주교 [jugyo] *n* bishop; 대주교 [daejugyo] *n* archbishop

주근깨 [jugeunkkae] *npl* freckles

주기 [jugi] *n* cycle (recurring period)

주다 [juda] *vt* give;...을 되돌려 주다 [... eul doedollyeo juda] *vi* return; 돌려주다 [dollyeojuda] *v* give back; 건네 주다 [geonne juda] *v* hand; 얼마나 줘야 되나요? [eolmana jwoya doenayo?] How much should I give?; 잔돈을 잘못 주신 것 같아요 [jandoneul jalmot jusin geot gatayo] I think you've given me the wrong change

주도권 [judogwon] *n* initiative

주류 [juryu] 주류판매 면허 [juryupanmae myeonheo] *n* off-licence

주름 [jureum] *n* crease; 주름살 [jureumsal] *n* wrinkle; 주름이 간 [jureumi gan] *adj* creased; 주름진 [jureumjin] *adj* wrinkled

주말 [jumal] *n* weekend; 주말동안 차를 빌리고 싶어요 [jumaldongan chareul billigo sipeoyo] I want to hire a car for the weekend

주머니 [jumeoni] *n* pocket; 향주머니 [hyangjumeoni] *n* sachet; 허리 주머니 [heori jumeoni] *n* bum bag

주먹 [jumeok] *n* fist

주목 [jumok] *n* yew

주문 [jumun] *n* spell (magic); 주문 제작한 [jumun jejakhan] *adj* customized; 주문서 [jumunseo] *n* order form; 주문하다 [jumunhada] *v* order (request)

주민 [jumin] *n* inhabitant, resident

주방 [jubang] *n* kitchen; 맞춤 주방 [matchum jubang] *n* fitted kitchen

주부 [jubu] *n* housewife

주사 [jusa] *n* injection; 주사기 [jusagi] *n* syringe; 주사하다 [jusahada] (편지) *v* inject; 주사를 놔 주세요 [jusareul nwa juseyo] Please give me an injection; 진통제 주사를 맞고 싶어요 [jintongje jusareul matgo sipeoyo] I want an injection for the pain; 진통제 주사를 원하지 않아요 [jintongje jusareul wonhaji anhayo] I don't want an injection for the pain

주사위 [jusawi] *npl* dice

주소 [juso] *n* address (location); 주소록 [jusorok] *n* address book; 웹 주소 [wep juso] *n* web address; 집주소 [jipjuso] *n* home address; 주소를 적어 주시겠어요? [jusoreul jeogeo jusigesseoyo?] Will you write down the address, please?; 웹사이트 주소는... 이에요 [wepsaiteu jusoneun...ieyo] The website address is...; 이 주소로 제 편지를 부쳐 주세요 [i jusoro je pyeonjireul buchyeo juseyo] Please send my mail on to this address; 이메일 주소가 어떻게 되세요? [imeil jusoga eotteoke doeseyo?] What is your email address?; 제 이메일 주소는...이에요 [je imeil jusoneun... ieyo] My email address is...

주스 [juseu] *n* juice; 과일 주스 [gwail juseu] *n* fruit juice

주연 [juyeon] *n* lead (in play/film); 주연하다 [juyeonhada] *v* star

주요 [juyo] 주요상품 [juyosangpum] *v* staple (commodity); 주요한 [juyohan] *adj* main, primary; 주요한 [juyohan] *adj* chief

주위 [juwi]...주위에 [...juwie] *prep* round; 주위에 [juwie] *adv* around

주유 [juyu] 주유소 [juyuso] *n* petrol station

주유기 [juyugi] 3번 주유기에 세우세요 [sambeon juyugie seuseyo] Pump number three, please

주유소 [juyuso] n service station

주의 [juui] n attention, care; 부주의한 [bujuuihan] adj sloppy; 비관주의자 [bigwanjuuija] n pessimist; 민주주의 [minjujuuui] n democracy; 주의깊은 [juuigipeun] adj observant; 주의하다 [juuihada] v mind, watch out; 자본주의 [jabonjuuui] n capitalism; 자연주의자 [jayeonjuuija] n naturalist; 국수주의 [guksujuuui] n nationalism; 국수주의자 [guksujuuija] n nationalist; 관료주의 [gwallyojuuui] n bureaucracy; 극단주의 [geukdanjuuui] n extremism; 극단주의자 [geukdanjuuija] n extremist

주인 [juin] n landlord, master; 상점 주인 [sangjeom juin] n shopkeeper; 술집 주인 [suljip juin] n publican; 여주인 [yeojuin] n landlady

주일 [juil] n week; 2주일간 [i juilgan] n fortnight; 일주일 입장권은 얼마예요? [iljuil ipjanggwoneun eolmayeyo?] How much is a pass per week?; 일주일 텐트 치는 데 얼마예요? [iljuil tenteu chineun de eolmayeyo?] How much is it per week for a tent?; 일주일에 얼마예요? [iljuire eolmayeyo?] How much is it for a week?

주장 [jujang] n allegation; 주장된 [jujangdoen] adj alleged; 주장하다 [jujanghada] v insist

주저 [jujeo] 주저하다 [jujeohada] v hesitate

주전자 [jujeonja] n jug, kettle

주정 [jujeong] 주정뱅이 [jujeongbaengi] n drunk

주제 [juje] n subject, theme, topic

주조 [jujo] 화폐 주조소 [hwapye jujoso] n mint (coins)

주주 [juju] n shareholder, stockholder

주차 [jucha] n parking; 주차요금 징수기 [juchayogeum jingsugi] n parking meter; 주차위반 딱지 [juchawiban ttakji] n parking ticket; 주차장 [juchajang] n car park; 주차하다

[juchahada] v park; 주차 미터기에 넣을 잔돈 있으세요? [jucha miteogie neoheul jandon isseuseyo?] Do you have change for the parking meter?; 주차 미터기가 고장났어요 [jucha miteogiga gojangnasseoyo] The parking meter is broken

주차권 [juchagwon] 주차권을 사야합니까? [juchagwoneul sayahamnikka?] Do I need to buy a car-parking ticket?

주차장 [juchajang] 트레일러 하우스 주차장 [teureilleo hauseu juchajang] n caravan site; 이 근처에 주차장 있어요? [i geuncheoe juchajang isseoyo?] Is there a car park near here?

주택 [jutaek] n house; 단독주택 [dandokjutaek] n detached house; 주택담보 융자 [jutaekdambo yungja] n mortgage; 주택을 담보로 융자를 받다 [jutaegeul damboro yungjareul batda] v mortgage; 이동 주택 [idong jutaek] n mobile home; 공영 주택 [gongyeong jutaek] n council house

주행 [juhaeng] 주행거리계 [juhaenggeorigye] n mileometer

죽 [juk] n porridge

죽다 [jukda] v die; 죽은 [jugeun] adj dead; 굶어죽다 [gurmeojukda] v starve

죽음 [jugeum] n death

죽이다 [jugida] v kill; 목 졸라 죽이다 [mok jolla jugida] v strangle

준 [jun] 준... [jun...] adj associate; 준결승전 [jungyeolseungjeon] n semifinal

준비 [junbi] n arrangement, preparation; 준비가 되어 있는 [junbiga doeeo inneun] adj prepared; 준비가 된 [junbiga doen] adj ready; 준비하다 [junbihada] v prepare; 준비하다 [junbihada] v arrange

줄 [jul] n file (tool), queue, row (line); 시곗줄 [sigyetjul] n watch strap; 줄서다 [julseoda] v queue; 줄이 있는 [juri inneun] adj stripy; 여기가 줄의 끝인가요? [yeogiga jurui kkeuchingayo?] Is this the end of the queue?

줄기 [julgi] 나무 줄기 [namu julgi] n trunk

줄다 [julda] 줄어들다 [jureodeulda] v shrink

줄다리기 [juldarigi] n tug-of-war

줄어들다 [jureodeulda] 줄어든 [jureodeun] adj shrunk

줄이다 [jurida] v diminish

줄자 [julja] n tape measure

줄질하다 [juljilhada] v file (smoothing)

중간 [junggan] n middle; 중간 크기의 [junggan keuguiui] adj medium-sized; 중간의 [jungganui] adj intermediate, medium (between extremes), mid; 경기 중의 중간 휴식 [gyeonggi jungui junggan hyusik] n half-time; 학기 중의 중간 방학 [hakgi jungui junggan banghak] n half-term

중개 [junggae] 중개인 [junggaein] n broker

중고 [junggo] 중고의 [junggoui] adj secondhand

중고교 [junggogyo] 사립 중고교 [sarip junggogyo] n public school

중국 [jungguk] n China; 중국 사람 [jungguk saram] n Chinese (person); 중국어 [junggugeo] n Chinese (language); 중국의 [junggugui] adj Chinese

중년 [jungnyeon] npl Middle Ages

중단 [jungdan] 중단시키다 [jungdansikida] v disrupt

중대 [jungdae] 중대한 [jungdaehan] adj critical, momentous; 중대한 [jungdaehan] adj crucial

중도 [jungdo] 중도하차 [jungdohacha] n stopover

중독 [jungdok] n addiction; 마약 중독자 [mayak jungdokja] n drug addict; 중독된 [jungdokdoen] adj addicted; 중독자 [jungdokja] n addict

중동 [jungdong] n Middle East

중등 [jungdeung] 중등학교 [jungdeunghakgyo] n secondary school

중량 [jungnyang] n weight; 수하물 허용 중량 [suhamul heoyong jungnyang] n

baggage allowance; 중량 초과의 [jungnyang chogwaui] adj overweight; 수하물 허용 중량은 얼마인가요? [suhamul heoyong jungnyangeun eolmaingayo?] What is the baggage allowance?

중립 [jungnip] n neutral; 중립의 [jungnibui] adj neutral

중사 [jungsa] n sergeant

중산 [jungsan] 중년의 [jungnyeonui] adj middle-aged; 중산 계급의 [jungsan gyegeubui] adj middle-class

중세 [jungse] 중세의 [jungseui] adj mediaeval

중심 [jungsim] n centre; 중심도로 [jungsimdoro] n main road; 중심의 [jungsimui] adj central

중심가 [jungsimga] 시내 중심가로 가 주세요 [sinae jungsimgaro ga juseyo] Please take me to the city centre

중앙 [jungang] 중앙 분리대가 있는 도로 [jungang bullidaega inneun doro] n dual carriageway; 중앙 난방 [jungang nanbang] n central heating; 중앙 아메리카 [jungang amerika] n Central America; 중앙 아프리카 공화국 [jungang apeurika gonghwaguk] n Central African Republic

중얼 [jungeol] 중얼거리다 [jungeolgeorida] v mutter

중요 [jungyo] 중요성 [jungyoseong] n importance, significance; 중요하다 [jungyohada] v matter; 중요하지 않은 [jungyohaji anheun] adj unimportant; 중요한 [jungyohan] adj important, major, significant

중위 [jungwi] n lieutenant

중재 [jungjae] n arbitration

중지 [jungji] 일시중지 [ilsijungji] n pause

중창단 [jungchangdan] 사중창단 [sajungchangdan] n quartet

중탄산소다 [jungtansansoda] n bicarbonate of soda

쥐 [jwi] n rat; 생쥐 [saengjwi] n mouse

즉 [jeuk] abbr i.e.

즉각 [jeukgak] 즉각적인 [jeukgakjeogin] adj prompt

즉시 [jeuksi] adv immediately, instantly,

promptly, readily; 즉시의 [jeuksiui] adj
immediate, instant

즐겁다 [jeulgeopda] 즐거운 [jeulgeoun]
adj merry, sweet (pleasing); 즐겁게
하다 [jeulgeopge hada] v amuse; 정말
즐거웠어요 [jeongmal
jeulgeowosseoyo] I've had a great
time; 함께 일해서 즐거웠어요
[hamkke ilhaeseo jeulgeowosseoyo]
It's been a pleasure working with you

즐기다 [jeulgida] v enjoy; 즐길 수 있는
[jeulgil su inneun] adj enjoyable

증 [jeung] 현기증 [hyeongijeung] n
vertigo

증가 [jeungga] n increase; 증가하다
[jeunggahada] v increase

증거 [jeunggeo] n evidence, proof;
증권거래소 [jeunggwongeoraeso] n
stock exchange

증권 [jeunggwon] n certificate, stock;
증권시장 [jeunggwonsijang] n stock
market; 증권중개인
[jeunggwonjunggaein] n stockbroker

증류 [jeungnyu] 증류소 [jeungnyuso] n
distillery

증명 [jeungmyeong] n demonstration;
증명자 [jeungmyeongja] n
demonstrator; 증명하다
[jeungmyeonghada] v demonstrate

증명서 [jeungmyeongseo] n certificate;
출생 증명서 [chulsaeng
jeungmyeongseo] n birth certificate; '
비행 적합' 증명서가 필요해요
['bihaeng jeokhab' jeungmyeongseoga
piryohaeyo] I need a 'fit to fly'
certificate

증상 [jeungsang] n symptom

증서 [jeungseo] 보험증서
[boheomjeungseo] n insurance
certificate; 보험증서를 볼 수
있을까요? [boheomjeungseoreul bol
su isseulkkayo?] Can I see your
insurance certificate please?

증오 [jeungo] n hatred

증인 [jeungin] n witness; 여호와의 증인
[yeohowaui jeungin] n Jehovah's
Witness; 증인이 돼 주시겠어요?
[jeungini dwae jusigesseoyo?] Can you

be a witness for me?

증폭 [jeungpok] 증폭기 [jeungpokgi] n
amplifier

증후군 [jeunghugun] 다운 증후군 [daun
jeunghugun] n Down's syndrome

지 [ji] 메모지 [memoji] n jotter; 출생지
[chulsaengji] n place of birth; 습지
[seupji] n swamp; 은박지 [eunbakji] n
tinfoil; 저수지 [jeosuji] n reservoir;
포장지 [pojangji] n wrapping paper

지갑 [jigap] n purse, wallet; 지갑을
잃어버렸어요 [jigabeul
ireobeoryeosseoyo] I've lost my wallet

지겹다 [jigyeopda] v bore (be dull)

지구 [jigu] n earth, globe; 지구 온난화
[jigu onnanhwa] n global warming

지금 [jigeum] n now; 지금 지불해야
하나요 아니면 나중에 지불해야 하나요?
[jigeum jibulhaeya hanayo animyeon
najunge jibulhaeya hanayo?] Do I pay
now or later?

지급 [jigeup] n pay, payment; 지급해야
할 [jigeuphaeya hal] adj payable

지나가다 [jinagada] v go by, go past

지나다 [jinada]...을 지나서 [...eul
jinaseo] prep past

지나치다 [jinachida] 도가 지나친 [doga
jinachin] adj overdone

지내다 [jinaeda] v be, pass time; 어떻게
지내세요? [eotteoke jinaeseyo?] How
are you?; 잘 지내요, 고마워요 [jal
jinaeyo, gomawoyo] Fine, thanks

지능 [jineung] 지능지수 [jineungjisu]
abbr IQ

지다 [jida] 해질녘 [haejillyeok] n dusk

지대 [jidae] n zone

지도 [jido] n map; 도로지도 [dorojido] n
road map; 지도책 [jidochaek] n atlas;
거리지도 [georijido] n street map;
개별지도 [gaebyeoljido] n tutorial;...
도로 지도가 필요해요 [... doro jidoga
pilyohaeyo] I need a road map of...;...
지도 있어요? [... jido isseoyo?] Have
you got a map of...?; 슬로프 지도
있어요? [seullopeu jido isseoyo?] Do
you have a map of the ski runs?; 시내
도로 지도가 필요해요 [sinae doro
jidoga pillyohaeyo] I want a street map

of the city; **시내지도를 어디에서 살 수 있어요?** [sinaejidoreul eodieseo sal su isseoyo?] Where can I buy a map of the city?; **이 지역 자전거 지도 있어요?** [i jiyeok jajeongeo jido isseoyo?] Is there a cycle map of this area?; **전국지도를 어디에서 살 수 있어요?** [jeongukjidoreul eodieseo sal su isseoyo?] Where can I buy a map of the country?; **지도 주시겠어요?** [jido jusigesseoyo?] Can I have a map?; **지도에서 어디에 있는지 알려 주시겠어요?** [jidoseo eodie inneunji allyeo jusigesseoyo?] Can you show me where it is on the map?; **지도에서 우리가 어디에 있는지 알려 주시겠어요?** [jidoseo uriga eodie inneunji allyeo jusigesseoyo?] Can you show me where we are on the map?; **지역지도를 어디에서 살 수 있나요?** [jiyeokjidoreul eodieseo sal su innayo?] Where can I buy a map of the region?; **지역지도를 어디에서 살 수 있어요?** [jiyeokjidoreul eodieseo sal su isseoyo?] Where can I buy a map of the area?

지도자 [jidoja] n leader

지렁이 [jireongi] n worm

지루 [jiru] **지루한** [jiruhan] adj bored, boring; **지루함** [jiruham] n boredom

지름길 [jireumgil] n shortcut

지리 [jiri] **지리학** [jirihak] n geography

지면 [jimyeon] n area, field; **작은 지면** [jageun jimyeon] n plot (piece of land)

지명 [jimyeong] n nomination; **지명하다** [jimyeonghada] v nominate

지문 [jimun] n fingerprint

지방 [jibang] n fat; **저지방의** [jeojibangui] adj low-fat

지불 [jibul] n payment; **보조금을 지불하다** [bojogeumeul jibulhada] v subsidize; **지불하다** [jibulhada] vi pay; **보험사가 지불해 주나요?** [boheomsaga jibulhae junayo?] Will the insurance pay for it?; **수표로 지불할 수 있나요?** [supyoro jibulhal su innayo?] Can I pay by cheque?; **신용카드로 지불할 수 있나요?** [sinyongkadeuro jibulhal su innayo?] Can I pay by credit card?;

어디에서 돈은 지불하나요 [eodieseo doneun jibulhanayo] Where do I pay?; **언제 돈을 지불해야 합니까??** [eonje doneul jibulhaeya hamnikka??] When do I pay?

지붕 [jibung] n roof; **차 지붕 위의 짐칸** [cha jibung wiui jimkan] n roof rack; **초가 지붕의** [choga jibungui] adj thatched; **지붕이 새요** [jibungi saeyo] The roof leaks

지성 [jiseong] n intelligence

지속 [jisok] **지속적** [jisokjeok] adv constantly; **지속적인** [jisokjeogin] adj persistent

지수 [jisu] n index (numerical scale)

지시 [jisi] npl directions, instructions

지식 [jisik] n knowledge; **지식인** [jisigin] n intellectual

지역 [jiyeok] n district, region; **지역의** [jiyeogui] adj regional; **지역 특산품 있어요?** [jiyeok teuksanpum isseoyo?] Do you have anything typical of this region?; **지역지도를 어디에서 살 수 있나요?** [jiyeokjidoreul eodieseo sal su innayo?] Where can I buy a map of the region?

지연 [jiyeon] n delay; **지연된** [jiyeondoen] adj delayed; **지연하다** [jiyeonhada] v delay, hold up; **비행기가 지연되었어요** [bihaenggiga jiyeondoeeosseoyo] The flight has been delayed

지옥 [jiok] n hell

지우다 [jiuda] v cross out, erase

지원 [jiwon] n support; **지원하다** [jiwonhada] v support

지위 [jiwi] n post (position)

지적 [jijeok] **지적인** [jijeogin] adj intellectual, intelligent; **지적하다** [jijeokhada] v point out

지정 [jijeong] **지정하다** [jijeonghada] v specify; **지정하다** [jijeonghada] v set

지중해 [jijunghae] n Mediterranean; **지중해의** [jijunghaeui] adj Mediterranean

지지 [jiji] **지지자** [jijija] n supporter

지진 [jijin] n earthquake

지질 [jijil] **지질학** [jijilhak] n geology

지출 [jichul] *n* expenditure

지팡이 [jipangi] *n* staff (*stick or rod*), walking stick

지퍼 [jipeo] *n* zip; 지퍼로 잠그다 [jipeoro jamgeuda] *vt* zip (up); 지퍼를 열다 [jipeoreul yeolda] *v* unzip

지평 [jipyeong] 지평선 [jipyeongseon] *n* horizon

지폐 [jipye] *n* banknote, note (*banknote*); 이 지폐를 동전으로 바꿀 수 있나요? [i jipyereul dongjeoneuro bakkul su innayo?] Do you have change for this note?

지푸라기 [jipuragi] *n* straw

지하 [jiha] 지하도 [jihado] *n* underpass; 지하실 [jihasil] *n* basement, cellar; 지하에 [jihae] *adv* underground; 지하의 [jihaui] *n* underground; 지하감옥 [jihagamok] *n* dungeon

지하철 [jihacheol] *n* subway; 지하철역 [jihacheollyeok] *n* metro station, tube station

지하철역 [jihacheollyeok] 가장 가까운 지하철역은 어디에 있어요? [gajang gakkaun jihacheollyeogeun eodie isseoyo?] Where is the nearest tube station?

지한 [jihan] 지한제 [jihanje] *n* antiperspirant

지혜 [jihye] *n* wisdom

지휘 [jihwi] 지휘자 [jihwija] *n* conductor

직각 [jikgak] *n* right angle

직경 [jikgyeong] *n* diameter

직관 [jikgwan] *n* intuition

직면 [jingmyeon] 직면하다 [jingmyeonhada] *v* face

직물 [jingmul] *n* fabric, textile

직불 [jikbul] 직불카드 [jikbulkadeu] *n* debit card; 직불 카드 받으세요? [jikbul kadeu badeuseyo?] Do you take debit cards?; 직불카드 받으세요? [jikbulkadeu badeuseyo?] Do you take debit cards?

직업 [jigeop] *n* job, occupation (*work*), profession; 직업상의 [jigeopsangui] *adj* vocational; 직업적으로 [jigeopjeogeuro] *adv* professionally; 직업적인 [jigeopjeogin] *adj* professional

직원 [jigwon] *n* personnel, staff (*workers*); 직원실 [jigwonsil] *n* staffroom

직접 [jikjeop] *adv* directly; 직접의 [jikjeobui] *adj* direct

직행 [jikhaeng] 직행 기차인가요? [jikhaeng gichaingayo?] Is it a direct train?; 직행이 더 좋아요 [jikhaengi deo johayo] I'd prefer to go direct

진 [jin] *n* gin; 진 앤 토닉 주세요 [jin aen tonik juseyo] I'll have a gin and tonic, please

진공 [jingong] 진공청소기 [jingongcheongsogi] *n* vacuum cleaner

진눈깨비 [jinnunkkaebi] *n* sleet; 진눈깨비가 내리다 [jinnunkkaebiga naerida] *v* sleet

진단 [jindan] *n* diagnosis

진료 [jillyo] 진료소 [jillyoso] *n* clinic, surgery (*doctor's*); 진료 예약을 할 수 있나요? [jillyo yeyageul hal su innayo?] Can I have an appointment with the doctor?

진수 [jinsu] (배를) 진수시키다 [(baereul) jinsusikida] *vt* launch

진술 [jinsul] 진술하다 [jinsulhada] *v* state

진실 [jinsil] 진실로 [jinsillo] *adv* truly; 진실한 [jinsilhan] *adj* sincere, true

진심 [jinsim] 진심으로 [jinsimeuro] *adv* sincerely

진열 [jinyeol] *n* exhibit, exhibition; 상점 진열장 [sangjeom jinyeoljang] *n* shop window; 상품 진열대 [sangpum jinyeoldae] *n* stall

진정 [jinjeong] *n* true feelings, suppression; 진정서 [jinjeongseo] *n* petition; 진정제 [jinjeongje] *n* sedative; 진정하다 [jinjeonghada] *v* calm down; 진정한 [jinjeonghan] *adj* authentic

진주 [jinju] *n* pearl

진짜 [jinjja] 진짜의 [jinjjaui] *adj* genuine

진창 [jinchang] *n* slush

진통 [jintong] 진통제 [jintongje] *n* painkiller

진통제 [jintongje] *n* painkiller; 진통제

주사를 맞고 싶어요 [jintongje jusareul matgo sipeoyo] I want an injection for the pain; 진통제 좀 주시겠어요? [jintongje jom jusigesseoyo?] Can you give me something for the pain?

진행 [jinhaeng] n progress

진화 [jinhwa] n evolution

진흙 [jinheulg] n mud; 진흙받이 [jinheurkbaji] n mudguard

질문 [jilmun] n enquiry, question; 자주 하는 질문 [jaju haneun jilmun] abbr FAQ; 질문하다 [jilmunhada] v query, question

질소 [jilso] n nitrogen

질식 [jilsik] 질식하다 [jilsikhada] v suffocate

질척 [jilcheok] 질척한 [jilcheokhan] adj muddy

질투 [jiltu] n envy; 질투하는 [jiltuhaneun] adj jealous; 질투하다 [jiltuhada] v envy

질풍 [jilpung] n gale

짐 [jim] n burden, load, pack; 짐을 내리다 [jimeul naerida] v unload; 지금 짐을 싸야 해요 [jigeum jimeul ssaya haeyo] I need to pack now

짐바브웨 [jimbabeuwe] n Zimbabwe; 짐바브웨 사람 [jimbabeuwe saram] n Zimbabwean; 짐바브웨의 [jimbabeuweui] adj Zimbabwean

짐수레 [jimsure] 짐수레가 있어요? [jimsurega isseoyo?] Are there any luggage trolleys?

집 [jip] n home; 두 채가 한 동을 이루고 있는 집 [du chaega han dongeul irugo inneun jip] n semi-detached house; 두꺼비집 [dukkeobijip] n fuse box; 시골집 [sigoljip] n cottage; 집 없는 [jip eomneun] adj homeless; 집주소 [jipjuso] n home address; 집에 [jibe] adv home; 집에 있다 [jibe itda] v stay in; 집에서 만든 [jibeseo mandeun] adj home-made; 거미집 [geomijip] n cobweb; 개집 [gaejip] n kennel; 아무 때나 집에 오세요 [amu ttaena jibe oseyo] Come home whenever you like; 언제 집에 가세요? [eonje jibe gaseyo?] When do you go home?; 오후

열한시까지 집에 오세요 [ohu yeolhansikkaji jibe oseyo] Please come home by 11p.m.; 집에 전화하시겠어요? [jibe jeonhwahasigesseoyo?] Would you like to phone home?; 집에 전화해도 될까요? [jibe jeonhwahaedo doelkkayo?] May I phone home?; 집에 가고 싶어요 [jibe gago sipeoyo] I'd like to go home

집게 [jipge] 족집게 [jokjipge] npl tweezers

집게손가락 [jipgesongarak] n index finger

집념 [jimnyeom] n obsession; 집념에 사로 잡힌 [jimnyeome saro japhin] adj obsessed

집다 [jipda] 집어 올리다 [jibeo ollida] v pick up; 꼬집다 [kkojipda] vt pinch

집단 [jipdan] n collective, group

집배 [jipbae] 여자 우편집배원 [yeoja upyeonjipbaewon] n postwoman; 우편집배원 [upyeonjipbaewon] n postman

집시 [jipsi] n gypsy

집중 [jipjung] n concentration; 집중적인 [jipjungjeogin] adj intensive; 집중하다 [jipjunghada] v concentrate

집표 [jippyo] 집표원 [jippyowon] n ticket collector

집필 [jippil] n writing

집합 [jiphap] 집합적인 [jiphapjeogin] adj collective; 집합하다 [jiphaphada] v round up

집회 [jiphoe] n assembly

짓누르다 [jitnureuda] v squash

짓다 [jitda] vt build

짓궂다 [jitgutda] 짓궂은 [jitgujeun] adj mischievous

짖다 [jitda] v howl

짜다 [jjada] v be salty, wring; 젖을 짜다 [jeojeul jjada] v milk; 짠 [jjan] adj salty; 음식이 너무 짜요 [eumsigi neomu jjayo] The food is too salty

짧다 [jjarpda] 짧은 [jjarbeun] adj short

짭다 [jjapda] 짭짤한 [jjapjjalhan] adj savoury

째 [jjae] 스무 번째의 [seumu beonjjaeui] adj twentieth; 열두 번째의 [yeoldu beonjjaeui] adj twelfth; 열세 번째의 [yeolse beonjjaeui] adj thirteenth

쪼개다 [jjogaeda] vt split

쪼들리다 [jjodeullida] 쪼들리는 [jjodeullineun] adj hard up

쪽 [jjok] n page

쫓다 [jjotta] 바짝 쫓다 [bajjak jjotta] v track down

쫓아내다 [jjochanaeda] v expel; (사람을) 쫓아내다 [(sarameul) jjochanaeda] v lock out

찌르다 [jjireuda] v poke, prick, stab

찔리다 [jjillida] vi stick

찢기 [jjitgi] n tear (split)

찢다 [jjitda] v tear, tear up; (물건을) 잡아 찢다 [(mulgeoneul) jaba jjitda] vt rip; 잡아 찢다 [jaba jjitda] v rip up

차 [cha] n tea, car; 순찰차 [sunchalcha] n patrol car; 승용차 [seungyongcha] n saloon, saloon car; 식당차 [sikdangcha] n buffet car, dining car; 오픈카 [opeunka] n convertible; 찻숟가락 [chassutgarak] n teaspoon; 찻잔 [chatjan] n teacup; 차 얻어 타기 [cha eodeo tagi] n hitchhiking; 차를 얻어 타다 [chareul eodeo tada] v hitchhike; 차량 [charyang] n vehicle; 구급차 [gugeupcha] n ambulance; 견인차 [gyeonincha] n breakdown van; 경주용차 [gyeongjuyongcha] n racing car; 티 타월 [ti tawol] n tea towel; 티백 [tibaek] n tea bag; 티타임 [titaim] n teatime; 티포트 [tipoteu] n teapot; 허브차 [heobeucha] n herbal tea; 회사차 [hoesacha] n company car; 차 주세요 [cha juseyo] A tea, please; 차 한 잔씩 더 주시겠어요? [cha han janssik deo jusigesseoyo?] Could we have another cup of tea, please?

차고 [chago] n garage; 차고 열쇠는 어느 것인가요? [chago yeolsoeneun eoneu geosingayo?] Which is the key for the garage?

차기 [chagi] n kick

차다 [chada] v be cold, fill up, kick; 빼곡히 찬 [ppaegokhi chan] adj crammed; (을) 차다 [(eul) chada] n kick; 꽉 찬 [kkwak chan] adj packed; 꽉찬 [kkwakchan] adj compact;

샤워물이 차요 [syawomuri chayo]The showers are cold; 와인이 찬가요? [waini changayo?] Is the wine chilled?; 음식이 너무 차요 [eumsigi neomu chayo]The food is too cold; 이 와인이 차지 않아요 [i waini chaji anhayo]This wine is not chilled; 고기가 차요 [gogiga chayo]The meat is cold

차단 [chadan] 자외선 차단제 [jaoeseon chadanje] n sunblock, sunscreen

차도 [chado] n driveway

차드 [chadeu] n Chad

차량 [charyang] n vehicle; 차량 연례 정비 [charyang yeollye jeongbi] abbr MOT; 오토 차량인가요? [oto charyangingayo?] Is it an automatic car?; 제 차량 서류예요 [je charyang seoryuyeyo] Here are my vehicle documents

차례 [charye] n sequence

차변 [chabyeon] n debit; 차변에 기입하다 [chabyeone giiphada] v debit

차별 [chabyeol] n discrimination; 남녀차별하는 [namnyeochabyeolhaneun] adj sexist; 성차별 [seongchabyeol] n sexism; 인종 차별주의 [injong chabyeoljuui] n racism; 인종 차별주의자 [injong chabyeoljuuija] n racist; 인종을 차별하는 [injongeul chabyeolhaneun] adj racist

차분 [chabun] 차분한 [chabunhan] adj relaxed

차원 [chawon] 3차원의 [samchawonui] adj three-dimensional

차월 [chawol] 차월한 [chawolhan] adj overdrawn

차이 [chai] 차이점 [chaijeom] n difference

차점 [chajeom] 차점자 [chajeomja] n runner-up

착륙 [changnyuk] n touchdown; 비상 착륙 [bisang changnyuk] n emergency landing; 착륙하다 [changnyukhada] n land

착색 [chaksaek] n colouring

착석 [chakseok] 착석하다 [chakseokhada] v sit down

착하다 [chakhada] 착한 [chakhan] adj good-natured

착휘 [chakhwi] 착취 [chakchwi] n exploitation

찬송 [chansong] 찬송가 [chansongga] n hymn

찬장 [chanjang] n cupboard, sideboard

참가 [chamga] 참가하다 [chamgahada] v participate; 파업참가자 [paeopchamgaja] n striker

참견 [chamgyeon] 참견하기 좋아하는 [chamgyeonhagi johahaneun] adj nosy

참다 [chamda] v bear, endure, tolerate; 참을 수 없는 [chameul su eomneun] adj unbearable

참조 [chamjo] n reference; 참조번호 [chamjobeonho] n reference number

참치 [chamchi] n tuna

참호 [chamho] n trench

창 [chang] n javelin, window; 베니션 블라인드 [benisyeon beullaindeu] n Venetian blind; 창쪽 좌석 [changjjok jwaseok] n window seat; 창유리 [changyuri] n window pane; 창턱 [changteok] n windowsill; 창쪽 좌석이 좋아요 [changjjok jwaseogi johayo] I'd like a window seat; 창을 닫아도 될까요? [changeul dadado doelkkayo?] May I close the window?; 창을 열어도 될까요? [changeul yeoreodo doelkkayo?] May I open the window?

창고 [changgo] n warehouse

창구 [changgu] 접수창구 [jeopsuchanggu] n reception

창문 [changmun] n window; 제가 창문을 깨뜨렸어요 [jega changmuneul kkaetteuryeosseoyo] I've broken the window; 창문이 안 열려요 [changmuni an yeollyeoyo] I can't open the window, The window won't open

창백 [changbaek] 창백한 [changbaekhan] adj pale

창자 [changja] n gut

창조 [changjo] n creation; 창조적인 [changjojeogin] adj creative; 창조하다 [changjohada] v create

찾다 [chatda] v find, look for, seek; 못 찾고 있는 [mot chatgo inneun] adj missing; 찾아보다 [chajaboda] v look up; 찾아내다 [chajanaeda] n spot; @ 표시를 찾을 수 없어요 [@ pyosireul chajeul su eopseoyo] I can't find the at sign; 우리는...을 찾고 있어요 [urineun...eul chatgo isseoyo] We're looking for...

채광 [chaegwang] n mining

채소 [chaeso] n vegetable

채식 [chaesik] n vegetarian diet; 채식주의의 [chaesikjuuiui] adj vegetarian; 채식주의자 [chaesikjuuija] n vegetarian; 절대 채식주의자 [jeoldae chaesikjuuija] n vegan; 채식 요리 있어요? [chaesik yori isseoyo?] Do you have any vegetarian dishes?; 채식주의자가 먹어도 될까요? [chaesikjuuijaga meogeodo doelkkayo?] Is this suitable for vegetarians?; 여기에 채식 식당이 있어요? [yeogie chaesik sikdangi isseoyo?] Are there any vegetarian restaurants here?; 완전 채식 요리 있나요? [wanjeon chaesik yori innayo?] Do you have any vegan dishes?; 완전 채식주의자가 먹어도 될까요? [wanjeon chaesikjuuijaga meogeodo doelkkayo?] Is this suitable for vegans?; 저는 채식주의자예요 [jeoneun chaesikjuuijayeyo] I'm vegetarian

채용 [chaeyong] n recruitment

채우다 [chaeuda] v fill up, fill; 다시 채우다 [dasi chaeuda] v refill

채점 [chaejeom] 채점하다 [chaejeomhada] v mark (grade)

채찍 [chaejjik] n whip

책 [chaek] n book; 만화책 [manhwachaek] n comic book; 책장 [chaekjang] n bookcase, bookshelf; 책가방 [chaekgabang] n schoolbag; 책갈피 [chaekgalpi] n bookmark; 서점 [seojeom] n bookshop; 스크랩북 [seukeuraepbuk] n scrapbook; 요리책 [yorichaek] n cookbook, cookery book; 전자책 [jeonjachaek] n e-book; 지도책 [jidochaek] n atlas; 영어로 된 안내책 있어요? [yeongeoro doen annaechaek isseoyo?] Do you have a guide book in English?

책상 [chaeksang] n desk; 당신의 책상을 쓸 수 있을까요? [dangsinui chaeksangeul sseul su isseulkkayo?] May I use your desk?

책임 [chaegim] n responsibility; 무책임한 [muchaegimhan] adj irresponsible; 책임이 있는 [chaegimi inneun] adj accountable, responsible

책자 [chaekja] 소책자 [sochaekja] n booklet, brochure, pamphlet

챔피언 [chaempieon] n champion; 챔피언쉽 [chaempieonswip] n championship

처 [cheo] 전처 [jeoncheo] n ex-wife

처녀 [cheonyeo] n virgin; 처녀자리 [cheonyeojari] n Virgo

처방 [cheobang] n prescription; 처방하다 [cheobanghada] v prescribe

처방약 [cheobangyak] n prescription drug; 어디에서 이 처방약을 조제할 수 있을까요? [eodieseo i cheobangyageul jojehal su isseulkkayo?] Where can I get this prescription made up?

처벌 [cheobeol] n penalty; 처벌하다 [cheobeolhada] v penalize

처음 [cheoeum] 처음으로 [cheoeumeuro] adv first;...에 처음 왔어요 [...e cheoeum wasseoyo] This is my first trip to...

척수 [cheoksu] n spinal cord

척추 [cheokchu] n spine

천 [cheon] n cloth; 1000분의 1 [cheon bunui il] n thousandth; 천 번째의 [cheon beonjjaeui] adj thousandth

천국 [cheonguk] n heaven

천년 [cheonnyeon] n millennium

천둥 [cheondung] n thunder; 천둥이 칠 것 같아요 [cheondungi chil geot gatayo] I think it's going to thunder

천막 [cheonmak] n tent; 천막 고정 말뚝 [cheonmak gojeong malttuk] n tent peg; 천막 기둥 [cheonmak gidung] n tent pole

천만 [cheonman] 천만에요 [cheonmaneyo] You're welcome

천문 [cheonmun] 천문학

[cheonmunhak] n astronomy

천사 [cheonsa] n angel

천식 [cheonsik] n asthma; 천식이 있어요 [cheonsigi isseoyo] I suffer from asthma

천연 [cheonyeon] 천연 자원 [cheonyeon jawon] npl natural resources; 천연 가스 [cheonyeon gaseu] n natural gas; 천연 그대로의 [cheonyeon geudaeroui] adj crude

천장 [cheonjang] n ceiling; 찬장 [chanjang] n dresser

천재 [cheonjae] n genius

천주교 [cheonjugyo] 천주교도 [cheonjugyodo] n Roman Catholic; 천주교의 [cheonjugyoui] adj Roman Catholic

천천히 [cheoncheonhi] adv slowly

천칭자리 [cheonchingjari] n Libra

철 [cheol] n iron; 스테인리스강 [seuteilliseugang] n stainless steel; 양철 [yangcheol] n tin; 철이 지나서 [cheori jinaseo] adv off-season; 철이 지난 [cheori jinan] adj off-season; 철하다 [cheolhada] v file (folder); 강철 [gangcheol] n steel

철단 [cheoldan] 절단 [jeoldan] n chop

철도 [cheoldo] n railway; 철도역 [cheoldoyeok] n railway station

철로 [cheollo] n rail

철물 [cheolmul] n hardware; 철물점 [cheolmuljeom] n ironmonger's

철사 [cheolsa] n wire

철자 [cheolja] 철자법 [cheoljabeop] n spelling; 철자검사 프로그램 [cheoljageomsa peurogeuraem] n spellchecker; 철자하다 [cheoljahada] v spell; 철자가 어떻게 되나요? [cheoljaga eotteoke doenayo?] How do you spell it?

철저 [cheoljeo] 철저하게 [cheoljeohage] adv thoroughly; 철저한 [cheoljeohan] adj thorough

철조 [cheoljo] 철조망 [cheoljomang] n barbed wire

철학 [cheolhak] n philosophy

철회 [cheolhoe] n withdrawal; 철회하다 [cheolhoehada] v call off; 철회하다

[cheolhoehada] v withdraw

첨가 [cheomga] 첨가물 [cheomgamul] n additive

첨탑 [cheomtap] n spire

첩 [cheop] n mistress

첩보 [cheopbo] 첩보 활동 [cheopbo hwaldong] n espionage; 첩보부 [cheopbobu] n secret service

첫번째 [cheotbeonjjae] 첫 번째의 [cheot beonjjaeui] adj first

첫째 [cheotjjae] n first; 첫째로 [cheotjjaero] adv firstly

청 [cheong] 보청기 [bocheonggi] n hearing aid

청각 [cheonggak] n hearing (sense); 저는 청각 장애인이에요 [jeoneun cheonggak jangaeinieyo] I'm deaf

청결 [cheonggyeol] n cleanliness; 아주 청결한 [aju cheonggyeolhan] adj spotless; 구강청결제 [gugangcheonggyeolje] n mouthwash

청과물 [cheonggwamul] 청과물상 [cheonggwamulsang] n greengrocer's

청구 [cheonggu] n appeal; 청구서 [cheongguseo] n claim form

청년 [cheongnyeon] 유스클럽 [yuseukeulleop] n youth club

청동 [cheongdong] n bronze

청바지 [cheongbaji] npl jeans

청소 [cheongso] n cleaning; 대청소 [daecheongso] n spring-cleaning; 진공 청소기로 청소하다 [jingong cheongsogiro cheongsohada] v hoover; 진공청소기로 청소하다 [jingongcheongsogiro cheongsohada] v vacuum; 청소 아줌마 [cheongso ajumma] n cleaning lady; 청소부 [cheongsobu] n cleaner, dustman; 청소기 [cheongsogi] n Hoover®

청소기 [cheongsogi] 진공 청소기로 청소하다 [jingong cheongsogiro cheongsohada] v hoover; 진공청소기 [jingongcheongsogi] n vacuum cleaner; 진공청소기로 청소하다 [jingongcheongsogiro cheongsohada] v vacuum

청소년 [cheongsonyeon] n adolescent, youth

청소부 [cheongsobu] 청소부는 언제 오나요? [cheongsobuneun eonje onayo?] When does the cleaner come?

청어 [cheongeo] *n* herring, kipper

청중 [cheongjung] *n* audience

청취 [cheongchwi] 청취자 [cheongchwija] *n* listener

체 [che] *n* sieve;...인 체하다 [...in chehada] *v* pretend

체계 [chegye] 면역체계 [myeonyeokchegye] *n* immune system

체벌 [chebeol] *n* corporal punishment

체스 [cheseu] *n* chess

체육 [cheyuk] 체육관 [cheyukgwan] *n* gym

체육관 [cheyukgwan] 체육관은 어디에 있어요? [cheyukgwaneun eodie isseoyo?] Where is the gym?

체조 [chejo] *n* keep-fit ▷ *npl* gymnastics; 체조 선수 [chejo seonsu] *n* gymnast

체첸 [chechen] 체첸 공화국 [chechen gonghwaguk] *n* Chechnya

체커 [chekeo] *npl* draughts

체코 [cheko] 체코 사람 [cheko saram] *n* Czech (*person*); 체코 공화국 [cheko gonghwaguk] *n* Czech Republic; 체코어 [chekoeo] *n* Czech (*language*); 체코의 [chekoui] *adj* Czech; 체코어 [chekoeo] Czech

체크 [chekeu] *n* tick; 체크 표시 [chekeu pyosi] *n* tick; 체크하다 [chekeuhada] *v* tick, tick off

체크아웃 [chekeuaut] *n* checkout; 체크아웃하다 [chekeuautada] *v* check out

체크인 [chekeuin] *n* check-in; 체크인하다 [chekeuinhada] *v* check in

체포 [chepo] *n* arrest; 체포하다 [chepohada] *v* arrest

첼로 [chello] *n* cello

초 [cho] *n* second; 양초 [yangcho] *n* candle

초가 [choga] 초가 지붕의 [choga jibungui] *adj* thatched

초과 [chogwa] 제한 초과 수하물 [jehan chogwa suhamul] *n* excess baggage; 중량 초과의 [jungnyang chogwaui] *adj* overweight; 초과 근무 시간 [chogwa geunmu sigan] *n* overtime

초급 [chogeup] 초급자 슬로프는 어딘가요? [chogeupja seullopeuneun eodingayo?] Where are the beginners' slopes?

초기 [chogi] 초기에 [chogie] *adv* initially; 초기의 [chogiui] *adj* initial

초대 [chodae] *n* invitation; 초대하다 [chodaehada] *v* invite

초라 [chora] 초라한 [chorahan] *adj* shabby

초보 [chobo] *n* the basics; 초보자 [choboja] *n* beginner; 초보자용 스키코스 [chobojayong seukikoseu] *n* nursery slope

초상 [chosang] 초상화 [chosanghwa] *n* portrait

초석 [choseok] *npl* foundations

초안 [choan] *n* draft

초음파 [choeumpa] *n* ultrasound

초인종 [choinjong] *n* doorbell

초자연 [chojayeon] 초자연의 [chojayeonui] *adj* supernatural

초점 [chojeom] *n* focus; 초점을 맞추다 [chojeomeul matchuda] *v* focus

초조 [chojo] 초조한 [chojohan] *adj* edgy

초콜릿 [chokollit] *n* chocolate

촉매 [chongmae] 촉매 변환 장치 [chongmae byeonhwan jangchi] *n* catalytic converter

촉진 [chokjin] 촉진하다 [chokjinhada] *v* promote

촛대 [chotdae] *n* candlestick

총 [chong] *n* gun; 산탄총 [santanchong] *n* shotgun; 소총 [sochong] *n* rifle; 권총 [gwonchong] *n* pistol; 기관총 [gigwanchong] *n* machine gun

총거래 [chonggeorae] 총거래액 [chonggeoraeaek] *n* turnover

총명 [chongmyeong] 총명한 [chongmyeonghan] *adj* brainy

총알 [chongal] *n* bullet

총회 [chonghoe] 연례 총회 [yeollye chonghoe] *abbr* AGM

최고 [choego] *n* ace; 최고 경영자 [choego gyeongyeongja] *abbr* CEO; 최고로 [choegoro] *adv* best; 최고의 [choegoui] *adj* best

최고조 [choegojo] 최고조의 부분 [choegojoui bubun] *n* highlight

최근 [choegeun] 최근에 [choegeune] *adv* recently; 최근의 [choegeunui] *adj* recent

최대 [choedae] *n* maximum; 최대량 [choedaeryang] *pron* most (*majority*); 최대의 [choedaeui] *adj* maximum

최루 [choeru] 최루가스 [choerugaseu] *n* teargas

최상 [choesang] 최상 품질 기한 [choesang pumjil gihan] *n* best-before date

최소 [choeso] *n* minimum; 최소의 [choesoui] *adj* least, minimum

최소량 [choesoryang] 최소량의 [choesoryangui] *adj* minimal

최소화 [choesohwa] 최소화하다 [choesohwahada] *v* minimize

최신 [choesin] 최신 설비 [choesin seolbi] *npl* mod cons; 최신의 [choesinui] *adj* up-to-date

최종 [choejong] 최종의 [choejongui] *adj* final, ultimate

최후 [choehu] 최후로 [choehuro] *adv* ultimately; 최후통첩 [choehutongcheop] *n* ultimatum

추가 [chuga] *n* addendum, supplement; 추가 시간 [chuga sigan] *n* injury time; 추가된 [chugadoen] *adj* additional; 추가요금 [chugayogeum] *n* surcharge; 추가하다 [chugahada] *v* add; 추가 비용이 있나요? [chuga biyongi innayo?] Is there a supplement to pay?; 추가 요금이 있어요? [chuga yogeumi isseoyo?] Is there a supplement to pay?;...을 추가해서 주세요 [...eul chugahaeseo juseyo] I'd like it with extra..., please; 전기 요금을 추가로 내야 하나요? [jeongi yogeumeul chugaro naeya hanayo?] Do we have to pay extra for electricity?

추구 [chugu] 추구하다 [chuguhada] *v* go after

추다 [chuda] *v* dance; 왈츠를 추다 [walcheureul chuda] *v* waltz

추락 [churak] *n* fall

추리 [churi] 추리 소설 [churi soseol] *n* thriller

추문 [chumun] *n* scandal

추방 [chubang] 국외로 추방하다 [gugoero chubanghada] *v* deport

추상 [chusang] 추상적인 [chusangjeogin] *adj* abstract

추세 [chuse] *n* trend

추월 [chuwol] 추월하다 [chuwolhada] *v* overtake

추적 [chujeok] *n* chase, pursuit; 추적하다 [chujeokhada] *v* chase, pursue

추정 [chujeong] 추정하다 [chujeonghada] *v* estimate, presume

추처 [chucheo] 추천하다 [chucheonhada] *v* recommend

추천 [chucheon] *n* recommendation

추첨 [chucheom] *n* raffle

추측 [chucheuk] *n* guess; 추측하다 [chucheukhada] *v* guess

축 [chuk] *n* axle

축구 [chukgu] *n* football; 축구 선수 [chukgu seonsu] *n* football player, footballer; 축구 경기 [chukgu gyeonggi] *n* football match; 월드컵 [woldeukeop] *n* World Cup; 축구 경기를 보고 싶어요 [chukgu gyeonggireul bogo sipeoyo] I'd like to see a football match; 축구합시다 [chukguhapsida] Let's play football

축복 [chukbok] *n* blessing; 축복하다 [chukbokhada] *v* bless

축소 [chukso] *n* reduction; 축소 모형 [chukso mohyeong] *n* miniature; 축소된 [chuksodoen] *adj* miniature; 축소하다 [chuksohada] *v* reduce

축제 [chukje] *n* festival

축축하다 [chukchukhada] 축축한 [chukchukhan] *adj* damp, moist

축하 [chukha] *n* celebration ▷ *npl* congratulations; 축하하다 [chukhahada] *v* congratulate

출구 [chulgu] *n* exit, way out; 출구는 어디에 있어요? [chulguneun eodie isseoyo?] Where is the exit?; 어느 출구가... 방향인가요? [eoneu chulguga... banghyangingayo?] Which exit for...?

출납 [chullap] 출납원 [chullabwon] n
cashier; 금전 출납기 [geumjeon
chullapgi] n cash register

출발 [chulbal] n departure, parting;
출발하다 [chulbalhada] v depart, set
off, start off; 출발하다 [chulbalhada] v
pull out

출산 [chulsan] 출산휴가 [chulsanhyuga]
n maternity leave; 5개월 후 출산해요
[ogaewol hu chulsanhaeyo] I'm due in
five months

출생 [chulsaeng] n birth; 출생 증명서
[chulsaeng jeungmyeongseo] n birth
certificate; 출생전의
[chulsaengjeonui] adj antenatal;
출생지 [chulsaengji] n birthplace,
place of birth

출석 [chulseok] n attendance; 출석하다
[chulseokhada] v attend

출신 [chulsin] 출신이다 [chulsinida] v
come from

출입구 [churipgu] n entrance; 휠체어를
이용할 수 있는 출입구는 어디인가요?
[hwilcheeoreul iyonghal su inneun
churipguneun eodiingayo?] Where is
the wheelchair-accessible entrance?

출입문 [churimmun] n doorway, entry;
회전식 출입문 [hoejeonsik
churimmun] n turnstile

출장 [chuljang] n business trip

출판 [chulpan] n publication; 출판하다
[chulpanhada] v publish

출항 [chulhang]... 가는 다음 출항은
언제인가요? [... ganeun daeum
chulhangeun eonjeingayo?] When is
the next sailing to...?;... 가는 마지막
출항은 언제인가요? [... ganeun
majimak chulhangeun eonjeingayo?]
When is the last sailing to...?; 언제
출항해요? [eonje chulhanghaeyo?]
When do we sail?

출현 [chulhyeon] n advent, appearance

출혈 [chulhyeol] 출혈하다
[chulhyeolhada] vi bleed

춤 [chum] n dance, dancing; 춤추는 사람
[chumchuneun saram] n dancer;
춤추다 [chumchuda] v dance; 사교춤
[sagyochum] n ballroom dancing; 춤

출래요? [chum chullaeyo?] Would you
like to dance?; 어디에 가면 춤출 수
있나요? [eodie gamyeon chumchul su
innayo?] Where can we go dancing?;
저는 춤 안 춰요 [jeoneun chum an
chwoyo] I don't really dance; 저는
춤추고 싶어요 [jeoneun chumchugo
sipeoyo] I feel like dancing

춥다 [chupda] 추운 [chuun] adj cold;
추위 [chuwi] n cold; 몹시 추워요
[mopsi chuwoyo] It's freezing cold;
방이 너무 추워요 [bangi neomu
chuwoyo] The room is too cold; 추워요
[chuwoyo] I feel cold, I'm cold; 오늘
밤에 추울까요? [oneul bame
chuulkkayo?] Will it be cold tonight?

충격 [chunggyeok] n shock; 충격을 주다
[chunggyeogeul juda] v shock;
충격적인 [chunggyeokjeogin] adj
shocking, traumatic

충돌 [chungdol] n bump, collision,
conflict, crash; 충돌하다
[chungdolhada] v clash, collide;
충돌하다 [chungdolhada] v crash; 연쇄
충돌 [yeonswae chungdol] n pile-up;
충돌이 있었어요 [chungdori
isseosseoyo] There's been a crash; 제
차가 충돌했어요 [je chaga
chungdolhaesseoyo] I've crashed my
car

충분 [chungbun] n plenty; 충분한
[chungbunhan] adj enough; 충분한 양
[chungbunhan yang] pron enough

충성 [chungseong] n loyalty

충전 [chungjeon] 충전기 [chungjeongi]
n charger; 충전하다 [chungjeonhada]
v charge (electricity); 재충전하다
[jaechungjeonhada] v recharge;
충전이 안 돼요 [chungjeoni an
dwaeyo] It's not charging; 어디에서
휴대전화를 충전할 수 있어요?
[eodieseo hyudaejeonhwareul
chungjeonhal su isseoyo?] Where can I
charge my mobile phone?; 가스
라이터를 충전해 주시겠어요? [gaseu
raiteoreul chungjeonhae
jusigesseoyo?] Do you have a refill for
my gas lighter?

충전물 [chungjeonmul] 충전물가 빠졌어요 [chungjeonmulga ppajyeosseoyo] A filling has fallen out

충전카드 [chungjeonkadeu] 어디에서 충전카드를 살 수 있어요? [eodieseo chungjeonkadeureul sal su isseoyo?] Where can I buy a top-up card?

취급 [chwigeup] 취급하다 [chwigeuphada] v treat

취미 [chwimi] n hobby

취소 [chwiso] n cancellation; 취소하다 [chwisohada] v back out, take back; 취소하다 [chwisohada] v cancel; 예약 취소된 표 있어요? [yeyak chwisodoen pyo isseoyo?] Are there any cancellations?

취약 [chwiyak] 취약한 [chwiyakhan] adj vulnerable

취지 [chwiji] 취지서 [chwijiseo] n prospectus

취침 [chwichim] 취침 시간 [chwichim sigan] n bedtime

취하다 [chwihada] 술 취하지 않은 [sul chwihaji anheun] adj sober; 술취한 [sulchwihan] adj drunk, tipsy

측면 [cheungmyeon] n aspect, side; 측면광 [cheungmyeongwang] n sidelight

측은 [cheugeun] 측은한 [cheugeunhan] adj pathetic

측정 [cheukjeong] npl measurements; 생물 측정학의 [saengmul cheukjeonghagui] adj biometric; 측정하다 [cheukjeonghada] v gauge, measure

측정기 [cheukjeonggi] 음주 측정기 상표명 [eumju cheukjeonggi sangpyomyeong] n Breathalyser®

층 [cheung] n layer; 1층 [il cheung] n ground floor; 아래층에 [araecheunge] adv downstairs; 아래층의 [araecheungui] adj downstairs; 오존층 [ojoncheung] n ozone layer

치 [chi] 칫솔 [chissol] n toothbrush; 치약 [chiyak] n toothpaste; 치통 [chitong] n toothache

치과 [chigwa] 치과 의사가 필요해요 [chigwa uisaga piryohaeyo] I need a dentist

치다 [chida] v run over, strike; 탁 치다 [tak chida] v thump; 한 대 치다 [han dae chida] v punch; 한대치기 [handaechigi] v punch (blow)

치료 [chiryo] n cure, treatment; 물리치료사 [mullichiryosa] n physiotherapist; 치료하다 [chiryohada] n cure; 응급 치료 [eunggeup chiryo] n first aid

치마 [chima] n skirt; 미니 스커트 [mini seukeoteu] n miniskirt; 앞치마 [apchima] n apron

치명 [chimyeong] 치명적인 [chimyeongjeogin] adj fatal

치수 [chisu] n dimension

치아 [chia] n tooth; 치실 [chisil] n dental floss; 치과의사 [chigwauisa] n dentist

치우다 [chiuda] v clear off, put away

치이다 [chiida] 누군가가 차에 치였어요 [nugungaga chae chiyeosseoyo] Someone has been knocked down by a car

치즈 [chijeu] n cheese; 코티지 치즈 [kotiji chijeu] n cottage cheese; 어떤 치즈인가요? [eotteon chijeuingayo?] What sort of cheese?

치질 [chijil] npl haemorrhoids, piles

치통 [chitong] 치통이 있어요 [chitongi isseoyo] I have toothache

칙칙하다 [chikchikhada] 칙칙한 [chikchikhan] adj drab

친구 [chingu] n friend, mate, pal; 남자 친구 [namja chingu] n boyfriend; 여자친구 [yeojachingu] n girlfriend; 친구들과 여기에 왔어요 [chingudeulgwa yeogie wasseoyo] I'm here with my friends

친밀 [chinmil] 친밀한 [chinmilhan] adj intimate

친절 [chinjeol] n kindness; 친절하게 [chinjeolhage] adv kindly; 친절한 [chinjeolhan] adj friendly, kind

친척 [chincheok] n relative ▷ npl in-laws

칠레 [chille] n Chile; 칠레 사람 [chille saram] n Chilean; 칠레의 [chilleui] adj Chilean

칠리 [chilli] n chilli

칠면조 [chilmyeonjo] n turkey

칠판 [chilpan] n blackboard

칠하다 [chilhada] v coat, paint; **니스를 칠하다** [niseureul chilhada] v varnish

침 [chim] n saliva, spit; **침뱉다** [chimbaetda] v spit; **침술** [chimsul] n acupuncture

침구 [chimgu] **침구류** [chimguryu] n bedding; **여분의 침구가 있어요?** [yeobunui chimguga isseoyo?] Is there any spare bedding?

침대 [chimdae] n bed, berth, bunk; **1 인용 침대** [il inyong chimdae] n single bed; **2인용 침대** [i inyong chimdae] n double bed; **침대 리넨** [chimdae rinen] n bed linen; **침대 맡의 램프** [chimdae matui raempeu] n bedside lamp; **침대 커버** [chimdae keobeo] npl bedclothes; **침대 곁의 보조 탁자** [chimdae gyeotui bojo takja] n bedside table; **침대보** [chimdaebo] n bedspread; **침대칸의 침대** [chimdaekanui chimdae] n couchette; **침대차** [chimdaecha] n sleeping car; **야전침대** [yajeonchimdae] n camp bed; **아기용 휴대 침대** [agiyong hyudae chimdae] n carrycot; **어린이 침대** [eorini chimdae] n cot; **이층 침대** [icheung chimdae] npl bunk beds; **킹사이즈 침대** [kingsaijeu chimdae] n king-size bed; **침대가 불편해요** [chimdaega bulpyeonhaeyo] The bed is uncomfortable; **기숙사 침대가 좋겠어요** [gisuksa chimdaega jokesseoyo] I'd like a dorm bed

침략 [chimnyak] **침략하다** [chimnyakhada] v invade

침례교 [chimnyegyo] **침례교도** [chimnyegyodo] n Baptist

침묵 [chimmuk] n silence

침배 [chimbae] **트윈 베드** [teuwin bedeu] npl twin beds

침실 [chimsil] n bedroom; **침실 겸 거실** [chimsil gyeom geosil] n bedsit; **트윈 베드가 있는 침실** [teuwin bedeuga inneun chimsil] n twin-bedded room; **일층에 침실이 있나요?** [ilcheunge chimsiri innayo?] Do you have any bedrooms on the ground floor?

침울 [chimul] **침울한** [chimulhan] adj moody

침입 [chimip] n break-in; **침입자** [chimipja] n intruder; **침입하다** [chimiphada] v break in, break in (on)

침팬지 [chimpaenji] n chimpanzee

칩 [chip] n chip (electronic); **마이크로칩** [maikeurochip] n microchip

칭찬 [chingchan] n admiration, compliment; **칭찬하는** [chingchanhaneun] adj complimentary; **칭찬하다** [chingchanhada] v admire, compliment, praise

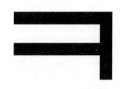

ㅋ

card?; **이 카드들을 어디에서 부칠 수 있어요?** [i kadeudeureul eodieseo buchil su isseoyo?] Where can I post these cards?; **이 현금 인출기에 제 카드를 사용할 수 있을까요?** [i hyeongeum inchulgie je kadeureul sayonghal su isseulkkayo?] Can I use my card with this cash machine?; **제 카드를 정지시켜야 해요** [je kadeureul jeongjisikyeoya haeyo] I need to cancel my card; **제 카드예요** [je kadeuyeyo] Here is my card; **직불 카드 받으세요?** [jikbul kadeu badeuseyo?] Do you take debit cards?; **직불카드 받으세요?** [jikbulkadeu badeuseyo?] Do you take debit cards?; **현금 인출기가 제 카드를 삼켰어요** [hyeongeum inchulgiga je kadeureul samkyeosseoyo] The cash machine swallowed my card

카락 [karak] **머리카락** [meorikarak] n hair

카레 [kare] n curry; **카레가루** [karegaru] n curry powder

카리브 [karibeu] **카리브 해** [karibeu hae] n Caribbean; **카리브 해의** [karibeu haeui] adj Caribbean

카메라 [kamera] n camera; **비디오 카메라** [bidio kamera] n video camera; **디지털 라디오** [dijiteol radio] n digital radio; **디지털 카메라** [dijiteol kamera] n digital camera; **카메라맨** [kameramaen] n cameraman; **카메라폰** [kamerapon] n camera phone; **제 카메라가 고장났어요** [je kameraga gojangnasseoyo] My camera is sticking

카메룬 [kamerun] n Cameroon

카세트 [kaseteu] n cassette

카스텔라 [kaseutella] n sponge (cake)

카우보이 [kauboi] n cowboy

카자흐스탄 [kajaheuseutan] n Kazakhstan

카타르 [katareu] n catarrh, Qatar

카페 [kape] **사이버 카페** [saibeo kape] n cybercafé

카페리 [kaperi]... **가는 카페리가 있어요?** [... ganeun kaperiga isseoyo?] Is there a car ferry to...?

카굴 [kagul] n cagoule

카나리아 [kanaria] n canary; **카나리아 제도** [kanaria jedo] npl Canaries

카네이션 [kaneisyeon] n carnation

카누 [kanu] n canoe; **카누타기** [kanutagi] n canoeing; **어디에서 카누 타기를 할 수 있나요?** [eodieseo kanu tagireul hal su innayo?] Where can we go canoeing?

카니발 [kanibal] n carnival

카드 [kadeu] n card, greetings card, playing card; **충전카드** [chungjeonkadeu] n top-up card; **카드 공중 전화** [kadeu gongjung jeonhwa] n cardphone; **신용카드** [sinyongkadeu] n credit card; **열차할인카드** [yeolchaharinkadeu] n railcard; **전화 카드** [jeonhwa kadeu] n phonecard; **직불카드** [jikbulkadeu] n debit card; **카드로 현금을 뽑을 수 있을까요?** [kadeuro hyeongeumeul ppobeul su isseulkkayo?] Can I use my card to get cash?; **카드를 도둑맞았어요** [kadeureul dodungmajasseoyo] My card has been stolen; **신용카드 받으세요?** [sinyongkadeu badeuseyo?] Do you take credit cards?; **신용카드로 지불할 수 있나요?** [sinyongkadeuro jibulhal su innayo?] Can I pay by credit card?; **어디에서 버스 카드를 살 수 있을까요?** [eodieseo beoseu kadeureul sal su isseulkkayo?] Where can I buy a bus

카페인 [kapein] *n* caffeine; **무카페인 커피** [mukapein keopi] *n* decaffeinated coffee; **무카페인** [mukapein] *adj* decaffeinated

카페테리아 [kapeteria] *n* cafeteria

카펫 [kapet] *n* carpet; **바닥 전체를 덮는 카펫** [badak jeonchereul deomneun kapet] *n* fitted carpet

카프카스 [kapeukaseu] **카프카스 산맥** [kapeukaseu sanmaek] *n* Caucasus

칵테일 [kakteil] *n* cocktail; **칵테일 파세요?** [kakteil paseyo?] Do you sell cocktails?

칸 [kan] **30호 칸은 어디에 있어요?** [samsibho kaneun eodie isseoyo?] Where is carriage number thirty?

칸나비스 [kannabiseu] *n* cannabis

칸막이 [kanmagi] *n* compartment

칼 [kal] *n* knife; **면도칼** [myeondokal] *n* razor; **펜나이프** [pennaipeu] *n* penknife

칼라 [kalla] *n* collar

칼로리 [kallori] *n* calorie

칼슘 [kalsyum] *n* calcium

캄보디아 [kambodia] *n* Cambodia; **캄보디아 사람** [kambodia saram] *n* Cambodian (*person*); **캄보디아의** [kambodiaui] *adj* Cambodian

캐나다 [kaenada] *n* Canada; **캐나다 사람** [kaenada saram] *n* Canadian; **캐나다의** [kaenadaui] *adj* Canadian

캐러멜 [kaereomel] *n* caramel

캐럴 [kaereol] *n* carol

캐럿 [kaereot] *n* carat

캐비닛 [kaebinit] *n* cabinet

캐서롤 [kaeseorol] *n* casserole

캐슈 [kaesyu] *n* cashew

캐시미어 [kaesimieo] *n* cashmere

캔디 [kaendi] *n* sweets; **아이스캔디** [aiseukaendi] *n* ice lolly

캔버스 [kaenbeoseu] *n* canvas

캠코더 [kaemkodeo] *n* camcorder

캠페인 [kaempein] *n* campaign

캠핑 [kaemping] **캠핑 가스** [kaemping gaseu] *n* camping gas

캠핑카 [kaempingka] *n* camper (van), caravan; **캠핑차 세울 곳이 있으면 좋겠어요** [kaempingcha seul gosi

isseumyeon jokesseoyo] We'd like a site for a camper (van), We'd like a site for a caravan; **캠핑차에 네 사람이면 얼마예요?** [kaempingchae ne saramimyeon eolmayeyo?] How much is it for a camper with four people?; **여기에 캠핑차를 주차해도 될까요?** [yeogie kaempingchareul juchahaedo doelkkayo?] Can we park our caravan here?

캡슐 [kaepsyul] *n* capsule

캥거루 [kaenggeoru] *n* kangaroo

커런트 [keoreonteu] **블랙커런트** [beullaekkeoreonteu] *n* blackcurrant

커서 [keoseo] *n* cursor

커스터드 [keoseuteodeu] *n* custard

커튼 [keoteun] *n* curtain

커틀릿 [keoteullit] *n* cutlet

커피 [keopi] *n* coffee; **무카페인 커피** [mukapein keopi] *n* decaffeinated coffee; **블랙 커피** [beullaek keopi] *n* black coffee; **커피 테이블** [keopi teibeul] *n* coffee table; **커피포트** [keopipoteu] *n* coffeepot; **라운지에서 커피를 마실 수 있을까요?** [raunjieseo keopireul masil su isseulkkayo?] Could we have coffee in the lounge?; **방금 만든 커피 있어요?** [banggeum mandeun keopi isseoyo?] Have you got fresh coffee?; **커피 주세요** [keopi juseyo] A coffee, please; **커피 한 잔씩 더 주시겠어요?** [keopi han janssik deo jusigesseoyo?] Could we have another cup of coffee, please?; **원두커피 있어요?** [wondukeopi isseoyo?] Have you got real coffee?; **크림만 넣은 커피 주세요** [keurimman neoheun keopi juseyo] A white coffee, please

컨디셔너 [keondisyeoneo] **컨디셔너 파세요?** [keondisyeoneo paseyo?] Do you sell conditioner?

컨설턴트 [keonseolteonteu] *n* consultant (*adviser*)

컬러 [keolleo] *adj* in colour

컬러 필름 [keolleo pilleum] **컬러 필름 주세요** [keolleo pilleum juseyo] A colour film, please; **이 카메라에 사용하는 컬러 필름이 필요해요** [i kamerae sayonghaneun keolleo pilleumi piryohaeyo] I need a colour film for this camera

컴퓨터 [keompyuteo] n computer; 랩톱 [raeptop] n laptop; 컴퓨터 사용 [keompyuteo sayong] n computing; 컴퓨터 과학 [keompyuteo gwahak] n computer science; 컴퓨터 게임 [keompyuteo geim] n computer game; 컴퓨터 좀 쓸 수 있을까요? [keompyuteo jom sseul su isseulkkayo?] May I use your computer?; 컴퓨터실은 어디에 있어요? [keompyuteosireun eodie isseoyo?] Where is the computer room?; 이 컴퓨터에서 CD를 만들 수 있을까요? [i keompyuteoeseo CDreul mandeul su isseulkkayo?] Can I make CDs at this computer?; 제 컴퓨터가 멈췄어요 [je keompyuteoga meomchwosseoyo] My computer has frozen

컵 [keop] n cup

케냐 [kenya] n Kenya; 케냐 사람 [kenya saram] n Kenyan; 케냐의 [kenyaui] adj Kenyan

케밥 [kebap] n kebab

케이블 [keibeul] n cable; 케이블카 [keibeulka] n cable car

케이크 [keikeu] n cake, gateau

케이터링 [keiteoring] n catering

케익 [keik] 케잉류 [keingnyu] n flan

케첩 [kecheop] n ketchup

켜다 [kyeoda] v switch on, turn on; 불켜도 돼요? [bulkyeodo dwaeyo?] Can I switch the light on?; 라디오 켜도 돼요? [radio kyeodo dwaeyo?] Can I switch the radio on?; 어떻게 켜야 될까요? [eotteoke kyeoya doelkkayo?] How do you switch it on?; 안 켜져요 [an kyeojyeoyo] It won't turn on

코 [ko] n nose; 코를 골다 [koreul golda] v snore; 코를 킁킁거리다 [koreul keungkeunggeorida] v sniff; 코피 [kopi] n nosebleed; 콧구멍 [kotgumeong] n nostril

코끼리 [kokkiri] n elephant; 바다코끼리 [badakokkiri] n walrus

고넷 [konet] n cornet

코란 [koran] n Koran

코르덴 [koreuden] n corduroy

코르크 [koreukeu] n cork; 코르크 마개뽑이 [koreukeu magaeppobi] n corkscrew

코미디 [komidi] n comedy; 코미디언 [komidieon] n comedian, comic

코소보 [kosobo] n Kosovo

코스타리카 [koseutarika] n Costa Rica

코치 [kochi] n coach (trainer)

코카인 [kokain] n cocaine; 강력 코카인 [gangnyeok kokain] n crack (cocaine)

코카콜라 [kokakolla] n Coke®

코코넛 [kokoneot] n coconut

코코아 [kokoa] n cocoa

코트 [koteu] n coat

콘 [kon] 콘플레이크 [konpeulleikeu] npl cornflakes

콘돔 [kondom] n condom

콘서트 [konseoteu] 어디에서 콘서트 표를 살 수 있어요? [eodieseo konseoteu pyoreul sal su isseoyo?] Where can I buy tickets for the concert?; 좋은 콘서트가 있어요? [joheun konseoteuga isseoyo?] Are there any good concerts on?

콘크리트 [konkeuriteu] n concrete

콘택트렌즈 [kontaekteurenjeu] 저는 콘택트렌즈를 껴요 [jeoneun kontaekteurenjeureul kkyeoyo] I wear contact lenses; 콘택트렌즈 세정액이요 [kontaekteurenjeu sejeongaegiyo] cleansing solution for contact lenses

콘텍트렌즈 [kontekteurenjeu] npl contact lenses

콜레스테롤 [kolleseuterol] n cholesterol

콜론 [kollon] n colon

콜롬비아 [kollombia] n Colombia; 콜롬비아 사람 [kollombia saram] n Colombian; 콜롬비아의 [kollombiaui] adj Colombian

콜리 [kolli] n collie

콜리플라워 [kollipeullawo] n cauliflower

콤팩트 [kompaekteu] 콤팩트디스크 [kompaekteudiseukeu] n compact disc, CD

콧 [kot] 콧수염 [kossuyeom] n moustache

콩 [kong] n bean, soya ▷ npl pulses;
병아리콩 [byeongarikong] n chickpea;
렌즈콩 [renjeukong] npl lentils; 완두콩
[wandukong] npl peas; 완두콩
[wandukong] npl mangetout; 잠두
[jamdu] n broad bean; 콩나물
[kongnamul] npl beansprouts; 깍지를
먹는 콩 [kkakjireul meongneun kong]
n runner bean; 강낭콩
[gangnangkong] npl French beans
콩고 [konggo] n Congo
쾌적 [kwaejeok] 쾌적한 [kwaejeokhan]
adj comfortable
쾌활 [kwaehwal] 쾌활한 [kwaehwalhan]
adj cheerful
쿠바 [kuba] n Cuba; 쿠바 사람 [kuba
saram] n Cuban; 쿠바의 [kubaui] adj
Cuban
쿠션 [kusyeon] n cushion
쿠웨이트 [kuweiteu] n Kuwait; 쿠웨이트
사람 [kuweiteu saram] n Kuwaiti;
쿠웨이트의 [kuweiteuui] adj Kuwaiti
퀘이커교 [kweikeogyo] 퀘이커교도
[kweikeogyodo] n Quaker
퀴즈 [kwijeu] n quiz
크기 [keugi] n size
크다 [keuda] 더 큰 [deo keun] adj
bigger; 소리가 큰 [soriga keun] adj
loud; 크고 무거운 [keugo mugeoun]
adj massive; 큰 [keun] adj big, large;
큰 소리로 [keun soriro] adv loudly;
키가 큰 [kiga keun] adj tall; 너무 커요
[neomu keoyo] It's too big; 집이 정말
커요 [jibi jeongmal keoyo] The house is
quite big
크래용 [keuraeyong] 크레용
[keureyong] n crayon
크래커 [keuraekeo] n cracker
크로아티아 [keuroatia] n Croatia;
크로아티아 사람 [keuroatia saram] n
Croatian (person); 크로아티아어
[keuroatiaeo] n Croatian (language);
크로아티아의 [keuroatiaui] adj
Croatian
크로커스 [keurokeoseu] n crocus
크롬 [keurom] n chrome
크리스마스 [keuriseumaseu] n
Christmas, Xmas; 크리스마스 카드

[keuriseumaseu kadeu] n Christmas
card; 크리스마스 이브 [keuriseumaseu
ibeu] n Christmas Eve; 크리스마스
트리 [keuriseumaseu teuri] n
Christmas tree; 메리 크리스마스!
[meri keuriseumaseu!] Merry
Christmas!
크리켓 [keuriket] n cricket (game)
크림 [keurim] n cream; 선크림
[seonkeurim] n suncream; 거품 낸
크림 [geopum naen keurim] n
whipped cream; 크림색의
[keurimsaegui] adj cream
클라리넷 [keullarinet] n clarinet
클러치 [keulleochi] n clutch
클럽 [keulleop] n club (group); 유스클럽
[yuseukeulleop] n youth club; 좋은
클럽은 어디있어요? [joheun
keulleobeun eodiisseoyo?] Where is
there a good club?
클레멘타인 [keullementain] n
clementine
클론 [keullon] n clone
클립 [keullip] n clip
키 [ki] n height; 키가 얼마인가요? [kiga
eolmaingayo?] How tall are you?
키보드 [kibodeu] n keyboard
키스 [kiseu] n kiss; 키스하다 [kiseuhada]
v kiss
키오스크 [kioseukeu] n kiosk
키우다 [kiuda] v bring up
키위 [kiwi] n kiwi
키프로스 [kipeuroseu] n Cyprus;
키프로스 사람 [kipeuroseu saram] n
Cypriot (person); 키프로스의
[kipeuroseuui] adj Cypriot
킬로 [killo] n kilo
킬로미터 [killomiteo] n kilometre
킬트 [kilteu] n kilt

ㅌ

타격 [tagyeok] n beat, hit, percussion, stroke (hit)

타다 [tada] v get on, ride; 차를 얻어 타다 [chareul eodeo tada] v hitchhike; 타는 사람 [taneun saram] n rider; 타기 [tagi] n ride

타당 [tadang] 타당한 [tadanghan] adj advisable

타라곤 [taragon] n tarragon

타맥 [tamaek] n tarmac

타박 [tabak] 타박상 [tabaksang] n bruise

타원 [tawon] 타원형의 [tawonhyeongui] adj oval

타월 [tawol] n towel; 타월을 빌려 주시겠어요? [taworeul billyeo jusigesseoyo?] Could you lend me a towel?; 타월을 더 갖다 주세요 [taworeul deo gatda juseyo] Please bring me more towels; 타월이 다 떨어졌어요 [tawori da tteoreojyeosseoyo] The towels have run out

타이 [tai] 넥타이 [nektai] n tie

타이어 [taieo] n tyre; 타이어 바람이 빠졌어요 [taieo barami ppajyeosseoyo] I have a flat tyre, I've a flat tyre; 타이어 압력이 얼마여야 하나요? [taieo amnyeogi eolmayeoya hanayo?] What should the tyre pressure be?; 타이어를 확인해 주시겠어요? [taieoreul hwaginhae jusigesseoyo?] Can you

check the tyres, please?; 타이어가 터졌어요 [taieoga teojyeosseoyo] The tyre has burst

타이완 [taiwan] n Taiwan; 타이완 사람 [taiwan saram] n Taiwanese; 타이완의 [taiwanui] adj Taiwanese

타이츠 [taicheu] npl tights

타이피스트 [taipiseuteu] n typist

타일 [tail] n tile; 타일을 붙인 [taireul buchin] adj tiled

타자 [taja] 타자기 [tajagi] n typewriter; 타자하다 [tajahada] v type

타조 [tajo] n ostrich

타지키스탄 [tajikiseutan] n Tajikistan

타트 [tateu] n tart

타협 [tahyeop] n compromise; 타협하다 [tahyeophada] v compromise

타히티 [tahiti] 타히티 섬 [tahiti seom] n Tahiti

탁구 [takgu] n table tennis

탁아 [taga] 탁아 서비스가 있어요? [taga seobiseuga isseoyo?] Is there a child-minding service?

탁아소 [tagaso] n crêche

탁자 [takja] 침대 곁의 보조 탁자 [chimdae gyeotui bojo takja] n bedside table

탄 [tan] 토탄 [totan] n peat

탄광 [tangwang] n colliery

탄력 [tallyeok] n elasticity, spring; 탄력근무제 [tallyeokgeunmuje] n flexitime

탄산 [tansan] 탄산수 [tansansu] n sparkling water

탄성 [tanseong] 탄성체 [tanseongche] n elastic

탄소 [tanso] n carbon; 탄소배출량 [tansobaechullyang] n carbon footprint

탄수화물 [tansuhwamul] n carbohydrate

탄약 [tanyak] n ammunition

탄자니아 [tanjania] n Tanzania; 탄자니아의 [tanjanaaui] adj Tanzanian; 탄자니아 사람 [tanjania saram] n Tanzanian

탄창 [tanchang] n cartridge, magazine (ammunition)

탈수 [talsu] 탈수 증상의 [talsu jeungsangui] *adj* dehydrated; 탈수기 [talsugi] *n* spin dryer

탈수기 [talsugi] 회전식 탈수기 [hoejeonsik talsugi] *n* tumble dryer

탈의 [tarui] 탈의실 [taruisil] *n* changing room, fitting room

탈의실 [taruisil] 탈의실은 어디에 있어요? [taruisireun eodie isseoyo?] Where are the changing rooms?

탈지 [talji] 반탈지유 [bantaljiyu] *n* semi-skimmed milk; 탈지유 [taljiyu] *n* skimmed milk

탈출 [talchul] *n* escape; 탈출하다 [talchulhada] *vi* escape

탈취 [talchwi] 탈취제 [talchwije] *n* deodorant

탈퇴 [taltoe] 탈퇴하다 [taltoehada] *v* opt out

탐색 [tamsaek] 탐색하다 [tamsaekhada] *v* pry

탐정 [tamjeong] *n* detective

탐폰 [tampon] *n* tampon

탐험 [tamheom] *n* expedition; 탐험가 [tamheomga] *n* explorer; 탐험하다 [tamheomhada] *v* explore

탑 [tap] *n* pylon, tower; 첨탑 [cheomtap] *n* steeple

탑승 [tapseung] 탑승권 [tapseunggwon] *n* boarding card, boarding pass;... 가는 비행기는 어디에서 탑승 수속을 하나요? [... ganeun bihaenggineun eodieseo tapseung susogeul hanayo?] Where do I check in for the flight to...?; 언제 탑승 수속을 해야 할까요? [eonje tapseung susogeul haeya halkkayo?] When do I have to check in?; 언제 탑승을 시작해요? [eonje tapseungeul sijakhaeyo?] When does boarding begin?; 언제까지 탑승 수속을 할 수 있어요? [eonjekkaji tapseung susogeul hal su isseoyo?] When is the latest I can check in?; 탑승 수속을 하고 싶어요 [tapseung susogeul hago sipeoyo] I'd like to check in, please

탑승권 [tapseunggwon] 제 탑승권이에요 [je tapseunggwonieyo] Here is my boarding card

탕파 [tangpa] *n* hot-water bottle

태국 [taeguk] *n* Thailand; 태국 사람 [taeguk saram] *n* Thai (person); 태국어 [taegugeo] *n* Thai (language); 태국의 [taegugui] *adj* Thai

태도 [taedo] *n* attitude

태만 [taeman] *v* skive

태생 [taesaeng] 태생의 [taesaengui] *adj* born

태아 [taea] *n* foetus

태양 [taeyang] *n* sun; 태양 에너지 [taeyang eneoji] *n* solar power; 태양의 [taeyangui] *adj* solar; 태양계 [taeyanggye] *n* solar system

태어나다 [taeeonada] *v* be born; 태어난 [taeeonan] *adj* native

태우다 [taeuda] 불태우다 [bultaeuda] *n* burn; (차에) 태워 주기 [(chae) taewo jugi] *n* lift (free ride)

태즈메이니아 [taejeumeinia] *n* Tasmania

태평양 [taepyeongyang] *n* Pacific

택배 [taekbae] *n* courier; 이것을 택배로 보내고 싶어요 [igeoseul taekbaero bonaego sipeoyo] I want to send this by courier

택시 [taeksi] *n* cab, taxi; 소형 콜택시 [sohyeong koltaeksi] *n* minicab; 택시 승차장 [taeksi seungchajang] *n* taxi rank; 택시 운전사 [taeksi unjeonsa] *n* taxi driver; 어디에서 택시를 탈 수 있어요? [eodieseo taeksireul tal su isseoyo?] Where can I get a taxi?; 여덟시에 택시를 불러 주세요 [yeodeopsie taeksireul bulleo juseyo] Please order me a taxi for 8 o'clock; 짐을 택시에 실어 주세요 [jimeul taeksie sireo juseyo] Please take my luggage to a taxi; 택시를 불러 주세요 [taeksireul bulleo juseyo] Please order me a taxi; 택시에 가방을 두고 내렸어요 [taeksie gabangeul dugo naeryeosseoyo] I left my bags in the taxi; 택시정류장 어디에 있어요? [taeksijeongnyujang eodie isseoyo?] Where is the taxi stand?; 택시가 필요해요 [taeksiga piryohaeyo] I need a taxi

탭댄스 [taepdaenseu] n tap-dancing
탱커 [taengkeo] n tanker
탱크 [taengkeu] n tank (combat vehicle), tank (large container)
터널 [teoneol] n tunnel
터득 [teodeuk] 터득하다 [teodeukhada] v master
터무니 [teomuni] 터무니 없는 [teomuni eomneun] adj extortionate
터치 [teochi] 터치라인 [teochirain] n touchline; 터치패드 [teochipaedeu] n touchpad
터키 [teoki] n Turkey; 터키 사람 [teoki saram] n Turk, Turkish; 터키의 [teokiui] adj Turkish
턱 [teok] n chin, jaw; 턱받이 [teokbaji] n bib; 턱수염 [teoksuyeom] n beard
턱시도 [teoksido] n tuxedo; 남자 턱시도 [namja teoksido] n dinner jacket
털 [teol] 양털 [yangteol] n fleece; 털이 많은 [teori manheun] adj hairy; 털기 [teolgi] n whisk
테너 [teneo] n tenor
테니스 [teniseu] n tennis; 테니스 라켓 [teniseu raket] n tennis racket; 테니스 치는 사람 [teniseu chineun saram] n tennis player; 테니스 코트 [teniseu koteu] n tennis court; 어디에서 테니스를 칠 수 있을까요? [eodieseo teniseureul chil su isseulkkayo?] Where can I play tennis?; 테니스 코트를 빌리는 데 얼마예요? [teniseu koteureul billineun de eolmayeyo?] How much is it to hire a tennis court?; 테니스를 치고 싶어요 [teniseureul chigo sipeoyo] We'd like to play tennis
테두리 [teduri] n rim
테라스 [teraseu] n patio, terrace
테러 [tereo] 테러 행위 [tereo haengwi] n terrorism; 테러리스트 [tereoriseuteu] n terrorist; 테러리스트 공격 [tereoriseuteu gonggyeok] n terrorist attack
테이블 [teibeul] n table (furniture)
테이프 [teipeu] n tape; 이 비디오 카메라에 사용하는 테이프 하나 주시겠어요? [i bidio kamerae sayonghaneun teipeu hana

jusigesseoyo?] Can I have a tape for this video camera, please?
테크노 [tekeuno] n techno
텐트 [tenteu] 여기에 텐트를 쳐도 될까요? [yeogie tenteureul chyeodo doelkkayo?] Can we pitch our tent here?; 일주일 텐트 치는 데 얼마예요? [iljuil tenteu chineun de eolmayeyo?] How much is it per week for a tent?; 텐트 칠 곳이 있으면 좋겠어요 [tenteu chil gosi isseumyeon jokesseoyo] We'd like a site for a tent; 하룻밤 텐트 치는 데 얼마예요? [harutbam tenteu chineun de eolmayeyo?] How much is it per night for a tent?
텔레비전 [tellebijeon] n television, telly; 디지털 텔레비전 [dijiteol tellebijeon] n digital television; 컬러 텔레비전 [keolleo tellebijeon] n colour television; 플라스마 TV [peullaseuma TV] n plasma TV; 텔레비전은 어디에 있어요? [tellebijeoneun eodie isseoyo?] Where is the television?
텔레비젼 [tellebijyeon] 유선 텔레비젼 [yuseon tellebijyeon] n cable television; 텔레비전 라운지가 있어요? [tellebijeon raunjiga isseoyo?] Is there a television lounge?
토 [to] 토하다 [tohada] v throw up
토고 [togo] n Togo
토끼 [tokki] n rabbit; 산토끼 [santokki] n hare
토너먼트 [toneomeonteu] n tournament
토네이도 [toneido] n tornado
토닉 [tonik] n tonic; 진 앤 토닉 주세요 [jin aen tonik juseyo] I'll have a gin and tonic, please
토대 [todae] n base, basis
토론 [toron] n discussion; 토론하다 [toronhada] v discuss
토마토 [tomato] n tomato; 토마토 소스 [tomato soseu] n tomato sauce
토막 [tomak] n stub; 고기 토막 [gogi tomak] n joint (meat)
토스트 [toseuteu] n toast (grilled bread)
토요일 [toyoil] 이번 토요일 [ibeon toyoil] this Saturday; 지난 토요일

[jinan toyoil] last Saturday; **토요일마다**
[toyoilmada] every Saturday, on
Saturdays; **토요일에** [toyoire] on
Saturday
토지 [toji] **토지소유자** [tojisoyuja] *n*
landowner
토피 [topi] *n* toffee
톤 [ton] *n* ton
톱 [top] *n* saw; **톱밥** [topbap] *n* sawdust
통 [tong] *n* barrel; **두통** [dutong] *n*
headache; **치통** [chitong] *n*
toothache; **쓰레기통** [sseuregitong] *n*
bin, dustbin; **여물통** [yeomultong] *n*
trough; **요통** [yotong] *n* back pain,
backache; **우체통** [uchetong] *n*
mailbox, postbox; **위통** [witong] *n*
stomachache; **통밀가루의**
[tongmilgaruui] *adj* wholemeal;
휴지통 [hyujitong] *n* wastepaper
basket
통가 [tongga] *n* Tonga
통계 [tonggye] **통계학** [tonggyehak] *npl*
statistics
통과 [tonggwa] **통과하다**
[tonggwahada] *vi* pass; **통과하다**
[tonggwahada] *vi* pass; **통과하여**
[tonggwahayeo] *prep* through
통근 [tonggeun] **통근자** [tonggeunja] *n*
commuter; **통근하다** [tonggeunhada]
v commute
통금 [tonggeum] *n* curfew; **통금 시간이
있어요?** [tonggeum sigani isseoyo?] Is
there a curfew?
통로 [tongno] *n* aisle, passage (*route*),
track; **통로쪽 좌석** [tongnojjok
jwaseok] *n* aisle seat; **통로쪽 좌석이
좋아요** [tongnojjok jwaseogi johayo]
I'd like an aisle seat
통보 [tongbo] **해고 통보** [haego tongbo]
n notice (*termination*)
통신 [tongsin] *n* correspondence,
communication; **내부 통신 시스템**
[naebu tongsin siseutem] *n* intercom;
원격통신 [wongyeoktongsin] *npl*
telecommunications
통역 [tongyeok] **통역사** [tongyeoksa] *n*
interpreter; **통역사가 필요해요**
[tongyeoksaga piryohaeyo] I need an

interpreter; **통역을 해 주시겠어요?**
[tongyeogeul hae jusigesseoyo?] Could
you act as an interpreter for us, please?
통제 [tongje] *n* control; **통제하다**
[tongjehada] *v* control; **통제할 수 없는**
[tongjehal su eomneun] *adj*
uncontrollable
통조림 [tongjorim] **통조림한**
[tongjorimhan] *adj* canned, tinned
통지 [tongji] *n* notice (*note*); **통지하다**
[tongjihada] *v* notify
통첩 [tongcheop] **최후통첩**
[choehutongcheop] *n* ultimatum
통치자 [tongchija] *n* ruler (*commander*)
통칭 [tongching]...**라는 통칭으로 알려진**
[...raneun tongchingeuro allyeojin]
prep alias
통통하다 [tongtonghada] **통통한**
[tongtonghan] *adj* plump
통행 [tonghaeng] *n* passage; **통행우선권**
[tonghaenguseongwon] *n* right of
way; **당신에게 통행 우선권이 없었어요**
[dangsinege tonghaeng useongwoni
eopseosseoyo] It wasn't your right of
way
통행료 [tonghaengnyo] **어디에서
통행료를 내나요?** [eodieseo
tonghaengnyoreul naenayo?] Where
can I pay the toll?
통화 [tonghwa] *n* currency; **통화 중 신호**
[tonghwa jung sinho] *n* busy signal;
통화중 신호음 [tonghwajung
sinhoeum] *n* engaged tone
통화중 [tonghwajung] **통화중이에요**
[tonghwajungieyo] It's engaged
퇴보 [toebo] *n* relapse
퇴원 [toewon] **저는 언제 퇴원하나요?**
[jeoneun eonje toewonhanayo?] When
will I be discharged?; **그는 언제
퇴원하나요?** [geuneun eonje
toewonhanayo?] When will he be
discharged?
퇴적 [toejeok] **퇴적물** [toejeongmul] *n*
pile
퇴직 [toejik] *n* retirement; **퇴직하다**
[toejikhada] *v* retire; **퇴직한**
[toejikhan] *adj* retired
투광 [tugwang] **투광 조명** [tugwang

jomyeong] n floodlight

투명 [tumyeong] 투명한 [tumyeonghan] adj see-through, transparent

투사 [tusa] 투사지 [tusaji] n tracing paper

투옥 [tuok] 투옥하다 [tuokhada] v jail

투자 [tuja] n investment; 투자자 [tujaja] n investor; 투자하다 [tujahada] v invest

투표 [tupyo] n vote; 투표하다 [tupyohada] v vote

튀기다 [twigida] v fry; 튀긴 [twigin] adj fried

튀니지 [twiniji] 튀니지 사람 [twiniji saram] n Tunisian; 튀니지의 [twinijiui] adj Tunisian; 튀니지의 [twinijiui] adj Tunisia

튀다 [twida] vi bounce; (물을) 튀기다 [(mureul) twigida] v splash

튜브 [tyubeu] n inner tube

튤립 [tyullip] n tulip

트랙터 [teuraekteo] n tractor

트랜지스터 [teuraenjiseuteo] n transistor

트램펄린 [teuraempeollin] n trampoline

트럭 [teureok] n lorry, truck; 소형 트럭 [sohyeong teureok] n van; 이삿짐 트럭 [isatjim teureok] n removal van; 트럭 운전사 [teureok unjeonsa] n lorry driver, truck driver

트럼펫 [teureompet] n trumpet

트레일러 [teureilleo] n trailer; 트레일러 하우스 [teureilleo hauseu] n caravan; 트레일러 하우스 주차장 [teureilleo hauseu juchajang] n caravan site

트로피 [teuropi] n trophy

트롤리 [teurolli] n trolley

트롬본 [teurombon] n trombone

트리니다드토바고 [teurinidadeutobago] n Trinidad and Tobago

트림 [teurim] n burp; 트림하다 [teurimhada] vi burp

특 [teuk] 특대의 [teukdaeui] adj outsize

특권 [teukgwon] n privilege

특급 [teukgeup] 특급 우편은 도착하는 데 얼마나 걸려요? [teukgeup upyeoneun dochakhaneun de culmana geollyeoyo?] How long will it

take by priority post?

특기 [teukgi] n speciality

특별 [teukbyeol] 특별한 [teukbyeolhan] adj special; 특별할인 [teukbyeolharin] n special offer; 특별히 [teukbyeolhi] adv specially; 주방장의 특별 요리는 무엇인가요? [jubangjangui teukbyeol yorineun mueosingayo?] What is the chef's speciality?; 이 집의 특별 요리는 무엇인가요? [i jibui teukbyeol yorineun mueosingayo?] What is the house speciality?

특산 [teuksan] 지역 특산 요리는 무엇인가요? [jiyeok teuksan yorineun mueosingayo?] What's the local speciality?; 지역 특산 요리가 있나요? [jiyeok teuksan yoriga innayo?] Is there a local speciality?; 지역 특산 음식을 먹어 보고 싶어요 [jiyeok teuksan eumsigeul meogeo bogo sipeoyo] I'd like to try something local, please

특산품 [teuksanpum] 도시 특산품 있어요? [dosi teuksanpum isseoyo?] Have you anything typical of this town?; 지역 특산품 있어요? [jiyeok teuksanpum isseoyo?] Do you have anything typical of this region?

특성 [teukseong] n character, characteristic

특유 [teugyu] 특유의 [teugyuui] adj particular; 특유한 [teugyuhan] adj peculiar

특징 [teukjing] n feature

특파원 [teukpawon] n correspondent

특허 [teukheo] n concession

특히 [teukhi] adv especially, particularly

튼튼하다 [teunteunhada] 튼튼한 [teunteunhan] adj tough

틀 [teul] n frame; 재봉틀 [jaebongteul] n sewing machine; 그림틀 [geurimteul] n picture frame

틀니 [teulli] npl dentures

틀리다 [teullida] 틀린 [teullin] adj wrong

티베트 [tibeteu] n Tibet; 티베트 사람 [tibeteu saram] n Tibetan (person); 티베트어 [tibeteueo] n Tibetan (language); 티베트의 [tibeteuui] adj Tibetan

티셔츠 [tisyeocheu] *n* T-shirt
티켓 [tiket] **전자티켓** [jeonjatiket] *n* e-ticket
티푸스 [tipuseu] **장티푸스** [jangtipuseu] *n* typhoid
팀 [tim] *n* team
팁 [tip] *n* tip *(reward)*; **팁을 주다** [tibeul juda] *vt* tip *(reward)*; **팁으로 얼마를 줘야 하나요?** [tibeuro eolmareul jwoya hanayo?] How much should I give as a tip?; **팁을 줘야 하나요?** [tibeul jwoya hanayo?] Is it usual to give a tip?

파 [pa] **실파** [silpa] *n* spring onion
파괴 [pagoe] *n* destruction; **공공시설 파괴 행위** [gonggongsiseol pagoe haengwi] *n* vandalism; **공공시설 파괴자** [gonggongsiseol pagoeja] *n* vandal; **파괴하다** [pagoehada] *v* destroy, ruin, vandalize, wreck
파나마 [panama] *n* Panama
파다 [pada] *vt* dig
파도 [pado] *n* wave; **밀려오는 파도** [millyeooneun pado] *n* surf; **파도타기를 하다** [padotagireul hada] *v* surf
파도타기 [padotagi] **어디에서 파도타기를 할 수 있나요?** [eodieseo padotagireul hal su innayo?] Where can you go surfing?
파라과이 [paragwai] *n* Paraguay; **파라과이 사람** [paragwai saram] *n* Paraguayan; **파라과이의** [paragwaiui] *adj* Paraguayan
파라세타몰 [parasetamol] **파라세타몰 주세요** [parasetamol juseyo] I'd like some paracetamol
파랗다 [parata] **파란** [paran] *adj* blue
파리 [pari] *n* fly
파마 [pama] *n* perm; **파마를 했어요** [pamareul haesseoyo] My hair is permed
파묻다 [pamutda] *v* bury
파산 [pasan] **파산한** [pasanhan] *adj* bankrupt

파상풍 [pasangpung] *n* tetanus

파손 [pason] *n* wreck

파스타 [paseuta] *n* pasta; 전채요리로 파스타를 주세요 [jeonchaeyoriro paseutareul juseyo] I'd like pasta as a starter

파슬리 [paseulli] *n* parsley

파업 [paeop] *n* strike; 파업을 하다 [paeobeul hada] *vi* strike *(suspend work)*; 파업참가자 [paeopchamgaja] *n* striker; 파업때문에요 [paeopttaemuneyo] because of a strike

파우더 [paudeo] 베이킹 파우더 [beiking paudeo] *n* baking powder; 탤컴 파우더 [taelkeom paudeo] *n* talcum powder

파운드 [paundeu] *n* pound, sterling; 영국 파운드 [yeongguk paundeu] *n* pound sterling

파이 [pai] *n* pie; 사과 파이 [sagwa pai] *n* apple pie

파인애플 [painaepeul] *n* pineapple

파인트 [painteu] *n* pint

파일 [pail] *n* file *(folder)*

파자마 [pajama] *npl* pyjamas

파장 [pajang] *n* wavelength

파충 [pachung] 파충류 [pachungnyu] *n* reptile

파키스탄 [pakiseutan] *n* Pakistan; 파키스탄 사람 [pakiseutan saram] *n* Pakistani; 파키스탄의 [pakiseutanui] *adj* Pakistani

파트너 [pateuneo] *n* partner; 제 파트너예요 [je pateuneoyeyo] This is my partner; 파트너가 있어요 [pateuneoga isseoyo] I have a partner

파티 [pati] *n* party *(social gathering)*; 총각파티 [chonggakpati] *n* stag night; 파티를 열다 [patireul yeolda] *v* party

파편 [papyeon] *n* splinter

파프리카 [papeurika] *n* paprika

판 [pan] *n* board *(go aboard)*, board *(wood)*, edition;...판 [...pan] *n* version; 난장판 [nanjangpan] *npl* shambles; 게시판 [gesipan] *n* bulletin board

판결 [pangyeol] *n* sentence *(punishment)*; 판결을 내리다 [pangyeoreul naerida] *v* sentence

판단 [pandan] *n* judgment; 잘못된 판단을 하다 [jalmotdoen pandaneul hada] *v* misjudge; 판단하다 [pandanhada] *v* judge

판매 [panmae] *n* sale; 주류판매 면허 [juryupanmae myeonheo] *n* off-licence; 여자 판매원 [yeoja panmaewon] *n* saleswoman; 자동 매표기 [jadong maepyogi] *n* ticket machine; 자동 판매기 [jadong panmaegi] *n* slot machine; 자동판매기 [jadongpanmaegi] *n* dispenser; 전화판매 [jeonhwapanmae] *npl* telesales; 판매대 [panmaedae] *npl* stands; 판매대표 [panmaedaepyo] *n* sales rep; 판매원 [panmaewon] *n* sales assistant, salesman, salesperson; 판매가격 [panmaegagyeok] *n* selling price

판매기 [panmaegi] 자동판매기 [jadongpanmaegi] *n* vending machine

판지 [panji] *n* cardboard

팔 [pal] *n* arm; 팔굽혀펴기 [palguphyeopyeogi] *n* press-up, push-up; 팔꿈치 [palkkumchi] *n* elbow; 팔을 움직일 수 없어요 [pareul umjigil su eopseoyo] I can't move my arm

팔다 [palda] *vt* sell; 다 팔아버리다 [da parabeorida] *v* sell out; 싸게 팔아치우다 [ssage parachiuda] *v* sell off

팔레스타인 [palleseutain] *n* Palestine; 팔레스타인 사람 [palleseutain saram] *n* Palestinian; 팔레스타인의 [palleseutainui] *adj* Palestinian

팔목 [palmok] *n* wrist

팔십 [palsip, yeodeun] *number* eighty

팔찌 [paljji] *n* bracelet

팝업 [pabeop] 팝업창 [pabeopchang] *n* pop-up

팝콘 [papkon] *n* popcorn

팟캐스트 [patkaeseuteu] *n* podcast

패드 [paedeu] *n* pad

패러글라이딩 [paereogeullaiding] 어디에서 패러글라이딩을 할 수 있어요? [eodieseo paereogeullaidingeul hal su isseoyo?] Where can you go paragliding?

패러센딩 [paereosending] 패러센딩을 하고 싶어요 [paereosendingeul hago sipeoyo] I'd like to go parascending

패배 [paebae] n defeat; **패배하다** [paebaehada] v defeat

패이다 [paeida] 움푹 패인 곳 [umpuk paein got] n dent

팩스 [paekseu] n fax; 당신의 팩스에 문제가 있어요 [dangsinui paekseue munjega isseoyo] There is a problem with your fax; 사용할 수 있는 팩스기가 있나요? [sayonghal su inneun paekseugiga innayo?] Is there a fax machine I can use?; 여기에서 팩스를 보낼 수 있을까요? [yeogieseo paekseureul bonael su isseulkkayo?] Can I send a fax from here?; 팩스 보내는 데 얼마입니까? [paekseu bonaeneun de eolmaimnikka?] How much is it to send a fax?; 팩스 번호가 무엇입니까? [paekseu beonhoga mueosimnikka?] What is the fax number?; 팩스 있어요? [paekseu isseoyo?] Do you have a fax?; 팩스를 보내고 싶어요 [paekseureul bonaego sipeoyo] I want to send a fax; 팩스를 다시 보내 주세요 [paekseureul dasi bonae juseyo] Please resend your fax

팬 [paen] n pan; 마지팬 [majipaen] n marzipan; 팬 구멍 [paen gumeong] n pothole; 팬케이크 [paenkeikeu] n pancake; 프라이팬 [peuraipaen] n frying pan

팬더 [paendeo] panda

팬티 [paenti] npl panties, pants; 사각팬티 [sagakpaenti] npl boxer shorts

팽팽하다 [paengpaenghada] 팽팽한 [paengpaenghan] adj tight

퍼덕거리다 [peodeokgeorida] v flap

퍼센트 [peosenteu] adv per cent

퍼즐 [peojeul] n puzzle; 조각 맞추기 퍼즐 [jogak matchugi peojeul] n jigsaw

펀치 [peonchi] n punch (hot drink)

펌프 [peompeu] n pump; 펌프로 퍼올리다 [peompeuro peoollida] v pump; 펌프 있어요? [peompeu isseoyo?] Do you have a pump?

페니 [peni] n penny

페니실린 [penisillin] n penicillin

페달 [pedal] n pedal

페러세일링 [pereoseilling] 어디에서 패러세일링을 할 수 있나요? [eodieseo paereoseillingeul hal su innayo?] Where can you go para-sailing?

페로스 [peroseu] 페로스 제도 [peroseu jedo] npl Faroe Islands

페루 [peru] n Peru; 페루 사람 [peru saram] n Peruvian; 페루의 [peruui] adj Peruvian

페르시아 [pereusia] 페르시아의 [pereusiaui] adj Persian

페리 [peri] n ferry; 카페리 [kaperi] n car-ferry

페미니스트 [peminiseuteu] n feminist

페이스트리 [peiseuteuri] n pastry; 퍼프 페이스트리 [peopeu peiseuteuri] n puff pastry

페인트 [peinteu] n paint

펜 [pen] n pen; 펜을 빌려 주시겠어요? [peneul billyeo jusigesseoyo?] Do you have a pen I could borrow?

펜던트 [pendeonteu] n pendant

펜치 [penchi] npl pliers

펜팔 [penpal] n penfriend

펠리컨 [pellikeon] n pelican

펠트 [pelteu] n felt; 펠트펜 [pelteupen] n felt-tip pen

펭귄 [penggwin] n penguin

펴다 [pyeoda] vt spread; (감긴 것을) 펴다 [(gamgin geoseul) pyeoda] v unroll; 펼치다 [pyeolchida] v spread out

편 [pyeon] 속편 [sokpyeon] n sequel

편견 [pyeongyeon] n prejudice; 편견을 가진 [pyeongyeoneul gajin] adj biased, prejudiced

편도 [pyeondo] n one-way, almond; 편도표 [pyeondopyo] n one-way ticket, single ticket;...까지 편도요 [...kkaji pyeondoyo] a single to...; 편도표는 얼마예요? [pyeondopyoneun eolmayeyo?] How much is a single ticket?

편도선 [pyeondoseon] npl tonsils; 편도선염 [pyeondoseonyeom] n

tonsillitis

편두통 [pyeondutong] n migraine

편리 [pyeolli] 편리한 [pyeollihan] adj convenient

편승 [pyeonseung] 자동차 편승 여행자 [jadongcha pyeonseung yeohaengja] n hitchhiker; 차 얻어 타기 [cha eodeo tagi] n hitchhiking

편의 [pyeonui] 편의 시설 [pyeonui siseol] npl amenities

편자 [pyeonja] n horseshoe

편지 [pyeonji] n letter (message); 받은 편지함 [badeun pyeonjiham] n inbox; 편지지 [pyeonjiji] n notepaper; 편지함 [pyeonjiham] n letterbox; 이 편지를 보내려고요 [i pyeonjireul bonaeryeogoyo] I'd like to send this letter; 저는 편지로 예약을 확인했어요 [jeoneun pyeonjiro yeyageul hwaginhaesseoyo] I confirmed my booking by letter

편집 [pyeonjip] 편집자 [pyeonjipja] n editor

편하다 [pyeonhada] 편하게 하는 [pyeonhage haneun] adj relaxing

평가 [pyeongga] 과대 평가하다 [gwadae pyeonggahada] v overestimate; 과소 평가하다 [gwaso pyeonggahada] v underestimate; 평가절하 [pyeonggajeolha] n devaluation; 평가하다 [pyeonggahada] v rate

평결 [pyeonggyeol] n verdict

평균 [pyeonggyun] n average; 평균의 [pyeonggyunui] adj average

평론 [pyeongnon] n review

평면 [pyeongmyeon] n flat, plane (surface)

평야 [pyeongya] n plain

평영 [pyeonggyeong] n breaststroke

평온 [pyeongon] 평온한 [pyeongonhan] adj restful

평일 [pyeongil] n weekday

평지 [pyeongji] n rape (plant)

평판 [pyeongpan] n reputation; 평판 스크린의 [pyeongpan seukeurinui] adj flat-screen; 평판이 좋은 [pyeongpani joheun] adj reputable

평평하다 [pyeongpyeonghada] 평평한

평평한 [pyeongpyeonghan] adj even, level, plain; 평평한 [pyeongpyeonghan] adj flat

평행 [pyeonghaeng] 평행인 [pyeonghaengin] adj parallel

평화 [pyeonghwa] n peace; 평화로운 [pyeonghwaroun] adj peaceful

폐 [pye] n lung; 폐렴 [pyeryeom] n pneumonia

폐쇄 [pyeswae] 폐쇄 회로 TV [pyeswae hoero TV] abbr CCTV

폐점 [pyejeom] 폐점 시간 [pyejeom sigan] n closing time

폐지 [pyeji] n abolition; 폐지하다 [pyejihada] v abolish

폐하 [pyeha] n majesty

폐허 [pyeheo] n ruin

포 [po] 방수포 [bangsupo] n tarpaulin; 박격포 [bakgyeokpo] n mortar (military)

포괄 [pogwal] 포괄적인 [pogwaljeogin] adj comprehensive, inclusive

포기 [pogi] 포기하다 [pogihada] v abandon, give up, waive; 포기하다 [pogihada] v give in

포낭 [ponang] n cyst

포도 [podo] n grape; 씨없는 건포도 [ssieomneun geonpodo] n redcurrant; 건포도 [geonpodo] n raisin; 포도원 [podowon] n vineyard

포도주 [podoju] 적포도주 [jeokpodoju] n red wine

포르노 [poreuno] n porn, pornography

포르투갈 [poreutugal] 포르투갈 [poreutugal] n Portugal; 포르투갈 사람 [poreutugal saram] n Portuguese (person); 포르투갈어 [poreutugareo] n Portuguese (language); 포르투갈의 [poreutugarui] adj Portuguese; 포르투갈어 [poreutugareo] Portuguese

포스터 [poseuteo] n poster

포옹 [poong] n cuddle, hug

포유 [poyu] 포유동물 [poyudongmul] n mammal

포일 [poil] n foil

포장 [pojang] n package, packaging; 포장지 [pojangji] n wrapping paper;

포장하다 [pojanghada] *vt* pack, wrap, wrap up

포크 [pokeu] *n* fork

포터 [poteo] *n* porter

포트폴리오 [poteupollio] *n* portfolio

포플러 [popeulleo] *n* poplar

포함 [poham] *n* inclusion;...을 포함하여 [...eul pohamhayeo] *prep* including; 포함된 [pohamdoen] *adj* included; 포함하다 [pohamhada] *v* include; 포함하다 [pohamhada] *v* contain, involve; 부가가치세 포함인가요? [bugagachise pohamingayo?] Is VAT included?; 봉사료 포함인가요? [bongsaryo pohamingayo?] Is service included?; 전기 요금이 포함되나요? [jeongi yogeumi pohamdoenayo?] Is the cost of electricity included?; 가격에 부츠가 포함되나요? [gagyeoge bucheuga pohamdoenayo?] Does the price include boots?; 가격에 막대가 포함되나요? [gagyeoge makdaega pohamdoenayo?] Does the price include poles?; 가격에는 무엇이 포함되나요? [gagyeogeneun mueosi pohamdoenayo?] What is included in the price?

폭 [pok] *n* width; 폭이 넓은 [pogi neorbeun] *adj* broad

폭격 [pokgyeok] *n* bombing; 폭격하다 [pokgyeokhada] *n* bomb

폭동 [pokdong] *n* riot; 폭동을 일으키다 [pokdongeul ireukida] *v* riot

폭력 [pongnyeok] *n* violence

폭발 [pokbal] *n* blast, explosion; 폭발성의 [pokbalseongui] *n* explosive; 폭발하다 [pokbalhada] *v* blow up, burst, explode

폭우 [pogu] *n* downpour

폭음 [pogeum] *n* binge drinking

폭탄 [poktan] *n* bomb; 시한폭탄 [sihanpoktan] *n* time bomb; 원자폭탄 [wonjapoktan] *n* atom bomb; 자살폭탄 테러범 [jasalpoktan tereobeom] *n* suicide bomber

폭포 [pokpo] *n* waterfall; 큰 폭포 [keun pokpo] *n* cataract (*waterfall*)

폭풍 [pokpung] *n* storm; 폭풍의

[pokpungui] *adj* stormy

폭풍우 [pokpungu] *n* rainstorm; 폭풍우가 쳐요 [pokpunguga chyeoyo] It's stormy; 폭풍우가 칠 것 같아요? [pokpunguga chil geot gatayo?] Do you think there will be a storm?

폴더 [poldeo] *n* folder

폴란드 [pollandeu] *n* Poland; 폴란드 사람 [pollandeu saram] *n* Pole; 폴란드어 [pollandeueo] *n* Polish; 폴란드의 [pollandeuui] *adj* Polish

폴리네시아 [pollinesia] *n* Polynesia; 폴리네시아 사람 [pollinesia saram] *n* Polynesian (*person*); 폴리네시아어 [pollinesiaeo] *n* Polynesian (*language*); 폴리네시아의 [pollinesiaui] *adj* Polynesian

표 [pyo] *n* ticket; 느낌표 [neukkimpyo] *n* exclamation mark; 당일 왕복표 [dangil wangbokpyo] *n* day return; 대차대조표 [daechadaejopyo] *n* balance sheet; 도표 [dopyo] *n* table (*chart*); 매표소 [maepyoso] *n* box office; 성적표 [seongjeokpyo] *n* report card; 시간표 [siganpyo] *n* timetable; 왕복표 [wangbokpyo] *n* return ticket; 전표 [jeonpyo] *n* slip (*paper*); 꼬리표 [kkoripyo] *n* tag; 가격표 [gagyeokpyo] *n* price list; 편도표 [pyeondopyo] *n* one-way ticket, single ticket; 다음주 금요일 표 두 장 주세요 [daeumju geumyoil pyo du jang juseyo] I'd like two tickets for next Friday; 어린이표 [eorinipyo] a child's ticket; 어디에서 발레 표를 살 수 있어요? [eodieseo balle pyoreul sal su isseoyo?] Where can I buy tickets for the ballet?; 어디에서 콘서트 표를 살 수 있어요? [eodieseo konseoteu pyoreul sal su isseoyo?] Where can I buy tickets for the concert?; 어디에서 표를 사나요? [eodieseo pyoreul sanayo?] Where can I get tickets?, Where can we get tickets?; 어디에서 표를 살 수 있을까요? [eodieseo pyoreul sal su isseulkkayo?] Where do I buy a ticket?; 여러 번 사용할 수 있는 표가 있어요? [yeoreo beon sayonghal su inneun pyoga isseoyo?] Do you have multi-journey tickets?; 여기서 표를 살 수 있어요? [yeogiseo pyoreul sal su isseoyo?] Can I buy the tickets here?; 오늘 밤 표 두 장이요 [oneul bam pyo du jangiyo] Two tickets for tonight, please; 오늘밤 표 두 장 주세요 [oneulbam pyo du jang juseyo] I'd like two tickets for tonight; 왕복표는 얼마예요? [wangbokpyoneun eolmayeyo?] How much is a return ticket?; 편도표는 얼마예요? [pyeondopyoneun eolmayeyo?] How much is a single ticket?; 표 두 장 주세요 [pyo du jang juseyo] I'd like two tickets, please; 표 한 장 주세요 [pyo han jang juseyo] A ticket, please; 표를 비싼 걸로 바꾸고 싶어요 [pyoreul bissan geollo bakkugo sipeoyo] I want to upgrade my ticket; 표를 바꾸고 싶어요 [pyoreul bakkugo sipeoyo] I want to change my ticket; 표를 예매해 주시겠어요? [pyoreul yemaehae jusigesseoyo?] Can you book the tickets for us?; 표를 잃어버렸어요 [pyoreul ireobeoryeosseoyo] I've lost my ticket; 표는 얼마예요? [pyoneun eolmayeyo?] How much are the tickets?; 표책자 한권 주세요 [pyochaekja hangwon juseyo] A book of tickets, please

표류 [pyoryu] n drift

표면 [pyomyeon] n surface

표백 [pyobaek] 표백제 [pyobaekje] n bleach; 표백한 [pyobaekhan] adj bleached

표범 [pyobeom] n leopard; 바다표범 [badapyobeom] n seal (animal); 흑표범 [heukpyobeom] n panther

표본 [pyobon] 도말 표본 검사 [domal pyobon geomsa] n smear test

표시 [pyosi] n mark, sign, token; 체크 표시 [chekeu pyosi] n tick; 표시기 [pyosigi] n indicator; 표시하다 [pyosihada] v mark (make sign)

표적 [pyojeok] n target

표제 [pyoje] n caption, headline

표준 [pyojun] n standard; 표준의

[pyojunui] adj standard

표지 [pyoji] 도로 표지 [doro pyoji] n road sign, signpost; 표지물 [pyojimul] n landmark

표현 [pyohyeon] n expression; 표현하다 [pyohyeonhada] v express

표효 [pyohyo] 으르렁거리다 [eureureonggeorida] v growl

푸들 [pudeul] n poodle

푸딩 [puding] n pudding

푸르다 [pureuda] 푸릇푸릇한 [pureutpureutan] adj lush

푸에르토리코 [puereutoriko] n Puerto Rico

풀 [pul] n glue, grass (plant), paste; 쐐기풀 [sswaegipul] n nettle; 장군풀 [janggunpul] n rhubarb; 고수풀 [gosupul] n coriander; 골풀 [golpul] n rush; 풀베는 기계 [pulbeneun gigye] n mower; 회향풀 [hoehyangpul] n fennel

풀다 [pulda] v untie, unwrap; (짐을) 풀다 [(jimeul) pulda] v unpack; (감은 것을) 풀다 [(gameun geoseul) pulda] vt unwind

풀이 [puri] 십자말풀이 [sipjamalpuri] n crossword

품 [pum] 목제품 [mokjepum] n woodwork; 기념품 [ginyeompum] n memento, souvenir; 화장품 [hwajangpum] npl toiletries

품목 [pummok] 품목 일람 [pummok illam] n inventory

품절 [pumjeol] 품절된 [pumjeoldoen] adj sold out

품종 [pumjong] n breed

품질 [pumjil] n quality

품질' 기한 [pumjir' gihan] 최상 품질 기한 [choesang pumjil gihan] n best-before date

풍선 [pungseon] n balloon; 풍선껌 [pungseonkkeom] n bubble gum

풍자 [pungja] n irony; 풍자적인 [pungjajeogin] adj ironic

풍진 [pungjin] n German measles

풍차 [pungcha] n windmill

퓨즈 [pyujeu] n fuse; 퓨즈를 바꿀 수 있나요? [pyujeureul bakkul su innayo?]

Can you mend a fuse?; 퓨즈가 나갔어요 [pyujeuga nagasseoyo] A fuse has blown

프랑스 [peurangseu] n France; 프랑스 사람 [peurangseu saram] n French, Frenchman; 프랑스 여자 [peurangseu yeoja] n Frenchwoman; 프랑스의 [peurangseuui] adj French

프로그램 [peurogeuraem] n program, programme; 컴퓨터용 회계처리 프로그램 [keompyuteoyong hoegyecheori peurogeuraem] n spreadsheet; 프로그래머 [peurogeuraemeo] n programmer; 프로그래밍 [peurogeuraeming] n programming; 프로그램을 짜다 [peurogeuraemeul jjada] v program; 메신저 프로그램을 사용할 수 있을까요? [mesinjeo peurogeuraemeul sayonghal su isseulkkayo?] Can I use messenger programmes?

프로젝터 [peurojekteo] n projector; 오버헤드 프로젝터 [obeohedeu peurojekteo] n overhead projector

프로젝트 [peurojekteu] n project

프리킥 [peurikik] n free kick

프린트 [peurinteu] 컬러 프린터 있어요? [keolleo peurinteo isseoyo?] Is there a colour printer?

플라밍고 [peullaminggo] n flamingo

플라스크 [peullaseukeu] n flask

플라스틱 [peullaseutik] n plastic; 플라스틱의 [peullaseutigui] adj plastic

플란넬 [peullannel] n flannel

플래시 [peullaesi] n flashlight

플랫폼 [peullaetpom] n platform

플러그 [peulleogeu] n plug; 플러그를 뽑다 [peulleogeureul ppopda] v unplug

플레이어 [peulleieo] DVD 플레이어 [DVD peulleieo] n DVD player; MP3 플레이어 [MP3 peulleieo] n MP3 player; MP4 플레이어 [MP4 peulleieo] n MP4 player

플레이크 [peulleikeu] 콘플레이크 [konpeulleikeu] npl cornflakes

플루트 [peulluteu] n flute

피 [pi] n blood; 수혈 [suhyeol] n blood

transfusion; 코피 [kopi] n nosebleed; 피를 보는 스포츠 [pireul boneun seupocheu] n blood sports; 피투성이의 [pituseongiui] adj bloody; 혈액 검사 [hyeoraek geomsa] n blood test; 이 얼룩은 피예요 [i eollugeun piyeyo] This stain is blood

피고 [pigo] n defendant; 피고인 [pigoin] n accused

피곤 [pigon] 피곤하게 하는 [pigonhage haneun] adj tiring; 피곤한 [pigonhan] adj tired; 피곤한 [pigonhan] adj exhausted; 좀 피곤해요 [jom pigonhaeyo] I'm a little tired; 피곤해요 [pigonhaeyo] I'm tired

피난 [pinan] 피난시키다 [pinansikida] v evacuate; 피난처 [pinancheo] n refuge; 화재 피난 장치 [hwajae pinan jangchi] n fire escape

피라미드 [piramideu] n pyramid

피로 [piro] 시차로 인한 피로 [sicharo inhan piro] n jet lag

피부 [pibu] n skin

피상 [pisang] 피상적인 [pisangjeogin] adj superficial

피스닙 [piseunip] n parsnip

피스톤 [piseuton] n piston

피아노 [piano] n piano; 피아니스트 [pianiseuteu] n pianist

피어싱 [pieosing] n piercing

피임 [piim] n contraception; 피임약 [piimyak] n contraceptive; 피임이 필요해요 [piimi piryohaeyo] I need contraception

피자 [pija] n pizza

피조물 [pijomul] n creature

피지 [piji] n Fiji

피하다 [pihada] v avoid

피해 [pihae] 피해자 [pihaeja] n victim

픽셀 [piksel] n pixel

핀 [pin] n pin; 머리핀 [meoripin] n hairgrip

핀란드 [pillandeu] n Finland; 핀란드 사람 [pillandeu saram] n Finn, Finnish; 핀란드의 [pillandeuui] adj Finnish

필기 [pilgi] 필기용지 [pilgiyongji] n writing paper

필름 [pilleum] 이 필름을 현상해

주시겠어요? [i pilleumeul hyeonsanghae jusigesseoyo?] Can you develop this film, please?; 필름이 걸렸어요 [pilleumi geollyeosseoyo] The film has jammed

필리핀 [pillipin] 필리핀 사람 [pillipin saram] n Filipino; 필리핀의 [pillipinui] adj Filipino

필사 [pilsa] 필사적으로 [pilsajeogeuro] adv desperately

필수 [pilsu] 필수의 [pilsuui] adj indispensable; 필수적인 [pilsujeogin] adj vital

필연 [pillyeon] 필연적인 [pillyeonjeogin] adj inevitable

필요 [pillyo] n need; 필요로 하다 [piryoro hada] v require; 필요조건 [piryojogeon] n requirement; 필요성 [piryoseong] n necessity; 필요하다 [piryohada] v need; 필요한 [piryohan] adj necessary; 봉투는 필요 없어요 [bongtuneun pillyo eopseoyo] I don't need a bag, thanks; 새 배터리가 필요해요 [sae baeteoriga pillyohaeyo] I need a new battery; 시트가 더 필요해요 [siteuga deo pillyohaeyo] We need more sheets; 오늘 밤에 아이들을 봐 줄 사람이 필요해요 [oneul bame aideureul bwa jul sarami piryohaeyo] I need someone to look after the children tonight; 필요하신 것이 있어요? [piryohasin geosi isseoyo?] Do you need anything?

필적 [piljeok] 필적하다 [piljeokhada] n match

필터 [pilteo] n filter

필통 [piltong] n pencil case

핑계 [pinggye] n pretext

하나 [hana] 단 하나의 [dan hanaui] adj single; 또 하나의 [tto hanaui] adj another; 어떤 하나의 [eotteon hanaui] art a, an

하녀 [hanyeo] n maid

하늘 [haneul] n sky

하다 [hada] vt do; ...하도록 [...hadorok] conj so (that); 다시 하다 [dasi hada] v redo; 뭐라고 하셨죠? [mworago hasyeotjyo?] excl pardon?; 감히...하다 [gamhi...hada] v dare; 할 수 있는 [hal su inneun] adj able; 할 수 있다 [hal su itda] v can; 어떻게 해야 합니까? [eotteoke haeya hamnikka?] What do I do?; 여기에서 할 만한 것이 있어요? [yeogieseo hal manhan geosi isseoyo?] What is there to do here?; 오늘 뭘 하시겠어요? [oneul mwol hasigesseoyo?] What would you like to do today?

하드보드 [hadeubodeu] n hardboard

하루 [haru] n day; 하루 입장권은 얼마예요? [haru ipjanggwoneun eolmayeyo?] How much is a pass for a day?; 하루 종일 우리 말고는 아무도 없으면 좋겠어요! [haru jongil uri malgoneun amudo eopseumyeon jokesseoyo!] We'd like to see nobody but us all day!

하마 [hama] n hippo, hippopotamus

하모니카 [hamonika] n mouth organ

하사 [hasa] n corporal

하수 [hasu] 하수구 [hasugu] n sewer

하숙 [hasuk] 하숙인 [hasugin] n lodger

하위 [hawi] 하위의 [hawiui] adj inferior

하이라이터 [hairaiteo] n highlighter

하이킹 [haiking] n hike, hiking

하이파이 [haipai] n hifi

하이픈 [haipeun] n hyphen

하이힐 [haihil] npl high heels; 하이힐의 [haihirui] adj high-heeled

하인 [hain] n servant

하차 [hacha] 중도하차 [jungdohacha] n stopover

하찮다 [hachanta] 하찮은 [hachanheun] adj rubbish

하키 [haki] n hockey; 아이스하키 [aiseuhaki] n ice hockey

하품 [hapum] 하품하다 [hapumhada] v yawn

하프 [hapeu] n harp

학 [hak] 물리학 [mullihak] npl physics; 물리학자 [mullihakja] n physicist; 동물학 [dongmulhak] n zoology; 사회학 [sahoehak] n sociology; 심리학 [simnihak] n psychology; 인류학 [illyuhak] n anthropology; 지리학 [jirihak] n geography; 지질학 [jijilhak] n geology; 통계학 [tonggyehak] npl statistics

학교 [hakgyo] n school; 야간 학교 [yagan hakgyo] n night school; 예술 학교 [yesul hakgyo] n art school; 중등학교 [jungdeunghakgyo] n secondary school; 초등학교 [chodeunghakgyo] n elementary school, primary school; 기숙학교 [gisukhakgyo] n boarding school; 스키 학교가 있어요? [seuki hakgyoga isseoyo?] Is there a ski school?

학기 [hakgi] n semester, term (division of year)

학년 [hangnyeon] 학년도 [hangnyeondo] n academic year

학대 [hakdae] 아동학대 [adonghakdae] n child abuse; 학대하다 [hakdaehada] v ill-treat

학동 [hakdong] n schoolchildren

학사 [haksa] abbr BA

학살 [haksal] 대학살 [daehaksal] n massacre

학생 [haksaeng] n pupil (learner), student; 남학생 [namhaksaeng] n schoolboy; 대학 재학생 [daehak jaehaksaeng] n undergraduate; 성인 학생 [seongin haksaeng] n mature student; 여학생 [yeohaksaeng] n schoolgirl; 학생할인 [haksaengharin] n student discount; 학생 할인이 있어요? [haksaeng harini isseoyo?] Are there any reductions for students?; 학생이에요 [haksaengieyo] I'm a student

학습 [hakseup] 학습자 [hakseupja] n learner

학원 [hagwon] n academy; 어학원 [eohagwon] n language school; 학원의 [hagwonui] adj academic

학자 [hakja] 심리학자 [simnihakja] n psychologist; 언어학자 [eoneohakja] n linguist; 경제학자 [gyeongjehakja] n economist

한계 [hangye] n limit

한국 [hanguk] n Korea, South Korea; 북한 [bukhan] n North Korea; 한국 사람 [hanguk saram] n Korean (person); 한국어 [hangugeo] n Korean (language); 한국의 [hangugui] adj Korean

한다 [handa] 해야 한다 [haeya handa] v must; 해야만 하다 [haeyaman hada] v have to

한번 [hanbeon] adv once

한산 [hansan] 한산한 때에 [hansanhan ttaee] adv off-peak

한숨 [hansum] 한숨 쉬다 [hansum swida] v sigh

한적 [hanjeok] 이 근처에 한적한 바닷가가 있나요? [i geuncheoe hanjeokhan badatgaga innayo?] Is there a quiet beach near here?

할당량 [haldangnyang] n quota

할만하다 [halmanhada] 할 만하다 [hal manhada] v deserve

할머니 [halmeoni] n grandma, grandmother, granny; 증조할머니 [jeungjohalmeoni] n great-grandmother

할부 [halbu] 할부금 [halbugeum] n
instalment
할수없다 [halsueopda]...할 수 없는 [...
hal su eomneun] adj unable to
할아버지 [harabeoji] n granddad,
grandfather, grandpa; 증조할아버지
[jeungjoharabeoji] n great-
grandfather
할인 [harin] n discount; 열차할인카드
[yeolchaharinkadeu] n railcard;
특별할인 [teukbyeolharin] n special
offer; 학생할인 [haksaengharin] n
student discount; 현금으로 내면
할인되나요? [hyeongeumeuro
naemyeon harindoenayo?] Do you
offer a discount for cash?
함 [ham] n box; 사물함 [samulham] n
locker; 용구함 [yongguham] n gear
box; 잠수함 [jamsuham] n submarine
함께 [hamkke] adv together;...과 함께 [...
gwa hamkke] prep with; 함께 살다
[hamkke salda] v live together
함대 [hamdae] n fleet
합 [hap] 다 합해서 주세요 [da
haphaeseo juseyo] All together, please
합격 [hapgyeok] n pass (meets standard);
합격하다 [hapgyeokhada] v pass (an
exam)
합계 [hapgye] n sum, total; 합계하다
[hapgyehada] v add up
합류 [hamnyu] 합류하다 [hamnyuhada]
vt join
합리 [hamni] 불합리한 [bulhamnihan]
adj absurd; 합리적으로
[hamnijeogeuro] adv reasonably;
합리적인 [hamnijeogin] adj rational
합법 [hapbeop] 합법적인
[hapbeopjeogin] adj legal
합병 [hapbyeong] n merger; 합병하다
[hapbyeonghada] v merge
합석 [hapseok] 합석해도 될까요?
[hapseokhaedo doelkkayo?] Can I join
you?
합승 [hapseung] v ride together, share a
ride; 합승할 수도 있어요 [hapseunghal
sudo isseoyo] We could share a taxi
합의 [habui] 합의를 얻은 [habuireul
eodeun] adj agreed

합창 [hapchang] 합창단 [hapchangdan]
n choir
합판 [happan] n plywood
핫도그 [hatdogeu] n hot dog
항 [hang] 항히스타민제
[hanghiseutaminje] n antihistamine
항공 [hanggong] 대기 항공권 [daegi
hanggonggwon] n stand-by ticket;
정기 항공편 [jeonggi hanggongpyeon]
n scheduled flight; 항공 관제사
[hanggong gwanjesa] n air-traffic
controller; 항공사 [hanggongsa] n
airline; 항공우편 [hanggongupyeon] n
airmail; 항공기 [hanggonggi] n
aircraft; 항공 우편은 도착하는 데
얼마나 걸려요? [hanggong upyeoneun
dochakhaneun de eolmana
geollyeoyo?] How long will it take by
air?
항구 [hanggu] n harbour, port (ships)
항목 [hangmok] n item; 항목별 광고
[hangmokbyeol gwanggo] npl small
ads
항법 [hangbeop] 위성항법
[wiseonghangbeop] n sat nav;
위성항법장치
[wiseonghangbeopjangchi] abbr GPS
항복 [hangbok] 항복하다
[hangbokhada] v surrender
항생 [hangsaeng] 항생 물질 [hangsaeng
muljil] n antibiotic
항아리 [hangari] n pot
항의 [hangui] n protest; 항의하다
[hanguihada] v protest
항체 [hangche] n antibody
항해 [hanghae] n sailing; 항해하다
[hanghaehada] v sail
해 [hae] n sun, year, harm, injury; 북극해
[bukgeukhae] n Arctic Ocean; 북해
[bukhae] n North Sea; 새해 [saehae] n
New Year; 선루프 [seollupeu] n
sunroof; 극히 해로운 [geukhi haeroun]
adj malignant; 해마다 [haemada] adv
annually, yearly; 해마다의
[haemadaui] adj annual; 해충
[haechung] n pest; 해치다 [haechida]
v harm; 해치다 [haechida] v hurt;
해질녘 [haejillyeok] n dusk; 다음 해

[daeum hae] next year; 올해 [olhae]
this year; 지난 해 [jinan hae] last year

해결 [haegyeol] n resolution, solution;
해결하다 [haegyeolhada] v solve, sort
out; 해결하다 [haegyeolhada] v figure
out

해고 [haego] n sack (dismissal); 해고 통보
[haego tongbo] n notice (termination);
해고하다 [haegohada] v dismiss;
해고하다 [haegohada] v lay off

해골 [haegol] n skeleton

해군 [haegun] n navy; 해군의 [haegunui]
adj naval

해독 [haedok] 해독제 [haedokje] n
antidote

해류 [haeryu] 해류가 있어요? [haeryuga
isseoyo?] Are there currents?

해머 [haemeo] n hammer

해먹 [haemeok] n hammock

해바라기 [haebaragi] n sunflower

해방 [haebang] n liberation, release;
해방하다 [haebanghada] v release

해법 [haebeop] n solution

해변 [haebyeon] n seaside

해사 [haesa] 해사의 [haesaui] adj
maritime

해산물 [haesanmul] n seafood; 해산물
좋아하세요? [haesanmul johahaseyo?]
Do you like seafood?; 해산물이
들어가지 않은 식사를 준비해
주시겠어요? [haesanmuri deureogaji
anheun siksareul junbihae
jusigesseoyo?] Could you prepare a
meal without seafood?

해석 [haeseok] 해석하다 [haeseokhada]
v interpret

해설 [haeseol] 해설자 [haeseolja] n
commentator

해수 [haesu] n sea water; 해수면
[haesumyeon] n sea level

해악 [haeak] n mischief

해안 [haean] n coast, seashore; 해안
경비대 [haean gyeongbidae] n
coastguard

해열제 [haeyeolje] 해열제 주세요
[haeyeolje juseyo] I'd like something
for a temperature

해외 [haeoe] 해외로 [haeoero] adv

overseas; 해외에 [haeoee] adv abroad

해일 [haeil] n tsunami

해적 [haejeok] n pirate

해초 [haecho] n seaweed

해치백 [haechibaek] n hatchback

해커 [haekeo] n hacker

해파리 [haepari] n jellyfish; 여기에
해파리가 있어요? [yeogie haepariga
isseoyo?] Are there jellyfish here?

해협 [haehyeop] n channel

핵 [haek] 핵의 [haegui] adj nuclear

핵심 [haeksim] n core

핸드백 [haendeubaek] n handbag

핸드볼 [haendeubol] n handball

핸들 [haendeul] 오른쪽 핸들 [oreunjjok
haendeul] n right-hand drive; 자동차
핸들 [jadongcha haendeul] n steering
wheel; 핸들바 [haendeulba] npl
handlebars

핸디캡 [haendikaep] 제 핸디캡은...
이에요 [je haendikaebeun...ieyo] My
handicap is...; 핸디캡이 얼마예요?
[haendikaebi eolmayeyo?] What's your
handicap?

핸즈프리 [haenjeupeuri] 핸즈프리 장치
[haenjeupeuri jangchi] n hands-free kit

햄 [haem] n ham

햄버거 [haembeogeo] n burger,
hamburger

햄스터 [haemseuteo] n hamster

햇볕 [haetbyeot] 햇볕에 탄 빛깔
[haetbyeote tan bitkkal] n tan; 햇볕에
탄 [haetbyeote tan] adj sunburnt;
햇볕에 탐 [haetbyeote tam] n sunburn

햇빛 [haetbit] n sunlight, sunshine;
햇빛이 밝은 [haetbichi balgeun] adj
sunny

행글라이딩 [haenggeullaiding] n
hang-gliding; 행글라이딩을 하고
싶어요 [haenggeullaidingeul hago
sipeoyo] I'd like to go hang-gliding

행동 [haengdong] n behaviour; 반사행동
[bansahaengdong] n reflex; 행동하다
[haengdonghada] v act, behave

행렬 [haengnyeol] n parade, procession

행복 [haengbok] n bliss, happiness;
행복하게 [haengbokhage] adv happily;
행복한 [haengbokhan] adj happy

행사 [haengsa] n event; 행사 장소 [haengsa jangso] n venue; 어느 스포츠 행사에 갈 수 있을까요? [eoneu seupocheu haengsae gal su isseulkkayo?] Which sporting events can we go to?

행상 [haengsang] 행상인 [haengsangin] n vendor

행성 [haengseong] n planet

행실 [haengsil] 행실이 바른 [haengsiri bareun] adj well-behaved

행운 [haengun] n luck; 운좋게 [unjoke] adv fortunately; 행운의 [haengunui] adj fortunate

행위 [haengwi] n act; 부도덕한 행위 [budodeokhan haengwi] n vice; 방해행위 [banghaehaengwi] v sabotage; 공공시설 파괴 행위 [gonggongsiseol pagoe haengwi] n vandalism; 강도 행위 [gangdo haengwi] n mugging

행정 [haengjeong] n administration; 행정 구역 [haengjeong guyeok] n ward (area); 행정상의 [haengjeongsangui] adj administrative; 행정관 [haengjeonggwan] n magistrate

행주 [haengju] n dish towel, dishcloth

행진 [haengjin] n march; 행진하다 [haengjinhada] v march

핥다 [hyartda] 핥다 [hartda] v lick

향 [hyang]...을 향하여 [...eul hyanghayeo] prep towards; 어떤 향이 있나요? [eotteon hyangi innayo?] What flavours do you have?

향료 [hyangnyo] n flavouring; 향료가 안 든 초콜릿 [hyangnyoga an deun chokollit] n plain chocolate

향수 [hyangsu] n perfume

향수병 [hyangsubyeong] 향수병에 걸린 [hyangsubyeonge geollin] adj homesick

향신 [hyangsin] 향료를 넣은 [hyangnyoreul neoheun] adj spicy; 향신료 [hyangsillyo] n spice

허가 [heoga] n leave, pass (permit); 노동허가증 [nodongheogajeung] n work permit; 주류판매 면허 [juryupanmae myeonheo] n off-licence; 허가증 [heogajeung] n permit

허락 [heorak] n permission; 입장을 허락하다 [ipjangeul heorakhada] v admit (allow in); 허락하다 [heorakhada] v allow, let

허리 [heori] n waist; 허리띠 [heoritti] n belt

허리케인 [heorikein] n hurricane

허브 [heobeu] npl herbs

허비 [heobi] 허비하다 [heobihada] v throw away

허세 [heose] n bluff; 허세를 부리다 [heosereul burida] v bluff

허수아비 [heosuabi] n scarecrow

허약 [heoyak] n weakness; 허약한 [heoyakhan] adj frail

허영 [heoyeong] 허영심이 강한 [heoyeongsimi ganghan] adj vain

허용 [heoyong] n allowance; 수하물 허용 중량은 얼마인가요? [suhamul heoyong jungnyangeun eolmaingayo?] What is the baggage allowance?; 허용치의 담배량을 가지고 있어요. [heoyongchiui dambaeryangeul gajigo isseoyo.] I have the allowed amount of tobacco to declare

허튼소리 [heoteunsori] 허튼 소리 [heoteun sori] n trash

헌법 [heonbeop] n constitution

헌신 [heonsin] n dedication; 헌신적인 [heonsinjeogin] adj dedicated, devoted

헐렁하다 [heolleonghada] 헐렁한 [heolleonghan] adj baggy, loose

험악 [heomak] 험악한 [heomakhan] adj thundery

헛간 [heotgan] n barn, shed

헛소리 [heossori] 헛소리하다 [heossorihada] v rave

헝가리 [heonggari] n Hungary; 헝가리 사람 [heonggari saram] n Hungarian; 헝가리의 [heonggariui] adj Hungarian

헝겊 [heonggeop] 깁는 헝겊 [gimneun heonggeop] n patch; 헝겊 조각 [heonggeop jogak] n rag

헤더 [hedeo] n heather

헤드폰 [hedeupon] npl headphones;

헤드폰이 있어요? [hedeuponi isseoyo?] Does it have headphones?

헤로인 [heroin] *n* heroin

헤르니아 [hereunia] *n* hernia

헤어 [heeo] 헤어 드라이어 [heeo deuraieo] *n* hairdryer; 헤어 스타일 [heeo seutail] *n* hairdo, hairstyle; 헤어 스프레이 [heeo seupeurei] *n* hair spray; 헤어 젤 [heeo jel] *n* hair gel

헤어드라이어 [heeodeuraieo] 헤어 드라이어가 필요해요 [heeo deuraieoga piryohaeyo] I need a hair dryer

헤어지다 [heeojida] *v* part with

헬리콥터 [hellikopteo] *n* helicopter

헬멧 [helmet] *n* helmet; 헬멧 주시겠어요? [helmet jusigesseoyo?] Can I have a helmet?

헹구다 [hengguda] *v* rinse; 헹구기 [henggugi] *n* rinse

혀 [hyeo] *n* tongue

혁명 [hyeongmyeong] *n* revolution; 혁명적인 [hyeongmyeongjeogin] *adj* revolutionary

혁신 [hyeoksin] *n* innovation; 혁신적인 [hyeoksinjeogin] *adj* innovative

현관 [hyeongwan] *n* porch; 현관 인터폰 [hyeongwan inteopon] *n* entry phone

현금 [hyeongeum] *n* cash; 현금 인출기 [hyeongeum inchulgi] *n* cash dispenser; 카드로 현금을 뽑을 수 있을까요? [kadeuro hyeongeumeul ppobeul su isseulkkayo?] Can I use my card to get cash?; 수표를 현금으로 바꿀 수 있을까요? [supyoreul hyeongeumeuro bakkul su isseulkkayo?] Can I cash a cheque?; 수표를 현금으로 바꾸고 싶어요 [supyoreul hyeongeumeuro bakkugo sipeoyo] I want to cash a cheque, please; 신용 카드로 현금 서비스를 받을 수 있을까요? [sinyong kadeuro hyeongeum seobiseureul badeul su isseulkkayo?] Can I get a cash advance with my credit card?; 여기에 현금 인출기가 있나요? [yeogie hyeongeum inchulgiga innayo?] Is there a cash machine here?; 가장 가까운 현금 인출기는 어디있어요? [gajang gakkaun hyeongeum inchulgineun eodiisseoyo?] Where is the nearest cash machine?; 현금으로 내면 할인되나요? [hyeongeumeuro naemyeon harindoenayo?] Do you offer a discount for cash?; 현금이 없어요 [hyeongeumi eopseoyo] I don't have any cash

현금인출기 [hyeongeuminchulgi] 이 현금 인출기에 제 카드를 사용할 수 있을까요? [i hyeongeum inchulgie je kadeureul sayonghal su isseulkkayo?] Can I use my card with this cash machine?

현기 [hyeongi] 현기증 [hyeongijeung] *n* vertigo

현기증 [hyeongijeung] 현기증 나는 [hyeongijeung naneun] *adj* dizzy; 현기증이 있어요 [hyeongijeungi isseoyo] I suffer from vertigo; 현기증이 계속 나요 [hyeongijeungi gyesok nayo] I keep having dizzy spells

현대 [hyeondae] *n* nowadays, the present time; 현대 언어 [hyeondae eoneo] *npl* modern languages; 현대의 [hyeondaeui] *adj* modern; 현대화하다 [hyeondaehwahada] *v* modernize

현명 [hyeonmyeong] 현명한 [hyeonmyeonghan] *adj* sensible, wise; 현명한 [hyeonmyeonghan] *adj* smart

현미 [hyeonmi] *n* brown rice

현미경 [hyeonmigyeong] *n* microscope

현상 [hyeonsang] *n* status quo

현수교 [hyeonsugyo] *n* suspension bridge

현실 [hyeonsil] *n* reality; 가상현실 [gasanghyeonsil] *n* virtual reality; 현실의 [hyeonsirui] *adj* real; 현실적인 [hyeonsiljeogin] *adj* realistic

현장 [hyeonjang] *n* scene, site

현재 [hyeonjae] *adv* currently, now ▷ *n* present *(time being)*; 현재의 [hyeonjaeui] *adj* current, present

현저 [hyeonjeo] 현저하게 [hyeonjeohage] *adv* remarkably; 현저한 [hyeonjeohan] *adj* noticeable, outstanding, remarkable

현판 [hyeonpan] *n* plaque

혈 [hyeol] 패혈증 [paehyeoljeung] n
blood poisoning

혈압 [hyeorap] n blood pressure

혈액 [hyeoraek] 혈액 검사 [hyeoraek
geomsa] n blood test; 혈액형
[hyeoraekhyeong] n blood group

혈액형 [hyeoraekhyeong] 제 혈액형은
O 플러스입니다. [je
hyeoraekhyeongeun O
peulleoseuhyeongimnida.] My blood
group is O positive

혈통 [hyeoltong] 혈통의 [hyeoltongui]
adj pedigree

혐오 [hyeomo] 혐오스러운
[hyeomoseureoun] adj disgusted;
혐오감을 일으키는 [hyeomogameul
ireukineun] adj repulsive

협동 [hyeopdong] n cooperation

협력 [hyeomnyeok] n collaboration,
cooperation; 협력하다
[hyeomnyeokhada] v collaborate

협박 [hyeopbak] n blackmail; 협박하다
[hyeopbakhada] v blackmail

협상 [hyeopsang] npl negotiations;
협상자 [hyeopsangja] n negotiator;
협상하다 [hyeopsanghada] v negotiate

협심증 [hyeopsimjeung] n angina

협정 [hyeopjeong] n agreement

협주 [hyeopju] 협주곡 [hyeopjugok] n
concerto

협회 [hyeophoe] n association

형 [hyeong] 삼각형 [samgakhyeong] n
triangle

형광 [hyeonggwang] 형광성의
[hyeonggwangseongui] adj
fluorescent

형식 [hyeongsik] n format; 형식적인
[hyeongsikjeogin] adj formal;
형식화하다 [hyeongsikhwahada] v
format

형용사 [hyeongyongsa] n adjective

형제 [hyeongje] n brother; 의붓형제
[uibutyeongje] n stepbrother;
형제자매 [hyeongjejamae] npl siblings

형태 [hyeongtae] n form

혜성 [hyeseong] n comet

호 [ho] 외호 [oeho] n moat

호기심 [hogisIm] 호기심이 강한
[hogisimi ganghan] adj curious

호두 [hodu] n walnut

호랑이 [horangi] n tiger

호르몬 [horeumon] n hormone

호른 [horeun] n horn; 프렌치 호른
[peurenchi horeun] n French horn

호박 [hobak] n amber, pumpkin, squash;
서양 호박 [seoyang hobak] n
courgette; 서양호박 [seoyanghobak] n
zucchini

호보크라프트 [hobokeurapeuteu]
호버크라프트 [hobeokeurapeuteu] n
hovercraft

호선 [hoseon]... 가려면 몇 호선 타야
되나요? [... garyeomyeon myeot
hoseon taya doenayo?] Which line
should I take for...?

호수 [hosu] n lake

호스 [hoseu] n hose, hosepipe

호스텔 [hoseutel] n hostel; 유스호스텔
[yuseuhoseutel] n youth hostel

호위 [howi] n convoy; 호위하다
[howihada] v escort

호의 [houi] n favour; 호의적이 아닌
[houijeogi anin] adj unfavourable

호주 [hoju] n Australia; 호주 사람 [hoju
saram] n Australian; 호주의 [hojuui]
adj Australian

호치키스 [hochikiseu] n stapler

호텔 [hotel] n hotel; 이 호텔에 가는 가장
좋은 방법은 무엇인가요? [i hotere
ganeun gajang joheun bangbeobeun
mueosingayo?] What's the best way to
get to this hotel?; 이 호텔까지 택시
요금이 얼마예요? [i hotelkkaji taeksi
yogeumi eolmayeyo?] How much is
the taxi fare to this hotel?; 그는 호텔을
운영해요 [geuneun hotereul
unyeonghaeyo] He runs the hotel;
호텔에 묵고 있어요 [hotere mukgo
isseoyo] I'm staying at a hotel; 호텔을
추천해 주시겠어요? [hotereul
chucheonhae jusigesseoyo?] Can you
recommend a hotel?; 호텔을 예약해
주시겠어요? [hotereul yeyakhae
jusigesseoyo?] Can you book me into a
hotel?; 호텔을 찾고 있어요 [hotereul
chatgo isseoyo] We're looking for a

hotel; 휠체어로 출입할 수 있는 호텔인가요? [hwilcheeoro churiphal su inneun hoteringayo?] Is your hotel accessible to wheelchairs?

호화 [hohwa] 호화로운 [hohwaroun] adj gorgeous, luxurious

호환 [hohwan] 호환성 있는 [hohwanseong inneun] adj compatible

호흡 [hoheup] n breathing

혹사 [hoksa] 혹사하다 [hoksahada] v slave

혹평 [hokpyeong] 혹평하다 [hokpyeonghada] v slag off

혹한 [hokhan] 혹한의 [hokhanui] adj freezing

혼돈 [hondon] n chaos; 혼돈된 [hondondoen] adj chaotic

혼동 [hondong] 혼동하다 [hondonghada] v confuse

혼란 [hollan] n confusion, mess, mix-up, muddle; 혼란시키는 [hollansikineun] adj confusing

혼수 [honsu] n coma

혼자 [honja] adv alone; 혼자 여기 왔어요 [honja yeogi wasseoyo] I'm here on my own; 혼자 있게 해 주세요! [honja itge hae juseyo!] Leave me alone!

혼합 [honhap] n mix; 혼합물 [honhammul] n mixture; 혼합된 샐러드 [honhapdoen saelleodeu] n mixed salad; 혼합된 [honhapdoen] adj mixed; 혼합하다 [honhaphada] v mix up

홀 [hol] n hall; 홀아비 [horabi] n widower

홀로 [hollo] adj alone

홈페이지 [hompeiji] n home page

홍보 [hongbo] 홍보활동 [hongbohwaldong] npl public relations

홍보실 [hongbosil] 홍보실이 있어요? [hongbosiri isseoyo?] Do you have a press office?

홍수 [hongsu] n flood

홍역 [hongyeok] npl measles; 최근에 홍역을 앓았어요 [choegeune hongyeogeul arasseoyo] I had measles recently

홍조 [hongjo] n flush

홍채 [hongchae] n iris

홍합 [honghap] n mussel

화 [hwa] n anger, flower; 발레화 [ballehwa] npl ballet shoes; 수채화 [suchaehwa] n watercolour; 수선화 [suseonhwa] n daffodil; 실내화 [sillaehwa] n slipper; 운동화 [undonghwa] npl sneakers; 초상화 [chosanghwa] n portrait; 화를 쉽게 내는 [hwareul swipge naeneun] adj irritable; 화를 잘 내는 [hwareul jal naeneun] adj touchy; 화나게 하는 [hwanage haneun] adj irritating; 화난 [hwanan] adj angry; 화난 [hwanan] adj mad (angry), upset

화가 [hwaga] n painter

화강암 [hwagangam] n granite

화랑 [hwarang] n gallery

화려 [hwaryeo] 화려한 [hwaryeohan] adj splendid

화면 [hwamyeon] n screen; 플라스마 화면 [peullaseuma hwamyeon] n plasma screen; 화면 보호기 [hwamyeon bohogi] n screen-saver

화물 [hwamul] n cargo, freight

화분 [hwabun] n plant pot; 화분에 심는 화초 [hwabune simneun hwacho] n pot plant

화사 [hwasa] 화산 [hwasan] n volcano

화살 [hwasal] n arrow; 가늘고 짧은 화살 [ganeulgo jjarbeun hwasal] n dart

화상 [hwasang] n burn

화씨 [hwassi] n degree Fahrenheit

화요일 [hwayoil] 화요일에 [hwayoire] on Tuesday

화장 [hwajang] n make-up; 화장복 [hwajangbok] n dressing gown; 화장대 [hwajangdae] n dressing table; 화장실 [hwajangsil] n loo; 화장품 [hwajangpum] npl cosmetics, toiletries

화장실 [hwajangsil] n lavatory, toilet; 남자 화장실 [namja hwajangsil] n gents'; 여자화장실 [yeojahwajangsil] n ladies'; 배에 화장실이 있어요? [baee hwajangsiri isseoyo?] Is there a toilet on board?; 장애인 화장실이 있어요? [jangaein hwajangsiri isseoyo?] Are

there any toilets for the disabled?;
차내에 화장실이 있어요? [chanae
hwajangsiri isseoyo?] Is there a toilet
on board?; **화장실은 어디있어요?**
[hwajangsireun eodiisseoyo?] Where
are the toilets?; **화장실을 사용해도
될까요?** [hwajangsireul sayonghaedo
doelkkayo?] Can I use the toilet?

화장장 [hwajangjang] n crematorium

화장지 [hwajangji] n toilet paper;
두루마리 화장지 [durumari hwajangji]
n toilet roll; **화장지가 없어요**
[hwajangjiga eopseoyo] There is no
toilet paper

화재 [hwajae] **화재 경보** [hwajae
gyeongbo] n fire alarm; **화재 피난 장치**
[hwajae pinan jangchi] n fire escape;
화재경보 [hwajaegyeongbo] n smoke
alarm

화창 [hwachang] **화창해요**
[hwachanghaeyo] It's sunny

화초 [hwacho] **화분에 심는 화초**
[hwabune simneun hwacho] n pot
plant

화폐 [hwapye] **화폐 주조소** [hwapye
jujoso] n mint (coins); **화폐의**
[hwapyeui] adj monetary

화학 [hwahak] n chemistry; **생화학**
[saenghwahak] n biochemistry; **화학
제품** [hwahak jepum] n chemical

확대 [hwakdae] n enlargement

확대경 [hwakdaegyeong] n magnifying
glass

확산 [hwaksan] n spread

확성 [hwakseong] **확성기**
[hwakseonggi] n loudspeaker

확신 [hwaksin] **확신하는**
[hwaksinhaneun] adj certain,
confident

확실 [hwaksil] **확실성** [hwaksilseong] n
certainty; **확실하게** [hwaksilhage] adv
surely; **확실한** [hwaksilhan] adj sure;
확실히 [hwaksilhi] adv certainly

확인 [hwagin] n check, confirmation,
identification; **미확인 비행물체**
[mihwagin bihaengmulche] abbr UFO;
확인하다 [hwaginhada] v confirm,
identify; **물을 확인해 주시겠어요?**

[mureul hwaginhae jusigesseoyo?] Can
you check the water, please?; **공기를
확인해 주시겠어요?** [gonggireul
hwaginhae jusigesseoyo?] Can you
check the air, please?; **타이어를 확인해
주시겠어요?** [taieoreul hwaginhae
jusigesseoyo?] Can you check the tyres,
please?

환 [hwan] **우편환** [upyeonhwan] n
postal order

환각 [hwangak] n illusion

환경 [hwangyeong] n environment ▷ npl
circumstances, surroundings;
친환경적인 [chinhwangyeongjeogin] adj
ecofriendly, environmentally friendly;
환경의 [hwangyeongui] adj
environmental

환기 [hwangi] n ventilation

환대 [hwandae] n hospitality

환불 [hwanbul] n rebate

환상 [hwansang] **환상적인**
[hwansangjeogin] adj fantastic

환승 [hwanseung] **환승 대기실**
[hwanseung daegisil] n transit lounge

환영 [hwanyeong] n welcome; **환영하다**
[hwanyeonghada] v welcome

환율 [hwanyul] n exchange rate, rate of
exchange; **환율이 어떻게 되나요?**
[hwanyuri eotteoke doenayo?] What's
the exchange rate?

환자 [hwanja] n patient; **난독증 환자**
[nandokjeung hwanja] n dyslexic;
노인병 환자 [noinbyeong hwanja] n
geriatric; **당뇨병 환자**
[dangnyobyeong hwanja] n diabetic;
중환자실 [junghwanjasil] n intensive
care unit; **간질 환자** [ganjil hwanja] n
epileptic

환전 [hwanjeon] **환전소** [hwanjeonso] n
bureau de change; **백...을...으로
환전하고 싶어요** [baek...eul...euro
hwanjeonhago sipeoyo] I'd like to
change one hundred... into...;
어디에서 환전할 수 있을까요?
[eodieseo hwanjeonhal su
isseulkkayo?] Where can I change some
money?; **...을...으로 환전하고 싶어요** [...
eul...euro hwanjeonhago sipeoyo] I

want to change some... into...

환전소 [hwanjeonso] 여기에 환전소가 있나요? [yeogie hwanjeonsoga innayo?] Is there a bureau de change here?; 환전소를 찾아야 해요 [hwanjeonsoreul chajaya haeyo] I need to find a bureau de change; 환전소는 언제 열어요? [hwanjeonsoneun eonje yeoreoyo?] When is the bureau de change open?

환풍기 [hwanpunggi] 방에 환풍기 있어요? [bange hwanpunggi isseoyo?] Does the room have a fan?

활 [hwal] n bow (weapon)

활공 [hwalgong] n gliding

활기 [hwalgi] 활기찬 [hwalgichan] adj lively

활동 [hwaldong] n action, activity; 홍보활동 [hongbohwaldong] npl public relations; 활동 휴가 [hwaldong hyuga] n activity holiday; 활동적인 [hwaldongjeogin] adj active; 어린이를 위한 활동이 있나요? [eorinireul wihan hwaldongi innayo?] Do you have activities for children?; 어떤 실내 활동이 있어요? [eotteon sillae hwaldongi isseoyo?] What indoor activities are there?; 어떤 야외 활동이 있어요? [eotteon yaoe hwaldongi isseoyo?] What outdoor activities are there?

활용 [hwallyong] 재활용하다 [jaehwallyonghada] v recycle

활주 [hwalju] 활주로 [hwaljuro] n runway

황달 [hwangdal] n jaundice

황동 [hwangdong] n brass

황량 [hwangnyang] 황량한 [hwangnyanghan] adj bleak, stark

황소 [hwangso] 황소자리 [hwangsojari] n Taurus

황야 [hwangya] n moor

황제 [hwangje] n emperor

황폐 [hwangpye] 황폐시키는 [hwangpyesikineun] adj devastating

회 [hoe] 1회성의 것 [han hoeseongui geot] n one-off

회견 [hoegyeon] 기자회견 [gijahoegyeon] n press conference

회계 [hoegye] n accountancy; 회계 연도 [hoegye yeondo] n financial year; 회계사 [hoegyesa] n accountant; 회계연도 [hoegyeyeondo] n fiscal year; 회계의 [hoegyeui] adj fiscal

회교 [hoegyo] 회교 사원 [hoegyo sawon] n mosque; 회교도 [hoegyodo] n Moslem; 회교의 [hoegyoui] adj Moslem

회로 [hoero] n circuit; 폐쇄 회로 TV [pyeswae hoero TV] abbr CCTV

회복 [hoebok] n recovery; 의식을 회복하다 [uisigeul hoebokhada] v come round; 회복하다 [hoebokhada] vi get over, recover

회사 [hoesa] n company, firm; 유제품 회사 [yujepum hoesa] n dairy; 자회사 [jahoesa] n subsidiary; 회사차 [hoesacha] n company car; 우리 회사에 관한 정보예요 [uri hoesae gwanhan jeongboyeyo] Here's some information about my company; 회사에 관한 정보를 받고 싶어요 [hoesae gwanhan jeongboreul batgo sipeoyo] I would like some information about the company

회수 [hoesu] 수하물 회수 [suhamul hoesu] n baggage reclaim

회원 [hoewon] n member; 회원 카드 [hoewon kadeu] n membership card; 회원 자격 [hoewon jagyeok] n membership; 회원이 되어야 하나요? [hoewoni doeeoya hanayo?] Do I have to be a member?, Do you have to be a member?

회의 [hoeui] n appointment, conference, council

회의장 [hoeuijang] 회의장으로 가 주세요 [hoeuijangeuro ga juseyo] Please take me to the conference centre

회의적 [hoeuijeok] 회의적인 [hoeuijeogin] adj sceptical

회전 [hoejeon] n turn; 회전 목마 [hoejeon mongma] n merry-go-round; 회전시키다 [hoejeonsikida] v turn round, turn around; 회전식 출입문

[hoejeonsik churimmun] n turnstile; 회전식 탈수기 [hoejeonsik talsugi] n tumble dryer; 회전하다 [hoejeonhada] vi turn

회칠 [hoechil] 회칠하다 [hoechilhada] v whitewash

회폐 [hoepye] n 컴퓨터용 회계처리 프로그램 [keompyuteoyong hoegyecheori peurogeuraem] n spreadsheet

회향 [hoehyang] 애기회향 [aegihoehyang] n cumin

획득 [hoekdeuk] 획득하다 [hoekdeukhada] v obtain

횡단 [hoengdan] 횡단 보도 [hoengdan bodo] n pedestrian crossing; 횡단보도 [hoengdanbodo] n zebra crossing; 횡단보도 [hoengdanbodo] n crossing

횡단보도 [hoengdanbodo] 보행자가 신호등을 조작하는 횡단보도 [bohaengjaga sinhodeungeul jojakhaneun hoengdanbodo] n pelican crossing

효과 [hyogwa] n effect; 효과적으로 [hyogwajeogeuro] adv effectively; 효과적인 [hyogwajeogin] adj effective

효모 [hyomo] n yeast

효율 [hyoyul] 효율적으로 [hyoyuljeogeuro] adv efficiently; 효율적인 [hyoyuljeogin] adj efficient

후 [hu]... 이후에 [... ihue] prep since;...한 후에 [...han hue] prep since;...후에 [... hue] prep after; 후에 [hue] prep after; 여름 후에 [yeoreum hue] after summer; 여덟시 후에 [yeodeopsi hue] after eight o'clock

후계 [hugye] 후계자 [hugyeja] n successor

후두 [hudu] 후두염 [huduyeom] n laryngitis

후보 [hubo] n candidate

후식 [husik] n dessert ▷ npl afters; 후식 메뉴 주세요 [husik menyu juseyo] The dessert menu, please; 후식을 주세요 [husigeul juseyo] We'd like a dessert

후원 [huwon] n backing, backup, sponsorship; 후원자 [huwonja] n sponsor; 후원하다 [huwonhada] v

back, back up, sponsor

후추 [huchu] n pepper; 후추 분쇄통 [huchu bunswaetong] n peppermill

후텁지근 [huteopjigeun] 후텁지근해요 [huteopjigeunhaeyo] It's muggy

후회 [huhoe] n regret; 깊은 후회 [gipeun huhoe] n remorse; 후회하다 [huhoehada] v regret

훈련 [hullyeon] n training; 피훈련자 [pihullyeonja] n trainee; 훈련 받은 [hullyeon badeun] adj trained; 훈련과정 [hullyeongwajeong] n training course; 훈련관 [hullyeongwan] n trainer; 훈련하다 [hullyeonhada] n train

훈제 [hunje] 훈제한 [hunjehan] adj smoked

훌륭 [hullyung] n admiration; 훌륭한 [hullyunghan] adj superb; 점심이 훌륭했어요 [jeomsimi hullyunghaesseoyo] The lunch was excellent

훔쳐가다 [humchyeogada] 누군가가 제 여행자 수표를 훔쳐 갔어요 [nugungaga je yeohaengja supyoreul humchyeo gasseoyo] Someone's stolen my traveller's cheques

훔치다 [humchida] v steal

휘발유 [hwibally u] n petrol; 무연 휘발유 [muyeon hwiballyu] n unleaded petrol

휘파람 [hwiparam] n whistle; 휘파람을 불다 [hwiparameul bulda] v whistle

휠체어 [hwilcheeo] n wheelchair; 저는 휠체어를 사용해요 [jeoneun hwilcheeoreul sayonghaeyo] I use a wheelchair; 휠체어 리프트가 있나요? [hwilcheeo ripeuteuga innayo?] Do you have a lift for wheelchairs?; 휠체어 있어요? [hwilcheeo isseoyo?] Do you have wheelchairs?; 휠체어로 출입할 수 있는 방이 필요해요 [hwilcheeoro churiphal su inneun bangi piryohaeyo] I need a room with wheelchair access; 휠체어로 출입할 수 있는 호텔인가요? [hwilcheeoro churiphal su inneun hoteringayo?] Is your hotel accessible to wheelchairs?; 휠체어로 열차에 타고 내릴 수 있을까요? [hwilcheeoro yeolchae tago naeril su isseulkkayo?] Is the train wheelchair-accessible?; **휠체어로...을 방문할 수 있나요?** [hwilcheeoro...eul bangmunhal su innayo?] Can you visit... in a wheelchair?; **휠체어를 이용할 수 있는 출입구는 어디인가요?** [hwilcheeoreul iyonghal su inneun churipguneun eodiingayo?] Where is the wheelchair-accessible entrance?

휠캡 [hwilkaep] n hubcap

휴가 [hyuga] n holiday, leave; **출산휴가** [chulsanhyuga] n maternity leave; **아버지의 육아 휴가** [abeojiui yuga hyuga] n paternity leave; **여름휴가** [yeoreumhyuga] npl summer holidays; **패키지 휴가** [paekiji hyuga] n package holiday; **활동 휴가** [hwaldong hyuga] n activity holiday; **여기 휴가차 왔어요** [yeogi hyugacha wasseoyo] I'm on holiday here; **휴가차 여기 왔어요** [hyugacha yeogi wasseoyo] I'm here on holiday

휴대 [hyudae] **휴대 세면백** [hyudae semyeonbaek] n sponge bag; **휴대 스테레오** [hyudae seutereo] n personal stereo; **휴대 계산기** [hyudae gyesangi] n pocket calculator; **휴대폰** [hyudaepon] n mobile phone; **휴대폰 번호** [hyudaepon beonho] n mobile number; **휴대폰 벨소리** [hyudaepon belsori] n ringtone; **휴대형의** [hyudaehyeongui] adj portable; **당신의 휴대 전화번호는 몇 번인가요?** [dangsinui hyudae jeonhwabeonhoneun myeot beoningayo?] What is the number of your mobile?; **제 휴대 전화 번호는... 이에요** [je hyudae jeonhwa beonhoneun...ieyo] My mobile number is...; **휴대전화 있어요?** [hyudaejeonhwa isseoyo?] Do you have a mobile?; **어디에서 휴대전화를 충전할 수 있어요?** [eodieseo hyudaejeonhwareul chungjeonhal su isseoyo?] Where can I charge my mobile phone?

휴대품 [hyudaepum] **휴대품 보관소**

[hyudaepum bogwanso] n cloakroom

휴식 [hyusik] n relaxation, rest, the rest; **경기 중의 중간 휴식** [gyeonggi jungui junggan hyusik] n half-time; **휴식시간** [hyusiksigan] n playtime, time off

휴양 [hyuyang] **휴양지** [hyuyangji] n resort

휴업 [hyueop] **휴업하다** [hyueophada] v shut down

휴일 [hyuil] n holiday; **휴일 잘 보내세요!** [hyuil jal bonaeseyo!] Enjoy your holiday!

휴전 [hyujeon] n ceasefire, truce

휴지 [hyuji] **휴지통** [hyujitong] n wastepaper basket

흉악 [hyungak] **흉악범** [hyungakbeom] n thug

흉터 [hyungteo] n scar

흐느끼다 [heuneukkida] v sob

흐르다 [heureuda] v flow

흐름 [heureum] n current (flow)

흐리다 [heurida] **잔뜩 흐린** [jantteuk heurin] adj overcast; **흐린** [heurin] adj cloudy

흑백 [heukbaek] x in black and white

흔들다 [heundeulda] vt shake; **쥐고 흔들다** [jwigo heundeulda] v boss around; **손흔들다** [sonheundeulda] v wave; **흔들리다** [heundeullida] vi shake

흔들리다 [heundeullida] **전후(좌우)로 흔들리다** [jeonhu(jwau)ro heundeullida] v sway; **흔들림** [heundeullim] n swing; **흔들린** [heundeullin] adj shaken

흙 [heulg] n soil; **흙손** [heurkson] n trowel

흠모 [heummo] **흠모하다** [heummohada] v adore

흡연 [heubyeon] n smoking; **비흡연자** [biheubyeonja] n non-smoker; **흡연자** [heubyeonja] n smoker; **흡연하지 않는** [heubyeonhaji annneun] adj non-smoking; **흡연실이 좋겠어요** [heubyeonsiri jokesseoyo] I'd like a smoking room; **흡연구역 좌석으로 주세요** [heubyeonguyeok jwaseogeuro juseyo] I'd like a seat in the smoking area

흡입 [heubip] **흡입기** [heubipgi] *n*
inhaler

흡혈 [heuphyeol] **흡혈귀**
[heuphyeolgwi] *n* vampire

흥 [heung] **흥을 깨는 사람** [heungeul
kkaeneun saram] *n* spoilsport

흥미 [heungmi] *n* interest; **흥미를 끄는**
[heungmireul kkeuneun] *adj* gripping;
흥미를 가진 [heungmireul gajin] *adj*
interested; **흥미를 갖게 하다**
[heungmireul gatge hada] *v* interest;
흥미있는 [heungmiinneun] *adj*
interesting; **흥미진진한**
[heungmijinjinhan] *adj* exciting

흥분 [heungbun] **흥분한** [heungbunhan]
adj excited

흥취 [heungchwi] *n* zest *(excitement)*

희다 [huida] **살결이 흰** [salgyeori huin]
adj fair *(light colour)*; **흰** [huin] *adj*
white

희망 [huimang] *n* hope; **희망없는**
[huimangeomneun] *adj* hopeless;
희망적인 [huimangjeogin] *adj* hopeful;
희망하다 [huimanghada] *v* hope;
희망하다 [huimanghada] *v* desire, wish

희미 [huimi] **희미한** [huimihan] *adj* faint

희미해지다 [huimihaejida] *v* fade

희생 [huisaeng] *n* sacrifice

희석 [huiseok] **희석된** [huiseokdoen] *adj*
diluted; **희석하다** [huiseokhada] *v*
dilute

히스타민 [hiseutamin] **항히스타민제**
[hanghiseutaminje] *n* antihistamine

히아신스 [hiasinseu] *n* hyacinth

히피 [hipi] *n* hippie

힌두교 [hindugyo] *n* Hinduism; **힌두교도**
[hindugyodo] *n* Hindu; **힌두교도의**
[hindugyodoui] *adj* Hindu

힌트 [hinteu] *n* hint, tip *(suggestion)*

힘 [him] *n* force, power, strength; **힘들게**
일하다 [himdeulge ilhada] *v* swot

힘들다 [himdeulda] *v* be hard, require
effort; **건너기 힘들었어요** [geonneogi
himdeureosseoyo] The crossing was
rough

힘줄 [himjul] *n* tendon

Korean Grammar

Introduction

This is a guide to some of the basic concepts and rules of Korean grammar. It is designed to enable you to form simple sentences. There are different levels of politeness in Korean, but polite forms, suitable for learners to use without being rude, are used in the example sentences in this grammar section.

Although the sentence structure of Korean is rather different from most European languages, learning Korean is not very difficult. In some ways, it is quite simple. For example: there is no grammatical gender and there are no definite or indefinite articles; there is no obligatory distinction between singular and plural; there are no relative pronouns, and verb forms do not change according to who is performing an action.

Sentence structure

The basic Korean sentence has a topic and a comment section. The topic (which is indicated by the topic marker 는 '(n)eun') usually comes at the beginning of the sentence, but if the topic can be understood among the speakers or from the context, it is often omitted.

> **(나는) 한국사람 입니다.**
> **(Na-neun) hanguksaram imnida.**
> *(I) am Korean.*

Because the subject is often omitted and the verb form does not change according to grammatical person, the sentence 서울에 갑니다 '**Seoule gamnida**' can mean *I/you/he/she/we/they will go to Seoul*, but the subject should be clear from the context.

Word order

Korean word order is: subject – object – verb. The verb comes at the end of the sentence. Therefore, *I eat kimchi* becomes *I kimchi eat*; 나는 김치를 먹습니다 'na-neun gimchireul meokseumnida'. Those elements that precede verbs have a rather free word order. In other words, except sentence-final verb, other elements are free to occur in almost any order.

> 아버지가 어머니께 선물을 드렸다.
> **Abeojiga eomeonikke seonmureul deuryeotda.**
> *My father gave my mother a present.*

> 어머니께 아버지가 선물을 드렸다.
> **Abeojiga eomeonikke seonmureul deuryeotda.**
> *My father gave my mother a present.*

Particles

The Korean language has small words called particles that show how different parts of the sentence relate to each other. Some work in a similar way to English prepositions, but in Korean they are typically attached to nouns. Sometimes, particles can attach to adverbs, adverbial particles, and other particles. These particles have the following functions.

-는 '(n)eun'	topic marker
-이/가 'i/ga'	subject marker
-를 '(r)eul'	direct object marker
-에게 'ege'	indirect object marker, goal, and location marker
-와 'wa'	connects nouns, means 'and' or 'with'
-에서 'eseo'	indicates the place where an action takes place

-의 'ui'	indicates that the second noun is described in some way by first, e.g. possession
-도 'do'	means 'too/also/as well'
-부터 'buteo'	means 'from/since'
-까지 'kkaji'	means 'until/as far as'

누가 사과를 먹었습니까?
Nuga sagwareul meogeosseumnikka?
Who ate the apple?

한국의 음식은 맛있습니다.
Hangugui eumsigeun masissseumnida.
Korean food is delicious.

프랑스의 음식도 맛있습니다.
Peurangseuui eumsikdo masissseumnida.
French food is also delicious.

Nouns

Nouns can have several functions in Korean. Most importantly, they can be subjects of sentences. Particles are attached to nouns to show grammatical case. Nouns can also take the plural marker 들 '**deul**'.

수지는 대학생 입니다.
Sujineun daehaksaeng imnida.
Suji is a university student.

선생님이 나에게 책을 선물로 주셨습니다.
Seonsaengnimi naege chaegeul seonmullo jusyeossseumnida.
My teacher gave me a book as a present.

우리들은 신입생 입니다.
Urideuleun sinipsaeng imnida.
We are freshmen.

Verbs

Verbs function as predicates in sentences and relate to the subject of the sentence. There are mainly two types of verbs in Korean: action verbs and descriptive verbs. Action verbs are used to represent activities, movements, and processes. Descriptive verbs refer to properties or states.

오빠가 도서관에 간다.
Oppaga doseogwane ganda.
My brother goes to a library.

아기가 노란색 옷을 입고 있습니다.
Agiga noransaek oseul ibeossseumnida.
The baby wore yellow clothes.

저 소녀는 아름답습니다.
Jeo sonyeoneun areumdapseumnida.
That girl is beautiful.

The copula verb -이다 '**-ida**' or -입니다 '**-imnida**' is usually used to link subjects and predicates in sentences. Normally, nouns or noun-like phrases precede -이다 '**-ida**'. Thus, nouns and noun-like words can act as predicates in sentences.

나는 이소연 입니다.
Naneun iseoyeon imnida.
I am Lee Seoyeon.

이것은 한국어 <u>교과서이다</u>.
Igeoseun hangugeo <u>gyogwaseoida</u>.
This is a Korean language textbook.

오늘은 <u>목요일 입니다</u>.
Oneureun <u>mogyoir imnida</u>.
It is Thursday today.

The verb - 있 다 '**-itda**' denotes existence of something or expresses ownership.

나는 집에 <u>있다</u>.
Naneun jibe <u>itda</u>.
I am at home.

(동생), 예산을 얼마나 가지고 <u>있어</u>?
(Dongseng), yesaneul eolmana gajigo <u>isseo</u>?
(Sister), how much of a budget do you have?

Tense

There are three tenses in Korean: past, present, and future depending on the time of utterance. Tense is expressed by different verb endings.

Present tense is used to express present actions, state of an object, habitual behaviours, and universal truths. It is also used for planned events.

학생이 학교에 <u>간다</u>.
Haksaengi hakgyoe <u>ganda</u>.
The student goes to school.

지구는 <u>돈다</u>.
Jiguneun <u>donda</u>.
The earth evolves.

그녀는 내일 아침 **떠난다**.
Geunyeoneun naeil achim tteonanda
She is leaving tomorrow morning.

Verb forms do not change according to who is performing an action, but do change for levels of politeness or when expressing a negative. The inflected forms of final endings of the *present tense* appear in the table below.

Plain form	-(는)다 '-(neun)da' (Plain Present Form)	-습니다 '-seumnida' (Polite Present Form)	-어(아, 여)요 '-eo(a, yeo)yo' (Casual Present Form)	-지 않아요 '-ji anhayo' (Negation Present Form)
가다 gada (go)	간다 ganda	갑니다 gamnida	가요 gayo	가지 않아요 gaji anhayo
보다 boda (see)	본다 bonda	봅니다 bomnida	봐요 bwayo	보지 않아요 Boji anhayo
먹다 meokda (eat)	먹는다 meongneunda	먹습니다 meokseumnida	먹어요 meogeoyo	먹지 않아요 meokji anhayo
배우다 baeuda (learn)	배운다 baeunda	배웁니다 baeumnida	배워요 baewoyo	배우지 않아요 baeuji anhayo
쓰다 sseuda (write)	쓴다 sseunda	씁니다 sseumnida	써요 sseoyo	쓰지 않아요 sseuji anhayo
하다 hada (do)	한다 handa	합니다 hamnida	해요 haeyo	하지 않아요 haji anhayo
좋다 jota (like)	좋다 jota	좋습니다 joseumnida	좋아요 johayo	좋지 않아요 jochi anhayo
이다 ida (is)	이다 ida	입니다 imnida	이에요 ieyo	이지 않아요 iji anhayo

The *past tense* expresses an event or state that is in the past. It is also used to express the completion or continuation of actions.

어제 비가 왔어요.
Eoje biga wasseoyo.
It rained yesterday.

지금 막 일을 다 끝냈습니다.
Jigeum mak ireul da kkeutnaessseumnida.
I have just finished my work.

The *past tense* form is represented by attaching the past verb ending 었 'eot', 았 'at', 였 'yeot' to the plain forms of verbs. The inflected forms of the verb endings of the *past tense* appear in the following table.

Plain form	-었(았, 였)다 '-eot (at, yeot)da' (Plain Past Form)	-었(았,였)습니다. '-eot (at, yeot) seumnida' (Polite Past Form)	-었(았, 였) 어요 '-eot (at, yeot) eoyo' (Casual Past Form)	-지 않아요 '-ji anhas-seoyo' (Negation Past Form)
가다 gada (go)	갔다 gatda	갔습니다 gassseumnida	갔어요 gasseoyo	가지 않았 어요 gaji anhasseoyo
보다 boda (see)	보았다 boatda	보았습니다 boassseumnida	봤어요 boasseoyo	보지 않았 어요 boji anhasseoyo
먹다 meokda (eat)	먹었다 meogeotda	먹었습니다 meogeoss-seumnida	먹었어요 meogeosseoyo	먹지 않았 어요 meokji anhasseoyo

Plain form	-었(았, 였)다 '-eot (at, yeot)da' (Plain Past Form)	-었(았,였)습니다. '-eot (at, yeot) seumnida' (Polite Past Form)	-었(았, 였)어요 '-eot (at, yeot) eoyo' (Casual Past Form)	-지 않아요 '-ji anhas-seoyo' (Negation Past Form)
배우다 baeuda (learn)	배웠다 baewotda	배웠습니다 baewossseum-nida	배웠어요 baewosseoyo	배우지 않았어요 baeuji anhas-seoyo
쓰다 sseuda (write)	썼다 sseotda	썼습니다 sseossseum-nida	썼어요 sseosseoyo	쓰지 않았어요 sseuji anhas-seoyo
하다 hada (do)	했다 haetda	했습니다 haessseumnida	했어요 haeseoyo	하지 않았어요 haji anhasseoyo
좋다 jota (like)	좋았다 johatda	좋았습니다 johasssseum-nida	좋았어요 johasseoyo	좋지 않았어요 jochi anhas-seoyo
이다 ida (is)	있었다 ieotda	있었습니다 ieossseumnida	있었어요 ieosseoyo	이지 않았어요 iji anhasseoyo

The *future tense* is expressed with 겠 'get', (-을) 겠/게 '(-eul) geot/geo' 겠 'get' implies the speaker's strong will and intention. (-을) 겠/게 '(-eul) geot/geo' express the simple future.

Plain form	-겠다 '-getda' (Plain Future Form)	-겠습니다 '-gess-seumnida' (Polite Future Form)	-겠어요 '-gesseoyo' (Casual Future Form)	-지 않겠어요 '-ji ankes-seoyo' (Negation Future Form)	-을 게요 '-eul geoeyo' (Casual Future Form)
가다 gada (go)	가겠다 gagetda	가겠습니다 gageess-seumnida	가겠어요 gagesseoyo	가지 않겠어요 gaji ankesseoyo	갈게요 gal geoeyo
보다 boda (see)	보겠다 bogetda	보겠습니다 bogess-seumnida	보겠어요 bogesseoyo	보지 않겠어요 boji ankes-seoyo	볼게요 bol geoeyo
먹다 meokda (eat)	먹겠다 meokgetda	먹겠습니다 meokgess-seumnida	먹겠어요 meokges-seoyo	먹지 않겠어요 meokji ankesseoyo	먹을게요 meogeul geoeyo
배우다 baeuda (learn)	배우겠다 baeugetda	배우겠습니다 baeugess-seumnida	배우겠어요 baeuges-seoyo	배우지 않겠어요 baeuji ankesseoyo	배울게요 baeul geoeyo

Questions

In Korean question sentences, word order does not change. For example, 입니다 'imnida' is a polite form of the declarative ending. You can create a question by simply adding 입니까 'imnikka' instead of the declarative marker 입니다 'imnida' at the end of the sentence.

서울 입니다.
Seoul imnida.
This is Seoul.

서울 <u>입니까</u>?
Seoul <u>imnikka</u>?
Is this Seoul?

당신의 생일은 언제 <u>입니까</u>?
Dangsinui saengireun eonje<u>imnikka</u>?
When is your birthday?

There are several question words in Korean. Unlike English, these words do not have to come at the beginning of the sentence.

그것이 <u>무엇</u> 입니까?
Geugeosi <u>mueot</u> imnikka?
What is that?

KOREAN question words	ENGLISH question words
누가 **nuga**	who
언제 **eonje**	when
어디서 **eodiseo**	where
무엇을 **mueoseul**	what
어떻게 **eotteoke**	how
왜 **wae**	why

Negatives

Negative Sentences are rather complicated in Korean. The sentences have several forms according to the types of sentences and kinds of verbs. This is summarised in the following table.

Verb Types	Sentence Types	Negation Forms
Action Verbs	Declarative	-지 않, -지 못 '-ji ant-, -ji mota-'
	Question	
	Imperative	-지 말 '-ji mal-'
	Suggestion	
Stative Verbs	Declarative	-지 않 '-ji ant-'
	Question	
Copula	Declarative	-이/가 아니다 '-i/ga anida'
	Question	

Action Declarative: 수미는 학교에 가<u>지</u> <u>못</u>했습니다.
Sumineun haggyoe gaji <u>mota</u>ssseumnida.
Sumi did not go to school.

Stative Declarative: 그 꽃은 아름답<u>지</u> <u>않</u>습니다.
Geu kkocheun areumdapuji <u>ant</u>seumnidaa.
The flower is not beautiful.

Action Suggestion: 집에 가<u>지</u> <u>말</u>자.
Jibe gaji <u>mal</u>ja
Let's not go home.

Adverbials

Adverbials can modify verbs, numerals, pronouns, other verbs, and sentences. Adverbs can be classified as: time adverbs, frequency adverbs, general adverbs, and degree adverbs.

Time adverbs convey information about time.

저는 <u>어제</u> 친구를 만났어요.
Jeoneun <u>eoje</u> chingureul mannasseoyo.
I met a friend yesterday.

이제 날씨가 추워집니다.
Ije nalssiga chuwojimnida.
The weather is getting cold now.

Frequency adverbs express frequency of actions or states.

어머니는 가끔 아버지와 영화보러 가십니다.
Eomeonineun gakkeum abeojiwa yeonghwaboreo gasimnida.
(My) mother sometimes goes to the movies with (my) father.

저는 그 사람을 자주 만납니다.
Jeoneun geusarameul jaju mannamnida.
I meet him often.

General adverbs refer to the most common adverbs with their own specific meanings.

우리는 모두 한국사람 입니다.
Urineun modu hanguksaram imnida.
We are all Koreans.

그들은 서로 좋아합니다.
Geudeureun seoro johahamnida.
They like each other.

Degree adverbs convey information about the degree or intensity of an action.

그 사람은 피아노를 아주 잘 칩니다.
Geu sarameun pianoreul aju jal chimnida.
He plays piano very well.

한강의 경치는 매우 아름답습니다.
Hangangui gyeongchineun maeu areumdapseumnida.
The scenery of Hangang is very beautiful.

Honorifics

In Korean grammar, extensive system of **honorific** forms are used to reflect the relationship between the subject and the speaker in the sentence. For the **subject honorification**, the most common way of marking honorification is to attach the honorific suffix -(으)시 '-(eu) si' to the verb. In order to use honorific expressions properly, it is important to understand the relationship between the subject, speaker, and listener. Age, degree of intimacy, social position, and personal relationship between speaker and target honorification should be considered.

Plain forms of Verbs	Honorific Forms
가다 gada (go)	가시다 gasida
읽다 irkda (read)	읽으시다 ilgeusida
좋다 jota (like)	좋으시다 joheusida
사다 sada (buy)	사시다 sasida

For example, even if the social position of the subject is higher than the speaker, when the social position of the listener is higher than the subject of the sentence, you do not need to use the honorific suffix.

> 할아버지, 아버지가 지금 왔습니다.
> **Harabeoji, abeojiga jigeum wassseumnida.**
> *Grandfather, father has just come back.*

The Korean language has a number of specific word forms called **honorific forms** which are used to show respect to the listener and/ or to the person they are speaking about by using appropriate noun, pronoun, verb or particle forms.

Category	Plain Form	Honorific Form
Noun	말 mal (word)	말씀 malsseum
	나이 nai (age)	연세 yeonse
	밥 bap (meal)	진지 jinji
	병 byeong (illness)	병환 byeonghwan
	집 jip (house)	댁 daek
Pronoun	그 사람 geu saram (he/she)	그 분 geu bun
	나 na (I)	
	우리 uri (we)	
Verb	주다 juda (give)	드리다 deurida
	묻다 mutda (ask)	여쭈다 yeojjuda
	만나다 mannada (meet)	뵙다 boepda
	자다 jada (sleep)	주무시다 jumusida
	먹다 meokda (eat)	잡수시다 japsusida
	있다 itda (is, exist)	계시다 gyesida
	배고프다 baegopeuda (hungry)	시장하다 sijanghada
Particle	이/가 i/ga (subject marker)	-께서 -kkeseo
	-에게 -ege (indirect object marker)	-께 -kke

선생님께서 그렇게 <u>말씀</u> 하셨어요.
Seonsaengnimi geureoke <u>malsseum</u> hasyeosseoyo.
The teacher said so.

할아버지, 아침 <u>진지</u> <u>드세요</u>.
Harabeoji, achim <u>jinji</u> <u>deuseyo</u>.
Grandfather, please eat your breakfast.

어머니<u>께</u> 드리려고 꽃을 샀어요.
Eomeoni<u>kke</u> deuriryeogo kkocheul sasseoyo.
I bought some flowers for my mother.

영어 문법

영어 문법

동사

동사는 사물의 동작이나 움직임, 상태, 성질,마음의 상태를
표현한다.

> John **was reading** Katherine's essay.
> 존은 캐서린의 에세이를 읽고 있었다.

> I **forgot** that it was your birthday.
> 네 생일인 것을 깜빡 잊어버렸어.

> Eleni **feels** much happier now.
> 엘레니는 이제 한결 더 행복함을 느낀다.

동사구는 문장에서 동사처럼 서술어 구실을 한다. 이는
동사만으로 구성되기도 하며, 관련된 여러 단어와 함께 쓰이기도
한다.

> he **walks**.
> 그는 걷는다.

> he **can walk**.
> 그는 걸을 수 있다.

타동사는 뒤에 목적어를 필요로 하지만, **자동사**는 뒤에 목적어를
필요로 하지 않는다.

> She **likes** cheese.
> 그녀는 치즈를 좋아한다.

> I **sneezed** loudly.
> 나는 큰소리로 재채기를 했다.

사전에서 동사를 찾을 경우에는, **동사원형**이 기본 형태이다. 아래 예문의 동사를 사전에서 찾는다면, 'encountered'가 아닌 **동사원형** 형태의 'encounter'를 찾아야 한다.

> She had **encountered** many problems.
> 그녀는 여러가지 어려움에 맞닥뜨렸었다.

조동사

조동사는 동사를 돕는 보조동사로, 주동사의 의미에 뜻을 더해준다. 시제나 태를 표현할때, 의문문이나 부정문을 만들때 사용한다.

Be동사나 **have**동사는 **1차 조동사**로 복합시제 표현에 사용된다.

Be동사는 현재 진행형, 과거진행형, 그리고 수동태 문장에 쓰인다

> I am **working**.
> 나는 일하고 있다

> We **were** all **wondering** about that.
> 우리 모두는 그것에 대해서 의아해 하고 있었다.

> Martin **was arrested** and held overnight
> 마틴은 체포되어 밤새 구금 되었다.

Have는 현재 완료형이나 과거 완료형에 사용된다.

> Sasha **has finished** fixing the car.
> 사샤는 차 수리를 막 끝냈다

> Amanda **had** already **eaten** when we arrived.
> 우리가 도착했을 때, 이미 아만다는 식사를 다 마쳤었다.

Do는 **보조 조동사**이다. 이는 부정문, 의문문 그리고 강조 구문에 사용된다.

> I **do** not **like** sausages at all.
> 나는 소시지를 전혀 좋아하지 않는다.
> **Do** you **like** prawns?
> 너는 새우를 좋아하니?
> You **do like** prawns, don't you?
> 너는 새우 좋아하지, 그렇지 않니?

법조동사

법조동사는 일반 동사 앞에 쓰이며 능력, 가능, 그리고 필요등과 같은 의미를 표현한다.

영어의 주요 법조동사는 다음과 같다. **can, could, may, might, must, ought, shall, will, would**.

법조동사는 다른 동사와 달리 형태변화가 없다.

> I **can** ride a horse.
> 나는 승마를 할 수 있다.

구어나, 비격식적인문어에서는 **'ll**(예, I'll)형으로 축약되기도 한다. **would**의경우는 **'d**(예, they'd)형으로 축약된다.

구동사

구동사는 본동사가 다른 품사와 결합하여 형성된다. 예를 들어, 본동사는 **부사, 전치사, 부사+전치사**와 결합하여 구동사가 된다.

> Verb+adverb: take off, give in, blow up
> 동사+부사:이륙하다, 항복하다, 폭파하다.

Verb+proposition: get at (someone), pick on (weaker children).
동사+전치사:(누군가를) 나무라다, (약한 아이를) 괴롭히다

Verb+adverb+proposition: put up with (insults)
동사+부사+전치사: (모욕을) 참고 견디다.

대개 구동사의 의미는 그를 구성하고 있는 동사, 부사 및 전치사의 각 문자 그대로의 의미와는 무관하다.

명사

명사는 사물의 이름을 나타내는 품사이다.

고유 명사는 사람이나 사물, 장소등의 고유한 이름을 나타내는 명사이다. 영어의 고유명사는 대문자로 시작한다.

John Lennon, China, Mount Everest
존 레논(사람 이름), 중국(나라 이름), 에베레스트 산(장소)

보통 명사는 고유명사 이외에 사물을 나타내는 모든 명사를 지칭한다. 보통명사는 추상명사와 구상명사로 나뉜다.

추상명사는 눈으로 보거나 만질 수 없는 것을 표현하는 명사이다.

honesty, anger, idea, time
정직함, 분노, 발상, 시간

구상 명사는 눈으로 보거나 만질 수 있는 구체적인 사물을 표현하는 명사이다. 구상명사는 생물과 무생물 모두를 지칭할 수 있다.

dog, teacher, stone, sugar
개, 선생님, 돌, 설탕

그 외의 명사로는, 사람이나 동물의 무리를 지칭하는 **집합 명사**가 있다.

a **herd** of cows
소떼

복합 명사는 두개 이상의 단어가 합쳐져 만들어진 명사이다. 이때, 한 단어로 합쳐지기도 하며, 두개의 단어가 따로 쓰이기도 하고, 두 단어가 하이픈으로 연결되기도 한다.

teapot, washing machine, break-in
찻주전자(한단어로 합쳐진 경우), 세탁기(두 단어가 따로 쓰인 경우), 침입(하이픈으로 연결된 경우)

가산 명사와 불가산 명사

가산 명사는 셀 수 있는 명사를 말한다. 영어의 가산 명사는 단수형과 복수형이 있으며, 복수형에는 –s를 붙인다. 단수형의 가산명사는 반드시 관사와 함께 쓰인다.

Dogs ran wild in the streets.
개들이 길에서 제멋대로 날뛰었다.
The dog is loose again.
저 개가 또 풀렸다.

불가산 명사는 셀 수 없는 명사를 말한다. 불가산 명사는 보통 복수형이 없으며 단수 취급을 받는다.

Sadia asked me for some **advice**.
사디아가 나에게 조언을 구했다.

물질 명사는 일정한 형태가 없고 셀 수 없는 물질을 나타내는 명사이다. 물질명사는 부정관사 'a(n)'과 함께 사용되지 않는다.

> I don't like **meat**.
> 저는 고기를 좋아하지 않아요.

대명사

대명사는 명사나 명사구를 대신하는 단어로, 한 문장이나 문단 내에서 같은 단어의 반복을 피하기 위해 사용한다. 이는 의미와 용법에 따라 일곱가지로 나뉜다.

　　사람을 지시하는 대명사를 **인칭 대명사**라고 한다. 인칭 대명사는 **주격**(I, you, he, she, it, we, they)과 **목적격**(me, you, him, her, us, them)이 있다.

> **We** saw **them** on Saturday.
> 우리는 토요일에 그들을 보았다.

재귀 대명사는 인칭대명사에 'self'를 붙인 형태로, '자기 자신'으로 해석된다. 문장에서 주어의 성분을 되가리키거나 강조할 때 쓰인다.

> Never mind. I'll do it **myself**.
> 신경쓰지마. 내가 스스로 알아서 할게.

소유 대명사는 소유를 나타낸다.

> Give it back, it's **mine**.
> 돌려줘, 그것 내 것이야.

지시 대명사는 화자로 부터의 물리적 거리를 나타낸다. 가까운 곳에 있는 사물을 가리킬 때는 *this*, 멀리 떨어진 곳에 있는 사물을 가리킬 때는 *that*을 쓴다.

This is mine and **that** is yours.
이것은 내 것이고, 저것이 네 것이야.

관계 대명사는 선행하는 어구를 받아 종속절과 연결시킨다.

Is there a doctor **who** speaks English?
영어 하는 의사가 있나요?

의문 대명사는 물음의 대상을 나타내는 대명사이다.

Where can I contact you?
어디로 연락 드리면 될까요?

부정 대명사는 특정하지 않은 사람이나 사물을 나타내는
대명사이다.

Much needs to be done.
많은 것들이 완료 되어야 한다.

형용사

형용사는 명사를 수식하며, 지시 대상에 대해 구체적으로
서술한다.

my new, wide-screen, 3D TV
내 새로 산 3D 평면TV.

형용사의 **비교급**은 두 개의 사물, 사람 혹은 상태를 비교하는데
사용된다.

She is **taller** than me.
그녀는 나보다 키가 더 크다.

형용사의 **최상급**는 두 개 이상의 사물, 사람 혹은 상태 중 하나가
다른 모든 것들보다 두드러지는 경우 쓰인다.

> That is the **smallest** camera I have ever seen.
> 그것은 내가 본 것 중에 최고로 작은 카메라이다.

형용사의 비교급과 최상급의 유형에는 두 가지가 있다.
첫번째로는, 비교급은 형용사에 **-er**을 붙이며, 최상급은 **-est**
를 붙인다. 보통 1음절의 단어의 경우에 이 방식이 적용된다.

	비교급	최상급
bright	brighter	the brightest
long	longer	the longest
sharp	sharper	the sharpest

형용사가 **-e**로 끝날 경우, **-e**는 삭제된다(wise-wiser-wisest). **-y**로
끝날 경우는 **-y**가 **-i**로 바뀌고 **-er**(비교급)나 **-est**(최상급)을
붙인다(pretty-prettier-prettiest).
두번째로는, 형용사가 3음절 이상의 단어일 경우 형용사에
앞에 **more**나 **most**를 붙여 비교급과 최상급을 만든다.

	비교급	최상급
fortunate	**more** fortunate	the **most** fortunate
relevant	**more** relevant	the **most** relevant

2음절의 형용사일 경우는 때에 따라 두 가지 방법을 모두
사용하기도 한다. 하지만 확실하지 않을 경우에는 **more/most** 를
붙이도록 한다.
비교급과 최상급 형용사에 불규칙 변화가 있다.

	비교급	최상급
good	better	the best
bad	worse	the worst
far	further	the furthest

부사

부사는 문장속에서 동사, 형용사, 혹은 다른 부사들을 수식한다. 문장에서 꼭 필요한 존재는 아니지만, 동사나 형용사 및 다른 부사에 시간, 빈도, 방법등의 구체적인 정보를 주는 기능을 한다.

　　부사의 형태는 기본적으로 관련된 형용사에 **-ly**를 붙여 완성한다(slow-slowly). **-ble**로 끝나는 형용사는, **-e**를 삭제하고 **-ly**를 붙인다(sensible-sensibly, true-truly). **-y**로 끝나는 형용사는 **-y**를 **-i**로 바꾸고 **-ly**를 붙인다(happy-happily).

　　문장 부사는 -ly로 끝나는 부사가 문장이나 구의 맨 앞에 놓이며 화자의 주관적인 판단을 나타낸다.

> **Actually** I don't mind.
> 사실, 난 괜찮아.

정도 부사란 rather(다소), quite(꽤), 및 almost(거의) 같은 단어들로, 형용사나 다른 부사들 앞에 쓰여 정도를 나타낸다.

> She began to cry, **quite** loudly.
> 그녀는 울기 시작했다, 꽤 크게 말이다.

장소 부사는 전치사와 같은 형태이지만, 이 경우 부사는 목적어를 취하지 않으며 보통은 문장의 마지막에 쓰인다.

> He hurried **over**.
> 그는 급히 일을 끝마쳤다.

한정사

한정사는 명사의 범위를 축소시키는 역할을 하며, 발화되고 있는 대상에 대해 좀 더 구체적인 정보를 준다.
한정사는 다음과 같은 종류를 포함한다.

- **부정관사(a)**와 **정관사(the)**
- **지시대명사(a)**: this(이것), that(저것), these(이것들), those (저것들)
- **소유격**: my(나의), your(너의), his(그의), their(그들의), our(우리의)
- **수량사**: some(약간), any(어떤), few(많지 않은, 약간의), enough(충분한)
- **기수**(하나, 둘, 셋, 등)와 **서수**(첫번째, 두번째, 세번째, 등)
- **배분사**: each(각각), every(모든), either(둘 중 하나), neither(어느것도 아닌)
- **감탄사**: what(정말, 얼마나), such(정말, 얼마나)

전치사

전치사는 명사나 대명사 혹은 그에 준하는 말 앞에 놓여 다른 명사와 대명사 와의 관계를 나타낸다. 단순 전치사는 in(-안에), on(-위에), under(-아래)와 같이 한 단어로 구성되어 있으며, 복합 전치사는 due to(-때문에), in spite of(-에도 불구하고) 처럼 두개 이상의 전치사로 구성되어 있다.

영어의 전치사는 아래 목록에 나와있다. 일부 단어는 함께 쓰인은 단어에 따라 전치사로도 사용되기도 하며, 부사로도 사용되기도 한다. 보통 전치사는 목적어를 필요로 한다.

aboard(-에 탄), about(-에 관한), above(-위에),
across(-건너), against(-에 반대하여), along(-을 따라),
among(-중에), around(-주변에), as(-처럼), at(-에서,-에),
before(-전에), behind(-뒤에), below(-아래), beside(-옆에),
between(-사이에), by(-옆에, -가에), during(-동안),

for(-위해), from(-로 부터), in(-안에), into(-안 쪽으로),
of(-의), opposite(-반대의), outside(-밖의), over(-너머),
regarding(-와 관련하여), since(-이후로),
through(-을 통해), till(-까지), to(-로,-쪽으로),
towards(-쪽으로, -을 향하여), under(-아래로),
until(-까지), up(위로), via(-을 통하여), with(-와 함께),
within(-안에), without(-없이)

접속사

접속사는 이어주는 말로, 단어와 단어를 이어주거나 구와 구를
이어주는 역할을 한다. 대표적인 접속사는 다음과 같다.

and는 '그리고'로 해석되며, 동등한 입장의 요소들을 서술할
때 사용된다.

> I went to the shop **and** bought some bread.
> 나는 장보러가서 빵을 좀 샀다.

but은 '그러나'로 해석되며, 앞 뒤의 요소들이 상반되는
내용일 때 사용된다.

> I bought some bread, **but** I forgot to get the milk.
> 나는 빵은 좀 샀지만, 우유를 깜빡했다.

or은 '또는', '그렇지 않으면'으로 해석되며, 선택해야 할 어,
구,절을 결합한다.

> Hurry up, **or** you will miss the bus.
> 서두르지 않으면 버스를 놓치게 될거야.

so는 이유를 나타내는 접속사로, '그래서', '그러므로'
등으로 해석된다.

I am so busy, **so** I can't go to the party.
나는 너무 바빠서, 파티에 가지 못할 것 같아.

시제

시제는 동사가 나타내는 동작이나 상태의 시간(현재, 과거, 미래등)을 나타내는 범주이다.
　　단순 시제에는, 현재, 과거, 미래형이 있다.

I **go** to a university in London.
나는 런던에 있는 대학에 다닌다.

He **cooked** a meal.
그가 식사 준비를 했다.

We **will phone** you later.
우리가 나중에 전화할게.

완료 시제에는, 현재완료, 과거완료, 미래완료형이 있다.

I **have ordered** a new sofa.
나는 새로운 소파 주문을 끝냈다.

He **had visited** London before.
그는 전에 런던에 가봤었던 적이 있다.

We **will have done** the work by then.
그때 까지는 우리가 그 일을 다 마쳤을 것이다.

진행 시세에는, 현재 진행, 과거 진행, 미래 진행형이 있다.

I **am waiting** for Gerry.
나는 제리를 기다리고 있는 중이다.

We **were trying** to see the queen.
우리는 여왕을 만나려고 노력하고 있었다.

Dad **will be worrying** about us.
아빠가 우리를 걱정하고있게 될거야.

완료 진행 시제에는, 현재 완료 진행, 과거 완료 진행, 미래 완료
진행형이 있다.

We **have been trying** to call you all morning.
오전 내내 너에게 전화 연결을 시도하고 있었어.

Anna **had been sitting** there all day.
안나는 하루 종일 거기 앉아 있어왔었다.

On Sunday, we **will have been living** together for 10 years.
일요일이되면, 우리가 함께 살아온지 10년이 될 것이다.

동사의 과거형은 보통 '-ed'를 붙이면 되지만, 일부의
동사들은 불규칙으로 변화한다.

현재형	과거형	과거 분사형
become(-가 되다)	became	become
go(가다)	went	been
swim(수영하다)	swam	swum

주어, 목적어와 간접 목적어

문장의 **주어**는 행위의 주체가 되는 명사나 그 상당어구이다.
모든 문장은 주어를 필요로 한다.

Her car broke down.
그녀의 차는 고장이 났다.

문장의 **목적어**는 동사가 나타내는 행위의 대상이 되는 존재를
나타내는 명사 및 상당어구로, 주로 동사 다음에 나타난다.

> I spilled **the milk**.
> 내가 우유를 쏟았다.

간접 목적어는 동사의 행위를 받는 사람을 지칭한다('- 에게')

> Mike gave **me** a box of chocolates.
> 마이크는 나에게 초콜릿 한 상자를 건넸다.

일 치

일치는 문장내 관계된 단어들이 서로 형태상 일정한 일치를
요구하는 일을 말한다.

주어 동사 일치
단수형 주어는 단수형 동사를 취하며, 복수형 주어는 복수형
동사를 취한다. 만약 단수형 동사가 'and'로 연결될 경우에는,
복수취급을 받는다. 하지만 두 단어가 연결되었을 경우라도, 그
개념이 단수일 경우에는 단수취급을 받는다.

> The house **is** very large.
> 그 집은 매우 크다.

> Fish and chips **is** my favourite food.
> 피쉬 앤 칩스는 내가 가장 좋아하는 음식이다.

'each(각)', 'every(모든)', 혹은 'no(어떤-도 없는)'와 함께 쓰인
주어는 단수 취급을 받는다. 책이름, 영화 및 음악의 제목 등은
복수형 일지라도 단수 취급을 받는다.

> Every seat **was** taken already.
> 자리가 이미 모두 찼다.

'Daffodils' **was** the first poem I learned at school.
'수선화' 는 내가 학교에서 배운 첫번째 시였다.

시제의 일치
한 문장 및 문단안의 시제는 일치하여야 한다.

While I was waiting, I **see** a film. (incorrect)
나는 기다리는동안, 영화를 본다.

While I was waiting, I **saw** a film. (correct)
나는 기다리는동안, 영화를 봤다.

ENGLISH – KOREAN
영 – 한

a

a [eɪ] *art* 어떤 하나의 [eotteon hanaui]
abandon [ə'bændən] *v* 포기하다 [pogihada]
abbey ['æbɪ] *n* 대수도원 [daesudowon]
abbreviation [ə,briːvɪ'eɪʃən] *n* 약어 [yageo]
abdomen ['æbdəmən; æb'dəʊ-] *n* 배 [bae]
abduct [æb'dʌkt] *v* 유괴하다 [yugoehada]
ability [ə'bɪlɪtɪ] *n* 능력 [neungnyeok]
able ['eɪbᵊl] *adj* 할 수 있는 [hal su inneun]
abnormal [æb'nɔːməl] *adj* 비정상적인 [bijeongsangjeogin]
abolish [ə'bɒlɪʃ] *v* 폐지하다 [pyejihada]
abolition [,æbə'lɪʃən] *n* 폐지 [pyeji]
abortion [ə'bɔːʃən] *n* 유산 [yusan]
about [ə'baʊt] *adv* 대략 [daeryak] ▷ *prep* ...에 대해 [...e daehae]
above [ə'bʌv] *prep* ...보다 위에 [...boda wie]
abroad [ə'brɔːd] *adv* 해외에 [haeoee]
abrupt [ə'brʌpt] *adj* 갑작스러운 [gapjakseureoun]
abruptly [ə'brʌptlɪ] *adv* 갑자기 [gapjagi]

abscess ['æbsɛs; -sɪs] *n* 종기 [jonggi]; **I have an abscess** 종기가 났어요 [jonggiga nasseoyo]
absence ['æbsəns] *n* 부재 [bujae]
absent ['æbsənt] *adj* 부재의 [bujaeui]
absent-minded [,æbsən't'maɪndɪd] *adj* 멍한 [meonghan]
absolutely [,æbsə'luːtlɪ] *adv* 절대적으로 [jeoldaejeoguro]
abstract ['æbstrækt] *adj* 추상적인 [chusangjeogin]
absurd [əb'sɜːd] *adj* 불합리한 [bulhamnihan]
Abu Dhabi ['æbuː 'dɑːbɪ] *n* 아부다비 [abudabi]
abuse *n* [ə'bjuːs] 남용 [namyong] ▷ *v* [ə'bjuːz] 남용하다 [namyonghada]; **child abuse** *n* 아동학대 [adonghakdae]
abusive [ə'bjuːsɪv] *adj* 욕설을 퍼붓는 [yokseoreul peobutneun]
academic [,ækə'dɛmɪk] *adj* 학원의 [hagwonui]; **academic year** *n* 학년도 [hangnyeondo]
academy [ə'kædəmɪ] *n* 학원 [hagwon]
accelerate [æk'sɛləˌreɪt] *v* 가속하다 [gasokhada]
acceleration [æk,sɛlə'reɪʃən] *n* 가속 [gasok]
accelerator [æk'sɛləˌreɪtə] *n* 가속기 [gasokgi]
accept [ək'sɛpt] *v* 받아들이다 [badadeurida]
acceptable [ək'sɛptəbᵊl] *adj* 받아들일 수 있는 [badadeuril su inneun]
access ['æksɛs] *n* 접근 [jeopgeun] ▷ *v* 접속하다 [jeopsokhada]
accessible [ək'sɛsəbᵊl] *adj* 접근하기 쉬운 [jeopgeunhagi swiun]
accessory [ək'sɛsərɪ] *n* 부속물 [busongmul]
accident ['æksɪdənt] *n* 사고 [sago]; **accident & emergency department** *n* 응급실 [eunggeupsil]; **accident insurance** *n* 상해보험 [sanghaeboheom]; **by accident** *adv* 우연히 [uyeonhi]; **I've had an accident** 사고를 당했어요 [sagoreul

danghaesseoyo]; **There's been an accident!** 사고가 있었어요! [sagoga isseosseoyo!]; **What do I do if I have an accident?** 사고가 나면 어떻게 해야 할까요? [sagoga namyeon eotteoke haeya halkkayo?]

accidental [ˌæksɪˈdɛntəl] *adj* 우연의 [uyeonui]

accidentally [ˌæksɪˈdɛntəlɪ] *adv* 우연히 [uyeonhi]

accommodate [əˈkɒməˌdeɪt] *v* 숙박처를 제공하다 [sukbakcheoreul jegonghada]

accommodation [əˌkɒməˈdeɪʃən] *n* 숙박 시설 [sukbak siseol]

accompany [əˈkʌmpənɪ; əˈkʌmpnɪ] *v* 동행하다 [donghaenghada]

accomplice [əˈkɒmplɪs; əˈkʌm-] *n* 공범 [gongbeom]

according [əˈkɔːdɪŋ] *prep* **according to** *prep*...에 따라 [...e ttara]

accordingly [əˈkɔːdɪŋlɪ] *adv* 따라서 [ttaraseo]

accordion [əˈkɔːdɪən] *n* 아코디언 [akodieon]

account [əˈkaʊnt] *n* (*in bank*) 은행계좌 [eunhaenggyejwa], (*report*) 보고 [bogo]; **account number** *n* 계좌번호 [gyejwabeonho]; **bank account** *n* 은행계좌 [eunhaenggyejwa]; **current account** *n* 당좌계좌 [dangjwagyejwa]; **joint account** *n* 공동 계좌 [gongdong gyejwa]

accountable [əˈkaʊntəbəl] *adj* 책임이 있는 [chaegimi inneun]

accountancy [əˈkaʊntənsɪ] *n* 회계 [hoegye]

accountant [əˈkaʊntənt] *n* 회계사 [hoegyesa]

account for [əˈkaʊnt fɔː] *v* 설명하다 [seolmyeonghada]

accuracy [ˈækjʊrəsɪ] *n* 정확성 [jeonghwakseong]

accurate [ˈækjərɪt] *adj* 정확한 [jeonghwakhan]

accurately [ˈækjərɪtlɪ] *adv* 정확하게 [jeonghwakhage]

accusation [ˌækjʊˈzeɪʃən] *n* 고소

[goso]

accuse [əˈkjuːz] *v* 고소하다 [gosohada] (법적 조치를 하다)

accused [əˈkjuːzd] *n* 피고인 [pigoin]

ace [eɪs] *n* 최고 [choego]

ache [eɪk] *n* 아픔 [apeum] ▷ *v* 아프다 [apeuda]

achieve [əˈtʃiːv] *v* 달성하다 [dalseonghada]

achievement [əˈtʃiːvmənt] *n* 성공 [seonggong]

acid [ˈæsɪd] *n* 산 [san]; **acid rain** *n* 산성비 [sanseongbi]

acknowledgement [əkˈnɒlɪdʒmənt] *n* 인정 [injeong]

acne [ˈæknɪ] *n* 여드름 [yeodeureum]

acorn [ˈeɪkɔːn] *n* 도토리 [dotori]

acoustic [əˈkuːstɪk] *adj* 소리의 [soriui]

acre [ˈeɪkə] *n* 에이커 [eikeo]

acrobat [ˈækrəˌbæt] *n* 곡예사 [gogyesa]

acronym [ˈækrənɪm] *n* 두문자어 [dumunjaeo]

across [əˈkrɒs] *prep* 가로질러서 [garojilleoseo]

act [ækt] *n* 행위 [haengwi] ▷ *v* 행동하다 [haengdonghada]

acting [ˈæktɪŋ] *adj* 대행의 [daehaengui] ▷ *n* 연기 [yeongi]

action [ˈækʃən] *n* 활동 [hwaldong]

active [ˈæktɪv] *adj* 활동적인 [hwaldongjeogin]

activity [ækˈtɪvɪtɪ] *n* 활동 [hwaldong]; **activity holiday** *n* 활동 휴가 [hwaldong hyuga]; **Do you have activities for children?** 어린이를 위한 활동이 있나요? [eorinireul wihan hwaldongi innayo?]

actor [ˈæktə] *n* 남자 배우 [namja baeu]

actress [ˈæktrɪs] *n* 여자 배우 [yeoja baeu]

actual [ˈæktʃʊəl] *adj* 실제의 [siljeui]

actually [ˈæktʃʊəlɪ] *adv* 실제로 [siljero]

acupuncture [ˈækjʊˌpʌŋktʃə] *n* 침술 [chimsul]

ad [æd] *abbr* 광고 [gwanggo]; **small ads** *npl* 항목별 광고 [hangmokbyeol gwanggo]

AD [eɪ di:] *abbr* 서기 [seogi] (년)
adapt [ə'dæpt] *v* 적응시키다 [jeoeungsikida]
adaptor [ə'dæptə] *n* 어댑터 [eodaepteo]
add [æd] *v* 추가하다 [chugahada]
addict ['ædɪkt] *n* 중독자 [jungdokja]; **drug addict** *n* 마약 중독자 [mayak jungdokja]
addicted [ə'dɪktɪd] *adj* 중독된 [jungdokdoen]
additional [ə'dɪʃənəl] *adj* 추가된 [chugadoen]
additive ['ædɪtɪv] *n* 첨가물 [cheomgamul]
address [ə'drɛs] *n (location)* 주소 [juso], *(speech)* 연설 [yeonseol]; **address book** *n* 주소록 [jusorok]; **home address** *n* 집주소 [jipjuso]; **web address** *n* 웹 주소 [wep juso]; **My email address is...** 제 이메일 주소는... 이에요 [je imeil jusoneun...ieyo]; **Please send my mail on to this address** 이 주소로 제 편지를 부쳐 주세요 [i jusoro je pyeonjireul buchyeo juseyo]; **The website address is...** 웹사이트 주소는...이에요 [wepsaiteu jusoneun...ieyo]; **What is your email address?** 이메일 주소가 어떻게 되세요? [imeil jusoga eotteoke doeseyo?]; **Will you write down the address, please?** 주소를 적어 주시겠어요? [jusoreul jeogeo jusigesseoyo?]
add up [æd ʌp] *v* 합계하다 [hapgyehada]
adjacent [ə'dʒeɪsənt] *adj* 인접한 [injeophan]
adjective ['ædʒɪktɪv] *n* 형용사 [hyeongyongsa]
adjust [ə'dʒʌst] *v* 조정하다 [jojeonghada]
adjustable [ə'dʒʌstəbəl] *adj* 조정할 수 있는 [jojeonghal su inneun]
adjustment [ə'dʒʌstmənt] *n* 조정 [jojeong]
administration [əd,mɪnɪ'streɪʃən] *n* 행정 [haengjeong]

administrative [əd'mɪnɪ,streɪtɪv] *adj* 행정상의 [haengjeongsangui]
admiration [,ædmə'reɪʃən] *n* 칭찬 [chingchan]
admire [əd'maɪə] *v* 칭찬하다 [chingchanhada]
admission [əd'mɪʃən] *n* 입장 [ipjang] (입장하다); **admission charge** *n* 입장료 [ipjangnyo]
admit [əd'mɪt] *v (allow in)* 입장을 허락하다 [ipjangeul heorakhada], *(confess)* 시인하다 [siinhada]
admittance [əd'mɪtəns] *n* 입장 [ipjang] (입장하다)
adolescence [,ædə'lɛsəns] *n* 사춘기 [sachungi]
adolescent [,ædə'lɛsənt] *n* 청소년 [cheongsonyeon]
adopt [ə'dɒpt] *v* 입양하다 [ibyanghada]
adopted [ə'dɒptɪd] *adj* 입양된 [ibyangdoen]
adoption [ə'dɒpʃən] *n* 입양 [ibyang]
adore [ə'dɔː] *v* 흠모하다 [heummohada]
Adriatic [,eɪdrɪ'ætɪk] *adj* 아드리아 해의 [adeuria haeui]
Adriatic Sea [,eɪdrɪ'ætɪk siː] *n* 아드리아 해 [adeuria hae]
adult ['ædʌlt; ə'dʌlt] *n* 성인 [seongin]; **adult education** *n* 성인 교육 [seongin gyoyuk]
advance [əd'vɑːns] *n* 전진 [jeonjin] ▷ *v* 전진시키다 [jeonjinsikida]; **advance booking** *n* 예약 [yeyak]
advanced [əd'vɑːnst] *adj* 앞선 [apseon]
advantage [əd'vɑːntɪdʒ] *n* 이점 [ijeom]
advent ['ædvɛnt; -vənt] *n* 출현 [chulhyeon]
adventure [əd'vɛntʃə] *n* 모험 [moheom]
adventurous [əd'vɛntʃərəs] *adj* 모험을 좋아하는 [moheomeul johahaneun]
adverb ['ædvɜːb] *n* 부사 [busa]
adversary ['ædvəsərɪ] *n* 적수 [jeoksu]
advert ['ædvɜːt] *n* 광고 [gwanggo]
advertise ['ædvə,taɪz] *v* 광고하다 [gwanggohada]

advertisement[əd'vɜːtɪsmənt;-tɪz-]*n* 광고 [gwanggo]

advertising ['ædvə,taɪzɪŋ] *n* 광고 [gwanggo]

advice [əd'vaɪs] *n* 조언 [joeon]

advisable [əd'vaɪzəbəl] *adj* 타당한 [tadanghan]

advise [əd'vaɪz] *v* 조언하다 [joeonhada]

aerial ['ɛərɪəl] *n* 안테나 [antena]

aerobics [ɛə'rəʊbɪks] *npl* 에어로빅 [eeorobik]

aerosol ['ɛərə,sɒl] *n* 에어로졸 [eeorojol]

affair [ə'fɛə] *n* 사건 [sageon]

affect [ə'fɛkt] *v* 영향을 미치다 [yeonghyangeul michida]

affectionate [ə'fɛkʃənɪt] *adj* 애정 어린 [aejeong eorin]

afford [ə'fɔːd] *v* 여유가 있다 [yeoyuga itda]

affordable [ə'fɔːdəbəl] *adj* 감당할 수 있는 [gamdanghal su inneun]

Afghan ['æfgæn; -gən] *adj* 아프가니스탄의 [apeuganiseutanui] ▷ *n* 아프가니스탄 사람 [apeuganiseutan saram]

Afghanistan [æf'gænɪ,stɑːn; -,stæn] *n* 아프가니스탄 [apeuganiseutan]

afraid [ə'freɪd] *adj* 두려워하여 [duryeowohayeo]

Africa ['æfrɪkə] *n* 아프리카 [apeurika]; **North Africa** *n* 북아프리카 [bugapeurika]; **South Africa** *n* 남아프리카 [namapeurika]

African ['æfrɪkən] *adj* 아프리카의 [apeurikaui] ▷ *n* 아프리카 사람 [apeurika saram]; **Central African Republic** *n* 중앙 아프리카 공화국 [jungang apeurika gonghwaguk]; **North African** *n* 북아프리카 사람 [bugapeurika saram], 북아프리카의 [bugapeurikaui]; **South African** *n* 남아프리카 사람 [namapeurika saram], 남아프리카의 [namapeurikaui]

Afrikaans [,æfrɪ'kɑːns; -'kɑːnz] *n* 아프리칸스어 [apeurikanseueo]

Afrikaner [afri'kɑːnə; ,æfrɪ'kɑːnə] *n* 아프리카너 [apeurikaneo]

after ['ɑːftə] *conj* 후에 [hue] ▷ *prep...* 후에 [...hue]; **after eight o'clock** 여덟시 후에 [yeodeopsi hue]

afternoon [,ɑːftə'nuːn] *n* 오후 [ohu]; **in the afternoon** 오후에 [ohue]; **tomorrow afternoon** 내일 오후 [naeil ohu]

afters ['ɑːftəz] *npl* 후식 [husik]

aftershave ['ɑːftə,ʃeɪv] *n* 면도한 후 바르는 로션 [myeondohan hu bareuneun rosyeon]

afterwards ['ɑːftəwədz] *adv* 나중에 [najunge]

again [ə'gɛn; ə'geɪn] *adv* 다시 [dasi]; **Can you try again later?** 나중에 다시 전화하시겠어요? [najunge dasi jeonhwahasigesseoyo?]

against [ə'gɛnst; ə'geɪnst] *prep* 반대하여 [bandaehayeo]

age [eɪdʒ] *n* 나이 [nai]; **age limit** *n* 나이 제한 [nai jehan]; **Middle Ages** *npl* 중년 [jungnyeon]

aged [eɪdʒɪd] *adj* 늙은 [neulgeun]

agency ['eɪdʒənsɪ] *n* 대행사 [daehaengsa]; **travel agency** *n* 여행사 [yeohaengsa]

agenda [ə'dʒɛndə] *n* 의제 [uije]

agent ['eɪdʒənt] *n* 대리인 [daeriin]; **estate agent** *n* 부동산 중개인 [budongsan junggaein]; **travel agent** *n* 여행사 직원 [yeohaengsa jigwon]

aggressive [ə'grɛsɪv] *adj* 공격적인 [gonggyeokjeogin]

AGM [eɪ dʒiː ɛm] *abbr* 연례 총회 [yeollye chonghoe]

ago [ə'gəʊ] *adv* **a month ago** 한 달 전에 [han dal jeone]; **a week ago** 일주일 전에 [iljuil jeone]

agony ['ægənɪ] *n* 고통 [gotong]

agree [ə'griː] *v* 동의하다 [donguihada]

agreed [ə'griːd] *adj* 합의를 얻은 [habuireul eodeun]

agreement [ə'griːmənt] *n* 협정 [hyeopjeong]

agricultural ['ægrɪ,kʌltʃərəl] *adj* 농업의 [nongeobui]

agriculture ['ægrɪ,kʌltʃə] *n* 농업 [nongeop]

ahead [əˈhɛd] *adv* 앞쪽에 [apjjoge]
aid [eɪd] *n* 원조 [wonjo]; **first aid** *n* 응급 치료 [eunggeup chiryo]; **first-aid kit** *n* 구급상자 [gugeupsangja]; **hearing aid** *n* 보청기 [bocheonggi]
AIDS [eɪdz] *n* 에이즈 [eijeu]
aim [eɪm] *n* 목적 [mokjeok] ▷ *v* 겨냥하다 [gyeonyanghada]
air [ɛə] *n* 공기 [gonggi] (바람); **air hostess** *n* 비행기 여승무원 [bihaenggi yeoseungmuwon]; **air-traffic controller** *n* 항공 관제사 [hanggong gwanjesa]; **Air Force** *n* 공군 [gonggun]; **Can you check the air, please?** 공기를 확인해 주시겠어요? [gonggireul hwaginhae jusigesseoyo?]
airbag [ɛəbæg] *n* 에어백 [eeobaek]
air-conditioned [ɛəkənˈdɪʃənd] *adj* 냉난방 장치를 한 [naengnanbang jangchireul han]
air conditioning [ɛə kənˈdɪʃənɪŋ] *n* 냉난방 장치 [naengnanbang jangchi]
aircraft [ˈɛəˌkrɑːft] *n* 항공기 [hanggonggi]
airline [ˈɛəˌlaɪn] *n* 항공사 [hanggongsa]
airmail [ˈɛəˌmeɪl] *n* 항공우편 [hanggongupyeon]
airport [ˈɛəˌpɔːt] *n* 공항 [gonghang]; **airport bus** *n* 공항버스 [gonghangbeoseu]; **How do I get to the airport?** 공항에 어떻게 갈 수 있을까요? [gonghange eotteoke gal su isseulkkayo?]; **How much is the taxi to the airport?** 공항까지 택시 요금이 얼마예요? [gonghangkkaji taeksi yogeumi eolmayeyo?]; **Is there a bus to the airport?** 공항 가는 버스가 있어요? [gonghang ganeun beoseuga isseoyo?]
airsick [ˈɛəˌsɪk] *adj* 비행기 멀미가 난 [bihaenggi meolmiga nan]
airspace [ˈɛəˌspeɪs] *n* 영공 [yeonggong]
airtight [ˈɛəˌtaɪt] *adj* 밀폐된 [milpyedoen]
aisle [aɪl] *n* 통로 [tongno]; **I'd like an aisle seat** 통로쪽 좌석이 좋아요 [tongnojjok jwaseogi johayo]
alarm [əˈlɑːm] *n* 비상 [bisang]; **alarm**

call *n* 비상 경보 [bisang gyeongbo]; **alarm clock** *n* 알람 시계 [allam sigye]; **false alarm** *n* 잘못된 경보 [jalmotdoen gyeongbo]; **fire alarm** *n* 화재 경보 [hwajae gyeongbo]; **smoke alarm** *n* 화재경보 [hwajaegyeongbo]
alarming [əˈlɑːmɪŋ] *adj* 놀라운 [nollaun]
Albania [ælˈbeɪnɪə] *n* 알바니아 [albania]
Albanian [ælˈbeɪnɪən] *adj* 알바니아의 [albaniaui] ▷ *n* (*language*) 알바니아어 [albaniaeo], (*person*) 알바니아 사람 [albania saram]
album [ˈælbəm] *n* 앨범 [aelbeom]; **photo album** *n* 사진 앨범 [sajin aelbeom]
alcohol [ˈælkəˌhɒl] *n* 알코올 [alkool]; **Does that contain alcohol?** 알코올이 들어있어요? [alkoori deureoisseoyo?]
alcohol-free [ˈælkəˌhɒlfriː] *adj* 무알코올의 [mualkoorui]
alcoholic [ˌælkəˈhɒlɪk] *adj* 알코올의 [alkoorui] ▷ *n* 알코올 중독자 [alkool jungdokja]
alert [əˈlɜːt] *adj* 경계하는 [gyeonggyehaneun] ▷ *v* 경고하다 [gyeonggohada]
Algeria [ælˈdʒɪərɪə] *n* 알제리 [aljeri]
Algerian [ælˈdʒɪərɪən] *adj* 알제리의 [aljeriui] ▷ *n* 알제리 사람 [aljeri saram]
alias [ˈeɪlɪəs] *adv* 가명 [gamyeong] ▷ *prep* ...라는 통칭으로 알려진 [...raneun tongchingeuro allyeojin]
alibi [ˈælɪˌbaɪ] *n* 알리바이 [allibai]
alien [ˈeɪljən; ˈeɪlɪən] *n* 외국인 [oegugin]
alive [əˈlaɪv] *adj* 살아있는 [sarainneun]
all [ɔːl] *adj* 모든 [modeun] ▷ *pron* 전부 [jeonbu]
Allah [ˈælə] *n* 알라 [alla]
allegation [ˌælɪˈɡeɪʃən] *n* 주장 [jujang]
alleged [əˈlɛdʒd] *adj* 주장된 [jujangdoen]
allergic [əˈlɜːdʒɪk] *adj* 알레르기의 [allereugiui]
allergy [ˈælədʒɪ] *n* 알레르기 [allereugi]; **peanut allergy** *n* 땅콩 알레르기

[ttangkong allereugi]
alley ['ælɪ] n 골목 [golmok]
alliance [ə'laɪəns] n 동맹 [dongmaeng]
alligator ['ælɪ,geɪtə] n 악어 [ageo]
allow [ə'laʊ] v 허락하다 [heorakhada]
all right [ɔːl raɪt] adv 잘 [jal]
ally ['ælaɪ; ə'laɪ] n 동맹국 [dongmaengguk]
almond ['ɑːmənd] n 아몬드 [amondeu]
almost ['ɔːlməʊst] adv 거의 [geoui]; **It's almost half past two** 거의 두시 반이에요 [geoui dusi banieyo]
alone [ə'ləʊn] adj 홀로 [hollo]
along [ə'lɒŋ] prep ...을 따라 [...eul ttara]
aloud [ə'laʊd] adv 소리내어 [sorinaeeo]
alphabet ['ælfə,bet] n 알파벳 [alpabet]
Alps [ælps] npl 알프스 산맥 [alpeuseu sanmaek]
already [ɔːl'redɪ] adv 이미 [imi]
alright [ɔːl'raɪt] adv **Are you alright?** 괜찮으세요? [gwaenchanheuseyo?]
also ['ɔːlsəʊ] adv 또한 [ttohan]
altar ['ɔːltə] n 제단 [jedan]
alter ['ɔːltə] v 바꾸다 [bakkuda]
alternate [ɔːl'tɜːnɪt] adj 교대의 [gyodaeui]
alternative [ɔːl'tɜːnətɪv] adj 양자택일인 [yangjataegirin] ▷ n 양자택일 [yangjataegil]
alternatively [ɔːl'tɜːnətɪvlɪ] adv 교대로 [gyodaero]
although [ɔːl'ðəʊ] conj 비록 [birok]
altitude ['æltɪ,tjuːd] n 고도 [godo]
altogether [,ɔːltə'ɡeðə; 'ɔːltə,ɡeðə] adv 완전히 [wanjeonhi]
aluminium [,æljʊ'mɪnɪəm] n 알루미늄 [alluminyum]
always ['ɔːlweɪz; -wɪz] adv 늘 [neul]
a.m. [eɪɛm] abbr 오전 [ojeon]
amateur ['æmətə; -tʃə; -,tjʊə; ,æmə'tɜː] n 아마추어 [amachueo]
amaze [ə'meɪz] v 놀라게 하다 [nollage hada]
amazed [ə'meɪzd] adj 놀란 [nollan]
amazing [ə'meɪzɪŋ] adj 놀라운 [nollaun]
ambassador [æm'bæsədə] n 대사 [daesa] (외교관)

amber ['æmbə] n 호박 [hobak]
ambition [æm'bɪʃən] n 야심 [yasim]
ambitious [æm'bɪʃəs] adj 야심적인 [yasimjeogin]
ambulance ['æmbjʊləns] n 구급차 [gugeupcha]; **Please call an ambulance** 구급차를 불러 주세요 [gugeupchareul bulleo juseyo]
ambush ['æmbʊʃ] n 매복 [maebok]
amenities [ə'miːnɪtɪz] npl 편의 시설 [pyeonui siseol]
America [ə'mɛrɪkə] n 미국 [miguk]; **Central America** n 중앙 아메리카 [jungang amerika]; **North America** n 북미 [bungmi]; **South America** n 남미 [nammi]
American [ə'mɛrɪkən] adj 미국의 [migugui] ▷ n 미국 사람 [miguk saram]; **American football** n 미식 축구 [misik chukgu]; **North American** n 북미 사람 [bungmi saram], 북미의 [bungmiui]; **South American** n 남미 사람 [nammi saram], 남미의 [nammiui]
ammunition [,æmjʊ'nɪʃən] n 탄약 [tanyak]
among [ə'mʌŋ] prep...사이에 [...saie]
amount [ə'maʊnt] n 양 [yang]
amp [æmp] n 암페어 [ampeeo]
amplifier ['æmplɪ,faɪə] n 증폭기 [jeungpokgi]
amuse [ə'mjuːz] v 즐겁게 하다 [jeulgeopge hada]; **amusement arcade** n 오락장 [orakjang]
an [ɑːn] art 어떤 하나의 [eotteon hanaui]
anaemic [ə'niːmɪk] adj 빈혈의 [binhyeorui]
anaesthetic [,ænɪs'θɛtɪk] n 마취제 [machwije]; **general anaesthetic** n 전신 마취 [jeonsin machwi]; **local anaesthetic** n 국소마취 [guksomachwi]
analyse ['ænə,laɪz] v 분석하다 [bunseokhada]
analysis [ə'nælɪsɪs] n 분석 [bunseok]
ancestor ['ænsɛstə] n 조상 [josang]
anchor ['æŋkə] n 닻 [dat]

anchovy ['æntʃəvɪ] *n* 안초비 [anchobi]

ancient ['eɪnʃənt] *adj* 고대의 [godaeui]

and [ænd; ənd; ən] *conj* 그리고 [geurigo]

Andes ['ændiːz] *npl* 안데스 산맥 [andeseu sanmaek]

Andorra [æn'dɔːrə] *n* 안도라 [andora]

angel ['eɪndʒəl] *n* 천사 [cheonsa]

anger ['æŋgə] *n* 분노 [bunno]

angina [æn'dʒaɪnə] *n* 협심증 [hyeopsimjeung]

angle ['æŋgəl] *n* 각 [gak]; **right angle** *n* 직각 [jikgak]

angler ['æŋglə] *n* 낚시꾼 [nakksikkun]

angling ['æŋglɪŋ] *n* 낚시질 [nakksijil]

Angola [æŋ'gəʊlə] *n* 앙골라 [anggolla]

Angolan [æŋ'gəʊlən] *adj* 앙골라의 [anggollaui] ▷ *n* 앙골라 사람 [anggolla saram]

angry ['æŋgrɪ] *adj* 화난 [hwanan]

animal ['ænɪməl] *n* 동물 [dongmul]

aniseed ['ænɪˌsiːd] *n* 아니스의 열매 [aniseuui yeolmae]

ankle ['æŋkəl] *n* 발목 [balmok]

anniversary [ˌænɪ'vɜːsərɪ] *n* 기념일 [ginyeomil]; **wedding anniversary** *n* 결혼기념일 [gyeolhonginyeomil]

announce [ə'naʊns] *v* 발표하다 [balpyohada]

announcement [ə'naʊnsmənt] *n* 발표 [balpyo]

annoy [ə'nɔɪ] *v* 귀찮게 하다 [gwichanke hada]

annoying [ə'nɔɪɪŋ; an'noying] *adj* 귀찮은 [gwichanheun]

annual ['ænjʊəl] *adj* 해마다의 [haemadaui]

annually ['ænjʊəlɪ] *adv* 해마다 [haemada]

anonymous [ə'nɒnɪməs] *adj* 익명의 [ingmyeongui]

anorak ['ænəˌræk] *n* 방한용 재킷 [banghanyong jaekit]

anorexia [ˌænɒ'rɛksɪə] *n* 식욕부진증 [sigyokbujinjeung]

anorexic [ˌænɒ'rɛksɪk] *adj* 식욕부진의 [sigyokbujinui]

another [ə'nʌðə] *adj* 또 하나의 [tto hanaui]

answer ['ɑːnsə] *n* 대답 [daedap] ▷ *v* 대답하다 [daedaphada]

answerphone ['ɑːnsəfəʊn] *n* 자동 응답기 [jadong eungdapgi]

ant [ænt] *n* 개미 [gaemi]

antagonize [æn'tægəˌnaɪz] *v* 적개심을 일으키다 [jeokgaesimeul ireukida]

Antarctic [æn'tɑːktɪk] *adj* 남극 대륙 [namgeuk daeryuk]; **the Antarctic** *n* 남극 [namgeuk]

Antarctica [ænt'ɑːktɪkə] *n* 남극 [namgeuk]

antelope ['æntɪˌləʊp] *n* 영양 [yeongyang] (동물)

antenatal [ˌæntɪ'neɪtəl] *adj* 출생전의 [chulsaengjeonui]

anthem ['ænθəm] *n* 국가 [gukga]

anthropology [ˌænθrə'pɒlədʒɪ] *n* 인류학 [illyuhak]

antibiotic [ˌæntɪbaɪ'ɒtɪk] *n* 항생 물질 [hangsaeng muljil]

antibody ['æntɪˌbɒdɪ] *n* 항체 [hangche]

anticlockwise [ˌæntɪ'klɒkˌwaɪz] *adv* 시계 반대 방향으로 [sigye bandae banghyangeuro]

antidepressant [ˌæntɪdɪ'prɛsənt] *n* 항우울제 [hanguulje]

antidote ['æntɪˌdəʊt] *n* 해독제 [haedokje]

antifreeze ['æntɪˌfriːz] *n* 부동액 [budongaek]

antihistamine [ˌæntɪ'hɪstəˌmiːn; -mɪn] *n* 항히스타민제 [hanghiseutaminje]

antiperspirant [ˌæntɪ'pɜːspərənt] *n* 지한제 [jihanje]

antique [æn'tiːk] *n* 골동품 [goldongpum]; **antique shop** *n* 골동품점 [goldongpumjeom]

antiseptic [ˌæntɪ'sɛptɪk] *n* 소독제 [sodokje]

antivirus ['æntɪˌvaɪrəs] *n* 안티바이러스 [antibaireoseu]

anxiety [æŋ'zaɪɪtɪ] *n* 불안 [buran]

any ['ɛnɪ] *pron* 어떤 [eotteon]

anybody ['ɛnɪˌbɒdɪ; -bədɪ] *pron* 아무도

[amudo]

anyhow [ˈɛnɪˌhaʊ] *adv* 어쨌든
[eojjaetdeun]

anyone [ˈɛnɪˌwʌn; -wən] *pron* 아무도
[amudo]

anything [ˈɛnɪˌθɪŋ] *pron* 아무것도
[amugeotdo]

anyway [ˈɛnɪˌweɪ] *adv* 어쨌든
[eojjaetdeun]

anywhere [ˈɛnɪˌwɛə] *adv* 어딘가에
[eodingae]

apart [əˈpɑːt] *adv* 따로따로 [ttarottaro]

apart from [əˈpɑːt frɒm] *prep* 제쳐 놓고
[jechyeo noko]

apartment [əˈpɑːtmənt] *n* 아파트
[apateu]; **We're looking for an
apartment** 아파트를 찾고 있어요
[apateureul chatgo isseoyo]; **We've
booked an apartment in the name
of...** ... 이름으로 아파트를 예약했어요
[... ireumeuro apateureul
yeyakhaesseoyo]

aperitif [ɑːˌpɛrɪˈtiːf] *n* 식전 반주
[sikjeon banju]; **We'd like an aperitif**
식전 반주를 주세요 [sikjeon banjureul
juseyo]

aperture [ˈæpətʃə] *n* 구멍 [gumeong]

apologize [əˈpɒləˌdʒaɪz] *v* 사과하다
[sagwahada]

apology [əˈpɒlədʒɪ] *n* 사과 [sagwa]

apostrophe [əˈpɒstrəfɪ] *n* 생략부호
[saengnyakbuho]

appalling [əˈpɔːlɪŋ] *adj* 무서운
[museoun]

apparatus [ˌæpəˈreɪtəs; -ˈrɑːtəs;
ˈæpəˌreɪtəs] *n* 기구 [gigu]

apparent [əˈpærənt; əˈpɛər-] *adj* 명백한
[myeongbaekhan]

apparently [əˈpærəntlɪ; əˈpɛər-] *adv*
명확히 [myeonghwakhi]

appeal [əˈpiːl] *n* 청구 [cheonggu] ▷ *v*
간청하다 [gancheonghada]

appear [əˈpɪə] *v* 나타나다 [natanada]

appearance [əˈpɪərəns] *n* 출현
[chulhyeon]

appendicitis [əˌpɛndɪˈsaɪtɪs] *n* 맹장염
[maengjangyeom]

appetite [ˈæpɪˌtaɪt] *n* 식욕 [sigyok]

applaud [əˈplɔːd] *v* 박수를 치다
[baksureul chida]

applause [əˈplɔːz] *n* 박수 [baksu]

apple [ˈæpl] *n* 사과 [sagwa]; **apple pie**
n 사과 파이 [sagwa pai]

appliance [əˈplaɪəns] *n* 기구 [gigu]

applicant [ˈæplɪkənt] *n* 신청자
[sincheongja]

application [ˌæplɪˈkeɪʃən] *n* 신청
[sincheong]; **application form** *n*
신청서 [sincheongseo]

apply [əˈplaɪ] *v* 신청하다
[sincheonghada]

appoint [əˈpɔɪnt] *v* 임명하다
[immyeonghada]

appointment [əˈpɔɪntmənt] *n* 회의
[hoeui]

appreciate [əˈpriːʃɪˌeɪt; -sɪ-] *v*
감사하다 [gamsahada]

apprehensive [ˌæprɪˈhɛnsɪv] *adj*
불안한 [buranhan]

apprentice [əˈprɛntɪs] *n* 견습생
[gyeonseupsaeng]

approach [əˈprəʊtʃ] *v* 접근하다
[jeopgeunhada]

appropriate [əˈprəʊprɪɪt] *adj* 적합한
[jeokhaphan]

approval [əˈpruːvəl] *n* 승인 [seungin]

approve [əˈpruːv] *v* 승인하다
[seunginhada]

approximate [əˈprɒksɪmɪt] *adj*
대략적인 [daeryakjeogin]

approximately [əˈprɒksɪmɪtlɪ] *adv*
대략 [daeryak]

apricot [ˈeɪprɪˌkɒt] *n* 살구 [salgu]

April [ˈeɪprəl] *n* 4월 [sawol]; **April
Fools' Day** *n* 만우절 [manujeol]

apron [ˈeɪprən] *n* 앞치마 [apchima]

aquarium [əˈkwɛərɪəm] *n* 수족관
[sujokgwan]

Aquarius [əˈkwɛərɪəs] *n* 물병자리
[mulbyeongjari]

Arab [ˈærəb] *adj* 아랍의 [arabui] ▷ *n*
아랍 사람 [arap saram]; **United Arab
Emirates** *npl* 아랍에미리트 연합국
[arabemiriteu yeonhapguk]

Arabic [ˈærəbɪk] *adj* 아라비아의
[arabiaui] ▷ *n (language)* 아라비아 사람

[arabia saram]

arbitration [ˌɑːbɪ'treɪʃən] n 중재 [jungjae]

arch [ɑːtʃ] n 아치 [achi]

archaeologist [ˌɑːkɪ'ɒlədʒɪst] n 고고학자 [gogohakja]

archaeology [ˌɑːkɪ'ɒlədʒɪ] n 고고학 [gogohak]

archbishop ['ɑːtʃ'bɪʃəp] n 대주교 [daejugyo]

architect ['ɑːkɪˌtɛkt] n 건축가 [geonchukga]

architecture ['ɑːkɪˌtɛktʃə] n 건축 [geonchuk]

archive ['ɑːkaɪv] n 기록 보관소 [girok bogwanso]

Arctic ['ɑːktɪk] adj 북극 [bukgeuk]; **Arctic Circle** n 북극권 [bukgeukgwon]; **Arctic Ocean** n 북극해 [bukgeukhae]; **the Arctic** n 북극 [bukgeuk]

area ['ɛərɪə] n 구역 [guyeok]; **service area** n 서비스 구역 [seobiseu guyeok]; **I'd like a seat in the smoking area** 흡연구역 좌석으로 주세요 [heubyeonguyeok jwaseogeuro juseyo]; **Is there a non-smoking area?** 금연 구역이 있나요? [geumyeon guyeogi innayo?]

Argentina [ˌɑːdʒən'tiːnə] n 아르헨티나 [areuhentina]

Argentinian [ˌɑːdʒən'tɪnɪən] adj 아르헨티나의 [areuhentinaui] ▷ n (person) 아르헨티나 사람 [areuhentina saram]

argue ['ɑːgjuː] v 논쟁하다 [nonjaenghada]

argument ['ɑːgjʊmənt] n 논쟁 [nonjaeng]

Aries ['ɛəriːz] n 양자리 [yangjari]

arm [ɑːm] n 팔 [pal]; **I can't move my arm** 팔을 움직일 수 없어요 [pareul umjigil su eopseoyo]

armchair ['ɑːmˌtʃɛə] n 안락 의자 [allak uija]

armed [ɑːmd] adj 무장한 [mujanghan]

Armenia [ɑː'miːnɪə] n 아르메니아 [areumenia]

Armenian [ɑː'miːnɪən] adj 아르메니아의 [areumeniaui] ▷ n (language) 아르메니아어 [areumeniaeo], (person) 아르메니아 사람 [areumenia saram]

armour ['ɑːmə] n 갑옷 [gabot]

armpit ['ɑːmˌpɪt] n 겨드랑이 [gyeodeurangi]

army ['ɑːmɪ] n 군대 [gundae]

aroma [ə'rəʊmə] n 방향 [banghyang]

aromatherapy [əˌrəʊmə'θɛrəpɪ] n 방향요법 [banghyangyobeop]

around [ə'raʊnd] adv 주위에 [juwie] ▷ prep 주위에 [juwie]

arrange [ə'reɪndʒ] v 준비하다 [junbihada]

arrangement [ə'reɪndʒmənt] n 준비 [junbi]

arrears [ə'rɪəz] npl 연체금 [yeonchegeum]

arrest [ə'rɛst] n 체포 [chepo] ▷ v 체포하다 [chepohada]

arrival [ə'raɪvəl] n 도착 [dochak]

arrive [ə'raɪv] v 도착하다 [dochakhada]

arrogant ['ærəgənt] adj 거만한 [geomanhan]

arrow ['ærəʊ] n 화살 [hwasal]

arson ['ɑːsən] n 방화죄 [banghwajoe]

art [ɑːt] n 예술 [yesul]; **art gallery** n 미술관 [misulgwan]; **art school** n 예술 학교 [yesul hakgyo]; **work of art** n 미술품 [misulpum]

artery ['ɑːtərɪ] n 동맥 [dongmaek]

arthritis [ɑː'θraɪtɪs] n 관절염 [gwanjeollyeom]; **I suffer from arthritis** 관절염이 있어요 [gwanjeollyeomi isseoyo]

artichoke ['ɑːtɪˌtʃəʊk] n 아티초크 [atichokeu]

article ['ɑːtɪkəl] n 기사 [gisa] (신문)

artificial [ˌɑːtɪ'fɪʃəl] adj 인공적인 [ingongjeogin]

artist ['ɑːtɪst] n 예술가 [yesulga]

artistic [ɑː'tɪstɪk; ɑr'tistɪk] adj 예술적인 [yesuljeogin]

as [əz] adv 마찬가지로 [machangajiro] ▷ conj 같이 [gachi] (유사한 것) ▷ prep... 로서 [...roseo]

asap [eɪsæp] *abbr* 가능한 한 빨리 [ganeunghan han ppalli]

ascent [ə'sɛnt] *n* **When is the last ascent?** 마지막 올라가기는 언제인가요? [majimak ollagagineun eonjeingayo?]

ashamed [ə'ʃeɪmd] *adj* 부끄러워하는 [bukkeureowohaneun]

ashore [ə'ʃɔː] *adv* **Can we go ashore now?** 지금 상륙해도 될까요? [jigeum sangnyukhaedo doelkkayo?]

ashtray ['æʃˌtreɪ] *n* 재떨이 [jaetteori]; **May I have an ashtray?** 재떨이 있어요? [jaetteori isseoyo?]

Asia ['eɪʃə; 'eɪʒə] *n* 아시아 [asia]

Asian ['eɪʃən; 'eɪʒən] *adj* 아시아의 [asiaui] ▷ *n* 아시아 사람 [asia saram]

Asiatic [ˌeɪʃɪ'ætɪk; -zɪ-] *adj* 아시아의 [asiaui]

ask [ɑːsk] *v* 묻다 [mutda] (질문)

ask for [ɑːsk fɔː] *v* 요청하다 [yocheonghada]

asleep [ə'sliːp] *adj* 잠들어 [jamdeureo]

asparagus [ə'spærəgəs] *n* 아스파라거스 [aseuparageoseu]

aspect ['æspɛkt] *n* 측면 [cheungmyeon]

aspirin ['æsprɪn] *n* 아스피린 [aseupirin]; **I can't take aspirin** 저는 아스피린을 못 먹어요 [jeoneun aseupirineul mot meogeoyo]; **I'd like some aspirin** 아스피린 주세요 [aseupirin juseyo]

assembly [ə'sɛmblɪ] *n* 집회 [jiphoe]

asset ['æsɛt] *n* 자산 [jasan]; **assets** *npl* 자산 [jasan]

assignment [ə'saɪnmənt] *n* 임무 [immu]

assistance [ə'sɪstəns] *n* 도움 [doum]

assistant [ə'sɪstənt] *n* 조수 [josu]; **personal assistant** *n* 비서 [biseo]; **sales assistant** *n* 판매원 [panmaewon]; **shop assistant** *n* 점원 [jeomwon]

associate *adj* [ə'səʊʃiːt] 준... [jun...] ▷ *n* [ə'səʊʃiːt] 제휴자 [jehyuja]

association [əˌsəʊsɪ'eɪʃən; -ʃɪ-] *n* 협회 [hyeophoe]

assortment [ə'sɔːtmənt] *n* 분류 [bullyu]

assume [ə'sjuːm] *v* 가정하다 [gajeonghada]

assure [ə'ʃʊə] *v* 보증하다 [bojeunghada]

asthma ['æsmə] *n* 천식 [cheonsik]

astonish [ə'stɒnɪʃ] *v* 놀라게 하다 [nollage hada]

astonished [ə'stɒnɪʃt] *adj* 놀란 [nollan]

astonishing [ə'stɒnɪʃɪŋ] *adj* 놀라운 [nollaun]

astrology [ə'strɒlədʒɪ] *n* 점성술 [jeomseongsul]

astronaut ['æstrəˌnɔːt] *n* 우주비행사 [ujubihaengsa]

astronomy [ə'strɒnəmɪ] *n* 천문학 [cheonmunhak]

asylum [ə'saɪləm] *n* 망명 [mangmyeong]; **asylum seeker** *n* 망명자 [mangmyeongja]

at [æt] *prep* ...에서 [...eseo]; **at least** *adv* 적어도 [jeogeodo]; **Do we stop at...?** ...에서 정차합니까? [...eseo jeongchahamnikka?]

atheist ['eɪθɪˌɪst] *n* 무신론자 [musinnonja]

athlete ['æθliːt] *n* 운동 선수 [undong seonsu]

athletic [æθ'lɛtɪk] *adj* 원기 왕성한 [wongi wangseonghan]

athletics [æθ'lɛtɪks] *npl* 운동경기 [undonggyeonggi]

Atlantic [ət'læntɪk] *n* 대서양 [daeseoyang]

atlas ['ætləs] *n* 지도책 [jidochaek]

atmosphere ['ætməsˌfɪə] *n* 대기 [daegi] (공기)

atom ['ætəm] *n* 원자 [wonja]; **atom bomb** *n* 원자폭탄 [wonjapoktan]

atomic [ə'tɒmɪk] *adj* 원자의 [wonjaui]

attach [ə'tætʃ] *v* 붙이다 [buchida]

attached [ə'tætʃt] *adj* 연결되어있는 [yeongyeoldoeeoinneun]

attachment [ə'tætʃmənt] *n* 애착 [aechak]

attack [ə'tæk] *n* 공격 [gonggyeok] ▷ *v*

공격하다 [gonggyeokhada]; **heart attack** n 심장마비 [simjangmabi]; **terrorist attack** n 테러리스트 공격 [tereoriseuteu gonggyeok]

attempt [ə'tɛmpt] n 시도 [sido] ▷ v 시도하다 [sidohada]

attend [ə'tɛnd] v 출석하다 [chulseokhada]

attendance [ə'tɛndəns] n 출석 [chulseok]

attendant [ə'tɛndənt] n **flight attendant** n 비행기 승무원 [bihaenggi seungmuwon]

attention [ə'tɛnʃən] n 주의 [juui]

attic ['ætɪk] n 다락방 [darakbang]

attitude ['ætɪ,tjuːd] n 태도 [taedo]

attorney [ə'tɜːnɪ] n 대리인 [daeriin]

attract [ə'trækt] v 끌어당기다 [kkeureodanggida]

attraction [ə'trækʃən] n 끌어당기기 [kkeureodanggigi]

attractive [ə'træktɪv] adj 마음을 끌어당기는 [maeumeul kkeureodanggineun]

aubergine ['əʊbəˌʒiːn] n 가지 [gaji]

auburn ['ɔːbən] adj 적갈색의 [jeokgalsaegui]

auction ['ɔːkʃən] n 경매 [gyeongmae]

audience ['ɔːdɪəns] n 청중 [cheongjung]

audit ['ɔːdɪt] n 감사 [gamsa] ▷ v 감사하다 [gamsahada]

audition [ɔː'dɪʃən] n 오디션 [odisyeon]

auditor ['ɔːdɪtə] n 감사관 [gamsagwan]

August ['ɔːgəst] n 8월 [parwol]

aunt [ɑːnt] n 고모,이모 [gomo,imo]

auntie ['ɑːntɪ] n 고모, 이모 [gomo, imo]

au pair [əʊ 'pɛə; o pɛr] n 오페어 [opeeo]

austerity [ɒ'stɛrɪtɪ] n 엄격함 [eomgyeokham]

Australasia [ˌɒstrə'leɪzɪə] n 오스트랄라시아 [oseuteurallasia]

Australia [ɒ'streɪlɪə] n 호주 [hoju]

Australian [ɒ'streɪlɪən] adj 호주의 [hojuui] ▷ n 호주 사람 [hoju saram]

Austria ['ɒstrɪə] n 오스트리아 [oseuteuria]

Austrian ['ɒstrɪən] adj 오스트리아의 [oseuteuriaui] ▷ n 오스트리아 사람 [oseuteuria saram]

authentic [ɔː'θɛntɪk] adj 진정한 [jinjeonghan]

author, authoress ['ɔːθə, 'ɔːθəˌrɛs] n 저자 [jeoja]

authorize ['ɔːθəˌraɪz] v 권한을 주다 [gwonhaneul juda]

autobiography [ˌɔːtəʊbaɪ'ɒgrəfɪ; ˌɔːtəbaɪ-] n 자서전 [jaseojeon]

autograph ['ɔːtəˌɡrɑːf; -ˌɡræf] n 서명 [seomyeong]

automatic [ˌɔːtə'mætɪk] adj 자동의 [jadongui]

automatically [ˌɔːtə'mætɪklɪ] adv 자동으로 [jadongeuro]

autonomous [ɔː'tɒnəməs] adj 자치의 [jachiui]

autonomy [ɔː'tɒnəmɪ] n 자치권 [jachigwon]

autumn ['ɔːtəm] n 가을 [gaeul]

availability [ə'veɪləbɪlɪtɪ] n 가용성 [gayongseong]

available [ə'veɪləbəl] adj 사용할 수 있는 [sayonghal su inneun]

avalanche ['ævəˌlɑːntʃ] n 사태 [satae]; **Is there a danger of avalanches?** 눈사태 위험이 있어요? [nunsatae wiheomi isseoyo?]

avenue ['ævɪˌnjuː] n 대로 [daero]

average ['ævərɪdʒ; 'ævrɪdʒ] adj 평균의 [pyeonggyunui] ▷ n 평균 [pyeonggyun]

avocado, avocados [ˌævə'kɑːdəʊ, ˌævə'kɑːdəʊs] n 아보카도 [abokado]

avoid [ə'vɔɪd] v 피하다 [pihada]

awake [ə'weɪk] adj 깨어 있는 [kkaeeo ltneun] ▷ v 잠깨다 [jamkkaeda]

award [ə'wɔːd] n 상 [sang]

aware [ə'wɛə] adj 알고 있는 [algo inneun]

away [ə'weɪ] adv 떨어져 [tteoreojyeo]; **away match** n 원정 경기 [wonjeong gyeonggi]

awful ['ɔːfʊl] adj 몹시 나쁜 [mopsi nappeun]

awfully ['ɔːfəlɪ; 'ɔːflɪ] adv 몹시 [mopsi]

awkward [ˈɔːkwəd] *adj* 서투른
[seotureun]
axe [æks] *n* 도끼 [dokki]
axle [ˈæksəl] *n* 축 [chuk]
Azerbaijan [ˌæzəbaɪˈdʒɑːn] *n*
아제르바이잔 [ajereubaijan]
Azerbaijani [ˌæzəbaɪˈdʒɑːnɪ] *adj*
아제르바이잔의 [ajereubaijanui] ▷ *n*
아제르바이잔 사람 [ajereubaijan
saram]

B&B [bi: ænd bi:] *n* 아침 제공 숙박
[achim jegong sukbak]
BA [bɑː] *abbr* 학사 [haksa]
baby [ˈbeɪbɪ] *n* 아기 [agi]; **baby milk** *n*
유아용 우유 [yuayong uyu]; **baby wipe**
n 유아용 수건 [yuayong sugeon];
baby's bottle *n* 아기 젖병 [agi
jeotbyeong]; **Are there facilities for
parents with babies?** 아기를 동반한
부모를 위한 시설이 있나요? [agireul
dongbanhan bumoreul wihan siseori
innayo?]
babysit [ˈbeɪbɪsɪt] *v* 아기를 보다
[agireul boda]
babysitter [ˈbeɪbɪsɪtə] *n* 아기 봐주는
사람 [agi bwajuneun saram]
babysitting [ˈbeɪbɪsɪtɪŋ] *n* 아기 보기
[agi bogi]
bachelor [ˈbætʃələ; ˈbætʃlə] *n* 미혼남
[mihonnam]
back [bæk] *adj* 뒤의 [dwiui] ▷ *adv* 뒤에
[dwie] ▷ *n* 등 [deung] ▷ *v* 후원하다
[huwonhada]; **back pain** *n* 요통
[yotong]; **I've got a bad back** 등이 안
좋아요 [deungi an johayo]; **I've hurt
my back** 등이 아파요 [deungi apayo]
backache [ˈbækˌeɪk] *n* 요통 [yotong]

backbone [ˈbækˌbəʊn] n 등뼈 [deungppyeo]
backfire [ˌbækˈfaɪə] v 실패하다 [silpaehada]
background [ˈbækˌɡraʊnd] n 배경 [baegyeong]
backing [ˈbækɪŋ] n 후원 [huwon]
back out [bæk aʊt] v 취소하다 [chwisohada]
backpack [ˈbækˌpæk] n 배낭 [baenang]
backpacker [ˈbækˌpækə] n 배낭여행자 [baenangyeohaengja]
backpacking [ˈbækˌpækɪŋ] n 배낭여행 [baenangyeohaeng]
backside [ˌbækˈsaɪd] n 엉덩이 [eongdeongi]
backslash [ˈbækˌslæʃ] n 백슬래시 [baekseullaesi]
backstroke [ˈbækˌstrəʊk] n 배영 [baeyeong]
back up [bæk ʌp] v 후원하다 [huwonhada]
backup [bækʌp] n 후원 [huwon]
backwards [ˈbækwədz] adv 뒤쪽으로 [dwijjogeuro]
bacon [ˈbeɪkən] n 베이컨 [beikeon]
bacteria [bækˈtɪərɪə] npl 박테리아 [bakteria]
bad [bæd] adj 나쁜 [nappeun]
badge [bædʒ] n 배지 [baeji] (핀)
badger [ˈbædʒə] n 오소리 [osori]
badly [ˈbædlɪ] adv 나쁘게 [nappeuge]
badminton [ˈbædmɪntən] n 배드민턴 [baedeuminteon]
bad-tempered [bædˈtɛmpəd] adj 기분이 상한 [gibuni sanghan]
baffled [ˈbæfˈld] adj 당황한 [danghwanghan]
bag [bæg] n 가방 [gabang]; **bum bag** n 허리 주머니 [heori jumeoni]; **carrier bag** n 쇼핑백 [syopingbaek]; **overnight bag** n 여행용 가방 [yeohaengyong gabang]; **plastic bag** n 비닐봉지 [binilbongji]; **polythene bag** n 비닐봉지 [binilbongji]; **shopping bag** n 쇼핑백 [syopingbaek]; **sleeping bag** n 침낭 [chimnang]; **tea bag** n 티백 [tibaek]; **toilet bag** n 세면가방 [semyeongabang]; **Could you watch my bag for a minute, please?** 잠깐만 제 가방을 봐 주시겠어요? [jamkkanman je gabangeul bwa jusigesseoyo?]; **Someone's stolen my bag** 누군가가 제 가방을 훔쳐 갔어요 [nugungaga je gabangeul humchyeo gasseoyo]
baggage [ˈbæɡɪdʒ] n 수하물 [suhamul]; **baggage allowance** n 수하물 허용 중량 [suhamul heoyong jungnyang]; **baggage reclaim** n 수하물 회수 [suhamul hoesu]; **excess baggage** n 제한 초과 수하물 [jehan chogwa suhamul]; **What is the baggage allowance?** 수하물 허용 중량은 얼마인가요? [suhamul heoyong jungnyangeun eolmaingayo?]
baggy [ˈbæɡɪ] adj 헐렁한 [heolleonghan]
bagpipes [ˈbæɡˌpaɪps] npl 백파이프 [baekpaipeu]
Bahamas [bəˈhɑːməz] npl 바하마 [bahama]
Bahrain [bɑːˈreɪn] n 바레인 [barein]
bail [beɪl] n 보석 [boseok]
bake [beɪk] v 굽다 [gupda] (요리)
baked [beɪkt] adj 구운 [guun]; **baked potato** n 구운 감자 [guun gamja]
baker [ˈbeɪkə] n 제빵사 [jeppangsa]
bakery [ˈbeɪkərɪ] n 빵집 [ppangjip]
baking [ˈbeɪkɪŋ] n 굽기 [gupgi] (요리); **baking powder** n 베이킹 파우더 [beiking paudeo]
balance [ˈbæləns] n 균형 [gyunhyeong]; **balance sheet** n 대차대조표 [daechadaejopyo]; **bank balance** n 은행잔고 [eunhaengjango]
balanced [ˈbælənst] adj 균형 잡힌 [gyunhyeong japhin]
balcony [ˈbælkənɪ] n 발코니 [balkoni]; **Do you have a room with a balcony?** 발코니 있는 방 있어요? [balkoni inneun bang isseoyo?]
bald [bɔːld] adj 대머리의 [daemeoriui]
Balkan [ˈbɔːlkən] adj 발칸 여러 나라의 [balkan yeoreo naraui]

ball [bɔːl] n (dance) 무도회 [mudohoe], (toy) 공 [gong] (라운드 게임)

ballerina [ˌbælə'riːnə] n 발레리나 [ballerina]

ballet ['bæleɪ; bæ'leɪ] n 발레 [balle]; **ballet dancer** n 발레 무용수 [balle muyongsu]; **ballet shoes** npl 발레화 [ballehwa]; **Where can I buy tickets for the ballet?** 어디에서 발레 표를 살 수 있어요? [eodieseo balle pyoreul sal su isseoyo?]

balloon [bə'luːn] n 풍선 [pungseon]

bamboo [bæm'buː] n 대나무 [daenamu]

ban [bæn] n 금지 [geumji] ▷ v 금지하다 [geumjihada]

banana [bə'nɑːnə] n 바나나 [banana]

band [bænd] n (musical group) 음악단 [eumakdan], (strip) 띠 [tti]; **brass band** n 관악대 [gwanakdae]; **elastic band** n 고무 밴드 [gomu baendeu]; **rubber band** n 고무밴드 [gomubaendeu]

bandage ['bændɪdʒ] n 붕대 [bungdae] ▷ v 붕대를 감다 [bungdaereul gamda]; **I'd like a bandage** 붕대를 감아 주세요 [bungdaereul gama juseyo]; **I'd like a fresh bandage** 붕대를 새로 감아 주세요 [bungdaereul saero gama juseyo]

Band-Aid® ['bændeɪd] n 반창고 [banchanggo]

bang [bæŋ] n 쾅하는 소리 [kwanghaneun sori] ▷ v 큰 소리가 나게 치다 [keun soriga nage chida]

Bangladesh [ˌbɑːŋglə'dɛʃ; ˌbæŋ-] n 방글라데시 [banggeulladesi]

Bangladeshi [ˌbɑːŋglə'dɛʃi; ˌbæŋ-] adj 방글라데시의 [banggeulladesiui] ▷ n 방글라데시 사람 [banggeulladesi saram]

banister ['bænɪstə] n 난간 [nangan]

banjo ['bændʒəʊ] n 밴조 [baenjo]

bank [bæŋk] n (finance) 은행 [eunhaeng] (금융), (ridge) 둑 [duk]; **bank account** n 은행계좌 [eunhaenggyejwa]; **bank balance** n 은행잔고 [eunhaengjango]; **bank charges** npl 은행 수수료 [eunhaeng susuryo]; **bank holiday** n 공휴일 [gonghyuil]; **bank statement** n 은행 계좌 통지서 [eunhaeng gyejwa tongjiseo]; **bottle bank** n 빈 병 수거함 [bin byeong sugeoham]; **merchant bank** n 상업 은행 [sangeop eunhaeng]; **How far is the bank?** 은행이 얼마나 먼가요? [eunhaengi eolmana meongayo?]; **I would like to transfer some money from my bank in...** ...에 있는 제 거래 은행에서 돈을 이체하고 싶어요 [...e inneun je georae eunhaengeseo doneul ichehago sipeoyo]; **Is the bank open today?** 오늘 은행 열어요? [oneul eunhaeng yeoreoyo?]; **Is there a bank here?** 여기에 은행이 있나요? [yeogie eunhaengi innayo?]; **When does the bank close?** 은행은 언제 닫나요? [eunhaengeun eonje datnayo?]

banker ['bæŋkə] n 은행가 [eunhaengga]

banknote ['bæŋkˌnəʊt] n 지폐 [jipye]

bankrupt ['bæŋkrʌpt; -rəpt] adj 파산한 [pasanhan]

banned [bænd] adj 금지된 [geumjidoen]

Baptist ['bæptɪst] n 침례교도 [chimnyegyodo]

bar [bɑː] n (alcohol) 술집 [suljip], (strip) 막대 [makdae]; **snack bar** n 스낵 바 [seunaek ba]

Barbados [bɑː'beɪdəʊs; -dəʊz; -dɒs] n 바베이도스 [babeidoseu]

barbaric [bɑː'bærɪk] adj 야만적인 [yamanjeogin]

barbecue ['bɑːbɪˌkjuː] n 바비큐 [babikyu]; **Where is the barbecue area?** 바비큐장소는 어디인가요? [babikyujangsoneun eodiingayo?]

barber ['bɑːbə] n 이발사 [ibalsa]

bare [bɛə] adj 발가벗은 [balgabeoseun] ▷ v 드러내다 [deureonaeda]

barefoot ['bɛəˌfʊt] adj 맨발의 [maenbarui] ▷ adv 맨발로 [maenballo]

barely ['bɛəlɪ] adv 간신히 [gansinhi]

bargain ['bɑːgɪn] n 거래 [georae]

barge [bɑːdʒ] n 바지선 [bajiseon]

bark [bɑːk] v 짖다 [jitda]

barley ['bɑːlɪ] n 보리 [bori]

barmaid ['bɑːˌmeɪd] n 여자 바텐더 [yeoja batendeo]

barman, barmen ['bɑːmən, 'bɑːmɛn] n 바텐더 [batendeo]

barn [bɑːn] n 헛간 [heotgan]

barrel ['bærəl] n 통 [tong]

barrier ['bærɪə] n 장벽 [jangbyeok]; **ticket barrier** n 개찰구 [gaechalgu]

bartender ['bɑːˌtɛndə] n 바텐더 [batendeo]

base [beɪs] n 토대 [todae]

baseball ['beɪsˌbɔːl] n 야구 [yagu]; **baseball cap** n 야구 모자 [yagu moja]

based [beɪst] adj ...을 바탕으로 한 [...eul batangeuro han]

basement ['beɪsmənt] n 지하실 [jihasil]

bash [bæʃ] n 강타 [gangta] ▷ v 강타하다 [gangtahada]

basic ['beɪsɪk] adj 기본의 [gibonui]

basically ['beɪsɪklɪ] adv 기본적으로 [gibonjeogeuro]

basics ['beɪsɪks] npl 기본 원리 [gibon wolli]

basil ['bæzəl] n 바질 [bajil]

basin ['beɪsən] n 대야 [daeya]

basis ['beɪsɪs] n 토대 [todae]

basket ['bɑːskɪt] n 바구니 [baguni]; **wastepaper basket** n 휴지통 [hyujitong]

basketball ['bɑːskɪtˌbɔːl] n 농구 [nonggu] (경기)

Basque [bæsk; bɑːsk] adj 바스크의 [baseukeuui] ▷ n (language) 바스크어 [baseukeueo], (person) 바스크 사람 [baseukeu saram]

bass [beɪs] n 베이스 [beiseu]; **bass drum** n 베이스 드럼 [beiseu deureom]; **double bass** n 더블베이스 [deobeulbeiseu]

bassoon [bə'suːn] n 바순 [basun]

bat [bæt] n (mammal) 박쥐 [bakjwi], (with ball) 방망이 [bangmangi]

bath [bɑːθ] n **bubble bath** n 거품 목욕 [geopum mogyok]

bathe [beɪð] v 목욕하다 [mogyokhada]

bathrobe ['bɑːθˌrəʊb] n 목욕 가운 [mogyok gaun]

bathroom ['bɑːθˌruːm; -ˌrʊm] n 욕실 [yoksil]; **Are there support railings in the bathroom?** 욕실에 장애인용 손잡이가 있어요? [yoksire jangaeinyong sonjabiga isseoyo?]; **Does the room have a private bathroom?** 방에 개인 욕실이 있어요? [bange gaein yoksiri isseoyo?]; **The bathroom is flooded** 욕실 물이 넘쳤어요 [yoksil muri neomchyeosseoyo]

baths [bɑːθz] npl 수영장 [suyeongjang]

bathtub ['bɑːθˌtʌb] n 욕조 [yokjo]

batter ['bætə] n 반죽 [banjuk]

battery ['bætərɪ] n 전지 [jeonji]

battle ['bætəl] n 전투 [jeontu]

battleship ['bætəlˌʃɪp] n 전함 [jeonham]

bay [beɪ] n 만 [man] (바다의 만); **bay leaf** n 월계수 잎 [wolgyesu ip]

BC [biː siː] abbr 기원전 [giwonjeon]

be [biː; bɪ] v 존재하다 [jonjaehada]

beach [biːtʃ] n 바닷가 [badatga]; **Are there any good beaches near here?** 이 근처에 좋은 바닷가가 있나요? [i geuncheoe joheun badatgaga innayo?]; **How far is the beach?** 바닷가가 얼마나 먼가요? [badatgaga eolmana meongayo?]; **I'm going to the beach** 바닷가에 갈 거예요 [badatgae gal geoyeyo]; **Is there a bus to the beach?** 바닷가 가는 버스가 있어요? [badatga ganeun beoseuga isseoyo?]

bead [biːd] n 구슬 [guseul]

beak [biːk] n 부리 [buri]

beam [biːm] n 환한 미소 [hwanhan miso]

bean [biːn] n 콩 [kong]; **broad bean** n 잠두 [jamdu]; **French beans** npl 강낭콩 [gangnangkong]; **runner bean** n 깍지를 먹는 콩 [kkakjireul meongneun kong]

beansprout ['biːnˌspraʊt] n **beansprouts** npl 콩나물 [kongnamul]

bear [bɛə] n 곰 [gom] ▷ v 받치다 [batchida]; **polar bear** n 북극곰 [bukgeukgom]; **teddy bear** n 곰인형 [gominhyeong]

beard [bɪəd] n 턱수염 [teoksuyeom]

bearded [bɪədɪd] adj 수염이 난 [suyeomi nan]

bear up [bɛə ʌp] v 견디다 [gyeondida]

beat [biːt] n 타격 [tagyeok] ▷ v (outdo) 능가하다 [neunggahada], (strike) 때리다 [ttaerida]

beautiful [ˈbjuːtɪfʊl] adj 아름다운 [areumdaun]

beautifully [ˈbjuːtɪflɪ] adv 아름답게 [areumdapge]

beauty n [ˈbjuːtɪ] n 미인 [miin]; **beauty salon** n 미용실 [miyongsil]; **beauty spot** n 명승지 [myeongseungji]

beaver [ˈbiːvə] n 비버 [bibeo]

because [bɪˈkɒz; -ˈkəz] conj 때문에 [ttaemune]; **because of a strike** 파업때문에요 [paeopttaemuneyo]

become [bɪˈkʌm] v...이 되다 [...i doeda]

bed [bɛd] n 침대 [chimdae]; **bed and breakfast** n 아침 제공 숙박 [achim jegong sukbak]; **bunk beds** npl 이층 침대 [icheung chimdae]; **camp bed** n 야전침대 [yajeonchimdae]; **double bed** n 2인용 침대 [i inyong chimdae]; **king-size bed** n 킹사이즈 침대 [kingsaijeu chimdae]; **single bed** n 1 인용 침대 [il inyong chimdae]; **sofa bed** n 소파식 침대 [sopasik chimdae]; **twin beds** npl 트윈 베드 [teuwin bedeu]; **I'd like a dorm bed** 기숙사 침대가 좋겠어요 [gisuksa chimdaega jokesseoyo]; **The bed is uncomfortable** 침대가 불편해요 [chimdaega bulpyeonhaeyo]

bedclothes [ˈbɛdˌkləʊðz] npl 침대 커버 [chimdae keobeo]

bedding [ˈbɛdɪŋ] n 침구류 [chimguryu]

bedroom [ˈbɛdˌruːm; -ˌrʊm] n 침실 [chimsil]; **Do you have any bedrooms on the ground floor?** 일층에 침실이 있나요? [ilcheunge chimsiri innayo?]

bedsit [ˈbɛdˌsɪt] n 침실 겸 거실 [chimsil gyeom geosil]

bedspread [ˈbɛdˌsprɛd] n 침대보 [chimdaebo]

bedtime [ˈbɛdˌtaɪm] n 취침 시간 [chwichim sigan]

bee [biː] n 벌 [beol]

beech [biːtʃ] n **beech (tree)** n 너도밤나무 [neodobamnamu]

beef [biːf] n 쇠고기 [soegogi]

beefburger [ˈbiːfˌbɜːgə] n 쇠고기 햄버거 [soegogi haembeogeo]

beer [bɪə] n 맥주 [maekju]; **another beer** 맥주 한 잔 더요 [maekju han jan deoyo]; **A draught beer, please** 생맥주 주세요 [saengmaekju juseyo]

beetle [ˈbiːtəl] n 딱정벌레 [ttakjeongbeolle]

beetroot [ˈbiːtˌruːt] n 비트 뿌리 [biteu ppuri]

before [bɪˈfɔː] adv 앞에 [ape] ▷ conj... 전에 [...jeone]

beforehand [bɪˈfɔːˌhænd] adv 미리 [miri]

beg [bɛg] v 구걸하다 [gugeolhada]

beggar [ˈbɛgə] n 거지 [geoji]

begin [bɪˈgɪn] v 시작하다 [sijakhada]

beginner [bɪˈgɪnə] n 초보자 [choboja]

beginning [bɪˈgɪnɪŋ] n 시작 [sijak]

behave [bɪˈheɪv] v 행동하다 [haengdonghada]

behaviour [bɪˈheɪvjə] n 행동 [haengdong]

behind [bɪˈhaɪnd] adv 뒤에 [dwie] ▷ n 엉덩이 [eongdeongi] ▷ prep...의 뒤에 [... ui dwie]; **lag behind** v 뒤떨어지다 [dwitteoreojida]

beige [beɪʒ] adj 베이지색의 [beijisaegui]

Beijing [ˈbeɪˈdʒɪŋ] n 베이징 [beijing]

Belarus [ˈbɛləˌrʌs; -ˌrʊs] n 벨로루시 [bellorusi]

Belarussian [ˌbɛləʊˈrʌʃən; ˌbjɛl-] adj 벨로루시의 [bellorusiui] ▷ n (language) 벨로루시어 [bellorusieo], (person) 벨로루시 사람 [bellorusi saram]

Belgian [ˈbɛldʒən] adj 벨기에의 [belgieui] ▷ n 벨기에 사람 [belgie saram]

Belgium [ˈbɛldʒəm] n 벨기에 [belgie]

belief [bɪˈliːf] n 믿음 [mideum]

believe [bɪ'liːv] vi 믿다 [mitda]
bell [bɛl] n 종 [jong] (울리다)
belly ['bɛlɪ] n 배 [bae]; **belly button** n 배꼽 [baekkop]
belong [bɪ'lɒŋ] v 속하다 [sokhada]; **belong to** v 속하다 [sokhada]
belongings [bɪ'lɒŋɪŋz] npl 소지품 [sojipum]
below [bɪ'ləʊ] adv 아래쪽에 [araejjoge] ▷ prep...보다 아래에 [...boda araee]
belt [bɛlt] n 허리띠 [heoritti]; **conveyor belt** n 컨베이어 벨트 [keonbeieo belteu]; **money belt** n 전대 [jeondae]; **safety belt** n 안전벨트 [anjeonbelteu]
bench [bɛntʃ] n 벤치 [benchi]
bend [bɛnd] n 굽은 부분 [gubeun bubun] ▷ v 굽히다 [guphida]; **bend down** v 굽히다 [guphida]; **bend over** v 굽히다 [guphida]
beneath [bɪ'niːθ] prep...의 밑에 [...ui mite]
benefit ['bɛnɪfɪt] n 이익 [iik] ▷ v 이익이 되다 [iigi doeda]
bent [bɛnt] adj (dishonest) 부정직한 [bujeongjikhan], (not straight) 굽은 [gubeun]
beret ['bɛreɪ] n 베레모 [beremo]
berry ['bɛrɪ] n 베리 [beri]
berth [bɜːθ] n 침대 [chimdae]
beside [bɪ'saɪd] prep...의 옆에 [...ui yeope]
besides [bɪ'saɪdz] adv 게다가 [gedaga]
best [bɛst] adj 최고의 [choegoui] ▷ adv 최고로 [choegoro]; **best man** n 신랑 들러리 [sillang deulleori]
bestseller [,bɛst'sɛlə] n 베스트셀러 [beseuteuselleo]
bet [bɛt] n 내기 [naegi] ▷ v 내기하다 [naegihada]
betray [bɪ'treɪ] v 배신하다 [baesinhada]
better ['bɛtə] adj 더 좋은 [deo joheun] ▷ adv 더 좋게 [deo joke]
betting ['bɛtɪŋ] n 내기 [naegi]; **betting shop** n 도박장 [dobakjang]
between [bɪ'twiːn] prep 사이에 [saie]
bewildered [bɪ'wɪldəd] adj 당황한 [danghwanghan]
beyond [bɪ'jɒnd] prep...의 너머에 [...ui neomeoe]

biased ['baɪəst] adj 편견을 가진 [pyeongyeoneul gajin]
bib [bɪb] n 턱받이 [teokbaji]
Bible ['baɪbəl] n 성경 [seonggyeong]
bicarbonate [baɪ'kɑːbənɪt; -,neɪt] n **bicarbonate of soda** n 중탄산소다 [jungtansansoda]
bicycle ['baɪsɪkəl] n 지전거 [jajeongeo]; **bicycle pump** n 자전거 펌프 [jajeongeo peompeu]
bid [bɪd] n 입찰 [ipchal] ▷ v (at auction) 입찰하다 [ipchalhada]
bifocals [baɪ'fəʊkəlz] npl 이중 초점 안경 [ijung chojeom angyeong]
big [bɪg] adj 큰 [keun]
bigger [bɪgə] adj 더 큰 [deo keun]; **Do you have a bigger one?** 더 큰 방 있어요? [deo keun bang isseoyo?]
bigheaded ['bɪg,hɛdɪd] adj 자만심이 강한 [jamansimi ganghan]
bike [baɪk] n 자전거, 오토바이 [jajeongeo, otobai]; **mountain bike** n 산악 자전거 [sanak jajeongeo]
bikini [bɪ'kiːnɪ] n 비키니 [bikini]
bilingual [baɪ'lɪŋgwəl] adj 이중 언어의 [ijung eoneoui]
bill [bɪl] n (account) 계산서 [gyesanseo], (legislation) 법안 [beoban]; **phone bill** n 전화요금 고지서 [jeonhwayogeum gojiseo]; **Please bring the bill** 계산서 갖다 주세요 [gyesanseo gatda juseyo]; **Please prepare the bill** 계산서를 준비해 주세요 [gyesanseoreul junbihae juseyo]; **Separate bills, please** 계산서를 각자 주세요 [gyesanseoreul gakja juseyo]; **The bill is wrong** 계산서가 잘못됐어요 [gyesanseoga jalmotdwaesseoyo]
billiards ['bɪljədz] npl 당구 [danggu]
billion ['bɪljən] n 10억 [sibeok]
bin [bɪn] n 쓰레기통 [sseuregitong]; **litter bin** n 쓰레기통 [sseuregitong]
binding ['baɪndɪŋ] n **Can you adjust my bindings, please?** 결속 장치를 조여 주시겠어요? [gyeolsok jangchireul joyeo jusigesseoyo?]; **Can you tighten my bindings, please?** 결속 장치를

조여 주시겠어요? [gyeolsok jangchireul joyeo jusigesseoyo?]

bingo ['bɪŋgəʊ] n 빙고 [binggo]

binoculars [bɪ'nɒkjʊləz; baɪ-] npl 쌍안경 [ssangangyeong]

biochemistry [ˌbaɪəʊ'kɛmɪstrɪ] n 생화학 [saenghwahak]

biodegradable [ˌbaɪəʊdɪ'greɪdəbᵊl] adj 생물분해성의 [saengmulbunhaeseongui]

biography [baɪ'ɒgrəfɪ] n 전기 [jeongi]

biological [ˌbaɪə'lɒdʒɪkᵊl] adj 생물학의 [saengmulhagui]

biology [baɪ'ɒlədʒɪ] n 생물학 [saengmulhak]

biometric [ˌbaɪəʊ'mɛtrɪk] adj 생물 측정학의 [saengmul cheukjeonghagui]

birch [bɜːtʃ] n 자작나무 [jajangnamu]

bird [bɜːd] n 새 [sae]; **bird flu** n 조류 독감 [joryu dokgam]; **bird of prey** n 맹금 [maenggeum]

birdwatching [bɜːdwɒtʃɪŋ] n 새 관찰 [sae gwanchal]

Biro® ['baɪrəʊ] n 볼펜 상표명 [bolpen sangpyomyeong]

birth [bɜːθ] n 출생 [chulsaeng]; **birth certificate** n 출생 증명서 [chulsaeng jeungmyeongseo]; **birth control** n 산아 제한 [sana jehan]; **place of birth** n 출생지 [chulsaengji]

birthday ['bɜːθˌdeɪ] n 생일 [saengil]; **Happy birthday!** 생일 축하해요! [saengil chukhahaeyo!]

birthplace ['bɜːθˌpleɪs] n 출생지 [chulsaengji]

biscuit ['bɪskɪt] n 비스킷 [biseukit]

bishop ['bɪʃəp] n 주교 [jugyo]

bit [bɪt] n 작은 조각 [jageun jogak]

bitch [bɪtʃ] n 암캐 [amkae]

bite [baɪt] n 물기 [mulgi] ▷ v 물다 [mulda]

bitter ['bɪtə] adj 쓴 [sseun]

black [blæk] adj 검은 [geomeun]; **black ice** n 도로의 살얼음 [doroui sareoreum]

blackberry ['blækbərɪ] n 검은딸기 [geomeunttalgi]

blackbird ['blækˌbɜːd] n 지빠귓과의

명금 [jippagwitgwaui myeonggeum]

blackboard ['blækˌbɔːd] n 칠판 [chilpan]

blackcurrant [ˌblæk'kʌrənt] n 블랙커런트 [beullaekkeoreonteu]

blackmail ['blækˌmeɪl] n 협박 [hyeopbak] ▷ v 협박하다 [hyeopbakhada]

blackout ['blækaʊt] n 등화관제 [deunghwagwanje]

bladder ['blædə] n 방광 [banggwang]; **gall bladder** n 담낭 [damnang]

blade [bleɪd] n 날 [nal] (날카로운); **razor blade** n 면도날 [myeondonal]; **shoulder blade** n 견갑골 [gyeongapgol]

blame [bleɪm] n 비난 [binan] ▷ v 비난하다 [binanhada]

blank [blæŋk] adj 빈 [bin] ▷ n 공백 [gongbaek]; **blank cheque** n 백지 수표 [baekji supyo]

blanket ['blæŋkɪt] n 담요 [damyo]; **electric blanket** n 전기 담요 [jeongi damyo]; **Please bring me an extra blanket** 담요를 하나 더 갖다 주세요 [damyoreul hana deo gatda juseyo]; **We need more blankets** 담요가 더 필요해요 [damyoga deo pillyohaeyo]

blast [blɑːst] n 폭발 [pokbal]

blatant ['bleɪtᵊnt] adj 분명한 [bunmyeonghan]

blaze [bleɪz] n 불꽃 [bulkkot]

blazer ['bleɪzə] n 블레이저 [beulleijeo]

bleach [bliːtʃ] n 표백제 [pyobaekje]

bleached [bliːtʃt] adj 표백한 [pyobaekhan]

bleak [bliːk] adj 황량한 [hwangnyanghan]

bleed [bliːd] v 출혈하다 [chulhyeolhada]

bleeper ['bliːpə] n 삐삐 [ppippi]

blender ['blɛndə] n 믹서 [mikseo]

bless [blɛs] v 축복하다 [chukbokhada]

blind [blaɪnd] adj 눈 먼 [nun meon] ▷ n 블라인드 [beullaindeu]; **Venetian blind** n 베니션 블라인드 [benisyeon beullaindeu]

blindfold ['blaɪndˌfəʊld] n 눈가리개

[nungarigae] ▷ v 눈을 가리다 [nuneul garida]

blink [blɪŋk] v 눈을 깜박이다 [nuneul kkambagida]

bliss [blɪs] n 행복 [haengbok]

blister ['blɪstə] n 수포 [supo]

blizzard ['blɪzəd] n 심한 눈보라 [simhan nunbora]

block [blɒk] n (buildings) 벽돌 [byeokdol], (obstruction) 장애물 [jangaemul], (solid piece) 덩어리 [deongeori] ▷ v 막다 [makda]

blockage ['blɒkɪdʒ] n 봉쇄 [bongswae]

blocked [blɒkt] adj 막힌 [makhin]

blog [blɒg] n 블로그 [beullogeu] ▷ v 블로그를 쓰다 [beullogeureul sseuda]

bloke [bləʊk] n 남 [nam]

blonde [blɒnd] adj 금발인 [geumbarin]

blood [blʌd] n 피 [pi]; **blood group** n 혈액형 [hyeoraekhyeong]; **blood poisoning** n 패혈증 [paehyeoljeung]; **blood pressure** n 혈압 [hyeorap]; **blood sports** n 피를 보는 스포츠 [pireul boneun seupocheu]; **blood test** n 혈액 검사 [hyeoraek geomsa]; **blood transfusion** n 수혈 [suhyeol]; **This stain is blood** 이 얼룩은 피예요 [i eollugeun piyeyo]

bloody ['blʌdɪ] adj 피투성이의 [pituseongiui]

blossom ['blɒsəm] n 꽃 [kkot] ▷ v 꽃이 피다 [kkochi pida]

blouse [blaʊz] n 블라우스 [beullauseu]

blow [bləʊ] n 강타 [gangta] ▷ v 불다 [bulda]

blow-dry [bləʊdraɪ] n 드라이어로 머리를 매만지기 [deuraieoro meorireul maemanjigi]

blow up [bləʊ ʌp] v 폭발하다 [pokbalhada]

blue [bluː] adj 파란 [paran]

blueberry ['bluːbərɪ; -brɪ] n 블루베리 [beulluberi]

blues [bluːz] npl 블루스 [beulluseu]

bluff [blʌf] n 허세 [heose] ▷ v 허세를 부리다 [heosereul burida]

blunder ['blʌndə] n 큰 실수 [keun sllsu]

blunt [blʌnt] adj 무딘 [mudin]

blush [blʌʃ] v 얼굴을 붉히다 [eolgureul burkhida]

blusher ['blʌʃə] n 볼터치 [bolteochi]

board [bɔːd] n (meeting) 위원회 [wiwonhoe], (wood) 판 [pan] ▷ v (go aboard) 판 [pan]; **board game** n 보드 게임 [bodeu geim]; **boarding card** n 탑승권 [tapseunggwon]; **boarding pass** n 탑승권 [tapseunggwon]; **boarding school** n 기숙학교 [gisukhakgyo]; **bulletin board** n 게시판 [gesipan]; **diving board** n 다이빙대 [daibingdae]; **draining board** n 식기 건조대 [sikgi geonjodae]; **half board** n 1박 2식 제공 [ilbak isik jegong]; **ironing board** n 다리미판 [darimipan]; **notice board** n 게시판 [gesipan]; **skirting board** n 굽도리널 [gupdorineol]

boarder ['bɔːdə] n 기숙생 [gisuksaeng]

boast [bəʊst] v 자랑하다 [jaranghada]

boat [bəʊt] n 배 [bae]; **fishing boat** n 어선 [eoseon]; **rowing boat** n 젓는 배 [jeotneun bae]; **sailing boat** n 범선 [beomseon]; **When is the first boat?** 첫 배는 언제 있어요? [cheot baeneun eonje isseoyo?]; **When is the last boat?** 마지막 배는 언제 있어요? [majimak baeneun eonje isseoyo?]; **Where does the boat leave from?** 배는 어디에서 출발하나요? [baeneun eodieseo chulbalhanayo?]

body ['bɒdɪ] n 몸 [mom]

bodybuilding ['bɒdɪˌbɪldɪŋ] n 보디빌딩 [bodibilding]

bodyguard ['bɒdɪˌgɑːd] n 경호원 [gyeonghowon]

bog [bɒg] n 늪 [neup]

boil [bɔɪl] vi 끓다 [kkeurta]

boiled [bɔɪld] adj 삶은 [sarmeun]; **boiled egg** n 삶은 달걀 [sarmeun dalgyal]

boiler ['bɔɪlə] n 보일러 [boilleo]

boiling ['bɔɪlɪŋ] adj 끓는 [kkeurnneun]

boil over [bɔɪl ˈəʊvə] v 끓어 넘치다 [kkeureo neomchida]

Bolivia [bəˈlɪvɪə] n 볼리비아 [bollibia]

Bolivian [bə'lɪvɪən] *adj* 볼리비아의 [bollibiaui] ▷ *n* 볼리비아 사람 [bollibia saram]

bolt [bəʊlt] *n* 빗장 [bitjang]

bomb [bɒm] *n* 폭탄 [poktan] ▷ *v* 폭격하다 [pokgyeokhada]; **atom bomb** *n* 원자폭탄 [wonjapoktan]

bombing [bɒmɪŋ] *n* 폭격 [pokgyeok]

bond [bɒnd] *n* 묶는 것 [mukkneun geot]

bone [bəʊn] *n* 뼈 [ppyeo]; **bone dry** *adj* 메마른 [memareun]

bonfire ['bɒn,faɪə] *n* 모닥불 [modakbul]

bonnet ['bɒnɪt] *n (car)* 보닛 [bonit]

bonus ['bəʊnəs] *n* 보너스 [boneoseu]

book [bʊk] *n* 책 [chaek] ▷ *v* 예약하다 [yeyakhada]; **address book** *n* 주소록 [jusorok]

bookcase ['bʊk,keɪs] *n* 책장 [chaekjang]

booking ['bʊkɪŋ] *n* 예약 [yeyak]; **advance booking** *n* 예약 [yeyak]; **booking office** *n* 매표소 [maepyoso]; **Can I change my booking?** 예약을 변경할 수 있을까요? [yeyageul byeongyeonghal su isseulkkayo?]; **I want to cancel my booking** 예약을 취소하고 싶어요 [yeyageul chwisohago sipeoyo]; **Is there a booking fee?** 예약 비용이 있어요? [yeyak biyongi isseoyo?]

booklet ['bʊklɪt] *n* 소책자 [sochaekja]

bookmark ['bʊk,mɑːk] *n* 책갈피 [chaekgalpi]

bookshelf ['bʊk,ʃɛlf] *n* 책장 [chaekjang]

bookshop ['bʊk,ʃɒp] *n* 서점 [seojeom]

boost [buːst] *v* 끌어올리다 [kkeureoollida]

boot [buːt] *n* 장화 [janghwa]

booze [buːz] *n* 술 [sul] (음료수)

border ['bɔːdə] *n* 경계 [gyeonggye] (가장자리)

bore [bɔː] *v (be dull)* 지겹다 [jigyeopda], *(drill)* 구멍을 뚫다 [gumeongeul tturta]

bored [bɔːd] *adj* 지루한 [jiruhan]

boredom ['bɔːdəm] *n* 지루함 [jiruham]

boring ['bɔːrɪŋ] *adj* 지루한 [jiruhan]

born [bɔːn] *adj* 태생의 [taesaengui]

borrow ['bɒrəʊ] *v* 빌리다 [billida]

Bosnia ['bɒznɪə] *n* 보스니아 [boseunia]; **Bosnia Herzegovina** *n* 보스니아 헤르체고비나 [boseunia hereuchegobina]

Bosnian ['bɒznɪən] *adj* 보스니아의 [boseuniaui] ▷ *n (person)* 보스니아 사람 [boseunia saram]

boss [bɒs] *n* 상사 [sangsa]

boss around [bɒs ə'raʊnd] *v* 쥐고 흔들다 [jwigo heundeulda]

bossy ['bɒsɪ] *adj* 오만한 [omanhan]

both [bəʊθ] *adj* 양쪽의 [yangjjogui] ▷ *pron* 양쪽 [yangjjok]

bother ['bɒðə] *v* 괴롭히다 [goerophida]

Botswana [bʊ'tʃwɑːnə; bʊt'swɑːnə; bɒt-] *n* 보츠와나 [bocheuwana]

bottle ['bɒtᵊl] *n* 병 [byeong]; **baby's bottle** *n* 아기 젖병 [agi jeotbyeong]; **bottle bank** *n* 빈 병 수거함 [bin byeong sugeoham]; **hot-water bottle** *n* 탕파 [tangpa]; **a bottle of mineral water** 생수 한 병 [saengsu han byeong]; **a bottle of red wine** 레드 와인 한 병 [redeu wain han byeong]; **Please bring another bottle** 한 병 더 갖다 주세요 [han byeong deo gatda juseyo]

bottle-opener ['bɒtᵊl,əʊpənə] *n* 병따개 [byeongttagae]

bottom ['bɒtəm] *adj* 바닥의 [badagui] ▷ *n* 바닥 [badak]

bought [bɔːt] *adj* 구입한 [guiphan]

bounce [baʊns] *v* 튀다 [twida]

bouncer ['baʊnsə] *n* 유흥업소 경비원 [yuheungeopso gyeongbiwon]

boundary ['baʊndərɪ; -drɪ] *n* 경계 [gyeonggye] (한계)

bouquet ['buːkeɪ] *n* 꽃다발 [kkottabal]

bow *n* [bəʊ] *(weapon)* 활 [hwal] ▷ *v* [baʊ] 절하다 [jeolhada]

bowels ['baʊəlz] *npl* 내장 [naejang]

bowl [bəʊl] *n* 그릇 [geureut]

bowling ['bəʊlɪŋ] *n* 볼링 [bolling]; **bowling alley** *n* 볼링 레인 [bolling rein]; **tenpin bowling** *n* 텐핀 볼링

[tenpin bolling]
bow tie [bəʊ] *n* **bow tie** *n* 나비 넥타이 [nabi nektai]
box [bɒks] *n* 상자 [sangja]; **box office** *n* 매표소 [maepyoso]; **call box** *n* 공중 전화 박스 [gongjung jeonhwa bakseu]; **fuse box** *n* 두꺼비집 [dukkeobijip]; **gear box** *n* 용구함 [yongguham]
boxer [ˈbɒksə] *n* 권투 선수 [gwontu seonsu]; **boxer shorts** *npl* 사각팬티 [sagakpaenti]
boxing [ˈbɒksɪŋ] *n* 권투 [gwontu]
boy [bɔɪ] *n* 소년 [sonyeon]
boyfriend [ˈbɔɪˌfrɛnd] *n* 남자 친구 [namja chingu]
bra [brɑː] *n* 브래지어 [beuraejieo]
brace [breɪs] *n (fastening)* 버팀대 [beotimdae]
bracelet [ˈbreɪslɪt] *n* 팔찌 [paljji]
braces [ˈbreɪsɪz] *npl* 멜빵 [melppang]
brackets [ˈbrækɪts] *npl* 괄호 [gwalho]
brain [breɪn] *n* 뇌 [noe]
brainy [ˈbreɪnɪ] *adj* 총명한 [chongmyeonghan]
brake [breɪk] *n* 브레이크 [beureikeu] ▷ *v* 브레이크를 걸다 [beureikeureul geolda]; **brake light** *n* 정지등 [jeongjideung]; **Does the bike have back-pedal brakes?** 자전거에 페달을 거꾸로 밟아 제동하는 브레이크가 있어요? [jajeongeoe pedareul geokkuro barba jedonghaneun beureikeuga isseoyo?]; **The brakes don't work** 브레이크가 작동하지 않아요 [beureikeuga jakdonghaji anhayo]
bran [bræn] *n* 왕겨 [wanggyeo]
branch [brɑːntʃ] *n* 가지 [gaji]
brand [brænd] *n* 상표 [sangpyo]; **brand name** *n* 상표명 [sangpyomyeong]
brand-new [brænd'njuː] *adj* 신상품 [sinsangpum]
brandy [ˈbrændɪ] *n* 브랜디 [beuraendi]; **I'll have a brandy** 브랜디 주세요 [beuraendi juseyo]
brass [brɑːs] *n* 황동 [hwangdong]; **brass band** *n* 관악대 [gwanakdae]
brat [bræt] *n* 꼬마 [kkoma]

brave [breɪv] *adj* 용감한 [yonggamhan]
bravery [ˈbreɪvərɪ] *n* 용기 [yonggi]
Brazil [brəˈzɪl] *n* 브라질 [beurajil]
Brazilian [brəˈzɪljən] *adj* 브라질의 [beurajirui] ▷ *n* 브라질 사람 [beurajil saram]
bread [brɛd] *n* 식빵 [sikppang]; **bread roll** *n* 롤 빵 [rol ppang]; **brown bread** *n* 흑빵 [heukppang]
bread bin [brɛdbɪn] *n* 빵 상자 [ppang sangja]
breadcrumbs [ˈbrɛdˌkrʌmz] *npl* 빵가루 [ppanggaru]
break [breɪk] *n* 깨짐 [kkaejim] ▷ *v* 깨다 [kkaeda] (금이 가다); **lunch break** *n* 점심시간 [jeomsimsigan]
break down [breɪk daʊn] *v* 고장나다 [gojangnada]
breakdown [ˈbreɪkdaʊn] *n* 고장 [gojang]; **breakdown truck** *n* 견인차 [gyeonincha]; **breakdown van** *n* 견인차 [gyeonincha]; **nervous breakdown** *n* 신경 쇠약 [singyeong soeyak]; **Call the breakdown service, please** 고장 서비스를 불러 주세요 [gojang seobiseureul bulleo juseyo]
breakfast [ˈbrɛkfəst] *n* 아침 식사 [achim siksa]; **bed and breakfast** *n* 아침 제공 숙박 [achim jegong sukbak]; **continental breakfast** *n* 대륙식의 아침식사 [daeryuksigui achimsiksa]; **What would you like for breakfast?** 아침 식사로 뭘 드시겠어요? [achim siksaro mwol deusigesseoyo?]
break in [breɪk ɪn] *v* 침입하다 [chimiphada]
break-in [ˈbreɪkɪn] *n* 침입 [chimip]
break up [breɪk ʌp] *v* 부수다 [busuda]
breast [brɛst] *n* 가슴 [gaseum]
breast-feed [ˈbrɛstˌfiːd] *v* 모유를 먹이다 [moyureul meogida]
breaststroke [ˈbrɛstˌstrəʊk] *n* 평영 [pyeongyeong]
breath [brɛθ] *n* 숨 [sum]
Breathalyser® [ˈbrɛθəˌlaɪzə] *n* 음주 측정기 상표명 [eumju cheukjeonggi sangpyomyeong]
breathe [briːð] *v* 숨을 쉬다 [sumeul

swida]

breathe in [bri:ð ɪn] v 들이쉬다 [deuriswida]

breathe out [bri:ð aʊt] v 내쉬다 [naeswida]

breathing ['bri:ðɪŋ] n 호흡 [hoheup]

breed [bri:d] n 품종 [pumjong] ▷ v 새끼를 낳다 [saekkireul nata]

breeze [bri:z] n 산들바람 [sandeulbaram]

brewery ['brʊərɪ] n 양조장 [yangjojang]

bribe [braɪb] v 뇌물을 주다 [noemureul juda]

bribery ['braɪbərɪ; 'bribery] n 뇌물 수수 [noemul susu]

brick [brɪk] n 벽돌 [byeokdol]

bricklayer ['brɪkˌleɪə] n 벽돌공 [byeokdolgong]

bride [braɪd] n 신부 [sinbu]

bridegroom ['braɪdˌgru:m; -ˌgrʊm] n 신랑 [sillang]

bridesmaid ['braɪdzˌmeɪd] n 신부 들러리 [sinbu deulleori]

bridge [brɪdʒ] n 다리 [dari]; **suspension bridge** n 현수교 [hyeonsugyo]

brief [bri:f] adj 잠시의 [jamsiui]

briefcase ['bri:fˌkeɪs] n 서류 가방 [seoryu gabang]

briefing ['bri:fɪŋ] n 브리핑 [beuriping]

briefly ['bri:flɪ] adv 간단히 [gandanhi]

briefs [bri:fs] npl 브리프 [beuripeu]

bright [braɪt] adj 밝은 [balgeun]

brilliant ['brɪljənt] adj 빛나는 [bitnaneun]

bring [brɪŋ] v 가져오다 [gajyeooda]

bring back [brɪŋ bæk] v 돌려주다 [dollyeojuda]

bring forward [brɪŋ 'fɔ:wəd] v 앞당기다 [apdanggida]

bring up [brɪŋ ʌp] v 키우다 [kiuda]

Britain ['brɪtən] n 영국 [yeongguk]

British ['brɪtɪʃ] adj 영국의 [yeonggugui] ▷ n 영국 사람 [yeongguk saram]

broad [brɔ:d] adj 폭이 넓은 [pogi neorbeun]

broadband ['brɔ:dˌbænd] n 광대역 [gwangdaeyeok]

broadcast ['brɔ:dˌkɑ:st] n 방송 [bangsong] ▷ v 방송하다 [bangsonghada]

broad-minded [brɔ:d'maɪndɪd] adj 너그러운 [neogeureoun]

broccoli ['brɒkəlɪ] n 브로콜리 [beurokolli]

brochure ['brəʊʃʊə; -ʃə] n 소책자 [sochaekja]

broke [brəʊk] adj 무일푼의 [muilpunui]

broken ['brəʊkən] adj 부서진 [buseojin]; **broken down** adj 고장난 [gojangnan]

broker ['brəʊkə] n 중개인 [junggaein]

bronchitis [brɒŋ'kaɪtɪs] n 기관지염 [gigwanjiyeom]

bronze [brɒnz] n 청동 [cheongdong]

brooch [brəʊtʃ] n 브로치 [beurochi]

broom [bru:m; brʊm] n 비 [bi]

broth [brɒθ] n 수프 [supeu]

brother ['brʌðə] n 형제 [hyeongje]

brother-in-law ['brʌðə ɪn lɔ:] n 시숙 [sisuk] (husband's brother)

brown [braʊn] adj 갈색의 [galsaegui]; **brown bread** n 흑빵 [heukppang]; **brown rice** n 현미 [hyeonmi]

browse [braʊz] v 훑어보다 [hurteoboda]

browser ['braʊzə] n 브라우저 [beuraujeo]

bruise [bru:z] n 타박상 [tabaksang]

brush [brʌʃ] n 솔 [sol] ▷ v 솔질하다 [soljilhada]

brutal ['bru:təl] adj 잔인한 [janinhan]

bubble ['bʌbəl] n 거품 [geopum]; **bubble bath** n 거품 목욕 [geopum mogyok]; **bubble gum** n 풍선껌 [pungseonkkeom]

bucket ['bʌkɪt] n 버킷 [beokit]

buckle ['bʌkəl] n 버클 [beokeul]

Buddha ['bʊdə] n 부처 [bucheo]

Buddhism ['bʊdɪzəm] n 불교 [bulgyo]

Buddhist ['bʊdɪst] adj 불교의 [bulgyoui] ▷ n 불교도 [bulgyodo]

budgerigar ['bʌdʒərɪˌgɑ:] n 잉꼬 [ingkko]

budget ['bʌdʒɪt] n 예산 [yesan]

budgie [ˈbʌdʒɪ] *n* 잉꼬 [ingkko]
buffalo [ˈbʌfələʊ] *n* 버팔로 [beopallo]
buffet [ˈbʊfeɪ] *n* 뷔페 [bwipe]; **buffet car** *n* 식당차 [sikdangcha]
bug [bʌg] *n* 벌레 [beolle]; **There are bugs in my room** 제 방에 벌레가 있어요 [je bange beollega isseoyo]
bugged [ˈbʌgd] *adj* 도청장치가 된 [docheongjangchiga doen]
buggy [ˈbʌgɪ] *n* 경마차 [gyeongmacha]
build [bɪld] *v* 짓다 [jitda]
builder [ˈbɪldə] *n* 건축업자 [geonchugeopja]
building [ˈbɪldɪŋ] *n* 건물 [geonmul]; **building site** *n* 건축 부지 [geonchuk buji]
bulb [bʌlb] *n* (electricity) 전구 [jeongu], (plant) 구근 [gugeun]
Bulgaria [bʌlˈgɛərɪə; bʊl-] *n* 불가리아 [bulgaria]
Bulgarian [bʌlˈgɛərɪən; bʊl-] *adj* 불가리아의 [bulgariaui] ▷ *n* (language) 불가리아어 [bulgariaeo], (person) 불가리아 사람 [bulgaria saram]
bulimia [bjuːˈlɪmɪə] *n* 과식증 [gwasikjeung]
bull [bʊl] *n* 황소 [hwangso]
bulldozer [ˈbʊlˌdəʊzə] *n* 불도저 [buldojeo]
bullet [ˈbʊlɪt] *n* 총알 [chongal]
bully [ˈbʊlɪ] *n* 불량배 [bullyangbae] ▷ *v* 약자를 괴롭히다 [yakjareul goerophida]
bum [bʌm] *n* 엉덩이 [eongdeongi]; **bum bag** *n* 허리 주머니 [heori jumeoni]
bumblebee [ˈbʌmbəlˌbiː] *n* 호박벌 [hobakbeol]
bump [bʌmp] *n* 충돌 [chungdol]; **bump into** *v* 우연히 만나다 [uyeonhi mannada]
bumper [ˈbʌmpə] *n* 범퍼 [beompeo]
bumpy [ˈbʌmpɪ] *adj* 울퉁불퉁한 [ultungbultunghan]
bun [bʌn] *n* 작은 빵 [jageun ppang]
bunch [bʌntʃ] *n* 송이 [songi] (꽃)
bungalow [ˈbʌŋgəˌləʊ] *n* 방갈로 [banggallo]

bungee jumping [ˈbʌndʒɪ] *n* 번지점프 [beonjijeompeu]
bunion [ˈbʌnjən] *n* 건막류 [geonmangnyu]
bunk [bʌŋk] *n* 침대 [chimdae]; **bunk beds** *npl* 이층 침대 [icheung chimdae]
buoy [bɔɪ; ˈbuːɪ] *n* 부표 [bupyo]
burden [ˈbɜːdən] *n* 짐 [jim]
bureaucracy [bjʊəˈrɒkrəsɪ] *n* 관료주의 [gwallyojuui]
bureau de change [ˈbjʊərəʊ də ˈʃɒnʒ] *n* 환전소 [hwanjeonso]; **I need to find a bureau de change** 환전소를 찾아야 해요 [hwanjeonsoreul chajaya haeyo]; **Is there a bureau de change here?** 여기에 환전소가 있나요? [yeogie hwanjeonsoga innayo?]; **When is the bureau de change open?** 환전소는 언제 열어요? [hwanjeonsoneun eonje yeoreoyo?]
burger [ˈbɜːgə] *n* 햄버거 [haembeogeo]
burglar [ˈbɜːglə] *n* 강도 [gangdo]; **burglar alarm** *n* 도난 경보기 [donan gyeongbogi]
burglary [ˈbɜːglərɪ] *n* 강도죄 [gangdojoe]
burgle [ˈbɜːgəl] *v* 강도질하다 [gangdojilhada]
Burma [ˈbɜːmə] *n* 버마 [beoma]
Burmese [bɜːˈmiːz] *adj* 버마의 [beomaui] ▷ *n* (language) 버마어 [beomaeo], (person) 버마 사람 [beoma saram]
burn [bɜːn] *n* 화상 [hwasang] ▷ *v* 불태우다 [bultaeuda]
burn down [bɜːn daʊn] *v* 전소하다 [jeonsohada]
burp [bɜːp] *n* 트림 [teurim] ▷ *v* 트림하다 [teurimhada]
burst [bɜːst] *v* 폭발하다 [pokbalhada]
bury [ˈbɛrɪ] *v* 파묻다 [pamutda]
bus [bʌs] *n* 버스 [beoseu]; **airport bus** *n* 공항버스 [gonghangbeoseu]; **bus station** *n* 버스 정류장 [beoseu jeongnyujang]; **bus stop** *n* 버스 정류장 [beoseu jeongnyujang]; **bus ticket** *n* 버스 승차권 [beoseu seungchagwon]; **Does this bus go to...?** 이 버스...

가나요? [i beoseu... ganayo?]; **Excuse me, which bus goes to…?** 실례합니다, 어느 버스가... 에 가나요? [sillyehamnida, eoneu beoseuga... e ganayo?]; **How often are the buses to…?** ... 가는 버스는 얼마나 자주 오나요? [... ganeun beoseuneun eolmana jaju onayo?]; **Is there a bus to the airport?** 공항 가는 버스가 있어요? [gonghang ganeun beoseuga isseoyo?]; **What time does the bus leave?** 버스는 몇 시에 떠나요? [beoseuneun myeot sie tteonayo?]; **What time is the last bus?** 마지막 버스는 몇 시에 있어요? [majimak beoseuneun myeot sie isseoyo?]; **When is the next bus to…?** ... 가는 다음 버스는 언제 있어요? [... ganeun daeum beoseuneun eonje isseoyo?]; **Where can I buy a bus card?** 어디에서 버스 카드를 살 수 있을까요? [eodieseo beoseu kadeureul sal su isseulkkayo?]; **Where can I get a bus to…?** 어디에서... 가는 버스를 탈 수 있어요? [eodieseo... ganeun beoseureul tal su isseoyo?]; **Where is the bus station?** 버스 정류장은 어디있어요? [beoseu jeongnyujangeun eodiisseoyo?]

bush [bʊʃ] n (shrub) 관목 [gwanmok], (thicket) 덤불 [deombul]

business ['bɪznɪs] n 사업 [saeop]; **business class** n 비즈니스 석 [bijeuniseu seok]; **business trip** n 출장 [chuljang]; **show business** n 쇼 비즈니스 [syo bijeuniseu]; **I'm here on business** 사업차 왔어요 [saeopcha wasseoyo]

businessman, businessmen ['bɪznɪs‚mæn; -mən, 'bɪznɪs‚mɛn] n 사업가 [saeopga]; **I'm a businessman** 사업가입니다 [saeopgaimnida]

businesswoman, businesswomen ['bɪznɪs‚wʊmən, 'bɪznɪs‚wimin] n 여성 사업가 [yeoseong saeopga]

busker ['bʌskə] n 노상 연예인 [nosang yeonyein]

bust [bʌst] n 여성의 가슴 [yeoseongui gaseum]

busy ['bɪzɪ] adj 바쁜 [bappeun]; **busy signal** n 통화 중 신호 [tonghwa jung sinho]

but [bʌt] conj 그러나 [geureona]

butcher ['bʊtʃə] n 정육점 주인 [jeongyukjeom juin]

butcher's ['bʊtʃəz] n 정육점 [jeongyukjeom]

butter ['bʌtə] n 버터 [beoteo]; **peanut butter** n 땅콩 버터 [ttangkong beoteo]

buttercup ['bʌtə‚kʌp] n 미나리아재비 [minariajaebi]

butterfly ['bʌtə‚flaɪ] n 나비 [nabi]

buttocks ['bʌtəks] npl 엉덩이 [eongdeongi]

button ['bʌtᵊn] n 단추 [danchu]; **belly button** n 배꼽 [baekkop]

buy [baɪ] v 사다 [sada]

buyer ['baɪə] n 구매자 [gumaeja]

buyout ['baɪ‚aʊt] n 매점 [maejeom]

by [baɪ] prep ...곁에서 [...gyeoteseo]

bye [baɪ] excl 안녕! [annyeong!]

bye-bye [baɪbaɪ] excl 안녕! [annyeong!]

bypass ['baɪ‚pɑːs] n 우회로 [uhoero]

C

cab [kæb] *n* 택시 [taeksi]

cabbage ['kæbɪdʒ] *n* 양배추 [yangbaechu]

cabin ['kæbɪn] *n* 선실 [seonsil]; **cabin crew** *n* 객실 승무원 [gaeksil seungmuwon]

cabinet ['kæbɪnɪt] *n* 캐비닛 [kaebinit]

cable ['keɪbəl] *n* 케이블 [keibeul]; **cable car** *n* 케이블카 [keibeulka]; **cable television** *n* 유선 텔레비전 [yuseon tellebijeon]

cactus ['kæktəs] *n* 선인장 [seoninjang]

cadet [kə'dɛt] *n* 생도 [saengdo]

café ['kæfeɪ; 'kæfɪ] *n* 카페 [kape]; **Internet café** *n* 인터넷 카페 [inteonet kape]; **Are there any Internet cafés here?** 여기에 인터넷 카페가 있나요? [yeogie inteonet kapega innayo?]

cafeteria [ˌkæfɪ'tɪərɪə] *n* 카페테리아 [kapeteria]

caffeine ['kæfiːn; 'kæfɪˌiːn] *n* 카페인 [kapein]

cage [keɪdʒ] *n* 새장 [saejang]

cagoule [kə'guːl] *n* 카굴 [kagul]

cake [keɪk] *n* 케이크 [keikeu]

calcium ['kælsɪəm] *n* 칼슘 [kalsyum]

calculate ['kælkjʊˌleɪt] *v* 계산하다 [gyesanhada]

calculation [ˌkælkjʊ'leɪʃən] *n* 계산 [gyesan]

calculator ['kælkjʊˌleɪtə] *n* 계산기 [gyesangi]; **pocket calculator** *n* 휴대 계산기 [hyudae gyesangi]

calendar ['kælɪndə] *n* 달력 [dallyeok]

calf, calves [kɑːf, kɑːvz] *n* 송아지 [songaji]

call [kɔːl] *n* 외침 [oechim] ▷ *v* 부르다 [bureuda]; **alarm call** *n* 비상 경보 [bisang gyeongbo]; **call box** *n* 공중 전화 박스 [gongjung jeonhwa bakseu]; **call centre** *n* 콜센터 [kolsenteo]; **roll call** *n* 점호 [jeomho]

call back [kɔːl bæk] *v* 다시 전화하다 [dasi jeonhwahada]

call for [kɔːl fɔː] *v* 요구하다 [yoguhada]

call off [kɔːl ɒf] *v* 철회하다 [cheolhoehada]

calm [kɑːm] *adj* 고요한 [goyohan]

calm down [kɑːm daʊn] *v* 진정하다 [jinjeonghada]

calorie ['kælərɪ] *n* 칼로리 [kallori]

Cambodia [kæm'bəʊdɪə] *n* 캄보디아 [kambodia]

Cambodian [kæm'bəʊdɪən] *adj* 캄보디아의 [kambodiaui] ▷ *n* (*person*) 캄보디아 사람 [kambodia saram]

camcorder ['kæmˌkɔːdə] *n* 캠코더 [kaemkodeo]

camel ['kæməl] *n* 낙타 [nakta]

camera ['kæmərə; 'kæmrə] *n* 카메라 [kamera]; **camera phone** *n* 카메라폰 [kamerapon]; **digital camera** *n* 디지털 카메라 [dijiteol kamera]; **video camera** *n* 비디오 카메라 [bidio kamera]

cameraman, cameramen ['kæmərəˌmæn; 'kæmrə-, 'kæmərəˌmɛn] *n* 카메라맨 [kameramaen]

Cameroon [ˌkæmə'ruːn; 'kæməˌruːn] *n* 카메룬 [kamerun]

camp [kæmp] *n* 야영지 [yayeongji] ▷ *v* 야영하다 [yayeonghada]; **camp bed** *n* 야전침대 [yajeonchimdae]

campaign [kæm'peɪn] *n* 캠페인

[kaempein]

camper ['kæmpə] n 야영자 [yayeongja]

camping ['kæmpɪŋ] n 야영 [yayeong]; **camping gas** n 캠핑 가스 [kaemping gaseu]

campsite ['kæmp,saɪt] n 야영지 [yayeongji]

campus ['kæmpəs] n 교정 [gyojeong]

can [kæn] v 할 수 있다 [hal su itda]; **watering can** n 물뿌리개 [mulppurigae]

Canada ['kænədə] n 캐나다 [kaenada]

Canadian [kə'neɪdɪən] adj 캐나다의 [kaenadaui] ▷ n 캐나다 사람 [kaenada saram]

canal [kə'næl] n 운하 [unha]

Canaries [kə'nɛəri:z] npl 카나리아 제도 [kanaria jedo]

canary [kə'nɛərɪ] n 카나리아 [kanaria]

cancel ['kænsəl] v 취소하다 [chwisohada]

cancellation [,kænsɪ'leɪʃən] n 취소 [chwiso]; **Are there any cancellations?** 예약 취소된 표 있어요? [yeyak chwisodoen pyo isseoyo?]

cancer ['kænsə] n (illness) 암 [am]

Cancer ['kænsə] n (horoscope) 게자리 [gejari]

candidate ['kændɪ,deɪt; -dɪt] n 후보 [hubo]

candle ['kændəl] n 양초 [yangcho]

candlestick ['kændəl,stɪk] n 촛대 [chotdae]

candyfloss ['kændɪ,flɒs] n 솜사탕 [somsatang]

canister ['kænɪstə] n 작은 깡통 [jageun kkangtong]

cannabis ['kænəbɪs] n 칸나비스 [kannabiseu]

canned [kænd] adj 통조림한 [tongjorimhan]

canoe [kə'nu:] n 카누 [kanu]

canoeing [kə'nu:ɪŋ] n 카누타기 [kanutagi]

can-opener ['kæn'əʊpənə] n 깡통따개 [kkangtongttagae]

canteen [kæn'ti:n] n 구내 식당 [gunae sikdang]

canter ['kæntə] v 느린 구보로 달리다 [neurin guboro dallida]

canvas ['kænvəs] n 캔버스 [kaenbeoseu]

canvass ['kænvəs] v 선거유세하다 [seongeoyusehada]

cap [kæp] n 모자 [moja]; **baseball cap** n 야구 모자 [yagu moja]

capable ['keɪpəbəl] adj ...할 능력이 있는 [...hal neungnyeogi inneun]

capacity [kə'pæsɪtɪ] n 수용량 [suyongnyang]

capital ['kæpɪtəl] n 수도 [sudo] (도시)

capitalism ['kæpɪtə,lɪzəm] n 자본주의 [jabonjuui]

Capricorn ['kæprɪ,kɔ:n] n 염소자리 [yeomsojari]

capsize [kæp'saɪz] v 뒤집히다 [dwijiphida]

capsule ['kæpsju:l] n 캡슐 [kaepsyul]

captain ['kæptɪn] n 선장 [seonjang]

caption ['kæpʃən] n 표제 [pyoje]

capture ['kæptʃə] v 붙잡다 [butjapda]

car [kɑ:] n 자동차 [jadongcha]; **buffet car** n 식당차 [sikdangcha]; **cable car** n 케이블카 [keibeulka]; **car hire** n 자동차 임대 [jadongcha imdae]; **car park** n 주차장 [juchajang]; **car rental** n 자동차 임대 [jadongcha imdae]; **car wash** n 세차 [secha]; **company car** n 회사차 [hoesacha]; **dining car** n 식당차 [sikdangcha]; **estate car** n 스테이션 왜건 [seuteisyeon waegeon]; **hired car** n 렌트카 [renteuka]; **patrol car** n 순찰차 [sunchalcha]; **racing car** n 경주용차 [gyeongjuyongcha]; **rental car** n 렌트카 [renteuka]; **saloon car** n 승용차 [seungyongcha]; **sleeping car** n 침대차 [chimdaecha]

carafe [kə'ræf; -'rɑ:f] n 유리 물병 [yuri mulbyeong]

caramel ['kærəməl; -,mɛl] n 캐러멜 [kaereomel]

carat ['kærət] n 캐럿 [kaereot]

caravan ['kærə,væn] n 트레일러 하우스 [teureilleo hauseu]; **caravan site** n 트레일러 하우스 주차장 [teureilleo hauseu juchajang]

carbohydrate [ˌkɑːbəʊˈhaɪdreɪt] *n* 탄수화물 [tansuhwamul]

carbon [ˈkɑːbᵊn] *n* 탄소 [tanso]; **carbon footprint** *n* 탄소배출량 [tansobaechullyang]

carburettor [ˌkɑːbjʊˈrɛtə; ˈkɑːbjʊˌrɛtə; -bə-] *n* 기화기 [gihwagi]

card [kɑːd] *n* 카드 [kadeu]; **boarding card** *n* 탑승권 [tapseunggwon]; **credit card** *n* 신용카드 [sinyongkadeu]; **debit card** *n* 직불카드 [jikbulkadeu]; **greetings card** *n* 카드 [kadeu]; **ID card** *abbr* 신분증 [sinbunjeung]; **membership card** *n* 회원 카드 [hoewon kadeu]; **playing card** *n* 카드 [kadeu]; **report card** *n* 성적표 [seongjeokpyo]; **top-up card** *n* 충전카드 [chungjeonkadeu]; **A memory card for this digital camera, please** 이 디지털 카메라에 사용하는 메모리 카드 주세요 [i dijiteol kamerae sayonghaneun memori kadeu juseyo]; **Can I use my card to get cash?** 카드로 현금을 뽑을 수 있을까요? [kadeuro hyeongeumeul ppobeul su isseulkkayo?]; **Do you sell phone cards?** 전화카드 파세요? [jeonhwakadeu paseyo?]; **Do you take credit cards?** 신용카드 받으세요? [sinyongkadeu badeuseyo?]; **Do you take debit cards?** 직불 카드 받으세요? [jikbul kadeu badeuseyo?]; **I need to cancel my card** 제 카드를 정지시켜야 해요 [je kadeureul jeongjisikyeoya haeyo]; **My card has been stolen** 카드를 도둑맞았어요 [kadeureul dodungmajasseoyo]; **Where can I post these cards?** 이 카드들을 어디에서 부칠 수 있어요? [i kadeudeureul eodieseo buchil su isseoyo?]

cardboard [ˈkɑːdˌbɔːd] *n* 판지 [panji]

cardigan [ˈkɑːdɪɡən] *n* 가디건 [gadigeon]

cardphone [ˈkɑːdfəʊn] *n* 카드 공중 전화 [kadeu gongjung jeonhwa]

care [kɛə] *n* 주의 [juui] ▷ *v* 돌보다 [dolboda]; **intensive care unit** *n* 중환자실 [junghwanjasil]

career [kəˈrɪə] *n* 경력 [gyeongnyeok]

careful [ˈkɛəfʊl] *adj* 조심스러운 [josimseureoun]

carefully [ˈkɛəfʊlɪ] *adv* 조심스럽게 [josimseureopge]

careless [ˈkɛəlɪs] *adj* 부주의한 [bujuuihan]

caretaker [ˈkɛəˌteɪkə] *n* 관리인 [gwalliin]

car-ferry [ˈkɑːfɛrɪ] *n* 카페리 [kaperi]

cargo [ˈkɑːɡəʊ] *n* 화물 [hwamul]

Caribbean [ˌkærɪˈbiːən; kəˈrɪbɪən] *adj* 카리브 해의 [karibeu haeui] ▷ *n* 카리브 해 [karibeu hae]

caring [ˈkɛərɪŋ] *adj* 돌보는 [dolboneun]

carnation [kɑːˈneɪʃən] *n* 카네이션 [kaneisyeon]

carnival [ˈkɑːnɪvᵊl] *n* 카니발 [kanibal]

carol [ˈkærəl] *n* 캐럴 [kaereol]

carpenter [ˈkɑːpɪntə] *n* 목수 [moksu]

carpentry [ˈkɑːpɪntrɪ] *n* 목수일 [moksuil]

carpet [ˈkɑːpɪt] *n* 카펫 [kapet]; **fitted carpet** *n* 바닥 전체를 덮는 카펫 [badak jeonchereul deomneun kapet]

carriage [ˈkærɪdʒ] *n* 객차 [gaekcha]

carriageway [ˈkærɪdʒˌweɪ] *n* **dual carriageway** *n* 중앙 분리대가 있는 도로 [jungang bullidaega inneun doro]

carrot [ˈkærət] *n* 당근 [danggeun]

carry [ˈkærɪ] *v* 운반하다 [unbanhada]

carrycot [ˈkærɪˌkɒt] *n* 아기용 휴대 침대 [agiyong hyudae chimdae]

carry on [ˈkærɪ ɒn] *v* 계속하다 [gyesokhada]

carry out [ˈkærɪ aʊt] *v* 실행하다 [silhaenghada]

cart [kɑːt] *n* 손수레 [sonsure]

carton [ˈkɑːtᵊn] *n* 상자 [sangja]

cartoon [kɑːˈtuːn] *n* 만화 [manhwa]

cartridge [ˈkɑːtrɪdʒ] *n* 탄창 [tanchang]

carve [kɑːv] *v* 새기다 [saegida]

case [keɪs] *n* 사례 [sarye] (보기); **pencil case** *n* 필통 [piltong]

cash [kæʃ] *n* 현금 [hyeongeum]; **cash dispenser** *n* 현금 인출기 [hyeongeum inchulgi]; **cash register** *n* 금전 출납기 [geumjeon chullapgi]; **Can I get a cash advance with my credit card?** 신용 카드로 현금 서비스를 받을 수 있을까요? [sinyong kadeuro hyeongeum seobiseureul badeul su isseulkkayo?]; **Do you offer a discount for cash?** 현금으로 내면 할인되나요? [hyeongeumeuro naemyeon harindoenayo?]; **I don't have any cash** 현금이 없어요 [hyeongeumi eopseoyo]; **I want to cash a cheque, please** 수표를 현금으로 바꾸고 싶어요 [supyoreul hyeongeumeuro bakkugo sipeoyo]; **Is there a cash machine here?** 여기에 현금 인출기가 있나요? [yeogie hyeongeum inchulgiga innayo?]; **Where is the nearest cash machine?** 가장 가까운 현금 인출기는 어디있어요? [gajang gakkaun hyeongeum inchulgineun eodiisseoyo?]

cashew ['kæʃuː; 'kæʃuː] *n* 캐슈 [kaesyu]

cashier [kæ'ʃɪə] *n* 출납원 [chullabwon]

cashmere ['kæʃmɪə] *n* 캐시미어 [kaesimieo]

casino [kə'siːnəʊ] *n* 도박장 [dobakjang]

casserole ['kæsə,rəʊl] *n* 캐서롤 [kaeseorol]

cassette [kæ'sɛt] *n* 카세트 [kaseteu]

cast [kɑːst] *n* 배역 [baeyeok]

castle ['kɑːsᵊl] *n* 성 [seong]

casual ['kæʒjʊəl] *adj* 우연한 [uyeonhan]

casually ['kæʒjʊəlɪ] *adv* 우연하게 [uyeonhage]

casualty ['kæʒjʊəltɪ] *n* 사상자 [sasangja]

cat [kæt] *n* 고양이 [goyangi]

catalogue ['kætə,lɒg] *n* 소책자 [sochaekja]

cataract ['kætə,rækt] *n* (*eye*) 백내장 [baengnaejang], (*waterfall*) 큰 폭포 [keun pokpo]

catarrh [kə'tɑː] *n* 카타르 [katareu]

catastrophe [kə'tæstrəfɪ] *n* 대참사 [daechamsa]

catch [kætʃ] *v* 잡다 [japda]

catching ['kætʃɪŋ] *adj* 전염성의 [jeonyeomseongui]

catch up [kætʃ ʌp] *v* 따라잡다 [ttarajapda]

category ['kætɪgərɪ] *n* 범주 [beomju]

catering ['keɪtərɪŋ] *n* 케이터링 [keiteoring]

caterpillar ['kætə,pɪlə] *n* 애벌레 [aebeolle]

cathedral [kə'θiːdrəl] *n* 대성당 [daeseongdang]; **When is the cathedral open?** 이 대성당은 언제 열어요? [i daeseongdangeun eonje yeoreoyo?]

Catholic ['kæθəlɪk; 'kæθlɪk] *adj* 가톨릭교의 [gatollikgyoui] ▷ *n* 가톨릭교도 [gatollikgyodo]; **Roman Catholic** *n* 천주교도 [cheonjugyodo], 천주교의 [cheonjugyoui]

cattle ['kætᵊl] *npl* 가축 [gachuk]

Caucasus ['kɔːkəsəs] *n* 카프카스 산맥 [kapeukaseu sanmaek]

cauliflower ['kɒlɪ,flaʊə] *n* 콜리플라워 [kollipeullawo]

cause [kɔːz] *n* (*ideals*) 원인 [wonin] (이상적), (*reason*) 원인 [wonin] ▷ *v* 원인이 되다 [wonini doeda]

caution ['kɔːʃən] *n* 조심 [josim]

cautious ['kɔːʃəs] *adj* 조심하는 [josimhaneun]

cautiously ['kɔːʃəslɪ] *adv* 조심스럽게 [josimseureopge]

cave [keɪv] *n* 동굴 [donggul]

CCTV [si: si: ti: vi:] *abbr* 폐쇄 회로 TV [pyeswae hoero TV]

CD [si: di:] *n* 콤팩트디스크 [kompaekteudiseukeu]; **CD burner** *n* CD 기록 장치 [CD girok jangchi]; **CD player** *n* CD 플레이어 [CD peulleieo]

CD-ROM [-'rɒm] *n* CD롬 [CDrom]

ceasefire ['siːsˈfaɪə] *n* 휴전 [hyujeon]

ceiling ['siːlɪŋ] *n* 천장 [cheonjang]

celebrate ['sɛlɪ,breɪt] *v* 경축하다 [gyeongchukhada]

celebration ['sɛlɪ,breɪʃən] *n* 축하 [chukha]

celebrity [sɪ'lɛbrɪtɪ] n 유명 인사 [yumyeong insa]

celery ['sɛlərɪ] n 셀러리 [selleori]

cell [sɛl] n 세포 [sepo]

cellar ['sɛlə] n 지하실 [jihasil]

cello ['tʃɛləʊ] n 첼로 [chello]

cement [sɪ'mɛnt] n 시멘트 [simenteu]

cemetery ['sɛmɪtrɪ] n 묘지 [myoji]

census ['sɛnsəs] n 인구 조사 [ingu josa]

cent [sɛnt] n 센트 [senteu]

centenary [sɛn'tiːnərɪ] n 100년 [baeng nyeon]

centimetre ['sɛntɪˌmiːtə] n 센티미터 [sentimiteo]

central ['sɛntrəl] adj 중심의 [jungsimui]; **central heating** n 중앙 난방 [jungang nanbang]; **Central America** n 중앙 아메리카 [jungang amerika]

centre ['sɛntə] n 중심 [jungsim]; **call centre** n 콜센터 [kolsenteo]; **city centre** n 도심 [dosim]; **job centre** n 구직센터 [gujiksenteo]; **leisure centre** n 레저 센터 [rejeo senteo]; **shopping centre** n 쇼핑센터 [syopingsenteo]; **town centre** n 도심 [dosim]; **visitor centre** n 관광 안내소 [gwangwang annaeso]; **How do I get to the centre of...?** ... 중심가에 어떻게 가나요? [... jungsimgae eotteoke ganayo?]

century ['sɛntʃərɪ] n 1 세기 [il segi]

CEO [siː iː əʊ] abbr 최고 경영자 [choego gyeongyeongja]

ceramic [sɪ'ræmɪk] adj 세라믹의 [seramigui]

cereal ['sɪərɪəl] n 시리얼 [sirieol]

ceremony ['sɛrɪmənɪ] n 의식 [uisik]

certain ['sɜːtən] adj 확신하는 [hwaksinhaneun]

certainly ['sɜːtənlɪ] adv 확실히 [hwaksilhi]

certainty ['sɜːtəntɪ] n 확실성 [hwaksilseong]

certificate [sə'tɪfɪkɪt] n 증명서 [jeungmyeongseo]; **birth certificate** n 출생 증명서 [chulsaeng jeungmyeongseo]; **marriage certificate** n 결혼 증명서 [gyeolhon jeungmyeongseo]; **medical certificate** n 의사소견서 [uisasogyeonseo]; **I need a 'fit to fly' certificate** '비행 적합' 증명서가 필요해요 ['bihaeng jeokhab' jeungmyeongseoga piryohaeyo]

Chad [tʃæd] n 차드 [chadeu]

chain [tʃeɪn] n 사슬 [saseul]

chair [tʃɛə] n (furniture) 의자 [uija]; **easy chair** n 안락 의자 [allak uija]; **rocking chair** n 흔들의자 [heundeuruija]; **Do you have a high chair?** 높은 의자 있어요? [nopeun uija isseoyo?]

chairlift ['tʃɛəˌlɪft] n 스키장 리프트 [seukijang ripeuteu]

chairman, chairmen ['tʃɛəmən, 'tʃɛəmɛn] n 의장 [uijang]

chalk [tʃɔːk] n 분필 [bunpil]

challenge ['tʃælɪndʒ] n 도전 [dojeon] ▷ v 도전하다 [dojeonhada]

challenging ['tʃælɪndʒɪŋ] adj 도전적인 [dojeonjeogin]

chambermaid ['tʃeɪmbəˌmeɪd] n 객실 담당 여직원 [gaeksil damdang yeojigwon]

champagne [ʃæm'peɪn] n 샴페인 [syampein]

champion ['tʃæmpɪən] n 챔피언 [chaempieon]

championship ['tʃæmpɪənˌʃɪp] n 챔피언쉽 [chaempieonswip]

chance [tʃɑːns] n 기회 [gihoe]; **by chance** adv 우연히 [uyeonhi]

change [tʃeɪndʒ] n 변화 [byeonhwa] ▷ vi 변하다 [byeonhada] ▷ vt 바꾸다 [bakkuda]; **changing room** n 탈의실 [taruisil]

changeable ['tʃeɪndʒəbəl] adj 변하기 쉬운 [byeonhagi siwun]

channel ['tʃænəl] n 해협 [haehyeop]

chaos ['keɪɒs] n 혼돈 [hondon]

chaotic ['keɪ'ɒtɪk] adj 혼돈된 [hondondoen]

chap [tʃæp] n 남자 [namja]

chapel ['tʃæpəl] n 예배당 [yebaedang]

chapter ['tʃæptə] n 장 [jang] (책)

character ['kærɪktə] n 특성

[teukseong]
characteristic [ˌkærɪktə'rɪstɪk] n 특성 [teukseong]

charcoal ['tʃɑːˌkəʊl] n 숯 [sut]

charge [tʃɑːdʒ] n (accusation) 고발 [gobal], (electricity) 전하 [jeonha] (전기), (price) 요금 [yogeum] ▷ v (accuse) 고발하다 [gobalhada], (electricity) 충전하다 [chungjeonhada], (price) (대금을) 부과하다 [(daegeumeul) bugwahada]; **admission charge** n 입장료 [ipjangnyo]; **cover charge** n 봉사료 [bongsaryo]; **service charge** n 서비스 요금 [seobiseu yogeum]; **Is there a charge for the service?** 서비스 요금이 있어요? [seobiseu yogeumi isseoyo?]; **Is there a mileage charge?** 주행거리에 따른 요금이 있어요? [juhaenggeorie ttareun yogeumi isseoyo?]

charger ['tʃɑːdʒə] n 충전기 [chungjeongi]

charity ['tʃærɪtɪ] n 자선 [jaseon]; **charity shop** n 자선 상점 [jaseon sangjeom]

charm [tʃɑːm] n 매력 [maeryeok]

charming ['tʃɑːmɪŋ] adj 매력적인 [maeryeokjeogin]

chart [tʃɑːt] n 도표 [dopyo]; **pie chart** n 원 그래프 [won geuraepeu]

chase [tʃeɪs] n 추적 [chujeok] ▷ v 추적하다 [chujeokhada]

chat [tʃæt] n 잡담 [japdam] ▷ v 잡담하다 [japdamhada]; **chat show** n 토크쇼 [tokeusyo]

chatroom ['tʃæt,ruːm; -,rʊm] n 대화방 [daehwabang]

chauffeur ['ʃəʊfə; ʃəʊ'fɜː] n 운전 기사 [unjeon gisa]

chauvinist ['ʃəʊvɪ,nɪst] n 열광적애국주의자 [yeolgwangjeogaegukjuuija]

cheap [tʃiːp] adj 싼 [ssan]; **Do you have anything cheaper?** 더 싼 거 있어요? [deo ssan geo isseoyo?]; **I'd like the cheapest option** 가장 싼 것이 좋아요 [gajang ssan geosi johayo]

cheat [tʃiːt] n 속임수 [sogimsu] ▷ v 속이다 [sogida]

Chechnya ['tʃɛtʃnjə] n 체첸 공화국 [chechen gonghwaguk]

check [tʃɛk] n 확인 [hwagin] ▷ v 점검하다 [jeomgeomhada]; **Can you check the water, please?** 물을 확인해 주시겠어요? [mureul hwaginhae jusigesseoyo?]

checked [tʃɛkt] adj 체크 무늬의 [chekeu munuiui]

check in [tʃɛk ɪn] v 체크인하다 [chekeuinhada]

check-in [tʃɛkɪn] n 체크인 [chekeuin]

check out [tʃɛk aʊt] v 체크아웃하다 [chekeuautada]

checkout ['tʃɛkaʊt] n 체크아웃 [chekeuaut]

check-up ['tʃɛkʌp] n 검사 [geomsa]

cheek [tʃiːk] n 뺨 [ppyam]

cheekbone ['tʃiːkˌbəʊn] n 광대뼈 [gwangdaeppyeo]

cheeky ['tʃiːkɪ] adj 무례한 [muryehan]

cheer [tʃɪə] n 갈채 [galchae] ▷ v 성원하다 [seongwonhada]

cheerful ['tʃɪəfʊl] adj 쾌활한 [kwaehwalhan]

cheerio [ˌtʃɪərɪ'əʊ] excl 안녕! [annyeong!]

cheers [tʃɪəz] excl 건배! [geonbae!]

cheese [tʃiːz] n 치즈 [chijeu]; **cottage cheese** n 코티지 치즈 [kotiji chijeu]; **What sort of cheese?** 어떤 치즈인가요? [eotteon chijeuingayo?]

chef [ʃɛf] n 요리사 [yorisa]

chemical ['kɛmɪkəl] n 화학 제품 [hwahak jepum]

chemist ['kɛmɪst] n 약사 [yaksa]; **chemist('s)** n 약국 [yakguk]

chemistry ['kɛmɪstrɪ] n 화학 [hwahak]

cheque [tʃɛk] n 수표 [supyo]; **blank cheque** n 백지 수표 [baekji supyo]; **traveller's cheque** n 여행자 수표 [yeohaengja supyo]; **Can I cash a cheque?** 수표를 현금으로 바꿀 수 있을까요? [supyoreul hyeongeumeuro bakkul su isseulkkayo?]; **Can I change my traveller's cheques here?**

여기에서 여행자 수표를 현금으로 바꿀 수 있을까요? [yeogieseo yeohaengja supyoreul hyeongeumeuro bakkul su isseulkkayo?]; **Can I pay by cheque?** 수표로 지불할 수 있나요? [supyoro jibulhal su innayo?]; **I want to change these traveller's cheques** 이 여행자 수표를 현금으로 바꾸고 싶어요 [i yeohaengja supyoreul hyeongeumeuro bakkugo sipeoyo]; **Someone's stolen my traveller's cheques** 누군가가 제 여행자 수표를 훔쳐 갔어요 [nugungaga je yeohaengja supyoreul humchyeo gasseoyo]

chequebook ['tʃɛk,bʊk] n 수표장 [supyojang]

cherry ['tʃɛrɪ] n 버찌 [beojji]

chess [tʃɛs] n 체스 [cheseu]

chest [tʃɛst] n (body part) 가슴 [gaseum], (storage) 상자 [sangja]; **chest of drawers** n 서랍장 [seorapjang]; **I have a pain in my chest** 가슴이 아파요 [gaseumi apayo]

chestnut ['tʃɛs,nʌt] n 밤 [bam]

chew [tʃuː] v 씹다 [ssipda]; **chewing gum** n 껌 [kkeom]

chick [tʃɪk] n 병아리 [byeongari]

chicken ['tʃɪkɪn] n 닭 [dalg]

chickenpox ['tʃɪkɪn,pɒks] n 수두 [sudu]

chickpea ['tʃɪk,piː] n 병아리콩 [byeongarikong]

chief [tʃiːf] adj 주요한 [juyohan] ▷ n 대표 [daepyo]

child, children [tʃaɪld, 'tʃɪldrən] n 아이 [ai]; **child abuse** n 아동학대 [adonghakdae]; **I don't have any children** 아이가 없어요 [aiga eopseoyo]; **I have three children** 아이가 셋 있어요 [aiga set isseoyo]; **I need someone to look after the children tonight** 오늘 밤에 아이들을 봐 줄 사람이 필요해요 [oneul bame aideureul bwa jul sarami piryohaeyo]; **I'm looking for a present for a child** 아이에게 줄 선물을 찾고 있어요 [aiege jul seonmureul chatgo isseoyo]; **Is it**

safe for children? 아이에게 안전한가요? [aiege anjeonhangayo?]; **My child is ill** 아이가 아파요 [aiga apayo]; **My child is missing** 아이가 없어졌어요 [aiga eopseojyeosseoyo]; **My children are in the car** 아이들이 차 안에 있어요 [aideuri cha ane isseoyo]; **The child is on this passport** 이 여권에는 아이가 등록되어 있어요 [i yeogwoneneun aiga deungnokdoeeo isseoyo]

childcare ['tʃaɪld,kɛə] n 육아 [yuga]

childhood ['tʃaɪldhʊd] n 어린 시절 [eorin sijeol]

childish ['tʃaɪldɪʃ] adj 유치한 [yuchihan]

childminder ['tʃaɪld,maɪndə] n 보모 [bomo]

Chile ['tʃɪlɪ] n 칠레 [chille]

Chilean ['tʃɪlɪən] adj 칠레의 [chilleui] ▷ n 칠레 사람 [chille saram]

chill [tʃɪl] v 식히다 [sikhida]

chilli ['tʃɪlɪ] n 칠리 [chilli]

chilly ['tʃɪlɪ] adj 쌀쌀한 [ssalssalhan]

chimney ['tʃɪmnɪ] n 굴뚝 [gulttuk]

chimpanzee [,tʃɪmpæn'ziː] n 침팬지 [chimpaenji]

chin [tʃɪn] n 턱 [teok]

china ['tʃaɪnə] n 도자기 [dojagi]

China ['tʃaɪnə] n 중국 [jungguk]

Chinese [tʃaɪ'niːz] adj 중국의 [junggugui] ▷ n (language) 중국어 [junggugeo], (person) 중국 사람 [jungguk saram]

chip [tʃɪp] n (electronic) 칩 [chip], (small piece) 조각 [jogak]; **silicon chip** n 실리콘 칩 [sillikon chip]

chips [tʃɪps] npl 감자칩 [gamjachip]

chiropodist [kɪ'rɒpədɪst] n 발치료 의사 [balchiryo uisa]

chisel ['tʃɪzəl] n 끌 [kkeul]

chives [tʃaɪvz] npl 부추 [buchu]

chlorine ['klɔːriːn] n 염소 [yeomso]

chocolate ['tʃɒkəlɪt; 'tʃɒklɪt; -lət] n 초콜릿 [chokollit]; **milk chocolate** n 밀크 초콜릿 [milkeu chokollit]; **plain chocolate** n 향료가 안 든 초콜릿 [hyangnyoga an deun chokollit]

choice [tʃɔɪs] n 선택 [seontaek]

choir [kwaɪə] n 합창단 [hapchangdan]

choke [tʃəʊk] v 숨이 막히다 [sumi makhida]

cholesterol [kə'lɛstə,rɒl] n 콜레스테롤 [kolleseuterol]

choose [tʃuːz] v 선택하다 [seontaekhada]

chop [tʃɒp] n 절단 [jeoldan] ▷ v 자르다 [jareuda]; **pork chop** n 돼지고기 토막 [dwaejigogi tomak]

chopsticks ['tʃɒpstɪks] npl 젓가락 [jeotgarak]

chosen ['tʃəʊzᵊn] adj 선발된 [seonbaldoen]

Christ [kraɪst] n 그리스도 [geuriseudo]

christening ['krɪsᵊnɪŋ] n 세례 [serye]

Christian ['krɪstʃən] adj 기독교의 [gidokgyoui] ▷ n 기독교도 [gidokgyodo]; **Christian name** n 세례명 [seryemyeong]

Christianity [,krɪstɪ'ænɪtɪ] n 기독교 신앙 [gidokgyo sinang]

Christmas ['krɪsməs] n 크리스마스 [keuriseumaseu]; **Christmas card** n 크리스마스 카드 [keuriseumaseu kadeu]; **Christmas Eve** n 크리스마스 이브 [keuriseumaseu ibeu]; **Christmas tree** n 크리스마스 트리 [keuriseumaseu teuri]; **Merry Christmas!** 메리 크리스마스! [meri keuriseumaseu!]

chrome [krəʊm] n 크롬 [keurom]

chronic ['krɒnɪk] adj 만성의 [manseongui]

chrysanthemum [krɪ'sænθəməm] n 국화 [gukhwa]

chubby ['tʃʌbɪ] adj 오동통한 [odongtonghan]

chunk [tʃʌŋk] n 큰 덩어리 [keun deongeori]

church [tʃɜːtʃ] n 교회 [gyohoe]; **Can we visit the church?** 교회를 방문할 수 있어요? [gyohoereul bangmunhal su isseoyo?]

cider ['saɪdə] n 사과즙 [sagwajeup]

cigar [sɪ'gɑː] n 시가 [siga] (담배를 피우다)

cigarette [,sɪgə'rɛt] n 담배 [dambae]; **cigarette lighter** n 라이터 [raiteo]

cinema ['sɪnɪmə] n 영화관 [yeonghwagwan]

cinnamon ['sɪnəmən] n 계피 [gyepi]

circle ['sɜːkᵊl] n 원 [won]; **Arctic Circle** n 북극권 [bukgeukgwon]

circuit ['sɜːkɪt] n 회로 [hoero]

circular ['sɜːkjʊlə] adj 원형의 [wonhyeongui]

circulation [,sɜːkjʊ'leɪʃən] n 순환 [sunhwan]

circumstances ['sɜːkəmstənsɪz] npl 환경 [hwangyeong]

circus ['sɜːkəs] n 서커스 [seokeoseu]

citizen ['sɪtɪzᵊn] n 시민 [simin]; **senior citizen** n 노인 [noin]

citizenship ['sɪtɪzən,ʃɪp] n 시민권 [simingwon]

city ['sɪtɪ] n 도시 [dosi]; **city centre** n 도심 [dosim]

civilian [sɪ'vɪljən] adj 민간의 [minganui] ▷ n 민간인 [minganin]

civilization [,sɪvɪlaɪ'zeɪʃən] n 문명 [munmyeong]

claim [kleɪm] n 요구 [yogu] ▷ v 요구하다 [yoguhada]; **claim form** n 청구서 [cheongguseo]

clap [klæp] v 박수치다 [baksuchida]

clarify ['klærɪ,faɪ] v 분명하게 하다 [bunmyeonghage hada]

clarinet [,klærɪ'nɛt] n 클라리넷 [keullarinet]

clash [klæʃ] v 충돌하다 [chungdolhada]

clasp [klɑːsp] n 걸쇠 [geolsoe]

class [klɑːs] n 계급 [gyegeup]; **business class** n 비즈니스 석 [bijeuniseu seok]; **economy class** n 이코노미 석 [ikonomi seok]; **second class** n 2류 [iryu]

classic ['klæsɪk] adj 전형적인 [jeonhyeongjeogin] ▷ n 고전 [gojeon] (오래된)

classical ['klæsɪkᵊl] adj 고전적인 [gojeonjeogin]

classmate ['klɑːs,meɪt] n 동급생 [donggeupsaeng]

classroom ['klɑːs,ruːm; -,rʊm] n 교실

[gyosil]; **classroom assistant** n 보조
교사 [bojo gyosa]

clause [klɔːz] n 조항 [johang]

claustrophobic [ˌklɔːstrəˈfəʊbɪk;
ˌklɒs-] adj 밀실 공포증의 [milsil
gongpojeungui]

claw [klɔː] n 발톱 [baltop]

clay [kleɪ] n 점토 [jeomto]

clean [kliːn] adj 깨끗한 [kkaekkeutan]
▷ v 깨끗하다 [kkaekkeutada]

cleaner [ˈkliːnə] n 청소부
[cheongsobu]; **When does the
cleaner come?** 청소부는 언제 오나요?
[cheongsobuneun eonje onayo?]

cleaning [ˈkliːnɪŋ] n 청소 [cheongso];
cleaning lady n 청소 아줌마
[cheongso ajumma]

cleanser [ˈklɛnzə] n 세척제 [secheokje]

clear [klɪə] adj 명백한
[myeongbaekhan]

clearly [ˈklɪəlɪ] adv 분명히
[bunmyeonghi]

clear off [klɪə ɒf] v 치우다 [chiuda]

clear up [klɪə ʌp] v 정돈하다
[jeongdonhada]

clementine [ˈklɛmənˌtiːn; -ˌtaɪn] n
클레멘타인 [keullementain]

clever [ˈklɛvə] adj 영리한 [yeongnihan]

click [klɪk] n 찰칵하는 소리
[chalkkakhaneun sori] ▷ v 찰칵 소리가
나다 [chalkkak soriga nada]

client [ˈklaɪənt] n 의뢰인 [uiroein]

cliff [klɪf] n 절벽 [jeolbyeok]

climate [ˈklaɪmɪt] n 기후 [gihu];
climate change n 기후 변화 [gihu
byeonhwa]

climb [klaɪm] v 등반하다
[deungbanhada]

climber [ˈklaɪmə] n 등산가
[deungsanga]

climbing [ˈklaɪmɪŋ] n 등반 [deungban]

clinic [ˈklɪnɪk] n 진료소 [jillyoso]

clip [klɪp] n 클립 [keullip]

clippers [ˈklɪpəz] npl 큰 가위 [keun
gawi]

cloakroom [ˈkləʊkˌruːm; -ˌrʊm] n
휴대품 보관소 [hyudaepum
bogwanso]

clock [klɒk] n 시계 [sigye]; **alarm clock** n
알람 시계 [allam sigye]

clockwise [ˈklɒkˌwaɪz] adv 시계
방향으로 [sigye banghyangeuro]

clog [klɒg] n 나막신 [namaksin]

clone [kləʊn] n 클론 [keullon] ▷ v
무성생식을 하다 [museongsaengsigeul
hada]

close adj [kləʊs] 가까운 [gakkaun] ▷ adv
[kləʊs] 가까이에 [gakkaie] ▷ v [kləʊz]
닫다 [datda]; **close by** adj 인접한
[injeophan]; **closing time** n 폐점 시간
[pyejeom sigan]

closed [kləʊzd] adj 닫힌 [dachin]

closely [kləʊslɪ] adv 밀접하게
[miljeophage]

closure [ˈkləʊʒə] n 종결 [jonggyeol]

cloth [klɒθ] n 천 [cheon]

clothes [kləʊðz] npl 옷 [ot]; **clothes line**
n 빨랫줄 [ppallaetjul]; **clothes peg** n
빨래 집게 [ppallae jipge]; **Is there
somewhere to dry clothes?** 옷을
건조시킬 곳이 있나요? [oseul
geonjosikil gosi innayo?]; **My clothes
are damp** 옷이 축축해요 [osi
chukchukhaeyo]

clothing [ˈkləʊðɪŋ] n 의복 [uibok]

cloud [klaʊd] n 구름 [gureum]

cloudy [ˈklaʊdɪ] adj 흐린 [heurin]; **It's
cloudy** 흐린 날씨에요 [heurin
nalssieyo]

clove [kləʊv] n 정향 [jeonghyang]

clown [klaʊn] n 어릿광대
[eoritgwangdae]

club [klʌb] n (group) 클럽 [keulleop],
(weapon) 무기 [mugi]; **golf club** n
(game) 골프채 [golpeuchae], (society)
골프 클럽 [golpeu keulleop]; **Where is
there a good club?** 좋은 클럽은
어디있어요? [joheun keulleobeun
eodiisseoyo?]

club together [klʌb təˈgɛðə] v 분담하다
[bundamhada]

clue [kluː] n 실마리 [silmari]

clumsy [ˈklʌmzɪ] adj 서투른
[seotureun]

clutch [klʌtʃ] n 클러치 [keulleochi]

clutter [ˈklʌtə] n 어질러진 물건

[eojilleojin mulgeon]

coach [kəʊtʃ] n (trainer) 코치 [kochi], (vehicle) 시외버스 [sioebeoseu]; **When does the coach leave in the morning?** 시외버스는 아침 언제 떠나요? [sioebeoseuneun achim eonje tteonayo?]

coal [kəʊl] n 석탄 [seoktan]

coarse [kɔːs] adj 거친 [geochin]

coast [kəʊst] n 해안 [haean]

coastguard [ˈkəʊstˌɡɑːd] n 해안 경비대 [haean gyeongbidae]

coat [kəʊt] n 코트 [koteu]; **fur coat** n 모피코트 [mopikoteu]

coathanger [ˈkəʊtˌhæŋə] n 옷걸이 [otgeori]

cobweb [ˈkɒbˌwɛb] n 거미집 [geomijip]

cocaine [kəˈkeɪn] n 코카인 [kokain]

cock [kɒk] n 수탉 [sutalg]

cockerel [ˈkɒkərəl; ˈkɒkrəl] n 수평아리 [supyeongari]

cockpit [ˈkɒkˌpɪt] n 조종실 [jojongsil]

cockroach [ˈkɒkˌrəʊtʃ] n 바퀴벌레 [bakwibeolle]

cocktail [ˈkɒkˌteɪl] n 칵테일 [kakteil]; **Do you sell cocktails?** 칵테일 파세요? [kakteil paseyo?]

cocoa [ˈkəʊkəʊ] n 코코아 [kokoa]

coconut [ˈkəʊkəˌnʌt] n 코코넛 [kokoneot]

cod [kɒd] n 대구 [daegu]

code [kəʊd] n 부호 [buho] (상징); **dialling code** n 국번 [gukbeon]; **Highway Code** n 교통규칙집 [gyotonggyuchikjip]

coeliac [ˈsiːlɪˌæk] adj 배의 [baeui]

coffee [ˈkɒfɪ] n 커피 [keopi]; **black coffee** n 블랙 커피 [beullaek keopi]; **decaffeinated coffee** n 무카페인 커피 [mukapein keopi]; **A white coffee, please** 크림만 넣은 커피 주세요 [keurimman neoheun keopi juseyo]; **Could we have another cup of coffee, please?** 커피 한 잔씩 더 주시겠어요? [keopi han janssik deo jusigesseoyo?]; **Have you got fresh coffee?** 방금 만든 커피 있어요? [banggeum mandeun keopi isseoyo?]

coffeepot [ˈkɒfɪˌpɒt] n 커피포트 [keopipoteu]

coffin [ˈkɒfɪn] n 관 [gwan]

coin [kɔɪn] n 동전 [dongjeon]; **I'd like some coins for the phone, please** 전화걸기 위해 동전을 바꾸고 싶어요 [jeonhwageolgi wihae dongjeoneul bakkugo sipeoyo]

coincide [ˌkəʊɪnˈsaɪd] v 동시에 일어나다 [dongsie ireonada]

coincidence [kəʊˈɪnsɪdəns] n 우연 [uyeon]

Coke® [kəʊk] n 코카콜라 [kokakolla]

colander [ˈkɒləndə; ˈkʌl-] n 여과기 [yeogwagi]

cold [kəʊld] adj 추운 [chuun] ▷ n 추위 [chuwi]; **cold sore** n 입가의 발진 [ipgaui baljin]

coleslaw [ˈkəʊlˌslɔː] n 양배추 샐러드 [yangbaechu saelleodeu]

collaborate [kəˈlæbəˌreɪt] v 협력하다 [hyeomnyeokhada]

collapse [kəˈlæps] v 무너지다 [muneojida]

collar [ˈkɒlə] n 칼라 [kalla]

collarbone [ˈkɒləˌbəʊn] n 쇄골 [swaegol]

colleague [ˈkɒliːɡ] n 동료 [dongnyo]

collect [kəˈlɛkt] v 모으다 [moeuda]

collection [kəˈlɛkʃən] n 수집 [sujip]

collective [kəˈlɛktɪv] adj 집합적인 [jiphapjeogin] ▷ n 집단 [jipdan]

collector [kəˈlɛktə] n 수집가 [sujipga]; **ticket collector** n 집표원 [jippyowon]

college [ˈkɒlɪdʒ] n 대학 [daehak]

collide [kəˈlaɪd] v 충돌하다 [chungdolhada]

collie [ˈkɒlɪ] n 콜리 [kolli]

colliery [ˈkɒljərɪ] n 탄광 [tangwang]

collision [kəˈlɪʒən] n 충돌 [chungdol]

Colombia [kəˈlɒmbɪə] n 콜롬비아 [kollombia]

Colombian [kəˈlɒmbɪən] adj 콜롬비아의 [kollombiaui] ▷ n 콜롬비아 사람 [kollombia saram]

colon [ˈkəʊlən] n 콜론 [kollon]

colonel [ˈkɜːnᵊl] n 육군 대령 [yukgun daeryeong]

colour ['kʌlə] n 색 [saek]; **Do you have this in another colour?** 다른 색 있어요? [dareun saek isseoyo?]; **I don't like the colour** 색이 마음에 들지 않아요 [saegi maeume deulji anhayo]

colour-blind ['kʌlə'blaɪnd] adj 색맹의 [saengmaengui]

colourful ['kʌləfʊl] adj 색채가 다양한 [saekchaega dayanghan]

colouring ['kʌlərɪŋ] n 착색 [chaksaek]

column ['kɒləm] n 기둥 [gidung]

coma ['kəʊmə] n 혼수 [honsu] (혼수상태)

comb [kəʊm] n 빗 [bit] ▷ v 빗다 [bitda]

combination [ˌkɒmbɪ'neɪʃən] n 결합 [gyeolhap]

combine [kəm'baɪn] v 결합시키다 [gyeolhapsikida]

come [kʌm] v 오다 [oda]

come back [kʌm bæk] v 돌아오다 [doraoda]

comedian [kə'miːdɪən] n 코미디언 [komidieon]

come down [kʌm daʊn] v 내려오다 [naeryeooda]

comedy ['kɒmɪdɪ] n 코미디 [komidi]

come from [kʌm frəm] v 출신이다 [chulsinida]

come in [kʌm ɪn] v 분명해지다 [bunmyeonghaejida]

come off [kʌm ɒf] v **The handle has come off** 손잡이가 빠졌어요 [sonjabiga ppajyeosseoyo]

come out [kʌm aʊt] v 밝혀지다 [barkhyeojida]

come round [kʌm raʊnd] v 의식을 회복하다 [uisigeul hoebokhada]

comet ['kɒmɪt] n 혜성 [hyeseong]

come up [kʌm ʌp] v 언급되다 [eongeupdoeda]

comfortable ['kʌmftəbəl; 'kʌmfətəbəl] adj 쾌적한 [kwaejeokhan]

comic ['kɒmɪk] n 코미디언 [komidieon]; **comic book** n 만화책 [manhwachaek]; **comic strip** n 만화 [manhwa]

coming ['kʌmɪŋ] adj 다가오는 [dagaoneun]

comma ['kɒmə] n 쉼표 [swimpyo]; **inverted commas** npl 따옴표 [ttaompyo]

command [kə'mɑːnd] n 명령 [myeongnyeong]

comment ['kɒmɛnt] n 논평 [nonpyeong] ▷ v 논평하다 [nonpyeonghada]

commentary ['kɒməntərɪ; -trɪ] n 논평 [nonpyeong]

commentator ['kɒmənˌteɪtə] n 해설자 [haeseolja]

commercial [kə'mɜːʃəl] n 광고 [gwanggo]; **commercial break** n 광고 [gwanggo]

commission [kə'mɪʃən] n 의뢰 [uiroe]

commit [kə'mɪt] v 저지르다 [jeojireuda]

committee [kə'mɪtɪ] n 위원회 [wiwonhoe]

common ['kɒmən] adj 공동의 [gongdongui]; **common sense** n 상식 [sangsik] (좋은 판단)

communicate [kə'mjuːnɪˌkeɪt] v 의사소통하다 [uisasotonghada]

communication [kəˌmjuːnɪ'keɪʃən] n 의사소통 [uisasotong]

communion [kə'mjuːnjən] n 성찬식 [seongchansik]

communism ['kɒmjʊˌnɪzəm] n 공산주의 [gongsanjuui]

communist ['kɒmjʊnɪst] adj 공산주의의 [gongsanjuuiui] ▷ n 공산주의자 [gongsanjuuija]

community [kə'mjuːnɪtɪ] n 공동체 [gongdongche]

commute [kə'mjuːt] v 통근하다 [tonggeunhada]

commuter [kə'mjuːtə] n 통근자 [tonggeunja]

compact [kəm'pækt] adj 꽉찬 [kkwakchan]; **compact disc** n 콤팩트디스크 [kompaekteudiseukeu]

companion [kəm'pænjən] n 동반자 [dongbanja]

company ['kʌmpənɪ] n 회사 [hoesa]; **company car** n 회사차 [hoesacha]; **I would like some information about**

the company 회사에 관한 정보를 받고 싶어요 [hoesae gwanhan jeongboreul batgo sipeoyo]

comparable ['kɒmpərəbəl] adj 비교되는 [bigyodoeneun]

comparatively [kəm'pærətɪvlɪ] adv 비교적 [bigyojeok]

compare [kəm'pɛə] v 비교하다 [bigyohada]

comparison [kəm'pærɪsən] n 비교 [bigyo]

compartment [kəm'pɑːtmənt] n 칸막이 [kanmagi]

compass ['kʌmpəs] n 나침반 [nachimban]

compatible [kəm'pætəbəl] adj 호환성 있는 [hohwanseong inneun]

compensate ['kɒmpɛnˌseɪt] v 보상하다 [bosanghada]

compensation [ˌkɒmpɛn'seɪʃən] n 보상 [bosang]

compere ['kɒmpɛə] n 사회자 [sahoeja]

compete [kəm'piːt] v 경쟁하다 [gyeongjaenghada]

competent ['kɒmpɪtənt] adj 유능한 [yuneunghan]

competition [ˌkɒmpɪ'tɪʃən] n 경쟁 [gyeongjaeng]

competitive [kəm'pɛtɪtɪv] adj 경쟁의 [gyeongjaengui]

competitor [kəm'pɛtɪtə] n 경쟁자 [gyeongjaengja]

complain [kəm'pleɪn] v 불평하다 [bulpyeonghada]

complaint [kəm'pleɪnt] n 불평하기 [bulpyeonghagi]

complementary [ˌkɒmplɪ'mɛntərɪ; -trɪ] adj 보충하는 [bochunghaneun]

complete [kəm'pliːt] adj 완전한 [wanjeonhan]

completely [kəm'pliːtlɪ] adv 완전히 [wanjeonhi]; **I want a completely new style** 완전히 새로운 스타일을 하고 싶어요 [wanjeonhi saeroun seutaireul hago sipeoyo]

complex ['kɒmplɛks] adj 복합적인 [bokhapjeogin] ▷ n 복합체 [bokhapche]

complexion [kəm'plɛkʃən] n 안색 [ansaek]

complicated ['kɒmplɪˌkeɪtɪd] adj 복잡한 [bokjaphan]

complication [ˌkɒmplɪ'keɪʃən] n 복잡 [bokjap]

compliment n ['kɒmplɪmənt] 칭찬 [chingchan] ▷ v ['kɒmplɪˌmɛnt] 칭찬하다 [chingchanhada]

complimentary [ˌkɒmplɪ'mɛntərɪ; -trɪ] adj 칭찬하는 [chingchanhaneun]

component [kəm'pəʊnənt] adj 구성하고 있는 [guseonghago inneun] ▷ n 성분 [seongbun]

composer [kəm'pəʊzə] n 작곡가 [jakgokga]

composition [ˌkɒmpə'zɪʃən] n 구성 [guseong]

comprehension [ˌkɒmprɪ'hɛnʃən] n 이해 [ihae]

comprehensive [ˌkɒmprɪ'hɛnsɪv] adj 포괄적인 [pogwaljeogin]

compromise ['kɒmprəˌmaɪz] n 타협 [tahyeop] ▷ v 타협하다 [tahyeophada]

compulsory [kəm'pʌlsərɪ] adj 강제적인 [gangjejeogin]

computer [kəm'pjuːtə] n 컴퓨터 [keompyuteo]; **computer game** n 컴퓨터 게임 [keompyuteo geim]; **computer science** n 컴퓨터 과학 [keompyuteo gwahak]; **May I use your computer?** 컴퓨터 좀 쓸 수 있을까요? [keompyuteo jom sseul su isseulkkayo?]; **My computer has frozen** 제 컴퓨터가 멈췄어요 [je keompyuteoga meomchwosseoyo]; **Where is the computer room?** 컴퓨터실은 어디에 있어요? [keompyuteosireun eodie isseoyo?]

computing [kəm'pjuːtɪŋ] n 컴퓨터 사용 [keompyuteo sayong]

concentrate ['kɒnsənˌtreɪt] v 집중하다 [jipjunghada]

concentration [ˌkɒnsən'treɪʃən] n 집중 [jipjung]

concern [kən'sɜːn] n 걱정 [geokjeong]

concerned [kən'sɜːnd] adj 걱정하는 [geokjeonghaneun]

concerning [kən'sɜːnɪŋ] prep ...에

관하여 [...e gwanhayeo]

concert ['kɒnsət] *n* 음악회 [eumakhoe]

concerto, concerti [kən'tʃɛətəʊ, kən'tʃɛətɪ] *n* 협주곡 [hyeopjugok]

concession [kən'sɛʃən] *n* 특허 [teukheo]

concise [kən'saɪs] *adj* 간결한 [gangyeolhan]

conclude [kən'kluːd] *v* 결말을 짓다 [gyeolmareul jitda]

conclusion [kən'kluːʒən] *n* 결론 [gyeollon]

concrete ['kɒnkriːt] *n* 콘크리트 [konkeuriteu]

concussion [kən'kʌʃən] *n* 뇌진탕 [noejintang]

condemn [kən'dɛm] *v* 비난하다 [binanhada]

condensation [ˌkɒndɛn'seɪʃən] *n* 응축 [eungchuk]

condition [kən'dɪʃən] *n* 조건 [jogeon]

conditional [kən'dɪʃənˀl] *adj* 조건부의 [jogeonbuui]

conditioner [kən'dɪʃənə] *n* 린스 [rinseu]

condom ['kɒndɒm; 'kɒndəm] *n* 콘돔 [kondom]

conduct [kən'dʌkt] *v* 실시하다 [silsihada]

conductor [kən'dʌktə] *n* 지휘자 [jihwija]; **bus conductor** *n* 버스 승무원 [beoseu seungmuwon]

cone [kəʊn] *n* 원뿔 [wonppul]

conference ['kɒnfərəns; -frəns] *n* 회의 [hoeui]; **press conference** *n* 기자회견 [gijahoegyeon]; **Please take me to the conference centre** 회의장으로 가 주세요 [hoeuijangeuro ga juseyo]

confess [kən'fɛs] *v* 고백하다 [gobaekhada]

confession [kən'fɛʃən] *n* 고백 [gobaek]

confetti [kən'fɛtɪ] *npl* 색종이 조각 [saekjongi jogak]

confidence ['kɒnfɪdəns] *n* (secret) 비밀 [bimil], (self-assurance) 자신감

[jasingam], (trust) 신뢰 [sinnoe]

confident ['kɒnfɪdənt] *adj* 확신하는 [hwaksinhaneun]

confidential [ˌkɒnfɪ'dɛnʃəl] *adj* 기밀의 [gimirui]

confirm [kən'fɜːm] *v* 확인하다 [hwaginhada]

confirmation [ˌkɒnfə'meɪʃən] *n* 확인 [hwagin]

confiscate ['kɒnfɪˌskeɪt] *v* 압수하다 [apsuhada]

conflict ['kɒnflɪkt] *n* 충돌 [chungdol]

confuse [kən'fjuːz] *v* 혼동하다 [hondonghada]

confused [kən'fjuːzd] *adj* 당황한 [danghwanghan]

confusing [kən'fjuːzɪŋ] *adj* 혼란시키는 [hollansikineun]

confusion [kən'fjuːʒən] *n* 혼란 [hollan]

congestion [kən'dʒɛstʃən] *n* 정체 [jeongche]

Congo ['kɒŋgəʊ] *n* 콩고 [konggo]

congratulate [kən'grætjʊˌleɪt] *v* 축하하다 [chukhahada]

congratulations [kənˌgrætjʊ'leɪʃənz] *npl* 축하 [chukha]

conifer ['kəʊnɪfə; 'kɒn-] *n* 구과 식물 [gugwa singmul]

conjugation [ˌkɒndʒʊ'geɪʃən] *n* 시간변화 [siganbyeonhwa]

conjunction [kən'dʒʌŋkʃən] *n* 결합 [gyeolhap]

conjurer ['kʌndʒərə] *n* 마술사 [masulsa]

connect [kə'nɛkt] *v* 연결하다 [yeongyeolhada]

connection [kə'nɛkʃən] *n* 연결 [yeongyeol]; **The connection seems very slow** 연결이 아주 느린 것 같아요 [yeongyeori aju neurin geot gatayo]

conquer ['kɒŋkə] *v* 정복하다 [jeongbokhada]

conscience ['kɒnʃəns] *n* 양심 [yangsim]

conscientious [ˌkɒnʃɪ'ɛnʃəs] *adj* 양심적인 [yangsimjeogin]

conscious ['kɒnʃəs] *adj* 의식하고 있는

[uisikhago inneun]
consciousness [ˈkɒnʃəsnɪs] *n* 의식
[uisik]
consecutive [kənˈsɛkjʊtɪv] *adj* 연속적인
[yeonsokjeogin]
consensus [kənˈsɛnsəs] *n* 일치 [ilchi]
consequence [ˈkɒnsɪkwəns] *n* 결과
[gyeolgwa]
consequently [ˈkɒnsɪkwəntlɪ] *adv*
따라서 [ttaraseo]
conservation [ˌkɒnsəˈveɪʃən] *n* 보존
[bojon]
conservative [kənˈsɜːvətɪv] *adj*
보수적인 [bosujeogin]
conservatory [kənˈsɜːvətrɪ] *n* 온실
[onsil]
consider [kənˈsɪdə] *v* 숙고하다
[sukgohada]
considerate [kənˈsɪdərɪt] *adj* 이해심
많은 [ihaesim manheun]
considering [kənˈsɪdərɪŋ] *prep* ...을
고려하면 [...eul goryeohamyeon]
consist [kənˈsɪst] *v* **consist of** *v*
구성되다 [guseongdoeda]
consistent [kənˈsɪstənt] *adj* 일관된
[ilgwandoen]
consonant [ˈkɒnsənənt] *n* 자음
[jaeum]
conspiracy [kənˈspɪrəsɪ] *n* 음모
[eummo] (계략)
constant [ˈkɒnstənt] *adj* 연속적인
[yeonsokjeogin]
constantly [ˈkɒnstəntlɪ] *adv* 지속적
[jisokjeok]
constipated [ˈkɒnstɪˌpeɪtɪd] *adj*
변비에 걸린 [byeonbie geollin]
constituency [kənˈstɪtjʊənsɪ] *n* 선거구
[seongeogu]
constitution [ˌkɒnstɪˈtjuːʃən] *n* 헌법
[heonbeop]
construct [kənˈstrʌkt] *v* 건설하다
[geonseolhada]
construction [kənˈstrʌkʃən] *n* 건설
[geonseol]
constructive [kənˈstrʌktɪv] *adj*
건설적인 [geonseoljeogin]
consul [ˈkɒnsəl] *n* 영사 [yeongsa]
consulate [ˈkɒnsjʊlɪt] *n* 영사관
[yeongsagwan]
consult [kənˈsʌlt] *v* 상의하다
[sanguihada]
consultant [kənˈsʌltªnt] *n* (*adviser*)
컨설턴트 [keonseolteonteu]
consumer [kənˈsjuːmə] *n* 소비자
[sobija]
contact *n* [ˈkɒntækt] 연락 [yeollak] ▷ *v*
[ˈkɒntækt] 접촉하다 [jeopchokhada];
contact lenses *npl* 콘텍트렌즈
[kontekteurenjeu]; **Where can I
contact you?** 어디로 연락 드리면
될까요? [eodiro yeollak deurimyeon
doelkkayo?]; **Who do we contact if
there are problems?** 문제가 있으면
누구에게 연락해야 할까요? [munjega
isseumyeon nuguege yeollakhaeya
halkkayo?]
contagious [kənˈteɪdʒəs] *adj* 전염성의
[jeonyeomseongui]
contain [kənˈteɪn] *v* 포함하다
[pohamhada]
container [kənˈteɪnə] *n* 용기 [yonggi]
contemporary [kənˈtɛmprərɪ] *adj*
동시대의 [dongsidaeui]
contempt [kənˈtɛmpt] *n* 모욕 [moyok]
content [ˈkɒntɛnt] *n* 내용 [naeyong];
contents (*list*) *npl* 목차 [mokcha]
contest [ˈkɒntɛst] *n* 경연
[gyeongyeon]
contestant [kənˈtɛstənt] *n* 경연 참가자
[gyeongyeon chamgaja]
context [ˈkɒntɛkst] *n* 맥락
[maengnak]
continent [ˈkɒntɪnənt] *n* 대륙
[daeryuk]
continual [kənˈtɪnjʊəl] *adj* 연속적인
[yeonsokjeogin]
continually [kənˈtɪnjʊəlɪ] *adv*
연속적으로 [yeonsokjeogeuro]
continue [kənˈtɪnjuː] *vi* 계속되다
[gyesokdoeda] ▷ *vt* 계속하다
[gyesokhada]
continuous [kənˈtɪnjʊəs] *adj* 연속적인
[yeonsokjeogin]
contraception [ˌkɒntrəˈsɛpʃən] *n* 피임
[piim]; **I need contraception** 피임이
필요해요 [piimi piryohaeyo]

contraceptive [ˌkɒntrə'sɛptɪv] n 피임약 [piimyak]

contract ['kɒntrækt] n 계약 [gyeyak]

contractor ['kɒntræktə; kən'træk-] n 계약자 [gyeyakja]

contradict [ˌkɒntrə'dɪkt] v 반박하다 [banbakhada]

contradiction [ˌkɒntrə'dɪkʃən] n 반박 [banbak]

contrary ['kɒntrərɪ] n 반대 [bandae]

contrast ['kɒntrɑːst] n 대조 [daejo]

contribute [kən'trɪbjuːt] v 기여하다 [giyeohada]

contribution [ˌkɒntrɪ'bjuːʃən] n 기여 [giyeo]

control [kən'trəʊl] n 통제 [tongje] ▷ v 통제하다 [tongjehada]; **birth control** n 산아 제한 [sana jehan]; **passport control** n 여권 검사 [yeogwon geomsa]; **remote control** n 리모컨 [rimokeon]

controller [kən'trəʊlə] n **air-traffic controller** n 항공 관제사 [hanggong gwanjesa]

controversial [ˌkɒntrə'vɜːʃəl] adj 논쟁의 [nonjaengui]

convenient [kən'viːnɪənt] adj 편리한 [pyeollihan]

convent ['kɒnvənt] n 수녀원 [sunyeowon]

conventional [kən'vɛnʃənəl] adj 전통적인 [jeontongjeogin]

conversation [ˌkɒnvə'seɪʃən] n 대화 [daehwa]

convert [kən'vɜːt] v 변하게 하다 [byeonhage hada]; **catalytic converter** n 촉매 변환 장치 [chongmae byeonhwan jangchi]

convertible [kən'vɜːtəbəl] adj 바꿀 수 있는 [bakkul su inneun] ▷ n 오픈카 [opeunka]

convict [kən'vɪkt] v 유죄를 입증하다 [yujoereul ipjeunghada]

convince [kən'vɪns] v 납득시키다 [napdeuksikida]

convincing [kən'vɪnsɪŋ; con'vincing] adj 설득력 있는 [seoldeungnyeok inneun]

convoy ['kɒnvɔɪ] n 호위 [howi]

cook [kʊk] n 요리사 [yorisa] ▷ v 요리하다 [yorihada]

cookbook ['kʊk,bʊk] n 요리책 [yorichaek]

cooker ['kʊkə] n 요리 기구 [yori gigu]; **gas cooker** n 가스레인지 [gaseureinji]

cookery ['kʊkərɪ] n 요리법 [yoribeop]; **cookery book** n 요리책 [yorichaek]

cooking ['kʊkɪŋ] n 요리 [yori]

cool [kuːl] adj (cold) 서늘한 [seoneulhan], (stylish) 멋진 [meotjin]

cooperation [kəʊˌɒpə'reɪʃən] n 협동 [hyeopdong]

cop [kɒp] n 경찰 [gyeongchal]

cope [kəʊp] v **cope (with)** v 대처하다 [daecheohada]

copper ['kɒpə] n 구리 [guri]

copy ['kɒpɪ] n (reproduction) 사본 [sabon], (written text) 원고 [wongo] ▷ v 복사하다 [boksahada]

copyright ['kɒpɪ,raɪt] n 저작권 [jeojakgwon]

coral ['kɒrəl] n 산호 [sanho]

cord [kɔːd] n **spinal cord** n 척수 [cheoksu]

cordless ['kɔːdlɪs] adj 무선의 [museonui]

corduroy ['kɔːdəˌrɔɪ; ˌkɔːdə'rɔɪ] n 코르덴 [koreuden]

core [kɔː] n 핵심 [haeksim]

coriander [ˌkɒrɪ'ændə] n 고수풀 [gosupul]

cork [kɔːk] n 코르크 [koreukeu]

corkscrew ['kɔːk,skruː] n 코르크 마개뽑이 [koreukeu magaeppobi]

corn [kɔːn] n 곡식 [goksik]

corner ['kɔːnə] n 모퉁이 [motungi]; **It's on the corner** 모퉁이에 있어요 [motungie isseoyo]; **It's round the corner** 모퉁이 근처에 있어요 [motungi geuncheoe isseoyo]

cornet ['kɔːnɪt] n 코넷 [konet]

cornflakes ['kɔːn,fleɪks] npl 콘플레이크 [konpeulleikeu]

cornflour ['kɔːn,flaʊə] n 옥수수 녹말 [oksusu nongmal]

corporal ['kɔːpərəl; -prəl] n 하사

[hasa]

corpse [kɔːps] n 시체 [siche]

correct [kəˈrɛkt] adj 옳은 [oreun] ▷ v 정정하다 [jeongjeonghada]

correction [kəˈrɛkʃən] n 정정 [jeongjeong]

correctly [kəˈrɛktlɪ] adv 정확하게 [jeonghwakhage]

correspondence [ˌkɒrɪˈspɒndəns] n 교신 [gyosin]

correspondent [ˌkɒrɪˈspɒndənt] n 특파원 [teukpawon]

corridor [ˈkɒrɪˌdɔː] n 복도 [bokdo]

corrupt [kəˈrʌpt] adj 부패한 [bupaehan]

corruption [kəˈrʌpʃən] n 부패 [bupae]

cosmetics [kɒzˈmɛtɪks] npl 화장품 [hwajangpum]

cost [kɒst] n 비용 [biyong] ▷ v 비용이 들다 [biyongi deulda]; **cost of living** n 생활비 [saenghwalbi]; **How much will the repairs cost?** 수리 비용은 얼마예요? [suri biyongeun eolmayeyo?]

Costa Rica [ˈkɒstə ˈriːkə] n 코스타리카 [koseutarika]

costume [ˈkɒstjuːm] n 복장 [bokjang]; **swimming costume** n 수영복 [suyeongbok]

cosy [ˈkəʊzɪ] adj 아늑한 [aneukhan]

cot [kɒt] n 어린이 침대 [eorini chimdae]; **Do you have a cot?** 어린이 침대 있어요? [eorini chimdae isseoyo?]

cottage [ˈkɒtɪdʒ] n 시골집 [sigoljip]; **cottage cheese** n 코티지 치즈 [kotiji chijeu]

cotton [ˈkɒtən] n 면 [myeon] (직물); **cotton bud** n 면봉 [myeonbong]; **cotton wool** n 솜 [som]

couch [kaʊtʃ] n 소파 [sopa]

couchette [kuːˈʃɛt] n 침대칸의 침대 [chimdaekanui chimdae]

cough [kɒf] n 기침 [gichim] ▷ v 기침하다 [gichimhada]; **cough mixture** n 기침약 [gichimyak]; **I have a cough** 기침이 나요 [gichimi nayo]

council [ˈkaʊnsəl] n 회의 [hoeui]; **council house** n 공영 주택 [gongyeong jutaek]

councillor [ˈkaʊnsələ] n 의원 [uiwon] (정치가)

count [kaʊnt] v 세다 [seda]

counter [ˈkaʊntə] n 계산대 [gyesandae]

count on [kaʊnt ɒn] v 의지하다 [uijihada]

country [ˈkʌntrɪ] n 국가 [gukga]; **developing country** n 개발도상국 [gaebaldosangguk]

countryside [ˈkʌntrɪˌsaɪd] n 시골 [sigol]

couple [ˈkʌpəl] n 한 쌍 [han ssang]

courage [ˈkʌrɪdʒ] n 용기 [yonggi]

courageous [kəˈreɪdʒəs] adj 용감한 [yonggamhan]

courgette [kʊəˈʒɛt] n 서양 호박 [seoyang hobak]

courier [ˈkʊərɪə] n 급사 [geupsa]

course [kɔːs] n 과정 [gwajeong]; **golf course** n 골프 코스 [golpeu koseu]; **main course** n 주 요리 [ju yori]; **refresher course** n 재교육 강습 [jaegyoyuk gangseup]; **training course** n 훈련과정 [hullyeongwajeong]

court [kɔːt] n 법원 [beobwon]; **tennis court** n 테니스 코트 [teniseu koteu]

courtyard [ˈkɔːtˌjɑːd] n 안뜰 [antteul]

cousin [ˈkʌzən] n 사촌 [sachon]

cover [ˈkʌvə] n 덮개 [deopgae] ▷ v 덮다 [deopda]; **cover charge** n 봉사료 [bongsaryo]

cow [kaʊ] n 암소 [amso]

coward [ˈkaʊəd] n 겁쟁이 [geopjaengi]

cowardly [ˈkaʊədlɪ] adj 겁많은 [geommanheun]

cowboy [ˈkaʊˌbɔɪ] n 카우보이 [kauboi]

crab [kræb] n 게 [ge]

crack [kræk] n (cocaine) 강력 코카인 [gangnyeok kokain], (fracture) 균열 [gyunyeol] ▷ v 금이 가다 [geumi gada]; **crack down on** v 단속하다 [dansokhada]

cracked [krækt] adj 금이 간 [geumi gan]

cracker [ˈkrækə] n 크래커 [keuraekeo]

cradle ['kreɪdᵊl] n 요람 [yoram] (아기)
craft [krɑːft] n 공예 [gongye]
craftsman ['krɑːftsmən] n 장인 [jangin]
(기술)
cram [kræm] v 과식하다 [gwasikhada]
crammed [kræmd] adj 빼곡히 찬
[ppaegokhi chan]
cranberry ['krænbərɪ; -brɪ] n 크란베리
[keuranberi]
crane [kreɪn] n (bird) 두루미 [durumi],
(for lifting) 기중기 [gijunggi]
crash [kræʃ] n 충돌 [chungdol] ▷ vi
충돌하다 [chungdolhada] ▷ vt
무너뜨리다 [muneotteurida]; **I've
crashed my car** 제 차가 충돌했어요
[je chaga chungdolhaesseoyo];
There's been a crash 충돌이 있었어요
[chungdori isseosseoyo]
crawl [krɔːl] v 기다 [gida]
crayfish ['kreɪˌfɪʃ] n 가재 [gajae] (생선)
crayon ['kreɪən; -ɒn] n 크레용
[keureyong]
crazy ['kreɪzɪ] adj 미친 [michin]
cream [kriːm] adj 크림색의
[keurimsaegui] ▷ n 크림 [keurim]; **ice
cream** n 아이스크림 [aiseukeurim];
shaving cream n 면도용 크림
[myeondoyong keurim]; **whipped
cream** n 거품 낸 크림 [geopum naen
keurim]
crease [kriːs] n 주름 [jureum]
creased [kriːst] adj 주름이 간 [jureumi
gan]
create [kriːˈeɪt] v 창조하다
[changjohada]
creation [kriːˈeɪʃən] n 창조 [changjo]
creative [kriːˈeɪtɪv] adj 창조적인
[changjojeogin]
creature ['kriːtʃə] n 피조물 [pijomul]
crêche [kreʃ] n 탁아소 [tagaso]
credentials [krɪˈdɛnʃəlz] npl 신임장
[sinimjang]
credible ['krɛdɪbᵊl] adj 신용할 수 있는
[sinyonghal su inneun]
credit ['krɛdɪt] n 신용 [sinyong]; **credit
card** n 신용카드 [sinyongkadeu]; **Can I
pay by credit card?** 신용카드로
지불할 수 있나요? [sinyongkadeuro

jibulhal su innayo?]; **Do you take
credit cards?** 신용카드 받으세요?
[sinyongkadeu badeuseyo?]
crematorium, crematoria
[ˌkrɛməˈtɔːrɪəm, ˌkrɛməˈtɔːrɪə] n
화장장 [hwajangjang]
cress [krɛs] n 다닥냉이 [dadangnaengi]
crew [kruː] n 승무원 [seungmuwon];
crew cut n 상고머리 [sanggomeori]
cricket ['krɪkɪt] n (game) 크리켓
[keuriket], (insect) 귀뚜라미
[gwitturami]
crime [kraɪm] n 범죄 [beomjoe]
criminal ['krɪmɪnᵊl] adj 범죄의
[beomjoeui] ▷ n 범인 [beomin]
crisis ['kraɪsɪs] n 위기 [wigi]
crisp [krɪsp] adj 바삭바삭한
[basakbasakhan]
crisps [krɪsps] npl 감자칩 [gamjachip]
crispy ['krɪspɪ] adj 바삭바삭한
[basakbasakhan]
criterion, criteria [kraɪˈtɪərɪən,
kraɪˈtɪərɪə] n 기준 [gijun]
critic ['krɪtɪk] n 비평가 [bipyeongga]
critical ['krɪtɪkᵊl] adj 중대한
[jungdaehan]
criticism ['krɪtɪˌsɪzəm] n 비평
[bipyeong]
criticize ['krɪtɪˌsaɪz] v 비평하다
[bipyeonghada]
Croatia [krəʊˈeɪʃə] n 크로아티아
[keuroatia]
Croatian [krəʊˈeɪʃən] adj 크로아티아의
[keuroatiaui] ▷ n (language)
크로아티아어 [keuroatiaeo], (person)
크로아티아 사람 [keuroatia saram]
crochet ['krəʊʃeɪ; -ʃɪ] v 코바늘로 뜨다
[kobaneullo tteuda]
crockery ['krɒkərɪ] n **We need more
crockery** 그릇이 더 필요해요
[geureutni deo pillyohaeyo]
crocodile ['krɒkəˌdaɪl] n 악어 [ageo]
crocus ['krəʊkəs] n 크로커스
[keurokeoseu]
crook [krʊk] n 사기꾼 [sagikkun],
(swindler) 사기꾼 [sagikkun]
crop [krɒp] n 농작물 [nongjangmul]
cross [krɒs] adj 교차된 [gyochadoen]

▷ *n* 십자가 [sipjaga] ▷ *v* 교차시키다 [gyochasikida]; **Red Cross** *n* 적십자 [jeoksipja]

cross-country ['krɒs'kʌntrɪ] *n* 크로스컨트리 경주 [keuroseukeonteuri gyeongju]

crossing ['krɒsɪŋ] *n* 횡단보도 [hoengdanbodo]; **level crossing** *n* 건널목 [geonneolmok]; **pedestrian crossing** *n* 횡단 보도 [hoengdan bodo]; **pelican crossing** *n* 보행자가 신호등을 조작하는 횡단보도 [bohaengjaga sinhodeungeul jojakhaneun hoengdanbodo]; **zebra crossing** *n* 횡단보도 [hoengdanbodo]

cross out [krɒs aʊt] *v* 지우다 [jiuda]

crossroads ['krɒs,rəʊdz] *n* 사거리 [sageori]

crossword ['krɒs,wɜːd] *n* 십자말풀이 [sipjamalpuri]

crouch down [kraʊtʃ daʊn] *v* 웅크리다 [ungkeurida]

crow [krəʊ] *n* 까마귀 [kkamagwi]

crowd [kraʊd] *n* 군중 [gunjung]

crowded [kraʊdɪd] *adj* 붐비는 [bumbineun]

crown [kraʊn] *n* 왕관 [wanggwan]

crucial ['kruːʃəl] *adj* 중대한 [jungdaehan]

crucifix ['kruːsɪfɪks] *n* 십자가상 [sipjagasang]

crude [kruːd] *adj* 천연 그대로의 [cheonyeon geudaeroui]

cruel ['kruːəl] *adj* 잔혹한 [janhokhan]

cruelty ['kruːəltɪ] *n* 잔혹함 [janhokham]

cruise [kruːz] *n* 만유 [manyu]

crumb [krʌm] *n* 부스러기 [buseureogi]

crush [krʌʃ] *v* 으깨다 [eukkaeda]

crutch [krʌtʃ] *n* 목발 [mokbal]

cry [kraɪ] *n* 울음 소리 [ureum sori] ▷ *v* 울다 [ulda]

crystal ['krɪstəl] *n* 수정 [sujeong]

cub [kʌb] *n* 짐승의 새끼 [jimseungui saekki]

Cuba ['kjuːbə] *n* 쿠바 [kuba]

Cuban ['kjuːbən] *adj* 쿠바의 [kubaui] ▷ *n* 쿠바 사람 [kuba saram]

cube [kjuːb] *n* 정육면체 [jeongyungmyeonche]; **ice cube** *n* 각얼음 [gageoreum]; **stock cube** *n* 고형수프 [gohyeongsupeu]

cubic ['kjuːbɪk] *adj* 입방의 [ipbangui]

cuckoo ['kʊkuː] *n* 뻐꾸기 [ppeokkugi]

cucumber ['kjuː,kʌmbə] *n* 오이 [oi]

cuddle ['kʌdəl] *n* 포옹 [poong] ▷ *v* 꼭 껴안다 [kkok kkyeoanda]

cue [kjuː] *n* (billiards) 신호 [sinho]

cufflinks ['kʌflɪŋks] *npl* 소매 단추 [somae danchu]

culprit ['kʌlprɪt] *n* 범인 [beomin]

cultural ['kʌltʃərəl] *adj* 문화의 [munhwaui]

culture ['kʌltʃə] *n* 문화 [munhwa]

cumin ['kʌmɪn] *n* 애기회향 [aegihoehyang]

cunning ['kʌnɪŋ] *adj* 교활한 [gyohwalhan]

cup [kʌp] *n* 컵 [keop]; **World Cup** *n* 월드컵 [woldeukeop]

cupboard ['kʌbəd] *n* 찬장 [chanjang]

curb [kɜːb] *n* 억제 [eokje]

cure [kjʊə] *n* 치료 [chiryo] ▷ *v* 치료하다 [chiryohada]

curfew ['kɜːfjuː] *n* 통금 [tonggeum]; **Is there a curfew?** 통금 시간이 있어요? [tonggeum sigani isseoyo?]

curious ['kjʊərɪəs] *adj* 호기심이 강한 [hogisimi ganghan]

curl [kɜːl] *n* 곱슬곱슬한 머리칼 [gopseulgopseulhan meorikal]

curler ['kɜːlə] *n* 헤어롤 [heeorol]

curly ['kɜːlɪ] *adj* 곱슬머리의 [gopseulmeoriui]

currant ['kʌrənt] *n* 건포도 [geonpodo]

currency ['kʌrənsɪ] *n* 통화 [tonghwa]

current ['kʌrənt] *adj* 현재의 [hyeonjaeui] ▷ *n* (electricity) 전류 [jeollyu], (flow) 흐름 [heureum]; **current account** *n* 당좌계좌 [dangjwagyejwa]; **current affairs** *npl* 시사 [sisa] (뉴스)

currently ['kʌrəntlɪ] *adv* 현재 [hyeonjae]

curriculum [kəˈrɪkjʊləm] *n* 교육과정 [gyoyukgwajeong]; **curriculum vitae**

n 이력서 [iryeokseo]

curry ['kʌrɪ] *n* 카레 [kare]; **curry powder** *n* 카레가루 [karegaru]

curse [kɜːs] *n* 저주 [jeoju]

cursor ['kɜːsə] *n* 커서 [keoseo]

curtain ['kɜːt³n] *n* 커튼 [keoteun]

cushion ['kʊʃən] *n* 쿠션 [kusyeon]

custard ['kʌstəd] *n* 커스터드 [keoseuteodeu]

custody ['kʌstədɪ] *n* 보관 [bogwan]

custom ['kʌstəm] *n* 관습 [gwanseup]

customer ['kʌstəmə] *n* 고객 [gogaek]

customized ['kʌstə͵maɪzd] *adj* 주문 제작한 [jumun jejakhan]

customs ['kʌstəmz] *npl* 관세 [gwanse]; **customs officer** *n* 세관원 [segwanwon]

cut [kʌt] *n* 절단 [jeoldan] ▷ *v* 절단하다 [jeoldanhada]; **crew cut** *n* 상고머리 [sanggomeori]; **power cut** *n* 정전 [jeongjeon]

cutback ['kʌt͵bæk] *n* 삭감 [sakgam]

cut down [kʌt daʊn] *v* 삭감하다 [sakgamhada]

cute [kjuːt] *adj* 귀여운 [gwiyeoun]

cutlery ['kʌtlərɪ] *n* 식기세트 [sikgiseteu]

cutlet ['kʌtlɪt] *n* 커틀릿 [keoteullit]

cut off [kʌt ɒf] *v* 잘라 버리다 [jalla beorida]

cutting ['kʌtɪŋ] *n* 절단 [jeoldan]

cut up [kʌt ʌp] *v* 잘게 자르다 [jalge jareuda]

CV [siː viː] *abbr* 이력서 [iryeokseo]

cybercafé ['saɪbə͵kæfeɪ; -͵kæfɪ] *n* 사이버 카페 [saibeo kape]

cybercrime ['saɪbə͵kraɪm] *n* 사이버 범죄 [saibeo beomjoe]

cycle ['saɪk³l] *n* (bike) 자전거 [jajeongeo], (recurring period) 주기 [jugi] ▷ *v* 순환하다 [sunhwanhada]; **cycle lane** *n* 자전거 도로 [jajeongeo doro]; **cycle path** *n* 자전거 도로 [jajeongeo doro]; **Where is the cycle path to...?** ...까지 가는 자전거 경로는 어디인가요? [...kkaji ganeun jajeongeo gyeongnoneun eodiingayo?]

cycling ['saɪklɪŋ] *n* 사이클링 [saikeulling]

cyclist ['saɪklɪst] *n* 자전거 타는 사람 [jajeongeo taneun saram]

cyclone ['saɪkləʊn] *n* 사이클론 [saikeullon]

cylinder ['sɪlɪndə] *n* 원통 [wontong]

cymbals ['sɪmb³lz] *npl* 심벌즈 [simbeoljeu]

Cypriot ['sɪprɪət] *adj* 키프로스의 [kipeuroseuui] ▷ *n* (person) 키프로스 사람 [kipeuroseu saram]

Cyprus ['saɪprəs] *n* 키프로스 [kipeuroseu]

cyst [sɪst] *n* 포낭 [ponang]

cystitis [sɪ'staɪtɪs] *n* 방광염 [banggwangyeom]

Czech [tʃɛk] *adj* 체코의 [chekoui] ▷ *n* (language) 체코어 [chekoeo], (person) 체코 사람 [cheko saram]; **Czech Republic** *n* 체코 공화국 [cheko gonghwaguk]

d

dad [dæd] n 아빠 [appa]
daddy ['dædɪ] n 아빠 [appa]
daffodil ['dæfədɪl] n 수선화 [suseonhwa]
daft [dɑːft] adj 어리석은 [eoriseogeun]
daily ['deɪlɪ] adj 매일의 [maeirui] ▷ adv 매일 [maeil]
dairy ['dɛərɪ] n 유제품 회사 [yujepum hoesa]; dairy produce n 유제품 [yujepum]; dairy products npl 유제품 [yujepum]
daisy ['deɪzɪ] n 데이지 [deiji]
dam [dæm] n 댐 [daem]
damage ['dæmɪdʒ] n 손상 [sonsang] ▷ v 손상하다 [sonsanghada]
damaged ['dæmɪdʒd] adj My luggage has been damaged 수하물이 손상되었어요 [suhamuri sonsangdoeeosseoyo]; My suitcase has arrived damaged 제 여행 가방이 손상되어 왔어요 [je yeohaeng gabangi sonsangdoeeo wasseoyo]
damn [dæm] adj 저주받은 [jeojubadeun]
damp [dæmp] adj 축축한 [chukchukhan]
dance [dɑːns] n 춤 [chum] ▷ v 춤추다 [chumchuda]; I don't really dance 저는 춤 안 춰요 [jeoneun chum an chwoyo]; I feel like dancing 저는 춤추고 싶어요 [jeoneun chumchugo sipeoyo]; Would you like to dance? 춤 출래요? [chum chullaeyo?]
dancer ['dɑːnsə] n 춤추는 사람 [chumchuneun saram]
dancing ['dɑːnsɪŋ] n 춤 [chum]; ballroom dancing n 사교춤 [sagyochum]; Where can we go dancing? 어디에 가면 춤출 수 있나요? [eodie gamyeon chumchul su innayo?]
dandelion ['dændɪ,laɪən] n 민들레 [mindeulle]
dandruff ['dændrəf] n 비듬 [bideum]
Dane [deɪn] n 덴마크 사람 [denmakeu saram]
danger ['deɪndʒə] n 위험 [wiheom]; Is there a danger of avalanches? 눈사태 위험이 있어요? [nunsatae wiheomi isseoyo?]
dangerous ['deɪndʒərəs] adj 위험한 [wiheomhan]
Danish ['deɪnɪʃ] adj 덴마크의 [denmakeuui] ▷ n (language) 덴마크어 [denmakeueo]
dare [dɛə] v 감히...하다 [gamhi...hada]
daring ['dɛərɪŋ] adj 대담한 [daedamhan]
dark [dɑːk] adj 어두운 [eoduun] ▷ n 어둠 [eodum]
darkness ['dɑːknɪs] n 어둠 [eodum]
darling ['dɑːlɪŋ] n 사랑스러운 사람 [sarangseureoun saram]
dart [dɑːt] n 가늘고 짧은 화살 [ganeulgo jjarbeun hwasal]
darts [dɑːts] npl 다트 게임 [dateu geim]
dash [dæʃ] v 돌진하다 [doljinhada]
dashboard ['dæʃ,bɔːd] n 계기판 [gyegipan]
data ['deɪtə; 'dɑːtə] npl 자료 [jaryo]
database ['deɪtə,beɪs] n 데이터베이스 [deiteobeiseu]
date [deɪt] n 날짜 [naljja]; best-before date n 최상 품질 기한 [choesang pumjil gihan]; expiry date n 만기일

[mangiil]; **sell-by date** n 유통만기일 [yutongmangiil]

daughter ['dɔːtə] n 딸 [ttal]; **My daughter is lost** 딸을 잃어버렸어요 [ttareul ireobeoryeosseoyo]; **My daughter is missing** 딸이 없어졌어요 [ttari eopseojyeosseoyo]

daughter-in-law ['dɔːtə ɪn lɔː] **(daughters-in-law)** n 며느리 [myeoneuri]

dawn [dɔːn] n 새벽 [saebyeok]

day [deɪ] n 하루 [haru]; **day return** n 당일 왕복표 [dangil wangbokpyo]; **Valentine's Day** n 밸런타인데이 [baelleontaindei]; **What are your rates per day?** 하루 요금이 얼마인가요? [haru yogeumi eolmaingayo?]

daytime ['deɪˌtaɪm] n 주간 [jugan]

dead [dɛd] adj 죽은 [jugeun] ▷ adv 완전히 [wanjeonhi]; **dead end** n 궁지 [gungji]

deadline ['dɛdˌlaɪn] n 마감 시간 [magam sigan]

deaf [dɛf] adj 귀가 들리지 않는 [gwiga deulliji annneun]

deafening ['dɛfªnɪŋ] adj 귀청이 터질 것 같은 [gwicheongi teojil geot gateun]

deal [diːl] n 거래 [georae]

dealer ['diːlə] n 상인 [sangin]; **drug dealer** n 마약상 [mayaksang]

deal with [diːl wɪð] v 다루다 [daruda]

dear [dɪə] adj (expensive) 비싼 [bissan], (loved) 사랑하는 [saranghaneun]

death [dɛθ] n 죽음 [jugeum]

debate [dɪ'beɪt] n 논쟁 [nonjaeng] ▷ v 논쟁하다 [nonjaenghada]

debit ['dɛbɪt] n 차변 [chabyeon] ▷ v 차변에 기입하다 [chabyeone giiphada]; **debit card** n 직불카드 [jikbulkadeu]; **direct debit** n 자동 이체 [jadong iche]

debt [dɛt] n 빚 [bit]

decade ['dɛkeɪd; dɪ'keɪd] n 10년간 [sim nyeongan]

decaffeinated [dɪ'kæfɪˌneɪtɪd] adj 무카페인 [mukapein]; **decaffeinated coffee** n 무카페인 커피 [mukapein keopi]

decay [dɪ'keɪ] v 썩다 [sseokda]

deceive [dɪ'siːv] v 속이다 [sogida]

December [dɪ'sɛmbə] n 12월 [shibiwol]

decent ['diːsªnt] adj 예절바른 [yejeolbareun]

decide [dɪ'saɪd] v 결심하다 [gyeolsimhada]

decimal ['dɛsɪməl] adj 십진법의 [sipjinbeobui]

decision [dɪ'sɪʒən] n 결심 [gyeolsim]

decisive [dɪ'saɪsɪv] adj 결정적인 [gyeoljeongjeogin]

deck [dɛk] n 갑판 [gappan]; **Can we go out on deck?** 갑판에 나가도 될까요? [gappane nagado doelkkayo?]; **How do I get to the car deck?** 차 싣는 갑판에 어떻게 갈 수 있어요? [cha sitneun gappane eotteoke gal su isseoyo?]

deckchair ['dɛkˌtʃɛə] n 접의자 [jeobuija]

declare [dɪ'klɛə] v 선언하다 [seoneonhada]

decorate ['dɛkəˌreɪt] v 장식하다 [jangsikhada]

decorator ['dɛkəˌreɪtə] n 장식자 [jangsikja]

decrease n ['diːkriːs] 감소 [gamso] ▷ v [dɪ'kriːs] 감소하다 [gamsohada]

dedicated ['dɛdɪˌkeɪtɪd] adj 헌신적인 [heonsinjeogin]

dedication [ˌdɛdɪ'keɪʃən] n 헌신 [heonsin]

deduct [dɪ'dʌkt] v 공제하다 [gongjehada]

deep [diːp] adj 깊은 [gipeun]

deep-fry [diːpfraɪ] v 기름에 튀기다 [gireume twigida]

deeply ['diːplɪ] adv 깊게 [gipge]

deer [dɪə] **(deer)** n 사슴 [saseum]

defeat [dɪ'fiːt] n 패배 [paebae] ▷ v 패배하다 [paebaehada]

defect [dɪ'fɛkt] n 결점 [gyeoljeom]

defence [dɪ'fɛns] n 수비 [subi]

defend [dɪ'fɛnd] v 방어하다 [bangeohada]

defendant [dɪˈfɛndənt] n 피고 [pigo]

defender [dɪˈfɛndə] n 방어자 [bangeoja]

deficit [ˈdɛfɪsɪt; dɪˈfɪsɪt] n 부족 [bujok]

define [dɪˈfaɪn] v 정의하다 [jeonguihada]

definite [ˈdɛfɪnɪt] adj 명확한 [myeonghwakhan]

definitely [ˈdɛfɪnɪtlɪ] adv 명확히 [myeonghwakhi]

definition [ˌdɛfɪˈnɪʃən] n 정의 [jeongui]

degree [dɪˈɡriː] n 정도 [jeongdo]; **degree centigrade** n 섭씨 [seopssi]; **degree Celsius** n 섭씨 [seopssi]; **degree Fahrenheit** n 화씨 [hwassi]

dehydrated [diahaɪˈdreɪtɪd] adj 탈수 증상의 [talsu jeungsangui]

de-icer [diːˈaɪsə] n 방빙제 [bangbingje]

delay [dɪˈleɪ] n 지연 [jiyeon] ▷ v 지연하다 [jiyeonhada]

delayed [dɪˈleɪd] adj 지연된 [jiyeondoen]

delegate n [ˈdɛlɪˌɡeɪt] 대표자 [daepyoja] ▷ v [ˈdɛlɪˌɡeɪt] 위임하다 [wiimhada]

delete [dɪˈliːt] v 삭제하다 [sakjehada]

deliberate [dɪˈlɪbərɪt] adj 고의적인 [gouijeogin]

deliberately [dɪˈlɪbərətlɪ] adv 고의적으로 [gouijeogeuro]

delicate [ˈdɛlɪkɪt] adj 섬세한 [seomsehan]

delicatessen [ˌdɛlɪkəˈtɛsən] n 조제식품 [jojesikpum]

delicious [dɪˈlɪʃəs] adj 맛있는 [masinneun]

delight [dɪˈlaɪt] n 기쁨 [gippeum]

delighted [dɪˈlaɪtɪd] adj 아주 기뻐하는 [aju gippeohaneun]

delightful [dɪˈlaɪtfʊl] adj 매우 기쁜 [maeu gippeun]

deliver [dɪˈlɪvə] v 전하다 [jeonhada]

delivery [dɪˈlɪvərɪ] n 배달 [baedal]; **recorded delivery** n 등기우편 [deunggiupyeon]

demand [dɪˈmɑːnd] n 요구 [yogu] ▷ v 요구하다 [yoguhada]

demanding [dɪˈmɑːndɪŋ] adj 지나치게 요구하는 [jinachige yoguhaneun]

demo, demos [ˈdɛməʊ, ˈdiːməʊz] n 데모 [demo]

democracy [dɪˈmɒkrəsɪ] n 민주주의 [minjujuui]

democratic [ˌdɛməˈkrætɪk] adj 민주적인 [minjujeogin]

demolish [dɪˈmɒlɪʃ] v 부수다 [busuda]

demonstrate [ˈdɛmənˌstreɪt] v 증명하다 [jeungmyeonghada]

demonstration [ˌdɛmənˈstreɪʃən] n 증명 [jeungmyeong]

demonstrator [ˈdɛmənˌstreɪtə] n 증명자 [jeungmyeongja]

denim [ˈdɛnɪm] n 데님 [denim]

denims [ˈdɛnɪmz] npl 데님제 옷 [denimje ot]

Denmark [ˈdɛnmɑːk] n 덴마크 [denmakeu]

dense [dɛns] adj 밀집한 [miljiphan]

density [ˈdɛnsɪtɪ] n 밀도 [mildo]

dent [dɛnt] n 움푹 패인 곳 [umpuk paein got] ▷ v 움푹 들어가게 하다 [umpuk deureogage hada]

dental [ˈdɛntəl] adj 이의 [iui]; **dental floss** n 치실 [chisil]

dentist [ˈdɛntɪst] n 치과의사 [chigwauisa]

dentures [ˈdɛntʃəz] npl 틀니 [teulli]

deny [dɪˈnaɪ] v 부정하다 [bujeonghada] (부정적)

deodorant [diːˈəʊdərənt] n 탈취제 [talchwije]

depart [dɪˈpɑːt] v 출발하다 [chulbalhada]

department [dɪˈpɑːtmənt] n 부 [bu]; **accident & emergency department** n 응급실 [eunggeupsil]; **department store** n 백화점 [baekhwajeom]

departure [dɪˈpɑːtʃə] n 출발 [chulbal]; **departure lounge** n 공항대기실 [gonghangdaegisil]

depend [dɪˈpɛnd] v 의존하다 [uijonhada]

deport [dɪˈpɔːt] v 국외로 추방하다 [gugoero chubanghada]

deposit [dɪˈpɒzɪt] n 예금 [yegeum]

depressed [dɪˈprɛst] *adj* 기운이 없는 [giuni eomneun]

depressing [dɪˈprɛsɪŋ] *adj* 기운을 잃게 하는 [giuneul irke haneun]

depression [dɪˈprɛʃən] *n* 우울 [uul]

depth [dɛpθ] *n* 깊이 [gipi]

descend [dɪˈsɛnd] *v* 내려가다 [naeryeogada]

describe [dɪˈskraɪb] *v* 묘사하다 [myosahada]

description [dɪˈskrɪpʃən] *n* 묘사 [myosa]

desert [ˈdɛzət] *n* 사막 [samak]; **desert island** *n* 무인도 [muindo]

deserve [dɪˈzɜːv] *v* 할 만하다 [hal manhada]

design [dɪˈzaɪn] *n* 디자인 [dijain] ▷ *v* 디자인하다 [dijainhada]

designer [dɪˈzaɪnə] *n* 디자이너 [dijaineo]; **interior designer** *n* 실내 장식가 [sillae jangsikga]

desire [dɪˈzaɪə] *n* 욕망 [yongmang] ▷ *v* 희망하다 [huimanghada]

desk [dɛsk] *n* 책상 [chaeksang]; **enquiry desk** *n* 안내 데스크 [annae deseukeu]; **May I use your desk?** 당신의 책상을 쓸 수 있을까요? [dangsinui chaeksangeul sseul su isseulkkayo?]

despair [dɪˈspɛə] *n* 절망 [jeolmang]

desperate [ˈdɛspərɪt; -prɪt] *adj* 절망적인 [jeolmangjeogin]

desperately [ˈdɛspərɪtlɪ] *adv* 필사적으로 [pilsajeogeuro]

despise [dɪˈspaɪz] *v* 경멸하다 [gyeongmyeolhada]

despite [dɪˈspaɪt] *prep* ...에도 불구하고 [...edo bulguhago]

dessert [dɪˈzɜːt] *n* 후식 [husik]; **dessert spoon** *n* 디저트스푼 [dijeoteuseupun]; **The dessert menu, please** 후식 메뉴 주세요 [husik menyu juseyo]; **We'd like a dessert** 후식을 주세요 [husigeul juseyo]

destination [ˌdɛstɪˈneɪʃən] *n* 목적지 [mokjeokji]

destiny [ˈdɛstɪnɪ] *n* 운명 [unmyeong]

destroy [dɪˈstrɔɪ] *v* 파괴하다 [pagoehada]

destruction [dɪˈstrʌkʃən] *n* 파괴 [pagoe]

detail [ˈdiːteɪl] *n* 세부 [sebu]

detailed [ˈdiːteɪld] *adj* 세밀한 [semilhan]

detective [dɪˈtɛktɪv] *n* 탐정 [tamjeong]

detention [dɪˈtɛnʃən] *n* 구류 [guryu]

detergent [dɪˈtɜːdʒənt] *n* 세제 [seje] (세척제)

deteriorate [dɪˈtɪərɪəˌreɪt] *v* 악화시키다 [akhwasikida]

determined [dɪˈtɜːmɪnd] *adj* 단호한 [danhohan]

detour [ˈdiːtʊə] *n* 우회 [uhoe]

devaluation [diːˌvæljuːˈeɪʃən] *n* 평가절하 [pyeonggajeolha]

devastated [ˈdɛvəˌsteɪtɪd] *adj* 망연자실한 [mangyeonjasilhan]

devastating [ˈdɛvəˌsteɪtɪŋ] *adj* 황폐시키는 [hwangpyesikineun]

develop [dɪˈvɛləp] *vi* 발전하다 [baljeonhada]; **developing country** *n* 개발도상국 [gaebaldosangguk]

development [dɪˈvɛləpmənt] *n* 개발 [gaebal] (향상)

device [dɪˈvaɪs] *n* 장치 [jangchi]

devil [ˈdɛvəl] *n* 악마 [angma]

devise [dɪˈvaɪz] *v* 궁리하다 [gungnihada]

devoted [dɪˈvəʊtɪd] *adj* 헌신적인 [heonsinjeogin]

diabetes [ˌdaɪəˈbiːtɪs; -tiːz] *n* 당뇨병 [dangnyobyeong]

diabetic [ˌdaɪəˈbɛtɪk] *adj* 당뇨병의 [dangnyobyeongui] ▷ *n* 당뇨병 환자 [dangnyobyeong hwanja]

diagnosis [ˌdaɪəgˈnəʊsɪs] *n* 진단 [jindan]

diagonal [daɪˈægənəl] *adj* 대각선의 [daegakseonui]

diagram [ˈdaɪəˌgræm] *n* 그림 [geurim]

dial [ˈdaɪəl; daɪl] *v* 전화를 걸다 [jeonhwareul geolda]; **dialling code** *n* 국번 [gukbeon]; **dialling tone** *n* 발신음 [balsineum]

dialect [ˈdaɪəˌlɛkt] *n* 방언 [bangeon]

dialogue [ˈdaɪəˌlɒg] *n* 대화 [daehwa]

diameter [daɪˈæmɪtə] *n* 직경 [jikgyeong]

diamond [ˈdaɪəmənd] *n* 다이아몬드 [daiamondeu]

diarrhoea [ˌdaɪəˈrɪə] *n* 설사 [seolsa]; **I have diarrhoea** 설사를 해요 [seolsareul haeyo]

diary [ˈdaɪərɪ] *n* 일기 [ilgi] (일지)

dice, die [daɪs, daɪ] *npl* 주사위 [jusawi]

dictation [dɪkˈteɪʃən] *n* 받아쓰기 [badasseugi]

dictator [dɪkˈteɪtə] *n* 독재자 [dokjaeja]

dictionary [ˈdɪkʃənərɪ; -ʃənrɪ] *n* 사전 [sajeon] (단어장)

die [daɪ] *v* 죽다 [jukda]

diesel [ˈdiːzəl] *n* 디젤기관 [dijelgigwan]

diet [ˈdaɪət] *n* 식이 요법 [sigi yobeop] ▷ *v* 다이어트하다 [daieoteuhada]

difference [ˈdɪfərəns; ˈdɪfrəns] *n* 차이점 [chaijeom]

different [ˈdɪfərənt; ˈdɪfrənt] *adj* 다른 [dareun]; **I would like something different** 다른 것을 사고 싶어요 [dareun geoseul sago sipeoyo]

difficult [ˈdɪfɪkəlt] *adj* 어려운 [eoryeoun]

difficulty [ˈdɪfɪkəltɪ] *n* 어려움 [eoryeoum]

dig [dɪg] *v* 파다 [pada]

digest [dɪˈdʒɛst; daɪ-] *v* 소화하다 [sohwahada] (음식)

digestion [dɪˈdʒɛstʃən; daɪ-] *n* 소화 [sohwa] (음식)

digger [ˈdɪgə] *n* 굴착기 [gulchakgi]

digital [ˈdɪdʒɪtəl] *adj* 디지털 방식의 [dijiteol bangsigui]; **digital camera** *n* 디지털 카메라 [dijiteol kamera]; **digital radio** *n* 디지털 라디오 [dijiteol radio]; **digital television** *n* 디지털 텔레비전 [dijiteol tellebijeon]; **digital watch** *n* 디지털 시계 [dijiteol sigye]

dignity [ˈdɪgnɪtɪ] *n* 존엄성 [joneomseong]

dilemma [dɪˈlɛmə; daɪ-] *n* 난관 [nangwan]

dilute [daɪˈluːt] *v* 희석하다 [huiseokhada]

diluted [daɪˈluːtɪd] *adj* 희석된 [huiseokdoen]

dim [dɪm] *adj* 어두운 [eoduun]

dimension [dɪˈmɛnʃən] *n* 치수 [chisu]

diminish [dɪˈmɪnɪʃ] *v* 줄이다 [jurida]

din [dɪn] *n* 소음 [soeum]

diner [ˈdaɪnə] *n* 식사 손님 [siksa sonnim]

dinghy [ˈdɪŋɪ] *n* 작은 보트 [jageun boteu]

dinner [ˈdɪnə] *n* 만찬 [manchan]; **dinner jacket** *n* 남자 턱시도 [namja teoksido]; **dinner party** *n* 만찬회 [manchanhoe]; **dinner time** *n* 저녁식사 시간 [jeonyeoksiksa sigan]

dinosaur [ˈdaɪnəˌsɔː] *n* 공룡 [gongnyong]

dip [dɪp] *n (food/sauce)* 딥 [dip] ▷ *v* 잠깐 담그다 [jamkkan damgeuda]

diploma [dɪˈpləʊmə] *n* 졸업장 [joreopjang]

diplomat [ˈdɪpləˌmæt] *n* 외교관 [oegyogwan]

diplomatic [ˌdɪpləˈmætɪk] *adj* 외교의 [oegyoui]

dipstick [ˈdɪpˌstɪk] *n* 유량계 [yuryanggye]

direct [dɪˈrɛkt; daɪ-] *adj* 직접의 [jikjeobui] ▷ *v* 이끌다 [ikkeulda]; **direct debit** *n* 자동 이체 [jadong iche]

direction [dɪˈrɛkʃən; daɪ-] *n* 방향 [banghyang]; **Can you draw me a map with directions?** 방향 약도를 그려 주시겠어요? [banghyang yakdoreul geuryeo jusigesseoyo?]

directions [dɪˈrɛkʃənz; daɪ-] *npl* 지시 [jisi]

directly [dɪˈrɛktlɪ; daɪ-] *adv* 직접 [jikjeop]

director [dɪˈrɛktə; daɪ-] *n* 관리자 [gwallija]; **managing director** *n* 사장 [sajang]

directory [dɪˈrɛktərɪ; -trɪ; daɪ-] *n* 전화번호부 [jeonhwabeonhobu]; **directory enquiries** *npl* 전화번호 문의 [jeonhwabeonho munui]; **telephone directory** *n* 전화번호부 [jeonhwabeonhobu]

dirt [dɜːt] *n* 더러움 [deoreoum]

dirty [ˈdɜːtɪ] *adj* 더러운 [deoreoun]
disability [ˌdɪsəˈbɪlɪtɪ] *n* 장애 [jangae]
disabled [dɪˈseɪbᵊld] *adj* 장애가 있는 [jangaega inneun] ▷ *npl* 장애인 [jangaein]; **Are there any toilets for the disabled?** 장애인 화장실이 있어요? [jangaein hwajangsiri isseoyo?]; **Do you provide access for the disabled?** 장애인이 이용할 수 있어요? [jangaeini iyonghal su isseoyo?]; **Is there a reduction for disabled people?** 장애인 할인이 있나요? [jangaein harini innayo?]; **What facilities do you have for disabled people?** 장애인을 위한 어떠한 시설이 있어요? [jangaeineul wihan eotteohan siseori isseoyo?]
disadvantage [ˌdɪsədˈvɑːntɪdʒ] *n* 불리 [bulli]
disagree [ˌdɪsəˈɡriː] *v* 의견이 맞지 않다 [uigyeoni matji anta]
disagreement [ˌdɪsəˈɡriːmənt] *n* 불일치 [burilchi]
disappear [ˌdɪsəˈpɪə] *v* 사라지다 [sarajida]
disappearance [ˌdɪsəˈpɪərəns] *n* 사라짐 [sarajim]
disappoint [ˌdɪsəˈpɔɪnt] *v* 실망시키다 [silmangsikida]
disappointed [ˌdɪsəˈpɔɪntɪd] *adj* 실망한 [silmanghan]
disappointing [ˌdɪsəˈpɔɪntɪŋ] *adj* 실망시키는 [silmangsikineun]
disappointment [ˌdɪsəˈpɔɪntmənt] *n* 실망 [silmang]
disaster [dɪˈzɑːstə] *n* 재난 [jaenan]
disastrous [dɪˈzɑːstrəs] *adj* 대재해의 [daejaehaeui]
disc [dɪsk] *n* 디스크 [diseukeu]; **compact disc** *n* 콤팩트디스크 [kompaekteudiseukeu]; **disc jockey** *n* 디스크 자키 [diseukeu jaki]; **slipped disc** *n* 변위 추간판 [byeonwi chuganpan]
discharge [dɪsˈtʃɑːdʒ] *v* **When will I be discharged?** 저는 언제 퇴원하나요? [jeoneun eonje toewonhanayo?]
discipline [ˈdɪsɪplɪn] *n* 규율 [gyuyul]

disclose [dɪsˈkləʊz] *v* 드러내다 [deureonaeda]
disco [ˈdɪskəʊ] *n* 디스코 [diseuko]
disconnect [ˌdɪskəˈnɛkt] *v* 분리하다 [bullihada]
discount [ˈdɪskaʊnt] *n* 할인 [harin]; **student discount** *n* 학생할인 [haksaengharin]; **Do you offer a discount for cash?** 현금으로 내면 할인되나요? [hyeongeumeuro naemyeon harindoenayo?]
discourage [dɪsˈkʌrɪdʒ] *v* 용기를 잃게 하다 [yonggireul irke hada]
discover [dɪsˈkʌvə] *v* 발견하다 [balgyeonhada]
discretion [dɪˈskrɛʃən] *n* 분별 [bunbyeol]
discrimination [dɪˌskrɪmɪˈneɪʃən] *n* 차별 [chabyeol]
discuss [dɪˈskʌs] *v* 토론하다 [toronhada]
discussion [dɪˈskʌʃən] *n* 토론 [toron]
disease [dɪˈziːz] *n* 병 [byeong]; **Alzheimer's disease** *n* 알츠하이머병 [alcheuhaimeobyeong]
disgraceful [dɪsˈɡreɪsfʊl] *adj* 수치스러운 [suchiseureoun]
disguise [dɪsˈɡaɪz] *v* 위장하다 [wijanghada]
disgusted [dɪsˈɡʌstɪd] *adj* 혐오스러운 [hyeomoseureoun]
disgusting [dɪsˈɡʌstɪŋ] *adj* 구역질나는 [guyeokjillaneun]
dish [dɪʃ] *n (food)* 음식 [eumsik], *(plate)* 접시 [jeopsi]; **dish towel** *n* 행주 [haengju]; **satellite dish** *n* 위성방송수신 접시 안테나 [wiseongbangsongsusin jeopsi antena]; **soap dish** *n* 비누 그릇 [binu geureut]
dishcloth [ˈdɪʃˌklɒθ] *n* 행주 [haengju]
dishonest [dɪsˈɒnɪst] *adj* 부정직한 [bujeongjikhan]
dishwasher [ˈdɪʃˌwɒʃə] *n* 식기 세척기 [sikgi secheokgi]
disinfectant [ˌdɪsɪnˈfɛktənt] *n* 소독제 [sodokje]
disk [dɪsk] *n* 디스크 [diseukeu]; **disk**

drive n 디스크 드라이브 [diseukeu deuraibeu]

diskette [dɪsˈkɛt] n 디스켓 [diseuket]

dislike [dɪsˈlaɪk] v 싫어하다 [sirheohada]

dismal [ˈdɪzməl] adj 음침한 [eumchimhan]

dismiss [dɪsˈmɪs] v 해고하다 [haegohada]

disobedient [ˌdɪsəˈbiːdɪənt] adj 순종치 않는 [sunjongchi annneun]

disobey [ˌdɪsəˈbeɪ] v 순종하지 않다 [sunjonghaji anta]

dispenser [dɪˈspɛnsə] n 자동판매기 [jadongpanmaegi]; **cash dispenser** n 현금 인출기 [hyeongeum inchulgi]

display [dɪˈspleɪ] n 전시 [jeonsi] (보여주다) ▷ v 전시하다 [jeonsihada]

disposable [dɪˈspəʊzəbᵊl] adj 일회용 [ilhoeyong]

disqualify [dɪsˈkwɒlɪˌfaɪ] v 실격시키다 [silgyeoksikida]

disrupt [dɪsˈrʌpt] v 중단시키다 [jungdansikida]

dissatisfied [dɪsˈsætɪsˌfaɪd] adj 불만스러운 [bulmanseureoun]

dissolve [dɪˈzɒlv] v 녹이다 [nogida]

distance [ˈdɪstəns] n 거리 [geori]

distant [ˈdɪstənt] adj 먼 [meon]

distillery [dɪˈstɪlərɪ] n 증류소 [jeungnyuso]

distinction [dɪˈstɪŋkʃən] n 구별 [gubyeol]

distinctive [dɪˈstɪŋktɪv] adj 독특한 [dokteukhan]

distinguish [dɪˈstɪŋgwɪʃ] v 구별하다 [gubyeolhada]

distract [dɪˈstrækt] v 산만하게 하다 [sanmanhage hada]

distribute [dɪˈstrɪbjuːt] v 분배하다 [bunbaehada]

distributor [dɪˈstrɪbjʊtə] n 분배자 [bunbaeja]

district [ˈdɪstrɪkt] n 지역 [jiyeok]

disturb [dɪˈstɜːb] v 방해하다 [banghaehada]

ditch [dɪtʃ] n 수로 [suro] ▷ v 버리다 [beorida]

dive [daɪv] n 다이빙 [daibing] ▷ v 다이빙하다 [daibinghada]; **I'd like to go diving** 다이빙을 하고 싶어요 [daibingeul hago sipeoyo]; **Where is the best place to dive?** 다이빙하기 가장 좋은 곳은 어디인가요? [daibinghagi gajang joheun goseun eodiingayo?]

diver [ˈdaɪvə] n 다이버 [daibeo]

diversion [daɪˈvɜːʃən] n 전환 [jeonhwan]

divide [dɪˈvaɪd] v 나누다 [nanuda]

diving [ˈdaɪvɪŋ] n 다이빙 [daibing]; **diving board** n 다이빙대 [daibingdae]; **scuba diving** n 스쿠버 다이빙 [seukubeo daibing]

division [dɪˈvɪʒən] n 분할 [bunhal]

divorce [dɪˈvɔːs] n 이혼 [ihon] ▷ v 이혼 [ihon]

divorced [dɪˈvɔːst] adj 이혼한 [ihonhan]

DIY [diː aɪ waɪ] abbr 손수 하는 일 [sonsu haneun il]

dizzy [ˈdɪzɪ] adj 현기증 나는 [hyeongijeung naneun]

DJ [diː dʒeɪ] abbr 디스크 자키 [diseukeu jaki]

DNA [diː ɛn eɪ] n 디옥시리보핵산 [dioksiribohaeksan]

do [dʊ] v 하다 [hada]

dock [dɒk] n 부두 [budu]

doctor [ˈdɒktə] n 의사 [uisa]; **Call a doctor!** 의사를 불러요! [uisareul bulleoyo!]; **I need a doctor** 의사가 필요해요 [uisaga piryohaeyo]; **Is there a doctor who speaks English?** 영어 하는 의사가 있나요? [yeongeo haneun uisaga innayo?]; **Please call the emergency doctor** 응급 의사를 불러 주세요 [eunggeup uisareul bulleo juseyo]

document [ˈdɒkjʊmənt] n 문서 [munseo]

documentary [ˌdɒkjʊˈmɛntərɪ; -trɪ] n 다큐멘터리 [dakyumenteori]

documentation [ˌdɒkjʊmɛnˈteɪʃən] n 문서화 [munseohwa]

documents [ˌdɒkjʊmɛnts] npl 문서

[munseo]

dodge [dɒdʒ] v 재빨리 몸을 비키다 [jaeppalli momeul bikida]

dog [dɒg] n 개 [gae]; **guide dog** n 맹인 안내견 [maengin annaegyeon]; **hot dog** n 핫도그 [hatdogeu]

dole [dəʊl] n 실업 수당 [sireop sudang]

doll [dɒl] n 인형 [inhyeong]

dollar [ˈdɒlə] n 달러 [dalleo]; **Do you take dollars?** 달러 받으세요? [dalleo badeuseyo?]

dolphin [ˈdɒlfɪn] n 돌고래 [dolgorae]

domestic [dəˈmɛstɪk] adj 국내의 [gungnaeui]

Dominican Republic [dəˈmɪnɪkən rɪˈpʌblɪk] n 도미니카 공화국 [dominika gonghwaguk]

domino [ˈdɒmɪˌnəʊ] n 도미노 [domino]

dominoes [ˈdɒmɪˌnəʊz] npl 도미노 [domino]

donate [dəʊˈneɪt] v 기증하다 [gijeunghada]

done [dʌn] adj 끝난 [kkeutnan]

donkey [ˈdɒŋkɪ] n 당나귀 [dangnagwi]

donor [ˈdəʊnə] n 기증자 [gijeungja]

door [dɔː] n 문 [mun]; **door handle** n 문 손잡이 [mun sonjabi]; **Keep the door locked** 문을 잠궈 두세요 [muneul jamgwo duseyo]; **The door handle has come off** 문 손잡이가 빠졌어요 [mun sonjabiga ppajyeosseoyo]; **The door won't close** 문이 안 닫혀요 [muni an datyeoyo]; **The door won't lock** 문이 안 잠겨요 [muni an jamgyeoyo]; **The door won't open** 문이 안 열려요 [muni an yeollyeoyo]; **Which is the key for the front door?** 앞문 열쇠는 어느 것인가요? [ammun yeolsoeneun eoneu geosingayo?]

doorbell [ˈdɔːˌbɛl] n 초인종 [choinjong]

doorman, doormen [ˈdɔːˌmæn; -mən, ˈdɔːˌmɛn] n 문지기 [munjigi]

doorstep [ˈdɔːˌstɛp] n 현관 계단 [hyeongwan gyedan]

dorm [dɔːm] n **Do you have any single sex dorms?** 남녀 공용이 아닌 기숙사 있나요? [namnyeo gongyongi anin gisuksa innayo?]

dormitory [ˈdɔːmɪtərɪ; -trɪ] n 기숙사 [gisuksa]

dose [dəʊs] n 복용량 [bogyongnyang]

dot [dɒt] n 점 [jeom]

double [ˈdʌb°l] adj 두 배의 [du baeui] ▷ v ...을 갑절로 하다 [...eul gapjeollo hada]; **double bass** n 더블베이스 [deobeulbeiseu]; **double bed** n 2인용 침대 [i inyong chimdae]; **double glazing** n 이중 유리 [ijung yuri]; **double room** n 2인실 [i insil]

doubt [daʊt] n 의심 [uisim] ▷ v 의심하다 [uisimhada]

doubtful [ˈdaʊtfʊl] adj 의심스러운 [uisimseureoun]

dough [dəʊ] n 반죽 [banjuk]

doughnut [ˈdəʊnʌt] n 도넛 [doneot]

do up [du ʌp] v 꾸리다 [kkurida] (포장)

dove [dʌv] n 비둘기 [bidulgi]

do without [du wɪˈðaʊt] v ...없이 지내다 [...eopsi jinaeda]

down [daʊn] adv 아래로 [araero]

download [ˈdaʊnˌləʊd] n 다운로드 [daunnodeu] ▷ v 다운로드하다 [daunnodeuhada]; **Can I download photos to here?** 여기로 사진을 다운로드할 수 있을까요? [yeogiro sajineul daunnodeuhal su isseulkkayo?]

downpour [ˈdaʊnˌpɔː] n 폭우 [pogu]

downstairs [ˈdaʊnˈstɛəz] adj 아래층의 [araecheungui] ▷ adv 아래층에 [araecheunge]

downtown [ˈdaʊnˈtaʊn] adv 도심지에 [dosimjie]

doze [dəʊz] v 졸다 [jolda]

dozen [ˈdʌz°n] n 다스 [daseu]

doze off [dəʊz ɒf] v 깜박 잠들다 [kkambak jamdeulda]

drab [dræb] adj 칙칙한 [chikchikhan]

draft [drɑːft] n 초안 [choan]

drag [dræg] v 끌다 [kkeulda]

dragon [ˈdrægən] n 용 [yong]

dragonfly [ˈdrægənˌflaɪ] n 잠자리 [jamjari] (곤충)

drain [dreɪn] n 배수 [baesu] (펌프질 하다) ▷ v 배출하다 [baechulhada]

(방출); **draining board** n 식기 건조대 [sikgi geonjodae]; **The drain is blocked** 배수구가 막혔어요 [baesuguga makhyeosseoyo]

drainpipe [ˈdreɪnˌpaɪp] n 배수관 [baesugwan]

drama [ˈdrɑːmə] n 극 [geuk]

dramatic [drəˈmætɪk] adj 극적인 [geukjeogin]

drastic [ˈdræstɪk] adj 과감한 [gwagamhan]; **I don't want anything drastic** 과감한 걸 원하지 않아요 [gwagamhan geol wonhaji anhayo]

draught [drɑːft] n 외풍 [oepung]

draughts [drɑːfts] npl 체커 [chekeo]

draw [drɔː] n (lottery) 제비뽑기 [jebippopgi], (tie) 동점 [dongjeom] ▷ v (equal with) 비기다 [bigida], (sketch) (그림 등을)그리다 [(geurim deungeul) geurida]

drawback [ˈdrɔːˌbæk] n 단점 [danjeom]

drawer [ˈdrɔːə] n 서랍 [seorap]; **The drawer is jammed** 서랍이 뻑뻑해요 [seorabi ppeokppeokhaeyo]

drawers [drɔːz] n **chest of drawers** n 서랍장 [seorapjang]

drawing [ˈdrɔːɪŋ] n 그림 [geurim]

drawing pin [ˈdrɔːɪŋ pɪn] n 압정 [apjeong]

dreadful [ˈdrɛdfʊl] adj 몹시 싫은 [mopsi sireun]

dream [driːm] n 꿈 [kkum] ▷ v 꿈꾸다 [kkumkkuda]

drench [drɛntʃ] v 흠뻑 적시다 [heumppeok jeoksida]

dress [drɛs] n 드레스 [deureseu] ▷ v 옷을 입다 [oseul ipda]; **evening dress** n 야회복 [yahoebok]; **wedding dress** n 웨딩드레스 [wedingdeureseu]; **Can I try on this dress?** 이 드레스 입어 볼 수 있어요? [i deureseu ibeo bol su isseoyo?]

dressed [drɛst] adj 옷을 입은 [oseul ibeun]

dresser [ˈdrɛsə] n 찬장 [chanjang]

dressing [ˈdrɛsɪŋ] n **salad dressing** n 샐러드 드레싱 [saelleodeu deuresing]

dressing gown [ˈdrɛsɪŋ gaʊn] n 화장복 [hwajangbok]

dressing table [ˈdrɛsɪŋ ˈteɪbəl] n 화장대 [hwajangdae]

dress up [drɛs ʌp] v 잘 차려입다 [jal charyeoipda]

dried [draɪd] adj 말린 [mallin]

drift [drɪft] n 표류 [pyoryu] ▷ v 떠돌다 [tteodolda]

drill [drɪl] n 드릴 [deuril] ▷ v 구멍을 뚫다 [gumeongeul tturta]; **pneumatic drill** n 공기압축기 [gonggiapchukgi]

drink [drɪŋk] n 음료 [eumnyo] ▷ v (음료를) 마시다 [(eumnyoreul) masida]; **binge drinking** n 폭음 [pogeum]; **drinking water** n 음료수 [eumnyosu]; **soft drink** n 청량 음료 [cheongnyang eumnyo]; **What non-alcoholic drinks do you have?** 어떤 무알코올 음료가 있나요? [eotteon mualkool eumnyoga innayo?]

drink-driving [ˈdrɪŋkˈdraɪvɪŋ] n 음주운전 [eumjuunjeon]

drip [drɪp] n 물방울 [mulbangul] ▷ v 똑똑 떨어지다 [ttokttok tteoreojida]

drive [draɪv] n 드라이브 [deuraibeu] ▷ v 운전하다 [unjeonhada]; **driving instructor** n 운전 강사 [unjeon gangsa]; **four-wheel drive** n 사륜구동 [saryungudong]; **left-hand drive** n 왼쪽 핸들 [oenjjok haendeul]; **right-hand drive** n 오른쪽 핸들 [oreunjjok haendeul]

driver [ˈdraɪvə] n 운전자 [unjeonja]; **learner driver** n 임시면허 운전자 [imsimyeonheo unjeonja]; **lorry driver** n 트럭 운전사 [teureok unjeonsa]; **racing driver** n 자동차 경주 선수 [jadongcha gyeongju seonsu]; **truck driver** n 트럭 운전사 [teureok unjeonsa]

driveway [ˈdraɪvˌweɪ] n 차도 [chado] (도로)

driving lesson [ˈdraɪvɪŋ ˈlɛsən] n 운전 교습 [unjeon gyoseup]

driving licence [ˈdraɪvɪŋ ˈlaɪsəns] n 운전 면허증 [unjeon myeonheojeung]; **Here is my driving licence** 제 운전

면허증이에요 [je unjeon myeonheojeungieyo]; **I don't have my driving licence on me** 저는 운전면허증이 없어요 [jeoneun unjeonmyeonheojeungi eopseoyo]; **My driving licence number is...** 제 운전 면허증 번호는....에요 [je unjeon myeonheojeung beonhoneun....eyo]

driving test ['draɪvɪŋ 'tɛst] n 운전 면허 시험 [unjeon myeonheo siheom]

drizzle ['drɪzəl] n 이슬비 [iseulbi]

drop [drɒp] n 방울 [bangul] ▷ v 똑똑 떨어트리다 [ttokttok tteoreoteurida]; **eye drops** npl 안약 [anyak]

drought [draʊt] n 가뭄 [gamum]

drown [draʊn] v 익사하다 [iksahada]

drowsy ['draʊzɪ] adj 졸리는 [jollineun]

drug [drʌg] n 약 [yak]; **drug addict** n 마약 중독자 [mayak jungdokja]; **drug dealer** n 마약상 [mayaksang]

drum [drʌm] n 드럼 [deureom]

drummer ['drʌmə] n 드러머 [deureomeo]

drunk [drʌŋk] adj 술취한 [sulchwihan] ▷ n 주정뱅이 [jujeongbaengi]

dry [draɪ] adj 건조한 [geonjohan] (젖지 않은) ▷ v 건조시키다 [geonjosikida]; **bone dry** adj 메마른 [memareun]

dry-cleaner's ['draɪ'kliːnəz] n 세탁소 [setakso]

dry-cleaning ['draɪ'kliːnɪŋ] n 드라이클리닝 [deuraikeullining]

dryer ['draɪə] n 건조기 [geonjogi]; **spin dryer** n 탈수기 [talsugi]; **tumble dryer** n 회전식 탈수기 [hoejeonsik talsugi]

dual ['djuːəl] adj **dual carriageway** n 중앙 분리대가 있는 도로 [jungang bullidaega inneun doro]

dubbed [dʌbt] adj...라고 불리는 [...rago bullineun]

dubious ['djuːbɪəs] adj 의심스러운 [uisimseureoun]

duck [dʌk] n 오리 [ori]

due [djuː] adj 만기가 된 [mangiga doen]

due to [djuː tʊ] prep...때문에 [...ttaemune]

dull [dʌl] adj 단조로운 [danjoroun]

dumb [dʌm] adj 말을 못하는 [mareul motanaeun]

dummy ['dʌmɪ] n 모형 [mohyeong]

dump [dʌmp] n 쓰레기 수거장 [sseuregi sugeojang] ▷ v 털썩 떨어뜨리다 [teolsseok tteoreotteurida]; **rubbish dump** n 쓰레기 수거장 [sseuregi sugeojang]

dumpling ['dʌmplɪŋ] n 만두 [mandu]

dune [djuːn] n **sand dune** n 모래 언덕 [morae eondeok]

dungarees [ˌdʌŋɡə'riːz] npl 멜빵 작업복 [melppang jageopbok]

dungeon ['dʌndʒən] n 지하감옥 [jihagamok]

duration [djʊ'reɪʃən] n 기간 [gigan]

during ['djʊərɪŋ] prep...동안 [...dongan]

dusk [dʌsk] n 해질녘 [haejillyeok]

dust [dʌst] n 먼지 [meonji] ▷ v 먼지를 털다 [meonjireul teolda]

dustbin ['dʌst‚bɪn] n 쓰레기통 [sseuregitong]

dustman, dustmen ['dʌstmən, 'dʌstmɛn] n 청소부 [cheongsobu]

dustpan ['dʌst‚pæn] n 쓰레받기 [sseurebatgi]

dusty ['dʌstɪ] adj 먼지투성이의 [meonjituseongiui]

Dutch [dʌtʃ] adj 네덜란드의 [nedeollandeuui] ▷ n 네덜란드 사람 [nedeollandeu saram]

Dutchman, Dutchmen ['dʌtʃmən, 'dʌtʃmɛn] n 네덜란드 사람 [nedeollandeu saram]

Dutchwoman, Dutchwomen [ˌdʌtʃwʊmən, 'dʌtʃ‚wɪmɪn] n 네덜란드 여자 [nedeollandeu yeoja]

duty ['djuːtɪ] n 임무 [immu]; **(customs) duty** n 관세 [gwanse]

duty-free ['djuːtɪ'friː] adj 면세의 [myeonseui] ▷ n 면세 [myeonse]

duvet ['duːveɪ] n 깃털 이불 [gittheol ibul]

DVD [di: vi: di:] n DVD [DVD]; **DVD burner** n DVD 기록 장치 [DVD girok jangchi]; **DVD player** n DVD 플레이어 [DVD peulleieo]

dwarf, dwarves [dwɔːf, dwɔːvz] n

난쟁이 [nanjaengi]
dye [daɪ] *n* 염료 [yeomnyo] ▷ *v* 염색하다 [yeomsaekhada]
dynamic [daɪ'næmɪk] *adj* 동적인 [dongjeogin]
dyslexia [dɪs'lɛksɪə] *n* 난독증 [nandokjeung]
dyslexic [dɪs'lɛksɪk] *adj* 난독증의 [nandokjeungui] ▷ *n* 난독증 환자 [nandokjeung hwanja]

each [iːtʃ] *adj* 각자의 [gakjaui] ▷ *pron* 각자 [gakja]
eagle ['iːgəl] *n* 독수리 [doksuri]
ear [ɪə] *n* 귀 [gwi]
earache ['ɪərˌeɪk] *n* 귀앓이 [gwiari]
eardrum ['ɪəˌdrʌm] *n* 고막 [gomak]
earlier ['ɜːlɪə] *adv* 더 일찍 [deo iljjik]
early ['ɜːlɪ] *adj* 이른 [ireun] ▷ *adv* 일찍 [iljjik]; **We arrived early/late** 우리가 일찍/ 늦게 도착했어요 [uriga iljjik/ neutge dochakhaesseoyo]
earn [ɜːn] *v* 벌다 [beolda]
earnings ['ɜːnɪŋz] *npl* 소득 [sodeuk]
earphones ['ɪəˌfəʊnz] *npl* 이어폰 [ieopon]
earplugs ['ɪəˌplʌgz] *npl* 귀마개 [gwimagae]
earring ['ɪəˌrɪŋ] *n* 귀고리 [gwigori]
earth [ɜːθ] *n* 지구 [jigu]
earthquake ['ɜːθˌkweɪk] *n* 지진 [jijin]
easily ['iːzɪlɪ] *adv* 쉽게 [swipge]
east [iːst] *adj* 동쪽의 [dongjjogui] ▷ *adv* 동쪽에 [dongjjoge] ▷ *n* 동쪽 [dongjjok]; **Far East** *n* 극동 [geukdong]; **Middle East** *n* 중동 [jungdong]
eastbound ['iːstˌbaʊnd] *adj* 동쪽으로 가는 [dongjjogeuro ganeun]

Easter ['iːstə] n 부활절 [buhwaljeol];
  Easter egg n 부활절 달걀 [buhwaljeol
  dalgyal]
eastern ['iːstən] adj 동쪽의
  [dongjjogui]
easy ['iːzɪ] adj 쉬운 [swiun]; **easy chair**
  n 안락 의자 [allak uija]
easy-going ['iːzɪ'gəʊɪŋ] adj 느긋한
  [neugeutan]
eat [iːt] v 먹다 [meokda]
e-book ['iːbʊk] n 전자책 [jeonjachaek]
eccentric [ɪk'sɛntrɪk] adj 별난
  [byeollan]
echo ['ɛkəʊ] n 메아리 [meari]
ecofriendly ['iːkəʊˌfrɛndlɪ] adj
  친환경적인 [chinhwangyeongjeogin]
ecological [ˌiːkə'lɒdʒɪkəl] adj 생태학의
  [saengtaehagui]
ecology [ɪ'kɒlədʒɪ] n 생태학
  [saengtaehak]
e-commerce ['iːkɒmɜːs] n 전자상거래
  [jeonjasanggeorae]
economic [ˌiːkə'nɒmɪk; ˌɛkə-] adj
  경제학의 [gyeongjehagui]
economical [ˌiːkə'nɒmɪkəl; ˌɛkə-] adj
  경제적인 [gyeongjejeogin]
economics [ˌiːkə'nɒmɪks; ˌɛkə-] npl
  경제학 [gyeongjehak]
economist [ɪ'kɒnəmɪst] n 경제학자
  [gyeongjehakja]
economize [ɪ'kɒnəˌmaɪz] v 절약하다
  [jeollyakhada]
economy [ɪ'kɒnəmɪ] n 경제 [gyeongje];
  economy class n 이코노미 석
  [ikonomi seok]
ecstasy ['ɛkstəsɪ] n 무아경
  [muagyeong]
Ecuador ['ɛkwəˌdɔː] n 에콰도르
  [ekwadoreu]
eczema ['ɛksɪmə; ɪg'ziːmə] n 습진
  [seupjin]
edge [ɛdʒ] n 가장자리 [gajangjari]
edgy ['ɛdʒɪ] adj 초조한 [chojohan]
edible ['ɛdɪbəl] adj 식용의 [sigyongui]
edition [ɪ'dɪʃən] n 판 [pan]
editor ['ɛdɪtə] n 편집자 [pyeonjipja]
educated ['ɛdjʊˌkeɪtɪd] adj 교육받은
  [gyoyukbadeun]

education [ˌɛdjʊ'keɪʃən] n 교육
  [gyoyuk]; **adult education** n 성인 교육
  [seongin gyoyuk]; **higher education** n
  고등교육 [godeunggyoyuk]
educational [ˌɛdjʊ'keɪʃənəl] adj 교육의
  [gyoyugui]
eel [iːl] n 뱀장어 [baemjangeo]
effect [ɪ'fɛkt] n 효과 [hyogwa]; **side**
  effect n 부작용 [bujagyong]
effective [ɪ'fɛktɪv] adj 효과적인
  [hyogwajeogin]
effectively [ɪ'fɛktɪvlɪ] adv 효과적으로
  [hyogwajeogeuro]
efficient [ɪ'fɪʃənt] adj 효율적인
  [hyoyuljeogin]
efficiently [ɪ'fɪʃəntlɪ] adv 효율적으로
  [hyoyuljeogeuro]
effort ['ɛfət] n 노력 [noryeok]
e.g. [iː dʒiː] abbr 예를 들면 [yereul
  deulmyeon]
egg [ɛg] n 달걀 [dalgyal]; **boiled egg** n
  삶은 달걀 [sarmeun dalgyal]; **egg**
  white n 달걀 흰자 [dalgyal huinja];
  egg yolk n 달걀 노른자 [dalgyal
  noreunja]; **Easter egg** n 부활절 달걀
  [buhwaljeol dalgyal]; **scrambled eggs**
  npl 스크램블드 에그
  [seukeuraembeuldeu egeu]
eggcup ['ɛgˌkʌp] n 달걀 그릇 [dalgyal
  geureut]
Egypt ['iːdʒɪpt] n 이집트 [ijipteu]
Egyptian [ɪ'dʒɪpʃən] adj 이집트의
  [ijipteuui] ▷ n 이집트 사람 [ijipteu
  saram]
eight [eɪt] number 여덟 [yeodeorp],
  (Sino-Korean) 팔 [pal]
eighteen ['eɪ'tiːn] number 열여덟
  [yeollyeodeorp], (Sino-Korean) 십팔
  [sippal]
eighteenth ['eɪ'tiːnθ] adj 열여덟
  번째의 [yeollyeodeol beonjjaeui]
eighth [eɪtθ] adj 여덟 번째의 [yeodeol
  beonjjaeui] ▷ n 8분의 1 [palbunui il]
eighty ['eɪtɪ] number 여든 [yeodeun],
  (Sino-Korean) 팔십 [palsip]
Eire ['ɛərə] n 아일랜드 [aillaendeu]
either ['aɪðə; 'iːðə] adv (with
  negative)...도 또한...아니다 [...do

ttohan...anida] ▷ *conj* (.. or)...이든 (아니면)... [...ideun (animyeon)...] ▷ *pron* 어느 쪽 하나 [eoneu jjok hana]; **either... or** *conj* ...거나 또는...거나 [...geona ttoneun...geona]

elastic [ɪˈlæstɪk] *n* 탄성체 [tanseongche]; **elastic band** *n* 고무 밴드 [gomu baendeu]

elbow [ˈɛlbəʊ] *n* 팔꿈치 [palkkumchi]

elder [ˈɛldə] *adj* 손위의 [sonwiui]

elderly [ˈɛldəlɪ] *adj* 나이가 지긋한 [naiga jigeutan]

eldest [ˈɛldɪst] *adj* 가장 나이 많은 [gajang nai manheun]

elect [ɪˈlɛkt] *v* 선출하다 [seonchulhada]

election [ɪˈlɛkʃən] *n* 선거 [seongeo]; **general election** *n* 총선거 [chongseongeo]

electorate [ɪˈlɛktərɪt] *n* 유권자 [yugwonja]

electric [ɪˈlɛktrɪk] *adj* 전기의 [jeongiui]; **electric blanket** *n* 전기 담요 [jeongi damyo]; **electric shock** *n* 감전 [gamjeon]

electrical [ɪˈlɛktrɪkəl] *adj* 전기의 [jeongiui]

electrician [ɪlɛkˈtrɪʃən; ˌiːlɛk-] *n* 전기 기사 [jeongi gisa]

electricity [ɪlɛkˈtrɪsɪtɪ; ˌiːlɛk-] *n* 전기 [jeongi]; **Do we have to pay extra for electricity?** 전기 요금을 추가로 내야 하나요? [jeongi yogeumeul chugaro naeya hanayo?]; **Is the cost of electricity included?** 전기 요금이 포함되나요? [jeongi yogeumi pohamdoenayo?]; **There is no electricity** 전기가 안 들어와요 [jeongiga an deureowayo]; **Where is the electricity meter?** 전기 계량기는 어디있어요? [jeongi gyeryanggineun eodiisseoyo?]

electronic [ɪlɛkˈtrɒnɪk; ˌiːlɛk-] *adj* 전자의 [jeonjaui]

electronics [ɪlɛkˈtrɒnɪks; ˌiːlɛk-] *npl* 전자공학 [jeonjagonghak]

elegant [ˈɛlɪɡənt] *adj* 우아한 [uahan]

element [ˈɛlɪmənt] *n* 요소 [yoso]

elephant [ˈɛlɪfənt] *n* 코끼리 [kokkiri]

eleven [ɪˈlɛvᵊn] *number* 열하나 [yeolhana], *(Sino-Korean)* 십일 [sibil]

eleventh [ɪˈlɛvᵊnθ] *adj* 열한 번째의 [yeolhan beonjjaeui]

eliminate [ɪˈlɪmɪˌneɪt] *v* 제거하다 [jegeohada]

elm [ɛlm] *n* 느릅나무 [neureumnamu]

else [ɛls] *adj* 그 밖에 [geu bakke]

elsewhere [ˌɛlsˈwɛə] *adv* 다른 곳에 [dareun gose]

email [ˈiːmeɪl] *n* 이메일 [imeil] ▷ *vt (a person)* 이메일을 보내다 [imeireul bonaeda]; **email address** *n* 이메일 주소 [imeil juso]; **Can I have your email?** 이메일 좀 알려 주시겠어요? [imeil jom allyeo jusigesseoyo?]; **Can I send an email?** 이메일 보내도 될까요? [imeil bonaedo doelkkayo?]; **Did you get my email?** 제 이메일 받았어요? [je imeil badasseoyo?]; **Do you have an email?** 이메일 있어요? [imeil isseoyo?]; **My email address is...** 제 이메일 주소는...이에요 [je imeil jusoneun...ieyo]; **What is your email address?** 이메일 주소가 어떻게 되세요? [imeil jusoga eotteoke doeseyo?]

embankment [ɪmˈbæŋkmənt] *n* 둑 [duk]

embarrassed [ˌɪmˈbærəst] *adj* 무안한 [muanhan]

embarrassing [ɪmˈbærəsɪŋ] *adj* 무안케 하는 [muanke haneun]

embassy [ˈɛmbəsɪ] *n* 대사관 [daesagwan]; **I need to call my embassy** 대사관에 전화해야 해요 [daesagwane jeonhwahaeya haeyo]

embroider [ɪmˈbrɔɪdə] *v* 자수를 놓다 [jasureul nota]

embroidery [ɪmˈbrɔɪdərɪ] *n* 자수 [jasu] *(바느질)*

emergency [ɪˈmɜːdʒənsɪ] *n* 비상 사태 [bisang satae]; **accident & emergency department** *n* 응급실 [eunggeupsil]; **emergency exit** *n* 비상구 [bisanggu]; **emergency landing** *n* 비상 착륙 [bisang changnyuk]

emigrate ['ɛmɪˌgreɪt] v 이주하다 [ijuhada]

emotion [ɪ'məʊʃən] n 감정 [gamjeong]

emotional [ɪ'məʊʃənəl] adj 감정의 [gamjeongui]

emperor, empress ['ɛmpərə, 'ɛmprɪs] n 황제 [hwangje]

emphasize ['ɛmfəˌsaɪz] v 강조하다 [gangjohada]

empire ['ɛmpaɪə] n 제국 [jeguk]

employ [ɪm'plɔɪ] v 고용하다 [goyonghada]

employee [ɛm'plɔɪiː; ˌɛmplɔɪ'iː] n 고용인 [goyongin]

employer [ɪm'plɔɪə] n 고용주 [goyongju]

employment [ɪm'plɔɪmənt] n 고용 [goyong]

empty ['ɛmptɪ] adj 빈 [bin] ▷ v (든 것을) 비우다 [(deun geoseul) biuda]

enamel [ɪ'næməl] n 에나멜 [enamel]

encourage [ɪn'kʌrɪdʒ] v 용기를 북돋우다 [yonggireul bukdoduda]

encouragement [ɪn'kʌrɪdʒmənt] n 격려 [gyeongnyeo]

encouraging [ɪn'kʌrɪdʒɪŋ] adj 격려가 되는 [gyeongnyeoga doeneun]

encyclopaedia [ɛnˌsaɪkləʊ'piːdɪə] n 백과 사전 [baekgwa sajeon]

end [ɛnd] n 끝 [kkeut] ▷ v 끝나다 [kkeutnada]; **dead end** n 궁지 [gungji]; **Is this the end of the queue?** 여기가 줄의 끝인가요? [yeogiga jurui kkeuchingayo?]

endanger [ɪn'deɪndʒə] v 위험에 빠뜨리다 [wiheome ppatteurida]

ending ['ɛndɪŋ] n 결말 [gyeolmal]

endless ['ɛndlɪs] adj 끝없는 [kkeuteomneun]

enemy ['ɛnəmɪ] n 원수 [wonsu]

energetic [ˌɛnə'dʒɛtɪk] adj 정력적인 [jeongnyeokjeogin]

energy ['ɛnədʒɪ] n 에너지 [eneoji]

engaged [ɪn'geɪdʒd] adj 약혼한 [yakhonhan]; **engaged tone** n 통화중 신호음 [tonghwajung sinhoeum]

engagement [ɪn'geɪdʒmənt] n 약속 [yaksok]; **engagement ring** n 약혼 반지 [yakhon banji]

engine ['ɛndʒɪn] n 엔진 [enjin]; **search engine** n 검색 엔진 [geomsaek enjin]; **The engine is overheating** 엔진이 과열됐어요 [enjini gwayeoldwaesseoyo]

engineer [ˌɛndʒɪ'nɪə] n 기술자 [gisulja]

engineering [ˌɛndʒɪ'nɪərɪŋ] n 공학 [gonghak]

England ['ɪŋglənd] n 잉글랜드 [inggeullaendeu]

English ['ɪŋglɪʃ] adj 잉글랜드의 [inggeullaendeuui] ▷ n 잉글랜드 사람 [inggeullaendeu saram]

Englishman, Englishmen ['ɪŋglɪʃmən, 'ɪŋglɪʃmɛn] n 잉글랜드 사람 [inggeullaendeu saram]

Englishwoman, Englishwomen ['ɪŋglɪʃwʊmən, 'ɪŋglɪʃwɪmɪn] n 잉글랜드 여자 [inggeullaendeu yeoja]

engrave [ɪn'greɪv] v 조각하다 [jogakhada]

enjoy [ɪn'dʒɔɪ] v 즐기다 [jeulgida]

enjoyable [ɪn'dʒɔɪəbəl] adj 즐길 수 있는 [jeulgil su inneun]

enlargement [ɪn'lɑːdʒmənt] n 확대 [hwakdae]

enormous [ɪ'nɔːməs] adj 거대한 [geodaehan]

enough [ɪ'nʌf] adj 충분한 [chungbunhan] ▷ pron 충분한 양 [chungbunhan yang]

enquire [ɪn'kwaɪə] v 문의하다 [munuihada]

enquiry [ɪn'kwaɪərɪ] n 질문 [jilmun]; **enquiry desk** n 안내 데스크 [annae deseukeu]

ensure [ɛn'ʃʊə; -'ʃɔː] v 보장하다 [bojanghada]

enter ['ɛntə] v 들어가다 [deureogada]

entertain [ˌɛntə'teɪn] v 대접하다 [daejeophada]

entertainer [ˌɛntə'teɪnə] n 연예인 [yeonyein]

entertaining [ˌɛntə'teɪnɪŋ] adj 재미있는 [jaemiinneun]

entertainment [ˌɛntə'teɪnmənt] n **What entertainment is there?** 어떤

오락거리가 있어요? [eotteon olageoliga iss-eoyo?]

enthusiasm [ɪnˈθjuːzɪˌæzəm] n 열의 [yeorui]

enthusiastic [ɪnˌθjuːzɪˈæstɪk] adj 열정적인 [yeoljeongjeogin]

entire [ɪnˈtaɪə] adj 전체의 [jeoncheui]

entirely [ɪnˈtaɪəlɪ] adv 완전히 [wanjeonhi]

entrance [ˈɛntrəns] n 입구 [ipgu]; **entrance fee** n 입장료 [ipjangnyo]; **Where is the wheelchair-accessible entrance?** 휠체어를 이용할 수 있는 출입구는 어디인가요? [hwilcheeoreul iyonghal su inneun churipguneun eodiingayo?]

entry [ˈɛntrɪ] n 입구 [ipgu]; **entry phone** n 현관 인터폰 [hyeongwan inteopon]

envelope [ˈɛnvəˌləʊp; ˈɒn-] n 봉투 [bongtu]

envious [ˈɛnvɪəs] adj 시기하는 듯한 [sigihaneun deutan]

environment [ɪnˈvaɪrənmənt] n 환경 [hwangyeong]

environmental [ɪnˌvaɪrənˈmɛntəl] adj 환경의 [hwangyeongui]; **environmentally friendly** adj 친환경적인 [chinhwangyeongjeogin]

envy [ˈɛnvɪ] n 질투 [jiltu] ▷ v 질투하다 [jiltuhada]

epidemic [ˌɛpɪˈdɛmɪk] n 유행병 [yuhaengbyeong]

epileptic [ˌɛpɪˈlɛptɪk] n 간질 환자 [ganjil hwanja]; **epileptic fit** n 간질 발작 [ganjilbaljjark]

episode [ˈɛpɪˌsəʊd] n 일화 [ilhwa]

equal [ˈiːkwəl] adj 같은 [gateun] ▷ v 같다 [gatda]

equality [ɪˈkwɒlɪtɪ] n 같음 [gateum]

equalize [ˈiːkwəˌlaɪz] v 같게하다 [gatgehada]

equation [ɪˈkweɪʒən; -ʃən] n 방정식 [bangjeongsik]

equator [ɪˈkweɪtə] n 적도 [jeokdo]

Equatorial Guinea [ˌɛkwəˈtɔːrɪəl ˈgɪnɪ] n 적도 기니 [jeokdo gini]

equipment [ɪˈkwɪpmənt] n 장비

[jangbi]; **Can we hire the equipment?** 장비를 빌릴 수 있나요? [jangbireul billil su innayo?]

equipped [ɪˈkwɪpt] adj 갖춘 [gatchun]

equivalent [ɪˈkwɪvələnt] n 동등한 것 [dongdeunghan geot]

erase [ɪˈreɪz] v 지우다 [jiuda]

Eritrea [ˌɛrɪˈtreɪə] n 에리트레아 [eriteurea]

erotic [ɪˈrɒtɪk] adj 성애의 [seongaeui]

error [ˈɛrə] n 오류 [oryu]

escalator [ˈɛskəˌleɪtə] n 에스컬레이터 [eseukeolleiteo]

escape [ɪˈskeɪp] n 탈출 [talchul] ▷ v 탈출하다 [talchulhada]; **fire escape** n 화재 피난 장치 [hwajae pinan jangchi]

escort [ɪsˈkɔːt] v 호위하다 [howihada]

especially [ɪˈspɛʃəlɪ] adv 특히 [teukhi]

espionage [ˈɛspɪəˌnɑːʒ] n 첩보 활동 [cheopbo hwaldong]

essay [ˈɛseɪ] n 수필 [supil]

essential [ɪˈsɛnʃəl] adj 근본적인 [geunbonjeogin]

estate [ɪˈsteɪt] n 부동산 [budongsan]; **estate agent** n 부동산 중개인 [budongsan junggaein]; **estate car** n 스테이션 왜건 [seuteisyeon waegeon]

estimate n [ˈɛstɪmɪt] 견적 [gyeonjeok] ▷ v [ˈɛstɪˌmeɪt] 추정하다 [chujeonghada]

Estonia [ɛˈstəʊnɪə] n 에스토니아 [eseutonia]

Estonian [ɛˈstəʊnɪən] adj 에스토니아의 [eseutoniaui] ▷ n (language) 에스토니아어 [eseutoniaeo], (person) 에스토니아 사람 [eseutonia saram]

etc [ɪt ˈsɛtrə] abbr 기타 등등 [gita deungdeung]

eternal [ɪˈtɜːnəl] adj 영원한 [yeongwonhan]

eternity [ɪˈtɜːnɪtɪ] n 영원 [yeongwon]

ethical [ˈɛθɪkəl] adj 윤리적인 [yullijeogin]

Ethiopia [ˌiːθɪˈəʊpɪə] n 에티오피아 [etiopia]

Ethiopian [ˌiːθɪˈəʊpɪən] adj 에티오피아의 [etiopiaui] ▷ n 에티오피아 사람 [etiopia saram]

ethnic [ˈɛθnɪk] *adj* 인종의 [injonguī]

e-ticket [ˈiːtɪkɪt] *n* 전자티켓 [jeonjatiket]

EU [iː juː] *abbr* 유럽연합 [yureobyeonhap]

euro [ˈjʊərəʊ] *n* 유로 [yuro]

Europe [ˈjʊərəp] *n* 유럽 [yureop]

European [ˌjʊərəˈpɪən] *adj* 유럽의 [yureobui] ▷ *n* 유럽 사람 [yureop saram]; **European Union** *n* 유럽연합 [yureobyeonhap]

evacuate [ɪˈvækjʊˌeɪt] *v* 피난시키다 [pinansikida]

eve [iːv] *n* 전야 [jeonya]

even [ˈiːvən] *adj* 평평한 [pyeongpyeonghan] ▷ *adv* ...이라도 [... irado]

evening [ˈiːvnɪŋ] *n* 저녁 [jeonyeok]; **evening class** *n* 야간 수업 [yagan sueop]; **evening dress** *n* 야회복 [yahoebok]; **in the evening** 저녁에 [jeonyeoge]; **The table is booked for nine o'clock this evening** 오늘 저녁 아홉시 테이블이 예약되었습니다 [oneul jeonyeok ahopsi teibeuri yeyakdoeeosseumnida]; **What are you doing this evening?** 오늘 저녁에 뭐 하실거예요? [oneul jeonyeoge mwo hasilgeoyeyo?]

event [ɪˈvɛnt] *n* 사건 [sageon]

eventful [ɪˈvɛntfʊl] *adj* 사건이 많은 [sageoni manheun]

eventually [ɪˈvɛntʃʊəlɪ] *adv* 결국 [gyeolguk]

ever [ˈɛvə] *adv* 이제까지 [ijekkaji]

every [ˈɛvrɪ] *adj* 모든 [modeun]

everybody [ˈɛvrɪˌbɒdɪ] *pron* 모두 [modu]

everyone [ˈɛvrɪˌwʌn; -wən] *pron* 모든 사람 [modeun saram]

everything [ˈɛvrɪθɪŋ] *pron* 모든 것 [modeun geot]

everywhere [ˈɛvrɪˌwɛə] *adv* 어디에나 [eodiena]

evidence [ˈɛvɪdəns] *n* 증거 [jeunggeo]

evil [ˈiːvəl] *adj* 사악한 [saakhan]

evolution [ˌiːvəˈluːʃən] *n* 진화 [jinhwa]

ewe [juː] *n* 암양 [amyang]

exact [ɪgˈzækt] *adj* 정확한 [jeonghwakhan]

exactly [ɪgˈzæktlɪ] *adv* 정확히 [jeonghwakhi]

exaggerate [ɪgˈzædʒəˌreɪt] *v* 과장하다 [gwajanghada]

exaggeration [ɪgˌzædʒəˌreɪʃən] *n* 과장 [gwajang]

exam [ɪgˈzæm] *n* 시험 [siheom]

examination [ɪgˌzæmɪˈneɪʃən] *n* (*medical*) 시험 [siheom], (*school*) 시험 [siheom]

examine [ɪgˈzæmɪn] *v* 조사하다 [josahada]

examiner [ɪgˈzæmɪnə] *n* 시험관 [siheomgwan]

example [ɪgˈzɑːmpl] *n* 예 [ye]

excellent [ˈɛksələnt] *adj* 우수한 [usuhan]

except [ɪkˈsɛpt] *prep* ...을 제외하고 [...eul jeoehago]

exception [ɪkˈsɛpʃən] *n* 예외 [yeoe]

exceptional [ɪkˈsɛpʃənəl] *adj* 예외적인 [yeoejeogin]

excessive [ɪkˈsɛsɪv] *adj* 과도한 [gwadohan]

exchange [ɪksˈtʃeɪndʒ] *v* 교환하다 [gyohwanhada]; **exchange rate** *n* 환율 [hwanyul]; **rate of exchange** *n* 환율 [hwanyul]; **stock exchange** *n* 증권거래소 [jeunggwongeoraeso]

excited [ɪkˈsaɪtɪd] *adj* 흥분한 [heungbunhan]

exciting [ɪkˈsaɪtɪŋ] *adj* 흥미진진한 [heungmijinjinhan]

exclude [ɪkˈskluːd] *v* 제외하다 [jeoehada]

excluding [ɪkˈskluːdɪŋ] *prep* ...을 제외하고 [...eul jeoehago]

exclusively [ɪkˈskluːsɪvlɪ] *adv* 독점적으로 [dokjeomjeogeuro]

excuse *n* [ɪkˈskjuːs] 변명 [byeonmyeong] ▷ *v* [ɪkˈskjuːz] 변명하다 [byeonmyeonghada]

execute [ˈɛksɪˌkjuːt] *v* 실행하다 [silhaenghada]

execution [ˌɛksɪˈkjuːʃən] *n* 실행 [silhaeng]

executive [ɪɡ'zɛkjʊtɪv] n 실행위원
[silhaengwiwon]

exercise ['ɛksəˌsaɪz] n 운동 [undong]

exhaust [ɪɡ'zɔːst] n **The exhaust is
broken** 배기관이 고장났어요
[baegigwani gojangnasseoyo]

exhausted [ɪɡ'zɔːstɪd] adj 피곤한
[pigonhan]

exhibition [ˌɛksɪ'bɪʃən] n 전시회
[jeonsihoe]

ex-husband [ɛks'hʌzbənd] n 전 남편
[jeon nampyeon]

exile ['ɛɡzaɪl; 'ɛksaɪl] n 망명
[mangmyeong]

exist [ɪɡ'zɪst] v 존재하다 [jonjaehada]

exit ['ɛɡzɪt; 'ɛksɪt] n 출구 [chulgu];
emergency exit n 비상구 [bisanggu];
Where is the exit? 출구는 어디에
있어요? [chulguneun eodie isseoyo?];
Which exit for...? 어느 출구가...
방향인가요? [eoneu chulguga...
banghyangingayo?]

exotic [ɪɡ'zɒtɪk] adj 이국적인
[igukjeogin]

expect [ɪk'spɛkt] v 기대하다
[gidaehada]

expedition [ˌɛkspɪ'dɪʃən] n 탐험
[tamheom]

expel [ɪk'spɛl] v 쫓아내다 [jjochanaeda]

expenditure [ɪk'spɛndɪtʃə] n 지출
[jichul]

expenses [ɪk'spɛnsɪz] npl 비용
[biyong]

expensive [ɪk'spɛnsɪv] adj 비싼
[bissan]

experience [ɪk'spɪərɪəns] n 경험
[gyeongheom]; **work experience** n
경력 [gyeongnyeok]

experienced [ɪk'spɪərɪənst] adj 노련한
[noryeonhan]

experiment [ɪk'spɛrɪmənt] n 실험
[silheom]

expert ['ɛkspɜːt] n 전문가 [jeonmunga]

expire [ɪk'spaɪə] v 만료되다
[mallyodoeda]

explain [ɪk'spleɪn] v 설명하다
[seolmyeonghada]

explanation [ˌɛksplə'neɪʃən] n 설명
[seolmyeong]

explode [ɪk'spləʊd] v 폭발하다
[pokbalhada]

exploit [ɪk'splɔɪt] v 이용하다
[iyonghada]

exploitation [ˌɛksplɔɪ'teɪʃən] n 착취
[chakchwi]

explore [ɪk'splɔː] v 탐험하다
[tamheomhada]

explorer [ɪk'splɔːrə] n 탐험가
[tamheomga]

explosion [ɪk'spləʊʒən] n 폭발
[pokbal]

explosive [ɪk'spləʊsɪv] n 폭발성의
[pokbalseongui]

export n ['ɛkspɔːt] 수출 [suchul] ▷ v
[ɪk'spɔːt] 수출하다 [suchulhada]

express [ɪk'sprɛs] v 표현하다
[pyohyeonhada]

expression [ɪk'sprɛʃən] n 표현
[pyohyeon]

extension [ɪk'stɛnʃən] n 연장
[yeonjang] (늘이다); **extension cable**
n 연장 케이블 [yeonjang keibeul]

extensive [ɪk'stɛnsɪv] adj 광대한
[gwangdaehan]

extensively [ɪk'stɛnsɪvlɪ] adv
광범위하게 [gwangbeomwihage]

extent [ɪk'stɛnt] n 범위 [beomwi]

exterior [ɪk'stɪərɪə] adj 외부의
[oebuui]

external [ɪk'stɜːnəl] adj 외부의 [oebuui]

extinct [ɪk'stɪŋkt] adj 멸종한
[myeoljonghan]

extinguisher [ɪk'stɪŋgwɪʃə] n 소화기
[sohwagi]

extortionate [ɪk'stɔːʃənɪt] adj 터무니
없는 [teomuni eomneun]

extra ['ɛkstrə] adj 여분의 [yeobunui]
▷ adv 여분으로 [yeobuneuro]

extraordinary [ɪk'strɔːdᵊnrɪ; -dᵊnərɪ]
adj 비범한 [bibeomhan]

extravagant [ɪk'strævɪgənt] adj
낭비하는 [nangbihaneun]

extreme [ɪk'striːm] adj 극도의
[geukdoui]

extremely [ɪk'striːmlɪ] adv 극도로
[geukdoro]

extremism [ɪk'stri:mɪzəm] n 극단주의
[geukdanjuui]
extremist [ɪk'stri:mɪst] n 극단주의자
[geukdanjuuija]
ex-wife [ɛks'waɪf] n 전처 [jeoncheo]
eye [aɪ] n 눈 [nun]; **eye drops** npl 안약
[anyak]; **eye shadow** n 아이섀도
[aisyaedo]; **I have something in my
eye** 눈에 뭐가 들어갔어요 [nune
mwoga deureogasseoyo]; **My eyes
are sore** 눈이 따가워요 [nuni
ttagawoyo]
eyebrow ['aɪ,braʊ] n 눈썹 [nunsseop]
eyelash ['aɪ,læʃ] n 속눈썹
[songnunsseop]
eyelid ['aɪ,lɪd] n 눈꺼풀 [nunkkeopul]
eyeliner ['aɪ,laɪnə] n 아이라이너
[airaineo]
eyesight ['aɪ,saɪt] n 시력 [siryeok]

fabric ['fæbrɪk] n 직물 [jingmul]
fabulous ['fæbjʊləs] adj 굉장히 좋은
[goengjanghi joheun]
face [feɪs] n 얼굴 [eolgul] ▷ v 직면하다
[jingmyeonhada]; **face cloth** n 수건
[sugeon]
facial ['feɪʃəl] adj 얼굴의 [eolgurui] ▷ n
미안술 [miansul]
facilities [fə'sɪlɪtɪz] npl 시설 [siseol];
Do you have facilities for children?
어린이를 위한 시설이 있나요?
[eorinireul wihan siseori innayo?];
**What facilities do you have for
disabled people?** 장애인을 위한
어떠한 시설이 있어요? [jangaeineul
wihan eotteohan siseori isseoyo?];
What facilities do you have here?
여기에는 어떤 시설이 있어요?
[yeogieneun eotteon siseori isseoyo?];
What sports facilities are there?
어떤 스포츠 시설이 있어요? [eotteon
seupocheu siseori isseoyo?]
fact [fækt] n 사실 [sasil]
factory ['fæktərɪ] n 공장 [gongjang]; **I
work in a factory** 공장에서 일해요
[gongjangeseo ilhaeyo]
fade [feɪd] v 희미해지다 [huimihaejida]

fag [fæg] n 고된 일 [godoen il]
fail [feɪl] v 실패하다 [silpaehada]
failure ['feɪljə] n 실패 [silpae] (성공적이 아님)
faint [feɪnt] adj 희미한 [huimihan] ▷ v 기절하다 [gijeolhada]
fair [fɛə] adj (light colour) 살결이 흰 [salgyeori huin], (reasonable) 공평한 [gongpyeonghan] ▷ n 박람회 [bangnamhoe]
fairground ['fɛəˌɡraʊnd] n 박람회장 [bangnamhoejang]
fairly ['fɛəlɪ] adv 상당히 [sangdanghi]
fairness ['fɛənɪs] n 공평함 [gongpyeongham]
fairy ['fɛərɪ] n 요정 [yojeong]
fairytale ['fɛərɪˌteɪl] n 동화 [donghwa]
faith [feɪθ] n 믿음 [mideum]
faithful ['feɪθfʊl] adj 성실한 [seongsilhan]
faithfully ['feɪθfʊlɪ] adv 성실하게 [seongsilhage]
fake [feɪk] adj 가짜의 [gajjaui] ▷ n 위조품 [wijopum]
fall [fɔːl] n 추락 [churak] ▷ v 떨어지다 [tteoreojida]
fall down [fɔːl daʊn] v 쓰러지다 [sseureojida]
fall for [fɔːl fɔː] v 반하다 [banhada] (매혹되다)
fall out [fɔːl aʊt] v 사이가 틀어지다 [saiga teureojida]
false [fɔːls] adj 그릇된 [geureutdoen]; **false alarm** n 잘못된 경보 [jalmotdoen gyeongbo]
fame [feɪm] n 명예 [myeongye]
familiar [fəˈmɪlɪə] adj 잘 알려져 있는 [jal allyeojyeo inneun]
family ['fæmɪlɪ; 'fæmlɪ] n 가족 [gajok]; **I want to reserve a family room** 가족실을 예약하고 싶어요 [gajoksireul yeyakhago sipeoyo]; **I'd like to book a family room** 가족실을 예약하고 싶어요 [gajoksireul yeyakhago sipeoyo]; **I'm here with my family** 가족과 여기에 왔어요 [gajokgwa yeogie wasseoyo]
famine ['fæmɪn] n 기근 [gigeun]

famous ['feɪməs] adj 유명한 [yumyeonghan]
fan [fæn] n 선풍기 [seonpunggi]; **fan belt** n 팬 벨트 [paen belteu]
fanatic [fəˈnætɪk] n 광신자 [gwangsinja]
fancy ['fænsɪ] v 공상하다 [gongsanghada]; **fancy dress** n 가장 무도회 의상 [gajang mudohoe uisang]
fantastic [fænˈtæstɪk] adj 환상적인 [hwansangjeogin]
FAQ [ɛf eɪ kjuː] abbr 자주 하는 질문 [jaju haneun jilmun]
far [fɑː] adj 먼 [meon] ▷ adv 멀리 [meolli]; **Far East** n 극동 [geukdong]; **How far is it?** 얼마나 먼가요? [eolmana meongayo?]; **How far is the bank?** 은행이 얼마나 먼가요? [eunhaengi eolmana meongayo?]; **Is it far?** 먼가요? [meongayo?]
fare [fɛə] n 승차 요금 [seungcha yogeum]
farewell [ˌfɛəˈwɛl] excl 안녕! [annyeong!]
farm [fɑːm] n 농장 [nongjang]
farmer ['fɑːmə] n 농부 [nongbu]
farmhouse ['fɑːmˌhaʊs] n 농가 [nongga]
farming ['fɑːmɪŋ] n 농사 [nongsa]
Faroe Islands ['fɛərəʊ 'aɪləndz] npl 페로스 제도 [peroseu jedo]
fascinating ['fæsɪˌneɪtɪŋ] adj 매혹적인 [maehokjeogin]
fashion ['fæʃən] n 유행 [yuhaeng]
fashionable ['fæʃənəbᵊl] adj 유행의 [yuhaengui]
fast [fɑːst] adj 빠른 [ppareun] ▷ adv 빨리 [ppalli]; **I think my watch is fast** 제 시계가 빠른 것 같아요 [je sigyega ppareun geot gatayo]
fat [fæt] adj 살찐 [saljjin] ▷ n 지방 [jibang] (기름)
fatal ['feɪtᵊl] adj 치명적인 [chimyeongjeogin]
fate [feɪt] n 운명 [unmyeong]
father ['fɑːðə] n 아버지 [abeoji]
father-in-law ['fɑːðə ɪn lɔː] **(fathers-in-law)** n 시아버지

[siabeoji] *(husband's father)*
fault [fɔːlt] *n (defect)* 실수 [silsu], *(mistake)* 실수 [silsu]
faulty ['fɔːltɪ] *adj* 결점이 있는 [gyeoljeomi inneun]
fauna ['fɔːnə] *npl* 동물군 [dongmulgun]
favour ['feɪvə] *n* 호의 [houi]
favourite ['feɪvərɪt; 'feɪvrɪt] *adj* 좋아하는 [johahaneun] ▷ *n* 좋아하는 것 [johahaneun geot]
fax [fæks] *n* 팩스 [paekseu] ▷ *v* 팩스 보내다 [paekseu bonaeda]; **Do you have a fax?** 팩스 있어요? [paekseu isseoyo?]; **How much is it to send a fax?** 팩스 보내는 데 얼마입니까? [paekseu bonaeneun de eolmaimnikka?]; **I want to send a fax** 팩스를 보내고 싶어요 [paekseureul bonaego sipeoyo]; **Is there a fax machine I can use?** 사용할 수 있는 팩스기가 있나요? [sayonghal su inneun paekseugiga innayo?]; **Please resend your fax** 팩스를 다시 보내 주세요 [paekseureul dasi bonae juseyo]; **There is a problem with your fax** 당신의 팩스에 문제가 있어요 [dangsinui paekseue munjega isseoyo]; **What is the fax number?** 팩스 번호가 무엇입니까? [paekseu beonhoga mueosimnikka?]
fear [fɪə] *n* 두려움 [duryeoum] ▷ *v* 두려워하다 [duryeowohada]
feasible ['fiːzəbəl] *adj* 실행할 수 있는 [silhaenghal su inneun]
feather ['fɛðə] *n* 깃털 [gittheol]
feature ['fiːtʃə] *n* 특징 [teukjing]
February ['fɛbrʊərɪ] *n* 2월 [iwol]
fed up [fɛd ʌp] *adj* 싫증이 난 [sircheungi nan]
fee [fiː] *n* 요금 [yogeum]; **entrance fee** *n* 입장료 [ipjangnyo]; **tuition fees** *npl* 수업료 [sueomnyo]
feed [fiːd] *v* 음식(먹이)을 주다 [eumsik(meogi)eul juda]
feedback ['fiːd,bæk] *n* 반응 [baneung]
feel [fiːl] *v* 느끼다 [neukkida]
feeling ['fiːlɪŋ] *n* 느낌 [neukkim]
feet [fiːt] *npl* 발 [bal]; **My feet are a size**

six 제 발은 육 사이즈예요 [je bareun yuk saijeuyeyo]; **My feet are sore** 발이 아파요 [bari apayo]
felt [fɛlt] *n* 펠트 [pelteu]
female ['fiːmeɪl] *adj* 여성의 [yeoseongui] ▷ *n* 여성 [yeoseong]
feminine ['fɛmɪnɪn] *adj* 여성스러운 [yeoseongseureoun]
feminist ['fɛmɪnɪst] *n* 페미니스트 [peminiseuteu]
fence [fɛns] *n* 울타리 [ultari]
fennel ['fɛnəl] *n* 회향풀 [hoehyangpul]
fern [fɜːn] *n* 고사리 [gosari]
ferret ['fɛrɪt] *n* 흰담비 [huindambi]
ferry ['fɛrɪ] *n* 페리 [peri]
fertile ['fɜːtaɪl] *adj* 비옥한 [biokhan]
fertilizer ['fɜːtɪ,laɪzə] *n* 비료 [biryo]
festival ['fɛstɪvəl] *n* 축제 [chukje]
fetch [fɛtʃ] *v* 가지고 오다 [gajigo oda]
fever ['fiːvə] *n* 열 [yeol]; **hay fever** *n* 꽃가루 알레르기 [kkotgaru allereugi]; **He has a fever** 열이 있어요 [yeori isseoyo]
few [fjuː] *adj* 소수의 [sosuui] ▷ *pron* 소수 [sosu]
fewer [fjuːə] *adj* 더 소수의 [deo sosuui]
fiancé [fɪˈɒnseɪ] *n* 약혼자 [yakhonja]
fiancée [fɪˈɒnseɪ] *n* 약혼녀 [yakhonnyeo]
fibre ['faɪbə] *n* 섬유 [seomyu]
fibreglass ['faɪbə,glɑːs] *n* 섬유 유리 [seomyu yuri]
fiction ['fɪkʃən] *n* 소설 [soseol]; **science fiction** *n* 공상과학 소설 [gongsanggwahak soseol]
field [fiːld] *n* 들판 [deulpan]; **playing field** *n* 경기장 [gyeonggijang]
fierce [fɪəs] *adj* 난폭한 [nanpokhan]
fifteen ['fɪfˈtiːn] *number* 열다섯 [yeoldaseot], *(Sino-Korean)* 십오 [sibo]
fifteenth ['fɪfˈtiːnθ] *adj* 열다섯 번째의 [yeoldaseot beonjjaeui]
fifth [fɪfθ] *adj* 다섯 번째의 [daseot beonjjaeui]
fifty ['fɪftɪ] *number* 쉰 [swin], *(Sino-Korean)* 오십 [osip]
fifty-fifty ['fɪftɪ,fɪftɪ] *adj* 절반의 [jeolbanui] ▷ *adv* 절반으로

fig | 262

[jeolbaneuro]

fig [fɪg] n 무화과 [muhwagwa]

fight [faɪt] n 싸움 [ssaum] ▷ v 싸우다 [ssauda]

fighting [faɪtɪŋ] n 싸움 [ssaum]

figure ['fɪgə; 'fɪgjər] n 숫자 [sutja]

figure out ['fɪgə aʊt] v 해결하다 [haegyeolhada]

Fiji ['fiːdʒiː; fiːˈdʒiː] n 피지 [piji]

file [faɪl] n (folder) 파일 [pail], (tool) 줄 [jul] ▷ v (folder) 철하다 [cheolhada], (smoothing) 줄질하다 [juljilhada]

Filipino, Filipina [ˌfɪlɪˈpiːnəʊ, ˌfɪlɪˈpiːna] adj 필리핀의 [pillipinui] ▷ n 필리핀 사람 [pillipin saram]

fill [fɪl] v 채우다 [chaeuda]

fillet ['fɪlɪt] n 살토막 [saltomakt] ▷ v 토막으로 썰다 [tomageuro sseolda]

fill in [fɪl ɪn] v 써넣다 [sseoneota]

filling ['fɪlɪŋ] n A filling has fallen out 충전물가 빠졌어요 [chungjeonmulga ppajyeosseoyo]; **Can you do a temporary filling?** 임시로 때워 주시겠어요? [imsiro ttaewo jusigesseoyo?]

fill up [fɪl ʌp] v 채우다 [chaeuda]

film [fɪlm] n 영화 [yeonghwa]; **film star** n 영화 배우 [yeonghwa baeu]; **horror film** n 공포 영화 [gongpo yeonghwa]; **Are there any films in English?** 영어로 된 영화가 있나요? [yeongeoro doen yeonghwaga innayo?]; **When does the film start?** 영화가 언제 시작해요? [yeonghwaga eonje sijakhaeyo?]; **Where can we go to see a film?** 어디에 가면 영화를 볼 수 있어요? [eodie gamyeon yeonghwareul bol su isseoyo?]; **Which film is on at the cinema?** 어떤 영화를 상영하나요? [eotteon yeonghwareul sangyeonghanayo?]

filter ['fɪltə] n 필터 [pilteo] ▷ v 거르다 [georeuda]

filthy ['fɪlθɪ] adj 불결한 [bulgyeolhan]

final ['faɪnᵊl] adj 최종의 [choejongui] ▷ n 결승전 [gyeolseungjeon]

finalize ['faɪnəˌlaɪz] v 마무리하다 [mamurihada]

finally ['faɪnəlɪ] adv 마침내 [machimnae]

finance [fɪˈnæns; ˈfaɪnæns] n 금융 [geumyung] ▷ v 자금을 공급하다 [jageumeul gonggeuphada]

financial [fɪˈnænʃəl; faɪ-] adj 재무상의 [jaemusangui]; **financial year** n 회계 연도 [hoegye yeondo]

find [faɪnd] v 찾다 [chatda]

find out [faɪnd aʊt] v 발견하다 [balgyeonhada]

fine [faɪn] adj 가느다란 [ganeudaran] ▷ adv 좋게 [joke] ▷ n 벌금 [beolgeum]; **How much is the fine?** 벌금이 얼마예요? [beolgeumi eolmayeyo?]; **Where do I pay the fine?** 어디에서 벌금을 내야 합니까? [eodieseo beolgeumeul naeya hamnikka?]

finger ['fɪŋgə] n 손가락 [songarak]; **index finger** n 집게손가락 [jipgesongarak]

fingernail ['fɪŋgəˌneɪl] n 손톱 [sontop]

fingerprint ['fɪŋgəˌprɪnt] n 지문 [jimun]

finish ['fɪnɪʃ] n 끝 [kkeut] ▷ v ...을 끝내다 [...eul kkeutnaeda]; **When does it finish?** 언제 끝나요? [eonje kkeutnayo?]; **When will you have finished?** 언제 끝나요? [eonje kkeutnayo?]

finished ['fɪnɪʃt] adj 끝낸 [kkeutnaen]

Finland ['fɪnlənd] n 핀란드 [pillandeu]

Finn ['fɪn] n 핀란드 사람 [pillandeu saram]

Finnish ['fɪnɪʃ] adj 핀란드의 [pillandeuui] ▷ n 핀란드 사람 [pillandeu saram]

fir [fɜː] n **fir (tree)** n 전나무 [jeonnamu]

fire [faɪə] n 불 [bul]; **fire alarm** n 화재 경보 [hwajae gyeongbo]; **fire brigade** n 소방대 [sobangdae]; **fire escape** n 화재 피난 장치 [hwajae pinan jangchi]; **fire extinguisher** n 소화기 [sohwagi]; **Fire!** 불이야! [buriya!]; **Please call the fire brigade** 소방대를 불러 주세요 [sobangdaereul bulleo juseyo]

fireman, firemen ['faɪəmən, 'faɪəmɛn] n 소방관 [sobanggwan]

fireplace ['faɪəˌpleɪs] n 벽난로 [byeongnanno]

firewall ['faɪəˌwɔːl] n 방화벽 [banghwabyeok]

fireworks ['faɪəˌwɜːks] npl 불꽃놀이 [bulkkotnori]

firm [fɜːm] adj 단단한 [dandanhan] ▷ n 회사 [hoesa]

first [fɜːst] adj 첫 번째의 [cheot beonjjaeui] ▷ adv 처음으로 [cheoeumeuro] ▷ n 첫째 [cheotjjae]; **first aid** n 응급 치료 [eunggeup chiryo]; **first name** n 이름 [ireum]

first-class ['fɜːstˈklɑːs] adj 제1급의 [je1geubui]

firstly ['fɜːstlɪ] adv 첫째로 [cheotjjaero]

fiscal ['fɪskəl] adj 회계의 [hoegyeui]; **fiscal year** n 회계연도 [hoegyeyeondo]

fish [fɪʃ] n 물고기 [mulgogi] ▷ v 낚시하다 [nakksihada]; **freshwater fish** n 민물고기 [minmulgogi]

fisherman, fishermen ['fɪʃəmən, 'fɪʃəmɛn] n 어부 [eobu]

fishing ['fɪʃɪŋ] n 어업 [eoeop]; **fishing boat** n 어선 [eoseon]; **fishing rod** n 낚싯대 [nakksitdae]; **fishing tackle** n 낚시 도구 [nakksi dogu]

fishmonger ['fɪʃˌmʌŋɡə] n 생선 장수 [saengseon jangsu]

fist [fɪst] n 주먹 [jumeok]

fit [fɪt] adj 알맞은 [almajeun] ▷ n 적합성 [jeokhapseong] ▷ v 적합하다 [jeokhaphada]; **epileptic fit** n 간질 발작 [ganjilbaljjark]; **fitted kitchen** n 맞춤 주방 [matchum jubang]; **fitted sheet** n 맞춤 시트 [matchum siteu]; **fitting room** n 탈의실 [taruisil]

fit in [fɪt ɪn] v 들어맞다 [deureomatda]

five [faɪv] number 다섯 [daseot], (Sino-Korean) 오 [o]

fix [fɪks] v 고정시키다 [gojeongsikida]

fixed [fɪkst] adj 고정된 [gojeongdoen]

fizzy ['fɪzɪ] adj 거품이는 [geopumineun]

flabby ['flæbɪ] adj 축 늘어진 [chuk neureojin]

flag [flæg] n 깃발 [gitbal]

flame [fleɪm] n 불꽃 [bulkkot]

flamingo [fləˈmɪŋɡəʊ] n 플라밍고 [peullaminggo]

flammable ['flæməbəl] adj 인화성의 [inhwaseongui]

flan [flæn] n 케익류 [keingnyu]

flannel ['flænəl] n 플란넬 [peullannel]

flap [flæp] v 퍼덕거리다 [peodeokgeorida]

flash [flæʃ] n 섬광 [seomgwang] ▷ v 번쩍이다 [beonjjeogida]

flashlight ['flæʃˌlaɪt] n 플래시 [peullaesi]

flask [flɑːsk] n 플라스크 [peullaseukeu]

flat [flæt] adj 평평한 [pyeongpyeonghan] ▷ n 평면 [pyeongmyeon]; **studio flat** n 원룸 아파트 [wollum apateu]

flat-screen ['flætˌskriːn] adj 평판 스크린의 [pyeongpan seukeurinui]

flatter ['flætə] v 아첨하다 [acheomhada]

flattered ['flætəd] adj 우쭐해진 [ujjulhaejin]

flavour ['fleɪvə] n 맛 [mat]

flavouring ['fleɪvərɪŋ] n 향료 [hyangnyo]

flaw [flɔː] n 결점 [gyeoljeom]

flea [fliː] n 벼룩 [byeoruk]; **flea market** n 벼룩시장 [byeoruksijang]

flee [fliː] v 달아나다 [daranada]

fleece [fliːs] n 양털 [yangteol]

fleet [fliːt] n 함대 [hamdae]

flex [flɛks] n 전선 [jeonseon] (연장)

flexible ['flɛksɪbəl] adj 구부릴 수 있는 [guburil su inneun]

flexitime ['flɛksɪˌtaɪm] n 탄력근무제 [tallyeokgeunmuje]

flight [flaɪt] n 비행 [bihaeng] (날다); **charter flight** n 전세기 [jeonsegi]; **flight attendant** n 비행기 승무원 [bihaenggi seungmuwon]; **scheduled flight** n 정기 항공편 [jeonggi hanggongpyeon]; **Are there any cheap flights?** 싼 비행기편이 있어요? [ssan bihaenggipyeoni isseoyo?]; **I would prefer an earlier flight** 더 이른 비행기편이 좋아요 [deo ireun bihaenggipyeoni johayo]; **I'd like to**

cancel my flight 비행기편을 취소하려고요 [bihaenggipyeoneul chwisoharyeogoyo]; **I'd like to change my flight** 비행기편을 바꾸려고요 [bihaenggipyeoneul bakkuryeogoyo]; **I've missed my flight** 비행기를 놓쳤어요 [bihaenggireul nochyeosseoyo]; **The flight has been delayed** 비행기가 지연되었어요 [bihaenggiga jiyeondoeeosseoyo]; **Where do I check in for the flight to...?** ... 가는 비행기는 어디에서 탑승 수속을 하나요? [... ganeun bihaenggineun eodieseo tapseung susogeul hanayo?]; **Where is the luggage for the flight from...?** ...발 비행기의 수하물은 어디에 있나요? [...bal bihaenggiui suhamureun eodie innayo?]; **Which gate for the flight to...?** ... 가는 비행기는 어느 출구인가요? [... ganeun bihaenggineun eoneu chulguingayo?]

fling [flɪŋ] v 던지다 [deonjida]

flip-flops ['flɪpˌflɒpz] npl 고무 슬리퍼 [gomu seullipeo]

flippers ['flɪpəz] npl 오리발 [oribal]

flirt [flɜːt] n 바람둥이 [baramdungi] ▷ v 장난 삼아 연애하다 [jangnan sama yeonaehada]

float [fləʊt] n 뜨는 것 [tteuneun geot] ▷ v 뜨다 [tteuda]

flock [flɒk] n 무리 [muri]

flood [flʌd] n 홍수 [hongsu] ▷ vi 범람하다 [beomramhada]

flooding ['flʌdɪŋ] n 범람 [beomnam]

floodlight ['flʌdˌlaɪt] n 투광 조명 [tugwang jomyeong]

floor [flɔː] n (방)바닥 [(bang)badak]; **ground floor** n 1층 [il cheung]

flop [flɒp] n 실패 [silpae]

floppy ['flɒpɪ] adj **floppy disk** n 플로피 디스크 [peullopi diseukeu]

flora ['flɔːrə] npl 식물군 [singmulgun]

florist ['flɒrɪst] n 꽃장수 [kkotchangsu]

flour ['flaʊə] n 가루 [garu]

flow [fləʊ] v 흐르다 [heureuda]

flower ['flaʊə] n 꽃 [kkot] ▷ v 꽃이 피다 [kkochi pida]

flu [fluː] n 독감 [dokgam]; **bird flu** n 조류 독감 [joryu dokgam]; **I had flu recently** 최근에 독감을 앓았어요 [choegeune dokgameul arasseoyo]; **I've got flu** 독감에 걸렸어요 [dokgame geollyeosseoyo]

fluent ['fluːənt] adj 유창한 [yuchanghan]

fluorescent [ˌfluəˈrɛsᵊnt] adj 형광성의 [hyeonggwangseongui]

flush [flʌʃ] n 홍조 [hongjo] ▷ v 얼굴이 붉어지다 [eolguri bulgeojida]

flute [fluːt] n 플루트 [peulluteu]

fly [flaɪ] n 파리 [pari] (곤충) ▷ v 날다 [nalda]

fly away [flaɪ əˈweɪ] v 날아가다 [naragada]

foal [fəʊl] n 망아지 [mangaji]

foam [fəʊm] n **shaving foam** n 면도용 거품 [myeondoyong geopum]

focus ['fəʊkəs] n 초점 [chojeom] ▷ v 초점을 맞추다 [chojeomeul matchuda]

foetus ['fiːtəs] n 태아 [taea]

fog [fɒg] n 안개 [angae]; **fog light** n 안개등 [angaedeung]

foggy ['fɒgɪ] adj 안개가 자욱한 [angaega jaukhan]

foil [fɔɪl] n 포일 [poil]

fold [fəʊld] n 접은 자리 [jeobeun jari] ▷ v 접다 [jeopda]

folder ['fəʊldə] n 폴더 [poldeo]

folding [fəʊldɪŋ] adj 접는 [jeomneun]

folklore ['fəʊkˌlɔː] n 민간전설 [minganjeonseol]

follow ['fɒləʊ] v 잇따르다 [itthtareuda]

following ['fɒləʊɪŋ] adj 다음의 [daeumui]

food [fuːd] n 식품 [sikpum]; **food poisoning** n 식중독 [sikjungdok]; **food processor** n 믹서 [mikseo]; **Do you have food?** 식품 있어요? [sikpum isseoyo?]

fool [fuːl] n 바보 [babo] ▷ v 속이다 [sogida]

foot, feet [fʊt, fiːt] n 발 [bal]; **My feet are a size six** 제 발은 육 사이즈예요 [je bareun yuk saijeuyeyo]

football ['fʊtˌbɔːl] n 축구 [chukgu];

American football n 미식 축구 [misik chukgu]; **football match** n 축구 경기 [chukgu gyeonggi]; **football player** n 축구 선수 [chukgu seonsu]; **I'd like to see a football match** 축구 경기를 보고 싶어요 [chukgu gyeonggireul bogo sipeoyo]; **Let's play football** 축구합시다 [chukguhapsida]

footballer ['fʊtˌbɔːlə] n 축구 선수 [chukgu seonsu]

footpath ['fʊtˌpɑːθ] n 보도 [bodo]

footprint ['fʊtˌprɪnt] n 발자국 [baljaguk]

footstep ['fʊtˌstɛp] n 걸음걸이 [georeumgeori]

for [fɔː; fə] prep...을 위하여 [...eul wihayeo]

forbid [fə'bɪd] v 금하다 [geumhada]

forbidden [fə'bɪdᵊn] adj 금지된 [geumjidoen]

force [fɔːs] n 힘 [him] ▷ v 강요하다 [gangyohada]; **Air Force** n 공군 [gonggun]

forecast ['fɔːˌkɑːst] n 예측 [yecheuk]

foreground ['fɔːˌgraʊnd] n 전경 [jeongyeong]

forehead ['fɒrɪd; 'fɔːˌhɛd] n 이마 [ima]

foreign ['fɒrɪn] adj 외국의 [oegugui]

foreigner ['fɒrɪnə] n 외국인 [oegugin]

foresee [fɔː'siː] v 예견하다 [yegyeonhada]

forest ['fɒrɪst] n 숲 [sup]

forever [fɔː'rɛvə; fə-] adv 영원히 [yeongwonhi]

forge [fɔːdʒ] v 단조하다 [danjohada] (금속)

forgery ['fɔːdʒərɪ] n 위조 [wijo]

forget [fə'gɛt] v 잊다 [itda]

forgive [fə'gɪv] v 용서하다 [yongseohada]

forgotten [fə'gɒtᵊn] adj 잊은 [ijeun]

fork [fɔːk] n 포크 [pokeu]; **Could I have a clean fork please?** 깨끗한 포크를 주시겠어요? [kkaekkeutan pokeureul jusigesseoyo?]

form [fɔːm] n 형태 [hyeongtae]; **application form** n 신청서 [sincheongseo]; **order form** n 주문서 [jumunseo]

formal ['fɔːməl] adj 형식적인 [hyeongsikjeogin]

formality [fɔː'mælɪtɪ] n 격식 [gyeoksik]

format ['fɔːmæt] n 형식 [hyeongsik] ▷ v 형식화하다 [hyeongsikhwahada]

former ['fɔːmə] adj 전의 [jeonui]

formerly ['fɔːməlɪ] adv 이전에는 [ijeoneneun]

formula ['fɔːmjʊlə] n 공식 [gongsik] (수학)

fort [fɔːt] n 요새 [yosae]

fortnight ['fɔːtˌnaɪt] n 2주일간 [i juilgan]

fortunate ['fɔːtʃənɪt] adj 행운의 [haengunui]

fortunately ['fɔːtʃənɪtlɪ] adv 운좋게 [unjoke]

fortune ['fɔːtʃən] n 재산 [jaesan]

forty ['fɔːtɪ] number 마흔 [maheun], (Sino-Korean) 사십 [sasip]

forward ['fɔːwəd] adv 앞으로 [apeuro] ▷ v 전송하다 [jeonsonghada]; **forward slash** n 포워드 슬래시 [powodeu seullaesi]; **lean forward** v 앞으로 굽히다 [apeuro guphida]

foster ['fɒstə] v 양육하다 [yangyukhada]; **foster child** n 수양 자녀 [suyang janyeo]

foul [faʊl] adj 더러운 [deoreoun] ▷ n 반칙 [banchik]

foundations [faʊn'deɪʃənz] npl 초석 [choseok]

fountain ['faʊntɪn] n 분수 [bunsu]; **fountain pen** n 만년필 [mannyeonpil]

four [fɔː] number 넷 [net], (Sino-Korean) 사 [sa]

fourteen ['fɔː'tiːn] number 열넷 [yeollet], (Sino-Korean) 십사 [sipsa]

fourteenth ['fɔː'tiːnθ] adj 열네 번째의 [yeolle beonjjaeui]

fourth [fɔːθ] adj 네 번째의 [ne beonjjaeui]

fox [fɒks] n 여우 [yeou]

fracture ['fræktʃə] n 골절 [goljeol]

fragile ['frædʒaɪl] adj 깨지기 쉬운 [kkaejigi swiun]

frail [freɪl] *adj* 허약한 [heoyakhan]
frame [freɪm] *n* 틀 [teul]; **picture frame** *n* 그림틀 [geurimteul]; **Zimmer® frame** *n* 보행 보조기 [bohaeng bojogi]
France [frɑːns] *n* 프랑스 [peurangseu]
frankly ['fræŋklɪ] *adv* 솔직히 [soljikhi]
frantic ['fræntɪk] *adj* 미칠 듯한 [michil deutan]
fraud [frɔːd] *n* 사기 [sagi]
freckles ['frɛkᵊlz] *npl* 주근깨 [jugeunkkae]
free [friː] *adj* (*no cost*) 무료의 [muryoui], (*no restraint*) 자유로운 [jayuroun] ▷ *v* 자유롭게 해주다 [jayuropge haejuda]; **free kick** *n* 프리킥 [peurikik]
freedom ['friːdəm] *n* 자유 [jayu]
freelance ['friːˌlɑːns] *adj* 자유계약의 [jayugyeyagui] ▷ *adv* 자유계약으로 [jayugyeyageuro]
freeze [friːz] *v* 얼다 [eolda]
freezer ['friːzə] *n* 냉동고 [naengdonggo]
freezing ['friːzɪŋ] *adj* 혹한의 [hokhanui]
freight [freɪt] *n* 화물 [hwamul]
French [frɛntʃ] *adj* 프랑스의 [peurangseuui] ▷ *n* 프랑스 사람 [peurangseu saram]; **French beans** *npl* 강낭콩 [gangnangkong]; **French horn** *n* 프렌치 호른 [peurenchi horeun]
Frenchman, Frenchmen ['frɛntʃmən, 'frɛntʃmɛn] *n* 프랑스 사람 [peurangseu saram]
Frenchwoman, Frenchwomen ['frɛntʃwʊmən, 'frɛntʃwɪmɪn] *n* 프랑스 여자 [peurangseu yeoja]
frequency ['friːkwənsɪ] *n* 빈도 [bindo]
frequent ['friːkwənt] *adj* 빈번한 [binbeonhan]
fresh [frɛʃ] *adj* 신선한 [sinseonhan]
freshen up ['frɛʃən ʌp] *v* 정리하다 [jeongnihada]
fret [frɛt] *v* 안달나다 [andallada]
Friday ['fraɪdɪ] *n* 금요일 [geumyoil]; **Good Friday** *n* 성 금요일 [seong geumyoil]; **on Friday the thirty-first of December** 십이월 삼십일일

금요일에 [sibiwol samsibiril geumyoire]; **on Friday** 금요일에 [geumyoire]
fridge [frɪdʒ] *n* 냉장고 [naengjanggo]
fried [fraɪd] *adj* 튀긴 [twigin]
friend [frɛnd] *n* 친구 [chingu]; **I'm here with my friends** 친구들과 여기에 왔어요 [chingudeulgwa yeogie wasseoyo]
friendly ['frɛndlɪ] *adj* 친절한 [chinjeolhan]
friendship ['frɛndʃɪp] *n* 우정 [ujeong]
fright [fraɪt] *n* 갑작스러운 놀람 [gapjakseureoun nollam]
frighten ['fraɪtᵊn] *v* 겁을 주다 [geobeul juda]
frightened ['fraɪtənd] *adj* 겁먹은 [geommeogeun]
frightening ['fraɪtᵊnɪŋ] *adj* 무서운 [museoun]
fringe [frɪndʒ] *n* 가장자리 [gajangjari]
frog [frɒg] *n* 개구리 [gaeguri]
from [frɒm; frəm] *prep* ...로부터 [... robuteo]
front [frʌnt] *adj* 앞의 [apui] ▷ *n* 앞 [ap]
frontier ['frʌntɪə; frʌn'tɪə] *n* 국경 [gukgyeong]
frost [frɒst] *n* 서리 [seori]
frosting ['frɒstɪŋ] *n* 설탕을 입힘 [seoltangeul iphim]
frosty ['frɒstɪ] *adj* 서리가 내릴 만큼 추운 [seoriga naeril mankeum chuun]
frown [fraʊn] *v* 눈살을 찌푸리다 [nunsareul jjipurida]
frozen ['frəʊzᵊn] *adj* 언 [eon]
fruit [fruːt] *n* (*botany*) 과일 [gwail], (*collectively*) 과일 [gwail]; **fruit juice** *n* 과일 주스 [gwail juseu]; **fruit machine** *n* 슬롯머신 [seullotmeosin]; **fruit salad** *n* 과일 샐러드 [gwail saelleodeu]; **passion fruit** *n* 시계풀의 열매 [sigyepurui yeolmae]
frustrated [frʌ'streɪtɪd] *adj* 좌절한 [jwajeolhan]
fry [fraɪ] *v* 튀기다 [twigida]; **frying pan** *n* 프라이팬 [peuraipaen]
fuel [fjʊəl] *n* 연료 [yeollyo]
fulfil [fʊl'fɪl] *v* 성취하다

[seongchwihada]

full [fʊl] *adj* 가득한 [gadeukhan]; **full moon** *n* 보름달 [boreumdal]; **full stop** *n* 마침표 [machimpyo]

full-time ['fʊl,taɪm] *adj* 전임의 [jeonimui] ▷ *adv* 전임으로 [jeonimeuro]

fully ['fʊlɪ] *adv* 완전히 [wanjeonhi]

fumes [fjuːmz] *npl* 연기 [yeongi]; **exhaust fumes** *npl* 배기 가스 [baegi gaseu]

fun [fʌn] *adj* 재미있는 [jaemiinneun] ▷ *n* 재미 [jaemi]

funds [fʌndz] *npl* 자금 [jageum]

funeral ['fjuːnərəl] *n* 장례식 [jangnyesik]; **funeral parlour** *n* 영안실 [yeongansil]

funfair ['fʌn,fɛə] *n* 유원지 [yuwonji]

funnel ['fʌnᵊl] *n* 깔때기 [kkalttaegi]

funny ['fʌnɪ] *adj* 우스운 [useuun]

fur [fɜː] *n* 모피 [mopi]; **fur coat** *n* 모피코트 [mopikoteu]

furious ['fjʊərɪəs] *adj* 격노한 [gyeongnohan]

furnished ['fɜːnɪʃt] *adj* 가구가 갖추어진 [gaguga gatchueojin]

furniture ['fɜːnɪtʃə] *n* 가구 [gagu]

further ['fɜːðə] *adj* 그 이상의 [geu isangui] ▷ *adv* 게다가 [gedaga]; **further education** *n* 성인 교육 [seongin gyoyuk]

fuse [fjuːz] *n* 퓨즈 [pyujeu]; **fuse box** *n* 두꺼비집 [dukkeobijip]; **A fuse has blown** 퓨즈가 나갔어요 [pyujeuga nagasseoyo]; **Can you mend a fuse?** 퓨즈를 바꿀 수 있나요? [pyujeureul bakkul su innayo?]

fusebox ['fjuːz,bɒks] *n* **Where is the fusebox?** 두꺼비집은 어디있어요?

fuss [fʌs] *n* 안달하기 [andalhagi]

fussy ['fʌsɪ] *adj* 야단법석하는 [yadanbeopseokhaneun]

future ['fjuːtʃə] *adj* 미래의 [miraeui] ▷ *n* 미래 [mirae]

Gabon [gəˈbɒn] *n* 가봉 [gabong] (국가)

gain [geɪn] *n* 이득 [ideuk] ▷ *v* 얻다 [eotda]

gale [geɪl] *n* 질풍 [jilpung]

gallery ['gælərɪ] *n* 화랑 [hwarang]; **art gallery** *n* 미술관 [misulgwan]

gallop ['gæləp] *n* 갤럽 [gaelleop] ▷ *v* 갤럽으로 달리다 [gaelleobeuro dallida]

gallstone ['gɔːl,stəʊn] *n* 담석 [damseok]

Gambia ['gæmbɪə] *n* 잠비아 [jambia]

gamble ['gæmbᵊl] *v* 도박을 하다 [dobageul hada]

gambler ['gæmblə] *n* 도박꾼 [dobakkun]

gambling ['gæmblɪŋ] *n* 도박 [dobak]

game [geɪm] *n* 게임 [geim]; **board game** *n* 보드 게임 [bodeu geim]; **games console** *n* 게임 콘솔 [geim konsol]; **Can I play video games?** 비디오 게임을 할 수 있을까요? [bidio geimeul hal su isseulkkayo?]

gang [gæŋ] *n* 갱 [gaeng]

gangster ['gæŋstə] *n* 갱단의 일원 [gaengdanui irwon]

gap [gæp] *n* 간격 [gangyeok]

garage ['gærɑːʒ; -rɪdʒ] *n* 차고 [chago];

Which is the key for the garage?
차고 열쇠는 어느 것인가요? [chago
yeolsoeneun eoneu geosingayo?]
garbage ['gɑːbɪdʒ] n 쓰레기 [sseuregi]
garden ['gɑːdⁿn] n 정원 [jeongwon];
garden centre n 원예점 [wonyejeom];
Can we visit the gardens? 정원을
방문할 수 있어요? [jeongwoneul
bangmunhal su isseoyo?]
gardener ['gɑːdnə] n 정원사
[jeongwonsa]
gardening ['gɑːdⁿnɪŋ] n 정원 가꾸기
[jeongwon gakkugi]
garlic ['gɑːlɪk] n 마늘 [maneul]; **Is
there any garlic in it?** 속에 마늘이
있나요? [soge maneuri innayo?]
garment ['gɑːmənt] n 의복 [uibok]
gas [gæs] n 가스 [gaseu]; **gas cooker** n
가스레인지 [gaseureinji]; **natural gas**
n 천연 가스 [cheonyeon gaseu]; **I can
smell gas** 가스 냄새가 나요 [gaseu
naemsaega nayo]; **Where is the gas
meter?** 가스 계량기는 어디있어요?
[gaseu gyeryanggineun eodiisseoyo?]
gasket ['gæskɪt] n 개스켓 [gaeseuket]
gate [geɪt] n 문 [mun]
gateau, gateaux ['gætəʊ, 'gætəʊz] n
케이크 [keikeu]
gather ['gæðə] v (끌어) 모으다
[(kkeureo) moeuda]
gauge [geɪdʒ] n 게이지 [geiji] ▷ v
측정하다 [cheukjeonghada]
gaze [geɪz] v 응시하다 [eungsihada]
gear [gɪə] n (equipment) 용구 [yonggu],
(mechanism) 기어 [gieo]; **gear box** n
용구함 [yongguham]; **gear lever** n
변속 레버 [byeonsok rebeo]; **gear
stick** n 변속 레버 [byeonsok rebeo];
Does the bike have gears? 자전거에
기어가 있어요? [jajeongeoe gieoga
isseoyo?]; **The gears don't work**
기어가 고장났어요 [gieoga
gojangnasseoyo]
gearbox ['gɪəˌbɒks] n **The gearbox is
broken** 변속기가 고장났어요
[byeonsoggiga gojangnass-eoyo]
gearshift ['gɪəˌʃɪft] n 변속 레버
[byeonsok rebeo]

gel [dʒɛl] n 겔 [gel]; **hair gel** n 헤어 젤
[heeo jel]
gem [dʒɛm] n 보석 [boseok]
Gemini ['dʒɛmɪˌnaɪ; -ˌniː] n 쌍둥이자리
[ssangdungijari]
gender ['dʒɛndə] n 성 [seong]
gene [dʒiːn] n 유전자 [yujeonja]
general ['dʒɛnərəl; 'dʒɛnrəl] adj
일반적인 [ilbanjeogin] ▷ n 장군
[janggun]; **general anaesthetic** n
전신 마취 [jeonsin machwi]; **general
election** n 총선거 [chongseongeo];
general knowledge n 일반 상식
[ilban sangsik]
generalize ['dʒɛnrəˌlaɪz] v 일반화하다
[ilbanhwahada]
generally ['dʒɛnrəlɪ] adv 일반적으로
[ilbanjeogeuro]
generation [ˌdʒɛnə'reɪʃən] n 세대
[sedae]
generator ['dʒɛnəˌreɪtə] n 발전기
[baljeongi]
generosity [ˌdʒɛnə'rɒsɪtɪ] n 관대
[gwandae]
generous ['dʒɛnərəs; 'dʒɛnrəs] adj 인심
좋은 [insim joheun]
genetic [dʒɪ'nɛtɪk] adj 유전의
[yujeonui]
genetically-modified
[dʒɪ'nɛtɪklɪ'mɒdɪˌfaɪd] adj 유전자
변형의 [yujeonja byeonhyeongui]
genetics [dʒɪ'nɛtɪks] n 유전학
[yujeonhak]
genius ['dʒiːnɪəs; -njəs] n 천재
[cheonjae]
gentle ['dʒɛntⁿl] adj 온화한
[onhwahan]
gentleman ['dʒɛntⁿlmən]
(gentlemen ['dʒɛntⁿlmɛn]**)** n 신사
[sinsa]
gently ['dʒɛntlɪ] adv 온화하게
[onhwahage]
gents' [dʒɛnts] n 남자 화장실 [namja
hwajangsil]; **Where is the gents?** 남자
화장실은 어디에 있어요? [namja
hwajangsireun eodie isseoyo?]
genuine ['dʒɛnjʊɪn] adj 진짜의
[jinjjaui]

geography [dʒɪˈɒɡrəfɪ] n 지리학 [jirihak]

geology [dʒɪˈɒlədʒɪ] n 지질학 [jijilhak]

Georgia [ˈdʒɔːdʒə] n (country) 그루지야 [geurujiya], (US state) 조지아 [jojia]

Georgian [ˈdʒɔːdʒən] adj 그루지야의 [geurujiyaui] ▷ n (inhabitant of Georgia) 그루지야 사람 [geurujiya saram]

geranium [dʒɪˈreɪnɪəm] n 제라늄 [jeranyum]

gerbil [ˈdʒɜːbɪl] n 게르빌루스쥐 [gereubilluseujwi]

geriatric [ˌdʒɛrɪˈætrɪk] adj 노인의 [noinui] ▷ n 노인병 환자 [noinbyeong hwanja]

germ [dʒɜːm] n 병균 [byeonggyun]

German [ˈdʒɜːmən] adj 독일의 [dogirui] ▷ n (language) 독일어 [dogireo], (person) 독일 사람 [dogil saram]; **German measles** n 풍진 [pungjin]

Germany [ˈdʒɜːmənɪ] n 독일 [dogil]

gesture [ˈdʒɛstʃə] n 몸짓 [momjit]

get [gɛt] v 얻다 [eotda], (to a place) 얻다 [eotda]

get away [gɛt əˈweɪ] v 벗어나다 [beoseonada]

get back [gɛt bæk] v 돌아오게 하다 [doraoge hada]

get in [gɛt ɪn] v 도착하다 [dochakhada]

get into [gɛt ˈɪntə] v 말려들다 [mallyeodeulda]

get off [gɛt ɒf] v 내리다 [naerida]

get on [gɛt ɒn] v 타다 [tada] (차량)

get out [gɛt aʊt] v 떠나다 [tteonada]

get over [gɛt ˈəʊvə] v 회복하다 [hoebokhada]

get through [gɛt θruː] v **I can't get through** 통화가 안돼요 [tonghwaga andwaeyo]

get together [gɛt təˈgɛðə] v 모이다 [moida]

get up [gɛt ʌp] v 일어나다 [ireonada]

Ghana [ˈgɑːnə] n 가나 [gana]

Ghanaian [gɑːˈneɪən] adj 가나의 [ganaui] ▷ n 가나 사람 [gana saram]

ghost [gəʊst] n 유령 [yuryeong]

giant [ˈdʒaɪənt] adj 거대한 [geodaehan] ▷ n 거인 [geoin]

gift [gɪft] n 선물 [seonmul]; **gift shop** n 선물가게 [seonmulgage]; **gift voucher** n 상품권 [sangpumgwon]; **Please can you gift-wrap it?** 선물 포장을 해 주시겠어요? [seonmul pojangeul hae jusigesseoyo?]; **This is a gift for you** 선물이에요 [seonmurieyo]; **Where can I buy gifts?** 어디에서 선물을 살 수 있어요? [eodieseo seonmureul sal su isseoyo?]

gifted [ˈgɪftɪd] adj 천부의 재능이 있는 [cheonbuui jaeneungi inneun]

gigantic [dʒaɪˈgæntɪk] adj 거대한 [geodaehan]

giggle [ˈgɪɡəl] v 낄낄웃다 [kkilkkirutda]

gin [dʒɪn] n 진 [jin]; **I'll have a gin and tonic, please** 진 앤 토닉 주세요 [jin aen tonik juseyo]

ginger [ˈdʒɪndʒə] adj 적갈색의 [jeokgalsaegui] ▷ n 생강 [saenggang]

giraffe [dʒɪˈrɑːf; -ˈræf] n 기린 [girin]

girl [gɜːl] n 소녀 [sonyeo]

girlfriend [ˈgɜːlˌfrɛnd] n 여자친구 [yeojachingu]; **I have a girlfriend** 여자친구가 있어요 [yeojachinguga isseoyo]

give [gɪv] v 주다 [juda]

give back [gɪv bæk] v 돌려주다 [dollyeojuda]

give in [gɪv ɪn] v 포기하다 [pogihada]

give out [gɪv aʊt] v 배포하다 [baepohada]

give up [gɪv ʌp] v 포기하다 [pogihada]

glacier [ˈglæsɪə; ˈgleɪs-] n 빙하 [bingha]

glad [glæd] adj 기쁜 [gippeun]

glamorous [ˈglæmərəs] adj 매혹적인 [maehokjeogin]

glance [glɑːns] n 흘끗 보기 [heulkkeut bogi] ▷ v 흘끗 보다 [heulkkeut boda]

gland [glænd] n 샘 [saem] (기관)

glare [glɛə] v 노려보다 [noryeoboda]

glaring [ˈglɛərɪŋ] adj 역력한 [yeongnyeokhan]

glass [glɑːs] n 유리 [yuri], (vessel) 유리 [yuri]; **magnifying glass** n 확대경 [hwakdaegyeong]; **stained glass** n

스테인드 글라스 [seuteindeu geullaseu]

glasses ['glɑːsɪz] npl 안경 [angyeong]; **Can you repair my glasses?** 제 안경을 고치실 수 있으세요? [je angyeongeul gochisil su isseuseyo?]

glazing ['gleɪzɪŋ] n **double glazing** n 이중 유리 [ijung yuri]

glider ['glaɪdə] n 글라이더 [geullaideo]

gliding ['glaɪdɪŋ] n 활공 [hwalgong]

global ['gləʊbəl] adj 세계적인 [segyejeogin]; **global warming** n 지구 온난화 [jigu onnanhwa]

globalization [ˌgləʊbəlaɪ'zeɪʃən] n 세계화 [segyehwa]

globe [gləʊb] n 지구 [jigu]

gloomy ['gluːmɪ] adj 우울한 [uulhan]

glorious ['glɔːrɪəs] adj 영광스러운 [yeonggwangseureoun]

glory ['glɔːrɪ] n 영광 [yeonggwang]

glove [glʌv] n 장갑 [janggap]; **glove compartment** n 수납함 [sunapham]; **oven glove** n 오븐용 장갑 [obeunyong janggap]; **rubber gloves** npl 고무장갑 [gomujanggap]

glucose ['gluːkəʊz; -kəʊs] n 글루코오스 [geullukooseu]

glue [gluː] n 풀 [pul] ▷ v 붙이다 [buchida]

gluten ['gluːtən] n 글루텐 [geulluten]; **Could you prepare a meal without gluten?** 글루텐이 들어가지 않은 식사를 준비해 주시겠어요? [geulluteni deureogaji anheun siksareul junbihae jusigesseoyo?]; **Do you have gluten-free dishes?** 글루텐이 없는 요리 있어요? [geulluteni eomneun yori isseoyo?]

GM [dʒiː ɛm] abbr 유전자 변형의 [yujeonja byeonhyeongui]

go [gəʊ] v 가다 [gada]

go after [gəʊ 'ɑːftə] v 추구하다 [chuguhada]

go ahead [gəʊ ə'hɛd] v 앞서 가다 [apseo gada]

goal [gəʊl] n 골 [gol] (골키퍼)

goalkeeper ['gəʊlˌkiːpə] n 골키퍼 [golkipeo]

goat [gəʊt] n 염소 [yeomso]

go away [gəʊ ə'weɪ] v 떠나다 [tteonada]

go back [gəʊ bæk] v 돌아오다 [doraoda]

go by [gəʊ baɪ] v 지나가다 [jinagada]

god [gɒd] n 신 [sin]

godchild, godchildren ['gɒdˌtʃaɪld, 'gɒdˌtʃɪldrən] n 대자녀 [daejanyeo]

goddaughter ['gɒdˌdɔːtə] n 대녀 [daenyeo]

godfather ['gɒdˌfɑːðə] n (baptism) 대부 [daebu], (criminal leader) 두목 [dumok]

godmother ['gɒdˌmʌðə] n 대모 [daemo]

go down [gəʊ daʊn] v 내려가다 [naeryeogada]

godson ['gɒdˌsʌn] n 대자 [daeja]

goggles ['gɒgəlz] npl 고글 [gogeul]; **I want to hire goggles** 고글을 빌리고 싶어요 [kogeu-eul billigo sip-eoyo]

go in [gəʊ ɪn] v 들어가다 [deureogada]

gold [gəʊld] n 금 [geum]

golden ['gəʊldən] adj 금색의 [geumsaegui]

goldfish ['gəʊldˌfɪʃ] n 금붕어 [geumbungeo]

gold-plated ['gəʊld'pleɪtɪd] adj 금도금한 [geumdogeumhan]

golf [gɒlf] n 골프 [golpeu]; **golf club** n (game) 골프채 [golpeuchae], (society) 골프 클럽 [golpeu keulleop]; **golf course** n 골프 코스 [golpeu koseu]; **Do they hire out golf clubs?** 골프채 빌려 주나요? [golpeuchae billyeo junayo?]; **Is there a public golf course near here?** 이 근처에 대중 골프장이 있나요? [i geuncheoe daejung golpeujangi innayo?]; **Where can I play golf?** 어디에서 골프를 칠 수 있어요? [eodieseo golpeureul chil su isseoyo?]

gone [gɒn] adj 사라진 [sarajin]

good [gʊd] adj 좋은 [joheun]

goodbye [ˌgʊd'baɪ] excl 안녕! [annyeong!]

good-looking ['gʊd'lʊkɪŋ] adj 잘생긴

[jalsaenggin]

good-natured ['gʊd'neɪtʃəd] *adj* 착한
[chakhan]

goods [gʊdz] *npl* 상품 [sangpum]

go off [gəʊ ɒf] *v* 끄다 [kkeuda]

Google® ['guːgᵊl] *v* 구글 [gugeul]

go on [gəʊ ɒn] *v* 계속하다
[gyesokhada]

goose, geese [guːs, giːs] *n* 거위
[geowi]; **goose pimples** *npl* 소름
[soreum]

gooseberry ['gʊzbəri; -bri] *n* 구스베리
[guseuberi]

go out [gəʊ aʊt] *v* 외출하다
[oechulhada]

go past [gəʊ pɑːst] *v* 지나가다
[jinagada]

gorgeous ['gɔːdʒəs] *adj* 호화로운
[hohwaroun]

gorilla [gə'rɪlə] *n* 고릴라 [gorilla]

go round [gəʊ raʊnd] *v* 골고루 돌아가다
[golgoru doragada]

gospel ['gɒspᵊl] *n* 복음 [bogeum]

gossip ['gɒsɪp] *n* 가쉽 [gaswip] ▷ *v*
수군거리다 [sugungeorida]

go through [gəʊ θruː] *v* 경험하다
[gyeongheomhada]

go up [gəʊ ʌp] *v* 올라가다 [ollagada]

government ['gʌvənmənt; 'gʌvəmənt]
n 정부 [jeongbu] (관청)

gown [gaʊn] *n* **dressing gown** *n* 화장복
[hwajangbok]

GP [dʒiː piː] *abbr* 일반 개업의 [ilban
gaeeobui]

GPS [dʒiː piː ɛs] *abbr* 위성항법장치
[wiseonghangbeopjangchi]

grab [græb] *v* 움켜잡다 [umkyeojapda]

graceful ['greɪsfʊl] *adj* 우아한 [uahan]

grade [greɪd] *n* 등급 [deunggeup]

gradual ['grædjʊəl] *adj* 점진적인
[jeomjinjeogin]

gradually ['grædjʊəlɪ] *adv* 점차
[jeomcha]

graduate ['grædjʊɪt] *n* 대학 졸업생
[daehak joreopsaeng]

graduation [,grædjʊ'eɪʃən] *n* 졸업
[joreop]

graffiti,graffito [græ'fiːtiː, græ'fiːtəʊ]

npl 낙서 [nakseo]

grain [greɪn] *n* 곡물 [gongmul]

grammar ['græmə] *n* 문법 [munbeop]

grammatical [grə'mætɪkᵊl] *adj* 문법의
[munbeobui]

gramme [græm] *n* 그램 [geuraem]

grand [grænd] *adj* 웅대한 [ungdaehan]

grandchild ['græn,tʃaɪld] *n* 손주
[sonju]; **grandchildren** *npl* 손주
[sonju]

granddad ['græn,dæd] *n* 할아버지
[harabeoji]

granddaughter ['græn,dɔːtə] *n* 손녀
[sonnyeo]

grandfather ['græn,fɑːðə] *n* 할아버지
[harabeoji]

grandma ['græn,mɑː] *n* 할머니
[halmeoni]

grandmother ['græn,mʌðə] *n* 할머니
[halmeoni]

grandpa ['græn,pɑː] *n* 할아버지
[harabeoji]

grandparents ['græn,pɛərəntz] *npl*
조부모 [jobumo]

grandson ['grænsʌn; 'grænd-] *n* 손자
[sonja]

granite ['grænɪt] *n* 화강암
[hwagangam]

granny ['grænɪ] *n* 할머니 [halmeoni]

grant [grɑːnt] *n* 보조금 [bojogeum]

grape [greɪp] *n* 포도 [podo]

grapefruit ['greɪp,fruːt] *n*
그레이프프루트 [geureipeupeuruteu]

graph [grɑːf; græf] *n* 그래프
[geuraepeu]

graphics ['græfɪks] *npl* 제도법
[jedobeop]

grasp [grɑːsp] *v* 붙잡다 [butjapda]

grass [grɑːs] *n* (*informer*) 정보 제공자
[jeongbo jegongja], (*marijuana*)
마리화나 [marihwana], (*plant*) 풀 [pul]

grasshopper ['grɑːs,hɒpə] *n* 메뚜기
[mettugi]

grate [greɪt] *v* 쇠살대 [soesaldae]

grateful ['greɪtfʊl] *adj* 고마워하는
[gomawohaneun]

grave [greɪv] *n* 무덤 [mudeom]

gravel ['grævᵊl] *n* 자갈 [jagal]

gravestone [ˈgreɪvˌstəʊn] n 묘비 [myobi]

graveyard [ˈgreɪvˌjɑːd] n 묘지 [myoji]

gravy [ˈgreɪvɪ] n 그레이비 [geureibi]

grease [griːs] n 기름 [gireum]

greasy [ˈgriːzɪ; -sɪ] adj 기름투성이의 [gireumtuseongiui]

great [greɪt] adj 위대한 [widaehan]

Great Britain [ˈgreɪt ˈbrɪtən] n 영국 [yeongguk]

great-grandfather [ˈgreɪtˈgrænˌfɑːðə] n 증조할아버지 [jeungjoharabeoji]

great-grandmother [ˈgreɪtˈgrænˌmʌðə] n 증조할머니 [jeungjohalmeoni]

Greece [griːs] n 그리스 [geuriseu] (국가)

greedy [ˈgriːdɪ] adj 욕심 많은 [yoksim manheun]

Greek [griːk] adj 그리스의 [geuriseuui] ▷ n (language) 그리스어 [geuriseueo], (person) 그리스 사람 [geuriseu saram]

green [griːn] adj (colour) 녹색의 [noksaegui], (inexperienced) 미숙한 [misukhan] ▷ n 녹색 [noksaek]; **green salad** n 야채 샐러드 [yachae saelleodeu]

greengrocer's [ˈgriːnˌgrəʊsəz] n 청과물상 [cheonggwamulsang]

greenhouse [ˈgriːnˌhaʊs] n 온실 [onsil]

Greenland [ˈgriːnlənd] n 그린란드 [geurillandeu]

greet [griːt] v 인사하다 [insahada]

greeting [ˈgriːtɪŋ] n 인사 [insa] (안녕하세요); **greetings card** n 카드 [kadeu]

grey [greɪ] adj 회색의 [hoesaegui]

grey-haired [ˌgreɪˈhɛəd] adj 백발의 [baekbarui]

grid [grɪd] n 격자 [gyeokja]

grief [griːf] n 슬픔 [seulpeum]

grill [grɪl] n 그릴 [geuril] ▷ v 그릴에 굽다 [geurire gupda]

grilled [grɪld] adj 그릴에 구운 [geurire guun]

grim [grɪm] adj 불길한 [bulgilhan]

grin [grɪn] n 싱긋 웃음 [singgeut useum] ▷ v 싱긋 웃다 [singgeut utda]

grind [graɪnd] v...을 갈아 (가루로) 만들다 [...eul gara (garuro) mandeulda]

grip [grɪp] v 단단히 잡다 [dandanhi japda]

gripping [ˈgrɪpɪŋ] adj 흥미를 끄는 [heungmireul kkeuneun]

grit [grɪt] n 모래알 [moraeal]

groan [grəʊn] v 신음하다 [sineumhada]

grocer [ˈgrəʊsə] n 식료품 상인 [singnyopum sangin]

groceries [ˈgrəʊsərɪz] npl 식료품 [singnyopum]

grocer's [ˈgrəʊsəz] n 식료품점 [singnyopumjeom]

groom [gruːm; grʊm] n 말 사육 담당자 [mal sayuk damdangja], (bridegroom) 신랑 [sillang]

grope [grəʊp] v 손으로 더듬다 [soneuro deodeumda]

gross [grəʊs] adj (fat) 심한 [simhan], (income etc.) 전체의 [jeoncheui]

grossly [ˈgrəʊslɪ] adv 심하게 [simhage]

ground [graʊnd] n 땅 [ttang] ▷ v 이륙을 금지하다 [iryugeul geumjihada]; **ground floor** n 1층 [il cheung]

group [gruːp] n 집단 [jipdan]

grouse [graʊs] n (complaint) 불평 [bulpyeong], (game bird) 들꿩 [deulkkwong]

grow [grəʊ] vi 성장하다 [seongjanghada] ▷ vt 기르다 [gireuda]

growl [graʊl] v 으르렁거리다 [eureureonggeorida]

grown-up [grəʊnʌp] n 성인 [seongin]

growth [grəʊθ] n 성장 [seongjang]

grow up [grəʊ ʌp] v 성숙하다 [seongsukhada]

grub [grʌb] n 음식 [eumsik]

grudge [grʌdʒ] n 원한 [wonhan]

gruesome [ˈgruːsəm] adj 무시무시한 [musimusihan]

grumpy [ˈgrʌmpɪ] adj 심술이 난 [simsuri nan]

guarantee [ˌgærənˈtiː] n 보증 [bojeung] ▷ v 보증하다 [bojeunghada];

It's still under guarantee 보증 기간이 끝나지 않았어요 [bojeung gigani kkeutnaji anhasseoyo]

guard [gɑːd] *n* 경호원 [gyeonghowon] ▷ *v* 보호하다 [bohohada]; **security guard** *n* 경호원 [gyeonghowon]

Guatemala [ˌgwɑːtəˈmɑːlə] *n* 과테말라 [gwatemalla]

guess [gɛs] *n* 추측 [chucheuk] ▷ *v* 추측하다 [chucheukhada]

guest [gɛst] *n* 손님 [sonnim]

guesthouse [ˈgɛstˌhaʊs] *n* 숙소 [sukso]

guide [gaɪd] *n* 안내자 [annaeja] ▷ *v* 안내자 [annaeja]; **guide dog** *n* 맹인 안내견 [maengin annaegyeon]; **guided tour** *n* 안내인이 딸린 여행 [annaeini ttallin yeohaeng]; **tour guide** *n* 관광 안내원 [gwangwang annaewon]

guidebook [ˈgaɪdˌbʊk] *n* 여행 안내서 [yeohaeng annaeseo]

guilt [gɪlt] *n* 유죄 [yujoe]

guilty [ˈgɪltɪ] *adj* 유죄의 [yujoeui]

Guinea [ˈgɪnɪ] *n* 기니 [gini]; **guinea pig** *n (for experiment)* 실험재료 [silheomjaeryo], *(rodent)* 기니피그 [ginipigeu]

guitar [gɪˈtɑː] *n* 기타 [gita]

gum [gʌm] *n* 아교 [agyo]; **chewing gum** *n* 껌 [kkeom]

gun [gʌn] *n* 총 [chong]; **machine gun** *n* 기관총 [gigwanchong]

gust [gʌst] *n* 돌풍 [dolpung]

gut [gʌt] *n* 창자 [changja]

guy [gaɪ] *n* 남자 [namja]

Guyana [gaɪˈænə] *n* 가이아나 [gaiana]

gym [dʒɪm] *n* 체육관 [cheyukgwan]; **Where is the gym?** 체육관은 어디에 있어요? [cheyukgwaneun eodie isseoyo?]

gymnast [ˈdʒɪmnæst] *n* 체조 선수 [chejo seonsu]

gymnastics [dʒɪmˈnæstɪks] *npl* 체조 [chejo]

gynaecologist [ˌgaɪnɪˈkɒlədʒɪst] *n* 부인과 의사 [buingwa uisa]

gypsy [ˈdʒɪpsɪ] *n* 집시 [jipsi]

habit [ˈhæbɪt] *n* 습관 [seupgwan]

hack [hæk] *v* 마구 자르다 [magu jareuda]

hacker [ˈhækə] *n* 해커 [haekeo]

haddock [ˈhædək] *n* 대구 [daegu]

haemorrhoids [ˈhɛmərɔɪdz] *npl* 치질 [chijil]

haggle [ˈhægəl] *v* 값을 끈질기게 깎다 [gapseul kkeunjilgige kkakkda]

hail [heɪl] *n* 우박 [ubak] ▷ *v* 우박이 내리다 [ubagi naerida]

hair [hɛə] *n* 머리카락 [meorikarak]; **hair gel** *n* 헤어 젤 [heeo jel]; **hair spray** *n* 헤어 스프레이 [heeo seupeurei]; **I have greasy hair** 제 머리카락은 기름기가 많아요 [je meorikarageun gireumgiga manhayo]

hairband [ˈhɛəˌbænd] *n* 머리띠 [meoritti]

hairbrush [ˈhɛəˌbrʌʃ] *n* 머리솔 [meorisol]

haircut [ˈhɛəˌkʌt] *n* 이발 [ibal]

hairdo [ˈhɛəˌduː] *n* 헤어 스타일 [heeo seutail]

hairdresser [ˈhɛəˌdrɛsə] *n* 미용사 [miyongsa]

hairdresser's [ˈhɛəˌdrɛsəz] *n* 미용실

[miyongsil]

hairdryer [ˈhɛəˌdraɪə] n 헤어 드라이어 [heeo deuraieo]

hairgrip [ˈhɛəɡrɪp] n 머리핀 [meoripin]

hairstyle [ˈhɛəstaɪl] n 헤어 스타일 [heeo seutail]

hairy [ˈhɛərɪ] adj 털이 많은 [teori manheun]

Haiti [ˈheɪtɪ; hɑːˈiːtɪ] n 아이티 [aiti]

half [hɑːf] adj 절반의 [jeolbanui] ▷ adv 반쯤 [banjjeum] ▷ n 절반 [jeolban]; **half board** n 1박 2식 제공 [ilbak isik jegong]

half-hour [ˈhɑːfˌaʊə] n 30분 [samsib bun]

half-price [ˈhɑːfˌpraɪs] adj 반값의 [bangapsui] ▷ adv 반값으로 [bangapseuro]

half-term [ˈhɑːfˌtɜːm] n 학기 중의 중간 방학 [hakgi jungui junggan banghak]

half-time [ˈhɑːfˌtaɪm] n 경기 중의 중간 휴식 [gyeonggi jungui junggan hyusik]

halfway [ˌhɑːfˈweɪ] adv 도중에 [dojunge]

hall [hɔːl] n 홀 [hol]; **town hall** n 시청 [sicheong] (건물)

hallway [ˈhɔːlˌweɪ] n 복도 [bokdo]

halt [hɔːlt] n 정지하다 [jeongjihada]

ham [hæm] n 햄 [haem]

hamburger [ˈhæmˌbɜːɡə] n 햄버거 [haembeogeo]

hammer [ˈhæmə] n 해머 [haemeo]

hammock [ˈhæmək] n 해먹 [haemeok]

hamster [ˈhæmstə] n 햄스터 [haemseuteo]

hand [hænd] n 손 [son] ▷ v 건네 주다 [geonne juda]; **hand luggage** n 수화물 [suhwamul]; **Where can I wash my hands?** 어디에서 손을 씻을 수 있을까요 [eodieseo soneul ssiseul su isseulkkayo]

handbag [ˈhændˌbæɡ] n 핸드백 [haendeubaek]

handball [ˈhændˌbɔːl] n 핸드볼 [haendeubol]

handbook [ˈhændˌbʊk] n 안내서 [annaeseo]

handbrake [ˈhændˌbreɪk] n 수동 브레이크 [sudong beureikeu]

handcuffs [ˈhændˌkʌfs] npl 수갑 [sugap]

handicap [ˈhændɪˌkæp] n **My handicap is...** 제 핸디캡은...이에요 [je haendikaebeun...ieyo]; **What's your handicap?** 핸디캡이 얼마예요? [haendikaebi eolmayeyo?]

handicapped [ˈhændɪˌkæpt] adj 장애가 있는 [jangaega inneun]

handkerchief [ˈhæŋkətʃɪf; -tʃiːf] n 손수건 [sonsugeon]

handle [ˈhændəl] n 손잡이 [sonjabi] ▷ v 다루다 [daruda]; **The door handle has come off** 문 손잡이가 빠졌어요 [mun sonjabiga ppajyeosseoyo]

handlebars [ˈhændəlˌbɑːz] npl 핸들바 [haendeulba]

handmade [ˌhændˈmeɪd] adj 손으로 만든 [soneuro mandeun]

hands-free [ˈhændzˌfriː] adj 손을 쓰지 않아도 되는 [soneul sseuji anhado doeneun]; **hands-free kit** n 핸즈프리 장치 [haenjeupeuri jangchi]

handsome [ˈhændsəm] adj 잘 생긴 [jal saenggin]

handwriting [ˈhændˌraɪtɪŋ] n 육필 [yukpil]

handy [ˈhændɪ] adj 가까이 있는 [gakkai inneun]

hang [hæŋ] vi 걸려 있다 [geollyeo itda] ▷ vt 걸다 [geolda]

hanger [ˈhæŋə] n 옷걸이 [otgeori]

hang-gliding [ˈhæŋˈɡlaɪdɪŋ] n 행글라이딩 [haenggeullaiding]; **I'd like to go hang-gliding** 행글라이딩을 하고 싶어요 [haenggeullaidingeul hago sipeoyo]

hang on [hæŋ ɒn] v 기다리다 [gidarida]

hangover [ˈhæŋˌəʊvə] n 숙취 [sukchwi]

hang up [hæŋ ʌp] v 전화를 끊다 [jeonhwareul kkeunta]

hankie [ˈhæŋkɪ] n 손수건 [sonsugeon]

happen [ˈhæpən] v 일어나다 [ireonada]

happily [ˈhæpɪlɪ] adv 행복하게

[haengbokhage]

happiness ['hæpɪnɪs] n 행복
[haengbok]

happy ['hæpɪ] adj 행복한
[haengbokhan]

harassment ['hærəsmənt] n 괴롭힘
[goerophim]

harbour ['hɑːbə] n 항구 [hanggu]

hard [hɑːd] adj (difficult) 어려운
[eoryeoun], (firm, rigid) 단단한
[dandanhan] ▷ adv 열심히 [yeolsimhi];
hard disk n 하드 디스크 [hadeu
diseukeu]; **hard shoulder** n 포장 갓길
[pojang gatgil]

hardboard ['hɑːdˌbɔːd] n 하드보드
[hadeubodeu]

hardly ['hɑːdlɪ] adv 거의...않다 [geoui...
anta]

hard up [hɑːd ʌp] adj 쪼들리는
[jjodeullineun]

hardware ['hɑːdˌwɛə] n 철물
[cheolmul]

hare [hɛə] n 산토끼 [santokki]

harm [hɑːm] v 해치다 [haechida]

harmful ['hɑːmfʊl] adj 유해한
[yuhaehan]

harmless ['hɑːmlɪs] adj 무해한
[muhaehan]

harp [hɑːp] n 하프 [hapeu]

harsh [hɑːʃ] adj 거친 [geochin]

harvest ['hɑːvɪst] n 수확 [suhwak] ▷ v
수확하다 [suhwakhada]

hastily [heɪstɪlɪ] adv 급히 [geuphi]

hat [hæt] n 모자 [moja]

hatchback ['hætʃˌbæk] n 해치백
[haechibaek]

hate [heɪt] v 미워하다 [miwohada]

hatred ['heɪtrɪd] n 증오 [jeungo]

haunted ['hɔːntɪd] adj 유령이 나오는
[yuryeongi naoneun]

have [hæv] v 가지고 있다 [gajigo itda]

have to [hæv tʊ] v 해야만 하다
[haeyaman hada]

hawthorn ['hɔːˌθɔːn] n 산사나무
[sansanamu]

hay [heɪ] n 건초 [geoncho]; **hay fever** n
꽃가루 알레르기 [kkotgaru allereugi]

haystack ['heɪˌstæk] n 건초 더미

[geoncho deomi]

hazelnut ['heɪzˀlˌnʌt] n 개암 [gaeam]

he [hiː] pron 그 남자 [geu namja]

head [hɛd] n (body part) 머리 [meori],
(principal) 사장 [sajang] ▷ v 나아가다
[naagada]; **deputy head** n 교감
[gyogam] (학교); **head office** n 본사
[bonsa]

headache ['hɛdˌeɪk] n 두통 [dutong];
I'd like something for a headache
두통약 주세요 [dutongyak juseyo]

headlamp ['hɛdˌlæmp] n 전조등
[jeonjodeung]

headlight ['hɛdˌlaɪt] n 전조등
[jeonjodeung]

headline ['hɛdˌlaɪn] n 표제
[pyoje]

headphones ['hɛdˌfəʊnz] npl 헤드폰
[hedeupon]; **Does it have
headphones?** 헤드폰이 있어요?
[hedeuponi isseoyo?]

headquarters [ˌhɛdˈkwɔːtəz] npl 본부
[bonbu]

headroom ['hɛdˌrʊm; -ˌruːm] n 머리위
공간 [meoriwi gonggan]

headscarf, headscarves ['hɛdˌskɑːf,
'hɛdˌskɑːvz] n 머리 스카프 [meori
seukapeu]

headteacher ['hɛdˈtiːtʃə] n 교장
[gyojang]

heal [hiːl] v (상처 등이) 낫다 [(sangcheo
deungi) natda]

health [hɛlθ] n 건강 [geongang]; **I don't
have health insurance** 저는
건강보험에 들지 않았어요 [jeoneun
geongangboheome deulji
anhasseoyo]; **I have private health
insurance** 저는 사설 건강보험에
들었어요 [jeoneun saseol
geongangboheome deureosseoyo]

healthy ['hɛlθɪ] adj 거친 [geochin]

heap [hiːp] n 무더기 [mudeogi]

hear [hɪə] v 듣다 [deutda]

hearing ['hɪərɪŋ] n 듣기 [deutgi];
hearing aid n 보청기 [bocheonggi]

heart [hɑːt] n 심장 [simjang]; **heart
attack** n 심장마비 [simjangmabi]; **I
have a heart condition** 심장병이

있어요 [simjangbyeongi isseoyo]
heartbroken ['hɑːt,brəʊkən] *adj*
비탄에 잠긴 [bitane jamgin]
heartburn ['hɑːt,bɜːn] *n* 가슴앓이
[gaseumari]
heat [hiːt] *n* 열 [yeol] ▷ *v* 가열하다
[gayeolhada]
heater ['hiːtə] *n* 가열기 [gayeolgi]
heather ['hɛðə] *n* 헤더 [hedeo]
heating ['hiːtɪŋ] *n* 가열 [gayeol];
central heating *n* 중앙 난방 [jungang
nanbang]
heat up [hiːt ʌp] *v* 가열되다
[gayeoldoeda]
heaven ['hɛvən] *n* 천국 [cheonguk]
heavily ['hɛvɪlɪ] *adv* 무겁게
[mugeopge]
heavy ['hɛvɪ] *adj* 무거운 [mugeoun]
hedge [hɛdʒ] *n* 생울타리 [saengultari]
hedgehog ['hɛdʒ,hɒg] *n* 고슴도치
[goseumdochi]
heel [hiːl] *n* 뒤꿈치 [dwikkumchi]; **high
heels** *npl* 하이힐 [haihil]
height [haɪt] *n* 높이 [nopi]
heir [ɛə] *n* 상속인 [sangsogin]
heiress ['ɛərɪs] *n* 상속녀
[sangsongnyeo]
helicopter ['hɛlɪ,kɒptə] *n* 헬리콥터
[hellikopteo]
hell [hɛl] *n* 지옥 [jiok]
hello [hɛ'ləʊ] *excl* 안녕! [annyeong!]
helmet ['hɛlmɪt] *n* 헬멧 [helmet]; **Can I
have a helmet?** 헬멧 주시겠어요?
[helmet jusigesseoyo?]
help [hɛlp] *n* 도움 [doum] ▷ *v* (남을) 돕다
[(nameul) dopda]
helpful ['hɛlpfʊl] *adj* 유용한
[yuyonghan]
helpline ['hɛlp,laɪn] *n* 상담전화
[sangdamjeonhwa]
hen [hɛn] *n* 암탉 [amtalg]; **hen night** *n*
여성만의 모임 [yeoseongmanui moim]
hepatitis [,hɛpə'taɪtɪs] *n* 간염
[ganyeom]
her [hɜː; hə; ə] *pron* 그 여자 [geu yeoja],
그 여자의 [geu yeojaui]
herbs [hɜːbz] *npl* 허브 [heobeu]
herd [hɜːd] *n* 무리 [muri]

here [hɪə] *adv* 여기에 [yeogie]
hereditary [hɪ'rɛdɪtərɪ; -trɪ] *adj*
유전성의 [yujeonseongui]
heritage ['hɛrɪtɪdʒ] *n* 유산 [yusan]
hernia ['hɜːnɪə] *n* 헤르니아 [hereunia]
hero ['hɪərəʊ] *n* 영웅 [yeongung]
heroin ['hɛrəʊɪn] *n* 헤로인 [heroin]
heroine ['hɛrəʊɪn] *n* 여자 영웅 [yeoja
yeongung]
heron ['hɛrən] *n* 백로과의 새
[baengnogwaui sae]
herring ['hɛrɪŋ] *n* 청어 [cheongeo]
hers [hɜːz] *pron* 그 여자 것 [geu yeoja
geot]
herself [hə'sɛlf] *pron* 그 여자 자신 [geu
yeoja jasin]
hesitate ['hɛzɪ,teɪt] *v* 주저하다
[jujeohada]
heterosexual [,hɛtərəʊ'sɛksjʊəl] *adj*
이성애의 [iseongaeui]
HGV [eɪtʃ dʒi: vi:] *abbr* 대형 수송차
[daehyeong susongcha]
hi [haɪ] *excl* 안녕! [annyeong!]
hiccups ['hɪkʌps] *npl* 딸꾹질
[ttalkkukjil]
hidden ['hɪdən] *adj* 숨겨진
[sumgyeojin]
hide [haɪd] *vi* 숨다 [sumda] ▷ *vt* 숨기다
[sumgida]
hide-and-seek [,haɪdænd'si:k] *n*
숨바꼭질 [sumbakkokjil]
hideous ['hɪdɪəs] *adj* 끔찍한
[kkeumjjikhan]
hifi ['haɪ'faɪ] *n* 하이파이 [haipai]
high [haɪ] *adj* 높은 [nopeun] ▷ *adv* 높이
[nopi]; **high heels** *npl* 하이힐 [haihil];
high jump *n* 높이뛰기 [nopittwigi];
high season *n* 성수기 [seongsugi]
highchair ['haɪ,tʃɛə] *n* 어린이용 높은
의자 [eoriniyong nopeun uija]
high-heeled ['haɪ,hiːld] *adj* 하이힐의
[haihirui]
highlight ['haɪ,laɪt] *n* 최고조의 부분
[choegojoui bubun] ▷ *v* 강조하다
[gangjohada]
highlighter ['haɪ,laɪtə] *n* 하이라이터
[hairaiteo]
high-rise ['haɪ,raɪz] *n* 고층 건물

[gocheung geonmul]

hijack ['haɪ,dʒæk] v 공중납치하다 [gongjungnapchihada]

hijacker ['haɪ,dʒækə] n 공중납치범 [gongjungnapchibeom]

hike [haɪk] n 하이킹 [haiking]

hiking [haɪkɪŋ] n 하이킹 [haiking]

hilarious [hɪ'lɛərɪəs] adj 몹시 재미있는 [mopsi jaemiinneun]

hill [hɪl] n 언덕 [eondeok]

hill-walking ['hɪl,wɔːkɪŋ] n 언덕 산책 [eondeok sanchaek]

him [hɪm; ɪm] pron 그 남자를 [geu namjareul]; **We must get him to hospital** 그 남자를 병원에 데려가야 해요 [geu namjareul byeongwone deryeogaya haeyo]

himself [hɪm'sɛlf; ɪm'sɛlf] pron 그 남자 자신 [geu namja jasin]

Hindu ['hɪnduː; hɪn'duː] adj 힌두교도의 [hindugyodoui] ▷ n 힌두교도 [hindugyodo]

Hinduism ['hɪndʊ,ɪzəm] n 힌두교 [hindugyo]

hinge [hɪndʒ] n 경첩 [gyeongcheop]

hint [hɪnt] n 힌트 [hinteu] ▷ v 암시하다 [amsihada]

hip [hɪp] n 엉덩이 [eongdeongi]

hippie ['hɪpɪ] n 히피 [hipi]

hippo ['hɪpəʊ] n 하마 [hama]

hippopotamus, hippopotami [,hɪpə'pɒtəməs, ,hɪpə'pɒtəmaɪ] n 하마 [hama]

hire ['haɪə] n 고용 [goyong] ▷ v 고용하다 [goyonghada]; **car hire** n 자동차 임대 [jadongcha imdae]; **hire car** n 렌트카 [renteuka]

his [hɪz; ɪz] adj 그 남자의 [geu namjaui] ▷ pron 그 남자 것 [geu namja geot]

historian [hɪ'stɔːrɪən] n 역사가 [yeoksaga]

historical [hɪ'stɒrɪkˀl] adj 역사적인 [yeoksajeogin]

history ['hɪstərɪ; 'hɪstrɪ] n 역사 [yeoksa] (연대기)

hit [hɪt] n 타격 [tagyeok] ▷ v 때리다 [ttaerida]

hitch [hɪtʃ] n 장애 [jangae]

hitchhike ['hɪtʃ,haɪk] v 차를 얻어 타다 [chareul eodeo tada]

hitchhiker ['hɪtʃ,haɪkə] n 자동차 편승 여행자 [jadongcha pyeonseung yeohaengja]

hitchhiking ['hɪtʃ,haɪkɪŋ] n 차 얻어 타기 [cha eodeo tagi]

HIV-negative [eɪtʃ aɪ viː 'nɛgətɪv] adj HIV 음성의 [HIV eumseongui]

HIV-positive [eɪtʃ aɪ viː 'pɒzɪtɪv] adj HIV 양성의 [HIV yangseongui]

hobby ['hɒbɪ] n 취미 [chwimi]

hockey ['hɒkɪ] n 하키 [haki]; **ice hockey** n 아이스하키 [aiseuhaki]

hold [həʊld] v 잡다 [japda]

holdall ['həʊld,ɔːl] n 큰 가방 [keun gabang]

hold on [həʊld ɒn] v 꽉 잡고 있다 [kkwak japgo itda]

hold up [həʊld ʌp] v 지연하다 [jiyeonhada]

hold-up [həʊldʌp] n 무장 강도 [mujang gangdo]

hole [həʊl] n 구멍 [gumeong]; **I have a hole in my shoe** 신발에 구멍이 났어요 [sinbare gumeongi nasseoyo]

holiday ['hɒlɪ,deɪ; -dɪ] n 휴일 [hyuil]; **activity holiday** n 활동 휴가 [hwaldong hyuga]; **bank holiday** n 공휴일 [gonghyuil]; **holiday home** n 별장 [byeoljang]; **holiday job** n 방학 중 아르바이트 [banghak jung areubaiteu]; **package holiday** n 패키지 휴가 [paekiji hyuga]; **public holiday** n 공휴일 [gonghyuil]; **Enjoy your holiday!** 휴일 잘 보내세요! [hyuil jal bonaeseyo!]

Holland ['hɒlənd] n 네덜란드 [nedeollandeu]

hollow ['hɒləʊ] adj 속이 빈 [sogi bin]

holly ['hɒlɪ] n 호랑가시나무 [horanggasinamu]

holy ['həʊlɪ] adj 신성한 [sinseonghan]

home [həʊm] adv 집에 [jibe] ▷ n 집 [jip]; **home address** n 집주소 [jipjuso]; **home match** n 홈경기 [homgyeonggi]; **home page** n 홈페이지 [hompeiji]; **mobile home** n

이동 주택 [idong jutaek]; **nursing home** n 양로원 [yangnowon]; **stately home** n 대저택 [daejeotaek]; **I'd like to go home** 집에 가고 싶어요 [jibe gago sipeoyo]; **Please come home by 11p.m.** 오후 열한시까지 집에 오세요 [ohu yeolhansikkaji jibe oseyo]; **When do you go home?** 언제 집에 가세요? [eonje jibe gaseyo?]; **Would you like to phone home?** 집에 전화하시겠어요? [jibe jeonhwahasigesseoyo?]

homeland ['həʊmˌlænd] n 고국 [goguk]

homeless ['həʊmlɪs] adj 집 없는 [jip eomneun]

home-made ['həʊm'meɪd] adj 집에서 만든 [jibeseo mandeun]

homeopathic [ˌhəʊmɪəʊ'pæθɪk] adj 동종 요법의 [dongjong yobeobui]

homeopathy [ˌhəʊmɪ'ɒpəθɪ] n 동종 요법 [dongjong yobeop]

homesick ['həʊmˌsɪk] adj 향수병에 걸린 [hyangsubyeonge geollin]

homework ['həʊmˌwɜːk] n 숙제 [sukje]

Honduras [hɒn'djʊərəs] n 온두라스 [onduraseu]

honest ['ɒnɪst] adj 정직한 [jeongjikhan]

honestly ['ɒnɪstlɪ] adv 정직하게 [jeongjikhage]

honesty ['ɒnɪstɪ] n 정직 [jeongjik]

honey ['hʌnɪ] n 벌꿀 [beolkkul]

honeymoon ['hʌnɪˌmuːn] n 신혼 여행 [sinhon yeohaeng]

honeysuckle ['hʌnɪˌsʌkəl] n 인동덩굴 [indongdeonggul]

honour ['ɒnə] n 명예 [myeongye]

hood [hʊd] n 두건 [dugeon]

hook [hʊk] n 갈고리 [galgori]

hooray [huː'reɪ] excl 만세! [manse!]

Hoover® ['huːvə] n 청소기 [cheongsogi]; **hoover** v 진공 청소기로 청소하다 [jingong cheongsogiro cheongsohada]

hope [həʊp] n 희망 [huimang] ▷ v 희망하다 [huimanghada]

hopeful ['həʊpfʊl] adj 희망적인 [huimangjeogin]

hopefully ['həʊpfʊlɪ] adv 바라건대 [barageondae]

hopeless ['həʊplɪs] adj 희망없는 [huimangeomneun]

horizon [hə'raɪzən] n 지평선 [jipyeongseon]

horizontal [ˌhɒrɪ'zɒntəl] adj 수평의 [supyeongui]

hormone ['hɔːməʊn] n 호르몬 [horeumon]

horn [hɔːn] n 뿔 [ppul]; **French horn** n 프렌치 호른 [peurenchi horeun]

horoscope ['hɒrəˌskəʊp] n 별자리 [byeoljari]

horrendous [hɒ'rɛndəs] adj 끔찍한 [kkeumjjikhan]

horrible ['hɒrəbəl] adj 끔찍한 [kkeumjjikhan]

horrifying ['hɒrɪˌfaɪɪŋ] adj 무서운 [museoun]

horror ['hɒrə] n 공포 [gongpo]; **horror film** n 공포 영화 [gongpo yeonghwa]

horse [hɔːs] n 말 [mal]; **horse racing** n 경마 [gyeongma]; **horse riding** n 승마 [seungma]; **rocking horse** n 흔들목마 [heundeulmongma]; **Can we go horse riding?** 말을 탈 수 있어요? [mareul tal su isseoyo?]

horseradish ['hɔːsˌrædɪʃ] n 고추냉이 [gochunaengi]

horseshoe ['hɔːsˌʃuː] n 편자 [pyeonja]

hose [həʊz] n 호스 [hoseu]

hosepipe ['həʊzˌpaɪp] n 호스 [hoseu]

hospital ['hɒspɪtəl] n 병원 [byeongwon]; **maternity hospital** n 산과병원 [sangwabyeongwon]; **mental hospital** n 정신 병원 [jeongsin byeongwon]; **How do I get to the hospital?** 병원에 어떻게 가나요? [byeongwone eotteoke ganayo?]; **I work in a hospital** 병원에서 일해요 [byeongwoneseo ilhaeyo]; **We must get him to hospital** 그 남자를 병원에 데려가야 해요 [geu namjareul byeongwone deryeogaya haeyo]; **Where is the**

hospital? 병원은 어디에 있나요? [byeongwoneun eodie innayo?]; **Will he have to go to hospital?** 병원에 가야 될까요? [byeongwone gaya doelkkayo?]

hospitality [ˌhɒspɪ'tælɪtɪ] n 환대 [hwandae]

host [həʊst] n (entertains) 사회자 [sahoeja], (multitude) 다수 [dasu]

hostage ['hɒstɪdʒ] n 인질 [injil]

hostel ['hɒstəl] n 호스텔 [hoseutel]; **Is there a youth hostel nearby?** 근처에 유스호스텔이 있어요? [geuncheoe yuseuhoseuteri isseoyo?]

hostess ['həʊstɪs] n **air hostess** n 비행기 여승무원 [bihaenggi yeoseungmuwon]

hostile ['hɒstaɪl] adj 적대적인 [jeokdaejeogin]

hot [hɒt] adj 뜨거운 [tteugeoun]; **hot dog** n 핫도그 [hatdogeu]

hotel [həʊ'tɛl] n 호텔 [hotel]; **Can you book me into a hotel?** 호텔을 예약해 주시겠어요? [hotereul yeyakhae jusigesseoyo?]; **Can you recommend a hotel?** 호텔을 추천해 주시겠어요? [hotereul chucheonhae jusigesseoyo?]; **He runs the hotel** 그는 호텔을 운영해요 [geuneun hotereul unyeonghaeyo]; **I'm staying at a hotel** 호텔에 묵고 있어요 [hotere mukgo isseoyo]; **Is your hotel accessible to wheelchairs?** 휠체어로 출입할 수 있는 호텔인가요? [hwilcheeoro churiphal su inneun hoteringayo?]; **We're looking for a hotel** 호텔을 찾고 있어요 [hotereul chatgo isseoyo]; **What's the best way to get to this hotel?** 이 호텔에 가는 가장 좋은 방법은 무엇인가요? [i hotere ganeun gajang joheun bangbeobeun mueosingayo?]

hour [aʊə] n 시간 [sigan]; **office hours** npl 근무 시간 [geunmu sigan]; **opening hours** npl 영업 시간 [yeongeop sigan]; **peak hours** npl 러시아워 [reosiawo]; **rush hour** n 러시아워 [reosiawo]; **visiting hours** npl 방문시간 [bangmunsigan]; **How much is it per hour?** 시간당 얼마예요? [sigandang eolmayeyo?]; **The journey takes two hours** 두 시간 여정이에요 [du sigan yeojeongieyo]; **When are visiting hours?** 면회 시간은 언제예요? [myeonhoe siganeun eonjeyeyo?]

hourly ['aʊəlɪ] adj 한 시간마다의 [han siganmadaui] ▷ adv 한 시간마다 [han siganmada]

house [haʊs] n 주택 [jutaek]; **council house** n 공영 주택 [gongyeong jutaek]; **detached house** n 단독주택 [dandokjutaek]; **semi-detached house** n 두 채가 한 동을 이루고 있는 집 [du chaega han dongeul irugo inneun jip]

household ['haʊsˌhəʊld] n 가족 [gajok]

housewife, housewives ['haʊsˌwaɪf, 'haʊsˌwaɪvz] n 주부 [jubu]

housework ['haʊsˌwɜːk] n 가사 [gasa] (허드렛일)

hovercraft ['hɒvəˌkrɑːft] n 호버크라프트 [hobeokeurapeuteu]

how [haʊ] adv 어떻게 [eotteoke]; **Do you know how to do this?** 이것을 어떻게 하는지 아세요? [igeoseul eotteoke haneunji aseyo?]; **How are you?** 어떻게 지내세요? [eotteoke jinaeseyo?]; **How do I get to...?** ...에 어떻게 가나요? [...e eotteoke ganayo?]; **How does this work?** 어떻게 작동하나요? [eotteoke jakdonghanayo?]; **How old are you?** 나이가 어떻게 되세요? [naiga eotteoke doeseyo?]

however [haʊ'ɛvə] adv 그러나 [geureona]

howl [haʊl] v 짖다 [jitda]

HQ [eɪtʃ kjuː] abbr 본부 [bonbu]

hubcap ['hʌbˌkæp] n 휠캡 [hwilkaep]

hug [hʌg] n 포옹 [poong] ▷ v 껴안다 [kkyeoanda]

huge [hjuːdʒ] adj 거대한 [geodaehan]

hull [hʌl] n 선체 [seonche]

hum [hʌm] v 윙윙거리다 [wingwinggeorida]

human ['hju:mən] *adj* 인간의 [inganui];
human being *n* 인간 [ingan]; **human
rights** *npl* 인권 [ingwon]
humanitarian [hju:ˌmænɪ'tɛərɪən] *adj*
인도주의자 [indojuuija]
humble ['hʌmbəl] *adj* 겸손한
[gyeomsonhan]
humid ['hju:mɪd] *adj* 습기 찬 [seupgi
chan]
humidity [hju:'mɪdɪtɪ] *n* 습기 [seupgi]
humorous ['hju:mərəs] *adj* 유머가
풍부한 [yumeoga pungbuhan]
humour ['hju:mə] *n* 유머 [yumeo];
sense of humour *n* 유머감각
[yumeogamgak]
hundred ['hʌndrəd] *number*
(Sino-Korean) 백 [baek]
Hungarian [hʌŋ'gɛərɪən] *adj* 헝가리의
[heonggariui] ▷ *n* 헝가리 사람
[heonggari saram]
Hungary ['hʌŋgərɪ] *n* 헝가리
[heonggari]
hunger ['hʌŋgə] *n* 굶주림 [gurmjurim]
hungry ['hʌŋgrɪ] *adj* 배고픈
[baegopeun]
hunt [hʌnt] *n* 사냥하다 [sanyanghada]
▷ *v* 사냥하다 [sanyanghada]
hunter ['hʌntə] *n* 사냥꾼 [sanyangkkun]
hunting ['hʌntɪŋ] *n* 사냥 [sanyang]
hurdle ['hɜ:dəl] *n* 장애물 [jangaemul]
hurricane ['hʌrɪkən; -keɪn] *n* 허리케인
[heorikein]
hurry ['hʌrɪ] *n* 서두름 [seodureum] ▷ *v*
서두르다 [seodureuda]
hurry up ['hʌrɪ ʌp] *v* 서두르다
[seodureuda]
hurt [hɜ:t] *adj* 다친 [dachin] ▷ *v* 해치다
[haechida]
husband ['hʌzbənd] *n* 남편
[nampyeon]; **This is my husband** 제
남편이에요 [je nampyeonieyo]
hut [hʌt] *n* 오두막 [odumak]
hyacinth ['haɪəsɪnθ] *n* 히아신스
[hiasinseu]
hydrogen ['haɪdrɪdʒən] *n* 수소 [suso]
hygiene ['haɪdʒi:n] *n* 위생학
[wisaenghak]
hymn [hɪm] *n* 찬송가 [chansongga]

hypermarket ['haɪpəˌmɑ:kɪt] *n* 대형
슈퍼마켓 [daehyeong syupeomaket]
hyphen ['haɪfən] *n* 하이픈 [haipeun]

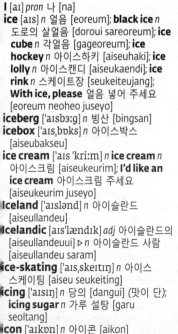

I [aɪ] *pron* 나 [na]

ice [aɪs] *n* 얼음 [eoreum]; **black ice** *n* 도로의 살얼음 [doroui sareoreum]; **ice cube** *n* 각얼음 [gageoreum]; **ice hockey** *n* 아이스하키 [aiseuhaki]; **ice lolly** *n* 아이스캔디 [aiseukaendi]; **ice rink** *n* 스케이트장 [seukeiteujang]; **With ice, please** 얼음 넣어 주세요 [eoreum neoheo juseyo]

iceberg ['aɪsbɜːɡ] *n* 빙산 [bingsan]

icebox ['aɪsˌbɒks] *n* 아이스박스 [aiseubakseu]

ice cream ['aɪs 'kriːm] *n* **ice cream** *n* 아이스크림 [aiseukeurim]; **I'd like an ice cream** 아이스크림 주세요 [aiseukeurim juseyo]

Iceland ['aɪslənd] *n* 아이슬란드 [aiseullandeu]

Icelandic [aɪs'lændɪk] *adj* 아이슬란드의 [aiseullandeuui] ▷ *n* 아이슬란드 사람 [aiseullandeu saram]

ice-skating ['aɪsˌskeɪtɪŋ] *n* 아이스 스케이팅 [aiseu seukeiting]

icing ['aɪsɪŋ] *n* 당의 [dangui] (맛이 단); **icing sugar** *n* 가루 설탕 [garu seoltang]

icon ['aɪkɒn] *n* 아이콘 [aikon]

icy ['aɪsɪ] *adj* 얼음의 [eoreumui]

idea [aɪ'dɪə] *n* 생각 [saenggak]

ideal [aɪ'dɪəl] *adj* 이상적인 [isangjeogin]

ideally [aɪ'dɪəlɪ] *adv* 이상적으로 [isangjeogeuro]

identical [aɪ'dɛntɪkəl] *adj* 동일한 [dongilhan]

identification [aɪˌdɛntɪfɪ'keɪʃən] *n* 확인 [hwagin]

identify [aɪ'dɛntɪˌfaɪ] *v* 확인하다 [hwaginhada]

identity [aɪ'dɛntɪtɪ] *n* 정체성 [jeongcheseong]; **identity card** *n* 신분증 [sinbunjeung]; **identity theft** *n* 명의 도용 [myeongui doyong]

ideology [ˌaɪdɪ'ɒlədʒɪ] *n* 이데올로기 [ideollogi]

idiot ['ɪdɪət] *n* 바보 [babo]

idiotic [ˌɪdɪ'ɒtɪk] *adj* 어리석은 [eoriseogeun]

idle ['aɪdəl] *adj* 놀고 있는 [nolgo inneun]

i.e. [aɪ iː] *abbr* 즉 [jeuk]

if [ɪf] *conj* 만일...이면 [manil...imyeon]

ignition [ɪɡ'nɪʃən] *n* 점화 [jeomhwa]

ignorance ['ɪɡnərəns] *n* 무식 [musik]

ignorant ['ɪɡnərənt] *adj* 무식한 [musikhan]

ignore [ɪɡ'nɔː] *v* 무시하다 [musihada]

ill [ɪl] *adj* 아픈 [apeun]

illegal [ɪ'liːɡəl] *adj* 불법의 [bulbeobui]

illegible [ɪ'lɛdʒɪbəl] *adj* 읽기 어려운 [irkgi eoryeoun]

illiterate [ɪ'lɪtərɪt] *adj* 문맹의 [munmaengui]

illness ['ɪlnɪs] *n* 병 [byeong]

ill-treat [ɪl'triːt] *v* 학대하다 [hakdaehada]

illusion [ɪ'luːʒən] *n* 환각 [hwangak]

illustration [ˌɪlə'streɪʃən] *n* 삽화 [saphwa]

image ['ɪmɪdʒ] *n* 이미지 [imiji]

imaginary [ɪ'mædʒɪnərɪ; -dʒɪnrɪ] *adj* 상상의 [sangsangui]

imagination [ɪˌmædʒɪ'neɪʃən] *n* 상상 [sangsang]

imagine [ɪ'mædʒɪn] *v* 상상하다 [sangsanghada]

imitate ['ɪmɪˌteɪt] *v* 모방하다

[mobanghada]

imitation [ˌɪmɪ'teɪʃən] *n* 모조품
[mojopum]

immature [ˌɪmə'tjʊə; -'tʃʊə] *adj* 미숙한
[misukhan]

immediate [ɪ'miːdɪət] *adj* 즉시의
[jeuksiui]

immediately [ɪ'miːdɪətlɪ] *adv* 즉시
[jeuksi]

immigrant ['ɪmɪgrənt] *n* 이주자 [ijuja]

immigration [ˌɪmɪ'greɪʃən] *n* 이민
[imin]

immoral [ɪ'mɒrəl] *adj* 부도덕한
[budodeokhan]

impact ['ɪmpækt] *n* 영향 [yeonghyang]

impaired [ɪm'pɛəd] *adj* **I'm visually impaired** 저는 시각 장애인이에요
[jeoneun sigak jangaeinieyo]

impartial [ɪm'pɑːʃəl] *adj* 공평한
[gongpyeonghan]

impatience [ɪm'peɪʃəns] *n* 성급함
[seonggeupham]

impatient [ɪm'peɪʃənt] *adj* 성급한
[seonggeuphan]

impatiently [ɪm'peɪʃəntlɪ] *adv*
성급하게 [seonggeuphage]

impersonal [ɪm'pɜːsənəl] *adj*
비개인적인 [bigaeinjeogin]

import *n* ['ɪmpɔːt] 수입 [suip] ▷ *v*
[ɪm'pɔːt] 수입하다 [suiphada]

importance [ɪm'pɔːtəns] *n* 중요성
[jungyoseong]

important [ɪm'pɔːtənt] *adj* 중요한
[jungyohan]

impossible [ɪm'pɒsəbəl] *adj* 불가능한
[bulganeunghan]

impractical [ɪm'præktɪkəl] *adj*
비실용적인 [bisillyongjeogin]

impress [ɪm'prɛs] *v* 감명을 주다
[gammyeongeul juda]

impressed [ɪm'prɛst] *adj* 감명받은
[gammyeongbadeun]

impression [ɪm'prɛʃən] *n* 인상 [insang]
(느낌)

impressive [ɪm'prɛsɪv] *adj* 인상적인
[insangjeogin]

improve [ɪm'pruːv] *v* 개선하다
[gaeseonhada] (보다 좋은)

improvement [ɪm'pruːvmənt] *n* 개선
[gaeseon] (보다 좋은)

in [ɪn] *prep* ...의 안에 [...ui ane]

inaccurate [ɪn'ækjʊrɪt; ɪn'accurate] *adj*
부정확한 [bujeonghwakhan]

inadequate [ɪn'ædɪkwɪt] *adj* 부적당한
[bujeokdanghan]

inadvertently [ˌɪnəd'vɜːtəntlɪ] *adv*
무심코 [musimko]

inbox ['ɪnbɒks] *n* 받은 편지함 [badeun
pyeonjiham]

incentive [ɪn'sɛntɪv] *n* 장려금
[jangnyeogeum]

inch [ɪntʃ] *n* 인치 [inchi]

incident ['ɪnsɪdənt] *n* 사건 [sageon]

include [ɪn'kluːd] *v* 포함하다
[pohamhada]

included [ɪn'kluːdɪd] *adj* 포함된
[pohamdoen]

including [ɪn'kluːdɪŋ] *prep* ...을
포함하여 [...eul pohamhayeo]

inclusive [ɪn'kluːsɪv] *adj* 포괄적인
[pogwaljeogin]

income ['ɪnkʌm; 'ɪnkəm] *n* 소득
[sodeuk]; **income tax** *n* 소득세
[sodeukse]

incompetent [ɪn'kɒmpɪtənt] *adj*
무능한 [muneunghan]

incomplete [ˌɪnkəm'pliːt] *adj* 불완전한
[burwanjeonhan]

inconsistent [ˌɪnkən'sɪstənt] *adj*
일관성이 없는 [ilgwanseongi
eomneun]

inconvenience [ˌɪnkən'viːnjəns;
-'viːnɪəns] *n* 불편 [bulpyeon]

inconvenient [ˌɪnkən'viːnjənt;
-'viːnɪənt] *adj* 불편한 [bulpyeonhan]

incorrect [ˌɪnkə'rɛkt] *adj* 부정확한
[bujeonghwakhan]

increase *n* ['ɪnkriːs] 증가 [jeungga] ▷ *v*
[ɪn'kriːs] 증가하다 [jeunggahada]

increasingly [ɪn'kriːsɪŋlɪ] *adv* 점차
[jeomcha]

incredible [ɪn'krɛdəbəl] *adj* 믿어지지
않는 [mideojiji annneun]

indecisive [ˌɪndɪ'saɪsɪv] *adj* 결단성이
없는 [gyeoldanseongi eomneun]

indeed [ɪn'diːd] *adv* 정말 [jeongmal]

independence [ˌɪndɪˈpɛndəns] n 독립 [dongnip]

independent [ˌɪndɪˈpɛndənt] adj 독립적인 [dongnipjeogin]

index [ˈɪndɛks] n (list) 색인 [saegin], (numerical scale) 지수 [jisu]; **index finger** n 집게손가락 [jipgesongarak]

India [ˈɪndɪə] n 인도 [indo] (국가)

Indian [ˈɪndɪən] adj 인도의 [indoui] ▷ n 인도 사람 [indo saram]; **Indian Ocean** n 인도양 [indoyang]

indicate [ˈɪndɪˌkeɪt] v 가리키다 [garikida]

indicator [ˈɪndɪˌkeɪtə] n 표시기 [pyosigi]

indigestion [ˌɪndɪˈdʒɛstʃən] n 소화 불량 [sohwa bullyang]

indirect [ˌɪndɪˈrɛkt] adj 간접의 [ganjeobui]

indispensable [ˌɪndɪˈspɛnsəbəl] adj 필수의 [pilsuui]

individual [ˌɪndɪˈvɪdjʊəl] adj 개인의 [gaeinui]

Indonesia [ˌɪndəʊˈniːzɪə] n 인도네시아 [indonesia]

Indonesian [ˌɪndəʊˈniːzɪən] adj 인도네시아의 [indonesiaui] ▷ n (person) 인도네시아 사람 [indonesia saram]

indoor [ˈɪnˌdɔː] adj 실내의 [sillaeui]

indoors [ˌɪnˈdɔːz] adv 실내에 [sillaee]

industrial [ɪnˈdʌstrɪəl] adj 산업의 [saneobui]; **industrial estate** n 산업 단지 [saneop danji]

industry [ˈɪndəstrɪ] n 산업 [saneop]

inefficient [ˌɪnɪˈfɪʃənt] adj 비능률적인 [bineungnyuljeogin]

inevitable [ɪnˈɛvɪtəbəl] adj 필연적인 [pillyeonjeogin]

inexpensive [ˌɪnɪkˈspɛnsɪv] adj 값싼 [gapssan]

inexperienced [ˌɪnɪkˈspɪərɪənst] adj 미숙한 [misukhan]

infantry [ˈɪnfəntrɪ] n 보병 [bobyeong]

infection [ɪnˈfɛkʃən] n 전염 [jeonyeom]

infectious [ɪnˈfɛkʃəs] adj 전염성인 [jeonyeomseongin]

inferior [ɪnˈfɪərɪə] adj 하위의 [hawiui]

▷ n 손아랫사람 [sonaraessaram]

infertile [ɪnˈfɜːtaɪl] adj 불임의 [burimui]

infinitive [ɪnˈfɪnɪtɪv] n 부정사 [bujeongsa]

infirmary [ɪnˈfɜːmərɪ] n 병원 [byeongwon]

inflamed [ɪnˈfleɪmd] adj 염증을 일으킨 [yeomjeungeul ireukin]

inflammation [ˌɪnfləˈmeɪʃən] n 염증 [yeomjeung]

inflatable [ɪnˈfleɪtəbəl] adj 부풀릴 수 있는 [bupullil su inneun]

inflation [ɪnˈfleɪʃən] n 인플레이션 [inpeulleisyeon]

inflexible [ɪnˈflɛksəbəl] adj 구부러지지 않는 [gubureojiji annneun]

influence [ˈɪnflʊəns] n 영향 [yeonghyang] ▷ v 영향을 미치다 [yeonghyangeul michida]

influenza [ˌɪnflʊˈɛnzə] n 인플루엔자 [inpeulluenja]

inform [ɪnˈfɔːm] v 알리다 [allida]

informal [ɪnˈfɔːməl] adj 비공식적인 [bigongsikjeogin]

information [ˌɪnfəˈmeɪʃən] n 정보 [jeongbo]; **information office** n 안내소 [annaeso]; **Here's some information about my company** 우리 회사에 관한 정보예요 [uri hoesae gwanhan jeongboyeyo]; **I'd like some information about...** ...에 관한 정보를 얻고 싶어요 [...e gwanhan jeongboreul eotgo sipeoyo]

informative [ɪnˈfɔːmətɪv] adj 정보를 주는 [jeongboreul juneun]

infrastructure [ˈɪnfrəˌstrʌktʃə] n 기반시설 [gibansiseol]

infuriating [ɪnˈfjʊərɪeɪtɪŋ] adj 격분시키는 [gyeokbunsikineun]

ingenious [ɪnˈdʒiːnjəs; -nɪəs] adj 독창적인 [dokchangjeogin]

ingredient [ɪnˈgriːdɪənt] n 성분 [seongbun]

inhabitant [ɪnˈhæbɪtənt] n 주민 [jumin]

inhaler [ɪnˈheɪlə] n 흡입기 [heubipgi]

inherit [ɪnˈhɛrɪt] v 물려받다

[mullyeobatda]

inheritance [ɪn'hɛrɪtəns] n 상속
[sangsok]

inhibition [ˌɪnɪ'bɪʃən; ˌɪnhɪ-] n 억제
[eokje]

initial [ɪ'nɪʃəl] adj 초기의 [chogiui] ▷ v
머리글자로 서명하다 [meorigeuljaro
seomyeonghada]

initially [ɪ'nɪʃəlɪ] adv 초기에 [chogie]

initials [ɪ'nɪʃəlz] npl 머리글자
[meorigeulja]

initiative [ɪ'nɪʃɪətɪv; -'nɪʃətɪv] n
주도권 [judogwon]

inject [ɪn'dʒɛkt] v 주사하다 [jusahada]
(약물)

injection [ɪn'dʒɛkʃən] n 주사 [jusa]
(주사를 놓다); **I want an injection for
the pain** 진통제 주사를 맞고 싶어요
[jintongje jusareul matgo sipeoyo];
Please give me an injection 주사를
놔 주세요 [jusareul nwa juseyo]

injure ['ɪndʒə] v 상처를 입히다
[sangcheoreul iphida]

injured ['ɪndʒəd] adj 상처 입은
[sangcheo ibeun]

injury ['ɪndʒərɪ] n 부상 [busang] (상처);
injury time n 추가 시간 [chuga sigan]

injustice [ɪn'dʒʌstɪs] n 부정 [bujeong]

ink [ɪŋk] n 잉크 [ingkeu]

in-laws [ɪnlɔːz] npl 친척 [chincheok]

inmate ['ɪnˌmeɪt] n 피수용자
[pisuyongja]

inn [ɪn] n 여인숙 [yeoinsuk]

inner ['ɪnə] adj 안의 [anui]; **inner tube**
n 튜브 [tyubeu]

innocent ['ɪnəsənt] adj 순결한
[sungyeolhan]

innovation [ˌɪnə'veɪʃən] n 혁신
[hyeoksin]

innovative ['ɪnəˌveɪtɪv] adj 혁신적인
[hyeoksinjeogin]

inquest ['ɪnˌkwɛst] n 심리 [simni]
(재판)

inquire [ɪn'kwaɪə] v 문의하다
[munuihada]

inquiry [ɪn'kwaɪərɪ] n 문의 [munui];
inquiries office n 안내소 [annaeso]

inquisitive [ɪn'kwɪzɪtɪv] adj 캐묻기

좋아하는 [kaemutgi johahaneun]

insane [ɪn'seɪn] adj 미친 [michin]

inscription [ɪn'skrɪpʃən] n 새겨진 것
[saegyeojin geot]

insect ['ɪnsɛkt] n 곤충 [gonchung];
insect repellent n 구충제
[guchungje]; **stick insect** n 대벌레
[daebeolle]

insecure [ˌɪnsɪ'kjʊə] adj 불안한
[buranhan]

insensitive [ɪn'sɛnsɪtɪv] adj 둔감한
[dungamhan]

inside adv [ˌɪn'saɪd] 내부에 [naebue]
▷ n ['ɪn'saɪd] 안쪽 [anjjok] ▷ prep...의
안쪽에 [...ui anjjoge]

insincere [ˌɪnsɪn'sɪə] adj 불성실한
[bulseongsilhan]

insist [ɪn'sɪst] v 주장하다 [jujanghada]

insomnia [ɪn'sɒmnɪə] n 불면증
[bulmyeonjeung]

inspect [ɪn'spɛkt] v 조사하다
[josahada]

inspector [ɪn'spɛktə] n 조사관
[josagwan]; **ticket inspector** n 검표원
[geompyowon]

instability [ˌɪnstə'bɪlɪtɪ] n 불안정
[buranjeong]

instalment [ɪn'stɔːlmənt] n 할부금
[halbugeum]

instance ['ɪnstəns] n 예 [ye]

instant ['ɪnstənt] adj 즉시의 [jeuksiui]

instantly ['ɪnstəntlɪ] adv 즉시 [jeuksi]

instead [ɪn'stɛd] adv 그 대신에 [geu
daesine]; **instead of** prep...대신에 [...
daesine]

instinct ['ɪnstɪŋkt] n 본능 [bonneung]

institute ['ɪnstɪˌtjuːt] n 연구소
[yeonguso]

institution [ˌɪnstɪ'tjuːʃən] n 기관
[gigwan]

instruct [ɪn'strʌkt] v 교육하다
[gyoyukhada]

instructions [ɪn'strʌkʃənz] npl 지시
[jisi]

instructor [ɪn'strʌktə] n 강사 [gangsa];
driving instructor n 운전 강사
[unjeon gangsa]

instrument ['ɪnstrəmənt] n 도구

[dogu]; **musical instrument** n 악기 [akgi]

insufficient [ˌɪnsəˈfɪʃənt] adj 불충분한 [bulchungbunhan]

insulation [ˌɪnsjʊˈleɪʃən] n 절연 [jeollyeon]

insulin [ˈɪnsjʊlɪn] n 인슐린 [insyullin]

insult n [ˈɪnsʌlt] 모욕 [moyok] ▷ v [ɪnˈsʌlt] 모욕하다 [moyokhada]

insurance [ɪnˈʃʊərəns; -ˈʃɔː-] n 보험 [boheom]; **accident insurance** n 상해보험 [sanghaeboheom]; **car insurance** n 자동차 보험 [jadongcha boheom]; **insurance certificate** n 보험증서 [boheomjeungseo]; **insurance policy** n 보험증권 [boheomjeunggwon]; **life insurance** n 생명보험 [saengmyeongboheom]; **third-party insurance** n 3자 보험 [samja boheom]; **travel insurance** n 여행보험 [yeohaengboheom]; **Can I see your insurance certificate please?** 보험증서를 볼 수 있을까요? [boheomjeungseoreul bol su isseulkkayo?]; **Do you have insurance?** 보험에 들었어요? [boheome deureosseoyo?]; **Give me your insurance details, please** 보험 정보를 알려 주세요 [boheom jeongboreul allyeo juseyo]; **Here are my insurance details** 제 보험 정보예요 [je boheom jeongboyeyo]; **How much extra is comprehensive insurance cover?** 종합 보험료로 얼마를 더 내야 할까요? [jonghap boheomnyoro eolmareul deo naeya halkkayo?]; **I don't have dental insurance** 저는 치과 보험에 들지 않았어요 [jeoneun chigwa boheome deulji anhasseoyo]; **I don't have health insurance** 저는 건강보험에 들지 않았어요 [jeoneun geonggangboheome deulji anhasseoyo]; **I have insurance** 저는 보험에 들었어요 [jeoneun boheome deureosseoyo]; **I'd like to arrange personal accident insurance** 개인보험을 들고 싶어요 [gaeinboheomeul deulgo sipeoyo]; **Is fully comprehensive insurance included in the price?** 가격에 종합 보험료가 포함되나요? [gagyeoge jonghap boheomnyoga pohamdoenayo?]; **Will the insurance pay for it?** 보험사가 지불해 주나요? [boheomsaga jibulhae junayo?]

insure [ɪnˈʃʊə; -ˈʃɔː] v 보증하다 [bojeunghada]

insured [ɪnˈʃʊəd; -ˈʃɔːd] adj 보험에 든 [boheome deun]

intact [ɪnˈtækt] adj 원래대로의 [wollaedaeroui]

intellectual [ˌɪntɪˈlɛktʃʊəl] adj 지능의 [jineungui] ▷ n 지식인 [jisigin]

intelligence [ɪnˈtɛlɪdʒəns] n 지성 [jiseong]

intelligent [ɪnˈtɛlɪdʒənt] adj 지적인 [jijeogin]

intend [ɪnˈtɛnd] v **intend to** v 작정이다 [jakjeongida]

intense [ɪnˈtɛns] adj 강렬한 [gangnyeolhan]

intensive [ɪnˈtɛnsɪv] adj 집중적인 [jipjungjeogin]; **intensive care unit** n 중환자실 [junghwanjasil]

intention [ɪnˈtɛnʃən] n 의도 [uido]

intentional [ɪnˈtɛnʃənºl] adj 고의적인 [gouijeogin]

intercom [ˈɪntəˌkɒm] n 내부 통신 시스템 [naebu tongsin siseutem]

interest [ˈɪntrɪst; -tərɪst] n (curiosity) 관심 [gwansim], (income) 이익 [iik] ▷ v 흥미를 갖게 하다 [heungmireul gatge hada]; **interest rate** n 금리 [geumni]

interested [ˈɪntrɪstɪd; -tərɪs-] adj 흥미를 가진 [heungmireul gajin]

interesting [ˈɪntrɪstɪŋ; -tərɪs-] adj 흥미있는 [heungmiinneun]

interior [ɪnˈtɪərɪə] n 내부 [naebu]; **interior designer** n 실내 장식가 [sillae jangsikga]

intermediate [ˌɪntəˈmiːdɪɪt] adj 중간의 [jungganui]

internal [ɪnˈtɜːnºl] adj 내부의 [naebuui]

international [ˌɪntəˈnæʃənºl] adj 국제적인 [gukjejeogin]

Internet ['ɪntəˌnɛt] n 인터넷 [inteonet]; **Internet café** n 인터넷 카페 [inteonet kape]; **Internet user** n 인터넷 사용자 [inteonet sayongja]; **Are there any Internet cafés here?** 여기에 인터넷 카페가 있나요? [yeogie inteonet kapega innayo?]; **Does the room have wireless Internet access?** 방에서 무선 인터넷 있어요? [bangeseo museon inteonet isseoyo?]; **Is there an Internet connection in the room?** 방에서 인터넷 되나요? [bangeseo inteonet doenayo?]

interpret [ɪn'tɜːprɪt] v 해석하다 [haeseokhada]

interpreter [ɪn'tɜːprɪtə] n 통역사 [tongyeoksa]; **I need an interpreter** 통역사가 필요해요 [tongyeoksaga piryohaeyo]

interrogate [ɪn'tɛrəˌgeɪt] v 심문하다 [simmunhada]

interrupt [ˌɪntə'rʌpt] v 방해하다 [banghaehada]

interruption [ˌɪntə'rʌpʃən] n 방해 [banghae]

interval ['ɪntəvəl] n 간격 [gangyeok]

interview ['ɪntəˌvjuː] n 면담 [myeondam] ▷ v 면담하다 [myeondamhada]

interviewer ['ɪntəˌvjuːə] n 면접원 [myeonjeobwon]

intimate ['ɪntɪmɪt] adj 친밀한 [chinmilhan]

intimidate [ɪn'tɪmɪˌdeɪt] v 위협하다 [wihyeophada]

into ['ɪntuː; 'ɪntə] prep ...안으로 [... aneuro]; **bump into** v 우연히 만나다 [uyeonhi mannada]

intolerant [ɪn'tɒlərənt] adj 관용성이 없는 [gwanyongseongi eomneun]

intranet ['ɪntrəˌnɛt] n 인트라넷 [inteuranet]

introduce [ˌɪntrə'djuːs] v 소개하다 [sogaehada]

introduction [ˌɪntrə'dʌkʃən] n 소개 [sogae] (프레젠테이션)

intruder [ɪn'truːdə] n 침입자 [chimipja]

intuition [ˌɪntjʊ'ɪʃən] n 직관 [jikgwan]

invade [ɪn'veɪd] v 침략하다 [chimnyakhada]

invalid ['ɪnvəˌlɪd] n 병약자 [byeongyakja]

invent [ɪn'vɛnt] v 발명하다 [balmyeonghada]

invention [ɪn'vɛnʃən] n 발명 [balmyeong]

inventor [ɪn'vɛntə] n 발명가 [balmyeongga]

inventory ['ɪnvəntərɪ; -trɪ] n 품목 일람 [pummok illam]

invest [ɪn'vɛst] v 투자하다 [tujahada]

investigation [ɪnˌvɛstɪ'geɪʃən] n 조사 [josa]

investment [ɪn'vɛstmənt] n 투자 [tuja]

investor [ɪn'vɛstə] n 투자자 [tujaja]

invigilator [ɪn'vɪdʒɪˌleɪtə] n 감독관 [gamdokgwan]

invisible [ɪn'vɪzəbəl] adj 보이지 않는 [boiji annneun]

invitation [ˌɪnvɪ'teɪʃən] n 초대 [chodae] (손님)

invite [ɪn'vaɪt] v 초대하다 [chodaehada]

invoice ['ɪnvɔɪs] n 송장 [songjang] (지불) ▷ v 송장을 보내다 [songjangeul bonaeda]

involve [ɪn'vɒlv] v 포함하다 [pohamhada]

iPod® ['aɪˌpɒd] n 아이팟 [aipat]

IQ [aɪ kjuː] abbr 지능지수 [jineungjisu]

Iran [ɪ'rɑːn] n 이란 [iran]

Iranian [ɪ'reɪnɪən] adj 이란의 [iranui] ▷ n (person) 이란 사람 [iran saram]

Iraq [ɪ'rɑːk] n 이라크 [irakeu]

Iraqi [ɪ'rɑːkɪ] adj 이라크의 [irakeuui] ▷ n 이라크 사람 [irakeu saram]

Ireland ['aɪələnd] n 아일랜드 [aillaendeu]; **Northern Ireland** n 북아일랜드 [bugaillaendeu]

iris ['aɪrɪs] n 홍채 [hongchae]

Irish ['aɪrɪʃ] adj 아일랜드의 [aillaendeuui] ▷ n 아일랜드 사람 [aillaendeu saram]

Irishman, Irishmen ['aɪrɪʃmən, 'aɪrɪʃmɛn] n 아일랜드 사람 [aillaendeu saram]

Irishwoman, Irishwomen
['aɪrɪʃwʊmən, 'aɪrɪʃwɪmɪn] *n*
아일랜드 여자 [aillaendeu yeoja]

iron ['aɪən] *n* 철 [cheol] (금속) ▷ *v*
다림질하다 [darimjilhada]

ironic [aɪ'rɒnɪk] *adj* 풍자적인
[pungjajeogin]

ironing ['aɪənɪŋ] *n* 다림질 [darimjil];
ironing board *n* 다리미판 [darimipan]

ironmonger's ['aɪən,mʌŋgəz] *n* 철물점
[cheolmuljeom]

irony ['aɪrənɪ] *n* 풍자 [pungja]

irregular [ɪ'rɛgjʊlə] *adj* 불규칙한
[bulgyuchikhan]

irrelevant [ɪ'rɛləvənt] *adj* 관계가 없는
[gwangyega eomneun]

irresponsible [,ɪrɪ'spɒnsəbᵊl] *adj*
무책임한 [muchaegimhan]

irritable ['ɪrɪtəbᵊl] *adj* 화를 쉽게 내는
[hwareul swipge naeneun]

irritating ['ɪrɪ,teɪtɪŋ] *adj* 화나게 하는
[hwanage haneun]

Islam ['ɪzlɑːm] *n* 이슬람교
[iseullamgyo]

Islamic [ɪz'lɑːmɪk] *adj* 이슬람교의
[iseullamgyoui]

island ['aɪlənd] *n* 섬 [seom]; **desert
island** *n* 무인도 [muindo]

isolated ['aɪsə,leɪtɪd] *adj* 격리된
[gyeongnidoen]

ISP [aɪ ɛs piː] *abbr* 인터넷 서비스 제공자
[inteonet seobiseu jegongja]

Israel ['ɪzreɪəl; -rɪəl] *n* 이스라엘
[iseurael]

Israeli [ɪz'reɪlɪ] *adj* 이스라엘의
[iseuraerui] ▷ *n* 이스라엘 사람 [iseurael
saram]

issue ['ɪʃjuː] *n* 쟁점 [jaengjeom] ▷ *v*
공포하다 [gongpohada]

it [ɪt] *pron* 그것 [geugeot]

IT [aɪ tiː] *abbr* 정보기술 [jeongbogisul]

Italian [ɪ'tæljən] *adj* 이탈리아의
[italliaui] ▷ *n* (language) 이탈리아어
[italliaeo], (person) 이탈리아 사람
[italliasaram]

Italy ['ɪtəlɪ] *n* 이탈리아 [italia]

itch [ɪtʃ] *v* 가렵다 [garyeopda]

itchy [ɪtʃɪ] *adj* 가려운 [garyeoun]

item ['aɪtəm] *n* 항목 [hangmok]

itinerary [aɪ'tɪnərərɪ; ɪ-] *n* 여행일정표
[yeohaengiljeongpyo]

its [ɪts] *adj* 그것의 [geugeosui]

itself [ɪt'sɛlf] *pron* 그것 자체 [geugeot
jache]

ivory ['aɪvərɪ; -vrɪ] *n* 상아 [sanga]

ivy ['aɪvɪ] *n* 담쟁이덩굴
[damjaengideonggul]

J

jab [dʒæb] n 재빠른 일격 [jaeppareun ilgyeok]

jack [dʒæk] n 잭 [jaek]

jacket ['dʒækɪt] n 재킷 [jaekit]; **dinner jacket** n 남자 턱시도 [namja teoksido]; **jacket potato** n 껍질째 구운 감자 [kkeopjiljjae guun gamja]; **life jacket** n 구명조끼 [gumyeongjokki]

jackpot ['dʒæk,pɒt] n 거액의 상금 [geoaegui sanggeum]

jail [dʒeɪl] n 감옥 [gamok] ▷ v 투옥하다 [tuokhada]

jam [dʒæm] n 잼 [jaem]; **jam jar** n 잼 병 [jaem byeong]; **traffic jam** n 교통마비 [gyotongmabi]

Jamaican [dʒə'meɪkən] adj 자메이카의 [jameikaui] ▷ n 자메이카 사람 [jameika saram]

jammed [dʒæmd] adj 끼여서 못움직이게 된 [kkiyeoseo mosumjigige doen]

janitor ['dʒænɪtə] n 수위 [suwi] (문지기)

January ['dʒænjʊərɪ] n 1월 [irwol]

Japan [dʒə'pæn] n 일본 [ilbon]

Japanese [ˌdʒæpə'niːz] adj 일본의 [ilbonui] ▷ n (language) 일본어 [ilboneo], (person) 일본 사람 [ilbon saram]

jar [dʒɑː] n 병 [byeong]; **jam jar** n 잼 병 [jaem byeong]

jaundice ['dʒɔːndɪs] n 황달 [hwangdal]

javelin ['dʒævlɪn] n 창 [chang]

jaw [dʒɔː] n 턱 [teok]

jazz [dʒæz] n 재즈 [jaejeu]

jealous ['dʒɛləs] adj 질투하는 [jiltuhaneun]

jeans [dʒiːnz] npl 청바지 [cheongbaji]

jelly ['dʒɛlɪ] n 젤리 [jelli]

jellyfish ['dʒɛlɪ,fɪʃ] n 해파리 [haepari]; **Are there jellyfish here?** 여기에 해파리가 있어요? [yeogie haepariga isseoyo?]

jersey ['dʒɜːzɪ] n 저지 [jeoji] (직물)

Jesus ['dʒiːzəs] n 예수 [yesu]

jet [dʒɛt] n 제트기 [jeteugi]; **jet lag** n 시차로 인한 피로 [sicharo inhan piro]; **jumbo jet** n 점보제트기 [jeombojeteugi]

jetty ['dʒɛtɪ] n 부두 [budu]

Jew [dʒuː] n 유태인 [yutaein]

jewel ['dʒuːəl] n 보석 [boseok]

jeweller ['dʒuːələ] n 보석상 [boseoksang]

jeweller's ['dʒuːələz] n 보석점 [boseokjeom]

jewellery ['dʒuːəlrɪ] n 보석류 [boseongnyu]

Jewish ['dʒuːɪʃ] adj 유태인의 [yutaeinui]

jigsaw ['dʒɪg,sɔː] n 조각 맞추기 퍼즐 [jogak matchugi peojeul]

job [dʒɒb] n 직업 [jigeop]; **job centre** n 구직센터 [gujiksenteo]

jobless ['dʒɒblɪs; 'jobless] adj 실직의 [siljigui]

jockey ['dʒɒkɪ] n 경마기수 [gyeongmagisu]

jog [dʒɒg] v 조깅하다 [joginghada]

jogging ['dʒɒgɪŋ] n 조깅 [joging]

join [dʒɔɪn] v 합류하다 [hamnyuhada]

joiner ['dʒɔɪnə] n 가구장이 [gagujangi]

joint [dʒɔɪnt] adj 공동의 [gongdongui] ▷ n (junction) 접합 부문 [jeophap bumun], (meat) 고기 토막 [gogi tomak]; **joint account** n 공동 계좌

[gongdong gyejwa]

joke [dʒəʊk] *n* 농담 [nongdam] ▷ *v*
농담하다 [nongdamhada]

jolly ['dʒɒlɪ] *adj* 명랑한
[myeongnanghan]

Jordan ['dʒɔːdⁿn] *n* 요르단 [yoreudan]

Jordanian [dʒɔːˈdeɪnɪən] *adj* 요르단의
[yoreudanui] ▷ *n* 요르단 사람
[yoreudan saram]

jot down [dʒɒt daʊn] *v* 메모하다
[memohada]

jotter ['dʒɒtə] *n* 메모지 [memoji]

journalism ['dʒɜːnⁿˌlɪzəm] *n* 저널리즘
[jeoneollijeum]

journalist ['dʒɜːnⁿlɪst] *n* 저널리스트
[jeoneolliseuteu]

journey ['dʒɜːnɪ] *n* 여행 [yeohaeng]

joy [dʒɔɪ] *n* 기쁨 [gippeum]

joystick ['dʒɔɪˌstɪk] *n* 조종간
[jojonggan]

judge [dʒʌdʒ] *n* 재판관 [jaepangwan]
▷ *v* 판단하다 [pandanhada]

judo ['dʒuːdəʊ] *n* 유도 [yudo] (운동)

jug [dʒʌg] *n* 주전자 [jujeonja]; **a jug of
water** 물 한 주전자 [mul han jujeonja]

juggler ['dʒʌglə] *n* 마술사 [masulsa]

juice [dʒuːs] *n* 주스 [juseu]; **orange
juice** *n* 오렌지 주스 [orenji juseu]

July [dʒuːˈlaɪ; dʒə-; dʒʊ-] *n* 7월
[chirwol]

jump [dʒʌmp] *n* 멀리뛰기 [meollittwigi]
▷ *v* 뛰다 [ttwida]; **high jump** *n*
높이뛰기 [nopittwigi]; **jump leads** *npl*
점프선 [jeompeuseon]; **long jump** *n*
멀리뛰기 [meollittwigi]

jumper ['dʒʌmpə] *n* 점퍼 [jeompeo]

jumping [dʒʌmpɪŋ] *n* **show-jumping** *n*
장애물 뛰어넘기 [jangaemul
ttwieoneomgi]

junction ['dʒʌŋkʃən] *n* 교차로
[gyocharo]

June [dʒuːn] *n* 6월 [yuwol]

jungle ['dʒʌŋgⁿl] *n* 정글 [jeonggeul]

junior ['dʒuːnjə] *adj* 손아래의
[sonaraeui]

junk [dʒʌŋk] *n* 쓰레기 [sseuregi]; **junk
mail** *n* 스팸메일 [seupaemmeil]

jury ['dʒʊərɪ] *n* 배심 [baesim]

just [dʒəst] *adv* 방금 [banggeum]; **I've
just arrived** 방금 도착했어요
[banggeum dochakhaesseoyo]

justice ['dʒʌstɪs] *n* 정의 [jeongui]

justify ['dʒʌstɪˌfaɪ] *v* 정당화하다
[jeongdanghwahada]

k

yeolsoe]; **Can I have a key?** 열쇠
주시겠어요? [yeolsoe jusigesseoyo?]; **I
left the keys in the car** 차에 열쇠를
두고 내렸어요 [chae yeolsoereul dugo
naeryeosseoyo]; **I'm having trouble
with the key** 열쇠에 문제가 있어요
[yeolsoee munjega isseoyo]; **I've
forgotten the key** 열쇠를 깜빡
잊었어요 [yeolsoereul kkamppak
ijeosseoyo]; **the key for room
number two hundred and two** 202
호 열쇠요 [ibaek-i ho yeolsoeyo]; **The
key doesn't work** 열쇠가 고장났어요
[yeolsoega gojangnasseoyo]; **We need
a second key** 보조 열쇠가 필요해요
[bojo yeolsoega pillyohaeyo]; **What's
this key for?** 이 열쇠는 어디 열쇠죠? [i
yeolsoenèun eodi yeolsoejyo?]; **Where
do we get the key...?** ... 열쇠는
어디에서 받을 수 있을까요? [...
yeolsoeneun eodieseo badeul su
isseulkkayo?]; **Where do we hand in
the key when we're leaving?** 나갈 때
어디에서 열쇠를 반납하나요? [nagal
ttae eodieseo yeolsoereul
bannaphanayo?]; **Which is the key for
the back door?** 뒷문 열쇠는 어느
것인가요? [dwitmun yeolsoeneun
eoneu geosingayo?]; **Which is the key
for this door?** 이 문 열쇠는 어느
것인가요? [i mun yeolsoeneun eoneu
geosingayo?]

kangaroo [ˌkæŋɡəˈruː] n 캥거루
[kaenggeoru]
karaoke [ˌkɑːrəˈəʊkɪ] n 노래방
[noraebang]
karate [kəˈrɑːtɪ] n 가라테 [garate]
Kazakhstan [ˌkɑːzɑːkˈstæn; -ˈstɑːn] n
카자흐스탄 [kajaheuseutan]
kebab [kəˈbæb] n 케밥 [kebap]
keen [kiːn] adj 열심인 [yeolsimin]
keep [kiːp] v 유지하다 [yujihada],
간직하다 [ganjikhada]
keep-fit [ˈkiːpˌfɪt] n 체조 [chejo]
keep out [kiːp aʊt] v 안에 들이지 않다
[ane deuriji anta]
keep up [kiːp ʌp] v 유지하다 [yujihada];
keep up with v 유지하다 [yujihada]
kennel [ˈkɛnəl] n 개집 [gaejip]
Kenya [ˈkɛnjə; ˈkiːnjə] n 케냐 [kenya]
Kenyan [ˈkɛnjən; ˈkiːnjən] adj 케냐의
[kenyaui] ▷ n 케냐 사람 [kenya saram]
kerb [kɜːb] n 연석 [yeonseok] (도로)
kerosene [ˈkɛrəˌsiːn] n 등유 [deungyu]
ketchup [ˈkɛtʃəp] n 케첩 [kecheop]
kettle [ˈkɛtəl] n 주전자 [jujeonja]
key [kiː] n (for lock) 열쇠 [yeolsoe],
(music/computer) 열쇠 [yeolsoe]; **car
keys** npl 자동차 열쇠 [jadongcha
keyboard [ˈkiːˌbɔːd] n 키보드 [kibodeu]
keyring [ˈkiːˌrɪŋ] n 열쇠고리
[yeolsoegori]
kick [kɪk] n 차기 [chagi] (발로) ▷ v (을)
차다 [(eul) chada]
kick off [kɪk ɒf] v 시작하다 [sijakhada]
kick-off [kɪkɒf] n 시작 [sijak]
kid [kɪd] n 아이 [ai] ▷ v 놀리다 [nollida]
kidnap [ˈkɪdnæp] v 유괴하다
[yugoehada]
kidney [ˈkɪdnɪ] n 신장 [sinjang]
kill [kɪl] v 죽이다 [jugida]
killer [ˈkɪlə] n 살인자 [sarinja]
kilo [ˈkiːləʊ] n 킬로 [killo]
kilometre [kɪˈlɒmɪtə; ˈkɪləˌmiːtə] n
킬로미터 [killomiteo]

kilt [kɪlt] n 킬트 [kilteu]
kind [kaɪnd] adj 친절한 [chinjeolhan] ▷ n 종류 [jongnyu]; **What kind of sandwiches do you have?** 어떤 종류의 샌드위치가 있으세요? [eotteon jongnyuui saendeuwichiga isseuseyo?]
kindly ['kaɪndlɪ] adv 친절하게 [chinjeolhage]
kindness ['kaɪndnɪs] n 친절 [chinjeol]
king [kɪŋ] n 왕 [wang]
kingdom ['kɪŋdəm] n 왕국 [wangguk]
kingfisher ['kɪŋ,fɪʃə] n 물총새 [mulchongsae]
kiosk ['kiːɒsk] n 키오스크 [kioseukeu]
kipper ['kɪpə] n 청어 [cheongeo]
kiss [kɪs] n 키스 [kiseu] ▷ v 키스하다 [kiseuhada]
kit [kɪt] n 도구 한 벌 [dogu han beol]; **hands-free kit** n 핸즈프리 장치 [haenjeupeuri jangchi]; **repair kit** n 수리도구 [suridogu]
kitchen ['kɪtʃɪn] n 주방 [jubang]; **fitted kitchen** n 맞춤 주방 [matchum jubang]
kite [kaɪt] n 연 [yeon]
kitten ['kɪtⁿn] n 새끼고양이 [saekkigoyangi]
kiwi ['kiːwiː] n 키위 [kiwi]
knee [niː] n 무릎 [mureup]
kneecap ['niː,kæp] n 슬개골 [seulgaegol]
kneel [niːl] v 무릎을 꿇다 [mureupeul kkurta]
kneel down [niːl daʊn] v 굴복하다 [gulbokhada]
knickers ['nɪkəz] npl 니커스 [nikeoseu]
knife [naɪf] n 칼 [kal]
knit [nɪt] v 뜨다 [tteuda] (스웨터)
knitting ['nɪtɪŋ] n 뜨개질 [tteugaejil]; **knitting needle** n 뜨개바늘 [tteugaebaneul]
knob [nɒb] n 손잡이 [sonjabi]
knock [nɒk] n 공격 [gonggyeok] ▷ v 두드리다 [dudeurida], (on the door etc.) 두드리다 [dudeurida]
knock down [nɒk daʊn] v 때려눕히다 [ttaeryeonuphida]
knock out [nɒk aʊt] v 의식을 잃게 하다 [uisigeul irke hada]
knot [nɒt] n 매듭 [maedeup]
know [nəʊ] v 알다 [alda]
know-all ['nəʊɔːl] n 아는 체하는 사람 [aneun chehaneun saram]
know-how ['nəʊ,haʊ] n 노하우 [nohau]
knowledge ['nɒlɪdʒ] n 지식 [jisik]
knowledgeable ['nɒlɪdʒəbᵊl] adj 박식한 [baksikhan]
known [nəʊn] adj 알려진 [allyeojin]
Koran [kɔːˈrɑːn] n 코란 [koran]
Korea [kəˈriːə] n 한국 [hanguk]; **North Korea** n 북한 [bukhan]; **South Korea** n 한국 [hanguk]
Korean [kəˈriːən] adj 한국의 [hangugui] ▷ n (language) 한국어 [hangugeo], (person) 한국 사람 [hanguk saram]
kosher ['kəʊʃə] adj 유태교 규칙에 따라 처리된 [yutaegyo gyuchige ttara cheoridoen]
Kosovo ['kɒsɒvɒ; 'kɒsəvəʊ] n 코소보 [kosobo]
Kuwait [kʊ'weɪt] n 쿠웨이트 [kuweiteu]
Kuwaiti [kʊ'weɪtɪ] adj 쿠웨이트의 [kuweiteuui] ▷ n 쿠웨이트 사람 [kuweiteu saram]
Kyrgyzstan ['kɪəgɪz,stɑːn; -,stæn] n 키르기스스탄 [kireugiseuseutan]

lab [læb] *n* 실험실 [silheomsil]

label ['leɪbᵊl] *n* 라벨 [rabel]

laboratory [lə'bɒrətərɪ; -trɪ; 'læbrətɔːrɪ] *n* 실험실 [silheomsil]; **language laboratory** *n* 어학실습실 [eohaksilseupsil]

labour ['leɪbə] *n* 노동 [nodong]

labourer ['leɪbərə] *n* 노동자 [nodongja]

lace [leɪs] *n* 레이스 [reiseu]

lack [læk] *n* 부족 [bujok]

lacquer ['lækə] *n* 래커 [raekeo]

lad [læd] *n* 젊은이 [jeormeuni]

ladder ['lædə] *n* 사다리 [sadari]

ladies ['leɪdɪz] *n* **ladies'** *n* 여자화장실 [yeojahwajangsil]; **Where is the ladies?** 여자 화장실은 어디에 있어요? [yeoja hwajangsil-eun urdie ittsuryo?]

ladle ['leɪdᵊl] *n* 국자 [gukja]

lady ['leɪdɪ] *n* 숙녀 [sungnyeo]

ladybird ['leɪdɪ,bɜːd] *n* 무당벌레 [mudangbeolle]

lag [læg] *n* **jet lag** *n* 시차로 인한 피로 [sicharo inhan piro]; **I'm suffering from jet lag** 시차 때문에 힘들어요 [sicha ttaemune himdeureoyo]

lager ['lɑːgə] *n* 저장맥주 [jeojangmaekju]

lagoon [lə'guːn] *n* 석호 [seokho]

laid-back ['leɪdbæk] *adj* 느긋한 [neugeutan]

lake [leɪk] *n* 호수 [hosu]

lamb [læm] *n* 어린양 [eorinyang]

lame [leɪm] *adj* 다리를 저는 [darireul jeoneun]

lamp [læmp] *n* 램프 [raempeu]; **bedside lamp** *n* 침대 맡의 램프 [chimdae matui raempeu]; **The lamp is not working** 램프가 작동하지 않아요 [raempeuga jakdonghaji anhayo]

lamppost ['læmp,pəʊst] *n* 가로등 기둥 [garodeung gidung]

lampshade ['læmp,ʃeɪd] *n* 램프의 갓 [raempeuui gat]

land [lænd] *n* 땅 [ttang] ▷ *v* 착륙하다 [changnyukhada]

landing ['lændɪŋ] *n* 층계 꼭대기의 마루 [cheunggye kkokdaegiui maru]

landlady ['lænd,leɪdɪ] *n* 여주인 [yeojuin]

landlord ['lænd,lɔːd] *n* 주인 [juin]

landmark ['lænd,mɑːk] *n* 표지물 [pyojimul]

landowner ['lænd,əʊnə] *n* 토지소유자 [tojisoyuja]

landscape ['lænd,skeɪp] *n* 경관 [gyeonggwan] (경치)

landslide ['lænd,slaɪd] *n* 산사태 [sansatae]

lane [leɪn] *n* 좁은 길 [jobeun gil], *(driving)* 좁은 길 [jobeun gil]; **cycle lane** *n* 자전거 도로 [jajeongeo doro]

language ['læŋgwɪdʒ] *n* 언어 [eoneo]; **language laboratory** *n* 어학실습실 [eohaksilseupsil]; **language school** *n* 어학원 [eohagwon]; **sign language** *n* 수화 [suhwa]

lanky ['læŋkɪ] *adj* 마르고 호리호리한 [mareugo horihorihan]

Laos [laʊz; laʊs] *n* 라오스 [raoseu]

lap [læp] *n* 무릎 [mureup]

laptop ['læp,tɒp] *n* 랩톱 [raeptop]

larder ['lɑːdə] *n* 식료품 저장실 [singnyopum jeojangsil]

large [lɑːdʒ] *adj* 큰 [keun]; **Do you have**

a large? 큰 사이즈 있어요? [keun saijeu isseoyo?]; **Do you have an extra large?** 아주 큰 사이즈 있어요? [aju keun saijeu isseoyo?]

largely ['lɑːdʒlɪ] adv 대부분 [daebubun]

laryngitis [ˌlærɪn'dʒaɪtɪs] n 후두염 [huduyeom]

laser ['leɪzə] n 레이저 [reijeo]

lass [læs] n 아가씨 [agassi]

last [lɑːst] adj 마지막의 [majimagui] ▷ adv 마침내 [machimnae] ▷ v 오래가다 [oraegada]; **I'm delighted to meet you at last** 마침내 뵙게 되어 기쁩니다 [machimnae boepge doeeo gippeumnida]

lastly ['lɑːstlɪ] adv 끝으로 [kkeuteuro]

late [leɪt] adj (dead) 사망한 [samanghan], (delayed) 늦은 [neujeun] ▷ adv 늦게 [neutge]

lately ['leɪtlɪ] adv 요즈음 [yojeueum]

later ['leɪtə] adv 나중에 [najunge]; **Can you try again later?** 나중에 다시 전화하시겠어요? [najunge dasi jeonhwahasigesseoyo?]; **I'll call back later** 나중에 다시 전화할께요 [najunge dasi jeonhwahalkkeyo]; **See you later** 나중에 뵙겠습니다 [najunge boepgesseumnida]; **Shall I come back later?** 나중에 다시 올까요? [najunge dasi olkkayo?]

Latin ['lætɪn] n 라틴어 [ratineo]

Latin America ['lætɪn ə'mɛrɪkə] n 라틴 아메리카 [ratin amerika]

Latin American ['lætɪn ə'mɛrɪkən] adj 라틴 아메리카의 [ratin amerikaui]

latitude ['lætɪˌtjuːd] n 위도 [wido]

Latvia ['lætvɪə] n 라트비아 [rateubia]

Latvian ['lætvɪən] adj 라트비아의 [rateubiaui] ▷ n (language) 라트비아어 [rateubiaeo], (person) 라트비아 사람 [rateubia saram]

laugh [lɑːf] n 웃음 [useum] ▷ v 웃다 [utda]

laughter ['lɑːftə] n 웃음 [useum]

launch [lɔːntʃ] v (배를) 진수시키다 [(baereul) jinsusikida]

Launderette® [ˌlɔːndə'rɛt; lɔːn'drɛt] n 빨래방 [ppallaebang]

laundry ['lɔːndrɪ] n 세탁소 [setakso]

lava ['lɑːvə] n 용암 [yongam]

lavatory ['lævətərɪ; -trɪ] n 화장실 [hwajangsil]

lavender ['lævəndə] n 라벤더 [rabendeo]

law [lɔː] n 법 [beop]; **law school** n 법과대학 [beopgwadaehak]

lawn [lɔːn] n 잔디밭 [jandibat]

lawnmower ['lɔːnˌməʊə] n 잔디 깎는 기계 [jandi kkakkneun gigye]

lawyer ['lɔːjə; 'lɔɪə] n 변호사 [byeonhosa]

laxative ['læksətɪv] n 완하제 [wanhaje]

lay [leɪ] v 눕히다 [nuphida]

layby ['leɪˌbaɪ] n 대피소 [daepiso]

layer ['leɪə] n 층 [cheung]; **ozone layer** n 오존층 [ojoncheung]

lay off [leɪ ɒf] v 해고하다 [haegohada]

layout ['leɪˌaʊt] n 배치계획 [baechigyehoek]

lazy ['leɪzɪ] adj 게으른 [geeureun]

lead¹ [liːd] n (in play/film) 주연 [juyeon], (position) 머릿글 [meoritgeul] ▷ v (남을) 인도하다 [(nameul) indohada]; **jump leads** npl 점프선 [jeompeuseon]; **lead singer** n 리드싱어 [rideusingeo]

lead² [lɛd] n (metal) 납 [nap] (금속)

leader ['liːdə] n 지도자 [jidoja]

lead-free [ˌlɛd'friː] adj 납이 없는 [nabi eomneun]

leaf [liːf] n 잎 [ip]; **bay leaf** n 월계수 잎 [wolgyesu ip]

leaflet ['liːflɪt] n 전단지 [jeondanji]

league [liːg] n 연맹 [yeonmaeng]

leak [liːk] n 새는 곳 [saeneun got] ▷ v 새다 [saeda]

lean [liːn] v 기대다 [gidaeda]; **lean forward** v 앞으로 굽히다 [apeuro guphida]

lean on [liːn ɒn] v 압력을 가하다 [amnyeogeul gahada]

lean out [liːn aʊt] v 밖으로 기울어지다 [bakkeuro giureojida]

leap [liːp] v 뛰다 [ttwida]; **leap year** n 윤년 [yunnyeon]

learn [lɜːn] v 배우다 [baeuda]

learner ['lɜːnə; 'learner] n 학습자 [hakseupja]; **learner driver** n 임시면허 운전자 [imsimyeonheo unjeonja]

lease [liːs] n 임대차계약 [imdaechagyeyak] ▷ v 임대(임차)하다 [imdae(imcha)hada]

least [liːst] adj 최소의 [choesoui]; **at least** adv 적어도 [jeogeodo]

leather ['lɛðə] n 가죽 [gajuk]

leave [liːv] n 허가 [heoga] ▷ v 떠나다 [tteonada]; **maternity leave** n 출산휴가 [chulsanhyuga]; **paternity leave** n 아버지의 육아 휴가 [abeojiui yuga hyuga]; **sick leave** n 병가 [byeongga]

leave out [liːv aʊt] v 빼놓다 [ppaenota]

leaves [liːvz] npl 잎들 [ipdeul]

Lebanese [ˌlɛbə'niːz] adj 레바논의 [rebanonui] ▷ n 레바논 사람 [rebanon saram]

Lebanon ['lɛbənən] n 레바논 [rebanon]

lecture ['lɛktʃə] n 강의 [gangui] ▷ v 강의하다 [ganguihada]

lecturer ['lɛktʃərə; 'lecturer] n 강사 [gangsa]

leek [liːk] n 리크 [rikeu]

left [lɛft] adj 왼쪽의 [oenjjogui] ▷ adv 왼쪽으로 [oenjjogeuro] ▷ n 왼쪽 [oenjjok]; **Go left at the next junction** 다음 사거리에서 왼쪽으로 가세요 [daeum sageorieseo oenjjogeuro gaseyo]; **Turn left** 왼쪽으로 꺾으세요 [oenjjogeuro kkeokkeuseyo]

left-hand [ˌlɛft'hænd] adj 왼쪽의 [oenjjogui]; **left-hand drive** n 왼쪽 핸들 [oenjjok haendeul]

left-handed [ˌlɛft'hændɪd] adj 왼손잡이의 [oensonjabiui]

left-luggage [ˌlɛft'lʌgɪdʒ] n 임시보관 수하물 [imsibogwan suhamul]; **left-luggage locker** n 임시보관 수하물함 [imsibogwan suhamulham]; **left-luggage office** n 수하물 임시보관소 [suhamul imsibogwanso]

leftovers ['lɛftˌəʊvəz] npl 나머지 [nameoji]

left-wing [ˌlɛft'wɪŋ] adj 좌익의 [jwaigui]

leg [lɛg] n 다리 [dari]; **I can't move my leg** 다리를 움직일 수 없어요 [darireul umjigil su eopseoyo]; **I've got cramp in my leg** 다리에 쥐가 났어요 [darie jwiga nasseoyo]; **My leg itches** 다리가 가려워요 [dariga garyeoweoyo]; **She has hurt her leg** 다리를 다쳤어요 [darireul dachyeosseoyo]

legal ['liːgəl] adj 합법적인 [hapbeopjeogin]

legend ['lɛdʒənd] n 전설 [jeonseol]

leggings ['lɛgɪŋz] npl 레깅스 [regingseu]

legible ['lɛdʒəbəl] adj 읽기쉬운 [irkgiswiun]

legislation [ˌlɛdʒɪs'leɪʃən] n 법률제정 [beomnyuljejeong]

leisure ['lɛʒə; 'liːʒər] n 레저 [rejeo]; **leisure centre** n 레저 센터 [rejeo senteo]

lemon ['lɛmən] n 레몬 [remon]; **with lemon** 레몬 넣어서요 [remon neoheoseoyo]

lemonade [ˌlɛmə'neɪd] n 레모네이드 [remoneideu]

lend [lɛnd] v 빌려주다 [billyeojuda]

length [lɛŋkθ; lɛŋθ] n 길이 [giri]

lens [lɛnz] n 렌즈 [renjeu]; **contact lenses** npl 콘택트렌즈 [kontekteurenjeu]; **zoom lens** n 줌 렌즈 [jum renjeu]; **cleansing solution for contact lenses** 콘택트렌즈 세정액이요 [kontaekteurenjeu sejeongaegiyo]; **I wear contact lenses** 저는 콘택트렌즈를 껴요 [jeoneun kontaekteurenjeureul kkyeoyo]

Lent [lɛnt] n 사순절 [sasunjeol]

lentils ['lɛntɪlz] npl 렌즈콩 [renjeukong]

Leo ['liːəʊ] n 사자자리 [sajajari]

leopard ['lɛpəd] n 표범 [pyobeom]

leotard ['lɪəˌtɑːd] n 레오타드 [reotadeu]

less [lɛs] adv 더 적게 [deo jeokge] ▷ pron 보다 적은 양 [boda jeogeun yang]

lesson ['lɛsən] n 수업 [sueop]; **driving**

lesson n 운전 교습 [unjeon gyoseup]
let [lɛt] v 허락하다 [heorakhada]
let down [lɛt daʊn] v 실망시키다 [silmangsikida]
let in [lɛt ɪn] v 안으로 들이다 [aneuro deurida]
letter ['lɛtə] n (a, b, c) 글자 [geulja], (message) 편지 [pyeonji]; **I'd like to send this letter** 이 편지를 보내려고요 [i pyeonjireul bonaeryeogoyo]
letterbox ['lɛtə,bɒks] n 편지함 [pyeonjiham]
lettuce ['lɛtɪs] n 상추 [sangchu]
leukaemia [luː'kiːmɪə] n 백혈병 [baekhyeolbyeong]
level ['lɛvəl] adj 같은 [gateun] ▷ n 수준 [sujun]; **level crossing** n 건널목 [geonneolmok]; **sea level** n 해수면 [haesumyeon]
lever ['liːvə] n 조종간 [jojonggan]
liar ['laɪə] n 거짓말쟁이 [geojitmaljaengi]
liberal ['lɪbərəl; 'lɪbrəl] adj 자유주의의 [jayujuuiui]
liberation [,lɪbə'reɪʃən] n 해방 [haebang]
Liberia [laɪ'bɪərɪə] n 라이베리아 [raiberia]
Liberian [laɪ'bɪərɪən] adj 라이베리아의 [raiberiaui] ▷ n 라이베리아 사람 [raiberia saram]
Libra ['liːbrə] n 천칭자리 [cheonchingjari]
librarian [laɪ'brɛərɪən] n 사서 [saseo]
library ['laɪbrərɪ] n 도서관 [doseogwan]
Libya ['lɪbɪə] n 리비아 [ribia]
Libyan ['lɪbɪən] adj 리비아의 [ribiaui] ▷ n 리비아 사람 [ribia saram]
lice [laɪs] npl 이 [i] (곤충)
licence ['laɪsəns] n 면허 [myeonheo]; **driving licence** n 운전 면허증 [unjeon myeonheojeung]; **I don't have my driving licence on me** 저는 운전면허증이 없어요 [jeoneun unjeonmyeonheojeungi eopseoyo]; **My driving licence number is...** 제 운전 면허증 번호는....에요 [je unjeon

myeonheojeung beonhoneun....eyo]
lick [lɪk] v 핥다 [hartda]
lid [lɪd] n 뚜껑 [ttukkeong]
lie [laɪ] n 거짓말 [geojitmal] ▷ v 거짓말하다 [geojitmalhada]
Liechtenstein ['lɪktən,staɪn; 'lɪçtənʃtain] n 리히텐슈타인 [rihitensyutain]
lie in [laɪ ɪn] v 늦잠 [neutjam]
lie-in ['laɪɪn] n **have a lie-in** v 늦잠 [neutjam]
lieutenant [lɛf'tɛnənt; luː'tɛnənt] n 중위 [jungwi]
life [laɪf] n 생명 [saengmyeong]; **life insurance** n 생명보험 [saengmyeongboheom]; **life jacket** n 구명조끼 [gumyeongjokki]
lifebelt ['laɪf,bɛlt] n 구명띠 [gumyeongtti]
lifeboat ['laɪf,bəʊt] n 구명정 [gumyeongjeong]
lifeguard ['laɪf,gɑːd] n 인명 구조원 [inmyeong gujowon]
life-saving ['laɪf,seɪvɪŋ] adj 구명의 [gumyeongui]
lifestyle ['laɪf,staɪl] n 사는 양식 [saneun yangsik]
lift [lɪft] n (free ride) (차에) 태워 주기 [(chae) taewo jugi], (up/down) 승강기 [seungganggi] ▷ v 올리다 [ollida]; **ski lift** n 스키 리프트 [seuki ripeuteu]; **Is there a lift in the building?** 건물에 승강기가 있나요? [geonmure seungganggiga innayo]
light [laɪt] adj (not dark) 밝은 [balgeun], (not heavy) 가벼운 [gabyeoun] ▷ n 불 [bul] ▷ v 불붙이다 [bulbuchida]; **brake light** n 정지등 [jeongjideung]; **hazard warning lights** npl 위험 경고등 [wiheom gyeonggodeung]; **light bulb** n 전구 [jeongu]; **pilot light** n 점화용 보조 버너 [jeomhwayong bojo beoneo]; **traffic lights** npl 교통신호등 [gyotongsinhodeung]; **Can I switch the light off?** 불꺼도 돼요? [bulkkeodo dwaeyo]; **Can I switch the light on?** 불켜도 돼요? [bulkyeodo

dwaeyo?]; **Have you got a light?** 불 있으세요? [bul isseuseyo?]

lighter ['laɪtə] n 라이터 [raiteo]; **Do you have a refill for my gas lighter?** 가스 라이터를 충전해 주시겠어요? [gaseu raiteoreul chungjeonhae jusigesseoyo?]

lighthouse ['laɪt,haʊs] n 등대 [deungdae]

lighting ['laɪtɪŋ] n 점화 [jeomhwa]

lightning ['laɪtnɪŋ] n 번개 [beongae]

like [laɪk] prep ...과 같이 [...gwa gachi] ▷ v 좋아하다 [johahada]

likely ['laɪklɪ] adj 가능한 [ganeunghan]

lilac ['laɪlək] adj 라일락색의 [raillaksaegui] ▷ n 라일락 [raillak]

Lilo® ['laɪləʊ] n 라일로 (에어매트리스) [raillo (eeomaeteuriseu)]

lily ['lɪlɪ] n 백합 [baekhap]; **lily of the valley** n 은방울꽃 [eunbangulkkot]

lime [laɪm] n (compound) 석회 [seokhoe], (fruit) 라임 [raim]

limestone ['laɪm,stəʊn] n 석회석 [seokhoeseok]

limit ['lɪmɪt] n 한계 [hangye]; **age limit** n 나이 제한 [nai jehan]; **speed limit** n 속도제한 [sokdojehan]

limousine ['lɪmə,ziːn; ,lɪmə'ziːn] n 리무진 [rimujin]

limp [lɪmp] v 다리를 절다 [darireul jeolda]

line [laɪn] n 선 [seon] (똑 바로); **washing line** n 빨랫줄 [ppallaetjul]; **Which line should I take for...?** 가려면 몇 호선 타야 되나요? [... garyeomyeon myeot hoseon taya doenayo?]

linen ['lɪnɪn] n 리넨 [rinen]; **bed linen** n 침대 리넨 [chimdae rinen]

liner ['laɪnə] n 정기선 [jeonggiseon]

lingerie ['lænʒərɪ] n 란제리 [ranjeri]; **Where is the lingerie department?** 란제리 매장은 어디에 있나요? [ranjeri maejangeun eodie innayo?]

linguist ['lɪŋgwɪst] n 언어학자 [eoneohakja]

linguistic [lɪŋ'gwɪstɪk] adj 언어학적인 [eoneohakjeogin]

lining ['laɪnɪŋ] n 안감 [angam]

link [lɪŋk] n 고리 [gori]; **link (up)** v 연결하다 [yeongyeolhada]

lino ['laɪnəʊ] n 리놀륨 [rinollyum]

lion ['laɪən] n 사자 [saja] (동물)

lioness ['laɪənɪs] n 암사자 [amsaja]

lip [lɪp] n 입술 [ipsul]; **lip salve** n 입술 연고 [ipsul yeongo]

lip-read ['lɪp,riːd] v 독순술로 이해하다 [doksunsullo ihaehada]

lipstick ['lɪp,stɪk] n 립스틱 [ripseutik]

liqueur [lɪ'kjʊə] n 리큐어 [rikyueo]; **What liqueurs do you have?** 어떤 리큐어가 있나요? [eotteon rikyueoga innayo?]

liquid ['lɪkwɪd] n 액체 [aekche]; **washing-up liquid** n 설거지용 세제 [seolgeojiyong seje]

liquidizer ['lɪkwɪ,daɪzə] n 믹서 [mikseo]

list [lɪst] n 목록 [mongnok] ▷ v 목록에 기재하다 [mongnoge gijaehada]; **mailing list** n 우편물 발송 주소 목록 [upyeonmul balsong juso mongnok]; **price list** n 가격표 [gagyeokpyo]; **waiting list** n 대기명단 [daegimyeongdan]; **wine list** n 와인 리스트 [wain riseuteu]; **The wine list, please** 와인 목록 주세요 [wain mongnok juseyo]

listen ['lɪsᵊn] v 듣다 [deutda]; **listen to** v 귀를 기울이다 [gwireul giurida]

listener ['lɪsnə] n 청취자 [cheongchwija]

literally ['lɪtərəlɪ] adv 글자 그대로 [geulja geudaero]

literature ['lɪtərɪtʃə; 'lɪtrɪ-] n 문학 [munhak]

Lithuania [,lɪθjʊ'eɪnɪə] n 리투아니아 [rituania]

Lithuanian [,lɪθjʊ'eɪnɪən] adj 리투아니아의 [rituaniaui] ▷ n (language) 리투아니아어 [rituaniaeo], (person) 리투아니아 사람 [rituania saram]

litre ['liːtə] n 리터 [riteo]

litter ['lɪtə] n 쓰레기 [sseuregi], (offspring) 한배의 새끼 [hanbaeui

saekki]; **litter bin** *n* 쓰레기통
[sseuregitong]

little ['lɪtəl] *adj* 작은 [jageun]

live¹ [lɪv] *v* 살다 [salda]

live² [laɪv] *adj* 살아있는 [sarainneun]

lively ['laɪvlɪ] *adj* 활기찬 [hwalgichan]

live on [lɪv ɒn] *v* 먹고 살다 [meokgo salda]

liver ['lɪvə] *n* 간 [gan] (내장)

live together [lɪv] *v* 함께 살다 [hamkke salda]

living ['lɪvɪŋ] *n* 생활 [saenghwal]; **cost of living** *n* 생활비 [saenghwalbi]; **living room** *n* 거실 [geosil]; **standard of living** *n* 생활수준 [saenghwalsujun]

lizard ['lɪzəd] *n* 도마뱀 [domabaem]

load [ləʊd] *n* 짐 [jim] ▷ *v* 싣다 [sitda]

loaf, loaves [ləʊf, ləʊvz] *n* 덩어리 [deongeori]

loan [ləʊn] *n* 대출금 [daechulgeum] ▷ *v* 빌려주다 [billyeojuda]

loathe [ləʊð] *v* 몹시 싫어하다 [mopsi sireohada]

lobby ['lɒbɪ] *n* **I'll meet you in the lobby** 로비에서 만나요 [robieseo mannayo]

lobster ['lɒbstə] *n* 바닷가재 [badatgajae]

local ['ləʊkəl] *adj* 국소적인 [guksojeogin]; **local anaesthetic** *n* 국소마취 [guksomachwi]

location [ləʊ'keɪʃən] *n* 위치 [wichi]; **My location is...** 여기 위치는...이에(예)요 [yeogi wichineun...ie(ye)yo]

lock [lɒk] *n* (*door*) 자물쇠 [jamulsoe], (*hair*) 머리타래 [meoritarae] ▷ *v* 잠그다 [jamgeuda]; **Can I have a lock?** 자물쇠 주시겠어요? [jamulsoe jusigesseoyo?]; **The lock is broken** 자물쇠가 고장났어요 [jamulsoega gojangnasseoyo]

locker ['lɒkə] *n* 사물함 [samulham]; **left-luggage locker** *n* 임시보관 수하물함 [imsibogwan suhamulham]; **Where are the clothes lockers?** 옷 넣는 사물함은 어디있어요? [ot neonneun samulhameun eodiisseoyo?]; **Which locker is mine?** 어느 사물함이 제 것인가요? [eoneu samulhami je geosingayo?]

locket ['lɒkɪt] *n* 작은 상자 [jageun sangja]

lock out [lɒk aʊt] *v* (사람을) 쫓아내다 [(sarameul) jjochanaeda]

locksmith ['lɒk,smɪθ] *n* 자물쇠 장수 [jamulsoe jangsu]

lodger ['lɒdʒə] *n* 하숙인 [hasugin]

loft [lɒft] *n* 다락방 [darakbang]

log [lɒg] *n* 통나무 [tongnamu]

logical ['lɒdʒɪkəl] *adj* 논리적인 [nollijeogin]

log in [lɒg ɪn] *v* 로그인하다 [rogeuinhada]

logo ['ləʊgəʊ; 'lɒg-] *n* 로고 [rogo]

log off [lɒg ɒf] *v* 로그오프하다 [rogeuopeuhada]

log on [lɒg ɒn] *v* 로그온하다 [rogeuonhada]

log out [lɒg aʊt] *v* 로그아웃하다 [rogeuautada]

lollipop ['lɒlɪ,pɒp] *n* 막대사탕 [makdaesatang]

lolly ['lɒlɪ] *n* 막대사탕 [makdaesatang]

London ['lʌndən] *n* 런던 [reondeon]

loneliness ['ləʊnlɪnɪs] *n* 고독 [godok]

lonely ['ləʊnlɪ] *adj* 고독한 [godokhan]

lonesome ['ləʊnsəm] *adj* 외로운 [oeroun]

long [lɒŋ] *adj* 긴 [gin] ▷ *adv* 길게 [gilge] ▷ *v* 몹시 그리워하다 [mopsi geuriwohada]; **long jump** *n* 멀리뛰기 [meollittwigi]

longer [lɒŋə] *adv* 더 길게 [deo gilge]

longitude ['lɒndʒɪ,tjuːd; 'lɒŋ-] *n* 경도 [gyeongdo] (지구)

loo [luː] *n* 화장실 [hwajangsil]

look [lʊk] *n* 모양 [moyang] ▷ *v* 보다 [boda]; **look at** *v* 고찰하다 [gochalhada]

look after [lʊk ɑːftə] *v* 돌보다 [dolboda]

look for [lʊk fɔː] *v* 찾다 [chatda]

look round [lʊk raʊnd] *v* 주변을 둘러보다 [jubyeoneul dulleoboda]

look up [lʊk ʌp] *v* 찾아보다 [chajaboda]

loose [luːs] *adj* 헐렁한 [heolleonghan]

lorry ['lɒrɪ] n 트럭 [teureok]; **lorry driver** n 트럭 운전사 [teureok unjeonsa]

lose [lu:z] vi 손해보다 [sonhaeboda] ▷ vt 잃다 [irta]

loser ['lu:zə] n 잃은 사람 [ireun saram]

loss [lɒs] n 손실 [sonsil]

lost [lɒst] adj 잃은 [ireun]; **lost-property office** n 분실물 보관소 [bunsilmul bogwanso]

lost-and-found ['lɒstænd'faʊnd] n 분실물 보관소 [bunsilmul bogwanso]

lot [lɒt] **a lot** n 무리 [muri] (많은)

lotion ['ləʊʃən] n 로션 [rosyeon]; **after sun lotion** n 볕에 탄 후 바르는 로션 [byeote tan hu bareuneun rosyeon]; **cleansing lotion** n 클렌징 로션 [keullenjing rosyeon]; **suntan lotion** n 선탠 로션 [seontaen rosyeon]

lottery ['lɒtərɪ] n 복권 [bogkwon]

loud [laʊd] adj 소리가 큰 [soriga keun]

loudly [laʊdlɪ] adv 큰 소리로 [keun soriro]

loudspeaker [,laʊd'spi:kə] n 확성기 [hwakseonggi]

lounge [laʊndʒ] n 라운지 [raunji]; **departure lounge** n 공항대기실 [gonghangdaegisil]; **transit lounge** n 환승 대기실 [hwanseung daegisil]; **Could we have coffee in the lounge?** 라운지에서 커피를 마실 수 있을까요? [raunjieseo keopireul masil su isseulkkayo?]; **Is there a television lounge?** 텔레비전 라운지가 있어요? [tellebijeon raunjiga isseoyo?]

lousy ['laʊzɪ] adj 비열한 [biyeolhan]

love [lʌv] n 사랑 [sarang] ▷ v 사랑하다 [saranghada]; **I love you** 사랑해요 [saranghaeyo]

lovely ['lʌvlɪ] adj 아주 매력적인 [aju maeryeokjeogin]

lover ['lʌvə] n 연인 [yeonin]

low [ləʊ] adj 낮은 [najeun] ▷ adv 낮게 [natge]; **low season** n 비성수기 [biseongsugi]

low-alcohol ['ləʊ,ælkə,hɒl] adj 알코올 농도가 낮은 [alkool nongdoga najeun]

lower ['ləʊə] adj 더 낮은 [deo najeun]

▷ v 낮추다 [natchuda]

low-fat ['ləʊ,fæt] adj 저지방의 [jeojibangui]

loyalty ['lɔɪəltɪ] n 충성 [chungseong]

luck [lʌk] n 행운 [haengun]

luckily ['lʌkɪlɪ] adv 다행히 [dahaenghi]

lucky ['lʌkɪ] adj 운좋은 [unjoheun]

lucrative ['lu:krətɪv] adj 수지맞는 [sujimatneun]

luggage ['lʌgɪdʒ] n 수화물 [suhwamul]; **hand luggage** n 수화물 [suhwamul]; **luggage rack** n 수화물 선반 [suhwamul seonban]; **luggage trolley** n 수화물 수레 [suhwamul sure]

lukewarm [,lu:k'wɔ:m] adj 미지근한 [mijigeunhan]

lullaby ['lʌlə,baɪ] n 자장가 [jajangga]

lump [lʌmp] n 덩어리 [deongeori]

lunatic ['lu:nætɪk] n 정신 이상자 [jeongsin isangja]

lunch [lʌntʃ] n 점심 [jeomsim]; **lunch break** n 점심시간 [jeomsimsigan]; **packed lunch** n 도시락 [dosirak]; **Can we meet for lunch?** 만나서 점심 먹을까요? [mannaseo jeomsim meogeulkkayo?]; **I'm free for lunch** 점심 때 시간 있어요 [jeomsim ttae sigan isseoyo]; **The lunch was excellent** 점심이 훌륭했어요 [jeomsimi hullyunghaesseoyo]; **When will lunch be ready?** 언제 점심이 준비되나요? [eonje jeomsimi junbidoenayo?]; **Where do we stop for lunch?** 점심 먹으러 어디에서 정차해요? [jeomsim meogeureo eodieseo jeongchahaeyo?]

lunchtime ['lʌntʃ,taɪm] n 점심시간 [jeomsimsigan]

lung [lʌŋ] n 폐 [pye] (내장)

lush [lʌʃ] adj 푸릇푸릇한 [pureutpureutan]

lust [lʌst] n 정욕 [jeongyok]

Luxembourg ['lʌksəm,bɜ:g] n 룩셈부르크 [ruksembureukeu]

luxurious [lʌg'zjʊərɪəs] adj 호화로운 [hohwaroun]

luxury ['lʌkʃərɪ] n 사치 [sachi]

lyrics ['lɪrɪks] npl 서정시 [seojeongsi]

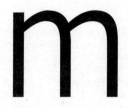

mac [mæk] *abbr* 레인코트 [reinkoteu]
macaroni [ˌmækəˈrəʊnɪ] *npl* 마카로니 [makaroni]
machine [məˈʃiːn] *n* 기계 [gigye]; **answering machine** *n* 자동 응답기 [jadong eungdapgi]; **machine gun** *n* 기관총 [gigwanchong]; **machine washable** *adj* 기계세탁이 가능한 [gigyesetagi ganeunghan]; **sewing machine** *n* 재봉틀 [jaebongteul]; **slot machine** *n* 자동 판매기 [jadong panmaegi]; **ticket machine** *n* 자동 매표기 [jadong maepyogi]; **vending machine** *n* 자동판매기 [jadongpanmaegi]; **washing machine** *n* 세탁기 [setakgi]
machinery [məˈʃiːnərɪ] *n* 기계류 [gigyeryu]
mackerel [ˈmækrəl] *n* 고등어 [godeungeo]
mad [mæd] *adj (angry)* 화난 [hwanan], *(insane)* 미친 [michin]
Madagascar [ˌmædəˈɡæskə] *n* 마다가스카르 [madagaseukareu]
madam [ˈmædəm] *n* 부인 [buin] (여성)
madly [ˈmædlɪ] *adv* 미친듯이 [michindeusi]

madman [ˈmædmən] *n* 미친 사람 [michin saram]
madness [ˈmædnɪs] *n* 정신이상 [jeongsinisang]
magazine [ˌmæɡəˈziːn] *n (ammunition)* 탄창 [tanchang], *(periodical)* 잡지 [japji]; **Where can I buy a magazine?** 어디에서 잡지를 살 수 있어요? [eodieseo japjireul sal su isseoyo?]
maggot [ˈmæɡət] *n* 구더기 [gudeogi]
magic [ˈmædʒɪk] *adj* 마술의 [masuleui] ▷ *n* 마술 [masul]
magical [ˈmædʒɪkəl] *adj* 마술적인 [masuljeogin]
magician [məˈdʒɪʃən] *n* 마술사 [masulsa]
magistrate [ˈmædʒɪˌstreɪt; -strɪt] *n* 행정관 [haengjeonggwan]
magnet [ˈmæɡnɪt] *n* 자석 [jaseok]
magnetic [mæɡˈnɛtɪk] *adj* 자석의 [jaseogui]
magnificent [mæɡˈnɪfɪsᵊnt] *adj* 거대한 [geodaehan]
magpie [ˈmæɡˌpaɪ] *n* 까치 [kkachi]
mahogany [məˈhɒɡənɪ] *n* 마호가니 [mahogani]
maid [meɪd] *n* 하녀 [hanyeo]
maiden [ˈmeɪdᵊn] *n* **maiden name** *n* 결혼 전의 성 [gyeolhon jeonui seong]
mail [meɪl] *n* 우편물 [upyeonmul] ▷ *v* 우송하다 [usonghada]; **junk mail** *n* 스팸메일 [seupaemmeil]; **Is there any mail for me?** 저한테 우편물 온 것 있어요? [jeohante upyeonmul on geot isseoyo?]
mailbox [ˈmeɪlˌbɒks] *n* 우체통 [uchetong]
mailing list [ˈmeɪlɪŋ ˈlɪst] *n* **mailing list** *n* 우편물 발송 주소 목록 [upyeonmul balsong juso mongnok]
main [meɪn] *adj* 주요한 [juyohan]; **main course** *n* 주 요리 [ju yori]; **main road** *n* 중심도로 [jungsimdoro]
mainland [ˈmeɪnlənd] *n* 본토 [bonto]
mainly [ˈmeɪnlɪ] *adv* 주로 [juro]
maintain [meɪnˈteɪn] *v* 유지하다 [yujihada]
maintenance [ˈmeɪntɪnəns] *n*

유지보수 [yujibosu]

maize [meɪz] n 옥수수 [oksusu]

majesty ['mædʒɪstɪ] n 폐하 [pyeha]

major ['meɪdʒə] adj 중요한 [jungyohan]

majority [mə'dʒɒrɪtɪ] n 대다수 [daedasu]

make [meɪk] v 만들다 [mandeulda]

makeover ['meɪk,əʊvə] n 개조 [gaejo]

maker ['meɪkə] n 조물주 [jomulju]

make up [meɪk ʌp] v 구성하다 [guseonghada]

make-up [meɪkʌp] n 화장 [hwajang] (화장품)

malaria [mə'lɛərɪə] n 말라리아 [mallaria]

Malawi [mə'lɑːwɪ] n 말라위 [mallawi]

Malaysia [mə'leɪzɪə] n 말레이시아 [malleisia]

Malaysian [mə'leɪzɪən] adj 말레이시아의 [malleisiaui] ▷ n 말레이시아 사람 [malleisia saram]

male [meɪl] adj 남성의 [namseongui] ▷ n 남성 [namseong]

malicious [mə'lɪʃəs] adj 악의 있는 [agui inneun]

malignant [mə'lɪgnənt] adj 극히 해로운 [geukhi haeroun]

malnutrition [,mælnjuː'trɪʃən] n 영양실조 [yeongyangsiljo]

Malta ['mɔːltə] n 몰타 [molta]

Maltese [mɔːl'tiːz] adj 몰타의 [moltaui] ▷ n (language) 몰타어 [moltaeo], (person) 몰타 사람 [molta saram]

mammal ['mæməl] n 포유동물 [poyudongmul]

mammoth ['mæməθ] adj 거대한 [geodaehan] ▷ n 매머드 [maemeodeu]

man, men [mæn, mɛn] n 남자 [namja]; **best man** n 신랑 들러리 [sillang deulleori]

manage ['mænɪdʒ] v 관리하다 [gwallihada]

manageable ['mænɪdʒəbʰl] adj 관리할 수 있는 [gwallihal su inneun]

management ['mænɪdʒmənt] n 관리 [gwalli]

manager ['mænɪdʒə] n 관리자

[gwallija]

manageress [,mænɪdʒə'rɛs; 'mænɪdʒə,rɛs] n 여성관리자 [yeoseonggwallija]

mandarin ['mændərɪn] n (fruit) 귤 [gyul], (official) 관리 [gwalli]

mangetout ['mɑ̃ʒ'tuː] n 완두콩 [wandukong]

mango ['mæŋgəʊ] n 망고 [manggo]

mania ['meɪnɪə] n 열광 [yeolgwang]

maniac ['meɪnɪ,æk] n 미치광이 [michigwangi]

manicure ['mænɪ,kjʊə] n 매니큐어 [maenikyueo] ▷ v 매니큐어를 하다 [maenikyueoreul hada]

manipulate [mə'nɪpjʊ,leɪt] v 조종하다 [jojonghada]

mankind [,mæn'kaɪnd] n 인류 [illyu]

man-made ['mæn,meɪd] adj 인공의 [ingongui]

manner ['mænə] n 방식 [bangsik]

manners ['mænəz] npl 관습 [gwanseup]

manpower ['mæn,paʊə] n 인력 [illyeok]

mansion ['mænʃən] n 대저택 [daejeotaek]

mantelpiece ['mæntʰl,piːs] n 벽난로 선반 [byeongnanno seonban]

manual ['mænjʊəl] n 안내서 [annaeseo]

manufacture [,mænjʊ'fæktʃə] v 제조하다 [jejohada]

manufacturer [,mænjʊ'fæktʃərə] n 생산자 [saengsanja]

manure [mə'njʊə] n 거름 [georeum]

manuscript ['mænjʊ,skrɪpt] n 원고 [wongo]

many ['mɛnɪ] adj 많은 [manheun] ▷ pron 다수 [dasu]

Maori ['maʊrɪ] adj 마오리의 [maoriui] ▷ n (language) 마오리어 [maorieo], (person) 마오리 사람 [maori saram]

map [mæp] n 지도 [jido]; **road map** n 도로지도 [dorojido]; **street map** n 거리지도 [georijido]; **Can I have a map?** 지도 주시겠어요? [jido jusigesseoyo?]; **Can you show me**

where it is on the map? 지도에서 어디에 있는지 알려 주시겠어요? [jidoeseo eodie inneunji allyeo jusigesseoyo?]; Do you have a map of the ski runs? 슬로프 지도 있어요? [seullopeu jido isseoyo?]; Have you got a map of...? ... 지도 있어요? [... jido isseoyo?]; I need a road map of... ... 도로 지도가 필요해요 [... doro jidoga pilyohaeyo]; Is there a cycle map of this area? 이 지역 자전거 지도 있어요? [i jiyeok jajeongeo jido isseoyo?]; Where can I buy a map of the area? 지역지도를 어디에서 살 수 있어요? [jiyeokjidoreul eodieseo sal su isseoyo?]

maple ['meɪpᵊl] n 단풍나무 [danpungnamu]

marathon ['mærəθən] n 마라톤 [maraton]

marble ['mɑːbᵊl] n 대리석 [daeriseok]

march [mɑːtʃ] n 행진 [haengjin] ▷ v 행진하다 [haengjinhada]

March [mɑːtʃ] n 3월 [samwol]

mare [mɛə] n 암말 [ammal]

margarine [ˌmɑːdʒəˈriːn; ˌmɑːgə-] n 마가린 [magarin]

margin ['mɑːdʒɪn] n 가장자리 [gajangjari]

marigold ['mærɪˌɡəʊld] n 금잔화 [geumjanhwa]

marijuana [ˌmærɪˈhwɑːnə] n 마리화나 [marihwana]

marina [məˈriːnə] n 선착장 [seonchakjang]

marinade n [ˌmærɪˈneɪd] 매리네이드 [maerineideu] ▷ v ['mærɪˌneɪd] 매리네이드에 담그다 [maerineideue damgeuda]

marital ['mærɪtᵊl] adj marital status n 결혼 상황 [gyeolhon sanghwang]

maritime ['mærɪˌtaɪm] adj 해사의 [haesaui]

marjoram ['mɑːdʒərəm] n 마저럼 [majeoreom]

mark [mɑːk] n 표시 [pyosi] ▷ v (grade) 채점하다 [chaejeomhada], (make sign) 표시하다 [pyosihada]; exclamation

mark n 느낌표 [neukkimpyo]; question mark n 의문부호 [uimunbuho]; quotation marks npl 인용부호 [inyongbuho]

market ['mɑːkɪt] n 시장 [sijang]; market research n 시장조사 [sijangjosa]; stock market n 증권시장 [jeunggwonsijang]; When is the market on? 시장은 언제 열려요? [sijangeun eonje yeollyeoyo?]

marketing ['mɑːkɪtɪŋ] n 마케팅 [maketing]

marketplace ['mɑːkɪtˌpleɪs] n 장터 [jangteo]

marmalade ['mɑːməˌleɪd] n 마멀레이드 [mameolleideu]

maroon [məˈruːn] adj 밤색의 [bamsaegui]

marriage ['mærɪdʒ] n 결혼 [gyeolhon]; marriage certificate n 결혼 증명서 [gyeolhon jeungmyeongseo]

married ['mærɪd] adj 기혼의 [gihonui]

marrow ['mærəʊ] n 골수 [golsu]

marry ['mærɪ] v 결혼하다 [gyeolhonhada]

marsh [mɑːʃ] n 습지 [seupji]

martyr ['mɑːtə] n 순교자 [sungyoja]

marvellous ['mɑːvᵊləs] adj 놀라운 [nollaun]

Marxism ['mɑːksɪzəm] n 마르크스주의 [mareukeuseujuui]

marzipan ['mɑːzɪˌpæn] n 마지팬 [majipaen]

mascara [mæˈskɑːrə] n 마스카라 [maseukara]

masculine ['mæskjʊlɪn] adj 남성적인 [namseongjeogin]

mask [mɑːsk] n 마스크 [maseukeu]

masked [mɑːskt] adj 마스크를 쓴 [maseukeureul sseun]

mass [mæs] n (amount) 덩어리 [deongeori], (church) 미사 [misa]; When is mass? 미사는 언제예요? [misaneun eonjeyeyo?]

massacre ['mæsəkə] n 대학살 [daehaksal]

massage ['mæsɑːʒ; -ɑːdʒ] n 마사지 [masaji]

massive ['mæsɪv] adj 크고 무거운 [keugo mugeoun]

mast [mɑ:st] n 기둥 [gidung]

master ['mɑ:stə] n 주인 [juin] ▷ v 터득하다 [teodeukhada]

masterpiece ['mɑ:stəpi:s] n 걸작 [geoljak]

mat [mæt] n 매트 [maeteu]; **mouse mat** n 마우스패드 [mauseupaedeu]

match [mætʃ] n (partnership) 쌍의 한쪽 [ssangui hanjjok], (sport) 경기 [gyeonggi] (시합) ▷ v 필적하다 [piljeokhada]; **away match** n 원정 경기 [wonjeong gyeonggi]; **home match** n 홈경기 [homgyeonggi]; **I'd like to see a football match** 축구 경기를 보고 싶어요 [chukgu gyeonggireul bogo sipeoyo]

matching [mætʃɪŋ] adj 어울리는 [eoullineun]

mate [meɪt] n 친구 [chingu]

material [mə'tɪərɪəl] n 재료 [jaeryo]; **What is the material?** 재료가 무엇인가요? [jaeryoga mueosingayo?]

maternal [mə'tɜ:nəl] adj 모성의 [moseongui]

mathematical [ˌmæθə'mætɪkəl; ˌmæθ'mæt-] adj 수학의 [suhagui]

mathematics [ˌmæθə'mætɪks; ˌmæθ'mæt-] npl 수학 [suhak]

maths [mæθs] npl 수학 [suhak]

matter ['mætə] n 사건 [sageon] ▷ v 중요하다 [jungyohada]

mattress ['mætrɪs] n 매트리스 [maeteuriseu]

mature [mə'tjʊə; -'tʃʊə] adj 성숙한 [seongsukhan]; **mature student** n 성인 학생 [seongin haksaeng]

Mauritania [ˌmɒrɪ'teɪnɪə] n 모리타니 [moritani]

Mauritius [mə'rɪʃəs] n 모리셔스 [morisyeoseu]

mauve [məʊv] adj 연한 자주색의 [yeonhan jajusaegui]

maximum ['mæksɪməm] adj 최대의 [choedaeui] ▷ n 최대 [choedae]

may [meɪ] v **May I call you tomorrow?** 내일 전화하면 될까요? [naeil jeonhwahamyeon doelkkayo?]; **May I open the window?** 창을 열어도 될까요? [changeul yeoreodo doelkkayo?]

May [meɪ] n 5월 [owol]

maybe ['meɪˌbi:] adv 아마 [ama]

mayonnaise [ˌmeɪə'neɪz] n 마요네즈 [mayonejeu]

mayor, mayoress [mɛə, 'mɛərɪs] n 시장 [sijang]

maze [meɪz] n 미로 [miro]

me [mi:] pron 나를 [nareul]

meadow ['mɛdəʊ] n 목초지 [mokchoji]

meal [mi:l] n 식사 [siksa]; **Could you prepare a meal without eggs?** 계란이 들어가지 않은 식사를 준비해 주시겠어요? [gyerani deureogaji anheun siksareul junbihae jusigesseoyo?]; **Could you prepare a meal without gluten?** 글루텐이 들어가지 않은 식사를 준비해 주시겠어요? [geulluteni deureogaji anheun siksareul junbihae jusigesseoyo?]

mealtime ['mi:lˌtaɪm] n 식사시간 [siksasigan]

mean [mi:n] adj 인색한 [insaekhan] ▷ v 의미하다 [uimihada]

meaning ['mi:nɪŋ] n 의미 [uimi]

means [mi:nz] npl 수단 [sudan]

meantime ['mi:nˌtaɪm] adv 그 동안에 [geu dongane]

meanwhile ['mi:nˌwaɪl] adv 그 동안에 [geu dongane]

measles ['mi:zəlz] npl 홍역 [hongyeok]; **German measles** n 풍진 [pungjin]; **I had measles recently** 최근에 홍역을 앓았어요 [choegeune hongyeogeul arasseoyo]

measure ['mɛʒə] v 측정하다 [cheukjeonghada]; **tape measure** n 줄자 [julja]

measurements ['mɛʒəmənts] npl 측정 [cheukjeong]

meat [mi:t] n 고기 [gogi]; **red meat** n 붉은 고기 [bulgeun gogi]; **Do you eat meat?** 고기 드세요? [gogi deuseyo?]; **I don't eat meat** 저는 고기 안 먹어요

[jeoneun gogi an meogeoyo]; **I don't eat red meat** 저는 붉은 고기를 안 먹어요 [jeoneun bulgeun gogireul an meogeoyo]; **I don't like meat** 저는 고기를 좋아하지 않아요 [jeoneun gogireul johahaji anhayo]; **The meat is cold** 고기가 차요 [gogiga chayo]; **This meat is off** 고기가 상했어요 [gogiga sanghaesseoyo]

meatball ['miːt,bɔːl] n 미트볼 [miteubol]

Mecca ['mɛkə] n 메카 [meka]

mechanic [mɪ'kænɪk] n 기계공 [gigyegong]

mechanical [mɪ'kænɪkəl] adj 기계적인 [gigyejeogin]

mechanism ['mɛkə,nɪzəm] n 장치 [jangchi]

medal ['mɛdəl] n 메달 [medal]

medallion [mɪ'dæljən] n 큰 메달 [keun medal]

media ['miːdɪə] npl 미디어 [midieo]

mediaeval [,mɛdɪ'iːvəl] adj 중세의 [jungseui]

medical ['mɛdɪkəl] adj 의학의 [uihagui] ▷ n 의사소견 [uisasogyeon]; **medical certificate** n 의사소견서 [uisasogyeonseo]

medication [,mɛdɪ'keɪʃən] n **I'm on this medication** 이미 이 약을 먹고 있어요 [imi i yageul meokgo isseoyo]

medicine ['mɛdɪsɪn; 'mɛdsɪn] n 약 [yak]; **I'm already taking this medicine** 이미 이 약을 먹고 있어요 [imi i yageul meokgo isseoyo]

meditation [,mɛdɪ'teɪʃən] n 명상 [myeongsang]

Mediterranean [,mɛdɪtə'reɪnɪən] adj 지중해의 [jijunghaeui] ▷ n 지중해 [jijunghae]

medium ['miːdɪəm] adj (between extremes) 중간의 [jungganui]

medium-sized ['miːdɪəm,saɪzd] adj 중간 크기의 [junggan keugiui]

meet [miːt] vi 만나다 [mannada]

meeting ['miːtɪŋ] n 만남 [mannam]

meet up [miːt ʌp] v 만나다 [mannada]

mega ['mɛɡə] adj 거대한 [geodaehan]

melody ['mɛlədɪ] n 멜로디 [mellodi]

melon ['mɛlən] n 멜론 [mellon]

melt [mɛlt] vi 녹다 [nokda] ▷ vt 녹이다 [nogida]

member ['mɛmbə] n 회원 [hoewon]; **Do I have to be a member?** 회원이 되어야 하나요? [hoewoni doeeoya hanayo?]

membership ['mɛmbəˌʃɪp] n 회원 자격 [hoewon jagyeok]; **membership card** n 회원 카드 [hoewon kadeu]

memento [mɪ'mɛntəʊ] n 기념품 [ginyeompum]

memo ['mɛməʊ] n 메모 [memo]

memorial [mɪ'mɔːrɪəl] n 기념물 [ginyeommul]

memorize ['mɛməˌraɪz] v 암기하다 [amgihada]

memory ['mɛmərɪ] n 기억 [gieok]; **memory card** n 메모리 카드 [memori kadeu]

mend [mɛnd] v 고치다 [gochida]

meningitis [,mɛnɪn'dʒaɪtɪs] n 수막염 [sumagyeom]

menopause ['mɛnəʊ,pɔːz] n 갱년기 [gaengnyeongi]

menstruation [,mɛnstrʊ'eɪʃən] n 생리 [saengni]

mental ['mɛntəl] adj 정신적인 [jeongsinjeogin]; **mental hospital** n 정신 병원 [jeongsin byeongwon]

mentality [mɛn'tælɪtɪ] n 사고 방식 [sago bangsik]

mention ['mɛnʃən] v 언급하다 [eongeuphada]

menu ['mɛnjuː] n 메뉴 [menyu]; **set menu** n 세트 메뉴 [seteu menyu]; **Do you have a children's menu?** 어린이 메뉴가 있나요? [eorini menyuga innayo?]; **Do you have a set-price menu?** 세트 가격 메뉴가 있나요? [seteu gagyeok menyuga innayo?]; **How much is the set menu?** 세트 메뉴는 얼마예요? [seteu menyuneun eolmayeyo?]; **The dessert menu, please** 후식 메뉴 주세요 [husik menyu juseyo]; **The menu, please** 메뉴 주세요 [menyu juseyo]; **We'll take the**

set menu 세트 메뉴 주세요 [seteu menyu juseyo]

mercury ['mɜːkjʊrɪ] n 수은 [sueun]

mercy ['mɜːsɪ] n 자비 [jabi] (은혜)

mere [mɪə] adj 단순한 [dansunhan]

merge [mɜːdʒ] v 합병하다 [happbyeonghada]

merger ['mɜːdʒə] n 합병 [happbyeong]

meringue [məˈræŋ] n 머랭 [meoraeng]

mermaid ['mɜːˌmeɪd] n 인어 [ineo]

merry ['mɛrɪ] adj 즐거운 [jeulgeoun]

merry-go-round ['mɛrɪɡəʊˈraʊnd] n 회전 목마 [hoejeon mongma]

mess [mɛs] n 혼란 [hollan]

mess about [mɛs əˈbaʊt] v 게으름피우다 [geeureumpiuda]

message ['mɛsɪdʒ] n 메시지 [mesiji]; **text message** n 문자 메시지 [munja mesiji]; **Can I leave a message with his secretary?** 그의 비서에게 메시지를 남길 수 있을까요? [geuui biseoege mesijireul namgil su isseulkkayo?]; **Can I leave a message?** 메시지를 남겨도 될까요? [mesijireul namgyeodo doelkkayo?]

messenger ['mɛsɪndʒə] n 메신저 [mesinjeo]

mess up [mɛs ʌp] v 망쳐놓다 [mangchyeonota]

messy ['mɛsɪ] adj 어질러진 [eojilleojin]

metabolism [mɪˈtæbəˌlɪzəm] n 신진대사 [sinjindaesa]

metal ['mɛtəl] n 금속 [geumsok]

meteorite ['miːtɪəˌraɪt] n 운석 [unseok]

meter ['miːtə] n 미터 [miteo]; **parking meter** n 주차요금 징수기 [juchayogeum jingsugi]; **Do you have a meter?** 미터기 있어요? [miteogi isseoyo?]; **Do you have change for the parking meter?** 주차 미터기에 넣을 잔돈 있으세요? [jucha miteogi neoheul jandon isseuseyo?]; **It's more than on the meter** 미터기에 나온 것보다 많아요 [miteogie naon geotboda manhayo]; **Please use the meter** 미터기를 사용해 주세요

[miteogireul sayonghae juseyo]; **The meter is broken** 미터기가 고장났어요 [miteogiga gojangnasseoyo]; **The parking meter is broken** 주차 미터기가 고장났어요 [jucha miteogiga gojangnasseoyo]

method ['mɛθəd] n 방법 [bangbeop]

Methodist ['mɛθədɪst] adj 감리교 신자의 [gamnigyo sinjaui]

metre ['miːtə] n 미터 [miteo]

metric ['mɛtrɪk] adj 미터법의 [miteobeobui]

Mexican ['mɛksɪkən] adj 멕시코의 [meksikoui] ▷ n 멕시코 사람 [meksiko saram]

Mexico ['mɛksɪˌkəʊ] n 멕시코 [meksiko]

microchip ['maɪkrəʊˌtʃɪp] n 마이크로칩 [maikeurochip]

microphone ['maɪkrəˌfəʊn] n 마이크 [maikeu]; **Does it have a microphone?** 마이크가 있어요? [maikeuga isseoyo?]

microscope ['maɪkrəˌskəʊp] n 현미경 [hyeonmigyeong]

mid [mɪd] adj 중간의 [jungganui]

midday ['mɪd'deɪ] n 정오 [jeongo]; **at midday** 정오에 [jeongoe]; **It's twelve midday** 정오 열두시예요 [jeongo yeoldusiyeyo]

middle ['mɪdəl] n 중간 [junggan]; **Middle Ages** npl 중년 [jungnyeon]; **Middle East** n 중동 [jungdong]

middle-aged ['mɪdəlˌeɪdʒɪd] adj 중년의 [jungnyeonui]

middle-class ['mɪdəlˌklɑːs] adj 중산 계급의 [jungsan gyegeubui]

midge [mɪdʒ] n 모기 [mogi]

midnight ['mɪdˌnaɪt] n 자정 [jajeong]

midwife, midwives ['mɪdˌwaɪf, 'mɪdˌwaɪvz] n 산파 [sanpa]

migraine ['miːgreɪn; 'maɪ-] n 편두통 [pyeondutong]

migrant ['maɪɡrənt] adj 이동성의 [idongseongui] ▷ n 이주자 [ijuja]

migration [maɪˈɡreɪʃən] n 이주 [iju]

mike [maɪk] n 마이크 [maikeu]

mild [maɪld] adj 순한 [sunhan]

mile [maɪl] n 마일 [mail]
mileage ['maɪlɪdʒ] n 총 마일수 [chong mailsu]
mileometer [maɪ'lɒmɪtə] n 주행거리계 [juhaenggeorigye]
military ['mɪlɪtəri; -tri] adj 군대의 [gundaeui]
milk [mɪlk] n 우유 [uyu] ▷ v 젖을 짜다 [jeojeul jjada]; **baby milk** n 유아용 우유 [yuayong uyu]; **milk chocolate** n 밀크 초콜릿 [milkeu chokollit]; **semi-skimmed milk** n 반탈지유 [bantaljiyu]; **skimmed milk** n 탈지유 [taljiyu]; **UHT milk** n 초고온살균우유 [chogoonsalgyunuyu]; **Do you drink milk?** 우유 마시세요? [uyu masiseyo?]; **Have you got real milk?** 생우유 있어요? [saenguyu isseoyo?]; **Is it made with unpasteurised milk?** 미살균 우유로 만든 것인가요? [misalgyun uyuro mandeun geosingayo?]; **with the milk separate** 우유는 따로 주세요 [uyuneun ttaro juseyo]
milkshake ['mɪlk,ʃeɪk] n 밀크셰이크 [milkeusyeikeu]
mill [mɪl] n 방앗간 [bangatgan]
millennium [mɪ'lɛnɪəm] n 천년 [cheonnyeon]
millimetre ['mɪlɪ,miːtə] n 밀리미터 [millimiteo]
million ['mɪljən] n 백만 [baengman]
millionaire [,mɪljə'nɛə] n 백만장자 [baengmanjangja]
mimic ['mɪmɪk] v 모방하다 [mobanghada]
mince [mɪns] v 저민 고기 [jeomin gogi]
mind [maɪnd] n 마음 [maeum] ▷ v 주의하다 [juuihada]
mine [maɪn] n 광산 [gwangsan] ▷ pron 내 것 [nae geot]
miner ['maɪnə] n 광부 [gwangbu]
mineral ['mɪnərəl; 'mɪnrəl] adj 광물성의 [gwangmulseongui] ▷ n 무기물 [mugimul]; **mineral water** n 광천수 [gwangcheonsu]
miniature ['mɪnɪtʃə] adj 축소된

[chuksodoen] ▷ n 축소 모형 [chukso mohyeong]
minibar ['mɪnɪ,bɑː] n 미니 바 [mini ba]
minibus ['mɪnɪ,bʌs] n 소형버스 [sohyeongbeoseu]
minicab ['mɪnɪ,kæb] n 소형 콜택시 [sohyeong koltaeksi]
minimal ['mɪnɪməl] adj 최소량의 [choesoryangui]
minimize ['mɪnɪ,maɪz] v 최소화하다 [choesohwahada]
minimum ['mɪnɪməm] adj 최소의 [choesoui] ▷ n 최소 [choeso]
mining ['maɪnɪŋ] n 채광 [chaegwang]
miniskirt ['mɪnɪ,skɜːt] n 미니 스커트 [mini seukeoteu]
minister ['mɪnɪstə] n (clergy) 목사 [moksa], (government) 장관 [janggwan] (정치가); **prime minister** n 수상 [susang] (통치자)
ministry ['mɪnɪstrɪ] n (government) 부 [bu], (religion) 사역 [sayeok]
mink [mɪŋk] n 밍크 [mingkeu]
minor ['maɪnə] adj 보다 작은 [boda jageun] ▷ n 미성년자 [miseongnyeonja]
minority [maɪ'nɒrɪtɪ; mɪ-] n 소수 [sosu]
mint [mɪnt] n (coins) 화폐 주조소 [hwapye jujoso], (herb/sweet) 박하 [bakha]
minus ['maɪnəs] prep ...을 뺀 [...eul ppaen]
minute adj [maɪ'njuːt] 미세한 [misehan] ▷ n ['mɪnɪt] 분 [bun]; **Can you wait here for a few minutes?** 여기서 몇 분만 기다려 주시겠어요? [yeogiseo myeot bunman gidaryeo jusigesseoyo?]; **We are ten minutes late** 우리가 십분 늦었어요 [uriga sipbun neujeosseoyo]
miracle ['mɪrəkəl] n 기적 [gijeok]
mirror ['mɪrə] n 거울 [geoul]; **rear-view mirror** n 백미러 [baengmireo]; **wing mirror** n 사이드 미러 [saideu mireo]
misbehave [,mɪsbɪ'heɪv] v 방탕하다 [bangtanghada]

miscarriage [mɪsˈkærɪdʒ] n 유산 [yusan]

miscellaneous [ˌmɪsəˈleɪnɪəs] adj 갖가지 잡다한 [gatgaji japdahan]

mischief [ˈmɪstʃɪf] n 해악 [haeak]

mischievous [ˈmɪstʃɪvəs] adj 짓궂은 [jitgujeun]

miser [ˈmaɪzə] n 구두쇠 [gudusoe]

miserable [ˈmɪzərəbᵊl; ˈmɪzrə-] adj 비참한 [bichamhan]

misery [ˈmɪzərɪ] n 비참 [bicham]

misfortune [mɪsˈfɔːtʃən] n 불운 [burun]

mishap [ˈmɪshæp] n 불행한 사건 [bulhaenghan sageon]

misjudge [ˌmɪsˈdʒʌdʒ] v 잘못된 판단을 하다 [jalmotdoen pandaneul hada]

mislay [mɪsˈleɪ] v 잘못 놓다 [jalmot nota]

misleading [mɪsˈliːdɪŋ] adj 오도하는 [odohaneun]

misprint [ˈmɪsˌprɪnt] n 오식 [osik]

miss [mɪs] v 놓치다 [nochida]

Miss [mɪs] n 양 [yang]

missile [ˈmɪsaɪl] n 미사일 [misail]

missing [ˈmɪsɪŋ] adj 못 찾고 있는 [mot chatgo inneun]

missionary [ˈmɪʃənərɪ] n 선교사 [seongyosa]

mist [mɪst] n 안개 [angae]

mistake [mɪˈsteɪk] n 실수 [silsu] ▷ v 실수하다 [silsuhada]

mistaken [mɪˈsteɪkən] adj 잘못된 [jalmotdoen]

mistakenly [mɪˈsteɪkənlɪ] adv 잘못 알고서 [jalmot algoseo]

mistletoe [ˈmɪsᵊlˌtəʊ] n 겨우살이 [gyeousari]

mistress [ˈmɪstrɪs] n 첩 [cheop]

misty [ˈmɪstɪ] adj 안개가 자욱한 [angaega jaukhan]

misunderstand [ˌmɪsʌndəˈstænd] v 오해하다 [ohaehada]

misunderstanding [ˌmɪsʌndəˈstændɪŋ] n 오해 [ohae]; **There's been a misunderstanding** 오해가 있었어요 [ohaega isseosseoyo]

mitten [ˈmɪtᵊn] n 벙어리 장갑 [beongeori janggap]

mix [mɪks] n 혼합 [honhap] ▷ v 섞다 [seokkda]

mixed [mɪkst] adj 혼합된 [honhapdoen]; **mixed salad** n 혼합된 샐러드 [honhapdoen saelleodeu]

mixer [ˈmɪksə] n 믹서 [mikseo]

mixture [ˈmɪkstʃə] n 혼합물 [honhammul]

mix up [mɪks ʌp] v 혼합하다 [honhaphada]

mix-up [mɪksʌp] n 혼란 [hollan]

MMS [ɛm ɛm ɛs] abbr 멀티미디어 메시지 서비스 [meoltimidieo mesiji seobiseu]

moan [məʊn] v 신음소리를 내다 [sineumsorireul naeda]

moat [məʊt] n 외호 [oeho]

mobile [ˈməʊbaɪl] adj 이동성의 [idongseongui]; **mobile home** n 이동 주택 [idong jutaek]; **mobile number** n 휴대폰 번호 [hyudaepon beonho]; **mobile phone** n 휴대폰 [hyudaepon]

mock [mɒk] adj 모조의 [mojoui] ▷ v 조롱하다 [joronghada]

mod cons [mɒd kɒnz] npl 최신 설비 [choesin seolbi]

model [ˈmɒdᵊl] adj 모범이 되는 [mobeomi doeneun] ▷ n 모형 [mohyeong] ▷ v 모형을 만들다 [mohyeongeul mandeulda]

modem [ˈməʊdɛm] n 모뎀 [modem]

moderate [ˈmɒdərɪt] adj 온건한 [ongeonhan]

moderation [ˌmɒdəˈreɪʃən] n 온건 [ongeon]

modern [ˈmɒdən] adj 현대의 [hyeondaeui]; **modern languages** npl 현대 언어 [hyeondae eoneo]

modernize [ˈmɒdəˌnaɪz] v 현대화하다 [hyeondaehwahada]

modest [ˈmɒdɪst] adj 겸손한 [gyeomsonhan]

modification [ˌmɒdɪfɪˈkeɪʃən] n 수정 [sujeong]

modify [ˈmɒdɪˌfaɪ] v 변경하다 [byeongyeonghada]

module [ˈmɒdjuːl] n 모듈 [modyul]

moist [mɔɪst] *adj* 축축한 [chukchukhan]

moisture ['mɔɪstʃə] *n* 습기 [seupgi]

moisturizer ['mɔɪstʃəraɪzə] *n* 보습제 [boseupje]

Moldova [mɒl'dəʊvə] *n* 몰도바 [moldoba]

Moldovan [mɒl'dəʊvən] *adj* 몰도바의 [moldobaui] ▷ *n* 몰도바 사람 [moldoba saram]

mole [məʊl] *n (infiltrator)* 스파이 [seupai], *(mammal)* 두더지 [dudeoji], *(skin)* 점 [jeom]

molecule ['mɒlɪ,kjuːl] *n* 분자 [bunja]

moment ['məʊmənt] *n* 순간 [sungan]

momentarily ['məʊməntərəlɪ; -trɪlɪ] *adv* 순간적으로 [sunganjeogeuro]

momentary ['məʊməntərɪ; -trɪ] *adj* 순간의 [sunganui]

momentous [məʊ'mɛntəs] *adj* 중대한 [jungdaehan]

Monaco ['mɒnə,kəʊ; mə'nɑː,kəʊ; mɒnako] *n* 모나코 [monako]

monarch ['mɒnək] *n* 군주 [gunju]

monarchy ['mɒnəkɪ] *n* 군주제 [gunjuje]

monastery ['mɒnəstərɪ; -strɪ] *n* 수도원 [sudowon]; **Is the monastery open to the public?** 이 수도원은 일반인에게 개방되나요? [i sudowoneun ilbaninege gaebangdoenayo?]

Monday ['mʌndɪ] *n* 월요일 [wollyoil]; **It's Monday the fifteenth of June** 유월 십오일 월요일이에요 [yuwol siboil woryoirieyo]; **on Monday** 월요일에 [woryoire]

monetary ['mʌnɪtərɪ; -trɪ] *adj* 화폐의 [hwapyeui]

money ['mʌnɪ] *n* 돈 [don]; **money belt** *n* 전대 [jeondae]; **pocket money** *n* 용돈 [yongdon]; **Can you arrange to have some money sent over urgently?** 돈을 급히 보내 줄 수 있나요? [doneul geuphi bonae jul su innayo?]; **Could you lend me some money?** 돈 좀 빌려 주시겠어요? [don jom billyeo jusigesseoyo?]; **I have no**

money 돈이 없어요 [doni eopseoyo]; **I have run out of money** 돈이 떨어졌어요 [doni tteoreojyeosseoyo]; **I would like to transfer some money from my account** 제 계좌에서 돈을 이체하고 싶어요 [je gyejwaeseo doneul ichehago sipeoyo]

Mongolia [mɒŋ'gəʊlɪə] *n* 몽골 [monggol]

Mongolian [mɒŋ'gəʊlɪən] *adj* 몽골의 [monggorui] ▷ *n (language)* 몽골어 [monggoreo], *(person)* 몽골 사람 [monggol saram]

mongrel ['mʌŋgrəl] *n* 잡종 [japjong]

monitor ['mɒnɪtə] *n* 모니터 [moniteo]

monk [mʌŋk] *n* 수도승 [sudoseung]

monkey ['mʌŋkɪ] *n* 원숭이 [wonsungi]

monopoly [mə'nɒpəlɪ] *n* 독점 [dokjeom]

monotonous [mə'nɒtənəs] *adj* 단조로운 [danjoroun]

monsoon [mɒn'suːn] *n* 우기 [ugi]

monster ['mɒnstə] *n* 괴물 [goemul]

month [mʌnθ] *n* 월 [wol]

monthly ['mʌnθlɪ] *adj* 매월의 [maeworui]

monument ['mɒnjʊmənt] *n* 기념비 [ginyeombi]

mood [muːd] *n* 기분 [gibun]

moody ['muːdɪ] *adj* 침울한 [chimulhan]

moon [muːn] *n* 달 [dal]; **full moon** *n* 보름달 [boreumdal]

moor [mʊə; mɔː] *n* 황야 [hwangya] ▷ *v* 정박하다 [jeongbakhada]

mop [mɒp] *n* 대걸레 [daegeolle]

moped ['məʊpɛd] *n* 모터 달린 자전거 [moteo dallin jajeongeo]; **I want to hire a moped** 모터 달린 자전거를 빌리고 싶어요 [moteo dallin jajeongeoreul billigo sipeoyo]

mop up [mɒp ʌp] *v* 대걸레로 닦다 [daegeollero dakkda]

moral ['mɒrəl] *adj* 도덕적인 [dodeokjeogin] ▷ *n* 도덕 [dodeok]

morale [mɒ'rɑːl] *n* 사기 [sagi]

morals ['mɒrəlz] *npl* 윤리 [yulli]

more [mɔː] *adj* 더 많은 [deo manheun] ▷ *adv* 더 많이 [deo manhi] ▷ *pron* 보다

많은 양 [boda manheun yang]
morgue [mɔːg] n 영안실 [yeongansil]
morning ['mɔːnɪŋ] n 아침 [achim];
  morning sickness n 입덧 [ipdeot]; **in
  the morning** 아침에 [achime]; **I will
  be leaving tomorrow morning at
  ten a.m.** 저는 내일 아침 10시에
  떠나요 [jeoneun naeil achim 1osie
  tteonayo]; **I've been sick since this
  morning** 오늘 아침부터 몸이 아파요
  [oneul achimbuteo momi apayo]; **Is
  the museum open in the morning?**
  이 박물관은 아침에 문 열어요? [i
  bangmulgwaneun achime mun
  yeoreoyo?]; **this morning** 오늘 아침
  [oneul achim]; **tomorrow morning**
  내일 아침 [naeil achim]
Moroccan [məˈrɒkən] adj 모로코의
  [morokoui] ▷ n 모로코 사람 [moroko
  saram]
Morocco [məˈrɒkəʊ] n 모로코
  [moroko]
morphine [ˈmɔːfiːn] n 모르핀
  [moreupin]
Morse [mɔːs] n 모스 [moseu]
mortar [ˈmɔːtə] n (military) 박격포
  [bakgyeokpo], (plaster) 모르타르
  [moreutareu]
mortgage [ˈmɔːgɪdʒ] n 주택담보 융자
  [jutaekdambo yungja] ▷ v 주택을
  담보로 융자를 받다 [jutaegeul
  damboro yungjareul batda]
mosaic [məˈzeɪɪk] n 모자이크
  [mojaikeu]
Moslem [ˈmɒzləm] adj 회교의
  [hoegyoui] ▷ n 회교도 [hoegyodo]
mosque [mɒsk] n 회교 사원 [hoegyo
  sawon]
mosquito [məˈskiːtəʊ] n 모기 [mogi]
moss [mɒs] n 이끼 [ikki]
most [məʊst] adj 가장 많은 [gajang
  manheun] ▷ adv (superlative) 가장 많이
  [gajang manhi] ▷ n (majority) 최대량
  [choedaeryang]
mostly [ˈməʊstlɪ] adv 대부분
  [daebubun]
MOT [ɛm əʊ tiː] abbr 차량 연례 정비
  [charyang yeollye jeongbi]

motel [məʊˈtɛl] n 모텔 [motel]
moth [mɒθ] n 나방 [nabang]
mother [ˈmʌðə] n 어머니 [eomeoni];
  mother tongue n 모국어 [mogugeo];
  surrogate mother n 대리모
  [daerimo]
mother-in-law [ˈmʌðə ɪn lɔː]
  (mothers-in-law) n (husband's
  mother) 시어머니 [sieomeoni]
motionless [ˈməʊʃənlɪs] adj 가만히
  있는 [gamanhi inneun]
motivated [ˈməʊtɪˌveɪtɪd] adj 동기를
  부여 받은 [donggireul buyeo badeun]
motivation [ˌməʊtɪˈveɪʃən] n
  동기부여 [donggibuyeo]
motive [ˈməʊtɪv] n 동기 [donggi]
  (장려금)
motor [ˈməʊtə] n 모터 [moteo]; **motor
  mechanic** n 자동차정비공
  [jadongchajeongbigong]; **motor
  racing** n 자동차경주
  [jadongchagyeongju]
motorbike [ˈməʊtəˌbaɪk] n 오토바이
  [otobai]; **I want to hire a motorbike**
  오토바이를 빌리고 싶어요 [otobaireul
  billigo sipeoyo]
motorboat [ˈməʊtəˌbəʊt] n 모터 보트
  [moteo boteu]
motorcycle [ˈməʊtəˌsaɪkᵊl] n 오토바이
  [otobai]
motorcyclist [ˈməʊtəˌsaɪklɪst] n
  오토바이를 타는 사람 [otobaireul
  taneun saram]
motorist [ˈməʊtərɪst] n 자동차 운전자
  [jadongcha unjeonja]
motorway [ˈməʊtəˌweɪ] n 고속도로
  [gosokdoro]; **How do I get to the
  motorway?** 고속도로에 어떻게
  갑니까? [gosokdoroe eotteoke
  gamnikka?]; **Is there a toll on this
  motorway?** 이 고속도로에는 요금소가
  있어요? [i gosokdoroeneun
  yogeumsoga isseoyo?]
mould [məʊld] n (fungus) 곰팡이
  [gompangi], (shape) 모형 [mohyeong]
mouldy [ˈməʊldɪ] adj 곰팡 슨
  [gompang seun]
mount [maʊnt] v 오르다 [oreuda]

mountain ['maʊntɪn] n 산 [san]; **mountain bike** n 산악 자전거 [sanak jajeongeo]; **Where is the nearest mountain rescue service post?** 가장 가까운 산악 구조대는 어디 있어요? [gajang gakkaun sanak gujodaeneun eodi isseoyo?]

mountaineer [,maʊntɪ'nɪə] n 등산자 [deungsanja]

mountaineering [,maʊntɪ'nɪərɪŋ] n 등산 [deungsan]

mountainous ['maʊntɪnəs] adj 산이 많은 [sani manheun]

mount up [maʊnt ʌp] v 장황하다 [janghwanghada]

mourning ['mɔːnɪŋ] n 애도 [aedo]

mouse [maʊs] **(mice)** n 생쥐 [saengjwi]; **mouse mat** n 마우스패드 [mauseupaedeu]

mousse [muːs] n 무스 [museu]

moustache [mə'stɑːʃ] n 콧수염 [kossuyeom]

mouth [maʊθ] n 입 [ip]; **mouth organ** n 하모니카 [hamonika]

mouthwash ['maʊθ,wɒʃ] n 구강청결제 [gugangcheonggyeolje]

move [muːv] n 이동 [idong] ▷ vi 움직이다 [umjigida]

move back [muːv bæk] v 뒤로 이동하다 [dwiro idonghada]

move forward [muːv fɔːwəd] v 앞으로 이동하다 [apeuro idonghada]

move in [muːv ɪn] v 이사하다 [isahada]

movement ['muːvmənt] n 운동 [undong]

movie ['muːvɪ] n 영화 [yeonghwa]

moving ['muːvɪŋ] adj 움직이는 [umjigineun]

mow [məʊ] v 베다 [beda] (깎다)

mower ['maʊə] n 풀베는 기계 [pulbeneun gigye]

Mozambique [,məʊzəm'biːk] n 모잠비크 [mojambikeu]

mph [maɪlz pə aʊə] abbr 시속 마일 수 [sisok mail su]

Mr ['mɪstə] n 씨 [ssi]

Mrs ['mɪsɪz] n 여사 [yeosa]

Ms [mɪz; məs] n 씨(여성) [ssi(yeoseong)]; **Can I speak to Ms…, please?** … 씨와 통화할 수 있을까요? [... ssiwa tonghwahal su isseulkkayo?]

MS ['ɛmɛs] abbr 다발성경화증 [dabalseonggyeonghwajung]

much [mʌtʃ] adj 많은 [manheun] ▷ adv 대량 [daeryang], 매우 [maeu]

mud [mʌd] n 진흙 [jinheulg]

muddle ['mʌdªl] n 혼란 [hollan]

muddy ['mʌdɪ] adj 질척한 [jilcheokhan]

mudguard ['mʌd,gɑːd] n 진흙받이 [jinheurkbaji]

muesli ['mjuːzlɪ] n 뮤즐리 [myujeulli]

muffler ['mʌflə] n 머플러 [meopeulleo]

mug [mʌg] n 머그 [meogeu] ▷ v 습격하다 [seupgyeokhada]

mugger ['mʌgə] n 노상 강도 [nosang gangdo]

mugging [mʌgɪŋ] n 강도 행위 [gangdo haengwi]

muggy ['mʌgɪ] adj **It's muggy** 후텁지근해요 [huteopjigeunhaeyo]

mule [mjuːl] n 노새 [nosae]

multinational [,mʌltɪ'næʃənªl] adj 다국적의 [dagukjeogui] ▷ n 다국적 기업 [dagukjeok gieop]

multiple ['mʌltɪpªl] adj **multiple sclerosis** n 다발성경화증 [dabalseonggyeonghwajung]

multiplication [,mʌltɪplɪ'keɪʃən] n 곱셈 [gopsem]

multiply ['mʌltɪ,plaɪ] v 곱하다 [gophada]

mum [mʌm] n 엄마 [eomma]

mummy ['mʌmɪ] n **(body)** 미이라 [miira], **(mother)** 엄마 [eomma]

mumps [mʌmps] n 볼거리 [bolgeori]

murder ['mɜːdə] n 살인 [sarin] ▷ v 살인하다 [sarinhada]

murderer ['mɜːdərə] n 살인자 [sarinja]

muscle ['mʌsªl] n 근육 [geunyuk]

muscular ['mʌskjʊlə] adj 근육이 발달한 [geunyugi baldalhan]

museum [mjuː'zɪəm] n 박물관 [bangmulgwan]; **Is the museum open every day?** 이 박물관은 매일 열어요? [i bangmulgwaneun maeil yeoreoyo?]; **When is the museum open?** 이

박물관은 언제 열어요? [i bangmulgwaneun eonje yeoreoyo?]

mushroom ['mʌʃruːm; -rʊm] n 버섯 [beoseot]

music ['mjuːzɪk] n 음악 [eumak]; **folk music** n 민속 음악 [minsok eumak]; **music centre** n 오디오 세트 [odio seteu]; **Where can we hear live music?** 어디에서 라이브 음악을 들을 수 있어요? [eodieseo raibeu eumageul deureul su isseoyo?]

musical ['mjuːzɪkᵊl] adj 음악적인 [eumakjeogin] ▷ n 뮤지컬 [myujikeol]; **musical instrument** n 악기 [akgi]

musician [mjuːˈzɪʃən] n 음악가 [eumakga]; **Where can we hear local musicians play?** 어디에서 지역 음악가의 연주를 들을 수 있어요? [eodieseo jiyeok eumakgaui yeonjureul deureul su isseoyo?]

Muslim ['mʊzlɪm; 'mʌz-] adj 이슬람교의 [iseullamgyoui] ▷ n 이슬람교 [iseullamgyo]

mussel ['mʌsᵊl] n 홍합 [honghap]

must [mʌst] v 해야 한다 [haeya handa]

mustard ['mʌstəd] n 겨자 [gyeoja]

mutter ['mʌtə] v 중얼거리다 [jungeolgeorida]

mutton ['mʌtᵊn] n 양 고기 [yang gogi]

mutual ['mjuːtʃʊəl] adj 상호간의 [sanghoganui]

my [maɪ] pron 나의 [naui]

Myanmar ['maɪænmɑː; 'mjænmɑː] n 미얀마 [miyanma]

myself [maɪˈsɛlf] pron 내 자신 [nae jasin]

mysterious [mɪˈstɪərɪəs] adj 신비한 [sinbihan]

mystery ['mɪstərɪ] n 신비 [sinbi]

myth [mɪθ] n 신화 [sinhwa]

mythology [mɪˈθɒlədʒɪ] n 신화 [sinhwa]

n

naff [næf] adj 구식의 [gusigui]

nag [næg] v 잔소리하다 [jansorihada]

nail [neɪl] n 못 [mot]; **nail polish** n 매니큐어 [maenikyueo]; **nail scissors** npl 손톱가위 [sontopgawi]; **nail varnish** n 매니큐어 [maenikyueo]; **nail-polish remover** n 매니큐어 제거제 [maenikyueo jegeoje]

nailbrush ['neɪlˌbrʌʃ] n 손톱솔 [sontopsol]

nailfile ['neɪlˌfaɪl] n 손톱 다듬는 줄 [sontop dadeumneun jul]

naive [nɑːˈiːv; nɑɪˈiːv] adj 순진한 [sunjinhan]

naked ['neɪkɪd] adj 발가벗은 [balgabeoseun]

name [neɪm] n 이름 [ireum]; **brand name** n 상표명 [sangpyomyeong]; **first name** n 이름 [ireum]; **maiden name** n 결혼 전의 성 [gyeolhon jeonui seong]; **I booked a room in the name of...** ... 이름으로 방을 예약했어요 [... ireumeuro bangeul yeyakhaesseoyo]; **My name is...** 제 이름은...이에요 [je ireumeun...ieyo]; **What's your name?** 당신의 이름은 무엇인가요? [dangsinui ireumeun mueosingayo?]

nanny ['nænɪ] n 보모 [bomo]

nap [næp] n 낮잠 [natjam]

napkin ['næpkɪn] n 냅킨 [naepkin]

nappy ['næpɪ] n 기저귀 [gijeogwi]

narrow ['nærəʊ] adj 좁은 [jobeun]

narrow-minded ['nærəʊ'maɪndɪd] adj 마음이 좁은 [maeumi jobeun]

nasty ['nɑːstɪ] adj 불쾌한 [bulkwaehan]

nation ['neɪʃən] n 민족 [minjok]; **United Nations** n 국제연합 [gukjeyeonhap]

national ['næʃənəl] adj 민족적인 [minjokjeogin]; **national anthem** n 애국가 [aegukga]; **national park** n 국립 공원 [gungnip gongwon]

nationalism ['næʃənə,lɪzəm; 'næʃnə-] n 국수주의 [guksujuui]

nationalist ['næʃənəlɪst] n 국수주의자 [guksujuuija]

nationality [,næʃə'nælɪtɪ] n 국적 [gukjeok]

nationalize ['næʃənə,laɪz; 'næʃnə-] v 국유화하다 [gugyuhwahada]

native ['neɪtɪv] adj 태어난 [taeeonan]; **native speaker** n 원어민 [woneomin]

NATO ['neɪtəʊ] abbr 북대서양조약기구 [bukdaeseoyangjoyakgigu]

natural ['nætʃrəl; -tʃərəl] adj 자연의 [jayeonui]; **natural gas** n 천연 가스 [cheonyeon gaseu]; **natural resources** npl 천연 자원 [cheonyeon jawon]

naturalist ['nætʃrəlɪst; -tʃərəl-] n 자연주의자 [jayeonjuuija]

naturally ['nætʃrəlɪ; -tʃərə-] adv 자연히 [jayeonhi]

nature ['neɪtʃə] n 자연 [jayeon]

naughty ['nɔːtɪ] adj 말썽꾸러기인 [malsseongkkureogiin]

nausea ['nɔːzɪə; -sɪə] n 구역질 [guyeokjil]

naval ['neɪvəl] adj 해군의 [haegunui]

navel ['neɪvəl] n 배꼽 [baekkop]

navy ['neɪvɪ] n 해군 [haegun]

navy-blue ['neɪvɪ'bluː] adj 진한 푸른색의 [jinhan pureunsaegui]

NB [ɛn biː] abbr (notabene) 주의 [juui]

near [nɪə] adj 가까운 [gakkaun] ▷ adv 가까이 [gakkai] ▷ prep 근접한 [geunjeophan]; **How do I get to the nearest tube station?** 가장 가까운 지하철역에 어떻게 가나요? [gajang gakkaun jihacheollyeoge eotteoke ganayo?]; **Where is the nearest bus stop?** 가장 가까운 버스 정류장은 어디있어요? [gajang gakkaun beoseu jeongnyujangeun eodiisseoyo?]

nearby adj ['nɪəbaɪ] 근처의 [geuncheoui] ▷ adv ['nɪə,baɪ] 근처에 [geuncheoe]; **Is there a bank nearby?** 근처에 은행이 있나요? [geuncheoe eunhaengi innayo?]

nearly ['nɪəlɪ] adv 거의 [geoui]

near-sighted [,nɪə'saɪtɪd] adj 근시의 [geunsiui]

neat [niːt] adj 깔끔한 [kkalkkeumhan]

neatly [niːtlɪ] adv 깔끔하게 [kkalkkeumhage]

necessarily ['nɛsɪsərɪlɪ; ,nɛsɪ'sɛrɪlɪ] adv 반드시 [bandeusi]

necessary ['nɛsɪsərɪ] adj 필요한 [piryohan]

necessity [nɪ'sɛsɪtɪ] n 필요성 [piryoseong]

neck [nɛk] n 목 [mok]

necklace ['nɛklɪs] n 목걸이 [mokgeori]

nectarine ['nɛktərɪn] n 승도복숭아 [seungdoboksunga]

need [niːd] n 필요 [pillyo] ▷ v 필요하다 [piryohada]; **Do you need anything?** 필요하신 것이 있어요? [piryohasin geosi isseoyo?]; **I don't need a bag, thanks** 봉투는 필요 없어요 [bongtuneun pillyo eopseoyo]; **I need assistance** 보조가 필요해요 [bojoga pillyohaeyo]; **I need contraception** 피임이 필요해요 [piimi piryohaeyo]

needle ['niːdəl] n 바늘 [baneul]; **knitting needle** n 뜨개바늘 [tteugaebaneul]; **Do you have a needle and thread?** 바늘과 실 있어요? [baneulgwa sil isseoyo?]

negative ['nɛgətɪv] adj 부정적인 [bujeongjeogin] ▷ n 부정적인 말(태도) [bujeongjeogin mal(taedo)]

neglect [nɪ'glɛkt] n 무시 [musi] ▷ v

무시하다 [musihada]
neglected [nɪˈglɛktɪd] *adj* 무시된 [musidoen]

negligee [ˈnɛglɪˌʒeɪ] *n* 네글리제 [negeullije]

negotiate [nɪˈgəʊʃɪˌeɪt] *v* 협상하다 [hyeopsanghada]

negotiations [nɪˌgəʊʃɪˈeɪʃənz] *npl* 협상 [hyeopsang]

negotiator [nɪˈgəʊʃɪˌeɪtə] *n* 협상자 [hyeopsangja]

neighbour [ˈneɪbə] *n* 이웃 [iut]

neighbourhood [ˈneɪbəˌhʊd] *n* 이웃 [iut]

neither [ˈnaɪðə; ˈniːðə] *adv*...도...도 아니다 [...do...do anida] ▷ *conj*...도 또한...아니다 [...do ttohan...anida] ▷ *pron* 어느 쪽도... 아니다 [eoneu jjokdo... anida]

neon [ˈniːɒn] *n* 네온 [neon]

Nepal [nɪˈpɔːl] *n* 네팔 [nepal]

nephew [ˈnɛvjuː; ˈnɛf-] *n* 조카 [joka]

nerve [nɜːv] *n* (*boldness*) 용기 [yonggi], (*to/from brain*) 신경 [singyeong]

nerve-racking [ˈnɜːvˈrækɪŋ] *adj* 신경을 거스르는 [singyeongeul geoseureuneun]

nervous [ˈnɜːvəs] *adj* 신경질적인 [singyeongjiljeogin]; **nervous breakdown** *n* 신경 쇠약 [singyeong soeyak]

nest [nɛst] *n* 둥지 [dungji]

net [nɛt] *n* 망 [mang]

Net [nɛt] *n* 인터넷 [inteonet]

netball [ˈnɛtˌbɔːl] *n* 네트볼 [neteubol]

Netherlands [ˈnɛðələndz] *npl* 네덜란드 [nedeollandeu]

nettle [ˈnɛtˀl] *n* 쐐기풀 [sswaegipul]

network [ˈnɛtˌwɜːk] *n* 네트워크 [neteuwokeu]

neurotic [njʊˈrɒtɪk] *adj* 신경증에 걸린 [singyeongjeunge geollin]

neutral [ˈnjuːtrəl] *adj* 중립의 [jungnibui] ▷ *n* 중립 [jungnip]

never [ˈnɛvə] *adv* 결코...않다 [gyeolko...anta]

nevertheless [ˌnɛvəðəˈlɛs] *adv* 그럼에도 불구하고 [geureomedo bulguhago]

new [njuː] *adj* 새로운 [saeroun]; **New Year** *n* 새해 [saehae]; **New Zealand** *n* 뉴질랜드 [nyujillaendeu]; **New Zealander** *n* 뉴질랜드 사람 [nyujillaendeu saram]

newborn [ˈnjuːˌbɔːn] *adj* 갓난 [gatnan]

newcomer [ˈnjuːˌkʌmə] *n* 신입 [sinip]

news [njuːz] *npl* 뉴스 [nyuseu]; **When is the news?** 뉴스는 언제 해요? [nyuseuneun eonje haeyo?]

newsagent [ˈnjuːzˌeɪdʒənt] *n* 신문 가게 [sinmun gage]

newspaper [ˈnjuːzˌpeɪpə] *n* 신문 [sinmun] (언론); **Do you have newspapers?** 신문 있어요? [sinmun isseoyo?]; **I would like a newspaper** 신문을 사고 싶어요 [sinmuneul sago sipeoyo]; **Where can I buy a newspaper?** 어디에서 신문을 살 수 있어요? [eodieseo sinmuneul sal su isseoyo?]; **Where is the nearest shop which sells newspapers?** 가장 가까운 신문 가게는 어디에 있어요? [gajang gakkaun sinmun gageneun eodie isseoyo?]

newsreader [ˈnjuːzˌriːdə] *n* 뉴스 아나운서 [nyuseu anaunseo]

newt [njuːt] *n* 영원 [yeongwon]

next [nɛkst] *adj* 다음의 [daeumui] ▷ *adv* 다음에 [daeume]; **next to** *prep* ...의 옆에 [...ui yeope]; **When do we stop next?** 다음에 언제 정차해요? [daeume eonje jeongchahaeyo?]

next-of-kin [ˈnɛkstɒvˈkɪn] *n* 근친자 [geunchinja]

Nicaragua [ˌnɪkəˈrægjʊə; nikaˈraɣwa] *n* 니카라과 [nikaragwa]

Nicaraguan [ˌnɪkəˈrægjʊən; -gwən] *adj* 니카라과의 [nikaragwaui] ▷ *n* 니카라과 사람 [nikaragwa saram]

nice [naɪs] *adj* 좋은 [joheun]

nickname [ˈnɪkˌneɪm] *n* 별명 [byeolmyeong]

nicotine [ˈnɪkəˌtiːn] *n* 니코틴 [nikotin]

niece [niːs] *n* 조카딸 [jokattal]

Niger [ˈnaɪdʒɪər] *n* 니제르 [nijereu]

Nigeria [naɪˈdʒɪərɪə] *n* 나이지리아

[naijiria]

Nigerian [naɪˈdʒɪərɪən] *adj* 나이지리아의 [naijiriaui] ▷ *n* 나이지리아 사람 [naijiria saram]

night [naɪt] *n* 밤 [bam]; **hen night** *n* 여성만의 모임 [yeoseongmanui moim]; **night school** *n* 야간 학교 [yagan hakgyo]; **stag night** *n* 총각파티 [chonggakpati]; **at night** 밤에 [bame]; **How much is it per night?** 하룻밤에 얼마예요? [harutbame eolmayeyo?]; **I want to stay an extra night** 하룻밤 더 묵고 싶어요 [harutbam deo mukgo sipeoyo]; **I'd like to stay for two nights** 이틀밤 묵고 싶어요 [iteulbam mukgo sipeoyo]; **last night** 지난 밤 [jinan bam]; **tomorrow night** 내일 밤 [naeil bam]

nightclub [ˈnaɪtˌklʌb] *n* 나이트 클럽 [naiteu keulleop]

nightdress [ˈnaɪtˌdrɛs] *n* 잠옷 [jamot]

nightie [ˈnaɪtɪ] *n* 잠옷 [jamot]

nightlife [ˈnaɪtˌlaɪf] *n* 야간 활동 [yagan hwaldong]

nightmare [ˈnaɪtˌmɛə] *n* 악몽 [angmong]

nightshift [ˈnaɪtˌʃɪft] *n* 야간 교대근무 [yagan gyodaegeunmu]

nil [nɪl] *n* 영 [yeong]

nine [naɪn] *number* 아홉 [ahop], *(Sino-Korean)* 구 [gu]

nineteen [ˌnaɪnˈtiːn] *number* 열아홉 [yeoarahop], *(Sino-Korean)* 십구 [sipgu]

nineteenth [ˌnaɪnˈtiːnθ] *adj* 열아홉 번째의 [yeorahop beonjjaeui]

ninety [ˈnaɪntɪ] *number* 아흔 [aheun], *(Sino-Korean)* 구십 [gusip]

ninth [naɪnθ] *adj* 아홉 번째의 [ahop beonjjaeui] ▷ *n* 9분의 1 [gubunui il]

nitrogen [ˈnaɪtrədʒən] *n* 질소 [jilso]

no [nəʊ] *pron*...이 하나도 없는 [...i hanado eomneun]; **no!** *excl* 아니오! [anio!]; **no one** *pron* 아무도... 않다(없다) [amudo... anta(eopda)]

nobody [ˈnəʊbədɪ] *pron* 아무도... 않다 [amudo... anta]

nod [nɒd] *v* 머리를 끄덕이다 [meorireul kkeudeogida]

noise [nɔɪz] *n* 소음 [soeum]

noisy [ˈnɔɪzɪ] *adj* 시끄러운 [sikkeureoun]

nominate [ˈnɒmɪˌneɪt] *v* 지명하다 [jimyeonghada]

nomination [ˌnɒmɪˈneɪʃən] *n* 지명 [jimyeong]

none [nʌn] *pron* 아무도... 않다 [amudo... anta]

nonsense [ˈnɒnsəns] *n* 허튼 소리 [heoteun sori]

non-smoker [nɒnˈsməʊkə] *n* 비흡연자 [biheubyeonja]

non-smoking [nɒnˈsməʊkɪŋ] *adj* 흡연하지 않는 [heubyeonhaji annneun]

non-stop [ˈnɒnˈstɒp] *adv* 쉬지 않고 [swiji anko]

noodles [ˈnuːdˀlz] *npl* 국수 [guksu] (식품)

noon [nuːn] *n* 정오 [jeongo]

nor [nɔː; nə] *conj*...도 아니고 또한...도 아니다 [...do anigo ttohan...do anida]

normal [ˈnɔːmˀl] *adj* 정상의 [jeongsangui]

normally [ˈnɔːməlɪ] *adv* 정상적으로 [jeongsangjeogeuro]

north [nɔːθ] *adj* 북쪽의 [bukjjogui] ▷ *adv* 북쪽으로 [bukjjogeuro] ▷ *n* 북쪽 [bukjjok]; **North Africa** *n* 북아프리카 [bugapeurika]; **North African** *n* 북아프리카 사람 [bugapeurika saram], 북아프리카의 [bugapeurikaui]; **North America** *n* 북미 [bungmi]; **North American** *n* 북미 사람 [bungmi saram], 북미의 [bungmiui]; **North Korea** *n* 북한 [bukhan]; **North Pole** *n* 북극 [bukgeuk]; **North Sea** *n* 북해 [bukhae]

northbound [ˈnɔːθˌbaʊnd] *adj* 북쪽으로 가는 [bukjjogeuro ganeun]

northeast [ˌnɔːθˈiːst; ˌnɔːˈriːst] *n* 북동쪽 [bukdongjjok]

northern [ˈnɔːðən] *adj* 북쪽의 [bukjjogui]; **Northern Ireland** *n* 북아일랜드 [bugaillaendeu]

northwest [ˌnɔːθˈwɛst; ˌnɔːˈwɛst] *n* 북서쪽 [bukseojjok]

Norway ['nɔːˌweɪ] n 노르웨이
[noreuwei]

Norwegian [nɔːˈwiːdʒən] adj
노르웨이의 [noreuweiui] ▷ n (language)
노르웨이어 [noreuweieo], (person)
노르웨이 사람 [noreuwei saram]

nose [nəʊz] n 코 [ko]

nosebleed ['nəʊzˌbliːd] n 코피 [kopi]

nostril ['nɒstrɪl] n 콧구멍
[kotgumeong]

nosy ['nəʊzɪ] adj 참견하기 좋아하는
[chamgyeonhagi johahaneun]

not [nɒt] adv... 아니다 [... anida]

note [nəʊt] n (banknote) 지폐 [jipye],
(message) 메모 [memo], (music) 음표
[eumpyo]; **sick note** n 병으로 인한
결석 통지 [byeongeuro inhan
gyeolseok tongji]; **Do you have
change for this note?** 이 지폐를
동전으로 바꿀 수 있나요? [i jipyereul
dongjeoneuro bakkul su innayo?]

notebook ['nəʊtˌbʊk] n 공책
[gongchaek]

note down [nəʊt daʊn] v 메모하다
[memohada]

notepad ['nəʊtˌpæd] n 메모장
[memojang]

notepaper ['nəʊtˌpeɪpə] n 편지지
[pyeonjiji]

nothing ['nʌθɪŋ] pron 아무것도 아닌 것
[amugeotdo anin geot]

notice ['nəʊtɪs] n (note) 통지 [tongji],
(termination) 해고 통보 [haego
tongbo] ▷ v 알아차리다 [aracharida];
notice board n 게시판 [gesipan]

noticeable ['nəʊtɪsəbəl] adj 현저한
[hyeonjeohan]

notify ['nəʊtɪˌfaɪ] v 통지하다
[tongjihada]

nought [nɔːt] n 영 [yeong]

noun [naʊn] n 명사 [myeongsa] (문법)

novel ['nɒvəl] n 소설 [soseol]

novelist ['nɒvəlɪst] n 소설가 [soseolga]

November [nəʊˈvɛmbə] n 11월
[sibilwol]

now [naʊ] adv 현재 [hyeonjae]

nowadays ['naʊəˌdeɪz] adv 요즘
[yojeueum]

nowhere ['nəʊˌwɛə] adv 아무데도...
없다(않다) [amudedo... eopda(anta)]

nuclear ['njuːklɪə] adj 핵의 [haegui]

nude [njuːd] adj 나체의 [nacheui] ▷ n
나체 [nache]

nudist ['njuːdɪst] n 나체주의자
[nachejuuija]

nuisance ['njuːsəns] n 귀찮은 존재
[gwichanheun jonjae]

numb [nʌm] adj 저린 [jeorin]

number ['nʌmbə] n 번호 [beonho];
account number n 계좌번호
[gyejwabeonho]; **mobile number** n
휴대폰 번호 [hyudaepon beonho];
number plate n 번호판 [beonhopan];
phone number n 전화번호
[jeonhwabeonho]; **reference number**
n 참조번호 [chamjobeonho]; **room
number** n 방 번호 [bang beonho];
wrong number n 잘못 걸린 전화
[jalmot geollin jeonhwa]; **Can I have
your phone number?** 전화번호 좀
알려 주시겠어요? [jeonhwabeonho
jom allyeo jusigesseoyo?]; **My mobile
number is...** 제 휴대 전화 번호는...
이에요 [je hyudae jeonhwa
beonhoneun...ieyo]; **What is the fax
number?** 팩스 번호가 무엇입니까?
[paekseu beonhoga mueosimnikka?];
**What is the number for directory
enquiries?** 전화번호 문의는 몇
번인가요? [jeonhwabeonho
munuineun myeot beoningayo?];
What is the number of your mobile?
당신의 휴대 전화번호는 몇 번인가요?
[dangsinui hyudae
jeonhwabeonhoneun myeot
beoningayo?]; **What's the telephone
number?** 전화번호가 무엇입니까?
[jeonhwabeonhoga mueosimnikka?]

numerous ['njuːmərəs] adj 매우 많은
[maeu manheun]

nun [nʌn] n 수녀 [sunyeo]

nurse [nɜːs] n 간호사 [ganhosa]; **I'd like
to speak to a nurse** 간호사에게
이야기하고 싶어요 [ganhosaege
iyagihago sipeoyo]

nursery ['nɜːsrɪ] n 육아실 [yugasil];

nursery rhyme *n* 동요 [dongyo];
nursery school *n* 유치원 [yuchiwon]
nursing home ['nɜːsɪŋ həʊm] *n*
nursing home 양로원 [yangnowon]
nut [nʌt] *n (device)* 너트 [neoteu], *(food)*
견과 [gyeongwa]; **nut allergy** *n* 견과
알레르기 [gyeongwa allereugi]; **Could
you prepare a meal without nuts?**
견과류가 들어가지 않은 식사를 준비해
주시겠어요? [gyeongwaryuga
deureogaji anheun siksareul junbihae
jusigesseoyo?]
nutmeg ['nʌtmɛg] *n* 육두구 [yukdugu]
nutrient ['njuːtrɪənt] *n* 영양제
[yeongyangje]
nutrition [njuːˈtrɪʃən] *n* 영양소
[yeongyangso]
nutritious [njuːˈtrɪʃəs] *adj* 영양이 되는
[yeongyangi doeneun]
nutter ['nʌtə] *n* 괴짜 [goejja]
nylon ['naɪlɒn] *n* 나일론 [naillon]

oak [əʊk] *n* 참나무 [chamnamu]
oar [ɔː] *n* 노 [no]
oasis, oases [əʊˈeɪsɪs, əʊˈeɪsiːz] *n*
오아시스 [oasiseu]
oath [əʊθ] *n* 서약 [seoyak]
oatmeal ['əʊtˌmiːl] *n* 오트밀 [oteumil]
oats [əʊts] *npl* 귀리 [gwiri]
obedient [əˈbiːdɪənt] *adj* 순종하는
[sunjonghaneun]
obese [əʊˈbiːs] *adj* 뚱뚱한
[ttungttunghan]
obey [əˈbeɪ] *v* 순종하다 [sunjonghada]
obituary [əˈbɪtjʊərɪ] *n* 사망기사
[samanggisa]
object ['ɒbdʒɪkt] *n* 물체 [mulche]
objection [əbˈdʒɛkʃən] *n* 이의 [iui]
objective [əbˈdʒɛktɪv] *n* 목적
[mokjeok]
oblong ['ɒbˌlɒŋ] *adj* 길게 늘여진 [gilge
neullyeojin]
obnoxious [əbˈnɒkʃəs] *adj* 불쾌한
[bulkwaehan]
oboe ['əʊbəʊ] *n* 오보에 [oboe]
obscene [əbˈsiːn] *adj* 음탕한
[eumtanghan]
observant [əbˈzɜːvənt] *adj* 주의깊은
[juuigipeun]

observatory [əbˈzɜːvətərɪ; -trɪ] *n*
관측소 [gwancheukso]
observe [əbˈzɜːv] *v* 관찰하다
[gwanchalhada]
observer [əbˈzɜːvə; obˈserver] *n* 관찰자
[gwanchalja]
obsessed [əbˈsɛst] *adj* 집념에 사로 잡힌
[jimnyeome saro japhin]
obsession [əbˈsɛʃən] *n* 집념
[jimnyeom]
obsolete [ˈɒbsəˌliːt; ˌɒbsəˈliːt] *adj* 쓸모
없어진 [sseulmo eopseojin]
obstacle [ˈɒbstəkᵊl] *n* 장애물
[jangaemul]
obstinate [ˈɒbstɪnɪt] *adj* 완고한
[wangohan]
obstruct [əbˈstrʌkt] *v* 방해하다
[banghaehada]
obtain [əbˈteɪn] *v* 획득하다
[hoekdeukhada]
obvious [ˈɒbvɪəs] *adj* 분명한
[bunmyeonghan]
obviously [ˈɒbvɪəslɪ] *adv* 분명하게
[bunmyeonghage]
occasion [əˈkeɪʒən] *n* 기회 [gihoe]
occasional [əˈkeɪʒənᵊl] *adj* 가끔의
[gakkeumui]
occasionally [əˈkeɪʒənəlɪ] *adv* 때때로
[ttaettaero]
occupation [ˌɒkjʊˈpeɪʃən] *n* (invasion)
점령 [jeomnyeong], (work) 직업
[jigeop]
occupy [ˈɒkjʊˌpaɪ] *v* 점유하다
[jeomyuhada]
occur [əˈkɜː] *v* 발생하다 [balsaenghada]
occurrence [əˈkʌrəns] *n* 발생
[balsaeng]
ocean [ˈəʊʃən] *n* 대양 [daeyang]; **Arctic
Ocean** *n* 북극해 [bukgeukhae]; **Indian
Ocean** *n* 인도양 [indoyang]
Oceania [ˌəʊʃɪˈɑːnɪə] *n* 오세아니아
[oseania]
o'clock [əˈklɒk] *adv* **after eight o'clock**
여덟시 후에 [yeodeopsi hue]; **at three
o'clock** 세시에 [se sie]; **I'd like to
book a table for four people for
tonight at eight o'clock** 오늘 밤
여덟시 네 명 테이블을 예약하고 싶어요

[oneul bam yeodeolbsi ne myeong
teibeul-eul yeyaghago sip-eoyo]; **It's
one o'clock** 한시예요 [hansiyeyo]; **It's
six o'clock** 여섯시예요 [yeoseosiyeyo]
October [ɒkˈtəʊbə] *n* 10월 [sirwol]
octopus [ˈɒktəpəs] *n* 문어 [muneo]
odd [ɒd] *adj* 이상한 [isanghan]
odour [ˈəʊdə] *n* 악취 [akchwi]
of [ɒv; əv] *prep* ...의 [...ui] (속하다)
off [ɒf] *adv* 떨어져 [tteoreojyeo] ▷ *prep*...
에서 떨어져 [...eseo tteoreojyeo]; **time
off** *n* 휴식시간 [hyusiksigan]
offence [əˈfɛns] *n* 위반 [wiban]
offend [əˈfɛnd] *v* 위반하다 [wibanhada]
offensive [əˈfɛnsɪv] *adj* 불쾌하게 하는
[bulkwaehage haneun]
offer [ˈɒfə] *n* 제공 [jegong] ▷ *v* 제공하다
[jegonghada]; **special offer** *n* 특별할인
[teukbyeolharin]
office [ˈɒfɪs] *n* 사무실 [samusil];
booking office *n* 매표소 [maepyoso];
box office *n* 매표소 [maepyoso]; **head
office** *n* 본사 [bonsa]; **information
office** *n* 안내소 [annaeso];
left-luggage office *n* 수하물
임시보관소 [suhamul imsibogwanso];
lost-property office *n* 분실물 보관소
[bunsilmul bogwanso]; **office hours**
npl 근무 시간 [geunmu sigan]; **post
office** *n* 우체국 [ucheguk]; **registry
office** *n* 등기소 [deunggiso]; **ticket
office** *n* 매표소 [maepyoso]; **tourist
office** *n* 여행사 [yeohaengsa]; **How do
I get to your office?** 당신 사무실에
어떻게 가지요? [dangsin samusire
eotteoke gajiyo?]; **I work in an office**
사무실에서 일해요 [samusireseo
ilhaeyo]
officer [ˈɒfɪsə] *n* 장교 [janggyo];
customs officer *n* 세관원
[segwanwon]; **police officer** *n* 경찰관
[gyeongchalgwan]; **prison officer** *n*
교도관 [gyodogwan]
official [əˈfɪʃəl] *adj* 공식적인
[gongsikjeogin]
off-licence [ˈɒfˌlaɪsəns] *n* 주류판매
면허 [juryupanmae myeonheo]
off-peak [ˈɒfˌpiːk] *adv* 한산한 때에

[hansanhan ttae]

off-season [ˈɒfˌsiːzˀn] *adj* 철이 지난 [cheori jinan] ▷ *adv* 철이 지나서 [cheori jinaseo]

offside [ˈɒfˈsaɪd] *adj* 오프사이드의 [opeusaideuui]

often [ˈɒfˀn; ˈɒftˀn] *adv* 자주 [jaju] (빈번한); **How often are the buses to…?** … 가는 버스는 얼마나 자주 오나요? [… ganeun beoseuneun eolmana jaju onayo?]

oil [ɔɪl] *n* 기름 [gireum] ▷ *v* 기름을 바르다 [gireumeul bareuda]; **olive oil** *n* 올리브 기름 [ollibeu gireum]; **This stain is oil** 이 얼룩은 기름이에요 [i eollugeun gireumieyo]

oil refinery [ɔɪl rɪˈfaɪnərɪ] *n* 정유 공장 [jeongyu gongjang]

oil rig [ɔɪl rɪg] *n* 유정의 굴착장치 [yujeongui gulchakjangchi]

oil slick [ɔɪl slɪk] *n* 물 위의 기름층 [mul wiui gireumcheung]

oil well [ɔɪl wɛl] *n* 유정 [yujeong]

ointment [ˈɔɪntmənt] *n* 연고 [yeongo] (크림)

OK [ˌəʊˈkeɪ] *excl* 좋아! [joha!]

okay [ˌəʊˈkeɪ] *adj* 괜찮은 [gwaenchanheun]; **okay!** *excl* 좋아! [joha!]

old [əʊld] *adj* 오래된 [oraedoen]; **old-age pensioner** *n* 노령의 연금수령자 [noryeongui yeongeumsuryeongja]

old-fashioned [ˈəʊldˈfæʃənd] *adj* 구식의 [gusigui]

olive [ˈɒlɪv] *n* 올리브 [ollibeu]; **olive oil** *n* 올리브 기름 [ollibeu gireum]; **olive tree** *n* 올리브 나무 [ollibeu namu]

Oman [əʊˈmɑːn] *n* 오만 [oman] (국가)

omelette [ˈɒmlɪt] *n* 오믈렛 [omeullet]

on [ɒn] *adv* 위에 [wie] ▷ *prep* …의 위에 […ui wie]; **on behalf of** *n* 대신 [daesin]; **on time** *adj* 정기적인 [jeonggijeogin]

once [wʌns] *adv* 한번 [hanbeon]

one [wʌn] *number* 하나 [hana], (Sino-Korean) 일 [il] ▷ *pron* 한 사람 [han saram]; **no one** *pron* 아무도… 않다(없다) [amudo… anta(eopda)]

one-off [ˈwʌnɒf] *n* 1회성의 것 [han

hoeseongui geot]

onion [ˈʌnjən] *n* 양파 [yangpa]; **spring onion** *n* 실파 [silpa]

online [ˈɒnˌlaɪn] *adj* 온라인의 [ollainui] ▷ *adv* 온라인으로 [ollaineuro]

onlooker [ˈɒnˌlʊkə] *n* 방관자 [banggwanja]

only [ˈəʊnlɪ] *adj* 유일한 [yuilhan] ▷ *adv* 다만…뿐 [daman…ppun]

open [ˈəʊpˀn] *adj* 열린 [yeollin] ▷ *v* 열다 [yeolda]; **opening hours** *npl* 영업 시간 [yeongeop sigan]

opera [ˈɒpərə] *n* 오페라 [opera]; **soap opera** *n* 연속극 [yeonsokgeuk]; **What's on tonight at the opera?** 오늘 밤 무슨 오페라를 공연해요? [oneul bam museun operareul gongyeonhaeyo?]

operate [ˈɒpəˌreɪt] *v* (to function) 작동하다 [jakdonghada], (to perform surgery) 수술하다 [susulhada]

operating theatre [ˈɒpəˌreɪtɪŋ ˈθɪətə] *n* 수술실 [susulsil]

operation [ˌɒpəˈreɪʃən] *n* (surgery) 수술 [susul], (undertaking) 시행 [sihaeng]

operator [ˈɒpəˌreɪtə] *n* 운전자 [unjeonja]

opinion [əˈpɪnjən] *n* 의견 [uigyeon]; **opinion poll** *n* 여론조사 [yeoronjosa]; **public opinion** *n* 여론 [yeoron]

opponent [əˈpəʊnənt] *n* 대항자 [daehangja]

opportunity [ˌɒpəˈtjuːnɪtɪ] *n* 기회 [gihoe]

oppose [əˈpəʊz] *v* 반대하다 [bandaehada]

opposed [əˈpəʊzd] *adj* 반대한 [bandaehan]

opposing [əˈpəʊzɪŋ] *adj* 반대하는 [bandaehaneun]

opposite [ˈɒpəzɪt; -sɪt] *adj* 반대쪽의 [bandaejjogui] ▷ *adv* 반대편에 [bandaepyeone] ▷ *prep* …의 맞은편에 […ui majeunpyeone]

opposition [ˌɒpəˈzɪʃən] *n* 반대 [bandae]

optician [ɒpˈtɪʃən] *n* 안경사 [angyeongsa]

optimism ['ɒptɪˌmɪzəm] n 낙천주의 [nakcheonjuui]

optimist ['ɒptɪˌmɪst] n 낙천가 [nakcheonga]

optimistic [ɒptɪ'mɪstɪk] adj 낙천적인 [nakcheonjeogin]

option ['ɒpʃən] n 선택권 [seontaekgwon]

optional ['ɒpʃənəl] adj 자유선택의 [jayuseontaegui]

opt out [ɒpt aʊt] v 탈퇴하다 [taltoehada]

or [ɔː] conj 또는 [ttoneun]; **either... or** conj ...거나 또는...거나 [...geona ttoneun...geona]

oral ['ɔːrəl; 'ɒrəl] adj 구두의 [guduui] ▷ n 구술시험 [gusulsiheom]

orange ['ɒrɪndʒ] adj 오렌지색의 [orenjisaegui] ▷ n 오렌지 [orenji]; **orange juice** n 오렌지 주스 [orenji juseu]

orchard ['ɔːtʃəd] n 과수원 [gwasuwon]

orchestra ['ɔːkɪstrə] n 관현악단 [gwanhyeonakdan]

orchid ['ɔːkɪd] n 난초 [nancho]

ordeal [ɔː'diːl] n 시련 [siryeon]

order ['ɔːdə] n 명령 [myeongnyeong] ▷ v (command) 명령하다 [myeongnyeonghada], (request) 주문하다 [jumunhada]; **order form** n 주문서 [jumunseo]; **postal order** n 우편환 [upyeonhwan]; **standing order** n 정기구독 [jeonggigudok]

ordinary ['ɔːdənrɪ] adj 보통의 [botongui]

oregano [ˌɒrɪ'gɑːnəʊ] n 오레가노 [oregano]

organ ['ɔːgən] n (body part) 기관 [gigwan] (신체부분), (music) 오르간 [oreugan]; **mouth organ** n 하모니카 [hamonika]

organic [ɔː'gænɪk] adj 유기의 [yuguui]

organism ['ɔːgəˌnɪzəm] n 유기체 [yugiche]

organization [ˌɔːgənaɪ'zeɪʃən] n 조직 [jojik]

organize ['ɔːgəˌnaɪz] v 조직하다 [jojikhada]

organizer ['ɔːgəˌnaɪzə] n **personal organizer** n 개인용 일정 수첩 [gaeinyong iljeong sucheop]

orgasm ['ɔːgæzəm] n 오르가슴 [oreugaseum]

Orient ['ɔːrɪənt] n 동양 [dongyang]

oriental [ˌɔːrɪ'ɛntəl] adj 동양의 [dongyangui]

origin ['ɒrɪdʒɪn] n 근원 [geunwon]

original [ə'rɪdʒɪnəl] adj 본래의 [bollaeui]

originally [ə'rɪdʒɪnəlɪ] adv 원래는 [wollaeneun]

ornament ['ɔːnəmənt] n 장식품 [jangsikpum]

orphan ['ɔːfən] n 고아 [goa]

ostrich ['ɒstrɪtʃ] n 타조 [tajo]

other ['ʌðə] adj 다른 [dareun]; **Do you have any others?** 다른 방 있어요? [dareun bang isseoyo?]

otherwise ['ʌðəˌwaɪz] adv 그렇지 않으면 [geureochi anheumyeon] ▷ conj 그렇지 않으면 [geureochi anheumyeon]

otter ['ɒtə] n 수달 [sudal]

ounce [aʊns] n 온스 [onseu]

our [aʊə] adj 우리의 [uriui]

ours [aʊəz] pron 우리 것 [uri geot]

ourselves [aʊə'sɛlvz] pron 우리 자신 [uri jasin]

out [aʊt] adj 밖의 [bakkui] ▷ adv 밖으로 [bakkeuro]

outbreak ['aʊtˌbreɪk] n 돌발 [dolbal]

outcome ['aʊtˌkʌm] n 결과 [gyeolgwa]

outdoor ['aʊt'dɔː] adj 옥외의 [ogoeui]

outdoors [ˌaʊt'dɔːz] adv 옥외에서 [ogoeeseo]

outfit ['aʊtˌfɪt] n 의상 [uisang]

outgoing ['aʊtˌgəʊɪŋ] adj 사교적인 [sagyojeogin]

outing ['aʊtɪŋ] n 소풍 [sopung]

outline ['aʊtˌlaɪn] n 개요 [gaeyo]

outlook ['aʊtˌlʊk] n 전망 [jeonmang]

out-of-date ['aʊtɒv'deɪt] adj 구식인 [gusigin]

out-of-doors ['aʊtɒv'dɔːz] adv 옥외에서 [ogoeeseo]

outrageous [aʊt'reɪdʒəs] adj 무례한

[muryehan]

outset ['aʊt‚sɛt] *n* 시작 [sijak]

outside *adj* ['aʊt‚saɪd] 외부의 [oebuui]
▷ *adv* [‚aʊt'saɪd] 바깥쪽으로
[bakkatjjogeuro] ▷ *n* ['aʊt'saɪd] 외부
[oebu] ▷ *prep*...의 밖에 [...ui bakke]

outsize ['aʊt‚saɪz] *adj* 특대의
[teukdaeui]

outskirts ['aʊt‚skɜːts] *npl* 변두리
[byeonduri]

outspoken [‚aʊt'spəʊkən] *adj* 솔직한
[soljikhan]

outstanding [‚aʊt'stændɪŋ] *adj* 현저한
[hyeonjeohan]

oval ['əʊvəl] *adj* 타원형의
[tawonhyeongui]

ovary ['əʊvərɪ] *n* 난소 [nanso]

oven ['ʌvən] *n* 오븐 [obeun];
microwave oven *n* 전자레인지
[jeonjareinji]; **oven glove** *n* 오븐용
장갑 [obeunyong janggap]

ovenproof ['ʌvən‚pruːf] *adj* 오븐에
넣어도 되는 [obeune neoheodo
doeneun]

over ['əʊvə] *adj* 위의 [wiui] ▷ *prep*... 위에
[... wie]

overall [‚əʊvər'ɔːl] *adv* 전반적으로
[jeonbanjeogeuro]

overalls [‚əʊvə'ɔːlz] *npl* 작업복
[jageopbok]

overcast ['əʊvə‚kɑːst] *adj* 잔뜩 흐린
[jantteuk heurin]

overcharge [‚əʊvə'tʃɑːdʒ] *v* 바가지
씌우다 [bagaji ssuiuda]

overcoat ['əʊvə‚kəʊt] *n* 외투 [oetu]

overcome [‚əʊvə'kʌm] *v* 극복하다
[geukbokhada]

overdone [‚əʊvə'dʌn] *adj* 도가 지나친
[doga jinachin]

overdose ['əʊvə‚dəʊs] *n* 과다 복용
[gwada bogyong]

overdraft ['əʊvə‚drɑːft] *n* 당좌 대월
[dangjwa daewol]

overdrawn [‚əʊvə'drɔːn] *adj* 차월한
[chawolhan]

overdue [‚əʊvə'djuː] *adj* 연체된
[yeonchedoen]

overestimate [‚əʊvər'ɛstɪ‚meɪt] *v*
과대 평가하다 [gwadae
pyeonggahada]

overheads ['əʊvə‚hɛdz] *npl* 경상비
[gyeongsangbi]

overlook [‚əʊvə'lʊk] *v* 간과하다
[gangwahada]

overnight ['əʊvə‚naɪt] *adv* **Can I park
here overnight?** 여기 밤새 주차해도
될까요? [yeogi bamsae juchahaedo
doelkkayo?]; **Can we camp here
overnight?** 여기서 밤새 야영해도
될까요? [yurkisur bamsae
yayeonghaedo doelkkayo?]; **Do I have
to stay overnight?** 오늘 밤에 여기
있어야 하나요? [neul bam-e yeogi
iss-eoya hanayo?]

overrule [‚əʊvə'ruːl] *v* 기각하다
[gigakhada]

overseas [‚əʊvə'siːz] *adv* 해외로
[haeoero]

oversight ['əʊvə‚saɪt] *n* (mistake)
부주의 [bujuui], (supervision) 감독
[gamdok]

oversleep [‚əʊvə'sliːp] *v* 너무 자다
[neomu jada]

overtake [‚əʊvə'teɪk] *v* 추월하다
[chuwolhada]

overtime ['əʊvə‚taɪm] *n* 초과 근무
시간 [chogwa geunmu sigan]

overweight [‚əʊvə'weɪt] *adj* 중량
초과의 [jungnyang chogwaui]

owe [əʊ] *v* 빚지다 [bitjida]

owing to ['əʊɪŋ tuː] *prep*... 때문에 [...
ttaemune]

owl [aʊl] *n* 올빼미 [olppaemi]

own [əʊn] *adj* 자기 자신의 [jagi jasinui]
▷ *v* 소유하다 [soyuhada]

owner ['əʊnə] *n* 소유자 [soyuja]

own up [əʊn ʌp] *v* 인정하다
[injeonghada]

oxygen ['ɒksɪdʒən] *n* 산소 [sanso]
(원소)

oyster ['ɔɪstə] *n* 굴 [gul]

ozone ['əʊzəʊn; əʊ'zəʊn] *n* 오존 [ojon];
ozone layer *n* 오존층 [ojoncheung]

p

PA [pi: eɪ] *abbr* 비서 [biseo]
pace [peɪs] *n* 보 [bo]
pacemaker ['peɪsˌmeɪkə] *n* 맥박 조정기 [maekbak jojeonggi]
Pacific [pə'sɪfɪk] *n* 태평양 [taepyeongyang]
pack [pæk] *n* 짐 [jim] ▷ *v* 포장하다 [pojanghada]; **I need to pack now** 지금 짐을 싸야 해요 [jigeum jimeul ssaya haeyo]
package ['pækɪdʒ] *n* 포장 [pojang]; **package holiday** *n* 패키지 휴가 [paekiji hyuga]; **package tour** *n* 패키지 여행 [paekiji yeohaeng]
packaging ['pækɪdʒɪŋ] *n* 포장 [pojang]
packed [pækt] *adj* 꽉 찬 [kkwak chan]; **packed lunch** *n* 도시락 [dosirak]
packet ['pækɪt] *n* 작은 꾸러미 [jageun kkureomi]
pad [pæd] *n* 패드 [paedeu]
paddle ['pæd³l] *n* 노 [no] ▷ *v* 젓다 [jeotda]
padlock ['pædˌlɒk] *n* 맹꽁이 자물쇠 [maengkkongi jamulsoe]
paedophile ['piːdəʊˌfaɪl] *n* 아동에 대한 이상 성욕자 [adonge daehan isang seongyokja]

page [peɪdʒ] *n* 쪽 [jjok] ▷ *v* 부르다 [bureuda]; **home page** *n* 홈페이지 [hompeiji]; **Yellow Pages®** *npl* 옐로우 페이지스 [yellou peijiseu]
pager ['peɪdʒə] *n* 삐삐 [ppippi]
paid [peɪd] *adj* 유급인 [yugeubin]
pail [peɪl] *n* 양동이 [yangdongi]
pain [peɪn] *n* 고통 [gotong]; **back pain** *n* 요통 [yotong]
painful ['peɪnfʊl] *adj* 아픈 [apeun]
painkiller ['peɪnˌkɪlə] *n* 진통제 [jintongje]
paint [peɪnt] *n* 페인트 [peinteu] ▷ *v* 그리다 [geurida]
paintbrush ['peɪntˌbrʌʃ] *n* 그림붓 [geurimbut]
painter ['peɪntə] *n* 화가 [hwaga]
painting ['peɪntɪŋ] *n* 그림 [geurim]
pair [pɛə] *n* 한 쌍 [han ssang]
Pakistan [ˌpɑːkɪ'stɑːn] *n* 파키스탄 [pakiseutan]
Pakistani [ˌpɑːkɪ'stɑːnɪ] *adj* 파키스탄의 [pakiseutanui] ▷ *n* 파키스탄 사람 [pakiseutan saram]
pal [pæl] *n* 친구 [chingu]
palace ['pælɪs] *n* 궁전 [gungjeon]
pale [peɪl] *adj* 창백한 [changbaekhan]
Palestine ['pælɪˌstaɪn] *n* 팔레스타인 [palleseutain]
Palestinian [ˌpælɪ'stɪnɪən] *adj* 팔레스타인의 [palleseutainui] ▷ *n* 팔레스타인 사람 [palleseutain saram]
palm [pɑːm] *n* (*part of hand*) 손바닥 [sonbadak], (*tree*) 야자나무 [yajanamu]
pamphlet ['pæmflɪt] *n* 소책자 [sochaekja]
pan [pæn] *n* 팬 [paen] (요리); **frying pan** *n* 프라이팬 [peuraipaen]
Panama [ˌpænə'mɑː; 'pænəˌmɑː] *n* 파나마 [panama]
pancake ['pænˌkeɪk] *n* 팬케이크 [paenkeikeu]
panda ['pændə] *n* 팬더 [paendeo]
panic ['pænɪk] *n* 공포 [gongpo] ▷ *v* 공포에 사로잡히다 [gongpoe sarojaphida]
panther ['pænθə] *n* 흑표범 [heukpyobeom]

panties ['pæntɪz] npl 팬티 [paenti]
pantomime ['pæntə,maɪm] n 무언극 [mueongeuk]
pants [pænts] npl 팬티 [paenti]
paper ['peɪpə] n 종이 [jongi]; **paper round** n 신문배달 [sinmunbaedal]; **scrap paper** n 메모 용지 [memo yongji]; **toilet paper** n 화장지 [hwajangji]; **tracing paper** n 투사지 [tusaji]; **wrapping paper** n 포장지 [pojangji]; **writing paper** n 필기용지 [pilgiyongji]
paperback ['peɪpə,bæk] n 페이퍼 백 [peipeo baek]
paperclip ['peɪpə,klɪp] n 종이클립 [jongikeullip]
paperweight ['peɪpə,weɪt] n 서진 [seojin]
paperwork ['peɪpə,wɜːk] n 문서작업 [munseojageop]
paprika ['pæprɪkə; pæ'priː-] n 파프리카 [papeurika]
paracetamol [,pærə'siːtə,mɒl; -'sɛtə-] n **I'd like some paracetamol** 파라세타몰 주세요 [parasetamol juseyo]
parachute ['pærə,ʃuːt] n 낙하산 [nakhasan]
parade [pə'reɪd] n 행렬 [haengnyeol]
paradise ['pærə,daɪs] n 낙원 [nagwon]
paraffin ['pærəfɪn] n 등유 [deungyu]
paragraph ['pærə,grɑːf; -,græf] n 문단 [mundan]
Paraguay ['pærə,gwaɪ] n 파라과이 [paragwai]
Paraguayan [,pærə'gwaɪən] adj 파라과이의 [paragwaiui] ▷ n 파라과이 사람 [paragwai saram]
parallel ['pærə,lɛl] adj 평행인 [pyeonghaengin]
paralysed ['pærə,laɪzd] adj 마비된 [mabidoen]
paramedic [,pærə'mɛdɪk] n 준의료 종사자 [junuiryo jongsaja]
parcel ['pɑːsᵊl] n 소포 [sopo]; **How much is it to send this parcel?** 이 소포 보내는 데 얼마예요? [i sopo bonaeneun de eolmayeyo?]; **I'd like to**

send this parcel 이 소포를 보내려고요 [i soporeul bonaeryeogoyo]
pardon ['pɑːdᵊn] n 용서 [yongseo]
parent ['pɛərənt] n 아버지 [abeoji]; **parents** npl 부모 [bumo]; **single parent** n 홀부모 [holbumo]
parish ['pærɪʃ] n 교구 [gyogu]
park [pɑːk] n 공원 [gongwon] (자연) ▷ v 주차하다 [juchahada]; **car park** n 주차장 [juchajang]; **national park** n 국립 공원 [gungnip gongwon]; **theme park** n 테마 공원 [tema gongwon]; **Is there a play park near here?** 이 근처에 놀이 공원이 있어요? [i geuncheoe nori gongwoni isseoyo?]
parking [pɑːkɪŋ] n 주차 [jucha]; **parking meter** n 주차요금 징수기 [juchayogeum jingsugi]; **parking ticket** n 주차위반 딱지 [juchawiban ttakji]; **Do I need to buy a car-parking ticket?** 주차권을 사야합니까? [juchagwoneul sayahamnikka?]; **Do you have change for the parking meter?** 주차 미터기에 넣을 잔돈 있으세요? [jucha miteogie neoheul jandon isseuseyo?]; **The parking meter is broken** 주차 미터기가 고장났어요 [jucha miteogiga gojangnasseoyo]
parliament ['pɑːləmənt] n 국회 [gukhoe]
parole [pə'rəʊl] n 가석방 [gaseokbang]
parrot ['pærət] n 앵무새 [aengmusae]
parsley ['pɑːslɪ] n 파슬리 [paseulli]
parsnip ['pɑːsnɪp] n 파스닙 [paseunip]
part [pɑːt] n 부분 [bubun]; **spare part** n 예비 부품 [yebi bupum]
partial ['pɑːʃəl] adj 부분적인 [bubunjeogin]
participate [pɑː'tɪsɪ,peɪt] v 참가하다 [chamgahada]
particular [pə'tɪkjʊlə] adj 특유의 [teugyuui]
particularly [pə'tɪkjʊləlɪ] adv 특히 [teukhi]
parting ['pɑːtɪŋ] n 출발 [chulbal]
partly ['pɑːtlɪ] adv 부분적으로

[bubunjeogeuro]

partner ['pɑːtnə] n 파트너 [pateuneo];
I have a partner 파트너가 있어요
[pateuneoga isseoyo]; **This is my
partner** 제 파트너예요 [je
pateuneoyeyo]

partridge ['pɑːtrɪdʒ] n 자고 [jago]

part-time ['pɑːtˌtaɪm] adj 시간제의
[siganjeui] ▷ adv 시간제로 [siganjero]

part with [pɑːt wɪð] v 헤어지다
[heeojida]

party ['pɑːtɪ] n (group) 단체 [danche],
(social gathering) 파티 [pati] ▷ v 파티를
열다 [patireul yeolda]; **dinner party** n
만찬회 [manchanhoe]; **search party** n
수색대 [susaekdae]

pass [pɑːs] n (in mountains) 오솔길
[osolgil], (meets standard) 합격
[hapgyeok], (permit) 허가 [heoga] ▷ v
(an exam) 합격하다 [hapgyeokhada]
▷ vi 통과하다 [tonggwahada];
boarding pass n 탑승권
[tapseunggwon]; **ski pass** n 스키장
시즌권 [seukijang sijeungwon]

passage ['pæsɪdʒ] n (musical) 악절
[akjeol], (route) 통로 [tongno]

passenger ['pæsɪndʒə] n 승객
[seunggaek]

passion ['pæʃən] n 열정 [yeoljeong];
passion fruit n 시계풀의 열매
[sigyepurui yeolmae]

passive ['pæsɪv] adj 수동적인
[sudongjeogin]

pass out [pɑːs aʊt] v 의식을 잃다
[uisigeul irta]

Passover ['pɑːsˌəʊvə] n 유월절
[yuwoljeol]

passport ['pɑːspɔːt] n 여권 [yeogwon]
(비자); **passport control** n 여권 검사
[yeogwon geomsa]; **Here is my
passport** 제 여권이에요 [je
yeogwonieyo]; **I've forgotten my
passport** 여권을 깜빡 잊었어요
[yeogwoneul kkamppak ijeosseoyo];
I've lost my passport 여권을
잃어버렸어요 [yeogwoneul
ireobeoryeosseoyo]; **My passport has
been stolen** 여권을 도둑맞았어요

[yeogwoneul dodungmajasseoyo];
Please give me my passport back 제
여권을 돌려주세요 [je yeogwoneul
dollyeojuseyo]; **The children are on
this passport** 이 여권에는 아이들이
등록되어 있어요 [i yeogwoneneun
aideuri deungnokdoeeo isseoyo]

password ['pɑːsˌwɜːd] n 암호 [amho]

past [pɑːst] adj 과거의 [gwageoui] ▷ n
과거 [gwageo] ▷ prep...을 지나서 [...eul
jinaseo]

pasta ['pæstə] n 파스타 [paseuta]; **I'd
like pasta as a starter** 전채요리로
파스타를 주세요 [jeonchaeyoriro
paseutareul juseyo]

paste [peɪst] n 풀 [pul]

pasteurized ['pæstəˌraɪzd] adj
저온살균한 [jeoonsalgyunhan]

pastime ['pɑːsˌtaɪm] n 오락 [orak]

pastry ['peɪstrɪ] n 페이스트리
[peiseuteuri]; **puff pastry** n 퍼프
페이스트리 [peopeu peiseuteuri];
shortcrust pastry n 쇼트크러스트
페이스트리 [syoteukeureoseuteu
peiseuteuri]

patch [pætʃ] n 깁는 헝겊 [gimneun
heonggeop]

patched [pætʃt] adj 기운 [giun]
(바느질)

path [pɑːθ] n 길 [gil]; **cycle path** n
자전거 도로 [jajeongeo doro]; **Keep to
the path** 길에서 벗어나지 마세요
[gireseo beoseonaji maseyo]; **Where
does this path lead?** 이 길은 어디로
이어지나요? [i gireun eodiro
ieojinayo?]

pathetic [pə'θɛtɪk] adj 측은한
[cheugeunhan]

patience ['peɪʃəns] n 인내 [innae]

patient ['peɪʃənt] adj 인내심이 있는
[innaesimi inneun] ▷ n 환자 [hwanja]

patio ['pætɪˌəʊ] n 테라스 [teraseu]

patriotic ['pætrɪəˌtɪk] adj 애국적인
[aegukjeogin]

patrol [pə'trəʊl] n 순찰 [sunchal];
patrol car n 순찰차 [sunchalcha]

pattern ['pætən] n 무늬 [munui]

pause [pɔːz] n 일시중지 [ilsijungji]

pavement ['peɪvmənt] n 인도 [indo]
pavilion [pə'vɪljən] n 별관 [byeolgwan]
paw [pɔ:] n 동물의 발 [dongmurui bal]
pawnbroker ['pɔ:n,brəʊkə] n 전당포 [jeondangpo]
pay [peɪ] n 지급 [jigeup] ▷ v 지불하다 [jibulhada]; **sick pay** n 병가 중 지급되는 급여 [byeongga jung jigeupdoeneun geubyeo]
payable ['peɪəbəl] adj 지급해야 할 [jigeuphaeya hal]
pay back [peɪ bæk] v 변제하다 [byeonjehada]
payment ['peɪmənt] n 지급 [jigeup]
payphone ['peɪ,fəʊn] n 공중전화 [gongjungjeonhwa]
peace [pi:s] n 평화 [pyeonghwa]
peaceful ['pi:sfʊl] adj 평화로운 [pyeonghwaroun]
peach [pi:tʃ] n 복숭아 [boksunga]
peacock ['pi:,kɒk] n 공작새 [gongjaksae]
peak [pi:k] n 뾰족한 끝 [ppyojokhan kkeut]; **peak hours** npl 러시아워 [reosiawo]
peanut ['pi:,nʌt] n 땅콩 [ttangkong]; **peanut allergy** n 땅콩 알레르기 [ttangkong allereugi]; **peanut butter** n 땅콩 버터 [ttangkong beoteo]; **Does that contain peanuts?** 땅콩이 들어 있나요? [ttangkongi deureo innayo?]; **I'm allergic to peanuts** 땅콩 알레르기가 있어요 [ttangkong allereugiga isseoyo]
pear [peə] n 배 [bae]
pearl [pɜ:l] n 진주 [jinju]
peas [pi:s] npl 완두콩 [wandukong]
peat [pi:t] n 토탄 [totan]
pebble ['pɛbəl] n 조약돌 [joyakdol]
peculiar [pɪ'kju:lɪə] adj 특유한 [teugyuhan]
pedal ['pɛdəl] n 페달 [pedal]
pedestrian [pɪ'dɛstrɪən] n 보행자 [bohaengja]; **pedestrian crossing** n 횡단 보도 [hoengdan bodo]; **pedestrian precinct** n 보행자 전용 구역 [bohaengja jeonyong guyeok]

pedestrianized [pɪ'dɛstrɪə,naɪzd] adj 보행자 전용의 [bohaengja jeonyongui]
pedigree ['pɛdɪ,gri:] adj 혈통의 [hyeoltongui]
peel [pi:l] n 껍질 [kkeopjil] ▷ v 껍질을 벗기다 [kkeopjireul beotgida]
peg [pɛg] n 못 [mot]
Pekinese [,pi:kɪŋ'i:z] n 발바리 [balbari]
pelican ['pɛlɪkən] n 펠리컨 [pellikeon]; **pelican crossing** n 보행자가 신호등을 조작하는 횡단보도 [bohaengjaga sinhodeungeul jojakhaneun hoengdanbodo]
pellet ['pɛlɪt] n 작은 공 [jageun gong]
pelvis ['pɛlvɪs] n 골반 [golban]
pen [pɛn] n 펜 [pen]; **ballpoint pen** n 볼펜 [bolpen]; **felt-tip pen** n 펠트펜 [pelteupen]; **fountain pen** n 만년필 [mannyeonpil]; **Do you have a pen I could borrow?** 펜을 빌려 주시겠어요? [peneul billyeo jusigesseoyo?]
penalize ['pi:nə,laɪz] v 처벌하다 [cheobeolhada]
penalty ['pɛnəltɪ] n 처벌 [cheobeol]
pencil ['pɛnsəl] n 연필 [yeonpil]; **pencil case** n 필통 [piltong]; **pencil sharpener** n 연필깎이 [yeonpilkkakki]
pendant ['pɛndənt] n 펜던트 [pendeonteu]
penfriend ['pɛn,frɛnd] n 펜팔 [penpal]
penguin ['pɛŋgwɪn] n 펭귄 [penggwin]
penicillin [,pɛnɪ'sɪlɪn] n 페니실린 [penisillin]
peninsula [pɪ'nɪnsjʊlə] n 반도 [bando]
penknife ['pɛn,naɪf] n 펜나이프 [pennaipeu]
penny ['pɛnɪ] n 페니 [peni]
pension ['pɛnʃən] n 연금 [yeongeum]
pensioner ['pɛnʃənə] n 연금 수령자 [yeongeum suryeongja]; **old-age pensioner** n 노령의 연금수령자 [noryeongui yeongeumsuryeongja]
pentathlon [pɛn'tæθlən] n 오종 경기 [ojong gyeonggi]
penultimate [pɪ'nʌltɪmɪt] adj 어미에서 두 번째(음절)의 [eomieseo du beonjjae(eumjeol)ui]
people ['pi:pəl] (**person** ['pɜ:sən]) npl

사람들 [saramdeul]

pepper ['pɛpə] *n* 후추 [huchu]

peppermill ['pɛpə‚mɪl] *n* 후추 분쇄통 [huchu bunswaetong]

peppermint ['pɛpə‚mɪnt] *n* 서양박하 [seoyangbakha]

per [pɜː; pə] *prep* ...당 [...dang] (각각); **per cent** *adv* 퍼센트 [peosenteu]

percentage [pə'sɛntɪdʒ] *n* 백분율 [baekbunyul]

percussion [pə'kʌʃən] *n* 타격 [tagyeok]

perfect ['pɜːfɪkt] *adj* 완벽한 [wanbyeokhan]

perfection [pə'fɛkʃən] *n* 완벽 [wanbyeok]

perfectly ['pɜːfɪktlɪ] *adv* 완벽하게 [wanbyeokhage]

perform [pə'fɔːm] *v* 수행하다 [suhaenghada]

performance [pə'fɔːməns] *n (artistic)* 수행 [suhaeng], *(functioning)* 수행 [suhaeng]

perfume ['pɜːfjuːm] *n* 향수 [hyangsu]

perhaps [pə'hæps; præps] *adv* 아마 [ama]

period ['pɪərɪəd] *n* 기간 [gigan]; **trial period** *n* 시용기간 [siyonggigan]

perjury ['pɜːdʒərɪ] *n* 위증죄 [wijeungjoe]

perm [pɜːm] *n* 파마 [pama]

permanent ['pɜːmənənt] *adj* 영구적인 [yeonggujeogin]

permanently ['pɜːmənəntlɪ] *adv* 영구히 [yeongguhi]

permission [pə'mɪʃən] *n* 허락 [heorak]

permit *n* ['pɜːmɪt] 허가증 [heogajeung] ▷ *v* [pə'mɪt] 허가증 [heogajeung]; **work permit** *n* 노동허가증 [nodongheogajeung]

persecute ['pɜːsɪ‚kjuːt] *v* 박해하다 [bakhaehada]

persevere [‚pɜːsɪ'vɪə] *v* 인내하다 [innaehada]

Persian ['pɜːʃən] *adj* 페르시아의 [pereusiaui]

persistent [pə'sɪstənt] *adj* 지속적인 [jisokjeogin]

person ['pɜːsən] **(people** ['piːpəl]**)** *n* 사람 [saram]

personal ['pɜːsənəl] *adj* 개인의 [gaeinui]; **personal assistant** *n* 비서 [biseo]; **personal organizer** *n* 개인용 일정 수첩 [gaeinyong iljeong sucheop]; **personal stereo** *n* 휴대 스테레오 [hyudae seutereo]

personality [‚pɜːsə'nælɪtɪ] *n* 성격 [seonggyeok]

personally ['pɜːsənəlɪ] *adv* 개인적으로 [gaeinjeogeuro]

personnel [‚pɜːsə'nɛl] *n* 직원 [jigwon]

perspective [pə'spɛktɪv] *n* 시각 [sigak]

perspiration [‚pɜːspə'reɪʃən] *n* 땀 [ttam]

persuade [pə'sweɪd] *v* 설득하다 [seoldeukhada]

persuasive [pə'sweɪsɪv] *adj* 설득력 있는 [seoldeungnyeok inneun]

Peru [pə'ruː] *n* 페루 [peru]

Peruvian [pə'ruːvɪən] *adj* 페루의 [peruui] ▷ *n* 페루 사람 [peru saram]

pessimist ['pɛsɪ‚mɪst] *n* 비관주의자 [bigwanjuuija]

pessimistic ['pɛsɪ‚mɪstɪk] *adj* 비관적인 [bigwanjeogin]

pest [pɛst] *n* 해충 [haechung]

pester ['pɛstə] *v* 괴롭히다 [goerophida]

pesticide ['pɛstɪ‚saɪd] *n* 살충제 [salchungje]

pet [pɛt] *n* 애완 동물 [aewan dongmul]

petition [pɪ'tɪʃən] *n* 진정서 [jinjeongseo]

petrified ['pɛtrɪ‚faɪd] *adj* 놀라서 멍해진 [nollaseo meonghaejin]

petrol ['pɛtrəl] *n* 휘발유 [hwiballyu]; **petrol station** *n* 주유소 [juyuso]; **petrol tank** *n* 휘발유 탱크 [hwiballyu taengkeu]; **unleaded petrol** *n* 무연 휘발유 [muyeon hwiballyu]

pewter ['pjuːtə] *n* 백랍 [baengnap]

pharmacist ['fɑːməsɪst] *n* 약사 [yaksa]

pharmacy ['fɑːməsɪ] *n* 조제 [joje]

PhD [piː eɪtʃ diː] *n* 박사 [baksa]

pheasant ['fɛzənt] *n* 꿩 [kkwong]

philosophy [fɪˈlɒsəfɪ] n 철학 [cheolhak]

phobia [ˈfəʊbɪə] n 공포증 [gongpojeung]

phone [fəʊn] n 전화 [jeonhwa] ▷ v 전화하다 [jeonhwahada]; **camera phone** n 카메라폰 [kamerapon]; **entry phone** n 현관 인터폰 [hyeongwan inteopon]; **mobile phone** n 휴대폰 [hyudaepon]; **phone back** v 다시 전화하다 [dasi jeonhwahada]; **phone bill** n 전화요금 고지서 [jeonhwayogeum gojiseo]; **phone number** n 전화번호 [jeonhwabeonho]; **smart phone** n 스마트 폰 [seumateu pon]; **Can I have your phone number?** 전화번호 좀 알려 주시겠어요? [jeonhwabeonho jom allyeo jusigesseoyo?]; **Can I phone from here?** 여기에서 전화를 해도 될까요? [yeogiseo jeonhwareul haedo doelkkayo?]; **Can I phone internationally from here?** 여기에서 국제 전화를 해도 될까요? [yeogiseo gukje jeonhwareul haedo doelkkayo?]; **Can I use your phone, please?** 전화 좀 쓸 수 있을까요? [jeonhwa jom sseul su isseulkkayo?]; **Do you sell international phone cards?** 국제 전화카드 파세요? [gukje jeonhwakadeu paseyo?]; **I must make a phone call** 전화를 해야 해요 [jeonhwareul haeya haeyo]; **I want to make a phone call** 전화를 하고 싶어요 [jeonhwareul hago sipeoyo]; **I'd like a twenty-five euro phone card** 25유로짜리 전화카드를 사고 싶어요 [ishibo yurojjari jeonhwakadeureul sago sipeoyo]; **I'd like some coins for the phone, please** 전화걸기 위해 동전을 바꾸고 싶어요 [jeonhwageolgi wihae dongjeoneul bakkugo sipeoyo]; **I'd like to phone my embassy** 대사관에 전화하고 싶어요 [daesagwane jeonhwahago sipeoyo]; **I'm having trouble with the phone** 전화에 문제가 있어요 [jeonhwae munjega isseoyo]; **May I phone home?** 집에 전화해도 될까요? [jibe jeonhwahaedo doelkkayo?]; **May I use your phone?** 전화 좀 쓸 수 있을까요? [jeonhwa jom sseul su isseulkkayo?]; **Where can I charge my mobile phone?** 어디에서 휴대전화를 충전할 수 있어요? [eodieseo hyudaejeonhwareul chungjeonhal su isseoyo?]; **Where can I make a phone call?** 어디에서 전화를 할 수 있을까요? [eodieseo jeonhwareul hal su isseulkkayo?]

phonebook [ˈfəʊnˌbʊk] n 전화번호부 [jeonhwabeonhobu]

phonebox [ˈfəʊnˌbɒks] n 공중 전화 [gongjung jeonhwa]

phonecall [ˈfəʊnˌkɔːl] n 전화 [jeonhwa]

phonecard [ˈfəʊnˌkɑːd] n 전화 카드 [jeonhwa kadeu]

photo [ˈfəʊtəʊ] n 사진 [sajin]; **photo album** n 사진 앨범 [sajin aelbeom]; **Can I download photos to here?** 여기로 사진을 다운로드할 수 있을까요? [yeogiro sajineul daunnodeuhal su isseulkkayo?]; **Can you put these photos on CD, please?** 이 사진들을 CD에 저장해 주시겠어요 [i sajindeureul CDe jeojanghae jusigesseoyo]; **How much do the photos cost?** 사진 요금은 얼마예요? [sajin yogeumeun eolmayeyo?]; **I'd like the photos glossy** 사진을 광택지로 뽑고 싶어요 [sajineul gwangtaekjiro ppopgo sipeoyo]; **I'd like the photos matt** 사진을 무광택지로 뽑고 싶어요 [sajineul mugwangtaekjiro ppopgo sipeoyo]; **When will the photos be ready?** 언제 사진이 준비될까요? [eonje sajini junbidoelkkayo?]

photocopier [ˈfəʊtəʊˌkɒpɪə] n 복사기 [boksagi]

photocopy [ˈfəʊtəʊˌkɒpɪ] n 복사 [boksa] ▷ v 복사하다 [boksahada]; **I'd like a photocopy of this, please** 이것을 복사하려고요 [igeoseul boksaharyeogoyo]; **Where can I get some photocopying done?** 어디에서

복사할 수 있을까요? [eodieseo boksahal su isseulkkayo?]

photograph ['fəʊtəɡrɑːf; -ɡræf] n 사진 [sajin] ▷ v 사진찍다 [sajinjjikda]

photographer [fə'tɒɡrəfə] n 사진사 [sajinsa]

photography [fə'tɒɡrəfɪ] n 사진술 [sajinsul]

phrase [freɪz] n 문구 [mungu]

phrasebook ['freɪz,bʊk] n 관용구 숙어집 [gwanyonggu sugeojip]

physical ['fɪzɪkəl] adj 신체의 [sincheui] ▷ n 신체검사 [sinchegeomsa]

physicist ['fɪzɪsɪst] n 물리학자 [mullihakja]

physics ['fɪzɪks] npl 물리학 [mullihak]

physiotherapist [,fɪzɪəʊ'θerəpɪst] n 물리치료사 [mullichiryosa]

physiotherapy [,fɪzɪəʊ'θerəpɪ] n 물리요법 [mulliyobeop]

pianist ['pɪənɪst] n 피아니스트 [pianiseuteu]

piano [pɪ'ænəʊ] n 피아노 [piano]

pick [pɪk] n 곡괭이 [gokgwaengi] ▷ v 선택하다 [seontaekhada]

pick on [pɪk ɒn] v 괴롭히다 [goerophida]

pick out [pɪk aʊt] v 고르다 [goreuda]

pickpocket ['pɪk,pɒkɪt] n 소매치기 [somaechigi]

pick up [pɪk ʌp] v 집어 올리다 [jibeo ollida]

picnic ['pɪknɪk] n 소풍 [sopung]

picture ['pɪktʃə] n 그림 [geurim]; **picture frame** n 그림틀 [geurimteul]

picturesque [,pɪktʃə'resk] adj 그림같은 [geurimgateun]

pie [paɪ] n 파이 [pai]; **apple pie** n 사과 파이 [sagwa pai]; **pie chart** n 원 그래프 [won geuraepeu]

piece [piːs] n 한 조각 [han jogak]

pier [pɪə] n 부두 [budu]

pierce [pɪəs] v 구멍뚫다 [gumeongtturta]

pierced [pɪəst] adj 구멍을 뚫은 [gumeongeul ttureun]

piercing ['pɪəsɪŋ] n 피어싱 [pieosing]

pig [pɪɡ] n 돼지 [dwaeji]; **guinea pig** n

(for experiment) 실험재료 [silheomjaeryo], (rodent) 기니피그 [ginipigeu]

pigeon ['pɪdʒɪn] n 비둘기 [bidulgi]

piggybank ['pɪɡɪ,bæŋk] n 돼지 저금통 [dwaeji jeogeumtong]

pigtail ['pɪɡ,teɪl] n 땋아늘인 머리 [ttahaneurin meori]

pile [paɪl] n 퇴적물 [toejeongmul]

piles [paɪlz] npl 치질 [chijil]

pile-up [paɪlʌp] n 연쇄 충돌 [yeonswae chungdol]

pilgrim ['pɪlɡrɪm] n 순례자 [sullyeja]

pilgrimage ['pɪlɡrɪmɪdʒ] n 순례 [sullye]

pill [pɪl] n 알약 [aryak]; **sleeping pill** n 수면제 [sumyeonje]

pillar ['pɪlə] n 기둥 [gidung]

pillow ['pɪləʊ] n 베개 [begae]; **Please bring me an extra pillow** 베개를 하나 더 갖다 주세요 [begaereul hana deo gatda juseyo]

pillowcase ['pɪləʊ,keɪs] n 베갯잇 [begaesit]

pilot ['paɪlət] n 비행사 [bihaengsa]; **pilot light** n 점화용 보조 버너 [jeomhwayong bojo beoneo]

pimple ['pɪmpəl] n 뾰루지 [ppyoruji]

pin [pɪn] n 핀 [pin]; **drawing pin** n 압정 [apjeong]; **rolling pin** n 밀방망이 [milbangmangi]; **safety pin** n 안전핀 [anjeonpin]; **I need a safety pin** 안전핀이 필요해요 [anjeonpini piryohaeyo]

pinafore ['pɪnə,fɔː] n 어린이용 앞치마 [eoriniyong apchima]

pinch [pɪntʃ] v 꼬집다 [kkojipda]

pine [paɪn] n 소나무 [sonamu]

pineapple ['paɪn,æpəl] n 파인애플 [painaepeul]

pink [pɪŋk] adj 분홍색의 [bunhongsaegui]

pint [paɪnt] n 파인트 [painteu]

pip [pɪp] n 씨 [ssi]

pipe [paɪp] n 도관 [dogwan]; **exhaust pipe** n 배기관 [baegigwan]

pipeline ['paɪp,laɪn] n 송유관 [songyugwan]

pirate ['paɪrɪt] *n* 해적 [haejeok]
Pisces ['paɪsiːz; 'pɪ-] *n* 물고기자리 [mulgogijari]
pistol ['pɪstəl] *n* 권총 [gwonchong]
piston ['pɪstən] *n* 피스톤 [piseuton]
pitch [pɪtʃ] *n* (sound) 음높이 [eumnopi], (sport) 경기장 [gyeonggijang] ▷ *v* 던지다 [deonjida]
pity ['pɪtɪ] *n* 동정 [dongjeong] ▷ *v* 불쌍히 여기다 [bulssanghi yeogida]
pixel ['pɪksəl] *n* 픽셀 [piksel]
pizza ['piːtsə] *n* 피자 [pija]
place [pleɪs] *n* 장소 [jangso] ▷ *v* 놓다 [nota]; **place of birth** *n* 출생지 [chulsaengji]
placement ['pleɪsmənt] *n* 배치 [baechi]
plain [pleɪn] *adj* 평평한 [pyeongpyeonghan] ▷ *n* 평야 [pyeongya]; **plain chocolate** *n* 향료가 안 든 초콜릿 [hyangnyoga an deun chokollit]
plait [plæt] *n* 땋은 것 [ttaheun geot]
plan [plæn] *n* 계획 [gyehoek] ▷ *v* 계획하다 [gyehoekhada]; **street plan** *n* 도로계획 [dorogyehoek]
plane [pleɪn] *n* (aeroplane) 비행기 [bihaenggi], (surface) 평면 [pyeongmyeon], (tool) 대패 [daepae]; **My plane leaves at...** 제가 탈 비행기는...에서 떠나요 [jega tal bihaenggineun...eseo tteonayo]
planet ['plænɪt] *n* 행성 [haengseong]
planning ['plænɪŋ] *n* 기획 [gihoek]
plant [plɑːnt] *n* 식물 [singmul], (site/ equipment) 공장 [gongjang] ▷ *v* 심다 [simda]; **plant pot** *n* 화분 [hwabun]; **pot plant** *n* 화분에 심는 화초 [hwabune simneun hwacho]
plaque [plæk; plɑːk] *n* 현판 [hyeonpan]
plaster ['plɑːstə] *n* (for wall) 회반죽 [hoebanjuk], (for wound) 반창고 [banchanggo]; **I'd like some plasters** 반창고 주세요 [banchanggo juseyo]
plastic ['plæstɪk; 'plɑːs-] *adj* 플라스틱의 [peullaseutigui] ▷ *n* 플라스틱 [peullaseutik]; **plastic bag** *n* 비닐봉지

[binilbongji]; **plastic surgery** *n* 성형외과 [seonghyeongoegwa]
plate [pleɪt] *n* 접시 [jeopsi]; **number plate** *n* 번호판 [beonhopan]
platform ['plætfɔːm] *n* 플랫폼 [peullaetpom]
platinum ['plætɪnəm] *n* 백금 [baekgeum]
play [pleɪ] *n* 연극 [yeongeuk] ▷ *v* (in sport) 경기를 하다 [gyeonggireul hada], (music) 연주를 하다 [yeonjureul hada]; **play truant** *v* 무단결석하다 [mudangyeolseokhada]; **playing card** *n* 카드 [kadeu]; **playing field** *n* 경기장 [gyeonggijang]; **Where can we go to see a play?** 어디에 가면 연극을 볼 수 있나요? [eodie gamyeon yeongeugeul bol su innayo?]
player ['pleɪə] *n* (instrumentalist) 연주자 [yeonjuja], (of sport) 선수 [seonsu]; **CD player** *n* CD 플레이어 [CD peulleieo]; **MP3 player** *n* MP3 플레이어 [MP3 peulleieo]; **MP4 player** *n* MP4 플레이어 [MP4 peulleieo]
playful ['pleɪfʊl] *adj* 재미있는 [jaemiinneun]
playground ['pleɪˌɡraʊnd] *n* 운동장 [undongjang]
playgroup ['pleɪˌɡruːp] *n* 사설 보육원 [saseol boyugwon]
PlayStation® ['pleɪˌsteɪʃən] *n* 플레이스테이션 [peulleiseuteisyeon]
playtime ['pleɪˌtaɪm] *n* 휴식시간 [hyusiksigan]
playwright ['pleɪˌraɪt] *n* 극작가 [geukjakga]
pleasant ['plɛzənt] *adj* 유쾌한 [yukwaehan]
please [pliːz] *excl* 제발! [jebal!]; **I'd like to check in, please** 탑승 수속을 하고 싶어요 [tapseung susogeul hago sipeoyo]
pleased [pliːzd] *adj* 기뻐하는 [gippeohaneun]
pleasure ['plɛʒə] *n* 기쁨 [gippeum]
plenty ['plɛntɪ] *n* 충분 [chungbun]
pliers ['plaɪəz] *npl* 펜치 [penchi]
plot [plɒt] *n* (piece of land) 작은 지면

[jageun jimyeon], *(secret plan)* 음모를 꾸미다 [eummoreul kkumida] ▷ v *(conspire)* 음모를 꾸미다 [eummoreul kkumida]

plough [plaʊ] n 쟁기 [jaenggi] ▷ v 쟁기로 갈다 [jaenggiro galda]

plug [plʌg] n 마개 [magae]; **spark plug** n 점화 플러그 [jeomhwa peulleogeu]

plughole ['plʌg,həʊl] n 마개 구멍 [magae gumeong]

plug in [plʌg ɪn] v 마개로 막다 [magaero makda]

plum [plʌm] n 서양자두 [seoyangjadu]

plumber ['plʌmə] n 배관공 [baegwangong]

plumbing ['plʌmɪŋ] n 배관 [baegwan]

plump [plʌmp] adj 통통한 [tongtonghan]

plunge [plʌndʒ] v 뛰어들다 [ttwieodeulda]

plural ['plʊərəl] n 복수 [boksu]

plus [plʌs] prep ...을 더하여 [...eul deohayeo]

plywood ['plaɪ,wʊd] n 합판 [happan]

p.m. [piː ɛm] abbr 오후 [ohu]; **Please come home by 11p.m.** 오후 열한시까지 집에 오세요 [ohu yeolhansikkaji jibe oseyo]

pneumonia [njuː'məʊnɪə] n 폐렴 [pyeryeom]

poached [pəʊtʃt] adj *(caught illegally)* 밀렵한 [millyeophan], *(simmered gently)* 서서히 끓인 [seoseohi kkeurin]

pocket ['pɒkɪt] n 주머니 [jumeoni]; **pocket calculator** n 휴대 계산기 [hyudae gyesangi]; **pocket money** n 용돈 [yongdon]

podcast ['pɒd,kɑːst] n 팟캐스트 [patkaeseuteu]

poem ['pəʊɪm] n 시 [si]

poet ['pəʊɪt] n 시인 [siin]

poetry ['pəʊɪtrɪ] n 시 [si]

point [pɔɪnt] n 요점 [yojeom] ▷ v 가리키다 [garikida]

pointless ['pɔɪntlɪs] adj 무의미한 [muuimihan]

point out [pɔɪnt aʊt] v 지적하다 [jijeokhada]

poison ['pɔɪzən] n 독 [dok] ▷ v 독을 넣다 [dogeul neota]

poisonous ['pɔɪzənəs] adj 유해한 [yuhaehan]

poke [pəʊk] v 찌르다 [jjireuda]

poker ['pəʊkə] n 부지깽이 [bujikkaengi]

Poland ['pəʊlənd] n 폴란드 [pollandeu]

polar ['pəʊlə] adj 극의 [geugui]; **polar bear** n 북극곰 [bukgeukgom]

pole [pəʊl] n 장대 [jangdae]; **North Pole** n 북극 [bukgeuk]; **pole vault** n 장대높이뛰기 [jangdaenopittwigi]; **South Pole** n 남극 [namgeuk]; **tent pole** n 천막 기둥 [cheonmak gidung]

Pole [pəʊl] n 폴란드 사람 [pollandeu saram]

police [pə'liːs] n 경찰 [gyeongchal]; **police officer** n 경찰관 [gyeongchalgwan]; **police station** n 경찰서 [kyungcharlsur]; **Call the police** 경찰을 불러 주세요 [gyeongchareul bulleo juseyo]; **I need a police report for my insurance** 보험 처리를 위한 경찰 보고서가 필요해요 [boheom cheorireul wihan gyeongchal bogoseoga pillyohaeyo]; **We will have to report it to the police** 경찰에 신고해야 합니다 [gyeongchare singohaeya hamnida]; **Where is the police station?** 경찰서는 어디있어요? [gyeongchalseoneun eodiisseoyo?]

policeman, policemen [pə'liːsmən, pə'liːsmɛn] n 경찰관 [gyeongchalgwan]

policewoman, policewomen [pə'liːswʊmən, pə'liːswɪmɪn] n 여자 경찰관 [yeoja gyeongchalgwan]

policy ['pɒlɪsɪ] n **insurance policy** n 보험증권 [boheomjeunggwon]

polio ['pəʊlɪəʊ] n 소아마비 [soamabi]

polish ['pɒlɪʃ] n 광택제 [gwangtaekje] ▷ v 닦다 [dakkda]; **nail polish** n 매니큐어 [maenikyueo]; **shoe polish** n 구두광택제 [gudugwangtaekje]

Polish ['pəʊlɪʃ] adj 폴란드의 [pollandeuui] ▷ n 폴란드어 [pollandeuo]

polite [pə'laɪt] *adj* 정중한 [jeongjunghan]

politely [pə'laɪtlɪ] *adv* 정중하게 [jeongjunghage]

politeness [pə'laɪtnɪs] *n* 정중함 [jeongjunghham]

political [pə'lɪtɪkəl] *adj* 정치적인 [jeongchijeogin]

politician [ˌpɒlɪ'tɪʃən] *n* 정치가 [jeongchiga]

politics ['pɒlɪtɪks] *npl* 정치학 [jeongchihak]

poll [pəʊl] *n* 여론조사 [yeoronjosa]; **opinion poll** *n* 여론조사 [yeoronjosa]

pollen ['pɒlən] *n* 꽃가루 [kkotgaru]

pollute [pə'luːt] *v* 오염시키다 [oyeomsikida]

polluted [pə'luːtɪd] *adj* 오염된 [oyeomdoen]

pollution [pə'luːʃən] *n* 오염 [oyeom]

Polynesia [ˌpɒlɪ'niːʒə; -ʒɪə] *n* 폴리네시아 [pollinesia]

Polynesian [ˌpɒlɪ'niːʒən; -ʒɪən] *adj* 폴리네시아의 [pollinesiaui] ▷ *n* (*language*) 폴리네시아어 [pollinesiaeo], (*person*) 폴리네시아 사람 [pollinesia saram]

pomegranate ['pɒmɪˌɡrænɪt; 'pɒmˌɡrænɪt] *n* 석류 [seongnyu]

pond [pɒnd] *n* 연못 [yeonmot]

pony ['pəʊnɪ] *n* 조랑말 [jorangmal]; **pony trekking** *n* 조랑말 등반 [jorangmal deungban]

ponytail ['pəʊnɪˌteɪl] *n* 말총머리 [malchongmeori]

poodle ['puːdəl] *n* 푸들 [pudeul]

pool [puːl] *n* (*resources*) 노동조합 [nodongjohap], (*water*) 웅덩이 [ungdeongi]; **paddling pool** *n* 얕은 수영장 [yateun suyeongjang]; **swimming pool** *n* 수영장 [suyeongjang]

poor [pʊə; pɔː] *adj* 가난한 [gananhan]

poorly ['pʊəlɪ; 'pɔː-] *adj* 건강이 나쁜 [geongangi nappeun]

popcorn ['pɒpˌkɔːn] *n* 팝콘 [papkon]

pope [pəʊp] *n* 교황 [gyohwang]

poplar ['pɒplə] *n* 포플러 [popeulleo]

poppy ['pɒpɪ] *n* 양귀비 [yanggwibi]

popular ['pɒpjʊlə] *adj* 인기있는 [ingiinneun]

popularity ['pɒpjʊlærɪtɪ] *n* 인기 [ingi]

population [ˌpɒpjʊ'leɪʃən] *n* 인구 [ingu]

pop-up [pɒpʌp] *n* 팝업창 [pabeopchang]

porch [pɔːtʃ] *n* 현관 [hyeongwan]

pork [pɔːk] *n* 돼지고기 [dwaejigogi]; **pork chop** *n* 돼지고기 토막 [dwaejigogi tomak]; **I don't eat pork** 저는 돼지고기를 안 먹어요 [jeoneun dwaejigogireul an meogeoyo]

porn [pɔːn] *n* 포르노 [poreuno]

pornographic [pɔː'nɒɡræfɪk] *adj* 외설적인 [oeseoljeogin]

pornography [pɔː'nɒɡrəfɪ] *n* 포르노 [poreuno]

porridge ['pɒrɪdʒ] *n* 죽 [juk]

port [pɔːt] *n* (*ships*) 항구 [hanggu], (*wine*) 포트와인 [poteuwain]

portable ['pɔːtəbəl] *adj* 휴대형의 [hyudaehyeongui]

porter ['pɔːtə] *n* 포터 [poteo]

portfolio [pɔːt'fəʊlɪəʊ] *n* 포트폴리오 [poteupollio]

portion ['pɔːʃən] *n* 부분 [bubun]

portrait ['pɔːtrɪt; -treɪt] *n* 초상화 [chosanghwa]

Portugal ['pɔːtjʊɡəl] *n* 포르투갈 [poreutugal]

Portuguese [ˌpɔːtjʊ'ɡiːz] *adj* 포르투갈의 [poreutugarui] ▷ *n* (*language*) 포르투갈어 [poreutugareo], (*person*) 포르투갈 사람 [poreutugal saram]

position [pə'zɪʃən] *n* 위치 [wichi]

positive ['pɒzɪtɪv] *adj* 적극적인 [jeokgeukjeogin]

possess [pə'zɛs] *v* 소유하다 [soyuhada]

possession [pə'zɛʃən] *n* 소유 [soyu]

possibility [ˌpɒsɪ'bɪlɪtɪ] *n* 가능성 [ganeungseong]

possible ['pɒsɪbəl] *adj* 가능한 [ganeunghan]; **as soon as possible** 가능한 한 빨리 [ganeunghan han ppalli]

possibly ['pɒsɪblɪ] *adv* 아마도 [amado]

post [pəʊst] *n* (mail) 우편 [upyeon], (position) 지위 [jiwi], (stake) 기둥 [gidung] ▷ *v* 우송하다 [usonghada]; **post office** *n* 우체국 [ucheguk]; **How long will it take by registered post?** 등기 우편은 도착하는 데 얼마나 걸려요? [deunggi upyeoneun dochakhaneun de eolmana geollyeoyo?]

postage ['pəʊstɪdʒ] *n* 우편요금 [upyeonyogeum]

postbox ['pəʊst,bɒks] *n* 우체통 [uchetong]

postcard ['pəʊst,kɑːd] *n* 우편엽서 [upyeonyeopseo]

postcode ['pəʊst,kəʊd] *n* 우편번호 [upyeonbeonho]

poster ['pəʊstə] *n* 포스터 [poseuteo]

postgraduate [pəʊst'grædjʊɪt] *n* 대학원생 [daehagwonsaeng]

postman, postmen ['pəʊstmən, 'pəʊstmɛn] *n* 우편집배원 [upyeonjipbaewon]

postmark ['pəʊst,mɑːk] *n* 소인 [soin] (편지)

postpone [pəʊst'pəʊn; pə'spəʊn] *v* 연기하다 [yeongihada]

postwoman, postwomen ['pəʊstwʊmən, 'pəʊstwɪmɪn] *n* 여자 우편집배원 [yeoja upyeonjipbaewon]

pot [pɒt] *n* 항아리 [hangari]; **plant pot** *n* 화분 [hwabun]; **pot plant** *n* 화분에 심는 화초 [hwabune simneun hwacho]

potato, potatoes [pə'teɪtəʊ, pə'teɪtəʊz] *n* 감자 [gamja]; **baked potato** *n* 구운 감자 [guun gamja]; **jacket potato** *n* 껍질째 구운 감자 [kkeopjiljjae guun gamja]; **mashed potatoes** *npl* 으깬 감자 [eukkaen gamja]; **potato peeler** *n* 감자 벗기는 기구 [gamja beotgineun gigu]

potential [pə'tɛnʃəl] *adj* 잠재적인 [jamjaejeogin] ▷ *n* 잠재성 [jamjaeseong]

pothole ['pɒt,həʊl] *n* 팬 구멍 [paen gumeong]

pottery ['pɒtərɪ] *n* 도기 [dogi]

potty ['pɒtɪ] *n* 유아용 변기 [yuayong byeongi]; **Do you have a potty?** 유아용 변기 있어요? [yuayong byeongi isseoyo?]

pound [paʊnd] *n* 파운드 [paundeu]; **pound sterling** *n* 영국 파운드 [yeongguk paundeu]

pour [pɔː] *v* 붓다 [butda]

poverty ['pɒvətɪ] *n* 가난 [ganan]

powder ['paʊdə] *n* 가루 [garu]; **baking powder** *n* 베이킹 파우더 [beiking paudeo]; **soap powder** *n* 가루비누 [garubinu]; **talcum powder** *n* 탤컴 파우더 [taelkeom paudeo]; **washing powder** *n* 가루 세탁 비누 [garu setak binu]

power ['paʊə] *n* 힘 [him]; **power cut** *n* 정전 [jeongjeon]; **solar power** *n* 태양 에너지 [taeyang eneoji]

powerful ['paʊəfʊl] *adj* 강력한 [gangnyeokhan]

practical ['præktɪkəl] *adj* 실용적인 [sillyongjeogin]

practically ['præktɪkəlɪ; -klɪ] *adv* 실제로는 [siljeroneun]

practice ['præktɪs] *n* 실행 [silhaeng]

practise ['præktɪs] *v* 실행하다 [silhaenghada]

praise [preɪz] *v* 칭찬하다 [chingchanhada]

pram [præm] *n* 유모차 [yumocha]

prank [præŋk] *n* 장난 [jangnan]

prawn [prɔːn] *n* 참새우 [chamsaeu]

pray [preɪ] *v* 기도하다 [gidohada]

prayer [prɛə] *n* 기도 [gido] (종교)

precaution [prɪ'kɔːʃən] *n* 예방조치 [yebangjochi]

preceding [prɪ'siːdɪŋ] *adj* 선행하는 [seonhaenghaneun]

precinct ['priːsɪŋkt] *n* 보행자 전용구역 [bohaengja jeonyongguyeok]; **pedestrian precinct** *n* 보행자 전용 구역 [bohaengja jeonyong guyeok]

precious ['prɛʃəs] *adj* 소중한 [sojunghan]

precise [prɪ'saɪs] *adj* 정확한 [jeonghwakhan]

precisely [prɪˈsaɪslɪ] *adv* 정확하게 [jeonghwakhage]

predecessor [ˈpriːdɪˌsɛsə] *n* 전임자 [jeonimja]

predict [prɪˈdɪkt] *v* 예측하다 [yecheukhada]

predictable [prɪˈdɪktəbəl] *adj* 예측 가능한 [yecheuk ganeunghan]

prefect [ˈpriːfɛkt] *n* 반장 [banjang]

prefer [prɪˈfɜː] *v* 선호하다 [seonhohada]

preferably [ˈprɛfərəblɪ; ˈprɛfrəblɪ] *adv* 가급적 [gageupjeok]

preference [ˈprɛfərəns; ˈprɛfrəns] *n* 선호도 [seonhodo]

pregnancy [ˈprɛgnənsɪ] *n* 임신 [imsin]

pregnant [ˈprɛgnənt] *adj* 임신중인 [imsinjungin]

prehistoric [ˌpriːhɪˈstɒrɪk] *adj* 선사시대의 [seonsasidaeui]

prejudice [ˈprɛdʒʊdɪs] *n* 편견 [pyeongyeon]

prejudiced [ˈprɛdʒʊdɪst] *adj* 편견을 가진 [pyeongyeoneul gajin]

premature [ˌprɛməˈtjʊə; ˈprɛməˌtjʊə] *adj* 시기상조의 [sigisangjoui]

premiere [ˈprɛmɪˌɛə; ˈprɛmɪə] *n* 첫 공연 [cheot gongyeon]

premises [ˈprɛmɪsɪz] *npl* 부동산 [budongsan]

premonition [ˌprɛməˈnɪʃən] *n* 예감 [yegam]

preoccupied [priːˈɒkjʊˌpaɪd] *adj* 몰두한 [molduhan]

prepaid [priːˈpeɪd] *adj* 선불한 [seonbulhan]

preparation [ˌprɛpəˈreɪʃən] *n* 준비 [junbi]

prepare [prɪˈpɛə] *v* 준비하다 [junbihada]

prepared [prɪˈpɛəd] *adj* 준비가 되어 있는 [junbiga doeeo inneun]

Presbyterian [ˌprɛzbɪˈtɪərɪən] *adj* 장로교회의 [jangnogyohoeui] ▷ *n* 장로교회 [jangnogyohoe]

prescribe [prɪˈskraɪb] *v* 처방하다 [cheobanghada]

prescription [prɪˈskrɪpʃən] *n* 처방 [cheobang]; **Where can I get this prescription made up?** 어디에서 이 처방약을 조제할 수 있을까요? [eodieseo i cheobangyageul jojehal su isseulkkayo?]

presence [ˈprɛzəns] *n* 존재 [jonjae]

present *adj* [ˈprɛz] 현재의 [hyeonjaeui] ▷ *n* [ˈprɛz] (*gift*) 선물 [seonmul], (*time being*) 현재 [hyeonjae] ▷ *v* [prɪˈzɛnt] 소개하다 [sogaehada]; **I'm looking for a present for my husband** 남편에게 줄 선물을 찾고 있어요 [nampyeonege jul seonmureul chatgo isseoyo]

presentation [ˌprɛzənˈteɪʃən] *n* 발표 [balpyo]

presenter [prɪˈzɛntə] *n* 뉴스 캐스터 [nyuseu kaeseuteo]

presently [ˈprɛzəntlɪ] *adv* 곧 [got]

preservative [prɪˈzɜːvətɪv] *n* 방부제 [bangbuje]

president [ˈprɛzɪdənt] *n* 대통령 [daetongnyeong]

press [prɛs] *n* 압축기 [apchukgi] ▷ *v* 누르다 [nureuda]; **press conference** *n* 기자회견 [gijahoegyeon]

press-up [prɛsʌp] *n* 팔굽혀펴기 [palguphyeopyeogi]

pressure [ˈprɛʃə] *n* 압력 [amnyeok] ▷ *v* 압력을 가하다 [amnyeogeul gahada]; **blood pressure** *n* 혈압 [hyeorap]; **What should the tyre pressure be?** 타이어 압력이 얼마여야 하나요? [taieo amnyeogi eolmayeoya hanayo?]

prestige [prɛˈstiːʒ] *n* 명성 [myeongseong]

prestigious [prɛˈstɪdʒəs] *adj* 유명한 [yumyeonghan]

presumably [prɪˈzjuːməblɪ] *adv* 아마 [ama]

presume [prɪˈzjuːm] *v* 추정하다 [chujeonghada]

pretend [prɪˈtɛnd] *v* ...인 체하다 [...in chehada]

pretext [ˈpriːtɛkst] *n* 핑계 [pinggye]

prettily [ˈprɪtɪlɪ] *adv* 예쁘게 [yeppeuge]

pretty [ˈprɪtɪ] *adj* 예쁜 [yeppeun] ▷ *adv* 꽤 [kkwae]

prevent [prɪˈvɛnt] *v* 예방하다

[yebanghada]
prevention [prɪ'vɛnʃən] n 예방 [yebang]
previous ['pri:vɪəs] adj 이전의 [ijeonui]
previously ['pri:vɪəslɪ] adv 전에 [jeone]
prey [preɪ] n 먹이 [meogi]
price [praɪs] n 가격 [gagyeok]; **price list** n 가격표 [gagyeokpyo]; **retail price** n 소매가격 [somaegagyeok]; **selling price** n 판매가격 [panmaegagyeok]; **Do you have a set-price menu?** 세트 가격 메뉴가 있나요? [seteu gagyeok menyuga innayo?]; **Does the price include boots?** 가격에 부츠가 포함되나요? [gagyeoge bucheuga pohamdoenayo?]; **Please write down the price** 가격을 적어 주세요 [gagyeogeul jeogeo juseyo]; **What is included in the price?** 가격에는 무엇이 포함되나요? [gagyeogeneun mueosi pohamdoenayo?]
prick [prɪk] v 찌르다 [jjireuda]
pride [praɪd] n 긍지 [geungji]
priest [pri:st] n 신부 [sinbu]
primarily ['praɪmərəlɪ] adv 주로 [juro]
primary ['praɪmərɪ] adj 주요한 [juyohan]; **primary school** n 초등학교 [chodeunghakgyo]
primitive ['prɪmɪtɪv] adj 원시적인 [wonsijeogin]
primrose ['prɪm,rəʊz] n 달맞이꽃 [dalmajikkot]
prince [prɪns] n 왕자 [wangja]
princess [prɪn'sɛs] n 공주 [gongju]
principal ['prɪnsɪpᵊl] adj 주된 [judoen] ▷ n 교장 [gyojang]
principle ['prɪnsɪpᵊl] n 원칙 [wonchik]
print [prɪnt] n 인쇄 [inswae] ▷ v 인쇄하다 [inswaehada]
printer ['prɪntə] n (machine) 인쇄기 [inswaegi], (person) 인쇄업자 [inswaeeopja]
printing ['prɪntɪŋ] n **How much is printing?** 인쇄하는 데 얼마예요? [inswaehaneun de eolmayeyo?]
printout ['prɪntaʊt] n 인쇄물

[inswaemul]
priority [praɪ'ɒrɪtɪ] n 우선순위 [useonsunwi]
prison ['prɪzᵊn] n 교도소 [gyodoso]; **prison officer** n 교도관 [gyodogwan]
prisoner ['prɪzənə] n 죄수 [joesu]
privacy ['prɪvəsɪ; 'praɪvəsɪ] n 사생활 [sasaenghwal]
private ['praɪvɪt] adj 사적인 [sajeogin]; **private property** n 사유재산 [sayujaesan]
privatize ['praɪvɪ,taɪz] v 사유화하다 [sayuhwahada]
privilege ['prɪvɪlɪdʒ] n 특권 [teukgwon]
prize [praɪz] n 상 [sang]
prize-giving ['praɪz,gɪvɪŋ] n 시상 [sisang]
prizewinner ['praɪz,wɪnə] n 수상자 [susangja]
probability [,prɒbə'bɪlɪtɪ] n 개연성 [gaeyeonseong]
probable ['prɒbəbᵊl] adj 있음직한 [isseumjikhan]
probably ['prɒbəblɪ] adv 아마도 [amado]
problem ['prɒbləm] n 문제 [munje]; **There's a problem with the room** 방에 문제가 있어요 [bange munjega isseoyo]; **Who do we contact if there are problems?** 문제가 있으면 누구에게 연락해야 할까요? [munjega isseumyeon nuguege yeollakhaeya halkkayo?]
proceedings [prə'si:dɪŋz] npl 소송 절차 [sosong jeolcha]
proceeds ['prəʊsi:dz] npl 수익금 [suikgeum]
process ['prəʊsɛs] n 과정 [gwajeong]
procession [prə'sɛʃən] n 행렬 [haengnyeol]
produce [prə'dju:s] v 생산하다 [saengsanhada]
producer [prə'dju:sə] n 생산자 [saengsanja]
product ['prɒdʌkt] n 제품 [jepum]
production [prə'dʌkʃən] n 생산 [saengsan]

productivity [ˌprɒdʌk'tɪvɪtɪ] n 생산성 [saengsanseong]

profession [prə'fɛʃən] n 직업 [jigeop]

professional [prə'fɛʃənᵊl] adj 직업적인 [jigeopjeogin] ▷ n 전문가 [jeonmunga]

professionally [prə'fɛʃənᵊlɪ] adv 직업적으로 [jigeopjeogeuro]

professor [prə'fɛsə] n 교수 [gyosu]

profit ['prɒfɪt] n 이익 [iik]

profitable ['prɒfɪtəbᵊl] adj 이로운 [iroun]

program ['prəʊgræm] n 프로그램 [peurogeuraem] ▷ v 프로그램을 짜다 [peurogeuraemeul jjada]

programme ['prəʊgræm] n 프로그램 [peurogeuraem]; **Can I use messenger programmes?** 메신저 프로그램을 사용할 수 있을까요? [mesinjeo peurogeuraemeul sayonghal su isseulkkayo?]

programmer ['prəʊgræmə] n 프로그래머 [peurogeuraemeo]

programming ['prəʊgræmɪŋ] n 프로그래밍 [peurogeuraeming]

progress ['prəʊgrɛs] n 진행 [jinhaeng]

prohibit [prə'hɪbɪt] v 금지하다 [geumjihada]

prohibited [prə'hɪbɪtɪd] adj 금지된 [geumjidoen]

project ['prɒdʒɛkt] n 프로젝트 [peurojekteu]

projector [prə'dʒɛktə] n 프로젝터 [peurojekteo]; **overhead projector** n 오버헤드 프로젝터 [obeohedeu peurojekteo]

promenade [ˌprɒmə'nɑːd] n 산책길 [sanchaekgil]

promise ['prɒmɪs] n 약속 [yaksok] ▷ v 약속하다 [yaksokhada]

promising ['prɒmɪsɪŋ] adj 전도 유망한 [jeondo yumanghan]

promote [prə'məʊt] v 촉진하다 [chokjinhada]

promotion [prə'məʊʃən] n 승진 [seungjin]

prompt [prɒmpt] adj 즉각적인 [jeukgakjeogin]

promptly ['prɒmptlɪ] adv 즉시 [jeuksi]

pronoun ['prəʊˌnaʊn] n 대명사 [daemyeongsa]

pronounce [prə'naʊns] v 발음하다 [bareumhada]

pronunciation [prəˌnʌnsɪ'eɪʃən] n 발음 [bareum]

proof [pruːf] n (evidence, for checking) 증거 [jeunggeo]

propaganda [ˌprɒpə'gændə] n 선전 [seonjeon]

proper ['prɒpə] adj 적합한 [jeokhaphan]

properly ['prɒpəlɪ] adv 적절하게 [jeokjeolhage]

property ['prɒpətɪ] n 재산 [jaesan]; **private property** n 사유재산 [sayujaesan]

proportion [prə'pɔːʃən] n 비율 [biyul]

proportional [prə'pɔːʃənᵊl] adj 비례하는 [biryehaneun]

proposal [prə'pəʊzᵊl] n 제안 [jean]

propose [prə'pəʊz] v 제안하다 [jeanhada]

prosecute ['prɒsɪˌkjuːt] v 기소하다 [gisohada]

prospect ['prɒspɛkt] n 전망 [jeonmang]

prospectus [prə'spɛktəs] n 취지서 [chwijiseo]

prosperity [prɒ'spɛrɪtɪ] n 번영 [beonyeong]

prostitute ['prɒstɪˌtjuːt] n 매춘부 [maechunbu]

protect [prə'tɛkt] v 보호하다 [bohohada]

protection [prə'tɛkʃən] n 보호 [boho]

protein ['prəʊtiːn] n 단백질 [danbaekjil]

protest n ['prəʊtɛst] 항의 [hangui] ▷ v [prə'tɛst] 항의하다 [hanguihada]

Protestant ['prɒtɪstənt] adj 개신교도의 [gaesingyodoui] ▷ n 개신교도 [gaesingyodo]

proud [praʊd] adj 자랑스러워 하는 [jarangseureowo haneun]

prove [pruːv] v 입증하다 [ipjeunghada]

proverb ['prɒvɜːb] n 격언 [gyeogeon]

provide [prə'vaɪd] v 제공하다 [jegonghada]; **provide for** v 대비하다 [daebihada]

provided [prə'vaɪdɪd] conj...(이라는) 조건으로 [...(iraneun) jogeoneuro]

providing [prə'vaɪdɪŋ] conj...(이라는) 조건으로 [...(iraneun) jogeoneuro]

provisional [prə'vɪʒənəl] adj 잠정적인 [jamjeongjeogin]

proximity [prɒk'sɪmɪtɪ] n 근접 [geunjeop]

prune [pruːn] n 말린 자두 [mallin jadu]

pry [praɪ] v 탐색하다 [tamsaekhada]

pseudonym ['sjuːdənɪm] n 가명 [gamyeong]

psychiatric [ˌsaɪkɪ'ætrɪk] adj 정신의학의 [jeongsinuihagui]

psychiatrist [saɪ'kaɪətrɪst] n 정신과 의사 [jeongsingwa uisa]

psychological [ˌsaɪkə'lɒdʒɪkəl] adj 심리학적인 [simnihakjeogin]

psychologist [saɪ'kɒlədʒɪst] n 심리학자 [simnihakja]

psychology [saɪ'kɒlədʒɪ] n 심리학 [simnihak]

psychotherapy [ˌsaɪkəʊ'θɛrəpɪ] n 심리요법 [simniyobeop]

PTO [pi: ti: əʊ] abbr 뒷면에 계속 [dwitmyeone gyesok]

pub [pʌb] n 술집 [suljip]

public ['pʌblɪk] adj 공공의 [gonggongui] ▷ n 대중 [daejung]; **public holiday** n 공휴일 [gonghyuil]; **public opinion** n 여론 [yeoron]; **public relations** npl 홍보활동 [hongbohwaldong]; **public school** n 사립 중고교 [sarip junggogyo]; **public transport** n 대중교통수단 [daejunggyotongsudan]

publican ['pʌblɪkən] n 술집 주인 [suljip juin]

publication [ˌpʌblɪ'keɪʃən] n 출판 [chulpan]

publish ['pʌblɪʃ] v 출판하다 [chulpanhada]

publisher ['pʌblɪʃə] n 발행자 [balhaengja]

pudding ['pʊdɪŋ] n 푸딩 [puding]

puddle ['pʌdəl] n 물웅덩이 [murungdeongi]

Puerto Rico ['pwɜːtəʊ 'riːkəʊ; 'pwɛə-] n 푸에르토리코 [pueureutoriko]

pull [pʊl] v 잡아당기다 [jabadanggida]

pull down [pʊl daʊn] v 부수다 [busuda]

pull out [pʊl aʊt] vi 출발하다 [chulbalhada] ▷ vt 끌어내다 [kkeureonaeda]

pullover ['pʊlˌəʊvə] n 풀오버 [purobeo]

pull up [pʊl ʌp] v 뽑다 [ppopda]

pulse [pʌls] n 맥박 [maekbak]

pulses [pʌlsɪz] npl 콩 [kong]

pump [pʌmp] n 펌프 [peompeu] ▷ v 펌프로 퍼올리다 [peompeuro peoollida]; **bicycle pump** n 자전거 펌프 [jajeongeo peompeu]; **Do you have a pump?** 펌프 있어요? [peompeu isseoyo?]

pumpkin ['pʌmpkɪn] n 호박 [hobak]

pump up [pʌmp ʌp] v 공기를 넣다 [gonggireul neota]

punch [pʌntʃ] n (blow) 한대치기 [handaechigi], (hot drink) 펀치 [peonchi] ▷ v 한 대 치다 [han dae chida]

punctual ['pʌŋktjʊəl] adj 시간을 엄수하는 [siganeul eomsuhaneun]

punctuation [ˌpʌŋktjʊ'eɪʃən] n 구두법 [gudubeop]

puncture ['pʌŋktʃə] n 구멍 [gumeong]

punish ['pʌnɪʃ] v 벌을 주다 [beoreul juda]

punishment ['pʌnɪʃmənt] n 벌 [beol]; **capital punishment** n 사형 [sahyeong]; **corporal punishment** n 체벌 [chebeol]

punk [pʌŋk] n 보잘것없는 사람 [bojalgeoseomneun saram]

pupil ['pjuːpəl] n (eye) 눈동자 [nundongja], (learner) 학생 [haksaeng]

puppet ['pʌpɪt] n 꼭두각시 [kkokdugaksi]

puppy ['pʌpɪ] n 강아지 [gangaji]

purchase ['pɜːtʃɪs] v 사다 [sada]

pure [pjʊə] adj 순수한 [sunsuhan]

purple ['pɜːpəl] adj 자줏빛의

[jajutbichui]

purpose [ˈpɜːpəs] *n* 목적 [mokjeok]
purr [pɜː] *v* 가르랑거리다
[gareuranggeorida]
purse [pɜːs] *n* 지갑 [jigap]
pursue [pəˈsjuː] *v* 추적하다
[chujeokhada]
pursuit [pəˈsjuːt] *n* 추적 [chujeok]
pus [pʌs] *n* 고름 [goreum]
push [pʊʃ] *v* 밀다 [milda]
pushchair [ˈpʊʃˌtʃɛə] *n* 유모차
[yumocha]
push-up [pʊʃʌp] *n* 팔굽혀펴기
[palguphyeopyeogi]
put [pʊt] *v* 놓다 [nota]
put aside [pʊt əˈsaɪd] *v* 한쪽에 두다
[hanjjoge duda]
put away [pʊt əˈweɪ] *v* 치우다 [chiuda]
put back [pʊt bæk] *v* 되돌리다
[doedollida]
put forward [pʊt ˈfɔːwəd] *v* 제출하다
[jechulhada]
put in [pʊt ɪn] *v* 삽입하다 [sabiphada]
put off [pʊt ɒf] *v* 연기하다 [yeongihada]
put up [pʊt ʌp] *v* 세우다 [seuda]
puzzle [ˈpʌzəl] *n* 퍼즐 [peojeul]
puzzled [ˈpʌzəld] *adj* 당황한
[danghwanghan]
puzzling [ˈpʌzlɪŋ] *adj* 당황하게 하는
[danghwanghage haneun]
pyjamas [pəˈdʒɑːməz] *npl* 파자마
[pajama]
pylon [ˈpaɪlən] *n* 탑 [tap]
pyramid [ˈpɪrəmɪd] *n* 피라미드
[piramideu]

q

Qatar [kæˈtɑː] *n* 카타르 [katareu]
quail [kweɪl] *n* 메추라기 [mechuragi]
quaint [kweɪnt] *adj* 기묘한 [gimyohan]
Quaker [ˈkweɪkə] *n* 퀘이커교도
[kweikeogyodo]
qualification [ˌkwɒlɪfɪˈkeɪʃən] *n* 자격
[jagyeok]
qualified [ˈkwɒlɪˌfaɪd] *adj* 자격 있는
[jagyeok inneun]
qualify [ˈkwɒlɪˌfaɪ] *v* 자격을 갖추다
[jagyeogeul gatchuda]
quality [ˈkwɒlɪtɪ] *n* 품질 [pumjil]
quantify [ˈkwɒntɪˌfaɪ] *v* 정량화하다
[jeongnyanghwahada]
quantity [ˈkwɒntɪtɪ] *n* 수량 [suryang]
quarantine [ˈkwɒrənˌtiːn] *n* 격리
[gyeongni]
quarrel [ˈkwɒrəl] *n* 말다툼 [maldatum]
▷ *v* 다투다 [datuda]
quarry [ˈkwɒrɪ] *n* 채석장
[chaeseokjang]
quarter [ˈkwɔːtə] *n* 4분의 1 [sabunui il];
quarter final *n* 8강전 [gangjeon]
quartet [kwɔːˈtɛt] *n* 사중창단
[sajungchangdan]
quay [kiː] *n* 선창 [seonchang]
queen [kwiːn] *n* 여왕 [yeowang]

query ['kwɪərɪ] *n* 의문 [uimun] ▷ *v*
질문하다 [jilmunhada]

question ['kwɛstʃən] *n* 질문 [jilmun] ▷ *v*
질문하다 [jilmunhada]; **question
mark** *n* 의문부호 [uimunbuho]

questionnaire [ˌkwɛstʃə'nɛə; ˌkɛs-] *n*
설문지 [seolmunji]

queue [kjuː] *n* 줄 [jul] ▷ *v* 줄서다
[julseoda]; **Is this the end of the
queue?** 여기가 줄의 끝인가요?
[yeogiga jurui kkeuchingayo?]

quick [kwɪk] *adj* 빠른 [ppareun]

quickly ['kwɪklɪ] *adv* 빨리 [ppalli];
Fetch help quickly! 빨리 도와주세요!
[ppalli dowajuseyo!]

quiet ['kwaɪət] *adj* 조용한 [joyonghan];
I'd like a quiet room 조용한 방이
좋겠어요 [joyonghan bangi
jokesseoyo]

quietly ['kwaɪətlɪ] *adv* 조용하게
[joyonghage]

quilt [kwɪlt] *n* 누비이불 [nubiibul]

quit [kwɪt] *v* 그만두다 [geumanduda]

quite [kwaɪt] *adv* 상당히 [sangdanghi]

quiz, quizzes [kwɪz, 'kwɪzɪz] *n* 퀴즈
[kwijeu]

quota ['kwəʊtə] *n* 할당량
[haldangnyang]

quotation [kwəʊ'teɪʃən] *n* 인용문
[inyongmun]; **quotation marks** *npl*
인용부호 [inyongbuho]

quote [kwəʊt] *n* 인용어구 [inyongeogu]
▷ *v* 인용하다 [inyonghada]

r

rabbi ['ræbaɪ] *n* 랍비 [rapbi]

rabbit ['ræbɪt] *n* 토끼 [tokki]

rabies ['reɪbiːz] *n* 공수병
[gongsubyeong]

race [reɪs] *n* (contest) 경주 [gyeongju],
(origin) 인종 [injong] ▷ *v* 경쟁하다
[gyeongjaenghada]

racecourse ['reɪsˌkɔːs] *n* 경주코스
[gyeongjukoseu]

racehorse ['reɪsˌhɔːs] *n* 경주마
[gyeongjuma]

racer ['reɪsə] *n* 경주자 [gyeongjuja]

racetrack ['reɪsˌtræk] *n* 경주장
[gyeongjujang]

racial ['reɪʃəl] *adj* 인종의 [injongui]

racing ['reɪsɪŋ] *n* **horse racing** *n* 경마
[gyeongma]; **motor racing** *n*
자동차경주 [jadongchagyeongju];
racing car *n* 경주용차
[gyeongjuyongcha]; **racing driver** *n*
자동차 경주 선수 [jadongcha gyeongju
seonsu]

racism ['reɪsɪzəm] *n* 인종 차별주의
[injong chabyeoljuui]

racist ['reɪsɪst] *adj* 인종을 차별하는
[injongeul chabyeolhaneun] ▷ *n* 인종
차별주의자 [injong chabyeoljuuija]

rack [ræk] n 선반 [seonban]; **luggage rack** n 수화물 선반 [suhwamul seonban]

racket ['rækɪt] n (racquet) 소동 [sodong]; **tennis racket** n 테니스 라켓 [teniseu raket]

racoon [rə'ku:n] n 너구리 [neoguri]

racquet ['rækɪt] n 라켓 [raket]

radar ['reɪdɑ:] n 레이더 [reideo]

radiation [ˌreɪdɪ'eɪʃən] n 복사 [boksa]

radiator ['reɪdɪˌeɪtə] n 방열기 [bangyeolgi]

radio ['reɪdɪəʊ] n 라디오 [radio]; **digital radio** n 디지털 라디오 [dijiteol radio]; **radio station** n 라디오 방송국 [radio bangsongguk]; **Can I switch the radio off?** 라디오 꺼도 돼요? [radio kkeodo dwaeyo?]; **Can I switch the radio on?** 라디오 켜도 돼요? [radio kyeodo dwaeyo?]

radioactive [ˌreɪdɪəʊ'æktɪv] adj 방사성의 [bangsaseongui]

radio-controlled ['reɪdɪəʊ'kən'trəʊld] adj 무선으로 조종되는 [museoneuro jojongdoeneun]

radish ['rædɪʃ] n 무 [mu]

raffle ['ræfəl] n 추첨 [chucheom]

raft [rɑ:ft] n 뗏목 [ttetmok]

rag [ræg] n 헝겊 조각 [heonggeop jogak]

rage [reɪdʒ] n 분노 [bunno]; **road rage** n 노상 분노 [nosang bunno]

raid [reɪd] n 급습 [geupseup] ▷ v 급습하다 [geupseuphada]

rail [reɪl] n 난간 [nangan], 철로 [cheollo]

railcard ['reɪlˌkɑ:d] n 열차할인카드 [yeolchaharinkadeu]

railings ['reɪlɪŋz] npl 난간 [nangan]

railway ['reɪlˌweɪ] n 철도 [cheoldo]; **railway station** n 철도역 [cheoldoyeok]

rain [reɪn] n 비 [bi] ▷ v 비내리다 [binaerida]; **acid rain** n 산성비 [sanseongbi]; **Do you think it's going to rain?** 비가 올 것 같아요? [biga ol geot gatayo?]; **It's raining** 비가 와요 [biga wayo]

rainbow ['reɪnˌbəʊ] n 무지개 [mujigae]

raincoat ['reɪnˌkəʊt] n 비옷 [biot]

rainforest ['reɪnˌfɒrɪst] n 열대 우림 [yeoldae urim]

rainy ['reɪnɪ] adj 비가 오는 [biga oneun]

raise [reɪz] v 올리다 [ollida]

raisin ['reɪzªn] n 건포도 [geonpodo]

rake [reɪk] n 갈퀴 [galkwi]

rally ['rælɪ] n 대회 [daehoe]

ram [ræm] n 숫양 [susyang] ▷ v 부딪치다 [buditchida]

Ramadan [ˌræmə'dɑ:n] n 라마단 [ramadan]

rambler ['ræmblə] n 도보 여행자 [dobo yeohaengja]

ramp [ræmp] n 사면 [samyeon]

random ['rændəm] adj 무작위의 [mujagwiui]

range [reɪndʒ] n (limits) 범위 [beomwi], (mountains) 방목장 [bangmokjang] ▷ v 변동하다 [byeondonghada]

rank [ræŋk] n (line) 열 [yeol], (status) 계층 [gyecheung] ▷ v 위치하다 [wichihada]

ransom ['rænsəm] n 배상금 [baesanggeum]

rape [reɪp] n (plant) 평지 [pyeongji], (sexual attack) 강간 [ganggan] ▷ v 강간하다 [gangganhada]

rapids ['ræpɪdz] npl 여울 [yeoul]

rapist ['reɪpɪst] n 강간범 [gangganbeom]

rare [rɛə] adj (uncommon) 드문 [deumun], (undercooked) 덜 익은 [deol igeun]

rarely ['rɛəlɪ] adv 드물게 [deumulge]

rash [ræʃ] n 발진 [baljin]

raspberry ['rɑ:zbərɪ; -brɪ] n 나무딸기 [namuttalgi]

rat [ræt] n 쥐 [jwi]

rate [reɪt] n 비율 [biyul] ▷ v 평가하다 [pyeonggahada]; **interest rate** n 금리 [geumni]; **rate of exchange** n 환율 [hwanyul]

rather ['rɑ:ðə] adv 상당히 [sangdanghi]

ratio ['reɪʃɪˌəʊ] n 비율 [biyul]
rational ['ræʃənəl] adj 합리적인 [hamnijeogin]
rattle ['rætəl] n 덜거덕 소리 [deolgeodeok sori]
rattlesnake ['rætəlˌsneɪk] n 방울뱀 [bangulbaem]
rave [reɪv] n 극찬 [geukchan] ▷ v 헛소리하다 [heossorihada]
raven ['reɪvən] n 큰까마귀 [keunkkamagwi]
ravenous ['rævənəs] adj 몹시 굶주린 [mopsi gurmjurin]
ravine [rə'viːn] n 계곡 [gyegok]
raw [rɔː] adj 날것의 [nalgeosui]
razor ['reɪzə] n 면도칼 [myeondokal]; **razor blade** n 면도날 [myeondonal]
reach [riːtʃ] v 도착하다 [dochakhada]
react [rɪ'ækt] v 반응하다 [baneunghada]
reaction [rɪ'ækʃən] n 반응 [baneung]
reactor [rɪ'æktə] n 원자로 [wonjaro]
read [riːd] v 읽다 [irkda]
reader ['riːdə] n 독자 [dokja] (잡지)
readily ['rɛdɪlɪ] adv 즉시 [jeuksi]
reading ['riːdɪŋ] n 독서 [dokseo]
read out [riːd] v 소리내어 읽다 [sorinaeeo irkda]
ready ['rɛdɪ] adj 준비가 된 [junbiga doen]
ready-cooked ['rɛdɪ'kʊkt] adj 이미 익혀진 [imi ikhyeojin]
real ['rɪəl] adj 진짜의 [jinjjaeui]
realistic [rɪə'lɪstɪk] adj 현실적인 [hyeonsiljeogin]
reality [rɪ'ælɪtɪ] n 현실 [hyeonsil]; **reality TV** n 리얼리티 TV 쇼 [rieolliti TV syo]; **virtual reality** n 가상현실 [gasanghyeonsil]
realize ['rɪəˌlaɪz] v 깨닫다 [kkaedatda]
really ['rɪəlɪ] adv 실제로 [siljero]
rear [rɪə] adj 뒤의 [dwiui] ▷ n 뒤 [dwi]; **rear-view mirror** n 백미러 [baengmireo]
reason ['riːzən] n 이유 [iyu]
reasonable ['riːzənəbəl] adj 이치에 맞는 [ichie matneun]
reasonably ['riːzənəblɪ] adv

합리적으로 [hamnijeogeuro]
reassure [ˌriːə'ʃʊə] v 안심시키다 [ansimsikida]
reassuring [ˌriːə'ʃʊərɪŋ] adj 안심시켜 주는 [ansimsikyeo juneun]
rebate ['riːbeɪt] n 환불 [hwanbul]
rebellious [rɪ'bɛljəs] adj 반항적인 [banhangjeogin]
rebuild [riː'bɪld] v 개축하다 [gaechukhada]
receipt [rɪ'siːt] n 영수증 [yeongsujeung]; **I need a receipt for the insurance** 보험 처리를 위한 영수증이 필요해요 [boheom cheorireul wihan yeongsujeungi pillyohaeyo]; **I need a receipt, please** 영수증이 필요해요 [yeongsujeungi piryohaeyo]
receive [rɪ'siːv] v 받다 [batda]
receiver [rɪ'siːvə] n (electronic) 수신기 [susingi], (person) 수령인 [suryeongin]
recent ['riːsənt] adj 최근의 [choegeunui]
recently ['riːsəntlɪ] adv 최근에 [choegeune]; **I had flu recently** 최근에 독감을 앓았어요 [choegeune dokgameul arasseoyo]
reception [rɪ'sɛpʃən] n 접수창구 [jeopsuchanggu]
receptionist [rɪ'sɛpʃənɪst] n 접수계원 [jeopsugyewon]
recession [rɪ'sɛʃən] n 불경기 [bulgyeonggi]
recharge [riː'tʃɑːdʒ] v 재충전하다 [jaechungjeonhada]
recipe ['rɛsɪpɪ] n 요리법 [yoribeop]
recipient [rɪ'sɪpɪənt] n 수령인 [suryeongin]
reckon ['rɛkən] v 간주하다 [ganjughada]
reclining [rɪ'klaɪnɪŋ] adj 여러 각도로 눕힐 수 있는 [yeoreo gakdoro nuphil su inneun]
recognizable ['rɛkəgˌnaɪzəbəl] adj 인식할수 있는 [insikhalsu inneun]
recognize ['rɛkəgˌnaɪz] v 인식하다 [insikhada]
recommend [ˌrɛkə'mɛnd] v 추천하다 [chucheonhada]

recommendation [ˌrɛkəmen'deɪʃən] n 추천 [chucheon]

reconsider [ˌriː.kən'sɪdə] v 재고하다 [jaegohada]

record n ['rɛkɔːd] 기록 [girok] ▷ v [rɪ'kɔːd] 기록하다 [girokhada]

recorded delivery [rɪ'kɔːdɪd dɪ'lɪvəri] n 등기우편 [deunggiupyeon]

recorder [rɪ'kɔːdə] n (music) 리코더 [rikodeo], (scribe) 기록자 [girokja]

recording [rɪ'kɔːdɪŋ] n 녹음 [nogeum]

recover [rɪ'kʌvə] v 회복하다 [hoebokhada]

recovery [rɪ'kʌvəri] n 회복 [hoebok]

recruitment [rɪ'kruːtmənt] n 채용 [chaeyong]

rectangle ['rɛkˌtæŋgəl] n 직사각형 [jiksagakhyeong]

rectangular [rɛk'tæŋjʊlə] adj 직사각형의 [jiksagakhyeongui]

rectify ['rɛktɪˌfaɪ] v 개정하다 [gaejeonghada]

recurring [rɪ'kʌrɪŋ] adj 다시 발생하는 [dasi balsaenghaneun]

recycle [riː'saɪkəl] v 재활용하다 [jaehwallyonghada]

recycling [riː'saɪklɪŋ] n 재활용 [jaehwallyong]

red [rɛd] adj 빨간 [ppalgan]; **red meat** n 붉은 고기 [bulgeun gogi]; **red wine** n 적포도주 [jeokpodoju]; **Red Cross** n 적십자 [jeoksipja]; **Red Sea** n 홍해 [honghae]

redcurrant ['rɛd'kʌrənt] n 씨없는 건포도 [ssieomneun geonpodo]

redecorate [riː'dɛkəˌreɪt] v 개장하다 [gaejanghada]

red-haired ['rɛd,hɛəd] adj 붉은 머리의 [bulgeun meoriui]

redhead ['rɛd,hɛd] n 머리털이 붉은 사람 [meoriteoribulgeun saram]

redo [riː'duː] v 다시 하다 [dasi hada]

reduce [rɪ'djuːs] v 축소하다 [chuksohada]

reduction [rɪ'dʌkʃən] n 축소 [chukso]

redundancy [rɪ'dʌndənsɪ] n 과잉 [gwaing]

redundant [rɪ'dʌndənt] adj 과다한 [gwadahan]

reed [riːd] n 갈대 [galdae]

reel [riːl; rɪəl] n 릴 [ril]

refer [rɪ'fɜː] v 언급하다 [eongeuphada]

referee [ˌrɛfə'riː] n 심판 [simpan]

reference ['rɛfərəns; 'rɛfrəns] n 참조 [chamjo]; **reference number** n 참조번호 [chamjobeonho]

refill [riː'fɪl] v 다시 채우다 [dasi chaeuda]

refinery [rɪ'faɪnərɪ] n 정제소 [jeongjeso]; **oil refinery** n 정유 공장 [jeongyu gongjang]

reflect [rɪ'flɛkt] v 반사하다 [bansahada]

reflection [rɪ'flɛkʃən] n 반사 [bansa]

reflex ['riːflɛks] n 반사행동 [bansahaengdong]

refreshing [rɪ'frɛʃɪŋ] adj 상쾌한 [sangkwaehan]

refreshments [rɪ'frɛʃmənts] npl 다과 [dagwa]

refrigerator [rɪ'frɪdʒəˌreɪtə] n 냉장고 [naengjanggo]

refuel [riː'fjuːəl] v 연료를 보급하다 [yeollyoreul bogeuphada]

refuge ['rɛfjuːdʒ] n 피난처 [pinancheo]

refugee [ˌrɛfjʊ'dʒiː] n 난민 [nanmin]

refund n ['riː.fʌnd] 반환금 [banhwangeum] ▷ v [rɪ'fʌnd] 반환하다 [banhwanhada]

refusal [rɪ'fjuːzəl] n 거절 [geojeol]

refuse¹ [rɪ'fjuːz] v 거절하다 [geojeolhada]

refuse² ['rɛfjuːs] n 쓰레기 [sseuregi]

regain [rɪ'geɪn] v 되찾다 [doechatda]

regard [rɪ'gɑːd] n 관련 [gwallyeon] ▷ v 간주하다 [ganjughada]

regarding [rɪ'gɑːdɪŋ] prep...에 관하여 [...e gwanhayeo]

regiment ['rɛdʒɪmənt] n 연대 [yeondae] (군인)

region ['riːdʒən] n 지역 [jiyeok]; **Do you have anything typical of this region?** 지역 특산품 있어요? [jiyeok teuksanpum isseoyo?]; **Where can I buy a map of the region?** 지역지도를 어디에서 살 수 있나요? [jiyeokjidoreul eodieseo sal su innayo?]

regional ['ri:dʒənºl] *adj* 지역의 [jiyeogui]

register ['rɛdʒɪstə] *n* 등록 [deungnok] ▷ *v* 등록하다 [deungnokhada]; **cash register** *n* 금전 출납기 [geumjeon chullapgi]

registered ['rɛdʒɪstəd] *adj* 등록된 [deungnokdoen]

registration [,rɛdʒɪ'streɪʃən] *n* 등록 [deungnok]

regret [rɪ'grɛt] *n* 후회 [huhoe] ▷ *v* 후회하다 [huhoehada]

regular ['rɛgjʊlə] *adj* 규칙적인 [gyuchikjeogin]

regularly ['rɛgjʊləlɪ] *adv* 규칙적으로 [gyuchikjeogeuro]

regulation [,rɛgjʊ'leɪʃən] *n* 규정 [gyujeong]

rehearsal [rɪ'hɜːsºl] *n* 예행 연습 [yehaeng yeonseup]

rehearse [rɪ'hɜːs] *v* 예행연습하다 [yehaengyeonseuphada]

reimburse [,ri:ɪm'bɜːs] *v* 변상하다 [byeonsanghada]

reindeer ['reɪn,dɪə] *n* 순록 [sunnok]

reins [reɪnz] *npl* 고삐 [goppi]

reject [rɪ'dʒɛkt] *v* 거절하다 [geojeolhada]

relapse ['ri:,læps] *n* 퇴보 [toebo]

related [rɪ'leɪtɪd] *adj* 관계가 있는 [gwangyega inneun]

relation [rɪ'leɪʃən] *n* 관계 [gwangye]; **public relations** *npl* 홍보활동 [hongbohwaldong]

relationship [rɪ'leɪʃənʃɪp] *n* 관계 [gwangye]

relative ['rɛlətɪv] *n* 친척 [chincheok]

relatively ['rɛlətɪvlɪ] *adv* 상대적으로 [sangdaejeogeuro]

relax [rɪ'læks] *v* 긴장을 풀다 [ginjangeul pulda]

relaxation [,ri:læk'seɪʃən] *n* 휴식 [hyusik]

relaxed [rɪ'lækst] *adj* 차분한 [chabunhan]

relaxing [rɪ'læksɪŋ] *adj* 편하게 하는 [pyeonhage haneun]

relay ['ri:leɪ] *n* 교대조 [gyodaejo]

release [rɪ'li:s] *n* 해방 [haebang] ▷ *v* 해방하다 [haebanghada]

relegate ['rɛlɪ,geɪt] *v* 좌천시키다 [jwacheonsikida]

relevant ['rɛlɪvənt] *adj* 관계가 있는 [gwangyega inneun]

reliable [rɪ'laɪəbºl] *adj* 신뢰할수 있는 [sinnoehalsu inneun]

relief [rɪ'li:f] *n* 안도 [ando]

relieve [rɪ'li:v] *v* 경감시키다 [gyeonggamsikida]

relieved [rɪ'li:vd] *adj* 안심한 [ansimhan]

religion [rɪ'lɪdʒən] *n* 종교 [jonggyo]

religious [rɪ'lɪdʒəs] *adj* 신앙심 깊은 [sinangsim gipeun]

reluctant [rɪ'lʌktənt] *adj* 마음이 내키지 않는 [maeumi naekiji annneun]

reluctantly [rɪ'lʌktəntlɪ] *adv* 억지로 [eokjiro]

rely [rɪ'laɪ] *v* **rely on** *v* 믿다 [mitda]

remain [rɪ'meɪn] *v* 남다 [namda]

remaining [rɪ'meɪnɪŋ] *adj* 남아 있는 [nama inneun]

remains [rɪ'meɪnz] *npl* 잔여물 [janyeomul]

remake ['ri:,meɪk] *n* 개조 [gaejo]

remark [rɪ'mɑːk] *n* 소견 [sogyeon]

remarkable [rɪ'mɑːkəbºl] *adj* 현저한 [hyeonjeohan]

remarkably [rɪ'mɑːkəblɪ] *adv* 현저하게 [hyeonjeohage]

remarry [ri:'mærɪ] *v* 재혼하다 [jaehonhada]

remedy ['rɛmɪdɪ] *n* 의약품 [uiyakpum]

remember [rɪ'mɛmbə] *v* 기억하다 [gieokhada]

remind [rɪ'maɪnd] *v* 생각나게 하다 [saenggangnage hada]

reminder [rɪ'maɪndə] *n* 생각나게 하는 것 [saenggangnage haneun geot]

remorse [rɪ'mɔːs] *n* 깊은 후회 [gipeun huhoe]

remote [rɪ'məʊt] *adj* 멀리 떨어진 [meolli tteoreojin]; **remote control** *n* 리모컨 [rimokeon]

remotely [rɪ'məʊtlɪ] *adv* 멀리서

[meolliseo]

removable [rɪ'muːvəbəl] *adj* 이동할수
있는 [idonghalsu inneun]

removal [rɪ'muːvəl] *n* 제거 [jegeo];
removal van *n* 이삿짐 트럭 [isatjim
teureok]

remove [rɪ'muːv] *v* 제거하다
[jegeohada]

remover [rɪ'muːvə] *n* **nail-polish
remover** *n* 매니큐어 제거제
[maenikyueo jegeoje]

rendezvous ['rɒndɪˌvuː] *n* 모임약속
[moimyaksok]

renew [rɪ'njuː] *v* 재생하다
[jaesaenghada]

renewable [rɪ'njuːəbəl] *adj* 재생가능한
[jaesaengganeunghan]

renovate ['rɛnəˌveɪt] *v* 쇄신하다
[swaesinhada]

renowned [rɪ'naʊnd] *adj* 유명한
[yumyeonghan]

rent [rɛnt] *n* 임대료 [imdaeryo] ▷ *v*
임대하다 [imdaehada]

rental ['rɛntəl] *n* 임대료 [imdaeryo]; **car
rental** *n* 자동차 임대 [jadongcha
imdae]; **rental car** *n* 렌트카 [renteuka]

reorganize [riːˈɔːɡəˌnaɪz] *v* 재조직하다
[jaejojikhada]

rep [rɛp] *n* 대표 [daepyo]

repair [rɪ'pɛə] *n* 수리 [suri] (고치다) ▷ *v*
수리하다 [surihada]; **repair kit** *n*
수리도구 [suridogu]; **Can you repair
it?** 수리할 수 있으세요? [surihal su
isseuseyo?]; **Do you have a repair kit?**
수리 공구 있어요? [suri gonggu
isseoyo?]; **How much will the repairs
cost?** 수리 비용은 얼마예요? [suri
biyongeun eolmayeyo?]; **Where is the
nearest bike repair shop?** 가장
가까운 자전거 수리점은 어디에 있어요?
[gajang gakkaun jajeongeo
surijeomeun eodie isseoyo?]

repay [rɪ'peɪ] *v* 상환하다
[sanghwanhada]

repayment [rɪ'peɪmənt] *n* 상환
[sanghwan]

repeat [rɪ'piːt] *n* 반복 [banbok] ▷ *v*
반복하다 [banbokhada]

repeatedly [rɪ'piːtɪdlɪ] *adv* 반복하여
[banbokhayeo]

repellent [rɪ'pɛlənt] *adj* 불쾌한
[bulkwaehan]; **insect repellent** *n*
구충제 [guchungje]

repercussions [ˌriːpəˈkʌʃənz] *npl* 영향
[yeonghyang]

repetitive [rɪ'pɛtɪtɪv] *adj* 반복적인
[banbokjeogin]

replace [rɪ'pleɪs] *v* 대신하다
[daesinhada]

replacement [rɪ'pleɪsmənt] *n* 교체
[gyoche]

replay *n* ['riːˌpleɪ] 재연 [jaeyeon] ▷ *v*
[riːˈpleɪ] 재연하다 [jaeyeonhada]

replica ['rɛplɪkə] *n* 복제품 [bokjepum]

reply [rɪ'plaɪ] *n* 대답 [daedap] ▷ *v*
대답하다 [daedaphada]

report [rɪ'pɔːt] *n* 보고 [bogo] ▷ *v*
보고하다 [bogohada]; **report card** *n*
성적표 [seongjeokpyo]; **I need a police
report for my insurance** 보험 처리를
위한 경찰 보고서가 필요해요 [boheom
cheorireul wihan gyeongchal
bogoseoga pillyohaeyo]

reporter [rɪ'pɔːtə] *n* 기자 [gija]

represent [ˌrɛprɪˈzɛnt] *v* 대표하다
[daepyohada]

representative [ˌrɛprɪˈzɛntətɪv] *adj*
대표적인 [daepyojeogin]

reproduction [ˌriːprəˈdʌkʃən] *n* 재생산
[jaesaengsan]

reptile ['rɛptaɪl] *n* 파충류
[pachungnyu]

republic [rɪ'pʌblɪk] *n* 공화국
[gonghwaguk]

repulsive [rɪ'pʌlsɪv] *adj* 혐오감을
일으키는 [hyeomogameul ireukineun]

reputable ['rɛpjʊtəbəl] *adj* 평판이 좋은
[pyeongpani joheun]

reputation [ˌrɛpjʊˈteɪʃən] *n* 평판
[pyeongpan]

request [rɪ'kwɛst] *n* 요청 [yocheong]
▷ *v* 요청하다 [yocheonghada]

require [rɪ'kwaɪə] *v* 필요로 하다
[piryoro hada]

requirement [rɪ'kwaɪəmənt] *n*
필요조건 [piryojogeon]

rescue ['rɛskjuː] n 구조 [gujo] ▷ v 구조하다 [gujohada]; **Where is the nearest mountain rescue service post?** 가장 가까운 산악 구조대는 어디 있어요? [gajang gakkaun sanak gujodaeneun eodi isseoyo?]

research [rɪ'sɜːtʃ; 'riːsɜːtʃ] n 연구 [yeongu]; **market research** n 시장조사 [sijangjosa]

resemblance [rɪ'zɛmbləns] n 유사 [yusa]

resemble [rɪ'zɛmbəl] v 닮다 [darmda]

resent [rɪ'zɛnt] v 분개하다 [bungaehada]

resentful [rɪ'zɛntfʊl] adj 분개하고 있는 [bungaehago inneun]

reservation [ˌrɛzə'veɪʃən] n 예약 [yeyak]; **I have a reservation** 예약했어요 [yeyakhaesseoyo]; **I have a seat reservation** 좌석을 예약했어요 [jwaseogeul yeyakhaesseoyo]; **I'd like to make a reservation for half past seven for two people** 일곱시 삼십분에 두 명 예약하고 싶어요 [ilgopsi samsipbune du myeong yeyakhago sipeoyo]

reserve [rɪ'zɜːv] n (land) 보류지 [boryuji], (retention) 보유 [boyu] ▷ v 예약하다 [yeyakhada]

reserved [rɪ'zɜːvd] adj 예약되어 있는 [yeyakdoeeo inneun]

reservoir ['rɛzəˌvwɑː] n 저수지 [jeosuji]

resident ['rɛzɪdənt] n 주민 [jumin]

residential [ˌrɛzɪ'dɛnʃəl] adj 거주의 [geojuui]

resign [rɪ'zaɪn] v 사임하다 [saimhada]

resin ['rɛzɪn] n 수지 [suji] (재료)

resist [rɪ'zɪst] v 저항하다 [jeohanghada]

resistance [rɪ'zɪstəns] n 저항 [jeohang]

resit [riː'sɪt] v 재시험 치르다 [jaesiheom chireuda]

resolution [ˌrɛzə'luːʃən] n 결심 [gyeolsim]

resort [rɪ'zɔːt] n 휴양지 [hyuyangji]; **resort to** v 의지하다 [uijihada]

resource [rɪ'zɔːs; -'sɔːs] n 자원 [jawon]; **natural resources** npl 천연 자원 [cheonyeon jawon]

respect [rɪ'spɛkt] n 존경 [jongyeong] ▷ v 존경하다 [jongyeonghada]

respectable [rɪ'spɛktəbəl] adj 존경할 만한 [jongyeonghal manhan]

respectively [rɪ'spɛktɪvlɪ] adv 각각 [gakgak]

respond [rɪ'spɒnd] v 응답하다 [eungdaphada]

response [rɪ'spɒns] n 응답 [eungdap]

responsibility [rɪˌspɒnsə'bɪlɪtɪ] n 책임 [chaegim]

responsible [rɪ'spɒnsəbəl] adj 책임이 있는 [chaegimi inneun]

rest [rɛst] n 휴식 [hyusik] ▷ v 쉬다 [swida]; **the rest** n 휴식 [hyusik]

restaurant ['rɛstəˌrɒn; 'rɛstrɒn; -rɒnt] n 식당 [sikdang]; **Are there any vegetarian restaurants here?** 여기에 채식 식당이 있어요? [yeogie chaesik sikdangi isseoyo?]

restful ['rɛstfʊl] adj 평온한 [pyeongonhan]

restless ['rɛstlɪs] adj 불안한 [buranhan]

restore [rɪ'stɔː] v 복원하다 [bogwonhada]

restrict [rɪ'strɪkt] v 제한하다 [jehanhada]

restructure [riː'strʌktʃə] v 재구성하다 [jaeguseonghada]

result [rɪ'zʌlt] n 결과 [gyeolgwa]; **result in** v 기인하다 [giinhada]

resume [rɪ'zjuːm] v 다시 시작하다 [dasi sijakhada]

retail ['riːteɪl] n 소매 [somae] ▷ v 소매하다 [somaehada]; **retail price** n 소매가격 [somaegagyeok]

retailer ['riːteɪlə] n 소매업자 [somaeeopja]

retire [rɪ'taɪə] v 퇴직하다 [toejikhada]

retired [rɪ'taɪəd] adj 퇴직한 [toejikhan]

retirement [rɪ'taɪəmənt] n 퇴직 [toejik]

retrace [rɪ'treɪs] v 되돌아가다 [doedoragada]

return [rɪ'tɜːn] n (coming back) 귀환 [gwihwan], (yield) 수확 [suhwak] ▷ vi

돌아오다 [doraoda] ▷ vt...을 되돌려 주다 [...eul doedollyeo juda]; **day return** n 당일 왕복표 [dangil wangbokpyo]; **return ticket** n 왕복표 [wangbokpyo]; **tax return** n 소득신고 [sodeuksingo]

reunion [riːˈjuːnjən] n 재회 [jaehoe]

reuse [riːˈjuːz] v 재사용하다 [jaesayonghada]

reveal [rɪˈviːl] v 드러내다 [deureonaeda]

revenge [rɪˈvɛndʒ] n 복수 [boksu]

revenue [ˈrɛvɪˌnjuː] n 세입 [seip]

reverse [rɪˈvɜːs] n 반대 [bandae] ▷ v 거꾸로 하다 [geokkuro hada]

review [rɪˈvjuː] n 평론 [pyeongnon]

revise [rɪˈvaɪz] v 수정하다 [sujeonghada]

revision [rɪˈvɪʒən] n 교정 [gyojeong]

revive [rɪˈvaɪv] v 소생시키다 [sosaengsikida]

revolting [rɪˈvəʊltɪŋ] adj 역하게 하는 [yeokhage haneun]

revolution [ˌrɛvəˈluːʃən] n 혁명 [hyeongmyeong]

revolutionary [ˌrɛvəˈluːʃənərɪ] adj 혁명적인 [hyeongmyeongjeogin]

revolver [rɪˈvɒlvə] n 회전식 연발 권총 [hoejeonsik yeonbal gwonchong]

reward [rɪˈwɔːd] n 보상 [bosang]

rewarding [rɪˈwɔːdɪŋ] adj 보람이 있는 [borami inneun]

rewind [riːˈwaɪnd] v 다시 감다 [dasi gamda]

rheumatism [ˈruːməˌtɪzəm] n 류머티즘 [ryumeotijeum]

rhubarb [ˈruːbɑːb] n 장군풀 [janggunpul]

rhyme [raɪm] n **nursery rhyme** n 동요 [dongyo]

rhythm [ˈrɪðəm] n 리듬 [rideum]

rib [rɪb] n 늑골 [neukgol]

ribbon [ˈrɪbən] n 리본 [ribon]

rice [raɪs] n 쌀 [ssal]; **brown rice** n 현미 [hyeonmi]

rich [rɪtʃ] adj 부유한 [buyuhan]

ride [raɪd] n 타기 [tagi] ▷ v 타다 [tada]

rider [ˈraɪdə] n 타는 사람 [taneun saram]

ridiculous [rɪˈdɪkjʊləs] adj 웃기는 [utgineun]

riding [ˈraɪdɪŋ] n 승마 [seungma]; **horse riding** n 승마 [seungma]

rifle [ˈraɪfᵊl] n 소총 [sochong]

rig [rɪg] n 굴착장치 [gulchakjangchi]; **oil rig** n 유정의 굴착장치 [yujeongui gulchakjangchi]

right [raɪt] adj (correct) 옳은 [oreun], (not left) 오른쪽의 [oreunjjogui] ▷ adv 바로 [baro] ▷ n 권리 [gwolli]; **civil rights** npl 시민권 [simingwon]; **human rights** npl 인권 [ingwon]; **right angle** n 직각 [jikgak]; **right of way** n 통행우선권 [tonghaenguseongwon]

right-hand [ˈraɪtˌhænd] adj 오른쪽의 [oreunjjogui]; **right-hand drive** n 오른쪽 핸들 [oreunjjok haendeul]

right-handed [ˈraɪtˌhændɪd] adj 오른손잡이의 [oreunsonjabiui]

rightly [ˈraɪtlɪ] adv 올바르게 [olbareuge]

right-wing [ˈraɪtˌwɪŋ] adj 우익의 [uigui]

rim [rɪm] n 테두리 [teduri]

ring [rɪŋ] n 반지 [banji] ▷ v 울리다 [ullida]; **engagement ring** n 약혼 반지 [yakhon banji]; **ring binder** n 링바인더 [ringbaindeo]; **ring road** n 순환도로 [sunhwandoro]; **wedding ring** n 결혼반지 [gyeolhonbanji]

ring back [rɪŋ bæk] v 다시 전화하다 [dasi jeonhwahada]

ringtone [ˈrɪŋˌtəʊn] n 휴대폰 벨소리 [hyudaepon belsori]

ring up [rɪŋ ʌp] v 전화하다 [jeonhwahada]

rink [rɪŋk] n 스케이트링크 [seukeiteuringkeu]; **ice rink** n 스케이트장 [seukeiteujang]; **skating rink** n 스케이트 링크 [seukeiteu ringkeu]

rinse [rɪns] n 헹구기 [henggugi] ▷ v 헹구다 [hengguda]

riot [ˈraɪət] n 폭동 [pokdong] ▷ v 폭동을 일으키다 [pokdongeul ireukida]

rip [rɪp] v (물건을) 잡아 찢다 [(mulgeoneul) jaba jjitda]
ripe [raɪp] adj 여문 [yeomun]
rip off [rɪp ɒf] v 사기치다 [sagichida]
rip-off [ˈrɪpɒf] n 바가지 [bagaji]
rip up [rɪp ʌp] v 잡아 찢다 [jaba jjitda]
rise [raɪz] n 상승 [sangseung] ▷ v 일어나다 [ireonada]
risk [rɪsk] n 위험 [wiheom] ▷ vt 위험을 무릅쓰다 [wiheomeul mureupsseuda]
risky [ˈrɪskɪ] adj 위험한 [wiheomhan]
ritual [ˈrɪtjʊəl] adj 의례적인 [uiryejeogin] ▷ n 의식 [uisik]
rival [ˈraɪvəl] adj 경쟁하는 [gyeongjaenghaneun] ▷ n 경쟁 상대 [gyeongjaeng sangdae]
rivalry [ˈraɪvəlrɪ] n 경쟁 [gyeongjaeng]
river [ˈrɪvə] n 강 [gang]; **Can one swim in the river?** 강에서 수영해도 될까요? [gangeseo suyeonghaedo doelkkayo?]
road [rəʊd] n 길 [gil]; **main road** n 중심도로 [jungsimdoro]; **ring road** n 순환도로 [sunhwandoro]; **road map** n 도로지도 [dorojido]; **road rage** n 노상 분노 [nosang bunno]; **road sign** n 도로 표지 [doro pyoji]; **road tax** n 도로세 [dorose]; **slip road** n 램프 [raempeu]; **Are the roads icy?** 길이 얼었어요? [giri eoreosseoyo?]; **Is the road to... snowed up?** ... 가는 길에 눈이 쌓였나요? [... ganeun gire nuni ssahyeonnayo?]; **When will the road be clear?** 길이 언제 뚫릴까요? [giri eonje tturrilkkayo?]; **Which road do I take for...?** ...에 가려면 어느 길을 타나요? [...e garyeomyeon eoneu gireul tanayo?]
roadblock [ˈrəʊdˌblɒk] n 노상 장애물 [nosang jangaemul]
roadworks [ˈrəʊdˌwɜːks] npl 도로 공사 [doro gongsa]
roast [rəʊst] adj 구운 [guun]
rob [rɒb] v 빼앗다 [ppaeatda]
robber [rɒbə] n 강도 [gangdo]
robbery [ˈrɒbərɪ] n 강도질 [gangdojil]
robin [ˈrɒbɪn] n 울새 [ulsae]
robot [ˈrəʊbɒt] n 로봇 [robot]
rock [rɒk] n 바위 [bawi] ▷ v 앞뒤(좌우)로

흔들다 [apdwi(jwau)ro heundeulda]; **rock climbing** n 암벽타기 [ambyeoktagi]
rocket [ˈrɒkɪt] n 로켓 [roket]
rod [rɒd] n 막대 [makdae]
rodent [ˈrəʊdənt] n 설치류 동물 [seolchiryu dongmul]
role [rəʊl] n 역할 [yeokhal]
roll [rəʊl] n 구르기 [gureugi] ▷ v 구르다 [gureuda]; **bread roll** n 롤 빵 [rol ppang]; **roll call** n 점호 [jeomho]
roller [ˈrəʊlə] n 굴림대 [gullimdae]
rollercoaster [ˈrəʊləˌkəʊstə] n 롤러코스터 [rolleokoseuteo]
rollerskates [ˈrəʊləˌskeɪts] npl 롤러스케이트 [rolleoseukeiteu]
rollerskating [ˈrəʊləˌskeɪtɪŋ] n 롤러스케이트 타기 [rolleoseukeiteu tagi]
Roman [ˈrəʊmən] adj 로마의 [romaui]; **Roman Catholic** n 천주교도 [cheonjugyodo], 천주교의 [cheonjugyoui]
romance [ˈrəʊmæns] n 로맨스 [romaenseu]
Romanesque [ˌrəʊməˈnɛsk] adj 로마네스크 양식의 [romaneseukeu yangsigui]
Romania [rəʊˈmeɪnɪə] n 루마니아 [rumania]
Romanian [rəʊˈmeɪnɪən] adj 루마니아의 [rumaniaui] ▷ n (language) 루마니아어 [rumaniaeo], (person) 루마니아 사람 [rumania saram]
romantic [rəʊˈmæntɪk] adj 로맨틱한 [romaentikhan]
roof [ruːf] n 지붕 [jibung]; **The roof leaks** 지붕이 새요 [jibungi saeyo]
roof rack [ˈruːfˌræk] n 차 지붕 위의 짐칸 [cha jibung wiui jimkan]
room [ruːm; rʊm] n 방 [bang]; **changing room** n 탈의실 [taruisil]; **dining room** n 식당 [sikdang]; **double room** n 2인실 [i insil]; **fitting room** n 탈의실 [taruisil]; **living room** n 거실 [geosil]; **room number** n 방 번호 [bang beonho]; **room service** n 객실서비스 [gaeksilseobiseu]; **single**

room *n* 1인용 방 [il inyong bang];
sitting room *n* 응접실 [eungjeopsil];
spare room *n* 빈 방 [bin bang]; **twin
room** *n* 트윈 룸 [teuwin rum];
twin-bedded room *n* 트윈 베드가
있는 침실 [teuwin bedeuga inneun
chimsil]; **utility room** *n* 다용도실
[dayongdosil]; **waiting room** *n* 대기실
[daegisil]; **Can I see the room?** 방을 볼
수 있을까요? [bangeul bol su
isseulkkayo?]; **Can I switch rooms?**
방을 바꿀 수 있나요? [bangeul bakkul
su innayo?]; **Can you clean the room,
please?** 방을 청소해 주시겠어요?
[bangeul cheongsohae jusigesseoyo?];
Do you have a room for tonight?
오늘 밤 방 있어요? [oneul bam bang
isseoyo?]; **Does the room have air
conditioning?** 방에 에어컨 있어요?
[bange eeokeon isseoyo?]; **How much
is the room?** 방이 얼마예요? [bangi
eolmayeyo?]; **I booked a room in the
name of...** ... 이름으로 방을
예약했어요 [... ireumeuro bangeul
yeyakhaesseoyo]; **I need a room with
wheelchair access** 휠체어로 출입할
수 있는 방이 필요해요 [hwilcheeoro
churiphal su inneun bangi piryohaeyo];
**I'd like a room with a view of the
sea** 바다가 보이는 방이 좋겠어요
[badaga boineun bangi jokesseoyo]; **I'd
like to rent a room** 방을 빌리고
싶어요 [bangeul billigo sipeoyo];
Please charge it to my room 제
방으로 청구하세요 [je bangeuro
cheongguhaseyo]; **The room is dirty**
방이 더러워요 [bangi deoreowoyo];
The room is too cold 방이 너무
추워요 [bangi neomu chuwoyo];
There's a problem with the room
방에 문제가 있어요 [bange munjega
isseoyo]
roommate ['ruːmˌmeɪt; 'rʊm-] *n*
룸메이트 [rummeiteu]
root [ruːt] *n* 뿌리 [ppuri]
rope [rəʊp] *n* 밧줄 [batjul]
rope in [rəʊp ɪn] *v* 권하다 [gwonhada]
rose [rəʊz] *n* 장미 [jangmi]

rosé ['rəʊzeɪ] *n* 로제 [roje]; **Can you
recommend a good rosé wine?** 좋은
로제 와인을 추천해 주시겠어요?
[joheun roje waineul chucheonhae
jusigesseoyo?]
rosemary ['rəʊzmərɪ] *n* 로즈메리
[rojeumeri]
rot [rɒt] *v* 썩다 [sseokda]
rotten ['rɒtᵊn] *adj* 썩은 [sseogeun]
rough [rʌf] *adj* 거친 [geochin]; **Is the
sea rough today?** 오늘 바다가
거친가요? [oneul badaga
geochingayo?]
roughly ['rʌflɪ] *adv* 대략 [daeryak]
roulette [ruːˈlɛt] *n* 룰렛 [rullet]
round [raʊnd] *adj* 둥근 [dunggeun] ▷ *n*
(*circle*) 원형 [wonhyeong], (*series*) 연속
[yeonsok] ▷ *prep*...주위에 [...juwie];
paper round *n* 신문배달
[sinmunbaedal]; **round trip** *n* 왕복여행
[wangbogyeohaeng]
roundabout ['raʊndəˌbaʊt] *n*
순환교차로 [sunhwangyocharo]
round up [raʊnd ʌp] *v* 집합하다
[jiphaphada]
route [ruːt] *n* 경로 [gyeongno]
routine [ruːˈtiːn] *n* 정해진 과정
[jeonghaejin gwajeong]
row¹ [rəʊ] *n* (*line*) 줄 [jul] ▷ *v* (*in boat*)
배를 젓다 [baereul jeotda]
row² [raʊ] *n* (*argument*) 말다툼
[maldatum] ▷ *v* (*to argue*) 다투다
[datuda]
rowing ['rəʊɪŋ] *n* 배젓기 [baejeotgi];
rowing boat *n* 젓는 배 [jeotneun bae]
royal ['rɔɪəl] *adj* 왕족의 [wangjogui]
rub [rʌb] *v* 문지르다 [munjireuda]
rubber ['rʌbə] *n* 고무 [gomu]; **rubber
band** *n* 고무밴드 [gomubaendeu];
rubber gloves *npl* 고무장갑
[gomujanggap]
rubbish ['rʌbɪʃ] *adj* 하찮은
[hachanheun] ▷ *n* 쓰레기 [sseuregi];
rubbish dump *n* 쓰레기 수거장
[sseuregi sugeojang]; **Where do we
leave the rubbish?** 쓰레기는 어디에
버릴까요? [sseuregineun eodie
beorilkkayo?]

rucksack ['rʌk,sæk] *n* 배낭 [baenang]
rude [ru:d] *adj* 무례한 [muryehan]
rug [rʌg] *n* 양탄자 [yangtanja]
rugby ['rʌgbɪ] *n* 럭비 [reokbi]
ruin ['ru:ɪn] *n* 폐허 [pyeheo] ▷ *v*
  파괴하다 [pagoehada]
rule [ru:l] *n* 규칙 [gyuchik]
rule out [ru:l aʊt] *v* 제외하다 [jeoehada]
ruler ['ru:lə] *n* (commander) 통치자
  [tongchija], (measure) 자 [ja]
rum [rʌm] *n* 럼 [reom]
rumour ['ru:mə] *n* 소문 [somun]
run [rʌn] *n* 뛰기 [ttwigi] ▷ *vi* 달리다
  [dallida] ▷ *vt* (길거리 등을) 달리다
  [(gilgeori deungeul) dallida]
run away [rʌn ə'weɪ] *v* 도망가다
  [domanggada]
runner ['rʌnə] *n* 경주자 [gyeongjuja];
  runner bean *n* 깍지를 먹는 콩
  [kkakjireul meongneun kong]
runner-up ['rʌnəʌp] *n* 차점자
  [chajeomja]
running ['rʌnɪŋ] *n* 달리기 [dalligi]
run out [rʌn aʊt] *v* **The towels have
  run out** 타월이 다 떨어졌어요 [tawori
  da tteoreojyeosseoyo]
run out of [rʌn aʊt ɒv] *v* 다 써버리다 [da
  sseoberida]
run over [rʌn 'əʊvə] *v* 치다 [chida]
runway ['rʌn,weɪ] *n* 활주로 [hwaljuro]
rural ['rʊərəl] *adj* 시골의 [sigorui]
rush [rʌʃ] *n* 골풀 [golpul] ▷ *v* 서두르다
  [seodureuda]; **rush hour** *n* 러시아워
  [reosiawo]
rusk [rʌsk] *n* 러스크 [reoseukeu]
Russia ['rʌʃə] *n* 러시아 [reosia]
Russian ['rʌʃən] *adj* 러시아의 [reosiaui]
  ▷ *n* (language) 러시아어 [reosiaeo],
  (person) 러시아 사람 [reosia saram]
rust [rʌst] *n* 녹 [nok]
rusty ['rʌstɪ] *adj* 녹슨 [nokseun]
ruthless ['ru:θlɪs] *adj* 잔인한
  [janinhan]
rye [raɪ] *n* 호밀 [homil]

S

Sabbath ['sæbəθ] *n* 안식일 [ansigil]
sabotage ['sæbə,tɑ:ʒ] *n* 방해행위
  [banghaehaengwi] ▷ *v* 사보타주하다
  [sabotajuhada]
sachet ['sæʃeɪ] *n* 향주머니
  [hyangjumeoni]
sack [sæk] *n* (container) 부대 [budae]
  (가방), (dismissal) 해고 [haego] ▷ *v*
  부대에 담다 [budaee damda]
sacred ['seɪkrɪd] *adj* 신성한
  [sinseonghan]
sacrifice ['sækrɪ,faɪs] *n* 희생
  [huisaeng]
sad [sæd] *adj* 슬픈 [seulpeun]
saddle ['sædªl] *n* 안장 [anjang]
saddlebag ['sædªl,bæg] *n* 새들백
  [saedeulbaek]
sadly [sædlɪ] *adv* 슬프게 [seulpeuge]
safari [sə'fɑ:rɪ] *n* 사파리 [sapari]
safe [seɪf] *adj* 안전한 [anjeonhan] ▷ *n*
  금고 [geumgo]; **I have some things in
  the safe** 금고에 넣어둔 것이 있어요
  [geumgoe neoheodun geosi isseoyo]; **I
  would like to put my jewellery in
  the safe** 제 장신구를 금고에 넣고
  싶어요 [je jangsingureul geumgoe
  neoko sipeoyo]; **Is it safe for children?**

아이에게 안전한가요? [aiege anjeonhangayo?]; **Is it safe to swim here?** 여기에서 수영해도 안전한가요? [yeogieseo suyeonghaedo anjeonhangayo?]; **Put that in the safe, please** 금고에 넣어 주세요 [geumgoe neoheo juseyo]

safety ['seɪftɪ] n 안전 [anjeon]; **safety belt** n 안전벨트 [anjeonbelteu]; **safety pin** n 안전핀 [anjeonpin]

saffron ['sæfrən] n 사프란 [sapeuran]

Sagittarius [ˌsædʒɪ'tɛərɪəs] n 궁수자리 [gungsujari]

Sahara [sə'hɑːrə] n 사하라 [sahara]

sail [seɪl] n 돛 [dot] ▷ v 항해하다 [hanghaehada]

sailing ['seɪlɪŋ] n 항해 [hanghae]; **sailing boat** n 범선 [beomseon]

sailor ['seɪlə] n 선원 [seonwon]

saint [seɪnt; sənt] n 성인 [seongin]

salad ['sæləd] n 샐러드 [saelleodeu]; **mixed salad** n 혼합된 샐러드 [honhapdoen saelleodeu]; **salad dressing** n 샐러드 드레싱 [saelleodeu deuresing]

salami [sə'lɑːmɪ] n 살라미 소시지 [sallami sosiji]

salary ['sælərɪ] n 월급 [wolgeup]

sale [seɪl] n 판매 [panmae]; **sales assistant** n 판매원 [panmaewon]; **sales rep** n 판매대표 [panmaedaepyo]

salesman, salesmen ['seɪlzmən, 'seɪlzmɛn] n 판매원 [panmaewon]

salesperson ['seɪlzpɜːs°n] n 판매원 [panmaewon]

saleswoman, saleswomen ['seɪlzwʊmən, 'seɪlzwɪmɪn] n 여자 판매원 [yeoja panmaewon]

saliva [sə'laɪvə] n 침 [chim]

salmon ['sæmən] n 연어 [yeoneo]

salon ['sælɒn] n **beauty salon** n 미용실 [miyongsil]

saloon [sə'luːn] n 승용차 [seungyongcha]; **saloon car** n 승용차 [seungyongcha]

salt [sɔːlt] n 소금 [sogeum]; **Pass the salt, please** 소금 좀 주세요 [sogeum jom juseyo]

saltwater ['sɔːltˌwɔːtə] adj 소금물의 [sogeummurui]

salty ['sɔːltɪ] adj 짠 [jjan]

salute [sə'luːt] v 인사하다 [insahada]

salve [sælv] n **lip salve** n 입술 연고 [ipsul yeongo]

same [seɪm] adj 동일한 [dongilhan]

sample ['sɑːmp°l] n 견본 [gyeonbon]

sand [sænd] n 모래 [morae]; **sand dune** n 모래 언덕 [morae eondeok]

sandal ['sænd°l] n 샌들 [saendeul]

sandcastle [sændkɑːs°l] n 모래성 [moraeseong]

sandpaper ['sændˌpeɪpə] n 사포 [sapo]

sandpit ['sændˌpɪt] n 모래상자 [moraesangja]

sandstone ['sændˌstəʊn] n 사암 [saam]

sandwich ['sænwɪdʒ; -wɪtʃ] n 샌드위치 [saendeuwichi]; **What kind of sandwiches do you have?** 어떤 종류의 샌드위치가 있으세요? [eotteon jongnyuui saendeuwichiga isseuseyo?]

San Marino [ˌsæn mə'riːnəʊ] n 산마리노 [sanmarino]

sapphire ['sæfaɪə] n 사파이어 [sapaieo]

sarcastic [sɑː'kæstɪk] adj 빈정대는 [binjeongdaeneun]

sardine [sɑː'diːn] n 정어리 [jeongeori]

satchel ['sætʃəl] n 멜빵 달린 가방 [melppang dallin gabang]

satellite ['sætəlaɪt] n 위성 [wiseong]; **satellite dish** n 위성방송수신 접시 안테나 [wiseongbangsongsusin jeopsi antena]

satisfaction [ˌsætɪs'fækʃən] n 만족 [manjok]

satisfactory [ˌsætɪs'fæktərɪ; -trɪ] adj 만족스러운 [manjokseureoun]

satisfied ['sætɪsˌfaɪd] adj 만족한 [manjokhan]

sat nav ['sæt næv] n 위성항법 [wiseonghangbeop]

Saturday ['sætədɪ] n 토요일 [toyoil]; **every Saturday** 토요일마다 [toyoilmada]; **last Saturday** 지난

토요일 [jinan toyoil]; **next Saturday**
다음 토요일 [daeum toyoil]; **on
Saturday** 토요일에 [toyoire]; **on
Saturdays** 토요일마다 [toyoilmada];
this Saturday 이번 토요일 [ibeon
toyoil]

sauce [sɔːs] n 소스 [soseu]; **soy sauce** n
간장 [ganjang] (식품); **tomato sauce** n
토마토 소스 [tomato soseu]

saucepan ['sɔːspən] n 냄비 [naembi]

saucer ['sɔːsə] n 받침 접시 [batchim
jeopsi]

Saudi ['sɔːdɪ; 'saʊ-] adj
사우디아라비아의 [saudiarabiaui] ▷ n
사우디아라비아 [saudiarabia]

Saudi Arabia ['sɔːdɪ; 'saʊ-] n
사우디아라비아 [saudiarabia]

Saudi Arabian ['sɔːdɪ ə'reɪbɪən] adj
사우디아라비아의 [saudiarabiaui] ▷ n
사우디아라비아 사람 [saudiarabia
saram]

sauna ['sɔːnə] n 사우나 [sauna]

sausage ['sɒsɪdʒ] n 소시지 [sosiji]

save [seɪv] v 구해주다 [guhaejuda]

save up [seɪv ʌp] v 저축하다
[jeochukhada]

savings ['seɪvɪŋz] npl 저축 [jeochuk]

savoury ['seɪvərɪ] adj 짭짤한
[jjapjjalhan]

saw [sɔː] n 톱 [top]

sawdust ['sɔːˌdʌst] n 톱밥 [topbap]

saxophone ['sæksəˌfəʊn] n 색소폰
[saeksopon]

say [seɪ] v 말하다 [malhada]

saying ['seɪɪŋ] n 말하기 [malhagi]

scaffolding ['skæfəldɪŋ] n 비계 [bigye]

scale [skeɪl] n (measure) 눈금
[nungeum], (tiny piece) 비늘 [bineul]

scales [skeɪlz] npl 저울 [jeoul]

scallop ['skɒləp; 'skæl-] n 국자가리비
[gukjagaribi]

scam [skæm] n 사기 [sagi]

scampi ['skæmpɪ] npl 가시발새우
[gasibalsaeu]

scan [skæn] n 정밀검사
[jeongmilgeomsa] ▷ v 자세히 살피다
[jasehi salpida]

scandal ['skænd°l] n 추문 [chumun]

Scandinavia [ˌskændɪ'neɪvɪə] n
스칸디나비아 [seukandinabia]

Scandinavian [ˌskændɪ'neɪvɪən] adj
스칸디나비아의 [seukandinabiaui]

scanner ['skænə] n 스캐너 [seukaeneo]

scar [skɑː] n 흉터 [hyungteo]

scarce [skɛəs] adj 부족한 [bujokhan]

scarcely ['skɛəslɪ] adv 겨우 [gyeou]

scare [skɛə] n 두려움 [duryeoum] ▷ v
겁주다 [geopjuda]

scarecrow ['skɛəˌkrəʊ] n 허수아비
[heosuabi]

scared [skɛəd] adj 겁먹은
[geommeogeun]

scarf, scarves [skɑːf, skɑːvz] n 스카프
[seukapeu]

scarlet ['skɑːlɪt] adj 주홍색의
[juhongsaegui]

scary ['skɛərɪ] adj 무서운 [museoun]

scene [siːn] n 현장 [hyeonjang]

scenery ['siːnərɪ] n 경치 [gyeongchi]

scent [sɛnt] n 냄새 [naemsae]

sceptical ['skɛptɪk°l] adj 회의적인
[hoeuijeogin]

schedule ['ʃɛdjuːl; 'skɛdʒʊəl] n 일정
[iljeong]

scheme [skiːm] n 계획 [gyehoek]

schizophrenic [ˌskɪtsəʊ'frɛnɪk] adj
정신분열증의
[jeongsinbunyeoljeunguiui]

scholarship ['skɒləʃɪp] n 장학금
[janghakgeum]

school [skuːl] n 학교 [hakgyo]; **art
school** n 예술 학교 [yesul hakgyo];
boarding school n 기숙학교
[gisukhakgyo]; **elementary school** n
초등학교 [chodeunghakgyo]; **infant
school** n 유치원 [yuchiwon];
language school n 어학원
[eohagwon]; **law school** n 법과대학
[beopgwadaehak]; **night school** n
야간 학교 [yagan hakgyo]; **nursery
school** n 유치원 [yuchiwon]; **primary
school** n 초등학교 [chodeunghakgyo];
public school n 사립 중고교 [sarip
junggogyo]; **school uniform** n 교복
[gyobok]; **secondary school** n
중등학교 [jungdeunghakgyo]

schoolbag ['sku:l,bæg] n 책가방 [chaekgabang]

schoolbook ['sku:l,bʊk] n 교과서 [gyogwaseo]

schoolboy ['sku:l,bɔɪ] n 남학생 [namhaksaeng]

schoolchildren ['sku:l,tʃɪldrən] n 학동 [hakdong]

schoolgirl ['sku:l,gɜ:l] n 여학생 [yeohaksaeng]

schoolteacher ['sku:l,ti:tʃə] n 교사 [gyosa]

science ['saɪəns] n 과학 [gwahag]; **science fiction** n 공상과학 소설 [gongsanggwahak soseol]

scientific [,saɪən'tɪfɪk] adj 과학적인 [gwahakjeogin]

scientist ['saɪəntɪst] n 과학자 [gwahakja]

sci-fi ['saɪ,faɪ] n 공상과학 소설 [gongsanggwahak soseol]

scissors ['sɪzəz] npl 가위 [gawi]; **nail scissors** npl 손톱가위 [sontopgawi]

sclerosis [sklɪə'rəʊsɪs] n **multiple sclerosis** n 다발성경화증 [dabalseonggyeonghwajeung]

scoff [skɒf] v 비웃다 [biutda]

scold [skəʊld] v 꾸짖다 [kkujitda]

scooter ['sku:tə] n 스쿠터 [seukuteo]

score [skɔ:] n (game/match) 득점 [deukjeom], (of music) 악보 [akbo] ▷ v 득점하다 [deukjeomhada]

Scorpio ['skɔ:pɪ,əʊ] n 전갈자리 [jeongaljari]

scorpion ['skɔ:pɪən] n 전갈 [jeongal]

Scot [skɒt] n 스코틀랜드 사람 [seukoteullaendeu saram]

Scotland ['skɒtlənd] n 스코틀랜드 [seukoteullaendeu]

Scots [skɒts] adj 스코틀랜드의 [seukoteullaendeuui]

Scotsman, Scotsmen ['skɒtsmən, 'skɒtsmɛn] n 스코틀랜드 사람 [seukoteullaendeu saram]

Scotswoman, Scotswomen ['skɒts,wʊmən, 'skɒts,wɪmɪn] n 스코틀랜드 여자 [seukoteullaendeu yeoja]

Scottish ['skɒtɪʃ] adj 스코틀랜드의 [seukoteullaendeuui]

scout [skaʊt] n 정찰 [jeongchal]

scrap [skræp] n (dispute) 싸움 [ssaum], (small piece) 조각 [jogak] ▷ v 버리다 [beorida]; **scrap paper** n 메모 용지 [memo yongji]

scrapbook ['skræp,bʊk] n 스크랩북 [seukeuraepbuk]

scratch [skrætʃ] n 긁기 [geurkgi] ▷ v 긁다 [geurkda]

scream [skri:m] n 비명 [bimyeong] (소리치다) ▷ v 비명지르다 [bimyeongjireuda]

screen [skri:n] n 화면 [hwamyeon]; **plasma screen** n 플라스마 화면 [peullaseuma hwamyeon]; **screen (off)** v 그늘지게 하다 [geuneuljige hada]

screen-saver ['skri:n,seɪvər] n 화면 보호기 [hwamyeon bohogi]

screw [skru:] n 나사못 [nasamot]

screwdriver ['skru:,draɪvə] n 나사돌리개 [nasadolligae]

scribble ['skrɪbəl] v 갈겨쓰다 [galgyeosseuda]

scrub [skrʌb] v 문지르다 [munjireuda]

sculptor ['skʌlptə] n 조각가 [jogakga]

sculpture ['skʌlptʃə] n 조각술 [jogaksul]

sea [si:] n 바다 [bada]; **North Sea** n 북해 [bukhae]; **Red Sea** n 홍해 [honghae]; **sea level** n 해수면 [haesumyeon]; **sea water** n 해수 [haesu]; **Is the sea rough today?** 오늘 바다가 거친가요? [oneul badaga geochingayo?]

seafood ['si:,fu:d] n 해산물 [haesanmul]; **Could you prepare a meal without seafood?** 해산물이 들어가지 않은 식사를 준비해 주시겠어요? [haesanmuri deureogaji anheun siksareul junbihae jusigesseoyo?]; **Do you like seafood?** 해산물 좋아하세요? [haesanmul johahaseyo?]

seagull ['si:,gʌl] n 갈매기 [galmaegi]

seal [si:l] n (animal) 바다표범

[badapyobeom], *(mark)* 도장 [dojang]
▷ *v* 봉인하다 [bonginhada]

seam [siːm] *n* 솔기 [solgi]

seaman, seamen [ˈsiːmən, ˈsiːmɛn] *n* 선원 [seonwon]

search [sɜːtʃ] *n* 검색 [geomsaek] ▷ *v* 검색하다 [geomsaekhada]; **search engine** *n* 검색 엔진 [geomsaek enjin]; **search party** *n* 수색대 [susaekdae]

seashore [ˈsiːˌʃɔː] *n* 해안 [haean]

seasick [ˈsiːˌsɪk] *adj* 뱃멀미의 [baetmeolmiui]

seaside [ˈsiːˌsaɪd] *n* 해변 [haebyeon]

season [ˈsiːzⁿn] *n* 계절 [gyejeol]; **high season** *n* 성수기 [seongsugi]; **low season** *n* 비성수기 [biseongsugi]; **season ticket** *n* 정기 승차권 [jeonggi seungchagwon]

seasonal [ˈsiːzənᵊl] *adj* 계절적인 [gyejeoljeogin]

seasoning [ˈsiːzənɪŋ] *n* 조미료 [jomiryo]

seat [siːt] *n (constituency)* 의석 [uiseok], *(furniture)* 의자 [uija]; **aisle seat** *n* 통로쪽 좌석 [tongnojjok jwaseok]; **window seat** *n* 창쪽 좌석 [changjjok jwaseok]

seatbelt [ˈsiːtˌbɛlt] *n* 좌석 벨트 [jwaseok belteu]

seaweed [ˈsiːˌwiːd] *n* 해초 [haecho]

second [ˈsɛkənd] *adj* 두번째의 [dubeonjjaeui] ▷ *n* 초 [cho] *(시간)*; **second class** *n* 2류 [iryu]

second-class [ˈsɛkəndˌklɑːs] *adj* 2류의 [iryuui]

secondhand [ˈsɛkəndˌhænd] *adj* 중고의 [junggoui]

secondly [ˈsɛkəndlɪ] *adv* 두번째로 [dubeonjjaero]

second-rate [ˈsɛkəndˌreɪt] *adj* 2등급의 [ideunggeubui]

secret [ˈsiːkrɪt] *adj* 비밀의 [bimirui] ▷ *n* 비밀 [bimil]; **secret service** *n* 첩보부 [cheopbobu]

secretary [ˈsɛkrətrɪ] *n* 비서 [biseo]

secretly [ˈsiːkrɪtlɪ] *adv* 비밀히 [bimilhi]

sect [sɛkt] *n* 분파 [bunpa]

section [ˈsɛkʃən] *n* 잘라낸 부분 [jallanaen bubun]

sector [ˈsɛktə] *n* 부문 [bumun]

secure [sɪˈkjʊə] *adj* 안전한 [anjeonhan]

security [sɪˈkjʊərɪtɪ] *n* 보안 [boan]; **security guard** *n* 경호원 [gyeonghowon]; **social security** *n* 사회보장 [sahoebojang]

sedative [ˈsɛdətɪv] *n* 진정제 [jinjeongje]

see [siː] *v* 보다 [boda]

seed [siːd] *n* 씨 [ssi]

seek [siːk] *v* 찾다 [chatda]

seem [siːm] *v* 보이다 [boida]

seesaw [ˈsiːˌsɔː] *n* 시소 [siso]

see-through [ˈsiːˌθruː] *adj* 투명한 [tumyeonghan]

seize [siːz] *v* 잡다 [japda]

seizure [ˈsiːʒə] *n* 발작 [baljak]

seldom [ˈsɛldəm] *adv* 드물게 [deumulge]

select [sɪˈlɛkt] *v* 선택하다 [seontaekhada]

selection [sɪˈlɛkʃən] *n* 선택 [seontaek]

self-assured [ˈsɛlfəˈʃʊəd] *adj* 자신있는 [jasininneun]

self-catering [ˈsɛlfˌkeɪtərɪŋ] *n* 자취 [jachwi]

self-centred [ˈsɛlfˌsɛntəd] *adj* 이기적인 [igijeogin]

self-conscious [ˈsɛlfˌkɒnʃəs] *adj* 자의식이 강한 [jauisigi ganghan]

self-contained [ˈsɛlfˌkənˈteɪnd] *adj* 자급식의 [jageupsigui]

self-control [ˈsɛlfˌkənˈtrəʊl] *n* 자제 [jaje]

self-defence [ˈsɛlfdɪˈfɛns] *n* 정당방위 [jeongdangbangwi]

self-discipline [ˈsɛlfˌdɪsɪplɪn] *n* 자기수양 [jagisuyang]

self-employed [ˈsɛlɪmˈplɔɪd] *adj* 자영업의 [jayeongeobui]

selfish [ˈsɛlfɪʃ] *adj* 이기적인 [igijeogin]

self-service [ˈsɛlfˌsɜːvɪs] *adj* 셀프서비스의 [selpeuseobiseuui]

sell [sɛl] *v* 팔다 [palda]; **sell-by date** *n* 유통만기일 [yutongmangiil]; **selling price** *n* 판매가격 [panmaegagyeok]

sell off [sɛl ɒf] *v* 싸게 팔아치우다

[ssage parachiuda]

Sellotape® ['sɛləˌteɪp] n 셀로테이프 [selloteipeu]

sell out [sɛl aʊt] v 다 팔아버리다 [da parabeorida]

semester [sɪ'mɛstə] n 학기 [hakgi]

semi ['sɛmɪ] n 두 채가 한 동을 이루고 있는 집 [du chaega han dongeul irugo inneun jip]

semicircle ['sɛmɪˌsɜːkəl] n 반원 [banwon]

semicolon [ˌsɛmɪ'kəʊlən] n 세미콜론 [semikollon]

semifinal [ˌsɛmɪ'faɪnəl] n 준결승전 [jungyeolseungjeon]

send [sɛnd] v 보내다 [bonaeda]

send back [sɛnd bæk] v 돌려보내다 [dollyeobonaeda]

sender ['sɛndə] n 발송인 [balsongin]

send off [sɛnd ɒf] v 떠나보내다 [tteonabonaeda]

send out [sɛnd aʊt] v 내보내다 [naebonaeda]

Senegal [ˌsɛnɪ'gɔːl] n 세네갈 [senegal]

Senegalese [ˌsɛnɪgə'liːz] adj 세네갈의 [senegarui] ▷ n 세네갈 사람 [senegal saram]

senior ['siːnjə] adj 연상의 [yeonsangui]; **senior citizen** n 노인 [noin]

sensational [sɛn'seɪʃənəl] adj 세상을 들끓게 하는 [sesangeul deulkkeurke haneun]

sense [sɛns] n 감각 [gamgak]; **sense of humour** n 유머감각 [yumeogamgak]

senseless ['sɛnslɪs] adj 무분별한 [mubunbyeolhan]

sensible ['sɛnsɪbəl] adj 현명한 [hyeonmyeonghan]

sensitive ['sɛnsɪtɪv] adj 민감한 [mingamhan]

sensuous ['sɛnsjʊəs] adj 감각적인 [gamgakjeogin]

sentence ['sɛntəns] n (punishment) 판결 [pangyeol], (words) 문장 [munjang] (쓰기) ▷ v 판결을 내리다 [pangyeoreul naerida]

sentimental [ˌsɛntɪ'mɛntəl] adj 감정적인 [gamjeongjeogin]

separate adj ['sɛpərɪt] 별개의 [byeolgaeui] ▷ v ['sɛpəˌreɪt] 분리하다 [bullihada]

separately ['sɛpərətlɪ] adv 분리하여 [bullihayeo]

separation [ˌsɛpə'reɪʃən] n 분리 [bulli]

September [sɛp'tɛmbə] n 9월 [guwol]

sequel ['siːkwəl] n 속편 [sokpyeon]

sequence ['siːkwəns] n 차례 [charye]

Serbia ['sɜːbɪə] n 세르비아 [sereubia]

Serbian ['sɜːbɪən] adj 세르비아의 [sereubiaui] ▷ n (language) 세르비아어 [sereubiaeo], (person) 세르비아 사람 [sereubia saram]

sergeant ['sɑːdʒənt] n 중사 [jungsa]

serial ['sɪərɪəl] n 연재물 [yeonjaemul]

series ['sɪəriːz; -rɪz] n 일련 [illyeon]

serious ['sɪərɪəs] adj 심각한 [simgakhan]; **Is it serious?** 심각한가요? [simgakhangayo?]

seriously ['sɪərɪəslɪ] adv 심각하게 [simgakhage]

sermon ['sɜːmən] n 설교 [seolgyo]

servant ['sɜːvənt] n 하인 [hain]; **civil servant** n 공무원 [gongmuwon]

serve [sɜːv] n 서브 [seobeu] ▷ v 섬기다 [seomgida]

server ['sɜːvə] n (computer) 서버 [seobeo], (person) 봉사자 [bongsaja]

service ['sɜːvɪs] n 서비스 [seobiseu] ▷ v 서비스를 하다 [seobiseureul hada]; **room service** n 객실서비스 [gaeksilseobiseu]; **secret service** n 첩보부 [cheopbobu]; **service area** n 서비스 구역 [seobiseu guyeok]; **service charge** n 서비스 요금 [seobiseu yogeum]; **service station** n 주유소 [juyuso]; **social services** npl 사회사업 [sahoesaeop]; **Call the breakdown service, please** 고장 서비스를 불러 주세요 [gojang seobiseureul bulleo juseyo]; **I want to complain about the service** 서비스에 대해 불만을 제기하고 싶어요 [seobiseue daehae bulmaneul jegihago sipeoyo]; **Is there a charge for the service?** 서비스 요금이 있어요? [seobiseu yogeumi isseoyo?];

Is there a child-minding service?
탁아 서비스가 있어요? [taga
seobiseuga isseoyo?]; **Is there room
service?** 룸 서비스가 있어요? [rum
seobiseuga isseoyo?]; **The service was
terrible** 서비스가 엉망이었어요
[seobiseuga eongmangieosseoyo]
serviceman, servicemen
['sɜːvɪsˌmæn; -mən, 'sɜːvɪsˌmɛn] n
군인 [gunin]
servicewoman, servicewomen
['sɜːvɪsˌwʊmən, 'sɜːvɪsˌwɪmɪn] n 여군
[yeogun]
serviette [ˌsɜːvɪˈɛt] n 식탁용 냅킨
[siktagyong naepkin]
session ['sɛʃən] n 기간 [gigan]
set [sɛt] n 한 벌 [han beol] ▷ v 지정하다
[jijeonghada]
setback ['sɛtbæk] n 방해 [banghae]
set menu [sɛt 'mɛnjuː] n 세트 메뉴
[seteu menyu]
set off [sɛt ɒf] v 출발하다 [chulbalhada]
set out [sɛt aʊt] v 설계하다
[seolgyehada]
settee [sɛˈtiː] n 소파 [sopa]
settle ['sɛtəl] v 정하다 [jeonghada]
settle down ['sɛtəl daʊn] v 자리잡다
[jarijapda]
seven ['sɛvən] number 일곱 [ilgop],
(Sino-Korean) 칠 [chil]
seventeen ['sɛvənˈtiːn] number 열일곱
[yeorilgop], (Sino-Korean) 십칠 [sipchil]
seventeenth ['sɛvənˈtiːnθ] adj 열일곱
번째의 [yeorilgop beonjjaeui]
seventh ['sɛvənθ] adj 일곱 번째의
[ilgop beonjjaeui] ▷ n 7분의 1
[chilbunui il]
seventy ['sɛvəntɪ] number 일흔 [ilheun],
(Sino-Korean) 칠십 [chilsip]
several ['sɛvrəl] adj 몇몇의
[myeotmyeochui] ▷ pron 몇몇
[myeotmyeot]
sew [səʊ] v 꿰매다 [kkwemaeda]
sewer ['suːə] n 하수구 [hasugu]
sewing ['səʊɪŋ] n 바느질 [baneujil];
sewing machine n 재봉틀
[jaebongteul]
sew up [səʊ ʌp] v 완전히 꿰매다

[wanjeonhi kkwemaeda]
sex [sɛks] n 성 [seong]
sexism ['sɛksɪzəm] n 성차별
[seongchabyeol]
sexist ['sɛksɪst] adj 남녀차별하는
[namnyeochabyeolhaneun]
sexual ['sɛksjʊəl] adj 성적인
[seongjeogin]; **sexual intercourse** n
성행위 [seonghaengwi]
sexuality [ˌsɛksjʊˈælɪtɪ] n 성별
[seongbyeol]
sexy ['sɛksɪ] adj 성적 매력이 있는
[seongjeok maeryeogi inneun]
shabby ['ʃæbɪ] adj 초라한 [chorahan]
shade [ʃeɪd] n 그늘 [geuneul]
shadow ['ʃædəʊ] n 그림자 [geurimja];
eye shadow n 아이섀도 [aisyaedo]
shake [ʃeɪk] vi 흔들리다 [heundeullida]
▷ vt 흔들다 [heundeulda]
shaken ['ʃeɪkən] adj 흔들린
[heundeullin]
shaky ['ʃeɪkɪ] adj 떨리는 [tteollineun]
shallow ['ʃæləʊ] adj 얕은 [yateun]
shambles ['ʃæmbəlz] npl 난장판
[nanjangpan]
shame [ʃeɪm] n 수치심 [suchisim]
shampoo [ʃæmˈpuː] n 샴푸 [syampu];
Do you sell shampoo? 샴푸 파세요?
[syampu paseyo?]
shape [ʃeɪp] n 모양 [moyang]
share [ʃɛə] n 몫 [mogt] ▷ v 나누다
[nanuda]
shareholder ['ʃɛəˌhəʊldə] n 주주 [juju]
share out [ʃɛə aʊt] v 분배하다
[bunbaehada]
shark [ʃɑːk] n 상어 [sangeo]
sharp [ʃɑːp] adj 날카로운 [nalkaroun]
shave [ʃeɪv] v 면도하다
[myeondohada]; **shaving cream** n
면도용 크림 [myeondoyong keurim];
shaving foam n 면도용 거품
[myeondoyong geopum]
shaver ['ʃeɪvə] n 전기 면도기 [jeongi
myeondogi]
shawl [ʃɔːl] n 숄 [syol]
she [ʃiː] pron 그 여자 [geu yeoja]
shed [ʃɛd] n 헛간 [heotgan]
sheep [ʃiːp] n 양 [yang]

sheepdog ['ʃiːp,dɒg] n 양 지키는 개 [yang jikineun gae]

sheepskin ['ʃiːp,skɪn] n 양가죽 [yanggajuk]

sheer [ʃɪə] adj 완전한 [wanjeonhan]

sheet [ʃiːt] n 시트 [siteu]; **balance sheet** n 대차대조표 [daechadaejopyo]; **fitted sheet** n 맞춤 시트 [matchum siteu]; **My sheets are dirty** 제 시트가 더러워요 [je siteuga deoreowoyo]; **The sheets are dirty** 시트가 더러워요 [siteuga deoreowoyo]; **We need more sheets** 시트가 더 필요해요 [siteuga deo pillyohaeyo]

shelf, shelves [ʃelf, ʃelvz] n 선반 [seonban]

shell [ʃɛl] n 껍질 [kkeopjil]; **shell suit** n 보온복 [boonbok]

shellfish ['ʃɛl,fɪʃ] n 조개 [jogae]; **I'm allergic to shellfish** 조개 알레르기가 있어요 [jogae allereugiga isseoyo]

shelter ['ʃɛltə] n 대피소 [daepiso]

shepherd ['ʃɛpəd] n 양치기 [yangchigi]

sherry ['ʃɛrɪ] n 셰리주 [syeriju]

shield [ʃiːld] n 방패 [bangpae]

shift [ʃɪft] n 이동 [idong] ▷ v 이동하다 [idonghada]

shifty ['ʃɪftɪ] adj 교활해 보이는 [gyohwalhae boineun]

Shiite ['ʃiːaɪt] adj 시아파의 [siapaui]

shin [ʃɪn] n 정강이 [jeonggangi]

shine [ʃaɪn] v 빛나다 [bitnada]

shiny ['ʃaɪnɪ] adj 빛나는 [bitnaneun]

ship [ʃɪp] n 선박 [seonbak]

shipbuilding ['ʃɪp,bɪldɪŋ] n 조선 [joseon]

shipment ['ʃɪpmənt] n 선적 [seonjeok]

shipwreck ['ʃɪp,rɛk] n 난파 [nanpa]

shipwrecked ['ʃɪp,rɛkt] adj 난파한 [nanpahan]

shipyard ['ʃɪp,jɑːd] n 조선소 [joseonso]

shirt [ʃɜːt] n 셔츠 [syeocheu]; **polo shirt** n 폴로 셔츠 [pollo syeocheu]

shiver ['ʃɪvə] v 덜덜 떨다 [deoldeol tteolda]

shock [ʃɒk] n 충격 [chunggyeok] ▷ v 충격을 주다 [chunggyeogeul juda]; **electric shock** n 감전 [gamjeon]

shocking ['ʃɒkɪŋ] adj 충격적인 [chunggyeokjeogin]

shoe [ʃuː] n 구두 [gudu]; **shoe polish** n 구두광택제 [gudugwangtaekje]; **shoe shop** n 구두가게 [gudugage]

shoelace ['ʃuː,leɪs] n 구두끈 [gudukkeun]

shoot [ʃuːt] v 쏘다 [ssoda]

shooting ['ʃuːtɪŋ] n 사격 [sagyeok]

shop [ʃɒp] n 상점 [sangjeom]; **antique shop** n 골동품점 [goldongpumjeom]; **gift shop** n 선물가게 [seonmulgage]; **shop assistant** n 점원 [jeomwon]; **shop window** n 상점 진열장 [sangjeom jinyeoljang]; **What time do the shops close?** 상점은 몇 시에 닫아요? [sangjeomeun myeot sie dadayo?]

shopkeeper ['ʃɒp,kiːpə] n 상점 주인 [sangjeom juin]

shoplifting ['ʃɒp,lɪftɪŋ] n 상점 절도 [sangjeom jeoldo]

shopping ['ʃɒpɪŋ] n 쇼핑 [syoping]; **shopping bag** n 쇼핑백 [syopingbaek]; **shopping centre** n 쇼핑센터 [syopingsenteo]; **shopping trolley** n 쇼핑카트 [syopingkateu]

shore [ʃɔː] n 바닷가 [badatga]

short [ʃɔːt] adj 짧은 [jjarbeun]; **short story** n 단편 소설 [danpyeon soseol]

shortage ['ʃɔːtɪdʒ] n 부족 [bujok]

shortcoming ['ʃɔːt,kʌmɪŋ] n 단점 [danjeom]

shortcut ['ʃɔːt,kʌt] n 지름길 [jireumgil]

shortfall ['ʃɔːt,fɔːl] n 부족 [bujok]

shorthand ['ʃɔːt,hænd] n 속기 [sokgi]

shortlist ['ʃɔːt,lɪst] n 최종선발 후보자 명단 [choejongseonbal huboja myeongdan]

shortly ['ʃɔːtlɪ] adv 곧 [got]

shorts [ʃɔːts] npl 반바지 [banbaji]

short-sighted ['ʃɔːt'saɪtɪd] adj 근시의 [geunsiui]

short-sleeved ['ʃɔːt,sliːvd] adj 반소매의 [bansomaeui]

shot [ʃɒt] n 발사 [balsa]

shotgun ['ʃɒt,gʌn] n 산탄총 [santanchong]

shoulder [ˈʃəʊldə] *n* 어깨 [eokkae]; **hard shoulder** *n* 포장 갓길 [pojang gatgil]; **shoulder blade** *n* 견갑골 [gyeongapgol]; **I've hurt my shoulder** 어깨가 아파요 [eokkaega apayo]

shout [ʃaʊt] *n* 고함 [goham] ▷ *v* 소리치다 [sorichida]

shovel [ˈʃʌvəl] *n* 삽 [sap]

show [ʃəʊ] *n* 쇼 [syo] ▷ *v* 보이다 [boida]; **show business** *n* 쇼 비즈니스 [syo bijeuniseu]; **Where can we go to see a show?** 어디에 가면 쇼를 볼 수 있나요? [eodie gamyeon syoreul bol su innayo?]

shower [ˈʃaʊə] *n* 샤워 [syawo]; **shower cap** *n* 샤워 캡 [syawo kaep]; **shower gel** *n* 샤워 젤 [syawo jel]; **Are there showers?** 샤워시설이 있어요? [syawosiseori isseoyo?]; **The shower doesn't work** 샤워기가 작동하지 않아요 [syawogiga jakdonghaji anhayo]; **The shower is dirty** 샤워기가 더러워요 [syawogiga deoreowoyo]; **The showers are cold** 샤워물이 차요 [syawomuri chayo]; **Where are the showers?** 샤워 시설은 어디있어요? [syawo siseoreun eodiisseoyo?]

showerproof [ˈʃaʊəˌpruːf] *adj* 방수의 [bangsuui]

showing [ˈʃəʊɪŋ] *n* 전시회 [jeonsihoe]

show off [ʃəʊ ɒf] *v* 과시하다 [gwasihada]

show-off [ˈʃəʊɒf] *n* 과시 [gwasi]

show up [ʃəʊ ʌp] *v* 보이다 [boida]

shriek [ʃriːk] *v* 비명을 지르다 [bimyeongeul jireuda]

shrimp [ʃrɪmp] *n* 새우 [saeu]

shrine [ʃraɪn] *n* 사당 [sadang]

shrink [ʃrɪŋk] *v* 줄어들다 [jureodeulda]

shrub [ʃrʌb] *n* 관목 [gwanmok]

shrug [ʃrʌg] *v* 어깨를 으쓱하다 [eokkaereul eusseukhada]

shrunk [ʃrʌŋk] *adj* 줄어든 [jureodeun]

shudder [ˈʃʌdə] *v* 떨다 [tteolda]

shuffle [ˈʃʌfəl] *v* 발을 끌며 걷다 [bareul kkeulmyeo geotda]

shut [ʃʌt] *v* 닫다 [datda]

shut down [ʃʌt daʊn] *v* 휴업하다 [hyueophada]

shutters [ˈʃʌtəz] *n* 덧문 [deotmun]

shuttle [ˈʃʌtəl] *n* 근거리 왕복 [geungeori wangbok]

shuttlecock [ˈʃʌtəlˌkɒk] *n* 배드민턴 공 [baedeuminteon gong]

shut up [ʃʌt ʌp] *v* 입 다물다 [ip damulda]

shy [ʃaɪ] *adj* 부끄럼 타는 [bukkeureom taneun]

Siberia [saɪˈbɪərɪə] *n* 시베리아 [siberia]

siblings [ˈsɪblɪŋz] *npl* 형제자매 [hyeongjejamae]

sick [sɪk] *adj* 병든 [byeongdeun]; **sick leave** *n* 병가 [byeongga]; **sick note** 병으로 인한 결석 통지 [byeongeuro inhan gyeolseok tongji]; **sick pay** *n* 병가 중 지급되는 급여 [byeongga jung jigeupdoeneun geubyeo]

sickening [ˈsɪkənɪŋ] *adj* 불쾌감을 주는 [bulkwaegameul juneun]

sickness [ˈsɪknɪs] *n* 병 [byeong]; **morning sickness** *n* 입덧 [ipdeot]; **travel sickness** *n* 멀미 [meolmi]

side [saɪd] *n* 측면 [cheungmyeon]; **side effect** *n* 부작용 [bujagyong]; **side street** *n* 골목길 [golmokgil]

sideboard [ˈsaɪdˌbɔːd] *n* 찬장 [chanjang]

sidelight [ˈsaɪdˌlaɪt] *n* 측면광 [cheungmyeongwang]

sideways [ˈsaɪdˌweɪz] *adv* 옆으로 [yeopeuro]

sieve [sɪv] *n* 체 [che]

sigh [saɪ] *n* 한숨 [hansum] ▷ *v* 한숨 쉬다 [hansum swida]

sight [saɪt] *n* 시력 [siryeok]

sightseeing [ˈsaɪtˌsiːɪŋ] *n* 관광 [gwangwang]; **Are there any sightseeing tours of the town?** 시내 관광 여행이 있어요? [sinae gwangwang yeohaengi isseoyo?]

sign [saɪn] *n* 표시 [pyosi] ▷ *v* 서명하다 [seomyeonghada]; **road sign** *n* 도로 표지 [doro pyoji]; **sign language** *n* 수화 [suhwa]; **I can't find the at sign** @ 표시를 찾을 수 없어요 [@ pyosireul chajeul su eopseoyo]

signal ['sɪgnᵊl] *n* 신호 [sinho] ▷ *v* 신호를 보내다 [sinhoreul bonaeda]; **busy signal** *n* 통화 중 신호 [tonghwa jung sinho]

signature ['sɪgnɪtʃə] *n* 서명 [seomyeong]

significance [sɪgˈnɪfɪkəns] *n* 중요성 [jungyoseong]

significant [sɪgˈnɪfɪkənt] *adj* 중요한 [jungyohan]

sign on [saɪn ɒn] *v* 등록하다 [deungnokhada]

signpost ['saɪnˌpəʊst] *n* 도로 표지 [doro pyoji]

Sikh [siːk] *adj* 시크교도의 [sikeugyodoui] ▷ *n* 시크교도 [sikeugyodo]

silence ['saɪləns] *n* 침묵 [chimmuk]

silencer ['saɪlənsə] *n* 소음기 [soeumgi]

silent ['saɪlənt] *adj* 조용한 [joyonghan]

silk [sɪlk] *n* 비단 [bidan]

silly ['sɪlɪ] *adj* 어리석은 [eoriseogeun]

silver ['sɪlvə] *n* 은 [eun]

similar ['sɪmɪlə] *adj* 비슷한 [biseutan]

similarity ['sɪmɪˈlærɪtɪ] *n* 비슷함 [biseutham]

simmer ['sɪmə] *v* 서서히 끓다 [seoseohi kkeurta]

simple ['sɪmpᵊl] *adj* 단순한 [dansunhan]

simplify ['sɪmplɪˌfaɪ] *v* 단순화하다 [dansunhwahada]

simply ['sɪmplɪ] *adv* 간단히 [gandanhi]

simultaneous [ˌsɪmᵊlˈteɪnɪəs; ˌsaɪmᵊlˈteɪnɪəs] *adj* 동시의 [dongsiui]

simultaneously [ˌsɪmᵊlˈteɪnɪəslɪ] *adv* 동시에 [dongsie]

sin [sɪn] *n* 죄 [joe]

since [sɪns] *adv* 그 이래 [geu irae] ▷ *conj* ...한 후에 [...han hue] ▷ *prep* ... 이후에 [... ihue]

sincere [sɪnˈsɪə] *adj* 진실한 [jinsilhan]

sincerely [sɪnˈsɪəlɪ] *adv* 진심으로 [jinsimeuro]

sing [sɪŋ] *v* 노래하다 [noraehada]

singer ['sɪŋə] *n* 가수 [gasu]; **lead singer** *n* 리드싱어 [rideusingeo]

singing ['sɪŋɪŋ] *n* 노래 [norae]

single ['sɪŋgᵊl] *adj* 단 하나의 [dan hanaui] ▷ *n* 1인용 방 [il inyong bang]; **single bed** *n* 1인용 침대 [il inyong chimdae]; **single parent** *n* 홀부모 [holbumo]; **single room** *n* 1인용 방 [il inyong bang]; **single ticket** *n* 편도표 [pyeondopyo]

singles ['sɪŋgᵊlz] *npl* 단식 경기 [dansik gyeonggi]

singular ['sɪŋgjʊlə] *n* 단수 [dansu] (하나)

sinister ['sɪnɪstə] *adj* 불길한 [bulgilhan]

sink [sɪŋk] *n* 개수대 [gaesudae] ▷ *v* 가라앉다 [garaantda]

sinus ['saɪnəs] *n* 굽이 [gubi]

sir [sɜː] *n* 경 [gyeong] (호칭)

siren ['saɪərən] *n* 경적 [gyeongjeok]

sister ['sɪstə] *n* 언니 [eonni] *(female's elder sister)*

sister-in-law ['sɪstə ɪn lɔː] *n* 시누이 [sinui] *(husband's sister)*

sit [sɪt] *v* 앉다 [antda]

sitcom ['sɪtˌkɒm] *n* 시트콤 [siteukom]

sit down [sɪt daʊn] *v* 착석하다 [chakseokhada]

site [saɪt] *n* 현장 [hyeonjang]; **building site** *n* 건축 부지 [geonchuk buji]; **caravan site** *n* 트레일러 하우스 주차장 [teureilleo hauseu juchajang]

situated ['sɪtjʊˌeɪtɪd] *adj* 위치한 [wichihan]

situation [ˌsɪtjʊˈeɪʃən] *n* 상황 [sanghwang]

six [sɪks] *number* 여섯 [yeoseot], *(Sino-Korean)* 육 [yuk]

sixteen ['sɪksˈtiːn] *number* 열여섯 [yeollyeoseot], *(Sino-Korean)* 십육 [sibyuk]

sixteenth ['sɪksˈtiːnθ] *adj* 열여섯 번째의 [yeollyeoseot beonjjaeui]

sixth [sɪksθ] *adj* 6분의 1 [yukbunui il]

sixty ['sɪkstɪ] *number* 예순 [yesun], *(Sino-Korean)* 육십 [yuksip]

size [saɪz] *n* 크기 [keugi]

skate [skeɪt] *v* 스케이트 [seukeiteu]; **Where can we go ice-skating?** 어니에서 스케이트를 탈 수 있어요?

[eodieseo seukeiteureul tal su isseoyo?]; **Where can we go roller skating?** 어디에서 롤러 스케이트를 탈 수 있어요? [eodieseo rolleo seukeiteureul tal su isseoyo?]

skateboard ['skeɪtˌbɔːd] *n* 스케이트보드 [seukeiteubodeu]; **I'd like to go skateboarding** 스케이트보드를 타고 싶어요 [seukeiteubodeureul tago sipeoyo]

skateboarding ['skeɪtˌbɔːdɪŋ] *n* 스케이트보드 타기 [seukeiteubodeu tagi]

skates [skeɪts] *npl* 스케이트 [seukeiteu]; **Where can we hire skates?** 어디에서 스케이트를 빌릴 수 있나요? [eodieseo seukeiteureul billil su innayo?]

skating ['skeɪtɪŋ] *n* 스케이트 타기 [seukeiteu tagi]; **skating rink** *n* 스케이트 링크 [seukeiteu ringkeu]

skeleton ['skɛlɪtən] *n* 해골 [haegol]

sketch [skɛtʃ] *n* 스케치 [seukechi] ▷ *v* 스케치하다 [seukechihada]

skewer ['skjʊə] *n* 꼬챙이 [kkochaengi]

ski [skiː] *n* 스키 [seuki] ▷ *v* 스키를 타다 [seukireul tada]; **ski lift** *n* 스키 리프트 [seuki ripeuteu]; **ski pass** *n* 스키장 시즌권 [seukijang sijeungwon]; **Can we hire skis here?** 여기에서 스키를 빌릴 수 있어요? [yeogieseo seukireul billil su isseoyo?]; **How much is a ski pass?** 스키장 입장권은 얼마예요? [seukijang ipjanggwoneun eolmayeyo?]; **I want to hire cross-country skis** 크로스컨트리 스키를 빌리고 싶어요 [keuroseukeonteuri seukireul billigo sipeoyo]; **I want to hire downhill skis** 활강 스키를 빌리고 싶어요 [hwalgang seukireul billigo sipeoyo]; **I want to hire ski poles** 스키막대를 빌리고 싶어요 [seukimakdaereul billigo sipeoyo]; **I want to hire skis** 스키를 빌리고 싶어요 [seukireul billigo sipeoyo]; **I'd like a ski pass for a day** 하루 스키장 입장권을 사고 싶어요 [haru seukijang ipjanggwoneul sago

sipeoyo]; **Is there a ski school?** 스키 학교가 있어요? [seuki hakgyoga isseoyo?]; **Where can I buy a ski pass?** 어디에서 스키장 입장권을 살 수 있을까요? [eodieseo seukijang ipjanggwoneul sal su isseulkkayo?]

skid [skɪd] *v* 미끄러지다 [mikkeureojida]

skier ['skiːə] *n* 스키 타는 사람 [seuki taneun saram]

skiing ['skiːɪŋ] *n* 스키 타기 [seuki tagi]

skilful ['skɪlfʊl] *adj* 숙련된 [sungnyeondoen]

skill [skɪl] *n* 수완 [suwan]

skilled [skɪld] *adj* 숙련된 [sungnyeondoen]

skimpy ['skɪmpɪ] *adj* 빈약한 [binyakhan]

skin [skɪn] *n* 피부 [pibu]

skinhead ['skɪnˌhɛd] *n* 스킨헤드족 [seukinhedeujok]

skinny ['skɪnɪ] *adj* 마른 [mareun]

skin-tight ['skɪnˌtaɪt] *adj* 꼭 끼는 [kkok kkineun]

skip [skɪp] *v* 가볍게 뛰어넘다 [gabyeopge ttwieoneomda]

skirt [skɜːt] *n* 치마 [chima]

skive [skaɪv] *v* 태만 [taeman]

skull [skʌl] *n* 두개골 [dugaegol]

sky [skaɪ] *n* 하늘 [haneul]

skyscraper ['skaɪˌskreɪpə] *n* 마천루 [macheollu]

slack [slæk] *adj* 느슨한 [neuseunhan]

slag off [slæg ɒf] *v* 혹평하다 [hokpyeonghada]

slam [slæm] *v* 쾅 닫다 [kwang datda]

slang [slæŋ] *n* 속어 [sogeo]

slap [slæp] *v* 찰싹 때리다 [chalssak ttaerida]

slash [slæʃ] *n* **forward slash** *n* 포워드 슬래시 [powodeu seullaesi]

slate [sleɪt] *n* 슬레이트 [seulleiteu]

slave [sleɪv] *n* 노예 [noye] ▷ *v* 혹사하다 [hoksahada]

sledge [slɛdʒ] *n* 썰매 [sseolmae]; **Where can we go sledging?** 어디에서 썰매 타기를 할 수 있나요? [eodieseo sseolmae tagireul hal su innayo?]

sledging ['slɛdʒɪŋ] *n* 썰매 타기 [sseolmae tagi]

sleep [sli:p] *n* 잠 [jam] ▷ *v* 자다 [jada]; **sleeping bag** *n* 침낭 [chimnang]; **sleeping car** *n* 침대차 [chimdaecha]; **sleeping pill** *n* 수면제 [sumyeonje]; **I can't sleep** 잠을 못 자요 [jameul mot jayo]; **I can't sleep for the heat** 더워서 잠을 잘 수 없어요 [deowoseo jameul jal su eopseoyo]; **I can't sleep for the noise** 시끄러워서 잠을 잘 수 없어요 [sikkeureowoseo jameul jal su eopseoyo]

sleep around [sli:p ə'raʊnd] *v* 동침하다 [dongchimhada]

sleeper ['sli:pə] *n* **Can I reserve a sleeper?** 침대칸을 예약할 수 있어요? [chimdaekan-eul yeyarkhal su iss-eoyo?]; **I want to book a sleeper to...** ...행 침대칸을 예약하고 싶어요 [...haeng chimdaekan-eul yeyaghago sip-eoyo]

sleep in [sli:p ɪn] *v* 늦잠 자다 [neutjam jada]

sleep together [sli:p tə'gɛðə] *v* 동침하다 [dongchimhada]

sleepwalk ['sli:pwɔ:k] *v* 자면서 돌아다니다 [jamyeonseo doradanida]

sleepy ['sli:pɪ] *adj* 졸리는 [jollineun]

sleet [sli:t] *n* 진눈깨비 [jinnunkkaebi] ▷ *v* 진눈깨비가 내리다 [jinnunkkaebiga naerida]

sleeve [sli:v] *n* 소매 [somae]

sleeveless ['sli:vlɪs] *adj* 소매가 없는 [somaega eomneun]

slender ['slɛndə] *adj* 날씬한 [nalssinhan]

slice [slaɪs] *n* 얇은 조각 [yarbeun jogak] ▷ *v* 얇게 베다 [yapge beda]

slick [slɪk] *n* **oil slick** *n* 물 위의 기름층 [mul wiui gireumcheung]

slide [slaɪd] *n* 미끄러지기 [mikkeureojigi] ▷ *v* 미끄러지다 [mikkeureojida]

slight [slaɪt] *adj* 약간의 [yakganui]

slightly ['slaɪtlɪ] *adv* 약간 [yakgan]; **We are slightly behind schedule** 예정보다 약간 늦고 있어요 [yejeongboda yakgan neutgo isseoyo]

slim [slɪm] *adj* 늘씬한 [neulssinhan]

sling [slɪŋ] *n* 삼각건 [samgakgeon]

slip [slɪp] *n* (mistake) 실수 [silsu], (paper) 전표 [jeonpyo], (underwear) 슬립 [seullip] ▷ *v* 미끄러지다 [mikkeureojida]; **slip road** *n* 램프 [raempeu]; **slipped disc** *n* 변위 추간판 [byeonwi chuganpan]

slipper ['slɪpə] *n* 실내화 [sillaehwa]

slippery ['slɪpərɪ; -prɪ] *adj* 미끄러운 [mikkeureoun]

slip up [slɪp ʌp] *v* 실수하다 [silsuhada]

slip-up [slɪpʌp] *n* 실수 [silsu]

slope [sləʊp] *n* 비탈 [bital]; **nursery slope** *n* 초보자용 스키코스 [chobojayong seukikoseu]

sloppy ['slɒpɪ] *adj* 부주의한 [bujuuihan]

slot [slɒt] *n* 동전 구멍 [dongjeon gumeong]; **slot machine** *n* 자동 판매기 [jadong panmaegi]

Slovak ['sləʊvæk] *adj* 슬로바키아의 [seullobakiaui] ▷ *n* (language) 슬로바키아어 [seullobakiaeo], (person) 슬로바키아 사람 [seullobakia saram]

Slovakia [sləʊ'vækɪə] *n* 슬로바키아 [seullobakia]

Slovenia [sləʊ'vi:nɪə] *n* 슬로베니아 [seullobenia]

Slovenian [sləʊ'vi:nɪən] *adj* 슬로베니아의 [seullobeniaui] ▷ *n* (language) 슬로베니아어 [seullobeniaeo], (person) 슬로베니아 사람 [seullobenia saram]

slow [sləʊ] *adj* 느린 [neurin]; **I think my watch is slow** 제 시계가 느린 것 같아요 [je sigyega neurin geot gatayo]; **The connection seems very slow** 연결이 아주 느린 것 같아요 [yeongyeori aju neurin geot gatayo]

slow down [sləʊ daʊn] *v* 속도가 떨어지다 [sokdoga tteoreojida]

slowly [sləʊlɪ] *adv* 천천히 [cheoncheonhi]; **Could you speak more slowly, please?** 천천히 말씀해 주시겠어요? [cheoncheonhi malsseumhae jusigesseoyo?]

slug [slʌg] *n* 민달팽이 [mindalpaengi]

slum [slʌm] n 빈민가 [binminga]

slush [slʌʃ] n 진창 [jinchang]

sly [slaɪ] adj 교활한 [gyohwalhan]

smack [smæk] v 세게 때리다 [sege ttaerida]

small [smɔːl] adj 작은 [jageun]; **small ads** npl 항목별 광고 [hangmokbyeol gwanggo]; **Do you have a small?** 작은 사이즈 있어요? [jageun saijeu isseoyo?]; **Do you have this in a smaller size?** 더 작은 사이즈 있어요? [deo jageun saijeu isseoyo?]

smart [smɑːt] adj 현명한 [hyeonmyeonghan]; **smart phone** n 스마트 폰 [seumateu pon]

smash [smæʃ] v 산산이 부수다 [sansani busuda]

smashing ['smæʃɪŋ] adj 아주 뛰어난 [aju ttwieonan]

smell [smɛl] n 냄새 [naemsae] ▷ vi 냄새를 맡다 [naemsaereul matda] ▷ vt 냄새가 나다 [naemsaega nada]; **I can smell gas** 가스 냄새가 나요 [gaseu naemsaega nayo]; **My room smells of smoke** 제 방은 담배 냄새가 나요 [je bangeun dambae naemsaega nayo]; **There's a funny smell** 이상한 냄새가 나요 [isanghan naemsaega nayo]

smelly ['smɛlɪ] adj 악취가 나는 [akchwiga naneun]

smile [smaɪl] n 미소 [miso] ▷ v 미소짓다 [misojitda]

smiley ['smaɪlɪ] n 웃음 기호 [useum giho]

smoke [sməʊk] n 연기 [yeongi] ▷ v 연기를 뿜다 [yeongireul ppumda]; **smoke alarm** n 화재경보 [hwajaegyeongbo]

smoked ['sməʊkt] adj 훈제한 [hunjehan]

smoker ['sməʊkə] n 흡연자 [heubyeonja]

smoking ['sməʊkɪŋ] n 흡연 [heubyeon]; **I'd like a seat in the smoking area** 흡연구역 좌석으로 주세요 [heubyeonguyeok jwaseogeuro juseyo]; **I'd like a smoking room** 흡연실이 좋겠어요 [heubyeonsiri jokesseoyo]

smoky ['sməʊkɪ] adj **It's too smoky here** 여기는 연기가 너무 자욱해요 [yeogineun yeongiga neomu jaughaeyo]

smooth [smuːð] adj 매끄러운 [maekkeureoun]

SMS [ɛs ɛm ɛs] n 문자메시지 [munjamesiji]

smudge [smʌdʒ] n 더러움 [deoreoum]

smug [smʌg] adj 잘난체하는 [jallanchehaneun]

smuggle ['smʌgᵊl] v 밀수하다 [milsuhada]

smuggler ['smʌglə] n 밀수업자 [milsueopja]

smuggling ['smʌglɪŋ] n 밀수 [milsu]

snack [snæk] n 가벼운 식사 [gabyeoun siksa]; **snack bar** n 스낵 바 [seunaek ba]

snail [sneɪl] n 달팽이 [dalpaengi]

snake [sneɪk] n 뱀 [baem]

snap [snæp] v 부서지다 [buseojida]

snapshot ['snæpˌʃɒt] n 스냅 사진 [seunaep sajin]

snarl [snɑːl] v 으르렁거리다 [eureureonggeorida]

snatch [snætʃ] v 낚아채다 [nakkachaeda]

sneakers ['sniːkəz] npl 운동화 [undonghwa]

sneeze [sniːz] v 재채기하다 [jaechaegihada]

sniff [snɪf] v 코를 킁킁거리다 [koreul keungkeunggeorida]

snigger ['snɪgə] v 킬킬 웃다 [kilkil utda]

snob [snɒb] n 속물 [songmul]

snooker ['snuːkə] n 스누커 [seunukeo]

snooze [snuːz] n 선잠 [seonjam] ▷ v 선잠 자다 [seonjam jada]

snore [snɔː] v 코를 골다 [koreul golda]

snorkel ['snɔːkᵊl] n 스노클 [seunokeul]; **I'd like to go snorkelling** 스노클링을 하고 싶어요 [seunokeullingeul hago sipeoyo]

snow [snəʊ] n 눈 [nun] ▷ v 눈이 내리다 [nuni naerida]; **Do you think it will snow?** 눈이 올 것 같아요? [nuni ol geot gatayo?]; **It's snowing** 눈이 와요 [nuni wayo]; **The snow is very heavy** 눈이 아주 많이 와요 [nuni aju manhi wayo]; **What are the snow conditions?** 눈 상태는 어떤가요? [nun sangtaeneun eotteongayo?]; **What is the snow like?** 눈은 어떤가요? [nuneun eotteongayo?]

snowball ['snəʊˌbɔːl] n 눈뭉치 [nunmungchi]

snowboard ['snəʊˌbɔːd] n **I want to hire a snowboard** 스노보드를 빌리고 싶어요 [seunobodeureul billigo sipeoyo]

snowflake ['snəʊˌfleɪk] n 눈송이 [nunsongi]

snowman ['snəʊˌmæn] n 눈사람 [nunsaram]

snowplough ['snəʊˌplaʊ] n 제설기 [jeseolgi]

snowstorm ['snəʊˌstɔːm] n 눈보라 [nunbora]

so [səʊ] adv 그렇게 [geureoke]; **so (that)** conj ...하도록 [...hadorok]; **Why are you charging me so much?** 왜 그렇게 비싸요? [wae geureoke bissayo?]

soak [səʊk] v 잠기다 [jamgida]

soaked [səʊkt] adj 흠뻑 젖은 [heumppeok jeojeun]

soap [səʊp] n 비누 [binu]; **soap dish** n 비누 그릇 [binu geureut]; **soap opera** n 연속극 [yeonsokgeuk]; **soap powder** n 가루비누 [garubinu]; **There is no soap** 비누가 없어요 [binuga eopseoyo]

sob [sɒb] v 흐느끼다 [heuneukkida]

sober ['səʊbə] adj 술 취하지 않은 [sul chwihaji anheun]

sociable ['səʊʃəbʰl] adj 사교적인 [sagyojeogin]

social ['səʊʃəl] adj 사회적인 [sahoejeogin]; **social security** n 사회보장 [sahoebojang]; **social services** npl 사회사업 [sahoesaeop]; **social worker** n 사회복지사 [sahoebokjisa]

socialism ['səʊʃəˌlɪzəm] n 사회주의 [sahoejuui]

socialist ['səʊʃəlɪst] adj 사회주의의 [sahoejuuiui] ▷ n 사회주의자 [sahoejuuija]

society [sə'saɪətɪ] n 사회 [sahoe]

sociology [ˌsəʊsɪ'ɒlədʒɪ] n 사회학 [sahoehak]

sock [sɒk] n 양말 [yangmal]

socket ['sɒkɪt] n 소켓 [soket]; **Where is the socket for my electric razor?** 전기면도기 소켓은 어디있어요? [jeongimyeondogi sokeseun eodiisseoyo?]

sofa ['səʊfə] n 소파 [sopa]; **sofa bed** n 소파식 침대 [sopasik chimdae]

soft [sɒft] adj 부드러운 [budeureoun]; **soft drink** n 청량 음료 [cheongnyang eumnyo]

softener ['sɒfᵊnə] n **Do you have softener?** 유연제 있어요? [yuyeonje isseoyo?]

software ['sɒftˌwɛə] n 소프트웨어 [sopeuteuweeo]

soggy ['sɒgɪ] adj 함빡 젖은 [hamppak jeojeun]

soil [sɔɪl] n 흙 [heulg]

solar ['səʊlə] adj 태양의 [taeyangui]; **solar power** n 태양 에너지 [taeyang eneoji]; **solar system** n 태양계 [taeyanggye]

soldier ['səʊldʒə] n 군인 [gunin]

sold out [səʊld aʊt] adj 품절된 [pumjeoldoen]

solicitor [sə'lɪsɪtə] n 변호사 [byeonhosa]

solid ['sɒlɪd] adj 고체의 [gocheui]

solo ['səʊləʊ] n 독주 [dokju]

soloist ['səʊləʊɪst] n 독주자 [dokjuja]

soluble ['sɒljʊbᵊl] adj 가용성의 [gayongseongui]

solution [sə'luːʃən] n 해법 [haebeop]

solve [sɒlv] v 해결하다 [haegyeolhada]

solvent ['sɒlvənt] n 용제 [yongje]

Somali [səʊ'mɑːlɪ] adj 소말리아의 [somalliaui] ▷ n (language) 소말리어 [somallieo], (person) 소말리족 [somallijok]

Somalia [səʊ'mɑːlɪə] n 소말리아

[somallia]

some [sʌm; səm] *adj* 어떤 [eotteon]
▷ *pron* 약간 [yakgan]

somebody ['sʌmbədɪ] *pron* 누군가 [nugunga]

somehow ['sʌm,haʊ] *adv* 어떻게든 [eotteokedeun]

someone ['sʌm,wʌn; -wən] *pron* 누군가 [nugunga]

someplace ['sʌm,pleɪs] *adv* 어딘가에 [eodingae]

something ['sʌmθɪŋ] *pron* 무언가 [mueonga]

sometime ['sʌm,taɪm] *adv* 언젠가 [eonjenga]

sometimes ['sʌm,taɪmz] *adv* 때때로 [ttaettaero]

somewhere ['sʌm,wɛə] *adv* 어딘가에 [eodingae]

son [sʌn] *n* 아들 [adeul]; **My son is lost** 아들을 잃어버렸어요 [adeureul ireobeoryeosseoyo]; **My son is missing** 아들이 없어졌어요 [adeuri eopseojyeosseoyo]

song [sɒŋ] *n* 노래 [norae]

son-in-law [sʌn ɪn lɔː] **(sons-in-law)** *n* 사위 [sawi]

soon [suːn] *adv* 곧 [got]; **See you soon** 곧 뵙겠습니다 [got boepgesseumnida]

sooner ['suːnə] *adv* 조만간 [jomangan]

soot [sʊt] *n* 검댕 [geomdaeng]

sophisticated [sə'fɪstɪ,keɪtɪd] *adj* 세련된 [seryeondoen]

soppy ['sɒpɪ] *adj* 감상적인 [gamsangjeogin]

soprano [sə'prɑːnəʊ] *n* 소프라노 [sopeurano]

sorbet ['sɔːbeɪ; -bɪt] *n* 셔벗 [syeobeot]

sorcerer ['sɔːsərə] *n* 마법사 [mabeopsa]

sore [sɔː] *adj* 아픈 [apeun] ▷ *n* 상처 [sangcheo]; **cold sore** *n* 입가의 발진 [ipgaui baljin]

sorry ['sɒrɪ] *interj* **sorry!** *excl* 미안! [mian!]; **I'm sorry** 미안합니다 [mianhamnida]; **I'm sorry to trouble you** 귀찮게해서 미안합니다 [gwichankehaeseo mianhamnida]; **I'm**
very sorry, I didn't know the regulations 죄송합니다만, 제가 규정을 몰랐어요 [joesonghamnidaman, jega gyujeongeul mollasseoyo]; **Sorry we're late** 늦어서 미안해요 [neujeoseo mianhaeyo]; **Sorry, I didn't catch that** 미안하지만 못 알아 들었어요 [mianhajiman mot ara deureosseoyo]; **Sorry, I'm not interested** 미안하지만, 관심없어요 [mianhajiman, gwansimeopseoyo]

sort [sɔːt] *n* 종류 [jongnyu]

sort out [sɔːt aʊt] *v* 해결하다 [haegyeolhada]

SOS [ɛs əʊ ɛs] *n* 위급신호 [wigeupsinho]

so-so [səʊsəʊ] *adv* 그럭저럭 [geureokjeoreok]

soul [səʊl] *n* 영혼 [yeonghon]

sound [saʊnd] *adj* 건전한 [geonjeonhan] ▷ *n* 소리 [sori]

soundtrack ['saʊnd,træk] *n* 배경음악 [baegyeongeumak]

soup [suːp] *n* 수프 [supeu]; **What is the soup of the day?** 오늘의 수프는 무엇인가요? [oneurui supeuneun mueosingayo?]

sour ['saʊə] *adj* 신 [sin]

south [saʊθ] *adj* 남쪽의 [namjjogui] ▷ *adv* 남쪽으로 [namjjogeuro] ▷ *n* 남쪽 [namjjok]; **South Africa** *n* 남아프리카 [namapeurika]; **South African** *n* 남아프리카 사람 [namapeurika saram], 남아프리카의 [namapeurikaui]; **South America** *n* 남미 [nammi]; **South American** *n* 남미 사람 [nammi saram], 남미의 [nammiui]; **South Korea** *n* 한국 [hanguk]; **South Pole** *n* 남극 [namgeuk]

southbound ['saʊθ,baʊnd] *adj* 남쪽으로 가는 [namjjogeuro ganeun]

southeast [,saʊθ'iːst; ,saʊ'iːst] *n* 남동쪽 [namdongjjok]

southern ['sʌðən] *adj* 남쪽의 [namjjogui]

southwest [,saʊθ'wɛst; ,saʊ'wɛst] *n* 남서쪽 [namseojjok]

souvenir [ˌsuːvəˈnɪə; ˈsuːvəˌnɪə] n
기념품 [ginyeompum]; **Do you have
souvenirs?** 기념품 있어요?
[ginyeompum isseoyo?]

soya [ˈsɔɪə] n 콩 [kong]

spa [spɑː] n 온천 [oncheon]

space [speɪs] n 공간 [gonggan]

spacecraft [ˈspeɪsˌkrɑːft] n 우주선
[ujuseon]

spade [speɪd] n 가래 [garae] (도구)

spaghetti [spəˈɡɛtɪ] n 스파게티
[seupageti]

Spain [speɪn] n 스페인 [seupein]

spam [spæm] n 스팸 메일 [seupaem
meil]

Spaniard [ˈspænjəd] n 스페인 사람
[seupein saram]

spaniel [ˈspænjəl] n 스패니얼
[seupaenieol]

Spanish [ˈspænɪʃ] adj 스페인의
[seupeinui] ▷ n 스페인 사람 [seupein
saram]

spank [spæŋk] v 찰싹 때리다 [chalssak
ttaerida]

spanner [ˈspænə] n 스패너
[seupaeneo]

spare [spɛə] adj 여분의 [yeobunui] ▷ v
용서하다 [yongseohada]; **spare part** n
예비 부품 [yebi bupum]; **spare room** n
빈 방 [bin bang]; **spare time** n
여가시간 [yeogasigan]; **spare tyre** n
예비 타이어 [yebi taieo]; **spare wheel**
n 예비 바퀴 [yebi bakwi]; **Is there any
spare bedding?** 여분의 침구가
있어요? [yeobunui chimguga isseoyo?]

spark [spɑːk] n 불꽃 [bulkkot]; **spark
plug** n 점화 플러그 [jeomhwa
peulleogeu]

sparrow [ˈspærəʊ] n 참새 [chamsae]

spasm [ˈspæzəm] n 경련
[gyeongnyeon]

spatula [ˈspætjʊlə] n 주걱 [jugeok]

speak [spiːk] v 말하다 [malhada]

speaker [ˈspiːkə] n 연사 [yeonsa];
native speaker n 원어민 [woneomin]

speak up [spiːk ʌp] v 털어놓고 얘기하다
[teoreonoko yaegihada]

special [ˈspɛʃəl] adj 특별한

[teukbyeolhan]; **special offer** n
특별할인 [teukbyeolharin]

specialist [ˈspɛʃəlɪst] n 전문가
[jeonmunga]

speciality [ˌspɛʃɪˈælɪtɪ] n 특기 [teukgi]

specialize [ˈspɛʃəˌlaɪz] v 전문으로 하다
[jeonmuneuro hada]

specially [ˈspɛʃəlɪ] adv 특별히
[teukbyeolhi]

species [ˈspiːʃiːz; ˈspiːʃɪˌiːz] n 종류
[jongnyu]

specific [spɪˈsɪfɪk] adj 구체적인
[guchejeogin]

specifically [spɪˈsɪfɪklɪ] adv
구체적으로 [guchejeogeuro]

specify [ˈspɛsɪˌfaɪ] v 지정하다
[jijeonghada]

specs [spɛks] npl 안경 [angyeong]

spectacles [ˈspɛktəkəlz] npl 안경
[angyeong]

spectacular [spɛkˈtækjʊlə] adj 장대한
[jangdaehan]

spectator [spɛkˈteɪtə] n 관중
[gwanjung]

speculate [ˈspɛkjʊˌleɪt] v 심사숙고하다
[simsasukgohada]

speech [spiːtʃ] n 언어 [eoneo]

speechless [ˈspiːtʃlɪs] adj 말을 못하는
[mareul motaneun]

speed [spiːd] n 속도 [sokdo]; **speed
limit** n 속도제한 [sokdojehan]; **What
is the speed limit on this road?** 이
도로는 제한 속도가 얼마인가요? [i
doroneun jehan sokdoga
eolmaingayo?]

speedboat [ˈspiːdˌbəʊt] n 고속 모터
보트 [gosok moteo boteu]

speeding [ˈspiːdɪŋ] n 속도내기
[sokdonaegi]

speedometer [spɪˈdɒmɪtə] n 속도계
[sokdogye]

speed up [spiːd ʌp] v 가속하다
[gasokhada]

spell [spɛl] n (magic) 주문 [jumun]
(마술), (time) 기간 [gigan] ▷ v 철자하다
[cheoljahada]

spellchecker [ˈspɛlˌtʃɛkə] n 철자검사
프로그램 [cheoljageomsa

peurogeuraem]
spelling ['spɛlɪŋ] n 철자법
[cheoljabeop]
spend [spɛnd] v 돈쓰다 [donsseuda]
sperm [spɜːm] n 정자 [jeongja]
spice [spaɪs] n 향신료 [hyangsillyo]
spicy ['spaɪsɪ] adj 향료를 넣은
[hyangnyoreul neoheun]
spider ['spaɪdə] n 거미 [geomi]
spill [spɪl] v 엎지르다 [eopjireuda]
spinach ['spɪnɪdʒ; -ɪtʃ] n 시금치
[sigeumchi]
spine [spaɪn] n 척추 [cheokchu]
spinster ['spɪnstə] n 미혼여성
[mihonyeoseong]
spire [spaɪə] n 첨탑 [cheomtap]
spirit ['spɪrɪt] n 정신 [jeongsin]
spirits ['spɪrɪts] npl 기분 [gibun]
spiritual ['spɪrɪtjʊəl] adj 정신적인
[jeongsinjeogin]
spit [spɪt] n 침 [chim] ▷ v 침뱉다
[chimbaetda]
spite [spaɪt] n 악의 [agui] ▷ v 괴롭히다
[goerophida]
spiteful ['spaɪtfʊl] adj 악의적인
[aguijeogin]
splash [splæʃ] v (물을) 튀기다 [(mureul)
twigida]
splendid ['splɛndɪd] adj 화려한
[hwaryeohan]
splint [splɪnt] n 부목 [bumok]
splinter ['splɪntə] n 파편 [papyeon]
split [splɪt] v 쪼개다 [jjogaeda]
split up [splɪt ʌp] v 분열하다
[bunyeolhada]
spoil [spɔɪl] v 망치다 [mangchida]
spoilsport ['spɔɪl,spɔːt] n 흥을 깨는
사람 [heungeul kkaeneun saram]
spoilt [spɔɪlt] adj 버릇 없는 [beoreut
eomneun]
spoke [spəʊk] n 스포크 [seupokeu]
spokesman, spokesmen
['spəʊksmən, 'spəʊksmɛn] n 대변인
[daebyeonin]
spokesperson ['spəʊks,pɜːsən] n
대변인 [daebyeonin]
spokeswoman, spokeswomen
['spəʊks,wʊmən, 'spəʊks,wɪmɪn] n

여자 대변인 [yeoja daebyeonin]
sponge [spʌndʒ] n (cake) 카스텔라
[kaseutella], (for washing) 스펀지
[seupeonji]; **sponge bag** n 휴대 세면백
[hyudae semyeonbaek]
sponsor ['spɒnsə] n 후원자 [huwonja]
▷ v 후원하다 [huwonhada]
sponsorship ['spɒnsəʃɪp] n 후원
[huwon]
spontaneous [spɒn'teɪnɪəs] adj
자발적인 [jabaljeogin]
spooky ['spuːkɪ; 'spooky] adj
공포스러운 [gongposeureoun]
spoon [spuːn] n 숟가락 [sutgarak];
Could I have a clean spoon, please?
깨끗한 숟가락을 주시겠어요?
[kkaekkeutan sutgarageul
jusigesseoyo?]
spoonful ['spuːn,fʊl] n 한 숟가락 가득
[han sutgarak gadeuk]
sport [spɔːt] n 스포츠 [seupocheu];
winter sports npl 겨울 스포츠 [gyeoul
seupocheu]; **What sports facilities
are there?** 어떤 스포츠 시설이 있어요?
[eotteon seupocheu siseori isseoyo?];
**Which sporting events can we go
to?** 어느 스포츠 행사에 갈 수
있을까요? [eoneu seupocheu
haengsae gal su isseulkkayo?]
sportsman, sportsmen
['spɔːtsmən, 'spɔːtsmɛn] n 스포츠맨
[seupocheumaen]
sportswear ['spɔːts,wɛə] n 운동복
[undongbok]
sportswoman, sportswomen
['spɔːts,wʊmən, 'spɔːts,wɪmɪn] n
스포츠우먼 [seupocheuumeon]
sporty ['spɔːtɪ] adj 경쾌한
[gyeongkwaehan]
spot [spɒt] n (blemish) 점 [jeom],
(place) 자리 [jari] ▷ v 찾아내다
[chajanaeda]
spotless ['spɒtlɪs] adj 아주 청결한 [aju
cheonggyeolhan]
spotlight ['spɒt,laɪt] n 스포트라이트
[seupoteuraiteu]
spotty ['spɒtɪ] adj 반점이 많은
[banjeomi manheun]

spouse [spaʊs] *n* 배우자 [baeuja]
sprain [spreɪn] *n* 접질림 [jeopjillim] ▷ *v* 삐다 [ppida]
spray [spreɪ] *n* 분무 [bunmu] ▷ *v* 분무하다 [bunmuhada]; **hair spray** *n* 헤어 스프레이 [heeo seupeurei]
spread [sprɛd] *n* 확산 [hwaksan] ▷ *v* 펴다 [pyeoda]
spread out [sprɛd aʊt] *v* 펼치다 [pyeolchida]
spreadsheet ['sprɛd,ʃiːt] *n* 컴퓨터용 회계처리 프로그램 [keompyuteoyong hoegyecheori peurogeuraem]
spring [sprɪŋ] *n* (coil) 용수철 [yongsucheol], (season) 봄 [bom]; **spring onion** *n* 실파 [silpa]
spring-cleaning ['sprɪŋ,kliːnɪŋ] *n* 대청소 [daecheongso]
springtime ['sprɪŋ,taɪm] *n* 봄철 [bomcheol]
sprinkler ['sprɪŋklə] *n* 살수기 [salsugi]
sprint [sprɪnt] *n* 단거리 경주 [dangeori gyeongju] ▷ *v* 전속력으로 달리다 [jeonsongnyeogeuro dallida]
sprinter ['sprɪntə] *n* 단거리 경주 선수 [dangeori gyeongju seonsu]
sprouts [spraʊts] *npl* 새싹 [saessak]; **Brussels sprouts** *npl* 양배추의 일종 [yangbaechuui iljong]
spy [spaɪ] *n* 스파이 [seupai] ▷ *v* 감시하다 [gamsihada]
spying ['spaɪɪŋ] *n* 정탐하기 [jeongtamhagi]
squabble ['skwɒbəl] *v* 쓸데없는 말다툼을 하다 [sseuldeeomneun maldatumeul hada]
squander ['skwɒndə] *v* 낭비하다 [nangbihada]
square [skwɛə] *adj* 정사각형의 [jeongsagakhyeongui] ▷ *n* 정사각형 [jeongsagakhyeong]
squash [skwɒʃ] *n* 호박 [hobak] ▷ *v* 짓누르다 [jitnureuda]
squeak [skwiːk] *v* 빽빽 울다 [ppaekppaek ulda]
squeeze [skwiːz] *v* 꽉 잡다 [kkwak japda]
squeeze in [skwiːz ɪn] *v* 비집고

들어가다 [bijipgo deureogada]
squid [skwɪd] *n* 오징어 [ojingeo]
squint [skwɪnt] *v* 눈을 가늘게 뜨고 보다 [nuneul ganeulge tteugo boda]
squirrel ['skwɪrəl; 'skwɜːrəl; 'skwʌr-] *n* 다람쥐 [daramjwi]
Sri Lanka [ˌsriː 'læŋkə] *n* 스리랑카 [seurirangka]
stab [stæb] *v* 찌르다 [jjireuda]
stability [stə'bɪlɪtɪ] *n* 안정성 [anjeongseong]
stable ['steɪbəl] *adj* 안정된 [anjeongdoen] ▷ *n* 마구간 [magugan]
stack [stæk] *n* 더미 [deomi]
stadium, stadia ['steɪdɪəm, 'steɪdɪə] *n* 경기장 [gyeonggijang]; **How do we get to the stadium?** 경기장에 어떻게 갈 수 있을까요? [gyeonggijange eotteoke gal su isseulkkayo?]
staff [stɑːf] *n* (stick or rod) 지팡이 [jipangi], (workers) 직원 [jigwon]
staffroom ['stɑːf,ruːm] *n* 직원실 [jigwonsil]
stage [steɪdʒ] *n* 무대 [mudae]
stagger ['stægə] *v* 비틀거리다 [biteulgeorida]
stain [steɪn] *n* 얼룩 [eolluk] ▷ *v* 얼룩지게 하다 [eollukjige hada]; **stain remover** *n* 얼룩 제거제 [eolluk jegeoje]; **Can you remove this stain?** 이 얼룩을 지울 수 있나요? [i eollugeul jiul su innayo?]; **This stain is coffee** 이 얼룩은 커피예요 [i eollugeun keopiyeyo]; **This stain is wine** 이 얼룩은 와인이에요 [i eollugeun wainieyo]
staircase ['stɛə,keɪs] *n* 계단 [gyedan]
stairs [stɛəz] *npl* 계단 [gyedan]
stale [steɪl] *adj* 신선하지 않은 [sinseonhaji anheun]
stalemate ['steɪl,meɪt] *n* 궁지 [gungji]
stall [stɔːl] *n* 상품 진열대 [sangpum jinyeoldae]
stamina ['stæmɪnə] *n* 스태미나 [seutaemina]
stammer ['stæmə] *v* 말을 더듬다 [mareul deodeumda]
stamp [stæmp] *n* 우표 [upyo] ▷ *v* 짓밟다

[jitbapda]; **Can I have stamps for four postcards to...** ...로 엽서를 네 장 보낼 건데 우표 좀 주세요 [...ro yeopseoreul ne jang bonael geonde upyo jom juseyo]; **Do you sell stamps?** 우표 파세요? [upyo paseyo?]; **Where can I buy stamps?** 어디에서 우표를 살 수 있나요? [eodieseo upyoreul sal su innayo?]; **Where is the nearest shop which sells stamps?** 가장 가까운 우표 가게는 어디에 있어요? [gajang gakkaun upyo gageneun eodie isseoyo?]

stand [stænd] v 서다 [seoda]

standard ['stændəd] adj 표준의 [pyojunui] ▷ n 표준 [pyojun]; **standard of living** n 생활수준 [saenghwalsujun]

stand for [stænd fɔː] v 대표하다 [daepyohada]

stand out [stænd aʊt] v 두드러지다 [dudeureojida]

standpoint ['stænd,pɔɪnt] n 관점 [gwanjeom]

stands ['stændz] npl 판매대 [panmaedae]

stand up [stænd ʌp] v 일어서다 [ireoseoda]

staple ['steɪpəl] n (commodity) 주요상품 [juyosangpum], (wire) 꺽쇠 [kkeoksoe] ▷ v 스테이플로 고정시키다 [seuteipeullo gojeongsikida]

stapler ['steɪplə] n 호치키스 [hochikiseu]

star [stɑː] n (person) 인기있는 사람 [ingiinneun saram], (sky) 별 [byeol] ▷ v 주연하다 [juyeonhada]; **film star** n 영화 배우 [yeonghwa baeu]

starch [stɑːtʃ] n 전분 [jeonbun]

stare [steə] v 응시하다 [eungsihada]

stark [stɑːk] adj 황량한 [hwangnyanghan]

start [stɑːt] n 시작 [sijak] ▷ vi 시작되다 [sijakdoeda] ▷ vt 시작하다 [sijakhada]; **The tour starts at about...** 관광은 약...에 시작합니다 [gwangwangeun yak...e sijakhamnida]; **When does the film start?** 영화가 언제 시작해요? [yeonghwaga eonje sijakhaeyo?]

starter ['stɑːtə] n 전채요리 [jeonchaeyori]; **I'd like pasta as a starter** 전채요리로 파스타를 주세요 [jeonchaeyoriro paseutareul juseyo]

startle ['stɑːtəl] v 깜짝 놀라게 하다 [kkamjjak nollage hada]

start off [stɑːt ɒf] v 출발하다 [chulbalhada]

starve [stɑːv] v 굶어죽다 [gurmeojukda]

state [steɪt] n 상태 [sangtae] ▷ v 진술하다 [jinsulhada]

statement ['steɪtmənt] n 성명서 [seongmyeongseo]; **bank statement** n 은행 계좌 통지서 [eunhaeng gyejwa tongjiseo]

station ['steɪʃən] n 정거장 [jeonggeojang]; **bus station** n 버스 정류장 [beoseu jeongnyujang]; **metro station** n 지하철역 [jihacheollyeok]; **petrol station** n 주유소 [juyuso]; **police station** n 경찰서 [kyungcharlsur]; **radio station** n 라디오 방송국 [radio bangsongguk]; **railway station** n 철도역 [cheoldoyeok]; **service station** n 주유소 [juyuso]; **tube station** n 지하철역 [jihacheollyeok]

stationer's ['steɪʃənəz] n 문구점 [mungujeom]

stationery ['steɪʃənərɪ] n 문방구 [munbanggu]

statistics [stə'tɪstɪks] npl 통계학 [tonggyehak]

statue ['stætjuː] n 상 [sang]

status ['steɪtəs] n **marital status** n 결혼 상황 [gyeolhon sanghwang]

status quo ['steɪtəs kwəʊ] n 현상 [hyeonsang]

stay [steɪ] n 거주 [geoju] ▷ v 머무르다 [meomureuda]

stay in [steɪ ɪn] v 집에 있다 [jibe itda]

stay up [steɪ ʌp] v 자지 않고 일어나 있다 [jaji anko ireona itda]

steady ['stedɪ] adj 안정된 [anjeongdoen]

steak [steɪk] n 스테이크 [seuteikeu]; **rump steak** n 럼프 스테이크

[reompeu seuteikeu]

steal [stiːl] v 훔치다 [humchida]

steam [stiːm] n 수증기 [sujeunggi]

steel [stiːl] n 강철 [gangcheol];
stainless steel n 스테인리스강
[seuteilliseugang]

steep [stiːp] adj 가파른 [gapareun]; **Is it very steep?** 아주 가파른가요? [aju gapareungayo?]

steeple [ˈstiːpəl] n 첨탑 [cheomtap]

steering [ˈstɪərɪŋ] n 조타 [jota];
steering wheel n 자동차 핸들
[jadongcha haendeul]

step [stɛp] n 걸음 [georeum]

stepbrother [ˈstɛpˌbrʌðə] n 의붓형제
[uibutyeongje]

stepdaughter [ˈstɛpˌdɔːtə] n 의붓딸
[uibutthtal]

stepfather [ˈstɛpˌfɑːðə] n 의붓아버지
[uibusabeoji]

stepladder [ˈstɛpˌlædə] n 접사다리
[jeopsadari]

stepmother [ˈstɛpˌmʌðə] n 의붓어머니
[uibuseomeoni]

stepsister [ˈstɛpˌsɪstə] n 의붓자매
[uibutjamae]

stepson [ˈstɛpˌsʌn] n 의붓아들
[uibusadeul]

stereo [ˈstɛrɪəʊ; ˈstɪər-] n 스테레오
[seutereo]; **personal stereo** n 휴대
스테레오 [hyudae seutereo]; **Is there a stereo in the car?** 차에 스테레오가
있어요? [chae seutereoga isseoyo?]

stereotype [ˈstɛrɪəˌtaɪp; ˈstɪər-] n
고정관념 [gojeonggwannyeom]

sterile [ˈstɛraɪl] adj 불모의 [bulmoui]

sterilize [ˈstɛrɪˌlaɪz] v 살균하다
[salgyunhada]

sterling [ˈstɜːlɪŋ] n 파운드 [paundeu]

steroid [ˈstɪərɔɪd; ˈstɛr-] n 스테로이드
[seuteroideu]

stew [stjuː] n 스튜 [seutyu]

steward [ˈstjʊəd] n 승무원
[seungmuwon]

tick [stɪk] n 나뭇가지 [namutgaji] ▷ v
찔리다 [jjillida]; **stick insect** n 대벌레
[daebeolle]; **walking stick** n 지팡이
[jipangi]

sticker [ˈstɪkə] n 스티커 [seutikeo]

stick out [stɪk aʊt] v 두드러지다
[dudeureojida]

sticky [ˈstɪkɪ] adj 끈적끈적한
[kkeunjeokkkeunjeokhan]

stiff [stɪf] adj 딱딱한 [ttakttakhan]

stifling [ˈstaɪflɪŋ] adj 답답한
[dapdaphan]

still [stɪl] adj 정지된 [jeongjidoen] ▷ adv
아직 [ajik]; **I'm still studying** 아직
공부하고 있어요 [ajik gongbuhago
isseoyo]

sting [stɪŋ] n 쏘인 상처 [ssoin
sangcheo] ▷ v 쏘다 [ssoda]

stingy [ˈstɪndʒɪ] adj 인색한 [insaekhan]

stink [stɪŋk] n 악취 [akchwi] ▷ v 악취가
나다 [akchwiga nada]

stir [stɜː] v 휘젓다 [hwijeotda]

stitch [stɪtʃ] n 한 바늘 [han baneul] ▷ v
깁다 [gipda]

stock [stɒk] n 재고품 [jaegopum]
(재고품 목록) ▷ v 들여놓다
[deullyeonota]; **stock cube** n 고형수프
[gohyeongsupeu]; **stock exchange** n
증권거래소 [jeunggwongeoraeso];
stock market n 증권시장
[jeunggwonsijang]

stockbroker [ˈstɒkˌbrəʊkə] n
증권중개인 [jeunggwonjunggaein]

stockholder [ˈstɒkˌhəʊldə] n 주주
[juju]

stocking [ˈstɒkɪŋ] n 스타킹 [seutaking]

stock up [stɒk ʌp] v **stock up on** v
사재다 [sajaeda]

stomach [ˈstʌmək] n 위 [wi] (내장)

stomachache [ˈstʌməkˌeɪk] n 위통
[witong]

stone [stəʊn] n 돌 [dol]

stool [stuːl] n 걸상 [geolsang]

stop [stɒp] n 정지 [jeongji] ▷ vi 멈추다
[meomchuda] ▷ vt 그만두다
[geumanduda]; **bus stop** n 버스 정류장
[beoseu jeongnyujang]; **full stop** n
마침표 [machimpyo]

stopover [ˈstɒpˌəʊvə] n 중도하차
[jungdohacha]

stopwatch [ˈstɒpˌwɒtʃ] n 스톱워치
[seutobwochi]

storage ['stɔːrɪdʒ] n 저장 [jeojang]
store [stɔː] n 상점 [sangjeom] ▷ v 저장하다 [jeojanghada]; **department store** n 백화점 [baekhwajeom]
storm [stɔːm] n 폭풍 [pokpung]; **Do you think there will be a storm?** 폭풍우가 칠 것 같아요? [pokpunguga chil geot gatayo?]
stormy ['stɔːmɪ] adj 폭풍의 [pokpungui]
story ['stɔːrɪ] n 이야기 [iyagi]; **short story** n 단편 소설 [danpyeon soseol]
stove [stəʊv] n 스토브 [seutobeu]
straight [streɪt] adj 똑바른 [ttokbareun]; **straight on** adv 똑바로 [ttokbaro]
straighteners ['streɪtⁿnəz] npl 스트레이트너 [seuteureiteuneo]
straightforward [,streɪt'fɔːwəd] adj 정직한 [jeongjikhan]
strain [streɪn] n 과로 [gwaro] ▷ v 긴장시키다 [ginjangsikida]
strained [streɪnd] adj 강요된 [gangyodoen]
stranded ['strændɪd] adj 오도가도 못하는 [odogado motaneun]
strange [streɪndʒ] adj 이상한 [isanghan]
stranger ['streɪndʒə] n 낯선사람 [natseonsaram]
strangle ['stræŋgⁿl] v 목 졸라 죽이다 [mok jolla jugida]
strap [stræp] n 끈 [kkeun]; **watch strap** n 시곗줄 [sigyetjul]
strategic [strə'tiːdʒɪk] adj 전략적인 [jeollyakjeogin]
strategy ['strætɪdʒɪ] n 전략 [jeollyak]
straw [strɔː] n 지푸라기 [jipuragi]
strawberry ['strɔːbərɪ; -brɪ] n 딸기 [ttalgi]
stray [streɪ] n 길잃은 동물 [girireun dongmul]
stream [striːm] n 개울 [gaeul]
street [striːt] n 거리 [geori]; **street map** n 거리지도 [georijido]; **street plan** n 도로계획 [dorogyehoek]
streetlamp ['striːt,læmp] n 가로등 [garodeung]

streetwise ['striːt,waɪz] adj 세상물정에 밝은 [sesangmuljeonge balgeun]
strength [strɛŋθ] n 힘 [him]
strengthen ['strɛŋθən] v 강화하다 [ganghwahada]
stress [strɛs] n 스트레스 [seuteureseu] ▷ v 강조하다 [gangjohada]
stressed ['strɛst] adj 스트레스를 받고 있는 [seuteureseureul batgo inneun]
stressful ['strɛsfʊl] adj 스트레스를 주는 [seuteureseureul juneun]
stretch [strɛtʃ] v 뻗어 있다 [ppeodeo itda]
stretcher ['strɛtʃə] n 들것 [deulgeot]
stretchy ['strɛtʃɪ] adj 신축성 있는 [sinchukseong inneun]
strict [strɪkt] adj 엄격한 [eomgyeokhan]
strictly [strɪktlɪ] adv 엄격하게 [eomgyeokhage]
strike [straɪk] n 파업 [paeop] ▷ vi 치다 [chida], (suspend work) 파업을 하다 [paeobeul hada]; **because of a strike** 파업때문에요 [paeopttaemuneyo]
striker ['straɪkə] n 파업참가자 [paeopchamgaja]
striking ['straɪkɪŋ] adj 인상적인 [insangjeogin]
string [strɪŋ] n 끈 [kkeun]
strip [strɪp] n 스트립쇼 [seuteuripsyo] ▷ v 벗기다 [beotgida]
stripe [straɪp] n 줄무늬 [julmunui]
striped [straɪpt] adj 줄무늬의 [julmunuiui]
stripper ['strɪpə] n 스트리퍼 [seuteuripeo]
stripy ['straɪpɪ] adj 줄이 있는 [juri inneun]
stroke [strəʊk] n (apoplexy) 발작 [baljak], (hit) 타격 [tagyeok] ▷ v 쓰다듬다 [sseudadeumda]
stroll [strəʊl] n 산책 [sanchaek]
strong [strɒŋ] adj 강한 [ganghan]; **I need something stronger** 더 강한 것이 필요해요 [deo ganghan geosi pillyohaeyo]
strongly [strɒŋlɪ] adv 강하게 [ganghage]

structure ['strʌktʃə] n 구조 [gujo]
struggle ['strʌgəl] v 열심히 노력하다 [yeolsimhi noryeokhada]
stub [stʌb] n 토막 [tomak]
stubborn ['stʌbən] adj 완고한 [wangohan]
stub out [stʌb aʊt] v 비벼 불을 끄다 [bibyeo bureul kkeuda]
stuck [stʌk] adj 곤경에 빠진 [gongyeonge ppajin]
stuck-up [stʌkʌp] adj 거만한 [geomanhan]
stud [stʌd] n 장식못 [jangsingmot]
student ['stjuːdənt] n 학생 [haksaeng]; **student discount** n 학생할인 [haksaengharin]; **Are there any reductions for students?** 학생 할인이 있어요? [haksaeng harini isseoyo?]; **I'm a student** 학생이에요 [haksaengieyo]
studio ['stjuːdɪ,əʊ] n 스튜디오 [seutyudio]; **studio flat** n 원룸 아파트 [wollum apateu]
study ['stʌdɪ] v 공부하다 [gongbuhada]
stuff [stʌf] n 물질 [muljil]
stuffy ['stʌfɪ] adj 답답한 [dapdaphan]
stumble ['stʌmbəl] v 걸려 넘어질 뻔하다 [geollyeo neomeojil ppeonhada]
stunned [stʌnd] adj 엄청난 [eomcheongnan]
stunning ['stʌnɪŋ] adj 매력적인 [maeryeokjeogin]
stunt [stʌnt] n 묘기 [myogi]
stuntman, stuntmen ['stʌntmən, 'stʌntmɛn] n 스턴트맨 [seuteonteumaen]
stupid ['stjuːpɪd] adj 바보같은 [babogateun]
stutter ['stʌtə] v 말을 더듬다 [mareul deodeumda]
style [staɪl] n 스타일 [seutail]; **I want a completely new style** 완전히 새로운 스타일을 하고 싶어요 [wanjeonhi saeroun seutaireul hago sipeoyo]
styling ['staɪlɪŋ] n **Do you sell styling products?** 스타일링 제품 파세요? [seutailling jepum paseyo?]

stylist ['staɪlɪst] n 스타일리스트 [seutailliseuteu]
subject ['sʌbdʒɪkt] n 주제 [juje]
submarine ['sʌbməˌriːn; ,sʌbmə'riːn] n 잠수함 [jamsuham]
subscription [səb'skrɪpʃən] n 구독 [gudok]
subsidiary [səb'sɪdɪərɪ] n 자회사 [jahoesa]
subsidize ['sʌbsɪ,daɪz] v 보조금을 지불하다 [bojogeumeul jibulhada]
subsidy ['sʌbsɪdɪ] n 보조금 [bojogeum]
substance ['sʌbstəns] n 물질 [muljil]
substitute ['sʌbstɪ,tjuːt] n 대리 [daeri] ▷ v 대신하다 [daesinhada]
subtitled ['sʌb,taɪtəld] adj 자막이 있는 [jamagi inneun]
subtitles ['sʌb,taɪtəlz] npl 자막 [jamak]
subtle ['sʌtəl] adj 미묘한 [mimyohan]
subtract [səb'trækt] v 빼다 [ppaeda]
suburb ['sʌbɜːb] n 교외 [gyooe]
suburban [sə'bɜːbən] adj 교외의 [gyooeui]
subway ['sʌb,weɪ] n 지하철 [jihacheol]
succeed [sək'siːd] v 성공하다 [seonggonghada]
success [sək'sɛs] n 성공 [seonggong]
successful [sək'sɛsfʊl] adj 성공한 [seonggonghan]
successfully [sək'sɛsfʊlɪ] adv 성공적으로 [seonggongjeogeuro]
successive [sək'sɛsɪv] adj 연속하는 [yeonsokhaneun]
successor [sək'sɛsə] n 후계자 [hugyeja]
such [sʌtʃ] adj 그런 [geureon] ▷ adv 그렇게 [geureoke]
suck [sʌk] v 입으로 빨다 [ibeuro ppalda]
Sudan [suː'dɑːn; -'dæn] n 수단 [sudan]
Sudanese [,suːdə'niːz] adj 수단의 [sudanui] ▷ n 수단 사람 [sudan saram]
sudden ['sʌdən] adj 갑작스러운 [gapjakseureoun]
suddenly ['sʌdənlɪ] adv 갑자기 [gapjagi]
sue [sjuː; suː] v 소송제기하다 [sosongjegihada]

suede [sweɪd] n 스웨이드 가죽 [seuweideu gajuk]

suffer [ˈsʌfə] v 괴로워하다 [goerowohada]

sufficient [səˈfɪʃənt] adj 불충분한 [bulchungbunhan]

suffocate [ˈsʌfəˌkeɪt] v 질식하다 [jilsikhada]

sugar [ˈʃʊgə] n 설탕 [seoltang]; **icing sugar** n 가루 설탕 [garu seoltang]; **no sugar** 무설탕 [museoltang]

sugar-free [ˈʃʊgəfriː] adj 무설탕의 [museoltangui]

suggest [səˈdʒɛst; səgˈdʒɛst] v 제안하다 [jeanhada]

suggestion [səˈdʒɛstʃən] n 제안 [jean]

suicide [ˈsuːɪˌsaɪd; ˈsjuː-] n 자살 [jasal]; **suicide bomber** n 자살폭탄 테러범 [jasalpoktan tereobeom]

suit [suːt; sjuːt] n 슈트 [syuteu] ▷ v 어울리다 [eoullida]; **bathing suit** n 수영복 [suyeongbok]; **shell suit** n 보온복 [boonbok]

suitable [ˈsuːtəbəl; ˈsjuːt-] adj 적합한 [jeokhaphan]

suitcase [ˈsuːtˌkeɪs; ˈsjuːt-] n 여행가방 [yeohaenggabang]

suite [swiːt] n 스위트 룸 [seuwiteu rum]

sulk [sʌlk] v 부루퉁해지다 [burutunghaejida]

sulky [ˈsʌlkɪ] adj 부루퉁한 [burutunghan]

sultana [sʌlˈtɑːnə] n 씨없는 건포도 [ssieomneun geonpodo]

sum [sʌm] n 합계 [hapgye]

summarize [ˈsʌməˌraɪz] v 요약하다 [yoyakhada]

summary [ˈsʌmərɪ] n 요약 [yoyak]

summer [ˈsʌmə] n 여름 [yeoreum]; **summer holidays** npl 여름휴가 [yeoreumhyuga]; **after summer** 여름 후에 [yeoreum hue]; **during the summer** 여름 동안에 [yeoreum dongane]; **in summer** 여름에 [yeoreume]

summertime [ˈsʌməˌtaɪm] n 여름철 [yeoreumcheol]

summit [ˈsʌmɪt] n 정상 [jeongsang] (맨 꼭대기)

sum up [sʌm ʌp] v 요약하다 [yoyakhada]

sun [sʌn] n 태양 [taeyang]

sunbathe [ˈsʌnˌbeɪð] v 일광욕을 하다 [ilgwangyogeul hada]

sunbed [ˈsʌnˌbɛd] n 일광욕 접이의자 [ilgwangyok jeobiuija]

sunblock [ˈsʌnˌblɒk] n 자외선 차단제 [jaoeseon chadanje]

sunburn [ˈsʌnˌbɜːn] n 햇볕에 탐 [haetbyeote tam]

sunburnt [ˈsʌnˌbɜːnt] adj 햇볕에 탄 [haetbyeote tan]

suncream [ˈsʌnˌkriːm] n 선크림 [seonkeurim]

Sunday [ˈsʌndɪ] n 일요일 [illyoil]; **Is the museum open on Sundays?** 이 박물관은 일요일마다 열어요? [i bangmulgwaneun iryoilmada yeoreoyo?]; **on Sunday** 일요일에 [iryoire]

sunflower [ˈsʌnˌflaʊə] n 해바라기 [haebaragi]

sunglasses [ˈsʌnˌglɑːsɪz] npl 선글라스 [seongeullaseu]

sunlight [ˈsʌnlaɪt] n 햇빛 [haetbit]

sunny [ˈsʌnɪ] adj 햇빛이 밝은 [haetbichi balgeun]

sunrise [ˈsʌnˌraɪz] n 일출 [ilchul]

sunroof [ˈsʌnˌruːf] n 선루프 [seollupeu]

sunscreen [ˈsʌnˌskriːn] n 자외선 차단제 [jaoeseon chadanje]

sunset [ˈsʌnˌsɛt] n 일몰 [ilmol]

sunshine [ˈsʌnˌʃaɪn] n 햇빛 [haetbit]

sunstroke [ˈsʌnˌstrəʊk] n 일사병 [ilsabyeong]

suntan [ˈsʌnˌtæn] n 선탠 [seontaen]; **suntan lotion** n 선탠 로션 [seontaen rosyeon]; **suntan oil** n 선탠 오일 [seontaen oil]

super [ˈsuːpə] adj 멋진 [meotjin]

superb [sʊˈpɜːb; sjʊ-] adj 훌륭한 [hullyunghan]

superficial [ˌsuːpəˈfɪʃəl] adj 피상적인 [pisangjeogin]

superior [suːˈpɪərɪə] adj 우수한

[usuhan] ▷ *n* 상사 [sangsa]

supermarket ['su:pə,mɑːkɪt] *n*
슈퍼마켓 [syupeomaket]; **I need to
find a supermarket** 슈퍼마켓을
찾아야 해요 [syupeomakeseul chajaya
haeyo]

supernatural [,su:pə'nætʃrəl;
-'nætʃərəl] *adj* 초자연의 [chojayeonui]

superstitious [,su:pə'stɪʃəs] *adj*
미신적인 [misinjeogin]

supervise ['su:pə,vaɪz] *v* 감독하다
[gamdokhada]

supervisor ['su:pə,vaɪzə] *n* 감독자
[gamdokja]

supper ['sʌpə] *n* 저녁식사
[jeonyeoksiksa]

supplement ['sʌplɪmənt] *n* 보충
[bochung]

supplier [sə'plaɪə] *n* 공급자
[gonggeupja]

supplies [sə'plaɪz] *npl* 공급품
[gonggeuppum]

supply [sə'plaɪ] *n* 공급 [gonggeup] ▷ *v*
공급하다 [gonggeuphada]; **supply
teacher** *n* 임시교사 [imsigyosa]

support [sə'pɔːt] *n* 지원 [jiwon] ▷ *v*
지원하다 [jiwonhada]

supporter [sə'pɔːtə] *n* 지지자 [jijija]

suppose [sə'pəʊz] *v* 가정하다
[gajeonghada]

supposedly [sə'pəʊzɪdlɪ] *adv* 아마
[ama]

supposing [sə'pəʊzɪŋ] *conj* ...이라고
가정하면 [...irago gajeonghamyeon]

surcharge ['sɜː,tʃɑːdʒ] *n* 추가요금
[chugayogeum]

sure [ʃʊə; ʃɔː] *adj* 확실한 [hwaksilhan]

surely ['ʃʊəlɪ; 'ʃɔː-] *adv* 확실하게
[hwaksilhage]

surf [sɜːf] *n* 밀려오는 파도
[millyeooneun pado] ▷ *v* 파도타기를
하다 [padotagireul hada]

surface ['sɜːfɪs] *n* 표면 [pyomyeon]

surfboard ['sɜːf,bɔːd] *n* 서핑보드
[seopingbodeu]

surfer ['sɜːfə] *n* 서핑하는 사람
[seopinghaneun saram]

surfing ['sɜːfɪŋ] *n* 서핑 [seoping]

surge [sɜːdʒ] *n* 격동 [gyeokdong]

surgeon ['sɜːdʒən] *n* 외과의사
[oegwauisa]

surgery ['sɜːdʒərɪ] *n* (*doctor's*) 진료소
[jillyoso], (*operation*) 수술 [susul];
cosmetic surgery *n* 미용 성형외과
[miyong seonghyeongoegwa]; **plastic
surgery** *n* 성형외과
[seonghyeongoegwa]

surname ['sɜː,neɪm] *n* 성 [seong]

surplus ['sɜːpləs] *adj* 잉여의 [ingyeoui]
▷ *n* 잉여 [ingyeo]

surprise [sə'praɪz] *n* 놀람 [nollam]

surprised [sə'praɪzd] *adj* 놀란 [nollan]

surprising [sə'praɪzɪŋ] *adj* 놀라운
[nollaun]

surprisingly [sə'praɪzɪŋlɪ] *adv*
놀랍게도 [nollapgedo]

surrender [sə'rɛndə] *v* 항복하다
[hangbokhada]

surround [sə'raʊnd] *v* 둘러싸다
[dulleossada]

surroundings [sə'raʊndɪŋz] *npl* 환경
[hwangyeong]

survey ['sɜːveɪ] *n* 조사 [josa]

surveyor [sɜː'veɪə] *n* 감독자
[gamdokja]

survival [sə'vaɪvəl] *n* 생존 [saengjon]

survive [sə'vaɪv] *v* 살아남다
[saranamda]

survivor [sə'vaɪvə] *n* 생존자
[saengjonja]

suspect *n* ['sʌspɛkt] 용의자 [yonguija]
▷ *v* [sə'spɛkt] 의심하다 [uisimhada]

suspend [sə'spɛnd] *v* 매달다
[maedalda]

suspenders [sə'spɛndəz] *npl* 멜빵
[melppang]

suspense [sə'spɛns] *n* 긴장감
[ginjanggam]

suspension [sə'spɛnʃən] *n* 정지
[jeongji]; **suspension bridge** *n* 현수교
[hyeonsugyo]

suspicious [sə'spɪʃəs] *adj* 수상한
[susanghan] (의심스러운)

swallow ['swɒləʊ] *n* 제비 [jebi] ▷ *vi*
삼키다 [samkida]

swamp [swɒmp] *n* 습지 [seupji]

swan [swɒn] n 백조 [baekjo]

swap [swɒp] v 바꾸다 [bakkuda]

swat [swɒt] v 찰싹 때리다 [chalssak ttaerida]

sway [sweɪ] v 전후(좌우)로 흔들리다 [jeonhu(jwau)ro heundeullida]

Swaziland ['swɑːzɪˌlænd] n 스와질란드 [seuwajillandeu]

swear [sweə] v 맹세하다 [maengsehada]

swearword ['sweəˌwɜːd] n 욕설 [yokseor]

sweat [swɛt] n 땀 [ttam] ▷ v 땀을 흘리다 [ttameul heullida]

sweater ['swɛtə] n 스웨터 [seuweteo]; **polo-necked sweater** n 폴로네크 스웨터 [pollonekeu seuweteo]

sweatshirt ['swɛtˌʃɜːt] n 스웨트셔츠 [seuweteusyeocheu]

sweaty ['swɛtɪ] adj 땀투성이의 [ttamtuseongiui]

swede [swiːd] n 순무 [sunmu]

Swede [swiːd] n 스웨덴 사람 [seuweden saram]

Sweden ['swiːdən] n 스웨덴 [seuweden]

Swedish ['swiːdɪʃ] adj 스웨덴의 [seuwedenui] ▷ n 스웨덴 사람 [seuweden saram]

sweep [swiːp] v 쓸다 [sseulda]

sweet [swiːt] adj (pleasing) 즐거운 [jeulgeoun], (taste) 단 [dan] (맛이 달콤한) ▷ n 사탕 [satang]

sweetcorn ['swiːtˌkɔːn] n 사탕옥수수 [satangoksusu]

sweetener ['swiːtnə] n 감미료 [gammiryo]; **Do you have any sweetener?** 감미료 있어요? [gammiryo isseoyo?]

sweets ['swiːtz] npl 사탕 [satang]

sweltering ['swɛltərɪŋ] adj 무더운 [mudeoun]

swerve [swɜːv] v 빗나가다 [bitnagada]

swim [swɪm] v 수영하다 [suyeonghada]

swimmer ['swɪmə] n 수영하는 사람 [suyeonghaneun saram]

swimming ['swɪmɪŋ] n 수영

[suyeong]; **swimming costume** n 수영복 [suyeongbok]; **swimming pool** n 수영장 [suyeongjang]; **swimming trunks** npl (남자) 수영복 [(namja) suyeongbok]; **Is there a swimming pool?** 수영장이 있어요? [suyeongjangi isseoyo?]; **Where is the public swimming pool?** 공용 수영장은 어디있어요? [gongyong suyeongjangeun eodiisseoyo?]

swimsuit ['swɪmˌsuːt; -ˌsjuːt] n 수영복 [suyeongbok]

swing [swɪŋ] n 흔들림 [heundeullim] ▷ v 흔들흔들 움직이다 [heundeulheundeul umjigida]

Swiss [swɪs] adj 스위스의 [seuwiseuui] ▷ n 스위스 사람 [seuwiseu saram]

switch [swɪtʃ] n 스위치 [seuwichi] ▷ v 교환하다 [gyohwanhada]

switchboard ['swɪtʃˌbɔːd] n 전화교환대 [jeonhwagyohwandae]

switch off [swɪtʃ ɒf] v 끄다 [kkeuda]

switch on [swɪtʃ ɒn] v 켜다 [kyeoda]

Switzerland ['swɪtsələnd] n 스위스 [seuwiseu]

swollen ['swəʊlən] adj 부푼 [bupun]

sword [sɔːd] n 검 [geom]

swordfish ['sɔːdˌfɪʃ] n 황새치 [hwangsaechi]

swot [swɒt] v 힘들게 일하다 [himdeulge ilhada]

syllable ['sɪləbəl] n 음절 [eumjeol]

syllabus ['sɪləbəs] n 강의 시간표 [gangui siganpyo]

symbol ['sɪmbəl] n 상징 [sangjing]

symmetrical [sɪ'mɛtrɪkəl] adj 대칭적인 [daechingjeogin]

sympathetic [ˌsɪmpə'θɛtɪk] adj 동정적인 [dongjeongjeogin]

sympathize ['sɪmpəˌθaɪz] v 동정하다 [dongjeonghada]

sympathy ['sɪmpəθɪ] n 동정 [dongjeong]

symphony ['sɪmfənɪ] n 교향곡 [gyohyanggok]

symptom ['sɪmptəm] n 증상 [jeungsang]

synagogue ['sɪnəˌgɒg] n 유태교

예배당 [yutaegyo yebaedang]

syndrome ['sɪndrəum] n **Down's syndrome** n 다운 증후군 [daun jeunghugun]

Syria ['sɪrɪə] n 시리아 [siria]

Syrian ['sɪrɪən] adj 시리아의 [siriaui] ▷ n 시리아 사람 [siria saram]

syringe ['sɪrɪndʒ; sɪ'rɪndʒ] n 주사기 [jusagi]

syrup ['sɪrəp] n 시럽 [sireop]

system ['sɪstəm] n 시스템 [siseutem]; **immune system** n 면역체계 [myeonyeokchegye]; **solar system** n 태양계 [taeyanggye]; **systems analyst** n 시스템 분석가 [siseutem bunseokga]

systematic [ˌsɪstɪ'mætɪk] adj 조직적인 [jojikjeogin]

table ['teɪbªl] n (chart) 도표 [dopyo], (furniture) 테이블 [teibeul]; **bedside table** n 침대 곁의 보조 탁자 [chimdae gyeotui bojo takja]; **coffee table** n 커피 테이블 [keopi teibeul]; **dressing table** n 화장대 [hwajangdae]; **table tennis** n 탁구 [takgu]; **table wine** n 식탁용 와인 [siktagyong wain]; **A table for four people, please** 네 명 테이블이요 [ne myeong teibeuriyo]; **I'd like to book a table for three people for tonight** 오늘 밤 세 명 테이블을 예약하고 싶어요 [oneul bam se myeong teibeureul yeyakhago sipeoyo]; **I'd like to book a table for two people for tomorrow night** 내일 밤 두 명 테이블을 예약하고 싶어요 [naeil bam du myeong teibeureul yeyakhago sipeoyo]; **The table is booked for nine o'clock this evening** 오늘 저녁 아홉시 테이블이 예약되었습니다 [oneul jeonyeok ahopsi teibeuri yeyakdoeeosseumnida]

tablecloth ['teɪbªlˌklɒθ] n 식탁보 [siktakbo]

tablespoon ['teɪbªlˌspuːn] n 테이블스푼 [teibeulseupun]

tablet ['tæblɪt] *n* 정제 [jeongje]

taboo [tə'buː] *adj* 금지된 [geumjidoen]
▷ *n* 금기 [geumgi]

tackle ['tækəl; 'teɪkəl] *n* 장비 [jangbi] ▷ *v*
다루다 [daruda]; **fishing tackle** *n* 낚시
도구 [nakksi dogu]

tact [tækt] *n* 재치 [jaechi]

tactful ['tæktfʊl] *adj* 재치있는
[jaechiinneun]

tactics ['tæktɪks] *npl* 전술 [jeonsul]

tactless ['tæktlɪs] *adj* 재치없는
[jaechieomneun]

tadpole ['tæd,pəʊl] *n* 올챙이
[olchaengi]

tag [tæg] *n* 꼬리표 [kkoripyo]

Tahiti [tə'hiːtɪ] *n* 타히티 섬 [tahiti
seom]

tail [teɪl] *n* 꼬리 [kkori]

tailor ['teɪlə] *n* 재단사 [jaedansa]

Taiwan ['taɪ'wɑːn] *n* 타이완 [taiwan]

Taiwanese [,taɪwɑː'niːz] *adj* 타이완의
[taiwanui] ▷ *n* 타이완 사람 [taiwan
saram]

Tajikistan [tɑː,dʒɪkɪ'stɑːn; -stæn] *n*
타지키스탄 [tajikiseutan]

take [teɪk] *v* 가지다 [gajida], *(time)* (
시간) 걸리다 [(sigan) geollida]

take after [teɪk 'ɑːftə] *v* 닮다 [darmda]

take apart [teɪk ə'pɑːt] *v* 분해하다
[bunhaehada]

take away [teɪk ə'weɪ] *v* 제거하다
[jegeohada]

takeaway ['teɪkə,weɪ] *n* 집에 사가지고
가는 요리 [jibe sagajigo ganeun yori]

take back [teɪk bæk] *v* 취소하다
[chwisohada]

taken ['teɪkən] *adj* **Is this seat taken?**
이 자리는 사용중인가요? [i jalineun
sayongjung-ingayo]

take off [teɪk ɒf] *v* 벗다 [beotda]

takeoff ['teɪk,ɒf] *n* 이륙 [iryuk]

take over [teɪk 'əʊvə] *v* 인계받다
[ingyebatda]

takeover ['teɪk,əʊvə] *n* 인수 [insu]

takings ['teɪkɪŋz] *npl* 소득 [sodeuk]

tale [teɪl] *n* 이야기 [iyagi]

talent ['tælənt] *n* 재능 [jaeneung]

talented ['tæləntɪd] *adj* 재능이 있는
[jaeneungi inneun]

talk [tɔːk] *n* 강연 [gangyeon] ▷ *v* 말하다
[malhada]; **talk to** *v* 말하다 [malhada]

talkative ['tɔːkətɪv] *adj* 말이 많은
[mari manheun]

tall [tɔːl] *adj* 키가 큰 [kiga keun]

tame [teɪm] *adj* 길들여진
[gildeullyeojin]

tampon ['tæmpɒn] *n* 탐폰 [tampon]

tan [tæn] *n* 햇볕에 탄 빛깔 [haetbyeote
tan bitkkal]

tandem ['tændəm] *n* 2인승 자전거 [i
inseung jajeongeo]

tangerine [,tændʒə'riːn] *n* 밀감
[milgam]

tank [tæŋk] *n* *(combat vehicle)* 탱크
[taengkeu], *(large container)* 탱크
[taengkeu]; **petrol tank** *n* 휘발유 탱크
[hwiballyu taengkeu]; **septic tank** *n*
정화조 [jeonghwajo]; **The petrol tank
is leaking** 연료 탱크가 새요 [yeollyo
taengkeuga saeyo]

tanker ['tæŋkə] *n* 탱커 [taengkeo]

tanned [tænd] *adj* 황갈색의
[hwanggalsaegui]

tantrum ['tæntrəm] *n* 고집 [gojip]
(고집부리다)

Tanzania [,tænzə'nɪə] *n* 탄자니아
[tanjania]

Tanzanian [,tænzə'nɪən] *adj*
탄자나아의 [tanjanaaui] ▷ *n* 탄자니아
사람 [tanjania saram]

tap [tæp] *n* 가볍게 두드리기 [gabyeopge
dudeurigi]

tap-dancing ['tæp,dɑːnsɪŋ] *n* 탭댄스
[taepdaenseu]

tape [teɪp] *n* 테이프 [teipeu] ▷ *v*
녹음하다 [nogeumhada]; **tape
measure** *n* 줄자 [julja]; **tape recorder**
n 녹음기 [nogeumgi]; **Can I have a
tape for this video camera, please?**
이 비디오 카메라에 사용하는 테이프
하나 주시겠어요? [i bidio kamerae
sayonghaneun teipeu hana
jusigesseoyo?]

target ['tɑːgɪt] *n* 표적 [pyojeok]

tariff ['tærɪf] *n* 관세 [gwanse]

tarmac ['tɑːmæk] *n* 타맥 [tamaek]

tarpaulin [tɑːˈpɔːlɪn] *n* 방수포
[bangsupo]

tarragon [ˈtærəgən] *n* 타라곤
[taragon]

tart [tɑːt] *n* 타트 [tateu]

tartan [ˈtɑːtən] *adj* 격자무늬의
[gyeokjamunuiui]

task [tɑːsk] *n* 과제 [gwaje]

Tasmania [tæzˈmeɪnɪə] *n* 태즈메이니아
[taejeumeinia]

taste [teɪst] *n* 맛 [mat] *▷ v* 맛보다
[matboda]; **Can I taste it?** 맛 좀 볼 수
있을까요? [mat jom bol su
isseulkkayo?]; **It doesn't taste very
nice** 맛이 별로예요 [masi byeolloyeyo]

tasteful [ˈteɪstfʊl] *adj* 고상한
[gosanghan]

tasteless [ˈteɪstlɪs] *adj* 맛없는
[maseomneun]

tasty [ˈteɪstɪ] *adj* 맛있는 [masinneun]

tattoo [tæˈtuː] *n* 문신 [munsin]

Taurus [ˈtɔːrəs] *n* 황소자리
[hwangsojari]

tax [tæks] *n* 세금 [segeum]; **income tax**
n 소득세 [sodeukse]; **road tax** *n*
도로세 [dorose]; **tax payer** *n* 납세자
[napseja]; **tax return** *n* 소득신고
[sodeuksingo]

taxi [ˈtæksɪ] *n* 택시 [taeksi]; **taxi driver**
n 택시 운전사 [taeksi unjeonsa]; **taxi
rank** *n* 택시 승차장 [taeksi
seungchajang]; **How much is the taxi
fare into town?** 시내까지 택시 요금이
얼마예요? [sinaekkaji taeksi yogeumi
eolmayeyo?]; **I left my bags in the
taxi** 택시에 가방을 두고 내렸어요
[taeksie gabangeul dugo
naeryeosseoyo]; **I need a taxi** 택시가
필요해요 [taeksiga piryohaeyo];
Please order me a taxi for 8 o'clock
여덟시에 택시를 불러 주세요
[yeodeopsie taeksireul bulleo juseyo];
Where can I get a taxi? 어디에서
택시를 탈 수 있어요? [eodieseo
taeksireul tal su isseoyo?]; **Where is
the taxi stand?** 택시정류장 어디에
있어요? [taeksijeongnyujang eodie
isseoyo?]

TB [tiː biː] *n* 결핵균 [gyeolhaekgyun]

tea [tiː] *n* 차 [cha] (음료수); **herbal tea**
n 허브차 [heobeucha]; **tea bag** *n* 티백
[tibaek]; **tea towel** *n* 티 타월 [ti tawol];
A tea, please 차 주세요 [cha juseyo];
**Could we have another cup of tea,
please?** 차 한 잔씩 더 주시겠어요?
[cha han janssik deo jusigesseoyo?]

teach [tiːtʃ] *v* 가르치다 [gareuchida]

teacher [ˈtiːtʃə] *n* 교사 [gyosa]; **supply
teacher** *n* 임시교사 [imsigyosa]; **I'm a
teacher** 교사입니다 [gyosaimnida]

teaching [ˈtiːtʃɪŋ] *n* 가르치기
[gareuchigi]

teacup [ˈtiːˌkʌp] *n* 찻잔 [chatjan]

team [tiːm] *n* 팀 [tim]

teapot [ˈtiːˌpɒt] *n* 티포트 [tipoteu]

tear¹ [tɪə] *n (from eye)* 눈물 [nunmul]

tear² [tɛə] *n (split)* 찢기 [jjitgi] *▷ v* 찢다
[jjitda]; **tear up** *v* 찢다 [jjitda]

teargas [ˈtɪəˌgæs] *n* 최루가스
[choerugaseu]

tease [tiːz] *v* 놀리다 [nollida]

teaspoon [ˈtiːˌspuːn] *n* 찻숟가락
[chassutgarak]

teatime [ˈtiːˌtaɪm] *n* 티타임 [titaim]

technical [ˈtɛknɪkəl] *adj* 기술적인
[gisuljeogin]

technician [tɛkˈnɪʃən] *n* 기술자
[gisulja]

technique [tɛkˈniːk] *n* 기법 [gibeop]

techno [ˈtɛknəʊ] *n* 테크노 [tekeuno]

technological [tɛkˈnɒlədʒɪkəl] *adj*
기술학상의 [gisulhaksangui]

technology [tɛkˈnɒlədʒɪ] *n* 기술
[gisul]

tee [tiː] *n* 티 [ti] (골프)

teenager [ˈtiːnˌeɪdʒə] *n* 십대 [sipdae]

teens [tiːnz] *npl* 십대 [sipdae]

tee-shirt [ˈtiːˌʃɜːt] *n* 티셔츠
[tisyeocheu]

teethe [tiːð] *v* 젖니가 나다 [jeotniga
nada]

teetotal [tiːˈtəʊtəl] *adj* 절대 금주의
[jeoldae geumjuui]

telecommunications
[ˌtɛlɪkəˌmjuːnɪˈkeɪʃənz] *npl* 원격통신
[wongyeoktongsin]

telegram ['tɛlɪˌgræm] n 전보 [jeonbo];
Can I send a telegram from here?
여기에서 전보를 보낼 수 있을까요?
[yeogieseo jeonboreul bonael su
isseulkkayo?]

telephone ['tɛlɪˌfəʊn] n 전화
[jeonhwa]; **telephone directory** n
전화번호부 [jeonhwabeonhobu]; **How
much is it to telephone…?** ...에
전화하려면 얼마예요? [...e
jeonhwaharyeomyeon eolmayeyo?]; **I
need to make an urgent telephone
call** 긴급 전화를 해야 해요 [gingeup
jeonhwareul haeya haeyo]; **What's
the telephone number?** 전화번호가
무엇입니까? [jeonhwabeonhoga
mueosimnikka?]

telesales ['tɛlɪˌseɪlz] npl 전화판매
[jeonhwapanmae]

telescope ['tɛlɪˌskəʊp] n 망원경
[mangwongyeong]

television ['tɛlɪˌvɪʒən] n 텔레비전
[tellebijeon]; **cable television** n 유선
텔레비전 [yuseon tellebijeon]; **colour
television** n 컬러 텔레비전 [keolleo
tellebijeon]; **digital television** n
디지털 텔레비전 [dijiteol tellebijeon];
Where is the television? 텔레비전은
어디에 있어요? [tellebijeoneun eodie
isseoyo?]

tell [tɛl] v 말하다 [malhada]

teller ['tɛlə] n 이야기하는 사람
[iyagihaneun saram]

tell off [tɛl ɒf] v 꾸짖다 [kkujitda]

telly ['tɛlɪ] n 텔레비전 [tellebijeon]

temp [tɛmp] n 임시고용 [imsigoyong]

temper ['tɛmpə] n 기분 [gibun]

temperature ['tɛmprɪtʃə] n 온도
[ondo]

temple ['tɛmpªl] n 신전 [sinjeon]

temporary ['tɛmpərərɪ; 'tɛmprərɪ] adj
임시의 [imsiui]

tempt [tɛmpt] v 유혹하다 [yuhokhada]

temptation [tɛmp'teɪʃən] n 유혹
[yuhok]

tempting ['tɛmptɪŋ] adj 유혹하는
[yuhokhaneun]

ten [tɛn] number 열 [yeol], (Sino-Korean)

십 [sib]

tenant ['tɛnənt] n 세입자 [seipja]

tend [tɛnd] v 경향이 있다
[gyeonghyangi itda]

tendency ['tɛndənsɪ] n 경향
[gyeonghyang]

tender ['tɛndə] adj 부드러운
[budeureoun]

tendon ['tɛndən] n 힘줄 [himjul]

tennis ['tɛnɪs] n 테니스 [teniseu]; **table
tennis** n 탁구 [takgu]; **tennis player** n
테니스 치는 사람 [teniseu chineun
saram]; **tennis racket** n 테니스 라켓
[teniseu raket]; **How much is it to
hire a tennis court?** 테니스 코트를
빌리는 데 얼마예요? [teniseu
koteureul billineun de eolmayeyo?];
Where can I play tennis? 어디에서
테니스를 칠 수 있을까요? [eodieseo
teniseureul chil su isseulkkayo?]

tenor ['tɛnə] n 테너 [teneo]

tense [tɛns] adj 긴장한 [ginjanghan] ▷ n
시제 [sije]

tension ['tɛnʃən] n 긴장 [ginjang]

tent [tɛnt] n 천막 [cheonmak]; **tent peg**
n 천막 고정 말뚝 [cheonmak gojeong
malttuk]; **tent pole** n 천막 기둥
[cheonmak gidung]

tenth [tɛnθ] adj 열 번째의 [yeol
beonjjaeui] ▷ n 10분의 1 [sim bunui il]

term [tɜːm] n (description) 용어
[yongeo], (division of year) 학기 [hakgi]

terminal ['tɜːmɪnªl] adj (병이) 말기의
[(byeongi) malgiui] ▷ n 종점
[jongjeom]

terminally ['tɜːmɪnªlɪ] adv 종말에
[jongmare]

terrace ['tɛrəs] n 테라스 [teraseu]; **Can
I eat on the terrace?** 테라스에서
먹어도 될까요? [teraseueseo
meogeodo doelkkayo?]

terraced ['tɛrəst] adj 계단식의
[gyedansigui]

terrible ['tɛrəbªl] adj 무서운 [museoun]

terribly ['tɛrəblɪ] adv 무섭게
[museopge]

terrier ['tɛrɪə] n 테리어 [terieo]

terrific [tə'rɪfɪk] adj 굉장한

[goengjanghan]

terrified ['tɛrɪ,faɪd] *adj* 겁에 질린 [geobe jillin]

terrify ['tɛrɪ,faɪ] *v* 겁나게 하다 [geomnage hada]

territory ['tɛrɪtərɪ; -trɪ] *n* 영토 [yeongto]

terrorism ['tɛrə,rɪzəm] *n* 테러 행위 [tereo haengwi]

terrorist ['tɛrərɪst] *n* 테러리스트 [tereoriseuteu]; **terrorist attack** *n* 테러리스트 공격 [tereoriseuteu gonggyeok]

test [tɛst] *n* 시험 [siheom] ▷ *v* 시험하다 [siheomhada]; **driving test** *n* 운전 면허 시험 [unjeon myeonheo siheom]; **smear test** *n* 도말 표본 검사 [domal pyobon geomsa]; **test tube** *n* 시험관 [siheomgwan]; **Can I test it, please?** 시험해 볼 수 있어요? [siheomhae bol su isseoyo?]

testicle ['tɛstɪkəl] *n* 고환 [gohwan]

tetanus ['tɛtənəs] *n* 파상풍 [pasangpung]; **I need a tetanus shot** 파상풍 주사가 필요해요 [pasangpung jusaga piryohaeyo]

text [tɛkst] *n* 본문 [bonmun] ▷ *v* 문자 메시지를 보내다 [munja mesijireul bonaeda]; **text message** *n* 문자 메시지 [munja mesiji]

textbook ['tɛkst,bʊk] *n* 교과서 [gyogwaseo]

textile ['tɛkstaɪl] *n* 직물 [jingmul]

Thai [taɪ] *adj* 태국의 [taegugui] ▷ *n* (language) 태국어 [taegugeo], (person) 태국 사람 [taeguk saram]

Thailand ['taɪ,lænd] *n* 태국 [taeguk]

than [ðæn; ðən] *conj*...보다 [...boda]

thank [θæŋk] *v* 감사하다 [gamsahada]

thanks [θæŋks] *excl* 감사! [gamsa!]

that [ðæt; ðət] *adj* 그 [geu] ▷ *conj*...라는 것 [...raneun geot] ▷ *pron* 저것 [jeogeot], 그 [geu]

thatched [θætʃt] *adj* 초가 지붕의 [choga jibungui]

thaw [θɔ:] *v* **It's thawing** 눈이 녹고 있어요 [nooni noggo itssuryou?]

the [ðə] *art* 그 [geu]

theatre ['θɪətə] *n* 극장 [geukjang]; **operating theatre** *n* 수술실 [susulsil]

theft [θɛft] *n* 도둑질 [dodukjil]; **identity theft** *n* 명의 도용 [myeongui doyong]

their [ðɛə] *pron* 그들의 [geudeurui]

theirs [ðɛəz] *pron* 그들의 것 [geudeurui geot]

them [ðɛm; ðəm] *pron* 그들을 [geudeureul]

theme [θi:m] *n* 주제 [juje]; **theme park** *n* 테마 공원 [tema gongwon]

themselves [ðəm'sɛlvz] *pron* 그들 자신 [geudeul jasin]

then [ðɛn] *adv* 그 때에 [geu ttaee] ▷ *conj* 게다가 [gedaga]

theology [θɪ'ɒlədʒɪ] *n* 신학 [sinhak]

theory ['θɪərɪ] *n* 이론 [iron]

therapy ['θɛrəpɪ] *n* 요법 [yobeop]

there [ðɛə] *adv* 거기에 [geogie]; **How do I get there?** 거기에 어떻게 가나요? [geogie eotteoke ganayo?]

therefore ['ðɛə,fɔ:] *adv* 그러므로 [geureomeuro]

thermometer [θə'mɒmɪtə] *n* 온도계 [ondogye]

Thermos® ['θɜ:məs] *n* 서모스 보온병 [seomoseu boonbyeong]

thermostat ['θɜ:mə,stæt] *n* 자동 온도 조절기 [jadong ondo jojeolgi]

these [ði:z] *adj* 이것들의 [igeotdeurui] ▷ *pron* 이것들 [igeotdeul]

they [ðeɪ] *pron* 그들 [geudeul]

thick [θɪk] *adj* 걸쭉한 [geoljjukan]

thickness ['θɪknɪs] *n* 두께 [dukke]

thief [θi:f] *n* 도둑 [doduk]

thigh [θaɪ] *n* 넓적다리 [neopjeokdari]

thin [θɪn] *adj* 얇은 [yarbeun]

thing [θɪŋ] *n* 물건 [mulgeon]

think [θɪŋk] *v* 생각하다 [saenggakhada]

third [θɜ:d] *adj* 세 번째의 [se beonjjaeui] ▷ *n* 3분의 1 [sambunui il]; **third-party insurance** *n* 3자 보험 [samja boheom]; **Third World** *n* 제3 세계 [je3segye]

thirdly ['θɜ:dlɪ] *adv* 세 번째로 [se beonjjaero]

thirst [θɜ:st] *n* 갈증 [galjeung]

thirsty ['θɜːstɪ] *adj* 목마른 [mongmareun]

thirteen ['θɜː'tiːn] *number* 열셋 [yeolset], *(Sino-Korean)* 십삼 [sipsam]

thirteenth ['θɜː'tiːnθ] *adj* 열세 번째의 [yeolse beonjjaeui]

thirty ['θɜːtɪ] *number* 서른 [seoreun], *(Sino-Korean)* 삼십 [samsip]

this [ðɪs] *adj* 이것 [igeot] ▷ *pron* 이것 [igeot]; **I'll have this** 이것 주세요 [igeot juseyo]

thistle ['θɪsᵊl] *n* 엉겅퀴 [eonggeongkwi]

thorn [θɔːn] *n* 가시 [gasi]

thorough ['θʌrə] *adj* 철저한 [cheoljeohan]

thoroughly ['θʌrəlɪ] *adv* 철저하게 [cheoljeohage]

those [ðəʊz] *adj* 그것들의 [geugeotdeurui] ▷ *pron* 그것들 [geugeotdeul]

though [ðəʊ] *adv* 그렇지만 [geureochiman] ▷ *conj* ...임에도 불구하고 [...imedo bulguhago]

thought [θɔːt] *n* 생각 [saenggak]

thoughtful ['θɔːtfʊl] *adj* 사려 깊은 [saryeo gipeun]

thoughtless ['θɔːtlɪs] *adj* 경솔한 [gyeongsolhan]

thousandth ['θaʊzənθ] *adj* 천 번째의 [cheon beonjjaeui] ▷ *n* 1000분의 1 [cheon bunui il]

thread [θrɛd] *n* 실 [sil]

threat [θrɛt] *n* 위협 [wihyeop]

threaten ['θrɛtᵊn] *v* 위협하다 [wihyeophada]

threatening ['θrɛtᵊnɪŋ] *adj* 위협적인 [wihyeopjeogin]

three [θriː] *number* 셋 [ses], *(Sino-Korean)* 삼 [sam]

three-dimensional [ˌθriːdɪ'mɛnʃənᵊl] *adj* 3차원의 [samchawonui]

thrifty ['θrɪftɪ] *adj* 검소한 [geomsohan]

thrill [θrɪl] *n* 전율 [jeonyul]

thrilled [θrɪld] *adj* 전율을 느끼는 [jeonyureul neukkineun]

thriller ['θrɪlə] *n* 추리 소설 [churi soseol]

thrilling ['θrɪlɪŋ] *adj* 감격적인 [gamgyeokjeogin]

throat [θrəʊt] *n* 목구멍 [mokgumeong]

throb [θrɒb] *v* 두근거리다 [dugeungeorida]

throne [θrəʊn] *n* 왕좌 [wangjwa]

through [θruː] *prep* 통과하여 [tonggwahayeo]

throughout [θruː'aʊt] *prep* ...의 전체에 [...ui jeonchee]

throw [θrəʊ] *v* 던지다 [deonjida]

throw away [θrəʊ ə'weɪ] *v* 허비하다 [heobihada]

throw out [θrəʊ aʊt] *v* 버리다 [beorida]

throw up [θrəʊ ʌp] *v* 토하다 [tohada]

thrush [θrʌʃ] *n* 개똥지빠귀 [gaettongjippagwi]

thug [θʌɡ] *n* 흉악범 [hyungakbeom]

thumb [θʌm] *n* 엄지손가락 [eomjisongarak]

thumb tack ['θʌmˌtæk] *n* 압핀 [appin]

thump [θʌmp] *v* 탁 치다 [tak chida]

thunder ['θʌndə] *n* 천둥 [cheondung]; **I think it's going to thunder** 천둥이 칠 것 같아요 [cheondungi chil geot gatayo]

thunderstorm ['θʌndəˌstɔːm] *n* 뇌우 [noeu]

thundery ['θʌndərɪ] *adj* 험악한 [heomakhan]

Thursday ['θɜːzdɪ] *n* 목요일 [mogyoil]; **on Thursday** 목요일에 [mogyoire]

thyme [taɪm] *n* 사향초 [sahyangcho]

Tibet [tɪ'bɛt] *n* 티베트 [tibeteu]

Tibetan [tɪ'bɛtᵊn] *adj* 티베트의 [tibeteuui] ▷ *n (language)* 티베트어 [tibeteueo], *(person)* 티베트 사람 [tibeteu saram]

tick [tɪk] *n* 체크 표시 [chekeu pyosi] ▷ *v* 체크하다 [chekeuhada]

ticket ['tɪkɪt] *n* 표 [pyo]; **bus ticket** *n* 버스 승차권 [beoseu seungchagwon]; **one-way ticket** *n* 편도표 [pyeondopyo]; **parking ticket** *n* 주차위반 딱지 [juchawiban ttakji]; **return ticket** *n* 왕복표 [wangbokpyo]; **season ticket** *n* 정기 승차권 [jeonggi seungchagwon]; **single ticket** *n*

편도표 [pyeondopyo]; **stand-by ticket** n 대기 항공권 [daegi hanggonggwon]; **ticket barrier** n 개찰구 [gaechalgu]; **ticket collector** n 집표원 [jippyowon]; **ticket inspector** n 검표원 [geompyowon]; **ticket machine** n 자동 매표기 [jadong maepyogi]; **ticket office** n 매표소 [maepyoso]; **a child's ticket** 어린이표 [eorinipyo]; **Can I buy the tickets here?** 여기서 표를 살 수 있어요? [yeogiseo pyoreul sal su isseoyo?]; **Can you book the tickets for us?** 표를 예매해 주시겠어요? [pyoreul yemaehae jusigesseoyo?]; **Do you have multi-journey tickets?** 여러 번 사용할 수 있는 표가 있어요? [yeoreo beon sayonghal su inneun pyoga isseoyo?]; **How much are the tickets?** 표는 얼마예요? [pyoneun eolmayeyo?]; **How much is a return ticket?** 왕복표는 얼마예요? [wangbokpyoneun eolmayeyo?]; **I want to upgrade my ticket** 표를 비싼 걸로 바꾸고 싶어요 [pyoreul bissan geollo bakkugo sipeoyo]; **I'd like two tickets for next Friday** 다음주 금요일 표 두 장 주세요 [daeumju geumyoil pyo du jang juseyo]; **I'd like two tickets, please** 표 두 장 주세요 [pyo du jang juseyo]; **I've lost my ticket** 표를 잃어버렸어요 [pyoreul ireobeoryeosseoyo]; **The ticket machine isn't working** 매표기가 고장났어요 [maepyogiga gojangnasseoyo]; **Two tickets for tonight, please** 오늘 밤 표 두 장이요 [oneul bam pyo du jangiyo]; **Where can I buy tickets for the concert?** 어디에서 콘서트 표를 살 수 있어요? [eodieseo konseoteu pyoreul sal su isseoyo?]; **Where can I get tickets?** 어디에서 표를 사나요? [eodieseo pyoreul sanayo?]; **Where is the ticket machine?** 매표기는 어디에 있어요? [maepyogineun eodie isseoyo?]

tickle ['tɪkəl] v 간질이다 [ganilieda]
ticklish ['tɪklɪʃ] adj 간지러운 [ganjirurun]

tick off [tɪk ɒf] v 체크하다 [chekeuhada]
tide [taɪd] n 조수 [josu]
tidy ['taɪdɪ] adj 단정한 [danjeonghan] ▷ v 정돈하다 [jeongdonhada]
tidy up ['taɪdɪ ʌp] v 정돈하다 [jeongdonhada]
tie [taɪ] n 넥타이 [nektai] ▷ v 매다 [maeda]; **bow tie** n 나비 넥타이 [nabi nektai]
tie up [taɪ ʌp] v 결속하다 [gyeolsokhada]
tiger ['taɪɡə] n 호랑이 [horangi]
tight [taɪt] adj 팽팽한 [paengpaenghan]
tighten ['taɪtən] v 단단히 죄다 [dandanhi joeda]
tights [taɪts] npl 타이츠 [taicheu]
tile [taɪl] n 타일 [tail]
tiled ['taɪld] adj 타일을 붙인 [taireul buchin]
till [tɪl] conj...까지 [...kkaji] ▷ n 계산대 [gyesandae]
timber ['tɪmbə] n 목재 [mokjae]
time [taɪm] n 시간 [sigan]; **closing time** n 폐점 시간 [pyejeom sigan]; **dinner time** n 저녁식사 시간 [jeonyeoksiksa sigan]; **on time** adj 정기적인 [jeonggijeogin]; **spare time** n 여가시간 [yeogasigan]; **time off** n 휴식시간 [hyusiksigan]; **time zone** n 시간대 [sigandae]; **Is it time to go?** 갈 시간인가요? [gal siganingayo?]; **Is the train on time?** 기차가 제 시간에 있어요? [gichaga je sigane isseoyo?]; **What's the minimum amount of time?** 최소 사용 시간은 얼마입니까? [choeso sayong siganeun eolmaimnikka?]
time bomb ['taɪm,bɒm] n 시한폭탄 [sihanpoktan]
timer ['taɪmə] n 타이머 [taimeo]
timeshare ['taɪm,ʃɛə] n 휴가시설의 공동 소유 [hyugasiseorui gongdong soyu]
timetable ['taɪm,teɪbəl] n 시간표 [siganpyo]; **Can I have a timetable, please?** 시간표 좀 주시겠어요?

[siganpyo jom jusigesseoyo?]
tin [tɪn] n 양철 [yangcheol]; **tin-opener**
n 깡통따개 [kkangtongttagae]
tinfoil ['tɪnˌfɔɪl] n 은박지 [eunbakji]
tinned [tɪnd] adj 통조림한
[tongjorimhan]
tinsel ['tɪnsəl] n 장식용 금속 조각
[jangsigyong geumsok jogak]
tinted ['tɪntɪd] adj 엷은 색깔의
[yeorbeun saekkkarui]
tiny ['taɪnɪ] adj 아주 작은 [aju jageun]
tip [tɪp] n (end of object) 끝 [kkeut],
(reward) 팁 [tip], (suggestion) 힌트
[hinteu] ▷ v (incline) 기울이다 [giurida]
(경사), (reward) 팁을 주다 [tibeul juda];
How much should I give as a tip?
팁으로 얼마를 줘야 하나요? [tibeuro
eolmareul jwoya hanayo?]; **Is it usual
to give a tip?** 팁을 줘야 하나요?
[tibeul jwoya hanayo?]
tipsy ['tɪpsɪ] adj 술취한 [sulchwihan]
tiptoe ['tɪpˌtəʊ] n 발끝 [balkkeut]
tired ['taɪəd] adj 피곤한 [pigonhan]
tiring ['taɪərɪŋ] adj 피곤하게 하는
[pigonhage haneun]
tissue ['tɪsjuː; 'tɪʃuː] n (anatomy) 조직
[jojik], (paper) 조직 [jojik]
title ['taɪtəl] n 제목 [jemok]
to [tuː; tʊ; tə] prep ...으로 [...euro] (방향)
toad [təʊd] n 두꺼비 [dukkeobi]
toadstool ['təʊdˌstuːl] n 독버섯
[dokbeoseot]
toast [təʊst] n (grilled bread) 구운 빵
[guun ppang], (tribute) 건배 [geonbae]
toaster ['təʊstə] n 토스터 [toseuteo]
tobacco [tə'bækəʊ] n 담배 [dambae]
tobacconist's [tə'bækənɪsts] n
담배가게 [dambaegage]
tobogganing [tə'bɒɡənɪŋ] n 썰매타기
[sseolmaetagi]
today [tə'deɪ] adv 오늘 [oneul]; **What
day is it today?** 오늘 무슨
요일이에요? [oneul museun yoirieyo?];
What is today's date? 오늘
며칠이에요? [oneul myeochirieyo?]
toddler ['tɒdlə] n 아장아장 걷는 아이
[ajangajang geotneun ai]
toe [təʊ] n 발가락 [balgarak]

toffee ['tɒfɪ] n 토피 [topi]
together [tə'ɡɛðə] adv 함께 [hamkke]
Togo ['təʊɡəʊ] n 토고 [togo]
toilet ['tɔɪlɪt] n 화장실 [hwajangsil];
toilet bag n 세면가방
[semyeongabang]; **toilet paper** n
화장지 [hwajangji]; **toilet roll** n
두루마리 화장지 [durumari hwajangji];
**Are there any toilets for the
disabled?** 장애인 화장실이 있어요?
[jangaein hwajangsiri isseoyo?]; **Can I
use the toilet?** 화장실을 사용해도
될까요? [hwajangsireul sayonghaedo
doelkkayo?]; **Is there a toilet on
board?** 차내에 화장실이 있어요?
[chanaee hwajangsiri isseoyo?]; **Where
are the toilets?** 화장실은 어디있어요?
[hwajangsireun eodiisseoyo?]
toiletries ['tɔɪlɪtriːs] npl 화장품
[hwajangpum]
token ['təʊkən] n 표시 [pyosi]
tolerant ['tɒlərənt] adj 관대한
[gwandaehan]
toll [təʊl] n 종치기 [jongchigi]
tomato, tomatoes [tə'mɑːtəʊ,
tə'mɑːtəʊz] n 토마토 [tomato];
tomato sauce n 토마토 소스 [tomato
soseu]
tomb [tuːm] n 무덤 [mudeom]
tomboy ['tɒmˌbɔɪ] n 말괄량이
[malgwallyangi]
tomorrow [tə'mɒrəʊ] adv 내일 [naeil];
Is it open tomorrow? 내일 열어요?
[naeil yeoreoyo?]; **tomorrow morning**
내일 아침 [naeil achim]
ton [tʌn] n 톤 [ton]
tone [təʊn] n **dialling tone** n 발신음
[balsineum]; **engaged tone** n 통화중
신호음 [tonghwajung sinhoeum]
Tonga ['tɒŋɡə] n 통가 [tongga]
tongue [tʌŋ] n 혀 [hyeo]; **mother
tongue** n 모국어 [mogugeo]
tonic ['tɒnɪk] n 강장제 [gangjangje]
tonight [tə'naɪt] adv 오늘밤
[oneulbam]
tonsillitis [ˌtɒnsɪ'laɪtɪs] n 편도선염
[pyeondoseonyeom]
tonsils ['tɒnsəlz] npl 편도선

[pyeondoseon]

too [tuː] *adv* ...도 또한 [...do ttohan]

tool [tuːl] *n* 도구 [dogu]

tooth, teeth ['tuːθ, tiːθ] *n* 치아 [chia];
wisdom tooth *n* 사랑니 [sarangni]

toothache ['tuːθˌeɪk] *n* 치통 [chitong];
I have toothache 치통이 있어요
[chitongi isseoyo]

toothbrush ['tuːθˌbrʌʃ] *n* 칫솔
[chissol]

toothpaste ['tuːθˌpeɪst] *n* 치약
[chiyak]

toothpick ['tuːθˌpɪk] *n* 이쑤시개
[issusigae]

top [tɒp] *adj* 맨 위의 [maen wiui] ▷ *n* 맨
위 [maen wi]

topic ['tɒpɪk] *n* 주제 [juje]

topical ['tɒpɪkəl] *adj* 시사적인
[sisajeogin]

top-secret ['tɒpˈsiːkrɪt] *adj* 일급기밀인
[ilgeupgimirin]

top up [tɒp ʌp] *v* **Can you top up the
windscreen washers?** 앞유리
세척액을 가득 채워 주시겠어요?
[apyuri secheogaegeul gadeuk
chaewo jusigesseoyo?]; **Where can I
buy a top-up card?** 어디에서
충전카드를 살 수 있어요? [eodieseo
chungjeonkadeureul sal su isseoyo?]

torch [tɔːtʃ] *n* 손전등 [sonjeondeung]

tornado [tɔːˈneɪdəʊ] *n* 토네이도
[toneido]

tortoise ['tɔːtəs] *n* 거북이 [geobugi]

torture ['tɔːtʃə] *n* 고문 [gomun]
(신체적 고통) ▷ *v* 고문하다
[gomunhada]

toss [tɒs] *v* 가볍게 던지다 [gabyeopge
deonjida]

total ['təʊtəl] *adj* 전체의 [jeoncheui] ▷ *n*
합계 [hapgye]

totally ['təʊtəlɪ] *adv* 완전히 [wanjeonhi]

touch [tʌtʃ] *v* 만지다 [manjida]

touchdown ['tʌtʃˌdaʊn] *n* 착륙
[changnyuk]

touched [tʌtʃt] *adj* 감동한
[gamdonghan]

touching ['tʌtʃɪŋ] *adj* 감동적인
[gamdongjeogin]

touchline ['tʌtʃˌlaɪn] *n* 터치라인
[teochirain]

touchpad ['tʌtʃˌpæd] *n* 터치패드
[teochipaedeu]

touchy ['tʌtʃɪ] *adj* 화를 잘 내는
[hwareul jal naeneun]

tough [tʌf] *adj* 튼튼한 [teunteunhan]

toupee ['tuːpeɪ] *n* (남성용) 가발
[(namseongyong) gabal]

tour [tʊə] *n* 여행 [yeohaeng] ▷ *v*
여행하다 [yeohaenghada]; **guided
tour** *n* 안내인이 딸린 여행 [annaeini
ttallin yeohaeng]; **package tour** *n*
패키지 여행 [paekiji yeohaeng]; **tour
guide** *n* 관광 안내원 [gwangwang
annaewon]; **tour operator** *n* 여행사
[yeohaengsa]; **Are there any
sightseeing tours of the town?** 시내
관광 여행이 있어요? [sinae
gwangwang yeohaengi isseoyo?]; **I
enjoyed the tour** 여행 재밌었어요
[yeohaeng jaemisseosseoyo]

tourism ['tʊərɪzəm] *n* 관광
[gwangwang]

tourist ['tʊərɪst] *n* 관광객
[gwangwanggaek]; **tourist office** *n*
여행사 [yeohaengsa]; **I'm here as a
tourist** 관광객으로 왔어요
[gwangwanggaegeuro wasseoyo]

tournament ['tʊənəmənt; 'tɔː-; 'tɜː-] *n*
토너먼트 [toneomeonteu]

towards [təˈwɔːdz; tɔːdz] *prep* ...을
향하여 [...eul hyanghayeo]

tow away [təʊ əˈweɪ] *v* 끌고가다
[kkeulgogada]

towel ['taʊəl] *n* 타월 [tawol]; **bath
towel** *n* 목욕 타월 [mogyok tawol];
dish towel *n* 행주 [haengju]; **sanitary
towel** *n* 생리대 [saengnidae]; **tea
towel** *n* 티 타월 [ti tawol]; **Could you
lend me a towel?** 타월을 빌려
주시겠어요? [taworeul billyeo
jusigesseoyo?]; **Please bring me more
towels** 타월을 더 갖다 주세요
[taworeul deo gatda juseyo]

tower ['taʊə] *n* 탑 [tap]

town [taʊn] *n* 도시 [dosi]; **town centre**
n 도심 [dosim]; **town hall** *n* 시청

[sicheong] (건물); **town planning** n
도시계획 [dosigyehoek]
toxic ['tɒksɪk] adj 유독한 [yudokhan]
toy [tɔɪ] n 장난감 [jangnangam]
trace [treɪs] n 자취 [jachwi]
tracing paper ['treɪsɪŋ 'peɪpə] n
  tracing paper n 투사지 [tusaji]
track [træk] n 통로 [tongno]
track down [træk daʊn] v 바짝 쫓다
[bajjak jjotta]
tracksuit ['træk,su:t; -,sju:t] n 운동복
[undongbok]
tractor ['træktə] n 트랙터 [teuraekteo]
trade [treɪd] n 무역 [muyeok]; **trade**
  union n 노동조합 [nodongjohap];
  trade unionist n 노동조합원
  [nodongjohabwon]
trademark ['treɪd,mɑ:k] n 상표
[sangpyo]
tradition [trə'dɪʃən] n 전통 [jeontong]
traditional [trə'dɪʃənᵊl] adj 전통적인
[jeontongjeogin]
traffic ['træfɪk] n 교통 [gyotong];
  traffic jam n 교통마비 [gyotongmabi];
  traffic lights npl 교통신호등
  [gyotongsinhodeung]; **traffic warden**
  n 교통감시관 [gyotonggamsigwan]; **Is**
  the traffic heavy on the motorway?
  고속도로에 교통이 복잡한가요?
  [gosokdoroe gyotongi
  bokjaphangayo?]
tragedy ['trædʒɪdɪ] n 비극 [bigeuk]
tragic ['trædʒɪk] adj 비극적인
[bigeukjeogin]
trailer ['treɪlə] n 트레일러 [teureilleo]
train [treɪn] n 기차 [gicha] ▷ v 훈련하다
[hullyeonhada]; **Does the train stop**
at...? 기차가...에서 서나요? [gichaga...
eseo seonayo?]; **How frequent are**
the trains to...? ... 가는 기차는
얼마나 자주 있어요? [... ganeun
gichaneun eolmana jaju isseoyo?]; **Is**
this the train for...? 이게...행
기차인가요? [ige...haeng gichaingayo?];
What time does the train arrive
in...? 기차는 몇 시에... 도착해요?
[gichaneun myeot sie...
dochakhaeyo?]; **What time does the**

train leave? 기차는 몇 시에 떠나요?
[gichaneun myeot sie tteonayo?];
What times are the trains to...?
... 가는 기차 시간표는 어떻게 되나요? [...
ganeun gicha siganpyoneun eotteoke
doenayo?]; **When is the first train**
to...? ... 가는 첫 기차는 언제 있어요?
[... ganeun cheot gichaneun eonje
isseoyo?]; **When is the last train**
to...? ... 가는 마지막 기차는 언제
있어요? [... ganeun majimak
gichaneun eonje isseoyo?]; **When is**
the next train to...? ... 가는 다음
기차는 언제 있어요? [... ganeun daeum
gichaneun eonje isseoyo?]; **When is**
the train due? 기차는 언제 도착해요?
[gichaneun eonje dochakhaeyo?];
Which platform does the train
leave from? 기차는 어느 승강장에서
떠나요? [gichaneun eoneu
seunggangjangeseo tteonayo?]
trained ['treɪnd] adj 훈련 받은
[hullyeon badeun]
trainee [treɪ'ni:] n 피훈련자
[pihullyeonja]
trainer ['treɪnə] n 훈련관
[hullyeongwan]
trainers ['treɪnəz] npl 운동화
[undonghwa]
training ['treɪnɪŋ] n 훈련 [hullyeon];
  training course n 훈련과정
  [hullyeongwajeong]
tram [træm] n 전차 [jeoncha]
tramp [træmp] n (beggar) 거지 [geoji],
(long walk) 장거리 도보 [janggeori
dobo]
trampoline ['træmpəlɪn; -,li:n] n
트램펄린 [teuraempeollin]
tranquillizer ['træŋkwɪ,laɪzə] n 신경
안정제 [singyeong anjeongje]
transaction [træn'zækʃən] n 교역
[gyoyeok]
transcript ['trænskrɪpt] n 사본
[sabon]
transfer n ['trænsf3:] 이동 [idong] ▷ v
[træns'f3:] 이동 [idong]
transform [træns'fɔ:m] v 변형시키다
[byeonhyeongsikida]

transfusion [træns'fju:ʒən] n 수혈 [suhyeol]; **blood transfusion** n 수혈 [suhyeol]

transistor [træn'zɪstə] n 트랜지스터 [teuraenjiseuteo]

transit ['trænsɪt; 'trænz-] n 운송 [unsong]; **transit lounge** n 환승 대기실 [hwanseung daegisil]

transition [træn'zɪʃən] n 변천 [byeoncheon]

translate [træns'leɪt; trænz-] v 번역하다 [beonyeokhada]

translation [træns'leɪʃən; trænz-] n 번역 [beonyeok]

translator [træns'leɪtə; trænz-] n 번역사 [beonyeoksa]

transparent [træns'pærənt; -'pɛər-] adj 투명한 [tumyeonghan]

transplant ['træns,plɑ:nt] n 이식 [isik]

transport n ['træns,pɔ:t] 운송 [unsong] ▷ v [træns'pɔ:t] 운송하다 [unsonghada]; **public transport** n 대중교통수단 [daejunggyotongsudan]

transvestite [trænz'vɛstaɪt] n 복장 도착자 [bokjang dochakja]

trap [træp] n 올가미 [olgami]

trash [træʃ] n 허튼 소리 [heoteun sori]

traumatic ['trɔ:mətɪk] adj 충격적인 [chunggyeokjeogin]

travel ['trævəl] n 여행 [yeohaeng] ▷ v 여행하다 [yeohaenghada]; **travel agency** n 여행사 [yeohaengsa]; **travel agent's** n 여행사 [yeohaengsa]; **travel sickness** n 멀미 [meolmi]; **I don't have travel insurance** 저는 여행자보험에 들지 않았어요 [jeoneun yeohaengjaboheome deulji anhasseoyo]; **I'm travelling alone** 혼자 여행하고 있어요 [honja yeohaenghago isseoyo]

traveller ['trævələ; 'trævlə] n 여행자 [yeohaengja]; **traveller's cheque** n 여행자 수표 [yeohaengja supyo]

travelling ['trævlɪŋ] n 여행 [yeohaeng]

tray [treɪ] n 쟁반 [jaengban]

treacle ['tri:kəl] n 당밀 [dangmil]

tread [trɛd] v 밟다 [barpda]

treasure ['trɛʒə] n 보물 [bomul]

treasurer ['trɛʒərə] n 경리 [gyeongni]

treat [tri:t] n 대접 [daejeop] (즐겁게 하다) ▷ v 취급하다 [chwigeuphada]

treatment ['tri:tmənt] n 치료 [chiryo]

treaty ['tri:tɪ] n 조약 [joyak]

treble ['trɛbəl] v 3배로 하다 [sambaero hada]

tree [tri:] n 나무 [namu]

trek [trɛk] n 길고 고된 여행 [gilgo godoen yeohaeng] ▷ v 고된여행하다 [godoenyeohaenghada]

trekking ['trɛkɪŋ] n **I'd like to go pony trekking** 조랑말 여행을 하고 싶어요 [jorangmal yeohaengeul hago sipeoyo]

tremble ['trɛmbəl] v 떨다 [tteolda]

tremendous [trɪ'mɛndəs] adj 거대한 [geodaehan]

trench [trɛntʃ] n 참호 [chamho]

trend [trɛnd] n 추세 [chuse]

trendy ['trɛndɪ] adj 유행을 좇는 [yuhaengeul jotneun]

trial ['traɪəl] n 재판 [jaepan]; **trial period** n 시용기간 [siyonggigan]

triangle ['traɪ,æŋgəl] n 삼각형 [samgakhyeong]

tribe [traɪb] n 부족 [bujok]

tribunal [traɪ'bju:nəl; trɪ-] n 법정 [beopjeong]

trick [trɪk] n 속임수 [sogimsu] ▷ v 속이다 [sogida]

tricky ['trɪkɪ] adj 애매한 [aemaehan]

tricycle ['traɪsɪkəl] n 세발자전거 [sebaljajeongeo]

trifle ['traɪfəl] n 사소한 것 [sasohan geot]

trim [trɪm] v 깎아 다듬다 [kkaka dadeumda]

Trinidad and Tobago ['trɪnɪ,dæd ænd tə'beɪgəʊ] n 트리니다드토바고 [teurinidadeutobago]

trip [trɪp] n 여행 [yeohaeng]; **business trip** n 출장 [chuljang]; **round trip** n 왕복여행 [wangbogyeohaeng]; **trip (up)** v 걸려 넘어지게 하다 [geollyeo neomeojige hada]; **Are there any boat trips on the river?** 강에서 하는

보트 여행이 있어요? [gangeseo haneun boteu yeohaengi isseoyo?]; **Do you run day trips to…?**…행 당일치기 여행 있어요? [...haeng dangilchigi yeohaeng isseoyo?]; **Have a good trip!** 여행 잘 하세요! [yeohaeng jal haseyo!]

triple ['trɪpᵊl] *adj* 3배의 [sambaeui]

triplets ['trɪplɪts] *npl* 세쌍둥이 [sessangdungi]

triumph ['traɪəmf] *n* 승리 [seungni] ▷ *v* 승리하다 [seungnihada]

trivial ['trɪvɪəl] *adj* 사소한 [sasohan]

trolley ['trɒlɪ] *n* 트롤리 [teurolli]; **luggage trolley** *n* 수화물 수레 [suhwamul sure]; **shopping trolley** *n* 쇼핑카트 [syopingkateu]

trombone [trɒm'bəʊn] *n* 트롬본 [teurombon]

troops ['truːps] *npl* 군대 [gundae]

trophy ['trəʊfɪ] *n* 트로피 [teuropi]

tropical ['trɒpɪkᵊl] *adj* 열대성의 [yeoldaeseongui]

trot [trɒt] *v* 빠른걸음으로 걷다 [ppareungeoreumeuro geotda]

trouble ['trʌbᵊl] *n* 곤란 [gollan]

troublemaker ['trʌbᵊl,meɪkə] *n* 말썽을 일으키는 사람 [malsseongeul ireukineun saram]

trough [trɒf] *n* 여물통 [yeomultong]

trousers ['traʊzəz] *npl* 바지 [baji]; **Can I try on these trousers?** 이 바지 입어봐도 될까요? [i baji ibeobwado doelkkayo?]

trout [traʊt] *n* 송어 [songeo]

trowel ['traʊəl] *n* 흙손 [heurkson]

truant ['truːənt] *n* **play truant** *v* 무단결석하다 [mudangyeolseokhada]

truce [truːs] *n* 휴전 [hyujeon]

truck [trʌk] *n* 트럭 [teureok]; **breakdown truck** *n* 견인차 [gyeonincha]; **truck driver** *n* 트럭 운전사 [teureok unjeonsa]

true [truː] *adj* 사실의 [sasirin]

truly ['truːlɪ] *adv* 진실로 [jinsillo]

trumpet ['trʌmpɪt] *n* 트럼펫 [teureompet]

trunk [trʌŋk] *n* 나무 줄기 [namu julgi]; **swimming trunks** *npl* (남자) 수영복 [(namja) suyeongbok]

trunks [trʌŋks] *npl* 남자 수영복 [namja suyeongbok]

trust [trʌst] *n* 신뢰 [sinnoe] ▷ *v* 신뢰하다 [sinnoehada]

trusting ['trʌstɪŋ] *adj* 신뢰하는 [sinnoehaneun]

truth [truːθ] *n* 진실 [jinsil]

truthful ['truːθfʊl] *adj* 신뢰하는 [sinnoehaneun]

try [traɪ] *n* 노력 [noryeok] ▷ *v* 시도하다 [sidohada]

try on [traɪ ɒn] *v* 입어보다 [ibeoboda]

try out [traɪ aʊt] *v* 시험해 보다 [siheomhae boda]

T-shirt ['tiː,ʃɜːt] *n* 티셔츠 [tisyeocheu]

tsunami [tsʊ'næmɪ] *n* 해일 [haeil]

tube [tjuːb] *n* 관 [gwan]; **inner tube** *n* 튜브 [tyubeu]; **test tube** *n* 시험관 [siheomgwan]; **tube station** *n* 지하철역 [jihacheollyeok]

tuberculosis [tjʊ,bɜːkjʊ'ləʊsɪs] *n* 결핵 [gyeolhaek]

Tuesday ['tjuːzdɪ] *n* 화요일 [hwayoil]; **Shrove Tuesday** *n* 오순절의 화요일 [osunjeorui hwayoil]; **on Tuesday** 화요일에 [hwayoire]

tug-of-war ['tʌgɒv'wɔː] *n* 줄다리기 [juldarigi]

tuition [tjuː'ɪʃən] *n* 수업 [sueop]; **tuition fees** *npl* 수업료 [sueomnyo]

tulip ['tjuːlɪp] *n* 튤립 [tyullip]

tummy ['tʌmɪ] *n* 배 [bae]

tumour ['tjuːmə] *n* 종양 [jongyang]

tuna ['tjuːnə] *n* 참치 [chamchi]

tune [tjuːn] *n* 곡조 [gokjo]

Tunisia [tjuː'nɪzɪə; -'nɪsɪə] *n* 튀니지의 [twinijiui]

Tunisian [tjuː'nɪzɪən; -'nɪsɪən] *adj* 튀니지의 [twinijiui] ▷ *n* 튀니지 사람 [twiniji saram]

tunnel ['tʌnᵊl] *n* 터널 [teoneol]

turbulence ['tɜːbjʊləns] *n* 난기류 [nangiryu]

Turk [tɜːk] *n* 터키 사람 [teoki saram]

turkey ['tɜːkɪ] *n* 칠면조 [chilmyeonjo]

Turkey ['tɜːkɪ] *n* 터키 [teoki]

Turkish ['tɜːkɪʃ] *adj* 터키의 [teokiui]

▷ *n* 터키 사람 [teoki saram]
turn [tɜːn] *n* 회전 [hoejeon] ▷ *v* 회전하다 [hoejeonhada]
turn around [tɜːn əˈraʊnd] *v* 회전시키다 [hoejeonsikida]
turn back [tɜːn bæk] *v* 되돌아가다 [doedoragada]
turn down [tɜːn daʊn] *v* 거절하다 [geojeolhada]
turning [ˈtɜːnɪŋ] *n* 모퉁이 [motungi]; **Take the first turning on your right** 첫 번째 모퉁이에서 오른쪽으로 꺾으세요 [cheot beonjjae motungieseo oreunjjogeuro kkeokkeuseyo]; **Take the second turning on your left** 두 번째 모퉁이에서 왼쪽으로 꺾으세요 [du beonjjae motungieseo oenjjogeuro kkeokkeuseyo]
turnip [ˈtɜːnɪp] *n* 순무 [sunmu]
turn off [tɜːn ɒf] *v* 끄다 [kkeuda]
turn on [tɜːn ɒn] *v* 켜다 [kyeoda]
turn out [tɜːn aʊt] *v* 끄다 [kkeuda]
turnover [ˈtɜːnˌəʊvə] *n* 총거래액 [chonggeoraeaek]
turn round [tɜːn raʊnd] *v* 회전시키다 [hoejeonsikida]
turnstile [ˈtɜːnˌstaɪl] *n* 회전식 출입문 [hoejeonsik churimmun]
turn up [tɜːn ʌp] *v* 나타나다 [natanada]
turquoise [ˈtɜːkwɔɪz; -kwɑːz] *adj* 청록색의 [cheongnoksaegui]
turtle [ˈtɜːtəl] *n* 거북 [geobuk]
tutor [ˈtjuːtə] *n* 가정교사 [gajeonggyosa]
tutorial [tjuːˈtɔːrɪəl] *n* 개별지도 [gaebyeoljido]
tuxedo [tʌkˈsiːdəʊ] *n* 턱시도 [teoksido]
TV [tiː viː] *n* TV [TV]; **plasma TV** *n* 플라스마 TV [peullaseuma TV]; **reality TV** *n* 리얼리티 TV 쇼 [rieolliti TV syo]; **Does the room have a TV?** 방에 TV 있어요? [bange TV isseoyo?]
tweezers [ˈtwiːzəz] *npl* 족집게 [jokjipge]
twelfth [twɛlfθ] *adj* 열두 번째의 [yeoldu beonjjaeui]
twelve [twɛlv] *number* 열둘 [yeoldul], *(Sino-Korean)* 십이 [sibi]

twentieth [ˈtwɛntɪɪθ] *adj* 스무 번째의 [seumu beonjjaeui]
twenty [ˈtwɛntɪ] *number* 스물 [seumur], *(Sino-Korean)* 이십 [isip]
twice [twaɪs] *adv* 두 번 [du beon]
twin [twɪn] *n* 쌍둥이 [ssangdungi]; **twin beds** *npl* 트윈 베드 [teuwin bedeu]; **twin room** *n* 트윈 룸 [teuwin rum]; **twin-bedded room** *n* 트윈 베드가 있는 침실 [teuwin bedeuga inneun chimsil]
twinned [twɪnd] *adj* 쌍을 이루는 [ssangeul iruneun]
twist [twɪst] *v* 비틀다 [biteulda]
twit [twɪt] *n* 바보 [babo]
two [tuː] *number* 둘 [dul], *(Sino-Korean)* 이 [i]
type [taɪp] *n* 유형 [yuhyeong] ▷ *v* 타이핑하다 [taipinghada]
typewriter [ˈtaɪpˌraɪtə] *n* 타자기 [tajagi]
typhoid [ˈtaɪfɔɪd] *n* 장티푸스 [jangtipuseu]
typical [ˈtɪpɪkəl] *adj* 전형적인 [jeonhyeongjeogin]
typist [ˈtaɪpɪst] *n* 타이피스트 [taipiseuteu]
tyre [ˈtaɪə] *n* 타이어 [taieo]; **spare tyre** *n* 예비 타이어 [yebi taieo]; **Can you check the tyres, please?** 타이어를 확인해 주시겠어요? [taieoreul hwaginhae jusigesseoyo?]; **I have a flat tyre** 타이어 바람이 빠졌어요 [taieo barami ppajyeosseoyo]; **The tyre has burst** 타이어가 터졌어요 [taieoga teojyeosseoyo]; **What should the tyre pressure be?** 타이어 압력이 얼마여야 하나요? [taieo amnyeogi eolmayeoya hanayo?]

u

UFO ['ju:fəʊ] *abbr* 미확인 비행물체 [mihwagin bihaengmulche]
Uganda [juːˈɡændə] *n* 우간다 [uganda]
Ugandan [juːˈɡændən] *adj* 우간다의 [ugandaui] ▷ *n* 우간다 사람 [uganda saram]
ugh [ʊx; ʊh; ʌh] *excl* 윽 [euk]
ugly ['ʌɡlɪ] *adj* 못생긴 [mossaenggin]
UK [juː keɪ] *n* 영국 [yeongguk]
Ukraine [juːˈkreɪn] *n* 우크라이나 [ukeuraina]
Ukrainian [juːˈkreɪnɪən] *adj* 우크라이나의 [ukeurainaui] ▷ *n* (language) 우크라이나어 [ukeurainaeo], (person) 우크라이나 사람 [ukeuraina saram]
ulcer ['ʌlsə] *n* 궤양 [gweyang]
Ulster ['ʌlstə] *n* 얼스터 [eolseuteo]
ultimate ['ʌltɪmɪt] *adj* 최종의 [choejongui]
ultimately ['ʌltɪmɪtlɪ] *adv* 최후로 [choehuro]
ultimatum [ˌʌltɪˈmeɪtəm] *n* 최후통첩 [choehutongcheop]
ultrasound ['ʌltrəˌsaʊnd] *n* 초음파 [choeumpa]
umbrella [ʌmˈbrɛlə] *n* 우산 [usan]

umpire ['ʌmpaɪə] *n* 심판 [simpan]
UN [juː ɛn] *abbr* 국제연합 [gukjeyeonhap]
unable [ʌnˈeɪbəl] *adj* **unable to** *adj*...할 수 없는 [...hal su eomneun]
unacceptable [ˌʌnəkˈsɛptəbəl] *adj* 용납할 수 없는 [yongnaphal su eomneun]
unanimous [juːˈnænɪməs] *adj* 만장일치인 [manjangilchiin]
unattended [ˌʌnəˈtɛndɪd] *adj* 내버려둔 [naebeoryeodun]
unavoidable [ˌʌnəˈvɔɪdəbəl] *adj* 불가피한 [bulgapihan]
unbearable [ʌnˈbɛərəbəl] *adj* 참을 수 없는 [chameul su eomneun]
unbeatable [ʌnˈbiːtəbəl] *adj* 무적의 [mujeogui]
unbelievable [ˌʌnbɪˈliːvəbəl] *adj* 불신한 [bulsinhan]
unbreakable [ʌnˈbreɪkəbəl] *adj* 깨지지 않는 [kkaejiji annneun]
uncanny [ʌnˈkænɪ] *adj* 신비로운 [sinbiroun]
uncertain [ʌnˈsɜːtən] *adj* 불확실한 [bulhwaksilhan]
uncertainty [ʌnˈsɜːtəntɪ] *n* 불확실 [bulhwaksil]
unchanged [ʌnˈtʃeɪndʒd] *adj* 불변의 [bulbyeonui]
uncivilized [ʌnˈsɪvɪˌlaɪzd] *adj* 야만적인 [yamanjeogin]
uncle ['ʌŋkəl] *n* 외삼촌 [oesamchon] (mother's brother)
unclear [ʌnˈklɪə] *adj* 불명확한 [bulmyeonghwakhan]
uncomfortable [ʌnˈkʌmftəbəl] *adj* 불편한 [bulpyeonhan]
unconditional [ˌʌnkənˈdɪʃənəl] *adj* 무조건적인 [mujogeonjeogin]
unconscious [ʌnˈkɒnʃəs] *adj* 무의식의 [muuisigui]
uncontrollable [ˌʌnkənˈtrəʊləbəl] *adj* 통제할 수 없는 [tongjehal su eomneun]
unconventional [ˌʌnkənˈvɛnʃənəl] *adj* 관습에 얽매이지 않는 [gwanseube eorngmaeiji annneun]

undecided [ˌʌndɪ'saɪdɪd] *adj* 결단을 내리지 못하는 [gyeoldaneul naeriji motaneun]

undeniable [ˌʌndɪ'naɪəbᵊl] *adj* 부정할 수 없는 [bujeonghal su eomneun]

under ['ʌndə] *prep*...의 밑에 [...ui mite]

underage [ˌʌndər'eɪdʒ] *adj* 미성년의 [miseongnyeonui]

underestimate [ˌʌndərestɪ'meɪt] *v* 과소 평가하다 [gwaso pyeonggahada]

undergo [ˌʌndə'gəʊ] *v* 경험하다 [gyeongheomhada]

undergraduate [ˌʌndə'grædjʊət] *n* 대학 재학생 [daehak jaehaksaeng]

underground *adj* ['ʌndəˌgraʊnd] 지하에 [jihae] ▷ *n* ['ʌndəˌgraʊnd] 지하의 [jihaui]

underline [ˌʌndə'laɪn] *v* 강조하다 [gangjohada]

underneath [ˌʌndə'niːθ] *adv* 밑에 [mite] ▷ *prep*...의 바로 밑에 [...ui baro mite]

underpaid [ˌʌndə'peɪd] *adj* 박봉의 [bakbongui]

underpants ['ʌndəˌpænts] *npl* 속바지 [sokbaji]

underpass ['ʌndəˌpɑːs] *n* 지하도 [jihado]

underskirt ['ʌndəˌskɜːt] *n* 속치마 [sokchima]

understand [ˌʌndə'stænd] *v* 이해하다 [ihaehada]

understandable [ˌʌndə'stændəbᵊl] *adj* 이해할 수 있는 [ihaehal su inneun]

understanding [ˌʌndə'stændɪŋ] *adj* 이해심 있는 [ihaesim inneun]

undertaker ['ʌndəˌteɪkə] *n* 장의사 [janguisa]

underwater ['ʌndə'wɔːtə] *adv* 물속에서 [mulsogeseo]

underwear ['ʌndəˌwɛə] *n* 속옷 [sogot]

undisputed [ˌʌndɪ'spjuːtɪd] *adj* 명백한 [myeongbaekhan]

undo [ʌn'duː] *v* 원상태로 돌리다 [wonsangtaero dollida]

undoubtedly [ʌn'daʊtɪdlɪ] *adv* 의심할 여지 없이 [uisimhal yeoji eopsi]

undress [ʌn'drɛs] *v* 옷을 벗다 [oseul beotda]

unemployed [ˌʌnɪm'plɔɪd] *adj* 실업의 [sireobui]

unemployment [ˌʌnɪm'plɔɪmənt] *n* 실직 [siljik]

unexpected [ˌʌnɪk'spɛktɪd] *adj* 뜻밖의 [tteutbakkui]

unexpectedly [ˌʌnɪk'spɛktɪdlɪ] *adv* 뜻밖에 [tteutbakke]

unfair [ʌn'fɛə] *adj* 불공평한 [bulgongpyeonghan]

unfaithful [ʌn'feɪθʊl] *adj* 불충실한 [bulchungsilhan]

unfamiliar [ˌʌnfə'mɪljə] *adj* 익숙지 않은 [iksukji anheun]

unfashionable [ʌn'fæʃənəbᵊl] *adj* 유행에 뒤떨어진 [yuhaenge dwitteoreojin]

unfavourable [ʌn'feɪvərəbᵊl; -'feɪvrə-] *adj* 호의적이 아닌 [houijeogi anin]

unfit [ʌn'fɪt] *adj* 부적당한 [bujeokdanghan]

unforgettable [ˌʌnfə'gɛtəbᵊl] *adj* 잊을 수 없는 [ijeul su eomneun]

unfortunately [ʌn'fɔːtʃənɪtlɪ] *adv* 유감스럽게도 [yugamseureopgedo]

unfriendly [ʌn'frɛndlɪ] *adj* 불친절한 [bulchinjeolhan]

ungrateful [ʌn'greɪtfʊl] *adj* 감사해 하지 않는 [gamsahae haji annneun]

unhappy [ʌn'hæpɪ] *adj* 슬픈 [seulpeun]

unhealthy [ʌn'hɛlθɪ] *adj* 병약한 [byeongyakhan]

unhelpful [ʌn'hɛlpfʊl] *adj* 도움이 되지 않는 [doumi doeji annneun]

uni ['juːnɪ] *n* 대학 [daehak]

unidentified [ˌʌnaɪ'dɛntɪˌfaɪd] *adj* 정체 불명의 [jeongche bulmyeongui]

uniform ['juːnɪˌfɔːm] *n* 제복 [jebok]; **school uniform** *n* 교복 [gyobok]

unimportant [ˌʌnɪm'pɔːtᵊnt] *adj* 중요하지 않은 [jungyohaji anheun]

uninhabited [ˌʌnɪn'hæbɪtɪd] *adj* 사람이 살지 않는 [sarami salji annneun]

unintentional [ˌʌnɪn'tɛnʃənᵊl] *adj*

본의아닌 [bonuianin]

union ['juːnjən] n 연합 [yeonhap];
European Union n 유럽연합
[yureobyeonhap]; **trade union** n
노동조합 [nodongjohap]

unique [juːˈniːk] adj 독특한
[dokteukhan]

unit ['juːnɪt] n 단위 [danwi]

unite [juːˈnaɪt] v 연합하다
[yeonhaphada]

United Kingdom [juːˈnaɪtɪd ˈkɪŋdəm]
n 영국 [yeongguk]

United States [juːˈnaɪtɪd steɪts] n
미국 [miguk]

universe ['juːnɪˌvɜːs] n 우주 [uju]

university [ˌjuːnɪˈvɜːsɪtɪ] n 대학
[daehak]

unknown [ʌnˈnəʊn] adj 알려지지 않은
[allyeojiji anheun]

unleaded [ʌnˈlɛdɪd] n 무연 [muyeon];
unleaded petrol n 무연 휘발유
[muyeon hwiballyu]; **...worth of
premium unleaded, please** 고급
무연...어치요 [gogeup muyeon...
eochiyo]

unless [ʌnˈlɛs] conj ...이 아니면 [...i
animyeon]

unlike [ʌnˈlaɪk] prep ...과는 다른 [...
gwaneun dareun]

unlikely [ʌnˈlaɪklɪ] adj 있을 법하지 않은
[isseul beophaji anheun]

unlisted [ʌnˈlɪstɪd] adj 목록에 없는
[mongnoge eomneun]

unload [ʌnˈləʊd] v 짐을 내리다 [jimeul
naerida]

unlock [ʌnˈlɒk] v (잠긴 것을) 열다
[(jamgin geoseul) yeolda]

unlucky [ʌnˈlʌkɪ] adj 불운한
[burunhan]

unmarried [ʌnˈmærɪd] adj 미혼의
[mihonui]

unnecessary [ʌnˈnɛsɪsərɪ; -ɪsrɪ] adj
불필요한 [bulpillyohan]

unofficial [ˌʌnəˈfɪʃəl] adj 비공식의
[bigongsigui]

unpack [ʌnˈpæk] v (짐을) 풀다 [(jimeul)
pulda]

unpaid [ʌnˈpeɪd] adj 무보수의

[mubosuui]

unpleasant [ʌnˈplɛzʰnt] adj 불쾌한
[bulkwaehan]

unplug [ʌnˈplʌɡ] v 플러그를 뽑다
[peulleogeureul ppopda]

unpopular [ʌnˈpɒpjʊlə] adj 인기가 없는
[ingiga eomneun]

unprecedented [ʌnˈprɛsɪˌdɛntɪd] adj
유례없는 [yuryeeomneun]

unpredictable [ˌʌnprɪˈdɪktəbʰl] adj
예측할 수 없는 [yecheukhal su
eomneun]

unreal [ʌnˈrɪəl] adj 비현실 [bihyeonsil]

unrealistic [ˌʌnrɪəˈlɪstɪk] adj
비현실적인 [bihyeonsiljeogin]

unreasonable [ʌnˈriːznəbʰl] adj
불합리한 [bulhamnihan]

unreliable [ˌʌnrɪˈlaɪəbʰl] adj 불신한
[bulsinhan]

unroll [ʌnˈrəʊl] v (감긴 것을) 펴다
[(gamgin geoseul) pyeoda]

unsatisfactory [ˌʌnsætɪsˈfæktərɪ; -trɪ]
adj 불만스러운 [bulmanseureoun]

unscrew [ʌnˈskruː] v 나사를 빼다
[nasareul ppaeda]

unshaven [ʌnˈʃeɪvʰn] adj 면도하지
않은 [myeondohaji anheun]

unskilled [ʌnˈskɪld] adj 미숙한
[misukhan]

unstable [ʌnˈsteɪbʰl] adj 불안정한
[buranjeonghan]

unsteady [ʌnˈstɛdɪ] adj 불안정한
[buranjeonghan]

unsuccessful [ˌʌnsəkˈsɛsfʊl] adj 실패한
[silpaehan]

unsuitable [ʌnˈsuːtəbʰl; ʌnˈsjuːt-] adj
부적당한 [bujeokdanghan]

unsure [ʌnˈʃʊə] adj 불확실한
[bulhwaksilhan]

untidy [ʌnˈtaɪdɪ] adj 단정치 못한
[danjeongchi motan]

untie [ʌnˈtaɪ] v 풀다 [pulda]

until [ʌnˈtɪl] conj ...까지 [...kkaji]

unusual [ʌnˈjuːʒʊəl] adj 유별난
[yubyeollan]

unwell [ʌnˈwɛl] adj 몸이 편치 않은
[momi pyeonchi anheun]

unwind [ʌnˈwaɪnd] v (감은 것을) 풀다

[(gameun geoseul) pulda]

unwise [ʌn'waɪz] *adj* 어리석은 [eoriseogeun]

unwrap [ʌn'ræp] *v* 풀다 [pulda]

unzip [ʌn'zɪp] *v* 지퍼를 열다 [jipeoreul yeolda]

up [ʌp] *adv* 위로 [wiro]

upbringing ['ʌp,brɪŋɪŋ] *n* 양육 [yangyuk]

update *n* ['ʌp,deɪt] 갱신하다 [gaengsinhada] ▷ *v* [ʌp'deɪt] 갱신하다 [gaengsinhada]

upgrade [ʌp'greɪd] *n* **I want to upgrade my ticket** 표를 비싼 걸로 바꾸고 싶어요 [pyoreul bissan geollo bakkugo sipeoyo]

uphill ['ʌp'hɪl] *adv* 위를 향하여 [wireul hyanghayeo]

upper ['ʌpə] *adj* 위의 [wiui]

upright ['ʌp,raɪt] *adv* 수직으로 [sujigeuro]

upset *adj* [ʌp'sɛt] 화난 [hwanan] ▷ *v* [ʌp'sɛt] 뒤엎다 [dwieopda]

upside down ['ʌp,saɪd daʊn] *adv* 거꾸로 [geokkuro]

upstairs ['ʌp'stɛəz] *adv* 위층으로 [wicheungeuro]

uptight [ʌp'taɪt] *adj* 긴장한 [ginjanghan]

up-to-date ['ʌptʊ,deɪt] *adj* 최신의 [choesinui]

upwards ['ʌpwədz] *adv* 위쪽으로 [wijjogeuro]

uranium [jʊ'reɪnɪəm] *n* 우라늄 [uranyum]

urgency ['ɜːdʒənsɪ] *n* 긴급 [gingeup]

urgent ['ɜːdʒənt] *adj* 긴급한 [gingeuphan]

urine ['jʊərɪn] *n* 소변 [sobyeon]

Uruguay ['jʊərə,gwaɪ] *n* 우루과이 [urugwai]

Uruguayan [,jʊərə'gwaɪən] *adj* 우루과이의 [urugwaiui] ▷ *n* 우루과이 사람 [urugwai saram]

us [ʌs] *pron* 우리를 [urireul]

use *n* [juːs] 사용 [sayong] ▷ *v* [juːz] 사용하다 [sayonghada]; **Please use the meter** 미터기를 사용해 주세요

[miteogireul sayonghae juseyo]

used [juːzd] *adj* 익숙한 [iksukhan]

useful ['juːsfʊl] *adj* 유용한 [yuyonghan]

useless ['juːslɪs] *adj* 무익한 [muikhan]

user ['juːzə] *n* 사용자 [sayongja]; **Internet user** *n* 인터넷 사용자 [inteonet sayongja]

user-friendly ['juːzə,frɛndlɪ] *adj* 사용하기 쉬운 [sayonghagi swiun]

use up [juːz ʌp] *v* 다 써버리다 [da sseobeorida]

usual ['juːʒʊəl] *adj* 보통의 [botongui]

usually ['juːʒʊəlɪ] *adv* 보통은 [botongeun]

U-turn ['juː,tɜːn] *n* U턴 [U teon]

Uzbekistan [,ʌzbɛkɪ'staːn] *n* 우즈베키스탄 [ujeubekiseutan]

V

vacancy ['veɪkənsɪ] n 공석 [gongseok]
vacant ['veɪkənt] adj 비어 있는 [bieo inneun]
vacate [və'keɪt] v 비우다 [biuda]
vaccinate ['væksɪˌneɪt] v 예방접종을 하다 [yebangjeopjongeul hada]
vaccination [ˌvæksɪ'neɪʃən] n 예방접종 [yebangjeopjong]
vacuum ['vækjʊəm] v 진공청소기로 청소하다 [jingongcheongsogiro cheongsohada]; **vacuum cleaner** n 진공청소기 [jingongcheongsogi]
vague [veɪg] adj 막연한 [magyeonhan]
vain [veɪn] adj 허영심이 강한 [heoyeongsimi ganghan]
valid ['vælɪd] adj 정당한 [jeongdanghan]
valley ['vælɪ] n 계곡 [gyegok]
valuable ['væljʊəb°l] adj 값비싼 [gabbissan]
valuables ['væljʊəb°lz] npl 귀중품 [gwijungpum]; **I'd like to put my valuables in the safe** 귀중품을 금고에 넣고 싶어요 [gwijungpumeul geumgoe neoko sipeoyo]; **Where can I leave my valuables?** 귀중품은 어디에 놓을 수 있을까요? [gwijungpumeun

eodie noheul su isseulkkayo?]
value ['væljuː] n 가치 [gachi]
vampire ['væmpaɪə] n 흡혈귀 [heuphyeolgwi]
van [væn] n 소형 트럭 [sohyeong teureok]; **breakdown van** n 견인차 [gyeonincha]; **removal van** n 이삿짐 트럭 [isatjim teureok]
vandal ['vænd°l] n 공공시설 파괴자 [gonggongsiseol pagoeja]
vandalism ['vændəˌlɪzəm] n 공공시설 파괴 행위 [gonggongsiseol pagoe haengwi]
vandalize ['vændəˌlaɪz] v 파괴하다 [pagoehada]
vanilla [və'nɪlə] n 바닐라 [banilla]
vanish ['vænɪʃ] v 사라지다 [sarajida]
variable ['vɛərɪəb°l] adj 변하기 쉬운 [byeonhagi swiun]
varied ['vɛərɪd] adj 다양한 [dayanghan]
variety [və'raɪɪtɪ] n 다양성 [dayangseong]
various ['vɛərɪəs] adj 다양한 [dayanghan]
varnish ['vɑːnɪʃ] n 니스 [niseu] ▷ v 니스를 칠하다 [niseureul chilhada]; **nail varnish** n 매니큐어 [maenikyueo]
vary ['vɛərɪ] v 변경하다 [byeongyeonghada]
vase [vɑːz] n 꽃병 [kkotbyeong]
VAT [væt] abbr 부가가치세 [bugagachise]; **Is VAT included?** 부가가치세 포함인가요? [bugagachise pohamingayo?]
Vatican ['vætɪkən] n 바티칸 궁전 [batikan gungjeon]
vault [vɔːlt] n **pole vault** n 장대높이뛰기 [jangdaenopittwigi]
veal [viːl] n 송아지 고기 [songaji gogi]
vegan ['viːgən] n 절대 채식주의자 [jeoldae chaesikjuuija]
vegetable ['vɛdʒtəb°l] n 채소 [chaeso]
vegetarian [ˌvɛdʒɪ'tɛərɪən] adj 채식주의의 [chaesikjuuiui] ▷ n 채식주의자 [chaesikjuuija]; **I'm vegetarian** 저는 채식주의자예요 [jeoneun chaesikjuuijayeyo]
vegetation [ˌvɛdʒɪ'teɪʃən] n 식물

[singmul]
vehicle ['viːɪkᵊl] n 차량 [charyang]
veil [veɪl] n 베일 [beil]
vein [veɪn] n 정맥 [jeongmaek]
Velcro® ['vɛlkrəʊ] n 벨크로 [belkeuro]
velvet ['vɛlvɪt] n 벨벳 [belbet]
vendor ['vɛndɔː] n 행상인 [haengsangin]
Venezuela [ˌvɛnɪ'zweɪlə] n 베네수엘라 [benesuella]
Venezuelan [ˌvɛnɪ'zweɪlən] adj 베네수엘라의 [benesuellaui] ▷ n 베네수엘라 사람 [benesuella saram]
venison ['vɛnɪzᵊn; -sᵊn] n 사슴 고기 [saseum gogi]
venom ['vɛnəm] n 독액 [dogaek]
ventilation [ˌvɛntɪ'leɪʃən] n 환기 [hwangi]
venue ['vɛnjuː] n 행사 장소 [haengsa jangso]
verb [vɜːb] n 동사 [dongsa] (문법)
verdict ['vɜːdɪkt] n 평결 [pyeonggyeol]
versatile ['vɜːsəˌtaɪl] adj 다재다능한 [dajaedaneunghan]
version ['vɜːʃən; -ʒən] n...판 [...pan]
versus ['vɜːsəs] prep... 대... [... dae...]
vertical ['vɜːtɪkᵊl] adj 수직의 [sujigui]
vertigo ['vɜːtɪˌɡəʊ] n 현기증 [hyeongijeung]
very ['vɛrɪ] adv 매우 [maeu]
vest [vɛst] n (남자용) 속 셔츠 [(namjayong) sok syeocheu]
vet [vɛt] n 수의사 [suuisa]
veteran ['vɛtərən; 'vɛtrən] adj 노련한 [noryeonhan] ▷ n 노병 [nobyeong]
veto ['viːtəʊ] n 거부권 [geobugwon]
via ['vaɪə] prep...을 거쳐 [...eul geochyeo]
vicar ['vɪkə] n 교구 목사 [gyogu moksa]
vice [vaɪs] n 부도덕한 행위 [budodeokhan haengwi]
vice versa ['vaɪsɪ 'vɜːsə] adv 반대로 [bandaero]
vicinity [vɪ'sɪnɪtɪ] n 근처 [geuncheo]
vicious ['vɪʃəs] adj 나쁜 [nappeun]
victim ['vɪktɪm] n 피해자 [pihaeja]
victory ['vɪktərɪ] n 승리 [seungni]
video ['vɪdɪˌəʊ] n 비디오 [bidio]; **video camera** n 비디오 카메라 [bidio kamera]
videophone ['vɪdɪəˌfəʊn] n 비디오 전화 [bidio jeonhwa]
Vietnam [ˌvjɛt'næm] n 베트남 [beteunam]
Vietnamese [ˌvjɛtnə'miːz] adj 베트남의 [beteunamui] ▷ n (language) 베트남어 [beteunameo], (person) 베트남 사람 [beteunam saram]
view [vjuː] n 견해 [gyeonhae]
viewer ['vjuːə] n 시청자 [sicheongja]
viewpoint ['vjuːˌpɔɪnt] n 관점 [gwanjeom]
vile [vaɪl] adj 비열한 [biyeolhan]
villa ['vɪlə] n 별장 [byeoljang]
village ['vɪlɪdʒ] n 마을 [maeul]
villain ['vɪlən] n 악한 [akhan]
vinaigrette [ˌvɪneɪ'ɡrɛt] n 비네그레트 소스 [binegeureteu soseu]
vine [vaɪn] n 덩굴식물 [deonggulsingmul]
vinegar ['vɪnɪɡə] n 식초 [sikcho]
vineyard ['vɪnjəd] n 포도원 [podowon]
viola [vɪ'əʊlə] n 비올라 [biolla]
violence ['vaɪələns] n 폭력 [pongnyeok]
violent ['vaɪələnt] adj 난폭한 [nanpokhan]
violin [ˌvaɪə'lɪn] n 바이올린 [baiollin]
violinist [ˌvaɪə'lɪnɪst] n 바이올리니스트 [baiolliniseuteu]
virgin ['vɜːdʒɪn] n 처녀 [cheonyeo]
Virgo ['vɜːɡəʊ] n 처녀자리 [cheonyeojari]
virtual ['vɜːtʃʊəl] adj 가상의 [gasangui]; **virtual reality** n 가상현실 [gasanghyeonsil]
virus ['vaɪrəs] n 바이러스 [baireoseu]
visa ['viːzə] n 비자 [bija]; **Here is my visa** 제 비자예요 [je bijayeyo]; **I have an entry visa** 입국 비자가 있어요 [ipguk bijaga isseoyo]
visibility [ˌvɪzɪ'bɪlɪtɪ] n 시계 [sigye]
visible ['vɪzɪbᵊl] adj 눈에 보이는 [nune boineun]
visit ['vɪzɪt] n 방문 [bangmun] ▷ v 방문하다 [bangmunhada]; **visiting hours** npl 방문시간 [bangmunsigan];

Can we visit the castle? 성을 방문할 수 있어요? [seongeul bangmunhal su isseoyo?]; **Do we have time to visit the town?** 시내를 방문할 시간이 있어요? [sinaereul bangmunhal sigani isseoyo?]; **I'm here visiting friends** 친구들을 방문하러 왔어요 [chingudeureul bangmunhareo wasseoyo]; **We'd like to visit…** …을(를) 방문하고 싶어요 [...eul(reul) bangmunhago sipeoyo]

visitor ['vɪzɪtə] n 방문객 [bangmungaek]; **visitor centre** n 관광 안내소 [gwangwang annaeso]

visual ['vɪʒʊəl; -zjʊ-] adj 시각의 [sigagui]

visualize ['vɪʒʊəˌlaɪz; -zjʊ-] v 시각화하다 [sigakhwahada]

vital ['vaɪtəl] adj 필수적인 [pilsujeogin]

vitamin ['vɪtəmɪn; 'vaɪ-] n 비타민 [bitamin]

vivid ['vɪvɪd] adj 선명한 [seonmyeonghan]

vocabulary [və'kæbjʊlərɪ] n 어휘 [eohwi]

vocational [vəʊ'keɪʃənəl] adj 직업상의 [jigeopsangui]

vodka ['vɒdkə] n 보드카 [bodeuka]

voice [vɔɪs] n 목소리 [moksori]

voicemail ['vɔɪsˌmeɪl] n 음성메일 [eumseongmeil]

void [vɔɪd] adj 텅 빈 [teong bin] ▷ n 공허감 [gongheogam]

volcano, volcanoes [vɒl'keɪnəʊ, vɒl'keɪnəʊz] n 화산 [hwasan]

volleyball ['vɒlɪˌbɔːl] n 배구 [baegu]

volt [vəʊlt] n 볼트 [bolteu]

voltage ['vəʊltɪdʒ] n 전압 [jeonap]; **What's the voltage?** 전압이 어떻게 되나요? [jeonabi eotteoke doenayo?]

volume ['vɒljuːm] n 부피 [bupi]

voluntarily ['vɒləntərɪlɪ] adv 자발적으로 [jabaljeogeuro]

voluntary ['vɒləntərɪ; -trɪ] adj 자발적인 [jabaljeogin]

volunteer [ˌvɒlən'tɪə] n 자원봉사자 [jawonbongsaja] ▷ v 자원하다 [jawonhada]

vomit ['vɒmɪt] v 구토하다 [gutohada]

vote [vəʊt] n 투표 [tupyo] ▷ v 투표하다 [tupyohada]

voucher ['vaʊtʃə] n 상품권 [sangpumgwon]; **gift voucher** n 상품권 [sangpumgwon]

vowel ['vaʊəl] n 모음 [moeum]

vulgar ['vʌlgə] adj 저속한 [jeosokhan]

vulnerable ['vʌlnərəbəl] adj 취약한 [chwiyakhan]

vulture ['vʌltʃə] n 독수리 [doksuri]

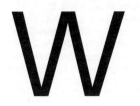

W

wafer [ˈweɪfə] n 웨이퍼 [weipeo]
waffle [ˈwɒfᵊl] n 와플 [wapeul] ▷ v 잡담하다 [japdamhada]
wage [weɪdʒ] n 임금 [imgeum]
waist [weɪst] n 허리 [heori]
waistcoat [ˈweɪsˌkəʊt] n 조끼 [jokki]
wait [weɪt] v 기다리다 [gidarida]; **wait for** v 기다리다 [gidarida]; **waiting list** n 대기명단 [daegimyeongdan]; **waiting room** n 대기실 [daegisil]
waiter [ˈweɪtə] n 웨이터 [weiteo]
waitress [ˈweɪtrɪs] n 웨이트리스 [weiteuriseu]
wait up [weɪt ʌp] v 대기하다 [daegihada]
waive [weɪv] v 포기하다 [pogihada]
wake up [weɪk ʌp] v 일어나다 [ireonada]
Wales [weɪlz] n 웨일스 [weilseu]
walk [wɔːk] n 걷기 [geotgi] (도보) ▷ v 걷다 [geotda]; **Are there any guided walks?** 가이드 딸린 걷기가 있어요? [gaideu ttallin geotgiga isseoyo?]; **Do you have a guide to local walks?** 현지 걷기 가이드가 있어요? [hyeonji geotgi gaideuga isseoyo?]
walkie-talkie [ˌwɔːkɪˈtɔːkɪ] n 워키토키 [wokitoki]
walking [ˈwɔːkɪŋ] n 걷기 [geotgi]; **walking stick** n 지팡이 [jipangi]
walkway [ˈwɔːkˌweɪ] n 보도 [bodo]
wall [wɔːl] n 벽 [byeok]
wallet [ˈwɒlɪt] n 지갑 [jigap]; **I've lost my wallet** 지갑을 잃어버렸어요 [jigabeul ireobeoryeosseoyo]; **My wallet has been stolen** 지갑을 도둑맞았어요 [jigabeul dodungmajasseoyo]
wallpaper [ˈwɔːlˌpeɪpə] n 벽지 [byeokji]
walnut [ˈwɔːlˌnʌt] n 호두 [hodu]
walrus [ˈwɔːlrəs; ˈwɒl-] n 바다코끼리 [badakokkiri]
waltz [wɔːls] n 왈츠 [walcheu] ▷ v 왈츠를 추다 [walcheureul chuda]
wander [ˈwɒndə] v 배회하다 [baehoehada]
want [wɒnt] v 원하다 [wonhada]
war [wɔː] n 전쟁 [jeonjaeng]; **civil war** n 내전 [naejeon] (폭동)
ward [wɔːd] n (area) 행정 구역 [haengjeong guyeok], (hospital room) 병실 [byeongsil]
warden [ˈwɔːdᵊn] n 관리인 [gwalliin]; **traffic warden** n 교통감시관 [gyotonggamsigwan]
wardrobe [ˈwɔːdrəʊb] n 옷장 [otjang]
warehouse [ˈwɛəˌhaʊs] n 창고 [changgo]
warm [wɔːm] adj 따뜻한 [ttatteutan]
warm up [wɔːm ʌp] v 따뜻하게 하다 [ttatteutage hada]
warn [wɔːn] v 경고하다 [gyeonggohada]
warning [ˈwɔːnɪŋ] n 경고 [gyeonggo]; **hazard warning lights** npl 위험 경고등 [wiheom gyeonggodeung]; **The oil warning light won't go off** 오일 경고등이 꺼지지 않아요 [oil gyeonggodeungi kkeojiji anhayo]
warranty [ˈwɒrəntɪ] n 보증 [bojeung]; **The car is still under warranty** 차 보증 기간이 끝나지 않았어요 [cha bojeung gigani kkeutnaji anhasseoyo]
wart [wɔːt] n 사마귀 [samagwi]

wash [wɒʃ] v 씻다 [ssitda]; **car wash** n 세차 [secha]

washable ['wɒʃəb°l] adj **machine washable** adj 기계세탁이 가능한 [gigyesetagi ganeunghan]; **Is it washable?** 물세탁 가능한가요? [mulsaetark ganeunghangayo?]

washbasin ['wɒʃˌbeɪs°n] n 세면대 [semyeondae]

washing ['wɒʃɪŋ] n 세탁 [setak]; **washing line** n 빨랫줄 [ppallaetjul]; **washing machine** n 세탁기 [setakgi]; **washing powder** n 가루 세탁 비누 [garu setak binu]; **Where can I do some washing?** 어디에서 세탁을 할 수 있을까요? [eodieseo setageul hal su isseulkkayo?]

washing-up ['wɒʃɪŋʌp] n 설거지 [seolgeoji]; **washing-up liquid** n 설거지용 세제 [seolgeojiyong seje]

wash up [wɒʃ ʌp] v 설거지하다 [seolgeojihada]

wasp [wɒsp] n 말벌 [malbeol]

waste [weɪst] n 낭비 [nangbi] ▷ v 낭비하다 [nangbihada]

watch [wɒtʃ] n 시계 [sigye] ▷ v 지켜보다 [jikyeoboda]; **digital watch** n 디지털 시계 [dijiteol sigye]; **Can you repair my watch?** 제 시계를 고치실 수 있으세요? [je sigyereul gochisil su isseuseyo?]; **I need a new strap for my watch** 새 시계줄이 필요해요 [sae sigyejuri pillyohaeyo]; **I think my watch is fast** 제 시계가 빠른 것 같아요 [je sigyega ppareun geot gatayo]; **I think my watch is slow** 제 시계가 느린 것 같아요 [je sigyega neurin geot gatayo]; **My watch has stopped** 제 시계가 멈췄어요 [je sigyega meomchwosseoyo]

watch out [wɒtʃ aʊt] v 주의하다 [juuihada]

water ['wɔːtə] n 물 [mul] ▷ v 물주다 [muljuda]; **drinking water** n 음료수 [eumnyosu]; **mineral water** n 광천수 [gwangcheonsu]; **sea water** n 해수 [haesu]; **sparkling water** n 탄산수 [tansansu]; **watering can** n 물뿌리개 [mulppurigae]; **a glass of water** 물 한 잔 [mul han jan]; **Can you check the water, please?** 물을 확인해 주시겠어요? [mureul hwaginhae jusigesseoyo?]; **How deep is the water?** 물이 얼마나 깊어요? [muri eolmana gipeoyo?]; **Please bring more water** 물을 더 갖다 주세요 [mureul deo gatda juseyo]

watercolour ['wɔːtəˌkʌlə] n 수채화 [suchaehwa]

watercress ['wɔːtəˌkrɛs] n 물냉이 [mullaengi]

waterfall ['wɔːtəˌfɔːl] n 폭포 [pokpo]

watermelon ['wɔːtəˌmɛlən] n 수박 [subak]

waterproof ['wɔːtəˌpruːf] adj 방수의 [bangsuui]

water-skiing ['wɔːtəˌskiːɪŋ] n 수상 스키 [susang seuki]; **Is it possible to go water-skiing here?** 여기에서 수상 스키를 타도 될까요? [yeogieseo susang seukireul tado doelkkayo?]

wave [weɪv] n 파도 [pado] ▷ v 손흔들다 [sonheundeulda]

wavelength ['weɪvˌlɛŋθ] n 파장 [pajang] (바다)

wavy ['weɪvɪ] adj 굽이치는 [gubichineun]

wax [wæks] n 밀랍 [millap]

way [weɪ] n 방법 [bangbeop]; **right of way** n 통행우선권 [tonghaenguseongwon]; **What's the best way to get to the railway station?** 기차역에 가는 가장 좋은 방법은 무엇인가요? [gichayeoge ganeun gajang joheun bangbeobeun mueosingayo?]

way in [weɪ ɪn] n 입구 [ipgu]

way out [weɪ aʊt] n 출구 [chulgu]

we [wiː] pron 우리 [uri]; **We live in...** 우리는...에 살아요 [urineun...e sarayo]

weak [wiːk] adj 약한 [yakhan]

weakness ['wiːknɪs] n 허약 [heoyak]

wealth [wɛlθ] n 부 [bu]

wealthy ['wɛlθɪ] adj 부유한 [buyuhan]

weapon ['wɛpən] n 무기 [mugi]

wear [wɛə] v 옷입다 [osipda]

weasel ['wiːzəl] n 족제비 [jokjebi]
weather ['wɛðə] n 날씨 [nalssi];
weather forecast n 일기예보
[ilgiyebo]; **Is the weather going to
change?** 날씨가 바뀔까요? [nalssiga
bakkwilkkayo?]; **What awful
weather!** 날씨가 아주 나빠요!
[nalssiga aju nappayo!]; **What will the
weather be like tomorrow?** 내일
날씨가 어떨까요? [naeil nalssiga
eotteolkkayo?]
web [wɛb] n 거미줄 [geomijul]; **web
address** n 웹 주소 [wep juso]; **web
browser** n 웹 브라우저 [wep
beuraujeo]
webcam ['wɛbˌkæm] n 웹캠
[wepkaem]
webmaster ['wɛbˌmɑːstə] n 웹마스터
[wemmaseuteo]
website ['wɛbˌsaɪt] n 웹사이트
[wepsaiteu]
webzine ['wɛbˌziːn] n 웹진 [wepjin]
wedding ['wɛdɪŋ] n 결혼식
[gyeolhonsik]; **wedding anniversary**
n 결혼기념일 [gyeolhoninyeomil];
wedding dress n 웨딩드레스
[wedingdeureseu]; **wedding ring** n
결혼반지 [gyeolhonbanji]
Wednesday ['wɛnzdɪ] n 수요일
[suyoil]; **Ash Wednesday** n 성회일
[seonghoeil]; **on Wednesday** 수요일에
[suyoire]
weed [wiːd] n 잡초 [japcho]
weedkiller ['wiːdˌkɪlə] n 제초제
[jechoje]
week [wiːk] n 주 [ju]; **a week ago**
일주일 전에 [iljuil jeone]; **How much is
it for a week?** 일주일에 얼마예요?
[iljuire eolmayeyo?]; **last week** 지난 주
[jinan ju]; **next week** 다음 주 [daeum
ju]
weekday ['wiːkˌdeɪ] n 평일 [pyeongil]
weekend [ˌwiːk'ɛnd] n 주말 [jumal]; **I
want to hire a car for the weekend**
주말동안 차를 빌리고 싶어요
[jumaldongan chareul billigo sipeoyo]
weep [wiːp] v 울다 [ulda]
weigh [weɪ] v 무게재다 [mugejaeda];

How much do you weigh? 몸무게가
얼마인가요? [mommugega
eolmaingayo?]
weight [weɪt] n 무게 [muge]
weightlifter ['weɪtˌlɪftə] n 역도 선수
[yeokdo seonsu]
weightlifting ['weɪtˌlɪftɪŋ] n 역도
[yeokdo]
weird [wɪəd] adj 별난 [byeollan]
welcome ['wɛlkəm] n 환영
[hwanyeong] (인사) ▷ v 환영하다
[hwanyeonghada]; **welcome!** excl
환영! [hwanyeong!] (인사)
well [wɛl] adj 건강한 [geonganghan]
▷ adv 잘 [jal] ▷ n 우물 [umul]; **oil well** n
유정 [yujeong]; **well done!** excl
잘했어요! [jalhaesseoyo!]; **Did you
sleep well?** 잘 주무셨어요? [jal
jumusyeosseoyo?]
well-behaved ['wɛl'bɪ'heɪvd] adj
행실이 바른 [haengsiri bareun]
wellies ['wɛlɪz] npl 고무장화
[gomujanghwa]
wellingtons ['wɛlɪŋtənz] npl 고무장화
[gomujanghwa]
well-known ['wɛl'nəʊn] adj 유명한
[yumyeonghan]
well-off ['wɛl'ɒf] adj 부유한 [buyuhan]
well-paid ['wɛl'peɪd] adj 보수가 좋은
[bosuga joheun]
Welsh [wɛlʃ] adj 웨일스의 [weilseuui]
▷ n 웨일스 사람 [weilseu saram]
west [wɛst] adj 서쪽의 [seojjogui] ▷ adv
서쪽으로 [sebjjogeuro] ▷ n 서쪽
[seojjok]; **West Indian** n 서인도제도
사람 [seoindojedo saram],
서인도제도의 [seoindojedoui]; **West
Indies** npl 서인도제도 [seoindojedo]
westbound ['wɛstˌbaʊnd] adj 서쪽으로
가는 [seojjogeuro ganeun]
western ['wɛstən] adj 서쪽의
[seojjogui] ▷ n 서부 [seobu]
wet [wɛt] adj 젖은 [jeojeun]
wetsuit ['wɛtˌsuːt] n 잠수복
[jamsubok]
whale [weɪl] n 고래 [gorae]
what [wɒt; wət] adj 무슨 [museun]
▷ pron 무엇 [mueot]; **What do you do?**

무슨 일하세요? [museun ilhaseyo?]; **What is the word for…?** … 무엇이라고 하나요? [...mueosirago hanayo?]

wheat [wiːt] n 밀 [mil]; **wheat intolerance** n 밀 알레르기 [mil allereugi]

wheel [wiːl] n 바퀴 [bakwi]; **spare wheel** n 예비 바퀴 [yebi bakwi]; **steering wheel** n 자동차 핸들 [jadongcha haendeul]

wheelbarrow ['wiːlˌbærəʊ] n 1륜 손수레 [illyun sonsure]

wheelchair ['wiːlˌtʃɛə] n 휠체어 [hwilcheeo]; **Can you visit… in a wheelchair?** 휠체어로...을 방문할 수 있나요? [hwilcheeoro...eul bangmunhal su innayo?]; **Do you have a lift for wheelchairs?** 휠체어 리프트가 있나요? [hwilcheeo ripeuteuga innayo?]; **Do you have wheelchairs?** 휠체어 있어요? [hwilcheeo isseoyo?]; **I need a room with wheelchair access** 휠체어로 출입할 수 있는 방이 필요해요 [hwilcheeoro churiphal su inneun bangi piryohaeyo]; **I use a wheelchair** 저는 휠체어를 사용해요 [jeoneun hwilcheeoreul sayonghaeyo]; **Is there wheelchair-friendly transport available to…?** 휠체어로...까지 갈 수 있는 교통 수단이 있나요? [hwilcheeoro...kkaji gal su inneun gyotong sudani innayo?]; **Is your hotel accessible to wheelchairs?** 휠체어로 출입할 수 있는 호텔인가요? [hwilcheeoro churiphal su inneun hoteringayo?]; **Where is the nearest repair shop for wheelchairs?** 가장 가까운 휠체어 수리점은 어디인가요? [gajang gakkaun hwilcheeo surijeomeun eodiingayo?]; **Where is the wheelchair-accessible entrance?** 휠체어를 이용할 수 있는 출입구는 어디인가요? [hwilcheeoreul iyonghal su inneun churipguneun eodiingayo?]

when [wɛn] adv 언제 [eonje] ▷ conj...인

때 [...in ttae]; **When does it begin?** 언제 시작해요? [eonje sijakhaeyo?]; **When does it finish?** 언제 끝나요? [eonje kkeutnayo?]; **When is it due?** 언제 도착해요? [eonje dochakhaeyo?]

where [wɛə] adv 어디에 [eodie] ▷ conj... 하는 곳에 [...haneun gose]; **Can you show me where we are on the map?** 지도에서 우리가 어디에 있는지 알려 주시겠어요? [jidoeseo uriga eodie inneunji allyeo jusigesseoyo?]; **Where are you staying?** 어디에 머무르세요? [eodie meomureuseyo?]; **Where can we meet?** 어디에서 만날까요? [eodieseo mannalkkayo?]; **Where can you go…?** 어디에 가면...을 할 수 있나요? [eodie gamyeon...eul hal su innayo?]; **Where do I pay?** 어디에서 돈은 지불하나요 [eodieseo doneun jibulhanayo]; **Where do I sign?** 어디에 서명하죠? [eodie seomyeonghajyo?]; **Where is…?** ...은 어디에 있어요? [... eun eodie isseoyo?],...은 어디에 있어요? [..eun eodie isseoyo?]; **Where is the gents?** 남자 화장실은 어디에 있어요? [namja hwajangsireun eodie isseoyo?]

whether ['wɛðə] conj...인지 어떤지 [... inji eotteonji]

which [wɪtʃ] pron 어느 [eoneu], 어느 것 [eoneu geot]; **Which is the key for this door?** 이 문 열쇠는 어느 것인가요? [i mun yeolsoeneun eoneu geosingayo?]

while [waɪls] conj...하는 동안에 [... haneun dongane] ▷ n 잠시 [jamsi]

whip [wɪp] n 채찍 [chaejjik]; **whipped cream** n 거품 낸 크림 [geopum naen keurim]

whisk [wɪsk] n 털기 [teolgi]

whiskers ['wɪskəz] npl 수염 [suyeom]

whisky ['wɪskɪ] n 위스키 [wiseuki]; **malt whisky** n 몰트 위스키 [molteu wiseuki]; **a whisky and soda** 위스키 앤 소다요 [wiseuki aen sodayo]; **I'll have a whisky** 위스키 주세요 [wiseuki juseyo]

whisper ['wɪspə] v 속삭이다 [soksagida]

whistle ['wɪsᵊl] *n* 휘파람 [hwiparam]
▷ *v* 휘파람을 불다 [hwiparameul bulda]

white [waɪt] *adj* 흰 [huin]; **egg white** *n* 달걀 흰자 [dalgyal huinja]

whiteboard ['waɪt,bɔːd] *n* 화이트보드 [hwaiteubodeu]

whitewash ['waɪt,wɒʃ] *v* 회칠하다 [hoechilhada]

whiting ['waɪtɪŋ] *n* 대구 [daegu]

who [huː] *pron* 누구 [nugu]; **Who am I talking to?** 전화하시는 분이 누구시죠? [jeonhwahasineun buni nugusijyo?]; **Who is it?** 누구세요? [nuguseyo?]; **Who's calling?** 누구시죠? [nugusijyo?]

whole [həʊl] *adj* 전체의 [jeoncheui] ▷ *n* 전체 [jeonche]

wholefoods ['həʊl,fuːdz] *npl* 자연식품 [jayeonsikpum]

wholemeal ['həʊl,miːl] *adj* 통밀가루의 [tongmilgaruui]

wholesale ['həʊl,seɪl] *adj* 도매의 [domaeui] ▷ *n* 도매 [domae]

whom [huːm] *pron* 누구에게 [nuguege]

whose [huːz] *adj* 누구의 [nuguui] ▷ *pron* 누구의 것 [nuguui geot]

why [waɪ] *adv* 왜 [wae]

wicked ['wɪkɪd] *adj* 사악한 [saakhan]

wide [waɪd] *adj* 넓은 [neorbeun] ▷ *adv* 넓게 [neopge]

widespread ['waɪd,sprɛd] *adj* 보편적 [bopyeonjeok]

widow ['wɪdəʊ] *n* 과부 [gwabu]

widower ['wɪdəʊə] *n* 홀아비 [horabi]

width [wɪdθ] *n* 폭 [pok]

wife, wives [waɪf, waɪvz] *n* 아내 [anae]; **This is my wife** 제 아내예요 [je anaeyeyo]

wig [wɪg] *n* 가발 [gabal]

wild [waɪld] *adj* 야생의 [yasaengui]

wildlife ['waɪld,laɪf] *n* 야생 생물 [yasaeng saengmul]; **We'd like to see wildlife** 야생 생물을 보고 싶어요 [yasaeng saengmureul bogo sipeoyo]

will [wɪl] *n* (document) 유서 [yuseo], (motivation) 의지 [uiji]

willing ['wɪlɪŋ] *adj* ...하고 싶은 마음이 드는 [...hago sipeun maeumi deuneun]

willingly ['wɪlɪŋlɪ] *adv* 기꺼이 [gikkeoi]

willow ['wɪləʊ] *n* 버드나무 [beodeunamu]

willpower ['wɪl,paʊə] *n* 의지력 [uijiryeok]

wilt [wɪlt] *v* 시들다 [sideulda]

win [wɪn] *v* 이기다 [igida]

wind¹ [wɪnd] *n* 바람 [baram] ▷ *vt* (with a blow etc.) 감다 [gamda]

wind² [waɪnd] *v* (coil around) 감다 [gamda]

windmill ['wɪnd,mɪl; 'wɪn,mɪl] *n* 풍차 [pungcha]

window ['wɪndəʊ] *n* 창 [chang]; **shop window** *n* 상점 진열장 [sangjeom jinyeoljang]; **window pane** *n* 창유리 [changyuri]; **window seat** *n* 창쪽 좌석 [changjjok jwaseok]; **I can't open the window** 창문이 안 열려요 [changmuni an yeollyeoyo]; **I'd like a window seat** 창쪽 좌석이 좋아요 [changjjok jwaseogi johayo]; **May I close the window?** 창을 닫아도 될까요? [changeul dadado doelkkayo?]; **May I open the window?** 창을 열어도 될까요? [changeul yeoreodo doelkkayo?]

windowsill ['wɪndəʊ,sɪl] *n* 창턱 [changteok]

windscreen ['wɪnd,skriːn] *n* 앞유리 [apyuri]; **windscreen wiper** *n* 창유리 닦개 [changyuri dakkgae]; **Can you top up the windscreen washers?** 앞유리 세척액을 가득 채워 주시겠어요? [apyuri secheogaegeul gadeuk chaewo jusigesseoyo?]; **Could you clean the windscreen?** 앞유리를 닦아 주시겠어요? [apyurireul dakka jusigesseoyo?]; **The windscreen is broken** 앞유리가 깨졌어요 [apyuriga kkaejyeosseoyo]

windsurfing ['wɪnd,sɜːfɪŋ] *n* 윈드서핑 [windeuseoping]

windy ['wɪndɪ] *adj* 바람이 센 [barami sen]

wine [waɪn] *n* 와인 [wain]; **house wine** *n* 하우스 와인 [hauseu wain]; **red wine** *n* 적포도주 [jeokpodoju]; **table wine** *n*

식탁용 와인 [siktagyong wain]; **wine list** n 와인 리스트 [wain riseuteu]; **a bottle of white wine** 화이트 와인 한 병 [hwaiteu wain han byeong]; **Can you recommend a good wine?** 좋은 와인을 추천해 주시겠어요? [joheun waineul chucheonhae jusigesseoyo?]; **Is the wine chilled?** 와인이 찬가요? [waini changayo?]; **The wine list, please** 와인 목록 주세요 [wain mongnok juseyo]; **This stain is wine** 이 얼룩은 와인이에요 [i eollugeun wainieyo]; **This wine is not chilled** 이 와인이 차지 않아요 [i waini chaji anhayo]

wineglass ['waɪnˌglɑːs] n 와인잔 [wainjan]

wing [wɪŋ] n 날개 [nalgae]; **wing mirror** n 사이드 미러 [saideu mireo]

wink [wɪŋk] v 윙크하다 [wingkeuhada]

winner ['wɪnə] n 승리자 [seungnija]

winning ['wɪnɪŋ] adj 승리의 [seungniui]

winter ['wɪntə] n 겨울 [gyeoul]; **winter sports** npl 겨울 스포츠 [gyeoul seupocheu]

wipe [waɪp] v 닦다 [dakkda]; **baby wipe** n 유아용 수건 [yuayong sugeon]

wipe up [waɪp ʌp] v 닦다 [dakkda]

wire [waɪə] n 철사 [cheolsa]; **barbed wire** n 철조망 [cheoljomang]

wisdom ['wɪzdəm] n 지혜 [jihye]; **wisdom tooth** n 사랑니 [sarangni]

wise [waɪz] adj 현명한 [hyeonmyeonghan]

wish [wɪʃ] n 소원 [sowon] (희망) ▷ v 희망하다 [huimanghada]

wit [wɪt] n 재치 [jaechi]

witch [wɪtʃ] n 마녀 [manyeo]

with [wɪð; wɪθ] prep...과 함께 [...gwa hamkke]

withdraw [wɪð'drɔː] v 철회하다 [cheolhoehada]

withdrawal [wɪð'drɔːəl] n 철회 [cheolhoe]

within [wɪ'ðɪn] prep (space)...의 안쪽에 [...ui anjjoge], (term)...의 안쪽에 [...ui anjjoge]

without [wɪ'ðaʊt] prep...없이 [...eopsi]

witness ['wɪtnɪs] n 증인 [jeungin]; **Jehovah's Witness** n 여호와의 증인 [yeohowaui jeungin]; **Can you be a witness for me?** 증인이 돼 주시겠어요? [jeungini dwae jusigesseoyo?]

witty ['wɪtɪ] adj 재치있는 [jaechiinneun]

wolf, wolves [wʊlf, wʊlvz] n 늑대 [neukdae]

woman, women ['wʊmən, 'wɪmɪn] n 여자 [yeoja]

wonder ['wʌndə] v 경탄하다 [gyeongtanhada]

wonderful ['wʌndəfʊl] adj 놀라운 [nollaun]

wood [wʊd] n (forest) 숲 [sup], (material) 목재 [mokjae]

wooden ['wʊdən] adj 목제의 [mokjeui]

woodwind ['wʊdˌwɪnd] n 목관 악기 [mokgwan akgi]

woodwork ['wʊdˌwɜːk] n 목제품 [mokjepum]

wool [wʊl] n 양모 [yangmo]; **cotton wool** n 솜 [som]

woollen ['wʊlən] adj 양모의 [yangmoui]

woollens ['wʊlənz] npl 모직물 [mojingmul]

word [wɜːd] n 단어 [daneo]

work [wɜːk] n 일 [il] ▷ v 일하다 [ilhada]; **work experience** n 경력 [gyeongnyeok]; **work of art** n 미술품 [misulpum]; **work permit** n 노동허가증 [nodongheogajeung]; **work station** n 작업 구역 [jageop guyeok]; **I hope we can work together again soon** 조만간 다시 함께 일할 수 있기를 바랍니다 [jomangan dasi hamkke ilhal su itgireul baramnida]; **I work in a factory** 공장에서 일해요 [gongjangeseo ilhaeyo]; **I'm here for work** 일 때문에 여기 왔어요 [il ttaemune yeogi wasseoyo]; **Where do you work?** 어디에서 일하세요? [eodieseo ilhaseyo?]

worker ['wɜːkə] n 노동자 [nodongja];
  social worker n 사회복지사
  [sahoebokjisa]
workforce ['wɜːkfɔːs] n 노동력
  [nodongnyeok]
working-class ['wɜːkɪŋklɑːs] adj
  노동자 계급의 [nodongja gyegeubui]
workman, workmen ['wɜːkmən,
  'wɜːkmɛn] n 노동자 [nodongja]
work out [wɜːk aʊt] v 성취하다
  [seongchwihada]
workplace ['wɜːkpleɪs] n 일터 [ilteo]
workshop ['wɜːkʃɒp] n 작업장
  [jageopjang]
workspace ['wɜːkspeɪs] n 작업공간
  [jageopgonggan]
workstation ['wɜːkˌsteɪʃən] n
  작업구역 [jageopguyeok]
world [wɜːld] n 세계 [segye]; **Third
  World** n 제3세계 [je3segye]; **World
  Cup** n 월드컵 [woldeukeop]
worm [wɜːm] n 지렁이 [jireongi]
worn [wɔːn] adj 낡은 [nalgeun]
worried ['wʌrɪd] adj 걱정스러운
  [geokjeongseureoun]
worry ['wʌrɪ] v 걱정하다
  [geokjeonghada]
worrying ['wʌrɪɪŋ] adj 걱정되는
  [geokjeongdoeneun]
worse [wɜːs] adj 더 나쁜 [deo
  nappeun] ▷ adv 더 나쁘게 [deo
  nappeuge]
worsen ['wɜːsən] v 악화되다
  [akhwadoeda]
worship ['wɜːʃɪp] v 숭배하다
  [sungbaehada]
worst [wɜːst] adj 가장 나쁜 [gajang
  nappeun]
worth [wɜːθ] n 가치 [gachi]; **Is it
  worth repairing?** 수리할 가치가
  있을까요? [surihal gachiga
  isseulkkayo?]
worthless ['wɜːθlɪs] adj 가치 없는
  [gachi eomneun]
would [wʊd; wəd] v **I would like to
  wash the car** 세차를 하려고요
  [sechareul haryeogoyo]; **We would
  like to go cycling** 자전거를 타고

싶어요 [jajeongeoreul tago sipeoyo]
wound [wuːnd] n 상처 [sangcheo]
  (부상) ▷ v 상처를 입히다 [sangcheoreul
  iphida]
wrap [ræp] v 포장하다 [pojanghada];
  wrapping paper n 포장지 [pojangji]
wrap up [ræp ʌp] v 포장하다
  [pojanghada]
wreck [rɛk] n 파손 [pason] ▷ v 파괴하다
  [pagoehada]
wreckage ['rɛkɪdʒ] n 잔해 [janhae]
wren [rɛn] n 굴뚝새 [gulttuksae]
wrench [rɛntʃ] n 렌치 [renchi] ▷ v
  비틀다 [biteulda]
wrestler ['rɛslə] n 레슬링 선수
  [reseulling seonsu]
wrestling ['rɛslɪŋ] n 레슬링 [reseulling]
wrinkle ['rɪŋkəl] n 주름살 [jureumsal]
wrinkled ['rɪŋkəld] adj 주름진
  [jureumjin]
wrist [rɪst] n 팔목 [palmok]
write [raɪt] v 글쓰다 [geulsseuda]
write down [raɪt daʊn] v 기재하다
  [gijaehada]
writer ['raɪtə] n 저자 [jeoja]
writing ['raɪtɪŋ] n 집필 [jippil]; **writing
  paper** n 필기용지 [pilgiyongji]
wrong [rɒŋ] adj 틀린 [teullin] ▷ adv
  잘못하여 [jalmotayeo]; **wrong
  number** n 잘못 걸린 전화 [jalmot
  geollin jeonhwa]

X y

Xmas [ˈɛksməs; ˈkrɪsməs] n 크리스마스 [keuriseumaseu]

X-ray [ɛksreɪ] n X선 [Xseon] ▷ v X선 사진을 찍다 [Xseon sajineul jjikda]

xylophone [ˈzaɪləˌfəʊn] n 실로폰 [sillopon]

yacht [jɒt] n 요트 [yoteu]

yard [jɑːd] n (enclosure) 마당 [madang], (measurement) 야드 [yadeu]

yawn [jɔːn] v 하품하다 [hapumhada]

year [jɪə] n 년 [nyeon]; **academic year** n 학년도 [hangnyeondo]; **financial year** n 회계 연도 [hoegye yeondo]; **leap year** n 윤년 [yunnyeon]; **New Year** n 새해 [saehae]

yearly [ˈjɪəlɪ] adj 1년간의 [illyeonganui] ▷ adv 해마다 [haemada]

yeast [jiːst] n 효모 [hyomo]

yell [jɛl] v 소리치다 [sorichida]

yellow [ˈjɛləʊ] adj 노란색의 [noransaegui]; **Yellow Pages®** npl 옐로우 페이지스 [yellou peijiseu]

Yemen [ˈjɛmən] n 예멘 [yemen]

yes [jɛs] excl 예 [ye]

yesterday [ˈjɛstədɪ; -ˌdeɪ] adv 어제 [eoje]

yet [jɛt] adv (interrogative) 아직 [ajik], (with negative) 아직 [ajik] ▷ conj (nevertheless) 아직 [ajik]

yew [juː] n 주목 [jumok]

yield [jiːld] v 산출하다 [sanchulhada]

yoga [ˈjəʊɡə] n 요가 [yoga]

yoghurt [ˈjəʊɡət; ˈjɒɡ-] n 요구르트

[yogureuteu]

yolk [jəʊk] *n* 노른자 [noreunja]

you [juː; jʊ] *pron (plural)* 당신 [dangsin], *(singular)* 너 [neo], *(singular polite)* 당신 [dangsin]

young [jʌŋ] *adj* 어린 [eorin]

younger [jʌŋə] *adj* 더 어린 [deo eorin]

youngest [jʌŋɪst] *adj* 가장 어린 [gajang eorin]

your [jɔː; jʊə; jə] *adj (plural)* 당신의 [dangsinui], *(singular)* 너의 [neoui], *(singular polite)* 당신의 [dangsinui]

yours [jɔːz; jʊəz] *pron (plural)* 당신의 것 [dangsinui geot], *(singular)* 너의 것 [neoui geot], *(singular polite)* 당신의 것 [dangsinui geot]

yourself [jɔːˈsɛlf; jʊə-] *pron* 너 자신 [neo jasin], *(intensifier)* 당신 자신 [dangsin jasin], *(polite)* 당신 자신 [dangsin jasin]

yourselves [jɔːˈsɛlvz] *pron (intensifier)* 여러분 자신 [yeoreobun jasin], *(polite)* 여러분 자신 [yeoreobun jasin], *(reflexive)* 여러분 자신 [yeoreobun jasin]

youth [juːθ] *n* 청소년 [cheongsonyeon]; **youth club** *n* 유스클럽 [yuseukeulleop]; **youth hostel** *n* 유스호스텔 [yuseuhoseutel]

Z

Zambia [ˈzæmbɪə] *n* 잠비아 [jambia]

Zambian [ˈzæmbɪən] *adj* 잠비아의 [jambiaui] ▷ *n* 잠비아 사람 [jambia saram]

zebra [ˈziːbrə; ˈzɛbrə] *n* 얼룩말 [eollungmal]; **zebra crossing** *n* 횡단보도 [hoengdanbodo]

zero, zeroes [ˈzɪərəʊ, ˈzɪərəʊz] *number* 공 [gong], *(Sino-Korean)* 영 [yeong]

zest [zɛst] *n (excitement)* 흥취 [heungchwi], *(lemon-peel)* 레몬 껍질 [remon kkeopjil]

Zimbabwe [zɪmˈbɑːbwɪ; -weɪ] *n* 짐바브웨 [jimbabeuwe]

Zimbabwean [zɪmˈbɑːbwɪən; -weɪən] *adj* 짐바브웨의 [jimbabeuweui] ▷ *n* 짐바브웨 사람 [jimbabeuwe saram]

zinc [zɪŋk] *n* 아연 [ayeon]

zip [zɪp] *n* 지퍼 [jipeo]; **zip (up)** *v* 지퍼로 잠그다 [jipeoro jamgeuda]

zit [zɪt] *n* 여드름 [yeodeureum]

zodiac [ˈzəʊdɪˌæk] *n* 12궁도 [sibi gungdo]

zone [zəʊn] *n* 지대 [jidae]; **time zone** *n* 시간대 [sigandae]

zoo [zuː] *n* 동물원 [dongmurwon]

zoology [zəʊˈɒlədʒɪ; zuː-] *n* 동물학
 [dongmulhak]
zoom [zuːm] *n* **zoom lens** *n* 줌 렌즈
 [jum renjeu]
zucchini [tsuːˈkiːnɪ; zuː-] *n* 서양호박
 [seoyanghobak]